Shirle Cameron
10 Feb. 2006

JESUS

JESUS

The Complete Guide

Edited by Leslie Houlden

continuum
LONDON • NEW YORK

Continuum International Publishing Group
The Tower Building, 11 York Road, London SE1 7NX
15 East 26th Street, New York NY 10010

First paperback edition by Continuum, 2005

The text of this book was previously published under the title *Jesus in History, Thought and Culture*, by the same author.

British Library Cataloguing-in-Publication Data
A catalogue record for this book is available from the British Library.

Library of Congress Cataloguing-in-Publication Data
A catalog record for this book is available from the Library of Congress.

ISBN: 0-8264-8011-X (paperback)

Printed and bound in Great Britain by MPG Books Lrd, Cornwall

DEDICATION

In memory of my Mother,

Lily Houlden

CONTENTS

CONTRIBUTORS AND THEIR ENTRIES

Prof. Efrain Agosto
Hartford Theological Seminary
Hartford, Connecticut, USA
AMERICAN (HISPANIC) CHRISTIANITY

Rev. Regis Armstrong
St. Fidelis Priory
Interlaken, New York, USA
FRANCIS OF ASSISI

Dr. Nigel Aston
University of Leicester, UK
FRENCH CHRISTIANITY

Rev. Prebendary Dr. Paul Avis
Council for Christian Unity
Church of England
ANGLICANISM
ECCLESIOLOGY
ESSENCE OF CHRISTIANITY

Rev. John Baggley
Corpus Christi Presbytery
Oxford, UK
ICONS AND THE ICON TRADITION

Prof. Peter Bouteneff
St. Vladimir's Orthodox Theological Seminary
Crestwood, New York, USA
ORTHODOX TRADITION

Rev. Dr. John Bowden
Highgate, London, UK
KÜNG, HANS (B. 1928)
SCHILLEBEECKX, EDWARD (B. 1914)

Rev. Michael Brierley
Diocese of Oxford, UK
KENOTICISM

Dr. Sebastian Brock
Oriental Institute, University of Oxford, UK
SYRIAC TRADITION

Prof. George J. Brooke
University of Manchester, UK
DEAD SEA SCROLLS

Dr. Brian J. Capper
Christ Church University College
Kent, UK
WEALTH

Dr. Brian R. Clack
St. Clare's College
Oxford, UK
NIETZSCHE, FRIEDRICH VON (1844–1900)
SCAPEGOAT
WITTGENSTEIN, LUDWIG (1889–1951)

Rev. Dr. John P. H. Clark
Greatham
Hartlepool
Teesside, UK
JULIAN OF NORWICH (C. 1342–1416 OR LATER)

Rev. Richard Coles
Grafton Underwood
Northants, UK
THE MEDIA

Dr. Sylvia Collins
University of Kingston, UK
ENGLISH CHRISTIANITY, MODERN

Dr. Richard Cross
Oriel College
University of Oxford, UK
FRANCISCAN THOUGHT AND PIETY

Prof. Tony Davies
University of Birmingham, UK
MILTON, JOHN (1608–1674)

Rev. Dr. William R. Davies
Thornton Cleveleys
Lancashire, UK
PENTECOSTALISM

Dr. Gregory W. Dawes
University of Otago
New Zealand
TROELTSCH, ERNST (1865–1923)

Dr. Andrew Dawson
Chester College
Merseyside, UK
AMERICAN (SOUTH) CHRISTIANITY

Rev. Paul Diemer OCSO
Mount St. Bernard Abbey, UK
BERNARD OF CLAIRVAUX (1090–1153)

Rev. Dr. Robert Dodaro OSA
Rome, Italy
AUGUSTINE OF HIPPO (354–430)

+ Rev. Canon Alan Dunstan
Truro
Cornwall, UK
HYMNS

Rev. Philip Endean, SJ
Campion Hall
University of Oxford, UK
IGNATIUS OF LOYOLA (C. 1491–1556)

Prof. Philip F. Esler
St. Mary's College
St. Andrews, UK
JESUS IN SOCIAL CONTEXT

Rev. Canon John Fenton
Oxford, UK
LIGHTFOOT, R. H. (1883–1953)

Rt. Rev. Dr. Peter. R. Forster
Bishop of Chester, UK
TORRANCE, T. F. (B. 1913)

Prof. Majella Franzmann
University of New England
Armidale
NSW, Australia
MANICHAEISM

Prof. Getatchew Haile
St. John's University
Collegeville, Minnesota, USA
ETHIOPIAN CHRISTIANITY

Dr. Douglas W. Geyer
Evanston, Illinois, USA
HELLENISTIC RELIGION

Dr. Hugh Goddard
University of Nottingham, UK
ISLAM

Rev. Prof. Clifford Green
Boston, Massachusetts, USA
BONHOEFFER, DIETRICH (1906–1945)

Douglas Gwyn
Pendle Hill Quaker Study Center
Philadelphia, Pennsylvania, USA
QUAKER THOUGHT

Rev. Prof. Emeritus S. G. Hall
St. Andrews University, UK
ANTIOCHENE THEOLOGY
CHALCEDON
GNOSTICISM
NICEA

Rev. Dr. Carolyn Hammond
Gamlingay, UK
MARY

Rt. Rev. Richard Harries
Bishop of Oxford, UK
ART

Rev. Canon Dr. A. E. Harvey
Broadway
Worcestershire, UK
JESUS AS A HISTORICAL FIGURE

Dr. Andrew W. Hass
University of Houston
Texas, USA
LITERATURE, WORLD

Prof. Emeritus John Hick
Birmingham, UK
INCARNATION IN CONTEMPORARY ANALYTIC PHILOSOPHY

Dr. Mike Higton
St. Luke's Campus
Exeter, UK
ENGLISH POPULAR CULTURE, MODERN

Rev. Dr. Barrie Hinksman
Temple Balsall, UK
PSYCHOTHERAPY

Dr. Nicholas Hope
University of Glasgow, UK
GERMAN CHRISTIANITY

Dr. B. L. Horne
(formerly King's College
University of London, UK)
DANTE ALIGHIERI (1265–1321)

Rev. Prof. Emeritus Leslie Houlden
Temple Balsall, UK
ADOPTIANISM
CADBURY, H. J. (1883–1974)
CHURCH
CREEDS
FAMILY
HENGEL, MARTIN (B. 1926)
HOLY SPIRIT
IRENAEUS (C. 130–C. 200)
JESUS, ABSENCES OF
JESUS, ACHIEVEMENT OF
JESUS, DEATH OF
JESUS, FAMILY OF
JESUS, MIRACLES OF
JESUS, NAME OF
JESUS, ORIGINS OF
JESUS, PARABLES OF
JESUS, TEACHING OF
JESUS AS PROPHET
JESUS AS SERVANT
JOHN, GOSPEL OF
KINGDOM OF GOD
LAW
LORD
LUKE, GOSPEL OF, AND ACTS OF THE APOSTLES
MARK, GOSPEL OF
MATTHEW, GOSPEL OF
NEW TESTAMENT AS A WHOLE
OLD AGE
POWER
PRAYER
PREEXISTENCE

REIMARUS, HERMANN SAMUEL (1694–1768)
SECOND COMING OF JESUS, ORIGINS OF
SECOND PERSON OF THE TRINITY
SEXUALITY
SON OF GOD
SON OF MAN
STRAUSS, D. F. (1808–1874)
TRANSFIGURATION
VERMES, GEZA (B. 1924)
WAR
WORK

Rev. Dr. David Hoyle
Gloucester Cathedral, UK
ENGLISH CHRISTIANITY, 1500–1750

Prof. David Jasper
University of Glasgow, UK
LITERATURE, ENGLISH

Prof. Gareth Jones
Canterbury Christ Church University College, UK
CHRISTOLOGY, MODERN

Prof. Emeritus John Kent
Bristol, UK
ENLIGHTENMENT

Rev. Fergus Kerr OP
Blackfriars
University of Oxford, UK
AQUINAS, THOMAS (1224/5–1274)

Dr. Edward Kessler
Centre for Jewish-Christian Relations
Cambridge, UK
JEWISH PERSPECTIVE
JEWISH SCHOLARSHIP

Dr. Frances Knight
University of Wales
Lampeter, UK
ENGLISH CHRISTIANITY, 1750–1940

Rev. Dr. Larry J. Kreitzer
Regent's Park College
University of Oxford, UK
FILM

Sophie, Lady Laws
London, UK
HEBREWS, LETTER TO THE

Prof. Dorothy Lee
Queen's College
Victoria
Australia
FEMINIST THEOLOGY

Rev. Dr. Kenneth Leech
St. Botolph's Church
London, UK
SPIRITUALITY

Rev. David Lindsay
Haberdashers Aske's School
Elstree, UK
RELIGIOUS EDUCATION IN BRITISH SCHOOLS

Prof. Dennis Ronald MacDonald
Claremont School of Theology
California, USA
HOMER

Prof. Emeritus James P. Mackey
Waterford
Ireland
IRISH CHRISTIANITY

Prof. Ian Markham
Hartford Theological Seminary
Connecticut, USA
AMERICAN (NORTH) CHRISTIANTY
ETHICS, MODERN

Prof. Thomas F. Mathews
New York University, USA
JESUS AS EMPEROR

Rev. Dr. Iain Matthew OCD
Carmelite Priory
Oxford, UK
JOHN OF THE CROSS (1542–1591)
TERESA OF AVILA

Prof. E. V. McKnight
Furman University
South Carolina, USA
WRIGHT, N. T. (b. 1948)

Prof. David McLellan
University of Kent
Canterbury, UK
MARXISM

Prof. Donald E. Meek
University of Edinburgh, UK
SCOTTISH (GAELIC) CHRISTIANITY

Dr. Justin Meggitt
Corpus Christi College
Cambridge University, UK
JOHN THE BAPTIST

Rev. Anthony Meredith, SJ
Farm Street Church
London, UK
ROMAN CATHOLICISM

Rev. Dr. R. W. L. Moberly
University of Durham, UK
HEBREW BIBLE

Dr. Roger Mohrlang
Whitworth College
Spokane, Washington, USA
PAUL

+ Rt. Rev. Hugh Montefiore
Wandsworth
London, UK
PARANORMAL

Dr. Peggy Morgan
Mansfield College
University of Oxford, UK
BUDDHISM

Rev. Dr. Robert Morgan
Linacre College
University of Oxford, UK
HARVEY, A. E. (B. 1930)
KECK, LEANDER E. (B. 1928)

Rev. Prof. Emeritus Colin Morris
Southampton, UK
HOLY SEPULCHRE

Prof. Emeritus Lewis S. Mudge
San Francisco Theological Seminary
California, USA
BULTMANN, RUDOLF (1884–1976)
CALVIN, JOHN (1509–1564)
LUTHER, MARTIN (1483–1546)
TILLICH, PAUL (1886–1965)

Very Rev. Gordon Mursell
Birmingham Cathedral, UK
SPIRITUALITY (PROTESTANT)

Dr. Stephen W. Need
(formerly La Sainte Union College of Higher Education
Southampton, UK)
MACQUARRIE, JOHN (B. 1919)
PANNENBERG, WOLFHART (B. 1928)

Dr. Vrej Nerses Nersessian
British Library
London, UK
ARMENIAN CHRISTIANITY

Rev. Prof. Kenneth G. C. Newport
Hope University
Liverpool, UK
SECOND COMING OF JESUS, IN CURRENT BELIEF
SEVENTH-DAY ADVENTISM
WESLEY, CHARLES (1707–1788) AND WESLEY, JOHN (1703–1791)

Rev. Vladimir Nikiforov
Royal Holloway College
University of London, UK
RUSSIAN CHRISTIANITY

Rev. Prof. Emeritus D. E. Nineham
Oxford, UK
SCHWEITZER, ALBERT (1875–1965)

Dr. Thomas O'Loughlin
University of Wales
Lampeter, UK
ANSELM (C. 1033–1109)
CELTIC AND EARLY ENGLISH CHRISTIANITY
DIDACHE
ERIUGENA, JOHN SCOTUS (D. 877)
ISIDORE OF SEVILLE (D. 636)
JESUS LETTERS
KEMPIS, THOMAS À (1380–1471)

Rev. Stuart Owen
Hendon
London, UK
GREAT WAR

Rev. Dr. D. C. Parker
University of Birmingham, UK
TEXTUAL CRITICISM

Dr. Paul Parvis
New College
Edinburgh, UK
ALEXANDRIAN THEOLOGY
APOLLINARIANISM
NESTORIANISM
ORIGEN (C. 185–254)

Rev. Dr. Graham Patrick
Northwich
Cheshire, UK
WESTCOTT, B. F. (1825–1901), LIGHTFOOT, J. B. (1828–1889), AND HORT, F. J. A. (1828–1892)

Rev. D. W. Peck
Diocese of Guildford, UK
AUDEN, W. H. (1907–1973)
ELIOT, T. S. (1888–1965)

Rt. Revd. Stephen Platten
Bishop of Wakefield, UK
BENEDICT (C. 480–C. 550)
PILGRIMAGE
RADICAL ORTHODOXY

Prof. Mark A. Powell
Trinity Lutheran Seminary
Columbus, Ohio, USA
BORG, J. M. (B. 1942)
CROSSAN, J. D. (B. 1934)
FUNK, ROBERT (B. 1926)
JESUS SEMINAR
MEIER, J. P. (B. 1942)
SANDERS, E. P. (B. 1937)

Rev. Dr. Brian G. Powley
York, UK
HARNACK, ADOLF VON (1851–1930)

Rev. Mark Pryce
Smethwick
Birmingham, UK
MASCULINITY

Dr. Ben Quash
Peterhouse
University of Cambridge, UK
BALTHASAR, HANS URS VON (1905–1988)

Rev. Alan Race
St. Andrew's Rectory
Leicester, UK
INTERFAITH THOUGHT AND RELATIONS

Rev. Paul Rout OFM
University of Kent
Canterbury, UK
BONAVENTURE (1217–1274)

Dr. Paul Spilsbury
University of Wales
Lampeter, UK
MESSIAH

Dr. C. Mary Stallings-Taney
Rowan University
New Jersey, USA
JOHN OF CAULIBUS

Rt. Rev. Dr. Kenneth Stevenson
Bishop of Portsmouth, UK
BAPTISM
EUCHARIST
LITURGY

Dr. Diane B. Stinton
Daystar University
Nairobi, Kenya
AFRICAN CHRISTIANITY

Prof. William F. Storrar
University of Edinburgh, UK
SCOTTISH (LOWLANDS) CHRISTIANITY

Rev. Roderick Strange
Collegio Beda
Rome, Italy
NEWMAN, JOHN HENRY (1801–1890)

Rev. Dr. William Strange
St. Michael's College
Cardiff, UK
CHILDREN

Prof. R. N. Swanson
University of Birmingham, UK
ENGLISH CHRISTIANITY, MEDIEVAL

Mr. Roderick Swanston
Royal College of Music
London, UK
MUSIC

Rev. Canon John P. M. Sweet
Selwyn College
University of Cambridge, UK
JOHN, REVELATION OF

Rev. Dr. Patrick Thomas
The Vicarage
Parc Penllwyn
Carmarthen, UK
WELSH CHRISTIANITY

Rev. Dr. Colin Thompson
St. Catherine's College
University of Oxford, UK
SPANISH CHRISTIANITY

Prof. Christine Trevett
University of Cardiff, UK
IGNATIUS OF ANTIOCH

Dr. Peter Vardy
Heythrop College
University of London, UK
KIERKEGAARD, SØREN (1813–1855)

Prof. Robert E. Van Voorst
Western Theological Seminary
Holland, Michigan, USA
JOSEPHUS
NONEXISTENCE HYPOTHESIS
RABBIS
THOMAS, GOSPEL OF

Rev. Dr. John H. Watson
Christchurch, UK
COPTIC CHRISTIANITY

Dr. Natalie K. Watson
Ripon College
Cuddesdon, UK
LIBERATION THEOLOGY

Revd. Prof. John Webster
University of Aberdeen, UK
BARTH, KARL (1886–1968)

Prof. Dr. A. J. M. Wedderburn
University of Munich
Germany
RESURRECTION

Revd. Maxine West
London, UK
SERAPION

Rev. R. Whyte
Tunbridge Wells, UK
CHINESE CHRISTIANITY

Rev. Trevor Williams
Trinity College
University of Oxford, UK
SCHLEIERMACHER, F. D. E. (1768–1834)
WILES, MAURICE (B. 1923)

Rev. Dr. Andrew Wingate
Leicester Cathedral, UK
HINDUISM
INDIAN CHRISTIANITY

Rev. Dr. James Woodward
Temple Balsall, UK
PASTORAL THEOLOGY, MODERN

†Rev. Dr. Edward Yarnold
Campion Hall
University of Oxford, UK
RAHNER, KARL (1904–1984)

ALPHABETICAL LIST OF ENTRIES

TOPICAL LIST OF ENTRIES

Biblical Scholarship (Nineteenth Century–Present)
- Borg, J. M. (b. 1942)
- Bultmann, Rudolf (1884–1976)
- Cadbury, H. J. (1883–1974)
- Crossan, J. D. (b. 1934)
- Funk, Robert (b. 1926)
- Harvey, A. E. (b. 1930)
- Hengel, Martin (b. 1926)
- Hort, F. J. A. (1828–1892) *See* Westcott, B. F. (1825–1901)
- Jesus Seminar
- Keck, Leander E. (b. 1928)
- Lightfoot, J. B. (1828–1889) *See* Westcott, B. F. (1825–1901)
- Meier, J. P. (b. 1942)
- Sanders, E. P. (b. 1937)
- Schillebeeckx, Edward (b. 1914)
- Schweitzer, Albert (1875–1965)
- Strauss, D. F. (1808–1874)
- Vermes, Geza (b. 1924)
- Westcott, B. F. (1825–1901)
- Wright, N. T. (b. 1948)

Books of the Bible and Other Early Writings
- Acts of the Apostles. *See* Luke, Gospel of, and Acts of the Apostles
- Dead Sea Scrolls
- *Didache*
- Hebrew Bible
- Hebrews, Letter to the
- Ignatius of Antioch (d. c. 110)
- John, Gospel of
- John, Revelation of
- Josephus
- Luke, Gospel of, and Acts of the Apostles
- Mark, Gospel of
- Matthew, Gospel of
- Paul
- Textual Criticism
- Thomas, Gospel of

Christianity: Major Forms and Styles
- Anglicanism
- Armenian Christianity
- Celtic and Early English Christianity
- Ethiopian Christianity
- Methodism. *See* Wesley, Charles (1707–1788) and Wesley, John (1703–1791)
- Orthodox Tradition
- Pentecostalism
- Roman Catholicism
- Seventh-day Adventism

Countries
- African Christianity
- American (Hispanic) Christianity
- American (North) Christianity
- American (South) Christianity
- Armenian Christianity
- Chinese Christianity
- Coptic Christianity
- English Christianity, Medieval

Culture

Ethical Topics

Jesus: Life and Times

Other Major Religions

Schools of Thought and Thinkers

INTRODUCTION

It is hard to think of a subject that lends itself more naturally than Jesus to presentation in an encyclopedia. There are so many ramifications of his influence, so many aspects of his effect on the world in the past twenty centuries, that, as this present work has developed, it has come to seem without end: new subjects kept coming into view, and so did the sense that many more could have been included. To take a basic matter, nobody else in the world's history has the distinction of having that history divided for most human beings at the supposed point of his entry into it. Whether we divide history into B.C. and A.D. ("before Christ" and "the year of the Lord") or the new and religiously neutral B.C.E. and C.E. ("before the common era" and "common era"), the point of division is the same; Jesus' effect seems to be ineradicable, despite all attempts to neutralize it! He has of course been the subject of innumerable books of many different kinds down the years, across a wide range of disciplines, and the millennium saw a particular surge of interest. But so wide-ranging and diverse (one could say encyclopedic) have been his effects that there is ample room for treatment in this flexible medium and format.

This book sets out to focus on as many aspects as possible of the phenomenon of Jesus in the past two thousand years: first, as a figure of the first century; then as the object of both thought and devotion in every succeeding period, giving rise to both brilliance and complexity; also as a major influence and subject in art, music, and literature, down to the present. Individual articles may fall into one of the three main categories (history, culture, thought), or they may crisscross as their subject demands. Much good can come from making connections across conventional boundaries.

Beginnings

The last two centuries in particular have seen an endless series of historically motivated inquiries into the "facts" about Jesus, seen in the light of "neutral" investigation. Jesus' towering religious role, giving rise to all kinds of reactions, has made academic neutrality often hard to achieve, and, especially in hindsight, we can see research affected by all kinds of ideological factors (see **Jesus as a Historical Figure; Schweitzer, Albert**). There is the added difficulty that, in his time, Jesus was utterly obscure. He lived in a remote corner of the Roman Empire, at a time long before government records of villagers were kept or in any case survived. In the attempt at objectivity, we can only work inward from such knowledge as is available—from public affairs and culture, and from archaeological discovery—to enable us to form a picture of his time and place (see **Jesus in Social Context**). Calendrical calculations have improved, and it seems (odd as it sounds) that Jesus was born between 6 and 4 B.C., probably in the village of Nazareth in Galilee, in the northern part of Palestine, itself part of the Roman province of Syria (though perhaps in Bethlehem, in Judea, in the southern part of the country). (See **Jesus, Family of; Jesus, Origins of.**) He probably had such education as was available, presumably in the setting of whatever meeting for worship and teaching of the Jewish Scriptures was present in the village, and he may possibly have been affected by the building nearby (never referred to in the Gospels) of the new Greek-style town of Sepphoris. In the late twenties, he embarked, probably through the influence of the dramatic reformist preaching of **John the Baptist,** on the fulfilling of a comparable but differently orientated mission of renewal. With associates, he embarked on preaching widely in the villages of Galilee the imminent realization, perhaps catastrophically, of God's "kingdom" or rule in the world. He also taught a return to simple, basic, but almost carefree duties, in an atmosphere of open fellowship, where burdens could be laid aside. He was known as a healer, a bringer of release from evils.

In due course, he traveled to Jerusalem, probably with a sense of a destiny to be fulfilled. This was the heartland of his Jewish faith, dominated by the great temple, recently rebuilt by Herod the Great and now effectively controlled by the high-priestly authorities, under the aegis (sometimes close, sometimes loose) of the Roman power. Here, probably in the early thirties of the first century, and triggered by some incident or series of happenings seen as provocative or seditious, he was arrested and put to death by crucifixion (see **Jesus, Death of**). Shortly afterward, he was seen as alive again by some of his close followers, and this was speedily interpreted in spectacular terms as demonstrating his role as indeed the central agent of God for the coming of the new age of joy and salvation (see **Resurrection**). No longer a simple local preaching and healing figure, his significance was now seen, albeit from the limited perspective of a small number, mainly of Galileans, as universal in scope. It would of course be a mistake to see this in modern terms: what could it mean in that period to uneducated people at the eastern end of the Mediterranean and at the farthest reaches of the Empire? It was the cosmic perspective of religious conviction: we see God as present and active in this man and in our group—this (and he) are therefore of widest and profoundest meaning for all. What is more, the purposes of God must surely soon be fulfilled in some almost unimaginable happening whose outcome would however be delight for his people. All this was given shape by Scriptural and other works circulating in the period. It was already the subject of intense study and speculation among Jews, and now, in a new form, among the followers of Jesus, with everything centering on him (see **Dead Sea Scrolls**).

So much can reasonably be said from a professional and detached historian's standpoint, though almost every detail can be controverted in one way or another, and there is ample room for expert disagreement. All (or most) of it can however also be seen from a quite different perspective, and it is from this other perspective alone that actual written evidence from something approaching the time is available. Here we find not the work of "dispassionate" historians but of committed believers. Apart from a brief reference in the late-first-century Jewish historian **Josephus,** we have for our resources in effect only the earliest Christian writings, eventually collected in the New Testament. This evidence has then a different character: it was written from faith, and it was written to faith—that is, both the writers and the readers or receivers were devoted to Jesus and "believed" in him. This does not at all mean that it is without historical value, but it is necessary always to recognize its character if we are to understand it and profit from it appropriately, using it for what it can do and not for what it cannot. We refer here first to the letters of **Paul** the apostle, the first of Christian writers, whose great work it was to get belief in and about Jesus into non-Jewish circles in ways that such "gentiles" could grasp and take to themselves. More than anyone, but with helpers, he took the faith to new territory, chiefly in Greece and Asia Minor (Turkey), work done mostly in the forties and fifties of the first century.

A little later, between A.D. 70 and the nineties, accounts of Jesus' life, death, and resurrection were written, and copies seem to have circulated quite quickly among the Christian communities (see **Church**), even as far as Egypt, where early examples have been discovered (see **Textual Criticism**). These writings are the four Gospels (**Mark, Matthew, Luke, John**; see also **Thomas, Gospel of**), which give us stories of Jesus' lifetime (see **Jesus, Miracles of**) and accounts of his teaching (see **Jesus, Teaching of**), notably his parables (see **Jesus, Parables of**), as well as majoring on the narrative of his suffering, death, and resurrection. It is interesting that Paul seems to have shown relatively little interest in the details of Jesus' actual life and teaching: Paul's faith centered on his coming, death, and resurrection. However, we need to read the Gospels themselves—though they read to us like biographies on modern lines and do indeed tell us much about what Jesus did and taught—as themselves writings of faith.

Paul and the Gospels alike express that faith partly by way of titles of honor used for Jesus, each of which has a pedigree, usually in the Old Testament, before it develops in application to this new and in many ways revolutionary figure (see **Jesus as Servant; Lord; Messiah; Son of God; Son of Man**). All of them express, in their different ways, the conviction that Jesus was God's decisive agent for the salvation of humankind: some go so far as to see him as God's fully empowered representative, standing for God himself among us. Each of these terms also, of course, had a future life, developing in its application in Christian worship and in formulations of belief—usually with little awareness, until recent times, that fresh nuances of meaning were coming on the scene.

Formative Times for Christian Beliefs

In the first four centuries of the Church, there was a ferment of development at both institutional and intellectual levels. The new faith was frowned on (to put it mildly) by the official life of the Roman Empire until the conversion of Emperor Constantine in the early fourth century, and was indeed subjected, especially toward the end of the period, to spasmodic severe persecution, with numerous martyrs, some still commemorated with devotion. Nevertheless, the Church, strong in its network of "branches" and "officers" (the bishops and their churches), and in its circulation of writings, made its way and maintained a remarkable record of vigorous thought and activity. It was in this period, spanning both sides of Constantine's inauguration of new favored status for the Church, that belief about Jesus came to be "defined" (better, refined), largely in terms that were seen, even if many of them were Scriptural (and so Jewish) in origin, through eyes chiefly formed by styles of Platonist philosophy (see entry for *Neoplatonism* in the glossary that begins on page 893). **Creeds** were formulated to sum up this belief, and leading teachers refined its terms (see **Irenaeus; Origen**). Some developments were rejected, often painfully (see **Apollinarianism**). In the fourth and fifth centuries, when such activities were more feasible, formal (and imperially sponsored) councils (**Nicea; Chalcedon**) arrived at agreed—up to a point—statements of faith, sometimes framed with considerable technicality and obscurity. It was the era of formulation and attempted settlement, and its fruits remain the official faith of the central, great churches. Some Christians, however, diverged, chiefly on issues concerned with Christ's divine status in relation to his humanness, and their inheritance remains (see **Armenian Christianity; Coptic Christianity; Ethiopian Christianity;** see also the glossary entry for word pairs *Divinity-Humanity; Divine nature–Human nature; Son of God–Son of man*).

The study of this period easily gives rise to the feeling that Christians (though liable to suffer martyrdom in the earlier part of it) spent their energy in furious thought and equally furious controversy with those Christians who took a different view, often on what may seem to us a minor point in an obscure, even unintelligible frame of reference. It is true that, especially in major centers like Antioch (in Syria) or (from the fourth century) Constantinople (now Istanbul), or, in some contexts, Rome, positions were held and argued with what may strike us as fierce tenacity and obstinacy; but it is a mistake to suppose that Christian life consisted of nothing else or was motivated by no different considerations. Quite the contrary; often, the theological points were controverted less for their own sake than for their bearing on fundamental personal reasons to do with salvation: it was vital to see as clearly as one could the bearing of one's beliefs on one's eternal standing before God in the light of Jesus. And matters of faith belonged in the context of Christian life, both moral and devotional. This life was centered on **Baptism**, for the person's solemn (and often dramatic, even frightening) entry into Christ and the community of his people, and on the Sunday-by-Sunday celebration of the **Eucharist,** when the community gathered to express and fortify its common life in Christ. The weekly gathering for worship was surrounded by frequent prayer and instruction or exhortation from bishops and priests, and by works of charity, modeled on acts of Jesus, for those in need (see glossary: *Sacrament*). By the end of this period, moreover, the monastic life, especially in Egypt and Syria, was growing in popularity—people (men and some women) giving themselves as "athletes for Christ" in a life of prayer and asceticism, sometimes taken to extremes. All this would have been felt to be in vain if Jesus could not be seen as "God among us," and that conviction was undoubtedly felt, in this period, to be a good deal more pressing than his simple, mere humanness—Jesus as one alongside us, as example and friend. It was in this total context that the difference between orthodoxy and heresy (see glossary discussion of these two terms) seemed vital to establish and maintain.

Middle Ages

In the following period there came about the gradual separation—for practical purposes, and often and in certain ways with great firmness—of the Church in the old Eastern half of the Roman Empire, centered on Constantinople (even when under Muslim authority after 1453) and gradually spreading from Greece and parts of the Balkan lands to Russia, from the Western Church, centered on Rome (see **Icons and the Icon Tradition; Orthodox Tradition**). For reasons of political and military development in the West, the latter came to be considerably more cohesive and powerful. There fell to its leaders, including many local bishops, much of the practical governing authority that the now departed empire in Western Europe no longer exercised, after the arrival of successive waves of Goths, Vandals, and other tribes. And the papacy itself drew to itself ever-increasing power to legislate for the Church in all lands where it could exercise authority, to appoint bishops and other higher clergy wherever it could win its way with local rulers (a constant struggle that still has echoes down to the present), and even to dictate policy to local kings and other princes, including (from A.D. 800) the Holy Roman Emperor (in practice, powerful chiefly in Germany).

It is not surprising that in such an ethos the worship of Jesus and the following of him took new turns. In part, and with important modifications, he came to be seen as himself king or emperor (see **Jesus as Emperor**), and images from the Revelation of John (see **John, Revelation of**) fortified such a doctrine; the Pope was then his chief officer, and the Church (in effect, the clergy) his local deputies for all spiritual—and many temporal—purposes.

At the same time, especially in monastic life (see **Benedict**), there developed a new tenderness in the picture of Jesus and in the following of him in prayer and discipleship (see **Bernard of Clairvaux; Franciscan Thought and Piety; Julian of Norwich; Prayer**). Crucifixes came to be made with vivid depictions of the suffering and dying rather than the triumphant, sovereign Jesus (see **Art**), and **Hymns** expressed this style of emotive spirituality. **Pilgrimage** developed, not just to the sites of saints' relics and tombs but especially to places where relics of Jesus or of **Mary** were to be found (e.g., the Crown of Thorns at La Sainte Chapelle, in Paris, or the Holy Shroud at Turin). This was a notable development of the much older pilgrimage to Jerusalem (and to Rome), centers of great happenings in the Church's beginnings. The **Eucharist** came to be seen, with ever more formal definition, as the very manifestation of Christ's continuing presence among his people (see **Aquinas, Thomas**), and churches were built to be above all the centers of eucharistic devotion and adoration (see **English Christianity, Medieval**).

Breakup and Reform

(See **Calvin, John; Ignatius of Loyola; Luther, Martin;** and see glossary: *Counter-Reformation; Reformed.*) In the later medieval period, there developed a reaction, in both some academic and some spiritually minded circles, against certain aspects of the recent development of the Western Church, in part its apparent overconcern with matters of property and rights, in part its loss of hold on gospel fundamentals. This sense was fortified by renewed study of the Bible, now possible in its original languages, and by the invention of printing. New ideas and perspectives could spread. The new climate was widespread but, with various local circumstances at work, found it easiest to make its way and to innovate in the prosperous cities of Northern Europe, especially in parts of Germany and Switzerland. Here, there was a special readiness to assert local independence, for example against a bishop (who might live some distance away) and property-owning monasteries, appearing not to make much of a contribution to the life of the place. Biblical study made it apparent that numerous traditional readings of New Testament texts carried senses cogently different from those hitherto believed: the Latin gave a flavor or even a sense quite other than the original Greek. Moreover, certain well-embedded church practices, such as the nonmarriage (ideally, the celibacy) of the clergy and the denial of the cup to the laity at the Eucharist, together with the customary infrequency (usually annual) of the receiving of Holy Communion by lay people, seemed quite ungrounded in Scripture and in early Church practice—they were mere customs that had bedded themselves down in the Church for reasons of dubious value. More deeply, the reading of Paul made people like Luther see that Christian life had become far too centered on a routine of meritorious observances, which, one could not help coming to feel (even if official doctrine said otherwise) was one's passport to salvation (and even then would it be recognized?). No, true faith said that one's acceptance by God was a free gift, quite beyond any necessity or possibility of one's earning of merit: it was a matter of grace.

These liberating doctrines set Jesus in a fresh light. The old piety, centering on meditation on the deeds of his life and the manner of his dying (see, for example, the patterns of stained-glass windows at Chartres Cathedral), was too far from the fundamental matters of the person's basic relationship with God through Christ and his dying "for us."

Catholic as well as what came to be called Protestant Christianity felt some of this wind, though in its own way. It showed, for example, in the radical obedience of **Ignatius of Loyola** and his new order, the Jesuits (see **Chinese Christianity**); in the reformed devotion visible in **John of the Cross** and **Teresa of Avila;** and in the missionary work of friars in the newly opened lands of the New World (see **American [South] Christianity**). With hindsight, many feel regret that these energies were not somehow held within a single community framework.

But there was, in some radical Protestant circles, especially in England, a further twist in the way Jesus was seen. Quakers (see **Quaker Thought**) and other groups in the mid-seventeenth century lost patience with the externals of religion. For them it was a question of holding not to "one crucified at Jerusalem 1600 years ago" but to "a Christ formed in us." It was the innerness of Jesus that alone mattered. It was, in a way, not far from much of the inspiration in the lives of many monks and nuns in the Catholic framework, but in its exclusive ferocity, it pointed in a quite different direction.

Rationality and History

The **Enlightenment** is the name for a broad movement of thought in the later seventeenth and especially the eighteenth centuries, marking philosophical and theological thought as far apart as East Prussia and Scotland (see **Christology, Modern**). It had the twin characteristics of empiricism (the following of rational thought and evidence as distinct from the established pronouncements of venerable authorities such as the Church) and candid historical enquiry. "Jesus," as received, was vulnerable from both directions. The Reformation had opened some of the doors—but turned out in reality to be, in some of its developments, a Pandora's box. In an atmosphere in which Platonist philosophical terminology no longer carried conviction or was beyond criticism, the traditional doctrines about Jesus were cast in doubt—all the more so, if one approached the past, including Jesus' own life and setting, with a new sense of reality and new imaginative (and, to some degree but with many more to come, physical) tools at one's disposal. No longer was it a matter of "Jesus was certainly divine, how then was he human?" but rather, "Jesus was a man, how then was he divine (and was he really)?" Theological discussion in fact centered less on Jesus than on the idea of God itself: for some already it was as much as one could do to hold to any kind of recognizable Christian faith. In such an atmosphere, religious feeling could easily seem at a discount, despite revivals such as that led by the **Wesleys** (see also **American [North] Christianity**). Christian confidence soon received a more substantial theological boost from the thought of **Schleiermacher** and **Kierkegaard**, but the march of skepticism persisted.

An important part of this movement of thought turned out to be the renewed and often skeptical study of the New Testament documents themselves and of the related subject, the life of Jesus, in the late eighteenth and nineteenth centuries. Heads rolled in German universities (see **Strauss, D. F.**); in England scholarship was more sober and, probably, in some ways more effective (see **Westcott, B. F.**). The articles in this volume on the Gospels and related topics show some of the fruits of more recent study in this tradition, and there are many individuals who have brief articles to themselves (see **Borg, J. M.; Bultmann, Rudolf; Crossan, J. D.; Funk, Robert; Harnack, Adolf von; Harvey, A. E.; Keck, Leander E.; Lightfoot, R. H.; Sanders, E. P.; Wright, N. T.**).

At the same time, there has been, especially since World War I, no shortage of thinkers seeking to reestablish, in a variety of ways and along fresh lines, something of the traditional thrust of Christian doctrine concerning Jesus: toweringly, Karl **Barth,** but see also **Balthasar, Hans Urs von; Bonhoeffer, Dietrich; Macquarrie, John; Pannenberg, Wolfhart; Rahner, Karl; Tillich, Paul**; and, more radically, **Wiles, Maurice**. More surprisingly, perhaps, Ludwig **Wittgenstein** approaches this category. And in the poetic idiom, we note the work of W. H. **Auden,** T. S. **Eliot,** and others who comment from a different angle on the more personal implications of these matters and on the experience they represent. More poignantly, there was the witness of the poets of the **Great War**.

It would be a mistake to suppose that Christian life has responded with immediate acclaim (or indeed notable rejection) to scholarly developments of the kind that has been described. As in some other periods, that life, with its habits of prayer and devotion and practical Christian living (not to speak of more humdrum aspects) in the Church, has often continued without undue disturbance; at the same time, some of the skeptical trends in relation to Jesus as a historical figure and in his doctrinal place have taken their toll, among the many factors that have led to the decline of Christian observance and understanding, especially in Western Europe. Depictions of Jesus in film (see **Film**) and the media (see **The Media**) illustrate some of the oddities of the present situation (see also **English Christianity, Modern; English Popular Culture, Modern**).

Others, of course, find faith rejuvenated by the imaginative "encounter" with the figure of Jesus made possible by realistic modern study of the period of his life and indeed study of the Gospels that first wrote about him in the light of faith, as it appeared in the days of its youth. And conservative styles of Christian belief and practice go on with huge vigor, apparently unaffected by the movements that have been discussed. Undoubtedly, what often seems to have been in the past a somewhat monolithic picture of belief about Jesus, promulgated and sanctioned by the Church and accepted by all (always somewhat illusory), certainly cannot stand. But faith continues, and is happy to face new tasks, not least the attempt to see how Jesus looks in the light of our awareness, in the global village, of the other great faiths of the world, which have undergone a quite different history and been subject to quite other developments and pressures (see **Interfaith Thought and Relations**). Some of these relationships of course go back a very long way, in the case of Christianity's parent and Jesus' homefaith, Judaism, right to the beginning, with a turbulent history to follow (see **Jewish Perspective**). Something of the same is true of the relationship with **Islam.**

Meanwhile, Jesus continues to evoke fresh works in the fields of artistic and literary endeavor (see **Art; Music; Literature, English; Literature, World**)—where the Welsh poet R. S. Thomas, stands out as a brooding and shrewd commentator on much that has been discussed. The question of Jesus remains alive. His elusiveness is notified at the start, by his leaving no writing that might tie him down. All we have is responses to him. It is as if he was determined to go on being endlessly rethought and freshly responded to.

On the other hand, time and again people seek to bind him to their own assumptions and hopes, often (nearly always!) supposed to derive from him. The left-hand panel of the cover of this book shows a painting of Jesus by Albrecht Dürer for which the artist used himself as model (it was a recognized devout practice). It is a parable of the tendency to make Jesus conform to one's own needs and aspirations. But as this book shows, Houdini-like, he escapes time after time. The name of Jesus still has wings. Jesus: who is he?

Travellers
I think of the continent
of the mind. At some stage
in the crossing of it a traveller
rejoiced. This is the truth,
he cried; I have won
my salvation!
What was it like
to be alive then? Was it a time
when two sparrows were sold
for a farthing? What recipe
did he bequeath us for the solution
of our problems other than the statement
of his condition? The territory
has expanded since then. We
see now that the journey is
without end, and there is no joy
in the knowledge. Going on, going
back, standing aside—the alternatives
are appalling, as is the imagining
of the lost traveller, what he would
say to us, if he were here
now, and how discredited we would find it.

—R. S. Thomas
Collected Poems, 1945–1990
(London: J. M. Dent, 1996, p. 308)

HOW TO USE THIS BOOK

Most readers will come to this book with a specific interest—in a topic or period or thinker or form of experience (like art or music or literature): what does this author or that say about Jesus? How may his resurrection be understood? How did they think about Jesus in medieval England or modern China? How has Jesus been depicted in the English-language poets?

But the use of a book like this tends to spread—and should be allowed to. One question begets another, either out of curiosity or out of ignorance now revealed. So each article is followed by a list of "see also" articles, which either take the subject into adjacent areas or elucidate matters referred to in the article just read. Encyclopedias are well designed for browsing, even idly.

Some readers, however, will turn to this book not so much to seek information or to browse out of general interest as to help them consider issues that arise in relation to Jesus and are currently the subjects of discussion and controversy. Here are some of these, and here are relevant articles and other sources of information in this book:

1. Miracle: both in general and in relation to particular events or acts where the question arises. See **Crossan, J. D.; Enlightenment; Jesus, Family of; Jesus, Miracles of; Jesus, Origins of; Resurrection; Strauss, D. F.; Wright, N. T.**

2. Jesus' status: how should we think of claims that he was "divine" or "God"? How do such claims relate to his human nature? How "human" was he? How about his being a male human being? See the glossary entries for *Christology* and for the word pairs *Divinity-Humanity; Divine nature–Human nature; Son of God–Son of man;* see also **Chalcedon; Enlightenment; Feminist Theology; Nicea.** See also entries presented under the subheading "Schools of Thought and Thinkers" in the Topical List of Entries in the front matter of this book (page xxi), as well as the Introduction that begins on page xxv.

3. Jesus as object of worship: what might this mean? How does it take place? See Topical List, under "Worship and Prayer" and many of those under the headings "Christianity: Major Forms and Styles" and "Countries."

4. Jesus' life: for recent discussions, see Topical List, scholars and subjects listed under Jesus: Life and Times. The article entitled **Jesus as a Historical Figure** makes a good starting place. See also **Enlightenment.**

5. Jesus' "uniqueness": there are other major faiths, related to Christianity in a range of ways. Partly for historical reasons and partly because of the

main line of Christian belief, Jesus has been held to be unique as the expression of God to humankind and as "savior." How should we think about this question? See Topical List: "Other Major Religions"; see also the article on **Interfaith Thought and Relations.** See also glossary entry for word pairs *Divinity-Humanity; Divine nature–Human nature; Son of God–Son of man*.

6. Jesus as "studied" and as "believed in" and "worshipped": the range of questions indicated here is most perplexing of all and goes to the roots of European and much of American culture in past and present. Jesus, as a figure or a topic, has come to demand two quite different kinds of approach or response: Are we to "give ourselves to" him in worship and allegiance, or are we to "study" him as we might study any other object in the world, past or present? The two responses make apparently contrary demands, and many find them incompatible, requiring choice. The preoccupation of modern Western education with varieties of the "study" approach makes it hard for many to change gear into a religious approach to Jesus without a sense of dishonesty in the mind. Yet even a rigorous "study" encounter with Jesus may evoke attraction or fascination that can tend toward "faith" or "worship"—though a multitude of problems may remain. This situation is not made easier because so much of the legacy of the past, much of it preserved in what may seem like intellectual aspic in the formulas of the Christian religion, is aware of no such difficulty: in its original day, it had simply not arisen. A development of historical and cultural "sympathy" may make the consideration of this issue more possible. So the articles in this book on Art, Literature, and Music may be more helpful than the more intellectual contributions. They may stimulate the imagination, often neglected in theological discussion, at the same time refining and disciplining it. The article on the **Enlightenment** helps to show how acute the difficulty came to be. And articles like those on **American (North) Christianity, Armenian Christianity, Coptic Christianity, Ethiopian Christianity,** and **Pentecostalism** may show that it is far from being universally felt. The article on **Radical Orthodoxy** points to a highly sophisticated intellectual attempt to respond to the situation with old Christian guns, refurbished, still blazing: even in the old Christian dogs there is still plenty of life, and some of the so-called liberal agonizing can seem to be futile in principle, intellectually and morally or religiously. For others, it is a necessary pain, or else an adventure of the spirit, that comes with living in the world of our time, God-given.

The articles fall, as we have seen, into the three broad areas of history, thought, and culture. Of course, many of them spread across the theoretical boundaries between these three areas, and no attempt has been made to say into which category a given article should be placed. Hence, articles appear in alphabetical order rather than in groups by subject matter. So the three areas represent a description of intended coverage—which is as wide as could reasonably be attempted, though of course, it will not be hard to spot omissions and instances of regrettable neglect.

The glossary is designed to illuminate either technical terms that crop up from time to time and may be unfamiliar or to throw light on half-understood terms that are relevant. At the end of the book, readers will find a thorough subject index to assist not only with locating specific information, but also with making connections among the various entries in more intricate fashion than can be accomplished by the end-of-entry cross-references.

Finally, it should be noted that the book is not a work of reference about "Christianity" or "Christian thought" as a whole, still less about "God" or "theology" in general. It is about Jesus. So the reader should add mentally to the titles of articles "Jesus in the thought of . . ." or "Jesus in relation to . . ." It would have been tedious for all articles to have begun with "J," so the number of those that begin with the name has been kept to a minimum.

The Contributors

For readers who would welcome a note on the contributors, a list is provided (see page ix). Any editor of a work of this kind encounters a similar range of issues, difficulties, and pleasures. Realities are liable to frustrate hopes: desired contributors are unable to help, but many lift the spirits by the excellence of their pieces. The editor is limited by the range of his acquaintance and knowledge, though he will consult as widely as he can. Naturally, neither his choices nor what they produce will please all readers or chime in with their own approach. Some contributors may even be horrified when they discover the bedfellows they have been given! These are hazards that can scarcely be helped. This editor has sought to enlist a wide range of writers, in terms of their academic background, religious affiliation, gender, and nationality. The editor may be felt to have contributed too many articles himself, though other editors of comparable works have written more. In defense, it is sometimes easier to write oneself than to recruit others. And, amid all the diversity, there may be advantage in having a number of articles that come from a single head—unless of course one is a reader who finds that head maddening.

Acknowledgments

I wish to express my warm appreciation to Tony Sloggett and Simon Mason of ABC-CLIO in Oxford and to Martha Whitt and her associates in ABC-CLIO's offices in Santa Barbara and Denver for the great smoothness and pleasure of working alongside them in the preparation of this work. Also, of course, to the large band of contributors for their ready cooperation, in some cases well beyond the call of duty.

—Leslie Houlden, October 2005

A

Acts of the Apostles

See Luke, Gospel of, and Acts of the Apostles; Second Coming of Jesus, Origins of

Adoptianism

Adoptianism (also commonly spelled *adoptionism)* is the modern technical term for a style of understanding the person and role of Jesus that can be identified classically in certain minor Christian thinkers (e.g., Theodotus of Byzantium, teaching in Rome; more famously, Paul of Samosata; and probably Marcellus of Ancyra) of the second, third, and fourth centuries. Their views were always overshadowed by other ways of thinking, and they soon came to be seen as deeply erroneous heretics, whose views were Jewish in provenance. They have never been rehabilitated, except, perhaps, in part and covertly, as the texts that lay behind them have come to be read more sympathetically and in their own right.

The heart of the adoptianist position is that Jesus was not "son of God" from all eternity, but this status was bestowed on him at a certain point in his human existence, most likely his baptism, when God is depicted (Mark 1.11, and parallels in Matthew and Luke) as solemnly giving him this title. It follows that in any discussion of the relationship between divine and human in the person of Jesus the adoptianist gives at least temporal priority to his humanness, and thereby breaks up any idea of his being always a union of human and divine. There was then a risk of joining up with the idea that after his human death, his divine self alone survived, and gone would be any belief that in Christ God had joined humanness forever with himself. The Incarnation, if that is a word that could still be used, was a transient phase in the divine "biography."

All the ancient and classical positions on the person of Jesus leaned upon a combination of Scriptural texts and underlying philosophical (or at any rate in some way intellectual) assumptions, often unconsciously affecting the way in which the texts themselves were read (even though they may originally have belonged to a different thought-world), and affecting too the choice of texts that stood out in bright lights in the context of the discussion. There can be no doubt that, because of its readier accessibility to being taken in the prevailing Platonic style of thought (misjudged in terms of its own milieu though this almost certainly was), the Gospel of John was the frontrunner when it came to formulating ideas on this question of Jesus' identity. The other Gospels might be quoted (though less than one might suppose) for Jesus' moral teaching, and, of course, massively, the Old Testament for essential prophetic backing, but John gave central (though, alas, not always unambiguous) teachings, even slogans, for doctrine concerning the nature of God and of Christ—in effect the classic orthodox teachings on the Trinity and the Person of Christ, the two great foci of Christian intellectual attention and controversy in the third, fourth, and fifth centuries. It was inevitable that in such a climate, adoptianist teaching should get short shrift, for it lacked any sense of the pre-existence of Christ, which became almost common ground by the later third century, especially in Alexandrian theology. Only its precise character remained to be defined—to the extent that in the Arian controversy, it can almost be said that the most theologically interesting thing Jesus ever did was to have pre-existed (i.e., before he ever entered this world at all).

This is a far cry from the main preoccupations of very many Christians of more recent times, and certainly from modern ways of reading the New Testament. For example, if we let each of the writers have his own voice, it is apparent that a belief in Jesus' pre-existence is to be found only in Paul (e.g., 1 Cor. 8.6; 2 Cor. 8.9) and John (1.1–14; 8.58; 17.24), and perhaps in Hebrews (1.3)—and even here the interpretation is not beyond challenge. It seems to stem from a Jewish manner of speaking of those items and factors (like the Law and the design of the Temple) that were crucial to Judaism: one could convey their vital character by holding that they had always existed—as it were, in the mind of God (cf. Exodus 25.40). For the Christian, the centrality of Jesus might, even must in some minds, be thus expressed.

Other New Testament writers walked in other (equally Jewish, of course) tracks—including the writers of the first three Gospels. Equally convinced of the centrality of Jesus in the good purposes of God, they expressed it in other ways, notably by the force of prophecy that gave infallible backing to all that Jesus was and did. In such a climate, it was inevitable that Jesus was soon seen, like heroic prophets of old, as one chosen for his vital role (cf. Psalm 2.7; 2 Samuel 7.14; Isa. 7.14). Not surprisingly, they could differ in identifying the episode in Jesus' life to which the call or authentication by God was attached, and there is a tendency to push it further and further back: in Mark the baptism, in Matthew the promise of birth (1.18ff.), in Luke the conception (1.26–35). (Finally, in John, the absolute "beginning," 1.1.)

But to call this way of thinking found in the first three Gospels by the heresy-branding term "adoptianism," with its implication that the real truth about Jesus was that he belonged in some "higher" and eternal position (e.g., as God's pre-existent Word), is wholly anachronistic. Better to see that different early Christian circles worked things out along different lines. Moreover, to differentiate in this qualitative way means giving to "son of God" a literal, biographical sense (leaving only the question when the "begetting" happened), rather than its being, surely, a matter of status, operating in the mode of poetry or symbolism. It was a statement of faith in what Jesus was in God's purposes—that is, his essential agent for salvation, not the record of a fact of history, let alone of an unusual biological event. But it is evident that the claim of some of the early adoptianists that their doctrine went back to the beginnings of Christianity seems now very hard wholly to deny. Perhaps we should say that by the time that doctrine was beginning to be defined and as other ideas came to have greater weight in the Church, their style of thinking had become something of a dinosaur—left over from an earlier time. Not that, given the poor sense of historical development at the time, people, on either side, saw it like that: there was little scope for such a style of discussion, only for deciding between "true" and "false." It is perhaps not surprising that the historical simplicity of adoptianist perspectives is likely now to raise sympathetic echoes; but it is as anachronistic to suppose that we now can really see as they saw as it is to condemn them for rejecting equally time-related views that happen to have had a longer and more prestigious shelf-life.

A modern, historically minded person may well feel some affinity with the adoptianist teaching: it is, after all, likely, as a matter of historical fact, that Jesus became aware of his prophetic vocation and mission at some stage in his life, which we cannot know for certain, though baptism at the hands of John the Baptist, already engaged in a preaching mission of repentance and regeneration, is a very good candidate. But adoptianism is highly unlikely to have arisen out of any such historical train of thought. It grew rather out of a conservative, Jewish-style strain of Christian thinking, seen, with variations, in each of the synoptic Gospels, which took for granted the oneness of God, king of all, and interpreted the place of Jesus in the light of that belief. It was the increasing elaborateness of Christian belief, arising from other strands, such as those found in embryo in Paul and John, that led to the ruling out of such a way of thinking. And that was perhaps only possible because the first three Gospels were read, not in the light of their theological standpoint, but simply as lives of Jesus, containing the precious record of his deeds and teaching.

Leslie Houlden

See also: Alexandrian Theology; Ignatius of Antioch; John, Gospel of; John the Baptist; Son of God; Textual Criticism

References

Kelly, J. N. D. 1958. *Early Christian Doctrines*. London: A. and C. Black.
Hurtado, Larry W. 1998. *One God, One Lord*. 2d ed. Edinburgh: T. and T. Clark.

African Christianity

Introduction

With Africa now a new heartland of the gospel, perceptions of Jesus in Africa today form a vital contribution to the history of Christian thought. Like believers from every church era and every continent, African Christians address the fundamental question of Jesus: "Who do you say that I am?" (Mark

8.29). Their responses, which make up contemporary African Christologies, reveal images of Jesus derived not only from biblical and Christian traditions but also from African realities, both past and present. In so doing, these Christologies offer fresh insights into the identity and significance of Jesus Christ at the turn of the third millennium.

This article introduces emergent African Christologies by first outlining various factors that shape their present formulation. Central images of Jesus in sub-Saharan Africa today are then identified, before considering the significance of contemporary African Christologies to the African context and for world Christianity.

Factors Shaping Contemporary African Christologies

Recent reflections on African Christianity stress the need for African believers to understand and appropriate Jesus in ways that are meaningful and relevant to their own mentality and experience. The call does not overlook the fact that indigenous Christians have perceived Jesus "through African eyes" ever since Christianity arrived on their continent. Examples of informal Christologies abound in the preaching, prayers, songs, rites, and iconography of African Christians, particularly among the so-called African Independent Churches or African Initiated Churches (AICs). Thus African believers have naturally interpreted Jesus in light of received biblical teaching *and* their own cultural heritage.

Nonetheless, it is only in recent decades that formal, academic expressions of Christology have become prominent in the writings of African theologians south of the Sahara. Charles Nyamiti, a leading theologian from Tanzania, defines African Christology more broadly as discourse on Christ that is consonant with African thinking and needs, and more narrowly as the systematic and scientific elaboration of reflections on Christ in keeping with African concerns and thought forms. Theologians acknowledge the danger of generalizations about Africa that lack sufficient regard for the diversity of peoples, languages, cultures, and histories represented. However, many assume enough homogeneity in the African experience to justify discussions of "African" Christology. Furthermore, theologians usually guard against generalizations by grounding their theological reflections in a particular group. Consequently, the plural form "Christologies" is widely used, with rationale for plurality found in biblical and historical precedents. Just as the New Testament and later Christian writers provide various portraits of Jesus, so too diverse Christologies arise in Africa today stemming from differences in political, cultural, linguistic, and denominational backgrounds. In addition, African theologians emphasize that Christology encompasses not only formal written expressions but also informal oral expressions located in the vital Christian experience presently manifest in Africa.

What accounts for the current Christological concentration in Africa? The rapid flourishing of Christologies since the 1980s, approximately, must be interpreted in light of political, cultural, and theological developments in twentieth-century Africa. African theology emerged as an intellectual discipline during the 1950s and 1960s, when many nations achieved political independence through widespread struggle against colonialism. Confronted by the assumed collusion between Christianity and colonialism, voiced especially by African intellectuals, African theologians strove to establish the case for being authentically African *and* Christian. Hence early efforts focused on formulating an apologetic for African theology in the face of nationalist critique and missionary domination of African churches. Christology was certainly inherent in this initial stage and then burgeoned once African theology gained recognition.

A cultural revolution accompanied the political "wind of change" that swept across the continent. Seeking to overcome the widespread denigration of traditional cultures during colonial times, Africans sought to reaffirm their identity and integrity by recovering indigenous names, dress, music, dance, and other art forms. Cultural revival was further reinforced through literary, historical, and philosophical writers. This ferment of revitalizing African cultures likewise stimulated efforts to indigenize local churches, thereby influencing emergent Christologies.

Theological developments, both globally and within Africa, also fostered creative Christological reflection. For example, the Second Vatican Council from 1962 to 1965 sanctioned a radical reappraisal of church life and re-evaluated non-Christian religions and cultures more positively. Consequently, Roman Catholic Christians in particular found greater freedom to articulate Christology from an African perspective. Pope Paul VI's visit to Kampala in 1969 spawned further theological reflection when he urged the bishops to cultivate an African Christianity. Moreover, new initiatives in Catholic and Protestant theologies coalesced through African participation in the wider context of Third World theology, including the Ecumenical Association of Third World Theologians (EATWOT) and the Ecumenical Association of African Theologians (EAAT). Finally, the remarkable rise of AICs throughout the twentieth century raised the profile of Christian presence in Africa and prompted African Christians from mission churches to reformulate their faith so as to be more meaningful to their members. In the process, nascent Christologies increasingly exhibited their origins in African contexts.

What factors have induced these new African Christologies? Ghanaian theologian John Pobee gives succinct expression to the complexity of issues when he describes African Christianity in terms of "the North Atlantic Captivity of the Church." That is to say, African Christians lament the ongoing domination of Western Christianity in Africa as manifest in theology and in church polity and practice. Within this general malaise, several elements bear upon the expressed Christologies.

In particular, historical and missiological issues prompt contemporary African Christologies. For instance, the strongly perceived historical collusion between missionaries and colonialists, plus the close association between Christianity and Western culture, have led some African Christians to perceive Jesus as being white, European, and consequently "foreign," as well as being submissive to the status quo. Theological issues then flow from this association of Christianity with Western civilization, which African believers now perceive to be a theological misconception. That is, Africans decry the "Judaizing" tendencies of Western missionaries to fashion the Christian faith according to their own heritage, and therefore seek to interpret Jesus authentically as Africans.

As a result of these factors, critical issues regarding African Christian identity come to light. Against the common experience of Africans straddling two seemingly disparate worlds of Christianity and African culture, described as African duality or "spiritual schizophrenia," efforts are made to appropriate Jesus as *African Christians*. Additionally, gender issues emerge from the lack of gender inclusiveness characteristic of the modern missionary movement, inspiring new efforts to glean women's perspectives on the person of Jesus. Finally, issues of language are crucial, for the continued domination of colonial languages urgently requires African Christologies to be articulated in the linguistic and conceptual categories appropriate to their contexts. These interrelated factors, whether stemming from Africa's past history or present realities, are therefore fundamental to the perceptions of Jesus articulated by African Christians today.

Thus what makes Christologies "African"? As African believers reflect on the identity and significance of Jesus today, they consciously appropriate Christ according to biblical revelation and in keeping with their own thought forms and contextual realities. In the process, they employ new sources and methods that lend distinctive shape to African Christologies. For example, among the sources currently advocated, the Bible is highlighted as primary and Christian tradition is acknowledged as essential. In addition, however, the African heritage features prominently, including aspects of traditional African cultures and religions plus the lived experience of the African Church, particularly that of the AICs. Likewise contemporary realities in Africa—whether political, economic, or social—elicit serious reflection, thereby marking African Christologies. Corresponding to these sources, Christological methods currently evidence two main approaches: (1) from the Bible to the African context(s), or moving from the biblical material about Christ to address specific issues in Africa; and (2) from the African context(s) to Christology, drawing upon the specified African cultural background or contemporary context as the locus for Christological formulation. In sum, African Christologies are prompted by the factors outlined above and distinguished by these particular sources and methods.

Central Images of Jesus in Africa Today

African Christologies are often presented according to the two main trends of African theology that emerged from the 1950s to the 1980s: "inculturation," which seeks to incarnate the Gospel in African cultures, and "liberation," which addresses socioeconomic and political ills in light of the Gospel. Although this broad twofold classification has been instructive in introducing the field of African theology, the dichotomy is increasingly called into question. Instead, theologians acknowledge that inculturation and liberation are intrinsically related to each other and equally necessary. Hence an integrative approach is currently advocated in constructing African Christologies. Correspondingly, a unified approach is adopted here in analyzing the vast array of contemporary African Christologies according to central themes. Four broad categories of images overlap with one another, and each category represents a cluster of related themes. Although the following outline is neither exclusive nor exhaustive, it offers a brief summary of central images of Jesus in Africa today.

Jesus as Life-Giver

Although "life" is a universal aspiration, it is especially prominent as a cardinal value in traditional African thought. Therefore how Jesus is perceived in relation to life, with respect to traditional thought and contemporary realities, features significantly in African Christianity. African concepts of life, as interpreted by Christians, provide the mental categories that converge with biblical affirmations to formulate images of Jesus as life-giver, or the one who fulfills African aspirations for life. For example, life, often designated "life-force" or "vital union," is a central focus of many African religions. Traditionally understood, life has its origin and fullness in God, and it is mediated through a hierarchical order of visible and invisible powers: from God through deceased clan and family members, through living leaders and family members, and even to the realm of nature. Participation in this common life is absolutely fundamental to individual and communal life, for the individual is thought to exist only in relation to the community. These facets of life in traditional African thought often lend shape to African Christians' perceptions of Jesus and the abundant life he brings (e.g., John 10.10; 14.6).

Contemporary realities in Africa, like the massive suffering from preventable diseases, AIDS, famine, poverty, injustice, ethnocentrism, and violence, further influence the expressed notions of Jesus as life-giver. In contrast to the respect traditionally accorded to life, widespread violations of the sacredness of life elicit sharp castigation from African theologians. Therefore, among the various images of Jesus in relation to life, such as creator, preserver, protector, and provider, a central image is undoubtedly that of Jesus as healer, or one who restores life. In preaching and prayers, testimony and songs, religious rites and theological texts, evidence abounds for the paramount importance of Jesus as healer. This is particularly the case among the AICs, which now inspire greater attentiveness to healing ministries among many Western-initiated churches that had previously neglected traditional African concepts of illness and ceded healing ministries to doctors and hospitals.

Rationale for appropriating Jesus as healer is found primarily in biblical teaching, particularly in the Gospel accounts of Jesus' healing ministry. Contemporary experience provides further grounds for the image, whether personal experience of healing attested by African believers or the prevalence of healing ministries in African Christianity today. Four main affirmations serve to summarize the meaning of the Christological image. First, the image of Jesus as healer corresponds to that of Jesus as life-giver, for it asserts that Jesus restores life wherever it has been diminished. Second, Jesus' healing is understood as the re-creation of wholeness in all aspects of life, encompassing the individual, communal, and cosmic spheres. Third, Jesus as healer signifies

Jesus' supremacy over all evil powers at play in the universe, whether manifest in the physical, psychological, spiritual, social, or any other realm. Finally, this Christological image is intrinsically related to other significant affirmations of Jesus as savior, liberator, and redeemer. Thus Jesus as healer is considered fundamental to inculturation and liberation.

One related, though controversial, image is that of Jesus as traditional healer. For example, some portray Jesus as *nganga*, the vernacular term (or its cognates) in many Bantu languages for the medicine person anachronistically translated "witch doctor." The Christological image is disputed, with objections stemming primarily from the negative connotations surrounding the term, often influenced by colonial and missionary hostilities toward this traditional figure, and the consequent fear of syncretism in associating Jesus with *nganga*. Conversely, evidence indicates that this image may potentially deepen African Christians' understanding of Jesus in relation to concepts from the African heritage. In other words, Jesus is perceived to accomplish the work of *nganga* in terms of healing, protecting from evil powers, and restoring community relations where disruption has occurred in the social fabric. Although the controversy is not readily resolved, it does illustrate the complex issues entailed in Christological formulation within the interface of Gospel and culture in Africa.

Jesus as Mediator

The concept of intermediaries is widespread throughout Africa. When a community experiences afflictions, such as illness, wrongdoing, or witchcraft, African religions look to intermediaries to discern the reasons for the disharmony evident in their universe and to rectify the problem, thereby mediating reconciliation. John Mbiti, an eminent Kenyan writer on African religions and Christianity, explains that the traditional notion of intermediaries is derived from common social and political custom in which people of higher status are approached indirectly through a third party. Consequently, while people certainly can and do approach God directly, they generally do so through the mediation of certain specialists or other beings. Mbiti identifies two types of intermediaries: human beings, such as priests, kings, healers, and diviners, and spiritual beings, believed to assist people in establishing closer contact with God. Although African peoples vary in their beliefs about the spirit world, most societies accord tremendous significance to the spirits of those recently deceased. Coined "the living-dead" by Mbiti, or "the ancestors" more generally, these spirits are often regarded as the best intermediaries, since they are believed to know the needs of humans and to have enhanced spiritual powers through closer proximity to God.

Given the significance of mediators in the African heritage, it is not surprising that African Christians have interpreted Jesus in relation to such notions. Depictions include Jesus as prophet, priest, lamb, sacrifice, reconciler, and peacemaker. One of the more significant images to emerge in this category is that of Jesus as ancestor. A brief outline of this admittedly controversial image illustrates the convergence of biblical and African traditions in current Christological formulation.

First, several critical issues emerge in examining Jesus as ancestor. Methodologically, the diversity of ethnic societies across Africa raises the danger of unwarranted generalizations about African beliefs concerning ancestors. Linguistically, problems stem from the word "ancestor" as the English translation for various African vernacular terms with different denotations and connotations. Theologically, important questions arise in relating Jesus to concepts of African ancestors: (1) the theological interpretation of the ancestors' identity, including the long-standing debate over whether African ancestors are actually worshipped or merely venerated; (2) the possible place of African ancestors within the Christian faith, especially with respect to certain doctrines regarding Christian saints; and (3) the role of African ancestors as mediators in relation to Christian claims of the sole mediation of Jesus Christ. The intricate issues involved account for the controversy surrounding the image of Jesus as ancestor.

Despite the challenges inherent in proposing this Christological portrait, an increasing number of African Christians affirm its meaning and significance to them. For example, Bénézet Bujo, a theologian from the Democratic Republic of Congo, advocates the image of Jesus as "Ancestor Par Excellence" or "Proto-Ancestor." Bujo develops a comprehensive ancestral theology by drawing parallels between ancestral beliefs and biblical teachings, in each case emphasizing that Jesus infinitely transcends the ideal of the God-fearing African ancestors. Other African believers likewise elucidate how Jesus fulfills the role that was traditionally played by the ancestors. Four main ancestral functions are delineated. First, Jesus is the mediator between God and humanity, analogous to the ancestors. Second, he is the founder of a new community of believers, and, as such, establishes its identity. Third, he continues to participate in the life of that community, in terms of his ongoing presence and power, which far exceed that of the ancestors. Finally, just as the goal of ancestral veneration in Africa is to foster abundant life, so Jesus is believed to provide the fullness of life that the ancestors sought for themselves and to transmit to their descendants.

Conversely, many African Christians object to the portrayal of Jesus as ancestor for various reasons. Historical and missiological factors hinder its appropriation, such as the negative connotations that became associated with the African ancestors through missionary denigration of them, plus the modernization and urbanization that often distance Christians from this aspect of their cultural heritage. The most serious objections, however, are theological. African ancestors are deemed inappropriate for analogous relationship with Jesus, on the grounds of contrasting definitions, qualifications, and characteristics of ancestors. Consequently, it is argued, to portray Jesus as ancestor or even "Proto-Ancestor" is to compromise his divinity.

Thus the controversy continues as some African Christians perceive Jesus as one who fits but also transcends the category of ancestors, while others firmly reject any such notion. Despite the current inconclusiveness, what lies beyond dispute is that in proposing this image from its own context of faith, Christianity in Africa is making a decisive impact upon the ongoing development of Christian thought.

Jesus as Loved One

Although core notions of kinship and communal life in Africa are foundational to all four categories of Christological themes, they are especially prominent in this third category, Jesus as loved one. In traditional African thought, as indicated above, the life of the individual is established and fulfilled only in relation to the life of the community. Thus to be is to participate in community, which encompasses the living, the dead, and the not-yet-born. Although this emphasis on family and community is not peculiarly African, it is characteristically African to conceive of family as "extended" rather than "nuclear." Hence theologians such as J. N. K. Mugambi from Kenya argue that the definition of family as a nuclear social unit is not strictly biblical, but rather a product of industrialization and urbanization. Despite the assault of modernization upon traditional family structures and communal life, these underlying values remain a typical feature of many African societies. Therefore family and communal experience undoubtedly influence how Jesus is appropriated by African Christians today.

This third category represents a cluster of relational images portraying Jesus as intimate family member and friend. For instance, Jesus is evidently perceived in Africa as brother, mother, father, and husband. Further examples convey consciousness of the companionship and personal presence of Christ as friend, guide, counselor, and comforter. Summary sketches of a few key images illustrate the interplay between biblical revelation and African existential realities in the expressed Christologies of African believers.

The image of Jesus as brother is found in formal and informal Christologies, based on New Testament evidence from Jesus' teaching and, for example, Paul's exhortations regarding believers being coheirs with Christ. Traditional African concepts of brotherhood also contribute to perceptions of Jesus, including notions of provision, protection, and being head of the family, particularly when assuming the role of the father. Thus when biblical teaching is appropriated through the experience of brotherhood in the African context, various facets of this Christological image come to light: the humanity of Jesus, his intimacy, availability, attentiveness, solidarity, and support. Furthermore, African Christians appeal to the image of Jesus as universal brother, who alone unites all humanity into a single clan and ethnic group, in order to overcome widespread ethnic hostilities across the continent.

African perceptions of Jesus as family member extend to parental images, notably that of Jesus as mother. For example, Kenyan theologian Anne Nasimiyu Wasike promotes this image, developing an analogy between Jesus' ministry and African concepts of motherhood. A mother is traditionally understood as one who nurtures life in all its dimensions, and one who symbolizes loving kindness, compassion, and mercy. Against the backdrop of life-diminishing forces in contemporary Africa, including structural adjustment programs, crippling economic debts, and civil wars, Nasimiyu Wasike asserts that Jesus as mother calls all believers—women *and* men—to protect and nurture life without discrimination on the basis of ethnicity, social, economic, or political ideology, or gender. This Christological image also emerges as an indigenous insight in certain prayers, songs, and sermons, particularly in vernacular languages. Since many African religions view God as mother and father, African Christians do not necessarily hesitate in extending the maternal imagery to Jesus. These believers insist that the Christological image is not tied to gender, but rather conveys the qualities associated with ideal motherhood. Other Christians, however, reject the image on the grounds of the historical Jesus being male. Yet they concede that the love of Christ, among other attributes, is akin to that of a mother. Thus the image of Jesus as mother not only illustrates indigenous perceptions of Christ in Africa but also serves to recover certain feminine aspects of the Triune God that may not be adequately acknowledged in Western Christologies.

Finally, various images related to Jesus as friend are extensive in African Christianity today. The depth of intimacy they convey reflects the universality and the particularity of the Christian faith. That is, the significance of the Incarnation lies not only in the Son of God's becoming human but also in his ongoing entrance into particular human communities as, for example, African Christians embrace him as family member and friend.

Jesus as Leader

Although concepts and practices of leadership vary throughout Africa, they provide powerful avenues for Christological reflection. Like the leadership roles discussed above, such as traditional healers or family heads who become ancestors, other governing functions in the sociopolitical and religious realms are applied analogously to Jesus. Two examples suffice to illustrate that these leadership images are derived from the gospel's encounter with the African heritage and contemporary realities.

Among the Akan people of Ghana, the image of Jesus as king/chief indicates the conviction of local believers that Jesus fulfills the leadership expectations in traditional thought. Exposition of the Akan king's role as "priest/chief/king," combining religious, social, and political leadership, serves to illuminate aspects of New Testament Christology. Hence Akan Christians ascribe traditional vernacular titles, honorifics, symbols, and leadership functions to Jesus, in each case highlighting Jesus' transcendence over human leaders (e.g., *Osagyefo*, traditionally a brave warrior or conquering king who delivers his people in battle). Consequently, Akan believers affirm that these images enhance their understanding and worship of Christ in ways that are meaningful within their cultural context.

Jesus as liberator forms a second significant leadership image that is not restricted to South Africa. On the contrary, theologians throughout the rest of sub-Saharan Africa call for liberation from cultural captivity, as well as from political, economic, and social structures that suffer enduring colonialism and neocolonialism. Cameroonian theologian Jean-Marc Ela is noteworthy for his incisive analysis of urgent problems in contemporary Africa, such as the oppressive structures of capitalist-driven globalization, as the necessary locus of theology. Among his Christological reflections that seek to recover the liberating dimensions of the gospel, he gives poignant expression to the cry of Africans' suffering throughout history being subsumed in Jesus' loud cry on the Cross. Similarly, Jesus as liberator typifies, though does not exhaust, African women's Christologies. Addressing various forms of oppression suffered under African religiocultural traditions, Western Christianity, and contemporary socioeconomic and political realities, women offer distinctive perspectives on the identity and significance of Jesus in Africa today. For example, Ghanaian theologian Mercy Oduyoye integrates biblical and African traditions in explicating a multidimensional portrait of Jesus as savior/liberator/redeemer. She then relates the significance of this image to the African context according to the goal of feminist theology, which she identifies to be women and men seeking together to become fully human.

Thus various images arise in the category of Jesus as leader. Yet a certain congruence emerges between African Christologies derived from traditional leadership and those advocated in contemporary liberation Christologies. Jesus therefore represents both the fulfillment of leadership expectations in traditional African thought and of current yearnings for liberation in all dimensions of life.

Conclusion

Contemporary African Christologies warrant serious attention on account of Africa's prominent place in world Christianity today. Christological reflections flourish across the continent, demonstrating the recent rise of "contextual" theologies that seek to engage seriously with the context or life situation of the people from whom and for whom they are written. As African believers increasingly appropriate Jesus in accordance with biblical and Christian tradition *and* historical and current realities in Africa, significance emerges both for African and for world Christianity.

In line with an axiom of Third World theology, African Christologies manifest an essential commitment to critical reflection and praxis, or committed action. Far from abstract, academic pursuits, these Christologies generally arise from believers witnessing to Jesus while grappling with the concrete issues of everyday life. Thus, parallel to first-century Christianity, Christological articulations evidently emerge through personal encounter with Jesus Christ, then expressed in the community of faith, particularly in the context of worship. Hence the creative Christologies voiced in the preaching, songs, prayers, and testimonial confessions not only attest to the vibrancy of African Christianity but also fuel the critical reflections of African theologians. Within this ongoing process of Christological formulation, the importance of vernacular comes to light. Likewise African women's Christologies are noteworthy, for in highlighting African women's experience as a locus of theology, they manifest the deep conviction of Jesus' suffering and solidarity with them in widespread situations of poverty, adversity, indignity, injustice, and violence. Altogether, then, African Christians attest to the significance of Jesus in their personal formation, social transformation, and ecclesiastical reformation. Notwithstanding the gravity of issues still in need of address in Africa, evidence indicates that African Christologies contribute substantially to the renewal of individuals and communities. In so doing, they characterize African Christianity in its efforts to integrate orthodoxy and orthopraxy.

The very dynamism of Christianity in Africa today suggests that the expressed Christologies bear significance for world Christianity. Most fundamentally, the present proliferation of Christology in Africa demonstrates the universality of the gospel, not only in principle but also in practice. In other words, emergent Christologies illustrate that Jesus truly "tabernacles" in every cultural context. Granted, the risk arises of misconstruing biblical teaching about Jesus' proper identity and significance by adopting insufficiently critical interpretations of him derived from indigenous concepts. The potential for misinterpretation increases because of the extensiveness of African Christianity and its multitudinous expressions. Generally speaking, however, the risk is countered by the biblical and ecumenical orientation of the African Christologies. Issues of biblical scholarship, particularly biblical hermeneutics, require due attention in Africa; nonetheless, the centrality of the Bible in the Christological reflection and praxis of African believers lies beyond dispute. Likewise, on the whole, African Christians uphold the humanity and the divinity of Jesus Christ as non-negotiables within their faith, thereby aligning themselves with Christian tradition from apostolic times to the present. Furthermore, African theologians increasingly emphasize the importance of Christological formulation within the local faith community as well as in dialogue with other faith communities across denominational, national, and religious borders. In fostering such engagement among faith communities across Africa and around the globe, African Christians confirm that no single cultural context can claim a monopoly on Christology. Rather, the multiplicity of local "faces of Jesus" in Africa enhances the discovery of the fullness of Christ that transcends all cultural constructs of the gospel. Consequently, images of Jesus in contemporary African Christianity duly enrich our corporate understanding of Christ in the worldwide Church.

Diane B. Stinton

See also: Christology, Modern; Coptic Christianity; Ethiopian Christianity; Liberation Theology; Literature, World

References

Appiah-Kubi, Kofi. 1987. "Christology." Pp. 69–81 in *A Reader in African Christian Theology*. Edited by John Parratt. London: SPCK.

Bediako, Kwame. 1990. *Jesus in African Culture: A Ghanaian Perspective*. Accra: Asempa.

Bujo, Bénézet. 1992. *African Theology in Its Social Context*. Translated by John O'Donohue. Nairobi: St. Paul.

Ela, Jean-Marc. 1994. "The Memory of the African People and the Cross of Christ." Pp. 17–35 in *The Scandal of a Crucified World: Perspectives on the Cross and Suffering*. Translated and edited by Yacob Tesfai. Maryknoll, NY: Orbis.

Manus, Ukachukwu Chris. 1998. "African Christologies: The Centre-Piece of African Christian Theology." *Zeitschrift für Missionswissenschaft und Religionswissenschaft* 82: 3–23.

Mbiti, John S. 1972. "Some African Concepts of Christology." Pp. 51–62 in *Christ and the Younger Churches*. Edited by Georg F. Vicedom. London: SPCK.

Mugambi, J. N. K., and Laurenti Magesa, eds. 1989. *Jesus in African Christianity: Experimentation and Diversity in African Christology*. African Christianity Series. Nairobi: Initiatives.
Nyamiti, Charles. 1984. *Christ as Our Ancestor: Christology from an African Perspective*. Mambo Occasional Papers—Missio-Pastoral Series, no. 11. Gweru, Zimbabwe: Mambo.
———. 1994. "Contemporary African Christologies: Assessment and Practical Suggestions." Pp. 62–77 in *Paths of African Theology*. Edited by Rosino Gibellini. London: SCM.
Oduyoye, Mercy Amba. 2001. *Introducing African Women's Theology*. Introductions in Feminist Theology, no. 6. Edited by Mary Grey et al. Sheffield: Sheffield Academic.
Pobee, John S. 1979. *Toward an African Theology*. Nashville: Abingdon.
———, ed. 1992. *Exploring Afro-Christology*. Frankfurt: Peter Lang.
Schreiter, Robert J., ed. 1991. *Faces of Jesus in Africa*. Faith and Cultures Series. Edited by Schreiter. Maryknoll, NY: Orbis.

Alexandrian Theology

The term "Alexandrian theology" is something of a shorthand expression. As used here, it refers to a vision of the person and work of Christ that was characteristic of, but not limited to, the thinkers and writers of the great city of Alexandria in the period between the beginning of the fourth century and the middle of the fifth. It was a crucial period in the development of classical Christological doctrine. In the last couple of decades of that period, the theology of Alexandria was locked in a bitter struggle with the rival theology of Antioch, a struggle that largely shaped the definition of the relation of the divine and human in Christ, which was to emerge from the Council of Chalcedon in 451.

It would be possible to begin the story of Alexandrian Christology further back and to include the theology of Origen from the middle of the third century. He was, after all, an Alexandrian, and his thought heavily influenced that of his successors, both positively and negatively—both when they followed him and when they reacted against him. But there are significant lines of discontinuity as well—above all a turning away from a highly Platonic and intellectualized scheme of things toward a greater concern with the physicality of fleshly existence.

As used here, then, "Alexandrian theology" describes a more or less coherent theological vision. It is the theology of Athanasius and Cyril. It is the vision that came to dominate the Christian East—Chalcedonian and non-Chalcedonian alike—and that at least from the time of Thomas Aquinas was to exert a powerful influence on the Latin West as well.

The Alexandrian picture of Christ can, using another piece of shorthand, be characterized as a Word/flesh (*Logos/sarx*) theology (using a schema developed above all by Aloys Grillmeier), in contrast to the Word/human (*Logos/anthropos*) pattern favored by the theologians of Antioch. This does *not* mean that writers like Athanasius and Cyril denied the humanity of Jesus; indeed, for both, the normal word for incarnation was, literally, "in-human-ment" rather than "in-flesh-ment." It does, however, mean that their language is characteristically shaped on the pattern of the Johannine prologue: "the Word became flesh" (John 1.14)—where, actually, "flesh" had its old Hebrew sense of "human." And it means that their vision of the work of Christ centers on the transforming and life-giving effect of the coming of the divine into our world of human, fleshly existence.

That marks a significant point of departure from Origen. By the beginning of the fourth century, the human soul of Jesus, which was of such importance to Origen, had virtually disappeared from the theological agenda. That can be seen in the thought of Athanasius.

Athanasius became bishop of Alexandria, just under the canonical age of thirty, in 328, and he held that great see—apart from five periods when he was exiled for his views—till his death on 2 May 373. It would be tempting but misleading to say that toward the end of his life, Athanasius' central concern shifted from Trinitarian questions to Christological ones. It would be tempting because there *was* a shift of focus; it would be misleading because they were not really separate problems. Throughout, his concern was to ensure that it was God who in Jesus was believed to have entered and transformed our world of human experience.

In Athanasius' scheme of things, the central human problem—that which must be overcome in Christ—is corruption. It is not primarily sin and certainly not (as in so much Western theology) primarily the guilt that flows from sin. It is rather decay, rotting, falling apart. Corruption has a moral component and moral consequences (because we are essentially unstable, our wills are unstable, too), but that is more of a by-product or an epiphenomenon than the central problem.

The solution is for the one who is Life itself to take flesh and make it his own. But his flesh is our flesh, and so it too is filled with life. The Word makes the body his, using it as an instrument. That means that human experiences, including suffering and death, become "his own"; thus, "being hungry, being thirsty, suffering, being weary, and things of that sort, of which the flesh is receptive" are said to be "his," since the body "was the body of God" (*Contra Arianos*, 3.31).

That is strong language, and it is important to see what is being claimed and what is not. For Athanasius, as for virtually the whole of patristic thought, it was axiomatic that God is "impassible." That does not mean that he is unconcerned or uninvolved. It does mean that he is never on the receiving end. He is not passively affected by things that happen outside, because he transcends our world of cause and effect. He stands at the head of the causal chain, but is not built into it.

Athanasius' thought was shaped by his lifelong struggle against what is conveniently if misleadingly labeled "Arianism." For Arius and his friends, the Son, or Word, was called into being from nonexistence at a point in pretime ("there was when he was not"). It can be said that he is "begotten" or "created" or "appointed." In the end it makes no difference, for those are all metaphors to describe the process by which God willed him into being. For Athanasius, on the other hand, the Father does not will to have a Son; he just does. The mysterious depth of the source of divine being that is the Father continually finds expression in a Son—eternally begotten from his very being—who is all that the Father is.

Among other things, that means that the Son is impassible; he transcends that liability to change imposed from without that marks the fragility of all created things. But "being impassible God, he assumed passible flesh" (ibid., 3.55). When we look, then, at the concrete figure of the earthly Jesus as presented in the Gospels, what we see is the Word made flesh. We see one subject—one "he"—capable of acting in two modes, divinely and humanly. "If we see him doing something or saying something, through the instrument which is his own body, *divinely*, we know that he is doing it inasmuch as he is God. And again, if we see him saying something or suffering something *humanly*, we are not unaware of the fact that, wearing flesh, he became a human being, and that is the way he is doing and saying these things" (ibid., 3.35).

Through the flesh, he undergoes human weakness and limitation and in the process reverses it. "The Word himself is impassible by nature but nonetheless, because of the flesh which he put on, these things are said about him, since these things belong to the flesh, and the body actually belonged to the Saviour. And he remains as he is, impassible by nature, and is not harmed by them, but rather makes them disappear and destroys them" (ibid., 3.34).

That includes even death and its ultimate cause, our liability to corruption. He undergoes death and reverses it through the resurrection, and thereby the power of death itself is—in principle—burned out.

That, for Athanasius, is the significance of the Cross. Although he can use the language of offering and sacrifice, it is not central to his thought. Thus, in his early work *On the Incarnation*, he asks himself why Jesus died on the Cross and not in some other way. His answer is that it was not appropriate for one who cured the diseases of others to succumb to disease himself, and it was right that his death be public so that no one would doubt that he had really died (*De Incarnatione*, 21–23). In other words, the Cross was *fitting*, but if Jesus had died of pneumonia, we would still have been saved.

In all of this Athanasius has been speaking only of the flesh or the body of Jesus. In fact he never talks about a human soul in Christ. The closest he ever comes to affirming the existence of one is in the letter issued at his direction by a synod that met in Alexandria in 362. Athanasius is trying to reconcile rival factions in the church of Antioch, and in the letter he acknowledges the validity of alternative theological expressions, some of which he does not particularly like himself. The synod asserts that "the Saviour had a body not unsouled nor without perception nor without rational mind" (*Tomus ad Antiochenos*, 7). But to use three negative adjectives ("un-souled," "un-perceptive," "un-minded") is not quite the same thing as to say explicitly that Jesus did indeed have a human, rational soul.

Athanasius never denies that there was a human soul in Christ, either—but he certainly never does anything with it theologically. He never gives it a job to do. In the Garden, for example, when Jesus prayed that the cup should pass from him (Matt. 26.39), he did so because "having been made human, he had flesh which was afraid." He himself—that is, the Word incarnate—willed the Passion, but "fear belonged to the flesh" (*C. Ar.*, 3.57).

From a post-Cartesian perspective or from the standpoint of modern psychology, that sounds distinctly odd. But two things must be said. The first is that Athanasius sees the human person very much as a psycho-physical unity. Jesus' flesh is animated and rational flesh, as the *Tome to the Antiochenes* affirms, and in that it is like our flesh.

The second point is that Athanasius was not interested in what he would have seen as the unanswerable question of what went on in Jesus' head. For that matter, he was not overly interested in what goes on in our heads, either. What he is concerned with is that in Jesus, God has broken into our world of corruption and decay and transformed it from within. And it is through our flesh that we are joined to the Word, through our flesh that we share in that transformation.

To be sure, the human mind should in principle provide the path back to God (*Contra Gentes*, 30). The Word is the image of the Father, and we are made *in* that image. That means that there is within each human person what Athanasius compares to a mirror; through introspection—by looking into that mirror—it should in principle be possible to see the Image and in him the Father (ibid., 8, 34). But in fact, in our world that path is blocked off; we are so mired in corruption that that very Platonic-sounding solution simply is not available. There is, for Athanasius, no short-circuiting of the saving significance of the physicality of God's presence in the world in Jesus.

When it comes to explaining how we as individuals plug into that salvation, Athanasius is rather more vague. Jesus had a teaching function. The testimony of the Word made flesh about the one God and his creation is irrefragably true, and we are meant to align ourselves with that truth. Beyond that, Athanasius has a residually Platonic vocabulary of "contemplating" God with a mind that is pure and free from distraction, and he can talk more loosely of "looking" to Jesus. But the transformation he is interested in is one that has in principle already been achieved and that in principle embraces the whole of humanity.

Around 357 Athanasius wrote—or caused to have written—the life of Antony the monk. Antony was presented as the type of the ideal human life. When he emerged from solitude after spending twenty years with no direct human contact, he looked just as he had before; he was neither fat nor thin, neither elated nor downcast (*Vita Antonii*, 14). And when he died at the age of 105, he had all his teeth (ibid., 93). Antony still dies, but he has achieved a foretaste of the incorruptibility that will be fully his—and ours—at the resurrection.

The great historian of doctrine Adolf von Harnack (q.v.) once said that Athanasius eliminates every aspect of the portrait of Christ that is evocative of the historical Jesus of Nazareth (*History of Dogma*, IV, 45). It might be truer to say that the historicity of the Word's taking flesh is of such centrality that the rest of human history has become a footnote.

A clearer and more sharply focused answer is given by Athanasius' great successor Cyril of Alexandria to the question how we as individuals come to share in the transformation achieved in Christ. Cyril became bishop of Alexandria in 412 and reigned—and the verb is not inappropriate in his case—till his death in 444. Cyril was a ruthless player in the bruising ecclesiastical power struggles of the fifth century. A hard man in a hard age, he was in his lifetime already the object of both adulation and hatred. But he was also a theologian of extraordinary depth and power whose picture of the Word made flesh came to dominate the thought and piety of the Greek-speaking East. Much of the theological controversy of the later fifth and sixth centuries involved the claims of rival schools to be the true heirs of Cyril.

Cyril's vision, like that of Athanasius, is dominated by the life-giving union of the Word with his flesh. Cyril, unlike Athanasius, is quite clear that there is a human, rational soul in Christ. He is, after all, writing after Apollinaris, and the condemnation of Apollinarianism as heretical had made the idea that there was no human soul untenable within the mainstream theological tradition. But that there is a human soul in Christ in often asserted almost parenthetically. Cyril will, for example, say that we "unite the Word from God the Father, in a way that is ineffable and beyond understanding, to the holy flesh, which has an intellectual soul" (*First Letter to Succensus*, 6). But with Cyril, as with Athanasius, the human, rational soul in Jesus does not really have anything to do, other than be there. That is, Cyril's Jesus is a man, but he is emphatically not a man standing in free moral decision before God. He is not a separate center of activity. He is not a separate subject of predication.

In the bitter controversy with Nestorius, which led to the latter's condemnation at the Council of Ephesus in 431, and in the confrontation with the theologians of Antioch, which simmered on for several years afterward, Cyril's central concern, the one thing he was not prepared to budge on, was the insistence that there were not two masculine subjects—two "he's"—in Christ. Thus, Cyril proclaims "one Son and Christ and Lord, the same God and man, not one thing and another, but being and being understood to be one and the same—both this and that," where "this" and "that" are neuter pronouns and "one" and "the same" are masculine. In that difference of gender lies the heart of Cyril's theology. To see why that is so and why it mattered so much to him and to the whole Greek tradition after him, we have to look at Cyril's vision of our salvation.

Cyril shares with Athanasius a picture of corruptible flesh that must be filled with life. If the man Jesus were an independently acting human subject, he would differ from the prophets only in degree, not in kind. If he were an independent moral agent or if he were some sort of specially honored friend of God, his achievement would have no effect on us. It is only if God himself shares the human condition of instability and vulnerability, it is only if God himself lives a human life and dies a human death, that human life is itself transformed.

God lives a human life because he takes flesh—endowed with a rational soul, Cyril will always remember to add. That flesh remains flesh—it is not swallowed up by the Godhead—but it is now "the flesh of God." If we want to engage in abstract intellectual analysis, "merely seeing with the eyes of the soul," we can distinguish in Christ two things, two realities, "two natures united," divinity and humanity (ibid., 6–7). But if we could actually see Jesus in the flesh, if we look to the Jesus of the Gospels, what actually confronts us is one living and life-giving reality, the "one nature of the Word made flesh" (and in that formula, so characteristic of Cyril's thought, the participle "made flesh" sometimes agrees with "nature" and sometimes with "Word").

Cyril is concerned throughout to work out a sort of grammar of the Incarnation. He consistently maintains that we cannot understand the *how* of the Incarnation. We have no access, from the inside as it were, to its structure, much less to what it felt like for Jesus to be God. What we do have access to are the accounts in the Creed and in the Gospels of what Jesus did.

Those accounts require us, Cyril thinks, to say that *who* Jesus is, is the Word or Son of God. There is no other "who" in the Incarnation. But that single subject now has two modes of activity. From all ages the Word of God, eternally begotten of the Father, has acted divinely, in creating and in sustaining his creation. But from a point in time, from the moment of the Incarnation, that same subject began also to act and to suffer humanly. It is the same subject, but two sets of predicates can now be applied to him.

So one has to say that the Word of God suffered and was crucified and died (*Anathema*, 12, in Cyril's *Third Letter to Nestorius*). He suffers and dies "in flesh" or "humanly" or "as man"—the qualification expresses the modality of the action—but the "he" who does it is God, the Word of God, for the simple reason that there is no other "he" in Jesus. Thus, Jesus' flesh "belongs to the very Word from God the Father" and not to "some other" (*Anathema*, 11), for there is no other to whom it could belong.

These two sets of predicates, these two languages that can be applied in parallel to the one subject who is Christ, can give rise to paradox. And Cyril and the whole devotional tradition that stems from him revels in such paradox. Thus, he delights to say that "even when he is seen as a babe and is in swaddling clothes and on the lap of the Virgin who bore him, he filled the whole of creation as God" (*Third Letter*, 3).

The Word in and of himself—the Word operating "divinely" or "as God"—remains impassible, but the sufferings are really his because the flesh that suffers is his. He "appropriates" our weakness and vulnerability and makes it his own, and by so doing "he as God made the weaknesses of flesh disappear" (*Scholia on the Incarnation*).

The Word is Life itself, and so Christ's flesh—the flesh the Word took from the Virgin, the flesh that walked around in Palestine, the flesh that now reigns with the Father—is welling with life, pulsing with life. "The flesh of the Lord is life-giving . . . since it belongs to the Word who has the power to give life to all things" (*Anathema*, 11). And that flesh we receive in the Eucharist, when "we celebrate the bloodless liturgy in the churches" (*Third Letter*, 7). Of course, we receive graced life in baptism. We feed (intellectually) on the Word in Scripture. But it is of a piece with Cyril's whole theological vision that there should above all be a very concrete and physical way in which we make that life our own.

For Cyril, as for Athanasius, the promised transformation is great. The blessing Jesus gives extends to the whole of human life. Indeed, Cyril can say—most unusually, in an ascetic age—that in going to Cana of Galilee Jesus sanctified the very beginnings of human life; in going to a wedding, he blessed and sanctified sex (ibid., 11; *Commentary on John*, 2.1).

The picture of Christ in Alexandrian theology was inevitably shaped by the problems and needs of the age. It sought to answer questions that may not be our own, and it shunned as impossible or inappropriate some characteristically modern questions, such as those concerning the psychology of Jesus or his consciousness of who he was. But it sought to give an account of how it could be said that in the man Jesus God himself had broken into our world of time and space. And it gave to the men and women of antiquity the hope and the promise of transformation—the transformation of their lives, of their bodies, and of their world.

Paul Parvis

See also: Antiochene Theology; Apollinarianism; Aquinas, Thomas; Chalcedon; Creeds; Ethiopian Christianity; Eucharist; Nicea; Origen

References

Primary

Newman, John Henry, trans. 1842–1844. *Select Treatises of St. Athanasius in Controversy with the Arians*. Oxford: John Henry Parker.

Robertson, Archibald, ed. 1892. *Select Writings and Letters of Athanasius, Bishop of Alexandria*. New York: Christian Literature.

Thomson, Robert W., ed. 1971. *Athanasius' Contra Gentes and De Incarnatione*. Oxford: Clarendon.

Wickham, Lionel R. 1983. *Cyril of Alexandria's Select Letters*. Oxford: Clarendon.

Secondary

Chadwick, Henry. 1951. "Eucharist and Christology in the Nestorian Controversy." Reprinted in *History and Thought of the Early Church*. By Chadwick. London: Variorum Reprints, 1983.

Grillmeier, Aloys. 1975. *Christ in Christian Tradition*. Vol. 1 of *From the Apostolic Age to Chalcedon (451)*. Translated by John Bowden. London: Mowbrays.

Hanson, R. P. C. 1988. *The Search for the Christian Doctrine of God: The Arian Controversy 318–381*. Edinburgh: T and T Clark.

Pettersen, A. L. 1985. "The Questioning Jesus in Athanasius' *Contra Arianos* III." Pp. 243–255 in *Arianism, Historical and Theological Reassessments, Papers from the Ninth International Conference on Patristic Studies, September 5–10, 1983, Oxford, England*. Edited by Robert C. Gregg. Philadelphia: Philadelphia Patristics Foundation.

Sellers, R. V. 1940. *Two Ancient Christologies*. London: SPCK.

American (Hispanic) Christianity

This essay addresses the question of Jesus in history, culture, and thought from the perspective of the Latino/Latina Christian community in the United States. Latin America per se is not the purview of this essay, but rather the immigrant community from Latin America, and their descendants, that now make the United States their home and the locus of their theological reflection. We can also refer to the individuals of this community as "Hispanic Americans" or simply "Hispanics." However, some debate remains around which term best fits this large and diverse population (De La Torre and Aponte, 15–16). Some prefer "Latino/a" (taking into account both genders) because of the largely Latin American roots; others use "Hispanic," which is the U.S. census term and recalls the community's European roots in Spain. Others, including many theologians, eschew the debate altogether and use the terms interchangeably, or prefer to refer to specific nationalities (for example, Puerto Rican, Mexican-American, Cubano, Dominican).

These questions are important in discussing Jesus because one of the major issues in Jesus scholarship is his identity. He was a Galilean Jew, but was he rural or urban, peasant or artisan? Issues surrounding his Gospel titles—Messiah, Son of Man, Son of God, and the like—also occupy studies of Jesus and Christology. Latino/Hispanics can relate to a Jesus that people—whether Gospel writers, historians, theologians, or followers—try to identify by means of titles, names, and descriptions prescribed by others. The Gospel question "Whom do you say that I am?" (Mark 8.27–30 and par.) intrigues the Latino or Latina Christian, because a similar question occupies talk and study of modern-day U.S. Hispanic reality.

Who Are U.S. Hispanics?

Indeed, almost any published work of Latino theology begins with a demographic presentation of Latino reality, another way of establishing identity. Thus, when we speak about Hispanic/Latino theology, including theological reflection on Jesus, we must identify the nature and size of this vast and diverse community. The 2000 U.S. census estimated a population of 36.4 million Hispanics. However, that does not include almost 4 million people on the U.S.-controlled island of Puerto Rico, and more than 5 million undocumented immigrants from Latin American countries in the United States. Therefore, with a population estimated to be well over 45 million individuals, Hispanics probably already constitute the largest "minority" in the United States. And because it is a young population that emphasizes family, children, and youth, it is also the fastest-growing community (De La Torre and Aponte, 16–28).

Another important factor in the identity of Latinos and Latinas is their diversity. The three largest Latino communities are Mexican Americans (64 percent of all U.S. Hispanics, mostly concentrated in the West and Southwest), Puerto Ricans (as many as 2 million, mostly in the Northeastern regions of the United States, not counting those who live in Puerto Rico), and Cubans (5 percent of all Latinos/as, concentrated in the Southeast). However, there are growing numbers of immigrants from other Latin American countries, including the Dominican Republic, Guatemala and San Salvador, and Colombia, Peru, and other South American nations. As a result, Spanish is spoken almost as much as English is in many parts of the United States, including many businesses, schools, and churches.

Religiously, Hispanics have traditionally been Roman Catholics, given the political and religious influence of Spain in Latin America for so many centuries. Thus much of U.S. Latino theological reflection, including reflection on

Jesus, comes from Roman Catholic Latino/a theologians. However, Hispanic presence in the United States, especially in the last hundred years, has produced an increased number of Protestants (Maldonado), including Hispanic Pentecostals (Villafañe). Moreover, recent efforts to dialogue as a joint community of Latino/a theologians, both Catholic and Protestant, have been most fruitful and promising, creating a "new ecumenism," including some common understandings of Jesus (Gonzalez, 9–20).

Finally, to understand the identity of the Latino theological community that reflects on Jesus, one must understand the socioeconomic status of the Latino community as a whole, just as we must understand the social conditions from which Jesus emerged. Latino reflection on Jesus recognizes social and economic hardships reflected in the Gospels and in the study of the historical Jesus. Hispanics in the United States suffer from relatively low incomes, poorer education than almost any other ethnic group, and the devastating effects of racism, including language barriers. All this is slowly improving, but still too many Hispanics, especially children and youth, lag behind in the normal indicators of quality of life in the United States (De La Torre and Aponte, 20–24).

This final aspect of Latino identity in the United States is particularly important for understanding Latino reflection on Jesus because many Hispanics find some common ground with Jesus, his followers, and their socioeconomic condition. Recent pictures of Jesus posit that he came from a poor, outcast Jewish community of Palestine—Galilee—and that the movement that he led was initially a religious and social response to abject oppression at the hands of Roman imperial forces and those that colluded with them—some of the elite, Jewish temple authorities in Jerusalem. In many ways that picture is the starting point (even before the most recent studies of the historical Jesus) for Latino/Latina theological reflection on the historical Jesus and the Gospels.

Elements of Latino/a Theological Reflection on Jesus

A survey of Latino/a theological reflection on Jesus could begin with the question of identity—"Who was Jesus?" Answers vary but seem to revolve around three issues—the relationship of Jesus to God, to his context, and to us. After many debates, the early Church's resolve to emphasize both the humanity and divinity of Jesus appeals to Hispanic theological sensibilities. It is important in Latino theology that Jesus be fully human because his true glory is to be found in his earthly ministry of healing and concern for the poor, and his willingness to die for their causes in the face of political oppression (Gonzalez, 140–143). At the same time, any focus on Jesus that belies his divinity, such as adoptionism, which argued that Jesus was only "adopted" as a son of God, is as unacceptable in Latino theology, as it was to the early Church, because it means that anybody can be God if they try hard enough. Hispanics in the United States have been told again and again that the only thing holding them back is their will, not the circumstances of social and economic injustice. Adoptionism speaks to the myth of equality and upward mobility, which has always been thrown in the face of minority communities in the United States, including Hispanics (ibid., 143–145). Thus the Chalcedonian definition of Jesus as fully human and fully divine makes sense to Latino theology because the humanity of Jesus ultimately identifies with our humanity, especially that of the poor and oppressed. Moreover a fully human Jesus shows that God is God when God's full humanity is on display. If Jesus suffered and Jesus is fully God, then God suffers as we do. For Hispanics, and all people who suffer oppression in this world, Jesus "must be divine, for otherwise his suffering has no power to redeem, and he must also be human, for otherwise his suffering has nothing to do with ours" (ibid., 149). In addition, both natures, the human and the divine, must remain intact; the humanity of Jesus is never swallowed up by his divinity.

These more theological considerations are supported by Latino theological reflection on the historical Jesus and its implications for Hispanic life and ministry today. Jesus' birth and upbringing in Nazareth of Galilee have significant historical and symbolic implications. "Galilee of the Gentiles," as the Jerusalem elite derisively called this northernmost region of Palestine, was noted for its influence from nearby Hellenistic cultures. Its status as a crossroads of various national and ethnic communities made Galilee a very cosmopolitan place (Elizondo, 51). It was both a crossroads for travel and the entry point for invasion. It had a "history of rejection," both from fellow Jews and from outsiders. From such a place came Jesus, hearing the taunt "Can anything good come out of Nazareth?" (John1.46).

Hispanics can relate to this Jesus. Latinos and Latinas know what it is to come from backwater *bajios* of Latin America or from the inner city barrios of the United States, and to be rejected by mainstream America, including mainstream religion, because of such origins. Yet, as with Jesus of Nazareth, "what the world rejects, God chooses as [God's] own" (Elizondo, 53). The theology of "the Galilean Christ" and his "mestizo" (mixed) ancestry and upbringing resonates well with U.S. Latino and Latina Christians.

However, this Jesus does not stay in Galilee. He travels to Jerusalem to challenge entrenched power there. He must confront the established leadership with his message of forgiveness and hope for the poor and marginalized of his home communities. It is this challenge and confrontation that ultimately results in the arrest and crucifixion of Jesus. However, for the Latino, such confrontation and suffering are necessary. How else can one bring relief to the oppressed, both in the time of Jesus and our own, if not by confronting established but unjust power, even to the point of death?

Latino reflection on Jesus conceives of a "hard-hitting Jesus" as well as a suffering one (Recinos). From the beginning of the Gospel record it is clear that Jesus will side with the marginalized against those in power. God selects Mary, the humble peasant girl with little social importance as the mother of Jesus. On her lips we hear the Magnificat, which "expresses how God remains faithful to the powerless" (ibid., 41). Many Latinos and Latinas in the low-income communities of the United States (the barrios) relate to this message to the poor and to Mary, who like so many poor Latina mothers suffers with her son, especially when he is beaten and put to death by supposedly trusted authorities. The veneration of the Virgin Mary, including local expressions like "Our Lady of Guadalupe" among Mexican Roman Catholics and other

Latinos and Latinas, celebrates this identification of all Hispanics everywhere with the suffering mother of Jesus, as well as Jesus himself (Goizueta, 37–46). Indeed, perhaps some Latina Christians relate better to the Virgin Mary than to the historical Jesus, as suggested, in part, by a *mujerista* (Latina womanist) theology (Isasi-Diaz, 50, 74, 120, 126).

Jesus clearly identified himself with the poor. He was born in a manger and raised in the city of Nazareth on the margins of Jewish and Roman society. He worked as a woodworker, menial labor most likely. Although not a trained theologian, this Jesus "showed concern primarily for the lowly people of the land who were rejected by dominant society" (Recinos, 42). Thus Latino/a theologians see parallels between many in the Latino community and the Jesus of the Gospels. In Jesus, who was reared in a poor family, far from the center of power, God shows his preferential option for the poor and powerless, including U.S. Latinos and Latinas. Jesus became a prophet of the people who proclaimed the inbreaking of the reign of God in an oppressive and unjust world. However, it was mostly the poor and marginalized themselves who recognized his prophetic role. To those in power, he was a threat; thus he had to be put to death.

This attention of Jesus to the poor and marginalized throughout his ministry included breaking down barriers for women. A Latino feminist theology recovers the active participation of women in the Jesus movement, noting several significant healings and miracles in the Gospels involving women. Only women disciples remained at the Cross and at the tomb, and they were the first to be charged by the Risen Christ to proclaim the good news of renewed life (Aquino, 138–149). Thus, "Jesus' compassion and solidarity with those who have less" included women in a significant way (ibid., 147).

For Latinas as well as Latinos, the Cross of Jesus is "a central symbol of Christianity" (Recinos, 62). North American theologians often decry Latino focus on the gory details of the crucifixion. Yet for many Hispanics, it is the broken, oppressed, crucified Jesus who demonstrates that God suffers with us. "An emaciated Christ is the sign that God is with those who hunger" (Gonzalez, 148). Many a Latino Holy Week includes dramatic representations of the Passion of Christ (Goizueta, 32–37). Latino/a theologians often remind us that crucifixion was reserved for threats to Roman power, and thus Jesus died for challenging imperial forces on behalf of the poor and oppressed of the Empire in Palestine (Recinos, 72–73). As Jesus died for confronting the political and religious powers of his day, so should this "hard-hitting Jesus" be a model for "barrio Christianity" today. The Latino barrios, where many in this community still live and work, places of crucifixion, marginality, and early death, cry out for hard-hitting followers of Jesus who challenge places of power. Jesus' vindication over death in the resurrection demonstrates that the abuses of the powerful that persecute and kill the powerless can be overturned into a life-giving power (ibid., 78).

The Intimate Jesus

Thus, from birth to life to death to life anew, the life and ministry of Jesus bears witness to the Latino/a Christian understanding of our life and responsibility today. Hispanic Christians identify with God through Jesus because of his full humanity. His suffering parallels that of many Hispanics today. His concern for the poor and marginalized means that God has a preference for those whom nobody else pays attention to, including the majority of Latinos and Latinas living in the United States today. Jesus' execution at the hands of those in power means that Latinos and Latinas today can also confront entrenched power on behalf of those in their number on the margins of U.S. society.

It is for these reasons that Latino theological reflection on Jesus today advocates *caminemos con Jesus*—"let us walk with Jesus" (Goizueta). He became like us "in every respect" (Hebrews 2.17). He is our brother, or as one Latino theologian puts it: "Jesús is my uncle," a reflection on the practice among Latino families to name their children after Jesus (Pedraja). Ultimately, then, Latino/a reflection on the historical Jesus celebrates the community's intimacy with him, even all these centuries after his earthly ministry.

Efrain Agosto

See also: Adoptianism; American (North) Christianity; American (South) Christianity; Chalcedon; Jesus, Death of; Jesus, Miracles of; Jesus in Social Context; Kingdom of God; Liberation Theology; Messiah; Pentecostalism; Roman Catholicism; Son of God; Son of Man

References

Aquino, Maria Pilar. 1993. *Our Cry for Life: Feminist Theology from Latin America*. Maryknoll, NY: Orbis.

De La Torre, Miguel, and Edwin Aponte. 2001. *Introducing Latino/a Theologies*. Maryknoll, NY: Orbis.

Elizondo, Virgilio. 1983. *Galilean Journey: The Mexican American Promise*. Maryknoll, NY: Orbis.

Goizueta, Roberto. 1995. *Caminemos con Jesús: Toward a Hispanic/Latino Theology of Accompaniment*. Maryknoll, NY: Orbis.

Gonzalez, Justo. 1990. *Mañana: Christian Theology from a Hispanic Perspective*. Nashville: Abingdon.

Isasi-Diaz, Ada Maria. 1993. *Elaborating a Mujerista Theology—En la Lucha, In the Struggle: A Hispanic Women's Liberation Theology*. Minneapolis: Fortress.

Maldonado, David. 1999. *Protestantes/Protestants: Hispanic Christianity within Mainline Traditions*. Nashville: Abingdon.

Pedraja, Luis. 1999. *Jesus Is My Uncle: Christology from a Hispanic Perspective*. Nashville: Abingdon.

Recinos, Harold. 1997. *Who Comes in the Name of the Lord: Jesus at the Margins*. Nashville: Abingdon.

Villafañe, Eldin. 1993. *The Liberating Spirit: Toward an Hispanic American Pentecostal Social Ethic*. Grand Rapids, MI: Wm. B. Eerdmans.

American (North) Christianity

This article, chiefly about the United States, will survey the following topics, mainly taking them in historical order: first, Jesus as a "problem" within Native American communities; second, Jesus in the setting of the deistic thinking of the Founding Fathers; third, Jesus in the churches, both mainstream denominations and the holiness and fundamentalist traditions; finally, "Jesus as liberator" in the African-American community. We shall show that in its public life, America tends to be much more theocentric than Christocentric, but in the experience of particular denominations, there is deep and vigorous devotion to Jesus.

Native Americans

Martin Marty writes: "From about 13,000 years ago until nearly 500 years ago, the descendants of Asian peoples who wandered across what is now a submerged land-bridge from Siberia spread across the Americas undisturbed. They developed numberless languages, cultures, and religious outlooks. Remains of their ways of life give evidence that, like all other human beings, they experienced conflict within and between their groups. The evidence also suggests that they reinforced their conflicts with religious dances, symbols, and motifs" (Bowden, ix). This is an important aspect of American experience. The so-called American Indians were able to live in harmony with nature; their relatively small numbers could roam over a vast landmass. With the European explorers arriving in 1492, followed by significant settlements from 1607, the gradually expanding European "exploitation" of the land, in terms of farming and control, led to a significant cultural conflict.

Within this conflict, Jesus became an important symbol. Henry Warner Bowden documents the different types of missions to the Native Americans. Spanish Franciscan missions went to New Mexico, and the combination of force and economic wealth fortified the preaching and led to significant numbers of conversions to Catholic Christianity. Bowden writes: "Enthusiastic missionaries listed a total of 7,000 converts in 1608, and they claimed 10,000 more baptized followers by 1620" (ibid., 45). This period of conversions was followed by a different phase, in which the stress was on the conceptual differences between two worldviews. The French Jesuit missions to the Hurons in the Great Lakes region were more willing to build connections between the Christian world view and the native religion. The stress on personal communication to the supernatural realm meant that "Christian prayers to Jesus found a ready counterpart in native ones to Iouskeha, who also blessed supplicants" (ibid., 79). By allowing these parallels to be made, the Jesuits wanted a form of Christianity to evolve that was acceptable to the indigenous faith and culture (compare Jesuit practice in China; see Chinese Christianity).

The English Puritan settlers in New England in the seventeenth century are interesting because, despite exhortations that mission to the estimated 150,000 Native Americans in the region should be undertaken, it was never a priority. This might have been partly because distinctively European diseases, transplanted to America, led to a significant reduction in population. It might also be due to the Calvinist theology of predestination, held by many of the settlers, which meant that missionary activities were considered less important than they were to the Roman Catholic orders, long at work further south. Whether it was in a context of confrontation (the Franciscans), accommodation (the Jesuits), or neglect (the Puritans), Jesus was primarily a problem for relations between Europeans and Native Americans.

Insofar as "Jesus as a problem" has in due course been transcended, development has taken a syncretistic form. Ake Hultkrantz has documented how, among Native American groups, certain beliefs (e.g., eschatology) and practices (e.g., the sun dance) have been influenced by Christianity. For example, among the Shoshoni we find a tradition involving "Christ, (who) after the crucifixion, had wandered up to the mountains to fast. Here he prayed to his Almighty Father that He should send his Holy Ghost down to the mountains to be at hand for those who could not read or write. And the Spirit appeared to the Indians in dreams at the rock drawings (where in the old days visions were sought by brave and lonely Shoshoni), and he gave them the Sun Dance" (Hultkrantz, 227). Here, an ancient Native American ritual has been linked with Jesus in an act of theological fusion.

The European Settlers and the Founding Fathers

For the settlers from Protestant Europe, centered on New England, the dominant motifs were taken from the Old Testament rather than the New. John Winthrop (1588–1649), for example, first governor of the Massachusetts Bay Colony, believed that his journey across the sea to the New World was analogous to the movement of the people of Israel from Egypt into the Promised Land. From persecution in England, to the many trials of the journey, to the struggles to make the land hospitable—it all seemed a fitting parallel. Winthrop talked of a particular covenant between the settlers and God, comparable to that between God and the people of Israel in the Old Testament. This covenant required, in practice, the construction of a theocracy—a people whose ruler was God. A theocentric covenant coupled with a sense of mission, to be God's people in the world, has remained part of the distinctive American worldview. Strikingly, in such a picture, Jesus is not prominent.

The Puritanism of the settlers was eventually modified into the deism of the Founders in the later eighteenth century. This sense of God as simply the rational creator and beneficent but remote power behind the universe was dominant among educated people in this period, under the influence of the philosophers of the Enlightenment. It is this spirit that dominates the two documents that define American identity: the Declaration of Independence (1776) and the subsequent Constitution. In the Declaration, we find God invoked, but no mention of Jesus: "We hold these truths to be self-evident, that all men are created equal, that they are endowed by their Creator with certain inalienable Rights."

A sense of the attitude toward Jesus is to be found in a letter written by Thomas Jefferson (1743–1826) to the English radical thinker and scientist Joseph Priestley, who moved to America in 1794. In it, he sketches his understanding of the "Christian system." He sees Jesus as a reformer of Jewish "deism and ethics":

> I should proceed to a view of the life, character, and doctrines of Jesus, who, sensible of the incorrectness of their [i.e., the Jews'] ideas of the Deity, and of morality, endeavoured to bring them to the principles of a pure deism, and juster notions of the attributes of God, to reform their moral doctrines to the standard of

> reason, justice and philanthropy, and to inculcate the belief of a future state. This view would purposely omit the question of his divinity, and even his inspiration. To do him justice, it would be necessary to remark the disadvantages his doctrines have to encounter, not having been committed to writing by himself, but by the most unlettered of men, by memory, long after they had heard them from him; when much was forgotten, much misunderstood, and presented in very paradoxical shapes. Yet such are the fragments remaining as to show a master workman, and that his system of morality was the most benevolent and sublime probably that has been ever taught, and consequently more perfect than those of any of the ancient philosophers. His character and doctrines have received still greater injury from those who pretend to be his special disciples, and who have disfigured and sophisticated his actions and precepts, from views of personal interest, so as to induce the unthinking part of mankind to throw off the whole system in disgust, and to pass sentence as an impostor on the most innocent, the most benevolent, the most eloquent and sublime character that ever has been exhibited to man (April 9, 1803; Jefferson, n.p.).

This is typical of the Founders: Jesus is seen as the supreme ethical exemplar, who needed to be slotted into a strong theocentric framework. So both from the early Puritans and the Founders, God has survived in public life much more effectively than Jesus. Despite the separation of Church from state and the official strict neutrality of the latter in religious matters, the phrase "In God we trust" is permitted to appear on the currency, and most public events are graced with references to God almost as a matter of course. But it is always God that is invoked, by the president, for example, never Jesus. The pluralism of America, greatly extended by the subsequent large-scale immigration of Jews and others, as well as both Protestant and Catholic Christians from many countries, is a theistic pluralism. The great majority of people believe in God, and most are content to shelter under his umbrella.

Jesus in the Churches

Although God, rather than Jesus, dominates the public space, it is a different matter within the churches. America is a deeply religious country. In the year 2000, the U.S. population was 276,000,000, of whom the two largest religious groups were the Roman Catholics, with 62,018,436, and the Southern Baptists, with 15,729,356 (Noll, app. A). Approximately 40 percent of Americans attend a place of worship in a typical week. Ninety percent of Americans insist that they have never doubted the existence of God and say that they pray some time in the week (Wills, 16). Given that there were no Christians in America five hundred years ago, it is worth noting that these groups are almost all the result of immigration during that period. The net result is that Catholicism, for example, is made up of vast groups of numerous different origins—Irish Catholics mix with English, Italian and Polish Catholics, and so on. The diversity of America is found within as well as across the denominations.

Furthermore, because of the wealth of America, it is not surprising that they manage to be major exporters of American views of Jesus. Mark Noll notes that "at the end of the twentieth century the churches of the United

States were sponsoring approximately 70,000 overseas missionaries, with another 8,400 from Canada and 2,400 from Mexico. As just one concrete example of America's reach overseas, the evangelistic organization, Campus Crusade for Christ, produced in 1979 a motion picture on the life of Christ, based on the Gospel of Luke. By early 2001, copies of the film had been distributed in 638 separate languages, it was being shown actively in more than a hundred countries, and it had been viewed by over four billion people" (Noll, 2).

Turning now to the congregations within the huge number and range of places of worship, we find that Jesus figures prominently. In many ways, the role Jesus plays in the various denominations within the United States is much the same as elsewhere: so Episcopalians, for example, following the English Anglican Church, make much of the Incarnation as a symbol for involvement, thereby justifying social action. However, there are distinctive uses of the figure of Jesus in certain traditions that are worth noting.

The first is the "holiness theology" of many in the Wesleyan tradition. Methodism continues to be strong in the United States: the United Methodist Church has 8,400,000 members, let alone the various splinter groups from mainstream Methodism. George Whitefield (1715–1770), the Anglican preacher who had been a member of John and Charles Wesley's "Holy Club" at Oxford, brought revivalism to the American colonies, together with Jonathan Edwards (1703–1758). They are credited with the Great Awakening (1735–1755) and the rise of evangelicalism in the States. Those attracted to their vision of Christianity became the source for the distinctive American emphasis on holiness. There was a "Second Great Awakening" at the turn of the century among Presbyterians, Baptists, and Congregationalists as well as Methodists throughout the country, and a "Third Great Awakening," striking similar revivalist chords, in the fifty years before 1914. A key writer in this tradition was Phoebe Palmer (1807–1874), who believed that, perhaps in reaction to the coldness of the nation's deistic ethos, it was important to cultivate an inward warmth of spirituality. Through her books, for example *The Way of Holiness* (1845), she advocated a program that would lead to "entire satisfaction" and "a closer walk with Christ."

The discourse of the holiness tradition has been felt beyond those linked to Methodism. Much of the language of revivalism and commitment has been shaped by a Jesus who requires holiness in those who follow him and has made it possible by sending the Holy Spirit.

The second (and related) example is the Jesus of the fundamentalist churches. Fundamentalism was a reaction against the so-called modernism of Arthur Cushman McGiffert (1861–1933), Shailer Mathews (1863–1941), and others. From the 1880s onward, evangelical Christians wanted to stress the "fundamentals" of the faith. In 1910–1915, a series of books called *The Fundamentals: A Testimony to the Truth* set out the key commitments. Mark Noll explains: "Among the fundamentals defended in these tracts were the reality of the Bible as the inspired Word of God, the incarnation of Jesus Christ as the Son of God in real human flesh, the substitutionary atonement of Christ on the cross as God's way of redeeming sinners, and the reality of a literal second coming of Christ to the earth at the end of the age" (Noll, 146). In relation to Christology, certain aspects were emphasized—in particular, the saving action of Jesus, in his death and resurrection; and the second coming became central to the preaching of fundamentalist churches. Both matters were significantly shaped by Dispensationalism. Dispensationalist theology, the work of John Nelson Derby (1800–1882), the founder of the Plymouth Brethren, and popularized by C. I. Scofield (1842–1921), divided human history into seven "dispensations," the two most important being those of "law" and "grace." The former ran from Moses to the death of Jesus and the latter is the period of the Church until the second coming. As James Barr has pointed out (1981), this meant that the ministry of Jesus and, in particular, the social radicalism of the Sermon on the Mount technically did not apply to the Church. Rather, the teaching of Jesus sets out the conditions for the end of the age, which did not come about because the Jewish Messiah was rejected.

This in part explains why the preoccupation of many in fundamentalist churches is with individual salvation and individual morality. It also explains how Jerry Falwell (b. 1933) and Pat Robertson (b. 1930) have linked their theology with many of the issues central to the Republican Party. This limited interest in and sense of social justice as Christian duty is coupled with a deep preoccupation with the end of the age. Hal Lindsey's phenomenal success in the 1970s with *The Late Great Planet Earth* has been followed by Jerry B. Jenkins's writings published in recent years. These books provide ample evidence for the way many Americans organize their lives around a strong expectation that the end of the present age is imminent. This interest extended to the president of the United States—although the scale of Ronald Reagan's actual concern was difficult to determine. Garry Wills is unsure how seriously Reagan took the considerable "hype" that many "prophecies were coming true" during his presidency. When Reagan was asked "in 1984 what he thought about Armageddon (a subject on which he had been warned to be circumspect), he showed agnosticism only about the date of the event, not about the event itself: 'No one knows whether those prophecies mean that Armageddon is a thousand years away or the day after tomorrow. So I have seriously warned and said we must plan according to Armageddon.' He changed the street number on the house he moved to after leaving the White House because it was the number of the Beast (666)" (Wills 1990, 150). Reagan probably shared the evangelical interest, but wisely was not prepared to commit himself to any particular interpretation of current events along those lines. It is to be noted that nowhere in this frame of reference is there the least sense of the historical criticism of Scripture that has been standard in nonfundamentalist theological studies for over a century and a half.

Finally in this section, we should refer to a number of more marginal but still substantial (and often high-profile) religious institutions that have arisen from the freedom of American religion. Most of them are, in their various different ways, close to the fundamentalists in general tone.

1. The Mormons (the Church of Jesus Christ of Latter-day Saints) date from the revelation to Joseph Smith in 1830, whereby the *Book of Mormon* (together with two other writings) was added to the canon of the Bible. With their headquarters in Salt Lake City, Utah, and by means of vigorous evangelistic work, the movement reached over 8 million by the end of the twentieth century. The Trinity is seen as consisting of three distinct deities, united in purpose. The risen Christ is believed to have ministered in America. They look forward eagerly to his second coming.

2. Jehovah's Witnesses (the Watch Tower Bible and Tract Society) is intensely apocalyptic or adventist in direction and ethos, from its beginnings in the 1870s. It is intensely evangelistic and fervent in its expectation of the coming of Christ to establish his millennial reign; it has forecast the "end events" on a number of occasions. It has spread widely, especially now in the developing world, and runs to over 4 million adherents.

3. Christian Science looks back to its founder, Mary Baker Eddy (1821–1910), and is chiefly concerned with healing through prayer (rather than through medical intervention), inspired by the example of Jesus' healing ministry.

Jesus and the African-American Churches

Although social justice issues tend to be neglected in certain fundamentalist churches, they are central in the African-American Church. The deep crime of slavery committed by white Europeans and settlers on the African has inevitably meant that Jesus the liberator is a key figure among African Americans. This Jesus is found in the famous Spirituals and in the exhilarating preaching in the churches. He is both a reassurance to the oppressed and a challenge to the oppressor. James Cone brings this out: "In reality the message of the Kingdom strikes at the very center of man's desire to define his own existence in the light of his own interest at the price of his brothers' enslavement. It means the irruption of a new age, an age that has to do with God's action in history on behalf of man's salvation. It is a message about the ghetto, Vietnam, and all other injustices done in the name of democracy and religion to further the social, political and economic interests of the oppressor. In Christ, God enters human affairs and takes sides with the oppressed, their suffering becomes his; their despair, divine despair. Through Christ the poor are offered freedom now to rebel against that which makes them other than human. It is ironical that America with its history of injustice to the poor (especially regarding the black man and the Indian) prides itself as a Christian nation (is there really such an animal?). It is even more ironical that officials within the body of the Church have passively or actively participated in injustices" (Cone, 8).

Cone talks about the need for a black revolution, which means "a radical break with the existing political and social structure and a redefinition of black life along the lines of black liberation" (ibid., 34). Perhaps the best known African-American theologian is Cornel West (currently at Princeton), who has argued that only a combination of Marxism and Christianity will overcome the intransigent racism of American life. In all this theology, Jesus figures as the great exemplar, leader, and teacher of God's liberating purpose.

Conclusion

This survey has described a number of the ways in which Jesus has figured and continues to do so. It is important to stress the range and diversity within American Christianity. There are significant examples of exceptions to some of the dominant trends that have been documented: for example, there are fundamentalists with a strong sympathy for social justice issues. Overall, however, in the public square of American life, the key concept is God rather than Jesus; within the churches, Jesus figures at the heart of enthusiasm, devotion, and personal religion, over a wide range of Christian denominations.

Ian Markham

See also: American (Hispanic) Christianity; American (South) Christianity; Chinese Christianity; Enlightenment; Liberation Theology; Second Coming of Jesus in Current Belief; Wesley, Charles; Wesley, John

References

Barr, James. 1981. *Fundamentalism*. London: SCM.

Bowden, Henry Warner. 1981. *American Indians* and *Christian Missions: Studies* in *Cultural Conflict*. Chicago: University of Chicago Press.

Cone, James H. 1999. *Risks of Faith: The Emergence of* a *Black Theology of Liberation, 1968–1998*. Boston: Beacon.

Hultkrantz, Ake. *Belief* and *Worship in Native North America*. New York: Syracuse University Press.

Jefferson, Thomas. "To Dr. Joseph Priestley Washington, Apr. 9, 1803." *The Letters of Thomas Jefferson: 1743–1826*. Retrieved July 31, 2003. http://odur.let.rug.nl/~usa/P/tj3/writings/brf/jefl152.htm

Markham, Ian. 1981. *Plurality and Christian Ethics*. 1994. Cambridge: Cambridge University Press.

Noll, Mark A. 2002. *The Old Religion: The History of North American Christianity*. Grand Rapids, MI: Eerdmans.

Wills, Gary. 1990. *Under God: Religion and American Politics*. New York: Simon and Schuster.

American (South) Christianity

Christianity arrived on the South American continent in the last decade of the fifteenth century, brought by the first waves of Franciscans and Dominicans traveling with the conquistadors of Catholic Spain. Much has changed since the landing of these first religious functionaries. Indigenous peoples, along with their religions, have disappeared, their cultures eradicated, with new and mixed ones taking their place. Over the course of the last five hundred years, the existence of Christianity in South America has offered both cause for celebration and reason for discomfort.

Closely allied with the European engineers of colonization and conquest, Christianity spread initially through coerced proselytization and enforced baptism of indigenous peoples and imported African slaves. Diplomatic arrangements (e.g., the *Patronato*) between a weakened papacy and the increasingly powerful Iberian monarchs subjected religious functionaries to direct political control, making the Christian Church, in effect, little more than an adjunct of nascent South American political structures. Through critics such as Bartolomé de las Casas (bishop of Chiapas, 1544–1547), Antonio de Valdivieso (bishop of Nicaragua, 1544–1550), Juan del Valle (bishop of Popayan, 1548–1560), and Diego Medellín (bishop of Santiago, 1574–1593), prophetic denunciation of European abuses made themselves heard. Little could be done in practical terms, however, to prevent Christian representatives being swept along with the tide of European aspirations to conquer and *civilize* the New World.

Part and parcel of ecclesiastical involvement in the colonial venture, representations of Jesus, however unwittingly, served to bolster the position and power of the European elites over the course of the first centuries of Christianity's presence in South America. Images of Jesus as one who bore passively his suffering and torment (e.g., "Jesus of a happy death") inevitably colluded with the fatalistic resignation of South America's poorest in accepting their "God-given" lot. Representations of Jesus as "Christ the celestial monarch" corresponded with the other end of the social scale. Correlating earthly power and those who wield it with eternal authority and heavenly grandeur, regal images of Jesus decked in the finery of Europe's aristocracy served to buttress existing hierarchies.

Despite the sporadic and short-lived existence of Protestant settlements (e.g., German Lutherans in Venezuela between 1529 and 1546, and Dutch Calvinists in Brazil from 1624 to 1654), Roman Catholicism enjoyed a virtual religious monopoly on the South American mainland for more than three hundred years. This religious monopoly came to an end in the nineteenth century owing to continentwide political and demographic change. Independence movements throughout South America wrested the continent's newborn nations from Spanish and Portuguese colonial control. Taking much of their cue from postrevolutionary France, postcolonial powers in South America viewed with suspicion an ecclesiastical institution that had been such a bulwark of the ancien regime. No longer integral to political aspirations, and thereby released from the state control of the Patronato, the Roman Catholic Church throughout South America was progressively "romanized" as it increasingly came under the sway of its European "Mother Church." At the same time, successive waves of northern European immigrants added to the diverse racial ethos of the continent. No longer legally inferior to Roman Catholicism, and buoyed by increasing numbers of non-Catholic immigrants, Protestant missionary movements were now able to make steady inroads within South America. In Chile, for example, the Anglican (1836), Lutheran (1846), Presbyterian (1872), Methodist (1877), and Baptist (1908) denominations established themselves successfully. The Christ of Roman ritual, calling upon his adherents to meet their sacramental obligations, and the Jesus of Protestant pietism, edifying individuals through moral example, would subsequently serve the South American faithful as mainstream Christological representations.

The two world wars of the last century did much to reconfigure the internal and external influences shaping the South American continent. Postwar rebuilding programs in Europe afforded opportunities for South American industrial development. South American industrialization soon escalated, giving rise to large-scale urbanization, population growth, and regional migration. In breaking old allegiances and established behavioral patterns, the social and cultural flux engendered by this rapid demographic change did much to turn over the ground for new ideas and practices to take root. Progressively eclipsing already weakened European leverage in South America, the rise of the United States as a global power ensured that many of these ideas and practices would have a North American provenance.

Although established for more than a hundred years, the nature of the Protestant presence in South America began to change substantially from the 1950s. Encouraged by North and South American political authorities alike, and empowered by Southern U.S. missionary funding and training, indigenous Pentecostal denominations increasingly made their evangelistic presence felt in the burgeoning South American conurbations. South American Pentecostalism emerged in the first decades of the twentieth century from transcontinental spiritual revival movements within traditional Protestant denominations. It was at that time, for example, that South America's two largest national Pentecostal churches (the Assemblies of God and the Christian Congregation in Brazil) were founded in Brazil. Initially bearing fruit in Argentina, Brazil, and Chile, Pentecostalism soon spread throughout the continent. The closure of East Asian missionary fields owing to events in China, Korea, and Vietnam did much to facilitate the concentration of Protestant missionary resources upon the South American continent. Coinciding with the aforementioned large-scale and rapid demographic shift, the coupling of Pentecostal missionary fervor with enhanced evangelistic resources did much to lay the foundations for Pentecostalism's continuing growth. Having found most success originally among the poorer sectors of South America, Pentecostal discourse and practice are now establishing a foothold among the continent's professional classes. The majority (approximately 80 percent) among Protestants in South America, Pentecostalism represents more than 10 percent of the population of those countries (Brazil, Guatemala, and Chile) in which it is most successful. Pentecostal churches represent the fastest growing sectors of Christianity in South America today.

Like its European and North American cousins, South American Pentecostalism is conservative in matters of biblical interpretation and theological reflection. Articulating a Spirit-based discipleship founded upon the charismatic gifts (e.g., speaking in tongues, prophecy, the casting out of unclean spirits), South American Pentecostalism worships a miracle-working, demon-exorcising Christ who, along with the Spirit, supports believers in their daily battles with the "principalities and powers of darkness." Emphasis upon the spiritual benefits of faith, especially that of divine healing through deliverance, is particularly pronounced within the more recent and fastest growing neo-Pentecostal churches, such as Brazil's Pentecostal Church "God is Love" and the Universal Church of the Kingdom of God.

Traditionally reticent in matters political, Protestant Christians are increasingly being mobilized through a variety of national parties (e.g., Venezuela's Authentic Renewal Organization and the Independent Christian Movement of Argentina), collective forums (e.g., the Brazilian Evangelical Association and Evangelical Progressive Movement of Brazil), and high-profile political successes through the elections of Protestant presidents Alberto Fujimori (Perú) and Jorge Serrano Elias (Guatemala). While programmatic participation in the formal political arena has in the past predominantly been undertaken by members of South America's traditional Protestant denominations, there is increasing evidence of ad hoc and coordinated Pentecostal engagement in both national and localized political campaigns. The majority of neo-Pentecostal church members, however, continue to subscribe to a spiritualized faith devoid of all but the most restricted sociopolitical outworkings.

Protestant representation on the South American continent is not the only sector of the Christian community to have undergone dramatic change. The contemporary Roman Catholic presence in South America has likewise altered in significant ways. The Second Vatican Council (Rome, 1962–1965) of the Roman Catholic Church officially sanctioned many of the progressive theological and ecclesiological trends emerging from liturgical renewal movements, biblical theological revitalization, and the advent of religious sociology in the 1950s. The impact of similar developments within the World Council of Churches must also not be overlooked. Neither intended nor anticipated by Vatican II reforms, the South American appropriation (e.g., the Second General Conference of Latin American Bishops, Medellín, 1968) of otherwise Eurocentric concerns fostered widespread pastoral renewal and theological innovation across the continent.

The results of rapid demographic change, escalating Protestant growth, perceived communist insurgence among the rural populace, a growing shortage of priests, and the findings of religious-sociological surveys had already alerted the Roman Catholic hierarchy in South America to the radically altered nature of its once central position as one of the three pillars (along with the land-owning oligarchies and the military) of traditional South American society. The growing realization that things had to change was further complemented by emerging theological emphases upon the status of the laity and their ecclesial rights to a fuller participation in the formal liturgical arena and decision-making processes of church life. Embracing each of these challenges in the reformist spirit of Vatican II, Roman Catholic authorities in South America set about formulating and implementing a wide-ranging program of institutional renewal and pastoral innovation.

Perhaps the best known pastoral phenomenon to emerge from this period of Roman Catholic renewal is the "base ecclesial community" (*comunidad[e] eclesial de base*). Base ecclesial communities (CEBs), sometimes called "base Christian communities," are extremely varied in kind, existing mainly among the poorest sectors of the South American continent, with anything between twenty and fifty committed members in each of the numerous communities making up an individual parish. Originally Roman Catholic in origin, growing numbers of Protestant base communities continue to establish themselves throughout the continent. While centered upon the worshipping life of the local community, CEBs serve principally as arenas of support throughout the whole week, providing opportunity for Bible study, catechesis, leadership training, and assorted other ways of living the Christian faith and accessing pastoral support in a more intimate medium than that allowed by the large-scale parish. Celebrating their faith collectively throughout the whole of the week, often without formal clerical presence, these small communities develop autochthonous forms of pastoral leadership and ecclesial expression tailored appropriately to the needs and aspirations of the prevailing social context. CEBs also encourage the Christian community to integrate further its life and witness within the surrounding locale by way of actively supporting, if not sometimes leading, localized support networks and campaigns. The ability of the base ecclesial communities to undertake this task, especially during the frequent periods of military repression in South America, has been central to their ongoing success.

Offering physical space, material support, personal commitment, and spiritual encouragement, base ecclesial communities are often at the forefront of food and clothing cooperatives, workers' unions, youth groups, parent associations, and local campaigns in pursuit of health clinics, sanitation facilities, educational ventures, and public transport provision. Indeed, the pastoral methods and reflective approaches used by many CEBs (e.g., See—Judge—Act) are designed with the specific intention of better integrating local needs and issues within the agenda of the Christian community. Although not as numerous as they were in the early 1980s, base ecclesial communities continue to represent the primary means of living the faith for millions of South American Christians.

Emerging under similar conditions as the base ecclesial community and, like the CEBs, existing in both Catholic and Protestant form, the theology of liberation is another distinctive manifestation of Christianity on the South American continent. Formulated initially by the likes of Gustavo Gutiérrez, Rubem Alves, Hugo Assmann, and Leonardo Boff, and maturing through the prolonged period of military rule in many South American countries, liberation theology flourished into one of the most influential expressions of post-war theological reflection in the global Christian community. Central to liberation theology's approach is an understanding of Jesus as the self-proclaimed herald of the Reign ("kingdom") of God who believed there to be no individual righteousness in the absence of meaningful and just relations with one's neighbors. Founded upon divine demands for justice and commencing with those considered least in society's eyes, the Reign of God constitutes the absolute fulfillment of the person that begins to unfold in this life but does not reach ultimate realization until the next. Manifesting itself *spiritually* in the breakdown of relations between humankind and God, *personally* in the estrangement of one person from another, and *structurally* through unjust societal mechanisms, sin's alienating effects are overcome by way of a holistic/integral salvation that redeems human beings in each of these dimensions. "Liberation" is the term favored to convey this multidimensional theological appreciation of salvation.

Multifaceted in nature, the contributions that liberation theology has made and continues to make to the Christian life in South America are myriad. The articulation of theological reflection with the lived experience of the poor in South America (more often than not members of base ecclesial communities) is carefully nurtured and zealously guarded by liberation theologians. Not least among the theological contributions made by liberation theology are the theoretical justifications offered in support of Christian engagement with social, economic, and political affairs. As salvation comprises the renewal of every aspect of our being, all matters that impact upon our integral well-being are legitimate objects of theological scrutiny and practical engagement. More than a privatized and inner spiritual relationship between the believer and God, faith holds for liberation theologians an ineluctably public dimension. Antithetical to the reign of justice heralded by Jesus, social structures perpetuating oppression and marginalization, economic mechanisms generating poverty and inequality, and political processes limiting participation and inclusion are subject to concerted Christian action. The practical resonance of liberation theology, along with its "preferential option for the poor," is not lost on those Christians living at the socioeconomic base of South American society.

Pastoral innovations and theological developments throughout South America have facilitated the emergence of a popular imaging of Jesus that is historically textured, not least thanks to people's increasing ability to access and read the Gospel narratives, yet readily amenable to contemporary appropriation through a variety of media. Hanging on a cross made from a lashed-together fork and spade, Jesus is pictured in a Salvadoran church office dressed in the hat and half-length trousers of the South American peasant. Connected by cords to each arm of the cross, men and women are bent double in their work upon the land. Crucified "once and for all" upon the implements of their labor, Jesus' cause is allied with the common people's daily struggle for survival. The theme of Jesus' alliance with the struggles of the poor is further explored by the imposing artwork of Santa María de los Angeles in Managua. Surrounded by representative motifs of Nicaraguan life, the Risen Christ is at the center of the largest painting in this church building. Below the Risen Jesus, for example, an empty cross is borne by a belabored assortment of individuals, while to their left a group of women stand holding photographs of loved ones "disappeared" by the security forces of pre-Sandinista Nicaragua. The message is clear. There is no travail of daily life of which Christ is unaware, no anguish caused by the daily grind of life to which the Risen Jesus has nothing to say. The people's struggle is Christ's struggle. In the same vein, a Colombian creed celebrates the resurrected Jesus' presence in those killed for their opposition, some of it armed, to injustice and oppression in South America. "We believe in Jesus, dead and raised in our martyred brothers Monsignor Oscar Arnulfo Romero, Camilo Torres, Alvaro Ulcué, Hector Gallego, and Misael Ramírez." Although the majority of Christians in South America would not countenance involvement in armed struggle, individuals such as Camilo Torres and disparate communities throughout the continent (e.g., Nicaragua's Sandinista revolution) have committed themselves to armed resistance in the face of state-sponsored oppression and other forms of institutionalized violence.

A Costa Rican statue of a newly resurrected Jesus, virtually naked and frail from his recent ordeal, conveys a dazed and disorientated vulnerability reflective of contemporary appreciations of Christ's humanity. In comparison, the 30-meter-high (and over 1,000-ton) *Cristo Redentor,* imperiously watching over Rio de Janeiro from the peak of Corcovado since 1931, reflects just how far the Christian community has come in such a short period of time. Indicative of an era in which popular images of Jesus were in short supply, and constructed in a period of Christian self-assuredness perhaps never to be recaptured, Rio's "Christ the Redeemer" embodies a bygone age. The words of the Nicaraguan Peasant Mass better echo the Christological aspirations of today's South American Christians: "You are the God of the poor, the human and humble God, the God who sweats in the street, the God with the worn face. That's why I speak with you, just as my people do. Because you are the laborer God, the working Christ."

Although Christianity continues to predominate the religious field of South America, a cultural diversity born of large-scale immigration (e.g., São Paulo has the largest Japanese community outside of Japan) and enhanced freedom of expression are progressively facilitating the emergence and establishment of non-Christian religions. In addition to the religious practices of Chinese, Japanese, and Near Eastern immigrants, South America is home to some of the fastest-growing communities of Mormons, Seventh-day Adventists, and Jehovah's Witnesses. Meanwhile, previously subdued "spiritist" (e.g., Candomblé and Umbanda in Brazil) and indigenous/preconquest (e.g., "Maya priests" in Guatemala) religions are steadily gaining ground. Along with New Age devotional practices (especially in Brazil), these formerly disenfranchised religions are being reinvigorated as increasing numbers of South Americans become open to alternative spiritualities, either as a complement to existing Christian adherence or as a wholesale replacement.

The product of former times, the towering statue of Jesus atop Corcovado stands as a reminder of the extent to which South America's multicultural present has been shaped by its Christian past. At the same time, the escalating growth of Pentecostalism among all sectors of society and the continued presence of Christian grassroots movements among the poor majority of the population are complemented by the increasingly innovative activity of Roman Catholic charismatic and Protestant renewal movements. Collectively, these religious phenomena point to the persisting presence of Christianity as a vibrant component of twenty-first-century life on the South American continent.

Andrew Dawson

See also: American (Hispanic) Christianity; American (North) Christianity; Holy Spirit; Kingdom of God; Liberation Theology; Pentecostalism; Seventh-day Adventism; Spanish Christianity

References

Cleary, Edward L., and Hannah W. Stewart-Gambino, eds. 1992. *Conflict and*

Competition: The Latin American Church in a Changing Environment. Boulder, CO: Lynne Rienner.

———, eds. 1997. *Power, Politics, and Pentecostals in Brazil*. Boulder, CO: Westview.

Cook, Guillermo, ed. 1994. *New Face of the Church in Latin America: Between Tradition and Change*. New York: Orbis.

Dawson, Andrew. 1998. *The Birth and Impact of the Base Ecclesial Community and Liberative Theological Discourse in Brazil*. Lanham, MD: International Scholars.

Dussel, Enrique. 1981. *A History of the Church in Latin America: Colonialism to Liberation (1492–1979)*. Grand Rapids, MI: Eerdmans.

Garrard-Burnett, Virginia, and David Stoll, eds. 1993. *Rethinking Protestantism in Latin America*. Philadelphia: Temple University Press.

Parker, Christian. 1996. *Popular Religion and Modernization in Latin America*. New York: Orbis.

Smith, Christian, and Joshua Prokopy, eds. 1999. *Latin American Religion in Motion*. New York: Routledge.

Anglicanism

At first glance the question of the place of Jesus in the Anglican tradition of theology and spirituality looks like a nonquestion. To very many Anglicans in the thirty-eight churches of the worldwide Anglican Communion it would be like asking what Jesus has got to do with life, the universe, and everything! The question is either rather pointless or else impossible to answer within finite limits. Anglicans would say that for them, as for other Christians, Jesus is presupposed in their belief, worship, and behavior. However, that assumption should not go unchallenged. The things that we take for granted are sometimes the very things that need to be probed and scrutinized.

This caution is borne out by the historic formularies of the Church of England, which have helped to shape Anglican ecclesial identity throughout the Communion. Neither the Book of Common Prayer (1662)—for all its Cranmerian glories—nor the Thirty-nine Articles of Religion offer much mileage for a distinctive Anglican perspective on Jesus of Nazareth. Even the striking words of the litany that evoke all that Jesus underwent as man for the salvation of humankind are drawn from the Latin of the old Anglo-Saxon Church: "By the mystery of thy holy Incarnation; by thy holy Nativity and Circumcision; by thy Baptism, Fasting and Temptation . . . By thine Agony and bloody Sweat; by thy Cross and Passion; by thy precious Death and Burial; by thy glorious Resurrection and Ascension; and by the coming of the Holy Ghost, *Good Lord deliver us*."

Where Is Jesus in the Study of Anglicanism?

This scepticism is reinforced if we consider what some standard works on Anglicanism have to say about Jesus. Surprisingly, they have said very little. The classic anthology of seventeenth-century Anglican writing (More and Cross, ed., 1935) devotes a mere 14 pages, out of more than 800, to the person of Jesus Christ. It does not include anything about his actual earthly ministry or his saving death. If they could have been challenged about this, the editors would probably have replied that Anglicanism did not have anything distinctive to say about those matters. But that argument could prove to be the thin end of a rather major wedge. In its beliefs, worship, structures, and spirituality, Anglicanism has much in common with various other branches of the Christian Church. That does not mean that Anglicanism does not have a distinctive slant on all these things. Our question here is whether it has a distinctive perspective on the person of Jesus Christ and his significance for Christian faith.

A recent anthology, on the theme of the Anglican quest for holiness, that covers the period from the beginning of the Reformation to the end of the twentieth century (Rowell, Stevenson, and Williams) is more rewarding. It includes several gems of intimate devotion to the figure of Jesus Christ. John Newton's hymn "How Sweet the Name of Jesus Sounds" reminds us that personal devotion to Jesus is authentic to Anglicanism, just as it is to other Christian traditions. William Law speaks of the Christian's calling to share the spirit and temper of Jesus' life and actions: "to walk as he walked." Scott Holland proclaims Jesus Christ as "the crown and sum of humanity." The American Anglican William Porcher DuBose writes: "Jesus Christ is to me, not a name, nor a memory or tradition, nor an idea or sentiment, nor a personification, but a living and personal reality, presence and power." A. H. Stanton reminds Anglicans that theirs is "the religion of a personal Saviour," and George Body points out that the Church's worship is "the worship of the Incarnate God, the man Christ Jesus." Others tell of the daily companionship, the unfailing friendship of Jesus Christ. But even so, these examples represent a tiny fraction of all that is included in a volume of 800 pages.

A widely used introduction to Anglicanism by several contributors, *The Study of Anglicanism*, contains one indexed reference to Jesus Christ and one to Christology, both in the same chapter. Louis Weil's contribution, "The Gospel in Anglicanism," addresses implicitly the significance of Jesus Christ for faith. But it does seem rather extraordinary that the study of Anglicanism should not lead us in any overt way to the study of Jesus Christ.

In the Anglican theologian John Macquarrie's standard work *Jesus Christ in Modern Thought*, Anglican theologians, with the exception of Charles Gore and John A. T. Robinson, are conspicuous by their absence. Although Macquarrie himself has made an estimable contribution, in this book and elsewhere, the gap that remains is at least partly understandable. Since Lionel Thornton's *The Incarnate Lord* (1928) there appears to have been no Anglican treatment of Christology comparable to the major treatises that have emerged from other Christian traditions, such as W. Pannenberg's *Jesus God and Man* (1964), E. Schillebeeckx's exhaustive two-volume treatment *Jesus* and *Christ*, or even W. Kasper's serviceable study *Jesus the Christ* (1974). The second volume of N. T. Wright's magnum opus on Christian origins, *Jesus and the Victory of God*, tackles the question of Jesus in the Synoptic Gospels, but quite properly it does not attempt to move beyond New Testament study to theological construction.

A further disappointment is that a general survey, *Jesus through the Centuries: His Place in the History of Culture*, by Jaroslav Pelikan (1985), contains only minimal references to Anglican writers. Shakespeare is mentioned in passing, as are T. S. Eliot and W. H. Auden. Charles Wesley and his hymns are there (he was never anything other than an Anglican). Pelikan also makes the arresting observation that "as respect for the organised church has declined, reverence for Jesus has grown." But by his account, the Anglican tradition has contributed little to turn our attention to Jesus.

At this point in our enquiry, two questions begin to become rather insistent. Is it the case, as the volumes mentioned above might suggest, that Anglicans have paid little attention to the founder of their religion? Or is it the case that, although Anglicans may have paid as much attention to Jesus Christ as anyone else has, this attention not been thought worth recording or retrieving? In order to answer these questions, it would be necessary to make a thorough historical survey of the literature written by Anglican theologians and to immerse oneself in the dusty tomes consigned to oblivion in cathedral and university libraries. This exercise is obviously quite impossible for our present purposes. There are, however, three areas where the significance of Jesus for faith has been explored by Anglican writers. These comprise first, the various attempts to develop a Christological metaphysic; second, the tradition of theological reflection on the humanity of Jesus; and third, the doctrine of the atonement.

The Quest for Meaning or the Longing for Redemption?

There is a distinguished tradition, in modern Anglican theology, of philosophical reflection on the Incarnation, the discursive elaboration of a worldview of which the Incarnation is the central focus. This tradition was influenced by the metaphysical confidence associated with philosophical idealism (in its personalist rather than absolute, Hegelian form). The keynote is struck in B. F. Westcott's *Christus Consummator* (1886), which begins with Plato's vision of reality and shows how it is fulfilled in Christ. The Incarnation completes nature and reconciles the contraries of modern thought. The exemplar of this genre is the collection *Lux Mundi* (1889), in which Gore and his associates set out to bring the Christian faith, as it had been received from the Fathers of the Church, into a closer relationship with modern thought. Gore can be said to have dedicated his life to this quest. His late works—*Belief in Christ* (1922) and *The Philosophy of the Good Life* (1930)—are an impressive exposition of the place of Jesus Christ, the incarnate Word of God, within a coherent worldview that brings together the insights of natural theology and the claims of divine revelation in Scripture.

The flowering of the metaphysical approach is seen in William Temple (successively Archbishop of York and of Canterbury; d.1944). Temple's early writings brashly assumed that Jesus Christ came merely to put the finishing touches to what Plato had already taught. His mature work, especially *Mens Creatrix* (1917) and *Christus Veritas* (1924), offered a more sober, though still speculative, approach to a Christ-centered worldview. One of the latest flourishings of the Anglican Christocentric metaphysic was Charles Raven's Gifford Lectures, entitled *Natural Religion and Christian Theology* (1953).

There was a perceptible shift, between the two world wars, from a focus on the search for a coherent meaning in the universe and seeing the person of Jesus Christ as the fulfillment of human aspirations and development, to a more tensive view of history and culture in which he is seen as bringing challenge and judgment into the world. This movement of the center of theological gravity is seen in Gore, for whom the biblical prophetic voice, from the eighth century B.C. through John the Baptist to Jesus himself, became ever more significant as a form of divine revelation. It is found in the impressive Gifford Lectures of the Anglican layman A. E. Taylor, *The Faith of a Moralist* (1930), which takes the reality of history more seriously than might have been the case forty or fifty years earlier.

The scholar who most consistently reshaped Anglican theology to a more prophetic mold was Sir Edwyn Hoskyns. Profoundly influenced by Karl Barth's early dialectical theology, Hoskyns translated into English the second edition of Barth's celebrated commentary on the Epistle to the Romans. In his contribution on the Gospels to *Essays Catholic and Critical* (1926) and more fully in *The Riddle of the New Testament* (1931), Hoskyns argued that the New Testament had been shaped primarily by Jesus' own interpretation of his mission and destiny. His Cross and Resurrection were the pivot of salvation history. Hoskyns reclaimed the New Testament literature, particularly the Gospels, from the liberal humanitarian and Hegelian evolutionary schools of theology and brought out the element of eschatological tension between the inauguration of the kingdom of God in the ministry of Jesus and its incomplete fulfillment in history. His *Cambridge Sermons* (1938) strike an unusual note with their themes of eschatology, sin, and the language of the New Testament being the language of the Church. The title of Hoskyns theological remains, *Crucifixion–Resurrection* (1981), sums up the distinctive twist that he gave to Anglican theology and Christology.

However, Hoskyns was not alone in his Christ-centered ecclesiology at this time. In 1936 the future archbishop A. M. Ramsey published *The Gospel and the Catholic Church*, which saw the Church as founded on the paschal mystery of Christ's death and resurrection. Ramsey was deeply influenced by the mid-nineteenth-century theologian F. D. Maurice, who had a knack of getting down to theological brass tacks and played a part in the rehabilitation of Reformation theology against the Tractarian (Oxford Movement) attack on the Reformers. Ramsey appealed to Luther's theology of the Cross and insisted, as Luther himself had done, that the Church stands or falls by its faithfulness to the gospel of grace. Ramsey united this concern with the impetus of the movement of liturgical renewal and showed how the Church both participates in Christ and shows forth his death and resurrection to the world through sacramental worship and in the structure of its ministry (particularly the episcopate).

The theme of prophetic judgment comes to urgent expression in Temple's introduction to the first report of the Church of England's Doctrine Commission, *Doctrine in the Church of England* (1938), in which he acknowledges the inadequacy of the Christocentric metaphysic, which had preoccupied Anglican scholars during his lifetime, in the face of the totalitarian threat to the democracies and the need "to sound the prophetic note" in a theology of redemption.

Reflecting on the Humanity of Jesus

Theological reflection on the Gospels, in the context of the whole New Testament, is of course as old as Christianity itself. At times it has been hamstrung by failure to do full justice to the true humanity of Jesus. In the modern period, Robert Wilberforce's *The Doctrine of the Incarnation of Our Lord Jesus Christ in Its Relation to Mankind and to the Church* (3d ed., 1850) stands out as an attempt to do precisely that, to address the theological significance of the humanity of Jesus (he is presented as the pattern of humanity) without falling into the rationalist reductionism that sees him as merely human.

Once we cross the watershed of the historical-critical method of biblical study, F. J. A. Hort's Hulsean Lectures for 1871, *The Way, the Truth, the Life*, stand out as an exposition of the tradition of the imitation of Christ that is both philosophical and ethical. Yet a more radical product of the historical approach was even then changing the way Anglicans thought about Jesus.

A revolution began with the publication, anonymously, in 1865 of *Ecce Homo* by Sir John Seeley. It offered an attractive presentation of Jesus in his real humanity as a moral reformer. Although its intention was doubtfully orthodox, *Ecce Homo* was a revelation to many orthodox Anglicans. It opened their eyes, as never before, to the Jesus of the Synoptic Gospels portrayed in his authentic humanity. To Gore, faithfulness to the humanity of "the figure of the Gospels" became a benchmark of theological integrity that had doctrinal consequences. Gore explored these in his essay in *Lux Mundi*, in his Bampton Lectures on the Incarnation, and in his *Dissertations* on the same theme. The main consequence of the human limitation of Jesus' knowledge (the absence of omniscience) was that the Incarnation must have entailed some discarding of the divine attributes of the eternal Word, the divine Son. This "kenotic" (from the New Testament Greek *kenosis*, emptying) theory of the Incarnation, though it could appeal not only to the evidence of the Gospels but also to St. Paul's hymn in Philippians 2, was regarded by conservative high churchmen, such as Liddon, as heterodox.

Steady, balanced work, combining biblical, historical, and philosophical methods, on the person and place of Jesus Christ was undertaken by such Anglican theologians as Oliver Quick, notably in *Doctrines of the Creed* (1938), and by Leonard Hodgson, notably in *And Was Made Man: An Introduction to the Study of the Gospels* (1928). Mainstream Anglican theologians and apologists though they both were, neither of them merely reproduced an uncritical orthodoxy. Both Quick and Hodgson accepted that the Incarnation entailed a genuinely human limitation on Jesus' knowledge, and both acknowledged that the belief in the virgin conception of Jesus involved serious difficulties.

Theological reflection on the humanity of Jesus recurred at the time of the Modernist movement in the Church of England. In 1921, J. F. Bethune-Baker argued that Christology should begin with what is known (we know that Jesus was a man) and proceed from that to what is unknown (in what sense he was also divine). The method of that hammer of Modernists, Charles Gore, was to work both inductively (from the evidence of history, the discoveries of science, and the arguments of philosophy) and deductively (through a critical examination of the teaching of the Church) simultaneously.

Some of the old arguments were reworked in the 1960s and are gathered together in Sykes and Clayton, *Christ, Faith and History: Cambridge Studies in Christology*. This mainly Anglican collection includes a debate between John A. T. Robinson and Stephen W. Sykes about the humanity of Jesus. Sykes attacks the assumption that to affirm the humanity of Jesus is a perfectly straightforward and uncomplicated matter. On the contrary, he claims, the humanity of Jesus must be considered theologically, just as his divinity must be, in the light of the unity of his person.

In *Jesus Christ in Modern Thought*, John Macquarrie (q.v.) addresses the humanity of Jesus (as well as his divinity). From a starting point in common human experience we can see Jesus as the one in whom the human potential for transcendence comes so close to the life of God that it can be said to have become "deified." Macquarrie demurs at the inevitable charge of adoptionism and Pelagianism. He believes that the humanity of Jesus is the proper starting point for method in Christology, though he insists that it is only half of the equation. It provokes us to ask where God is in all this. With DuBose, Macquarrie affirms that, as the representative human being, Jesus reveals the truth about humanity and in so doing points us to God.

Jesus and the Atonement in Modern Anglicanism

A collateral enterprise of Anglican theology, with links to Christology and the critical study of the New Testament, is the study of the atonement, particularly of the redemptive significance of the death of Jesus. Not uniquely but nevertheless characteristically, modern Anglican theologians have been drawn back repeatedly to wrestle with this question. Often they have believed that they were liberating the Church from views that obscured the real Jesus, the servant and agent of God's unfathomable love. Benjamin Jowett's essay on the atonement (1855, revised 1859, published in *Theological Essays*) begins with an outburst of moral revulsion against juridical, substitutionary doctrines of atonement. Jowett insists that the death of Jesus should not be abstracted from his life and ministry: "Christ died for us in no other sense than he lived or rose again for us." Redemption is effected through our identification and communion with the living Christ.

F. D. Maurice's *Theological Essays* (1853) presented the atonement as an act of divine self-giving. In Jesus, God offered himself for the sins of the world. In him, divine love and human suffering were brought together. Maurice's *The Doctrine of Sacrifice* (1854, new ed. 1879) vindicated this stance against criticism. Maurice claimed to be recovering the reality of God's loving work of salvation from the fog of human error. We are not delivered, Maurice proclaimed, from any threat emanating from God, but from dark and slavish notions, arising from our own fears, that we have projected onto God.

R. C. Moberly's *Atonement and Personality* (1901) reinterpreted the death of Christ in the tradition of Abelardian exemplarism but without falling into a subjectivizing of the atonement (rather he overobjectified it by not doing justice to the necessity of the appropriate human response to make atonement effective). Moberly gave fresh acknowledgment to the personhood of Jesus and to the personal appropriation of the atonement by developing the idea of the representative role of Jesus as both human and divine. Jesus perfectly expressed both God's just purpose and the human act of penitence. He was indeed "the perfect penitent." Moberly's doctrine escaped from mechanical transaction models of the atonement by emphasizing the real dynamic relation between Jesus and humanity through creation and re-creation.

Hastings Rashdall's *The Idea of Atonement in Christian Theology* (1919) was a major restatement of the Abelardian or exemplarist view of the atonement. Rashdall had already savaged Moberly's logic in a major review (1902). His method in this treatise is to start from the teaching of Jesus in the Gospels. Rashdall's is a simplistic interpretation of that teaching; he overlooks the eschatological, dramatic, and sacrificial elements. For him, all that needs to change is the human heart: repentance alone is needed to enter the kingdom of God's forgiveness. God is compassionately involved in the world and seeks the transformation of human attitudes into conformity with the divine.

In *Christus Veritas*, William Temple developed a slightly tougher version of the moral influence theory. In the suffering of Jesus on the Cross, we see both what sin costs God and the strength of God's loving purpose to restore us to communion with himself. Temple's approach is also reflected in *Doctrine in the Church of England*.

The 1995 report of the Doctrine Commission of the Church of England, *The Mystery of Salvation*, dwells on the vicarious or representative-sacrificial interpretation of the death of Jesus, linking it with twentieth-century insights into the compassionate solidarity of God with human suffering, but it does not come down on the side of any single model of the atonement. An appendix makes a critical comparison between the views of the atonement presupposed in the *Book of Common Prayer* (1662) and in the *Alternative Service Book 1980*, respectively.

Conclusion

At the outset of our brief enquiry we raised the question of whether Anglicanism has been deficient in giving theological attention to the person of Jesus. We suspected that if Anglicans were accused of neglecting the founder, source, and inspiration of their faith, they would reply that he is presupposed in all they do and say. At the end of our admittedly cursory consideration of Jesus in Anglicanism, we are faced with the uncomfortable conclusion that, although Anglicans are second to none in their personal devotion to Jesus, the Anglican theological enterprise is not, on the whole, adequately focused on Jesus, not sufficiently Christocentric. Perhaps this encyclopedia, initiated and edited by an Anglican biblical scholar who has not himself been remiss in giving attention to the identity of Jesus, will help to redress the balance.

Paul Avis

See also: Adoptianism; Auden, W. H.; Barth, Karl; Eliot, T. S.; Incarnation in Contemporary Analytic Philosophy; Jesus, Achievement of; Kenoticism;

Kingdom of God; Luther, Martin; Macquarrie, John; Pannenberg, Wolfhart; Schillebeeckx, Edward; Wesley, Charles; Wesley, John; Westcott, B. F., Lightfoot, J. B., and Hort, F. J. A.; Wiles, Maurice; Wright, N. T.

References

Avis, P. 1988. "The Atonement." In *Keeping the Faith: Essays to Mark the Centenary of Lux Mundi*. Edited by G. Wainwright. Philadelphia: Fortress; Allison Park, PA: Pickwick.

Doctrine Commission of the Church of England. 1995. *The Mystery of Salvation*. London: Church House.

More, P. E., and F. L. Cross, eds. 1935. *Anglicanism*. London: SPCK.

Rowell, G., K. Stevenson, and R. Williams, eds. 2001. *Love's Redeeming Work: The Anglican Quest for Holiness*. Oxford: Oxford University Press.

Sykes, S. W., and J. Clayton, eds. 1972. *Christ, Faith and History: Cambridge Studies in Christology*. Cambridge: Cambridge University Press.

Weil, L. 1998. "The Gospel in Anglicanism." In *The Study of Anglicanism*. Rev. ed. Edited by S. W. Sykes, J. Booty, and J. Knight. London: SPCK; Minneapolis: Fortress.

Wright, N. T. 1996. *Jesus and the Victory of God*. London: SPCK.

Anselm (c. 1033–1109)

Anselm was a medieval theologian whose writings are respected for their contribution to theology and philosophy even today. A native of Aosta in northern Italy, in 1056 he traveled to the abbey of Bec (Normandy) to study. He became a monk there (c. 1060) and later its abbot (1070). During that time he gained a reputation as both an abbot and a teacher, and Bec became an important school of theology. He left Bec in 1093 to travel to Norman England to become Archbishop of Canterbury. His time as archbishop was troubled because he, a supporter of Pope Gregory VII's views on relations between ecclesiastics and lay leaders, disputed with two kings: William Rufus and Henry I. This led to several periods of exile, and he finally returned to Canterbury only in 1106. His last three years were disturbed by a dispute with the archbishop of York over primacy in England. Despite the administrative tasks of abbot and bishop (a large administrative correspondence survives), and many travels to Rome and elsewhere, he managed to write books while in both offices, and his works on Christology were produced during his exiles.

Anselm differed from other writers of his time in that he saw theology not primarily as an attempt to arrange authorities and positions within a suitable framework (for either teaching or internal coherence—generally seen as theology's task in the West since Isidore of Seville), but as a search using the powers of the human mind for a deeper understanding of that which underlies what is held by faith. This process he described as "faith seeking insight" (*fides quaerens intellectum*), where this insight was a "seeing" into the mystery beyond human imagination, which is more luminous and clear than what is known by faith, but less than the "sight" granted to the saints in heaven (the beatific vision). There is a ladder of understanding: from faith, to insight, to vision. Insight, he believed, would show the seeker beauty and give joy, but while it was attained by reason this was not set in opposition to authorities (i.e., the Scriptures and the Fathers), but was independent until it could proceed no further. He used this process, famously, not only to examine the content of the notion of God so as to appreciate in the more profound way what it meant to say that the divine existence was more real than anything we experience—the basis of the so-called ontological argument—but also to examine two central tenets of Christian faith about Jesus: that he was God become man (the Incarnation) and that he restored man to divine friendship (redemption).

The key work in which he sought a new insight into the Christ-event is the dialogue *Cur Deus homo* (*Why the God-man*). Written during an exile, it represents his mature thought. It took up the patristic question of what "prompted" the Son to become incarnate in Jesus, which had been examined by Irenaeus and Athanasius among many. The standard Western reasoning, more especially since Augustine's time, was that the Incarnation took place as a result of sin, the Original Sin of Adam, which had lost humanity its claim to life with God: "Adam used his immortality badly and so we die, Christ used his mortality well and so we live" (Augustine). Thus the questions of incarnation and redemption were united as cause and effect. Anselm accepted this Western stand but broke new ground by reducing the number of assumptions used in its theological formulation. The standard position prior to him was that the devil had a claim on humanity from the first sin, and that Christ "bought back" humans from the devil by his death on the Cross. Anselm denied that the devil had any claim, and indeed that such a claim was necessary to explain why Christ had to suffer; instead, he explained both redemption and the Cross using his "theology of satisfaction." Anselm argued that any sin, such as Adam's (which was then transmitted, so making humanity sinful), is an infinite offense to God (infinite because the goodness offended is infinite), and this requires an infinite atonement, or, in the liturgical language of his day, "satisfaction." Since a mere pardon by God would not accord with his justice, some human being would have to make the satisfaction. But who could provide it, since all the children of Adam were themselves offenders? It would require a perfect human, but one capable of an infinite act of love—yet such an infinite act is impossible to a finite creature, even a perfect one. To redeem humanity, God himself would have to make the satisfaction as a human being—hence God becoming a man in Jesus Christ. Only by this process of satisfaction could God, being just, fulfill his original plan for human happiness and not have his purposes frustrated. And, since sin must not touch this human (or he would be incapable of making satisfaction), Jesus had to have a virginal conception (the theme he pursued in his other major Christological work, *De conceptu virginali*), because a human father would pass on the taint of Adam's sin in making Mary pregnant.

Although Anselm's theory had critics, from the outset, particularly as it appeared that one could deduce what God *had* to do, it became the basis of later Western Christology where soteriology was the driving force, until, at least, the nineteenth century. Moreover, through Anselm's widely used meditations, the theory, but in more accessible forms, became a standard part of Western spirituality whereby Jesus was focused upon as "the God-Man" and a "perfect human," "the sinless one slain for the sinner," rather than the individual human being Jesus who is the Word incarnate.

Thomas O'Loughlin

See also: Augustine of Hippo; Irenaeus; Isidore of Seville

References

Luscombe, David E., and Gillian R. Evans, eds. 1996. *Anselm, Aosta, Bec and Canterbury*. Sheffield: Academic Press.

McIntyre, John. 1954. *St. Anselm and His Critics: A Re-interpretation of the Cur Deus Homo*. Edinburgh: Oliver and Boyd.

Southern, R. W. 1990. *Saint Anselm: A Portrait in a Landscape*. Cambridge: Cambridge University Press.

Antichrist

See Second Coming of Jesus in Current Belief

Antiochene Theology

Antioch, on the Orontes, in Syria, was a center of Christian mission from earliest times (Acts 11.19–26; 13.1–4), and various Christian writings are associated with its flourishing church—for example, the Gospel of Matthew, the letters of Ignatius, and the Apology of a second-century bishop, Theophilus. Historians, beginning with Friedrich Loofs (1858–1928), associate particular ideas about Christ with a number of Antiochene churchmen, beginning with its bishop, Paul of Samosata, condemned for heresy about 268, and including Eustathius (bishop c. 324–327), the theologians Diodore of Tarsus (d. 390) and Theodore of Mopsuestia (c. 350–428); also the controversial monk promoted to the bishopric of Constantinople, Nestorius (d. soon after 451), and Nestorius's supporter, Theodoret of Cyros (c. 395–c. 460). The Council of Chalcedon took up elements of the Antiochene tradition, as did the so-called Nestorian churches in the East.

The classification of Christology into Alexandrian and Antiochene is somewhat arbitrary, especially from a geographical point of view. Notable "Alexandrians" operated in and around Antioch (such as Apollinaris Severus [bishop 512–538]). Further, there are overlaps and variations in the thought of those who represent the "schools." Broadly speaking, Antiochenes are associated with a down-to-earth preference for the literal meaning of Scripture, against allegorical interpretation, and a tendency to keep the humanity of Jesus distinct from his divinity without confusion or mixture.

It is too crude to assert that Alexandria began with the deity of Jesus, and Antioch with his humanity. It is true, however, that whereas Alexandrians such as Origen and Cyril of Alexandria (c. 376–444) thought of Jesus as the eternal divine Word clothed in flesh (Word-Flesh Christology), the later Antiochenes contemplated the one Jesus Christ and saw him as simultaneously God and Man (Word-Man Christology). Scholars (notably Grillmeier) now take the view that what is usually called "Antiochene Christology" did not exist before Theodore of Mopsuestia.

Paul of Samosata is known to us only from his enemies and critics. The bishops who assembled to condemn him were mostly connected with the teaching of Origen, and Paul seems to have disagreed with them in two ways. First, he held that God is a single being, and his Word or *Logos* not a distinct person beside the Father; second, he seemed to say that Jesus Christ was an ordinary man ("from below"), who was inspired by that divine Word, whereas his opponents saw him as a divine being clothed in flesh or humanity. Either way, Paul was condemned for denying that Christ was truly divine.

The first Antiochene reaction to Arianism (see Nicea) was strongly hostile. Eustathius affirmed the unity of God as one Being (*ousia*, "substance") against the view shared by Arius and others that God was three beings, Father, Son, and Holy Spirit. It is this one God who acts to reveal himself in Jesus. Eustathius alone of the early opponents of Arianism noted that Arians thought of Jesus as without a human rational soul: they saw him as the Word with a vulnerable "passible" body, and therefore not perfectly or absolutely divine. Eustathius deployed Origen's notion that Jesus had a created soul with which the divine Word was united and claimed that his mental growth and sufferings were to be attributed to that. Jesus is thus a whole man, body and soul, growth and suffering included, and his deity is unimpaired by human experience and weakness. After Eustathius was deposed, his successors, whether conventionally labeled Arians or Orthodox, would condemn his views. Part of the church at Antioch, however, separated themselves from the others and upheld his teaching.

The next phase in Antiochene Christology is marked by the resistance of Diodore of Tarsus first to the Emperor Julian's neopagan assault on Christianity (361–363), and second to Arianism and Apollinarianism. The notion that the divine *Logos*, the pure spiritual mind of God himself, could be manifested in a fleshly man who was born, grew, and suffered was absurd to Julian, as it had been to earlier anti-Christian controversialists. Modern research shows (against Loofs, who read Diodore in the light of his successors) that Diodore started from a Word-Flesh Christology, very exposed to Julian's critique. Diodore responded by distinguishing the divine Word from the Flesh: it was not the divine Word that grew in wisdom and stature (Luke 2.52), but the Flesh he took, on which the Word bestowed wisdom bit by bit. Similarly Diodore distinguishes between various biblical titles of Jesus. He is "Only-begotten" as born of God from eternity, "First-born" as a created Man destined to be promoted to God's right hand. Divinely he is Son of God, humanly Son of David. Later Diodore engaged with Apollinaris, whose teaching he saw as confusing Jesus into a hybrid, neither God nor Man. Diodore held that the two natures or essences (*ousiai*) must be kept apart in the one person, or else the godhead is compromised. It is probable that in the end Diodore recognized that Apollinaris was wrong to deny a created human rational soul in Jesus, but the surviving texts do not say this.

A disciple of Diodore, however, was the great master of the Antiochene school, who in a sense defines it: Theodore (c. 350–428), who became bishop of Mopsuestia in 392. Like Diodore, he died in honor as a pillar of orthodoxy, but came to be hated after Nestorius was condemned; only a few of his writings survive. Theodore held that the Man Jesus was complete with soul and mind; Arianism and Apollinarianism were wrong on that point. Jesus was one being or person, but with two natures (*phuseis*) that must be distinguished and not confused. Church tradition might affirm paradoxes such as "God died" or "Mary is mother of God," but these were shorthand for a richer truth. If Mary is "Godbearer" she is also "Manbearer"—but it is best to say "Christbearer," because "Christ" implies at once God and Man. The eternal Word took flesh in the sense that he took a Man for his own use, like a robe to put on or a temple to dwell in. The Word "takes" or "assumes," and the Man is "taken" or "assumed." Word and Man are to be worshipped as one, just as homage is paid to the king, not to his soul or body separately. None of the weakness, growth, ignorance, learning, suffering, or death attributed to Jesus in Scripture is artificial or feigned, and equally none of it infringes his godhead in any way. Theodore develops in detail Diodore's emphasis that different Scripture texts attribute to Jesus divine features, others human, and that they are to be understood with that distinction.

The indwelling of God in Christ (Colossians 2.9) was explained in terms of "good pleasure" or "will" (*eudokia*). It could not be part of God's "essence" (*ousia*) to dwell in men, or indwelling would apply to all things; nor is it simply his "activity" (*energeia*), since that applies to all his works. To distinguish some persons, as Scripture does, as the place where God dwells involves choice on the part of God. So by good pleasure he dwells in holy people and the righteous, and supremely in the case of Jesus Christ. But Christ is exceptional: there are different kinds of indwelling, and God dwells in him as in a Son (cf. Mark 1.11). This meant ultimately a union so close that the man Jesus ascends to the throne of God and will come to judge the world. But just as the indwelling of the Spirit is incomplete in our human experience and is to be perfected hereafter, so Jesus, before he died, was being prepared for total union with the Word, but it was not yet achieved. For that there is a good reason: through all his growth and activity before his Passion, Christ was a free agent, choosing the good, and rewarded for his virtue. Without that human freedom and development he could not have become the model for others. In the end Word and Man are totally one in the Risen Christ.

The death of Theodore coincided with the rise of the Antiochene monk Nestorius (c. 381–after 451) to become archbishop of Constantinople in 428. Politically inept, Nestorius's sharp presentation of a theology like Theodore's led to his condemnation for heresy. The title *theotokos*, or "Godbearer," was customary in honoring St. Mary the Virgin. One of Nestorius's followers from Antioch attacked this custom in Constantinople, and Nestorius was asked to adjudicate. His first response was technically correct: Mary cannot be the mother of God, or she would be older than God himself; she is "Manbearer." Some people in the court and churches of the capital, and in the two greatest bishoprics of Rome and Alexandria, had already been offended by Nestorius, and they were easily persuaded that he was a heretic who denied Christ's deity. Too late he made clear that (like Theodore) he saw Mary as the bearer of the Man who is God, best called "Christbearer." Cyril of Alexandria, who feared the effects on his own position of the rising power of the bishop in the capital city, organized a brilliant and expensive assault on Nestorius, winning Celestine of Rome to his side: Nestorius was required to subscribe to a rather extreme set of *Twelve Anathemas*, or be deposed. The Emperor Theodosius II, who supported Nestorius, was unable to save him from trial at the Council of Ephesus in 431. Armed with Rome's authority, Cyril led a council that condemned Nestorius for distorting the Creed of Nicea: he had refused to accept Cyril's view that the sole subject of all the actions and experiences of Jesus was the divine Son of God, Creator of the world; Nestorius had turned him into an inspired man. The Syrian bishops, led by John of Antioch, were late arriving, and they were appalled by Cyril's apparently unlawful actions, and especially by his extreme *Twelve Anathemas*; their "Little Council" condemned Cyril and his ally Memnon of Ephesus. The frustrated Emperor upheld the condemnations of both parties, and Cyril was exiled as well as Nestorius. Constructive attempts followed to heal the consequent divisions, and peace was achieved in 433 when Cyril regained his see on the basis of a "*Formula of Union*," which had started life as an Antiochene document at Ephesus. The *Formula* acknowledged Mary as *theotokos* but also affirmed (against Cyril's *Anathemas*) that there are two natures in Christ, divine and human, and that pious writers attributed some sayings and actions of Christ to his human nature, others to his divine. This was accepted by Cyril, and by the bishops of Rome, Constantinople, and Antioch.

Nestorius would spend the rest of his life in exile, and he wrote a book, which survives under the disguise-title *The Book of Heraclides*, in which he explains and defends his views and actions. It becomes clear that he differed little from his master Theodore, affirming that Christ is to be seen as one being in whom the whole Word and the whole Man are united, each subsisting as a distinct being (*ousia*, *hypostasis*), but sharing a single outward manifestation (*prosopon*, inadequately rendered "person" or "role"). Nestorius was defended, though finally disowned in the interests of the peace of the Church, by his friend Theodoret of Cyros. Theodoret criticized Cyril's extreme *Twelve Anathemas* and defended the Antiochene doctrine of "two natures" as it came under attack after Cyril died in 444. His *Eranistes* is a remarkably learned and moderate exposition of his position. Theodoret may have been responsible for the *Formula of Union* of 433, the classic expression of the Antiochene method of setting out the one Lord Jesus Christ with his two natures, divine and human, which is annexed to and authorized in the *Definition* of Chalcedon. Cyril himself, after agreeing to the compromise of that *Formula*, appeased his own extremists by attacking the past Antiochene worthies, Diodore and Theodore, a course that led a century later to their posthumous condemnation and the loss of most of their books.

The chief legacy of Antiochene Christology is the inclusion of its principles in the *Formula* of Chalcedon: Christ is one individual person with two whole natures, divine and human. It also survives in the Nestorian Church (officially known as "The Holy, Catholic and Apostolic Assyrian Church of the East"), once extensive in Persia and across central Asia, but now sadly diminished. Some modern critics, including Loofs, found in Antiochene Christology a model and justification for critical historical study of the human Jesus. That should be treated with caution, since they were no less concerned with his absolute deity and interpreted many words and deeds attributed to him in the Gospels as direct expressions of the divine *Logos*. Scholars debate whether, in terms of the traditional faith of the Church, Nestorius was rightly condemned. His own claim that Chalcedon had vindicated him, and some of the material in *The Bazaar of Heraclides*, discovered in the twentieth century, suggests that he was not. This debate is documented in Grillmeier (559–568), who would guardedly acquit him.

S. G. Hall

See also: Alexandrian Theology; Apollinarianism; Chalcedon; Ignatius of Antioch; Nestorianism; Nicea; Son of God

References

Grillmeier, Aloys. 1975. *Christ in Christian Tradition I: From the Apostolic Age to Chalcedon (AD 451)*. London: Mowbrays.
Hall, Stuart G. 1991. *Doctrine and Practice in the Early Church*. London: SPCK.
Kelly, J. N. D. 1960. *Early Christian Doctrines*. London: Methuen.
Stevenson, James, ed. 1987. *A New Eusebius*. London: SPCK.
———, ed. 1989. *Creeds, Councils and Controversies*. London: SPCK.

Apollinarianism

Apollinarianism may be defined as the heresy that denies the existence of a human soul or mind in Christ. It assumes that the Son or Word of God took flesh (only) and directly fulfilled in Jesus the role that the human mind or soul fulfills in an ordinary human being. But the process by which that position came to be labeled as heretical was a lengthy one, and it is only if we can see why Apollinarianism seemed to so many such an attractive option that we can understand why thinking about the humanity of Jesus developed the way it eventually did in the early Church.

Around the year 360, Apollinaris became bishop of Laodicea, on the Syrian coast about fifty miles south of the great city of Antioch. Much of his work as a Christian teacher was carried on in Antioch, and it was there that Jerome heard him lecture in 377.

But Apollinaris's roots in many ways lay not in Antioch but in its theological and ecclesiastical rival, Alexandria. Apollinaris's father had come from Alexandria, and Apollinaris's thought—indeed, his whole career—was shaped by devotion to the person and thought of Athanasius. In 346, Athanasius passed through Laodicea on his journey back to Alexandria at the end of his second exile. Apollinaris entertained him in his home and was excommunicated for his trouble by the then bishop of Laodicea, George, who was one of Athanasius's many enemies. In antiquity an extensive correspondence between Athanasius and Apollinaris was known, though none of it survives. And Apollinaris always professed to be following in the footsteps of his "teacher," Athanasius (Apollinaris, *To the Bishops in Diocaesarea*, 1).

For Athanasius, it was crucial for our salvation that the Word had taken flesh. He had no interest in the human soul of Jesus. Indeed, he never affirmed that there was one, though he never denied it either. Apollinaris took the fateful step of formally denying the existence of a human, rational soul in Jesus. "We confess . . . that the Word himself became flesh, without assuming a human mind" (ibid., 2). Thus Jesus is no more—and no less—than "God enfleshed," as Apollinaris is fond of saying.

A great deal of confusion has been caused by a remark of Rufinus of Aquileia. Writing at the very beginning of the fifth century, he says that Apollinaris at first taught that what was lacking in Jesus was the entire human soul but that, in response to criticism, Apollinaris backtracked slightly and began to claim that there was in Jesus a human *animal* soul but that the divine *Logos* took the place of the mind or human *rational* soul (*Historia Ecclesiastica*, 2.18). In that Rufinus is almost certainly wrong. What is involved is an ambiguity in the use of the word "soul" (*psuche*). For Apollinaris and his contemporaries, every living thing is "ensouled." The soul is the life principle that makes all living things grow and that lets animals move. Human animals are unique in having a special part of the soul that is endowed with reason. Sometimes Apollinaris thinks in terms of a simple two-way opposition between body and soul. Sometimes he thinks of the distinction between the lower (animal) part of the soul and the higher (intellectual) part. And sometimes he contrasts animated (living) flesh with the rational soul that is meant to govern it. So Rufinus has picked up a slippage in terminology and rationalized it by distinguishing two periods in the evolution of Apollinaris's thought. But what Apollinaris means is that in Jesus there is no separate human thinking and decision-making faculty.

"Those who teach two minds in the case of Christ—I mean a divine one and a human one—are like people who try to carve stones with their fingers. . . . It is impossible that in one and the same concrete being two minds coexist, willing things opposite to one another" (Lietzmann, fragment 150). It is impossible in general because the mind—any mind—is essentially "self-moved": it is self-determining and chooses its own direction. There cannot, Apollinaris thinks, be two self-determining principles in the same subject.

But in the case of Christ the coexistence of two minds is impossible for the further reason that it would undermine the very idea of incarnation. To say that there was in Jesus a human, rational soul would be to say, not that the word became flesh, but that "the Word of God sojourned in a holy man, as was the case with the prophets" (*To the Bishops in Diocaesarea*, 2). If the Word—the *Logos*—were not himself the mind that is enfleshed in Jesus, "what you would have," Apollinaris says, "would be Wisdom enlightening the mind of a human being. But that is the case with all human beings. And if it were so, the coming of Christ was not the sojourning of God, but only the birth of a human being" (ibid., frag. 70).

Why would Apollinaris want to say that sort of thing? Although both the human mind and the divine mind are "self-moved," the latter is consistently so, while the former is not ("identically moved" is Apollinaris's word; ibid., frag. 151). The human mind is wobbly and unstable. It is "changeable and taken captive by foul thoughts" and often submits to the flesh through weakness. That means that the natural order of things is perverted, and the human person becomes out of joint. The flesh is meant to be "ruled," but all too often it gains the upper hand. But the mind of Christ is "divine, unchangeable, heavenly," and the flesh is submissive to it, as it was meant to be (*To the Bishops in Diocaesarea*, 2; Lietzmann, frag. 76). Through this reintegration of the human person, "sin was loosed in Christ and death, which is from sin, was dissolved, and we, sharing in the accomplishment, are saved by faith" (*Tomus Synodicus*).

Apollinaris's picture of Jesus is often accused of throwing away the fullness of the Incarnation and the fullness of our salvation. The Incarnation is said to be impugned because Jesus did not become fully man. And the fullness of salvation is said to be impugned because the human mind is not affected. Apollinaris, of course, would not see it that way.

In the first place, Apollinaris thinks that he is asserting—indeed, that he is safeguarding the assertion—that God became man. "A human being is, according to Paul, a mind in flesh" (Lietzmann, frag. 72; he is thinking of a passage like Rom. 7.25), and that is precisely what Apollinaris thinks he sees in Christ. But in Christ the mind is not a human mind, but rather the divine mind, which is the *Logos*. So in assuming flesh—"flesh consubstantial with our flesh" (*Tomus Synodicus*)—the Word *became* human; he did not come into a human being. "If complete God was joined to a complete human being, there would be two of them" (ibid., frag. 76b).

The classic statement of the second accusation—that our minds need healing as well as our bodies—is the maxim that Gregory of Nazianzen hurled at Apollinaris in the year 382: "What is not assumed is not healed, but it is what is united to God that is saved" (*Letter 101, to Cledonius*, 30). But again, for Apollinaris, that misses the point. The problem that must be overcome is the inherent instability of our minds, darting about erratically amid the manifold attractions and distractions of our world of time and space. What is needed is a "mind which cannot be conquered by psychological or physical disturbances and that leads the flesh and the impulses of the flesh divinely and sinlessly and is not only undefeated by death but in fact overthrows it" (*Kata Meros Pistis*, 30). If Jesus had been the subject of normal human psychological processes, he would have remained like one of the prophets of old—an exceptionally good man. No matter how virtuous his actions, his achievement would have been contingent; the inherent instability would have remained. Instead, Christ opens up a new possibility of human life, a newly restored pattern of human existence. The work of salvation was accomplished by the flesh of Christ, controlled by the divine mind within him; "the self-moved mind in us shares in the overthrow, insofar as it assimilates itself to Christ" (Lietzmann, frag. 74).

Where did Apollinaris go wrong? It might be thought that he simply went too far. He carried the thought of Athanasius to its logical (or illogical) conclusion and made explicit what Athanasius had been content to leave in decent and fuzzy obscurity. But there is a sense in which in trying to explicate Athanasius's theology he overturned some of its key elements. For Athanasius, the human person is a close-knit psychophysical entity. That was true of

Christ and it is true of us. And salvation is for Athanasius understood primarily as the gift of incorruptibility to our perishable flesh.

Apollinaris lays much more stress on stability of mind—on the unchangeability of the divine mind in Christ and on the need for our human minds to be conformed to the pattern of his. Perhaps Apollinaris claims to know too much about the nature of the psychological processes in Jesus and to demand too much of ours.

In any event, Apollinaris for most of his life managed to remain on good terms with most of the defenders of Nicene orthodoxy. But condemnations began in the late 370s, including one by the Second Ecumenical Council at Constantinople in 381 (*Canons*, 1 and 7). He became a favored target for the three great Cappadocian Fathers—Basil, his friend Gregory of Nazianzen, and his brother Gregory of Nyssa—who redefined or reappropriated Nicene orthodoxy in the 370s and 380s. Apollinaris himself died around 392. In 425 most of the remaining Apollinarian community in Antioch was finally reunited with the mainstream Church.

Apollinarianism, in the sense of a denial of the reality of the full humanity of Jesus, remains one of the perennial temptations of Christian thought and devotion. But perhaps its real danger is a tendency to devalue the complexity and ambiguity of human existence.

Paul Parvis

See also: Alexandrian Theology; Creeds; Nicea

References

Primary Source

Lietzmann, Hans, ed. 1904. *Apollinaris von Laodicea und seine Schule, Texte und Untersuchungen* I. Tübingen: J. C. B. Mohr.

Secondary Sources

Chadwick, H., ed. 1956. *St. Basil the Great and Apollinaris of Laodicea*. Oxford: Clarendon.

Grillmeier, Aloys. 1975. *Christ in Christian Tradition*. Vol. 1 of *From the Apostolic Age to Chalcedon (451)*. Translated by John Bowden. London: Mowbrays.

Mühlenberg, Ekkehard. 1969. "Apollinaris von Laodicea." Pp. 362–371 in *Apollinaris von Laodicea*. Edited by Mühlenberg. Forschungen zur Kirchen- und Dogmengeschichte 23. Göttingen: Vandenhoeck and Ruprecht.

Norris, R. A., Jr. 1963. *Manhood and Christ: A Study in the Christology of Theodore of Mopsuestia*. Oxford: Clarendon.

Raven, C. E. 1923. *Apollinarianism: An Essay on the Christology of the Early Church*. Cambridge: Cambridge University Press.

Aquinas, Thomas (1224/5–1274)

Thomas Aquinas, as a friar of the Order of Preachers, had a personal devotion to Jesus Christ; he based several outlines of Christian doctrine on the Creed ("The Christian faith consists above all in the confession of the Holy Trinity, and it glories especially in the cross of our Lord Jesus Christ"). In the *Summa Theologiae*, his best known work, he regards the consideration of "the

Saviour of all and the benefits conferred by him on human kind" as the "consummation of the whole theological enterprise."

Most of Aquinas's career was devoted to expounding Scripture. He could not have imagined students of Christian doctrine whose days were not shaped by worship and ascetical practices. The friars, in particular, understood the liturgy as continuous meditation on, and re-creation of, the realities declared in the articles of the Creed: their daily lives immersed them in "following Christ."

Aquinas never discloses his personal piety, but in the numerous apologias he composed against opponents of the mendicant friars we find him highlighting the theme of "following Christ." Indeed, in a phrase familiar from Jerome (c. 345–420), regarded as an authority on the essence of monastic (religious) life, Aquinas speaks of "following the naked Christ naked."

In the *Summa Theologiae*, Aquinas seems to take Jesus as the prototype of the mendicant friar: Jesus is said to have chosen an active life of preaching and teaching, passing on to others the fruits of his own contemplation. In other words, he was not simply a monk, engaged in contemplation, but also a preacher, ready to share the Good News with others. Aquinas's life, and conception of the friars' way of life, was centered on imitating the Jesus of the Gospels.

When we turn to the *Summa Theologiae*, it might look as if the Jesus of the Gospels disappears. No one would expect Aquinas to work out his Christology in terms of the post-Enlightenment Quest of the Historical Jesus, by reconstructing the history of Jesus of Nazareth. He opens his Christology with questions about "the mystery of the Incarnation: God has become man for our salvation."

The first question is whether it was appropriate for God to become incarnate at all. Given that the Son of God has in fact taken a human nature, as Aquinas supposes, his task as a theologian is to show that there is nothing inappropriate about this. It was neither expected nor required, yet if we think about it, the Incarnation is not utterly arbitrary and unintelligible. For Aquinas, as for medieval theology as a whole, the chief purpose of theological argument was to bring out how fitting the events of God's dealings with the world turn out to be—once what has happened can be taken in and reflected on in a contemplative spirit.

Aquinas, as usual, thinks dialectically. He begins by setting out four reasons for regarding the Incarnation as scandalous: God should not be united to anything physical; God is infinitely distant from us; God should not become entangled with evil; and God, who transcends the entire universe, should not be contained in a woman's womb. In short, it is not difficult to see, these are the objections that would be felt by those—particularly, at the time, the Cathars—who regarded matter, flesh, and the body as radically incompatible with the divine.

Aquinas appeals to a particular conception of God: citing John of Damascus (d. c. 750) and Pseudo-Dionysius the Areopagite (fifth century), whom he takes to voice the doctrine of the undivided Church, Aquinas contends that it fits with the idea of God as the supreme good that God should communicate himself to the creature in the highest way. The Incarnation is one more communication of divine goodness, continuing the process inaugurated in God's creation of the world from nothing, and the process promised to culminate in the "total participation in divinity which is the true beatitude of man and the goal of human life, granted us by Christ's humanity": "God became man so that man might become God."

Aquinas at once moves on to consider the ontological implications of God's becoming incarnate, taking his stand, unsurprisingly, on the decisive formulation of the Council of Chalcedon (451): "two natures in one person." In the middle of this highly metaphysical exposition, however, he offers an account of "the singular human being" Jesus Christ, drawing on the Gospels and portraying him, in effect, as the paradigm of the moral agent described at great length in the previous part of the *Summa*.

Primarily, Aquinas is resisting Docetist temptations. In his day, the temptation was to regard Christ as solely divine, God only "seeming" to be human (Greek *dokein:* "to seem"). Moreover, since Christ's human nature is an "instrument of divinity," in the phrase from John of Damascus that Thomas will make much use of, it is appropriate that he should offer a description of the Jesus of the Gospels. He needs to counter what he obviously takes to be a tempting view that Christ's human nature must be united to the divinity in such a way that the man Jesus, if not just a puppet, could only be a conduit of divine grace. On the contrary, as human, Christ is sanctified like any holy person, only more so. He has the virtues like any other human being, excluding faith and hope, however, since he never completely loses or lacks the vision of God, but certainly including the gifts of the Holy Spirit, the gift of fear of the Lord, and the charisms including prophecy.

This particular individual, who is the man Jesus, as radically and totally holy, is then the "source of grace," as "head of the church" and as head of the human race as a whole. The discussion here is pervaded with New Testament references: Eph. 1.22, Rom. 8.29, 12.4, etc.; 1 Tim. 4.10, 1 John 2.2, etc. The people of Israel are included: "[T]he patriarchs, by observing the sacraments of the Law, were carried to Christ by the same faith and love by which we [Christians] also are brought to him."

Aquinas next turns to consider "what the Son of God incarnate in the human nature united to himself did or suffered." First we consider Christ's "entry into the world," his conception, birth, baptism, and so forth, including questions about the Mother of God. (For Aquinas, Mariology is a subsection of Christology, and, famously, while he allows that other traditions of celebrating the conception of the Virgin liturgically should be tolerated, he sees no need to hold any doctrine of her "immaculate conception": she was sanctified in the womb like John the Baptist.)

Then, on Christ's life in the world, we return to the Synoptic Gospels: Christ's mode of life; the resisting temptation; his preaching; and his miracles. Compared with modern historical-critical reconstructions, obviously, these considerations are very elementary.

That the Christian faith "glories especially in the cross of Christ" emerges in the questions on the Passion. The first question—"whether

Christ had to suffer in order to redeem the human race" (*Summa Theologiae* 3.46.1)—is a meditation on John 3.14 and Luke 24, insisting that God was not compelled to save humankind this way and that Christ chose to die. God could have redeemed us otherwise (ibid., 46.2) but this way provides an example of obedience (ibid., 46.3). Asking why Christ's death was by crucifixion, thus on a cross, Thomas brings together several patristic motifs: the multiple symbolism of the Cross as Tree of Life, that on which Christ was lifted up, the sign that embraces the whole world; the wood of the Cross anticipated by Noah's wooden ark, Moses' rod, and the Ark of the Covenant (ibid., 46.4). The time was right, even though Thomas cannot decide whether it was the Passover (ibid., 46.9); the place was appropriate, Jerusalem (ibid., 46.10). In retrospect, being crucified between two thieves was extremely significant—quoting from Isa. 53:12 as well as Chrysostom, Jerome, Leo, Hilary, Bede, Origen, and Augustine, in another tapestry of patristic allusions.

Thomas turns to the question of who was responsible for Christ's death: he laid down his life willingly (ibid., 47.1–2); out of obedience to the Father's will (ibid., 47.3); but he died at the hands of men (ibid., 47.4–6)—with the "leaders of the Jews," *principes Judaeorum*, bearing the heaviest guilt, the "uneducated Jews," *minores de populo*, being forgiven because of their ignorance, and the pagans including Pontius Pilate being "much more excusable still, since they had no knowledge of the Law."

By far the most contentious question here, from the earliest days of Christian reflection, revolves round the thesis that the man Jesus Christ was caught up in the beatific vision of God throughout his life and even as he died on the Cross (ibid., 3.46.8; but see also 3.9.2 and 3.10.1–4). Thomas cites John of Damascus, always his principal authority in delicate doctrinal matters: Christ's divinity "allowed his flesh to act and suffer whatever was appropriate." In effect, there is no contradiction between Christ's undergoing the *dolor passionis* (pain of the Passion) and enjoying the *gaudium fruitionis* (joy of fruition). The cry of dereliction (Matt.27.46), Thomas will claim, means that God "abandoned Christ in death inasmuch as he exposed him to the power of his persecutors"—"he withdrew his protection, but maintained the union" (*Summa Theologiae*, 3.50.2 ad 1).

That is to say, the cry of dereliction is that of a holy man who, in his suffering, remains certain of the love of his Father. The psalm from which the cry comes needs to be read through to the end, when it will turn out that the psalmist foresees salvation in the midst of his affliction (Ps. 21 [22]).

It is one thing to read Psalm 21 through to the end: thus to put the cry of dereliction in a context that deprives it of the horror of believing Christ to be abandoned by God. It is another matter to interpret the abandonment as meaning no more than that at last the protection against his enemies that he had enjoyed so far was now withdrawn.

In traditional language, Jesus was simultaneously a *viator* and a *comprehensor:* walking the earth while having the vision that the blessed have of God in heaven. For Thomas, the continuous union with God implied in the beatific vision is only an implication of the hypostatic union: if the divine nature and a human nature are to be united in the Incarnation, then there can be no suspension or cessation of the divine nature's being what it is without breaking up the union altogether. Finally, for Thomas, as in the tradition, Jesus is of the same divine nature as the Father: Christ's union with the Father could not be dissolved. This is a logical issue: no Person of the Trinity can exist deprived of relationship in communion with the other two.

In question 48, Thomas considers how Christ's death brought salvation, listing the traditional themes of merit, satisfaction, sacrifice, and redemption. In question 49, Thomas discusses the "results" of Christ's death: freeing humankind from sin; from the power of the devil; from the debt of punishment; reconciling us to God and opening heaven's gate to us.

Thomas devotes a question to the burial and to the sepulchre (*Summa Theologiae*, 3.51), here again citing mainly patristic themes: the appropriateness of the garden, the tomb/womb symbolism.

Finally, considering Christ's descent into hell, Thomas holds that Christ delivered the patriarchs and saints of the Old Testament but did not descend into the hell of the damned (ibid., 52.6) and could do nothing about infants who had died unbaptized (ibid., 52.7).

This takes us to Christ's resurrection, the nature of his risen body, the witnesses, the effects on us, his ascension, his being seated at the Father's right hand, and his being judge of the living and the dead (ibid., 3.53–58).

The question on Christ as judge, and thus the entire Christology, concludes with these words (ibid., 3.59.6): "For this reason God has established none other over the whole earth, since the Lord Jesus Christ is one and the same God and man—let this be enough for the present about the mystery of his Incarnation."

The Christological considerations that begin with the appropriateness of the Incarnation; continue with the logical implications of the hypostatic union (ibid., 3.2–19); the New Testament and largely Pauline themes (as Aquinas thinks) of obedience to the Father, prayer, priesthood, sonship, predestination, worship, and mediation (ibid., 20–26); the events from conception to death, burial, and descent into hell (ibid., 27–52); thus culminate with a relatively lengthy account of Christ in glory, and finally with Christ as judge (ibid., 53–59).

Here Thomas discusses only what bears on Christ's position as judge, as he notes, deferring consideration of the Last Judgment as such (but not living to write it). The text is a tapestry of biblical citations. "In the court where God judges, through Jesus Christ he will judge the secrets of mankind" (Rom. 2.16). The focus is entirely eschatological: "God alone makes souls blessed through participation in him; but Christ is the one who leads us to beatitude" (*Summa Theologiae*, 3.59.2 ad 2). The "consummation of the whole theological project," as Thomas says, is consideration of "the Saviour and what he has done for the human race" (ibid., 3, prologue). Christ, for Thomas as for the tradition, is always also Christ in and with the Church. True enough, no doubt because he lived before divisions in the Church gave rise to questions about the identity and location of "the true Church" (the schism between

East and West did not pose such questions), Thomas has no explicit doctrine of the Church.

For Thomas, Christology does not conclude with the enthronement of the risen Christ as judge of all the earth. After considering the mysteries of the Word incarnate, as he says, we continue with the "Church's sacraments, which have their efficacy from the incarnate Word himself" (ibid., 3.60, prologue). It soon emerges that the sacraments of the Church, and particularly baptism and the Eucharist, have been instituted for two main purposes: "to perfect human beings in what pertains to the worship of God according to the religion of the Christian life and also to counter the failures by sin" (e.g., ibid., 3.65.1). It then turns out, entirely in accordance with tradition, that baptism is "the sacrament of the death and Passion of Christ as regenerating the human creature in Christ in virtue of his Passion," while the Eucharist is "the sacrament of his Passion as perfecting one in union with the Christ who suffered" (e.g., ibid., 3.73.3)—baptism as the sacrament of faith and thus the foundation of the spiritual life, the Eucharist as the sacrament of charity, being the bond of perfection (Col. 3.14).

Thomas does not regard the Church or the sacraments as any kind of continuation or prolongation of the presence of the incarnate Word. The *sacramenta fidei* certainly cause grace and effect salvation, doing so however always in virtue of the Passion of Christ. In the end of the day, Thomas's Christological considerations bring the reader to the Cross. It would not be a difficult exercise to trace the frequency of phrases appealing in one form or other to *Christus passus*: the Christ who suffered, once for all, as we may add, and "to save his people from their sins," albeit glossing that immediately as "showing us in himself the way of truth through which, by rising, we can reach the beatitude of immortal life" (*Summa Theologiae*, 3, prologue).

Fergus Kerr

See also: Baptism; Chalcedon; Enlightenment; Eucharist

References

Primary Sources

Aquinas, St. Thomas. 1965–1976. *Summa Theologiae*, vols. 48–55. Latin text and English translation, with introductions, notes, appendices, and glossaries. London: Blackfriars, in conjunction with Eyre and Spottiswoode; New York: McGraw-Hill.

Secondary Sources

Cessario, Romanus. 1990. *The Godly Image: Christ and Salvation in Catholic Thought from Anselm to Aquinas*. Petersham, MA: St. Bede's.

Levering, Matthew. 2002. *Christ's Fulfilment of Torah and Temple: A Thomastic Theology of Salvation*. Notre Dame, IN: University of Notre Dame Press.

Arius, Arianism

See Nicea

Armenian Christianity

According to the *Epic Histories* of P'awstos Buzand and the *Acts of Addai*, Christianity was first introduced into Armenia from Edessa by Thaddeus, who "set up the great and first church . . . the mother-church of all Armenia," in Taron. Moses Khorenatsi speaks of the "throne of the apostle Thaddeus" (III.liv). From the seventh century, the name of the apostle Bartholomew is also introduced into the apostolocity claim within Armenian historiography. In the *Commentary on the Acts of the Apostles* by Tertullian, Armenians are mentioned among those peoples present at Pentecost. By the third century, the Armenian Christian community was sufficiently organized to attract the attention of Bishop Dionysius of Alexandria, who wrote a letter *On Repentance* to their bishop named Meruzanes (Eusebius, *Ecclesiastical History*, Bk. VI).

The second, more successful evangelization is credited to St. Gregory the Enlightener and the See of Cappadocia in the fourth century. Agat'angeghos links the preaching of the Gospel in Armenia by St. Gregory to the martyrdom of St. Thaddeus in the district of Artaz near Maku.

Sozomen in his *Ecclesiastical History* (Bk. II) says that "the Armenians were the first to embrace Christianity through the conversion of their king Tiridates." Eusebius in his *History* confirms this by recording that "the tyrant [Maximianus Daia] had the further trouble of the war against the Armenians who were Christians and exceedingly earnest in their piety towards the Deity." This persecution of the Armenians took place in A.D. 312. Tiridates's conversion took place in 306/7, and St. Gregory's consecration in 314 provided a period of eight or nine years during which time the church of Armenia was established.

The invention of the Armenian alphabet in 406 and the first translation of the Bible between 407 and 413 were considered important events. Koriwn stresses the value of the Armenian version, stating that Moses, the prophets, the evangelists, and the apostles "became Armenian speakers." The Armenians alone call the Bible *Astuadsashountch*—that is, the "breath of God."

An event of major significance took place in 451, when the Armenians fought the battle of Avarayr against Sassanian Persia. For the first time a Christian nation made a declaration of the principle of the inviolability of freedom of conscience. "From this belief no one can move us, neither angels, nor men, nor sword, nor water, nor any tortures that can be conceived or devised. . . . We will, here below, choose no other lord in thy place [referring to the king of Persia], and in heaven we will honour no other God than Jesus Christ, for there is no other God save Him."

The Fathers of the Armenian Church regard the doctrinal decisions of the Councils of Nicea (325), Constantinople (381), and Ephesus (431) "to be the basis of life and guide to the path leading to God." The Nicene Creed, brought to Armenia by Aristakes, who represented the Armenian Church at the Council of Nicea, has the following anathema added to it: "As for those who say there was a time when the Son was not or there was a time when the Holy Spirit was not or that they came into being out of nothing, or who say that the Son of God or the Holy Spirit are of different substance and that they are changeable or alterable, such the catholic and apostolic holy Church doth anathematize." This statement refutes Arianism, Macedonianism, Apollinarianism, and Nestorianism. St. Gregory added to the Creed his prayer, "As for us, we glorify Him who was before all ages, adoring the Holy Trinity, and the one Godhead of the Father, the Son, and the Holy Ghost, now and ever through ages of ages. Amen."

According to the Armenian Church, the Orthodox faith is that Our Lord Jesus is perfect in his Godhead and perfect in his Manhood. He is *God Incarnate*. Nerses IV Klayetsi (1102–1173), in his *Encyclical Letter*, says: "[T]he Son is begotten of the nature of the Father, but outside time. His begetting is not in the manner of the birth of man, subject to passion and transitory. . . . Rather he is begotten like light from light, fire from fire, for they do not become foreign to each other in individuation, but remain one ray and one warmth of fire and of light both in the one who is generated and in the one from whom he is generated; and there is one nature for both, although they are distinguished from each other in person. In the same way the light of the Son came forth from the light of the Father and the fire of the divinity of the Son came forth from the fire of the Father, they are not other but of one and the same nature."

The Armenian doctrine of the Virgin birth and redemption is also consistent with the above exposition. Mary is "Godbearer" (*Astuadsadsin* = *Theotokos*) and not "bearer of Christ" (*K'ristosadsin*), a term preferred by the Antiochene school. In a hymn sung during the feast of Nativity and Epiphany, the birth of Christ is described by Gregory of Narek (945–1003) thus: "[T]he first-born, of the Mother of God, Virgin Bearer of the Lord, creator becoming a true man as originally created, not in the fallen state of mortals" (Prayer 34), or "The uncontainable in Earth and Heaven is wrapped within swaddling clothes/From the Father inseparate he seats himself in the Holy altar." To refute the accusation that Armenian doctrine is Monophysite in the Eutychian sense the Trisagion as recited in the Armenian Liturgy has: "Holy God, Holy and powerful, Holy and immortal, who wast crucified for us." The crucial clause is: "who wast crucified for us." This phrase is replaced by other phrases: "who didst rise from the dead" at Easter, or "who was born and manifested for us" at the Nativity and Epiphany. Step'anos Siwnetsi (680–735), in his *Commentary on the Divine Liturgy*, says that as the Godhead was present in Christ incarnate, it "was legitimate to say that God was crucified for us, has risen from the dead and was born and manifested for us." The tenor of Armenian theology is daring in accepting that God does suffer and die on the Cross. St. Gregory of Narek (951–1003) speaks of "the crucified God," anticipating the theology of *The Crucified God* by Jürgen Moltmann (1973) by a thousand years.

David the Invincible (590–660) defines the Cross with the predicate *Astuadsenkal* (God-receiving) since, for the Armenian theologian, "the tree of life" in the Book of Revelation becomes the wood of life in the shape of the Cross, "for Abraham saw in the Sabek tree the Cross of Christ."

The *khatchk' ar* (= cross + stone) in Armenian sculpture or the Glorified Cross in Armenian miniatures representing the Life of Christ are among the most original symbols of religious piety. The Cross as the "sign" of God or the "wood" of life is a symbol not of death but life. One of the chants composed by Gregory of Narek and sung on Easter Sunday invokes the powerful image of Christ as a lion on the Cross: "I tell of the voice of the lion/Who roared on the four-winged cross. On the four-winged cross he roared,/His voice resounding in Hades." The lion is king over all the beasts, and Christ is king over all creation.

Vrej Nerses Nersessian

See also: Apollinarianism; Chalcedon; Creeds; Nestorianism; Nicea

References

Aghat'angeghos. 1976. *History of the Armenians*. Translated by Robert W. Thomson. Albany: State University of New York.

Buzand, P'awstos. 1989. *The Epic Histories*. Translation and commentary by Nina G. Garsoian. Cambridge: Harvard University Press.

Frivold, Leif. 1981. *The Incarnation: A Study of the Doctrine of the Incarnation in the Armenian Church in the 5th and 6th Centuries according to the Book of Letters*. Oslo: Universitetsforlaget.

Khorenatsi, Moses. 1978. *History of the Armenians*. Translation and commentary on the literary sources by Robert W. Thomson. Cambridge: Harvard University Press.

Narekats'i, Grigor, St. 2001. *Speaking with God from the Depths of the Heart*. English translation and introduction by Thomas J. Samuelian. Yerevan: Vem.

Nersessian, V. 2001. *The Bible in the Armenian Tradition*. London: British Library.

———. 2001. *Treasures from the Ark: 1700 Years of Armenian Christian Art*. London: British Library.

Thompson, R. W. 1970. *The Teaching of Saint Gregory: An Early Armenian Catechism*. Translation and commentary by Robert W. Thomson. Cambridge: Harvard University Press.

Art

It is possible to look at how Jesus is depicted in art in a narrow sense, whether he had a beard, the length of his hair, and so on. More important than that are the dominant Christian beliefs with which his image was associated at a particular time. Those beliefs are related to the political circumstances of the Church in the culture in which it was set: but they also express theological insights about the meaning of Jesus for that age, insights expressed in its art. All these aspects are kept in mind here.

For most of Christian history the meaning of Jesus was expressed not only in images in which he is the central figure but also through the representation of stories in the Hebrew Scriptures and scenes in which his mother Mary is dominant. For all was seen under the providence of God, Old Testament scenes prefiguring Jesus and those of Mary and the Saints carrying his transfiguring life into Christian believers. However, in this article the focus will be only on those works of art in which Jesus is central, except in such instances as the catacombs, where Old Testament scenes are integral to the presentation of his meaning.

According to the fourth-century church historian Eusebius, King Agbar of

Edessa (the modern Urfa in southwest Turkey) received a letter from Jesus. By the sixth century, it was also believed that he had received a towel with the image of Christ on it, miraculously imprinted, to cure his illness. Two images have been claimed to be this mandylion, or holy towel, one in the Vatican and one in Genoa. But although an image that was claimed to be the mandylion was in Constantinople from 944 to 1203, from where it was seized by the Crusaders, there is no hard evidence to link the surviving images with an image that may or may not have been in existence in the sixth century. Nevertheless this alleged portrait of Jesus has been very influential in later centuries, shaping Christian understanding of how Jesus looked. Shown in Illustration 1 is an icon of the tenth century now in St. Catherine's Monastery, Sinai, depicting Agbar holding the mandylion with the face of Christ imprinted on it. Jesus, with long brown hair and a short beard, is looking at the viewer. Until the 1914 war this image was carried on banners by soldiers in Orthodox countries.

This image is one of three that are termed acheiropaeic or "not made by hands." The equivalent image in the West is that of St. Veronica with the Sudarium or cloth with which Veronica wiped the sweat from the brow of Jesus as he carried the Cross. This incident is first recorded in the fourth century, and copies of the scene are known from the thirteenth. For many centuries this was the most widely revered image of Christ in the West, highly popular not only because of its devotional impact but also because prayers said even with reproductions could earn an indulgence. The most widely known image "not made by hands" today is the Turin shroud, now carbon-dated to between 1260 and 1390. Although these images have been highly influential in the way that Jesus has been depicted for more than a thousand years, we begin here with the earliest Christian art that has survived.

Before the Great Destruction of Art (Iconoclasm) in the Eighth and Ninth Centuries

The Great Deliverer

Although there is imagery in Jewish art that has survived in the synagogue dating from the second century at Dura Europos, the frontier town between the Roman and Persian empires, Judaism officially forbade images, and there is no evidence of its visual influence on Christian art. The contrary is the case as far as Roman art is concerned. The earliest Christian art of the catacombs in the second century and first half of the third took over familiar Roman symbols, such as the anchor and the fish, and gave them a Christian meaning. Especially it adopted the popular theme of a shepherd with a sheep over his shoulders. There are literally hundreds of depictions of this theme, and it is not always easy to tell whether a particular piece is pre-Christian or Christian. Other images that appear but were not developed include Jesus as the new Orpheus and Christ ascending to heaven as the Sun God, depicted in a way similar to the apotheosis of the emperor, and dating from the second century. It has survived in the mausoleum of the Julii under St. Peter's in Rome. The story of Jonah and the whale was a popular Christian theme, and here too familiar classical imagery was taken over. The final scene in the story of Jonah under the gourd, symbolizing Jonah in paradise, has a proto-

Illustration 1: Icon of King Abgar of Edessa portrayed holding the mandylion, or holy towel, of Christ. St. Catherine's Monastery, Sinai, tenth century. (The Art Archive/Monastery of Saint Catherine, Sinai, Egypt/Dagli Orti)

type in the scene of Endymion sleeping and waiting for his lover Selene.

It was in the third century that Old Testament scenes began to appear: those extant, including the Jonah cycle and scenes such as Daniel in the lions' den, the three Hebrews in the fiery furnace, and the overthrow of Pharaoh in the Red Sea, outnumber those from the New Testament, such as Jesus healing and the raising of Lazarus, by three to one. These images conveyed a simple, direct message: God could protect, heal, and save. He could even raise the dead to eternal life, for he himself, the resurrection and the life, had also been raised from death. Those who brought their dead to these burial places came in hope.

One important feature of these scenes, not congenial to the modern mind, is that Jesus is depicted as a divine miracle worker who could outperform the magicians of the ancient world. In nearly every scene to do with the raising of Lazarus and the healing of the sick, Jesus has a magician's wand in his hand. It is this that accounts for the presence of a particular selection of Old Testament scenes. For example, there are twenty-eight sarcophagi in Rome showing the overthrow of Pharaoh in the Red Sea. Pharaoh in the Bible is depicted as the great magician but Moses is an even greater one, and in the confrontation at the Red Sea Pharaoh's chariots are overthrown. Persia was also associated with magic, and not only do the three boys in the fiery furnace wear Persian costume with the distinctive "Phrygian" cap but so do the three magi or magicians as they come to worship the Christ child on the lap of Mary. This is the reason that the magi appear, rather than for example the nativity's being depicted through the annunciation or the birth of Christ. All the magic forces of the ancient world, from Persia, symbolized in the magi, and Egypt, whose overthrow is symbolized in Moses, the prototype of Christ, meet their match in Jesus. As New Testament themes become predominant in the fourth century, it is stories of healings above all that are most frequent. They even appear on everyday objects such as plates and garments. The ancient world had many healing shrines, particularly those of Asclepius, but they appear to have had no images. The Christian Church assured people that Christ the great healer and miracle-worker was everywhere present to meet human need. Through images of Christ healing the woman with the haemorrhage, the blind man, or the paralytic, and through the scenes of the miraculous loaves and the wedding at Cana, it was evident that he could overcome every obstacle.

The Philosopher God

When Christianity became first legal and then the official religion of the Roman Empire in the fourth century, it was natural that Christian artists should appropriate some imperial imagery to celebrate the new order. Indeed, this iconographic idea dominated art history for seventy years. It has now been shown, however, that far more significant in understanding how Jesus was seen in that period is imagery drawn from the gods and from the ancient ideal of the philosopher, and this was often used in an anti-imperialistic way. Ancient philosophers could be people of influence, and Jesus is depicted as such a philosopher, teaching his assembled disciples, in scenes in the catacombs, on sarcophagi, and in the apse mosaic of St. Pudenziana in Rome from about 400. In depictions of Christ's entry into Jerusalem, in the West, he is shown sitting on a donkey dressed in tunic and pallium, his right arm enclosed in the sling of the pallium in the way philosophers traditionally wore the garment, with a hand raised in speech or blessing.

One feature that suggests Jesus was seen not so much as an emperor but as a god is the fact that he is shown sitting on the divine throne of Jupiter, not the imperial stool, as in the apse mosaic of St. Pudenziana, referred to above. Furthermore, he takes on the features of Jupiter, with beard and long dark hair. At the same time it has been argued that in other depictions of Jesus at this time, when he is depicted beardless, he shows certain feminine features that were again associated with the gods. This is markedly so in the scene of the baptism of Jesus in the Arian baptistry in Ravenna in the first half of the sixth century, and in the apse mosaic of the Church of Holy David in Thessaloniki of about 450. Furthermore, in scenes of the entry into Jerusalem in the East, Jesus is always depicted sitting side-saddle on the donkey, the way women rode. Femininity in the gods was associated with divine fecundity and was linked, for example in the apse mosaic in Thessaloniki, with the rivers of paradise streaming out to bring life to the world.

The early depictions of Jesus in the catacombs and on the sarcophagi show him as a handsome, beardless Roman youth, usually with long curly hair (again, a sign of the gods). This is true not only of the apse mosaic in the church of Holy David in Thessaloniki referred to above but also of the so-called Passion Sarcophagus. Such an image was probably associated in people's minds with Apollo and Dionysius. This image of Jesus as a beardless Roman youth persisted until the sixth century. In S. Apollinare Nuovo in Ravenna (557–570), scenes of the life of Jesus that surround the upper half show him sometimes beardless and sometimes with dark beard and hair. This latter image first appeared in the catacombs in the late fourth century and, as already stated, may reflect the imagery of Jupiter. There is a sixth-century icon at St. Catherine's Monastery, Sinai, one of the very few portable icons that survived iconoclasm, which shows Jesus in this way, in the form that came to be called Pantocrator, the ruler of all things (see Illustration 2). He has a Bible in his left hand and is lifting his right in blessing. He has a dark beard and hair. This became the standard form for the Eastern Church and came to dominate the dome in Byzantine churches, albeit in a somewhat fiercer form. It is an interesting question, at the moment unanswerable, how far this taking up of features from pagan deities reflects ideas (our Christ is better than your Apollo or your Jupiter), and how far it is a case of artists using visual images with which they were familiar, items in their repertoire.

Christus Victor

When Christianity emerged triumphant in the Roman world, not surprisingly, the victory of Jesus was depicted in art. For example, the mid-fourth-century sarcophagus known as the Passion Sarcophagus from the catacomb of Domitilla, already referred to, shows the wreath of victory in four out of its five scenes. The crown that a Roman soldier is putting on Jesus is not of thorns but of laurel, and a similar crown overhangs Pilate as he interrogates a large Jesus. The central panel has a cross on which is imposed a large wreath, inside of which is the Chi Rho sign, the symbol that Constantine used for the banners of his soldiers. Below the crossbeam of the Cross are two soldiers sleeping outside the tomb of Christ. Cross and resurrection are seen together as one great victory. When Jesus was first depicted on the Cross, he was shown with arms outstretched and his eyes open, very much alive and

Illustration 2: Sixth-century icon of Christ Pantocrator, or ruler of all things, in St. Catherine's Monastery, Sinai. Christ as Pantocrator is usually represented with a Gospel in the left hand, with the right hand raised in blessing. (Ancient Art and Architecture Collection, Ltd.)

victorious, as on an ivory relief in the British Museum dated from 430 pictured in Illustration 3.

The scene of Pilate interrogating Jesus is frequent and, in juxtaposition with the other scenes on this and other sarcophagi, clearly indicates that the old Roman order has been displaced by a new one made possible by the sacrifice of Jesus, usually symbolized by the story of Abraham about to sacrifice Isaac. Jesus is often shown in a central panel handing over scrolls to Peter and Paul on either side of him, delegating his authority. The supreme authority is no longer the emperor but the Church that has received its authority from the new lawgiver.

Christ in Glory

From the fourth century, New Testament scenes predominate, with occasional prototypes or pointers to these from the Old Testament. Some images remained definitive for all subsequent Christian art, both East and West. For

Illustration 3: An ivory relief of the crucifixion dated 420–430 and now housed in the British Museum portrays the image of Christ victorious. (British Museum)

example, the apse mosaic in St. Catherine's Monastery, Sinai, of the Transfiguration, dating from the sixth century, faithfully depicts the biblical scene with Jesus in a *mandorla* ("body halo"), with Moses on one side and Elijah on the other and the three disciples sprawling on the ground (see illustration on page 375 of this encyclopedia). At this time the resurrection of Christ was shown by a scene of the three women coming to the tomb and finding it empty. This is an image that may go back to the third century and that appears in a small Christian church in Dura Europos as well as on the same British Museum ivory as the crucifixion referred to above and in a mosaic in Ravenna. The tomb in this scene is an *aedicule*, or "little house," and it was based on the actual building erected over the tomb of Jesus in Jerusalem in the fourth century. Pilgrims began to come to Jerusalem in large numbers and, seeing such monuments, could be assured that Jesus had actually lived, died, and been raised from the dead. In a similar way when Christians in Ravenna and elsewhere saw the scene of the three women before the reproduction of that building, they could visually and spiritually enter into the scene. They themselves could become partakers of this saving event.

When major Christian churches began to be built in the fourth century, they took the form of Roman public buildings, basilicas with an apse at the east end. Processions were important for the liturgical life of the ancient world, both for the cult of the pagan gods and the Christian liturgy. In churches the central nave could be filled with mosaics of the martyrs in procession, as is the case in St. Apollinare Nuovo in Ravenna. But the focal point for all these basilicas was the apse. Romans made very frequent use of floor mosaic, but Christians made mosaics of glass as well as marble and covered the walls of the apse with these tesserae (small glass or marble cubes) in vivid colors and especially in gold. Here they could see Christ in glory. In the apse mosaic of the Church of Holy David in Thessaloniki, already referred to, Jesus is depicted in terms of the vision of Ezek. 1.4–28 in a circular aureole of light, seated upon a rainbow. Around him are the four beasts of the apocalypse representing the evangelists, with Ezekiel on one side and Habakkuk on the other, with the rivers of paradise flowing out. This is probably what the apses of Constantinople, now all lost, looked like. These body halos, or *mandorlas*, seem to have come by trade routes from the East, from Buddhist art. They were used by Christians to depict the divinity of Jesus, and the inscription on this mosaic makes it clear that this is his full divinity, not the view of the Arianizing emperors. The Church of Saints Cosmas and Damian in Rome (526–530) shows a standing Jesus in clouds of glory with right hand upraised and his left hand holding a scroll, with saints on either side and scenes of paradise below their feet. Here Christ is even now in paradise rewarding his saints and martyrs, but the viewer is also reminded that this is the one who will come again in clouds of glory. In the Church of St. Vitale in Ravenna (547), Jesus is seated on the globe, handing out a martyr's crown with paradise below his feet. Glory and the reward of paradise get the emphasis, not judgment. There was no wholly definitive image for decorating the apse at this stage, but in one way or another the Christian eye would be drawn along the long aisle of the basilica to an image of Jesus in glory who would reward his own.

So in this period we see an evolution of the image of Jesus drawn from pre-Christian symbols to seeing him as the divine miracle-worker who had defeated the magicians of the ancient world on their own ground. Then, by the fourth century, the old gods had given way to a Jesus of both youthful beauty and ancient wisdom. The Church had also become intellectually supreme, so Jesus was a philosopher god imparting his wisdom to his apostles. It was to these apostles that authority had now been given, not the emperor, and the bishops were their spiritual heirs. This authority came from Jesus, light of light, true God of true God, who could be seen in glory before your very eyes in the apse of the church.

The Early Medieval Period: East, West, and Beyond the Edge of Empire

Byzantium

For two centuries (640–843) there was fierce controversy in the Eastern empire over the legitimacy of Christian images, a period in which many were destroyed, hence the name Iconoclasm. However, the seventh council of Nicea in 747 and "The triumph of Orthodoxy" in 843 established that images are an essential expression of Christian faith. As John of Damascus (c. 655—c. 750) argued, the material world has been created good by God and therefore can and should be used to express his glory. Moreover, although the invisible

God cannot and should not be represented, God had made himself visible in Jesus Christ and therefore Christian art is a witness to the Incarnation. By this time the Church had also resolved, in its official doctrines, how Christians were to think about the relations of the humanity and divinity of Jesus. This gave artistic confidence to depict Christ dead on the Cross, which artists had been wary of doing before in case this failed to disclose his divinity. So, for example, in a mosaic in the monastery of Osios Loukas in Greece of 1022, Jesus is shown with his eyes closed, head fallen to one side, the body sagging and blood flowing from his hands and feet, shown in Illustration 4. Such images came as a shock to some Western Christians. Cardinal Humbert (d. 1061), in his anathema of the Eastern Church, asked: "How do you come to fasten to Christ's Cross the picture of a dying man?" The balancing image to this was that of the *anastasis*, the Greek word for resurrection, a scene in the West that is usually called the descent into hell, one of the great achievements of orthodox iconography. It shows Christ, banner in hand, trampling down Hades under his feet, the bars and locks of hell all broken. With one hand he pulls out Adam, while Eve waits for her turn (or is pulled out by Christ's other hand). To one side there are King David and King Solomon, signifying the royal human descent of Jesus, and on the other side is John the Baptist, pointing the way, and sometimes Abel, the first to be killed and

Illustration 4: The Byzantine mosaic of Christ crucified in the narthex of the main church of the monastery of Osios Loukas in Greece, dated 1022, reflects the development of artists' confidence to depict Christ dead on the cross. (Erich Lessing/Art Resource)

therefore one of the first to rise again. Again, a mosaic of this can be seen at Osios Loukas, as well as at Daphni in Greece (1030), as shown in Illustration 5, and one at Nea Moni on Chios from about the same time.

By the tenth century, the scenes from the New Testament that were authorized for depiction in church had become standardized around the great festivals of the Christian year, both those to do with Jesus and those to do with Mary. These included the annunciation, the nativity, the presentation in the temple, the baptism of Jesus, the Transfiguration, the entry into Jerusalem, the crucifixion, the women finding the tomb empty, and the Resurrection. At the same time as this cycle became established, so did the layout and design of classical Byzantine churches. In the dome is the dominating figure of Christ pantocrator, ruler of all, surrounded by cherubim, seraphim, and angels. Round the walls of the church are scenes from the life of Jesus with some of the major feasts, such as the nativity, in the squinches. The apse (in mosaic) is dominated by Mary holding the Christ-child, while the inside of the west wall shows a fresco of the *koimesis*, or dormition, the "falling asleep" of the Virgin Mary. This last is another of the great achievements of Orthodox iconography. It depicts Jesus bending tenderly over the dying Mary and taking her soul to himself, as in the tenth-century ivory from Constantinople (see Illustration 6). What this schema impressed upon the mind of the Christian worshipper were the main Christian truths, not arid dogmas but beautiful, deeply spiritual realities that were to encompass and

Illustration 5: The anastasis (resurrection) mosaic (11th cen.) in the monastery of Daphni, Greece, involves the rescue from hell of holy people of old. (The Art Archive/Dagli Orti)

Illustration 6: Icon of the koimesis, or falling asleep, of the Virgin in ivory—such images stressed the beauty and deep spirituality of Christian belief that were to pervade all aspects of life. (The Metropolitan Museum of Art, Gift of J. Pierpont Morgan, 1917. [17.190.132])

pervade all aspects of life. As Patriarch Germanus (c. 640—c. 733) said, "The Church is the earthly heaven in which the heavenly God lives and moves."

After iconoclasm there were two artistic revivals, first under the Macedonian dynasty of emperors in Constantinople from 843 to 1025, and then under the Comneni from 1025 to 1180. Both looked back to the artistic achievements of the classical world and in many works created art no less elegant and harmonious in the service of Christian truth. Examples of these two periods can be seen in some of the icons at St. Catherine's Monastery,

Sinai; in what remains of the mosaics in the great church of Hagia Sophia in Istanbul; in the monasteries of Osios Loukas and Daphni already mentioned; and in many painted churches, especially those in Cyprus, where under unpretentious sloping roofs there opens up a world of spiritual and artistic wonder.

The West

On Christmas Day 800, Charlemagne was crowned Holy Roman Emperor by the pope. During the reign of his dynasty (768–900), there was a conscious attempt at *renovatio*, the re-creation of the classical culture of the old Roman Empire: not the pagan empire but the Christian Roman Empire of Constantine and Theodosius. Charlemagne encouraged learning and the arts from his capital at Aachen, though we have to remember that at this time the West was greatly inferior, both economically and culturally, to Byzantium and its Islamic neighbors. Nevertheless, we know from the *Libri Carolini* that there was disagreement in court circles about the appropriateness of religious images and a particular dislike of their veneration, which was associated with Byzantium. There are eleven surviving Gospel books from Charlemagne's time, but they contain few representations of Christ. They do have however some magnificent pictures of the evangelists themselves, writing and drawing inspiration from the symbols associated with them. It seems that Charlemagne wanted readers to concentrate on studying the actual word of Scripture and on taking it deeply into themselves. The surviving ivories, in sharp contrast, are replete with scenes of Jesus. One reason for this is that they are nearly all based on late antique prototypes. One Gospel book-cover in Oxford (MS Douce 176) has eleven scenes of Jesus of which nine are accounted for by earlier ivories. On these ivories we see the Christianized Roman winged victory, the magi still dressed as Persians, and Jesus himself for the most part as a Roman youth. The style of these ivories is not as accomplished as the late antique prototypes, and they, like the Gospels, show the influence of the more linear Germano-Celtic art. These ivories very often provided the book-covers for the Gospels. As such they would have been in front of the reader before he opened the pages, the image of Christ providing a spur to meditation.

The Old Testament meant a very great deal to Charlemagne. He saw himself as an anointed king, after the pattern of David, and there are Davidic scenes in the illustrations. Indeed in the illustrations of Psalm 23 in the Utrecht Psalter, Christ is shown as leader of the army of the apostles, an iconography that sought to absorb Christ into the Germanic warrior ethic. The Carolingian court and artists were also happy to incorporate mythological figures into scenes with Christ in order to show him as Lord over the many fearful things in a fearful world. For example, a ninth-century ivory of the crucifixion made in Metz and now in the British Museum shows not only a personified sun and moon looking down from the top but also a personified earth and sea looking up from the bottom, while a snake winds itself round the bottom of the Cross. In other examples, Christ is shown trampling down the asp and the basilisk under his feet (alluding to the Psalms, notably 91).

After the collapse of the Carolingian Empire with its consequent chaos, there came a new period of relative order and stability under the Ottonian emperors (919–1024). Like Charlemagne they saw themselves as re-creating the Christian world of the fourth century, and in art they used models from that time as well as those from the Carolingian period. There may also have been some direct Byzantine influence, because Theophano, who married Otto II, was a Byzantine princess. However, particularly in the illuminated Gospels, there is more evidence of the late antique style, but with brilliant colors that may have been influenced by the enamel workshops. These clear outlines and great swaths of bright color create an effect that is at once stark and mysterious. This art was expressed not only in illuminated manuscripts and ivories but also in jewelry and bronze doors.

The Ottonian kings were more concerned than Charlemagne to stress the sacred nature of their kingship under the overall kingship of Christ. So Christ is shown in a sacramentary of 1002–1014 crowning King Henry II, attended by angels; in other illustrations, crowned kings and queens are shown kneeling before Christ as ruler of all.

The Ottonians in their understanding of kingship, both that of Christ and their own, wanted to stress both majesty and humility. One vivid way in which they did this can be seen from the Lothar cross in Aachen Cathedral (1000). As the cross was carried in procession down the aisle, people saw finely worked gold studded with jewels. In the center was a fine cameo of the Emperor Augustus crowned with a wreath. On the other side of the cross, however, the side that faced the emperor in the Imperial Gallery at the West End, is a relief of Christ crucified. Christ is shown with his head falling to one side and the body twisted, dead with blood flowing from hands and side and feet. The people saw the majesty and the king was reminded of the humility.

This humble side found expression in the most moving work of art of the Ottonian period, the Gero crucifix, commissioned by Archbishop Gero of Cologne about 975, shown in Illustration 7. In this crucifix there is no concentration on suffering as such. Rather, what is caught is the sheer weight of Christ's body, hanging down yet in repose. The body is sheer weight, helpless and passive, yet at the same time there is dignity and serenity conveyed in fine graceful lines. There is a poignancy without any suggestion of emotional bludgeoning. As quoted above, Cardinal Humbert was surprised to see a dead Christ on the Cross in the East. But in Germany this same tradition developed in the tenth century and found sublime expression in the free-standing wooden sculpture of Gero, which is still in Cologne.

Beyond the Edge of Empire

From the fourth century a large wooden cross, covered in precious metal and jewels, stood on Golgotha in Jerusalem. Pilgrims took the image of it back home with them to the edges of the empire, east and west, and beyond its frontiers. Jerusalem was captured by the Persians in 629 but not long after recaptured by the Emperor Heraclius, who triumphantly returned the cross to its proper place and held it up to be honored. This feast of the uplifting or exaltation of the cross (in due course an annual observance, on 14 September) made the symbol even more important. Today, stone crosses dating from the

Illustration 7: The Cross of Gero in Cologne Cathedral emphasizes serenity as opposed to suffering. (Erich Lessing/Art Resource)

sixth to the twelfth centuries can be found in Georgia and Armenia to the east and in Ireland, Wales, Cornwall, the north of England, and Scotland to the west. Some of these crosses—for example, many in Ireland—were erected in conscious imitation of what the pilgrims saw in Jerusalem, the stepped mound on which such crosses were erected representing Golgotha and the carving on the stone reflecting the fact that the cross in Jerusalem was covered in metal, with its metal studs and jewels. On the top there is very often a little canopy or miniature house, representing what pilgrims had seen built over the tomb of Jesus. These stone crosses, some large and magnificently carved, are not there to represent the crucifixion so much as the person of Christ and his victory, as the Gospel was spreading to all parts of the known world. The scenes carved on the crosses do very often show the crucifixion and other scenes connected with the passion and resurrection, as in the early tenth-century cross of Muiredach at Monasterboice, in Ireland, the west face of which appears in Illustration 8. But they also contain scenes of Daniel in the lions' den and the three boys in the fiery furnace, giving continuity with the art of the catacombs, as well as other scenes familiar from all periods of Christian art, such as the soldiers before the empty tomb, doubting Thomas, the baptism of Jesus, and the wedding at Cana. There are also depictions of Christ in majesty and the last judgment.

Illuminated manuscripts also date from this early period, in Ireland notably the Book of Kells (c. 800). The art from the Book of Kells shown in Illustration 9 renders Jesus with long, blond, curly hair, a red beard, and blue eyes. The figures are often intertwined with the interlocking, Celtic linear decoration. Other important illuminated Gospels survive from the northeast of England, most famously among them the Lindisfarne Gospels.

Georgia, to the east of the Roman Empire, became Christian very early, with the royal household being converted about 350. It has a long tradition of Christian art, very much influenced by Byzantium, but also by Syria. There are vivid, colorful, cloisonne enamels from the early medieval period: an eighth-

Illustration 8: The cross of Muiredach at Monasterboice, Ireland. The cross's elaborately carved scenes convey the force of Christ's passion and victory, in part through Old Testament foreshadowings. (Photo courtesy Richard Harries)

century Christ on the Cross, shown strong and alive, and a tenth-century one showing him dead. There are some of the earliest forms of the *anastasis*. There are also repousse icons from this period and even earlier reliefs on the very distinctive Georgian churches from as early as the sixth century. The iconography of the art is on the whole Byzantine, but the style and the medium, particularly the enamels, give an effect of simple charm and vitality.

Armenia, Georgia's neighbor, became officially Christian even earlier, when the king was baptized about 330. Armenian architecture is different from that of Georgia but no less distinctive. Its early simple crosses on stones developed into the characteristic stone monument of Armenia, the *khatchk'ar*. This often has a cross of life carved on it, with great leaves going up either side of the cross. They nearly always have linear interlacing, providing a wide surround.

Again, as in Georgia, Byzantine influence has been very marked both in iconography and style, though the Syrian influence shows itself in Gospel illustrations where the outlines of the figures are clear. There is little detail, and there are large areas of color. Armenian Gospel illumination reached a peak in the thirteenth century and again in the early sixteenth, when a large community of Armenians was moved from what is now South Turkey to New Julfa in Isfahan. The Gospel-book of Queen Mlk'e of 851 depicts the ascension of Christ. Mary is in the center of the lower register in an orans position (i.e., standing with hands raised in prayer), with the apostles on either side of her, all signifying the Church. Above is Christ in a *mandorla*, upheld by two angels with other angels on either side of him. This can be compared with a similar scene of the ascension in the Syrian Rabbula Gospels of 586, an ampulla at Monza in Italy, and a Coptic fresco of Baouit in Egypt,

Illustration 9: The arrest of Christ in the Book of Kells (ca. 800), folio 114r at Trinity College, Dublin. (The Granger Collection, New York)

the last two also dating from the sixth century, when this iconography became established.

The Eleventh to the Fourteenth Centuries

Romanesque and Gothic Sculpture and Carving

The main period of Romanesque art, 1050–1150, was shaped by a number of factors. Western Europe had recovered its strength and confidence after the earlier disintegration following the Carolingian period. Christian forces had advanced through Spain and confined Muslims in the south, while in 1099 a Latin kingdom had been set up in Palestine. It was a profoundly religious period, with a monastic revival driven from Cluny, the Burgundian headquarters of the most highly developed form of religious life at the time. By 1100, the Order of Cluny had more than a thousand religious houses. This monastic zeal went with serious attempts to reform the Church.

It was Cluny, with its emphasis on glorifying God in worship, that brought about the revival of sculpture; sculpture was part and parcel of the great cathedrals and monastic buildings that were being built in many parts of Europe. This sculpture is an essential part of these buildings, whether as capitals in the cloisters, within the church to enrich the setting of the liturgy, as figures on the west front, or as reliefs above and around the doors. Most scenes from the life of Jesus are represented in Romanesque sculpture, but some from this period are perhaps of particular interest. First is the depiction of the risen Christ with disciples on the road to Emmaus. This was a great period for pilgrimage, particularly to Santiago de Compostela, and churches were built at many of the pilgrim sites on the route. Jesus is shown as a fellow pilgrim on the road to Emmaus in the cloister of Santo Dominigo de Silos, complete with pilgrim's hat, scrip, and stave (see Illustration 10), and also on another capital at Autun. On Tuesday of Easter week there was often the performance of a play about Christ's appearance on the road to Emmaus, and it has been suggested that these carvings took their images from that. Jesus raising Lazarus had been an important theme in the catacombs, and it became even more prominent in the Middle Ages. There is a particularly fine example in a relief of Chichester Cathedral (c. 1140) in which the face of Jesus is at once concerned, sorrowful, and authoritative.

The most characteristic and striking Romanesque images of Jesus, however, are those that appear in the portals or on the tympanum above one of the main doors of churches. In such scenes Christ is depicted in a *mandorla* of glory, either ascending, sending out the apostles, or judging the world. The typical visual image here is sometimes that taken from an eighth-century illuminated commentary on the Revelation of St. John from Beatus, Abbot of Liebana. And at Moissac a crowned Christ in glory dominates the tympanum with symbols of the evangelists holding their Gospels around him and two seraphs engaged in ecstatic worship. The rest of the tympanum is filled by the four-and-twenty elders of Rev. 4–5. Each looks up with earnest and adoring gaze, holding a viol and a vial or chalice. The emphasis is on glory and praise, not judgment. In the tympanum at Vézelay, a Christ in glory is shown sending the Holy Spirit on the apostles, who in their turn are being sent out on

Illustration 10: This carving of the walk to Emmaus in the cloister at Santo Domingo de Silos in Spain portrays Christ as a fellow pilgrim on the road (eleventh–twelfth c.). (Archivo Iconografico S.A./Corbis)

mission. On the Prior's door at Ely Cathedral, Christ is simply shown in glory in a *mandorla* surrounded by supporting angels, but at Autun and Conques we have Christ the judge, surrounded by the blessed on one side and the damned on the other.

Romanesque relief work and carving were also outstanding in other media, for example metal doors, fine examples of which can be seen in Verona, Pisa, and Hildesheim, on which many scenes from the life of Jesus

Illustration 11: The Volto Santo at Lucca, Italy, is the best known free-standing wooden cross that offers the image of Christ as priest/king. (Scala/Art Resource, New York)

are shown. The mosaics at the church of St. Clemente in Rome and at Monreale in Sicily show how East and West could come together with a common iconography—and magnificent craftsmanship.

During this period there developed the image of Christ on the cross as priest/king, the best known free-standing wooden carving being the *Volto Santo* at Lucca in Italy, as shown in Illustration 11. It was well known by the eleventh century, and recent research suggests that it may be much earlier. There are similar, no less striking versions of this in Catalonia, where it is known as the Majestad. There is a particularly fine example in Borgo San Sepolcro in Italy, which recent carbon dating puts not later than the early ninth century. Christ is shown at Lucca with a long-sleeved robe and a distinctive knotted belt. His arms are held out straight, and his head is only slightly tilted. As already indicated, the Revelation of St. John played an important part in the spiritual life of this time and, in particular, from an artistic point of view the description of the exalted Christ as a high priest, "clothed with a long robe and with a golden girdle round his breast" (Rev. 1.13). At the same time there were many metal crosses showing Christ with a loincloth, not a priestly robe, and his head falling to one side, yet crowned. Many of these have survived from both Germany and Scandinavia, which became Christian only comparatively late. In an illuminated manuscript from Regensburg (c. 1020), Jesus is depicted in a long, purple, priestly robe, with a crown on his head and a stole round his neck. Christ reigns as both priest and king. At Langford in West Oxfordshire there are two relief carvings reset on the outside of the church, one showing Christ in a long robe like that at Lucca and the other showing him in a loincloth with head falling sideways and with something resembling a crown on his head.

The great cathedrals that went up from 1140 onward and the art associated with them are usually termed Gothic, as opposed to the contemporary developments in Italy. The cathedrals, with their pointed arches and soaring space, allowed for the development of stained glass by which the faithful could be taught. Inside the churches of this period there could be wall paintings, especially a great doom above the chancel arch to remind worshipers of Jesus the judge of all things. Outside, very often on the west front, there would be statuary to bring the faith home. On the north portal at Chartres there are early-thirteenth-century statues of Old Testament figures, hieratic, elongated, with wise, soulful faces. Each figure bears a symbol that represents Jesus in traditional Old Testament terms: Melchizedek has a chalice, Abraham rests his hand upon the head of Isaac, Samuel has a sacrificial lamb, David a crown of thorns, and so on. Sculpture of this period became distinguished by its classic pose and truthfulness to nature, by its lyric flow, and the vigor of its individual characterization. The same features distinguish the goldsmith's work and ivories. At the same time as Giotto (1266–1337) was emphasizing the humanity of Jesus in painting, there was a similar concern to depict human emotion in carving—for example, that by Nicola Pisano (active 1258 to 1278) and his son Giovanni (active 1265 to 1314) on their carved pulpits in Pisa, Pistoia, and Siena.

Mystical Humanism in Early Italian Painting

In this period in Italy there are three main influences on the way Jesus is portrayed. First, the religious revival brought about by the preaching and teaching of the Franciscans and Dominicans. This encouraged a greater intensity of religious emotion. Franciscan preachers in particular encouraged believers to imagine that they were actually present at the Gospel event being depicted. In their imagination they would hold the infant Christ or see the blood flowing down from the Cross. Second, there was the beginning of a return to the style and ethos of classical Rome that came to dominate the art of the fifteenth and early sixteenth centuries. Third, there was a growing interest in the human, both in the depiction of the human figure and in the expression of human emotions, an interest that had also characterized Romanesque and early Gothic art in the twelfth century, as already mentioned.

In the church of St. Domenico in Arezzo there is a painted crucifix by Cimabue (1240–1302). The face of Christ falling on one side with eyes closed conveys a powerful sense of inner concentration and repose. This is not a crucifix that emphasizes the suffering of Christ, but it manages to convey both beauty and spiritual intensity. The body tilts gracefully against the background of red and black triangles. Both Franciscans and Dominicans rejected an art of extraneous decoration and urged a concentration on essentials. One of the essentials was the crucifix above the altar.

Duccio (1255/60–1315/18) is best known for his *Maesta* of the Virgin Mary in Siena. But behind and around this were twenty-six scenes of the Passion of Jesus and other panels that show events in his life. Like Cimabue's crucifix, there is still an iconic quality about these scenes with their Byzantine Italian style. They invite the viewer to contemplate and pray to the Jesus before them. This Jesus is at once human and authoritative. For example, he stands before Pilate in a long robe, passive but unperturbed. He looks at Pilate with eyes that authoritatively question the one who questions him. In a similar scene, in which Jesus is before King Herod, the eyes of Jesus look out to question the viewer. Among the panels there was one (now in New York) that showed Christ rejecting the temptation of the devil to give him the kingdoms of the world. The temptations of Christ were not often depicted, and this is a rare, powerful example.

The humanity of Jesus that developed with Cimabue and Duccio flowers with Giotto (1266–1337), especially in his paintings of the life of Jesus in the Scrovegni chapel in Padua. Since the time of Vasari (1511–1574), Giotto has been regarded as the initiator of the more realistic, human tradition in Western art, as opposed to the "Primitive Greek style." The Orthodox Church, on the other hand, regards this as the point when religious art in the West began to degenerate. It is likely that Giotto continues to appeal because he still holds together the Byzantine, iconic dimension with the new emphasis on human psychology and expression. In his painting, the expressions on the faces and the gestures of the arms and hands convey drama and emotion: but as whole compositions they are still subservient to the religious spirit. This is not drama for its own sake. It is controlled by the figure of Jesus, who arouses intense emotions, both human and religious, in both the other characters in the painting and in the spectator. A good example of this is Giotto's fresco *The Lamentation over the Dead Christ*, shown in Illustration 12. This scene was derived from the Byzantine liturgical icon of the *threnos* and became important in this period.

Romanesque sculpture and the painting of the early Italian Renaissance were appreciated anew during the twentieth century. This may be because they both managed to convey something of the transcendent. The Romanesque does it by combining the classical, or Roman, with the more linear, abstract native tradition of Europe: Giotto does it by retaining the Byzantine sense of another, spiritual world, while at the same time depicting human characters with intense emotions. As Italian art developed and became more technically accomplished, something of this numinous dimension, which is still there in Giotto and which remained in Siena for some time after Duccio, was lost.

The Fourteenth to the Sixteenth Centuries

The Ideal Human Beauty

After Giotto, Fra Angelico (1387/1400–1455) continued in the tradition of the uncluttered, devotional image. In the Convent of St. Mark in Florence, he painted a fresco in each of the forty cells to help the meditations of the Dominican friars, of which he was one. The Jesus he painted, with his light brown hair and beard divided in the middle, has a stillness and serenity. His eyes are gentle, even when looking at Judas. In the fresco depicting the three Marys at the tomb, the risen Christ appears above the women emerging from a *mandorla* of light. He is present, but not of this world. By contrast, the rising Christ of Piero della Francesca (1410–1492) at Borgo San Sepolcro is very much a human figure. The early Church was always reticent about depicting the mystery of the resurrection itself. It was suggested either by the women discovering the tomb empty or through the *anastasis*. In the late medieval West and Renaissance Italy, no such reticence was shown. Jesus, in

Illustration 12: Lamentation over the Dead Christ *(1305) by Giotto in the Scrovegni Chapel, Padua. Giotto synthesized the Byzantine, iconic dimension with the new emphasis on human psychology and expression. (Archivo Iconografico S.A./Corbis)*

Piero's painting, with one foot on the ledge of the tomb, climbs out with a classically beautiful body and eyes haunted by what he has been through. Even more startling is the risen Christ of Bramantino (1465–1530), portrayed with his ghostly pale white skin with its veins showing, his face drawn, and his eyes red with tears and suffering (see Illustration 13). This seems not so much the "spiritual body" of St. Paul, referred to in 1 Cor. 15, as a dead body that has come alive again.

Like Piero della Francesca and other Italian artists of the fifteenth century, Mantegna (1431–1506) displays great skill in his use of perspective. He paints Christ dead from the standpoint of a spectator looking along the dead body from Christ's feet at the same level. Whereas the traditional scene of the Lamentation has prominent figures mourning either side of the body, Mantegna shows only the profiles of two, one with a handkerchief to her eye, in the top left-hand corner. He also uses perspective to dramatic effect, and again radically alters the traditional image, in his painting of Christ's descent into hell. Instead of showing Christ in hell itself, facing either the viewer or Adam, he shows Christ's back as he is about to disappear down a dark underground cave.

Illustration 13: Bramantino's Cristo Resusitado *in Museo Thyssen-Bornemisza, Madrid, exemplifies the willingness of artists in the late Medieval period to communicate the subject of the resurrection directly, rather than by oblique suggestion. (Coleccion Thyssen-Bornemisza, Madrid)*

For the early Church, the Magi represented the magic of the East offering its allegiance to the Christ child. As a result of the Franciscans, the nativity of Christ became more prominent in Christian devotion and art, and over the course of time the Magi had turned into three kings with different names, races, and ages. Late Medieval and Renaissance artists loved to depict the kings, in all their finery, offering their gifts. Gozzoli (1421–1497), who shared a love of pageantry and ceremonial with his patron, distributed the procession of the three kings over three walls in the chapel of the Medici Palace in Florence. In the nativity of Botticelli (1445–1510), the Christ child is on the ground with Mary kneeling in adoration before him, an image that had entered Christian art in the late fourteenth century. Above the makeshift stable, angels dance in a circle, and in the foreground they embrace human beings. This mystical dance joining heaven and earth may have

Illustration 14: Michelangelo's Risen Christ *(1519) in Santa Maria Sopra Minerva, Rome, is an Apollo figure free from wounds or suffering. (Araldo de Luca/Corbis)*

been derived from the Platonic philosophy, which influenced some of Botticelli's patrons.

Michelangelo (1475–1564) was also influenced by Neoplatonism. He not only observed nature, like other Renaissance artists, but also aspired to an ideal beauty. There is a symmetry and sweetness about his first Pietà in St. Peter's Rome, as well as a poignancy. This image had developed as a liturgical icon in twelfth-century Byzantine art. As a variant of the Lamentation, it developed in the West in German art and moved to Italy via France, reaching its spiritual fullness in Michelangelo. His risen Christ, illustrated here, is an Apollo figure without wounds or suffering. Again, his Christ at the last judgment is a heroic figure with classical torso (see Illustration 14). Personally devout, Michelangelo sought to express divine beauty in and through the beauty of the human body, and this included the body of Jesus.

The earliest surviving example of a depiction of the Last Supper is a sixth-century mosaic from Ravenna. It has always been a popular subject, and in Leonardo da Vinci (1452–1519) it had dramatic tension when he painted it for the refectory at S. Maria delle Grazie in Milan. For he focuses on the moment of Jesus' announcement that one of his apostles would betray him, and on their reaction.

Devotional Images

Flemish painters of the Renaissance were no less talented or innovative than their Italian counterparts. However, their style is less classical and their mood more religiously intense and expressive. Hubert van Eyck (d. 1426) and his brother Jan (1390–1441) painted the *Adoration of the Lamb* based on the description in Rev. 14. A council of the Church in 692 had in fact said that the ancient image of the lamb should be set aside in favor of actual figures of Jesus, but because of its biblical authority it recurs, particularly in Western art, as in van Eyck's magisterial painting. An influential image from this time depicted in a variety of ways by a number of Flemish and Netherlandish artists is "The Man of Sorrows." A mosaic icon showing a half-length figure of the suffering Christ in front of the cross, with arms folded on his breast, was produced in Constantinople about 1300 and taken to a church in Rome. The Carthusians who owned the church wanted to publicize it, and so they had a print made of it by Israhel van Meckenem. In the period 1300 to 1500 religious art ceased to be a purely public matter. It went into people's homes and with them on their travels. Devotional books encouraged people to imagine themselves before the Man of Sorrows and themselves as the cause of the sorrow. It has been said that the Man of Sorrows is the most precise visual expression of late-medieval piety, and printing ensured its widespread distribution.

During the fifteenth century, a new image entered the repertoire of Christian art, Christ seated upon Calvary, a sorrowful figure summing up the whole Passion. Naked, exhausted, Christ is seated upon a hillock. His feet and his hands are bound with cords. The crown of thorns tears his forehead, and what blood is left in him slowly oozes away. He seems to wait, and an unspeakable weariness fills the half-closed eyes. Christ has already been mocked, crowned with thorns, and scourged. He has carried his cross along the way to Calvary. His robe has been torn away. Now he simply waits. Michelangelo affirmed divine love through the beauty of Jesus. Other fifteenth-century artists affirmed divine love through the willingness of Jesus to plumb the depths of human suffering. This theme was also very much present in the lime-wood sculptures of Germany, which were either free-standing or which formed part of an altar. These are finely carved with expressive faces and gestures.

The Sixteenth to the Early Nineteenth Centuries

Religious Fervor

Constantinople fell in 1453, bringing the great Byzantine tradition to an end. But 500 years before that Christianity had been preached in Russia, and Byzantine influence continued through the tradition of Russian Orthodoxy, including icons. After the fall of Constantinople some Byzantine artists fled to Crete, where an unusually creative fusion of Western and Eastern art emerged for a period. It was from here that El Greco (Domenikos Theotocopoulos, 1541–1614) came. After study under Titian and influenced by Tintoretto in Venice and a period in Rome, he made his life in Spain. He made a number of versions of Christ driving the traders from the temple, one of which is illustrated here and which, like all his pictures, shows an extraordinary energy and intensity. The elongated Jesus, with determined eyes and spiritual force, drives the traders out (see Illustration 15). Influenced by the spirituality of the Catholic Reformation, especially Ignatius Loyola and John of the Cross, his figures are like flames driven by the Spirit. It is likely that this scene was used to represent the drive to reform the Church.

Titian (1490–1576) painted as many mythological scenes as biblical ones, all with color and beauty. Especially memorable among the latter is his *Noli Me Tangere*, inspired by John 20.17. Tintoretto (1518–1594), however, concentrated on biblical subjects. A devout Catholic, sympathetic to the Catholic reform movement, he painted scenes of great drama. Over twenty-five years he painted the life of Jesus on the walls of the Scuola Grande di San Rocco in Venice. His crucifixion, for example, is full of figures moving and active. In the center, Jesus raised high above them on the Cross looks down in a halo of spiritual power. The movement below and around is more than matched by the movement from God to humanity.

The sense of drama in the paintings of Caravaggio (1573–1610) is equally obvious. Their effect is even more immediate because he cut out much extraneous detail in order to concentrate on essentials. In the *Calling of Saint Matthew*, a scene not often depicted and one that perhaps had a particular meaning for Caravaggio, who led a somewhat wild and tempestuous existence, the light falls on the young, lean face of Jesus, following his eyes along his raised arm and pointing hand, which is directed at Matthew, slumped over a table before his money. The faces of other characters in the painting point either to Jesus or to Matthew. They are dressed in contemporary costume, and the faces are those of people with whom Caravaggio mixed daily. Here and in *The Supper at Emmaus* he makes full use of chiaroscuro,

Illustration 15: El Greco's Christ Driving the Traders from the Temple *(c. 1600) shows an extraordinary energy and intensity. (National Gallery Collection. By kind permission of the Trustees of the National Gallery, London/Corbis)*

contrasts of dark and light to obtain theatrical effects. *The Supper at Emmaus* became prominent as a theme in Christian art at this time, because of theological disputes over the Eucharist. In Caravaggio's painting (shown in Illustration 16), the light comes from one side to fall on the moment when the two disciples recognize who he is, in the breaking of bread. One grips the arms of his chair, the other throws his arms akimbo, and both, with their realistic peasant faces, gaze in amazement. The face of Jesus is that of a young Jew, perhaps one of his models. Caravaggio tried to get away from idealized forms of beauty to show the natural truth.

In the north of Europe natural truth tended to be depicted in even more stark terms, sometimes grotesque and caricatured. Bosch had set out a series of powerful religious allegories in this way. He influenced Pieter Bruegel the elder (1525–1569). In his *Adoration of the Kings* there is scarcely a figure that is not caricatured. A mob of soldiers and peasants press forward with stupid curiosity. The peasants have ugly yokel faces. What is more surprising is that the kings, far from being glorious, are old and wizened, with long straggly hair, which is white in the case of one of them. They seem scarcely able to bend down. It is into this unadorned, unromantic world that the Incarnate Word is born.

Illustration 16: Caravaggio's The Supper at Emmaus *(c. 1596–1602) uses contemporary dress and a realistic approach in a move away from idealized forms of beauty. (*The Art Archive/National Gallery, London*)*

The world in which these artists worked was a very troubled one, deeply divided by the religious reformers. This sense of anxiety is conveyed in the work of Dürer (1471–1528). In addition to his famous *Apocalypse*, he produced three sets of prints on the Passion in which the so-called small Passion has thirty-seven items. The prints went with poems, which encouraged readers not only to concentrate on the patient suffering of Jesus but also to consider how much their continuing sins contributed to his continuing suffering. Dürer was trained as a goldsmith, as well as being influenced by the art of Italy, and his meticulous, clear line on engravings and woodcuts made his understanding of Jesus widely known throughout Europe. He appears to have remained a loyal Catholic but found solace through the writings of Martin Luther. His individual prints, engravings, and plates later accompanied the writings of reformed theologians, including Luther and Melanchthon.

Europe continued to be a continent of suffering, and the heightened awareness of this in the fifteenth century continued into the sixteenth. Mathias Grünewald (1470/80–1528) painted the Isenheim altarpiece with its central figure of Christ on the Cross, once described as the greatest of all German paintings. Jesus is shown racked with pain, his body seared by the flagellation and with thorns still sticking into his flesh. The painting was commissioned by a religious order that specialized in caring for people suffering from a severe skin disease. They were placed in the chapel before this painting, and if no miracle occurred and they were not healed, they could at least console themselves with the thought that the God who was with them was one whose skin and flesh had been equally tormented.

The leading Roman Catholic painter of the Flemish Baroque was Peter Paul Rubens (1577–1640). A good example of his style is *The Descent from the Cross*, with its emphasis on the drama, movement, and heightened emotion of the scene. Rembrandt (1606–1669) began by painting biblical scenes in a similarly grandiose manner. However, a series of personal tragedies, the death of his children, followed by that of his wife, Saskia, then the death of his devoted partner and his son, together with heavy debts and having to sell all his possessions, reduced Rembrandt to nothing in worldly terms. But his art took on a new, profoundly spiritual dimension. The Jesus of his paintings is not grandiose but diminutive and still, surrounded by people who are in need of his healing and teaching. He paints the adoration of the shepherds, a scene that began to replace the adoration of the kings at this time, the shepherds and the holy family kneeling in a stable, their bodies conveying gentle, supportive love. He painted the prodigal son, another Gospel scene that became prominent at this time. The returning son kneels before the father who puts his gentle hands on his back. When a child asked where the mother was in this story, she received the reply: "He is a father who loves like a mother." It is this love that is expressed in the Jesus of the so-called *Hundred Guilder Print*, in which the sick and the lame, women who want their children blessed, and all manner of other people come before a Jesus of quiet dignity. This work, summing up all those in need who come to Jesus (see Matt.19.13–15), is reproduced in Illustration 17. This was the most popular of Rembrandt's images and, like many of his other illustrations, it was repro-

Illustration 17: In Rembrandt's Hundred Guilder Print, *all manner of people come before a Jesus of quiet dignity. Amsterdam, Rijksprentenkabinet. (Burstein Collection/Corbis)*

duced in many Protestant bibles. It is probably his view of Jesus, more than any other, that has entered into Protestant consciousness.

Beyond the Bounds of Reason

There were talented artists in the first part of the eighteenth century, but they have left no lasting religious images. In the last half, however, we have the extraordinary figure of William Blake (1757–1827). The Bible was a major source of inspiration for Blake's paintings and engravings, but it seems likely that he saw Jesus Christ, the divine human, not only in the figure of the Gospels but also in a range of archetypes of free humanity. For he claimed to communicate directly with the spiritual world. His figure of Jesus in Gospel scenes is, however, very conventional, with a long, flowing white robe and bearded face, much as many Victorians would later picture him. Among the less usual scenes that Blake paints are *Christ in the Carpenter's Shop* and the *Hymn of Christ and the Apostles*. The young Jesus in the carpenter's shop has a pair of large compasses in one hand, compasses that appear again in Blake's depiction both of Newton and of the Ancient of Days creating the world. For Blake they may signify a synthesis of the capacity to measure things, reason, and what was for him even more important, the imagination. In his scenes of the resurrection, the risen Christ floats free and liberated, a classical, joyous figure, but very similar to *Albion Rose* or *Glad Day*, his symbol of the people of England liberated.

Another painter who wanted to move beyond the limits of rationality and also beyond conventional eighteenth-century landscape painting was Caspar David Friedrich (1774–1840). The Romantic Movement, in which he may be placed, has been described as "spilt religion." Friedrich painted landscapes with a hallucinatory quality, full of symbols that evoke a strong sense of closeness and distance, precise detail and sublime aura. He did not paint Jesus directly, but a great number of his landscapes contain a crucifix: most famously *Cross in the Mountains*, *Morning in the Riesengebirge*, *Cross on the Baltic*, *Pilgrimage at Sunrise*, *Winter Landscape*, and *Cross and Cathedral in the Mountains*. Against the background of a mysterious, haunting landscape, the Cross stands stark and solitary, in nearly every case with the figure of Jesus on it clearly visible. This is a Jesus who shares human solitariness.

From the Nineteenth Century to Today: Europe and Beyond

During this period, depictions of Jesus reflect the major artistic movements, with increasing emphasis during the twentieth century on the brutality and suffering of the world in which Jesus lived. A few artists, such as Stanley Spencer (1891–1959), consciously stood apart from the dominant stylistic trends. It is therefore a period characterized by a great variety of forms of artistic expression: but also one of greater Christian richness than is sometimes recognized.

From Medievalism to Modernism

For the Pre-Raphaelites, Christian themes were central to their project, which they executed in stained glass and tapestry as well as in painting. Millais (1829–1896), like Blake, painted the boy Jesus in the carpenter's shop of his father, a scene that may also have been intended to emphasize the importance of craft at a time of rapid industrialization. We would see this picture as somewhat overidealized and romantic, but it aroused the most extraordinary hostility for its alleged brutal realism. Ford Madox Brown (1821–1893) painted Jesus washing the feet of Peter, an event included within the Passion cycle in Byzantine, Medieval, and Renaissance art but rarely depicted as an independent topic. Brown shows Jesus, with stubbly beard and long, straight hair, going over his neck, concentrating hard on the drying of Peter's feet. Again it was objected to, even in art journals, on the grounds of its coarseness and indignity. William Holman Hunt (1827–1910) is best known for the *Light of the World* in which Jesus is shown in semidarkness carrying a lantern and knocking at an ancient door over which weeds have grown. The painting, shown in Illustration 18, is based on Rev. 3.20: "Behold, I stand at the door and knock." Hunt also painted the risen Christ appearing to the two Marys. Jesus with long auburn, almost ginger, hair, throwing off his grave clothes that are still twined around his arms, appears within a circular rainbow against the background of a red sky. Another Hunt picture showed Jesus as a young man in the carpenter's shop with the shadow of death falling on the wall behind him.

The Pre-Raphaelites had a dreamlike quality about some of their work, and that is even more true of the French Symbolists. Odilon Redon (1840–1916) found himself confronted with Christ during years of personal crisis, and the image of Jesus dominated his work between 1895 and 1900. This is expressed in *Christ with Red Thorns*, *Christ in Silence*, *The Sacred Heart*, and his depiction of Calvary, all in pastel with a soft, mystical feel about them.

Although some of the Impressionists and Post-Impressionists were devout (Manet, for example, and Cézanne, who attended Mass daily), paintings on Christian themes are rare. Van Gogh (1853–1890) was certainly devout, had been a preacher, and a sense of religious ecstasy imbues most of his painting. He painted the *Raising of Lazarus* after Rembrandt and a Pietà after Delacroix in which the yellow green of the body of Jesus stands out against the other blues. Paul Gauguin (1848–1903) was one of the first to be influenced by primitive art. He painted both *Christ in the Garden of Olives* and *The Yellow Christ*, showing Jesus on the cross, using strong, unusual colors to evoke a particular religious feeling. Emil Nolde (1867–1956) was the most gifted exponent of Expressionism in Germany. One of the concerns of the school was a vision of new human beings who would be reunited with both nature and their lost origins. Nolde painted a number of traditional Christian themes to express this vision, and he regarded his religious works as central to his art. He painted a nine-part polyptych on the life of Christ, a Last Supper, an Entombment, and a Pentecost. Best known, however, is his *Christ among the Children*. This theme had become a popular topic among northern artists following its representations by Lucas Cranach as a visual defense for Martin Luther's controversy with the Anabaptists over the validity of infant baptism. Nolde's painting, shown in Illustration 19, shows Jesus bending toward the group of children who smile and clasp him joyously. Georges

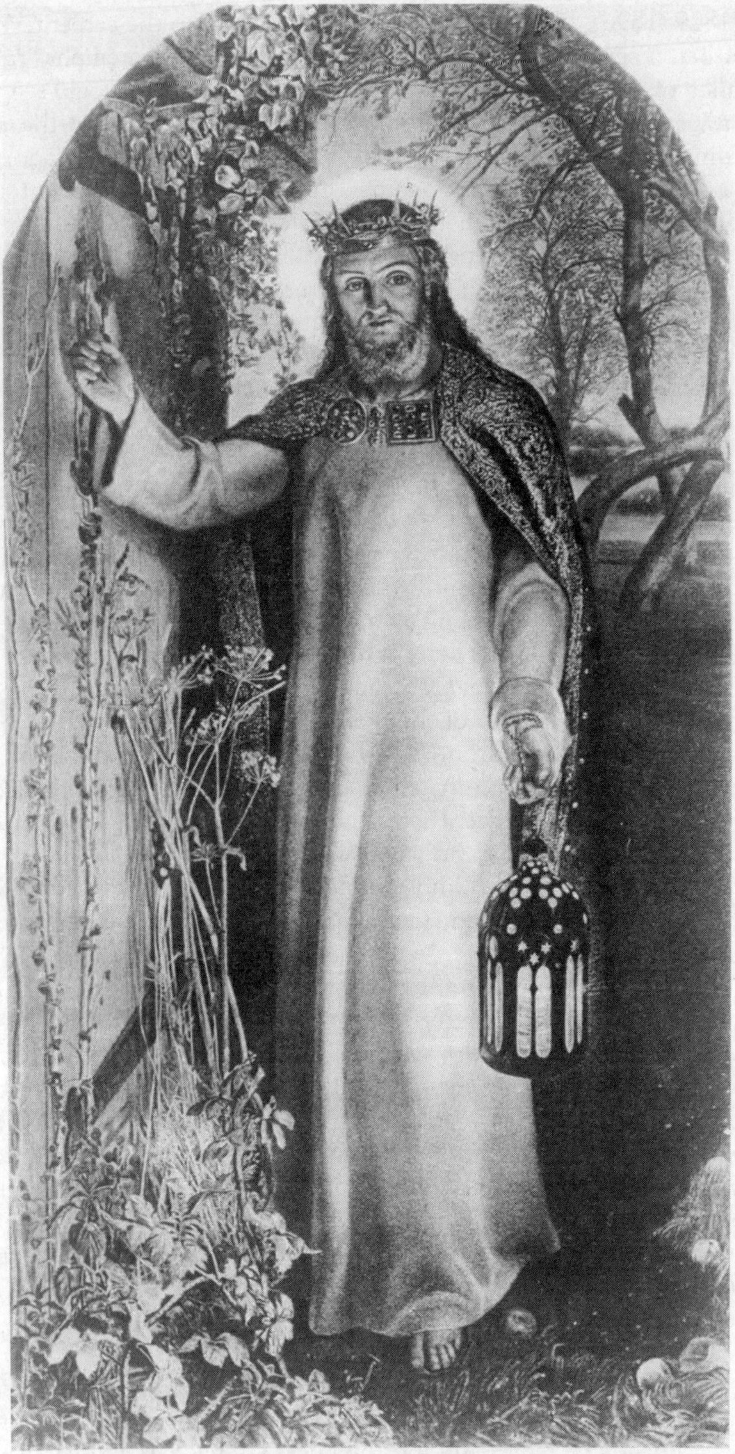

Illustration 18: William Holman Hunt's Christ, the Light of the World *is based on Rev. 3.20: "Behold, I stand at the door and knock." Keble College, Oxford. (Foto Marburg/Art Resource, New York)*

Illustration 19: Christ among the Children *(1910) is perhaps the best-known religious-themed painting by the German Expressionist Emil Nolde. Museum of Modern Art, New York. (Digital Image © MOMA/Licensed by Scala/Art Resource, New York)*

Illustration 20 (left): Christ on the Cross *(1939) by Georges Rouault. Portrayals of Christ by the devoutly Catholic Rouault are imbued with a sense of darkness and suffering. (Museé National d'Art Moderne, Centre Charles Pompidou [CNAC/MNAM/Dist. Réunion des Museés Nationaux/Art Resource, New York)*

Rouault (1871–1958) was apprenticed to a stained-glass maker, and his paintings and prints reflect this early influence. A devout Catholic, profoundly aware of the tragedy of life, he has a sense of darkness and suffering in his paintings, particularly in those of Christ. He gave one of his pictures a quotation from Pascal: "Christ suffers until the end of the world." In his *Christ on the Cross* (see Illustration 20), the pale but strong body of Jesus looms out of a somber background. The head of Jesus falls sideways; his eyes are half-closed, yet include the viewer in a tender gaze.

The twentieth century was rich in sculpture, and Henry Moore did a number of sculptures of the *Madonna and Child*. But it was Jacob Epstein (1880–1959) who focused on Jesus. Epstein, of Jewish background, was much influenced by African and Pacific art, of which he owned more than a thousand examples. He carved *Risen Christ*, now in the Scottish Gallery of Modern Art in Edinburgh, as his private memorial to World War I. Jesus is shown as a tall, columnar figure with a still, stern face, pointing to the wound in one of his hands. This dignified figure was viciously attacked in the press as being like "some degraded Chaldean or African . . . some Asiatic, American or Hun-Jew . . . some emaciated Hindu or badly grown Egyptian." Epstein's *Behold the Man* received a similar response, but his *Christ in Majesty* (see Illustration 21), made for Llandaff Cathedral in 1953, was better received. Again it shows Jesus as tall and columnar, this time with arms slightly moved away from the body and palms opened to the viewer. In Germany the Expressionist sculptor Ernst Barlach (1870–1938) developed, in his later work, wood carving in the Gothic tradition with great tragic power. Unfortunately his work was condemned, and much was destroyed during the Nazi regime. His carving of *Christ and Thomas* shows Thomas holding on to the shoulders of Jesus and looking up at him. Jesus supports Thomas in a tender embrace at the same time looking at the viewer.

Illustration 21: Jacob Epstein's Christ in Majesty *was made for Llandaff Cathedral, Wales, in 1953. (With grateful thanks to the Dean and Chapter of Llandaff Cathedral)*

As already mentioned, outside

Illustration 22: Stanley Spencer. The Scorpion, *from his eight-painting series on the theme of Christ in the Wilderness. (© 2003 Artists Rights Society [ARS], New York/DACS, London)*

the main currents of twentieth-century art were a number of artists working with Christian themes, including Stanley Spencer (1891–1959), whose reputation has continued to grow. He painted Jesus throughout his life both in contemporary scenes, such as preaching at Cookham Regatta, and in biblical scenes relocated to Cookham. Among many outstanding works are eight paintings on the theme of Christ in the Wilderness. For example, *The Scorpion* (see Illustration 22) shows a large, bulky, bearded Jesus gazing on a scorpion in his cupped hands. Jesus looks on it with great gentleness, with an infinite pity. Marc Chagall (1887–1985) was Jewish but influenced by a group of Russian artists who wished to show Jesus as a Jew. In *The White Crucifixion,* painted in 1938 after he had observed the pogroms in Europe, he depicts scenes of synagogues burning and Jews fleeing. In the center of the picture, illuminated by white light coming from an unfurled Torah, is Jesus on the Cross, with a Jewish prayer shawl round his waist rather than a loincloth: Jesus suffering with and among his own people.

Gustav van de Woestyne (1881–1947), a Belgian, painted Christ in the desert. He is a solitary figure against a yellow background, thin and wearing an unshaped, seamless white garment. Most remarkable are the face and eyes. One eye looks ahead to the horizon, seeing all that is there, the other is swiveled around to look at the viewer, except that it seems lost inside its head, evoking an inner world of profound stillness. James Ensor (1860–1949), also a Belgian, said: "Except for rare moments I have been in league with bitterness and disillusion." One of the rare moments is in his painting of Christ calming the storm. A group of German painters reacted against Expressionism and what had gone before, striving instead for an honest objectivity (*Neue Sachlichkeit*). Max Beckman (1884–1950) painted *The Descent from the Cross* in 1917. It shows a larger than life Jesus, emaciated and stiff, part of Beckman's protest against suffering and the war. Otto Dix (1891–1969) in *Ecce Homo II* reflected his own experience as a prisoner of war in World War II and the terrible conditions in Germany immediately afterward. Jesus is shown as very thin, suffering, with a large, gaunt head and green eyes. He also painted *Jesus and Veronica,* in which Jesus, surrounded by thuggish soldiers, looks gratefully at Veronica. His work, like Beckman's, was suppressed by the Nazis. Max Ernst (1891–1976), like the other Germans of his time, drew on German traditions, and in his painting of the crucifixion in 1913 seemed to anticipate the horrors of World War I. He became a founding member of the Surrealist Group, out of which came one of the best known images of Jesus in the twentieth century, *Christ of St. John of the Cross* by Salvador Dalí (1904–1989). Equally well known were some images by Graham Sutherland (1903–1980), his crucifixions, his tapestry of Christ in glory in Coventry Cathedral, and his painting of Christ appearing to Mary Magdalene in Chichester Cathedral.

The twentieth century was dominated by suffering, and inevitably paintings of Jesus tended to concentrate on his sharing in that suffering. Nevertheless, there were various artists who in their own distinctive styles sought to convey other aspects as well. Eric Gill (1882–1940) engraved, drew, and carved in a way that was at once sharply linear and sensual. His carvings of the *Stations of the Cross* show a Jesus strikingly handsome in appearance, with full lips, prominent nostrils, and large eyes, with flowing robes and graceful gestures. His friend David Jones (1895–1974), a poet as well as a painter and engraver, shows Jesus' grace even in the midst of suffering. Quite distinctive is the work of Cecil Collins (1908–1989). Collins stood in the tradition of William Blake and the poet Kathleen Raine in seeking to express eternal spiritual realities through particular artistic symbols. For Collins the major symbol was that of the fool whose true wisdom puts to rout the folly of the world. So Jesus is often depicted as the supreme fool. In *Christ before the Judge* he stands supremely confident and untouched. On the Cross, clowns dance around him and beat their tambourines on one side, while on the other figures with spikes look menacing. In *The Resurrection*, Christ soars upward from the tomb, a graceful whirl of rising light, a crown of thorns turned into a crown of glory on his head. The spikes of spiky people on the ground are rendered helpless. Other artists who depicted Jesus include Roy de Maistre (1894–1968), William Roberts (1895–1980), Hans Feibusch (1898–1998),

Elizabeth Frink (1930–1993), and Ceri Richards (1903–1971), who painted a particularly striking *Supper at Emmaus* for the chapel of St. Edmund Hall, Oxford.

Contemporary British Depictions of Jesus

A sculpture by Marc Wallinger (b. 1959), *Ecce Homo*, depicts Jesus as a frail, human figure, a crown of thorns circling his shaven head. In a world of grandiose and often brutal schemes it brings out the vulnerability and beauty of what it is to be a human being. Other talented artists who have sought to show Jesus include Norman Adams (b. 1927), who has done a remarkable set of *Stations of the Cross* with the face of Christ like an agonized mask yet moving on to a resurrection in nonfigurative terms; Craigie Aitchison (b. 1927), who has consistently painted a tiny cross with a figure slumped over it against a wide background; Maggi Hambling (b. 1945), who every Good Friday seeks to make a study of the Passion; Albert Herbert (b. 1925), who in diminutive, childlike figures manages to convey both charm and spiritual truth in his paintings of Jesus and other biblical figures; Francis Hoyland (b. 1930); Mark Cazalet (b. 1964); John Hayward, who in 1965 painted *Christ the Worker*, for the Southwark Ordination Course; and Roger Wagner (b. 1957), who paints scenes from the Old Testament as well as the New in a style that is at once visionary and realistic, meticulous and hallucinatory. His *Menorah*, reproduced in Illustration 23, depicts the crucifixion against the background of

Illustration 23: The Menorah, *by Roger Wagner, who paints in a style that is simultaneously realistic and hallucinatory. (Courtesy of Roger Wagner)*

Didcot power station, which stands in at the same time for the gas ovens of Auschwitz. John Reilly conveys a sense of movement and dance even at the crucifixion, and Nicholas Mynheer (b. 1958) depicts Jesus and the disciples in curious curves that are at once elegant and sharp, as well as being powerfully expressive of religious feelings. Mynheer carves as well as paints. Other carvers and sculptors include Jean Lamb (b. 1957), Fenwick Lawson (b. 1932), and Peter Eugene Ball (b. 1943), whose carved Christs, in a Romanesque style very often colored or gilded, powerfully evoke sorrow and glory. His work is a special feature in Winchester Cathedral, as are the icons of Sergei Federov. David Wynne (b. 1926) has made three life-size versions of the risen Christ with Mary Magdalene at the moment when he is saying: "Go to my brothers and tell them I am ascending to my father and your father, my God and your God."

Worldwide

In recent decades especially real attempts have been made to express the Christian faith in terms of the culture in which it is set. What follows is indicative of such attempts in just a few cultures. During the 1930s, for example, a Roman Catholic university in China held exhibitions of Christian art by Chinese artists. These paintings on silk show the fineness of touch characteristic of Chinese art at its best, with all the distinctive features of trees, bamboos, and mountains. Jesus is a Chinese figure in a Chinese landscape, and there are some unusual features, such as in the flight to Egypt, in which the Holy Family is shown in a punt, and the house where the Last Supper is held is richly furnished, because it would have been degrading to think of Jesus as poor. Some of these paintings were by Luke Ch'en, a well-known Chinese painter, and others were by some of his pupils. In Australia, Miriam-Rose Ungunmerr-Boumann has painted a set of stations of the Cross in her Aboriginal style; another Aboriginal work by George Mung Mung depicted *Mary of Warmum,* the pregnant Mary, with the Christ child dancing on a shield on her chest. Arthur Boyd (b. 1920) painted Jesus as a woman on the Cross, the Cross standing in a still river against a harsh white Australian landscape. It is entitled *Crucifixion Shoalhaven.* James Brown (b. 1951) has painted a masklike face of Christ in greens and grays. Colin McCahon (1919–1987), sometimes claimed as New Zealand's outstanding artist, painted biblical scenes, including the resurrection of Lazarus.

India has had a longer, if unnoticed, tradition of indigenous Christian art, with Jamini Roy (1887–1972) being one of the pioneers. He found inspiration in the folk art of Bengal villages. He uses clear outlines, bright colors, and Jesus, like the other characters, has prominent fish eyes. Solomon Raj has done many fine woodcuts and lithographs, including one of Jesus sitting cross-legged like a Hindu holy man on a lotus surrounded by fishes and flowers, as seen in Illustration 24. The lotus is Asia's main religious symbol for the true self, and the picture suggests that Christ is the true self of every person. A series of paintings on the life of Christ by Alfred Thomas, from a Hindu family, depicts Jesus as a beautiful young man, his hair up in a bun and moving with the grace of a Hindu dancer. African Christian art is distin-

Illustration 24: Solomon Raj's lithograph Christ on the Lotus *fuses Christ with the lotus, the Asian religious symbol of the true self. (Courtesy Richard Harries)*

guished by its carving in the styles of its different regions. In Japan, Sadao Watanabe has painted almost 400 works on biblical themes in a Japanese idiom, and the same point can be made in relation to other countries in Asia. In Latin America in recent years there has been an attempt to encourage paintings of Jesus closely related to the theme of liberation for both individuals and society.

If we discount the image "not made by hands" discussed at the beginning of the article, we have no record of what Jesus actually looked like. So every artist has imagined him in terms of his or her own culture and ideals: the resulting image has reflected changes in artistic fashion and the dominant feeling of each age. In Europe from the fourteenth century but especially in the twentieth century, Christian artists have been aware of the extent of human suffering and how God in Jesus has entered into and shares this as a fellow human. But this has set up a corresponding challenge, as to how the victory of the Cross and in particular the resurrection can be conveyed in artistic terms in a way that does not take away from the reality of human agony. Not many artists have been able to hold together both these aspects. Even more testing, from a visual point of view, is how to depict Jesus as a human being in a human culture while at the same time indicating that, from the standpoint of Christian faith, he is more than a human being. Very few artists manage to convey a sense of his true human-ness while at the same time doing justice to a divine dimension. Both challenges remain.

Richard Harries

See also: Armenian Christianity; Chinese Christianity; Francis of Assisi; Holy Sepulchre; Icons and the Icon Tradition; Ignatius of Loyola; Jesus, Death of; Jesus as Emperor; John of the Cross; Liberation Theology; Luther, Martin; Pilgrimage; Resurrection; Sexuality; Transfiguration

References

Apostolos-Cappadona, Diane. 1994. *Dictionary of Christian Art*. New York: Continuum; London: Lutterworth.

Barasch, Moshe. 1987. *Giotto and the Language of Gesture*. Cambridge: Cambridge University Press.

Baxandall, Michael. 1980. *The Lime Wood Sculptors of Renaissance Germany*. London: Yale University Press.

Beckwith, John. 1969. *Early Medieval Art*. London: Thames and Hudson.

Collins, Judith. 1989. *Cecil Collins*. London: Tate Gallery.

Cormack, Robin. 2000. *Byzantine Art*. Oxford: Oxford University Press.

Crumlin, Rosemary. 1998. *Beyond Belief: Modern Art and the Religious Imagination*. National Gallery of Victoria.

Day, Michael. 1984. *Modern Art in English Churches*. London: Mowbray.

De Borchgrave, Helen. 1999. *A Journey into Christian Art*. London: Lion.

Derbes, Anne. 1996. *Picturing the Passion in Late Medieval Italy*. Cambridge: Cambridge University Press.

Devonshire-Jones, Tom, ed. 1993. *Images of Christ*. St. Matthew's (Northampton) Centenary Art Committee.

Drury, John. 1999. *Painting the Word: Christian Pictures and Their Meanings*. London: Yale University Press.

Elsner, Jas. 1995. *Art and the Roman Viewer*. Cambridge: Cambridge University Press.

Hamlyn, Robin, and Michael Phillips. 2000. *William Blake*. London: Tate Gallery.
Harries, Richard. 1995. *A Gallery of Reflections: The Nativity of Christ*. London: Lion Publishing and the Bible Reading Fellowship.
Hoekstra, Hidde. 1990. *Rembrandt and the Bible*. Weerts, Netherlands: Royal Smeets Offset.
Image of Christ. 2000. London: The National Gallery.
Jensen, Robin Margaret. 2000. *Understanding Early Christian Art*. London: Routledge.
Kartsonis, Anna D. 1986. *Anastasis: The Making of an Image*. Princeton: Princeton University Press.
Koerner, Joseph Leo. 1990. *Caspar David Fridrich and the Subject of Landscape*. London: Reaktion.
Mâle, Emile. 1982. *Religious Art: From the 12th to the 18th Century*. Princeton: Princeton University Press.
Maney, W. S., in association with the Henry Moore Centre for the Study of Sculpture. 1989. *Jacob Epstein, Sculpture and Drawings*.
Mathews, Thomas F. 1993. *The Clash of Gods*. Princeton: Princeton University Press.
Murray, Peter and Linda. 1998. *The Oxford Companion to Christian Art and Architecture*. Oxford: Oxford University Press.
O'Grady, Ron, ed. 2001. *Christ for all People*. New York: Orbis.
Pre-Raphaelites. 1984. London: Tate Gallery Publishing.
Schiller, Gertrud. 1971. *Iconography of Christian Art*. London: Lund Humphries.
Spencer, Stanley. 1991. *The Apotheosis of Love*. Edited by Jane Alison. London: Barbican Art Gallery.
Takenaka, Masao, and Ron O'Grady. 1991. *The Bible through Asian Eyes*. Auckland, New Zealand: Pac.
Thomas, Denis. 1979. *The Face of Christ*. London: Hamlyn.
van Os, Henk. 1995. *The Art of Devotion*. London: Merrell Holberton.
Young, Brian. 1990. *The Villein's Bible*. London: Barrie and Jenkins.

Athanasius

See Alexandrian Theology

Atonement

See Jesus, Achievement of

Auden, W. H. (1907–1973)

Despite living in the critical shadow of T. S. Eliot, his former editor, Wystan Hugh Auden was a poet of equal standing whose conversion to Christianity had as profound an effect on his poetry as it did on his life. Although more academic work focuses on the place of theology in the poetry of Eliot, it is Auden's work that is more accessible and Christologically focused. Yet, according to Auden, "there can no more be Christian art than there can be Christian science or a Christian diet, only a Christian spirit in which the artist or scientist does or does not work" (Auden 1948, 458). Though both he and Eliot shared the Anglo-Catholic tradition of the Church of England, they

W. H. Auden (1907–1973) (Library of Congress, Prints and Photographs Division [LC-USZ62-110212])

came to the theological conclusion of the centrality of the Incarnation by very different routes. Eliot's path was primarily mystical, whereas Auden's was rooted in a search for social justice. As a result, Auden criticized Eliot's elitism and anti-Semitism as being unworthy of his theology. Auden's intellectual concerns and life mirrored the progress of the twentieth century and its great movements. Perhaps unusual for a poet, he was well versed in the sciences and in philosophy and studied intensely the work of Sigmund Freud, Karl Marx, and Søren Kierkegaard. The works of each left an indelible mark on his spiritual development and poetry as he struggled to make sense of his sexuality in the 1920s, to stand against fascism in the 1930s, and to explore the nature of sin and redemption in a world immersed in the global conflicts of the 1940s.

Many critics watched in dismay as Auden, a popular left-wing poet, abandoned England to pursue a new life in America in 1939. With England on the brink of war, some regarded Auden's flight as tantamount to treason. Others found even more disturbing his return to the devout Anglican faith of his childhood. One of the key factors that led to his disillusionment with the Left was its defense of Stalin despite the known facts of his reign of terror. More personal was the shock he experienced during the Spanish Civil War when the Republicans kept churches locked shut on ideological grounds.

His experience as a war correspondent in China and as a poet in Spain made plain to him that it was the individual who suffers and the individual who causes the suffering, and thus, who must remain liable to judgment by external forces. It was unsatisfactory that Adolf Hitler and the horrors of fascism could be excused or condemned by general theories of nature, history, economics, or psychology. Equally important for Auden was his need to identify the source of love and a remedy for guilt, sin, and suffering in the world. For these, Auden, like Eliot, turned to the life and death of Jesus Christ.

Jesus as man and savior appealed to Auden because his teaching was neither technical nor moralistic, but relational and personal. Auden did not talk much about his personal faith, and when he did in prose it was usually in abstract terms. This tendency to veil the personal through abstraction in his poetry resulted in a hiddenness that has led some commentators to overlook the importance of Christology in his verse. Yet the figure of Jesus was a regular presence in his poetry even after he left the Church at sixteen. One of his earliest poems, written a year earlier, is "Pardon" (1922), a commentary on Jesus forgiving the woman taken in adultery. Here, Jesus appears as a radical teacher who unmasks bourgeois convention and hypocrisy. "A Summer Night" (1933) recounts a sudden mystical encounter with agape love that Auden experienced while lying on the grass after dinner one evening with fellow teachers. This transforming vision of love and hope undermined many of his secular convictions. In "Musée des Beaux Arts" (1938), written just before he left England, Auden used Pieter Brueghel's paintings, notably *Icasus*, as a means of reinterpreting classical mythology with a Christian understanding. The banality of suffering does not render it meaningless, but precisely because it occurs at the edge of the canvas it must be addressed in a similarly oblique manner.

Auden's fear that his early success in England would lead to a stultification of his poetry and a narrowing of his mind led him to leave for America in early 1939 with his friend and fellow poet Christopher Isherwood. Soon after he arrived in New York he met his lifelong homosexual partner Chester Kallman, a Jewish university student and poet, with whom Auden later collaborated on several major projects.

Auden's first major American work was published both as *New Year Letter* and *The Double Man* (1940). It is a thirty-page open letter at whose heart is a diagnosis and description of the vast spiritual disorder of the world. A witty description of the existential loneliness of man despite the various and wholly inadequate attempts by great men through the ages to cover up this fact, the poem demands that readers hear the howling and see the horrors of China, Spain, Abyssinia, and Germany—particularly, in the latter, in Jewish prison cells. It deconstructs Auden's and others' faith in Freud, Marx, or poetry to make things better, concluding that one must have faith to understand the real condition facing man: "true democracy begins / With free confession of our sins" (Auden 1991 [1976], 241). In surveying the world, Auden felt the reality of sin was so great that redemption could not come from within the world. Though passing reference is made in the poem to "blind Christs and mad Madonnas," they are objects that man fails to understand. Significantly, the poem concludes with Auden finding Christ, in a prayer addressed, in circumlocutory terms, to him as "unicorn," "ichthus," and the "one before whom nothing was." A few months later, in "The Dark Years" (October 1940), the name "Jesus" appears, as the antithesis of Judas, for the first time in Auden's work since his childhood.

In the same month Auden started going to church again. His next publication, the long poem *For the Time Being: A Christmas Oratorio* (1945), has Jesus, as both babe and man, at its center. Throughout this work, Auden's first major postconversion poem, he conflates modernity and antiquity. The narrator sets the scene of the Incarnation in terms easily recognized by English speakers: unemployment, disrupted travel, and gender politics. This direction is in no small part due to the theological influence of Reinhold Niebuhr and Søren Kierkegaard, thinkers who located moral authority in the radically free will of individuals, who would be judged by God on the basis of the good they sought to achieve and the moral proximity of their intentions and actions to Christ's life and teaching.

Auden believed the reality and power of the Incarnation needed to be apprehended by each age and culture. The Word, though only made flesh in one generation long ago, is still addressed personally to each generation through the Spirit. The poem captures the mood of the new age of anxiety. The uncertainty with which modernity must hold to its certainties is illustrated throughout as well-known biblical characters articulate their fears, inadequacies, and hope in contemporary speech rather than dress.

This bifocal theological perspective on time and timelessness continued in Auden's most mature poems with Christological themes, such as "Horae Canonicae" (1952–1954), the realization of his desire of many years to write a secular poetry sequence based on the monastic hours, or services, of each day, which are themselves based on the events of Good Friday. As with poems such as "Musée des Beaux Arts" and "Friday's Child" (dedicated to Dietrich Bonhoeffer), the central theme in "Horae Canonicae" is the guilt of the bystander and the collusion of the crowd. It is the death of Christ that redeems all sinners, whether their guilt is rooted in the activity that causes suffering or in equally serious passivity, which fails to stop it.

D.W. Peck

See also: Eliot, T. S.; Kierkegaard, Søren; Marxism

References

Auden, W. H. 1948. *The Dyer's Hand*. London: Faber.
———. 1990 [1948]. *Forewords and Afterwords*. New York: Vintage.
———. 1991 [1976]. *Collected Poems*. New York: Vintage.
Hecht, Anthony. 1993. *The Hidden Law*. Cambridge: Harvard University Press.
Mendelson, Edward. 1999. *Later Auden*. London: Faber and Faber.

Augustine of Hippo (354–430)

Against earlier, less appreciative evaluations, scholars over the past half-century have affirmed the significance of Jesus Christ in the thought of the Latin Church Father Augustine of Hippo as well as the importance of his general contribution to the classical Christian tradition. Despite the fact that he authored no specific work on Christ, it is now generally accepted that his views on Christ evolved during his lifetime, that he arrived at a formulation of the doctrine of the unity of divine and human natures in the unique person of Christ that strongly influenced Pope Leo the Great's representation of this doctrine to the Council of Chalcedon in 451, and that Christ played a central role in the African bishop's thought.

At the beginning of the twentieth century, the German scholar Otto Scheel concluded that under the compelling influence of Neoplatonist philosophy, Augustine held an asymmetrical view of Christ in which the qualities attributed to the eternal, divine Word *(Verbum, Logos)* obscured his human nature and historical reality. Opposition to Scheel's thesis by a succession of scholars culminated in a groundbreaking study by Tarcisius van Bavel (1954) that traced Augustine's efforts to give proper weight to Christ's human emotions and knowledge. Bavel maintained that Augustine gradually developed an account of the unity of Christ's divine and human natures, first in terms of a union of grace, but later as a substantial union theologically expressed through the category of a single person (*una persona*). Finally, the Dutch scholar argued that within his account of the unity of natures in Christ, Augustine promoted the concept of an "exchange of characteristics" proper to each nature, a position later expressed in the patristic doctrine of the hypostatic union and of the *communicatio idiomatum* (*circuminsessio*, *perichoresis*). This complex portrait of Christ emphasizes those human qualities by virtue of which he is judged capable of experiencing and redeeming the fullest range of human suffering, physical and spiritual. Other scholars have further elaborated Augustine's understanding of the Incarnation and its consequences for the development of Latin Christian interpretations of Christ. As a result, it is increasingly accepted that broad philosophical and theological questions in Augustine's thought concerning the triune God, human knowledge, psychology, human action and divine agency, history, salvation, scriptural interpretation, the Church, ethics, politics, aesthetics, and eschatology are better understood when examined in relation to his conception of the unity of natures in Christ.

Augustine acknowledged believing in Christ continually from his early youth. During a serious childhood illness, he asked his mother to allow his baptism in "Christ your God," and at age nineteen he was saddened not to find Christ mentioned in Cicero's *Hortensius*, the book that awakened in him a search for wisdom (*Confessiones* 1.11.17; 3.4.8). This spiritual quest took him first to the Manichaeans, where he found that the name of Christ was revered (*Confessiones* 3.6.10), even though their refusal to accept the doctrine of the Incarnation or the existence of purely spiritual reality led him to imagine the divine Son of God in the limited terms of a luminous, ethereal substance detached from the Father (*Confessiones* 5.10.19–20). Manichaeans venerated Jesus as preeminent among human beings, a spiritually gifted prophet without equal who nevertheless was not the divine Son. Augustine claimed that his passage from Manichaeism to academic skepticism did not lead him to abandon his faith in Christ as the savior of his soul (*Confessiones* 5.14.25; 7.7.11). At Milan, after reading a number of Platonist writings, he was able to accept the existence of spiritual substance and, hence, to begin to understand the Catholic doctrine of the triune nature of God (*Confessiones* 7.10.16). He first thought of Christ as a unique human being of outstanding wisdom, the more so because of his miraculous birth from the Virgin Mary. However, on account of his difficulty reconciling divine immutability with changeable, human nature, he could not accept the idea of a substantial unity between the divine Word and Jesus.

Instead, he accepted an explanation based in Platonist metaphyics that limited their relationship to a "participation" by Christ's human soul and intellect *(anima, mens)* in the wisdom proper to the divine Word. In adopting this position (which he later ascribed to Photinus), he admitted that he had yet to understand the mystery *(sacramentum)* by which the Word was made flesh (*Confessiones* 7.19.25). From the epistles of Paul and the prologue to John's Gospel, he gained an initial appreciation, which he did not find in his Platonist readings, that in the self-abasement by which the divine Word became a human being, God displayed a humility that provides the only way for believers to accept the Incarnation (*Confessiones* 7.20.26–21.27; cf. *De beata vita* 1.4). Prior to his baptism in 387, Augustine acknowledged that in Christ the eternal Word descended from on high, took on human flesh, and acted in a human being (*De Academicis* 3.19.42–20.43; *De ordine* 2.5.16; 2.9.27; cf. Mallard 1980, 85–89). This understanding of the Incarnation was sufficiently orthodox for its time, although it suggested that the "person" of Christ consisted in the divine Word, which had assumed a human being as its exterior manifestation.

During the ten years following his baptism, Augustine deepened his study of the Pauline epistles and became even more convinced of the necessity for humility in the face of the divine initiative (grace) through which believers are enabled to apprehend the Incarnation as mystery. Within this same period, he preached and wrote against the docetic view adopted by the Manichaeans, which denied that the Son of God was incarnate in Jesus, as well as against the Apollinarian doctrine, which held that in uniting itself with Jesus' body in the womb of the Virgin Mary, the divine Word substituted itself for the functions proper to Christ's rational, human soul (*Contra Faustum Manicheum* 29–30; *Sermo* 182.2.2; *De agone christiano* 18.20–20.22; *De diversis quaestionibus* 83.80). Moreover, against the emmanationist explanations for the origin of the universe preferred by the Manichaeans, Augustine argued the Christian position that God created the universe out of nothing through the divine Word (*De Genesi contra Manicheos* 1.2.3). From this perspective he concluded that by means of the Incarnation, the Word through whom God created man was the same Word through whom man was healed and restored from sin and death. In this context, Augustine frequently preached and wrote about Christ as the "humble physician." This leitmotif responded to the appeal that the image of the divine physician already exerted in African and Manichaean religious consciousness; it also enabled Augustine to argue, against the Manichaean belief in the divinity of the human soul, that the latter was created good by God but was inherently weakened by sinful pride, which Adam introduced into human nature, so that the soul requires the humility of God as the medicine that heals it (Studer, 27).

Repeated emphasis on the interaction between Christ's two natures led Augustine, in the years between 400 and 411, to search out a more cogent explanation for the unity of the divine Word with Jesus. He concluded at first that this unity was paralleled in the unity between the human soul and body in general, which he understood along Neoplatonist lines. Accordingly, the divine Word united itself with Christ's human nature by virtue of an "intention" *(intentio)* in the divine will that corresponded on the human plane to an intention within the soul uniting it with the body (*Epistula* 137.11; 157.4;

In Iohannis evangelium tractatus 47.11). Sometime after 411, Augustine perceived that this account resulted in an overemphasis on the divine Word as the primary subject within the unity of the two natures.

At the same time, he was developing his understanding of the term "person" in the context of the unity of natures in Christ. Initially, he employed the term in a dramatic context rooted in the image of a "mask" *(prosopon)*. This use of "person" allowed him to signify the identities of the various speakers within a given biblical passage, in particular, within the Psalms. For example, on one hand, Christ could be said to be speaking "in his person" and "for himself" *(in persona sua)*;or, on the other hand, "in our person" or "for us" *(in persona nostra)*, as when he cried out on the cross, "My God, my God, why have you abandoned me?" (Matt. 27.46; cf. Ps. 22). Here, Christ is the speaker; however, he speaks vicariously on behalf of sinful man, whose nature, but not whose sin, he shares (*Enarrationes in Psalmos* 30.2.1.11; 37.6, 27). Gradually, Augustine reasoned in theological terms from this rhetorical usage of "person" that the voices or speakers in Christ, which represented the two natures, had to be united substantially in one subject *(unitas personae)*, but in such a way that neither nature would lose its integrity.

Sometime prior to 411, he concluded that the concept of "person" was capable of supporting this transformation from a rhetorical to a metaphysical category. Beginning in 411, he began to express the unity of the divine and human natures in Christ through the formula "two natures conjoined in one person *[una persona]*." By this he meant to indicate that the God-man is a unique, specific being, that he is equal in divinity with God the Father and at the same time completely human, but that in his human nature he differed from all other men insofar as he was entirely free of sin, original or personal (*De peccatorum meritis et remissione et de baptismo parvulorum* 1.31.60; *Epistula* 187.10; *Enchiridion de fide spe et caritate* 10.34–12.40; *Contra sermonem Arrianorum* 9.7). In 449, Pope Leo the Great sent to Flavian, the bishop of Constantinople, a letter (the "Tome of Leo") proposing a version of this formula derived in part, directly or indirectly, from Augustine (cf. *Contra sermonem Arrianorum* 8.6; Leo I, *Epistula* 28). Later, in 451, Leo urged the bishops gathered at the Council of Chalcedon in order to resolve the Christological controversy surrounding Eutyches, to accept the formula for the unity of two natures in the one person of Christ that the pope had earlier sent in the letter to Flavian. His letter and the formula it proposed were viewed as orthodox by the council.

Augustine's emphasis on the oneness of Christ's "person" enabled him to employ the concept of the communication of idioms in order to oppose in clearer terms both the Apollinarian denial of the presence in Christ of a human soul and Arian arguments against the divinity of Christ. In formal terms, this teaching, which was already developed in the Christian East, asserted that attributes proper to one of Christ's natures could be predicated of the other nature as well. Thus, Augustine claimed that, in Christ, God assumed human flesh and died, but also that man could be called God (*In Iohannis euangelium tractatus* 27.4; *Sermo* 80.5; 265B.3; *Contra sermonem Arrianorum* 8.6; cf. Studer, 42–43). In this regard, Augustine also referred to a "wondrous exchange" *(mira commutatio)*, by which he meant that through his redemptive activity, Christ extends the qualities proper to his divine nature to members of his body, the Church (*Enarrationes in Psalmos* 30.2.1.3). In making this point, Augustine joined the result of his sustained effort to understand the unity of Christ's natures with another strand in his decade-long reflection on Christ, the unity between Christ and his Church.

Augustine deepened his concept of the "whole Christ" *(Christus totus)* in the context of his preaching and writing against the Donatists, a substantial body of North African Christians who argued that the Church exists only where it can be found "without stain or wrinkle" (Eph. 5.27). In other words, the true Church exists only where its members, particularly its ordained ministers, are completely free of serious sin. Against this view, Augustine insisted that the holiness of the Church, including that of its ministers and sacraments, exists only in Christ, who, as "head of the body, the Church" (Col. 1.18), purifies the members of his body of sin and its consequences (*Contra litteras Petiliani* 2.239; *Sermo Dolbeau* 22.19; *Enarrationes in Psalmos* 118.22.4; *Sermo* 157.3; *De trinitate* 1.12.24). During his controversy with Pelagius and his associates following 411, Augustine further clarified his position that it is only by virtue of its unity with Christ's divine nature that his human nature is completely free of sin (*Enchiridion de fide, spe et caritate* 12.40; *De praedestinatione sanctorum* 15.30). Christian doctrine is thus obliged to affirm that Christ is the only man in history who is completely just *(unicus iustus)*, and that he alone can make others just.

Augustine's formulation of the doctrines concerning the unity of natures in the one person of Christ and of the "whole Christ, head and body," by which the members of the Church are conjoined with and justified by Christ, deepened his understanding of Christ as the one mediator, the point of conjunction, between God and man. Central to this understanding of Christ's mediatorial role is the concept of mystery *(mysterium, sacramentum)* through which God, in Christ, reveals himself. Man arrives at knowledge of God and of those attributes, such as wisdom and virtue, which Augustine held as having their source in God, by means of a philosophical speculation grounded not only in the investigation of perennial truths but in the experience of grace and of the moral conversion that grace effects in the human soul. It is with these dynamics in mind that Augustine deepened over time his understanding of Christ as the "interior teacher," the "humble physician," the principle of divine illumination of the human intellect, the union of human knowledge *(scientia)* and divine wisdom *(sapientia)*, the sacrament *(sacramentum)* and the exemplar *(exemplum)* of the moral life, the true priest, the founder and ruler of the city of God. No human activity can be understood apart from the knowledge and love of the triune God, which is mediated to man under the form of mystery in the life of Christ. Although Augustine held that man's participation in this mystery is made possible by God continually and primarily in the teaching and sacraments of the Catholic Church, he did not exclude the possibility that Christ could still reveal himself as the savior to other spiritually inclined individuals outside of the Christian dispensation (*Sermo Dolbeau* 26.37). In this case, however, as in the case of the baptized members of Christ's Church, Augustine concluded that only those individuals will enjoy the full benefits of this divine grace who are predestined by God to practice the way of humility first exemplified in the Incarnation.

Robert Dodaro

See also: Apollinarianism; Chalcedon; Jesus, Origins of; John, Gospel of; Manichaeism; Son of God

References

Babcock, William S. 1972. *The Christ of the Exchange: A Study in the Christology of Augustine's* Enarrationes in Psalmos. Ann Arbor, MI: University Microfilms.

Bavel, Tarcisius van. 1954. *Recherches sur la christologie de saint Augustin. L'humain et le divin dans le Christ d'après saint Augustin.* Fribourg: Éditions universitaires.

McWilliam, Joanne E. 1992. "The Study of Augustine's Christology in the Twentieth Century." Pp. 183–205 in *Augustine: From Rhetor to Theologian.* Edited by Joanne McWilliam. Waterloo, Ontario: Wilfrid Laurier University Press.

Mallard, William. 1980. "The Incarnation in Augustine's Conversion." *Recherches augustiniennes* 15: 80–98.

———. 1999. "Jesus Christ." Pp. 463–470 in *Augustine through the Ages: An Encyclopedia.* Edited by Allan D. Fitzgerald. Grand Rapids, MI: William B. Eerdmans.

Studer, Basil. 1997. *The Grace of Christ and the Grace of God in Augustine of Hippo.* Translated by Matthew J. O'Connell. Collegeville, MN: The Liturgical Press.

B

Balthasar, Hans Urs von (1905–1988)

Von Balthasar, a Swiss Jesuit and a major figure in modern Catholic thought, follows Karl Barth in being a thoroughly Christocentric theologian. God is revealed in Jesus Christ's human form (the *Gestalt Christi*) and in the form or shape of his lived life. This form is mediated in the scriptural form that communicates the shape of Jesus' person and work to us, and in the ecclesial or Church form, which also has a Christlike shape (manifesting Cross, resurrection, and *eschaton* in its existence and witness). But more than this, the form of Christ is the key to reading the creation itself, in all its formations. Like Barth, von Balthasar understands Christ in his particularity to be the touchstone of reality. Christ is the *concretissimum* by whose particularity the absolutely glorious, good, and true come to light; he it is who animates and gives meaning to everything else: Scripture, tradition, and dogma, as well as the life of the creation in its ordering to (or for the sake of) the covenant between Christ and his Church.

Von Balthasar thinks that the historical-critical approach to Jesus, and the demythologization that often accompanies it, can be blind to what is a full, formed expression of the truth of Christ in Scripture. His emphasis on the integrity of the scriptural revelation, in which all the many parts of the canonical whole mediate the *Gestalt Christi*, "presupposes an understanding of totality that is spiritual and not literary and philological" (von Balthasar 1982, 550). We should not dismantle it with alien instruments of our own devising. The life is in the whole. He sees here an important aesthetic analogy with the way we come to appreciate a work of art. Investigating the circumstances of its production, the biography of the artist, or the techniques required to carry it off are all very well, but can never be a substitute for finding oneself claimed by the work in its final, given form. This involves a more receptive and contemplative attitude on the part of the viewer.

How is the Jesus Christ of dogmatics related to the Jesus Christ brought to our eyes by New Testament exegesis? In *Theo-Drama* 3, von Balthasar argues that in each case an overlay of interpretation is apparent where Jesus is concerned. The history of Christian theological thought about Jesus (dogmatics) yields a body of interpretation about the meaning of his person and the nature of his work (his "mission," to use von Balthasar's term of choice) that seems to go well beyond what was immediately apparent at the time. But the New Testament suggests that Jesus himself had a self-understanding beyond what would have already been evident in his own situation; he had a strange and unique expectation of the End and identified with it in an extraordinary way. Von Balthasar recommends that the exceptional character of Jesus' own self-consciousness and the exceptional character of theology's later reflections on him be allowed to inform each other, and he does not anticipate that they will be found to be in tension.

Von Balthasar's is a deeply Johannine Christology. He insists that the combined witness of the New Testament writings finds its summation and interpretative key in John's Gospel. On this Johannine basis, von Balthasar makes two of his key claims about Jesus. First, Jesus is orientated to his "hour" (the *eschaton,* taking shape historically in the specific form of the Cross, the descent into Hell, and the resurrection, although in his incarnate state of "economic ignorance" Jesus does not know the historical details in advance). Second, he has a certainty, in the Holy Spirit, of doing the Father's will at every particular moment and of being in relationship with him.

In accord with these claims (and in similarly Johannine vein), von Balthasar asserts that Jesus is (and could never be other than) the "One Sent": (1) This is the ground of his uniqueness, but also of his inclusivity, for what he is sent to do has universal reach and leaves nothing and no one untouched. (2) His being the "One Sent" determines his dominant characteristic in his incarnate life: obedience. (3) His being the "One Sent" becomes the uniting term of (a) his Trinitarian relation to the Father (his person), and (b) his soteriological goal (his work). There is no break between the immanent procession of the Son from the Father in the life of the Trinity and the economic mission of the Son in his incarnate life. They are the single, indivisible movement of the "One Sent." In this way, von Balthasar gives the doctrine of the two natures of Christ in the hypostatic union a dramatic expression, preferring the language of "actions" to that of "natures." He also leaves room for the idea of "movement" or "dynamism" in God's being.

Jesus' mission is different from that of other human beings because he always has and is his mission, whereas others only receive their mission on the basis of their coming to faith. His mission indicates the economic revelation of a decision freely made in concert by the whole Trinity. Von Balthasar believes that in his incarnate state Jesus knew (though initially only in a latent way) of his identity as the Son of God, but holds that he did not know the details of what the Father through the Spirit would set before him from moment to moment for the fulfillment of his mission. He is aware of the formal scope of his mission but uncertain of its content. Instead, he utterly abandons himself to the Father who guides him by the Spirit and in whom he has complete trust. He acts in a certain "economic ignorance." Von Balthasar writes that "in not anticipating the hour . . . he formally embraces the totality of the world that is to be reconciled, whereas the changing details of the Passion render this formal embrace concrete in the most diverse ways" (von Balthasar 1994, 234). But for just this reason we can ascribe obedience and faith to him, and the perfection of his obedience (dependent as it is to some extent upon "not-knowing") is, paradoxically, one of the best demonstrations of his divine character as the "One Sent"—receiving himself wholly from the Father through the Spirit. Jesus' apparently passive "letting-things-happen" is in fact the "superaction" of his obedience, "in which he is at one with a demand that goes beyond all limits, a demand that could only be made of *him*" (ibid., 237).

The latent awareness that Christ has of his mission and person (these being inseparable, as the title "One Sent" makes clear) must nevertheless be awakened, just as self-consciousness would for any person. This is the logic of the incarnation. Von Balthasar holds it to be an elementary truth of human nature that "unless a child is awakened to I-consciousness through the instrumentality of a Thou, it cannot become a human child at all" (von Balthasar 1992, 175). At this point, the assertion that Mariology is an inner component of Christology makes an appearance. Jesus' inner initiation, in relationship to his heavenly Father, takes place in harmony with his external, historical initiation in the human world, as Mary teaches him Israel's religious traditions and hopes. Mary is also the perfect respondent to Christ's mission—his necessary counterpart in the divine-human drama, though wholly dependent on the grace his work makes available. She models the creature's ideal response to grace and is the core around which the Church develops.

In von Balthasar's view, the startling, apparently hyperbolic attributes given to Jesus Christ by Paul and John (primacy over all things, pre-existence, etc.) should be understood as diverse assertions about his *mission*. Statements of Christ's primacy (namely, that everything has been created "for him" and "in him") are ways of saying that it is through Christ's being and work that true meaning is imparted to all things. Statements about Christ's pre-existence are ways of saying that his incarnate existence is identical with the actual implementation of God's eternal plan for the world—his incarnation was the eternal decision of God; he was "with God" when God drew up the world plan to reconcile all things to himself. For this reason, as Karl Barth also asserted, there is not a single moment when the *Logos* can be held to be *asarkos* (without flesh); there is no question of prescinding from Christ's incarnation. The assumption of human flesh is an integral part of God's original plan for the world and seen from eternity is timeless. In these examples, we see von Balthasar's essential strategy of showing how all Christological claims are outworkings (ripplings out) from the central affirmation that *Jesus Christ is the One Sent by the Father*. Nothing is gained by beginning with speculations about (for example) the possibility of pre-existence in the abstract; the starting point must be paying proper attention to Christ's person and action. He speaks and acts in a way that shows him to be unique. In Cross and resurrection, he acts beyond the boundaries that ordinarily circumscribe finite human life. He elicits ecclesial faith, because no sense can be made of him unless he is understood as the Word of God.

The figure of Jesus Christ is, for von Balthasar, the key to a knowledge of the Trinity, of which he is the valid exposition and presence in the world. His mission, properly understood in faith, presupposes an origin and a goal. To put it another way, the performance of his dramatic role as the One Sent (*der*

Gesendete) presupposes someone who sends (*der Sendende*), to whom the "accomplished" mission (*die Sendung*) is handed over. The Spirit is the one who mediates this mission, in the bond of obedience and love that unites Son to Father; he delivers the mission to the One Sent and delivers it back in its completion to the One-who-sends. In Jesus' Christ attitude of total, free availability, we also glimpse the utter perichoretic, or intertwining, self-donation (and simultaneous mutual constitution) of the Trinitarian persons in the perfection of their love. The analogy between human obedience and Trinitarian self-donation must be disciplined by the principle of immeasurable dissimilarity between creature and Creator, human and divine, but there is nevertheless a correspondence between the two things. Thus, by appearing as the Son, Jesus Christ interprets the triune God and makes him present. Access to God is made possible through his being made visible in the human history of Jesus Christ.

In his discussions of soteriology in *Theo-Drama* 4, von Balthasar insists that Christ's saving work cannot be reduced to a "system." What takes place in Jesus' "hour" remains mysterious. However, von Balthasar identifies what are five main features of the atonement in the New Testament and suggests that any adequate soteriology must do justice to all five, and no aspect must be allowed to dominate the others unduly: (1) Jesus Christ *gives himself up freely* as God's only Son. (2) An *exchange of places* occurs (the *sacrum commercium* of the Fathers). (3) This means *liberation* (from sin; from the world; from the devil). (4) The Holy Spirit is thereby imparted and *we are drawn into the divine, Trinitarian life*. (5) The entire process of reconciliation flows from that primary source, which is God's gracious *love*.

For von Balthasar, the mystery of salvation involves both incarnation and cross in an inseparable unity, but the decisive dramatic element in soteriology is the *sacrum commercium*, made supremely visible on the Cross. God's entire world drama is concentrated on this moment: "[T]his is the theo-drama into which the world *and* God have their ultimate input; here absolute freedom enters into created freedom, interacts with created freedom and acts *as* created freedom. . . . This is the climax and the turning point of the theo-drama, and as such it already contains and anticipates the final act, the 'eschatology'" (von Balthasar 1994, 318).

The order of creation and the order of redemption or grace are intrinsically related to each other, in von Balthasar's view, and are not artificially to be prized apart or mutually opposed. Christ comes to judge but also to fulfill creation. But this does not mean that God "owes" it to natural man to raise him to the state of grace; God only "owes" it to himself to be faithful to the order and consistency of his "unitary world plan." That said, von Balthasar allows room (a room that Barth seems not to have) for an abundance of transpositions of Christ's work, and even his characteristics, into the lives of the saints (meaning, in the end, all Christians with their manifold missions, though von Balthasar retains a special exemplary place for the canonized saints). Individual missions interact with the mission of Christ, and share many of its features, so that they become vehicles of revelation in their own (relative) right. To be called by Jesus Christ is to be called by and into his mission. For von Balthasar, this call will always be mediated by the concrete Church.

Ben Quash

See also: Barth, Karl; Holy Spirit; John, Gospel of; Mary; Paul; Son of God

References

Oakes, Edward T. 1994. *Pattern of Redemption: The Theology of Hans Urs von Balthasar*. New York: Continuum.

O'Hanlon, G. F. 1990. *The Immutability of God in the Theology of Hans Urs von Balthasar*. Cambridge: Cambridge University Press.

von Balthasar, Hans Urs. 1982 [1961]. *The Glory of the Lord*. Vol. 1, *Seeing the Form*. Edinburgh: T. and T. Clark.

———. 1989 [1969]. *The Glory of the Lord*. Vol. 7, *Theology: The New Covenant*. Edinburgh: T. and T. Clark.

———. 1992 [1978]. *Theo-Drama: Theological Dramatic Theory*. Vol. 3, *Dramatis Personae: Persons in Christ*. San Francisco: Ignatius Press.

———. 1994 [1980]. *Theo-Drama: Theological Dramatic Theory*. Vol. 4, *The Action*. San Francisco: Ignatius Press.

Baptism

Baptism is a Greek word that means washing, which Christianity took over to describe the washing that marks the entry of the new Christian into the Church. "I believe in one baptism" are words taken from one of the oldest formulations of the Christian faith, the so-called so-called Apostles' Creed. Each of those words is weighted: the individual profession of faith, the reality of baptism as a sacramental washing, and the fact that it takes place only once in an individual's life—in contrast to the ritual washings of other religions. The "once-and-for-all" character of baptism means a tension with Christian experience, one of the reasons why there have been differing practices regarding the appropriate age for baptism, with supplementary rites such as confirmation taking place at a later age when infants and young children are baptized. Baptismal teaching, often referred to by the Greek word "catechesis," has a long history; it usually applies to those being baptized as adults or those being confirmed. One baptism once only contrasts with the Eucharist, which by its very nature is repeatable. But the fundamental issue underlying baptism is the extent to which it is Christological or pneumatological; most Christian writers regard it as both, but there have been times, for example in the medieval West, when the role of the Holy Spirit has been associated more emphatically with confirmation. A small family gathering around a pedestal font on a Sunday afternoon for the baptism of an infant is clearly a far cry from the baptism of an adult believer in a large tank of water during a Sunday-morning liturgy.

Metaphors and Narratives

There are many ways of approaching the ideas that underline the meaning of baptism, of which three predominate and have their origin in the New Testament. The first is the most obvious, washing (1 Cor. 6.11), indicated by the use of the word "baptism." The second is that of dying and rising (Rom. 6.3–11), a central part of Paul's teaching about new life in Christ, which is strongly paschal in tone, where the waters suggest drowning, in order to live anew. The third is about new birth (John 3.5), suggesting the waters of the womb of the Church; this metaphor is more pentecostal, the new birth being in the Spirit. But in all three, Christ is the agent, whether it is of the washing, the dying and rising, or the giving of the new birth—as the encounter between Jesus and Nicodemus indicates. Most of the classical liturgies keep all these three together in the various prayers used. For example, in the prayer for the blessing of the water at the Easter Vigil in the Roman rite, washing and dying and rising and rebirth commingle, although there was a tendency in some of the liturgical revision in the second part of the twentieth century to accentuate the motif of dying and rising, thanks partly to the emphasis given in the preaching of Cyril of Jerusalem (c. 315–387), who had the responsibility of baptizing new Christians in the Church of the Holy Sepulchre built on the supposed site of Jesus' burial. On the other hand, some of the hymns of Ephrem the Syrian (c. 306–373) draw out strongly the theme of rebirth in the Spirit.

It is not possible to say everything in a prayer, nor a sermon, nor indeed a doctrinal treatise. But the balance of these three metaphors can be critical. A baptismal piety based largely on one to the exclusion of others misses out on important truths. To emphasize the washing away of sin runs the risk of making baptism retrospective; the Christian can only be washed once in baptism and yet keeps committing more sins, and that needs its own explanation. To emphasize dying and rising with Christ runs the risk of underplaying the forward-looking work of the Holy Spirit. And to emphasize the waters of rebirth at the expense of washing and of dying and rising can underplay the Cross in the Christian life.

But there are also two different narratives in the New Testament that influence baptismal preaching and liturgy. The first is the baptism of Jesus himself, which is recounted in all four Gospels (Matt. 3.13–17; Mark 1.9–11; Luke 3.21–22; John 1.31–34), though ambiguously in John. The second is when Jesus takes children into his arms (Matt. 19.13–15; Mark 10.13–16; Luke 18.15–17). Whereas the Eastern liturgies employ the former almost as a kind of "institution narrative" of baptism and identify Christ as the agent of the baptizing, the medieval Roman liturgy shifted toward the latter, as a warrant for baptizing infants—a warrant and a practice taken over in some of the Reformation churches. For example, the English Prayer Books use Mark 10.13–16 at infant baptism, which is probably the most pronounced of the three versions, with Jesus rebuking the disciples when they try to turn the children away, and the children taken up into his arms for blessing; but when the form of baptism "for those of riper years" was introduced in the 1662 Prayer Book, the reading is altered to John 3.1–8, Jesus and Nicodemus. Whether it is Jesus and the children or Jesus and Nicodemus, the approach to biblical narrative is different. Whereas the older, patristic view of Jesus' baptism as being in some sense an archetype for Christian baptism, a drama into which the new believer is drawn, the later medieval and Reformation view of Jesus encountering either children or an adult enquirer like Nicodemus is more a scene in which the sponsor (or in the case of Jesus and Nicodemus, the adult believer) is being taught by Jesus.

Another factor is the way sacrament and experience are handled in the baptismal life. The washing, dying and rising, and rebirth are frequently taken to be realities in the life of the new Christian, but it is rare for the experience of conversion and commitment to Christ to coincide exactly in time with one's baptism. This caused the Church in the fourth century to place increasing weight on the importance of catechesis, to the extent of trying to restrict baptism to certain specific occasions in the liturgical year, such as Epiphany, Pentecost, and above all, Easter. But by the late medieval period, this elaborate scheme had long broken down, giving rise to the more private family scene of infant baptism, with a strongly objective view of sacramental rebirth. The Reformation was bound to produce a counter-reaction, which in its more radical manifestations wrestled with these metaphors. The Swiss Reformer Ulrich Zwingli (1484–1531) drew a sharp contrast between spiritual and ritual baptism, between the experience of salvation and its liturgical expression, in a way that could be described as symbolic memorialism. The English Puritan William Perkins (1558–1602), on the other hand, took a more moderate line, in which he allowed Christian experience and liturgical worship to have some kind of interplay, in a way that could be described as symbolic parallelism. More conservative Reformers, including John Calvin (q.v.) himself (1509–1564), hold that baptism does what it is intended to do—namely, convey the gifts of God to the new believer. This latter view adapts the more objective view of the Latin, Greek, and other ancient Eastern churches.

Liturgy and Catechesis

The New Testament gives many accounts of baptism, whether of individuals, such as Paul (Acts 9.18), or of households, such as that of Lydia (Acts 16.15). Sometimes there is a clear indication of catechesis, as in the example of Philip's encounter with the Ethiopian eunuch, where the sheep led to the slaughter (Isa. 53.7–8) is explained by Philip to refer to Jesus—an encounter that leads straightaway to baptism. But an elaborate scheme soon developed. In the *Apostolic Tradition* of Hippolytus, which probably reflects liturgical practice at Rome in the early third century, the time of preparation for baptism is three years, and the candidates have to make a public profession of faith, along the lines of what is now known as the Apostles' Creed. And in addition to being baptized in water, they are first of all anointed all over with the oil of exorcism and then anointed on the forehead with the oil of thanksgiving. Hippolytus may or may not be typical of custom at the time. Later evidence suggests a great degree of variation, involving the kind of catechesis given, and the exact meaning of the anointings, which appear to have grown out of ancient bathing practices, the first anointing corresponding to the oil rubbed all over the body to act like a soap, and the second functioning as a perfume—that is exactly what chrism oil, as it came to be called, is like. Other customs included the clothing of the newly baptized as a sign of having put on Christ (Gal. 3.27). The first anointing was often associated with the baptismal renunciations, wherein the candidates renounced evil before turning to Christ. The chrismation was usually associated with the new life given in baptism, and at the time of Ambrose of Milan (339–397) a prayer was used mentioning the gifts of the Spirit (Isa. 11.2ff.), which came later on to be referred to as the "confirmation prayer."

The great preachers of the fourth century, such as John Chrysostom (c. 347–407) and Theodore of Mopsuestia (c. 350–428), set great store by the privilege of being appointed baptismal preacher during Lent leading up to the baptism at the Easter Vigil. Candidates had to learn the Lord's Prayer and the Apostles' Creed by heart and recite both publicly on an occasion before the baptism itself. Augustine (354–430) was gentler on the Lord's Prayer, since it was an integral part of public worship; but the Creed was used only at baptism, and therefore the candidates needed to get the words right. There was considerable scope, too, for instructing candidates in the individual character of each of the four Gospels, resulting in an imaginative practice of teaching them about the opening words of each Gospel through the traditional symbolism of the four living creatures (Rev. 4.7), with Matthew as the man, Mark as the lion, Luke as the ox, and John as the eagle, all four of them pointing to Christ himself, as the preachers often pointed out. Considerable emphasis was placed on the path to baptism as a walk of faith with Christ, to the extent that some of the teachings recounted in the Gospels were sometimes included in the catechesis liturgies, probably linked with the liturgical readings themselves. For example, salt was blessed and placed in the mouth of the candidate, recalling that followers of Christ are to be salt of the earth (Matt. 5.13). Miracles were sometimes used in the same way, with the liturgical president breathing over the candidates with the word "Ephphatha" (Mark 7.34), suggesting that the new faith would enable the new Christians to lose their dumbness and give them tongues with which to praise and witness to Christ.

Such a liturgy of encounter relied heavily on communal backup, imaginative celebration, and lively preaching, and the same is true in its revival in the Roman Catholic Church since the Second Vatican Council. Attenuation is the way the death knell is sounded for these rites; for example, the rites of catechesis in the medieval West were prefixed to the baptism service itself on every occasion, so that an infant was given the salt and was breathed over with "Ephphatha"; and then the chrismation and its accompanying prayer for the gifts of the Spirit, originally an inseparable feature of the baptism service, became detached in order to form the rite of confirmation by a bishop only. In such a jumble of different elements, with or without proper catechesis, it is not surprising that the Reformers swept away a great deal of such an elaborate scheme in order to concentrate on conscious and intelligent faith in a simple liturgy, in which the primary symbolism of water could stand out clearly without having to do battle with what were regarded as secondary symbolisms such as anointing and clothing. The Reformers, however, returned to the patristic emphasis on catechesis, whether of adult candidates or of parents and sponsors or before confirmation. Now, it is often seen also as a continuing pastoral process in parish life.

Twentieth-century liturgical revision has had to wrestle with many other issues, over and above a greater knowledge of antiquity, in an increasingly secular world that has often been compared to the society in which Christianity itself was born. The Christ who is the same, yesterday, today, and forever (Heb. 13.8), as is recalled when the paschal candle is blessed at the Easter Vigil, may not invariably be witnessed to in an authentic way by trying to turn the clock back. Many of the new liturgies, however, show signs of attraction to the older forms of catechesis, using the gospel narratives in an imaginative manner and reintroducing some of the old symbolism, including the chrism oil and the baptismal robe, as ways of highlighting the primary symbolism of water. But if history teaches anything about baptism, it is that the bold lines of the liturgy are always more effective when they stand out clearly. "Is this your faith?" asks the president of each candidate just before the water is poured over each in the baptism service of the Church of England's *Common Worship* (2000), a service that sets out, through the use of seasonal material, including the blessing of the water, to draw out those three New Testament metaphors—of washing, dying and rising, and rebirth—in equal measure.

It is clear that the renewed focus on baptism in many churches shows an increasing awareness of the meaning of baptism in a much changed world. But it can be a mixed blessing, because what is seen as a privilege of the Christian community can easily become a prize to be won by those on the outside. This in turn projects the image of a Church that is proprietorial about its sacraments, which in turn overthrows the messy, rough-edged kind of community who followed Jesus of Nazareth, as the Gospels recount. Any tests for membership of the Church, in Gospel terms, could perhaps be pointed in another direction: is it worth joining? The culture of exclusiveness, which is not the same thing as trying to combine affection with demand, does not earn much praise in the New Testament.

Architecture and Iconography

Methods of baptizing vary according to circumstances as well as tradition. Broadly speaking, there are three. Submersion (often confused with immersion), whereby the whole body of the person being baptized is "submerged" under the water; that is what Cyril of Jerusalem describes in his catecheses, and it was clearly envisaged in the large baptisteries constructed, for example, at Pisa. Immersion, on the other hand, involves the person kneeling in the font, with water reaching only part of the body, water then being poured over the head, sometimes in large quantities; there are many more examples of this kind surviving, sometimes as archaeological remains, from antiquity, and there is a modern example in Portsmouth Cathedral.

Then there is affusion, whereby the candidate is sprinkled with water while standing (or being held) over the font, which could be quite small. Each of these methods corresponds with the three metaphors from the New Testament: submersion expressing dying and rising, immersion washing, and affusion the waters of rebirth. While submersion, regarded by many Baptists as normative, was not as extensive in the earliest times as is sometimes thought, affusion is clearly the most popular method in recent centuries in the Roman Catholic and Protestant West. Indeed, the large bronze fifteenth-century font in Aarhus Cathedral, Denmark, with its four legs decorated with the symbols of the evangelists, is of a size in which an infant or small child could have been placed upright for immersion if not submersion; it has since been covered with a large silver dish in which a much smaller amount of water is placed for affusion. There is a tendency nowadays to construct larger fonts, in which immersion and lavish affusion are both possible. Christian art often serves as an interpretative accompaniment.

Icons of the baptism of Christ interpret the "narrative" in different ways; for example, there is usually a dove above the head of Christ, symbolizing the Holy Spirit, and a "glory" symbol at the top, symbolizing God the Father, thus turning the whole scene into the action of the Trinity, given further emphasis by John the Baptist's often sideways, detached posture; the River Jordan is often deliberately shaped like a womb. Such icons suggest either submersion or immersion, whereas the later, medieval depiction of the scene by Piero della Francesca (1415/20–1492) has Jesus standing by the side of the Jordan, and John the Baptist pouring a small amount of water from a shell, echoing the increasing practice of affusion, to the extent of its being no more than a sprinkling, harbinger of the practice of renewal of baptismal vows that has become popular in recent times. The contemporary emphasis on baptism, in a context of ecumenical agreements, relies increasingly on the older traditions of baptismal theology and practice.

Kenneth Stevenson

See also: Augustine of Hippo; Calvin, John; Creeds; Eucharist; Holy Sepulchre; Holy Spirit; Icons and the Icon Tradition; John the Baptist

References

Church of England. 2000. *Common Worship*. London: Church House Publishing.

Johnson, Maxwell E., ed. 1995. *Living Water, Sealing Spirit*. New York: Pueblo.

Kavanagh, Aidan. 1974. *The Shape of Baptism: The Rite of Christian Initiation*. Studies in the Reformed Rites of the Catholic Church, vol. I. New York: Pueblo.

Mazza, Enrico. 1989. *Mystagogy: A Theology of Liturgy in the Patristic Age*. New York: Pueblo.

Robinson, P. G. A. 1997. "Baptism in Ritual Perspective: Myth, Symbol and Metaphor as Anthropological Foundations for a Baptismal Theology." Ph.D. dissertation, Durham University.

Stevenson, Kenneth. 1998. *The Mystery of Baptism in the Anglican Tradition*. Norwich: Canterbury; Harrisburg: Morehouse.

Thurian, Max, and Geoffrey Wainwright, eds. 1983. *Baptism and Eucharist: Ecumenical Convergence in Celebration*. Geneva: World Council of Churches; Grand Rapids, MI: Eerdmans.

Yarnold, Edward, S.J. 1994. *The Awe-Inspiring Rites of Initiation*. Edinburgh: T. and T. Clark.

Baptism of Jesus

See Son of God

Barth, Karl (1886–1968)

Karl Barth was the most influential reformed theologian since Schleiermacher, and his work remains one of the indispensable reference points for contemporary constructive reflection on the identity and mission of Jesus. The son of a moderate Swiss pastor and theologian, Barth studied with leading German liberal theologians at the turn of the twentieth century before a decade of pastoral work in Switzerland (1911–1921). In the middle of World War I, Barth's operative liberal theology, under strain for some time, finally collapsed, and he underwent an intense period of theological critique and reconstruction, centered on a rediscovery of the sovereign freedom of God in revelation and salvation. The most noteworthy fruit of this reorientation is the two editions of his commentary *The Epistle to the Romans* (1919, 1921). In 1921, Barth took up a chair of Reformed theology in Göttingen. Here, and later in Münster, he consolidated his rediscovery through deep and broad study of the classical traditions of theology, and he was widely regarded as the leader of the "dialectical theology" movement in the 1920s. From 1930 to 1935 he taught at Bonn and was a central figure in Protestant protest against National Socialism. Dismissed from his chair in Germany, Barth returned to Switzerland and his native Basel, where he taught until retirement in 1961. A voluminous writer, his chief literary work is the massive *Church Dogmatics*, along with biblical commentaries, a large number of controversial and occasional writings, interpretations of creedal and confessional texts, and academic lecture cycles on biblical, historical, and doctrinal tropics, many of them published posthumously. In most of this material, Christological issues lie near the center of Barth's concerns; his work forms the most sustained effort on the part of a modern Protestant thinker to give an account of Jesus Christ as determinative for all reality and as the one through whom the truth of all reality may be perceived.

Karl Barth (Library of Congress, Prints and Photographs Division [LC-USZ62-122917])

Analysis of Barth's work has suffered from a conventional but misleading periodization of the development of his thought. His thinking is commonly held to fall into three periods: an early liberal phase (up to 1916); a so-called dialectical phase, lasting from then until the end of the 1920s, in which Barth's disavowal of Protestant liberalism led him into a sharply polarized account of God and created reality dominated by a rigorous doctrine of divine transcendence; and a "mature" phase, associated with the *Church Dogmatics*, in which Barth undertook a rich description of the fellowship between God and creation, centered increasingly on the redemptive action of Christ. On this account of Barth, it is only in the third phase that Christology takes full control of his thought; in the "dialectical" phase, the necessary rediscovery of divine transcendence draws attention away from God's identity with the man Jesus. However, the posthumous publication of material from the 1920s (notably Barth's Göttingen dogmatics lectures) has undermined this conventional picture by showing that much of Barth's later thinking, including his thinking on Christology, was already sketched out very early on in his theological career. The Christology of the *Church Dogmatics* is thus more an amplification and refinement of his earlier thought than a fresh departure or radical revision. Barth's statement in his first *Romans* commentary—"our subject-matter is our knowledge of God realised in Christ"—could thus stand as the rubric for his entire theological work.

Barth received his theological formation in the liberal tradition of Ritschl and Harnack. Reflection upon the history and teaching of Jesus was fundamental to that tradition and led to some characteristic preoccupations: a concern with Jesus as human historical figure; a corresponding distaste for "metaphysical" speculations about Christ's person, states, and offices as found in Protestant dogmatics; a strong interest in Jesus as ethical guide; an interpretation of the "high" ontological categories of the Christological tradition as indications of human moral evaluation of Jesus or of ethical dependence upon him. Barth broke with this liberal Christology largely under the impact of his rediscovery of the biblical gospel of Christ, which he came to see as utterly discontinuous with human moral and religious aspiration. Rather than symbolizing the coalescence of the divine and the human, Jesus came to be seen by Barth as the point at which their estrangement is both signaled and overcome. In his biblical interpretation in this early period, Barth emphasized that, because God is not a modulation of worldly reality or a determinate object, Jesus is "on the frontier of what is observable"; he cannot be known by historical reconstruction or moral sympathy, but only indirectly, after the manner of God. The motif of "resurrection" proved especially resourceful in establishing the mode of Jesus' presence as a miraculous gift beyond direct historical, moral, or spiritual perception.

Alongside this early critique of the moral immanentism of liberal Protestant Christology and his replacement of it by a depiction of Jesus as revelatory miracle, Barth also explored patristic Christological teaching in his first dogmatics lectures in the mid-1920s. The patristic materials, along with their refinement by the post-Reformation Lutheran and Reformed divines, offered Barth a conceptuality to articulate his Christological instincts about the free majesty of God's self-revelation in Christ without endangering the full reality of Jesus' sharing in contingent historical existence. Barth's appeal to patristic teaching about Jesus' humanity as enhypostatic (that is, about its subsistence in the divine Word) enabled him to speak more firmly of Jesus as the historical (though not directly intuitable) embodiment of God. Further, Barth established early on a decided preference for a Reformed doctrine of the Incarnation over a Lutheran one. This involved asserting that the union of divinity and humanity in the incarnate one is best understood as an event rather than a state, and that the union is properly located in the person of the incarnate one, not at the level of the natures. Both assertions underscore the sheer sovereignty of God's act in the Incarnation and help distinguish historical incarnation from immanence within history. These clarifications, which form the basis for Barth's later theology of incarnation, show that already at this relatively early stage his thinking about Jesus was not trapped within an antithesis of eternity and history. Rather, Barth was seeking ways of talking of Jesus as the one in and as whom God is graciously present in history. Some recent interpreters have associated Barth's rejection of liberal immanence Christology with postmodern censure of the metaphysics and "ontotheology" of presence; such interpretations lack plausibility largely because they give insufficient weight to the genuinely positive interests of Barth's early Christology. Indeed, in important respects Barth continued the Christological project of his liberal forebears (whom he always regarded with deep respect); like them, he considered Jesus to be constitutive of the *relation* of God and humankind. Where he differed from his teachers was in a refusal to make Jesus a function or, perhaps, the perfect exemplification of the human side of that relation, and in his insistence that the relation is established and maintained from outside humankind in a wholly nonreversible way.

The fullest statement of Barth's theological convictions about Jesus is, of course, in the *Church Dogmatics*. This work was planned to run to five volumes (each subdivided into parts), on the doctrines of revelation, God, creation, reconciliation, and redemption; the fourth volume remained unfinished at Barth's death, and the fifth was never begun. Barth is often described as a "Christocentric" thinker, in that he deduces teaching in all areas of Christian theology from prior Christological doctrine. That is substantially true and is particularly evident in the most revisionary sections of the *Dogmatics*, such as the treatments of divine election, creation, or theological anthropology. Indeed, throughout the work Barth envisages all parts of Christian theology as established, shaped, and corrected by reflection upon the identity of Jesus Christ, and in an important sense, therefore, the *Dogmatics* in its entirety is a Christology.

Two important qualifications should be noted, however. First, for Barth Christology is inseparable from the doctrine of the Trinity, without which it would be mere "Jesusology." All Barth's Christological affirmations have a Trinitarian basis, and his Christology cannot be expounded in isolation from what he has to say of the eternal will of the Father or of the applicative and transformative work of the Holy Spirit. Second, attention to the person and work of Jesus Christ is inseparable from attention to the realm of human history and action. This is not—as Barth feared had happened in the liberal tradition—because Jesus is placed within a greater reality that encompasses him; its roots are rather in Barth's commitment to that which is indicated by the doctrine of the hypostatic union. To speak of the union of divinity and humanity in Jesus Christ is, in part, to consider Jesus as the central agent in the drama of the covenant between God and humankind. In a wholly unique way, what takes place in Jesus is the restoration of fellowship between God and his human partners, Jesus Christ acting as the divine judge and reconciler and as the obedient human partner. Talk of Jesus Christ is thus incomplete unless it leads to talk of the human world that he redeems and of which he is the head. Because God is in Christ, and because Christ sums up humankind in himself, the theme of Christian theology is twofold: the differentiated fellowship of God and the creature. Barth's "Christocentrism" is thus very different from the "Christomonism" with which he is sometimes charged.

The first volume of the *Church Dogmatics* weaves together the doctrines of Trinity and revelation, expounding revelation as the self-communicative presence of the Holy Trinity in which God wills, establishes, and perfects knowledge of himself through his work as creator, reconciler, and redeemer. The exposition contains two substantial accounts of Christological doctrine. Paragraph 11, on "God the Son," presents Jesus as the "axiomatic presupposition" of all thinking about himself (the echoes of Anselm are strong) and gives an initial description of the Son's eternal, antecedent deity. Both points emphasize that Jesus is a basic, rather than a derivative, reality and is only knowable through his own revelatory action. This orientation forms the context of a detailed exposition of the Nicene Creed. In paragraph 15, on "The Mystery of Revelation," Barth turns to a more precise description of the relation of divinity and humanity in the incarnate one. He follows the Reformed emphasis on the freedom and transcendence of the Word in assuming flesh, not in order to subtract from the genuineness of Jesus' humanity but in order to emphasize its derivation in the omnipotence of the Word who is the sole ground of Jesus' existence. The way in which Barth insists on the indivisibility of the doctrines of Trinity and incarnation thus prevents both a humanistic picture of Jesus as moral prototype and also an abstract idea of God's freedom as other than his freedom to take flesh.

Barth's use of Christology to banish abstraction from theology is especially apparent in the doctrine of God in the second volume of *Church Dogmatics*. The Christological corrective is everywhere at work: in Barth's recasting of the attributes of God in which God's "freedom" and God's "loving" are brought together on a Christological basis in order to call into question the traditional distinction between immanent and relative attributes; or in the highly original doctrine of election, according to which the subject of election is God himself in Christ.

In a similar way, Christology functions as the organizing center for the doctrines of creation, humanity, and providence in the third volume. Thus, rather than starting from general anthropological considerations drawn from the human and natural sciences, Barth begins his theological anthropology from the humanity of Christ: "The ontological determination of humanity is grounded in the fact that among all others is the man Jesus." Because Jesus Christ is ingredient within the being of God, and so the source of human being, humankind subsists in him. Yet Barth insists that to affirm this is not to rob Jesus of a specific historical identity by turning him into an archetype. He is simply pressing the logic of incarnation, bringing together Jesus' sheer particularity with the universally constitutive force of his being and action as God. The universal scope of Jesus, once again, is not such that all other human being is resolved back into him and robbed of its proper identity. Although Barth is sometimes considered to collapse anthropology into Christology, the lengthy account of human action in the ethics of creation (in the final part of the third volume) shows that Jesus is considered the ground, not the suspension, of human agency.

The fourth volume of the *Church Dogmatics*, on the doctrine of reconciliation, extends the method and substance of the earlier work. Its structure is very complex, interweaving an account of the person and work of Christ with a doctrine of sin and a theology of the Holy Spirit, the church, and the Christian life. The material does not follow the traditional dogmatic sequential arrangement but is assembled into three immense passages of argument. Each part-volume begins with a substantial presentation of an aspect of the integrated reality of Jesus' person and work as the incarnate savior who is the actuality of God's work of reconciliation in which the broken covenant is restored. Although Barth's imagination is deeply shaped by older Christological categories (the "states" of Christ as the humiliated and exalted one, and the "offices" of Christ as king, priest, and prophet), he reworks them with extraordinary vividness, using them to gain conceptual purchase on the singular and irreducible reality of Jesus. The account of the being and action of Jesus is followed by a treatment of sin as the antithesis of the movement of Jesus (to his humility there corresponds sin as pride; to his exaltation there corresponds sin as misery; to his truth there corresponds sin as falsehood). The overcoming of sin is then propounded as justification, sanctification, and vocation; the Spirit's work in the Church is set out in terms of the gathering, upbuilding, and sending of the community, with the individual Christian life as faith, hope, and love. A final section, spelling out the ethical dimensions of the person and work of Christ through an account of baptism, the Lord's Prayer, and the Eucharist, was laid aside by Barth in an unfinished state.

Barth's mature Christology is notable in at least three respects. First, its sheer scale, range, and depth make it one of the most significant pieces of writing about Jesus in the Western Christian tradition. Second, its deep structure is narrative or dramatic rather than conceptual, attempting to indicate the history of Jesus as both utterly particular and of universal scope; it was in the matter of Christology that Barth exercised to the full his remarkable powers as a descriptive theologian. Third, it is extremely innovative, not scrupling to refashion tracts of theological teaching to give more adequate expression to the conviction that Jesus is definitive of the ways and works of God. And so, for example, he knits together lordship and servanthood in such a way that Jesus' lowliness is intrinsic to, not contradictory of, his deity; or again, he shifts the locus of Jesus' prophetic office from his earthly ministry to his work as the exalted one who is communicatively present in the world.

From the beginning of his theological work, Barth displayed a marked tendency to appeal to Christian teaching about Jesus in order to perform functions that other theologians more naturally assigned to different Christian doctrines. Where liberal Protestant theologians spoke of the presence of God by talk of human religious and moral consciousness, or existential theologians spoke of God as "realized" through human selfhood, Barth believed that the Church's talk of Jesus is the necessary and sufficient condition for truth in all other areas of inquiry. The burden of much criticism of Barth is to ask whether his project can maintain itself in a more pluralistic, less stable religious and theological culture. That he undertook his project without transforming Jesus into an abstract principle, and without absorbing all creaturely being and time into this singular figure, at once wholly unique and wholly without measure, is the significance of his Christological teaching.

John Webster

See also: Anselm; Calvin, John; Chalcedon; Creeds; Harnack, Adolf von; Holy Spirit; Jesus as a Historical Figure; Jesus as Servant; Luther, Martin; Resurrection; Schleiermacher, F. D. E.; Second Person of the Trinity

References

Barth, K. 1933. *The Epistle to the Romans*. Oxford: Oxford University Press.
———. 1956–1975. *Church Dogmatics*. Edinburgh: T. and T. Clark.
Hunsinger, G. 2000. *Disruptive Grace*. Grand Rapids, MI: Eerdmans.
Marshall, B. 1987. *Christology in Conflict*. Oxford: Blackwell.
Thompson, J. 1978. *Christ in Perspective*. Edinburgh: St. Andrew.
Webster, J. 2000. *Barth*. London: Continuum.
———, ed. 2000. *The Cambridge Companion to Karl Barth*. Cambridge: Cambridge University Press.

Benedict (c. 480–c. 550)

Both tradition and historical analysis date the birth of St. Benedict as c. 480, in Nursia, in central Italy; he died c. 550 at his monastery at Monte Cassino, to the south of Rome. Benedict's key role in Western monasticism was to produce a brief rule whereby monks might live together in community. The earlier monastic tradition exemplified by St. Jerome in the Judaean desert and St. Antony in Egypt, comprised a solitary life wherein the monks came together only for corporate worship in a conventual church. Benedict was not the first to compile a monastic rule. His rule is thought by most scholars to be dependent upon the early-sixth-century *Regula Magistri* (Rule of the Master).

The significance of Jesus in the Rule of St. Benedict is clear both from Benedict's use of Scripture and the centrality of the figure of Christ in the teaching of the Rule. Implicitly the vows themselves (e.g., renunciation of property and family life) appear to derive from Jesus' teaching; so, obedience may be based on John 15.14: "You are my friends if you do what I command you." The Rule is permeated with Scriptural references and quotations; from the Gospels alone there are almost eighty allusions and a few direct quotations. The centrality of the example and teaching of Jesus is clear from the beginning and ending of the Rule. The first paragraph of the prologue concludes with an assumption that the reader is "taking up the strong and glorious weapons of obedience in order to do battle in the service of the Lord Christ, the true King." The final paragraph of the prologue begins: "We propose, therefore, to establish a school of the Lord's service . . ." Once again, the reference is to Jesus as *Christ the Lord*. The Rule is aimed at forming a discipline that will allow both individual monks and the community as a whole to return to God by patterning their lives on the model of Christ. This aim is classically expressed in the instruction to monks in chapter 53 on the reception of guests at the monastery: "All who arrive as guests are to be welcomed like Christ, for he is going to say, 'I was a stranger and you welcomed me.'" This is a direct quotation from Matt. 25.35. The method whereby this aim will be achieved is to pattern one's life on the Christ of faith. In chapter 73, the epilogue of the Rule, Benedict exhorts his monks: "Do you with Christ's help fulfil this little Rule written for beginners." The abbot, as the head of the community, is a key figure in the process of monastic formation. He represents Christ, so in chapter 2: "[He] [the abbot] is believed to act in the place of Christ in the monastery, since he is called by *his* title." Here Benedict makes reference to Paul's teaching about Abba, as father, in Rom. 8.15, although Paul is directing his readers to God the Father rather than Christ.

The modern reader engaging with the Rule of St. Benedict will need to view the text not only from the point of view of nourishment in regard to Christian spirituality but also from a theological standpoint. Inevitably Benedict is writing in a precritical era, but more significant still, his references are not specifically to Jesus' earthly life. Instead Jesus is viewed from a Christological point of view. Benedict's monks are to be formed after the manner of Jesus—that is, after the example of the "Christ of faith." It is only in this sense that a follower of Benedict is asked to shape his life after the manner of Jesus. Benedict and his world have already assumed the credal figure of Jesus as *Logos*. The frequent references to the Gospel are therefore not even proof texts but simply references that catch up the metaphysical figure after whom good monks are to fashion themselves.

In the later Middle Ages new patterns developed—there is no doubt that St. Francis of Assisi intended his friars literally to follow the pattern dictated in the Gospel by Jesus of giving up all that they had and following the way of the Cross. Here the Christocentric teaching relates to Francis's literal following of the Gospel injunction to poverty; friars will have nowhere to lay their heads, they are itinerants. Benedict would have abhorred Francis's pattern of teaching, even though it can be squared more directly with the earthly life of Jesus. His Rule sharply warns against such a life: "Finally, there are the monks called gyrovagues, who spend their entire lives drifting from region to region. . . . Always on the move, they never settle down" (chapter 1). The Rule of Benedict is no less Christocentric than that of Francis, but it is a Christocentricity based on the Christ of faith—and so the manner and outcome of the teaching are different. The Franciscan way implies a direct engagement with and mission in the world, after the manner of Jesus' life and teaching. Benedict's community is committed to a life of prayer and stability.

The impact of Jesus in Benedict, then, is aspirational, both through the call to prayer and through the exemplary life of the community that is to manifest Christ's own discipleship. In chapter 72 Benedict teaches: "They (the monks) should prefer nothing whatever to Christ. May he bring us all alike to life everlasting." Part of the means by which these virtues are to be inculcated is through the prayerful reading of Scripture itself, which is designated as *lectio divina* (godly reading); the discipline of *lectio divina* again indicates how Scripture is used as a metaphysical canvas where Christ is almost a symbolic figure for the monastic life. In the Rule of St. Benedict, the prologue and epilogue act as a frame setting the life that is patterned on Christ the Lord within a clear context of learning. Listening, obedience (from the Latin meaning to listen carefully; and see John 15.14), and discipleship, including renouncing private property and family life, are the key words for translating the teaching and life of Christ into the formation of a community. The prologue concludes: "Let us then never withdraw from this discipleship to him [Jesus], but persevering in his teachings in the monastery till death, let us share the sufferings of Christ through patience, and so deserve also to share in his kingdom."

Stephen Platten

See also: Creeds; Franciscan Thought and Piety

References

de Waal, Esther. 1995–2000. *A Life-Giving Way (A Commentary on the Rule of St. Benedict)*. London: Mowbray.

Fry, Timothy, OSB. 1981. *The Rule of St. Benedict*. In Latin and English, with Notes. Collegeville: Liturgical Press.

Parry, David, OSB. 1980. *Households of God*. London: Darton Longman and Todd.

———. 1990. *The Rule of St. Benedict*. Translated by Abbot David Parry OSB. Leominster: Gracewing.

Bernard of Clairvaux (1090–1153)

St. Bernard of Clairvaux was one of the early leaders of the Cistercian reform of Benedictine monasticism that swept northern Europe in the early twelfth century. Although he was not one of the founders of the Order, it was largely because of his enthusiasm for the Cistercian life and his magnetic personality in drawing young men to its abbeys that the Cistercian "Way" spread so rapidly. Through his writings and commentaries, especially on the "Song of Songs," which reflected his own spiritual experiences, he is recognized as one of the major monastic theologians of the Middle Ages and is often referred to as "the last of the Fathers."

His teaching on Jesus is at the heart of his spirituality, and he wrote in his Sermon 15 on the Song of Songs that when he named Jesus, he set before himself a Man who was meek and humble of heart, kind, prudent, chaste, without sin, and holy in the eyes of all; and that this same Man was also the all-powerful God whose way of life healed him, and whose support was his strength.

For Bernard the great moment in history is the moment of the Incarnation, when the Word, the second person of the Blessed Trinity, comes from the heart of the Father in heaven to the womb of the Virgin Mary on earth and becomes flesh in Jesus Christ to redeem the human race and to share his divine life with us. This is the fundamental Christian mystery of God's love, "from which all the other Christian mysteries unfold." Bernard is astounded at such a love that can set its heart on mere humans. He can never forget that God first loved us while we were still sinners and before we came to know and love him. And Bernard wanted his whole life to respond to such love with a love that was without measure. He looks at Jesus to learn how to love. He sees in him a love that is affectionate, balanced, and constant. He goes to meet Jesus on a basic human level as one human being to another. He is attracted to him, drawn to him as a Friend and Companion, and he recognizes that this friendship is a great gift of the Holy Spirit. But although his heart goes out to the humanity of this Man, his ultimate desire is to be united with the divine Person of the Word to whom this humanity belongs. Bernard never tries to separate the humanity from the divinity in Jesus, but he recognizes that his human love for the humanity of the God-Man leads him through faith to the spiritual love of the Word.

He sees Jesus not as a remote savior but as a dear friend, a wise counselor, a strong helper, who has come into our world to dwell not only with us but also in us through faith, and to help us in our needs. Bernard is one of us, a man of God but still a man with human weaknesses, and above all he knows our human needs. He says that Jesus comes to give what everyone needs at times, his personal and powerful guidance, help, and protection.

Bernard took it for granted that we are made in the image and likeness of God, and so are *capax dei*. This means that not only are we "capable" of a union with God as close as that of a husband and wife, but that we are *made* for it. It is only through such a union, in this life or the next, that we find our completion and fulfillment as persons. The image of God in us may be tarnished through the Fall, sin, and human frailty, but Bernard insists that no matter how low we may have fallen, however much we are in the gutter, as long as there is a spark of free will left in us, the closest union with the Word is always possible.

His whole spiritual program lies in trying to remove the tarnish of our selfishness from the "image" of God that we carry within us. We do this, he says, especially through the reordering of our love and the redirecting of our will. Bernard was a Cistercian, and as a theologian of the Cistercian life he knew that was precisely what the Cistercian life with its prayer and asceticism was intended to do—to make its monks and nuns more Christlike. Love for Jesus was the motive for his asceticism, which helped him to become more like Jesus; it was also a way of sharing Jesus' sufferings and gave him something to offer as a token of his love. He speaks of following Jesus and imitating him as a man (for example in his humility), but he is not thinking simply of an external imitation; he is looking for a deeper kind of union that comes from a sharing in his divine life. This for him is the crux of the matter. The divine life of Jesus, says Bernard, is a healing life: it is like a powerful medicine that can curb anger, heal the wounds of envy, quench lust. It is kind, merciful, and prudent and can even bring new resolution to the will. But we have to grasp the medicine, take it and make it our own.

Then it becomes an injection of spiritual health that makes union with Jesus the way to the Father.

Bernard centers his whole spirituality around the life of Jesus. When he speaks of being enriched by meditating on Jesus, he is speaking not simply of an intellectual enrichment but rather of his attempt to unite himself with the love and the motives expressed in the various events in Jesus' life—so that in this way the power of Jesus' everyday virtues of humility, compassion, frugality, and mercy might become a way of salvation leading from the fleshly humanity of Jesus to his divine Person: the Word.

We see this in the way he meditated on the Passion. He does not dwell in detail on the physical sufferings of Jesus; rather he was obsessed with Jesus' motives, with the great love that inspired him to drink this chalice as the price of our redemption. That is what moved Bernard, and he is often depicted with the instruments of the Passion in his arms. They were like the bundle of myrrh, in a favorite text of his from the Song of Songs: "[My] beloved is like a bundle of myrrh between my breasts."

The myrrh stands for the redeeming grace of the Passion, and for Jesus himself, with whom he is united as closely as someone with their beloved. It is almost a mystical sharing. It is a sharing that is alive, driven by the love and free choice of both Jesus and Bernard, which has the power to change and transform Bernard the lover into Jesus the Beloved.

Bernard insisted that the spiritual life is a journey in faith. It is not enough to recognize the God-Man in Jesus as he went about doing good, or even in the Risen Jesus in the Garden; one has to go further and recognize and be united in spirit and in faith with the glorified-and-ascended-Jesus who is now in heaven. That is the union to which Bernard leads us, a union in faith brought about by the Holy Spirit who brings to us all those things that belong to Jesus.

Was there anything new in Bernard's approach? He builds on the patristic tradition of the past, but he expresses his devotion and intimate feelings in a way that is tender and personal, drawing on his own experience. It is not simply an emotional outpouring but something that draws deep, spiritual, and redemptive life from the mysteries in Jesus' life to an extent that had not been done in quite the same way before.

Bernard was not alone among his contemporary Cistercians in writing about Jesus. The thoughts of Aelred of Rievaulx (1109–1166) on Jesus found their way into the life of Christ by Ludolph of Saxony, which so influenced Ignatius Loyola in the sixteenth century. Blessed Guerrics, Abbot of Igny in France, became well known for his spiritual teaching on conformity to the Word-Incarnate and on the formation of Christ within us, and one should also mention Abbot John of Ford in Devon at the end of the twelfth century.

Bernard's devotion to Jesus especially influenced the Franciscan St. Bonaventure (1221–1274), whose treatise on the Mystic Vine was for centuries attributed to Bernard. And he became a source of inspiration for the Franciscan movement in their devotion to the Man Christ Jesus. It was through reading St. Bernard that the German mystic St. Gertrude (1256–1301) came to appreciate that it was the surpassing love that Jesus had for us that moved him to suffer and die for us, and this led her to the source and symbol of that love—his Sacred Heart. Bernard himself maintained that anything he read that was not about Jesus was dry and insipid, while the very name of Jesus was like honey in the mouth, like music in the ear, and a song in the heart.

Paul Diemer

See also: Bonaventure; English Christianity, Medieval; Ignatius of Loyola; Roman Catholicism; Second Person of the Trinity; Spirituality

References

Le Bail, Anselm, OCSO. 1937. *Dictionnaire de Spiritualite*. Paris: Beauchesne.
Leclercq, Jean, OSB. 1957–1977. *Sancti Bernadi Opera*. Edited with H. M. Rochais and C. H. Talbot. Rome: Editiones Cistercienses.
McGinn, Bernard. 1995. *The Growth of Mysticism*. London: SCM.

Black Christianity

See African Christianity; American (North) Christianity; Pentecostalism; Seventh-day Adventism

Bonaventure (1217–1274)

The person of Jesus Christ lies at the center of Bonaventure's theology. His Christological reflections lead us to a cosmic vision of universal peace and reconciliation when the circle of creation history is drawn with Christ as its center. Bonaventure was born in 1217 in Bagnoregio, near Orvieto. As a theologian, he acted as regent master in the Franciscan school of theology at the University of Paris. As a member of the Franciscan Order, he served as its seventh minister-general. He died in 1274, and his legacy includes many works of theology and spirituality written both during his university tenure and later as minister general.

The Franciscan theological tradition can be said to have originated in the writings of Bonaventure. Its inspiration, however, and its constant source of creativity are to be found in the one from whose spirit Bonaventure drank so deeply, St. Francis of Assisi. It is impossible to properly understand Bonaventure and indeed the whole of the Franciscan theological tradition without a recognition of its foundation in the life and experience of Francis. It is because Christ featured as the experiential center of the life of Francis that Christ becomes the theological center of Bonaventure's metaphysics.

Bonaventure's theology begins with God, the Trinitarian God of Christian revelation. The source of the Trinitarian life is the Father, the *fontalis plenitudo*, the fountain fullness, the infinite abyss of the good. The life of the Father is that of limitless self-emptying love and the expression of this is to be found in the Eternal Word. The Word expresses all that the Father is and does and so becomes the pattern for all that the Father creates. As the Word spoken from the depths of the Godhead, the Word is the center of the Trinity. As the Word spoken in the act of creation, a creation that reflects its origin in the Godhead, the Word is the center of all that is.

In the Incarnation, the Eternal Word is enfleshed in human history in the person of Jesus, the Christ. Christ is the fullest expression within time of the eternal mystery that is the foundation of all being, the Trinitarian life of the Godhead. That is why Bonaventure insists that Christ is definitive for unlocking the meaning and purpose of the cosmos. Just as the Eternal Word continually returns love to the Father as origin source, so the meaning of history is found in the return of all creatures to God from whom they have their origin.

Bonaventure's model is that of a circle whereby all things emanate from God and are destined to return to God. For humanity to achieve its proper destiny, it is vital that this circle be completed. If the tracing of a circle is to be successfully completed, it is necessary to locate the center. In his *Collations on the Six Days*, a series of lectures delivered by Bonaventure in 1273, he powerfully develops his understanding of Christ as the center of all that is, Christ in whom there occurs the coincidence of opposites, the harmony of the divine and the human. Humanity is called to realize its image, to be like God. Christ is the one who reveals what it is to be like God, since Christ is the expression in time of who God is.

Bonaventure's emphasis on the example of the humanity of Christ is based precisely on this conviction—that Jesus reveals the nature of what it is to be like God. Just as the source of the Godhead is the *fontalis plenitudo*, the eternal self-emptying goodness and love, so the one who desires to be like God must embrace a life of emptying self-giving love. This is the meaning of *kenosis*, the eternal self-emptying of the Father expressed in history in the *kenosis* of the Son. But humanity, through pride, is blinded to what it is to become like God. Pride involves a turning inward to focus upon self and the importance of self, rather than the turning to the other that is the life of love, exemplified in Trinitarian love. Pride disrupts the tracing of the circle and, hampered by the blindness of pride, humanity cannot locate the center in order to complete the journey of the return to God.

It is here that the mystery of Trinitarian love takes the initiative. God reaches out and in love finds the center for sinful humanity. This is the meaning of the Incarnation, the meaning of the life of Christ, manifest particularly in the self-giving love that finds expression in the Cross. "How marvellous is divine wisdom, for it brought forth salvation through the cinders of humility. For the centre is lost in the circle, and it cannot be found except by two lines crossing each other at right angle" (*Collations on the Six Days* 1.24). It is in the imitation of this self-giving love revealed in Jesus that one lives at the center and so is able to complete the circle of the journey into God.

Paul Rout

See also: Francis of Assisi; John, Gospel of; Kenoticism; Spirituality

References

Bonaventure. 1970. *Collations on the Six Days*. Translated by J. de Vinck. Paterson, NJ: St. Anthony Guild.

Delio, Ilia. 2001. *Simply Bonaventure: An Introduction to His Life, Thought and Writings*. New York: New City.

Hayes, Zachary. 1992. *The Hidden Centre: Spirituality and Speculative Christology in St. Bonaventure*. New York: Franciscan Institute.
Rout, Paul. 1996. *Francis and Bonaventure*. London: Harper Collins. Reprinted in *Great Christian Thinkers: The Spiritual Heritage of Six Key Theologians*. Edited by Peter Vardy. London: Fount, 1999.

Bonhoeffer, Dietrich (1906–1945)

In a famous letter from Tegel Prison a few months before he was murdered by the Nazis for his part in trying to overthrow the Hitler regime and bring peace to Europe, Dietrich Bonhoeffer asked: "Who is Christ really, for us, today?" (*Letters and Papers from Prison*, 279). The answer he gave throughout his short but brilliant life (1906–1945) is that Jesus Christ embodies God's freedom for humanity. God is not free *from* humanity and the world, God is free *for* humanity, *for* the world. Jesus reveals that God is not absent, but present, not remote, but near, not against us, but for us. And because God freely became human, authentic humanity is God's gift to the people of a godless world. Like Luther, who said, "You are to look at this little baby in the crib and this poor man on the cross and say: This is God," Bonhoeffer boldly asked: "Who is this person, of whom it is declared that he is God?" (*Christ the Center*, 98). He replied: the truly human Jesus of Nazareth is none other than the eternal God become human. That is what the name Jesus Christ means to Bonhoeffer. The man Jesus cannot be understood apart from God; God cannot be understood apart from Jesus.

This answer rests on the biblical witness to Jesus, understood through the classical Christian teaching of the Councils of Nicea (325) and Chalcedon (451), and distinctively interpreted through Bonhoeffer's both Lutheran and modern eyes. Christology is the center and animating heart of his theology. Like a diamond whose light flashes in all directions, so different facets of Christ and his meaning for human life are stressed in writings that came from different contexts in Bonhoeffer's life.

The social significance of Christ is decisive for Bonhoeffer. In his first book, *Sanctorum Communio* (1927), Christ both represents and reveals God to humanity and personifies all human beings before God. What happens in him and to him affects everyone. In his cross, Christ vicariously bears God's judgment on self-seeking human beings; in his resurrection the triumph of God's vicarious love is revealed and the new humanity is re-created from the old. The Church-community is the social form of God's revelation and thus the social form of Christ's living presence in the world. It is Christ existing as Church-community. In active-being-for-one-another the members of the Church-community embody the freedom God has for humanity that is revealed in Jesus.

The Christology lectures of 1933 (see *Christ the Center*) begin with a dramatic exchange. A person asks Jesus an abstract question, trying to capture him by human reason: "How can God be truly and fully present in a human being? How can a man who is God incarnate be really and truly human?" But Jesus reverses the question and counters: "Who are you, that you want to categorize and control me?" To question Jesus is to be existentially questioned oneself in return. Jesus is a person, not an intellectual puzzle. He reveals himself and is known only in personal encounter. And personal encounter requires presence, the presence of the resurrected and living Lord.

Just as God is the God who is free for humanity, so Jesus is personally present in freedom "for us, for me" (*pro nobis, pro me*); that is the very structure of his person. But in what form is Christ present? In the form of the Church-community—as word of Gospel address, as sacrament, as community. This presence in the human form of the Church-community is just as paradoxical and scandalous—but no more so—than the Incarnation of God as a Jewish man in ancient Palestine. Indeed, God is humiliated as well as exalted by being present in a community of believing yet sinful people.

The present Christ is the Mediator, the one who is in the center, mediating the transforming presence of God to all reality. Specifically Christ is the center of human historical existence, of politics and the state, and of nature. Christ is the universal mediator, not confined to the Church. In history, politics, and nature Christ is hidden; in the Church, however, Christ's presence is revealed and believed. As the mediator of existence, Christ frees those who are imprisoned from the self-seeking of their own power into mutual love for and with others; as the mediator of the state Christ judges the false messianic pretensions of politics and gives promises and signs of God's coming kingdom; as the mediator of nature, which since the Fall does not unambiguously proclaim and glorify its creator, Christ's presence in the sacraments frees nature to praise its creator and to signal the proper dignity and service of nature in human spiritual-bodily life.

In his widely influential book *Discipleship* (1937), Bonhoeffer focused on Jesus and the Sermon on the Mount. Calling the Church away from "cheap grace," a Church long acculturated that had finally been seduced by Nazism, Jesus calls Christians really to follow him, to be disciples, to be obedient. Faith and obedience are the two sides of discipleship: only those who are obedient really believe, and only those who believe are really obedient.

Discipleship was a highly personal book for Bonhoeffer, as well as a manifesto in the Church struggle against Nazism. As the Sermon on the Mount presents Jesus calling and teaching his first followers, Bonhoeffer believed that Jesus speaks just as directly today through his word in the Church-community. He wants his readers to hear not harsh laws, false hopes, or difficult concepts from the Church, but the very voice of Jesus calling them to follow and obey him in their real world. Discipleship—following Jesus—is highly personal and urgently public; it is both spiritual and political. The words of Jesus, "Love your enemies," and the commandment, "You shall not kill," made a powerful impact on Bonhoeffer so that he regarded Christian pacifism as self-evident, a rare and dangerous position in the Germany of the 1930s.

The figure of Jesus Christ is equally central to Bonhoeffer's *Ethics* (1940–1943), the posthumous book aimed at the reconstruction of Christian life and of German society after peace was won (it also includes the ethical analysis that underlay Bonhoeffer's participation in the anti-Hitler conspiracy and attempted coup d'état). Fundamental to its theology is the reconciliation of God and the world through God's becoming human in Jesus Christ, God taking on humanity in the flesh (incarnation). Pithily, Bonhoeffer says: "The name Jesus contains within itself the whole of humanity and the whole of God" (*Ethics*, 74). The reality of the world is understood not by doctrines of "realism" or "idealism," nor by principles or ideologies; the real world is the world as it is reconciled from its abysmal godlessness by God's reconciliation in Christ. This reconciliation has no other ground than the perfect love of God.

Repeatedly Bonhoeffer focuses on Christ in the threefold form of his incarnation, crucifixion, and resurrection. And these are not abstract events of ancient history, but the form in which the living Christ encounters contemporary human beings. The theme of Jesus being *pro nobis* and *pro me* is carried through in the *Ethics*. *Jesus the incarnate* reveals that God loves real human beings, who are created to be not less than human nor more than human, but truly human—to live free for God and free for their human companions, creatures of God who should neither be scorned nor idolized. *Jesus the crucified* reveals that God executes and suffers judgment upon God's own self, judgment that belongs to sinful human beings. A truly human person, reconciled with God, lives continually under this judgment; those who accept this judgment are set free to live before God a life of genuine worldliness, liberated from the temptations to deify the world or to deny its godlessness. *Jesus the resurrected* reveals that God's love for humanity is stronger than judgment and death, and that humanity is re-created as a new humanity. Human beings henceforth may live free from the fear of death or the idolizing of death; mortal life can be lived with its good and evil, its joy and sorrow, knowing that the ultimate power in the world and the ultimate destiny of humanity are in the hands of its Creator, Reconciler, and Redeemer.

In light of this understanding of Jesus, Christian ethics is ultimately not about moral principles, laws, duty, virtue, or even conscience, and still less is it about a perennial conflict between what is "Christian" and what is "worldly." It is, Bonhoeffer says disarmingly, about "doing the will of God." In keeping with his catholic vision that in Christ God is dealing with the whole of humanity, good people, even if they are not believers, may discover that Christ is the origin and guarantor of those humane values they hold most dear—justice, truth, reason, and peace.

It was in his famous prison meditations that Bonhoeffer posed this question: "Who is Christ really, for us, today?" (*Letters and Papers from Prison*, 279). It was prompted by the observation that many modern people had developed a whole range of strengths through scientific knowledge, through technologies to control nature from medicine to agriculture, and through social planning from insurance to population control. The development of these strengths Bonhoeffer summarized as humanity's "coming of age," referring to adulthood as the stage of solving one's own problems and taking responsibility for one's own life, no longer dependent upon parents. As a result, the type of religion wherein people expected God to be their ultimate problem-solver (the *deus ex machina*) was obsolete. Even more critically from a theological perspective, such religion, rooted in human weakness, led to projecting a God of power who was the counterpart to human need. Jesus, Bonhoeffer argued, did not fit into this religious mold—a mold that had been similarly diagnosed by Freud in canny psychological terms. Given this definition of religion, a "religious" Jesus would be an idol designed to serve the needs of the self, would be marginalized on the edges of life, and would be powerless to transform human life and society.

In contrast, a "non-religious" Jesus was not an avatar of the power-God of human wishfulness and illusion. Instead Bonhoeffer stresses God's weakness and suffering in all the paradox of the Lutheran *theologia crucis*, theology of the Cross. The limpid formula in which the essence of Bonhoeffer's teaching is summarized in his prison letters is this: Jesus is "the one for others." This is the final formulation in which Bonhoeffer distills his central theme of God's freedom for humanity. As the one who exists for others, Jesus is not consigned to life's margins but is life's center and Lord. Formed in the image of Jesus, the Christian life is "existing for others," and the Church is truly the Church only in "being for others." Faith, then, is not being "religious," or subscribing to orthodox dogma, but participating in this being of Jesus, in his incarnation, Cross, and resurrection, in a new life of "existing for others." Through faith of this sort, Bonhoeffer concludes, one becomes human and Christian.

Clifford Green

See also: Chalcedon; Christology, Modern; German Christianity; Nicea; Resurrection

References

Bethge, Eberhard. 2000. *Dietrich Bonhoeffer: A Biography*. Rev. ed. Minneapolis: Fortress.

Bonhoeffer, Dietrich. 1978. *Christ the Center*. San Francisco: Harper and Row.

———. 1995. *Ethics*. New York: Simon and Schuster.

———. 1996. *Works*. English ed. Minneapolis: Fortress.

———. 1997. *Letters and Papers from Prison*. New York: Simon and Schuster.

De Gruchy, John W., ed. 1999. *The Cambridge Companion to Dietrich Bonhoeffer*. Cambridge: Cambridge University Press.

Feil, Ernst, and Barbara Fink. 1998. *International Bibliography on Dietrich Bonhoeffer*. Gütersloh: Chr. Kaiser-Gütersloher Verlagshaus.

Green, Clifford. 1999. *Bonhoeffer: A Theology of Sociality*. Rev. ed. Grand Rapids, MI: Eerdmans.

Kelly, Geffrey B., and F. Burton Nelson, eds. 1995. *A Testament to Freedom: The Essential Writings of Dietrich Bonhoeffer*. Rev. ed. San Francisco: HarperSanFrancisco.

Borg, J. M. (b. 1942)

Marcus Borg, professor of religion and culture at Oregon State University, has taken a multidisciplinary approach to historical Jesus studies and communicated his work in a popular vein to a widespread audience. A student of world religions, Borg takes a special interest in varieties of spirituality and mysticism, as well as in the sociological aspects of religious movements and the inevitable relationships between those movements and their political environs. Although he has written numerous scholarly works, Borg became best known in America for a popular volume called *Meeting Jesus Again for the First Time*. A spiritual autobiography, the latter work traces the author's own faith-journey from precritical naiveté to agnosticism and then to a recovery of what he presents as an intellectually responsible piety. Borg has also gained notoriety as one of the most high-profile members of the controversial Jesus Seminar.

Borg understands Jesus to have been a complex figure, incorporating several religious types discernible in many cultures; the combination of these types in a single individual is what makes him especially interesting and perhaps unique. Borg's overarching category for Jesus is "Spirit Person"—that is, a human being who was believed to be in touch with the realm of the divine and who was recognized by those about him (friends and foes) as serving as something of a conduit to that other world. Thus, Borg emphasizes the mystical and charismatic aspects of Jesus' personality in a way that is atypical for most Jesus scholars. Jesus was a devout man of prayer; he enjoyed an intense intimacy with God, saw visions, and claimed that God spoke directly to him.

As a charismatic Spirit Person, Jesus was regarded as one who could work miracles, especially acts of healing and exorcism. But Jesus also presented himself as a sage—that is, as a teacher of wisdom comparable to Buddha or Lao Tsu who challenged conventional understandings and invited his followers to see the world in new terms. Jesus encouraged people to see reality as nourishing and supportive rather than as hostile or indifferent; he did not teach doctrine or ethics as such, but his vision of reality encouraged an orientation of trust as opposed to an obsession with self-preservation.

There was also a distinct social/political aspect to Jesus' life and ministry. He initiated a reform movement within Israel that sought to replace the "politics of holiness," which segregated people, with an inclusive ethos based on compassion. Thus, Jesus openly associated with women and outcasts, encouraged redistribution of wealth, and in other ways challenged cultural paradigms that he thought sought to preserve the status quo at the expense of justice and mercy. As such, he also became known as a social prophet whose message was directed against the ruling urban elites. It was the latter role that ultimately determined his fate, as prophetic acts performed in Jerusalem (entering the city on a donkey, overturning tables in the temple court) were interpreted as posing a threat to the social order.

Like many of his colleagues in the Jesus Seminar, Borg argues that Jesus did not have a pronounced eschatological vision, and he does not regard the Gospel material predicting a final judgment or the coming of the Son of Man as authentic. He interprets sayings about the kingdom of God as expressive of present-day experience rather than as indicative of an imminent future consummation. Critics of Borg's presentation often capitalize on this aspect, believing that the Gospels' portrayal of an eschatological Jesus is not incompatible with the socially conscious Spirit Person Borg otherwise describes. Similarly, some are dismayed by Borg's claim that the historical Jesus probably did not think of himself as the Messiah, since they feel that the figure he describes would have been likely to accept such an identification. Other critics, however, have felt that Borg's multifaceted image is already too comprehensive, that the actual historical figure may have been some of these things (Spirit Person, healer, sage, reformer, social prophet) but is not likely to have been all of them.

Mark A. Powell

See also: Jesus, Miracles of; Jesus, Teaching of; Jesus in Social Context; Jesus Seminar; Kingdom of God; Messiah; Prayer; Wealth

References

Borg, Marcus J. 1984. *Conflict, Holiness, and Politics in the Teaching of Jesus*. New York: Edwin Mellen.

———. 1988. *Jesus: A New Vision*. San Francisco: Harper and Row.

———. 1994a. *Jesus in Contemporary Scholarship*. Valley Forge, PA: Trinity Press International.

———. 1994b. *Meeting Jesus Again for the First Time: The Historical Jesus and the Heart of Contemporary Faith*. San Francisco: HarperSanFrancisco.

Borg, Marcus J., and N. T. Wright. 1998. *The Meaning of Jesus: Two Visions*. San Francisco: HarperSanFrancisco.

Buddhism

There are two main groups of people who have been and are interested in investigating possible ways in which Jesus might be related to Buddhism or Buddhism to Jesus. The first group look at that relationship through Christian and the second through Buddhist eyes.

Buddhism as a religio-philosophical system began in northwest India at least some 500 years before the birth of Jesus. There are, therefore, no references to Jesus or Christianity in the Buddhist scriptures of the Pali Canon, which Theravada Buddhists claim to be the earliest material that dates from this time. Nor does the New Testament make any reference to Buddhism, so there is no early scriptural material on which either group can build. Later, there were almost certainly cultural contacts between Christians and Buddhists through trade and other forms of travel, and the transmission of fables such as that of St. Barlaam and St. Josaphat have been traced back to the stories of Gautama Buddha in his previous births ("jataka" stories) as a being on the path to enlightenment, a bodhisattva (see Smith, 6–11). Some more recent work has been done on possible cultural parallels and interactions after the rise of Christianity (Derrett), but there is overall hardly any documentary evidence, and certainly no uncontested material, that is explicitly or implicitly relevant to the task of relating Jesus to Buddhism until the late nineteenth century, when colonial and missionary contact and textual translations made people from the two traditions more aware of each other's ideas. These nineteenth-century observations and comparisons laid the foundations for the dialogues of the twentieth century, and by the late twentieth century substantial movements in Buddhist-Christian contact and dialogue were producing sophisticated material from scholars and practitioners in both traditions, including reflections on the relationship between Jesus and Buddhism.

In 1873 in Sri Lanka, the Buddhist monk the Venerable Gunanada entered into a two-day debate (*vada*) with the Sinhalese Christian minister, David de Silva, as a response to what were perceived as aggressive Christian missionary tactics. Each presented four lectures, and the Buddhist critique set a high moral tone, contrasting, for example, the good omens that accompany the birth of the Buddha, according to the Pali texts, with the massacre of the innocents that accompanies the birth of Jesus, according to the New Testament (Kloppenberg, 7).

In the West, Edwin Arnold's poem about the Buddha called "The Light of Asia," which was published in 1879, had immediate and popular impact. It led many people in Western Christian contexts to compare Jesus with the Buddha. These comparisons were both positive and negative. One liberal Anglican clergyman saw people's positive interest in Gautama Buddha as presenting them with a feeling that "they have been confronted with a formidable rival to Jesus Christ," and that was very challenging for many Western Christians (Almond, 2). Others saw both Jesus and the Buddha as "men whose lives, stripped of the halo of legend and enthusiasm that has surrounded them, have come down to us unsullied by the suspicion of a single evil deed, and illumined by patience and courage, by fixity of purpose and stern devotion, by the most heroic self-denial and the most perfect charity" (ibid., 69). Some Westerners thought that the stories of Jesus must have influenced the stories of the Buddha for the moral resonances to be so strong, and some that the life of Jesus was obviously more historical and not so couched in myth and legend. This last response shows the contemporary disparity in scholarly investigation of the sources of the lives of the two figures. Later scholarly analyses of the textual stories of the life of Gautama Buddha have been influenced by those focused on the quest for the historical Jesus in the unraveling of the layers of history, legend, and myth (see Pye 1979). There has also been work demonstrating that the texts, traditions of interpretation, and essence of Buddhism have been explored in ways parallel to and probably influenced by scholarship on the teaching and traditions surrounding Jesus (see Pye and Morgan, 9–58).

The stories of the lives and work of Gautama the Buddha and Jesus the Christ have been compared and contrasted in different ways by many people, including: B. H. Streeter (*The Buddha and The Christ*. London: Macmillan, 1932); Ninian Smart (in Brandon, S. G. F., ed., *The Saviour God*. Manchester: University Press, 1963); Leo Lefebure (1993); Thich Nhat Hanh (1995), and most recently in the Dalai Lama's dialogue at the John Main seminars. There are, of course, also interesting parallels in the narratives of the two figures. Both have miraculous births; the future greatness of both is recognized by sages at religious ceremonies (Jesus' presentation in the temple and Gautama's naming at his father's court); both undergo a period of testing or temptation; and both perform miracles. In contrast to the Christian idea of inherited or original sin as the background to Jesus' task, Buddhism presents the core problem as ignorance. This means that the related language worlds that describe the tasks of atonement/salvation and wisdom/enlightenment are very different. Jesus Christ saves humanity through his death, Gautama Buddha enlightens humanity through his teaching. Jesus is unique in Christian teaching, whereas for Buddhists every aeon and cosmos has its Buddha. The central iconic images of the two faiths present these contrasting emphases in a variety of ways. The death of the eighty-year-old Gautama Buddha lying peacefully between two sal trees and accepting final Nirvana is very different from the agonizing death of the thirty-three-year-old Jesus Christ crucified as a common criminal.

Two other images that indicate differences of emphasis are the "Christ in Majesty" paintings and mosaics so common in the domes or apses of Byzantine churches and the statues of the Buddha in the full lotus posture of meditation and enlightenment so common throughout the Buddhist world. These images are easily misunderstood by members of the other tradition; for example, the Japanese lay Buddhist D. T. Suzuki (*Mysticism: Christian and Buddhist*. London: George Allen and Unwin, 1957, p. 136) thought the figure of the crucified Christ "sadistic," and many Christians find images of the Buddha inactive and inward-looking. Masao Abe, the Japanese Zen Buddhist philosopher, who has worked in America for many years, has been engaged in a very rich movement of Buddhist Christian dialogue that began with his discussions with John Cobb but is now spread more extensively. In a lecture given to Christian missionaries in Kyoto, Japan, in 1974, he contrasts the Christian views of God and faith and the Zen ideas of Nothingness and enlightenment. He says of the Christian and Buddhist understandings of Jesus: "Jesus is the mediator between man and God. He has the nature of *homoousios*, consubstantiality, in which the immanence and transcendence are paradoxically one. Thus Jesus Christ may be said to be a symbol of the Buddhist idea of relationality or independent causation. With full justification Buddhists regard Jesus as a Buddha or as an Awakened one. The new life through death is clearly realised in him." But "from a Zen point of view, the Christian realisation of man's finitude in terms of sinfulness, and consequently the idea of salvation through Jesus Christ, does not seem thoroughgoing enough to reach the ultimate Reality. Can man's finitude in terms of sinfulness be fully overcome through faith?" (Abe 1995, 189). The discussions begun by Abe and Cobb have grown into an international association for Buddhist-Christian studies and dialogue with regular conferences and a journal, *The Journal of Buddhist-Christian Studies*.

When Buddhists hear the story of Jesus' life and death, it often brings to mind the Buddhist concept of a bodhisattva. Bodhisattvas place the enlightenment of other beings as their priority and make a vow that they will attend to that rather than their own aspiration to Nirvana; indeed, it can be said that the happiness (the opposite of suffering) of other beings *is* the bodhisattvas' path. So the classical text by Shantideva, *The Guide to the Bodhisattva's Way of Life*, shows that the bodhisattva seeks to be the doctor, nurse, and medicine for those who are sick, until they are healed; to be food and drink for the hungry; is willing to give up his/her body for the sake of benefiting all and be a lamp for those desiring light. From the Christian point of view this seems to illustrate the idea of self-giving love that is so central to the doctrine of the Incarnation and Jesus' sacrifice on the Cross. This self-giving love that can be said to be the essence of the life and death of Jesus also has a close parallel in the Buddhist idea of compassion. For Christians, Jesus' love is closely connected with forgiveness and is the opposite of hatred, and they therefore find that his teachings resonate with the words from the Pali text, the Dhammapada (Dharmapada in Sanskrit), that "hatred is never appeased by hatred in this world; it is appeased by love" (v. 5; translated in W. Rahula, *What the Buddha Taught*. London: Gordon Fraser, 1959, p. 125).

In chapter 2 of the letter to the Philippians in the New Testament, Paul exhorts Christians to have the "mind" of Christ Jesus, and he characterizes this mind in the Greek word *kenosis*, which is usually translated as "self-emptying." It indicated that the very nature of God as love, a nature that Christians recognize in the figure of Jesus and that they affirm by saying that Jesus is God incarnate, is self-emptying, kenotic. For Christians, God is the Ultimate Reality, an Ultimate Reality that is thus identified as *kenosis*, empty. Both Christians and Buddhists in dialogue with each other have seen in this concept of *kenosis* a possible parallel not only to the Buddhist idea of being a "selfless person" but, more significantly, to the Buddhist concept of *sunyata*, the Sanskrit term for "emptiness." *Sunyata* is one of the many Buddhist terms that are used for "Ultimate Reality" or "The Real." Nirvana is the most commonly known of these terms, and when Buddhists are asked to define or describe Nirvana the task is seen to be as difficult as describing to a blind man the colors of a rainbow or to a fish what it is like to live on dry land. Silence is perhaps the best response, for what it is *not* is easier to say than what it is. Here, in these two terms, *kenosis* and *sunyata*, we find a style of discourse that Christians call apophatic, or negative theology. The Buddhist Masao Abe has explored this comparison (Cobb and Ives), and the Christian Donald W. Mitchell explores these ideas in the following way: "This Void is experienced in Christian spirituality as the ground of Being and beings. It is an absolute non-being that seems to give form to all things including the personal trinitarian forms of God in one's religious experience. It could be considered a final darkness beyond the light, a final Silence beyond all words, a final Godhead beyond the Trinity. If this were true, as Meister Eckhart may have believed, then this mystical void may also be similar to Buddhist Emptiness, especially if the Void were to be understood as a kenotic reality that is *not* an absolute transcendent reality apart from the world" (Mitchell, 23).

The Christian encounter with Buddhists and Buddhist ideas, and the understanding of Jesus in this context, can be seen to be a modern parallel to the Christian encounter with Greek thought and its use of Greek philosophical categories in the seminal early centuries of Christian self-definition. In the third and fourth centuries, Christians were formulating doctrines using the language world of Greek philosophy, which was quite different from that of the Hebraic world in which Christianity has its roots. Some, like Tertullian, thought that process misguided and asked the rhetorical question: "What has Athens to do with Jerusalem?" In reality, however, as the example of the Christological definitions of the Council of Chalcedon and other early doctrinal formulations show, Christians did use the Greek worldview to express Christian truths in the ways they saw most appropriate at the time.

In a comparable way, some Christian theologians are re-expressing Christian ideas, including their understanding of who Jesus is, their Christology, in categories derived from Buddhism, especially Mahayana Buddhist philosophy. In Burma, the rich Greek term *Logos* ("word") in John's Gospel is translated by the rich Buddhist term "dharma," thus asserting Jesus as dharma, a term that is variously translated into English as truth, teaching, or law. John Keenan uses Mahayana Buddhist philosophical categories and sees Jesus as empty of self and of any essence, and as culturally immersed in the conditions of his time (linking with the Buddhist idea of dependent co-arising). He embodies two truths, one that is experienced as ultimate and one that is experienced as provisional. "He embodied ultimate meaning in his contingent, dependently co-arisen living and dying" (Keenan, 233).

The above exercise of expressing Christological truths in Buddhist terms naturally leads to what John Cobb has called the area beyond dialogue, that of creative transformation and mutual transformation. This emphasizes that the explorations are not just a matter of using different terms but also of engaging with a whole new way of thinking about things. As some Christians and Buddhists enter into each other's language worlds and share spiritual practices, they are influencing in a very deep way each other's understanding and presentation of their faiths, including that of their key figures. For Christians that means having new insights into the figure of Jesus and experimenting with diverse cultural ways of presenting them. These insights can be expressed in visual images such as the making of a Tibetan-style *thangka* (painted wall hanging) with Jesus as the central figure and events from his life around the outside; or painting Jesus' temptation so that the figures of Mara and his daughters from the Buddhist story are the images of the tempter. The female bodhisattva of compassion from the Far East can also be used as a "type" of the Madonna and Child. There can also be a greater use of stories of Jesus set apart in meditative prayer and silence and a greater emphasis on his invitation to others to "leave father and mother" for a celibate and world-renouncing life that is for the sake of the world. The monastic dialogues between the two communities that build on that aspect of Jesus as a model for life have been particularly rich. The salvation experience of dying and rising with Christ is likened by the influential Christian monk Thomas Merton to the Zen experience of the Great Death that is associated with satori or enlightenment. The Buddhist emphasis on ahimsa (nonharming) of all sentient beings is challenging Christians to rethink their anthropocentrism and develop models of Jesus that place more emphasis on ecological concerns, positive human potential, and nonharming than some of those of the past. The encounter with Buddhists is one of many factors in this creative process of Christological expression.

Peggy Morgan

See also: Chalcedon; Incarnation in Contemporary Analytic Philosophy; Interfaith Thought and Relations; Jesus, Achievement of; Kenoticism; Spirituality

References

Abe, Masao. 1995. *Buddhism and Interfaith Dialogue*. London: Macmillan.

Almond, Philip. 1988. *The British Discovery of Buddhism*. Cambridge: Cambridge University Press.
Cobb, John B., and Christopher Ives, eds. 1990. *The Emptying God*. New York: Orbis.
Corless, Roger, and Paul Knitter, eds. 1990. *Buddhist Emptiness and Christian Trinity*. New Jersey: Paulist.
Derrett, J., and M. Duncan. 2000. *The Bible and the Buddhists*. Sardini: Edetrice Centro Studi.
Griffiths, Paul J. 1990. *Christianity through Non-Christian Eyes*. New York: Orbis.
Keenan, John P. 1989. *The Meaning of Christ: A Mahayana Theology*. New York: Orbis.
Kloppenberg, Ria. 1994. *A Buddhist-Christian Encounter in Sri Lanka: The Panadura Vada*. Leeds: University, BASR Occasional Paper.
Mitchell, Donald W. 1991. *Spirituality and Emptiness*. New York: Paulist.
Pye, M. 1979. *The Buddha*. London: Duckworth.
Pye, M., and R. Morgan, eds. 1973. *The Cardinal Meaning*. The Hague: Mouton.
Smith, W. Cantwell. 1981. *Towards a World Theology*. London: Macmillan.
Thich Nhat Hanh. 1995. *Living Buddha, Living Christ*. New York: Rivermead.

Bultmann, Rudolf (1884–1976)

Rudolf Bultmann argues that the Gospel accounts of Jesus are not history or biography, but rather theological constructions by later generations of the Church. For this University of Marburg Scripture scholar and theologian, the search for the historical reality of Jesus of Nazareth discloses an eschatological prophet who interpreted the world in apocalyptic terms all but impossible for modern human beings to credit. Hence the need to "demythologize" (a term Bultmann himself uses sparingly) the core message so that it becomes a call to existential decision. This call, and our response to it, is rearticulated with the aid of twentieth-century existentialist thought: in particular, that of Martin Heidegger.

The underlying problem here is that of constructive theology in every age: finding adequate words for describing our relationship to God, who is "wholly other." The ancients wrestle with this conundrum in the language and conceptuality of "myth," which objectifies God as "up there." To think of God as residing in "heaven" is to treat the abstract idea of transcendence in objectifying, mythological terms. For Bultmann, such a conceptuality is not only dated. It is also intrinsically inadequate. Christian preaching of Jesus Christ as the Word of God must not be understood as demanding a sacrifice of the modern intellect in favor of an out-of-date cosmology. The essence of the *kerygma*, or proclamation, is not intrinsically tied to any such cosmology. Expressed in such first-century terms, it becomes a misleading, indeed false, stumbling block to modern human beings. We can both modernize our conception of God, and indeed come closer to the truth about God, by thinking in terms of the existential faith-event that underlies all access to God and all God-language of whatever sort.

Bultmann finds evidence in the New Testament itself of a transition from Jesus as historical figure to a very different Christ of faith. The transition begins when the Kingdom of God, the politico-religious apocalypse Jesus was understood by his immediate followers to have proclaimed, failed to come in their lifetimes. The necessary adjustment of perspective eventually turned Jesus into a Hellenistic redeemer figure. In such terms the Church began to proclaim Jesus as crucified and risen Messiah, the Lord of a time between proclamation and consummation.

In the opening paragraphs of his magisterial *Theology of the New Testament*, Bultmann sets forth with great clarity the implications for New Testament interpretation of this movement from "Jesus of history" to "Christ of faith." Jesus' own message is "a presupposition for the theology of the New Testament rather than a part of that theology itself. . . . Christian faith did not exist until there was a Christian *kerygma:* that is, a *kerygma* proclaiming Jesus Christ—specifically Jesus Christ the crucified and risen One—to be God's eschatological act of salvation. He was first so proclaimed in the *kerygma* of the earliest Church, not in the message of the historical Jesus" (Bultmann 1952, 3).

It is not surprising, then, that Bultmann gives little attention to discovering who this historical personage in fact was. He rather traces the sources concerning Jesus through oral tradition that is already reassembling and shaping them theologically to the theological compositions known as the Gospels and to the constructive theological work of the early Christian communities, some of it earlier than the Gospels, some of it later. Bultmann can be read as justifying his own demythologization program by finding something very like it in the process described. The bulk of his *Theology* indeed consists of accounts of the thought of the New Testament's two great constructive theologians, Paul and John. In these writers we have early demythologizations of the faith-terminology of the generation of Jesus' immediate followers. If New Testament writers themselves can demythologize Jesus' apocalyptic teachings, so can we, using our own philosophical categories.

Bultmann's reconstruction of the genesis of the New Testament witness from relatively unexplored "presuppositions" to Christ proclaimed as divine savior owes much to the practice of "form criticism." Using this method, Bultmann argues from the literary characteristics of different "forms" or genres of the text (e.g., narratives, hymns, parables, wisdom sayings, liturgies, creedlike formulas, theological treatises, etc.) to conclusions about the settings and uses of these passages in the faith communities that composed, employed, and conserved them. He was thus able, by inference, to reconstruct the formative processes behind the texts as we have them.

Bultmann finds strong influences in these processes from sources such as gnosticism, Hellenistic Judaism, and the mystery religions. Even the Gospel of Mark, long thought to tell a relatively straightforward story independent of Hellenistic influence, is interpreted by Bultmann as a product of the Hellenistic Church far removed from Jesus' own time. The community behind Mark's Gospel, in Bultmann's view, must have taken pieces of the mostly oral Jesus-tradition and pieced them together into a synthetic narrative designed to make a theological point. Other New Testament documents also become mythical reconstructions driven by Greek ideas of a heavenly redeemer figure.

In turn, these Greek ideas must themselves be demythologized before they will speak to modern human beings. And Bultmann sees existential categories as key to understanding the modern human condition. He sets aside both Jewish apocalyptic and Hellenistic redeemer categories in favor of an understanding that first makes the *kerygma* intensely challenging and personal. He then expresses this challenge in formal philosophical terms. On the one hand, the modern individual's self-understanding is seen as dominated by the awareness of finitude and contingency and an accompanying concern about security against the future threat of annihilation. At this personally lived level, faith is not assent to a series of either historical or doctrinal propositions but rather an overcoming of the flawed, anxious, lack of confidence one finds in attachment to the things of this world in favor of a security found only in God, mediated by the figure of Jesus Christ.

This "existential" interpretation of the Gospel message then finds elucidation and support in the "existentia*list*" categories of Martin Heidegger as found in *Being and Time*. It does not seem that Bultmann takes aboard this work as a whole in the terms Heidegger himself intended. (One could, for example, call it a brilliantly innovative statement in the tradition of Western ontology from Plato onward, passing through Kant's notion of the "transcendental self" in Husserl's phenomenological version of it, all flowing into the category of *Dasein*, the expression of "being" in whose awareness arises the very question of being.) Although Bultmann is fully aware of all this, it seems that he appropriates only such items of Heideggerian terminology as lend themselves to formulating an appropriate "preunderstanding" for approaching the New Testament and for proclaiming its message to the middle-twentieth century. Bultmannian borrowings from Heidegger include such terms as *Fragestellung* ("putting of the question"), *Geworfenheit* ("thrownness"), *Existenz* (the "being" of human beings), *Vorhandenheit* (the "being" of things), *eigentlich* ("authentic"), *Sorge* ("care"), *Verfallenheit* ("fallenness"), *Sein-zum-Tode* ("being-unto-death"), and numerous others.

Thus, Bultmann would claim, the biblical Word remains the controlling category and the terminology from Heidegger only a means for penetrating and expounding its true meaning. It is not as if the Word itself were being trimmed to conform with the spirit of an age destined itself soon to pass away, but rather that this process uncovers what the New Testament message is truly about for any age. The Gospel addresses existential questions, Bultmann argues, whatever the terms used for articulating such questions.

Still, an implication of the demythologizing procedure is that truth needs to be rearticulated within the limits of the language and conceptuality of each particular place and time. But, as Bultmann carries out this rearticulation, something is lost. It has been said of the Marburg scholar (i.e., by Paul Ricoeur and others) that he does not take seriously the expressive power of biblical language itself. He rather jumps directly from the *kerygma,* stated in barest terms, that "God has drawn near to us in Jesus Christ," to faith understood starkly as the surrender of my self-will, that I may stand radically before

God. This distinguishes Bultmann from Tillich, who gives much more attention to the communicative capacity of symbolic expressions.

The New Testament proclamation of Jesus as the Word of God, once liberated from outdated cosmologies, is thus a message calling upon us to die to anxiety about our future security, finding in Christ's crucifixion a message of liberation from self-concern and reliance upon the grace of God the "wholly other" one. The message calls upon us to renounce, in an existential (not necessarily existential*ist*) decision the conceit that we stand self-sufficiently in the center of reality, turning to trust in the God who stands beyond any possible objectivizing description.

The Bultmannian vision passed through several subsequent stages and permutations among his pupils in the German universities (Bornkamm, Käsemann, and others) and among interpreters such as John Macquarrie and Schubert Ogden. Bultmannian influence began to wane in Europe and America by the 1970s—if not earlier—as the vogue of Heideggerian existentialism diminished and new theological issues took the stage. Still, the intrinsic problems of New Testament interpretation articulated by this scholar, even if expressed in different theological and philosophical terms, remain for future investigators to wrestle with.

Lewis S. Mudge

See also: Christology, Modern; Gnosticism; Jesus as a Historical Figure; John, Gospel of; Kingdom of God; Macquarrie, John; Messiah; Paul; Resurrection; Tillich, Paul

References

Bultmann, Rudolf Karl. 1952. *Theology of the New Testament*. 2 vols. London: SCM.

———.1958a. *Jesus Christ and Mythology*. New York: Scribner.

———. 1958b. *Jesus and the Word*. New York. Scribner.

Kegley, Charles W., ed. 1966. *The Theology of Rudolf Bultmann*. New York: Harper and Row.

Painter, John. 1987. *Theology as Hermeneutics: Rudolf Bultmann's Interpretation of the History of Jesus*. Sheffield: Almond.

Ricoeur, Paul. 1974. "Preface to Bultmann." In *The Conflict of Interpretations: Essays on Hermeneutics*. Edited by Don Ihde. Evanston: Northwestern University Press.

C

Cadbury, H. J. (1883–1974)

Henry Joel Cadbury was an American New Testament scholar of Quaker allegiance—his name would almost compel it, and especially toward the end of his life he wrote much on Quaker history. He taught at a number of universities, notably Bryn Mawr College and finally Harvard. He is known chiefly for his book *The Making of Luke-Acts* (1927), which was refreshing in its width of outlook and anticipated later trends in the study of these writings. But he also wrote two brief books about Jesus, *The Peril of Modernizing Jesus* (1937) and *Jesus, What Manner of Man* (1947), both more significant in their teaching than their size might indicate. The first was the more critical, not to say relentless, in its hammering of common assumptions, in both academic and lay circles. The second was the more positive and constructive, though not all readers would see much light between it and its predecessor.

In a way, the first book was a follow-up to Schweitzer's celebrated exposure of the tendency to arrive at a picture of the historical Jesus that makes him congenial to the aspirations of one's own time and outlook. But whereas Schweitzer was chiefly concerned with the work of German (and some other) scholars of the nineteenth century, famous for their high-minded liberal assumptions, and with showing how distant they were from the Jesus of first-century Galilee, Cadbury was also interested in exposing the less refined tendencies of much American opinion on the subject. He could be scathing, for example, in his account of the businessman who confidently claimed Jesus as the patron of go-getting capitalist money-making, with its ethic of ruthless hard work. Cadbury's enemy was anachronism, spawning self-serving invention or at least flagrant partiality of judgment. But he was equally clear about the comparable behavior of theologians, such as the American writers of the early twentieth century who claimed Jesus as author of "the social gospel," with the kingdom of God, preached by Jesus, defined as "an ideal social order."

Cadbury was ahead of his time in his insistence on the sheer difficulty we have in grasping the thought-forms or mentality of cultures other than our own, not to speak of our reluctance to do so—all the more so if assumptions derived from faith seem to be under threat. Such a "distortion" of Jesus was surely at work already, Cadbury held, in the writing of the Gospels, where church interests and needs modify the telling of the story of Jesus.

In other words, Cadbury was protesting against the many-shaped determination, by people of all kinds of convictions, either to have a Jesus after their own heart or a timeless and static Jesus, aloof from social and cultural circumstances of a particular time and place. He was relentless in exposing the often insidious and ingenious character of our wish to have a Jesus corresponding to our own beliefs or prejudices, and to use him as a way of appealing for or against later Christianity or the Church, according to our own purpose. The depiction of Christ in official dogma was an early instance of the perennial modernizing tendency.

Cadbury's openness and candor reached a rare level in his encouraging of readiness to admit in relation to this or that aspect of Jesus that we simply do not know. In his attempts to "place" Jesus in his time and place (e.g., in his Jewishness), Cadbury, it turned out, was a forerunner of many later writers, but he is perfectly aware that the tendency to modernize has its counterpart in a tendency also to overarchaize, so in effect outlawing originality. He is then a beacon of warning to all those many scholars who have given the world a more or less complete portrait of the person, life, and teaching of Jesus, even when they are out to avoid the perils of cutting him to some favored pattern.

The later book, presented as more constructive, might not be recognized as such by all readers. It makes no concessions to those unsure of the lessons of its predecessor, and it cannot be said to produce a full-blown description of Jesus (we simply do not know). It may be all the more impressive to note his positive claims—for example, that Jesus stands for the principle of unenforceable obligation; that he acts with rare inner assurance; that his teaching stems not from general rules but from particular instances. Sometimes indeed later critics might think Cadbury a shade too credulous on one point or another. He would surely see their point.

Leslie Houlden

See also: Jesus as a Historical Figure; Kingdom of God; Schweitzer, Albert

References

Cadbury, Henry J. 1962a [1937]. *The Peril of Modernizing Jesus*. London: Macmillan; London: SPCK.

———. 1962b [1947]. *Jesus, What Manner of Man?* London: Macmillan; London: SPCK.

Caiaphas

See Jesus in Social Context

Calvin, John (1509–1564)

John Calvin is at one with the historic tradition of Christian faith in confessing Jesus of Nazareth to be the Christ (i.e., God's agent for salvation). The Geneva reformer's Christology, set within the whole argument of his *Institutes of the Christian Religion*, closely follows the traditions of Nicea and Chalcedon, while tending to substitute relational language for the ancient

Greek terminology of substance, nature, and personhood. Although not the inventor of what has come to be called the "reformed tradition" (for the latter is already to be found in essence in figures such as Augustine, Chrysostom, and Bernard of Clairvaux), Calvin provides an able summing up and focusing of earlier Christological teaching, albeit with certain distinctive characteristics, such as the doctrine of "accommodation." Calvin's work has won its way over the centuries owing not to its conceptual originality but rather to its orderliness, clarity, and power of expression.

Calvin's doctrine of Christ is most fully articulated in *Institutes*, book II. The exposition begins with an analysis of human sinfulness, making clear that one can only truly know the sinfulness of sin in the light of redemption by Christ the mediator. With respect to both sin and its resolution, Calvin is a faithful Augustinian. We are free to will what we desire, but not free of our own power to attain what we most need: the restoration of our freedom to live with integrity before God. It is Jesus Christ who, by virtue of his atoning death and empowering resurrection, offers us this power. The Second Adam is thus the clue to the meaning of the First (Rom. 5.12).

This insight has obvious consequences for our understanding of the law. Luther characteristically expounds law before Gospel; Calvin reverses that order, intending to convey that just as we truly know the meaning of Adam only in Christ, so Christ's gospel is the basis for knowing what it means to keep the commandments (including, certainly, life under Torah's moral, as opposed to ritual, demands and perhaps the whole tradition of medieval law in which Calvin was schooled). Here is the Christological ground for the famous "third use of the law," in which Torah "finds its place among believers in whose hearts the Spirit of God already lives and reigns" (*Institutes* II, vii, 12). The final (1559) edition of the *Institutes* (in contrast to previous editions) places this exposition of law in the light of the Gospel prior to Calvin's discussion of the Ten Commandments, rather than before.

It follows that faith in Jesus Christ is decisive for a knowledge of God unto salvation. "The whole knowledge of God the creator . . . would be useless unless faith also followed, setting forth for us God our Father in Christ" (ibid., vi, 1.). That is, the knowledge of God we may naturally possess (in the form, say, of awe toward creation) is limited. The limit Calvin has in mind consists not only in the sinful corruption of natural knowledge but also in humanity's essential incapacity, unaided, for knowing God's true benevolence toward us. We do indeed have a certain wisdom (knowledge of God and knowledge of ourselves, as Calvin says in the opening chapter of the *Institutes*), but, apart from Christ, we do not have an inkling of what *saving* knowledge is.

God in Jesus Christ has addressed this human limit by having "accommodated himself to our little measure" (Irenaeus). The notion of God's "accommodation" to our capacities in Jesus Christ is one of the distinctives of Calvin's Christological doctrine. In classical rhetoric, *accommodatio* means adapting a discourse to the capabilities, needs, and situation of its hearers. The term is not unknown in patristic literature, finding mention especially with reference to difficulties in Scripture. But Calvin employs it in connection with

John Calvin. (Library of Congress, Prints and Photographs Division [LC-USZ262-77315])

most of the relationships between God and humanity, and especially with reference to Jesus Christ. God "lisps" in speaking to us of who God is (*Institutes* I, xiii, 1). Or God addresses us as a mother speaking to her child, "so as not to leave us behind in our weakness" (ibid. III, xxi, 4). "In Christ God so to speak makes himself little in order to lower himself to our capacity" (*Commentary on I Peter*, I, 20a).

Indeed, God's love for us *demands* that God become "God with us" in Jesus Christ. Here Calvin introduces an elaborate reflection on Isa. 7.14 and Matt. 1.23 (Reist, 41f.). "Hence it was necessary for the Son of God to become for us Immanuel, that is, God with us, and in such a way that His divinity and our human nature might by mutual connection grow together. Otherwise the nearness might not have been near enough, nor the affinity sufficiently firm, for us to hope that God might dwell with us" (*Institutes* II, xii, 1). For the first time, in the edition of 1559, Calvin asserts that God and we "by mutual connection grow together." No longer does revelation impress us with the distance between God and ourselves, the contrast between God's Spirit and our defilement, but rather with the closeness of "mutual connection."

Here the larger implications of the doctrine of "accommodation" become clear. It is not that only a part of Godself is to be found in Christ, but that God limits his whole self, makes himself finite, in order to allow us to comprehend God's nature as we grow together with God. God is *with* us in God's essential being. Human beings may claim to worship God the creator, but without the Mediator it is "not possible for them truly to taste God's mercy, and thus be persuaded that he [is] their father" (ibid., 4).

Here Benjamin Reist finds grounds for calling Calvin's Christology "processive" because it is "relational." "Dare we to say," writes Reist, "that for Calvin it was becoming clear that as God grows, so do we? If so, dare we say that in the light of Calvin's insights we may now risk the view that our own growth is the result of, even a clue to, God's growth?" (Reist, 43).

This interpretation is controversial. But it underlines the apparent difference between some of Calvin's own formulations and those of later Calvinism. In later works the distance between creatures and their creator is strenuously maintained. See, for example, the *Westminster Confession of*

Faith, chapters II and VIII. Clearly at this point Calvin's thought was still developing. One can only speculate what might have become of this passage had the writer lived to write yet another edition of the *Institutes* (ibid.).

There follows the well-known exposition of the three offices of Jesus Christ as "prophet, king, and priest." As prophet, Jesus was anointed by the Holy Spirit to be herald and witness of the Father's grace, not as other teachers were so called, but in a unique way. Furthermore, this anointing was not for Jesus' own ministry alone but for his entire body, the Church, in order that the power of the Spirit might be continuously present in the Church's preaching (*Institutes* II, xv, 2). With Jesus, prophecy in the Old Testament sense comes to an end, but it gives way to a continuing proclamation of the gospel through the ages. This, too, Reist claims to be "processive" in the sense that the task of Christ's first office is not completed by him in the days of his flesh but continues in the ongoing life of his Body, presumably growing and deepening in the light of historical experience.

As for the kingly role, Calvin stresses that it is spiritual, not political (ibid., xv, 3). Again, implications for ecclesiology are in view. In his kingly office, Christ protects the Church and guarantees its perpetuity (ibid., xv, 3). Similarly Christ in this role guarantees the eternal life of the individual person (ibid.). "What, then, would it profit us to be gathered under the reign of the Heavenly King unless beyond this earthly life we were certain of enjoying its benefits?" (ibid., 4).

Finally, in Christ's priestly role we come upon the connection Calvin makes between the person of the Mediator and his work of atonement. Apart from the priestly office, Christ's work as prophet and king can have no efficacy for us. We have no access to God without Christ as priestly mediator. "God's righteous curse bars our access to him, and God in his capacity as judge is angry toward us. Hence, an expiation must intervene in order that Christ as priest may obtain God's favor for us and appease his wrath. Thus Christ to perform this office had to come with a sacrifice" (ibid., 6). The echoes of Anselm's *Cur Deus Homo* are plain here. And once again the ecclesiological reference is discernible. Christ plays the priestly role in order to render God propitious toward us but also to receive us as companions in the priestly office. "For we who are defiled in ourselves yet are priests in Him" (ibid.).

It is clear from these formulas that Calvin brings the "person" and the "work" of Christ close together. Who Christ is relates to what he accomplishes. On this basis (and because he is a traditionalist) the reformer accepts and defends the classic Nicene and Chalcedonian formulas without rearguing them except in relation to those he regarded as the heretics of his own day. He rejects the Eutychian teaching that Christ really did not take flesh from Mary, as well as the position of Servetus that Christ is not coequal and consubstantial with the Father. He is opposed to all forms of Docetism, insisting that Jesus had a real human soul and real human flesh and that he suffered real pain. The impression is of a theologian who, had he lived in the fifth century, would have been more at home in the Antiochene school of thought than in the Alexandrian.

This tendency marks a contrast with Luther, who particularly emphasized the unity of Christ's personhood. Calvin rather stresses the integrity of each of the two natures, fearing that one could destroy both natures' integrity by insisting too much on their unity. Calvin, moreover, opposes the Lutheran interpretation of the *communicatio idiomatum* (the "communication of properties" between the divine and human natures of Christ), arguing that the human nature as such was not capable of being divinized and thus given the property of omnipresence. When the *Logos* becomes incarnate as Jesus he does not give up the divine attribute of omnipresence but continues to fill the whole cosmos, and thus to be outside as well as inside the human nature he has assumed. The glorified human nature of Christ is indeed at God's right hand in heaven, but even there remains localized, in contrast to his infinite and eternal divine nature that is at all times omnipresent. Yet, even so, the omnipresent divine nature is always perfectly united with the localized human nature.

Here are the roots of the doctrine that came to be known (especially to opponents) in the early seventeenth century as the *extra Calvinisticum* ("that Calvinistic extra"). As more explicitly developed, it states that, in the course of the Incarnation and beyond it, the Word by whom all things were made continues to be present and active beyond the flesh to which it is united in Jesus Christ. Luther and his followers tended to say that the divine nature's power to be everywhere was communicated to the human nature as well, but kept hidden during the earthly ministry.

Lewis S. Mudge

See also: Alexandrian Theology; Anselm; Antiochene Theology; Augustine of Hippo; Bernard of Clairvaux; Chalcedon; Christology, Modern; Jesus, Death of; Luther, Martin; Nicea; Resurrection

References

Calvin, John. 1559. *Institutes of the Christian Religion*. Translated and edited by Ford Lewis Battles and John T. McNeill. *Library of Christian Classics*, XX and XXI. London: SCM.

Dowey, Edward A. 1952. *The Knowledge of God in Calvin's Theology*. New York: Columbia University Press.

Hoogland, Marvin P. 1966. *Calvin's Perspective on the Exaltation of Christ*. Kampen, Netherlands: J. H. Kok.

Jansen, John Frederick. 1956. *Calvin's Doctrine of the Work of Christ*. London: J. Clark.

McNeill, John T. 1954. *The History and Character of Calvinism*. New York: Oxford University Press.

Reist, Benjamin A. 1991. *A Reading of Calvin's Institutes*. Louisville, KY: Westminster/John Knox.

Wallace, Ronald S. 1953. *Calvin's Doctrine of Word and Sacrament*. Edinburgh: Oliver and Boyd.

Celtic and Early English Christianity

Christianity is first mentioned as being present in Britain (most of the island being then a Roman province) in the later second century, and at some time soon after that it spread among the native Celtic-language-speaking population within the province. When Christianity first appeared in Ireland is unknown, but by 431 there was a community of sufficient size there—probably many of those Christians were slaves captured in Britain—that the bishop of Rome, Celestine I, sent them a bishop, Palladius; there is evidence of continuing concern in Rome for the welfare of these Christians during the fifth century. There is no evidence that Christianity spread north of the Roman area of Britain, among the Picts, at this time. These early generations of Christians, whether their cultural background was Latin or Celtic, appear to be no different from other Western Christians at the time with regard to their views of Jesus. The one Christian who stands out in the period is Pelagius (prominent c. 410–15)—often said to be from Britain, although Jerome says that he was Irish, in which case Augustine's description of him as "British" would be a cultural description indicating a non-Roman family. He is famous as a heretic opposed by Augustine and others. But there is nothing to suggest that he had any radically different view of Jesus; and if he did hold the views on the relation of divine grace and the freedom of the will ascribed to him by Augustine, then it would simply imply that he was less concerned with Jesus as a savior and more concerned with Jesus as a demanding master.

In the course of the fifth century, a sequence of events radically altered the cultural and religious landscape of the British Isles: the Roman legions withdrew, there was an increase in raiding from west and north, and new settlers, the Angles and the Saxons, arrived from northern Germany. Although we know that many of the Irish raiders were Christians—the name of one such war-band leader has survived: Coroticus—and that Christianity was spreading among the native Irish population, the German settlers were wholly pagan and brought their native religion with them. It is at this period—later fifth to early sixth centuries—that we encounter both our first textual evidence for Christianity in the writings of St. Patrick (a Briton working as a bishop in Ireland) and Gildas (among those British being pushed back toward modern-day Wales by the Germanic invaders), and the fundamental problem of interpretation that dogs all discussion of the Christianity that is found in Celtic and early English societies. Both Patrick and Gildas see themselves simply as Western Christians and stress their lack of regional specificity vis-à-vis the Latin world, and yet the religious perceptions—and so for Christians, the view of Jesus—of individuals and societies are not immune from the cultural landscape in which they find themselves. Put simply, we should not expect to find a radically different view of Jesus in these societies—the notion that there is "the Jesus of Celtic Christianity" is a modern illusion—and certainly not in their formal theology, where they used, broadly, the same Latin liturgy, doctrinal formulae, and authorities as the rest of Western Christianity. But we do find subtle shifts of emphasis that reflect their more local concerns.

Both Patrick and Gildas see themselves as Romans, but they differ from earlier generations of Christians in stressing a view of Christ as the one who comes at the end of history as the rewarding and condemning judge. For Gildas the plague of pagan settlers is a punishment sent from

Christ's courtroom (see 2 Cor. 5.10) on his compatriots for their sins. Patrick believes that Christ will return as judge very soon, and that he himself is one of the final witnesses working at "the ends of the earth" (cf. Acts 1.8); when he has finished his preaching, "the end will come" (Matt. 24.14). However, if both Patrick and Gildas share an apocalyptic outlook, in their liturgy and formal preaching they are part of the Latin Christianity of late antiquity. Thus Patrick preserves a baptismal creed from the British liturgy of his time containing this section on Jesus:

> And his Son, Jesus Christ, whom we declare to have always existed with the Father. He was with the Father spiritually before the world came into being; begotten of the Father before the beginning of anything in a way that is beyond our speech. And "through him all things were made," all things visible and invisible. He was made man, and having conquered death was taken back into the heavens to the Father. "And he has bestowed on him all power above every name in heaven and on earth and under the earth, so that every tongue may confess that our Lord and God is Jesus Christ." In him we believe, looking forward to his coming in the *very near* [these words are without parallel in other creeds, yet fit Patrick's theology and should be seen as his adaptation] future when he will judge the living and the dead, and "will repay each according to his works." (*Confessio*, 4 [see in O'Loughlin, 52–92])

Scholars have devoted much labor to relating this to the creed of Nicea, but in fact that is unnecessary: both Nicea and Patrick just took over standard baptismal formulae from their regions—and there were regional variations within a general form—and adapted them to the precise theological point they wanted to make.

During the sixth and seventh centuries Christianity became a more powerful force in Irish society, apparently the dominant force in the remnants of British society (Wales). It also began to make progress among the Picts (eastern Scotland) and among the Germanic tribes in England through the work of missionaries from Ireland. This was a new experience for Western Christianity, whose liturgy and most important texts were in Latin, in that for the first time it was establishing itself in a culture without a Latin substrate: they had to engage in a process of cultural and linguistic translation. With regard to perceptions of Jesus, this had several effects. First, the highest terminology of their social scale was applied to Jesus; thus in Irish he gained the title "High King of Heaven," while in Anglo-Saxon societies Christ is likened to the leader of a tribal band. Second, aspects of society affected pastoral practice with a consequent shift in understandings of Christ. The one truly distinctive contribution from the clergy of the Celtic lands was a new approach to sins committed after baptism, which avoided the pastoral impasse of "public penance." This was based on insular (i.e., as distinct from mainland European) legal practice and a system of correction for monks derived from Cassian (the fifth-century monastic teacher in southern France), but it was underpinned theologically by the notion of sin as sickness, with Christ as savior being "the divine physician." This was a notion that became a common element first in insular preaching—despite hesitations by some Anglo-Saxon clergy working with Archbishop Theodore (c. 602–690, at Canterbury from c. 670)—and eventually became common in the West.

Any attempt to identify other characteristic features of local insular perceptions of Jesus are fraught: one can fix on a particular image, then (1) by ignoring the fact that such images were common across the West *at that time*, and (2) contrasting the image with a later understanding, perhaps from after the fourteenth century, arrive at a position whereby the Christianity of the Celtic lands and Anglo-Saxon England appears sui generis and exotic. For example, when one looks at saints' lives from the period one can be struck by the way they imagine Jesus as a model for imitation; but similar views of Jesus, both positive and negative, can be found across Europe at the time. Thus, with one possible exception, when one examines their classroom theology—textbooks, exegesis—or their surviving collections of homilies, it is impossible to identify its origins on the basis of any distinctive theology. And, while they were aware of current disputes in Christology—for example, monothelitism, the belief that Christ had only a divine will (see Bede, *Historia ecclesiastica* 4, 1 and 17–18), or the "Three Chapters" debate (see Columbanus, and items in bibliography)—they always remain firmly within the Western orthodox camp. The one possible exception is their interest in Christ as "Lord of History," wherein the insular writers of the seventh and eighth centuries are different from Continental writers on the theme (e.g., Julian of Toledo, d. 690). Bede (c. 673–735) arranges his view of time in a far more organized way than Augustine's "ages of the world," so that his people were living in the "age of Christ" at the optimal point in human history, just before the time when Christ will be "all in all" (cf. Eph. 1.23). This finds other expressions in the way that they keep annalistic records, in their concern to produce vernacular versions of the "six ages of the world," and the concern of the Irish exegete Ailerán (d. 665) to study the genealogy of Christ. They were keen to show that they were living in "the age of Christ" as chosen holy nations—acknowledging Jesus as their king and becoming his royal followers, a theme based on 1 Pet. 2.9—in the period of "the law of the letter" (Scripture), which comes after a long period of preparation (when God worked providentially among their non-Christian ancestors) and precedes the conclusion of the world's history. One other interesting contribution of the insular world to the image of Christ is a series of texts, known today by scholars as "the ordinals of Christ," whereby incidents in Jesus' life are identified as tantamount to his taking on the task of each order of clergy.

In devotions focused on Jesus the insular world is not markedly different from the general Western pattern, and it exhibits both mainstream Christian devotions (e.g., the Irish "Litanies of Jesus," which implore his help), as well as some of the more exotic forms such as the *Carta dominica*, known in Ireland and Anglo-Saxon England, which presents Jesus as a stern observer/judge. In the former case, Jesus is the object of petition, and the assembly calls on the Church's saints and the holy figures of their Old Testament to make intercession for them with Jesus—for example, "I beg of you [Jesus] through [the intercession] of all your sons of true virginity throughout the world, both of the Old and New Testament, with John the youth, your bosom fosterchild." In other litanics Jesus is addressed by a series of titles—for example, "O morning star, O giver of the Law, O final judge." In the case of the *Carta*, both main "Jesus Letters" were widely known in insular circles; Jesus is one who enforces a strict sabbatarianism and demands penitence from his followers.

Thomas O'Loughlin

See also: Augustine of Hippo; Creeds; Irish Christianity; Jesus Letters; Welsh Christianity; Glossary: *pelagianism*

References

Atherton, Mark, ed. 2002. *Celts and Christians*. Cardiff: University of Wales Press.
Bischoff, Bernhard, and Michael Lapidge. 1994. *Biblical Commentaries from the Canterbury School of Theodore and Hadrian*. Cambridge: Cambridge University Press.
Clancy, Finbarr. 1998. "*Vive in Christo, ut Christus in te*: The Christology of St. Columbanus." Pp. 163–195 in *Studies in Patristic Christology*. Edited by Thomas Finan and Vincent Twomey. Dublin: Four Courts.
Gray, Patrick T. R., and Michael W. Herren. 1994. "Columbanus and the Three Chapters Controversy—A New Approach." *Journal of Theological Studies* 45: 160–170.
Jones, Charles W. 1969. "Some Introductory Remarks on Bede's Commentary on Genesis." *Sacris Erudiri* 19: 115–198.
O'Loughlin, Thomas. 1999. *Saint Patrick: The Man and His Works*. London: SPCK.
———. 2000a. *Celtic Theology: Humanity, World and God in Early Irish Writings*. London: Continuum.
———. 2000b. *Journeys on the Edges: The Celtic Tradition*. London: Darton, Longman and Todd.

Chalcedon

In 451 a Council met at Chalcedon in Asia Minor in order to settle disputes over the person of Jesus Christ (Christology). The Council of Ephesus in 431 (see Antiochene Theology) had left unresolved questions, and a solution was patched up in 433 on the basis of the *Formula of Union*. This confessed that

> the Lord Jesus Christ was complete God and complete Man, with rational soul and body; born before the ages of his Father as regards deity, the same born at the end of days from Mary the Virgin as regards humanity; the same in being as the Father as regards deity, and the same in being as ourselves as regards humanity; for a union occurred of two natures, and therefore we confess one Christ, one Son, one Lord. In this sense of unconfused union we confess the holy Virgin as Godbearer [Greek.: *theotokos*], since God the Word was enfleshed and became man, and from the very conception united with himself the shrine [cf. John 2.19–21] taken from her. As to the expressions used of the Lord by the gospel-writers and apostles, we recognize that theologians apply some in common, referring to the one outward manifestation, others separately, referring to two natures, and making it customary to use terms of divine honour for the deity of Christ, and lowly ones for his humanity.

In this *Formula* both Antiochenes on the one side and Cyril on the other allow major features of each other's positions: the Antiochenes accept *Theotokos* and emphasize the unity; Cyril allowed "two natures" and the separate application of Scripture texts, and that the union is "unconfused," not an Apollinarian hybrid of god-and-man. Disquiet remained. Many Antiochenes, including their leading theologian, Theodoret of Cyros (c. 395–c. 460), thought that Nestorius had been unjustly condemned, and that the real heretic was Cyril (see Alexandrian Theology). Cyril himself was pilloried for his concessions by some who were attached to the "One Nature" doctrine, and in defending himself he started attacking the dead heroes of Antiochene Christology, Diodore of Tarsus and Theodore of Mopsuestia. In 444 Cyril was succeeded by Dioscorus (also spelled Dioscuros), who was prepared to ditch the settlement of 433 and lead the Church in a "Monophysite" direction—that is, one based on the principle of "One Nature" in Jesus Christ.

The word "nature" (*phusis*) has important ambiguities in Greek. As in English, it can mean "the natural world" (the subject of "natural" science) and can also mean the collection of features, which make up a thing or person ("It's in her *nature*"). But unlike English it can also mean a concrete being or entity: *phusis* originally meant "growth" or "a growth." When Diodore of Tarsus and others defended the deity of Christ by speaking of his two "beings" (*ousiai*), Apollinaris (Apollinarianism) had responded by insisting that Christ is "One nature, that of the divine Word, enfleshed": whatever Jesus does is done by the pre-existent Word of God, not by some man he took, and that includes accommodating himself to suffering and death. Apollinaris had been generally condemned in 381 for denying a created human rational soul in Jesus, but some of his works, powerful and apparently orthodox, were circulating under the names of honored fathers of the recent past. Cyril, brought up in this tradition, at first found the Antiochene principle of "two natures" unacceptable, as implying two persons: it made Jesus a mere man, inhabited or inspired by the divine *Logos*. He insisted that Jesus was the one "nature," the divine *Logos* who took on the characteristics of a human being. There was a "natural" or "hypostatic" union, since the *Logos* had united human nature to his own *nature* (*kata phusin*) or *essentially* (*kath' hupostasin*). Only in this sense did he concede "two natures" in the *Formula of Union*.

Dioscorus preferred the earlier Cyril to the Cyril who in 433 had compromised to get his archbishopric restored. He began a campaign against those who in the Antiochene area still defended Nestorius and were suppressing Cyrilline views. These included Theodoret of Cyros (c. 395–c. 460), who was confined to his diocese by the Emperor. Thus encouraged, one Eutyches, a revered monastic leader in Constantinople more than seventy years old, spoke out against the doctrine of two natures in Christ. In November 448 Eutyches was accused before the local court of Flavian, archbishop of Constantinople (446–150). His judges used a variety of formulae about the constitution of Jesus Christ: Flavian suggested "of [or "from"; Greek: *ek*] two natures after he became man"; others suggested "two natures with (*en*) one outward manifestation (*prosopon*)" or "made known with (*en*) two natures." Eutyches, however, insisted that: "after the Word became man, that is after the birth of our Lord Jesus Christ, . . . one nature, that of God who has been enfleshed and made man." He had difficulty with "same in being (*homoousios*) as us in his manhood," which the *Formula of Union* asserted, for Christ's flesh is divine, and he rejected any formula other than the Creed of Nicea, which of course meant the *Formula*. Eutyches was condemned. He appealed to Rome and Alexandria, as well as to members of the imperial court. There he had a strong ally in his godson the eunuch Chrysaphius, who managed most of the business of the emperor Theodosius II (408–450).

Dioscorus rose to his defense, and a great council gathered at the emperor's command in Ephesus in August 449 to review the case. The proceedings against Eutyches were read out, and the judgment reversed. The catchwords were, "After the Union, One," and "One from two": when God the Son became Man, he remained a single nature or being, though he had added human nature to the divine. Flavian was deposed for Nestorianism, as were Theodoret and another leading Antiochene, Ibas of Edessa. The bishops, including Flavian's former supporters, approved. It would later be alleged that pressure and violence were used; Leo I, bishop of Rome (440–461), would call it the *Latrocinium*, or "Robbery," and Flavian's death soon after came to be viewed as a martyrdom. For the moment, the combination of Alexandrian authority, imperial power, hatred of Nestorianism, and the political instability of Western Europe left Dioscorus, and the one-nature doctrine, triumphant.

The victory was short-lived, however. Theodosius II died in a riding accident a year after the council met, and his clever sister Pulcheria took over, marrying as consort a competent soldier named Marcian. These new emperors exiled Eutyches again, struck down his protector Chrysaphius, and honored the memory and bones of Flavian. One motive was to raise the status of the imperial city of Constantinople as against the primacy in the Church of Alexandria. Another was to restore unity with the Western Church and Empire. The Pope, Leo I (rightly dubbed "the Great"), had received appeals from both Eutyches and Flavian against their condemnations, and he came down for Flavian. Rome perceived that an agreement based on the *Formula of Union* had been unilaterally broken. Leo set out his doctrinal judgment in a letter to Flavian, commonly known as *The Tome of Leo*. This was intended as a formula that would resolve the issue for the universal Church. It was written before the council of 449, and Dioscorus deliberately made sure that it was not seen or heard by most of the bishops present. It remains an important document of traditional Christology.

Leo insists that God the Son took real and total humanity from the Virgin: "With the proper character of each nature and being [Latin: *substantia*] preserved and combining in one Person, humility was embraced by majesty, weakness by strength, mortality by eternity; . . . an inviolable nature was united with one that could suffer, so that, as necessary for our healing, one and the same Mediator of God and men, the Man Jesus Christ [1 Tim. 2.5] might be able to die because of the one, and not able to die because of the other. In the entire and complete nature of a man true God was born." Leo stresses the distinction visible in Christ's words and deeds: "Each kind [*forma*] does what is proper to it in communion with the other, the Word performing what belongs to the Word, and the flesh carrying out what belongs to flesh. One of these is brilliant with miracles, the other succumbs to injuries." This principle, which we can find in other writers from about A.D. 200 onward, is illustrated by Leo from each part of Christ's life: "A baby's infancy is revealed by the humble cradle, the greatness of the Most High is declared by angel-voices. . . . To hunger, to thirst, to be weary and to sleep are evidently human. To feed thousands of people with five loaves, to offer the Samaritan woman living water, such that its drinking makes one never thirst again, to walk on the surface of the sea with feet that do not sink, and to calm the rising waves when the storm arises, is indubitably divine." His conclusion is: "Although in the Lord Jesus Christ there is one person of God and Man, yet the abuse suffered in common has one basis, the glory common to both has another: humanity less than the Father comes to him from us, divinity equal with the Father from the Father." There is a final attack on the Eutychian formula, which allowed two natures before the union, one afterward. Quite the reverse, says Leo: there was one Son of God, who added human nature to his own in the incarnation.

With the favorable change of imperial policy, Leo hoped the Easterns would accept his *Tome* and be satisfied. But neither state nor church in Constantinople was prepared to accept the implications of the bishop of Rome resolving an Eastern dispute. A council was therefore called at Chalcedon in 451, near Nicea, with the reluctant agreement of Leo, to review the events of 448 and 449. In a series of sessions the trial of Eutyches and the actions of Dioscorus were reviewed. Dioscorus was condemned, both for his behavior and for his doctrine: his favored formula, "One out of two," was specifically condemned. Theodoret condemned Nestorius and was reinstated; when misgivings were expressed about some of the stronger statements in Leo's *Tome*, he helped the council by finding parallel expressions in Cyril's more moderate writings. Most of those who had voted with Dioscorus in 449 now changed sides, alleging that they had been compelled against their will; it was the only way to hold on to their offices in the Church and in the state. A number of problems in canon law were resolved, and in particular the position of Constantinople as the second see of Christendom was reinforced and extended, over the older tradition that Alexandria came after Rome. This same movement would not allow Leo's *Tome* alone to settle the dogmatic issue: a new formula was needed, and Constantinople's part would be large.

All paid lip service to the rule that the only creed for settling doctrine was that of Nicea: Cyril and Nestorius both alleged it, as did both parties at Ephesus in 431, and Eutyches at his trial. Further definitions or interpretations had however been added, such as Cyril's *Twelve Anathemas* and the *Formula of Union*. Those who planned a new formula at Chalcedon recognized the problem, and, while giving absolute pre-eminence to Nicea, they proposed accepting other documents as authoritative applications of it to new questions. They discovered, presumably in the archives at Constantinople itself, a copy of the creed used by the Council of Constantinople of 381 (for text, see Nicea). This, they claimed, had been formulated to deal with the question of the deity of the Holy Spirit. Similarly, against Nestorius they received Cyril's letters to Nestorius and to "the Easterns," and against Eutyches the *Tome* of Leo. The documents intended were all related to the credal question: Cyril's *Second Letter to Nestorius* had expounded Cyril's interpretation of Nicea; his *Letter to John of Antioch* both quoted and accepted the *Formula of Union;* and Leo drew specific attention to the traditional creed in his argument. Thus a precedent was set, and the traditional creed was stated anew:

> The Synod resists those who try to split the mystery of the Dispensation [*oikonomia*] into a pair of sons; it ejects from the roll of priests those who presume to say that the godhead of the Only-begotten is subject to passion; it opposes those who think of mixture or confusion in connexion with the two natures of Christ; it repudiates those who discordantly claim that the form of a servant, taken from us by him, was of a heavenly or some other substance; and it condemns those who invent stories of two natures of the Lord before the union, while imagining one after the union.
>
> Following therefore the holy fathers, we confess one and the same Son, our Lord Jesus Christ, and unanimously we all teach, one and the same to be complete in godhead, the same complete in manhood, truly God and truly Man, the same composed of rational soul and body, *homoousios* [same-in-being] with the Father as regards godhead, and the same *homoousios* [same-in-being] with ourselves as regards manhood, in every thing like us except for sin; born as regards godhead from his Father before all ages, and as regards manhood, the same at the end of days for us and for our salvation from the Virgin Mary, the Godbearer; one and the same Christ, Son, Lord, Only-begotten, acknowledged with two natures unconfusedly, immutably, indivisibly, inseparably; the difference between the natures being in no way abolished by the union, but rather the character of each nature being preserved, and combining in one outward manifestation (*prosopon*) and one entity (*hupostasis*), not dividing or distinguishing into two outward manifestations, but one and the same Son and Only-begotten, God, Word, Lord, Jesus Christ.

This *Definition* rejects views attributed to Nestorius and especially Eutyches, and then affirms its faith: the one Lord Jesus Christ in his two natures (the characteristic approach of Antiochene Christology), which are complete in every particular, the one divine and eternal, the other human and mortal. The one Christ is twofold in nature, and neither nature is reduced. The godhead does not suffer or get diluted in a mixture, and the manhood is not infringed by divine powers. There was a particular debate over "acknowledged with two natures." The original draft had "of [*ek:* "out of" or "from"] two natures"; but that might allow "one out of two," the formula of Eutyches and Dioscuros. Leo's representatives insisted on *en*, "with" or "in" two natures, to make it clear that the manhood is entire and undiminished in the incarnate Lord.

This new creed was rejected by large parts of the Eastern Church. Those usually called Monophysites rejected the "two-headed idol of Chalcedon." They stood by Dioscorus at first, but developed important theological traditions of their own through brilliant writers such as Timothy Aeluros (d. 477), Philoxenus of Mabbug (c. 450–523), and Severus of Antioch (c. 456–538).

These repudiated the notion (of Eutyches) that Christ's humanity was heavenly and not like ours, and elaborated doctrines based on Cyril's principles of "One nature, that of the divine Word, enfleshed" and "hypostatic union" (i.e., that the humanity of Jesus is not a man, but belongs to the person of the divine Word). In Egypt most rejected the imperially imposed bishops, and the Coptic Orthodox Church is traditionally Monophysite. In the next century a new denomination opposed to Chalcedon was formed in Syria, chiefly through the work of Jacob Baradeus (c. 500–578), whence the nickname "Jacobites" for the correctly named "Syrian Orthodox Church"; it still subsists in the Middle East and India. The Armenians were not involved at Chalcedon and have never accepted the *Definition*. These churches survive the vicissitudes of history, which include various attempts to reform or detach them by Western churches both Catholic and Protestant. Efforts at reconciliation began in the ancient church, notably under the Emperor Justinian (r. 527–565). He favored giving a "Cyrilline" twist to Chalcedonian doctrine and condemning Antiochene Christology; he even tried the extreme doctrine called "Aphthartodocetism," which argued that Christ's flesh was always immune to corruption, a view that the Monophysite leaders themselves repudiated as Eutychian. Such efforts failed, because compromise in the East invariably upset relations with Rome, where the matter was regarded as settled when Chalcedon accepted the *Tome* of Leo. The same applied also to the attempts in the seventh century to appease the Monophysites by interpreting the Two Natures doctrine in terms of a single Activity ("Monenergism") or a single Will ("Monothelitism"). Although they rejected Chalcedon as a Nestorian division of Christ's person, Monophysites generally strove to make clear that his humanity is complete.

In modern times some doctrinal rapprochement between these Eastern dissenters and the mainstream Orthodox Churches has been possible. What they have in common, including centuries of living under the dominion of Islam as well as much liturgy and spirituality, makes it questionable whether division over "One Christ with two natures," or "One nature, of the divine Word, enfleshed," makes any sense.

Not only this unhappy history, but other factors have called into question the whole development of Christology in the early centuries. William Temple once wrote that the Chalcedonian *Definition* represented "the bankruptcy of Greek patristic theology." He later qualified this as meaning that the whole debate, which tries to define Christ in terms of substance, essence, nature, and the like, leads nowhere (Temple, 134). Some scholars think the process of defining, both at Chalcedon and in what followed, was disastrous to the spirit of Greek Christianity: "Jesus Christ disappears in the smokescreen of the two-nature philosophy. Formalism triumphs, and the living figure of the evangelical Redeemer is desiccated to a logical mummy" (Prestige, 147). "The Church of the East had been deprived of its faith. The *henosis physike*, the natural union, was not mentioned; no one could any longer teach that the God-Logos had taken up the human nature into the unity of his unique substance and made it the perfect organ of his deity" (Harnack IV, 222 [*Dogmengeschichte* II, 396]). It is certainly true that for most ancient

Christians the moral teachings of Jesus, and the practice of personal involvement with his life, death, and resurrection through the sacraments, meant far more than the technicalities of Christological definition. Modern Protestant theology has generally tried to base Christology more directly on the New Testament itself, bypassing the Fathers of the Church. That is not true for all, however: David Jenkins bases a radical apologetic for Christianity upon the discovery that Chalcedon represents: "a union has been achieved between that evolutionary product of cosmic dust which is a human being and that transcendent and wholly other purposeful personalness who is God. . . . In this there is discovered the personal fulfilment both of God and of man" (Jenkins, 55). Aloys Grillmeier repudiates Harnack, averring that the problem of expressing the unity of Christ who is fully God and Man was at Chalcedon resolved. Another leading Roman Catholic, Karl Rahner, goes further, finding in the repudiation of Eutyches by the council a key that opens the door to the modern investigation of the historical Jesus and the incorporation of that research into an intelligible modern Christology. Whatever the merits of these writers, one might regard the decisions of the ancient Councils, that Jesus Christ is fully God, that he is fully Man, and that these distinct natures are fully united in one Person, give guidelines for valid praying and preaching; the *Highway Code* is not the same as driving well, but the good driver will know it. Perhaps also some of the woodenness we sense in patristic debates about Jesus derives from their literalism in reading Scripture, and historical criticism gives us the opportunity and call to do better.

Stuart George Hall

See also: Alexandrian Theology; Antiochene Theology; Armenian Christianity; Coptic Christianity; Creeds; Harnack, Adolf von; Nestorianism; Nicea; Rahner, Karl; Son of God

References

Primary

Creeds, Councils and Controversies. 1989. Edited by James Stevenson, revised with additional documents by W. H. C. Frend. London: SPCK.

The Oecumenical Documents of the Faith. 1950. Edited by T. Herbert Bindley, revised by F. W. Green. London: Methuen.

Secondary

Frend, William H. C. 1984. *The Rise of Christianity*. London: Darton, Longman and Todd.

Grillmeier, Aloys. 1975. *Christ in Christian Tradition*. Vol. I: *From the Apostolic Age to Chalcedon (AD 451)*. London/Oxford: A. R. Mowbray.

Hall, Stuart George. 1991. *Doctrine and Practice in the Early Church*. London: SPCK.

Harnack, Adolph von. 1961 [1894–1899]. *History of Dogma*. New York: Dover.

Jenkins, David E. 1967. *The Glory of Man*. London: SCM.

Kelly, John N. D. 1960. *Early Christian Doctrines*. London: A. and C. Black.

Prestige, G. L. 1940. *Fathers and Heretics*. London: SPCK.

Rahner Reader. 1975. Edited by Gerald A. McCool. London: Darton, Longman and Todd.

Temple, William. 1924. *Christus Veritas*. London: Macmillan.

Children

The prominence of children in the Gospel accounts of Jesus' ministry indicates that Jesus gave a particular significance to children. Not only do the Gospels contain specific sayings and stories in which children are the focus of attention (see below), but they also include incidental references to the world of children (Matt. 11.16–19; Luke 11.7) and draw on imagery from the experience of children (Matt. 7. 9–11). Jesus' interest in children is unlikely merely to have been imagined by his first followers—early Christian writings show little concern with children and develop their ideas on childhood in ways distinct from the teaching in the Gospels. Nor can we account for this interest as simply part of Jesus' Jewish background—Jews certainly took a more benevolent view of children than most gentiles did, but Jesus' interest in children for their own sake (rather than for their potential) seems to set him apart from his contemporaries. In Jesus' proclamation of the kingdom of God there is a special significance accorded to children, as models for adults who wish to enter the kingdom of God and as objects of care identified with Jesus himself.

One of the most striking passages involving children is the story of people bringing children to Jesus (Matt. 19.13–15; Mark 10.13–16; Luke 18.15–17). In Mark and Luke the request made to Jesus is that he touch them, and in Matthew that he lay hands on them and pray for them. The disciples rebuke the people, but Jesus replies: "Let the little children come to me; do not stop them, for it is to such as these that the Kingdom of God belongs." Some interpreters understand Jesus' words here to be pointing to an inherent subjective quality in children, such as innocence or implicit faith, which means that the kingdom of God belongs to such as them. Most interpreters today favor the view that these words point to an objective status as the key feature: children exemplify the vulnerability and powerlessness of those to whom the kingdom belongs.

In Mark and Luke, Jesus then continues with teaching that relates children to adult disciples: "Truly I tell you, whoever does not receive the kingdom of God as a little child will never enter it." Matthew has a similar saying, placed in the context of the dispute about greatness in the kingdom of heaven (Matt. 18.3–4). This saying sets out one of the great reversals of life in the kingdom of God. Whereas in ordinary life, children learn from adults and have adulthood as a goal, in the kingdom of God children supply the model for adults. If the key characteristic of the child is his or her objective status, then "to receive the kingdom of God as a little child" (or "change and become like children": Matt.) may mean that the way into the kingdom of God is by accepting a childlike place of least consequence in the power structure of society.

The ancient world had no concept of a general responsibility to care for children other than one's own. In this respect, too, Jesus' teaching proposed a great reversal of values in the kingdom of God. At the end of the scene in Mark 10.13–16, Jesus did what was requested and not only "touched" the children but also "embraced" them (Mark 10.16; see also Mark 9.36). Jesus' embrace of the children symbolizes his identification with them, which he makes explicit in several sayings.

In response to the disciples' dispute about who was the greatest, Jesus takes a child and places him or her among them and says, "Whoever welcomes one such child [Luke: "this child"] in my name welcomes me, and whoever welcomes me welcomes not only me but the one who sent me" (Mark 9.33–37; parallels with differences: Matt. 18.1–5; Luke 9.46–48). "Welcoming" in this passage implies acting with the hospitable care of a host. In one sense this saying is enjoining on disciples the care that Jesus himself shows to children. But the saying goes further by portraying the child as Jesus' representative, and by identifying action toward the child as action toward himself. As the apostles are commissioned to be Jesus' representatives by what they do (Matt. 10.40–42), so children are described as Jesus' representatives by what is done to them (and see also Matt. 18.6–7, 10; Mark 9.42).

One of the problems in interpreting Gospel sayings about children is to know when "child" or "little one" is being used merely as a metaphor for adult disciples, and when such terms are to be taken literally, or whether such terms might have both a literal and a metaphorical reference. For instance, in Matt. 11.25 (parallel Luke 10.21), Jesus gives thanks to his Father "because you have hidden these things from the wise and intelligent and have revealed them to infants." It might seem mainly or exclusively a metaphorical reference to the unlearned disciples, but later in Matthew there is an instance of children showing insight into the identity of Jesus when the religious leaders show no such insight (Matt. 21.14–16). This example may suggest that references to children or "little ones" may have a literal reference, even if they also could be applied metaphorically to adults.

We should finally note what Jesus did not say about children. Unlike some contemporaries, he did not use the term "child" disparagingly. He did not address any teaching to them in particular. He did not call children to the changes demanded by discipleship, but affirmed them as children.

William Strange

See also: Family; Kingdom of God

References

Francis, James. 1996. "Children and Childhood in the New Testament." Pp. 65–85 in *The Family in Theological Perspective*. Edited by Stephen C. Barton. Edinburgh: T. and T. Clark.

Gundry-Volf, Judith M. 2001. "The Least and the Greatest: Children in the New Testament." Pp. 29–60 in *The Child in Christian Thought*. Edited by Marcia J. Bunge. Grand Rapids, MI/Cambridge: William B. Eerdmans.

Strange, William A. 1996. *Children in the Early Church*. Carlisle, Cumbria, UK: Paternoster.

Chinese Christianity

The long history of Chinese Christianity is not always appreciated by the outside world, and the Christian impact on China is more complex than its outward expressions seem to suggest.

Images of Jesus displayed in countless churches and in the homes of both Catholic and Protestant believers in China are startlingly reminiscent of Western religious art. It is easy to conclude with Chinese critics of Christianity down the centuries that it is a religion alien to Chinese culture and tradition, imported from the West. The occasional portrayals of Jesus in Chinese guise such as the illustrations in *The Life of Christ, by Chinese Artists*, published in the 1940s (London: Society for the Propagation of the Gospel, 1945) or the contemporary work of artists associated with the Christian Art Centre in Nanjing are noteworthy, but remain exceptional.

Trying to assess the significance of the person of Jesus for China is by no means easy, but there are certain themes that have persisted through the centuries and that can help in understanding the contemporary situation.

China's First Christians

It was a Persian bishop, Aloben, who first brought Christianity to China, arriving in the cosmopolitan capital of Tang China, Chang'an (modern Xi'an in Shaanxi Province). This "Nestorian" Christianity flourished for a while, dying out in the ninth century. It is significant because of its attempt to relate the person of Jesus to Chinese tradition. The famous stela in Xi'an, together with documents from Dunhuang on the Silk Road, use Chinese terminology to describe Jesus: he is the "Illustrious Honoured One who hid his true majesty and came into the world of men," the Sage who follows the "Way" (Chinese: *Dao*). Chinese Christians in future ages continued to relate Jesus to the Confucian ideal of the "wise man" living a life of moral rectitude, and this remains a powerful image for many even today. *Dao* is a term common to various Chinese philosophies, including Confucianism and, of course, Daoism, but its usage is varied and subtle. The Daoist classic the *Dao De Jing* begins with justly famous words: "The *Dao* that can be named is not the eternal *Dao*." Some Christians have suggested translating *dao* as "God," but that obscures the elusive nature of the text. On the other hand, the use of *dao* in the Chinese Union version of the Bible to translate the Greek *Logos* in the opening of John's Gospel is entirely appropriate.

Jesus the Sage, or the Lord of Heaven?

Christianity established a lasting presence in China with the arrival in 1583 of the Jesuits, led by Fr. Matteo Ricci. Their mission was aimed at the scholar-officials (literati) who constituted China's ruling elite, men deeply committed to the humanist principles of Confucius (551–479 B.C.), even if in their private lives they might also espouse Buddhist or Daoist beliefs. Confucius was mainly concerned with the proper ordering of society, showing little interest in the "gods." The values of filial devotion, loyalty, harmony, love, sexual propriety, and sobriety were central to Confucianism. Recognizing its importance, the Jesuits endeavored to portray Jesus as the sage whose teaching embraced and transcended that of Confucius.

The Jesuits' theology stressed the supernatural status of Jesus, and that was difficult to reconcile with a Confucian humanist interpretation of Jesus as a supremely wise man. From a Confucian perspective the assertion that the "Lord of Heaven" (Chinese: *Tianzhu*) took human form and died the death of a common criminal seemed incredible. Consequently, for apologetic purposes, the Jesuits in their initial teaching deliberately downplayed the Incarnation and Crucifixion. The attempt to portray Jesus as a Confucian sage was difficult to reconcile with Jesus, the Lord from Heaven, and that basic contradiction was never satisfactorily resolved.

The Jesuit mission reached its high point in 1692, when, in the early years of the Qing Dynasty (1644–1911), the Kangxi emperor issued an Edict of Toleration, elevating Christianity to the same status as Buddhism and Daoism. The emperor even wrote a poem in which he spoke of the crucified Jesus as

> Six-footer hanging at the same height as two thieves.
> It is suffering that moves the whole world and all ranks.

However, the controversy over Chinese ancestral rites, so fundamental to Chinese culture, led the Vatican to overrule the Jesuits' acceptance of the veneration of ancestors, with the result that Kangxi in 1721 issued an edict banning Christianity. The attempt to win the scholar-officials to the faith had failed.

The negative attitude of the elite was to harden in the period after 1721. The Catholic Church retreated into China's great rural hinterland, turning in on itself, surviving in secret in the villages. Personal piety expressed in a fervent devotion to Jesus and to the cult of Mary helped the Church to survive through to the time when foreign missionaries returned in the mid-nineteenth century. From the 1840s until the expulsion of missionaries in the early 1950s, China's Catholics continued to exist in comparative isolation from the rest of society, an isolation that only intensified under communism. Today it is proving difficult for such traditional communities to come to terms with the growing impact of economic modernization.

Changing Elite Responses to Jesus in the Twentieth Century

The anti-Christian attitudes of elite culture hardened in the early twentieth century as a potent blend of nationalism and Marxism rejected religion. The writer Lu Xun summed up in *Wild Grass* the intellectuals' view of Jesus, writing of the crucifixion: "God has forsaken him, and so he is the son of man after all." There remains here a hint of respect for Jesus as a wise man, although belief in God is rejected in the name of revolutionary struggle: "[A] rebellious fighter has arisen from mankind," but "[t]he creator, the weakling, hides himself in shame."

The communist victory in 1949 led many Christian intellectuals either to abandon their faith, accepting "Marxism, Leninism, Mao Zedong-Thought," or to seek to align their faith with communism. Ordinary believers, facing a series of fierce campaigns against religious belief, kept their counsel, sustained by a simple pietism that nurtured them through the terrible years. The Cultural Revolution of 1966–1976 seemed to sound the death knell for Chinese Christianity, but at that very time the seeds of revival were being sown—a revival that exploded into the "Jesus Fever" of recent years, when Christianity has flourished as never before.

After 1976, most of China's intellectuals abandoned Marxism. A search for new moral foundations has started, and the failure of indigenous traditions to prevent the disasters of the Maoist era has led to a new openness to foreign ideas. Many are finding in the figure of the New Testament Jesus an attractive moral exemplar. Some philosophers argue that it is the Christian respect for the individual person that lies at the heart of the Western respect for human and civil rights, leading to a reevaluation of Christianity. For most, however, Jesus is respected as a teacher and sage, not as God incarnate.

Popular Attitudes toward Jesus

The study of the thought of the literati omits a vital part of the story of the interaction between Jesus and Chinese culture. Some Buddhists argued that Jesus' appearance on earth could be understood as an *avatar*, an incarnation of divine consciousness on earth. In reality the Christian doctrine of the Incarnation is denied, for an *avatar* only has the appearance of being human. Nevertheless, it is probable that such ideas contributed to popular views of who Jesus was. Educated Buddhists dismissed the idea, arguing—like the influential sixteenth-century Buddhist monk, Ruchun—for the reality of the humanity of Jesus, suggesting that it points to the truth of the doctrine of the transmigration of souls: Jesus as a man remains caught up within the cycle of death and rebirth and remains inferior to the Buddhas who have moved beyond duality.

The Daoist religion offered its practitioners ways to attain a form of material immortality. It was believed that some of these semidivine figures continued to dwell on earth, living in forests and mountains. The veneration of recent historical figures led in some cases to their elevation to the status of local deities (such as the eight immortals of Daoism). From the Southern Song Dynasty (1127–1279) through to the Yuan (Mongol) period in the fourteenth century, various messianic cults emerged, drawing on a mixture of foreign and indigenous teachings. The Maitreya or the Buddha of all encompassing love was transformed into belief in a Future Buddha reigning in Heaven from whence he will descend to relieve the sufferings of mankind, bringing about a state of untroubled joy. Such, for example, were the teachings of the White Lotus movement, which combined the Pure Land School of Buddhism with Manichaean and other non-Buddhist beliefs. Its influence continued into the twentieth century and possibly persists in China today.

Popular culture was more open to aspects of Christian teaching about Jesus than elite culture. In the past two centuries Jesus has sometimes assumed the role traditionally taken by various Chinese deities. He becomes the source of healing and exorcism and of supernatural help, especially for the poor and for women with their lower social status. Belief in semidivine "saviors" who would prepare the way for the millenarian event became widespread. When the doctrinal and worship practices of Chinese sects are compared with those of Christianity there are surprising parallels: belief in a creator god; the alienation of humankind from the deity; the coming of a compassionate savior; rest for the saved in paradise; women afforded high status, even assuming leadership roles. Congregational in nature, they are led by a charismatic leader claiming miraculous powers, including healing and exorcism. In the nineteenth century Catholic and Protestant converts often came from a sectarian background. As one sinologist writes: "A large number of Chinese sectarians, including many from the White Lotus tradition became Christian converts." Shandong Province and the North China Plain in particular were "a hotbed of sectarian-Christian fusion" (Daniel Bays in Wilson Barnett and Fairbank, 123).

Recent interest in popular culture enables a more holistic understanding of the role of Jesus within Chinese culture. But the elite/nonelite dichotomy is itself too simplistic. There is always an intermediate group of educated figures who act as mediators between elite and popular culture. Such was Liang A Fa, one of the first converts to Protestant Christianity in the nineteenth century. He imbibed popular ideas expressed in morality books that combined Buddhist and Daoist ideas with the moral tenets of Confucianism and was dismayed by the decadence of late Qing China. Initially he sought salvation through Buddhism but was unhappy with the lax morality of many Buddhists. He found in Protestant Christianity both moral seriousness and a way to salvation.

Liang's book, *Good Words Exhorting Mankind,* directly influenced Hong Xiuquan, leader of the Taiping Heavenly Kingdom, which swept China into an appalling civil war between 1850 and 1864. He claimed to be the Heavenly King, younger brother of Jesus Christ. Such heterodox doctrines were rooted in the long history of Chinese sectarianism, and Hong's view of Jesus fits well into these traditions.

Jesus in Contemporary China

It is out of this general background of popular culture and its range of beliefs that belief in Jesus took on a particular Chinese expression. Circumstantial evidence from contemporary China suggests that similar ideas still appeal to significant groups of the poor. Millennial movements can attract large numbers of the poor. In the 1980s Hua Xuehe proclaimed himself as the Second Jesus, attracting support from at least ten provinces and founding the *Lingling Jiao* (the Religion of the Spirit). Wu Yangming claimed to be the Established King (*Beili Wang*), who had come to replace Jesus. In 2001, "Lightning from the East," a millenarian group, was flourishing.

An increasingly fragmented society needs sources of inspiration and hope for the future. Fervent devotion to Jesus as savior and a strong belief in the power of the Spirit to bring about inner and outer transformation is characteristic of Catholic and Protestant spirituality. Claims of a miraculous release from physical and mental illness in a society all too often unable to provide adequate health provision are widespread. In a society in which the disparities of wealth have grown more stark, strong millenarian beliefs are a source of hope and comfort to a world offering an uncertain future. Chinese indigenous groups like the Little Flock and the True Jesus Church as well as groups such as the Seventh-day Adventists and independent congregations like that run by Pastor Lin Xiangao in Guangzhou embrace millenarian beliefs.

The "religion of Jesus" (Chinese: *Jidu Jiao*)—Chinese Protestant Christianity—takes many forms in China today. Regardless of whether that religion is espoused by those who worship in state-registered buildings or in unregistered places of worship, the nature of belief is similar. Rooted in the moral outlook of traditional culture, in which Confucian ideas are deeply embedded, and emerging out of a context of diverse beliefs associated with Buddhist, Daoist, and sectarian ideas, Christianity is taking on its own particular Chinese forms. The "religion of the Lord of Heaven" (*Tianzhu Jiao*)—Chinese Catholicism—also offers hope within a rapidly changing society, but its slower rate of growth is most likely related to its problems in emerging from its self-contained communities to face a radically different social reality. One thing is certain: the influence of Jesus on Chinese history, culture, and thought has never been greater than it is today.

Bob Whyte

See also: Buddhism; Incarnation in Contemporary Analytic Philosophy; Manichaeism; Marxism; Nestorianism; Seventh-day Adventism

References

Bays, Daniel H., ed. 1999. *Christianity in China: From the Eighteenth Century to the Present*. Stanford: Stanford University Press.

Madsen, Richard. 1998. *China's Catholics: Tragedy and Hope in an Emerging Civil Society*. Berkeley: University of California Press.

Palmer, Martin. 2001. *The Jesus Sutras: Rediscovering the Lost Scrolls of Taoist Christianity*. London: Piatkus.

Standaert, Nicholas, ed. 2000. *Handbook of Christianity in China*. Vol. 1: *635–1800*. Leiden, Netherlands: Brill.

Uhalley, Stephen, Jr., and Xiaoxin Wu, eds. 2000. *China and Christianity: Burdened Past, Hopeful Future*. New York and London: M. E. Sharpe.

Whyte, Bob. 1988. *Unfinished Encounter: China and Christianity*. London: Collins Fount.

Wilson Barnett, Suzanne, and John King Fairbank, eds. 1985. *Christianity in China: Early Protestant Missionary Writings*. Cambridge: Harvard University Press.

Christology

See Adoptianism; Alexandrian Theology; Chalcedon; Christology, Modern; Hebrews; Incarnation in Contemporary Analytic Philosophy; John, Gospel of; Nicea; Paul

Christology, Modern

One of the most significant questions in the development of modern Christology and theology is that of the historical Jesus—that is, who Jesus is, and what his significance or meaning is as a historical individual. If "modernity" is often defined philosophically as a period beginning soon after the Enlightenment in the seventeenth century and ending with the onset of postmodernity in the final quarter of the twentieth century, however, the question of the historical Jesus demonstrates that modern Christology and theology begin earlier. In fact, the decisive shift in modern Christology and theology occurred in the sixteenth century, predating philosophical developments by up to one hundred years.

In the Wittenberg Sermons of 1522, Martin Luther (1483–1546) outlined the Reformation's underlying theology. Addressing his congregation's violent unrest, exacerbated by too hasty a rejection of the mediation of the Church, Luther teased out the primary role of Jesus Christ as the sole mediator between God and the world, the medium by which God and the world are joined. In so doing, Luther cast the Church's medieval heritage into sharp relief and brought center stage a new figure for theological reflection: Jesus of Nazareth. This was a new development and the true start of modern Christology and theology.

This statement is not meant to suggest that theology had never before thought about the status or meaning of Jesus, or that such a discipline as Christology was unknown in Christianity before the sixteenth century. What Luther did, however, was to argue that Christian belief centers on a range of questions that can only be answered by reference to Jesus of Nazareth, and that those questions, and those answers, are the proper subject matter of Christian reflection. Luther's successors—for example, John Calvin (1509–1564) and Huldrych Zwingli (1484–1531) in Switzerland and Thomas Cranmer (1489–1556) in England—adopted Luther's position with alacrity, thereby having a lasting influence upon the shape of modern Christology and theology.

Starting with such figures is important, because the temptation with any discussion of modernity is to think philosophically, to begin with René Descartes (1596–1650) and to move quickly to Immanuel Kant (1724–1804). Modern theology, however, begins when people like Luther start to think about the status of mediation between God and humanity in ways that are not limited or defined by the Church alone. What this means for theology is that modernity begins with thinking about how individuals know they are saved—by knowing Jesus in particular—and then moves on to thinking about what it is to know anything in general.

"Modernity," consequently, is best defined as that period in which human reflection has been concerned with the science of knowledge, and modern theology, in this sense, is the science of how we know God in relation to humanity. Modern Christology is how we know Jesus in the context of the knowledge of God, and against the background of how we know anything at all. Thus, in modernity Christology and theology are intelligible in terms of human self-understanding, but reflected back upon the question of the historical Jesus, a process Luther recognized in 1522, and that thereafter was central to Christian reflection.

Although the indicated general movement in thought is encountered in the work of Descartes, it is best exemplified by Kant's philosophy, which sought to understand the conditions that make it possible for humans to know the world they live in, and to make cognitive, moral, and aesthetic decisions about that world. Kant's emphasis upon the conditions of possibility of knowledge is important, because for Kant Jesus' abiding significance is in showing people how to behave ethically—that is, as a teacher of morals. The role of theology, therefore, is to elucidate this aspect of Jesus' ministry, which is something Kant establishes in texts like *Religion within the Limits of Reason Alone* (1793).

This Kantian shift is important because it gives methodological structure to the religious development that Luther introduced in 1522. Whereas Luther's position was based upon an explicit understanding of the meaning of the Bible, Kant's thought focuses upon how we understand the meaning of the Bible and make it effective in our lives. It is a subtle distinction, one that takes its place within a consistent scheme of modern Protestant thought. It is key to the development of modern Christology, however, because it shifts attention away from Jesus' role in relation to the Church, toward Jesus' role in relation to the human capacity to recognize his significance.

Writing in the final quarter of the eighteenth century, Kant was able to concentrate upon the logical or purely cognitive dimensions of theological epistemology's recognition of Jesus and its capacity to locate his significance in relation to human reason. That theme of recognition, however, also had other aspects in the eighteenth century, most notably the discovery of the strictly *historical* character of the raw materials from which we learned of Jesus. This discovery heralded the onset of what came to be known as the historical-critical movement, and its two most significant progenitors were Hermann Reimarus (1694–1768) and Gotthold Lessing (1729–1781).

As has been argued, if Luther saw Jesus as Messiah and Teacher, Kant reduced that understanding to Jesus' teaching of a specific set of moral precepts. Reimarus, writing in the period from 1744 to 1767, effectively asked the question "What do we know about Jesus, so that we might think we understand his meaning and message?" Reimarus's answer, mediated through the editing work and philosophical refraction of Lessing (the Wolfenbüttel Fragments of 1774–1778), was: "Very little, because Jesus belonged to a time and place very different from our own." Kant had intuitively recognized this issue, but had sought to overcome it by concentrating solely upon a philosophical appropriation of Jesus' message. Lessing argued, in effect, that such a move was impossible, or rather that such a move did violence to the historical circumstances relating to the origin of Jesus' message.

Although the apparent contradiction here is considerable, in fact Kant and Lessing are working toward two very different, though equally significant, goals. Stated bluntly, Lessing wants to know what really happened and argues that this is practically very difficult to know because of what he calls the "dirty great ditch" of history that separates Jesus' time from our own. Lessing's mediation of Reimarus's thought has signal repercussions throughout all subsequent Christology and theology, because it brings Christian doctrine into intimate contact with its historical and thereby contextual dimensions. It is impossible to think through the structure and development of modern Christology and theology without reference to the critical work of Reimarus and Lessing.

In contrast to Reimarus and Lessing, Kant originates the philosophical interpretation of the historical Jesus, because Kant is more interested in what Jesus means than what actually happened, and because he thinks that what Jesus means can best be answered with reference to moral philosophy. Kant, too, originated a very significant line of thinking, as is most clearly exemplified in the work of two of his near contemporaries, Friedrich Schleiermacher

(1768–1834) and Georg Hegel (1770–1831), figures who developed theological reflection on this question in relation to philosophical idealism. Schleiermacher argued that Jesus' significance could best be understood in terms of his supreme embodiment of what he called "absolute God consciousness." Hegel reasoned that Jesus' relevance to human understanding resided in his proclamation of a religion of revelation. Both, in their own ways, typified an intellectual response that sought to go beyond historical fact, toward theological and philosophical meaning.

The period between the 1830s and 1890s was dominated by this tension between two very different ways of understanding, and this period in European theology, particularly in German-speaking states, was dominated by countless attempts either to discover the true historic character of Jesus' mission and message, or its deepest theological and philosophical significance. Typical of those persuaded by the historical-critical method was David Friedrich Strauss (1808–1874), whose *Life of Jesus* in 1835 argued passionately that Jesus was an apocalyptic prophet whose claims on nineteenth-century Europe were minimal.

The major academic centers, by contrast, were dominated by a movement known as neo-Kantianism that, as its name suggests, took its lead from the work of Kant. The foremost figures here were Albrecht Ritschl (1822–1889), whose influence was at its peak in the period from 1870 to 1900, and later Adolf von Harnack (1851–1930). Both Ritschl and Harnack argued strongly that Jesus was the teacher of a superior ethical message—indeed, the greatest religious ethics that the world had ever known.

Some would argue that liberal Protestant attempts to arrive at the genuine philosophical or theological significance of Jesus continue today. By contrast, however, the historical-critical approach took a decisive turn in 1906 when Albert Schweitzer (1875–1965) published his epochal *Quest of the Historical Jesus*, which both demolished many of the more fanciful liberal images of Jesus and established once and for all the historical significance of biblical material for any understanding of Jesus' authentic gospel. Schweitzer's argument was a revisiting of Strauss's thesis of 1835, albeit with a far higher degree of critical scholarship and a more jaundiced (and extensive) attack upon the perceived "inventions" of liberal Protestant life-of-Jesus theologies.

Although Schweitzer's attack on these theological images was effective, far more significant was his work on eschatology, an emphasis that had been prefigured in the thought of such figures as William Wrede (1859–1906) and Franz Overbeck (1837–1905). Understood from this perspective, Schweitzer regarded Jesus as an apocalyptic prophet, a figure who proclaimed the kingdom of God as the judgment and end of this world, and the imminent arrival of God's rule from beyond space and time. This other-worldly emphasis had a profound influence upon all subsequent Christology and theology, because it argued that Jesus was no longer to be viewed as a synthesizing element, but rather as a divisive *Krisis* in the relationship between God and the world, a *Krisis* of judgment and decision.

If Schweitzer's work had its initial effects in the world of biblical scholarship, those were soon felt throughout theology. The quandary facing theology was, however, significant and long lasting. Effectively, nineteenth-century theologies had decided between the historical-critical method and the liberal images of Jesus schools—either the one or the other, but not both. Now, at the beginning of the twentieth century, theology was faced by the realization that its Christology was inherently paradoxical, and that Jesus was simultaneously an eschatological prophet from a very different historical time and place *and* the Redeemer whom the Church had to proclaim as the Savior of the world.

The task facing modern Christology and theology, therefore, was not to elide this tension, but rather to understand what it really means. Central to such efforts was Martin Kähler's (1835–1912) important study, *The So-called Historical Jesus and the Historic, Biblical Christ* (1892/96), in which he argued that these two qualities—history and theology—came together in the one eschatological mission and message of Jesus. Henceforth, the challenge facing modern Christology and theology was not to choose between these two, but rather to understand eschatology itself as the bridge between God and the world.

It would be wrong to suggest, however, that this turn changed everything at the end of the nineteenth century. On the contrary, liberal Protestantism continued to be the dominant force in Europe until the end of World War I, when Karl Barth's (1886–1968) *Commentary on Romans* (1919/22), supported by the work of such figures as Rudolf Bultmann (1884–1976) and Emil Brunner (1889–1966), established dialectical theology and thereby effected a lasting shift in the way in which people understood the place of Jesus in modern Christology. In many respects this was not due to the absolute novelty of Barth's position, which was heavily influenced by the work of Schweitzer and Overbeck as well as Kähler. There was, however, a change of emphasis in Barth's work, one that addressed the eschatological role of Jesus Christ as Mediator between God and the world, and which in turn diminished liberal Protestantism's emphasis upon regaining the "real," historical Jesus. Indeed, Bultmann went as far as to reject any attempt to discover the historical Jesus, though Brunner never fully agreed with Barth and Bultmann, and the latter two softened their position in later years.

If Barth and Bultmann had any lasting influence upon the understanding of Jesus' place in modern Christology and theology, it was in terms of the primacy of eschatology over history, a way of understanding the problem that predominated in Europe until the 1950s. Then a return to the question of the historical Jesus, led in New Testament studies by Ernst Käsemann and in systematics by Wolfhart Pannenberg (1928–), redressed the balance very positively, arguing that in order to understand the Christ of faith properly, one also had to understand the historical Jesus as well as possible. In short, figures like Käsemann and Pannenberg argued for a renewed attempt to appreciate the significance of the concept of history itself, something that echoed the concerns of Barth and Bultmann, but came to very different conclusions. The lasting significance of Pannenberg's work in particular was to demonstrate the complexity of the concept of history, and history's role in theological and philosophical reflection, something that had not been achieved in the same way since Hegel's work in the 1830s.

The turn toward a more complex understanding of history paved the way for another significant development in the 1960s, when theologians began to reflect seriously upon its diverse character in terms of social, political, and economic considerations. In part this was encouraged by the Second Vatican Council (1962–1965), which recognized such changes in society in the 1960s, and in part by the explosion of a wide range of political movements that were relevant to theologians keen to explore the perceived character and significance of Jesus' proclamation of the kingdom of God. Obvious examples of this development include feminist, environmental, political, and liberation theologies.

Judged with hindsight, it is easy to conclude somewhat pejoratively that such theologies had forgotten Bultmann's and Schweitzer's strictures against creating images of Jesus in one's own likeness, and Barth's warning against underestimating the sheer Otherness of Christ, God's Word. The real emphasis in 1960s Christology and theology, however, was upon what could be achieved by claiming Jesus for one's own time and place, a process of hermeneutic retrieval that was motivated primarily by profoundly therapeutic ambitions, as perhaps most clearly recognized in the writings of Jürgen Moltmann (1926–), but also exemplified in the work of a wide range of contemporary theologians.

What emerged in the 1960s as a concerted attempt to think through the social and historical character of Christology and theology became, in the 1970s and 1980s, a commitment to the genuine diversity of Christian witness and reflection. This recognition in turn led in the 1990s to a profound commitment to theological pluralism, a commitment that, notwithstanding certain reactions against it from more conservative quarters, is now widely accepted. The lasting significance of diversity and pluralism lies not only in the recognition of contextual and ecclesial distinction but also in the now intellectual willingness to appreciate the legitimacy of approaching, and describing, Jesus in ways that are attractive and intelligible to one's audience. Thus Jesus the liberator, the black Jesus, and the woman Jesus (to name just a few) have all become designations with legitimacy at the beginning of the twentieth century. These developments are a very long way from the homogeneity of Barth's Christology, Kant's philosophically neutral take on Jesus and morals, and even the overly sentimental images of liberal Protestantism.

One can recognize, therefore, that certain trends in modern Christology and theology are cyclical, with distinct tendencies recurring, albeit in ways that are subtly transformed by wider social and historical considerations. It would be wrong, consequently, to attempt to identify any general theory of progression in these disciplines, even if, rightly, one can argue that the intellectual situation now is far more sophisticated than it was, say, in the early eighteenth or early nineteenth century. If such a development has occurred as a reflection of greater Christian responsibility, albeit against the background of philosophical developments that now embrace postmodernity and its clear challenges to critical reflection, then it can only enhance the credibility of Christian reflection upon the question of its historical origins in the mission and message of Jesus of Nazareth.

At the same time, however, Christology must protect itself against an endless diversity that tends toward a simply fragmented understanding of Jesus and his eternal significance. Christianity faces diverse contemporary challenges, ones that confront its ability to think and act therapeutically for the sake of the Gospel and the mission of the Church. Properly understood, it is such concerns that ought to predominate in Christology and theology, rather than the conceptual acrobatics of solely intellectual endeavor. In this respect, while one might acknowledge the partiality of certain contemporary images of Jesus, it is that very partiality that makes them effective and legitimate contributions.

In conclusion, one should reason that the most significant developments in modern Christology and theology have been methodological rather than particularly substantive—that it is more a question of learning how to understand and thereby appropriate Jesus, rather than discovering certain incontrovertible "facts" about the man or his historical setting. Modernity has brought responsibility and insight to Christology and theology, and a realization that Jesus' role—to be savior—is greater than any constraint upon the theories that allow one to prefer one image over another.

It is this very practical and liberative character that makes an understanding of the place of Jesus in modern Christology and theology so important. Reading through the significant developments since Luther's sermons in Wittenberg, one recognizes that the really important question centers on what efforts one can make to facilitate the work of the Risen Lord. Without that realization, modern Christology and theology can be seen to be simply a long series of responses to developments in philosophy and social thought, rather than the decisive contribution in the modern effort to relate God's Word to the world.

Gareth Jones

See also: Barth, Karl; Bultmann, Rudolf; Calvin, John; Enlightenment; Harnack, Adolf von; Jesus as a Historical Figure; Kingdom of God; Liberation Theology; Luther, Martin; Pannenberg, Wolfhart; Reimarus, Hermann Samuel; Schleiermacher, F. D. E.; Schweitzer, Albert; Strauss, D. F.

References

Hick, John. 1993. *The Metaphor of God Incarnate: Christology in a Pluralistic Age*. London: SCM.

Jones, Gareth. 1995. *Critical Theology: Questions of Truth and Method*. Cambridge: Polity.

Jungel, Eberhard. 1983. *God as the Mystery of the World: On the Foundation of the Theology of the Crucified One in the Dispute between Theism and Atheism*. Edinburgh: T. and T. Clark.

Kasper, Walter. 1976. *Jesus the Christ*. London: Sheed and Ward.

Keuss, Jeffrey. 2002. *A Poetics of Jesus: The Search for Christ through Writing in the Nineteenth Century*. Cambridge: Ashgate.

Macquarrie, John. 1998. *Christology Revisited*. London: SCM.

McGrath, Alister. 1986. *The Making of Modern German Christology*. Oxford: Blackwell.
McIntyre, John. 1998. *The Shape of Christology: Studies in the Doctrine of the Person of Christ*. Edinburgh: T. and T. Clark.
Marshall, Bruce. 1987. *Christology in Conflict*. Oxford: Blackwell.
O'Collins, Gerald. 1995. *Christology: A Biblical, Historical, and Systematic Study of Jesus Christ*. Oxford: Oxford University Press.
Ogden, Schubert. 1992. *The Point of Christology*. Dallas: Southern Methodist University Press.
Schillebeeckx, Edward. 1981. *Jesus: An Experiment in Christology*. London: Collins.
Webster, John. 2002. *Word and Church*. Edinburgh: T. and T. Clark.

Church

This article is not concerned with the ways Jesus has been perceived in the Church down the years nor the ways Christian communities have seen themselves as relating to him: many other articles in this volume bear on those matters in a variety of ways. The purpose here is narrower but fundamental. It relates to the roots of those many later developments—whose links to origins are infinitely complex and sometimes strange, though usually with claims that the later ideas and practice have New Testament validation. We shall survey the main New Testament writings, seeking to identify the various ways they see the place of Jesus in relation to the diverse communities that owed their existence to him in the early years of the Christian movement.

1. Paul, whose life was over before any of the Gospels were written (though not of course before many of the traditions they contain were in circulation), devotes much attention in his letters to the counseling of the small urban, mainly gentile Christian communities to whom he writes. In the course of his writing, he reveals, implicitly or explicitly, how he perceived their character and role. Paul and his colleagues had established most of the groups he writes to, and Paul himself was the main visible sign of their common allegiance. He deals, often in a very practical way, with problems that have their analogies in any similar group (e.g., arguments over admired leaders: 1 Cor. 1.11–12; precedence: 1 Cor. 12). Yet nearly always there is a special feature: they must stop bickering because of their unity "in Christ" (ibid., 1.13); they must not devalue the less exciting members of the group because all of them are vital "limbs and organs" of Christ's "body" (ibid., 12.1–30).

In other words, these communities, for all their variety, are essentially a single entity, both in their local manifestations (the focus in ch. 12) and more widely (the focus in ch. 1). Their oneness goes deeper than their having certain ideas or aims in common (for in some important ways they were, in Paul's own experience, deeply divided; cf. Gal., Phil., 2 Cor.). It is, we might say, existential. Christ is not simply the originator of a school of thought to which they subscribe (like, for example, Plato for Platonists), nor the dead founder of their movement. He is the sole principle and animator of their life; so that the image of body and limbs (applied commonly to political units like cities) is natural to express Paul's sense of their true position. It can be put even more boldly: they live "in Christ" and (less commonly, Col. 1.27) he "in them." They have no "meaning" without him.

Paul sees himself less as "a servant of the Church" (though he would by no means deny it) or a Christian leader, but, most typically, as the "agent (apostle) of Jesus Christ" (e.g., 1 Cor. 1.1; 2 Cor. 1.1). It is, as it were, his proud badge of office or authentication. In a sense therefore he stands at a remove from the communities themselves, the visible human factor binding the scattered groups together. Just as Jesus had been a mediator, a middle man, so, in his different way, was the apostle.

The term "church" (Greek: *ekklesia)* is the word for a civic or other community, especially as assembled for its common purposes. In Paul's undoubted letters, it applies mostly to a particular congregation, or groups of them (1 Cor. 1.2; Gal. 1.22). But in Ephesians and Colossians, perhaps written by a follower of Paul, there is a development that has only a few anticipations, in terms of word-usage, in the genuine letters (1 Cor. 12.28?). Here, the Church is seen as a quasi-mystical and universal entity, one with Christ and his expression of salvation's present fruit, with a universal and heavenly destiny ahead of it (Eph. 1–2). It is these writings that sow the seeds of later "high" doctrines of the Church's role and destiny, in a variety of empirical manifestations but most obviously and powerfully in the Catholic Church as centered in the long flow of history, on the Christian community in Rome, and its leader.

Yet also, for Paul at least, though centered on Christ, the new community is still the old people of God (Israel), renewed and on the way to its age-old destiny, so often disturbed and disrupted. In tension (and perhaps inconsistency) with his "in Christ" teaching and emphasis, Paul, the Jew, does not abandon his more visceral "Israel" perspective and seeks to give it formal expression. In Rom. 9–11, in an elaborate and tortuous (and historically implausible?) argument that treats "Jews" and "gentiles" as solid masses who somehow move as totalities, he tries to show how, ultimately, and as a fruit of his own mission to gentiles, the Jews, provoked to jealousy of gentile entry into God's people, will enjoy the new universal fulfillment of God's design for all humanity. Inevitably, this sense of the Church receded, more in practice than in theology, as time passed; and often less positive (to say the least) attitudes toward the Jews (the "old Israel") took over as the Church became both more dominant and more widespread.

2. Mark is the most problematic of the early Christian writers in relation to our subject. There is no doubt that, like the other early writings, this work comes out of a Christian community, such as we see depicted, often vividly, in Paul's letters. The Gospel will have been written for recitation to such a church at its meetings. Our instinct is to look to his portrayal of Jesus' first followers ("the disciples," chiefly the Twelve) as showing us "the Church." Yet it works here only with great difficulty. The picture of people who are called and indeed "follow" Jesus (1.16–20; 3.14) and receive "the secret of the kingdom of God" (4.11–12) is otherwise so unedifying as to make them a deterrent, or at the least a warning, to all others who share the allegiance to which they were called. If "follow" is the crucial Marcan word for adherence to Jesus, then the "purer," more edifying examples here are those of Levi (2.13–14) and Bartimaeus (10.52), both self-contained episodes, surely

vignettes of what it should be to live within this community attached to Jesus and living in his light.

In the plot of the Gospel, the Twelve and their leaders, like Peter, appear more and more as blunderers, failures, and traitors, hopeless as "followers" and as models for the Church (6.52; 8.14–21, 27–33; 14.10–11, 50, 66–72). There has been endless discussion about how to take, in any plausible historical context, this intensely negative picture of men who would soon arrive as, practically if not officially, the foundation saints of the Church, figures for imitation and veneration. That process would begin with Mark's immediate successors, Matthew and Luke. It may be that we are simply to see Mark as giving expression to antipathy to the Jerusalem church, led by members of the Twelve, in Mark's more gentile-Christian circle. Or else he was teaching a profound spiritual lesson: to be a Christian "leader" is always perilous, and Jesus is the true model (10.35–45). Or the disciples are not meant in their real selves at all, but as warning figures of the spiritual dangers of following Jesus, while other characters in the Gospel (like Bartimaeus, 10.52, the woman who anoints Jesus, 14.3–9, and Simon who carries his cross, 15.41) are models and examples to Christian readers—though such a reading, however edifying, may seem oversophisticated to be present in Mark's intention.

The most obvious "meaning" of the Twelve continues to be some kind of reference to Jesus as renewer of Israel, with his followers representing the twelve tribes; and their problematic character is not dissimilar to that of Israel in the wilderness under Moses whom Jesus supersedes (9.2–9). Other "twelves" in Mark, if less explicit, fortify the thought: 5.25, 42: Jesus cures a debilitated Israel and brings new life; 6.43: Jesus' provision for Israel is inexhaustible. The more one follows this line of thought, the more it seems that, for Mark (and probably in historical reality), Jesus was little concerned to do anything that one could call "founding the Church": rather, he was leading a renewal movement in Israel, in a rural Galilean context (like others before and after him), with the renewal of God's covenant with his people as his central aim (cf. 14.22–25) and the kingdom of God his central proclamation. Even a passage often quoted as conveying a sense of a new people of God, 10.28–31, where one's old community (whether Judaism or some gentile allegiance) is replaced by the new community centered on Jesus (cf. Paul's "body of Christ"), may better be read in the light of covenant-renewal.

3. Matthew is, fortunately, less problematic in this regard. Giving us a kind of life-line, he actually uses the word *ekklesia,* and it is plain that the character and conduct of the Christian community is of central concern to him. He is aware of "church" both in a universal sense (though we may reasonably doubt how informed or how wide his knowledge was), as in 16.18, and in a local sense, as in 18.17. In the former passage, he sees the people of Jesus ("my Church") as engaged in a war against the powers of evil, as Jesus was in his ministry—and victory is assured. In the latter, we see Matthew the practical churchman, providing for the community's role in the guidance and discipline of its members. As we should expect, there is good reason to believe that he sees the Christian communities or congregations in counterpoint with their Jewish counterparts, which are regularly referred to as "their

synagogues" (e.g., 4.23; 13.54—five times in all, two of them from Mark). It is often said that we should imagine Matthew's congregation as engaged in lively and surely hostile controversy with "non-Jesus" Jewish congregations nearby. It may also be that the use of *ekklesia* (here and perhaps already in Paul) was deliberate, to differentiate from the preferred Jewish term for religious (and other) gatherings, *sunagoge* ("synagogue"). And we must recognize that Matthew's strongly Jewish-Christian community had in many respects (e.g., observance of the Law, 5.17–19) more in common with the synagogue than with some other manifestations of the Jesus movement (such as the gentile congregations stemming from Paul's mission). Finally, Matthew's view of Christian life was, we should recognize, firmly institutional, and his Jesus is a provider of structure for his followers, for teaching, and ultimately for judgment, even to the very end of the age (19.28; 28.20).

4. Luke-Acts shows us a writer who, as we should expect, given his practical historical perspective, is more conscious than any other in the New Testament of Christianity as a movement that expresses itself in local communities or congregations: the word *ekklesia* appears twenty-three times in Acts (once for the old Israel, 7.38)—never in the Gospel: for Luke, it belongs to the post-Jesus mission; and in this separation, Luke is surely correct. What is chiefly interesting is the question of his own concerns in this matter. We may conjecture (though not idly) that in his own day, Luke looked back on "the story so far" with a mixture of gratitude and wonder at the extraordinary spread of the Gospel stemming from Jesus and centering on him, and of anxiety that it was in danger of falling apart in disagreements over true teaching (a fear voiced by Paul, Acts 20.28–30). In his telling of the tale, Luke did his best to heal the major rift in early Christianity, that between the Pauline mission ("liberal" in its terms of admission of gentiles) and the less indulgent (and less imaginative?) Jewish-Christians centered (until A.D. 70) on the Jerusalem church. From the start of his story of Jesus, he had held to a mediating position: Jesus' role was for both the renewal of Israel and the salvation of the gentile world (see notably Luke 2.29–32; 3.4–6). In that sense, the Church was a renewed Israel. Luke's strategy reaches its climax in Acts 15, where he gives his view of what he thought, or wished, had been the attempted basis for unity between the two versions of Christian mission: a reasoned and scripturally rooted compromise on Law-observance. It is likely that there was in this account a measure of hoping against hope, and it is not really borne out by Paul's letters, closer to the events. In historical reality, the swift decline of Jewish Christianity after A.D. 70 changed the shape of the problem, and it fell to Luke's successors to hold on to a "Jewish contribution" to the Church's heritage, notably in the old Scriptures, as vital to its true validity.

5. John is sometimes held to have no "doctrine of the Church," and in some formal terms this may be so; but from a deeper point of view, he is wholly convinced of the essentially and intensely corporate character of the mission of Jesus. Above all in the supper discourses (chs. 13–17) and, most memorably, in the two images of flock and vine (chs. 10 and 15), Jesus forms "his own" as one with himself and as perpetuating his own work and identity.

Jesus' "own" have no significance apart from him, and he is their principle of life; as complement, the continuing of Jesus' "life" is in them, indwelt by the Spirit. Certainly, the Johannine movement expressed itself in congregational terms, as the three epistles make plain. Johannine Christianity was no mere philosophical school, for all the sophistication and depth of its thinking. It was indeed exposed to some of the meaner aspects of church life: power struggles and squabbles-to-the-death about the formulation of belief.

6. The Revelation of John accentuates an aspect of understanding of the Christian community present, no doubt, in the other writers we have considered, sometimes explicitly—for example, Matt. 19.28: its ultimate life when God fulfills his purposes at "the End." Rev. 21–22 shows us the Church as the center of the goal of world history, yet still "Israel-like" and indeed "Eden-like" in its forms and in the imagery that describes it: so the ideas of the beginnings (in Genesis) are fulfilled in the ending. At the same time, this book's uses of the word "church" relate to the congregations (in Asia Minor) known to the seer-author himself (chs. 1–3; 22.16).

The likelihood may be (as suggested above in relation to Mark) that Jesus himself was less concerned with establishing a structured movement (e.g., with a central headquarters and local branches, complete with authorized officers) than with preaching the rule of God amid the villagers of Galilee. This does not invalidate in the least the adaptation of his message to different circumstances and settings, or its being couched in quite different verbal and organizational forms. Nor does it render improper the ways in which, from Paul onward, Christians have expressed, sometimes admittedly in extravagant terms, their sense of corporate existence and dependence on him who is their sole ultimate basis for existing. Such "thinking out" of who and what they are and signify in the world has been essential, and it was under way virtually from the start. Adaptation is, here as so often, the condition of survival. But the sober realities of Jesus' mission are a standing warning against the risk of travesty when his name is claimed.

Leslie Houlden

See also: John, Gospel of; John, Revelation of; Kingdom of God; Luke, Gospel of, and Acts of the Apostles; Paul

References

Banks, Robert. 1980. *Paul's Idea of Community*. Exeter: Paternoster.
Brown, R. E. 1979. *The Community of the Beloved Disciple*. Dublin: Geoffrey Chapman.
Houlden, J. L. 1997. *The Public Face of the Gospel*. London: SCM.
Kee, Howard C. 1977. *Community of the New Age*. London: SCM.
Meeks, W. A. 1983. *The First Urban Christians*. New Haven: Yale University Press.

Coptic Christianity

The Coptic Orthodox Church, centered in Egypt, where it is the dominant Christian body, is a conservative community. For at least fifteen centuries, in the long period before the dissemination of the Scriptures in the vernacular, Alexandrian Christology and a tenacious eucharistic devotion formed the image of Jesus in the Egyptian Church. These enduring traditions are vital for the contemporary church.

Two Copts determined the lasting indigenous conception of Jesus Christ. St. Athanasius the Apostolic (c. 296–373) defended Orthodoxy against Arianism and is identified with the affirmations of the Creed of Nicea. St. Cyril (d. 444) emphasized the primary Coptic Christological formula: *mia phusis tou theou Logou sersarkomene* (or, interchangeably, *sersarkomenou*): "the one nature of God the Word incarnate." Rejecting the Chalcedonian definition of "one person in two natures" (451), the Copts and other Oriental Orthodox (Ethiopian, Armenian, Syrian, and Indians) have been described as Monophysites and identified with the heresiarch Eutyches (c. 378–454) and sometimes with the Docetists, denying the reality of the human nature of Jesus and of his sufferings. For the Copts, talk of two natures implies duality, and their position should be defined by the term Miaphysite rather than Monophysite. *Mia* means one as a unity, one out of two natures, while *mono* implies one only, simply one, a single one. The Copts do not want to say that Christ is God and Man joined together, for that implies separation. He is rather God Incarnate: Godhead and Manhood are united in a perfect union, in being and in nature. There is neither separation nor division in Christ. In his devotions, the Copt most often prays in union with God Incarnate: One being, One nature, and One person. Egyptian theologians may affirm that Christ is One nature out of two natures. They may speak of two natures before the union took place. But after the union there is but One nature: One nature having the properties of the two natures. Nothing less than Coptic self-identity is involved in this Christological declaration.

Declaration of faith and of devotion are inseparable. A defining moment is in the Liturgy of St. Basil when the celebrant elevates the paten and exclaims:

> Amen. Amen. Amen. I believe. I believe. I believe, and confess to my last breath, that this is the life-giving Body which your Only-begotten Son, our Lord, God and Saviour Jesus Christ took from our Lady and Queen of us all, the *Theotokos*, the pure Saint Mary. He made it one with His divinity, without mingling, nor confusion nor alteration. . . . Truly, I believe that His divinity never parted from His humanity not even for a single moment nor the twinkling of an eye. He gave Himself for us . . . in the expectation of eternal life for all those who participate in Him. . . . Truly, I believe that this is so. Amen.

There is a powerful sense of community and loving care in the celebration of the liturgy, with added significance in a country where Christians have been a minority for over a millennium, but Holy Communion is the supreme expression of individual, intimate communion with Jesus Christ. The Holy Gifts are spooned into the mouth of the faithful, and the communicant protectively covers the mouth with a cotton napkin. Bread and wine have become the pure Body and precious Blood of Christ. The Copts are fearful of using philosophical terms concerning the real presence of Christ in the Eucharist, preferring uncritical appeals to biblical passages like 1 Cor. 10.16; 11.23–29 or the discourse in John 6.26–58.

The most influential Christian text in the Middle East is the Arabic Bible, the work of the American Arabists Eli Smith (1801–1857) and Cornelius Van Dyck (1818–1895) with their Syrian colleagues Butrus al-Bustani (1819–1893) and Nasif al-Yaziji (1800–1871). The accessibility and ubiquity of this text has produced a defensive biblical literalism. Islam is the context. The final recension of the Qur'an dates from the seventh century. If Islam has an infallible, unchangeable *Um al-Kitab*, the Mother of the Book, at *Allah's* side, then the Bible must be equally inerrant. The Bible is a library and does not easily compare with the chapters (*surahs*) of the Qur'an, but since infallibility is claimed for the Islamic text, the Copts must "*quranize*" the Bible. The distinction between the Jesus of the New Testament and the equivalent *Isa* of the Qur'an is expressed in Egypt as the deepest divergence between a prophet in Islam and the Divine Word (*Logos*) of the Christians. Most Middle Eastern Christians are equally uncomfortable with considerations of "Jesus the Jew." In 1965, when the Second Vatican Council promulgated the declaration *Nostra Aetate* absolving the Jewish people of deicide and condemning anti-Semitism, the reigning Coptic patriarch (Kyrillos the Sixth, r. 1959–1971) condemned the declaration as an imperialist-Zionist plot against the Arab nations and their churches. The Arabic word *Isra'iliyun* refers not only to the Old Testament Jews but also to the people of the modern State of Israel. Recent attempts to expunge the word from liturgical texts are highly problematic, considering the Jewish provenance of the Gospel. Jesus as an authoritative preacher is, after all, not unlike a prophet in Islamic tradition, and Jesus is not wholly unlike a rabbinical teacher of Judaism. But for the Coptic exegete the *Logos* of the Fourth Gospel, which is regarded as a historical narrative and authoritative, even marginalizes Jesus as miracle-worker, healer, and exorcist. The Bible is read as confirming the insights of Alexandrian Christology.

The Egyptian national renaissance led to the Republican Revolution of 1952, which encouraged the exploration of ancient civilization and the historical process. Confronted with the archaeological rediscovery of pharaonic imagery in the nineteenth and twentieth centuries, Egypt's Christian minority recovered an interest in their past. It was proposed that if Egyptians had a pharaonic lineage then they also had a Christian ancestry, and the Copts became enthusiastic about applying the sobriquet "the sons of the Pharaohs" to their community. Parallels between pharaonic religion and Christian faith are widely studied, and an outline is suggestive. Akhenaten (1383–1365 B.C.) in the eighteenth dynasty was an acknowledged heretic because of his monotheistic beliefs. He could be seen as pointing long ago to Coptic Egypt. Jesus is paralleled with Osiris, who was both god and man, whose resurrection narrative is comparable with Christian thought, and whose wife, Isis, suckling her son Horus, provided the pattern for the icon of the Mother and Child in Coptic iconography. Apis and Horemheb, god and pharaoh, are both described as the subjects of virgin birth through the intervention of Ptah and Amon. The extreme anthropomorphism in pharaonic tradition is perceived as a preparation for the Gospel. Although the Cross is believed to have become the principal symbol of the Christian religion after the events

Christ and the Abbot Ména. Seventh century. Louvre. (Réunion des Musées Nationaux/Art Resource, New York)

at the Milvian Bridge (312) and the accession of Constantine the Great (d. 337), the Copts claim that the early Church of Alexandria had long used the ancient *Ankh* symbol as Egypt's cross. The *Ankh* is a cross with a hollow oval head and symbolizes the key to paradise and pharaonic sign of eternal life. The Copts also attribute special meaning to the flight of the Holy Family from its persecutors in Palestine to safety in Egypt (Matt. 2.15; Hos. 11.1; Exod. 4.22). According to Coptic tradition, Joseph, Mary, and Jesus traveled from Sinai in the East to the Wadi Natroun in the West and southward to Old Cairo and eventually to Assyut in the heart of Upper Egypt. Coptic susceptibility has survived to the extent that the Holy Family has been perceived as virtually naturalized Egyptians, an identity of real consequence in Nasserite Egypt and especially at the turn of the millennium.

The Coptic icon of *Christ Protecting Abba Mina*, from the sixth-century

Coptic Qursi (literally "throne"), which houses the Communion vessels on the altar. It has icons on all sides; shown here are St. Michael and St. Mark. (Photograph courtesy John Watson)

Bawit and now in the Louvre, is one of the most famous images in Christian art. Important icons survive from all epochs of Egyptian history, but they are not as significant in Coptic devotion as they are among other Orthodox. Islam has naturally had an impact on Coptic Art. Islam is aniconic and sometimes iconoclastic, but the worst acts of Coptic iconoclasm were implemented in the nineteenth century when the reforming patriarch Kyrillos the Fourth, who had been educated by the English Church Missionary Society, burned icons outside his cathedral in 1854. A century later Kyrillos the Sixth reversed the iconoclastic development and appointed Isaac Fanous to lead a renaissance in Coptic iconography. Kyrillos was acting upon his instinct that iconography is a badge of Orthodoxy, which had been often neglected by the Copts. Isaac Fanous successfully reinstated ancient techniques and historical symbolism. He applied elements of pharaonic tradition and occasionally referred to the Fayoum portraits of the Greco-Roman period. He has painted the life of Christ in hundreds of icons throughout Egypt and the Coptic Diaspora. The Neo-Coptic School of Isaac Fanous has dominated Coptic visual arts in the second half of the twentieth century, creating images that affirm the spiritual, ascetic, and social traditions of the Copts. A parallel development was witnessed in the long life of the Coptic musicologist Ragheb Moftah (1898–2001), who transposed Coptic music into Western notation and recovered Coptic hymnody, including numerous collections concentrated upon the Liturgy of St. Basil the Great, the Incarnation, and the *Theotokos*.

The Coptic calendar begins on 11 September and is calculated from the accession of the Roman Emperor Diocletian (284) as marking the beginning of the Era of the Martyrs. The Coptic Church has often described itself as a church under the Cross. Centuries of fierce persecution or persistent discrimination against the Copts has occasionally resulted in a doctrine of salvation tested at a historical, communal, and individual level. An outstanding modern example is found in the writings of the Alexandrian theologian Bishoi Kamel Isaac (1931–1979).

Antony the Great (c. 251–356), the father of monasticism, Paul of Thebes (d. 340), called the Hermit, and Pachomius (c. 290–346), monastic pioneers, were all Copts. From the third century to the Coptic Renaissance of the twentieth century, Egyptian monasticism has left an indelible mark on the spiritual and institutional life of the Church at large. Coptic monastic teaching affirms a spirituality of *imitatio Christi*—the imitation of Christ. Solitude is acknowledged in Mark 1.35, 6.46; Luke 4.42; and is seen as implied by the Apostle Paul in Gal. 1.17. Asceticism is witnessed in the wilderness experiences of Jesus—for example, Mark 1.12–13; Matt. 4.1–11 and 8.18–22; Luke 4.1–13 and 9.57–62. Solitariness, even alienation, is confirmed in Matt. 26.36–46; Mark 14.32–42; and Luke 22.39–46. Christ is the model for the monk. Hermits are the finest of the monks because they have chosen asceticism and separation. Monastic lives, which illustrate the Incarnation of the Son of God, are poised at the intersection between the divine and the world. They are angelic. The Jesus Prayer, believed to be of Coptic origin from the seventh century, has been revived as a means of expressing a relationship with the Savior. Monks and nuns are celibate because the virgin Christ and

Mary the *Theotokos* have consecrated the pattern of virginity for both sexes, so the Copts recognize monks as ideal Christians. In April 1959 a hermit was summoned from his cell to be patriarch. He was Mina *al-Muttawahd* (lit.: the solitary), and he reigned for twelve years. Amba Abram, Bishop of Fayoum (d. 1936), an extreme recluse and spiritual director who rarely preached a sermon, was canonized in the popular imagination on the day of his death. Matta El-Meskeen (b. 1919), a major ascetic and ecumenical theologian, is the spiritual father of Abu Makar in ancient Scetis and has led an enclosed life for more than fifty years. Contemporary Coptic nuns have identified the austere and silent Abba Justus Al-Antouni (1910–1976) as their patron. Professed and consecrated religious are the pride of Coptic Orthodoxy, and their inspiration is ubiquitous.

The Coptic Catholic Church (in common with Rome) and Coptic Evangelical congregations are minorities within a minority. Generally uninfluenced by Orthodoxy, the former have a devotion to Jesus shaped by the thought and spirituality of the western Mediterranean, the latter by a call to personal decision derived from American revivalism. In Coptic Orthodoxy, recognition of the Christ of the creed, who has received definitive exposition in Coptic art, life, and thought, is preferred to any putative historical Jesus. Deconstruction and reconstruction of the image of Jesus Christ is always deplored. But so many elements have contributed to the creation of the contemporary Coptic icon of God Incarnate that it is possible to imagine some creative developments in the future.

John H. Watson

See also: Alexandrian Theology; Benedict; Chalcedon; Creeds; Ethiopian Christianity; Eucharist; Icons and the Icon Tradition; Islam; Nicea; Orthodox Tradition

References

Atiya, Aziz. 1968. A *History of Eastern Christianity*. London: Methuen.

Cragg, Kenneth. 1991. *The Arab Christian*. Louisville, KY: Westminster.

Doorn-Harder, Pieternella van. 1995. *Contemporary Coptic Nuns*. Columbia: University of South Carolina Press.

Meinardus, Otto F. A. 1999. *Two Thousand Years of Coptic Christianity*. Cairo: American University Press.

Sadek, Ashraf and Bernadette. 2000. *L'Incarnation de la Lumière: Le renouveau iconographique copte à travers l'oeuvre d'Isaac Fanous*. Limoges: Le Monde Copte.

Watson, John. 2000. *Among the Copts*. Brighton: Sussex Academic Press.

Young, Frances. 1983. *From Nicaea to Chalcedon*. London: SCM.

Creeds

A creed is a formal statement of official religious belief, used in services and for a number of other purposes in church life. It is commonly seen as a kind of test of church membership. The mainstream Christian churches use two accredited creeds, the Apostles' Creed and the Nicene Creed. Despite its name, the former can be traced back, not to the original apostles but to the

Old Roman Creed, known in the church of that city at the end of the second century. It reached its present form in the early eighth century. The latter comes into view at the important Council of Nicea in 325 and received its present, longer form in 381 at the Council of Constantinople. Both creeds fall into three sections, probably taking the hint from the instruction at the end of the Gospel of Matthew to baptize "in the name of the Father and of the Son and of the Holy Spirit." The three sections follow this Trinitarian structure, but in both cases the middle section, containing belief concerning Jesus, is the longest and in older versions predominated even more.

This testifies to two facts. First, in the early centuries, when these documents took their form, there was more controversy concerning the nature of Jesus than about any other subject, and it was therefore felt to be important to define carefully. But, perhaps more important and certainly what is more fundamental, it was belief about Jesus, which was the most plainly differentiating feature of the Christian religion, as distinct from either its parent Judaism or the Greco-Roman religions of various kinds that dominated its environment in that first period of its life.

Indeed, if we look back to the earliest Christian writings, we find quasi-credal statements relating to Jesus quoted, and it is surely correct to see them as having a number of roles in the life of the early Church. For example, in 1 Cor. 12.3, we find what seems to be an accepted slogan, quoted by Paul: "Jesus is Lord." Here, it seems, is one of the first brief statements of what was at the heart of the Christians' distinctive belief—the centrality and supremacy of Jesus as God's agent for salvation and so as the heart of the believer's life. Here was what made him and her different from those around. We cannot tell precisely what range of use the formula had: was it used in ecstatic worship, or at baptism when commitment to the Christian cause was made, or when called to account by outsiders?

In this early period, the concept of "a creed" was of course not present, and we can see a number of passages from the time having the role of a summary of belief, used for purposes such as those referred to, and some of them can as easily be referred to as hymns or confessions as creeds. See, for example, 1 Cor. 15.3–5, Phil. 2.5–11, and 1 Tim. 3.16. In such cases there is every likelihood that these are familiar formulations, and we notice their diversity of structure and their poetic quality. By the time of the close ancestors of our later creeds, some decades later, there was more uniformity and more structure—and, it seems, a more practical approach: what needs to be affirmed by our members, and especially by new members at their baptism? The Old Roman Creed, for example, demonstrates these qualities. It is both practical and down to earth. And in its second section, about Jesus, it simply recites the main outline of his career, from conception to ascension and with the prospect of return in power and for judgment. In fact, it is light on doctrinal concepts; it seems to be thought sufficient to affirm what we may call the great saving acts that he performed or underwent at God's hand. Interpretation was to be had elsewhere and in other contexts.

What strikes the modern Christian as surprising is the total omission of any reference to the deeds of Jesus' lifetime and his teaching—that is, the main content of the Gospels. There is a total gap between his birth and his suffering and death. There is also no reference here, or in the third section, more concerned with aspects of Christian life, to his gift of the Eucharist, the central act of Christian worship. The creed we have here in the Old Roman Creed, and the same was true elsewhere, was used first at baptisms, where (adult) candidates were required to answer to the creed in question form: "Do you believe . . . ?" (And such a use of the creed is often revived in modern practice.)

The Nicene Creed has a similar early history, but its central section, about Christ, included more abstract and technical material, simply because of contested beliefs on the subject, especially in Eastern Christianity. Only later did it become the practice to recite one or other of the traditional creeds in the course of regular services (more so in the Anglican Prayer Books of the sixteenth and seventeenth centuries than elsewhere). The Nicene Creed, with its strong Christological emphasis, became (and remains) that said or sung at the Sunday Eucharist.

Leslie Houlden

See also: Baptism; Chalcedon; Eucharist; Lord; Nicea

References

Doctrine Commission of the Church of England. 1976. *Christian Believing*. London: SPCK.

Kelly, J. N. D. 1950. *Early Christian Creeds*. London: Longmans Green.

Cross, Crucifixion

See Great War; Holy Sepulchre; Jesus, Death of

Crossan, J. D. (b. 1934)

John Dominic Crossan became one of the most prominent American scholars to publish works on the historical figure of Jesus in the late twentieth century. He is noted for being among the first to develop a fully multidisciplinary approach to the subject, integrating contributions from cultural anthropology, archaeology, sociology, psychohistorical studies, literary criticism, and many other fields of inquiry. He is controversial for ascribing more validity to the historical witness of certain apocryphal writings (the Gospel of Thomas, the Gospel of Peter) than most scholars would allow. Ultimately, Crossan presents Jesus as an itinerant, countercultural peasant whose teaching and lifestyle had more in common with that of Greek Cynic philosophers than with Jewish prophets, priests, or rabbis.

An Irish immigrant, Crossan grew up in Roman Catholicism to become a monk, a priest, and a professor. He eventually left the priesthood, in part to marry but also out of an admitted dissatisfaction with ordained ministry. He continued, however, to teach at DePaul University until retirement and published seminal studies on parables and apocryphal writings. Active in numerous scholarly guilds, he also served as cofounder of the Jesus Seminar. His magnum opus, *The Historical Jesus*, presents the culmination of a lifetime of study; *The Origins of Christianity* serves to refine some of the arguments, respond to criticisms, and advance theories as to how nonhistorical understandings of Jesus developed in the years between his crucifixion and the writing of the Gospels.

Crossan's reconstruction of Jesus presents him as "a peasant Jewish Cynic"—that is, as a countercultural, uneducated philosopher who dispensed folk wisdom in ways that threatened the social ethos of his day; though it is fair to say that recently Crossan has played down the idea of Jesus' Cynic, philosophical connections. Jesus sought to subvert the patron-client systems of the time by encouraging everyone, especially the lowest classes, to have unmediated relationships with God and with each other. Thus he opposed any form of hierarchy—not only overtly political ones but also traditional family structures and religious systems that sought to mediate access to God through priests, parents, or teachers. Jesus spread his radical ideas not only by speaking in aphorisms and parables but also through symbolic ritual acts, among which "magic" and "meals" were primary. Jesus became known as a healer and as an exorcist because he performed a sort of folk magic to effect psychosomatic cures that demonstrated direct accessibility of God. He also initiated community meals in which people of all classes, including outcasts, would partake equally, illustrating (and in part effecting) the abolition of "patrons" and "clients." Thus Jesus was a social revolutionary, attempting to transform society from the bottom up. Crossan does not believe that Jesus performed supernatural miracles or that he claimed any special status for himself. A pacifist, Jesus espoused an "ethical eschatology" that calls for nonviolent human action to redeem the world as opposed to apocalyptic, violent acts of God. Jesus never would have allowed himself to be viewed as a mediator; he did not have disciples as such, but only "companions." He was executed in Jerusalem without a trial and, most likely, his body was never even placed in a tomb but was abandoned and "eaten by dogs."

Crossan's critics focus especially on what they regard as an idiosyncratic use of sources and on what they consider to be an incredible gulf between Crossan's reconstruction of the historical Jesus and the presumably unreliable early witness of the Church. First, Crossan regards material in the Gospel of Thomas as earlier and more reliable than anything in the four New Testament Gospels except material ascribed to the hypothetical Q source. He likewise believes that the Gospel of Peter contains a Passion story that predates any of the canonical Passion narratives. Very few scholars agree with these decisions. Second, Crossan's understanding of Jesus demands not only that the New Testament Gospels be viewed as containing very little eyewitness testimony but also that the process of oral tradition prior to their writing be understood as an occasion for gross alteration and outright fabrication. His reconstruction requires that by the time of Paul (who knew many of the original followers of Jesus) the historical figure of Jesus had ceased to be known or relevant, replaced by a mythological construct. For Crossan's opponents, the likelihood of such changes occurring so quickly and so completely seems remote.

Mark A. Powell

See also: Family; Jesus, Miracles of; Jesus, Parables of; Jesus in Social Context; Jesus Seminar; Thomas, Gospel of

References

Crossan, John Dominic. 1991. *The Historical Jesus: The Life of a Mediterranean Jewish Peasant*. San Francisco: HarperSanFrancisco.

———. 1998. *The Birth of Christianity: Discovering What Happened in the Years Immediately after the Execution of Jesus*. San Francisco: HarperSanFrancisco.

Crossan, John Dominc, and J. L. Reed. 2002. *Excavating Jesus: Beneath the Stones, Behind the Texts*. London: SPCK.

Cynics

See Jesus in Social Context

Cyril of Alexandria

See Alexandrian Theology; Chalcedon

D

Dante Alighieri (1265–1321)

The truth of the observation that every work of art both reflects and transcends its own era is nowhere more vividly demonstrated than in the case of Dante. In him we encounter a writer whose universal genius is more firmly anchored in his own age than almost any other great artist in the history of Western European civilization. Few others have been able to, or have wanted to, incorporate the preoccupations of their own society so directly into his or her work as this late medieval Florentine. To read his writings is to enter into and gain purchase on an entire culture at a particular moment of its development. He was the author of works in a number of different literary genres, but it is chiefly as the creator of the *Divine Comedy*, universally acknowledged as one of the greatest achievements of the poetic imagination, that he is remembered and celebrated. It tells the story of the author's visionary journey to God through the three realms of the afterlife as found in the teachings of the Catholic Church: Hell (*Inferno*), Purgatory (*Purgatorio*), and Heaven (*Paradiso*). Although often ferociously anticlerical, Dante remained an unwaveringly devout son of the Church, and the entire poem is steeped in the doctrine and practices of medieval Catholicism.

Given this fact, it comes as a surprise to many readers to find that there seem to be so few references to the person of Jesus Christ in Dante's writings. Perhaps we should not expect Jesus to figure prominently in much of the early, or so-called minor, works, but the *Comedy* is overtly Christian in both intention and structure, and its theme is redemption. Yet in this poem of nearly five thousand lines, there are only fifty-six clear references to Jesus Christ, and the holy name itself is uttered only twice. In nearly all other instances he is referred to either by a title such as "Word of God," "Son of God," "Lamb of God," "Spouse of the Church," or, most frequently, simply as Christ. Occasionally he appears in elaborate allegorical form, as in the scene at the top of the mountain of Purgatory where, in the midst of the pageant, the mythical beast—the griffin—drawing the triumphal car, signifies the divine and human nature of the Incarnate Lord (*Purgatorio* XXIX, 106–114). In yet other places the references to Jesus are periphrastic—as, for example, in *Inferno* IV, 52: "I saw a Mighty One [*un possente*] come here crowned with victory," or "[It] was a little before He came who took from Dis the great spoil of the uppermost circle" (ibid., XII 38). And it is not insignificant, as we shall

Dante Alighieri (Corel)

see, that thirty-nine of these fifty-six references occur in the third section of the poem: *Paradiso*.

It is, perhaps, even more surprising when Dante is set in his historical context: the late thirteenth and early fourteenth centuries, a period that was witnessing a great surge of popular devotion to the sacred humanity of the Lord. Seen against this background, Dante's treatment of the figure of Jesus Christ takes on a puzzling aspect. G. L. Prestige in his essay on this subject ("Eros: Or Devotion to the Sacred Humanity," in *Fathers and Heretics*) observed that "during the twelfth century a revolutionary change passed over the devotion of the Western Church." Jesus Christ was coming to be regarded not only as "deliverer and illuminator . . . but still more as companion, friend, and brother. . . . He is sought not so much as the temporal revelation of the Father as for the sake of his own perfect human qualities" (p. 85). Doubtless devotion to the person of the Savior can be found in other periods of the Church's history and has roots that stretch back to the earliest days of the Christian community, but it is undeniably the case that the spread and flowering of the devotion occurred in the very era to which Dante belonged, and that two of the driving spirits of this devotion were two men to whom the poet was to accord the highest honor in his poem: Bernard of Clairvaux and Francis of Assisi. It is known that Dante received part of his early education at the hands of the Franciscans and may even have been a tertiary of that order. Yet, for all his emphasis on love, there is no trace of the typical Franciscan devotion with its mystical identification with the human suffering of Jesus. Bernard, regarded as the medieval source of much of the devotion, actually appears in the final cantos of *Paradiso* to take the place of Beatrice at Dante's side and act as the poet's last guide on his journey to the beatific vision. Yet there is nothing of Bernard's distinctive mysticism, his suspicion of intellectual religion, or his characterization of Christ as the supreme lover of the individual soul.

In view of all this it seems we have, in Dante's presentation of Jesus Christ, a portrayal that, in some significant sense, is running counter to the spirit of his age: the creation of a man who never showed the slightest interest in the mystical devotion to the sacred humanity of the Lord and never presented a picture of Jesus that expressed the passionate spirit found in the hymns, sermons, and prayers of his own day. This may partly be explained by his own temperament: the value he placed on the power of the intellect and the use of reason, and his refusal to make of religion primarily a matter of heart and will. In this he showed himself as much a disciple of Thomas Aquinas and the Dominican tradition as of the Bernardine and Franciscan teachings. His Christian mysticism was one in which there was an unflinching determination to marry intellect and feeling, reason and love; and nowhere is this clearer than in the work of his mature genius, the *Divine Comedy*. But there is something else that impinged upon his portrayal of Christ that will have to be considered: the place he gave to the figure of Beatrice, that mysterious center of his creative and religious life. Having said all this, however, only a superficial reader of the *Comedy* will leave it with the impression that the person of Jesus Christ is other than central to its purpose. It may not be a meditation on the sacred humanity in the manner of his contemporaries, but it does present a distinctive picture of Jesus Christ and demonstrates a sensibility that is not only interested in the historical person of the Lord but also committed to his doctrinal significance. The *Comedy* is in fact a profoundly Christological poem.

It is not until the *Comedy* that Dante's thought becomes centered in this way. Apart from the earliest work, the *Vita Nuova,* the minor works have very little to say about Christ. *Il Convivio* (c. 1303–1307) is a philosophical piece, a series of commentaries on some of his own poems. In its disquisition on a number of philosophical matters—the constitution of the soul, the nature of human happiness, cosmology—there are a few scattered references to Jesus Christ that seem, to a modern reader, merely quaint. So, for example, a discussion of the relationship between God the Father and God the Son in the Holy Trinity is introduced primarily with the purpose of substantiating a theory about angelic intelligences (II, 5). In a later passage the supposed age at which Christ's death occurred is put to curious use as proof of an Aristotelian argument about the "highest point" of the arc of a man's life (IV, 23). However, even here, in a text that is saturated with the philosophical precepts of the ancients, especially Aristotle, Dante indicates an unshakable reliance on the figure of his Lord whose teaching is regarded as surpassing in truth and nobility that of all the philosophers (II, 8). In the later work on political theory, *De Monarchia* (c. 1312), there is to be detected, perhaps, an aspect of that Franciscan spirituality with which he must have been familiar. The worldliness, wealth, and secular power of his own day are regarded with such disapproval that Dante proposes a radical solution to the corruption of the ecclesiastical institution: the separation of Church and state and the complete renunciation of secular rule by the Church.

The earliest of the minor works, *Vita Nuova,* is a more complicated case. It is, ostensibly, an autobiographical work that recounts in poetry and prose his early love for, and loss of, Beatrice. Its peculiar form need not detain us; its content must, for the journey to God that is the subject of the *Comedy* begins here in the houses and streets of thirteenth-century Florence. Beatrice, the girl with whom Dante tells us he fell in love at the age of nine in 1274, is clothed with Christlike connotations. "Beatrice, the object of Dante's praise, is *like* Christ. She is like him in her provenance, in her salvific purpose, in the perfection of her being and example, and in her claim to obedience" (Took, 54). It is true that the person of Jesus Christ makes no appearance, nor is the holy name invoked, yet the text is replete with the language of revelation and salvation, nearly all of which is related to Beatrice, and is pregnant with meanings that will only be unveiled decades in the future, in the *Divina Commedia*.

As I have said, it would seem that we are unlikely to find in the *Comedy* the expression of any devotion to the person of Jesus Christ that is comparable to that which was becoming so widespread in the Catholic Christianity of Dante's own age. There is no urge to the imitation of Christ, no mystical union with the sufferings of the earthly Lord, no extended contemplation of his Passion and death, no outpourings of adoration in the terms a lover might use, no sense, even, of Jesus as companion and friend. Instead there is a portrayal of Christ, which could be said to be closer to the spirituality of a much earlier era: that of the patristic age—even perhaps of the age of the New Testament, for like the author of the epistle to the Colossians, it could accurately be said of Dante that his affections were fixed on "things above where Christ is seated at the right hand of God" and that he believed himself to be someone whose life "is hid with Christ in God" (Col. 3.1–3). It is for this reason that most of the allusions to Christ in the *Comedy* are to be found in the final section, *Paradiso*, as Dante, anticipating the ecstasy of the beatific vision, is guided by Beatrice through the heavenly spheres to the glorious sight of the Holy Trinity.

But that the glorified Christ of the Holy Trinity is also the historical Jesus, crucified and risen, is a fact of which Dante is perfectly well aware and that he is intent on keeping before his readers' consciousness in all parts of the poem. Its very structure is, so to speak, both Christological and liturgical, for it holds its reader fast in the narrative of the last days of Jesus' earthly life. The story begins on Good Friday, the time of the crucifixion. Dante and Virgil descend into hell as Jesus descended into hell on Good Friday, and they emerge into the sunlight of the mountain of Purgatory on the morning of the third day, Easter. The journey up the mountain and through the celestial spheres takes a week. The end is reached on the Sunday of the octave of Easter: the completion, in the medieval Church's calendar, of the celebration of the Feast of the resurrection. The Comedy is, in fact, a Resurrection poem. In *Inferno* the references to Christ are nearly all to do with the theme of Christ's victory over sin and death. Jesus, here, is the triumphant Christ who in his death entered hell to harrow it. This popular medieval theme of the harrowing of hell is introduced a number of times. The reader (in the persons of Dante and Virgil) encounters scenes that are dramatic reminders of the passage of the Son of God through hell as he entered the infernal regions over Holy Saturday to deliver the myriad souls who had been awaiting his appearing. This liberation of mankind, living and dead, is, for Dante, the purpose of the crucifixion, and the landscape of hell is littered with the rubble of Christ's victorious progress as his descent literally breaks things apart (XII, 41–45; XI, 106–114). Little mention is made of the life of Jesus in this section, but there are terse allusions to the teachings of Christ and an acute sensitivity to the ways in which human beings, especially the members of the hierarchy of the Church, have ignored and flouted them (XIX, 90–96).

The awareness of the details of Christ's life and the content of his teaching in the Gospels is, deliberately, more evident in the second part, *Purgatorio*, for it is in this place that those who have genuinely tried but failed to conform to the mind of Christ are confronted with the teachings of the Gospel as they repent and are purged of their sins in their progress to the divine light. We find, also, that there is a shift in the perspective on the purpose of the crucifixion of Jesus. The interpretation of the death here points forward to the long presentation of the doctrine of the Atonement in the seventh canto of *Paradiso*. One notes again that the allusions to the Passion have none of the warm, intimate quality so characteristic of contemporary devotion; such events as are described are recounted with a cool objectivity and are there chiefly to illustrate a theological or political point (XX, 88–93; XXIII, 73–77). The whole *Comedy* is rich in biblical allusion, and the sayings are woven into the narrative with great confidence and dexterity.

Thus Christ can be said to be present in the text in the form of his teachings, even though his name is not often mentioned. As Dante and Virgil climb the terraces of the mountain, the guardian angels of the terraces pronounce blessings using the words of the Beatitudes, and at the beginning of the eleventh canto the Lord's Prayer appears in a form in which each clause is followed by a meditation on its meaning. On the evidence of *Purgatory* alone we must conclude that the Jesus of Dante was not only the eternal Son of God whose love drew souls irresistibly toward the beatific vision but was also the greatest of all the teachers of morality.

As we enter heaven in the final section of the poem, the figure of Jesus takes on further dimensions. In the seventh canto he appears as the divine sacrificial victim in an extended presentation of the doctrine of the Atonement. Beatrice is now Dante's guide, and in answer to his puzzled question as to how exactly "just vengeance" could be "justly avenged," she outlines the classical exposition of the salvific work of Christ as expounded two centuries earlier by Anselm of Canterbury in *Cur Deus Homo*. The crucifixion is to be understood as the "just vengeance" on human nature borne willingly by the God-Man Jesus Christ (VII, 19–120). It is entirely characteristic of Dante that he should be attracted to this juridical explanation of the saving work of his Lord: his passion for justice in human affairs is complemented by his unshakable conviction in the ultimate triumph of the justice of God. But this justice will not be in conflict with his love; it is, in fact, to be seen as an expression of his love. That point has already been made in the words of the inscription over the gates through which Dante and Virgil entered hell at the beginning of the journey. In the end it is Dante's belief that it is God's love—a love that sets in order everything—that moves the universe (XXX, 143–145) and that love is shown specifically toward men and women in the person of Jesus Christ. At the very end of his journey, Dante sees the Holy Trinity, and within the depths of the Godhead he is able to distinguish the outlines of a human face, "our image," *nostra effige;* it is the face of Christ (XXX, 129–132). Christ is the supremely loving one.

But throughout the *Comedy*, the language of passionate adoration has been reserved for Beatrice alone. Readers who have wanted Dante to be more obviously orthodox (including those of his own day) have frequently found this heightened rhetoric of love objectionable, even idolatrous. But such a simplistic reading of the work does scant justice to its poetic complexity. However theological the poem may be, it is still poetry and not theology; and the person of Beatrice is a literary trope, even though she may have been a real person with whom the poet fell in love. As such she is both the Florentine girl and the image of Christ. Furthermore, Dante will not separate human and divine love. He does not identify them, but he will not separate them, and for this he is regarded by some as suspiciously unorthodox. But for him, human love, properly understood and without losing any of its own distinctiveness or beauty, will lead to divine love. Beatrice, properly understood, will lead to Christ. At the beginning of the story she comes to his aid; in the end she leaves his side to take her place in the communion of the saints, the Celestial Rose. She is not the originator of her own beauty nor the ultimate cause of Dante's love, and her departure from him confirms this; but by this time she has received, as the image of her source, Christ, the adoration of her passionate lover, Dante, and it is to him, Christ, through her, that Dante's own love has been offered. In the story it is Beatrice who is the recipient of these outpourings; in the allegory, it is Christ. When this is grasped, it can be seen in how profound a sense we can call Dante a man of his own age: the Jesus of Dante is not as far from the Jesus of his contemporaries as was imagined. The *Comedy* read in this light may truly be regarded as a celebration of the sacred humanity of Christ, but the genius of the poet was such that its expression was transformed into "something rich and strange."

B. L. Horne

See also: Anselm; Aquinas, Thomas; Bernard of Clairvaux; Creeds; English Christianity, Medieval; Francis of Assisi; Jesus, Achievement of; Roman Catholicism

References

Alighieri, Dante. *La Vita Nuova*. 1969. Translated by Barbara Reynolds. Harmondsworth: Penguin.

———. *The Divine Comedy (Divina Commedia)*. 1980. Edited and translated by C. S. Singleton. 3 vols. Bollingen Series 80. Princeton: Princeton University Press.

———. 1989. *The Banquet (Il Convivio)*. Translated by Christopher Ryan. Stanford French and Italian Studies 61. Saratoga, CA: Anima Libri.

———. *Monarchia*. 1995. Edited and translated by Prue Shaw. Cambridge Medieval Classics 4. Cambridge: Cambridge University Press.

Anderson, William. 1980. *Dante the Maker*. London: Routledge and Kegan Paul.

Balthasar, Hans Urs von. 1986. *The Glory of the Lord: A Theological Aesthetics*. Vol. III: *Studies in Theological Styles: Lay Styles*. Translated by Louth Saward and Simon Williams. Edited by J. Riches. Edinburgh: T. and T. Clark.

Botterill, Stephen. 1994. *Dante and the Mystical Tradition: St. Bernard of Clairvaux in the "Commedia."* Cambridge: Cambridge University Press.

Brooke, Rosalind and Christopher. 1984. *Popular Religion in the Middle Ages*. London: Thames and Hudson.

Foster, Kenelm. 1977. *The Two Dantes*. London: Darton, Longman and Todd.
Gilson, Etienne. 1948. *Dante the Philosopher*. Translated by David Moore. London: Sheed and Ward.
Jacoff, R., ed. 1993. *The Cambridge Companion to Dante*. Cambridge: Cambridge University Press.
Prestige, G. L. 1963. *Fathers and Heretics*. London: SPCK.
Took, J. F. 1990. *Dante: Lyric Poet and Philosopher: An Introduction to the Minor Works*. Oxford: Clarendon.

Dead Sea Scrolls

The term "Dead Sea Scrolls" (DSS) refers to manuscripts discovered in several places since 1947 in the region of the Dead Sea, from Wadi ed-Daliyeh about fourteen kilometers north of Jericho to Masada near the southwest shore of the Dead Sea. These manuscripts date from between the fourth century B.C. and the seventh century A.D. Most commonly, however, the term DSS is used to refer to the collection of about 850 manuscripts found between 1947 and 1956 in eleven caves at or near Qumran on the northwest shore of the Dead Sea. The Qumran scrolls seem to be the remains of a library that consisted of authoritative texts (many of which would later be included in the Hebrew Bible), sectarian compositions, and general Jewish literature. The owners of this library are most often and most suitably identified with some part of the Essenes. Some Essenes lived at Qumran between 100 B.C. and A.D. 68; others lived throughout Judea in small conventicles.

Nowhere in any of the scrolls is Jesus mentioned, nor are there any references to any early Christians. Furthermore it is highly unlikely that any of the Greek fragments found in Qumran Cave 7 are copies of any of the books of the New Testament. Likewise, nowhere in the New Testament are there any unambiguous references to the Essenes. Nevertheless, there are several striking parallels between the Gospel portrayals of what Jesus said and did and the DSS. These parallels have enjoyed much prominence, especially among those who have been interested in reconstructing the Jewish world in which Jesus lived, a feature of Jesus research that was prompted in part by wanting to assert the Jewishness of Jesus in face of the Holocaust. The interest has also been exploited by scholars, motivated more by faith than reason, who have had narrow historicist concerns linked with the desire to demonstrate the veracity of divine revelation as that is supposed to reside in the writings of the New Testament.

At each stage in the scholarly discussion of the significance of the DSS for understanding Jesus there have been three approaches. Most of this article will consider the dominant view that there is some significant relationship, even if only because the DSS are the largest body of Jewish textual evidence from Palestine that is contemporary with Jesus. They thus speak eloquently of much of the character of Palestinian Judaism at the time of Jesus. The other less widespread views are that Jesus and the DSS have no relationship at all, and that such a lack should be noted forcefully, or that the relationship is so close that Jesus can be viewed as akin to an Essene.

A. There have been at least four principal ways of construing that there is some kind of relationship between Jesus and the DSS, and that the DSS enhance how Jesus' Jewishness is best understood. (1) First and most often, in some of his deeds and words Jesus is thought merely to be echoing contemporary Jewish teachings and practices, which are also coincidentally found in the scrolls. For example, Jesus' emphasis on the reign ("kingdom") of God echoes in some ways the declaration of the sovereignty of God found in the Qumran Songs for the Sabbath Sacrifice; the debates about his messianic self-understanding can be informed by the kinds of messianic hopes present in many of the sectarian scrolls; the organization of his close followers as a group of twelve echoes the way the Qumran community also tried to be heirs of the tribes of Israel; and his celibacy has its nearest counterpart in the asceticism of some Essenes. Or, more precisely, 4Q525.2 ii 1–6 contains a poetic set of beatitudes, one of which mentions the "pure in heart" and the last of which is a meditation on persecution; in Matt. 5.8, Jesus' sixth beatitude concerns the "pure in heart," and the eighth and ninth concern persecution. Here seems to be a common Jewish form of wisdom instruction with no necessary dependence of one text upon the other. Or again, both the authors of the DSS and Jesus seem to be the heirs of a common exegetical tradition concerning the vineyard in Isa. 5 (the motif is developed in similar ways in 4Q500 1; and Luke 20.9–19) and the anointed proclaimer of good news of Isa. 52 and 61 (the author of 11QMelchizedek and Jesus in Luke 4.18–19 both understand the figure eschatologically). In terms of religious practices, Jesus' exorcisms reflect common Jewish views of the link between sickness and demons, a view also known at Qumran (e.g., 4Q242), as was the therapeutic technique of laying on of hands (1QapGen 20.29). This overall approach is often neglected by those who research the life and teachings of Jesus because of the common abuse of the criterion of dissimilarity; however, it should not be thought that the authentic Jesus can only be found in items for which there is no parallel elsewhere, otherwise Jesus would never have been understood by his Jewish contemporaries.

(2) Second, some scholars have argued that Jesus adopted certain insights from compositions that the Essenes preserved or even composed; this approach to Jesus commonly stresses the eclectic character of his teaching, proposing that it is his combination of ideas (especially those of the Pharisees and Essenes) that is distinctive, rather than any particular element. Four examples indicate the range of Jesus' possible dependence on Essene ideas. In Luke (Q) 7.22 Jesus answers the disciples of John the Baptist about his identity by quoting Isa. 61 in an adapted form; the same adaptation can only be found elsewhere in 4Q521.2 ii + 4.2: "[T]he dead are raised, the poor have good news brought to them." In Mark 10.2–9 Jesus justifies his strict interpretation of divorce law by appealing to Gen. 1.27 and 2.24; in the sectarian Damascus Document (CD 4.20–5.1) a similar justification is given for monogamy and against divorce. In Matt. 5.33 Jesus advises against endorsing oaths by appealing to the deity, a practice also attacked in CD 15.1–2. Jesus' use of "Abba," "Father," as an address to God is matched most closely in contemporary Palestinian Jewish prayer in 4Q372 1.16 ("my Father and my God") and 4Q460.9 i 6 ("my Father and my Lord").

(3) Third, some scholars have stressed the view that rather than being directly dependent on Essene teaching Jesus may have known it and reacted against it. In Matt. 5.43 Jesus reproaches those who love their neighbors and hate their enemies, as seems to be the case in some sectarian compositions (e.g., 1QS 1.10). In Luke 16.8 Jesus appears to be telling the parable of the dishonest manager to discourage imitation of the "sons of light," a term used as a self-designation of the community of the DSS. The quasi-sectarian 4QInstruction (4Q416.2 iii 3–5) teaches that it is better not to touch money entrusted to one than to risk losing it; Jesus seems to teach just the opposite (Matt. 25.14–30; Luke 19.11–27). Whereas MMT (4Q394 8 iii 19-iv 4), the War Rule (1QM 7.4–5), and the Rule of the Congregation (1QSa 2.5–8) all variously speak against the blind, deaf, and lame, Jesus seems to go out of his way to demonstrate through his healing ministry and eating practices that God is concerned that just such people should be restored to the worshipping community.

Some scholars have combined both the second and third approaches outlined above to show that Jesus was part of first-century Jewish debates, knowingly agreeing and disagreeing with Essene views as suited his own principles; this approach has been taken not least by several prominent Jewish scholars.

(4) Fourth, some scholars have suggested that Jesus capitalized on the model of leadership provided by the Teacher of Righteousness of the sectarian DSS (especially as described in the Damascus Document and the Pesharim [biblical commentaries]). In its most controversial and least substantiated form this view proposes that Jesus was recognized as the Teacher returned from the dead; though few if any would hold to this nowadays, its possibility shows how some of the parallels between the DSS and Jesus can be construed. More generally, the Teacher can be viewed as an embodiment of the eschatological prophet and/or priest expected by some Jews; Jesus likewise may have embodied some aspects of such a role for himself (Mark 6.4; John 6.14).

Explanations for these parallels between the DSS and Jesus have taken various routes. Most often it is proposed that it was Jesus' encounter with John the Baptist that provided his link to Essene teaching and practice. Although John was probably not an Essene, the geographical proximity of his ministry to Qumran and his attention to divine judgment, repentance, and ritual washing show that John is likely to have known about Essene teachings and rituals, and possibly even adapted them for his own purposes.

While not denying that Essene views could have been mediated through John the Baptist, other scholars suggest that Jesus encountered Essenes during his ministry and that he particularly approved of some of their ethical views, such as those on divorce and poverty. In light of this, it is supposed by some that Jesus used buildings close to the Essene quarter when he stayed in Jerusalem and that the house used for the Last Supper was possibly owned by an Essene.

Rather than speaking of "Jesus and the DSS," other scholars have preferred to analyze the many parallels between the DSS and the writings of the New Testament. Since none of the written works of the New Testament are earlier than the 50s A.D., the main point of contact between the Essenes and early Christianity can be portrayed as taking place in the second half of the first century A.D. Any supposed Essene influence in the teaching of Jesus can then be explained as the later influence of Essene views on the second generation of Christians who were attempting to record Jesus' deeds and sayings; Essene influence on the New Testament authors was read back into earlier layers of the tradition. On the one hand this view makes some satisfactory sense of the dominant historical reconstructions, which locate Jesus chiefly in Galilee and stress his message of the inclusiveness and immediacy of the kingdom of God; the influence of the ideas in the DSS is seen as minimal. On the other hand this approach conveniently preserves much of the distinctiveness of Jesus' message and his likely self-understanding. Some Christian scholars have been happy to adopt this approach as an implicit way of protecting Jesus' uniqueness.

B. The second overall approach to assessing the significance of the DSS for understanding Jesus has been to deny any connection between the two. Several factors support the view. Most obviously, nowhere in the DSS is there mention of Jesus or any of his disciples; conversely, nowhere in the New Testament is there any clear reference to the Essenes or their texts. Furthermore, Jesus was from Galilee and apparently of lower artisan status; the scrolls from Qumran belonged to an educated and predominantly priestly elite whose main focus was Jerusalem. Jesus preached a message of inclusivity and probably regularly ate with many Jews whom others marginalized; the Qumran Essenes were among those most ready to maintain purity through rigid rules of exclusion. Thus for geographical, sociological, and theological reasons Jesus can be distanced from the collectors and authors of the DSS. This lack of clear evidence has resulted in some overly skeptical conclusions that reflect an unrealistic construction of first-century Judaism as if its distinctive groupings seldom interacted.

C. The third approach, the opposite of the second, has asserted that in some way Jesus and his followers should be identified with those who collected the scrolls. The lack of explicit evidence permits those who take this approach to present elaborate and largely unverifiable (and therefore also irrefutable) reconstructions of Palestinian Judaism and Jesus' place in it. The general public's yearning for historical certainties, however unlikely, and its fascination with conspiracy theories have often given pride of place to approaches such as those of B. Thiering (for whom Jesus is a disgraced member of the Qumran community). More plausible, but suffering from vast oversimplification, is the approach of R. Eisenman: he sweepingly classifies all first-century Judaism as either nationalist (like the Zealots) or assimilationist (like Paul). For Eisenman there are hints in the Gospels and Acts that Jesus and his first followers were nationalist xenophobic Jews like the Essenes; only after Paul's victory in early Christianity were the sources adapted to minimize these features and stress that Jesus was outward-looking and inclusive in his preaching and practice.

George J. Brooke

See also: Jesus in Social Context; Kingdom of God

References

Betz, Otto, and Rainer Riesner. 1994. *Jesus, Qumran and the Vatican*. London: SCM.

Carmignac, Jean. 1962. *Christ and the Teacher of Righteousness: The Evidence of the Dead Sea Scrolls*. Baltimore, MD and Dublin: Helicon.

Charlesworth, James H., ed. 1992. *Jesus and the Dead Sea Scrolls*. New York: Doubleday.

Eisenman, Robert. 1996. *The Dead Sea Scrolls and the First Christians: Essays and Translations*. Shaftesbury, Dorset, UK: Element Books.

Evans, Craig A. 1994. "The Recently Published Dead Sea Scrolls and the Historical Jesus." Pp. 547–565 in *Studying the Historical Jesus: Evaluations of the State of Current Research*. Edited by Bruce Chilton and Craig A. Evans. Leiden, Netherlands: Brill Academic.

García Martínez, Florentino. 1996. *The Dead Sea Scrolls Translated*. 2d ed. Leiden, Netherlands and Grand Rapids, MI: Eerdmans.

Kuhn, Heinz-Wolfgang. 2000. "Jesus." Pp. 404–408 in *Encyclopedia of the Dead Sea Scrolls*. Edited by Lawrence H. Schiffman and James C. VanderKam. New York: Oxford University Press.

Sanders, E. P. 1985. *Jesus and Judaism*. London: SCM; Philadelphia: Fortress.

Thiering, Barbara. 1992a. *Jesus and the Riddle of the Dead Sea Scrolls*. San Francisco: HarperSan Francisco.

———. 1992b. *Jesus the Man*. London: Doubleday.

Vermes, G. 1995. *The Dead Sea Scrolls in English*. 4th ed. London: Penguin.

Didache

Written probably in the first century but only discovered in 1873, the *Didache* ("The Teaching of the Twelve Apostles") is a composite of practical texts—instructions, liturgical prayers, regulations—reflecting the practices and beliefs of an early Jewish-Christian community where no book of the canonical New Testament is clearly known, but where many of the sayings of Jesus, to be included in the Synoptic Gospels and Matthew in particular, were known. Because it shows a community's social makeup and practices *prior* to the Gospels, it holds a unique place for understanding the early church developments. Given that it contains teaching material—a moral instruction (1.1–6.2) and a homily (16)—it is surprising that there is no formal teaching on what this community, which made a definite break with Judaism (cf. 8.1) to follow "Jesus Christ" (e.g., 9.4 or 12.5) as "Lord" (e.g., 4.1 or 4.12), believed about Jesus, except for stating that whenever a preacher "speaks about the Lord [Jesus], he is present" (4.1). This apparent silence has meant that the *Didache* does not figure in most studies of early beliefs about Jesus; yet it is a witness to those beliefs, especially in its liturgical texts, and shows the importance of Jewish models of latter-day salvific figures for the first Christians in imagining whom they were following.

The central motif for understanding Jesus is that he is the final and definitive prophet—probably the earliest strand of Christological belief—and has been sent to gather into unity scattered Israel (9.4, cf. Jer. 31.10 and Ezek. 28.25). As such, Jesus is God's "servant" (*pais*) (e.g., 9.2) and "the holy vine of the servant David" (9.2). By making Jesus comparable with David, and in particular presenting him as David's vine (cf. Jer. 33.15), they see him as the one who realizes in his life the whole salvific economy of the history of Israel. Thus the community thank God for Jesus at the same time as they thank God for all that has been given them "through (*dia*) Jesus Christ" (e.g., 9.2), for he is the one who has revealed the Father's "holy name" (10.2). This revelation by Jesus was done at the Father's bidding; so Jesus gives life and knowledge of the Father (9.3), makes it possible for the Father's name "to dwell in their hearts," and gives them "knowledge, faith and immortality" (10.2). Jesus also makes it possible for the community to offer the Father praise and thanksgiving: for they thank the Father through (*dia*) him (10.4), and he makes the community at prayer the new temple (10.5 and 14.3). Jesus as prophetic servant is both the means of the divine gift and the one who brings about the Father's will. This evidence's value is, partially, that, since it comes from a eucharistic prayer, we know it had wide currency among Christians as a picture of Jesus, and through that prayer's structure and its lack of dependence on the Last Supper we know that it was probably in use prior to practice underlying Mark's Gospel.

A further aspect of *Didache*'s view of Jesus as servant-prophet is that he is the future judge who will come at the End. Thus it uses *Maranatha* (cf. 1 Cor. 16.22) in prayers (10.6), and the homily's theme (16) is that "the Lord is coming" in an apocalyptic manner—similar to the "coming of the Son of man" in Matt. 24.30.

The *Didache* uses several titles for Jesus, and, implicitly, the images of priest, king, prophet, and judge show a community with a complex, already developed theology of Jesus as what-he-means-for-them. Liturgy is the driving force in this elaboration, and *Didache*'s most developed statement is liturgical: they baptize "in the name of the Father and of the Son and of the Holy Spirit" (7.1 and 7.3; identical with Matt. 28.19)—the only times it refers to "the Son" or treats Jesus equally with "the Father." By contrast, *Didache* shows no interest in the historical Jesus, except for seeing him as the source of teaching (6.2), commandments (e.g., 4.13 or 9.5), sayings, and prayers making up his Gospel (8.2), and their regular gathering for the Eucharist (14.1–3).

Thomas O'Loughlin

See also: Eucharist; Jesus as Servant; Kingdom of God; Matthew, Gospel of

References

Draper, Jonathan A. 2000. "Ritual Process and Ritual Symbols in Didache 7–10." *Vigiliae Christianae* 54: 121–158.

Louth, A., ed. 1987. *Early Christian Writings*. London: Penguin.

Mazza, Enrico. 1995. *The Origins of the Eucharistic Prayer*. Collegeville, MN: Liturgical Press.

Niederwimmer, Kurt. *The Didache*. Minneapolis, MN: Augsburg Fortress.

Divinity

See Barth, Karl; Chalcedon; Macquarrie, John; Nicea; Pannenberg, Wolfhart; Schleiermacher, F. D. E.

Docetism

See Ignatius of Antioch; Gnosticism; Schleiermacher, F. D. E.

E

Ecclesiology

This article is concerned with the relation of Jesus Christ to the Church in history and in theology. The central question is this: What connects the historical figure of Jesus Christ, confessed by Christians as savior and Lord, with the great institution, spreading out geographically and historically, that bears his name? The specific historical question is, Did Jesus found the Church? The crucial theological question is, How is the Church's life at all times grounded on Jesus Christ?

Did Jesus Found the Church?

Did Jesus intend there to be a Christian Church? Did he foresee the emergence of a great international institution with enduring structures of government, with its own laws and complex traditions? In answering this question, theologians tend to become rather paradoxical. Wright says: "The question is hopeless. Of course he didn't; of course he did" (Wright, 275). Knox claims that the issue is "largely irrelevant." "The important thing is not what Jesus intended or expected, but what God did" (Knox, 35).

Modern scholarship (pioneered in this respect by Johannes Weiss and Albert Schweitzer at the turn of the twentieth century) has rediscovered the eschatological (related to the *eschaton*, the end time of history) horizon that bounded the ministry of Jesus. He expected a decisive divine intervention to bring about the end of the present age or world order (though not "the end of the world") either imminently or within a few years. He interpreted his sufferings and those that he anticipated for his disciples as belonging to the great tribulation that would serve as the birth pangs of the new age (John 16.16).

Jesus himself linked his death with the coming of the kingdom (Luke 22.28; Mark 14.25). Future hope is drawn down by the New Testament writers and located in the event of Jesus Christ. Expectations about the future course of history are rerouted, passing through his death and resurrection. Jesus and the earlier New Testament writers did not anticipate that history would continue for thousands of years. Does the eschatological crisis proclaimed and inaugurated by Jesus preclude any intention on his part to found an ongoing institutional structure for his followers? To give a nuanced answer to this question we must look a little more closely at the eschatological framework of the New Testament. A century of study has arrived at a number of fairly secure conclusions.

First, the primary orientation of Jesus' eschatology was to the future. J. Weiss's *Jesus' Proclamation of the Kingdom of God* (1892) overturned the liberal theological consensus, represented by A. Ritschl, that the kingdom of God was a realm of progressive moral attainment that was slowly but surely permeating world history. On the contrary, claimed Weiss, the kingdom of God according to Jesus was wholly supernatural and transcendent. It would come only by a decisive act of divine intervention. The coming of the kingdom would be sudden, universal, destructive, and transforming. Jesus' eschatology was radically dualistic: "The kingdom of God is a radically superworldly entity which stands in diametric opposition to this world" (Weiss, 114). Although Weiss's futurist absolutism was modified by subsequent scholarship, he had drawn attention to strong evidence in the Gospels that is only capable of sustaining a futurist interpretation (e.g., "Your kingdom come!": Matt. 6.10).

Second, Jesus' eschatology included a crucial element of present realization. A bold reversal of Weiss's theory was attempted by C. H. Dodd with his theory of "realised eschatology." In *The Parables of the Kingdom* (1935, rev. ed. 1961), Dodd argued that the central text concerning Jesus' proclamation of the kingdom, Mark 1.14–15, should be translated: "The kingdom of God has come." Dodd claimed that Jesus intended to proclaim the kingdom of God not as something to come in the near future, but as a matter of present experience. The kingdom was not merely imminent, but had arrived. Dodd insisted that, in the life and death of Jesus, the kingdom of God had come without remainder (cf. Matt. 12.28). There was no outstanding eschatological agenda to be fulfilled. Dodd was seconded by T. F. Glasson's *The Second Advent* (1945, 3d ed. 1963). Glasson argued that Jesus did not teach a futurist eschatology in any sense—though the evangelists, influenced by Pauline ideas (for example, in 1 Thess.), interpreted him as doing so. As far as Glasson is concerned, we have to discount both Paul and the evangelists in order to arrive at the original—entirely realized—eschatology of the New Testament.

Third, the future and present aspects in Jesus' eschatology are not in conflict but in tension: they are dialectically related. W. G. Kümmel (1961), among others, attempted a position that mediated between the future (Weiss) and present (Dodd) aspects of the kingdom in the teaching of Jesus. The kingdom was neither remotely future nor entirely present, but imminent. For Kümmel, Jesus expected the kingdom soon, say within a lifetime, but not immediately. Kümmel rules out both purely futurist and purely presentist interpretations. Kümmel frankly admits that Jesus was mistaken about the imminence of the kingdom. He discards eschatology and collapses the kingdom into the person of Jesus. Kümmel takes up a mediating position between futurist and presentist interpretations.

A similar compromise is found in E. P. Sanders's restorationist eschatology. Sanders believes that Jesus looked for the imminent direct intervention of God in history, the elimination of evil and evildoers, the building of a new temple, and the reconstitution of Israel. He finds evidence of both present and future references, and if forced to choose, would put the emphasis on the kingdom as immediately future. Sanders does not think that present and future references to the kingdom refer to two aspects of the same reality.

A more dialectical and theologically fruitful concept was developed by J. Jeremias, who spoke of "an eschatology in process of realisation." This points to the notion of an inaugurated eschatology: already impinging, unfolding now, but with a future agenda of some sort still to be revealed.

The eschatological horizon of the New Testament seems to rule out any intention on the part of the historical Jesus to found the Christian Church as a structured organization spanning the centuries. But it does not preclude the possibility that Jesus entertained a purpose for his followers after his death—indeed, it calls for it. Texts such as Luke 12.35 ("Be dressed for action and have your lamps lit") and Mark 10.39 (where Jesus foretells that James and John will come to share his sufferings) show that Jesus saw a role for a community of his followers after his death (Rowland). Jesus' proclamation of the kingdom involved a particular community. This sparse conclusion cannot in itself provide a basis for the developed ecclesiology of the Christian Church, which must be constructed, if at all, on more indirect and sophisticated grounds than a direct appeal to the supposed intention of the historical Jesus. However, the eschatological horizon of the New Testament, far from inhibiting all ecclesiology deriving from Jesus himself, actually demands a particular form of it. For biblical eschatology (taking the intertestamental period into account also) includes the idea of the messianic community of the last days, the gathered elect, the faithful remnant, who will be the instrument of God's saving purpose for the world.

A. Loisy said that Jesus foretold the kingdom and it was the Church that came. Although Jesus looked for the reign of God in a renewed heaven and earth, where human beings would be as the angels in heaven, loosed from carnal and earthly ties, the movement that emerged after his death and resurrection consisted of a miscellaneous collection of men and women who were patently mortal, sinful, and implicated in the ways and means of the world, whose common life was significantly determined by human and social factors and developed in a diversity of ways. This fact is incompatible with any simplistic appeal to a God-given pattern for the Church and its structures, whether they are papal, episcopal, or presbyterian. How do modern theologians respond to this dilemma?

Jesus and the Church in Modern Theology

Reflection among modern Roman Catholic theologians on the question, "Did Jesus found the Church?" inevitably takes its cue from Loisy's *The Gospel and the Church* (1902). Loisy argued that it was the kingdom of God, not the Church, that Jesus was concerned with. It was certain, he argued, that Jesus did not provide systematically for the constitution of a Church established on earth and destined to endure for many centuries. However, Loisy believed that the Gospel of the kingdom entailed social and organizational implications. These were the seeds from which grew the great tree of the

[Roman] Catholic Church. Although Jesus foretold the kingdom, it was intentional that it was the Church that came.

Partly as a result of the debate that Loisy generated, Catholic theology—Anglican as well as Roman—has undergone a development that has moderated traditional Catholic claims that Jesus Christ explicitly instituted the Church as a visible, structured society with officers who were at first the apostles and subsequently those ordained by them in personal succession. For Roman Catholics, of course, Peter and his presumed successors, the popes, have been preeminent among these officers.

K. Rahner (1904–1984) claimed that the Church was indeed founded by Jesus and is not merely self-validating. In the light of the eschatological horizon of the New Testament, Rahner was unable to claim that the essential structures of Catholicism—the episcopate and the Petrine office—could be traced back to the words or deeds of the historical Jesus. His tactics then were twofold. First, he argued that there is a genetic connection between the historical structures of later Catholicism, such as the papacy and the historic episcopate, and the developments of the formative apostolic period. Second, he set out an a priori argument, drawing out what is entailed in uncontroversial basic theological axioms, to show that the salvation announced by Jesus entailed a corporate dimension that corresponded to an essential characteristic of human nature—namely, that it is grounded in interpersonal communication. Religion therefore could not be based on mere subjective human experience, but must confront us with objective authority. So Rahner was able to claim that the hierarchical Church with an authoritative (and under certain conditions, infallible) teaching office (magisterium) sprang from the very essence of Christianity (Rahner, 322–344).

E. Schillebeeckx, on the other hand, abandoned even Rahner's subtle and sophisticated reinterpretation of the divine foundation of the Church's structure. Schillebeeckx pointed out that it was clear historically that Jesus did not intend to found a new religion or even a new community. He addressed the whole of Israel (symbolized by the twelve apostles), and the earliest Christians were conscious of being simply a community within the fold of the Jewish Church. It is, Schillebeeckx says, historically untenable and a sign of ideological fundamentalism to claim, as many Christians still do, that the historical forms of the Church can be derived from Jesus' own institution, and that the historical and contingent growth of the Church represents a necessary development willed by God. However, Jesus certainly did intend, according to Schillebeeckx, that there should be faith in his message that led to communal discipleship. So Schillebeeckx seems to be saying: if we cannot claim that the Church was founded *by* Jesus, we can at least insist that the Church is founded *on* Jesus (Schillebeeckx, 154ff.).

G. Tavard seems to side with Schillebeeckx in adopting a minimalist interpretation of Jesus' intentions for the Church. The institution of the Church as a social and spiritual entity cannot be traced directly to the recorded words of Jesus. Tavard concedes that the formation of a distinct community by his followers did correspond to Jesus' intention. But it remains hazardous to claim that his intention was explicitly formulated in his teaching. So the idea that Jesus instituted the Church is to be taken "with a grain of salt" (Tavard, 31, 50).

The Protestant theologian F. D. E. Schleiermacher (1768–1834) located the Church's raison d'être in the realm of feeling ("piety")—a consciousness of God mediated by the redeeming work of Christ. The distinctive Christian form of being dependent on God is conducive to fellowship or communion, in which believers communicate their self-consciousness through speech and so edify each other. In the Christian understanding of redemption, Christ assumes believers into the power of his God-consciousness and the fellowship of his unclouded blessedness. The inner essence of the Church, expressed in word and sacrament and focused in Jesus Christ, never varies. The outward form of the Church is subject to variation, but this is a matter of indifference. In returning in this way to the unchanging center or essence of the Church's existence, Schleiermacher could be regarded as (and certainly saw himself as) picking up again the dominant ecclesiological concern of the sixteenth-century reformers who insisted that Christ is present in the Church through word and sacrament and that these are sufficient to guarantee the authentic existence of the Church, quite apart from empirical historical continuity.

Karl Barth's (1886–1968) treatise on the Church in his *Church Dogmatics* (IV.1.62) developed the impulse of his early theology (seen particularly in the second edition of the commentary on Romans) of divine grace as intersecting the world vertically from above and as qualitatively different from all human spiritual aspirations. Barth's approach is what might be called an "ecclesiological actualism," whereby the Church emerges into existence sporadically, spasmodically, and temporarily, as it is called into being by God. The positive substance of this is that the Church is Christ's "earthly-historical form of existence." Barth was here developing Bonhoeffer's insight in his youthful work of 1930 *Sanctorum Communio* that "Christ exists as the Church." But, as Barth insisted, precisely because it is the mode of Christ's being, the Church remains transcendent. It exists only as a definite history takes place—not the history of popes, bishops, and councils, but the history of faith in the Gospel.

The Christian Church, Barth stresses, is not a human, social, and historical institution—a divine society on earth that spans the centuries—but only exists as and when it "takes place," so to speak. Therefore no concrete form of the Christian community can be as such the object of faith. Barth was highly critical of the virtual identification, which he believed he could detect in the more triumphalist forms of Roman Catholic theology, between the mystery of the Church as the Body of Christ and the empirical Church with its history, law, and organization. However, having asserted the priority of the mystical Church, Barth then goes on to insist on the imperative of concrete, visible unity that could only be attained by traditions taking their historical identity seriously and not trading it in for the sake of ecumenical goodwill. Barth comes remarkably close to Schleiermacher by insisting that the catholicity of the Church is the persistence of its true inner identity and essence through all the many changes of outward form.

J. Moltmann objects to any talk of Jesus as either the "founder" or the "foundation" of Christianity. "Founder" suggests that the Church merely looks back to Jesus, who, as it were, laid the foundation stone for what came later, so that the Church can go on its way without troubling itself to remember Jesus and his way. "Foundation" suggests the idea of Jesus laying down a quasi-legal constitution for the Church and continuing to dominate it through this his "last will and testament," but through his dead hand not his living spirit. Both ideas of founder and foundation see the Church emanating from a historical person but not from a living contemporary (Moltmann, 70f.).

Modern Anglican theology began with Charles Gore (1853–1932). His *The Church and the Ministry* (1886, 2d ed. 1889, rev. 1919) stressed historical and institutional continuity from Jesus and the apostles. Gore defined the apostolic Church as spiritual hierarchy of graduated orders. He supported this view from the Pastoral Epistles that he believed were written by Paul himself. Gore believed that Jesus deliberately planned a Church that would perpetuate his work through the centuries.

An example of the assumption that Jesus laid down a blueprint for the Church and in particular instituted the pattern of its ministry, is the claim made by the Roman Catholic Church and by some Anglo-Catholics who are opposed to the admission of women to the priesthood, that women cannot be priests because Jesus chose only male apostles. Such persons are unlikely to be persuaded by the argument that not only did Jesus not institute an all-male ministry, he did not institute an ordained ministry as such at all.

The Anglican–Roman Catholic International Commission (ARCIC) abandoned the standard Roman Catholic claim that Jesus instituted a church ruled by the apostles and their successors the bishops and presided over by Peter and his successors the popes. ARCIC acknowledged that this claim could not be supported from the New Testament or the very early Church. In its place, ARCIC proposed an appeal to God's providential government of the Church, which had seen fit to allow the office of the bishop of Rome to develop into that of universal pastor.

The Gospel of Christ and the Renewal of the Church

Movements of renewal in the Church have been marked consistently by a return to the Gospel (the "good news") and to the origins of the Church in Jesus and the apostles. In the early centuries individuals took themselves to the desert in imitation of John the Baptist and Jesus. The medieval reforming movements in the Western church, such as the Franciscans, were an attempt to return to the radical simplicity of disciples of Jesus Christ. The sixteenth-century reformers were fired by a passion for the pure Gospel that they believed had been rediscovered through scholarly, critical attention to the text of the Greek New Testament. They made the Gospel all in all and set it over against the visible Church in judgment and reformation. In his Ninety-five Theses, Luther proclaimed: "The true treasure of the Church is the holy gospel of the glory and the grace of God." For Luther, the Church is constituted by the living presence of Christ effected through the words and sacraments of the Gospel. Where the Gospel is found, Christ is present, and where Christ is present, the Church must truly exist.

In the middle decades of the twentieth century, the biblical theology movement, the liturgical renewal movement, and the ecumenical movement all pointed the Church back to its origins in the Gospel of God. In one of the finest expressions of this theological renewal, Michael Ramsey's *The Gospel and the Catholic Church* (1936), the future archbishop of Canterbury looked back to the Reformation and asserted that its themes of the word, faith, and grace were truly Catholic: "These are Catholicism's own themes, and out of them it was born." The Church and its structures are inseparable from the Gospel. The doctrine of the Church is included within the knowledge of Christ crucified.

The mid-twentieth century theological renewal inspired the ecumenical movement and ensured that the World Council of Churches, when it came into being in 1948, was founded on the Gospel and centered on the person of Christ. As a fellowship of churches that confess the Lord Jesus Christ as God and Savior, the WCC has a Christological focus and pursues a Christological method. A memorandum drafted by Archbishop William Temple, inviting churches to become members of the proposed council, affirmed that the council stood on faith in the Lord Jesus Christ as God and savior and that this basis was an affirmation of the Incarnation and the atonement. The evangelical and Christological method of the ecumenical movement was restated at the second assembly, at Lund in 1952: as we seek to draw closer to Christ we come closer to one another.

Ecclesiological renewal was also taking place in the Roman Catholic Church. The Second Vatican Council (1962–1965) saw the Church as founded on the Gospel of Christ. Jesus inaugurated the Church by preaching the good news, the coming of God's kingdom. By preaching the gospel, the apostles gathered together the Church. The Church is a miracle of divine grace, created by the preaching of the Gospel. Christians are incorporated into the Church through baptism. The Eucharist forms and builds up the Church. Hans Küng's *The Church* (1976) was an exposition of the ecclesiology of Vatican II and at the same time a radicalization of it. We can only know what the Church should be now if we know what the Church was originally. The Church must return to its origin, to Jesus and his Gospel.

The Groupe des Dombes has recently called on the churches to find their true identity in continual conversion to God as they heed anew the call of Christ in the Gospel. More fundamental than our identity as members of the Church, and certainly much more fundamental than our identity as members of a particular confessional tradition, is our identity as those who respond to Christ's call in the Gospel to be converted. This conversion is required by the coming and the resurrection of Jesus Christ.

Paul Avis

See also: Barth, Karl; Bonhoeffer, Dietrich; Church; Essence of Christianity; Kingdom of God; Luther, Martin; Schleiermacher, F. D. E.; Schweitzer, Albert

References

Knox, John. 1963. *The Church and the Reality of Christ*. London: Collins.

Kümmel, W. G. 1961. *Promise and Fulfilment: The Eschatological Message of Jesus*. London: SCM.

Küng, Hans. 1976. *The Church*. London: Search.

Meyer, Ben. 1979. *The Aims of Jesus*. London: SCM.

Moltmann, J. 1977. *The Church in the Power of the Spirit*. London: SCM.

Perrin, Norman. 1963. *The Kingdom of God in the Teaching of Jesus*. London: SCM.

Rahner, Karl. 1978. *Foundations of Christian Faith*. London: Darton, Longman and Todd.

Rowland, Christopher. 1985. *Christian Origins*. London: SPCK.

Schillebeeckx, Edward. 1990. *Church: The Human Story of God*. London: SCM.

Tavard, George. 1992. *The Church: Community of Salvation: An Ecumenical Ecclesiology*. Collegeville, MN: Liturgical Press.

Weiss, Johannes. 1971. *Jesus' Proclamation of the Kingdom of God*. London: SCM; Philadelphia: Fortress.

Wright, N. T. 1996. *Jesus and the Victory of God*. London: SPCK.

Eliot, T. S. (1888–1965)

T. S. Eliot is one of the twentieth century's most accomplished, devout, and orthodox Christian poets. Yet Eliot did not think of himself as a religious poet, and the absence of any direct writing on the person of Jesus, whether in poetry or prose, strengthens his case. Even those poems that are considered his most religious are not so much about Jesus as concerned with other people who struggle with the implications of the birth and death of Jesus in their lives.

Born in 1888 in St. Louis, Missouri, Thomas Stearns Eliot came from a highly respected New England family who were steeped in the piety of Unitarianism, a liberal congregational theistic tradition that did not require of its members a belief in the core Christian doctrine of the Trinity. Eliot's grandfather William Greenleaf Eliot was one of the great American preachers of the nineteenth century, and his mother, a frequently published poet, wrote mostly on religious themes. In 1915 he married Vivienne Haigh-Wood, who suffered repeated bouts of mental illness and drug addiction, eventually causing the couple to live apart until her death. After Eliot's conversion to Christianity in 1927 at the age of thirty-nine, he became a harsh critic of Unitarianism and any attempt to make Christianity appear "reasonable" by diluting its traditional doctrines. In his mystical faith he was deeply influenced by the conservative Anglo-Catholic tradition of the Church of England.

Eliot embodied in his poetry and life the existential dilemma faced by intellectuals in the early twentieth century. But in 1910, while walking near Harvard University, he had a mystical experience in which light and silence overwhelmed him and seemed to suffuse the entire world. The traces of this experience are evident thirty years later in sections of the *Four Quartets* (1943).

Trained as a philosopher, Eliot was deeply frustrated by the modern tendency to separate philosophy from the study of religion, which he felt must be interrelated. Thus his concern for metaphysics and his highest regard for

Dante and Lancelot Andrewes, whose literary creations reflect so fully the philosophical systems that they devoted their lives to studying and following. Nevertheless, in 1917, a decade before his conversion, Eliot's doctoral dissertation made clear his belief that the subjective world of consciousness was the only sphere of truth. The struggle to apprehend the doctrines of the Church would take many years.

Many regarded his conversion in 1927 as a betrayal, coming as it did several years after the publication of the bleak but magnificent poem *The Waste Land* (1922). But even in his earliest poems Eliot was consistently writing on the themes of redemption, suffering, and sacrifice, as well as the faith of the saints and martyrs. In his fourth *Prelude* (1912) an insomniac man on his bed, amid a thousand sordid images, clings to "the notion of some infinitely gentle, infinitely suffering thing." Early drafts of *The Waste Land* contained a significant passage on the resurrection of Jesus that Ezra Pound, in his role as editor, advised be cut.

Significantly, the poem *Gerontion* (1919) was at one point considered by Eliot to be a prelude to *The Waste Land*. In *Gerontion* Eliot uses one of his favorite Christological sources, the writings of Lancelot Andrewes. In this still early poem, Eliot's diagnoses and judgment of the world are entirely biblical. In the world, though the Word made flesh struggles to speak, it could become a terrifying and rejuvenating power. Other works of this period—such as *The Hippopotamus* (1917) and *Mr Eliot's Sunday Morning Service* (1918)—treat the institutional Church with derision, but scenes from the life of Christ and reflections of Jesus as the Word or *Logos* of God are kept in sharp contrast.

The Waste Land is seen by many to be a diagnosis of the spiritual state of Western civilization. It is a poem of judgment, which, for Eliot, retains the possibility of new life at the end. In the final part of the poem, "What the Thunder Said," Jesus appears first in the Garden of Gethsemane and then on the road to Emmaus. Critics such as Lyndall Gordon have made the connection that the biblical paradigm for salvation comes through the Exodus experience: one only arrives at the Promised Land by first going through the Waste Land. She sees *The Waste Land* in a genre similar to nineteenth-century spiritual autobiographies with which Eliot's mother and grandfather were so familiar.

For more than ten years Eliot had read the works of Dante and Andrewes and meditated on the Incarnation, ultimately concluding that sin is an objective condition of humankind from which an objective saving act is necessary. He had known since his years as a philosophy student that orthodox Christianity stood or fell on belief in the fact that Jesus Christ was the Son of God and actually born of a virgin. In 1926, while in St. Peter's Church in Rome, Eliot shocked his family by falling to his knees in front of a *pietà*. One year later he would astonish his closest friends by announcing his conversion, after the fact, having been baptized and confirmed in secret. Part of his reticence was the result of his fear of being out of step with his friends—Ezra Pound, Virginia Woolf, and the rest of the Bloomsbury Group, who were deeply antipathetic to Christianity and on whom Eliot depended heavily for approval and support.

His first postconversion poem, *Journey of the Magi* (1927), is not a confident confession of personal faith, but a dramatized meditation on the ambiguity of life and death, which were both so clearly present in the mind of a Magus who encountered the Christ-child. The fusion of birth and death forms the climax of the discovery that the Magi had made. This paradox of Incarnation, in which the temporal world is ruptured by eternity, is the crux of Eliot's faith. "Only through time is time conquered," he writes in *Burnt Norton*, one of the *Four Quartets* (1936–1943). Rarely does Eliot address Jesus directly apart from the *Logos* Christology of the Gospel of John and the Neoplatonist philosophers. Eliot reaches out to an unknowable God through the *via negativa*.

The hope that stands over against the wrong turnings and missed opportunities—global and personal—that are addressed in the *Four Quartets* is that the coming of Christ breaks the existential cycle that he describes in *East Coker* (1940) as one of "eating and drinking, dung and death." In *East Coker* one gets a rare glimpse of the benefits of Christ's Passion when he appears as "the wounded surgeon" who applies the scalpel to the diseased parts so that, "beneath the bleeding hands we feel / the sharp compassion of the healer's art." But the cure (salvation) is not complete until the sickness grows worse. For Eliot, the discovery in *Little Gidding* (1942) is that behind the appearance of absurd suffering it is possible that a charismatic pattern of love exists. The love is a purgative power, symbolized by fire. It is the inability to be detached from one's life and the world that blinds humanity from the truth. For Eliot it is Christ who shows the way that through death alone, the ultimate detachment, can one grasp the fullness of life.

D. W. Peck

See also: American (North) Christianity; Dante Alighieri; John, Gospel of; Literature, English; Spirituality

References

Bergonzi, Bernard, ed. 1969. *T. S. Eliot: Four Quartets*. London: Macmillan.
Eliot, T. S. 1971. *The Complete Poems and Plays*. San Diego: Harcourt Brace Jovanovich.
Gordon, Lyndall. 1998. *T. S. Eliot: An Imperfect Life*. London: Vintage Random House.
Williamson, George. 1967. *A Reader's Guide to T. S. Eliot*. 2d ed. London: Thames and Hudson.

English Christianity, Medieval

Theological and devotional appreciations of Jesus are central to understanding the cultural and spiritual life of any Christian society. This applies as much to England between 1066 and the Reformation as to anywhere else. Jesus was part of the general cultural baggage, as shown by his frequent invocation in late medieval vernacular letters.

The Norman invasion and conquest of 1066 fundamentally changed England's relations with the rest of the Catholic Church, integrating it much more firmly than before into Continental movements. After 1066 England was unavoidably affected by the transformations of Continental Catholicism caused by the growth of the papal monarchy, a revolution in monasticism, and the new intellectual climate of the twelfth-century Renaissance. In later centuries, Continental links and influences continued to affect English religion at all levels. Following the rise of the universities in the twelfth century, English scholars regularly studied theology at Paris (at least until c. 1300); Continental spiritual and devotional currents were constantly being imported, and English trends exported. The complex interdependencies and interrelationships within Catholicism make it hard to see Jesus' role in England's theological, spiritual, and devotional history in distinctly insular terms between 1066 and the Reformation; it is almost impossible to discern a specifically "English" Jesus.

Nevertheless, there were some specific developments. It was in his early years as Archbishop of Canterbury, between 1095 and 1098, that St. Anselm developed his resolution of the major issue in salvation history, "Why did God become Man?" (*Cur deus homo?*), rewriting understanding of the process of redemption to make Christ's sacrifice an act of satisfaction to God the Father in atonement for the Fall, to replace the idea (dating from the late fourth century) that it was a payment to the Devil in recompense for being deprived of his rights to humankind in perpetuity. However, while Anselm's reformulation significantly transformed theological understanding, it did not automatically sweep the board. English theologians in later centuries, like their Continental colleagues, still responded to the question of salvation in terms of "the devil's rights."

Theological understandings were essentially academic and intellectual; for most English people their relationship with Jesus was less intellectualized, more devotional. Throughout the later Middle Ages it was essential to that relationship that God had become Man: medieval Catholicism as a religion centered on the fact of Incarnation. Yet that same religion also emphasized Christ's sacrifice: while posited on the fact of Incarnation, at its heart was the fact of Passion, that Christ had died in the welter of pain and suffering that was the crucifixion, an event of such magnitude that it could not be comprehended. The Passion dominates late-medieval English attitudes to and relationships with Christ, as portrayed through affective (or emotional) piety.

The spiritual and devotional relationships established with Christ were many and complex. They usually resist any attempts to make them explicitly "English" in any sense other than their being recorded in English or in England. One of the most important devotional texts of the fifteenth century, Nicholas Love's *Mirror of the Blessed Life of Jesus Christ*, was in essence a translation of a Continental Latin work, wrongly attributed to St. Bonaventure but interpolated to make it a vehicle for resistance to the contemporary English heresy of Lollardy. The process of importation affected the chronology of influence: difficulties of communication and textual reproduction meant a time lag in England's adoption of some Continental trends. Thomas à Kempis's *Imitation of Christ* (originally produced around 1420) was first translated into English around 1450 but became widely available only after

1500; some of the mystical Jesus feasts, including the Transfiguration, had not fully taken root when Henry VIII broke with Rome.

The incarnate Jesus offered a potent devotional focus, in his life as a whole, or in particular aspects of it. His life might be treated as part of the full history of salvation, as in the lengthy thirteenth-century poem, *Cursor mundi*, which integrates Christ's life into a world history from the Creation to the Apocalypse. In the various cycles of mystery plays Christ's life fits into the overall retelling of biblical history from Creation to Last Judgment. English writers throughout the later Middle Ages produced a range of texts that recounted Christ's life in whole or in part, and at varying length, to stimulate mental and affective involvement. They often focused specifically on the Passion. However, although the Passion was important, as the leading element in a widespread tradition of affective piety, it did not totally overshadow other phases of Christ's life. Nicholas Love's text, for instance, covered the whole life, and it or a similar text perhaps stimulated the imagination of Margery Kempe in the early fifteenth century, for whom Christ's humanity was reflected in boy children and young men. The concreteness of the incarnational emphasis was important: Margery Kempe's quasi-autobiographical account of her religious experiences reveals a very homely, human, and conversational relationship with Christ. When she experienced her mystical marriage with the Godhead it was in a state of fear—she could cope with Christ in his humanity, but the Godhead was overwhelming.

Passion devotion emphasized the enormity of Christ's self-sacrifice, its pain and humiliation, as a focus for meditation. It also integrated contemporary chivalric mentalities, with Christ being seen as the Lover-Knight and the Passion as a joust with death and the Devil. Manuscript illuminations and woodcuts depicted the *arma Christi*, the instruments of the Passion, as objects for imaginative meditation. A quantitative approach to spirituality totted up indulgences acquired for reciting prayers before images like those of Christ as Man of Sorrows, or a *pietà* (an image insecurely located in Christocentric and Marian devotion). Likewise, medieval calculation constructed devotional routines around the five wounds (a very specific and ubiquitous devotional focus), and the number of lashes in the scourging, or of drops of blood shed by Christ during the Passion. Christ was seen as blood-soaked and blood-drained (the latter graphically described in the mystic Julian of Norwich's recollection of her initial vision of Christ as the prelude to her Showings).

Rendered pictorially, such devotions challenge modern sensibilities and squeamishness, yet they had a real meaning, in deepening a sense of the scale of Christ's self-sacrifice for humanity. One representation of this, which is markedly if not exclusively English, is the "charter of Christ," in which Christ identifies his terrestrial sufferings in a charter of manumission for humanity. For his was a death with a purpose. One reaction should be empathy, in mental reenactment and personal involvement with the events of Christ's terrestrial life (again revealed strikingly in the recollections of Margery Kempe). Another should be gratitude: an awareness of the debt that humanity, collectively and individually, owed to the self-sacrificed incarnate deity.

Modern squeamishness is often also repelled by the verbal expression of medieval English devotional relationships with Christ, which respond to the Passion in terms that often seem blatantly erotic. This strand pervades medieval devotional mystical writing. In the twelfth century, it was expressed in the Passion meditation written by Aelred of Rievaulx for his sister as she prepared to become an anchoress and separate herself from the world. In the fourteenth century, it is stated most emphatically in some of the lyrics of Richard Rolle, one of that small group usually identified as the "middle English mystics."

While providing an important stimulus to affective piety, Jesus also influenced other medieval English religious practice. The Seven Corporal Acts of Mercy (see Matt. 25.31–46) were seen as addressed to Christ reflected in ordinary humans. In particular, Christ's Passion infused all seven sacraments. Stained glass windows and manuscript illustrations link the crucifixion to each of the sacraments through the blood flowing from the suffering Christ. The link was most clear in the Mass: at its heart was the symbolic repetition of Christ's sacrifice in the act of consecration, which according to the doctrine of transubstantiation promulgated at the Fourth Lateran Council (1215) marked a substitution of the body and blood of Christ for the preexisting bread and wine of the unconsecrated elements. That in turn encouraged the late-medieval devotion to Corpus Christi. Yet the Mass was much more than a mere reenactment of the Last Supper: medieval deconstructions made it a veritable reenactment of the complete Passion, with each movement and gesture by the celebrant, each article of his clothing, meant to stimulate participants and onlookers by their specific symbolic evocations. Consecration and transubstantiation, by making Christ actually present, allowed all involved in the celebration, laity and clergy, to establish direct and personal contact with divinity. Instructions to the laity about their behavior during the Mass sought to channel devotion appropriately, directing thoughts firmly toward Christ, as in the *Layfolks' Mass Book*. The totality and complexity of such symbolic reading of the Mass as a representation of Christ's life was exemplified, on the eve of England's Reformation, in *The Interpretation and Signification of the Mass* (originally issued in Flemish in 1509 and published in English translation in 1532). As part of its extensive commentary, this tract divided Christ's life and the Mass jointly into three sections. The first, covering Christ's life from Nativity to Passion, was recapitulated in the early stages of the Mass, through to the preface and sanctus. The second section saw correspondence between the period from Passion to resurrection and that segment of the Mass lasting from the sanctus until the priest had received the sacrament. Finally, the remainder of the Mass through to its end signified Christ's time on earth from the resurrection to the ascension.

Such mental reenactment in the Mass was encouraged in other devotions. The Hours of the Cross used the sevenfold division of the daily divine office as the skeleton for a sectionalized meditative Passion devotion. The scheme appears frequently in Books of Hours, with versions also being anglicized to allow greater participation.

Devotion to Jesus was also reflected in other ways. In the fifteenth century, several guilds and fraternities were founded in his honor, including the guild of the Name of Jesus in St. Paul's Cathedral, London. In the early sixteenth century this became one of England's leading fraternities, with nationwide membership. Other Jesus guilds included those founded in the cathedrals of York and Lichfield. The Jesus Mass also became one of the most popular Masses, with priests being appointed specifically for its recitation.

Relics also stimulated devotion. In the thirteenth century, England gained three important cult sites based on portions of Christ's blood: at Westminster, Hailes, and Ashridge. (Other places, such as Norwich Cathedral, also possessed Holy Blood relics, but did not promote them to attract pilgrims.) The origins of these relics were obscure, with some suggestions that the blood was not a relic of the actual crucifixion, but resulted from a eucharistic miracle (to prove the transubstantiation of the wine into blood) or had been produced from a miraculously bleeding crucifix. Westminster, which did explicitly claim that its blood was a relic of the crucifixion, fared worst of the leading English Holy Blood sites. Of the three, Hailes became the most important. Its relic was acquired in 1270, and thereafter Hailes was a major shrine and pilgrimage center until the sixteenth century. With the Reformation, and the attack on shrines and superstition, the Hailes relic was publicly vilified as a forgery and destroyed in London to eliminate its power.

There is considerable evidence to support assertions that late-medieval English spirituality became increasingly Christocentric. This evolution may have paved the way for part of the fundamental religious transformation at the Reformation. As the theological emphasis shifted from the Gospels and the incarnate Christ to the epistles (especially the Pauline texts), and to a Christianity with a more intellectualized view of Christ's role and relationship with humankind, so a climate was created that would permit Reformation. The importance of Jesus and his Passion would not be undermined by these changes, but their meaning would transform.

R. N. Swanson

See also: Anselm; Bonaventure; Eucharist; Incarnation in Contemporary Analytic Philosophy; Jesus, Death of; Julian of Norwich; Kempis, Thomas à; Roman Catholicism; Transfiguration

References

Anselm, St. 1974–76. *Cur deus homo* ["Why God Became Man"]. Pp. 39–137 in *Anselm of Canterbury*. Edited by Jasper Hopkins and Herbert Richardson. Toronto and New York: Edwin Mellen.

Beckwith, Sarah. 1993. *Christ's Body: Identity, Culture and Society in Late Medieval Writings*. London: Routledge.

Bennett, J. A. W. 1982. *Poetry of the Passion: Studies in Twelve Centuries of English Verse*. Oxford: Clarendon.

Glasscoe, Marion. 1993. *English Medieval Mystics: Games of Faith*. London and New York: Longman.

Marx, C. W. 1995. *The Devil's Rights and Redemption in the Literature of Medieval England*. Cambridge: D. S. Brewer.

Ross, Ellen M. 1997. *The Grief of God: Images of the Suffering Jesus in Late Medieval England*. New York and Oxford: Oxford University Press.

Rubin, Miri. 1991. *Corpus Christi: The Eucharist in Late Medieval Culture*. Cambridge: Cambridge University Press.
Sargent, Michael G., ed. 1992. *Nicholas Love's Mirror of the Blessed Life of Jesus Christ: A Critical Edition Based on Cambridge University Library Additional MSS 6578 and 6686*. New York and London: Garland.
Spalding, Mary C. 1914. *The Middle English Charters of Christ*. Bryn Mawr College Monographs, Monograph Series 15. Bryn Mawr, PA: Bryn Mawr College Press.
Vincent, Nicholas. 2001. *The Holy Blood: King Henry III and the Westminster Blood Relic*. Cambridge: Cambridge University Press.

English Christianity, 1500–1750

Catholics and Protestants both agree that salvation depends on Christ, but disagree about how men and women share in the benefits of Christ's work. Between 1500 and 1700 arguments about the relationship between Christ and his Church dominated English religious life. In 1500, England was a Catholic country with a faith that concentrated on the human sufferings of Christ and on the Mass, in which individual Christians were incorporated into Christ. New learning was sharpening biblical studies but did not significantly change that faith. The Protestant Reformation, in the 1530s, swept away images of the suffering Christ. There was a greater emphasis on knowing Christ through Scripture then, and rather less was said about sharing in Christ through Communion. Catholics held up Christ's sufferings as an example to the faithful, urging them to join in the great work of human redemption. Protestants talked of the Cross of Christ in order to remind Christians that this was the price that he alone could pay for their sin. After the Protestant Reformation, human beings were left with little to offer to God. By the close of the sixteenth century, Puritan writers were insisting that all religion rested on God's sovereign will, and the work of Christ was pushed to one side. Critics of Puritanism wrote passionately about the Incarnation and the Communion service, and the argument escalated in the years before the Civil War. Puritan views triumphed in that war, but by the end of the seventeenth century there was a new and very different stress on holy living that gave men and women a more active faith but threatened to undermine Christ's work in a different way, by giving too much attention to the way men and women can help themselves.

In 1500, the figure of Christ crucified was set firmly before the English people. The Cross and its victim (known as the "rood") were seen in parish churches across the country, high above the chancel screen. The faithful would kneel at Mass, quite literally at the foot of the Cross, and there they were encouraged to brood over the pains that Christ endured. The anonymous poem *Woefully Arrayed* gives a glimpse of the devotion offered there: "Remember my tender heart-root for thee brake, With paines my veines constrained to crack. Thus was I defaced."

Christ's human suffering was central to English religious life. Each year, on Good Friday, the events of the Passion were rehearsed in the parish with barefoot creeping to the Cross and the "burial" of a consecrated host in an Easter sepulchre (there is a good example surviving at Heckington in Lincolnshire).

One of the most popular images in late-medieval England was of the Mass of St. Gregory, a vision of Christ appearing over the altar at Mass surrounded by the implements of the Passion. At the Mass, English Christians consistently made the connection between Christ broken on the Cross and the host broken at the altar. Each Mass was another Calvary in which the faithful received Christ's broken and risen body and prayed to be made like Christ. Devotion to Christ in the sacrament was so intense as to irritate Cranmer, who objected to the enthusiasm for seeing the host elevated: "[T]hey worshiped that visible thing that they saw with their eyes and took it for very God" (Cranmer, 442).

English Catholics in the early sixteenth century also insisted that Christ was judge of the sinful. They pictured him seated, watching the archangel Michael weigh souls, while Mary and John pleaded for the righteous and demons clamored. At Wenhaston in Suffolk, and in many other places, the rood stood against a huge "doom" painting of the day of judgment. Elsewhere, as in Fairford in Gloucestershire, the same scene was depicted in the west window. Even in these scenes, though, it was still made clear that Christ was a human being, and his hands showed the marks of the nails. Christ was worshipped as savior and judge, but popularly he was known best as part of the human family, one of our kith and kin, our "brother," as Bishop John Fisher put it.

The windows at Fairford and those at King's College, Cambridge, were based on designs found in a medieval text known as the *Biblia Pauperum*. This book paired each scene from the life of Christ (except for his unique death) with an Old Testament parallel. Thus at King's, above the annunciation and Mary's obedience, is a picture of the Fall and Eve's disobedience, while above the Last Supper are the Israelites fed with manna in the wilderness. The Old Testament scenes were known as "types," and this approach is thus known as typology. Christ's life had been interpreted in this way for generations, but by the 1520s new learning and different ways of interpreting Scripture were becoming fashionable. Textual studies became more critical and more acute. Even so, the old stress on Christ's humanity and our need of his help were sustained. Fisher, Bishop of Rochester, who eagerly promoted new learning, could still insist that the human body was "a sachell full of dunge." He urged penitence and tears, described the pains of purgatory with urgency, and depended on Christ and the sacraments to save him. In a famous Good Friday sermon on the crucifix, Fisher suggested that the Cross is a "book" we must read (an idea made familiar by Richard Rolle and others): "Seest thou not his eyes, how they be fylled with blood and bitter teares? Seest thou not his eares, how they be filled with blasphemous rebukes. . . . O most unkinde sinner, all this he suffred for thy sake" (Fisher, 400).

Fisher, More, Colet, and other devout Catholics were all steeped in this piety. In that sense their attachment to Christ had a deeply medieval character. They coupled this piety, though, with modern scholarship and with a passionate desire to share their learning with others through the printing press and preaching.

The Protestant reformers of the early sixteenth century were brought up in this same culture. In 1549 Hugh Latimer, bishop of Worcester and soon to be a Protestant martyr, preached a detailed account of the agonies of Christ memorably calling them "the scalding house." Catholics would say the same, but there was a difference. Latimer, Cranmer, and the other reformers wanted to teach Christians that no amount of such piety and penitence would help them. Protestants never tired of explaining that we are justified by faith alone. In principle the reformers had nothing new to say about the person of Christ, but they understood what he had achieved in a new way, removing all sense of human contribution to our salvation. Their real interest was in showing the extent of human sinfulness and arguing that we must depend on God who alone can rescue men and women from depravity. In practice, though, because they said so much about sin, they had to say a great deal about the remedy for sin, and that caused them to pay an even greater and possibly narrower attention to the Cross than their Catholic critics. So, *The Sermon of the Misery of all Mankind*, from the Protestant *First Book of Homilies* (1547), concludes:

> We have heard how that, of ourselves and by ourselves, we are not able either to think a good thought, or work a good deed: so that we can find in ourselves no hope of salvation, but rather whatsoever maketh unto our destruction. Again we have heard the tender kindness and great mercy of God the Father toward us, and how beneficial he is to us for Christ's sake.

Thus theology was dominated by talk of sin and redemption. Joyful meditation on the wounds of Christ, which had been a means of access to his loving heart, was swept away. The rigorous insistence that salvation comes from Christ and is not worked by us shut down any piety that hinted at human effort or achievement. In the Catholic Mass Christ had been made present and had drawn close. Now, in *The Book of Common Prayer* (1549 and 1552), the faithful stopped praying that the bread and wine might become the body and blood of Christ and stopped thinking about his physical proximity. Faith was what mattered; Christ came only in faith, and even then only to the truly faithful.

Catholic prayer books, called primers, had insisted that men and women can become part of Christ's body. The prayer *Salve salutaris hostia* asked: "May You be my head, that I may remain in You, and You in me." The *Book of Common Prayer,* in 1549, said something similar, for example, in the collect for the Sunday next before Easter: "Mercifully grant, that we may both follow the example of his patience, and be made partakers of his resurrection." Even so there was a subtle change of language. Cranmer put more emphasis on the fact that Christ saves us and less on the fact that we share his life. He also preferred to think of the faithful as the servants of God rather than as children of God and brothers and sisters of Christ, as in the collect for the Third Sunday in Lent: "We beseech thee, Almighty God, look upon the hearty desires of thy humble *servants*."

Protestant Reformation proceeded with the destruction of rood screens and images, and ended the rituals of the Catholic year. It must have seemed at times that Christ had been driven away from daily life. On the title page of *The Great Bible*, first published in 1539, the central figure is King Henry VIII, and Christ can only peer over his shoulder as the great work of reformation goes on. It was this Great Bible that Cranmer, the first Protestant archbishop of Canterbury, intended to put in the place of the old devotion. Scripture was the heart of the matter for the Protestant reformers. William Tyndale translated the New Testament, and in his Preface called it the "covenant made with us of God in Christ's blood." The reformers believed that the English Scriptures were not just a book of words, but God's power and Christ's salvation. So England got to know Christ as the word of God and words themselves became more and more important. The English Reformation was a change carried forward partially by force but also by preaching, and soon the attention to word produced outstanding writers and preachers.

John Donne (1572–1631) was a convert from Catholicism who gave powerful expression to Protestant ideas about human sinfulness and need. He turned to Christ as his only hope:

> I have a sinn of feare yt when I have spun
> My last thred, I shall perish on the shore.
> *A Hymn to Christ*

In "Goodfriday, 1613, Riding Westward," however, Donne made it clear that Christ is not just the remedy for sin (though this is profoundly important to him); he describes Christ crucified as someone that imagination strains to understand:

> Could I behold those hands which span the poles,
> *And turne all spheares at once, peirc'd with those holes?*

Donne's was a distinctive voice. In other Protestant writers the stress was different. Donne wrote about the mystery of God and revelation in Christ. Others, usually called "Puritan," wrote about the sovereignty of God and salvation in Christ. The Cross was central, but not, as it had been in Catholic writing, as a stimulus to devotion and a call to grieve over Christ's sufferings. Now Christ was described as the only one capable of saving us, and his Cross was set before Christians to require them to acknowledge their need. Richard Sibbes memorably drew upon the preaching of John the Baptist to lay bare our absolute need of Christ: "The first condition of men whom he has to deal withal is, that they were bruised reeds, and smoking flax; not trees, but reeds; and not whole, but bruised reeds" (*The Bruised Reed and the Smoking Flax* I).

At its best this Puritan writing had real intensity that brought believers to the foot of the Cross and set Christ firmly before them. It also contained a massive emphasis on the doctrines of election and predestination. As a consequence, some Puritan writers seemed to suggest that the life and work of Christ were merely the necessary consequence of decisions God made before the foundation of the world. Here the stress on human dependence on God reached its logical conclusion. Everything hinged on God's decisions. So it became almost commonplace to argue that Christ did not die for all people, but only for the elect (because Christ could not be said to have died in vain for one whom God had not predestined to salvation). In the writings and preaching of men like William Perkins (1558–1602), the work of Christ was utterly subordinated to the decrees of God.

This approach was not universally welcome. A generation after John Donne another poet, George Herbert (1593–1633), wrote about the passion of Christ and made again the connection between Calvary and the Eucharist.

> Love is that liquor sweet and most divine,
> Which my God feels as blood; but I as wine.
> ("The Agony")

The same point is made again in the most famous of Herbert's poems, which presents Christ as a loving savior gently coaxing a sinful soul not to the Cross, but to the altar for Communion:

> *Let my shame*
> Go where it doth deserve.
> And know you not, says Love, who bore the blame?
> My dear, then I will serve.
> You must sit down, says Love, and taste my meat.
> So I did sit and eat.
> ("Love III")

So, while one group of English Protestants concentrated on the salvation that Christ won for human beings who can do nothing for themselves, another group paid increasing attention to the Incarnation and to Christ's abiding presence in the world and in the sacraments. Puritans, interested in predestination, thought Christ important because he revealed the eternal purposes of God. Others brought Christ rather closer to home. In an immensely influential book produced in this period, *The Laws of Ecclesiastical Polity*, Richard Hooker (1554–1600) insisted that human nature is Christ's "own inseparable habitation" (V.54.5). Like George Herbert, Hooker believed that humanity and divinity meet in the Eucharist, which "invisibly yet really work our communion or fellowship with the person of Jesus Christ" (V.67.11).

In Lancelot Andrewes (1555–1626), one of the most powerful and charismatic figures in the Jacobean church, there was an almost identical emphasis. His sermons on the Nativity and Incarnation are now famous.

> He was *Christus anonymous*, "Christ unchristened," as it were. "For his name came not till He became One 'with us' in person. . . . And then, name the Child, and give Him this name 'Immanuel.' For thus He was a right 'Immanuel,' truly 'with us.'" (*Sermons of the Nativity*, 47)

He too made the connection that Hooker made between the theology of Incarnation and the doctrine of the Eucharist and urged a devotion that participated in Christ through Communion.

Differences of opinion and approach become impossible to contain. In the 1630s and 1640s the Church of England argued about altars, bowing, bishops, and a great deal more. There were also substantial and significant theological disagreements over grace, the sacraments, and election. With the triumph of the parliamentary cause in the Civil War, one style of theology became dominant and it was one that stressed the wrath of God and an absolute dependence on Christ to rescue the elect from inevitable judgment. Parliament's new prayer book, *The Westminster Directory* of 1644, emphasized "the Mortification of sinne" and "the quickening of our dead spirits." This kind of teaching was challenged at the Restoration but survived in the works of Dissenters like John Bunyan (see, for example, *Grace Abounding to the Chief of Sinners*) and, in a gentler form, Richard Baxter. At its best it had a magnificent insistence on the sovereignty of God; at its worst it set such a distance between the human Christ and the eternal Father as to collapse the doctrine of the Trinity. This was a mistake that John Milton made and expressed in the curious conversations between Father and Son in *Paradise Lost*.

After the Civil War the clergy of the Church of England, who had now seen schism and rebellion firsthand, were more anxious than ever about the dangers of human sinfulness. Intellectual argument had not changed human nature, and they put their efforts instead into preaching a practical and rather intolerant piety. In 1658 a book was published that virtually became the voice of English Christianity for the rest of the century. *The Whole Duty of Man* was an intensely practical manual that provided "rules for godly living" and urged repentance. After the arguments about grace and election, this was a welcome change of emphasis, but the disputes had not really gone away; in the universities, they raged on in the works of men like George Bull and Thomas Barlow. Holy living was all very well, but English divinity now implied that men and women could save themselves—and the role of Christ became controversial all over again. William Sherlock, for example, insisted that repentance and the love of God were the beginning of justification, a point that the Protestant reformers of the sixteenth century had always refused to concede, arguing instead that Christ alone is the formal cause of justification.

Catholics and Protestants alike had been clear that our highest hope is to be incorporated in Christ. Now the idea of some sort of mystical union with Christ came under attack as clergy insisted that salvation begins with moral action. As the clergy encouraged Christians to shake off their base nature and strive for perfection, they spoke of the powers of human reason. This tendency, coupled with the influence of Hobbes and Descartes, gave a new emphasis to the use of reason in theology. That in turn produced some important work, but also had less welcome consequences. In 1689 Arthur Bury, the rector of Exeter College, Oxford, published a book that accepted the Arian heresy, that God the Son is subordinate to God the Father. Bury was condemned, and the century ended in vigorous and vicious arguments about the person and work of Christ.

David Hoyle

See also: English Christianity, Medieval; Eucharist; Jesus, Achievement of; Jesus, Death of; Jesus, Name of; Spirituality

References

Andrewes, Lancelot, ed., and J. P. Wilson. 1841–1843. *Ninety-Six Sermons by the Right Honourable and Reverend Father in God, Lancelot Andrewes*. Oxford: Parker.

Collinson, Patrick. 1990 [1967]. *The Elizabethan Puritan Movement*. Oxford: Oxford University Press.

Cranmer, Thomas. 1846. *Miscellaneous Writings*.

Davies, Horton. 1996 [1970]. *Worship and Theology in England*. Vols. I and II. Princeton: Princeton University Press.

Dickens, A. G. 1989 [1964]. *The English Reformation*. London: Batsford.

Duffy, Eamon. 1992. *The Stripping of the Altars*. New Haven: Yale University Press.

Ford, David, and Mike Higton. 2002. *Jesus*. Oxford: Oxford University Press.

Mayor, J. E. B., ed. [1876] 1935. *The English Works of John Fisher*. Publisher unknown.

McCulloch, Diarmaid. 1996. *Thomas Cranmer*. New Haven: Yale University Press.

Mursell, Gordon. 2001. *English Spirituality*. London: SPCK.

Spurr, John. 1991. *The Restoration Church of England*. New Haven: Yale University Press.

Tyacke, Nicholas. 1987. *Anti-Calvinists*. Oxford: Oxford University Press.

English Christianity, 1750–1940

Throughout the period 1750 to 1940, Jesus was the subject of many English hymns, devotional works, full-length biographies, and works of art. In late-eighteenth-century England, Christian books about Jesus were either devotional or adopted the approach of the "harmony," which tried to explain away all inconsistencies in the Gospel accounts, in the manner that had been traditional for centuries. In the nineteenth century, depictions of Jesus were radically altered by the impact of critical thought, and some writers began to question the miraculous elements in his story. There was a new emphasis on setting Jesus in his first-century Palestinian setting, and this was also reflected in the naturalistic mid-nineteenth-century depictions of him by the Pre-Raphaelite artists. There was a large demand for devotional works on Jesus in the mid-Victorian years, stimulated by the conventions of the mid-Victorian Sunday, which many Christians devoted partly to religious reading. Their increased consumption of religious books was made possible by cheaper paper and printing. The decline in the Victorian Sunday partly explains the shrinking market for books about Jesus in the late nineteenth and early twentieth centuries, together with changing approaches to the New Testament. Although in the first half of the twentieth century leading Christian thinkers continued to write biographies and other devotional and theological works about Jesus, they were not as widely read as in previous decades. For many English Christians in the period 1750 to 1940, however, their image of Jesus remained largely based on what they derived from the Gospels, hymns, religious prints, sermons, and Sunday schools, despite the undoubted impact of religious publishing.

John Fleetwood's *Life of Our Lord*, first published in 1767, and reprinted regularly until the 1850s, is an example of a popular early life of Jesus that ignored Enlightenment rationalism. It was written in easy-to-read continuous prose, with dialogue lifted from the words recorded in the Gospels, which gave the text a sense of familiarity and authority. Authorial speculation, although not absent, was kept to a minimum. The biblical story was interpreted in its literal form. Thus the temptation of Christ was a real meeting with the Devil, not a psychological struggle, and demoniacs were literally possessed, not mentally ill. The overall impression was of a much fuller account of the Gospel episodes than that provided in the Gospels themselves. Fleetwood sometimes provided embellishments designed to make events more comprehensible. Mary, he claimed, "had long indulged the hope of being selected by God to be the honoured mother of the saviour of Israel." Fleetwood continued to be popular until well into the nineteenth century.

The growth in popularity of hymn singing among dissenting evangelicals in the eighteenth century meant that Christians began increasingly to sing about their belief in Jesus. This promoted a spirituality that stressed the immediacy and continuing power of his presence. Charles Wesley and Isaac Watts wrote many hymns that continued to be popular throughout the period reviewed here, as did William Cowper and John Newton. Hymns such as "When I Survey the Wondrous Cross" (Watts), "Lo! He Comes with Clouds Descending," "Hark! the Herald Angels Sing," and "Hail the Day That Sees Him Rise" (all Wesley) encouraged meditation on the central episodes of the life of Christ, whereas "Jesus Shall Reign Where'er the Sun" (Watts) and "Christ, Whose Glory Fills the Skies" (Wesley) emphasized his cosmic power and majesty. Other hymns emphasized the relationship of joy and intimacy between the Savior Jesus Christ and the individual believer, together with the forgiveness of sin; examples included "Jesu, Lover of My Soul" and "O for a Thousand Tongues to Sing" (both Wesley), "Jesus, Where'er Thy People Meet" and "There Is a Fountain Filled with Blood" (both Cowper), and "How Sweet the Name of Jesus Sounds" (Newton).

Hymn singing proved immensely popular among Nonconformist worshippers, and by the 1840s it was becoming widely accepted by members of the Church of England. The most notable Anglican hymn writer and translator was John Mason Neale, who consciously reacted against the subjective emotionalism of evangelical hymns by producing more restrained works such as "Christ Is Gone Up; Yet Ere He Passed." Nevertheless, much Victorian hymn writing continued in a sentimental vain, assisting the development of the "gentle Jesus, meek and mild" tradition that was initially expressed in a hymn by Charles Wesley and became deeply embedded in English understandings of Jesus. Some of these hymns were intended for children—for example, "Jesus, Good above All Other" and "Loving Shepherd of Thy Sheep"; but others such as "Jesu, Meek and Gentle" and "Jesu, Meek and Lowly" were intended to be sung by adult congregations. These hymns involved the projection of qualities the Victorians associated with childhood or womanhood onto the adult Jesus, in a manner that produced an anodyne, benign, and ultimately rather powerless figure. They reflected a strand of liberal Protestantism that was also reinforced in much of the ephemeral tract literature of the mid-nineteenth century and in many of the more substantial Victorian lives of Jesus.

The first life of Jesus to make a major impact in England was D. F. Strauss's *Leben Jesu*, which was translated into English by George Eliot in 1846. Strauss argued that Jesus' life was not simply the unfolding of a sequence of miraculous events and fulfilled prophecies, nor was it simply a chain of natural events that the Gospel writers had wrongly interpreted. Rather, the Gospels represented a type of religious writing known as "myth"—the genre of primitive religious literature in which certain events were magnified to illustrate and make sense of religious beliefs. Strauss's denial of miracles and the doubts that he cast on the reliability of the evangelists prompted a backlash from more conservative theologians, who produced a flurry of orthodox "harmony" lives of Jesus. Another, and more significant reaction came in the desire to counter Strauss by learning more about the historical Jesus, and thus making him a more multidimensional figure, set in a distinct geographical and social context. This was facilitated by travel possibilities to the Near East that began to emerge in the mid-nineteenth century. Suddenly scholars were able to visit the biblical sites for themselves and let their descriptive powers run riot as they made the imaginative leap into first-century Palestine. Such visits were now seen as an indispensable part of understanding the authentic background of the historical Jesus. This approach was epitomized by Ernest Renan, whose *Vie de Jésus* was almost immediately translated into English in 1863 and became a very widely read classic. Renan wrote the book during an extended visit to Palestine, and his evocation of the scenery, flora, and fauna of Galilee, described in vivid and elegant prose, proved immensely popular. Like Fleetwood, he was very readable, but unlike Fleetwood the Jesus he portrayed was an entirely human figure, a man of charm and charisma, of "pure and sweet beauty"; Renan's account left no room for the supernatural or the miraculous. This offended many English readers, as did Renan's suggestion that Jesus had misled people into thinking that he performed miracles and had then become the victim of his own deceptions. English theologians of all outlooks set about reasserting the inspiration of Scripture, the validity of miracles, and, most important, the deity of Christ.

Nevertheless, the next major volley in the battle over the presentation of Jesus was also fired from the side of the skeptics. The anonymously published *Ecce Homo: A Survey of the Life and Work of Christ* (1865), in fact by J. R. Seeley, professor of Latin at University College, London, caused offense on account of the ambiguity of its presuppositions. The author claimed that he was postponing all theological questions for some future volume, and he avoided the need to discuss the miraculous or nonmiraculous status of the infancy narratives by beginning his account with the baptism of Jesus. In fact, the book contained no appeals to miracle (but no denials either) and no assertions of Christ's divinity, or discussions of the inspiration of Scripture, or of the resurrection or the atonement. Greater attention was given to the exposition of Christian moral principles, a trend that continued in the following decades. Jesus was presented as a magnetic personality, with a single-minded mission to restore the fortunes of Israel. Yet the author adopted a reverential tone toward his subject, which helped to allay some fears that Seeley was just an English Strauss or Renan. The book sold 8,000 copies in the first four months and was frequently reprinted. The publication of F. W. Farrar's *Life of Christ* in 1874 marked a significant reassertion of a more traditional view of Christ. Farrar's work was scholarly, attractively written, and orthodox. It was also based on his firsthand observations in the Holy Land. Within a short time it had sold thirty editions and 100,000 copies. The Jesus portrayed by Farrar was nothing less than the Son of God and the Savior of the world. He was recognizably the same figure who emerges from the theology of Paul and who is described in the creeds of the Church. At the same time, Farrar used his descriptive powers, and his firsthand experience of Palestine, to convey the reality of Jesus' humanity and his first-century setting.

For the rest of the nineteenth century, every successful British life of Jesus was molded in the shape supplied by Farrar. Many authors turned their hand to the task of attempting to satisfy what seemed to be an insatiable demand for books about Jesus, and more literature was devoted to him than to any other sacred subject. Although the subject matter remained the same, authors varied in their approach. Some, such as Thomas Hughes, author of *The Manliness of Christ* (1879), sought to address one of the central themes in mid-Victorian religion, the debate about Christian manliness, at the same time endeavoring to combat the feminine qualities that he believed had been wrongly attributed to Jesus. He portrayed him instead as a manly warrior, doing battle with a variety of adversaries. Others, such as Alfred Edersheim, who wrote the massive *Life and Times of Jesus the Messiah* (1883), developed an encyclopedic approach to describing the details of Jesus' Jewish background.

The British public's voracious appetite for books about Jesus lasted until about 1900, when the climate changed decisively. More skeptical strands of German criticism began to make an impact, and synoptic studies became a great deal more complicated. The professional biblical scholar and the devotional writer went their separate ways, whereas the roles had previously been combined with little strain. The ideas of the deceased neo-Hegelian philosopher T. H. Green were also making an impact. He had stressed that what mattered was the idea of Christ, the God-man reconciling God and his creatures, rather than the somewhat antiquarian accounts of his historical life. There began to be a renewed emphasis on the teaching of Jesus, rather than the details of his life. Albert Schweitzer, whose influential work *The Quest of the Historical Jesus* was translated into English in 1910, was particularly responsible for casting doubt on the notion that much could be known about the historical Jesus, or that his world could be reconstructed for the modern mind. In the early years of the twentieth century, the distinction between the Jesus of history and the Christ of faith began to be made far more forcefully than before. The simple Galilean Jesus and the divinized eternal Christ started to walk in different directions, and to be studied by different people at different times. A. E. Garvie's *Studies in the Inner Life of Christ* (1907) struck out in a different direction by tracing the development of Jesus' personality, rather than the details of his life: "[E]nough is being written about the scenery, the upholstery, and drapery of the life of Jesus" (Garvie, vi). Scholars continued to publish books with titles like *Jesus of Nazareth* (Charles Gore, 1929) and *The Life and Teaching of Jesus Christ* (Charles and Eleanor Raven, 1933). These books were aimed at the general reader and might have looked as if they were in the old-fashioned lives of Jesus tradition, but in fact they took account of recent scholarly developments, asked questions like "Are our Gospels trustworthy?" and gave great attention to source criticism.

Throughout the period, the illustrations in religious books and Bibles were important sources for conveying a physical portrait of Jesus, which became embedded in the English Christian mind. John Fleetwood's *Life of Our Lord* was produced with engravings, and although the engravings differed in later editions, the iconography remained the same. Bibles were frequently illustrated, sometimes lavishly. Eighteenth-century editions such as Goadby's *Illustration of the New Testament* (1759) were expensive, but John Cassell's *Illustrated Family Bible* (1859) had more than a thousand illustrations and sold 300,000 copies a week at a penny a time. Early-nineteenth-century Bibles often favored engraved reproductions of classic artworks by Reynolds, Rembrandt, Poussin, and others. The late-nineteenth-century watercolors of William Hole also influenced the way in which generations of British Christians envisioned Jesus. The Jesus who emerged was of consistent appearance: robed, unshod, bearded, with an intense but rather agonized expression. The eighteenth-century engravings depicted a more round-faced, curly-haired Jesus, often set against imposing classical architecture. The faces of the other biblical characters tended to be drawn identically, in a way, which robbed them of personality. Later illustrations paid much more attention to facial expressions and to "authentic" backdrops, and Jesus developed a thinner face, usually with straighter hair. The Sacred Heart iconography of Roman Catholicism was also immensely popular during the nineteenth century and portrayed a tender, suffering figure, which was intended to evoke a response of compassion in the viewer.

The mid-Victorian enthusiasm for placing Jesus in his first-century Palestinian context was reflected in the art of the Pre-Raphaelites, who developed a naturalistic style that at first seemed shocking, as if showing the full implications of the Incarnation was somehow a pictorial blasphemy. Joseph's carpenter's shop was the carefully detailed background for both John Everett Millais's *Christ in the House of His Parents* (1849–1850) and William Holman Hunt's *The Shadow of Death* (1873), which was painted in Palestine. Both paintings combined elaborate symbolism with realist attention to detail, suggesting both the historical reality of Jesus and also his theological significance. The most famous and frequently reproduced depiction of Jesus was Holman Hunt's *Light of the World* (first exhibited in 1854 and engraved in 1860). Inspired by Rev. 3.20—"Behold, I stand at the door and knock," it showed Christ at night, knocking at a weed-choked, handleless door, dressed in the robes of the high priest with a crown of gold and a crown of thorns, the moon behind his head forming a nimbus. The image of Christ knocking on the door of the human heart suggested a closeness between Christ and the believer and depicted the moment at which he waits for a response. The picture, which was championed by the art critic John Ruskin, touched something deep in the popular religious imagination, and it was admired far more frequently than it was criticized. It was copied and recopied until it hung, like a visual tract, in many homes in nineteenth-century Britain. A later version of the painting was sent on a tour of the British Empire, where it was seen by seven million people between 1905 and 1907. In the twentieth century the painting fell out of favor, and Pre-Raphaelite images of Jesus began to be seen as cloying and sentimental. World War I was a decisive turning point, and interwar artistic representations were markedly different. An example is in Stanley Spencer's *The Resurrection of the Soldiers*, in which Christ sits in the middle distance, inconspicuously receiving the soldiers' crosses.

Frances Knight

See also: Art; Creeds; Enlightenment; Great War; Hymns; Jesus, Miracles of; Jesus, Origins of; Jesus in Social Context; Resurrection; Schweitzer, Albert; Strauss, D. F.

References

Carleton Paget, James. 2001. "Quests for the Historical Jesus." Pp. 138–155 in *The Cambridge Companion to Jesus*. Edited by Markus Bockmuehl. Cambridge: Cambridge University Press.

Landow, George P. 1979. *William Holman Hunt and Typological Symbolism*. New Haven and London: Yale University Press.

Maas, Jeremy. 1984. *Holman Hunt and the Light of the World*. London and Berkeley: Scolar.

Pals, Daniel L. 1982. *The Victorian "Lives" of Jesus*. San Antonio, TX: Trinity University Press.

Pelikan, Jaroslav. 1997. *The Illustrated Jesus through the Centuries*. New Haven and London: Yale University Press.

English Christianity, Modern

Christianity and the Church, both in England and indeed elsewhere, have undergone major changes since World War II, and the place of Jesus cannot be taken for granted in the popular imagination of the general public. Indeed, John Lennon said of the Beatles in 1966, "We're more popular than Jesus now; I don't know which will go first, rock 'n' roll or Christianity" (Lennon). For many people both then and now, Lennon's comments may not be too far from the truth. Sociological studies of what "ordinary" men and women believe and say about Jesus give the impression of uncertainty, confusion, doubt, and irrelevance for large numbers of self-identifying Christians, whether or not they are churchgoers. Relatively few people consciously place Jesus at the center of their lives in any significant way, or hold to traditional Christian beliefs such as the divinity of Christ (as well as his humanity), his ability to perform miracles, the virgin birth, and Jesus' physical resurrection from the dead. This article draws on social research to explore popular views of Jesus in the context of wider social change in the postwar period.

There have been numerous surveys of religious beliefs and behavior in

England since the first religious census in 1851. These usually ask about church attendance or membership, concepts of God, and opinions on moral issues, but relatively few have been more specifically concerned with popular beliefs about Jesus. This makes it difficult to get a clear picture of lay perceptions of him. Indeed, the fact that "Jesus questions" get asked so infrequently may in itself suggest that Christ is no longer considered a prominent figure in most people's worldview (Brown, 4).

The surveys that have been conducted show that whatever views people may have of Jesus, they are held in a context of decreasing Christian practice. Since the mid-1950s church membership fell from around 25 percent of the British adult population to 12 percent in the 1990s (Bruce, 37). Weekly church attendance fell from approximately 20 percent of the population to just under 10 percent in the same period (ibid., 40). Correspondingly, the number of people believing in a personal God (the traditional Christian conception of God) and Jesus as the Son of God also fell. Table 1 shows the popularity of these beliefs compared with others since the 1940s.

Table 1 Traditional Religious Belief in Britain (taken from Gill, 1999: 70)

	Percentage of British Population				
	1940s/50s	*1960s*	*1970s*	*1980s*	*1990s*
Belief					
Jesus as Son of God	68	62	–	49	–
God as personal	43	39	32	32	31
God	–	79	74	72	67
God as spirit or life force	38	39	38	39	40
Life after death	49	49	37	43	44
Heaven	–	–	52	55	52
Hell	–	–	21	26	25
Devil	24	28	20	24	26
Disbelief					
Jesus is just a man/story	18	22	–	38	–
God	–	10	15	18	27
Life after death	21	23	42	40	42
Heaven	–	–	33	35	39
Hell	–	–	68	65	66
Devil	54	52	70	64	67

Other surveys have shown that during the 1990s about 50 percent of adults agreed that "Jesus really rose from the dead" (*Sunday Times* newspaper poll of 1,500 people conducted in 1996; Brierley 1997, 2.5). And while around 57 percent of teenagers in England agreed that "Jesus is the Son of God," only 40 percent agreed that "Jesus really rose from the dead," 33 percent that they "wanted to love Jesus," 31 percent that they "knew Jesus helped them," and 26 percent that they "knew Jesus was very close to them" (based on a survey of 3,863 twelve- to sixteen-year-olds; Francis, 346). Table 2 shows the results of another teenage survey (1,090 young people aged thirteen to sixteen years, conducted in 1993 and 1994).

Table 2 Young People's Beliefs about Jesus (percentages rounded up to the nearest whole number) (taken from Collins, 1997: 288)

	Percent Agree	*Percent Not Certain*	*Percent Disagree*
Jesus is the Son of God	58	29	13
Jesus really rose from the dead	36	42	22
Jesus Christ is God	18	40	42
Jesus really did walk on water	20	46	34

These figures indicate that popular opinions about Jesus have moved away from traditional church teaching in the postwar period, but not entirely. Yet, while statistical data give some indication of general beliefs, it is difficult to know what people really mean when they agree or disagree with "Jesus statements" on a questionnaire. What does it mean, for instance, to agree that Jesus is the Son of God? What is the significance of this belief for day-to-day living? Again there is relatively little empirical evidence to be sure. The research does, however, suggest that it is wise to treat such belief statements with caution and not simply at face value. For example, many more people say they believe that Jesus is the "Son of God" than in a "personal God," or that Jesus was himself God (or divine). It may be, therefore, that when people agree "Jesus is the Son of God," this is more a recognition of a cultural title than a statement of faith within a wider Christian framework.

The research also shows that uncertainty and confusion underlie many of the belief statements noted in surveys, and relatively large numbers of people tick the "don't know" box on questionnaires or give a set of answers that appear internally contradictory at least from an orthodox Christian perspective. A study conducted in the 1940s commented: "Of those who attend Church of England services regularly or intermittently, one-quarter do not believe in an after-life—on the other hand one-fifth of those who don't go to church at all do believe. Of those who don't believe in a Deity or are agnostic nearly a quarter tend to think that Christ was "something more than a man"; on the other hand, a rather larger proportion of Church of England churchgoers say he was *only* a man. Of those who say he was only a man, one in five also say they believe he was born of a virgin. But of those who attend Church of England services one in four doubt the doctrine of the Virgin Birth, and only one in three give quite definite assent to it" (Mass Observation, 18).

Similarly, a study carried out in the 1980s of religious attitudes among white, working-class men and women on a housing estate in London commented: "Only about a quarter of the [24] interviewees seem to have believed Jesus was the Son of God." A naturalistic theme emerged: "I believe-like he was there." Jesus was "just an ordinary person"; stories about him "could be by Enid Blyton"; and "He might have been a madman for all they know, and they believed in him. It's like that Billy Graham, because everyone believes that he's something really good, don't they?" . . . There was also an ethical theme, and even an ethical analogy: Jesus was God "for all the good work he's done" (Ahern, 112).

The uncertainty and fragmented nature of beliefs about Jesus is indicative of a broader move away from traditional Christian teaching. This is largely a consequence of church decline, since up until the mid-1950s the Church had managed to keep the traditional Christian narrative alive among the general population. The 1960s, however, saw a sharp decline in church affiliation as people became disillusioned with old institutional authorities, and new technological, political, intellectual, and social developments opened up alternative worldviews. Communications and information technology, ease of travel, and the expansion of higher education gave people (particularly young people) the time and resources to think about other religious and philosophical traditions. Consequently, the late 1960s and 1970s saw the development of a range of new religious movements with an Eastern influence. Alongside this, liberal theological ideas that challenged and reinterpreted traditional church teaching in line with modern philosophy, science, and social scientific perspectives began to make their way into public discourse. For example, Bishop John Robinson's controversial book *Honest to God* (1963) was readily accessible to a large readership. While relatively few people were directly affected by non-Christian new religious movements or liberal theology beyond what they read in the newspapers, these developments helped to undermine the plausibility of traditional beliefs.

More significantly, the 1950s and 1960s saw the beginning of mass consumerism and the development of the leisure industry, which competed with church commitments. Increasingly people began to define themselves in terms of what they spent their money on and did in their spare time outside of work and church. The introduction of the contraceptive pill and general liberalization of moral values also made church teaching appear outdated for many people. By the 1980s and 1990s Christianity had itself become a consumer choice. Beliefs, including those about Jesus, came to be adopted on a more selective and individualistic basis.

In short, the 1960s marked the beginnings of a cultural change that continued to develop through subsequent decades, and largely sidelined Christianity and Jesus in the popular imagination. Consequently, the memory of Jesus has faded among the 37 million people (65 percent of the population; Davie, 48) who still call themselves Christian. Hornsby-Smith refers to the uncertain, selective, and heterodox nature of beliefs that have emerged as a result of this cultural shift as "customary Christianity": "derived from 'official' religion but without being under its continuing control . . . the beliefs and practices that make up customary religion are the product of formal religious socialisation [children are still taught about Jesus in schools, public holidays continue to nominally mark the life of Jesus, and so on], but subject to trivialization, conventionality, apathy, convenience and self-interest" (Hornsby-Smith, 90).

General beliefs about Jesus held by many lay Christians over the last fifty years have therefore largely been confused, uncertain, and irrelevant to daily life. There are, however, some exceptions among committed Christians of all denominations. A minority have worked out a coherent view of Jesus based on developments in modern, sometimes liberal, theology. Others have stood against the tide and held onto more traditional beliefs about Jesus. Numerically the most significant group in the latter category are evangelical Christians from various denominations. While all major Christian churches have declined, evangelical congregations have declined at a much slower rate and now constitute the most striking type of churchmanship in English Christianity (Brierley 2000, 150). This is potentially very significant for lay perceptions of Jesus, because the evangelical tradition places a heavy emphasis on an individual's "personal relationship with Christ"—the idea of being "born again" is central. To be a Christian within an evangelical framework it is not enough simply to be born into, and brought up in, the Church; Jesus cannot be taken for granted. Rather, the believer has to make a conscious, individual decision of commitment to Christ. This is reflected in a distinctive type of language used within evangelical circles that keeps the name of Jesus very salient in day-to-day talk. For example, people talk about "accepting Jesus into their hearts," "coming to Christ," and so on. There is some evidence that such phrases enable evangelical believers to discuss openly their faith and Jesus in a way that might be difficult or even embarrassing in other Christian circles (Stringer, 156–157). This means that many believers locate their identity squarely in relation to Jesus, and as a person he is central to their lives. As one young evangelical put it, Jesus is "probably the best friend that I've got really, because he's always there for me and he always listens and he died for me, which is an amazing thing. Even if I'd been the only person on earth he still would have died for me" (Collins, 75).

What people believe and say about Jesus in contemporary English Christianity at a "grassroots" level is, therefore, multifaceted. On the one hand, most people do not know what to believe and do not give him much thought. Yet Jesus remains a part of English culture and periodically attracts attention (for example, the National Gallery's millennium exhibition *Seeing Salvation* generated considerable interest, attracting an average of 5,002 visitors per day [Thorpe]), and even "customary Christians" may pray to Jesus in times of crisis. On the other hand, a smaller number hold Jesus very central to their lives and relate to him on a very personal, almost "familiar," basis. To summarize, the collapse of traditional Church authority from the 1960s onward has located Christian belief in a "spiritual marketplace" subject to individual choice, selectivity, and personal interpretation. This has resulted in a greater commitment to Jesus for some Christians, but wider uncertainty, doubt, and indifference about him for many more.

Sylvia Collins

See also: English Popular Culture, Modern; Film; Jesus, Miracles of; Jesus, Origins of; Mary; The Media; Resurrection; Son of God

References

Ahern, Geoffrey. 1987. "'I Do Believe in Christmas': White Working-Class People and Anglican Clergy in Inner-City London." Pp. 73–133 in *Inner City God*. By Geoffrey Ahern and Grace Davie. London: Hodder and Stoughton.
Brierley, Peter. 2000. *The Tide Is Running Out: What the English Church Attendance Survey Reveals*. London: Christian Research.
———, ed. 1997. *UK Christian Handbook: Religious Trends No. 1, 1998/99 Edition*. London: Christian Research.
Brown, Callum G. 2001. *The Death of Christian Britain*. London: Routledge.
Bruce, Steve. 1995. *Religion in Modern Britain*. Oxford: Oxford University Press.
Collins, Sylvia. 1997. "Young People's Faith in Late Modernity." Ph.D. dissertation, University of Surrey, Guildford.
Davie, Grace. 1994. *Religion in Britain since 1945: Believing without Belonging*. Oxford: Blackwell.
Francis, Leslie J. 1992. "Christianity Today: The Teenage Experience." Pp. 340–368 in *The Contours of Christian Education*. Edited by Jeff Astley and David Day. Great Wakering, UK: McCrimmon.
Gill, Robin. 1999. *Churchgoing and Christian Ethics*. Cambridge: Cambridge University Press.
Hornsby-Smith, Michael P. 1991. *Roman Catholic Beliefs in England: Customary Catholicism and Transformations of Religious Authority*. Cambridge: Cambridge University Press.
Lennon, John. 1966. *London Evening Standard*. 4 March.
Mass Observation. 1948. *Puzzled People*. London: Gollanz.
Stringer, Martin D. 1999. *On the Perception of Worship*. Birmingham, UK: University of Birmingham Press.
Thorpe, Vanessa. 2002. "Why Art Is the Nation's Big Draw." http://www.observer.co.uk/uk_news/story/0,6903,639987,00.html (accessed 22 July 2002).

English Popular Culture, Modern

In modern English popular culture, representations of Jesus play a deeply contested role, subject to many incompatible interpretations. Portrayals of Jesus have played such an important part so many times in the complex cultural evolution of the West that any modern representation of him cannot avoid a messy inheritance of diverse expectations, sensitivities, and questions. In such a context, there is no such thing as a standard or normal or inoffensive public portrayal of Jesus. He can be portrayed at one moment as the representative of established religious or moral institutions, at another as the bearer of a challenge to those institutions, and at yet another as the representative of a religiousness or spirituality to which those institutions are irrelevant. Any public portrayal of or reference to Jesus within popular culture cannot avoid being caught in such multiple fields of sensitivity and expectation, and is almost bound to generate unexpected responses as its meaning is refracted through them. To trace the full story of the deployment and reception of any one portrayal of Jesus would thus involve becoming fluent in many opposing discourses, and the story will almost inevitably be one of meanings passing like ships in the night. Nevertheless, in various ways this ongoing contest of interpretations has a tendency to reproduce itself: many of the most obvious forms of portrayal of

Jesus feed off or are reinforced by forms to which they are apparently thoroughly opposed.

Survey

If we take "Jesus in modern English popular culture" at its broadest, it refers to all representations of or allusions to Jesus in expressive forms dispersed widely around English society in the present or recent past. Even to catalog the media in which relevant portrayals might be found, from T-shirts to television and Christmas cards to computer games, would be a mammoth task, and no comprehensive study of the field exists. Nevertheless, a good many of the representations of or allusions to Jesus in modern English popular culture fall into four broad categories, according to the main purposes that they appear to serve.

The Sensational Jesus

Some representations of Jesus in popular culture explicitly relish the contested nature of the field. These are portrayals of Jesus that seek dramatically to strip away pious and ecclesial interpretations and lay bare the true, and utterly incompatible, reality underneath. Very often drawing on the rhetoric (if not always the expertise) of scholarly historical criticism—while sometimes setting themselves against the supposed vested interests of the guilds of professional scholars—such portrayals deliberately try to shock, upset, or challenge. Timothy Freke's and Peter Gandy's best-seller, *The Jesus Mysteries: Was the Original Jesus a Pagan God?* is a good recent example. For some of these sensationalist portrayals, "Jesus" is nothing but an invention of spiritual need or institutional power (see, for instance, Phyllis Graham's *The Jesus Hoax*); for others an original, innocent Jesus has been made to bear the sins of the Church and awaits rescue (see, for instance, F. P. Rout's website, "The Search for the Real Jesus"). Sometimes the aim appears to be primarily the debunking of Christianity; at other times the aim is to claim Jesus for some other group or project (see, for example, Misha'al ibn Abdullah's website "What Did Jesus Really Say?" or Tin Htut's "Is Jesus a Buddhist?"). Many milder portrayals, such as the supposed computerized reconstruction of Jesus' face on BBC Television's April 2001 program *Son of God*, play on similar sensational possibilities of unconventional portrayals.

Such sensational portrayals cannot be thought of simply as battling against more conventional representations, however. To a certain extent, the presence of these sensational portrayals in the public sphere calls forth responses or reassertions, thus indirectly increasing the numbers of more conventional portrayals and to some extent setting some of the terms that those portrayals use.

The Radical Jesus

Many portrayals of Jesus can be found in popular culture that have their origin in the attempts by various individuals or groups to reform or purify Christianity. Such portrayals are often presented amid a rhetoric very similar to that of the sensational Jesus just described: calls for a return to the *real* Jesus, calls for the uncovering of a long-hidden Jesus; but whereas the sensational portrayals emerge from an atmosphere of debunking or rejecting Christianity, these radical portrayals appear initially as a call for faithful authenticity.

There are, of course, any number of different versions of "authenticity": the authenticity of biblical literalism, the authenticity of historical criticism, the authenticity of personal relationship, the authenticity of political activism, or the authenticity of Jewish roots, for example. The portrayals that most obviously fit this description in contemporary English culture, though, most often emerge from what has been called the "postevangelical" movement or the alternative worship scene: a tendency within existing denominations or at their fringes and beyond that is in part fed by attempts to reevaluate a broadly evangelical Jesus along more socially and culturally radical terms. An example at the fringes is the web magazine *Stranger Things*, which described itself as the "lovechild of pop culture and ultimate reality," and which described Jesus as "the most seditious of all"; in the Christian mainstream, the Churches' Advertising Network (CAN)'s 1999 "Meek. Mild. As If. Discover the Real Jesus" posters aped a familiar icon of Che Guevara.

That poster illustrates another feature of this category of depictions, however: the tendency, once the group or movement responsible for the portrayal begins to develop a public identity of its own beyond the simple fact of reaction, for its portrayals to shift from primarily being challenges to well-established Christian groupings to being representatives or champions of newly established ones. The CAN poster's slogan finished "Come to Church, April 14."

The Proselytizing Jesus

Many portrayals of Jesus that find their way into popular culture are the result of one or another form of Christian mission: they are placed in the public sphere deliberately by Christian groups for the purposes of evangelism. As a result, in modern English popular culture the Jesus encountered is very often a proselytizing Jesus, part of the self-presentation and advertising of some Christian grouping or other. The most visible versions of this are often—though by no means always—from the evangelical wing of English Christianity, whether that be from very conservative evangelicals (see, for example, "The Revelation Website"), or from more moderate groups (such as the "Jesus Christ: Saviour of the World" site). In many of these evangelistic representations of Jesus, it is clearer than elsewhere that the identification of Jesus is deeply entwined with the relevant group's self-definition: Jesus becomes a standard-bearer for the group, and the one to whom the boundary-policing of the group is referred. For the more conservative of these groups, the portrayal tends to be inseparable from a denunciation of many aspects of popular culture media (see, for example, the "Blessed Hope Ministries" website and its Harry Potter page). On the other hand, many portrayals of Christ dedicated to Christian mission represent Christian identities, which are markedly more porous and less conflictual (compare "The Revelation Website" or "Blessed Hope Ministries" with "Webjesus," for instance, and compare both with "Jesus in the City").

There is a strange alliance between many of these portrayals of Jesus and the sensational portrayals described above. Proselytizing representations of Jesus are often couched in apologetic terms, and often explicitly framed as rebuttals of the skeptical messages of sensational portrayals. In turn, these proselytizing portrayals are often precisely the kinds of depiction of Jesus that the authors of sensational portrayals are most eager to debunk. The argument between the two tendencies has an internal dynamism; it reproduces itself constantly, with each side feeding and being fed by the other. Many of the radical portrayals of Jesus described above are also similarly fed by their opposition to the less subtle proselytizing portrayals: they work precisely by trying to rediscover a gap between Jesus and the group identity that he is being made to serve.

The Devotional Jesus

Even if they are consumed very largely by members of various Christian groupings, the presence on shop shelves and window displays of worship CDs and devotional books meshes with the presence of church poster boards and churchyard statues, half-remembered school assembly hymns and prayers, glimpsed religious programs at Easter and Christmas, repeated exposure to Thought for the Day on BBC Radio 4, and hundreds of other forms to ensure that thousands of devotional images of Jesus find their way into popular consciousness and form part of the visual and aural background of popular culture.

It is difficult even to begin to summarize the actual content of devotional portrayals of Jesus, and two initial comments will have to suffice here. On the one hand, it seems to be the case that many of the newer devotional portrayals of or references to Jesus that become publicly visible, but that clearly emerge from genuine individual or communal devotional practices, belong to a broadly evangelical piety: they focus on personal relationship to Jesus as friend, guide, and savior (see, for instance, the "Our Devotions" website or think of WWJD—"What Would Jesus Do?"—bracelets). On the other hand, swamping all other forms of devotional portrayals of Christ within popular culture is that vast body of devotional or pseudodevotional material we call religious kitsch, whether it be cheap postcards of Jesus of the Sacred Heart, plastic statues of the Virgin and Child, or a range of watches named after Jesus (see the "Jesus Watches" website or the "Ship of Fools" "Gadgets for God" pages).

One effect of all this is that, for all the contesting and proselytizing surrounding representations of him, Jesus continues in modern English popular culture to have an unmistakable aura of sanctity or holiness, or at least a suggestion of deep personal commitments that should not be toyed with. This does not, of course, mean that in English popular culture everybody feels bound to submit to that ban; indeed, one of the ways in which this devotional background becomes visible is precisely when it is transgressed. The naming of a band "Creaming Jesus," for instance, still has the power to generate disapproval or distaste—not simply among those who have an explicit commitment to Christianity, but also among those who feel that something important is being cheapened for the sake of personal publicity. In this way, the presence of devotional portrayals of Jesus feeds the sensational portrayals that gain energy from trying to puncture or rubbish them; at the same time, the overwhelming profusion of kitsch itself feeds portrayals of the radical Jesus, as some seek to recover the difficult, challenging Jesus from underneath airbrushed layers of sentimentality.

Sources

Typing "Jesus" into one of the larger Internet search engines, and restricting the results to domains registered in the United Kingdom, yields a very diverse list of websites in which many of the other media or expressive forms that make up popular culture are represented. Such a search on Google (http://www.google.com) in January 2002 yielded 273,000 such websites, many of which described or advertised books, television programs, films, organizations, magazines, and consumer goods of various kinds. The results of such a survey are, of course, ephemeral, like the popular culture they represent: some of the websites listed among the sources below (drawn from among the first 100 or so relevant sites returned) will very likely have vanished by the time this article is read, and their places will have been taken by others. All websites are cited as accessed on 20 January 2002.

Mike Higton

See also: Art; Media, the

References

Anonymous. 2001. "Jesus Christ: Saviour of the World." http://www.lordjesuschrist.co.uk

Brown, Chris. 2001. "Webjesus." http://www.webjesus.co.uk/

Churches' Advertising Network. 1999. "Easter Campaign 1999." http://www.ely.anglican.org/advertising/

Davie, Grace. 1994. *Religion in Britain since 1945: Believing without Belonging.* Oxford: Blackwell.

Ford, David F., and Mike Higton. 2002. *Jesus.* Oxford: Oxford University Press.

Freke, Timothy, and Peter Gandy. 2000. *The Jesus Mysteries: Was the Original Jesus a Pagan God?* London: HarperCollins.

Gaston, Leslie C. "Blessed Hope Ministries." http://www.bhm.dircon.co.uk

Goodnews Internet Church. 2001. "Our Devotions." http://www.devotions.co.uk

Graham, Phyllis. 1974. *The Jesus Hoax.* London: Leslie Frewin.

Htut, Tin. 2000. "Is Jesus a Buddhist?" http://web.ukonline.co.uk/buddhism/jesus.htm

ibn Abdullah, Misha'al. 1996. "What Did Jesus Really Say?" http://www.ummah.org.uk/jesussay/

Jackson, Wayne. 2001. "The Revelation Website." http://www.revelationwebsite.co.uk

Jesus Watches. 2001. "Jesus Watches." http://www.jesuswatches.co.uk

Jungle Records. 2000. "Creaming Jesus." http://www.jungle-records.demon.co.uk/bands/creamingjesus.htm

Miller, D. 2001. "Christianity Deconstructed #5: Worship." In *Stranger Things.* http://www.strangerthingsmag.com/deconstructed5.html

Rout, F. P. 2001. "The Search for the Real Jesus." http://www.therealjesus.co.uk

Storey, John. 1997. *Cultural Theory and Popular Culture.* London: Prentice-Hall.

Strinati, Dominic. 1995. *Introduction to Theories of Popular Culture*. London: Routledge.
Tomlinson, David. 1995. *The Post Evangelical*. London: Triangle.
Urban Mission Congress. 2002. "Jesus in the City." http://www.jitc.org.uk

Enlightenment

The Enlightenment is the modern English name for a social and intellectual transformation, whose chief religious consequence was that the figure of Jesus Christ and the vast system of ideas and institutions that had grown around his story as told in the Bible lost much of the political and cultural influence that they had built up in Europe during the medieval period. This upheaval took place between the sixteenth century, during the European Renaissance and Reformation, and the French Revolution. It happened because increasing numbers of people, inside and outside the churches, began to question the value of traditional authority, whether written or spoken, classical or Christian, in the areas of government, science, and religion. There was a developing cultural crisis that became acute in the eighteenth century and that generated a partially new, less Christian social order. The cultural change toward a secular society was decisive and has never been reversed. The American (1776) and French (1789) Revolutions, for example, left no specific role for either Jesus or the Christian churches in the political system. When orthodox theologians wrote about Christ they found that the authority of the Bible, the Fathers, and tradition was declining. In the long run the ethical teaching of Jesus came to matter more than its broad theological context. The prestige of Newtonian science obliged universities in Europe and the Americas to modify curricula that for centuries had combined Christian theology and scholastic Aristotelian philosophy. The New Testament narratives about Jesus were historicized—that is, treated like any other historical documents, a process that continued through the nineteenth century and removed much of the supernatural aura that had surrounded the figure of Jesus, though there was no concerted campaign to reduce him to a mythical figure comparable to the old Greek and Roman deities.

A further source of the Enlightenment's reconsideration of the work of Jesus was the new information about the rest of the planet that exploration and trade were making available: more and more became known about other religions and cultures, so that even in Europe Jesus lost some of his preeminence and became in some circles one of a group of major religious figures. According to the ecclesiastical interpretation of what had happened since 1500, preaching the Gospel of Jesus had softened the hearts of barbarians and savages in South America, for example, and had made it possible to lift them into a superior, Christian culture. Eighteenth-century commentators like the French philosopher Charles de Montesquieu (1689–1755) regarded the developments brought about by the introduction of the religion of Jesus as also involving loss and alienation.

These changes did not mean that there was a single "enlightened" attitude to the figure of Jesus Christ. But whereas for a seventeenth-century orthodox Roman Catholic theologian like Blaise Pascal (1623–1662), the one true religion, Christianity, was revealed through the mission of the divine-human Jesus Christ to a world that would otherwise have remained tragically ignorant of the way of salvation, by the end of the eighteenth century the sophisticated treated Jesus as one possible source, and that human and fallible, of religious insight and teaching. Instead of accepting Jesus' authority as final, they preferred to trust their own minds, which most of them still believed had a supernatural origin, as the proper source of information about the kind of behavior that was required of them, and to think of religion in practical terms rather than in terms of dogma, ritual, and ecstatic experience. Above all, they began to think positively about the pursuit of happiness in this life, a subject about which Jesus had said little in comparison with what he said about the happiness of the saved. A powerful ascetic tradition, established in the first five centuries of the Christian era, had interpreted Jesus as saying that people should give up the world: increasingly, people felt entitled to embrace it without loss of moral status. The burning of witches stopped, and belief in the recorded miracles of Jesus declined.

At the intellectual level much of what happened had precedents in the classical skepticism of men like Michel de Montaigne (1533–1592), in the philosophical materialism of a small group of late-sixteenth- and seventeenth-century Italian and French "libertines" or freethinkers, and in the intense intellectual life of later seventeenth-century Protestant Holland, which sheltered exiles like the pantheistic Jewish philosopher Benedict Spinoza (1632–1677) and the skeptical Calvinist Pierre Bayle (1647–1706). Such writers pleaded, without much initial success, for greater official toleration of philosophical and religious diversity in Europe; the churches found it hard to reconcile this attitude with what they understood as Jesus' exclusive claim to be the Way, the Truth, and the Life.

A more general demand for intellectual freedom broke through in England in the 1690s, as the country started to recover its balance after a long period of social and religious division that had led to civil war. Radical material published in England was circulating in Europe by the 1720s, usually in manuscript for safety, and a second wave of critical thought appeared in France; the movement, as one may call it by that time, spread to Germany and Italy by the middle of the century and had affected all of Europe by 1789. In England the radicals were influenced by the new picture of the universe that Newtonian science offered and by the theology of John Locke (1632–1704), who sought to reduce the demands of Jesus' teaching to a slender minimum that might unite instead of divide all sensible men. Neither Newton (1642–1727), who was obsessed with calculating the date of the second coming of Jesus, nor Locke advocated the traditional doctrine of the divinity of Christ, though both still accepted Jesus as having a high degree of religious authority—and the former showed himself a biblical literalist in areas that would later be surprising.

A more anti-Christian wave of feeling, whose origins were as much social as theological, passed through the next generation of English radicals, for whom Jesus became a specific target. Anthony Collins (1676–1729), for example, rejected the traditional claim that one of the proofs of the truth of

Christianity was that Jesus fulfilled Old Testament prophecy; he also dismissed the New Testament stories that attributed miracles to Jesus as the product of human invention and superstition. At the heart of this radical criticism of the biblical account of Jesus was the rejection of the story of his resurrection. For Collins, Jesus was no more than a religious teacher who had started a new sect that had happened to prosper.

At their mildest the radicals, who were usually called deists by their opponents, regarded Christianity as one of the many varieties of a basic natural religion that a God closer to the mind of Locke and Newton than to that of Pascal had made available to all mankind, but that had been perverted by priesthoods for their own profit. When Matthew Tindal (1657–1733) said that the essence of Christianity was as old as the creation, he meant that Jesus had not been the bearer of a unique revelation. Such writers echoed Locke in their rejection as irrational of the dogma of the original sin of Adam and Eve and of the alleged divine condemnation of the human race based on it, and they therefore dismissed as superfluous the orthodox picture of Jesus Christ as the God-man who alone was able to save humanity from eternal punishment, a scale of retribution that the radicals dismissed as out of all proportion to human wickedness. The situation differed in France because there religious nonconformity was still persecuted for much of the eighteenth century, and so a major concern of the French radicals was to reduce the great wealth and political influence of the Roman Catholic Church and to end its active religious censorship of thought and publication. The activities of Jesus Christ as described in the New Testament were criticized in order to weaken the authority of the Church. The French materialist Denis Diderot (1713–1784), for example, dismissed the Temptation Narrative, according to which Jesus Christ, the Son of God, had been tempted by the Devil, as a story worthy of the Thousand and One Nights. When he wrote this in 1762, Diderot was drawing on a campaign against the historical truth of the Temptation Narrative and against the existence of the Devil, which already went back to the Holland of the 1690s.

This steady and often contemptuous eighteenth-century French attack on the value of the whole Bible, in which Voltaire (1694–1778) played a leading role, helped to marginalize the influence of Jesus on the modem development of Western, and in the longer run global, culture, as well as to undermine the intellectual standing of the Church. This general reaction against the authority of Jesus was supported from the late seventeenth century by the growth of new techniques of biblical scholarship, which combined research into the text and meaning of the New Testament with a radically fresh approach to what was now seen as the complex history of its production.

In Germany, for example, in the mid-eighteenth century, the distinguished Hebraist H. S. Reimarus (1694–1768) showed that it was possible to find two historical layers in the Gospels, one that reflected a primitive tradition about Jesus and showed that he had aimed unsuccessfully at a religiopolitical revolution in Judea, and another, later layer, produced after Jesus' death by his disappointed disciples, who rewrote history so as to refloat his mission on a spiritual basis and to throw his triumph into the future. Reimarus argued that it was still possible to detect points in the accounts at which the original intentions of Jesus showed through the work of the apostles. This interpretation of the history of the Gospel texts was published in the 1770s after Reimarus's death by the German philosopher G. E. Lessing (1729–1781): it was by no means the last reconstruction of what had happened, but it marked a significant moment in the history of the Enlightenment's campaign against the theological picture of Jesus, because no subsequent scholar was able to restore the unity of the Gospels as a supernaturally given story about Jesus who was both the Man of Sorrows and the Lamb of God. Lessing himself went further, arguing that even if the stories about the resurrection of Jesus and about Jesus himself raising a dead man to life were true, they did not logically oblige one to believe that Jesus was the Son of God. And Immanuel Kant (1724–1804), the outstanding philosopher of the period, based his argument in support of religious belief in moral action, not in the figure or teaching of Jesus as such. By the end of the eighteenth century, the Enlightenment reaction against the traditional version of the meaning of the story of Jesus had done its work. Stridency was no longer appropriate, and radical thinkers no longer denounced him as an impostor or as a fiction of the apostles: the defenders of the orthodox interpretation of Jesus had lost the struggle for the high ground of European culture, even before geology and biology had begun to transform the temporal history of both the planet and of all life upon it.

These cultural changes did not, however, entail the disappearance of Jesus from the collective European imagination, or the collapse of the Christian churches that invoked his authority to justify their existence. What tended to replace the older doctrine of a divine-human savior in popular Protestantism was a positive, uncritical picture of Jesus as a supremely human and compassionate advocate of mutual forgiveness and love, themes that themselves were implicit in some forms of Enlightenment thought—for example, in the *Testament of the Savoyard Vicar,* which Jean-Jacques Rousseau included in his novel *Emile* (1762), and in Voltaire's constant contrast between the tolerant attitudes of Jesus and the intolerant behavior of the churches. In the Roman Catholic Church the equivalent reaction was the further development of the theology and piety surrounding the New Testament figure of the Mother of Jesus.

John Kent

See also: Interfaith Thought and Relations; Jesus, Miracles of; Jesus as a Historical Figure; Reimarus, Hermann Samuel; Resurrection; Roman Catholicism; Son of God

References

Cottret, B. 1990. *Le Christ des Lumières: Jésus de Newton à Voltaire*. Paris: Editions du Cerf.

Gray, J. 1998. *Voltaire and the Enlightenment*. London: Phoenix.

Harrison, P. 1990. *"Religion" and the Religions in the English Enlightenment*. Cambridge: Cambridge University Press.

Israel, J. I. 2001. *Radical Enlightenment: Philosophy and the Making of Modernity*.

O'Higgins, J. 1970. *Anthony Collins, the Man and His Works*. The Hague: Martinus Nijhof.
Porter, R. 2001. *The Enlightenment*. Basingstoke, UK: Palgrave.
Ugrinsky, A., ed. 1986. *Lessing and the Enlightenment*. New York: Greenwood.

Eriugena, John Scotus (d. 877)

John Scotus Eriugena was an Irish scholar who first comes to notice when asked by Hincmar of Rheims to refute Gottschalk, who proposed a "double predestination" (i.e., either to salvation or to its opposite) (851). From then until his death he can be linked to Rheims, Soissons, Laon, and Charles the Bald's palace at Compiègne. Eriugena was a typical teacher of the period: teaching the arts, exegesis, and the standard theological questions. While handling these areas with originality, he stands apart from contemporaries in translating and using a range of Greek patristic sources—for example, the pseudo-Dionysius and Maximus the Confessor. However, it is upon his masterpiece, entitled the *Periphyseon* (on the division of reality) that his reputation as a distinctive theologian rests. In it he put forth a systematic theology that views all reality as coming forth from, and returning to, the transcendent source of being.

The *Periphyseon*, in five books, uses the form of the pupil interrogating his teacher about the whole of reality. This format, for Eriugena, mimics the human quest for knowledge and salvation: like the disciples around Jesus the Word. The quest is for an understanding of the relationships between all that is and is not, and within the realm of being, between the creator and the creation. Thus Eriugena sees what can be spoken of *(natura)* divided into four: (1) uncreated and creating (God); and (2) its contradictory, uncreated and uncreating (nothing); (3) created and creating (the primordial causes located in the Word); and (4) its contradictory, created and uncreating (the material universe). Divisions 3 and 4 proceed from God and have as their destiny—fulfilled in the Word incarnate—the return to God. This process Eriugena refers to as *deificatio* (rendering the Greek *theosis*). This approach has led some scholars to present him as a pantheist *antenomen;* however, this accusation fails to note both the distance he sees between God and the creation, and how he focuses on the tradition of *creatio ex nihilo*—expressed in his use of patristic Genesis commentaries. Moreover, there has been a tendency to see him solely in philosophical terms as a Christian Neoplatonist, hence his engagement with theology has not received due attention. And, because its strangeness distanced it from its own academic milieu, Eriugena's work had little impact: appreciation would suppose a systematic framework such as appeared in the twelfth century. Then, however, its form differs from Eriugena, and consequently his work raised suspicions of heresy: it was neither like recent developments nor like older works then being bypassed. Consequently, historians of theology have bypassed him, as he is not seen as a contributor to any long-running Western debates.

However, within his sacramental view of the creation—influenced by pseudo-Dionysius along with Augustine—he has a very definite Christology. Seen, above all, in the culmination of the *Periphyseon*, book 5, the whole activity of God in creation is viewed in relation to the Incarnation of the Word. This is the pivotal point of history (both of creation and salvation): the high point of creation going out from God and the beginning and means of its return. For some scholars this understanding of the Incarnation seems but an ahistorical cosmic event without concern for history, but Eriugena's scheme fails without the historical event of Jesus as the Word becoming flesh, to complete what was begun in history in Adam. Now, after the events of Eden, Christ is the signal to fallen humanity, calling it back to its source and healing human transgressions (book 3, 684A). The Word descends to redeem those created realities that have their origin in the Word (see John 1.3), and so are in him and called back to their destiny. When all creation is unified at the End, this is a Christological reality: "[T]he common end of the whole of creation is the Word of God" (book 5, 893A). In this "bringing back," because the Word assumes humanity, humanity is assumed and raised up to a union "above the things that are and the things that are not" (ibid., 895B). This whole process is foreshadowed in the Transfiguration (Matt. 17.1–8 and parallels): in communion with the risen Christ, risen humanity is transfigured to be like him; and it is offered to humanity to show that Christ is the summit of contemplation (see his prayer to Christ at ibid., 1010C).

Thomas O'Loughlin

See also: Augustine of Hippo; Glossary: *Neoplatonism*

References

Carabine, Deirdre. 2000. *John Scotus Eriugena*. Oxford: Oxford University Press.
Eriugena. 1987. *Periphyseon (Division of Nature)*. Translated by I. P. Sheldon-Williams and John J. O'Meara. Montreal: Bellarmin.

Eschatology

See Church; John, Revelation of; Kingdom of God; Second Coming of Jesus, in Current Belief; Second Coming of Jesus, Origins of

Essence of Christianity

The question of the essence of Christianity is a perennial issue for theology and one to which no agreed answer is available. It is undisputed that the essence of Christianity must have something seriously to do with Jesus, but exactly what remains a subject for debate. The term "essence of Christianity" has been employed by theologians for centuries. But nineteenth-century liberal Protestant theology saw a creative flowering of the discussion. This was partly prompted by the challenge posed by the historical-critical method of Bible study to any straightforward reading of beliefs from the text of the New Testament. More recent explorations of the issue have grappled with the question of whether a postliberal appropriation of the concept of "the essence of Christianity" is possible and fruitful.

As a point of entry into the discussion we could take the catchphrase "Christianity is Christ." This expression is a truism, a statement of the obvious, but it is also theologically teasing, almost provocative. Christianity is of course about Jesus Christ, but it is also about a great deal more. If Christianity is Christ, it has an anchorage point in history, in the fact or event of a person who lived and died (and according to Christian belief, rose again) on this earth. But the statement implies more than merely a historical reference point. It would not make sense to say: "Christianity is Jesus of Nazareth," because that would be a bare, minimally theological historical reference. Although the name "Jesus" (by way of the etymology of the Hebrew version, "Joshua") points to his work of salvation (Matt. 1.21: "You are to name him Jesus, for he shall save his people from their sins"), it does not provide a full theological identity. The title "Christ" (Messiah), however, locates Jesus of Nazareth in the faith, the hopes, and the destiny of his people. It implies that it is precisely as Jesus is received, believed in, and followed in the community of faith that he becomes the essential identifying figure of Christianity.

The problem of the essence of Christianity is raised in theological reflection at times of crisis and heart searching for the Christian faith. It may be prompted by the challenge of the claims of other religions and worldviews to the uniqueness of the Christian revelation. It may be stimulated by truth claims that are made on behalf of the physical, social, or human sciences, or on behalf of a method of philosophical analysis that appears to threaten Christian beliefs. The question of the essence of Christianity also arises in situations of interchurch conflict ("Should we really be arguing/fighting/divided over this?") or of ecumenical convergence ("What do we as churches hold in common that is greater than our differences? What bonds of communion hold us together?"). In these circumstances Christian theologians soon begin to ask: "What is fundamental, crucial, or essential in Christianity? Where does the heart, the very core of the faith lie? What makes it what it is? What is ultimately nonnegotiable in Christian belief?"

The concept of the essence of Christianity is second cousin to the notion of "fundamentals of the faith" or "the foundation of faith," debated by the sixteenth- and seventeenth-century divines, including Anglicans. "Essence" language is found in post-Reformation Protestant theology. A classic statement of it is found in the seminal Anglican divine Richard Hooker (c. 1554–1600) in his *Laws of Ecclesiastical Polity*. In discussing the unity of the Church, Hooker points to the "one Lord, one faith, one baptism" of Eph. 4.4–6 and claims that the profession of these truths "supernaturally appertain to the very essence of Christianity and are necessarily required in every particular Christian man." He comes close to asserting that "Christianity is Christ" when he proposes that "the principal thing which is believed" is "Christ crucified for the salvation of the world" and several variations on that theme. Using the metaphor of the foundation on which the Gospel is built, Hooker points to "that very Jesus whom the Virgin conceived of the Holy Ghost, whom Simeon embraced in his arms, whom Pilate condemned, whom the Jews crucified, whom the apostles preached, he is Christ, the only Saviour of the world."

The liberal Protestant discussion of the essence of Christianity begins with F. D. E. Schleiermacher (1768–1834). For Schleiermacher the touchstone of truth is not primarily intellectual or moral but experiential. Its locus is human consciousness, individual and communal. He places the question of the essence of Christianity itself between the question of the essence of religion as such ("the sense of absolute dependence") and the question of the essence of Protestantism (that the individual's relation to God precedes their relation to the Church). Schleiermacher concludes that Christianity, as a monotheistic faith belonging to the type of religion that is orientated to the moral task, is distinguished from other monotheistic, moral faiths by the fact that in it "everything is related to the redemption accomplished by Jesus of Nazareth." That redemption is accomplished in believers as they are drawn to share the God-consciousness that Jesus enjoyed.

A. Sabatier's (1839–1901) account of the essence of Christianity presupposes Schleiermacher's revolution in Christian theology that transposed doctrine into terms of consciousness or spirit. For Sabatier, the religious experience of Jesus Christ, the consciousness of God that he enjoyed, is the foundation of Christianity. The religious and moral content of his consciousness may be assimilated by our own. The spirit of Christ in our consciousness, appropriated by a faculty of spiritual discernment (faith), is of the "permanent essence" of Christianity. The focus of the essence is a "state of soul," and the primary method of theology is therefore psychological. Sabatier thus attempts to free the essence of Christianity from the constraints of scientific and historical knowledge and to locate it in Jesus' self-authenticating experience, not in any details of what may or may not have happened to him.

A. Ritschl (1822–1889) builds on Schleiermacher's work and supersedes him in the attempt to identify "the specifically peculiar nature of Christianity." In his view Schleiermacher's interpretation of the essence was not sufficiently integrated with the biblical witness to Jesus Christ. For Ritschl, Christianity is "a culmination of the monotheistic, spiritual and teleological religion of the Bible" and is "based on the life of its Author as Redeemer and as Founder of the Kingdom of God." Jesus Christ is both savior and Lord. Christianity can be seen as "an ellipse with two foci": spiritual redemption and moral endeavor, freedom, and service.

For E. Troeltsch (1865–1923) the quest for the absoluteness of Christianity is bound up with the defense of the definitiveness or absoluteness of Christianity as a revealed religion that is complete and cannot be superseded. Troeltsch's method is neither purely historical nor purely metaphysical. The relativities of history can never answer the question of the absoluteness of Christianity, because the answer must transcend the contingent historical process. But an idealist (Hegelian) scheme of the evolution of religious consciousness cannot answer it either because it is an a priori approach that sits light to the specific insights of the great religious traditions.

Troeltsch's engagement with those traditions, which he divides into religions of law and religions of redemption, results in a characterization of Christianity as the religion in which redemption is received "through faithful, trusting participation in the person-like character of God, the ground of all life and of all genuine value." Troeltsch eventually came to the conclusion that only a formal, transcendental concept of the essence of Christianity was possible, because the essence differs from one age to another and is refracted by each culture and reinterpreted within it. It could be argued that, at this point, he lost his theological grip on the determining figure of Jesus Christ.

A. von Harnack (1851–1930) represents the culmination of the "liberal Protestant" quest for the essence of Christianity. His book of that title (1900) finds it in the ethical value of the Fatherhood of God, the brotherhood of man, and the infinite value of every human soul. Harnack draws this conclusion from a particular reading of the teachings of Jesus, notably the Sermon on the Mount. It is what Jesus taught, not who he was or what he underwent, that is decisive for Harnack.

In 1902 the American Protestant theologian W. A. Brown published *The Essence of Christianity*. He argues that a succinct definition of Christianity had been required for apologetic reasons from the earliest times, in order to prove either that Christianity was religion itself (up to the Enlightenment) or that it was the ultimate, absolute religion (in Schleiermacher, Hegel, and Ritschl). The absolute religion is one that meets every human religious need and therefore does not need to be altered or superseded. Brown draws out what is already evident from the discussions of his predecessors—that no answer can be given to the question of the essence of Christianity that confines itself to Christianity. A purely internal approach to the essence of Christianity does not work. Having said that, however, Brown advocates a Christ-centered account of the essence: "It is in Jesus Christ . . . [his] life, character, authority, gospel . . . that we find the distinctive mark of Christianity." In a nutshell, it is his "transforming influence" that is the very essence of Christianity.

From World War I to almost the end of the Cold War, the essence of Christianity project was under a cloud. Its liberal presuppositions were discredited, but its questions would not go away. K. Barth (1886–1968) attacked Harnack, Ritschl, and Schleiermacher and would have found "essence" language much too nebulous. Yet even he was compelled to speak (in more positivistic language) of "the centre" of Christianity.

During the 1960s and 1970s the Anglican theologian S. W. Sykes wrestled with the legacy of liberal Protestantism, particularly with issues of historical relativism and cultural pluralism, but within a modern rather than postmodern framework that saw these issues as threat rather than promise. In his early work Sykes took as the focus of theological method "the character of Christ" within a pluriformity of expressions of Christian belief. In *The Identity of Christianity* (1984) the emphasis shifted to the character of God, as known in Christ, for it is the doctrine of God that "contextualises" the life and destiny of Jesus Christ. "The identity of Christianity is given in the identity of God." Nevertheless, Sykes believes—on account of the cultural factors that Troeltsch highlighted—that no single statement of the essence of Christianity can serve for all times. Indeed, it is not clear that Sykes is confident that any definition will meet with general acceptance at any time. Adopting an idea from the philosophy of science, he suggests that the essence of Christianity is "an essentially [*sic*] contested concept."

Sykes moves away from his mentors Schleiermacher and Barth and comes under the sway of Newman in stressing, as "a theological necessity," the need for "the maximum amount of visible continuity" in the institutional life of the Church. He finds this continuity particularly in a church's liturgy and canon law. For Schleiermacher and Barth, it was the inner life of Christianity that was unchanging. Like Luther, they sat light to its infinitely varied outward expression. It is a Catholic (Roman, Anglican, or Orthodox) preoccupation to attempt to discern visible continuity and to believe that this links the Church of today with Christ himself. The inner essence of Christianity is a typically Protestant concern; its visible identity and continuity is a typically Catholic one. The essence quest probes to the heart, the bedrock of the faith, stripping away all that is derivative and secondary. It is evangelically motivated, seeking "the pearl of great price," the true treasure of the Gospel. The identity quest, on the other hand, seeks a view of the whole; it embraces plenitude, fullness. Essence is a critical principle, prophetic, iconoclastic, reforming. Identity is an integrative principle, conservative, inclusive, consolidating.

Several aspects of the essence quest await further exploration. Is it to be found in doctrine or practice? in form or content? in origin or destiny? Can it be confined to a central focus—the person of Jesus Christ and his redeeming work—or does it ultimately entail a broad cognitive framework, the whole agenda of theology, and so come into dialogue with other disciplines and other faiths? It seems likely that the question of the essence of Christianity will continue to fascinate theologians for generations to come.

Paul Avis

See also: Anglicanism; Barth, Karl; Enlightenment; Harnack, Adolf von; Jesus, Name of; Luther, Martin; Messiah; Newman, John Henry; Schleiermacher, F. D. E.; Troeltsch, Ernst

References

Sykes, S. W. 1984. *The Identity of Christianity*. London: SPCK.
Troeltsch, E. 1977. "What Does 'Essence of Christianity' Mean?" In *Writings on Theology and Religion*. Edited by R. Morgan and M. Pye. Atlanta: John Knox.

Ethical Issues

See Ethics, Modern; Family; Jesus, Teaching of; Sexuality; War; Wealth; Work

Ethics, Modern

Jesus is primarily a problem for modern social and political ethics. Many aspects of the picture that we have of Jesus in the New Testament are difficult to apply to the modern social and political realm. The first problem is that there are passages that seem to imply a disinterest in the political realm of this world. In John's Gospel, Jesus explains to Pilate: "My kingship is not of this world; if my kingship were of this world, my servants would fight, that I might not be handed over to the Jews; but my kingship is not from the world" (John 18.36). Understanding precisely what Jesus meant by "kingdom of

God" is a matter of considerable scholarly dispute. However, at least the understanding of "kingship" in this passage in John's Gospel is not conducive to a strong affirmation of social and political ethics. The second problem is that some of the injunctions are difficult for the political ruler to implement. "Judge not, that you be not judged" (Matt. 7.1) is virtually impossible to apply in the political realm. The general drift toward pacifism (for example, "Do not resist one who is evil. But if any one strikes you on the right cheek, turn to him the other also," Matt. 5.39) is difficult for those called to be responsible for the internal and external security of a modern nation-state.

The third problem is that the Jesus emerging from the modern quest for the historical Jesus does not suggest that the political realm ought to be a particular priority. Edward Sanders, for example, in his highly regarded study *Jesus and Judaism*, sees Jesus as a prophet, primarily interested in the end of the age, calling the faithful in Israel to a state of holiness. Although there is a radical edge to the teaching of Jesus (for example, his commitment to inclusivity by reaching out to those that many insist are outside the faithful remnant), it is not suggestive of an endorsement of the management of a state. As a result of these problems many of the sayings and teachings of Jesus, from the perspective of the social and the political, are either irrelevant or unrealistic.

Yet despite these problems, the figure of Jesus and the social and political realm did in due course engage with each other. And as they did so, the problems were both confronted and accommodated. This article will briefly outline some of the ways in which Jesus was handled historically. This will include the countercultural approach of the very early Church, followed by the Constantinian turn (where Jesus and the political state are merged), culminating in the Christendom project of the Middle Ages, and then briefly the impact of the Reformation. In the second section, the article will explore five ways that Jesus is handled in the modern period. These five ways are (a) the historical Jesus as an inspiration to a radical politics, (b) the Jesus of deism and the influence on American politics, (c) the Christological shift and the radical politics of Karl Barth, (d) Jesus as a perpetual challenge to the social order as seen in Reinhold Niebuhr, and (e) Jesus and the reaffirmation of politics as seen in the work of the British theologian Oliver O'Donovan.

Historical Background

For many commentators in this area, "Constantinianism" is the pivotal issue. It describes the "fall" of the Church from a persecuted sect to an established religion. However, before turning to this, there is another significant division that warrants mention. The Church became divided (culturally and in due course institutionally) into a Latin-Western Church and a Greek-Eastern Church. One of the differences between West and East was over the relationship between Church and state. Ambrose and Eusebius are often seen as representatives for these two distinct traditions, even leading "some thinkers to speak of a 'republican' tradition in the West as opposed to a 'monarchist' tradition in the East, the one asserting the independent responsibility of church and individual, the other seeing earthly government as part of the divine economy" (O'Donovan). It is beyond the scope of this article to develop the implicit differences in Christology; suffice it to say that Christology did play a significant difference in the emergence of these two contrasting accounts.

Turning then to the conversion of Constantine: although his conversion to Christianity in A.D. 313 is important, the narrative that a radical, pacifist, unconforming Church suddenly became established and conservative is a vast oversimplification. What is true is that the initial impact of the teaching of Jesus on the early Church was to encourage tendencies toward both pacifism and a suspicion of wealth and property. A sense of these radical tendencies is seen in "A Plea Regarding Christians," which according to tradition was written by Athenagoras in A.D. 177. The author is explaining that it is irrational to persecute Christians, because they are good citizens of the empire and:

> The injury we suffer from our persecutors does not concern our property or our civil rights or anything of less importance. For we hold these things in contempt, although they appear weighty to the crowd. We have learned not only not to return blow for blow, nor to sue those who plunder and rob us, but to those who smite us on one cheek to offer the other also, and to those who take away our coat to give our overcoat as well. But when we have given up our property, they plot against our bodies and souls, pouring upon us a multitude of accusations which have not the slightest foundation, but which are the stock in trade of gossips and the like.

However, this radical reading of the Sermon on the Mount is already being modified by Clement of Alexandria, writing over a hundred years prior to the conversion of Constantine. Clement of Alexandria suggests that Jesus' injunctions against riches should not be taken too literally:

> Riches, then, which benefit also our neighbours, are not to be thrown away. For they are possessions, inasmuch as they are possessed, and goods, inasmuch as they are useful and provided by God for the use of men; and they lie to our hand, and are put under our power, as material and instruments which are for good use to those who know the instrument.

Certainly by the time of Constantine's conversion, this trend is established and develops in impetus. After Constantine's conversion the radicalism of the Church is expressed in the emergence of the monastic ideal (see, for example, the Rule of St. Benedict). And the fact that Christianity became the religion of the empire meant that the relationship of Jesus to political thought became a matter of some importance.

The primary issue for the Church was the relationship of Jesus' teaching on violence to the need for the empire to defend itself. The theologian who confronts this question overtly is Augustine of Hippo. In his *Reply to Faustus the Manichaean*, Augustine formulates his famous Just War doctrine and needs to circumvent the Sermon on the Mount. So he writes: "If it is supposed that God could not enjoin warfare, because in after times it was said by the Lord Jesus Christ, 'I say unto you, That ye resist not evil: but if any one strike thee on the right cheek, turn to him the left also' (Matt. 5:39), the answer is, that what is required is not a bodily action, but an inward disposition." In other words, Augustine is interpreting Jesus in such a way that he does not conflict with the manifest fact that throughout the Hebrew Bible God repeatedly calls the Jewish people to kill other nations by suggesting that his teaching is less to do with the actual action and more to do with the intention surrounding the action.

Such hermeneutical maneuvers enabled a relatively harmonious relationship between Church and state to emerge, at least as far as theory was concerned. Indeed, the medieval period, with the emergence of the ideal of Christendom, meant that there was a growing sense in which the sacred power of the Church could extend to and embrace the secular realm. Thomas Aquinas's affirmation of the political realm as a divinely intended aspect of the natural order entailed an inevitable interest by the Church in all matters. Although the actual logistics of such involvement of the Church in the activities of the emperor and regional rulers in Europe at that time was never smooth, there was recognition that the Church was entitled to be involved.

In the history of political theory, the Reformation is viewed as the pivotal event. And Jesus was as ever in this area a problem and difficulty for many of the reformers. The Reformation is pivotal because it gave overt credence to the idea of national sovereignty. The sense that a prince and people, who identify with a particular culture within a particular area, are entitled to rule themselves, without outside interference, is a consequence of the Reformation. As the various Reformation movements attracted the support of the princes, so Christendom started to disintegrate, and the princes affirmed their national autonomy from the Bishop of Rome. Given that Reformation movements were calling for a "return to the Bible," one might expect Jesus to be central. However, it was the Pauline theme of "justification by faith" and the right of the state to total obedience (Rom. 13) that proved more significant than the Sermon on the Mount. Luther's "Two Kingdoms" doctrine called on Christians to acknowledge the paradox that as salvation from sin runs parallel with the reality of sin in the Christian's life and will continue to do so until the End, so the Church will run parallel with the kingdom of this world until the End. This meant in practice that the radical exhortations in the Sermon on the Mount apply to the Kingdom of God but do not apply to the kingdom of this world. This enabled Luther to insist that the rebellion of the German peasants against the unjust rule of the princes was wrong.

Modern Period

Three examples will now be offered of the way that Jesus can be seen to operate in political and social ethics in the modern period (i.e., the 1600s onward). The first is the way in which the historical Jesus has operated as an inspiration to a radical politics. This is seen visibly in the Quakers and the Mennonites, which were both groups inspired by the example of Jesus to live in a way that is countercultural. We also have the historical Jesus playing a prominent role in Liberation Theology and its related political theologies. However, two modern theologians have made the radicalism of Jesus central to their social and political thought. John Howard Yoder, in what has become a classic, *The Politics of Jesus*, argues that Jesus embodied and taught that violence is always wrong. And such a disposition is seen as not contradicted by Rom. 13 (with its injunction to obey rulers who are appointed by God). Yoder writes:

> Romans 12–13 and Matthew 5–7 are not in contradiction or in tension. They both instruct Christians to be nonresistant in all their relationships, including the social. They both call on the disciples of Jesus to renounce participation in the interplay of egoisms which this world calls "vengeance" or "justice." They both call Christians to respect and be subject to the historical process in which the sword continues to be wielded and to bring about a kind of order under fire, but not to perceive in the wielding of the sword their own reconciling ministry.

For Yoder, it is part of Christian orthodoxy to be committed to nonviolence. Another theologian who has been taking a similar track, although in a much more obviously evangelical way, is Ronald Sider. His two books, *Rich Christians in an Age of Hunger* and *Christ and Violence*, were a significant influence on evangelicals and therefore a challenge to the religious right in the United States. For Sider, following Christ really does mean a simple lifestyle that is committed to nonviolence.

The second very significant contribution of Jesus to social and political thought in the modern period is the Jesus that emerged through deism and was so influential on the Founding Fathers of the American Constitution. Thomas Jefferson, for example, describes himself as a Christian "in the only sense in which he [i.e., Jesus Christ] wished anyone to be." However, this Jesus was one who had developed the Jewish view of God and provided more robust notions of God's qualities and the structures of government. In addition, this Jesus saw the need for the moral circle of social obligation to extend beyond just family to all society. H. Richard Niebuhr sums up the Jesus of deism thus:

> The philosophers, statesmen, reformers, poets, and novelists who acclaim Christ with Jefferson all repeat the same theme; Jesus Christ is the great enlightener, the great teacher, the one who directs all men in culture to the attainment of wisdom, moral perfection, and peace. Sometimes he is hailed as the great utilitarian, sometimes as the great idealist, sometimes as the man of reason, sometimes as the man of sentiment. But whatever categories are by means of which he is understood, the things for which he stands are fundamentally the same—a peaceful, cooperative society achieved by moral training. (Niebuhr, 92)

This Jesus undoubtedly contributed to what Robert Bellah called "American Civil Religion." This is the widespread set of attitudes that invest certain aspects of American political social life (e.g., the flag and the American presidency) with a virtually religious status. In this deistic sense, Jesus has had a very direct impact on the political life of America.

The third and final example of Jesus operating in political thought comes from the work of an English theologian at Oxford University—Oliver O'Donovan. His book *The Desire of Nations* is widely perceived as a defense of Christendom. Although O'Donovan would probably hesitate at such a description, it is an attempt to construct an overtly Christian political theory that creates the possibility of a Christian government. It is driven by a missiological commitment to bring political structures under the lordship of Christ. He derives certain themes from the Old Testament, which he then finds reflected in the ministry of Jesus. Interestingly, he takes seriously the insights of contemporary New Testament scholars into the nature and ministry of Jesus; he discusses, for example, at some length the work of Edward Sanders. The overall impact is that Christian theology can provide a rich set of political concepts that can and should shape the Christian view of the world.

Conclusion

The impact of Jesus in social and political thought has been seen in two ways: first, there has been a historical impact. Jesus has been a key issue for Christians as they discovered increasing power after the conversion of Constantine. Second, those involved in the issue of social and political thought from the vantage point of Christian ethics have been forced to engage with Jesus, although it should be noted that this is not the case for those involved in mainstream secular social and political theory. Even Jean Elshtain, who is a political theorist with a keen interest in religion, mentions Jesus only in passing.

Ultimately Jesus should be seen as an appropriate challenge to the ways in which humanity is inclined to manage and order our social and political life. The organization of our social life often requires pragmatic compromises that reach calculated ends that enable broad harmony and coexistence among people. The teaching of Jesus is an endless challenge to such compromises and a perpetual exhortation that we always ensure that we do not lose sight of the demanding ideal of love and justice in our management of our social life.

Ian Markham

See also: American (North) Christianity; Aquinas, Thomas; Augustine of Hippo; Barth, Karl; Benedict; Kingdom of God; Liberation Theology; Luther, Martin; Quaker Thought; Sanders, E. P.

References

Niebuhr, H. Richard. 1951. *Christ and Culture*. New York: Harper.

O'Donovan, O. 1999. *The Desire of Nations*. Cambridge: Cambridge University Press.

O'Donovan, O., and Joan Lockwood O'Donovan, eds. 1999. *From Irenaeus to Grotius*. Grand Rapids, MI: Eerdmans.

Sanders, E. P. 1985. *Jesus and Judaism*. London: SCM.

Sider, Ronald. 1977. *Rich Christians in an Age of Hunger*. London: Hodder and Stoughton.

———. 1980. *Christ and Violence*. London: Lion.

Yoder, John H. 1944. *The Politics of Jesus*. Grand Rapids, MI: Eerdmans.

Ethiopian Christianity

Introduction

This article focuses on points specific to the Ethiopian Orthodox Täwah_do Church about Jesus and makes only a brief statement about what it has in common with other churches. (The significance of the word "Täwaḥədo" [meaning "unity"] in its name will be clear in the course of the article.)

A Christian whose faith is strong might believe that the introduction of Christianity into Ethiopia was a providential act. Rufinus, the fifth-century historian, tells us that in the early fourth century, a certain teacher, called Meropius, and two of his students, Frumentius and Aedesius, boarded a (Roman) boat at Tyre (in today's Lebanon) intending to visit countries on the shores of the Red Sea and the Indian Ocean. When the boat arrived at

St. George and the Dragon. Ethiopian miniature of the C17. (British Library [Or. 516 fo. 99V]. By kind permission of the British Library)

an Ethiopian seaport (confused with an Indian port), the coast guards attacked it for violating their country's territory, as the treaty of friendship between Aksum/Ethiopia and Rome had been abrogated at that time. The travelers were all killed save for the two boys, whom the guards captured and took to the palace to present to the king.

The king took the boys in, and Frumentius ultimately became the secretary of the state. He took advantage of his position at the royal court to look for the Christian merchants (probably fellow Syrians) in the city and encourage them to organize themselves as a worshipping community. He advised them to build an oratory with a school attached to it. The seed of the new faith was sown in the Horn of Africa when the Christians did as Frumentius advised them; subsequent events show that the soil was fertile.

Years later, when Frumentius and Aedesius had the opportunity to leave the country, Frumentius went to Alexandria, the nearest center of Christianity, to connect the young Church in Ethiopia with the rest of the Christian world. In Alexandria he pleaded with Archbishop Athanasius to send a bishop to Ethiopia. Athanasius chose and ordained Frumentius himself to be that bishop—a sensible choice, as Frumentius knew the people and the people knew him. In Aksum, Frumentius was received as the apostle of Ethiopia. The Ethiopian Orthodox Täwaḥədo Church remembers him as Abba Sälama Käśate Bərhan, "Father Sälama, The Illuminator."

The nomination and ordination of a nonnative metropolitan for Ethiopia by the Church of Alexandria, which began accidentally with St. Frumentius in the middle of the fourth century, became a tradition, codified in the Pseudo-Nicene Decrees, and continued until the middle of the twentieth century. These decrees, which made Ethiopia one of the dioceses of the Coptic Church, were uncritically accepted by the Ethiopian Church and became a part of its canon law.

The consequence of accepting these decrees was that the local church was made dependent on the Coptic Church for spiritual leadership, its liturgical tradition, the theological interpretation of the faith, and answers to questions concerning Christology. Following the Coptic Church's leadership, the Ethiopian Church became one of the churches that rejected the decisions taken at the Council of Chalcedon in A.D. 451. The particular issue of discord discussed at that time, relevant to this article, was the relationship between divinity and humanity in Jesus Christ.

Jesus as the Foundation of the Church

As in other churches, Jesus is the foundation of the Christian faith of the Ethiopian Orthodox Täwaḥədo Church. For the Church, he is God Incarnate. In accordance with the Scriptures of the New Testament, the Nicene Creed, and the writings of ante-Chalcedonian Fathers, he is the Son of God (John 1.14), one of the three persons of the Trinity. The Church teaches that salvation and the way to the Father are through Jesus Christ alone, who died to save man from original sin (John 14.6). The Nicene Creed is not only an important part of the liturgy, but also of the daily prayers of the faithful. Jesus' mother, the Blessed Virgin Mary, is called *Wäladitä Amlak*,

"Mother of God," though not (at least not officially, except indirectly in the Trisagion) *Wäladitä Ǝgzi'abḥer* (*amlak* is "God," while *Ǝgzi'abḥer* is "The Lord God").

The Church's other sources of teaching on Jesus include the *Testament of Our Lord*, the *Testament of Our Lord in Galilee*, the *Miracles of Jesus*, the *Story of Mary*, and the *Miracles of Mary*. The stories about Jesus told in the *Gospel of the Childhood of Our Lord Jesus Christ* are preserved scattered in these sources. Although apocryphal as in many Oriental churches, in Ethiopia they are part of the Church's scriptural readings and rituals and are considered more or less equal with the canonical books. The difference between "apocryphal" and "canonical" is basically conceptual. In practice and teaching, they are all holy books from which evidence can be quoted for any theological arguments.

To these sources on Jesus, one may add the Pseudo-Apostolic Constitutions, composed of the *Synodicon* and the *Didascalia*, and two collections of homilies, the *Qerəlos* or *Cyril*, and the *Haymanotä Abäw*, or *Faith of the Fathers* (treatises and homilies by the Church Fathers). Except for the *Qerəlos*, which is from the Greek, all of these are translations from the Christian Arabic literature of the Coptic Church. Local theologians, too, have written extensively to interpret and elaborate on what these sources have to say about the nature of Jesus.

Conception and Nativity

There is more than one apocryphal version of the story of the annunciation of the birth of Jesus from a virgin. All versions show that the Lord took all necessary precautions so that the apparition and strange message related in the annunciation would not startle or shock the Blessed Virgin. In the story, the Archangel Gabriel is depicted as an old man with whom she could speak without fear and suspicion, which might have happened if he had appeared as a young man approaching a young woman. Mary was so pure that the thought of man never crossed her mind at any time in her life. She is called "The Virgin in Both" (body and mind).

In one of the stories Mary first heard only the voice of the annunciation, without the appearance of the announcer. This happened as she was coming back from a spring where she and the other girls of the village fetched water. She brought the water home and went immediately to the Temple to ask the Lord for an explanation of the strange message. As she was praying, the archangel appeared to her and repeated the annunciation she had heard earlier and answered her inquiries about the message, along the line of Luke 1.26–38.

The disciples of Jesus reported on what their teacher later told them about the messenger of the glad tidings:

> He said to (us), "Do you know that the angel Gabriel came and made the annunciation to Mary?" We said to him, "Yes, Lord." He answered saying, "Do you not remember what I told you earlier, how for the angels I became like an angel?" We said to him, "Yes, Lord." He said to us, "At that time, I appeared to Mary in the likeness of the Archangel Gabriel and spoke to her. Her heart accepted (what I told her) and believed and smiled, and (I) the Word, entered her and

> became flesh. I became a messenger for myself in the likeness of the image of an angel." (Guerrier, 197–198)

What he told them "earlier" is also recorded in the same source:

> When I came from the Father, for the angels and the archangels I became like them, passing through them in their likeness and as one of them. I passed through the orders, the powers and the principalities; and the Archangels Michael, Gabriel, Uriel and Raphael followed me as far as the fifth firmament of the heavens, it seeming to them that (I) was one of them. (ibid., 196–197)

The attitude in the story about the relationship between Mary and Joseph is similar to that of the annunciation. None of the stories, including the Ethiopic (or Gə'əz) version of the Gospels, admits unequivocally that Joseph was Mary's husband. The tradition is that Mary, as a child dedicated to God, grew up residing in the Temple, the angel of God bringing her meals every day at a regular time.

When she reached the age of maturity, the high priest and the rest of the clergy decided that she should live with a family, rather than in the Temple, where menstruating women were not allowed. They used lots to learn God's choice of a righteous family for her. The high priest collected the staffs of the elderly among them and prayed on them in the Temple. Then he returned all of them to their owners, except the last one, which was Joseph's. When the high priest returned it to Joseph, a dove came out of it and rested on his head (Chaîne, 8). St. Joseph took the Blessed Virgin to his house to take care of her and protect her "as her guardian." He was indeed a righteous man (Matt. 1.19).

When Jesus was born, Salome, the midwife, who was in the service of the Holy Family, wanted to verify that Mary indeed gave birth to a child in virginity and that she was still a virgin after delivery. She approached Mary to probe her body by inserting her finger. She accepted the veracity of what she had been told when her hand was instantly but temporarily paralyzed for doubting (Grébaut, 585–586).

Childhood

The questions of how Jesus was brought up and where he lived until he "came from Galilee to the Jordan to John to be baptized by him" (Matt. 3.13) are not raised in the tradition of Ethiopian theological scholarship as they are in others. The Church's three religious books, the *Story of Mary* (the *Nägärä Maryam*), the *Miracles of Mary* (the *Tä'ammərä Marayam*), and the *Miracles of Jesus* (the *Tä'ammərä Iyyäsus*), provide most of the answers.

Jesus grew up in Galilee in his family with the children of Joseph (from an earlier marriage) as his brothers and sisters. His clothes grew up with him. Like all children, he showed some behaviors that parents do not appreciate. Even in the Gospel, it has been reported how "the boy Jesus stayed behind in Jerusalem but his parents did not know it" (Luke 2.43–48). He did other such things early in his life. For example, he rode the rays of sunshine that came into the house through some holes. His playmates fell to the ground and were hurt when they tried to imitate him; in fact, one of them died. His mother punished him when the dead child's parents held the boy responsible for the death of their child.

On another occasion, while he was playing by a river on a Saturday, he took mud and fashioned twelve birds, which he ordered to fly. The molds changed into live birds and flew. His playmates tried to do the same, but they were disappointed and their feelings were hurt when their clay birds could not fly. The Jews complained to his parents, making the accusation that he did not observe the Sabbath. Joseph admonished him.

When Jesus reached school age, his parents took him to a teacher. There was discord between him and the teacher on the very first day. The teacher was irritated when the boy asked him the meaning of *alfa* and *beth*—the names of the first two letters in the alphabet—instead of repeating them after him as ordered, because challenging a teacher was considered disrespectful. Nevertheless, the teacher was astonished when he discovered that his pupil already knew the alphabet and much more (cf. Mark 1.22; Luke 2.47).

One day Mary sent Jesus to the spring to fetch water for the family. He accidentally broke the water jar. But he brought water home anyway, carrying it with his garment. When his mother was angry with him for breaking the jar, he went back to the spring, collected the broken pieces of clay, and restored the jar (Grébaut, 626–637).

Blessed with the Blood of Jesus

An anonymous homily in honor of the Archangel Uriel, which seems to be a recent composition, states that every site in the world where a church is, or will be built, has been blessed by the blood of Jesus. It may be remembered that when Jesus was on the Cross, one of the Roman soldiers, Longinus, pierced him on his right side. The Archangel Uriel brought a cup and received the blood in it. Carrying the cup, he and the Archangel Michael rushed into the world and sprinkled the blood on many places to sanctify them for building churches. The reason for their haste was to be back in time to escort Jesus when he went down to Sheol to raise "the bodies of the saints who had fallen asleep" (Matt. 27.52).

The Body of Jesus

Christ's orders, "Take, eat; this is my body," and "Drink of it, all of you; for this is my blood of the covenant" (Matt. 26.26–28), are understood in the literal sense of the words and are obeyed (cf. John 6.51). When taking the Holy Communion in the form of bread and wine, the faithful eat the real flesh of Jesus and drink his real blood. The body and blood look like bread and wine only in one's imagination; they cease to be bread and wine after the institution narrative and the transubstantiation. The religious literature contains stories about how certain holy men have seen with their naked eyes how the oblation was transformed into baby Jesus being slaughtered when the priest broke it for Communion.

Monophysitism

The concept of the manner of the union of humanity and divinity in Christ caused a serious controversy in the Universal Church in the fourth to the sixth centuries, resulting in dissension and schisms. The decision taken at the Council of Chalcedon in 451, that Jesus Christ has two natures—human and divine—was rejected by five churches, including the Ethiopian Orthodox Täwaḥədo Church, as a diocese of the Orthodox Church of the Church of Alexandria. These non-Chalcedonian churches maintained then, as they do now, that, after the union of divinity and humanity, one should not speak of two natures but of one. Although both groups believed that Jesus is perfect man and perfect God, instead of resolving their minor differences they chose to accuse each other of heresy. Each side coined a term to label the opponent. One side was labeled Diophysite (like Nestorius, who believed that Jesus was a man in whom the Son of God dwelt by grace) and the other Monophysite (like Eutyches who believed that, after Incarnation, Christ had only one divine nature).

Defending the one-nature-out-of-the-union-of-the-two theology (or Täwaḥədo) has drained the energy of the Ethiopian Orthodox Church. To begin with, in the 1520s the country's authorities established contact with Portugal (whose people were Diophysites) when their Christian kingdom was besieged by Ottoman Turks and was later overrun by its revolting Muslim subjects. The Church, whose existence was seriously threatened, was saved with help from Portugal, which sent a contingent of 400 well-armed soldiers.

At the end of fifteen years of warfare with the invading Muslim forces, the Portuguese demanded that the Ethiopian Church change its faith in Christ and be under Rome, rather than under Alexandria. The king (Gälawdewos, 1540–1559) and the clergy refused, but the Portuguese were allowed to stay in certain regions of the country and propagate their faith to the people among whom they settled.

The continued Islamic pressure forced King Susənyos (1607–1632) not only to request material help from the Portuguese, but finally also to ask for a bishop ordained in Rome. The bishop came and the king officially embraced Catholicism, but the faithful, led by the monks, revolted. After the loss of an untold number of lives in the revolt, the king abdicated and the Portuguese missionaries were either driven out of the country or hanged. That, however, was not the end of the story.

The Christological controversy that they sowed took on a local character and continued into the eighteenth century (some say that it still continues, though clandestinely). At that time, the issue in contention was the significance of the anointing of Jesus Christ as stated in Luke 4.18/Isa. 61.1; Acts 4.27; Heb. 1.9/ Ps. 45.7. Priests are anointed to be endued with authority to perform the ritual of the Eucharist and to loosen and bind the faithful in cases of sin. Kings are anointed to receive divine power to rule. But why is the Son, who is God, anointed to become King, Priest, and Prophet? The discussion divided the Church into three schools of thought, each with several subdivisions.

The theologians called Qəb'at, "Unctionists," maintain that Jesus became "the natural Son of God by the unction (= anointing) of the Holy

Spirit." For them, the flesh that the Son took was created by the Holy Spirit at the annunciation/conception.

The Täwaḥədo, "Unionists," saw a subordination of one of the three persons in the Trinity, the Son, in the Unctionists' concept of the role played by the Holy Spirit in the Incarnation. They insisted on replacing the formula of the Unctionists, "natural Son of God by the unction of the Holy Spirit," with their own, "natural Son by the union" (of humanity and divinity). They maintain that unction is a role played by all three persons of the Trinity. If the Holy Spirit is unction, they say, the Son too is unction. This makes the Son a participant in the creation of his flesh.

The Unctionists and the Unionists agree in the view that Jesus Christ, or the Word Incarnate, is the natural Son of the Father in his divinity as well as in his humanity. Their disagreement is in the process. They are what the Chalcedonians would call Monophysites.

The third view is that of the ṣägga, "Gracist" or "Adoptionists," who teach that Jesus Christ in his humanity became the Son of God by grace or adoption through the Holy Spirit either in the womb of the Blessed Virgin at conception or at baptism in the River Jordan. The Adoptionists are equated with those who teach "Three Births" for Jesus Christ, the eternal birth from the Father, his temporal birth from Mary, and his presumed birth by adoption. The ṣägga are very close to the Chalcedonians, influenced by the Catholics' attempts to put the Ethiopian Orthodox Church under Rome. They were excommunicated in 1878 at a council attended by all prominent authorities of Church and state (Getatchew 1986, 205–206).

Delegating Power

In the Middle Ages, the Blessed Virgin became so powerful that she shared authority with her Son. In theory, it all started when the Holy Family was in Ethiopia as part of the flight from "those who sought the child's life" (Matt. 2.20). During their sojourn of three and a half years in Ethiopia, "the most honored country of all those under the sky," she noticed that "her son was always blessing southward." She asked him, "My son, why are you blessing southward?" He said, "I have a nation there who love me; they love you even more. They quench their thirst without water when they call you "Our Lady Mary." Our lady Mary asked, "Give that nation to me." He said, "Let them be your tithe." The south exemplifies Ethiopia and the queen of the south, Mary (Matt. 12.42).

This, they say, is the reason why Mary reigns over Christian Ethiopia. King Zär'a Ya'əqob (1434–1468), for one, was certain whom his country belonged to. While arguing against the presence of Jews in his kingdom, he once said, "And if you come here to the land of Ethiopia, a wide country of Jesus Christ, Son of David, and a country of Mary, who is holy in virginity . . . you will be consumed by spear and knife because of your filthy religion" (Wendt, 5).

The real reason for the great reverence of Mary may be the Church's acceptance of a collection of short stories of miracles she worked in Europe and Palestine that made its way to Ethiopia via Egypt. A number of stories about how Mary healed the sick and raised the dead were modeled after those worked by Jesus as narrated in the Gospels. She was addressed as "Holy Virgin in Both" (body and mind), while Jesus was called Wäldä Maryam, "Son of Mary," a common tradition of naming children in Ethiopia.

In another story, Mary asks Jesus, "Give me a covenant, that is, promise me that you will forgive the sins of whoever observes my memorial, invokes my name, has faith in me, builds a church for me, gives enough food to the hungry, and water to the thirsty for my sake, clothes the naked, receives the poor—every one who observes my memorial according to his ability, having faith in me." When the merciful Savior heard the request, the story continues, he agreed to forgive [such sinners] for the sake of his mother, the pure Mary. On that blessed day, he gave her the Covenant of Mercy (*Kidanä Mḥərät*), that he would do for her without delay whatever she asked. *Kidanä Mḥərät* is another name of Mary (EMML 2044, ff. 137a–139a; Getatchew and Macomber, 36).

The body of Christ that the Christians eat, it was affirmed, is nothing else but the flesh that he took from Mary. One of the supplications in the liturgy states that worshipping her with her Son is proper. This was, however, banned at the council of 1878, although the decision may have not reached all churches and monasteries. In some monasteries, the reverence given to Mary reaches the level of a cult.

The Likeness of God

St. Paul tells us that Jesus is "the image of God" (2 Cor. 4.4). This, of course, is said in a spiritual sense. In the Middle Ages, however, Jesus' physical image was used to defeat a serious heresy of some theologians who taught that God has no form.

King Zär'a Ya'əqob, the head of state and the theologian of the Church, maintained that God has a form and that that form looks like that of man because man was created after his likeness (Gen. 1.26). He wrote a homily to be read annually on the day John the Evangelist is commemorated, refuting his opponents who, quoting the Evangelist (John 1.18), taught that God has no form. In the homily he said:

> O John, virgin and priest, come to us today and give us of the milk of your Gospel to drink. We seek you and inquire of you; tell us, what does it mean what you said in your Gospel, "No one has ever seen God; the only Son, who is in the bosom of his Father, told us"? For on the basis of these words, Zämika'el Gämaləyel and Aṣqa said, "God has no form like man's. God did not create in his image and likeness the form of Adam's body, which is palpable and visible." (Getatchew 1983, 159)

The leader of the opposition was Zämika'el. But Gämaləyel testimony in support of Zämika'el was difficult to refute. He said, "I agree with Zämika'el. As the Gospel said, "No one has ever seen God. Whom shall I say he looks like, if no one has ever seen him?"

The argument took place at an assembly where the clergy of the royal camp and the teachers at the famous educational centers were present. The assembly was called by the king himself to decide on the issue.

When the king heard Gämaləyel response, he said: "Do you abide by this statement?" Gämaləyel said, "Yes, I do." The king said (to the assembly), "Be my witnesses, O clergy of the royal camp, that he may not deny." The clergy said, "We have heard." The king's response as a refutation, which follows, became the Church's official teaching on the image of God:

> Wasn't Christ incarnated? Wasn't he born in a perfect form of man? Didn't he grow up gradually to the size of perfect man? Didn't he bear passion for our sake? Wasn't he hit on the head with reeds? Wasn't he crucified on the cross? Wasn't he nailed by his hands and feet? Didn't he drink vinegar with gall? Didn't he taste death in flesh? Wasn't he pierced on his side with a spear? Wasn't he buried in a tomb? Didn't he rise from the dead? Didn't he ascend to heaven? Didn't he sit on the right side of the Father? If the Son of God is now sitting on the side of the Father in a perfect form of man, which he took from the perfect Virgin, do the forms of the Father and the Holy spirit, who were not incarnated, resemble the perfect form of man, which is manifested in the Son or do they not resemble it? (ibid.)

The Gospel of Jesus Christ

In the book *The Miracles of Jesus*, the Lord supplements extensively the Beatitudes (Matt. 5.1–12) and adds a list of important warnings to sinners:

> Blessed are those who hate the comfort of this world, fight for me, die for the sake of my name, argue in support of my teaching, do not judge others, honor my priests, make their children priests, give clothes to my priests, fight the heretics, build churches in the name of Mary, pray in church rather than at home, share their money with my priests, invite my priests once every forty days, give their houses to the priests, do not rule their brothers, open their treasures to the poor, and hasten to come to church for prayer.
>
> Woe to them who deny me, mock my faithful, allow the plunder of churches, marry someone who is not faithful, agree with the Jews, violate orphans and widows, mock my priests, erase my name from the books, accuse their brethren before kings and rulers, do not share with the poor their comfortable life, tell lies about their brethren to defame them, are satiated when the poor are hungry, pollute their bodies with strange people, display the vain of others and hide the truth about them, do not help their Christian brethren when they are in trouble, watch my priests when they come near them sitting down instead of standing up to receive them. (EMML 2050, ff. 72a–77b; Getatchew and Macomber, 58)

Jesus was also present at the Ecumenical Council of Nicea in 325 to guide the discussion in the Orthodox way. The Church Fathers summoned by Emperor Constantine for the council were 318 bishops and archbishops. But the number of the participants at the conference was 319. Emperor Constantine ordered that that number of chairs (319) be prepared at the meal table for the participants. Those who came to the dining hall were, however, only 318. The riddle was solved for the emperor when the Holy Fathers told him that Jesus Christ, who would not come for the dinner, chaired the meeting and guided the discussion.

Names of Jesus

The Blessed Virgin is called Mother of God (Amlak), of the Savior (Mädḫən), of Life (Ḥəywät), of Jesus (Iyyäsus), of Christ (Krəstos), of Emmanuel (Amanu'el), of the Right Hand (Yäman), of Truth (Ṣədq), and of the Day (Mä'alt). He is called also Son of God and Son of Mary. His most common names are, however, Jesus, Christ, Emmanuel, and Savior of the World.

This last group of names makes Jesus, in the mind of the faithful, more than one person. That is, a prayer to Emmanuel, for example, might not mean a prayer to Jesus or the Savior of the World. This can be noticed even in the fact that a *mälkə'* (image) has been composed for each of these names. A *mälkə'* is a collection of rhyming hymns of five lines praising the parts of the body of the holy and saintly person, including Jesus Christ, Savior of the World, and Emmanuel.

Some of the sources state that Jesus himself used such names when he prayed to the Father, healed the sick, and raised the dead. The example they give are "Eli Eli, lamasabachthani" (Matt. 27.46), and "Talitha cumi" (Mark 6.41). These sources further claim that "the keys of the kingdom of heaven that (Jesus) gave to his disciples so that whoever (they) bind on earth shall be bound in heaven, and whoever (they) loose on earth shall be loosed in heaven" (Matt. 18.18), and "the authority (he) gave them over unclean spirits, to cast them out, and to heal every disease and every infirmity" (Matt. 10.1) are his and his Father's secret names. The Church's position on what is tantamount to invoking "spells," or practicing magic, is equivocal. It condemns an aspect, but not all of it, since rejecting such prayers totally would entail the exclusion of the story of Mary and the funeral ritual from the Church's religious books or editing them drastically, deleting all such prayers in them.

Getatchew Haile

See also: Adoptianism; Alexandrian Theology; Chalcedon; Coptic Christianity; Creeds; Mary; Nestorianism; Nicea; Second Person of the Trinity

References

Arras, Victor. 1972. *De Transitu Mariae: Apocrypha Aethiopica*. Vol. 342/66. Louvain.

Chaîne, M. 1962. *Apocrypha de Beate Maria Virgine*. Vol. 39/22. Louvain: CSCO.

Ethiopian Manuscript Microfilm Library (EMML), cataloged by Getatchew and Macomber.

Getatchew Haile. 1983. "The Homily of Zär'a Ya'əqob in Honor of St. John the Evangelist." EMML 1480, ff. 48r–52v. Pp. 44–166 in *Oriens Christianus*, Vol. 67.

———. 1986. "Materials on the Theology of Qəb'at or Unction." Pp. 205–250 in *Ethiopian Studies*. Edited by Gideon Goldenberg. Boston: Rotterdam.

Getatchew Haile, and William F. Macomber, 1982. *A Catalogue of Ethiopian Manuscripts Microfilmed for the Ethiopian Manuscript Microfilm Library, Addis Ababa, and for the Hill Monastic Manuscript Library, Collegeville*. Vol. VI. Collegeville, MN.

Grébaut, Sylvain. 1919. *Les Miracles de Jésus*. P.O., Vol. 12, Paris.

Guerrier, L. 1913. *Le Testament en Galilée de Notre-Seigneur Jésus-Christ*. P.O., Vol. 9/3, Paris.

Rufini Aquileiensis Presbyteri. *Historia Ecclesiastica*. Edited by J. P. Migne. Patrologia Latina 21, cols. 478–480.
Wendt, Kurt. 1962. *Das Maṣḥafa Milad (Liber Nativitatis) und Maṣḥafa Sellāasē (Liber Trinitatis) des Kaisers Zar'a Yāā'qob*, CSCO, Vol. 221/41. Louvain: CSCO.

Eucharist

The Eucharist is the regular meal for Christians, at which they gather for spiritual sustenance. Eucharist is the Greek word for "thanksgiving," and it is the most common word used, as the celebration looks back in thanksgiving for the work of Christ, his ministry and teaching, but above all his death as the means whereby new life is experienced and extended to others. There are other terms as well, which provide other nuances. The term "Lord's Supper" points to the institution of the Eucharist on the first Maundy Thursday. Holy Communion indicates the mutual sharing that takes place in breaking the bread and giving the cup. Liturgy (meaning "work of the people" in Greek) is the term most used in the Christian East (Orthodox) and expresses the communal activity in offering worship. And "Mass," traditionally most used in the Roman Catholic Church and among many Lutherans and a few Anglicans, points to the offering of the service as a way of being equipped—"dismissed"—to serve the Lord in the world. Unlike baptism, which is not repeated, the Eucharist has from the very beginning been intended for frequent, constant celebration, the meaning of the command to repeat recorded by Jesus (1 Cor. 11.26; Luke 22.19). Given the inbuilt adverse factor of repetition, which in some reformed traditions has given rise to the practice of infrequent celebration, and given the many different pastoral and theological contexts in which the Eucharist has taken place across the ages, the variations are considerable.

Origins and Theological Themes

There are four accounts of the Last Supper in the New Testament. Although each is slightly different (Matt. 26.26–29; Mark 14.22–25; Luke 22.15–20; 1 Cor. 11.23–26), there is a common structure: the disciples gather for a meal of bread and wine, which is expressed by the words of Jesus, the context of his impending death providing a new meaning altogether to what was probably their customary meal-fellowship hitherto. The Jewish origins of the Last Supper figured prominently in twentieth-century scholarship. Although the Gospels themselves do not agree on whether it was a Passover meal (the Fourth Gospel, exceptionally, depicts Jesus' death the next day as happening on the Passover; John 19.14), increasing interest is focusing on the ritual background, both Jewish (the regular eve of Sabbath meals) as well as Hellenistic (the vegetarian meals of communities such as the Stoics). The Eucharist emerges from this wider context as a new kind of fellowship meal, retaining the Jewish elements of blessing, the germs of the "eucharistic prayer," and the important theological notion of covenant, which is mentioned in all four narratives in reference to the cup in Christ's blood (Matt. 26.28; Mark 14.24; Luke 22.20; 1 Cor. 11.25). The new covenant thus replaces the Old Testament covenants, establishing a new relationship between God and his people, those who follow Christ. There is thus an inherently personal quality to this covenant, as it embodies the words and work of Jesus, linking with his death, and pointing forward to repetition in the life of the Church. In Jewish terms, this replaces the Passover sacrifice, and makes the Eucharist both a common point of origin and an inevitable point of departure in Jewish-Christian dialogue. Among the significant differences in the accounts of the Last Supper is the way in which, on the one hand, Jesus indicates his refusal to drink the cup again until with his disciples in the kingdom (Matt. 26.29; Mark 14.25; Luke 22.28), and, on the other hand, the command to repeat is explicitly given (Luke 22.19; 1 Cor. 11.25).

How to interpret the notion of memorial in the command to repeat brings us face-to-face with theological issues comparable to those relating to baptism. For among the important repertoire of ideas surrounding the Eucharist are the way Christ is perceived to be present and how the Eucharist is seen to be sacrificial. Both these notions can be traced back to the very beginning, for the Last Supper is interpreted by the New Testament writers as taking place in Jesus' presence, with words identifying himself sacrificially with the bread and wine. It was thus inevitable that when prayers were formulated and teaching of any kind given, language came to be used that was both symbolically charged and realist in tone. Irenaeus (c. 130–c. 200), Bishop of Lyon, sought to hold these trends in tension, seeing them as echoes of how needful it was to see Jesus as both earthly (a fully human being) and heavenly (the Son of God). Eucharistic prayers soon developed formulations that spoke of offering the bread and wine, so that they might become for the communicants the body and blood of Christ. Exactly how this was expressed varied to the point of becoming controversial in time. Historians have often seen two complementary tendencies: a "realist" and a "symbolic" view of both the presence of Christ and of the offering itself. And as with baptism, the role of the Holy Spirit becomes significant too. In the fourth-century East, it was becoming universal to understand the consecration of the gifts of bread and wine in terms of the action of the Holy Spirit, an expression of the East's sensitivity to Trinitarian theology. In the Catholic West, on the other hand, consecration was generally seen as effected by the Godhead, not specifically the Holy Spirit. Also in the East, the notion of sacrifice was regarded as closely tied up with memorial, whereas in the West, sacrifice became a stronger theme, the single eucharistic prayer of the Roman rite ("the Roman Canon") resounding with this approach throughout.

Eucharistic faith goes hand in hand with practice, and a Eucharist strong on sacrifice celebrated repeatedly at a side altar for the departed in a monastery in the fifteenth century with few if any communicants stands in something of a contrast to the grand scale, corporate Eucharist described in the basilicas of Rome in the seventh century, with Communion for everyone. The term "transubstantiation," inspired by the revival of interest in Aristotelian philosophy, first coined in France in the twelfth century, was fully worked out by Thomas Aquinas (c. 1225–1274), whereby the metaphysical "substance" (as opposed to the physical "accidents") of the bread and wine become the body and blood of Christ. As with many new developments, it is one thing to coin a term, another altogether to allow it to gather new resonances; and two centuries later, it was understood in a somewhat stronger sense than Aquinas originally intended. In any case, the dislocation from collective to individual between the patristic and the medieval period was a subtle development; but it meant that the reformers would make a radical exploration of new possibilities, which involved softening the language of presence and sacrifice in different ways: Martin Luther (1483–1546) found the former easier to deal with by propounding the notion of "consubstantiation," the bread and wine remaining what they were but conveying the spiritual realities of the body and blood of Christ; John Calvin (1509–1564) spiritualized both terms in a realist way, making the action of the Eucharist that of Christ himself in heaven. This is a feature developed powerfully with much patristic learning by many of the Anglican writers of the seventeenth century, such as Lancelot Andrewes (1555–1626). The Eucharist is thus understood fundamentally as the work of Christ now in the Church, and not by the Church for something or someone else.

The period since the Reformation has seen remarkable rapprochement as the churches learn to understand each other better, and, in the West, in a secular culture that can be deeply critical of the negative social legacies of an institution that is supposed to gather together and proclaim the new covenant of forgiveness and reconciliation. Ecumenical writers such as Michael Ramsey, archbishop of Canterbury (1904–1988), and Geoffrey Wainwright (b. 1939), a leading Methodist theologian, toiled hard to work out a constructive synthesis that walks with the paradoxes of the Eucharist imaginatively and also takes history seriously. For Wainwright, the eucharistic hymns of Charles Wesley (1707–1788) put some of this kind of theology in the language of poetry. The Second Vatican Council heralded a new era in the Roman Catholic Church, which recovered much of what was lost of the ecclesial character of the Eucharist in patristic writers, notably Augustine of Hippo (354–430). The Christian East became increasingly a stronger influence in this ecumenical endeavor, not only in international dialogue, in the World Council of Churches Faith and Order Agreement on Baptism, Eucharist and Ministry (1982) but also in the way the churches of the West continued to look to the Eastern Fathers—for example, Basil of Caesarea (c. 330–379) and John Chrysostom (c. 347–407)—for ways of understanding the Eucharist that were dynamic without being mechanistic, and personal without being entirely subjective. But in some ways the divisions of the past remain—and resurface. Radical Protestantism continues to find untenable the language of realism of the eucharistic presence, and traditional Catholics often find it impossible to countenance a Christian community that does not "reserve" the eucharistic elements, not just for those who are prevented for reasons of sickness from receiving Communion at church but also for the purposes of adoration.

Liturgy

There is a discernible consensus on what should form part of the liturgy, and this holds good for a Coptic service in Egypt, a Roman Catholic Mass in Guatemala, a Lutheran celebration in the U.S. Midwest, a Baptist Lord's Supper in Moscow, or an Anglican Eucharist in South Africa. Most liturgies consist of two main parts, the first being an encounter with the Word of God, and the second, an encounter at the eucharistic table. The person of Jesus Christ is central to both, whether the Word is read or preached, or whether one is considering the prayer over the bread and wine before the elements are shared together. In the ecumenical consensus of our own time, there is an argument for contrasting two sets of high points in the liturgy: the reading of the Gospel corresponds with the eucharistic prayer, in being a recounting of the narrative of the community, whereas the preaching of the sermon and the distribution of the gifts at Communion are both about "making" the food of life, in the words of the preacher and in the consecrated bread and wine made freely available. That is one reason why, for example, at the start of many a service in the Scots Presbyterian Kirk the Bible is brought in by the parish beadle and placed on the pulpit-desk before the entry of the minister, in the same way that for centuries in the East the deacon has brought in the Book of Gospels and laid it on the altar—a practice now widespread in the Roman Catholic Church, as well as many Anglican and Lutheran churches. In one of the earliest accounts of the Eucharist, written in Rome for the benefit of outsiders to the Christian faith, Justin Martyr (c. 100–c. 165) tells us that the people gather; they listen to readings from Scripture and a sermon; they stand for the prayers of intercession; after which the table is prepared, prayers of thanksgiving are offered by the one who presides over the assembly, and the eucharistic gifts are shared, some being taken away to the homes of those unable to be present. Most Christians anywhere in the world today will recognize their own practice in that simple account.

The details necessarily vary. In some traditions, the preliminaries can be complex, such as the widespread custom of private confession before receiving Communion in the Orthodox churches, akin to the practice of intending communicants coming forward for absolution with the laying on of hands at the altar rail in some Lutheran churches: the forgiveness offered by Christ has to be extended in this special way before the encounter at the Lord's table. The reading of the Gospel is usually treated as distinct from other lections, with the congregation standing up before hearing the work and words of Jesus read to them. The intercessions that follow are the community's way of wrestling with their Christian faith in the context of the world they live in, which perhaps explains why they often abound in words when the strait-jacket of traditional forms is cast aside in the interests of freedom of expression: it may be easy to pray for the government of the day, but it can be quite hard to pray for someone who is dying of cancer. But Jesus does not give us many hints in the Gospels that faith is always going to be easy. The greeting of Peace, which usually acts as a hinge between the Word and the Sacrament, recalls the appearance of Christ to the disciples in the Upper Room on the evening of the first Easter Day (John 20.26). The preparation of the table can take many forms, as like many actions it can be interpreted either in functional or symbolic terms. But the eucharistic prayer, or its equivalent, which comes next, is an item that often varies from one occasion to another. It is necessarily Christocentric, placing Christ's life in the context of salvation-history and in many traditions drawing out the particular feature of the occasion—for example, his birth at Christmas, or the Cross at Passiontide. Central to the prayer, however, is the narrative of the institution of the Last Supper, which some Reformation traditions recite separately, in order to give it greater prominence. In that prayer, too, will be found the differences of theological emphasis that have been noted, such as the role of the Spirit, how far the Eucharist is seen as entering into Christ's eternal sacrifice, and how Christ's presence is referred to by the use of such words as "be," "be for us," and "become." How the gifts are distributed also varies. The East and most of the Protestant West use ordinary bread, whereas the Roman Catholic Church, as well as many Anglicans and Lutherans, use wafer bread; the use of large wafers means that the bread can be broken, so that when each person sees what they are about to receive, they are aware of being part of a wider whole. But in some Protestant churches, the bread is already broken into small pieces, and the (unfermented) wine may be distributed in small glasses, an indication of an individualistic piety that is in contrast with the communitarian approach of many of the modern liturgies.

Architecture, Art, and Setting

What a church building looks like inside expresses some of the differences so far described. A large stone table suggests the sacrifice of Christ recalled in the Eucharist, whereas a small, movable wooden table suggests with equal clarity the gathering of the community for its family meal. Similarly, a church that has only one altar-table, even if it is a large building, places strong prominence on the unity of its communal celebration, whereas a multiplicity of altars expresses a more fragmented sense of identity, where people come along to meet the Lord. In addition to the altar-table there is the focus of where the readings and sermon are given from. A large pulpit, especially if decorated with Gospel-motifs, suggests a special emphasis on the encounter of the congregation with Christ through the preaching of the Word. On the other hand, an ad hoc lectern resembling a music-stand immediately speaks of a provisionalness to the enterprise that may not be intended. Paintings of the Last Supper sometimes bring out these emphases, the disciples usually painted as a motley crew and Judas easily identifiable as the betrayer. Signs of contemporaneity are often not far from the surface—for example, with Stanley Spencer's oil painting in which the disciples recline back in the seats so that their feet obtrude into the central space between the tables, conveying the immediate impression that they are waiting for their feet to be washed, and thereby recalling the Fourth Gospel's unique drama at the Supper (John 13.1–20).

The sight lines of a building can speak volumes. Medieval Gothic churches, such as Winchester Cathedral in England, were often built in a cruciform style, in order the better to support a central tower, and also to express in themselves the sacrifice of Christ. But in one and the same building, the chancel and sanctuary can be remote and distant, acting almost like the iconostasis (icon screen) in an Orthodox Church, so that worship has a sense of mystery, especially at the consecration of the eucharistic gifts. All this contrasts considerably with the desire for accessibility and openness, the president standing behind the table facing the rest of the community. Liturgical vesture, too, can add further resonances. The absence of them brings out further the sense of Christ being in the community, whereas the elaboration of them helps to make the president and the other ministers look distant—and different. Different understandings of ordination are part of this area of debate; the late-medieval understanding of the priest standing at the altar "in persona Christi" ("in the person of Christ"), with the Mass as an allegory of Christ's life, is a far cry from the priest clad in simple vestments presiding over an assembly in which different ministries are offered, in welcome, reading, praying the intercessions, preparing the table, and serving eucharistic gifts to the communicants.

Kenneth Stevenson

See also: Aquinas, Thomas; Augustine of Hippo; Calvin, John; Holy Spirit; Irenaeus; Liturgy; Luther, Martin; Wesley, Charles and John

References

Crockett, William R. 1989. *Eucharist: Symbol of Transformation*. New York: Pueblo.

Gorringe, Timothy. 1997. *The Sign of Love: Reflections on the Eucharist*. London: SPCK.

Jasper, R. C. D., and G. J. Cuming, eds. 1980. *The Prayers of the Eucharist: Early and Reformed*. New York: Pueblo.

McAdoo, H. R., and Kenneth Stevenson. 1997. *The Mystery of the Eucharist in the Anglican Tradition*. Norwich, UK: Canterbury.

McGowan, Andrew. 1999. *Ascetic Eucharists: Food and Drink in Early Christian Ritual Meals*. Oxford: Clarendon.

Power, David N. 1992. *The Eucharistic Mystery: Revitalizing the Tradition*. New York: Crossroad.

Stevenson, Kenneth. 2002. *Do This: The Shape, Style and Meaning of the Eucharist*. Norwich, UK: Canterbury.

Thurian, Max, and Geoffrey Wainwright, eds. 1983. *Baptism and Eucharist: Ecumenical Convergence in Celebration*. Geneva: World Council of Churches/Grand Rapids, MI: Eerdmans.

F

Family

The teaching of Jesus on the subject of the family is less than and other than common assumption would suppose. It can be divided into three categories, partly overlapping, partly distinct. First: sayings and episodes concerned with Jesus and his own family. Second: teaching concerning the attitude that followers of his should have to their families. Third: teaching apparently affecting people in general, or any rate the community that will attend to it. There is of course the difficulty that affects our reading of the Gospels in general and Jesus' teaching in particular. Are we to read that teaching as if straight from Jesus' lips? If so, what if there is disagreement, or at any rate difference between one passage and another? Or should we test it for use in Christian communities and perhaps bearing signs of that use? Or might it be that it also carries marks of, even stems from, the evangelist who writes it? And might this be the case where one evangelist may be thought to have altered the teaching as found in the work of a predecessor—for example, Matthew or Luke in their taking over of something in Mark? All this makes for some complexity and uncertainty. But we should begin by surveying what is to be found in each category.

Jesus' Family

This is surveyed in a separate article (Jesus, Family of), and that article should be consulted. But it needs to be noted here because it may bear on other aspects of our subject. In particular, whatever differences appear between the evangelists—with Matthew and Luke showing a much more positive approach to Jesus' family than Mark—it can hardly be said that in any of the Gospels Jesus works from the bosom of his family and he seems largely to cut free from them. So it comes as no surprise when he enjoins similar conduct upon his followers.

Jesus' Teaching for His Followers

The call to follow Jesus is one to forsake all, including one's family. One must be ready for a family-less life of itinerant mission. In Mark, the call of the first disciples in 1.16–20 sets the norm. Mark sees Jesus taking the point wider in 10.28–31. To follow is to forsake. We should note that, here, wives are not included in the list of kinsfolk who are to be renounced by those who follow

Jesus. Is this because we have read, in 10.1–12, that divorce is not permitted to those who follow him? They are to live, with marriage unbroken, in the manner of Adam and Eve in paradise, which is now restored in the kingdom of God: divorce was a concession to human weakness in the interim that Moses provided for. Yet when the mission is described in 3.13–19 and 6.7–13; 30, there is no mention of wives, and for all we can tell, the disciples went out unescorted, except by the fellow-member of the team of two. But how far was this in part an idealized picture—or did it apply only to those engaged, perhaps temporarily, in itinerant evangelism? In fact, Peter is the only disciple whose wife gets a mention, and that is indirect (1.29–31); he may be a widower, for all we can tell (but there is 1 Cor. 9.5). Certainly Mark gives no encouragement for the marriage of the followers of Jesus. Family is something they forsake, for the good of the urgent mission. All the same, when the last times come, there will be family division, with parents turning against children and brother against brother (13.12); so not all contact will have been lost. What we cannot tell is how far Mark's picture relates to the tradition of Jesus' own lifetime and how far to Christian life at the time of writing. The latter is less plausible, unless we suppose that Mark wrote at a time of great crisis, perhaps the revolt of Jews against Rome in Palestine. But if Mark wrote for Christian communities, then the teaching has the character of a wake-up call: you need not be exactly like this, but you must not sag into the comforts of the home. The kingdom may demand all, without further notice. Matt. 19.10–12 explicitly favors celibacy, at least for some.

Matthew is content to reproduce this stringent teaching in the parallel passages (19.27–30), and so is Luke. The latter, in fact, for all his gentleness, intensifies Mark's picture: at 18.29, in the list of those to be renounced by Jesus' followers, wives are added. Indeed, some manuscripts of both Matthew and Mark add wives into the list, and there is fluidity among manuscripts about the order of family members listed. That the theme caused flutters among copyists is not in the least surprising; nor is it strange that, as abstinence from marriage became more of an ideal among Christian "athletes," especially when monasticism began to take hold in the fourth century, a reference to wives should be added. That is not quite the ethos of the Gospels, whose eye is more on the mission in Jesus' day or perhaps at the time of writing, when the End draws near.

Matthew and Luke both include another strenuous antifamily saying: at Matthew 10.37, Jesus' disciples are told they must not love their parents or children more than they love Jesus; and at Luke 14.26, we read that one cannot be Jesus' disciple unless one hates mother, siblings, children, and (as at 18.29) wives. This extreme statement may be put down to the quite frequent phenomenon of Semitic exaggeration (compare the prophets denouncing sacrifice), but there is no denying the tone; and the "hate" can hardly be said to be "family-friendly."

The upshot has to be that, as far as the Gospels are concerned (and where else can we look?), Jesus is scarcely an encourager of "the Christian family." For that concept we have to turn to the more direct evidence of Christian communities in the post-Jesus years. In the epistles of Paul and his successors, we find plenty of evidence and guidance for "the Christian family," both the whole church in a place seen in household terms and the institution of Christian families, parents, and children (see Eph. 5.21–6.9; 1 Peter 3.1–7). We also find partly Christian families—1 Cor. 7.10–14—though nonmarriage is still encouraged (vv. 8–9). Yet none of this is referred to Jesus, except the forbidding of divorce if at all possible (though non-Christian partners present both a problem and a loophole). This material, directed to stability in the family, has, not surprisingly, been found more helpful for the ordering of Christian family life than anything in the teaching of Jesus; so it came to the fore in the Reformation, when the preferring of celibacy as the better Christian path dropped away and Christian family life began to come into its own as the great good.

Exception in the Teaching of Jesus

The single exception in the teaching of Jesus is the material concerning divorce, scarcely applicable if family life was nonexistent in Jesus' circle. So there is some obscurity. Here, whether from Jesus or from the developing tradition, we find Jesus saying that his followers must not divorce at all (Mark 10) or only in special circumstances (Matt. 19; 5.31–32). Here we do have what we may now see (and churches have long seen) as provision for society at large, or at any rate insofar as it seeks the Church's ministry in the area of marriage and then comes into problems.

The material we have surveyed is not without its surprises in view of the accepted view that the Church (and so Jesus) is solidly behind families. Perhaps it should be, and there is no doubt that the nearness of the End surely presupposed in the Gospels scarcely compels in the long term. But the antifamily teaching still has its voice and hovers in the air if we feel inclined to make "the family" into an absolute. For Jesus it might be an obstacle to the kingdom of God, and freedom from its ties has a serious role to play.

Leslie Houlden

See also: Jesus, Family of; Jesus, Origins of; Kingdom of God; Sexuality; War

Reference

Barton, S. C. 1994. *Discipleship and Family Ties in Mark and Matthew.* Cambridge: Cambridge University Press.

Feminist Theology

The attitude of feminist theology to the person and work of Jesus is an ambiguous and complex one. Christology itself is confusing enough, but theological feminism is equally complicated and increasingly diverse. Not all women concerned with women's well-being wish to call themselves "feminist." In cultures outside the Western tradition, many women resent being grouped together with Western women regardless of differences of race, culture, and class. Even within the one culture, women's voices are pluralistic. For a number of women, issues of gender are only one element in a cluster of other concerns, including racism and ecology. Linked to this is the increasing emphasis in some circles on context as the only adequate ground for theology, so that it becomes difficult (if not impossible) on this view to make universal statements about Christology; everything depends on how different cultural or racial groups experience Jesus. Indeed, in some forms of feminist theology, the question of Jesus' identity seems almost illegitimate. For others, the fact that Jesus continues to be experienced by women as savior, brother, lover, and liberator begs the question of his identity.

In classical terms, Christology is concerned with the identity of Jesus Christ—his relationship both to God and to humankind—from the perspective of salvation and his role as savior. The Christian tradition believes that since Jesus is both divine and human, he functions as the bridge between God and the world, redeeming men and women from sin and death. Jesus' eschatological return signals the fulfillment of salvation for the world, the divine pronouncement of judgment against evil, and the final advent of God's reign. This portrait of Jesus' identity and mission is grounded in the biblical witness, although the New Testament has a range of diversity in its understanding of the person and work of Christ. The same understanding is developed in early Christian writings, which wrestled with the question of Jesus' identity from within the economy of salvation.

Feminist theology sees its role as critiquing the Christian tradition through the lens of women's experience. For many Christian feminists, classical Christology has been formulated exclusively by men, women being barred from the debates and councils of the early Church; even the Scriptures are written from a male perspective, reflecting male interests and male experience. Thus, according to this critique, women's experience is given markedly less prominence than men's within the tradition. This critique raises sharply the question of whether the Christian theological inheritance is adequate to incorporate women in its Christology. The question is not primarily one of equal rights; more fundamental is the scope of salvation and women's place within the household of faith. Questions of Christology—as the early Church recognized—have vital implications for anthropology and ecclesiology: for the Christian understanding of human nature and for the self-understanding of the Church.

The doctrine of the Incarnation is central to this debate. If God has become human in male form, where does that leave females? How can women relate to a God who, in becoming human, does not share the uniqueness of their flesh or their experience? Is women's nature or the female body of lesser importance by reason of the divine choice? The issue is fundamentally a symbolic one: women in the Jewish and Christian traditions are made in the image of God, and in Christian theology remade in the image of the Risen Christ through baptism. Where the archetypal symbol or icon of God in Christian theology is male, the female remains marginal and invisible.

Equally significant are concerns relating to the significance of the Cross. In feminist thinking, there are considerable theological problems with the view that the death of Jesus is a selfless sacrifice to appease a demanding and angry God. Equally problematical is the related view that salvation manifests itself in the movement of the soul from pride and self-assertion to humility and self-abasement before God. For feminist theology, such a model leads women not to humility but to a fundamental loss of identity and a timorous self-esteem. The notion of Christ's death as exemplary condemns women, in this view, to a lifetime of self-sacrifice that leaves them empty and bereft, enslaved to the needs and demands of others. Salvation in these terms seems far from liberating for women.

Part of the issue is the fact that God is portrayed in Scripture and tradition through largely masculine language and imagery. Trinitarian theology, with its roots in the New Testament, appears to some feminist eyes a largely male construction. The Incarnation exacerbates the masculinity of Christian iconography and provides a sacred canopy for patriarchal structures that oppress and constrain women's lives: God looks like a male deity, incarnate in male form, giving "headship" to males within Church and family; only males can represent Christ in the life of the Church. For feminist theology, this is an unacceptable equation, confirming women's marginalization, if not exclusion, from the household of faith on the basis of fundamental Christian dogma.

The clearest expression of the feminist critique of the Christian tradition has been enunciated by Rosemary Radford Ruether, with the question "Can a male Saviour save women?" The answer to this critical question has been varied. If answered in the affirmative (which is by no means agreed upon), it raises the further question of *how* such a savior can save women. Post-Christian feminism rejects outright the Christian doctrines of the Incarnation and the atonement: the male, incarnate Christ is an inadequate God-figure for women's salvation. In different ways, Mary Daly and Daphne Hampson both answer Ruether's question in the negative. Daly believes that arguments for male supremacy are based on Jesus as the divinization of maleness. In her view, women need to find salvation within themselves, not from without; if it is from men that they need to be saved, then a male savior is a contradiction in terms. Hampson has a more nuanced awareness of orthodox Christology but argues that it is irredeemably flawed: it is dominated by male imagery, despite attempts to the contrary, and it is based on a philosophical belief that the particular can function as a universal. At the same time, Hampson argues (from outside Christianity) that Christian theology needs to establish a case for the uniqueness of Jesus, otherwise it ceases to be Christian.

Ruether's answer to her own question is that the maleness of Jesus has no theological significance in itself. She argues that the center of Christology lies not so much in the person of Jesus as in his liberating, prophetic message as lived out in his own actions—a message that is in continuity with the Old Testament prophets and found in the supposedly "low" Christology of the Synoptic Gospels. Yet Ruether is reluctant to reject the notion of Jesus as Redeemer, even though she regards the view of Jesus as Messiah and incarnate Son as mythological in the negative sense. She wants to hold to the view that Jesus is in some sense unique, without explaining how he is able to redeem women (as well as men). Priority, in any case, lies in Jesus' message; the question of his identity is secondary, if not irrelevant.

The New Testament scholar Elisabeth Schüssler Fiorenza has made a striking contribution to feminist Christology from a hermeneutical basis. Schüssler

Fiorenza recognizes the problem of Jesus' maleness and believes that individualistic interpretations of Jesus as the revealed Son of the Father and divine Lord are dangerous and oppressive. She rejects the uniqueness of Jesus and sees him as standing in a line of prophetic figures, messengers of Sophia (Wisdom). Whereas the later traditions of the New Testament present a patriarchal (or, in her language, "kyriarchal") view of God, early traditions behind the biblical text give insight into what she perceives as more helpful patterns of Christology. For her, the center of Christian faith lies in Jesus' liberating message of the reign of the Kingdom of God, with its critique of sociopolitical structures of oppression in regard to gender, race, and class. What Schüssler Fiorenza offers is not strictly speaking the Jesus of the Gospels, nor of the New Testament as a whole, but a reconstruction of early traditions that is shaped by her understanding of the feminist agenda.

A popular Christian feminist response to the Christological problem is to shift the focus from the person of Jesus, not just to his message but to a corporate understanding of his identity. Sallie McFague's work tends in this direction. She understands the world metaphorically as the "body" of God. The Incarnation relates not so much to the divine presence in Jesus but rather to God's closeness to all creation. Incarnation now becomes a cosmic statement of that which has always existed. The theological locus of incarnation moves from redemption to creation, from the particular humanity of Jesus to the generality of the world. Although Jesus is an important figure, he is not unique. Indeed, everyone can be involved in the ongoing work of salvation, for McFague, a salvation that is coextensive with creation; nothing is ontologically different or cosmic about the person or work of Christ.

Other forms of feminist Christology prefer to speak of "Christa" rather than Christ, taking as far as possible the divide between the historical Jesus and the Christ of faith. Carter Heyward and Rita Nagashaki Brock employ the term of the community and the spirit it embodies. "Christa" has many dimensions for Heyward: creation, the sacredness of community and friendship, the hope of renewal for the earth, the strength to change the world, the freedom and spiritedness of all creatures, the power of erotic love. For Brock, the concept of "Christa" is also linked to community. Although both still speak of "incarnation," they do so in an abstract sense, divorced from the embodiment of Jesus.

In a similar vein, Brock and other feminist theologians reject what they see as the destructive myth of the heroic individual who saves others by his courage and daring. The notion of God demanding Jesus' death as an atonement for sin is a form of child abuse, in this view, its origins lying in the ancient Roman patriarchal understanding of the power of the father to dispense life and death over his household. In this version of feminist theology, women do not require to be saved from the sin of pride, as they are more sinned against than sinning: in any case, their basic sinfulness lies in self-negation rather than self-assertion. These perspectives reject classical Trinitarian formulations and challenge any understanding of Jesus' death as atoning.

Other forms of feminist theology have attempted to understand the person and work of Christ from within the tradition, accepting both his divine origins and fully realized human life. According to this view, the New Testament—not only the Fourth Gospel but also the Synoptic Gospels and the Pauline corpus—does not separate the message of the reign of God from Jesus, the messenger. For them, Jesus bears the message in a way that is dependent on his divine origins and his bodily, human reality. Jesus' ministry is viewed from the lens of the Cross and the resurrection, and within the defining question of his identity. From this angle, the stretching of "incarnation" to mean little more than the vague, ongoing presence of God within the world is humanist rather than Christian, with a pedagogical and ethical focus rather than a belief in the human need for divine transformation. The complex identity of Jesus is what enables such a transfiguration to become a reality, both in human life and structures (including in the relations between men and women) and within the wider scope of creation.

Janet Martin Soskice has argued that feminist theologians who try to distance themselves from the Incarnation embodied in Jesus undermine their own concerns to take seriously the human body. Feminism in general is highly critical of an ontological dualism that downplays or ignores the body in favor of the soul. Other theologians influenced by classical Christian understandings of Jesus as well as by feminist theology include Patricia Wilson-Kastner, Catherine LaCugna, and Elizabeth Johnson. These theologians argue that a genuinely embodied Christology—in the historical person of Jesus of Nazareth—provides the groundwork for a holistic theology that embraces and transforms the diversity of human experience in all its richness and breadth. Jacqueline Grant provides a much-needed emphasis on the racism of much Western Christology and points to Jesus as the divinely human cosufferer whose divinity overthrows any human attempts (white or male) to supplant him.

In this view, the body of Jesus has as much relevance for women as for men: all humanity, male and female, is incorporated into the divine. In the Gospels, the body of Jesus has the capacity to transpose itself across a variety of human boundaries, including that of gender. In the Fourth Gospel, for example, the notion of "flesh" moves beyond the actual embodiment of the historical Jesus and takes on a wider symbolic and sacramental meaning that comprehends women as well as men, extending to all creation. This kind of feminist theology is wary of what it sees as a gender fundamentalism that defines what it means to be human along impassable lines. For these theologians, such fundamentalism leads to narcissistic self-promotion, wherein gender is projected onto the divine.

Those feminist theologians who believe that the tradition can be retrieved in new ways argue that the Incarnation is both contextual and cosmic, intersecting with the specificities of human life in space and time. It is universal because it is divine. The divine humanity in Jesus Christ—incarnate, crucified, and risen—has the capacity to touch every human life, to embrace every creature who inhabits the same dimensions, sharing mortal flesh though in infinitely diverse ways. It is not that the male Jesus is deified at some point in his life—such an adoptianist Christology is much more problematical for feminism, because it proposes the divinization of a solitary, male human being. The point is rather that the eternal Word becomes flesh in the person of Jesus of Nazareth. This is not the deification of male humanity but, in a more radical inversion, the divine enfleshment of God within the bounds of a human life, which in turn leads to the deification of all human beings. In this reading of feminist theology, the early Patristic maxim "What he did not take up, he did not redeem" confirms the reality of salvation in Christ for all human beings, regardless of gender, race, class, or culture (Gal. 3.28–29).

It follows that those who attempt to make too much of the maleness of Christ, whether post-Christian or fundamentalist Christian, accord it an unwarranted status. It is not the maleness of Jesus that is salvific but his divine humanity, which in his risen life extends infinitely beyond the boundaries and limitations of his pre-Easter life. Within the classical interpretation of the Incarnation, moreover, Jesus' sacrificial death is not the harsh demand of a human father for the sacrifice of his son. Rather, the Cross is an act of divine self-giving love in which God is fully present. Trinitarian theology, according to Patricia Wilson-Kastner, interprets the Cross as the suffering love of God, in which the death of God is transformed to become the profoundest statement of the joyful, life-giving power of God. It parallels the song sung at creation, in which the Trinity participates in the creative act that gives birth to the world. The triune God who created the world is the same God who redeems it.

This kind of theology rules out a narrow and one-sided definition of sin. Angela West has argued that the feminist attempt to declare women innocent, in the face of the patriarchal tendency to blame Eve for human sinfulness, is understandable but ultimately unhelpful. Men and women are equal in their inheritance of the divine image, both its ongoing presence and its disfiguration; more to the point, they are mutual participants in divine grace. Whether pride or sloth is the basic form of sin—if sin has a gender focus at all—is secondary to the need to emphasize the way in which sin has distorted relationships between God and humankind, between human beings themselves (including on the level of gender), and between humankind and nature. Salvation, from this point of view, signifies the reconciliation ("at-onement") of all that is fragmented and alien.

The question in this kind of Christology is whether the biblical and Patristic understanding of the Incarnation, interpreted anew, has the possibility not only for including women but also for healing those divisions that have dogged the Western tradition: the dualistic split between body and soul, matter and spirit, nature and history, sexuality and spirituality, the political and personal, masculine and feminine. The split has been particularly damaging for women, identified in each case with the "lesser" element. In this view, according to Wilson-Kastner and others, salvation is concerned with the healing of divisions and the liberation of a true humanity, embodied in Jesus. The Incarnation is the confirmation, transformation, and unification of all things in Christ.

The obvious objection to such an affirmation of the cosmic Christ is the male language used of God and Christ throughout the Christian tradition, which seems to weaken its inclusive intentions. Alongside masculine categories, however, feminist theologians have sought other images within (and sometimes beyond) the tradition to complement the seemingly masculine slant of Christological language and imagery. The Wisdom-Sophia language of the New Testament offers a different kind of imagery for Christ, with more obviously feminine overtones. The same is true for imagery of Jesus as Mother, implicit in the New Testament and explicit in the writings, for example, of Clement of Alexandria and Julian of Norwich. The body of Jesus is understood theologically as giving birth and giving suck to believers, particularly through the sacraments. Even some of the masculine language, properly understood, can be utilized in new ways that challenge—rather than reinforce—those forms of ideology and idolatry that are associated with gender.

Although Christian theology knows that God is beyond all mortal categories, including that of gender, the point has been insufficiently emphasized in the tradition. The Incarnation cannot be used to support the idolatrous exalting of one gender over the other. Feminist theology needs to continue struggling with Jesus' identity, not as an abstract proposition but from within the narrative and economy of salvation. Without an understanding that Jesus' identity is contiguous both with God and with human beings, no genuinely Christian theology is possible. It is vital that Christian women understand that their salvation is assured, that they are not second-class citizens within the household of faith, and that their humanity is taken up into God, through the Incarnation, the death, and the Resurrection of Jesus Christ.

Dorothy Lee

See also: Adoptianism; John, Gospel of; Julian of Norwich; Kingdom of God; Mary; Messiah

References

Brock, Rita Nagashaki. 1988, 1992. *Journeys by Heart: A Christology of Erotic Power*. New York: Crossroad.

Daly, Mary. 1973, 1985. *Beyond God the Father: Towards a Philosophy of Women's Liberation*. Boston: Beacon.

Grant, Jacqueline. 1989. *White Woman's Christ and Black Women's Jesus: Feminist Christology and Womanist Response*. Atlanta: Scholars.

Hampson, Daphne. 1990. *Theology and Feminism*. Oxford: Blackwell.

Heyward, Carter. 1989. *Touching Our Strength: The Erotic as Power and the Love of God*. San Francisco: Harper and Row.

Johnson, Elizabeth A. 1992. *She Who Is: The Mystery of God in Feminist Theological Discourse*. New York: Crossroad.

LaCugna, Catherine Mowry. 1993. *God for Us: The Trinity and Christian Life*. San Francisco: Harper.

Lee, Dorothy. 2002. *Flesh and Glory: Symbol, Gender and Theology in the Gospel of John*. New York: Crossroad.

McFague, Sallie. 1987. *Models of God: Theology for an Ecological Nuclear Age*. London: SCM.

———. 1993. *The Body of God: An Ecological Theology*. Minneapolis: Fortress.

Ruether, Rosemary Radford. 1983, 1993. *Sexism and God-Talk: Toward a Feminist Theology*. Boston: Beacon.

Schüssler Fiorenza, Elisabeth. 1994. *Miriam's Child, Sophia's Prophet: Critical Issues in Feminist Christology*. London: SCM.

———. 2000. *Jesus: The Politics of Interpretation*. London: Continuum.

Soskice, Janet Martin. 2000. "Blood and Defilement: Reflections on Jesus and the Symbolics of Sex." Pp. 285–303 in *The Convergence of Theology: Festschrift Honoring Gerald O'Collins*. Edited by D. Kendell and S. T. Davis. New York: Paulist.

West, Angela. 1995. *Deadly Innocence: Feminism and the Mythology of Sin*. London: Cassell.

Wilson-Kastner, Patricia Faith. 1983. *Feminism and the Christ*. Philadelphia: Fortress.

Film

Although filmmaking is a relatively recent artistic endeavor, which began only a little over a century ago, it might well be described as *the* art form of the twentieth century, both in terms of its popular appeal and its worldwide influence. Not surprisingly, the story of the life of Jesus of Nazareth has been the subject of fascination for filmmakers from the earliest days of cinema right down to the present. In this sense, the continuing production of so-called Jesus films, driven by both overtly religious and secular interests, serves as an illustration of the continuing interest that there is in the life of Jesus. Most of the fashions, trends, and assumptions informing twentieth-century interpretations of Jesus are also mirrored in the various "Jesus films" that have been produced over the years. Insofar as filmmaking serves as a two-way mirror, both challenging and illustrating the prevailing values and beliefs of the day, it remains an important feature of the modern world. Virtually every Western country with a filmmaking industry has produced "Jesus films," and although the majority are from the United States and Europe, a significant number have been produced in Latin America. Most "Jesus films" present what is in effect a harmonized version of the life of Jesus of Nazareth; only in rare instances are films made that follow one particular Gospel writer's account.

A number of significant "Jesus films" from the era of black-and-white silent films have survived, some of which were based in large measure on selected passages from the New Testament Gospel accounts, while others were based on works of historical fiction that were set in the first-century world and effectively used Jesus Christ as a minor character in their overall storyline. Thus the French film production company Pathé released *The Life and Passion of Jesus Christ* in 1902; the film ran for nineteen minutes and presented thirty-one scenes from the New Testament. D. W. Griffith's classic *Intolerance* (1916) presents the life of Jesus as one of four interweaving storylines illustrating religious intolerance throughout human history (the other historical periods are the Babylonian, the French Revolution, and the Modern). Griffith was very selective in the scenes from the life of Jesus depicted within the film, with the most effective being the changing of the water into wine at the wedding of Cana in John 2.1–11 (the film was severely criticized by the temperance movement in the United States at the time). Another example is Cecil B. DeMille's *King of Kings* (1927), which lasted two hours and is perhaps best remembered for its attempt to spice up the rather drab and overly familiar New Testament story with its insertion of a sexual subplot involving a scantily clad Mary Magdalene.

Among the most important "Jesus films" based on works of historical fiction was DeMille's *Ben Hur* (1925), based on the best-selling novel by General Lew Wallace and in 1959 remade by William Wyler into the Oscar-winning vehicle that helped launch the career of Charlton Heston and burned images of the chariot race forever into the minds of the moviegoing public. Interestingly, great controversy existed over the depiction of Jesus within many of these early silent films; as it was thought by some conservative groups that it was blasphemous to have an actor portray the person of Jesus, many other cinematic techniques were used, including using a bright light rather than an actor to represent his divine presence. Similar reservations applied for later films, including the 1959 *Ben-Hur*, which never gives a close-up of the face of Jesus but uses over-the-shoulder shots and concentrates on the impact that the personality of Jesus has on those who are looking at him (and the camera).

The heyday of "Jesus film" production came in the 1950s and 1960s as part of the emphasis on the "sword and sandal epics" that dominated Hollywood's production interests. A number of films portraying the life of Jesus appeared during these decades, including Nicholas Ray's *King of Kings* (1961), George Stevens's *The Greatest Story Ever Told* (1965), and Pier Paolo Pasolini's *The Gospel According to St. Matthew* (1966). The era also saw a number of films based on widely read novels of historical fiction, works that were set in the first century A.D. and had the life of Jesus as a necessary backdrop for the story related. Included were such films as Mervyn LeRoy's *Quo Vadis* (1951), based on the novel by Henryk Sankiewicz; Henry Koster's *The Robe* (1953), based on the novel by Lloyd C. Douglas; Victor Saville's *The Silver Chalice* (1954), based on the novel by Thomas B. Costain; Irving Pichel's *Day of Triumph* (1954); William Wyler's *Ben-Hur* (1959), based on the novel by Lew Wallace; and Richard Fleischer's *Barabbas* (1962), based on the novel by the Nobel Prize–winning author Pär Lagerkvist. Generally, "Jesus films" from this period are lavish productions, with vast budgets and enormous crowd scenes, but with little of theological or dramatic interest as far as the character of Jesus is concerned. They tend to play fast and loose with the Gospel accounts, and frequently concentrate on fictional characters who are only tangentially related to it. Occasionally there is some quirky feature about the acting or the circumstances of shooting one of these films that causes it to be remembered, such as John Wayne's playing the Roman centurion at the crucifixion in *The Greatest Story Ever Told;* or Richard Burton's obsessive hand-washing after touching the blood-splattered Cross of Christ in *The Robe;* or the fact that the crucifixion scene in *Barabbas* was shot during an actual eclipse in Italy in order to depict the "darkness at noon" motif as a literal phenomenon. However, few would identify the portrayal of Jesus himself as a groundbreaking performance by any of the actors who played this role.

This changed with the release of what many viewers consider to be one of the most reverential "Jesus films" produced—Franco Zeffirelli's *Jesus of Nazareth* (1977), a film that made Robert Powell a major star and that defined the visual image of Jesus in the minds of a viewing audience perhaps more than any other single "Jesus film." A simple but effective psychological ploy was used to help achieve this effect within the film—Powell's Jesus never once blinks through the entire eight hours of the film; scenes in which the actor blinked were either reshot or edited out. The result is that the audience is presented with penetrating, unrelenting eye contact with a blue-eyed(!) Jesus throughout the picture. Zeffirelli's film was a major media event, and the fact that it was originally aired in the United States on National Broadcasting Corporation (NBC) television over two nights during Easter (3 and 10 April 1977) gave it an unprecedented audience.

Other made-for-TV movies depicting aspects of the life of Jesus were to follow the success of *Jesus of Nazareth*. In 1978 the American Broadcasting Corporation (ABC) aired Bernard L. Kowalski's *The Nativity*, while in 1979 NBC broadcast its version of the birth narratives in the form of Eric Till's *Mary and Joseph: A Story of Faith*. The year 1979 also saw the release of Peter Sykes's *Jesus*, a film based solely on the Gospel according to Luke and produced by a religious production company known as the Genesis Project. The film boasted on-site locations in the Holy Land and a cast that was made up almost completely of Israelis (the actor playing Jesus was an exception); however, the film lacks a dramatic edge and plods rather mechanically through the narrative of Luke. A more entertaining project is Roger Young's *Jesus* (1999), a television miniseries aired by the Columbia Broadcasting System (CBS) in the United States that achieved some critical acclaim (it was nominated for an Emmy award).

Two films from 1973 also are worth special notice, for they testify to the attraction that Jesus of Nazareth held for a younger generation of viewers: David Greene's *Godspell* and Norman Jewison's *Jesus Christ Superstar*. Both had enjoyed immense popularity as musical stage productions and combined an accessible Jesus-figure with modern pop/rock music. *Jesus Christ Superstar* in particular was a visually striking film that updated the "Jesus story" to modern times, substituting Kalashnikov rifles for Roman spears and American tanks for chariots. The film also offered an interesting theological interpretation of the betrayal of Jesus by Judas Iscariot, a theme that continues to fascinate modern audiences and was, no doubt, partly responsible for the revival of the production on stages around the world in the late 1990s.

Special note must also be made of Terry Jones's film *Monty Python's Life of Brian* (1979), which strictly speaking is not a film about Jesus of Nazareth as such (the only direct connections to the New Testament Gospels are in the opening sequences, involving the Magi going to the wrong dwelling in Bethlehem, and a brief sequence in which crowd members mishear Jesus' words spoken at the Sermon on the Mount). However, the film has an important contribution to make as a satirical critique of the so-called Quest for the Historical Jesus movement that has waxed and waned within New Testament scholarship over the years. The film has rightly earned a place as one of the best-loved of all "religious" films, even though it generated an enormous amount of public criticism when it was released and still remains the object of disdain within some conservative circles.

Public controversy was also to focus on Martin Scorsese's *The Last Temptation of Christ* (1988), based on the best-selling book from 1955 by the Cretan writer Nikos Kazantzakis. The film offers an intriguing interpretation of the humanity of Jesus of Nazareth and has been the object of calls to censor it because of the suggestions that it makes about the sexual relationship between Jesus and Mary Magdalene. Nevertheless, it remains one of the most interesting "Jesus films" of the past twenty years, mainly because of the challenge it offers to traditional interpretations of the dual nature of Jesus Christ. It also is one of the few films to depict an imagined encounter between Jesus of Nazareth and Paul the Apostle.

Another important trend within "Jesus films" over the past twenty years or so is exemplified by those that either present an allegorical study of the life of Jesus, or present cinematic images of a Christ-figure who serves as a savior or redeemer. One of the most influential of the allegorical studies is Denys Arcand's *Jesus of Montreal* (1989), which presents us with a modern version of a Passion play set in Montreal in Canada. The film succeeds remarkably well, presenting a story-within-a-story format and bridging the gap between the first-century world of Jesus and the twentieth-century world of a Western city with power and style. In this regard, the film's allegorical equation of the money-changers in the temple of Jerusalem with the financial money-men who control the business deals of pornographic films is a memorable case in point. Much more difficult to quantify, but much more prevalent and influential for the general viewing audience, are those films that do not attempt to present an explicit image of Jesus of Nazareth but are content to offer a vision of a savior-figure or a redeemer of some sort who faces opposition at the cost of self-sacrifice. Some notable examples include George Stevens's *Shane* (1953), a classic western in which a former gunslinger comes to the assistance of a struggling family; Andrei Tarkovsky's *The Sacrifice* (1986), about a man's desperate attempts to save his family from what he feels is annihilation; Gabriel Axel's *Babette's Feast* (1987), in which a Parisian refugee effects reconciliation within a family by means of providing an elaborate meal for them (the eucharistic subtheme is striking); and Tim Robbins's *Dead Man Walking* (1995), which chronicles the self-sacrifice of a nun for the cause of a man on death row. This approach to "Jesus films" offers endless opportunities for future generations of filmmakers and their audiences.

Larry J. Kreitzer

See also: Art; Jesus as a Historical Figure; The Media

References

Baugh, Lloyd. 1997. *Imaging the Divine: Jesus and Christ-Figures in Film*. Kansas City, MO: Sheed and Ward.

Kinnard, Roy, and Tim Davis. 1992. *Divine Images: A History of Jesus on the Screen*. New York: Citadel.

Kreitzer, Larry J. 2002. *Gospel Images in Fiction and Film: On Reversing the Hermeneutical Flow*. Sheffield, UK: Sheffield Academic.

Stern, Richard C., Clayton N. Jefford, and Guerric Debona. 1999. *Savior on the Silver Screen*. Mahwah, NJ: Paulist.
Tatum, W. Barnes. 1997. *Jesus at the Movies: A Guide to the First Hundred Years*. Santa Rosa, CA: Polebridge.

Flusser, D.

See Jewish Scholarship

Francis of Assisi

Francis of Assisi (d. 1226) was preoccupied with Jesus Christ, so much so that his first biographer, Thomas of Celano (d. 1260), described him as being "always with Jesus." Much of this most popular saint's Christology, however, has emerged through the rich hagiographic material that surrounds him, and, because of it, his images and understanding of Christ have been filtered through the lenses of his biographers. From Thomas of Celano, his classical medieval hagiographer, on to Bonaventure of Bagnoreggio (d. 1274), the brilliant theological craftsman of Paris, and to Bartholomew of Pisa (d. 1401), the prolific compiler of the monumental and controversial *Book of the Conformities*, biographers have tapped their own theologies and images to describe Francis's concentration on Christ. Only recently have authors, most notably Norbert Nguyyên-Van-Khanh, turned to his writings to determine how the saint speaks for himself.

It may be argued that Francis was simply building on the theology of Bernard of Clairvaux (d. 1153) and the first Cistercians, who ushered in a new era of spirituality focusing on the mysteries of the Incarnate Word. Nonetheless, Francis's writings focus so intently on the person of Jesus that they bring new dimensions and intensity to Cistercian thought. Of all his writings, Francis's *Earlier Rule*, written between 1209 and 1221, is replete with his Gospel thought. In light of the chronicler, Jordan of Giano (d. 1262), the strongly "Synoptic Gospels" flavor of that document emerges as influenced by Caesar of Speyer, whom Francis requested to "adorn [his work] with words from the Gospel." When it is compared with Francis's other writings, the *Earlier Rule* stands out as uniquely Synoptic; the others are strongly Johannine and provide insights into his Christological thought.

In the first place, it was Johannine thought that shaped Francis's sensitivity to Jesus as the Word of the Father. His writings repeatedly urge his followers to be attentive to "words of our Lord Jesus Christ" that are also "the words of the Holy Spirit" offering "spirit and life." Unlike the monastic and apostolic spiritualities of the religious life of the first twelve centuries of Christian life, Francis proposed an evangelical spirituality focused on the Word alone, the "food of the poor" (cf. Isa. 55). There is a unique "sacramental" dimension to Francis's reverence for the Word: it is revealed in his repeated call to respect "the Lord's most holy words," to "administer" them to others, and to "make a home and a dwelling place" for them. How innate this is in his own life became clear in his dramatic stripping of himself before his father, Pietro Bernardone, and his embrace of "Our Father in heaven."

From that moment, however, a second Johannine influence manifests itself in Francis's vision of Christ as the "beloved Son." Having taken such a strong stance before his father and the people of Assisi, Francis emerges as someone driven to become "the beloved" of his heavenly Father—that is, to become like Christ. If God's name is essentially, for Francis, that of Father, then that of Christ is primarily that of Son, the Father's "blessed and glorious," "most holy beloved Son," and "the most high Son." Conforming to that Son by focusing intently on the Gospels became the major endeavor of Francis's life and, as a result, Christ became his Brother, as did those who, like him, centered their lives on the beloved Son. When his writings are read from this perspective, it is clear that Francis understood that he and his followers constituted a family, a gathering of brothers centered on the beloved Son, all of whom were making their way to the Father.

Although he never lost sight of his divinity, the drive to become like and to focus on the beloved Son, Jesus, encouraged Francis to develop images of Christ that stressed the depths of his self-emptying in the Incarnation. Thus Francis never lets his readers lose sight of the Jesus who is "true God and true man" or of the contrast in his glory and his sufferings. These dimensions of Christ's life remain intimately entwined in Francis's thought, prompting him to describe Christ not only as the Lord of glory and the supreme judge of all, but also in terms of the suffering servant who washes feet, of the one who became a poor beggar, a stranger, a lamb, and, most shockingly, a worm. At a time when the image of the Good Shepherd was neglected, Francis revives in his followers its consciousness, once more in the terms of John's Gospel, of the one who lays down his life for his sheep.

Two events in Francis's later life impacted upon his images of Christ: his celebration of Christmas at Greccio in 1223 and his vision of the Seraph on LaVerna in 1224. His love for the poverty of the Christ-child emerges in his earlier writings. The celebration at Greccio, however, clearly demonstrated his desire to etch the wonder of the Word becoming flesh on the minds of everyone. Although there is evidence that enactments of the Nativity were taking place at this period, Francis's celebration captured the hearts of all and through his biographies spread throughout the world. Thomas of Celano's description suggests that this Christmas ritual was a reality as early as 1228, less than two years after the saint's death. The mystical experience of LaVerna in which the six-winged Seraph enveloping one like the crucified appeared to Francis and imprinted on him the sacred stigmata, Bonaventure interpreted as verification of the adage "Such is the power of love that it transforms the lover into the Beloved," and as the culmination of the leitmotif of his official life of Francis: his unswerving devotion to the crucified Christ. Franciscan spirituality will always be remembered for its accentuation of these two images of Christ. When seen in light of Francis's total embrace of the mystery of the Incarnate Word, however, they remarkably bring into focus its depth.

Regis Armstrong

See also: Bernard of Clairvaux; Bonaventure; Franciscan Thought and Piety; John, Gospel of

References

Armstrong, Regis J., et al., eds. 1999–2002. *Francis of Assisi: Early Documents I, II, III*. New York, London, Manila: New City.

Nguyyên-Van-Khanh, Norbert. 1994. *The Teacher of His Heart: Jesus Christ in the Thought and Writings of St. Francis*. St. Bonaventure, New York: Franciscan Institute.

Franciscan Thought and Piety

The Franciscan Order was founded in 1209 by St. Francis of Assisi (c. 1182–1226), as a group of friars distinguished by a life of complete poverty. Two distinct but related trends are characteristic of Franciscan Christology, in both its theological and its spiritual modes: first, a strong emphasis on the humanity of Christ, and secondly, a powerfully Christocentric understanding of reality. Both of these features developed in different ways from the insights of St. Francis himself.

Francis had no formal theological training. But his Christological thinking was dramatically symbolized by his public renunciation of his worldly way of life, in the market square in Assisi in 1206, stripping himself completely of his clothes. Francis thenceforward undertook a vocation of the imitation of Christ in a life of poverty. From this moment the first feature of Franciscan spirituality and theology was firmly established: a focus on the humanity of Christ as the object of imitation. Francis himself acted out this theological insight in dramatic form, reenacting various episodes in Christ's life and allegedly receiving the marks of the stigmata near the end of his life.

The emphasis on the humanity of Christ had its origin in the teaching of the Cistercian St. Bernard of Clairvaux (1090–1153) but was taken out of the monastic cloister by Francis and his followers. Underlying both Bernard's engagement with the human life of Christ and that of the later Franciscans was a powerfully *affective* spirituality. Contemplating Christ's life springs from *desire:* a desire to be united to Christ by living a life of the imitation of Christ, a desire that is satisfied by the active life of preaching and witness, and by the contemplative life of mystical identification with Christ. Francis added a very distinctive feature of his own. Christ as the poor man who owned nothing, but lived by mendicancy is the model of the life of the friar, the poor man who owns nothing and lives by begging. In line with Francis's stress on Christ's humility was a particular devotion to the Infant Jesus and to Christ crucified: aspects of Christ's life that reveal him as weak and powerless.

Coupled with Francis's views on poverty and Christ's humanity, however, were the beginnings of the second very distinctive feature of Franciscan Christology: the sense of the centrality of Christ. In an obvious sense, a strong devotion to the humanity of Christ makes Christ central to theology and spirituality. But Franciscan Christocentrism went much further than this, and manifested itself in more sophisticated ways. Francis's particular contribution here was an understanding that we are made in the "image" and "likeness" of Christ: our body is made in the image of the (incarnate) Son, just as our soul is made in his likeness. (The traditional distinction derives from Gen. 1.26.) Christ is the model for all human beings from Adam onward.

These two features of Franciscan Christology were developed in various ways by Francis's followers. Francis's beliefs concerning poverty proved deeply problematic in the history of the order. The remarkable popularity of Francis's teaching during the thirteenth century led to a huge growth throughout Europe in the numbers of friars, and with this increase immediately arose the trappings of a large and powerful ecclesiastical institution. The compromise effectively settled by Bonaventure (c. 1217–1274, minister general of the order from 1257 to 1274) and finally confirmed by John XXII in 1317—allowing communal but not personal possessions—left the more extreme followers of Francis's vision of the religious life dissatisfied. Foremost among these "Spiritual" Franciscans were Peter John Olivi (c. 1248–1298) and, later, Michael of Cesena (c. 1270–1342, minister general from 1316 to 1329). Many of these Spiritual Franciscans adopted a strongly eschatological understanding of history, derived from the writings of the Trappist reformer Joachim of Fiore (c. 1132–1202). Central to Joachim's understanding of history was a threefold periodization: the age of the Father (the Old Testament), the age of the Son (the New Testament), and the age of the Spirit (the future age when poverty and contemplation would become central to the Christian life, and new religious orders would convert the whole world to the spiritual life). Joachim calculated that the age of the Spirit was to be inaugurated c. 1260, and Franciscans and others identified the inauguration of the third age with the advent of the Franciscan Order. On this view of history, Christology assumes a new significance: Christ marks the beginning of a new epoch and will intervene again as judge of the world, ending all time.

For some Franciscans, such as William of Ockham (c. 1280–c. 1349), the emphasis on poverty led to a new theory of property. Adam in the Garden of Eden owned nothing but had the free use of everything. After the fall, God gave ownership of things to people, to protect their well-being against other fallen and sinful human beings. Christ, and his Franciscan followers, since they are permitted to own nothing but rather only to use what they need, are like Adam—prelapsarian ("pre-fall") men living the life of perfection. These insights clearly derive from the fundamental emphasis on Christ's poverty, an emphasis that in many ways set the agenda for the whole Franciscan Order. The ideals of the Spiritual Franciscans, even though they were arguably closer to those of Francis himself, proved too impractical for existence in the midst of the world—the sort of existence that was central to the Franciscan vision—and the Spirituals remained alienated from the Order. But the ideal of poverty continued in the Middle Ages, and with it the Christology that motivated it.

Unlike the rival Dominicans, the Franciscans did not initially set themselves up as a teaching order. But with the massive growth of the Order in its earliest days, the development of a distinctive technical theology was perhaps inevitable in the highly professional and academic climate of thirteenth-century theology. Unlike the Dominicans (with their adoption of the doctrines of Thomas Aquinas), however, the Franciscans did not officially declare the teachings of any one of their theologians normative. The result of this was that, of all the theological groupings in the late thirteenth and early fourteenth centuries—arguably the richest and most important period in Franciscan theology—the Franciscans were the most creative and productive. Nevertheless, the basic insights of the Franciscan theologians in the period tended to conform to the fundamental pattern of Franciscan Christology, taking its lead from Francis himself.

Of the two characteristic Franciscan Christological foci, Christocentrism took rather longer to find coherent theological expression. Dominant in the thought of the greatest thirteenth-century Franciscan theologian, Bonaventure, was the notion of Christ as exemplar and hierarch: the spiritual life is construed as a journey to God; Christ is both the example and the leader on this journey. Theologically, Bonaventure, in common with all the medieval Schoolmen, tended to stress the great spiritual gifts of the human Jesus: despite the awful reality of his suffering and death, the Word in his human nature enjoyed the beatific vision and maximal human knowledge. As one writer has put it, Bonaventure sees Christ not as a mere example but as Exemplar, the normative pattern of human life, possessing every possible human excellence. The Franciscan stress on the humanity of Christ remained central in medieval Franciscan spirituality after Bonaventure. In the tradition of Francis and Bonaventure, the early-fourteenth-century *Meditations on the Life of Christ*, written by John de Caulibus of San Gemignano, recounts in minute and imaginative detail the life of Christ, focusing on Christ's sufferings and the central importance in the friar's life of imitating those sufferings. The friar is exhorted to meditate on the events of Christ's life, becoming like Christ by imagining himself actually undergoing Christ's sufferings. Such an approach was typical of Franciscan spiritual writing throughout the Middle Ages and beyond.

Theologically, the greatest and most historically significant Franciscan thinker was beyond doubt John Duns Scotus (c. 1266–1308); perhaps more than any of his predecessors Scotus found a way of integrating Francis's distinctive vision into a theological system constructed on principles of rigorous philosophical consistency. While, like Bonaventure, Scotus held that Christ had all spiritual gifts, he emphasized to a greater extent the autonomy of Christ's human nature and will. Unlike many of his predecessors, Franciscan and non-Franciscan alike, Scotus held that the Incarnation as such does not affect Christ's human will, which remains free just as it would do if it were not united to the divine person. It is important not to overemphasize this: the difference between Scotus and his predecessors is that Scotus developed—for philosophical reasons—the sort of analysis of reality that could consistently allow him to maintain the relative autonomy of Christ's human nature. His predecessors—again for largely nontheological reasons—did not accept the sort of philosophical analysis that allows for such autonomy: thus, to the extent that they asserted some sort of autonomy (e.g., in their claiming that Christ's soul knows things, rather than, or in addition to, their asserting that the Word knows things in a human way), they tended toward inconsistency. For philosophical reasons, then, Scotus found himself in a position to defend Francis's stress on the concrete reality of Christ's humanity.

Indeed, this emphasis found expression in Scotus's Christology in other ways too. All medieval theologians maintained that Christ's human nature is an individual in itself. This position requires an account of the conditions under which individual natures subsist (i.e., are persons). For if every individual nature is a person, it follows that Christ's human nature is a person, and thus that there are two persons in the incarnate Christ. This would amount to the Nestorian heresy. The general solution was to assert that a necessary condition for subsistence is independent existence (i.e., failing to be united to, for example, the second person of the Trinity). Theologians posited various accounts of what this independence might amount to. For example, some supposed that independence is a *mode* added to an individual nature, or a *relation*, or some other kind of reality such as *esse* (existence). Following some hints in Peter John Olivi, Scotus held that independence is simply a negation. Thus, he reasoned, Christ's human nature, actually united to the second person of the Trinity, lacks no reality that every other human nature possesses. And this, as Scotus saw the matter, allowed him to assert the true reality of Christ's human nature in the strongest possible sense. Thus, as Scotus understood it, he more than almost any other of his contemporaries was in a position to affirm the reality of the redemption. He quotes in his support Gregory of Nazianzus (known to Scotus through John of Damascus): "[W]hat is not assumed is not healed." No kind of human reality is such that it cannot be assumed; every kind, therefore, can be redeemed.

Scotus's best-known Christological idea is his claim that the second person of the Trinity would have become incarnate irrespective of the fall of Adam and consequent need of the human race for redemption. This position could be found occasionally before Scotus in both Franciscan and non-Franciscan sources. Prior to the Franciscans, the Benedictine Rupert of Deutz (c. 1075–1139/40) defended the claim on scriptural grounds. Among Franciscans, the position was defended in the *Summa fratris Alexandri*, compiled by Alexander of Hales (c. 1185–1245), John of la Rochelle (c. 1200–1245), and others. These writers defended the position on the basis of the pseudo-Dionysian principle that the good is self-diffusive: the Incarnation is the highest form of the self-diffusion of good, and thus necessary. Scotus proposed a more philosophical argument in defense of the position, and thus found a powerful philosophical and theological justification for Francis's spiritually motivated Christocentrism. Basically, Scotus argued that a perfectly good agent, such as God, always wills greater goods "prior" to willing lesser goods, and prior to his permitting his creatures to perform bad actions. So God wills the greater good of Christ's Incarnation prior to his permitting Adam to fall. The basic insight is that the greatest of all good actions cannot be dependent upon a bad action.

With Scotus, the basic theological contours of a distinctively Franciscan Christology were fully established. Indeed, textbooks of Scotist theology continued to be written until well into the eighteenth century, itself a century of unparalleled popularity for the Franciscan Order. Nevertheless, the influence of Scotus and older forms of theology could hardly continue in an intellectual climate set by the eighteenth-century Enlightenment, and for a period of nearly two hundred years the Franciscans lacked obvious doctrinal homogeneity. (An exception to this is the persistent teaching on the Immaculate Conception of Mary, a view that triumphed in 1854 with Pope Pius IX's infallible declaration of the dogma.) Although Leo XIII's choice of Aquinas as the authoritative guide to Catholic theology and philosophy (*Aeterni Patris*, 1882) was a blow for the Franciscans, the result was an increased interest, in the early twentieth century, in all sorts of scholastic thought, including that of Bonaventure and Scotus. In this way, distinctive Franciscan insights were recovered. This sometimes led to difficulties: notoriously, the reinterpretation of Scotus's very robust account of the reality of Christ's assumed human nature proposed by the Franciscan Déodat de Basly during the first decades of the twentieth century resulted in the condemnation by Pius XII, in 1951, of the proposed "assumed man" *(assumptus homo)* Christology, wrongly ascribed by Déodat de Basly to Scotus. Nevertheless, an assertion of the psychological independence of the assumed nature, arguably pioneered in Déodat de Basly's "Scotist" Christology and an aspect of this Christology that escaped condemnation, has become a commonplace in modern Roman Catholic thought.

Richard Cross

See also: Bernard of Clairvaux; Bonaventure; Enlightenment; Francis of Assisi; John of Caulibus

References

Burger, Maria. 1994. *Personalität im Horizont absoluter Prädestination: Untersuchungen zur Christologie des Johannes Duns Scotus und ihrer Rezeption in modernen theologischen Ansätzen*. Beiträge zur Geschichte der Philosophie und Theologie des Mittelalters, N. F., 40. Münster: Aschendorff.

Cross, Richard. 2002. *The Metaphysics of the Incarnation: Thomas Aquinas to Duns Scotus*. Oxford: Oxford University Press.

Hayes, Zachary. 1981. *The Hidden Center: Spirituality and Speculative Christology in Bonaventure*. St. Bonaventure, NY: Franciscan Institute.

Lambert, Malcolm. 1998. *Franciscan Poverty: The Doctrine of the Absolute Poverty of Christ and the Apostles in the Franciscan Order 1210–1323*. Rev. ed. St. Bonaventure, NY: Franciscan Institute.

McElrath, Damian, ed. 1980. *Franciscan Christology: Selected Texts, Translations and Introductory Essays*. Franciscan Sources, 1. St. Bonaventure, NY: Franciscan Institute.

Moorman, John R. H. 1968. *A History of the Franciscan Order: From Its Origins to the Year 1517*. Oxford: Clarendon.

Osborne, Kenan B., ed. 1994. *The History of Franciscan Theology*. St. Bonaventure, NY: Franciscan Institute.

French Christianity

Christianity spread slowly in third- and fourth-century Gaul: indeed, only one Gallic bishop attended the Council of Nicea in 325. Orthodoxy had to compete against both a tenacious rural paganism and a variety of non-Trinitarian heresies so that a focus upon the person of Christ as both human and divine endowed Catholicism with a distinctive identity and appeal. Hence the enduring popularity of that episode in the life of the fourth-century prelate Martin of Tours, a former soldier and ascetic, when he cut his cloak to clothe a nearly naked beggar at Amiens, and then dreamed that Jesus appeared to him dressed in the cloak that he had given away. Martin had been a follower of Hilary, bishop of Poitiers (c. 315–c. 68), often described as "the Athanasius of the West," who, more than anyone, worked tirelessly against the spread of Arianism in Gaul and preached that Jesus was the eternal and incarnate Word of God, of one substance with the Father. However, it was not until after the conversion of Clovis, king of the Franks, in 496 that Catholic Christianity's progress in Gaul was ensured, a process illustrated in the writings of Gregory of Tours. By that date many shrines and baptistries were under construction, and monasticism was growing in popularity in much of France.

Monasticism was an important agency for encouraging Christocentric fervency within the regular Orders at the height of their influence in the eleventh and twelfth centuries. The Cluniac reform movement was of significance in this respect, and so was St. Anselm. In works like his treatise on the Incarnation, *Cur Deus Homo?*, and his *Méditation pour exciter la crainte* (c. 1070), he initiated the trend of regarding Jesus Christ less as Judge Eternal than as pleader for errant mankind before the throne of the Father. This text had a vast influence on monastic piety as expounded in the thought of the great Cistercian, St. Bernard of Clairvaux, celebrated for his fervent mystical devotion to Christ as the Bridegroom of the Soul; the first of his three sermons for the Feast of the Circumcision of Christ celebrates the divine worth of "the name before all other names." When his follower, a Cistercian abbot, was elected Eugenius III in 1145, Bernard sent him *On Consideration (De consideratione)*, beseeching him not to allow administrative detail to distract him from what was primary in the Church: the person of Jesus Christ.

Devotional trends in the later medieval period owed much to the spread of the mendicant orders. The peripatetic preacher and Dominican friar Vincent Ferrer (1350–1419) had a major impact on the crowds who heard him in France (he was equally popular in Spain and Italy) and proposed that the name of Jesus be inscribed and honored in each Christian house. His suggestion built on the Franciscan observance of devotion to the name of Jesus Christ, a usage that the work of St. Bonaventure (the minister-general of the Franciscans) at the Council of Lyon (summoned to effect a reunion between the Western and Eastern churches in 1274) had helped to secure, and one hallowed by St.-Louis (Louis IX) himself. The observance spread throughout the Gallican Church. Thus, in 1461, the chapter-general of the Order of Cluny prescribed that the "Mass of the Name of Jesus" be inserted into the missal. Just as personal devotions to the Virgin Mary flourished in late-medieval France, so did those to Jesus. It was unsurprising that at Troyes in 1429, Jeanne d'Arc had "Jesus Maria" inscribed on the standard that she would lead victoriously from Orleans to Rome. She was executed with a cross placed before her, calling on the name of Jesus.

The surviving visual evidence also tells us much about the place of Jesus in French medieval Christianity and provides a countercurrent to literary and verbal emphasis on Jesus' humanity. The figure of Christ in Majesty was frequently placed in the tympanum of the doorway of great abbey and cathedral churches, with or without the representation of the Last Judgment. An eighteenth-century engraving of Cluny, before it was largely destroyed during the French Revolution, depicts Jesus seated in a mandorla held by angels, with cherubim flying around, a design of c. 1110. In the cloisters at Moissac, Christ sits in majesty above the scene of the Last Judgment, just as he does at Autun, Vézelay, and at other Benedictine sites, while at Chartres the central portal bears Christ in Majesty on the tympanum, flanked to the right by the Incarnation and to the left by the Ascension.

Iconoclasm was a feature of the sixteenth-century French Wars of Religion, when Huguenots (French Protestants) sought to destroy images considered to have no scriptural justification. In its earlier manifestations, evangelical religion had not appeared to challenge an outpouring of creative achievement in all the arts. This era, c. 1475–1530, was one that saw an intensification of lay religious life in France, as the *devotio moderna*, requiring a personal commitment to a life of piety in the world according to the example of Christ, made its full impact felt. Guides and handbooks to such a life poured from the new printing presses. The influence of Erasmus was as considerable in France as elsewhere in Europe, with highly placed patrons in the circle of Protestant humanists around François I's sister, Marguerite de Navarre; their belief in the possibility of human perfection was increasingly at odds with the emphasis of the Lutheran Reformation, which began to make inroads in French elite circles during the 1520s. Like Calvin subsequently, Luther denied that man had any autonomous power of self-determination for good. Sixteenth-century French Protestantism was consistently insistent that salvation was uniquely available through grace rather than works, and that a believer must nourish his or her own devotional life in Jesus Christ, whose redemptive work alone rescued them from the penalty of the fall. It rejected the characteristic late-fifteenth-century Catholic forms such as the Rosary, the Litanies, the Stations of the Cross, and the Angelus as having any devotional meaning, or works as having any salvific value as opposed to grace. Access to the Bible through literacy was essential. The first French translation of the whole Bible was published by the humanist Jacques Lefèvre d'Étaples in 1530; Olivétan published the first Protestant translation five years later.

The prevailing form of French Protestantism was Calvinism, well placed for implanting inside the Valois state from having its center just across the Swiss frontier in Geneva. It has often been alleged that Calvin established a "moral reign of terror" in Geneva, but that should be set against Calvin's own devotional commitment to the person of Jesus Christ. Although ruthless against any departure from Athanasian norms (as the notorious burning of the Socinian, Servetus, underlined), Calvinist preachers commended the reality of Christ's humanity to their congregations, and Calvin was constantly at pains to stress how much Jesus was fully God and fully man, and to demonstrate the unity and the distinction between his two natures. The depth of his love for the figure of Jesus as friend and pattern, quite as much as judge, is obvious in most of his published writings. His magnum opus, the *Institutes*, were written, as he said, in "hunger and thirst for Christ" and were intended as an exposition grounded in Christian teaching. Indeed, Calvin, in the first edition, the most humanistic version, actually refers to his text as trying to embody the "philosophy of Christ."

In the Wars of Religion, Huguenots, like other contemporary Protestant groupings, found inspiration as much in Old Testament analogies to the Israelites as in the figure of Jesus. Their Catholic opponents, however, saw Jesus within the context of a whole range of devotions sanctioned by the Council of Trent (1545–1564), and particularly as the central figure within the Holy Family. After the former Huguenot, Henri IV, the first Bourbon sovereign, signed the Treaty of Nantes with members of the reformed religion in 1598, the return of stable conditions inside France permitted an extraordinary outpouring of Catholic spiritual energies as a range of exceptional Christian figures, men and women, worked to secure the triumph of Tridentine values across the kingdom, ending the dubious cults of dubious saints endemic in rural France, and to convert Huguenots back to Catholicism. Meditation was inseparable from practical action.

The "metaphysic of the saints," as Henri Bremond in his classic *Histoire du sentiment religieux en France* (1921) called the beliefs of the leaders of the French Catholic Reformation, was orientated primarily toward the figure of Christ. This metaphysic was immensely fashionable throughout the century, and it often found literary expression, as in Jean de La Ceppède's (1548–1623) long sonnet-sequence on Christ's Passion, *Théorèmes sur le sacré mystère de notre Rédemption* (1613 and 1623); it is full of religious symbolism, biblical learning, and elaborate conceits that suggest comparisons to John Donne. The original inspiration for this renaissance of the Christian life in France was perhaps Pierre, Cardinal de Bérulle (1575–1629), first superior-general of the Oratory (founded to train clergy on the model of the Oratory of Filippo Neri); those who shared and transmitted this spirituality included Mother Madeleine of St.-Joseph (1578–1637), the first French prioress of the Great Carmel in Paris; St. Jean Eudes (1601–1680), founder in 1643 of the Congregation of Jesus and Mary (Eudists) for the education of priests in seminaries; St. Jean-Baptiste de la Salle (1651–1719), founder of the Brothers of the Christian Schools; and the missionary revivalist of rural France, St. Louis-Marie Grignion de Montfort (1673–1716), founder of the Company of Mary and of the Daughters of Wisdom. Even those who rejected Jesuit teaching and culture, such as Blaise Pascal, were drawn into the same spiritual milieu: this great Jansenist and mathematician invoked Christ in his Passion in his own extraordinary conversion experience, his "night of fire," 23 November 1654.

The influence of the Berullian School on the formation of the parish clergy and the instruction of the laity in seventeenth-century France according to Tridentine norms was immeasurable. Although Marian inspirations were always prominent—Bérulle's *Life of Jesus* (1629) emphasizes her unique status in the created order as Mother of God—they should be seen in invariable relationship to a profoundly Christocentric understanding of God. Jesus was the incarnate Word, whom we are called to imitate and follow in all things. It was by so doing that the believer could enter into communion with God. As St. John Eudes expressed it in *The Life and Kingdom of Jesus in Christian Souls* (1637): "We should be clothed with his sentiments and inclinations, perform all our actions with the same dispositions and intentions he brought to his."

Missionary priests working in the countryside to teach and nurture the populace in the faith incorporated much of this stress in their own instructions. For instance, they recommended that the prayer beginning "O Good and Sweetest Jesus" should be recited kneeling before the crucifix as a form of convenient devotion for any man or woman. This was part of their wider program for the faithful of obtaining illumination in the Passion and death of Jesus, and finding in his agonies an inspiration for managing the vicissitudes of an individual's life.

One of the enduring features of this spiritual flowering was the cult of the Sacred Heart of Jesus. It was zealously promoted by St. John Eudes, who composed an office for it in 1670 and, two years later, established the Feast of the Sacred Heart in all Eudist houses. By his efforts the doctrinal basis for the new devotion was successfully stabilized. Its refounder (the cult had its origins in the Middle Ages) was Marguerite-Marie Alacoque (1647–1690), a Visitandine nun, who experienced a series of visions of Christ by which she was led to remind Catholics of his love for all mankind, a basic truth enshrined in devotion to the Sacred Heart of Jesus. Marguerite-Marie had many critics among French clergy and bishops, so her attempts to establish a feast across France were often obstructed; it was not until the eighteenth century that the Sacred Heart was actively fostered throughout the Gallican Church (the leaders of the French Church formally commended it to the faithful in 1765), when its usefulness as a means of weaning the rural populace away from the cult of dubious minor and local saints was fully appreciated. It spread, as Jean de Viguerie wrote in *Le Catholicisme des français dans l'ancienne France*, "like a fertilizing wave."

The Sacred Heart was not popular in all quarters. Jansenist spirituality, more refined, more austere, had its adherents, despite the condemnation under which the cult lay after publication of the highly controversial Bull Unigenitus in 1713. For Jansenists, the Sacred Heart was close to idolatrous and they rejected any observance of its feast day. However, Jansenist influence on the continuing Catholic renewal of the eighteenth century (especially effective in the west of France) was marginal. The enterprise had by 1750 produced a laity that was better instructed and therefore more properly "Christian" according to Tridentine norms, than any previous generation. The missionary and parochial clergy worked constantly to have men and women focus their devotional lives on Christ himself, the Virgin Mary, and the leading saints. Vital agencies for achieving this were the confraternities, and though their power was less in the prerevolutionary period than it had been two centuries earlier, they remained a force to be reckoned with. Confraternities dedicated to the Holy Sacrament and the Sacred Heart were centers of sociability as well as devotion, with a hardcore bourgeois membership.

Their religious devotion blended well with the cult of sensibility that swept through France from the 1750s onward, fanned by the writings of Rousseau.

Rousseau was not an orthodox Christian, but the spiritual intensity of so much of his writing and his unambiguous appreciation of the life and ministry of Jesus Christ ensured his vast impact on the mass of literate French men and women who remained Catholics. There was a definite compatibility between his insistence on spiritual rebirth and that of the mystic strain in much post-Reformation Catholic teaching. The vivid testimony of the Savoyard priest in Rousseau's best-selling *Émile* (1762) to the divinity disclosed in Nature may have discomforted the orthodox (and led to the book's condemnation by the Sorbonne), but this had to be set alongside the author's endorsement of a benevolence partly inspired by Jesus' example. Once the revolution began in 1789, Rousseau's influence was claimed exclusively by the Revolutionaries who, by 1793, had turned the revolution into its own cult intended to supplant Christianity in the affections of the French nation. For much of the 1790s the churches were closed, Catholics risked their lives by meeting covertly for worship, the only expression of attachment to Jesus Christ by the authorities was to the "Sans-culotte Jésus," and exaltation of the Sacred Heart of Jesus was abolished in favor of the sacred heart of the revolutionary leader Marat.

French men and women (especially women) were too thoroughly Christianized to make the state-sanctioned dismantling of Catholicism feasible. The situation was regularized by Napoleon Bonaparte in the Concordat of 1801, the instrument that governed Church-state relations in France for the next 104 years. Nevertheless, the cultural rupture opened up by the revolution endured and ensured that republicanism and Christianity remained at odds with each other until at least the mid-twentieth century. After 1801, Catholicism struggled to regain its former influence with the French public and was most successful in commending itself to the rural masses. Mariological innovations were the great success story of the century, but taking place alongside devotions that focused on Jesus. Thus the clergy and devotional manuals continued to make the Christocentric emphasis, which had been so successful before the revolution, with that of the Sacred Heart, if anything, growing in popularity. It became an emblem of the political right, associated with the counterrevolutionary resistance of the Vendée (in western France) to the regicide republic in the 1790s, and was adopted afresh after France's defeat in the war with Prussia in 1870–1871, whereupon royalists and Catholics insisted that the whole country stood in need of repentance for its disobedience over many decades to the divine will. This provided the impetus behind the construction of the church of the Sacred Heart in Paris, situated at Montmartre on the site traditionally associated with the martyrdom of St.-Denis. The basilica now constitutes a visual focal point for modern French Catholicism.

Among the educated, the romantic revival and the reaction against the bloodshed and the vandalism of the revolution led to a revival of religion under Napoleon and, particularly, during the Restored Monarchy of 1814/15–1830, but it was already ebbing by the revolution of July 1830. The anticlerical tradition of the bourgeois elite had reasserted itself and, in combination with an Enlightenment distrust of dogma, had led many men to abandon recognition of Christ's divinity while retaining a profound regard for the former savior's ethical values. The book for them was Ernest Renan's (1823–1892) *Vie de Jésus*, published in 1863, part of a twelve-volume work on the origins and growth of Christianity and by far the most controversial in its rejection of a transcendental Christ. It was a celebration of what Renan called "the poetry of the soul—faith, liberty, virtue, devotion," as this had been voiced by Jesus, "this sublime person," for whom Renan foretold a rosy future: "[H]is worship will constantly renew its youth, the tale of his life will cause endless tears, his sufferings will soften the best of hearts." The book's influence in France was far-reaching: it sold more than 60,000 copies in the first six months.

The work scandalized as much as it edified and promptly led to Renan's dismissal as a professor at the Collège de France in 1864. Nevertheless, the Renan version of Christ is that which has been most dominant among educated, middle-class Frenchmen (except in areas like the west, the southwest, and the northeast, where Catholicism has remained stronger than most parts of the country), so that it has paradoxically become a nondogmatic orthodoxy in its own right. In the twentieth century, political commitments were more popular than Christian ones among French males, with devotional enthusiasm to Jesus typically to be encountered more strongly among their mothers, wives, and daughters.

Yet one should be careful not to overstate this so-called feminization of religion, or Catholicism's inability to win intellectuals in every generation—such as Verlaine, Péguy, Claudel, Mauriac, and Green. Other male role models include Charles de Foucauld (d. 1916), who wished to be known only as "Charles de Jésus." Against Foucauld's pious simplicity may be set the attempt by Catholic progressivists at the turn of the twentieth century to engage with modernist currents. It was not always successful and could sit uneasily with the Thomism that had been officially adopted as its philosophy by the Church in 1879. Thus the biblical critic Alfred Loisy (1857–1940), professor of history at the Collège de France 1909–1913, in his *L'Evangile et l'église* (1902), denied that the Church was explicitly established by Christ and saw the Savior's teachings essentially in moral terms. He was excommunicated in 1907, the same year that Pius X condemned modernism as heresy. It did not stop its adherents trying to engage with contemporary thinkers such as Bergson and Blondel and allowing it to modify their own Christologies.

Since World War II, France, like other European states, has undergone a process of rapid secularization. Christian witness is a distinctly minority activity, yet where it is professed, it is undertaken from genuine commitment rather than social pressures; an underlying belief in Jesus Christ's unique nature as God and man is not at the expense of a vigorous, questioning faith. Two figures have been especially influential. The first, Gabriel Marcel, has famously combined existentialism with Christianity in a creative synthesis that defied papal condemnation of existentialism in 1950. Marcel's interpretation of belief as in essence focused on one person, Jesus Christ, was quite influential in the 1950s and 1960s, though he had less of a popular following than did, posthumously, the Jesuit priest Teilhard de Chardin (1881–1955). A process-theologian, Chardin wrote visionary books published after his death, about a Christ-centered understanding of evolution, that have a continuing appeal.

Nigel Aston

See also: Anselm; Bernard of Clairvaux; Bonaventure; Calvin, John; English Christianity, Medieval; Enlightenment; Francis of Assisi; Luther, Martin; Mary; Nicea; Roman Catholicism

References

Bowman, Frank Paul. 1987. *Le Christ des barricades 1789–1848*, Paris: Le Cerf.
Evans, G. R. 1983. *The Mind of St. Bernard of Clairvaux*. Oxford: Clarendon.
Evans, Joan. 1948. *Art in Medieval France, 987–1498*. London: Oxford University Press.
Grimsley, R. 1968. *Rousseau and the Religious Quest*. Oxford: Clarendon.
Jonas, Raymond. 2000. *France and the Cult of the Sacred Heart: An Epic Tale for Modern Times*. Berkeley: University of California Press.
Po-Chia Hsia, R. 1998. *The World of Catholic Renewal 1540–1770*. Cambridge: Cambridge University Press.
Poulat, E. 1962. *Histoire, dogme et critique dans la crise moderniste*. Tournai: Casterman.
Southern, Sir Richard. 1990. *St. Anselm*. Cambridge: Cambridge University Press.
Speaight, Robert. 1967. *Teilhard de Chardin: A Biography*. London: Collins.
Thompson, William, and M. Glendon Lowell. 1989. *Bérulle and the French School: Selected Writings*. New York: Paulist.
Van Dam, R. 1983. *Saints and Their Miracles in Late Antique Gaul*. Princeton: Princeton University Press.
Wallace Hadrill, J. M. 1983. *The Frankish Church*. Oxford: Clarendon.
Wardman, H. W. 1964. *Ernest Renan: A Critical Biography*. London: Athlone.

Fulfilment

See Hebrew Bible; John, Gospel of; Luke, Gospel of; Mark, Gospel of; Matthew, Gospel of

Funk, Robert (b. 1926)

Robert W. Funk is best known as the founder of the controversial Jesus Seminar, and his work on Jesus draws heavily on the findings of that group. Funk stands in the skeptical tradition of William Wrede and regards much of the biblical witness to Jesus as unauthentic. He describes the actual person of Jesus as an iconoclastic poet and sage, who had no eschatological vision and who would have shunned attributions of status that would make him a messiah, a prophet, or the founder of a new religion.

Funk was raised as the child of fundamentalist evangelists and, initially, led revivals as such an evangelist himself. He eventually rejected what he came to regard as religious fanaticism and earned international respect as a New Testament scholar, teaching at Texas Christian, Harvard, and Emory

Universities and producing a number of significant works, including a popular grammar for the study of New Testament Greek and several books on literary interpretation of the Gospels. For a time he was executive director of the Society of Biblical Literature. Since the early 1980s he has served as director of the Westar Institute and of Polebridge Press, both of which produce a variety of materials for biblical studies. In 1985, Funk founded the Jesus Seminar under the sponsorship of the Westar Institute.

Funk lays out his understanding of the historical Jesus in his book *Honest to Jesus*. He believes that Jesus started as a disciple of John the Baptist but eventually rejected both the ascetic and eschatological orientations of his mentor. Instead of talking about a coming judgment, Jesus described the kingdom of God as a present reality, visible in an egalitarian community life in which he called all people to participate. Jesus fraternized shamelessly with those who were considered outcasts and ridiculed what he considered to be the empty values of his society. Favorite targets of his wit were reliance on wealth, uncritical respect for blood relatives, and the pomposity of religion. He became a traveling sage, known for his facility at telling parables and at coining paradoxical aphorisms that challenged conventional ways of thinking.

In Funk's view, Jesus' philosophy was mainly secular: he did not make theological statements about God or call on people to repent or to fast or to keep the sabbath. Furthermore, even though Jesus was a social critic, he did not offer any prescription for how to solve the world's problems. Indeed, he made fun of those who claimed to have answers, and he did not put forward any program of his own beyond what he regarded as "common sense" observations about life. Thus, he encouraged communal sharing, radical compassion, and inclusive hospitality, but he was reticent to speak at all about himself, and he did not offer any particular vision for the future. Notably, Funk does not think that Jesus enlisted disciples, and he suggests that "starting a new religion would have been the furthest thing from his mind." Still, Jesus did attract followers, some of whom came to regard him as a healer and an exorcist. Eventually he made his way to Jerusalem, where he instigated some kind of protest prank in the temple. As a result, he was arrested and swiftly executed without a trial.

Besides offering this description of Jesus, Funk has argued for a "new reformation" in Christianity that would reject the "creedalism" built around what he considers to be nonhistorical supernatural events (virgin birth, miracles, resurrection). Funk hopes that Christianity will embrace the faith *of* Jesus rather than just being a religion *about* him; he encourages Christians to practice the inclusivity and reciprocal forgiveness that Jesus taught, while rejecting most of the historic doctrines that churches have taught concerning him. He disparages the view that Jesus is to be regarded as a divine figure whose life or death is in any way connected with such mythological phenomena as "blood atonement" or "cosmic judgment."

The criticisms of Funk's work follow largely from those that are leveled against the Jesus Seminar. In addition, Funk is often regarded as unnecessarily negative in his evaluation of church traditions, summarily dismissing the ideas of early Christians like Paul and the Gospel authors as representing quick imposition of foreign ideas. Funk's opponents wonder whether the gaps between Jesus and these witnesses could really have been as great as his construal demands. To them, it seems unlikely that devoted followers would have fabricated so many stories concerning their leader and almost completely lost any faithfulness to his vision in such a short span of time.

Mark A. Powell

See also: Crossan, J. D.; Jesus, Miracles of; Jesus, Origins of; Jesus as a Historical Figure; Jesus Seminar; John the Baptist; Kingdom of God; Paul; Resurrection; Wealth

Reference

Robert W. Funk. 1996. *Honest to Jesus: Jesus for a New Millennium*. San Francisco: HarperSanFrancisco.

G

Galilee

See Jesus in Social Context

German Christianity

The "Jesus of history" can be identified in modern times, especially before 1900, as an almost specifically Protestant German scholarly quest. Its appearance in the late eighteenth century was facilitated by the deposition of the supernatural Christ by Enlightenment philosophy. What is striking thereafter was the way it developed into a national task among Protestant German university theologians, church historians, and philosophers after German university realignment and reform c. 1790–1815. This favored Protestant theology and state higher education at the expense of Catholic Germany before the short-lived movement called Catholic modernism (c. 1900–1910). A new romantic cult of personality in German literature and philosophy favored this quest, too. The notable exception to a Protestant German claim to Jesus was Renan, whose 1863 *Vie de Jésus* was published in five different German editions within the year. Also remarkable was the successful popularization of this scholarship both in Germany and in Western Europe, if at first anonymously for fear of official reprisals in an age when blasphemy was still a criminal offense: Lessing's publication of Reimarus as the "anonymous" *Wolfenbüttel Fragments* (1774–1778) may be compared to George Eliot's anonymous translation of Strauss's *Life of Jesus* (1846) and Feuerbach's *Essence of Christianity* (1854).

This entry is concerned with the recent period c. 1880–1945, which was catastrophic in Germany for the Jesus Christ of faith. These times began with Jesus standing for the Protestant spirit of free inquiry and social conscience propagated by the great turn-of-the-century generation of "liberal Protestant" theologians such as Ritschl, Adolf Harnack, and Schweitzer. However, their very successful popularization of the human Jesus is a cautionary tale about the dangers inherent in making Jesus relevant for the present. The Jesus Christ of faith slipped all too easily into the shade provided by a new nation's cultivation of Germanic cultural and pseudoreligious values.

Liberal patristics and theology tried to address the modern citizen who had become alien to the institutional Church, but might nevertheless be open to an informal Christianity, if what Jesus stood for could be seen clearly as relevant to modern needs. Access to Jesus, the simple preacher of love toward God and man, was personal and not mediated by the institutional Church and its dogma and creed. This is what lay behind the Synoptic Gospels of Mark, Luke, and Matthew. If you accepted the Fatherhood of God, you accepted its corollary, the brotherhood of man. You could be a serious Christian without going to church. The Christian Enlightenment's struggle for humanity seemed to gain a new lease of life, though Schweitzer did strike a fresh path in pushing aside the obvious emphasis by his colleagues on the ethical teaching of Jesus. He considered such teaching only an interim before the imminent catastrophe that the coming of the Kingdom of God implied. All three liberal theologians were, however, very successful in modeling Jesus to suit a modern Christian practical pastorate of action in a new industrial world in which religion was considered, if at all, a private matter. Schweitzer's great Strasburg summary, *The Quest of the Historical Jesus* (1906), complemented by Harnack's equally popular Berlin lectures (1899–1900), *What Is Christianity?* (1901), became twentieth-century basic theological household equipment. There is even a current rebirth of interest in Harnack and his generation, which is remarkable after the burial of liberal Protestantism and the historical approach by Barth and by the Nazi German dictatorship. Remarkable too, but forgotten today, is the comment in the 1929 entry "Jesus and the Present" in the standard second edition of *Die Religion in Geschichte und Gegenwart:* it can be said with certainty that "within the Christian congregation the importance of Jesus Christ and research on Him has at no point in church history been greater than today." Symptomatic was the best-seller *The Century of the Church* (1926), published by the general superintendent of the Prussian Kurmark (1925–1933), Otto Dibelius.

Striking after c. 1880 is the way a Protestant liberal upper-middle class, and in the decade before 1914 social-democratic left and nationalistic right intelligentsia, appropriated Jesus to manage the sudden crisis produced by Germany's urban-industrial revolution. The *Kulturkampf*, and the condemnation of a brief decade of German Catholic modernism by the pope in 1910, excluded the German Catholic Church, a third of the German population. It clung fortresslike to tradition before a new self-consciousness dawned in the 1920s. A Protestant hyphenated Jesus and Christianity became very popular because it gave hope that dependency on prince or patron, and amateur Christian family-based charity, could be changed and improved. In a new German associational climate, hyphens appeared in turn, such as "Christian-Social" in opposition to Marxist Social Democracy (1878: Adolf Stoecker's labor party); "Evangelical-Social" (1890: the social action congress chaired by Harnack, 1902–1912, and uniting gurus such as Max Weber and Troeltsch); and "Community-Christianity" (1888: the Gnadau Whitsun conference, which introduced the lay "Brotherhood"). We may call this "hyphenated Christianity." If not homogeneous in theology, all shared the values of the contemporary Anglo-American Social Gospel movement. Individual Christian self-realization within the socially just modern community demanded a Jesus who taught an undogmatic Christianity, stood for modern relative values, preached in colloquial idiom on situational subjects drawn from daily life, gathered the congregation in a service of informal worship, and supported modern professional social care. This progressive and utopian cast of mind was, in the words of Berlin's Zola, Max Kretzer, in his best-seller *The Sermon on the Mount* (ten editions, 1890–1920), a Jesus who "wanted to remove conflict in the world; natural and divine law were one for Him; (Jesus) made the fulfilment of His commandments dependent on the equality of all men." Industrial labor too, if it looked to Jesus, produced a new, agnostic, "socialism of the heart" Jesus literature and poetry (*Arbeiterdichtung*, c. 1910–1930). Jesus stood for the sanctity of labor and the oppressed, for brotherhood on the factory shop-floor, for spiritual elevation gained in weekend pursuits and on Sunday as a rest day, and for turning away from a naive belief in progress toward an expectation of change that appeared in an eschatological sense suddenly as a dispensation, particularly as comradeship learned in the trenches and in the griefs of 1918–1919.

Ecclesiology expressed by church architects and artists moved in a similar direction. They derided the derivative Eisenach neo-Gothic norms (1861) for church architecture with their standardized Nazarene altar pictures depicting the crucifixion or Last Supper. Tradition was not a straitjacket. Instead they tried to represent the variety they associated with the gathered congregation of the informal early Church. The outsized, monumental church was past. Modern industrial materials such as cement, steel, and glass were used to suit the changing urban parish congregation, which wanted access to Jesus in a place of worship allowing for spiritual intimacy. Squares, circles, and ovals united in one informal congregational room that could also be used for meetings and other parish events, combining space and worship, architecture and theology, sermon and communion. Jesus and God were present, architect Otto Bartning argued in *New Church Architecture* (1919), in the space filled by the congregation. Bartning's steel church built for the 1928 Cologne Pressa exhibition is one of the most striking models among many idiosyncratic new Protestant parish churches begun in the decade before 1914. In religious art, the new mood of individual Christian self-realization sought to break free from the soft-tone Nazarene and the folksy Dürer woodcut style of popular Bible illustrators like Ludwig Richter or Rudolf Schäfer. Expression of modern spiritual crisis turned to primitive and apocalyptic art forms like Emil Nolde's woodcut *The Prophet* and his oil on canvas *Crucifixion* triptych, as well as Ernst Barlach's rough-hewn massive oak carving *The Vision*—all executed in 1912. Theirs was a church art that designed a Jesus to serve the spiritual needs of uprooted modern Everyman. Of the crucifixion scene Nolde wrote later reflectively (1934) that if "priests reveal how small their own souls are when they weep and wail over Christ's death . . . isn't the death of every ordinary person, in pain and misery, in sickness or war, or in the fulfilment of his own destiny, a much harder death? I couldn't help thinking about this."

There was a much darker side to hyphenated Jesus in the person of the Germanic ideologue opposed to the liberal Jesus of history, to progressive Christian social action, and to this recent return to informal Christian worship and fellowship. Even an expressionist church artist like Nolde, who was an early member of his local Nazi Party, found that this did not prevent the inclusion of his works in the 1937 Munich Degenerate Art Exhibition. A resurgence of the primitive, irrational, and superstitious, captured in Schweitzer's metaphor the "primeval forest," which he gave to his postwar account (1921) of his African mission, caught on in both Protestant and Catholic Germany shortly before 1914, and especially during the brutal war years. Linked to this was a return to the values of the village hearth and church. Colloquial writing like the lapsed Dithmarsh pastor Gustav Frenssen's (d. 1945) *Hilligenlei* (1905)—"Nazareth" situated on the Lower Saxon heath—had a wide readership. Here Jesus was the local hero testifying to the eternal value of the human soul and the proximity of the unknowable power of God. Such resonance is also explicable in an old Christian culture wherein many still accepted the Gospels without reflection, and believed in a personal, almost corporeal *Der Herr* who has suffered and died for me, either as an often Moravian-inspired "blood and wounds" piety, or in the tradition of late-medieval Bernardine mysticism. Schäfer's illustrations in pre- and postwar family Bibles, published by Stuttgart's Bible Institute, also drew upon such thinking.

The "speculative" Jesus of Hegelian and Fichtean German religious philosophy revived too, as Germanic uniqueness and heroic action colored by Nordic and social Darwinist hues, served as a replacement for Christian divine goodness, in new populist writing by lapsed Protestant publicists. Seminal were Paul de Lagarde (Bötticher), *German Writings* (1878); Friedrich Langbehn, *Rembrandt as Educator* (1890); and especially Houston Stewart Chamberlain, Wagner's son-in-law, in his Aryan mission statement, *Foundations of the Nineteenth Century* (1899). Their "Germanization of Christianity," a term coined in 1911 by another disenchanted Protestant, a former parish clergyman, Arthur Bonus (d. 1941), was to be the stuff of a "new myth." It drew inspiration from an imaginary spiritually intact Germanic village community and the warlike gods of Norse Saga literature, rejected the "Jewish" Old Testament and Palestine of Jesus and St. Paul, and shunned Christian universality as an alien intrusion in German culture. German-religious rather than Christian renewal would come with this revival of a male Germanic spirit whose basic drive was the will to power, to self-assertion, and to world domination. This new myth preaching German organic wholeness and an unquestioning belief in an "eternal Germany," or "Reich" (the old Catholic empire before 1806 was recalled by a large postwar Catholic literature based on a corporatist social order), became so potent in 1918, because it also gave hope to a new neoconservative generation who wanted, like their liberal and socialist opponents, to end aristocratic supremacy and moral pressures exerted by leading social circles. They spoke for the ordinary man. The radical difference, apparent first in the 1920s, was this neoconservative demand for a complete revaluation of man's place in society. They had a vision of the fall that required total leadership and frequent blood-letting.

Sermons and devotional literature from 1914 to 1918, which naturally enhanced the prewar trend toward the situational and occasional, also boosted, at the expense of the Jesus of faith and Christian universality, the idea of German male fellowship and sacrifice expressed by the German nation at war. Catholic bishops and military chaplains, anxious to show their patriotism for fear of being branded disloyal, preached a Jesus in German battle-dress like their Protestant colleagues. War was the great instructor and innovator. Notably bishops Faulhaber and Bertram, future Catholic leaders under Hitler, spoke of the Eucharist as "a war seminary" teaching the German soldier the spirit of sacrifice; of Christ's destiny (Luke 24.26) as best answered by the heroic death of the German soldier. This was the key to the mystery of Christ. Given such thinking, the proximity of the Russian Revolution to German collapse and revolution unleashed a widespread mood of betrayal of common German sacrifice at the expense of the Christian Cross.

Especially in flourishing German youth culture in the 1920s, a hunger for German rather than Christian wholeness, a preference for the spiritual in other religions like Hinduism and Buddhism and even the old Norse gods, and a new obsession with Dostoevsky's or Kierkegaard's psychoanalytic approach as a means to a deeper understanding of the irrational in the human condition rather than the use of reason and source criticism of the Gospels, eased the way for the use of myth and symbol by postwar radical-right ideologues in a new German republic that allowed for the greatest possible freedom of expression in its constitution. Their mediocre writings denying the Christian Jesus could only be taken as furthering this doctrine.

Protestant university theology became a dominant postwar force defining what it meant to be a Christian once again. But the popularity of Harnack (d. 1930) and his liberal Protestant generation was passing, and it was matched in revolutionary times by a pessimistic "theology in crisis." A radical solution was advocated by both the Germanic right and Protestant theologians and clergy who suspected the spiritual worth of hyphenated Christianity. In particular, the latter denied the efficacy of human reason in the interpretation of Jesus' relationship with God.

Postwar disestablishment of German Protestantism and the resultant search—special to those speculative times—for the existential meaning *(Seinsbegriff)* of a postwar Protestant People's Church *(Volkskirche)*, in ecclesiology and theology, produced a pervasive extreme nationalist and antiliberal *Volksnomos* theology. Wartime experience questioned the Jesus of history and faith. "Back to the young Luther," who personified lonely German spiritual and heroic struggle in a basically irrational and evil world order, became a preferred path. Luther's German will and self-assertion, it was argued, made the German Reformation unique in European culture, and it could be unique as a force for German national renewal after 1918. Big names in Lutheran theology ensured wide dissemination of this radical interpretation written up as cheap tracts for the times. One of the most successful popularizers was Emanuel Hirsch, a Göttingen authority on Fichte and Kierkegaard, who, in frequently reprinted tracts such as *Germany's Fate* (1921), called for a social and ethical revolution that recognized, as a new natural theology, the organic orders "People" and "Nation." They personified God's will in creation. Individual Christian conscience and action, as seen in the Sermon on the Mount, was made subservient to that of a given People. From here it was no distance to a populist "German Christian movement" in the late 1920s, and obscurantist religious philosophics like that of Alfred Rosenberg's *Myth of the Twentieth Century* (1930). These vocalized a German Aryan Jesus, demanded the elimination of the "Rabbi" St. Paul (in flat contradiction to Luther's debt to Romans and the other Pauline letters), the eradication of everything Jewish or "servile" in the Gospels, and praised the heroic Aryan German war dead as a more potent modern symbol of sacrifice for Germans than the crucifixion.

Obedience to Jesus Christ on the Cross and the Fatherhood of God came as a shock, as highlighted in Karl Barth's graphic *Commentary on Romans* (1919). Barth and Dialectical Theology's radicalism originated too in wartime disaffection: among reformed Swiss and Swabian "Religious-Socialist" colleagues who argued for the compatibility of Christian conscience and action with Social Democracy as a prophetic force speaking for all outside the old institutional churches. Barth preached the chasm between God and man; and Jesus' humanity in a liberal Protestant or Pietist sense was to be questioned. Jesus was not a hero but a Dostoevskyan figure; there was no such thing as a divine core in Everyman that allowed Jesus to become a real presence in every person. Jesus alone revealed God. Barth wrote thus in his preface to the second edition of his *Commentary* (1921): "If I have a system, it is limited to a recognition of what Kierkegaard called the 'infinite qualitative distinction' between time and eternity, and to my regarding this as possessing negative as well as positive significance: 'God is in heaven, and thou art on earth.' The relation between such a God and such a man, and the relation between such a man and such a God, is for me the theme of the Bible and the essence of philosophy." We are essentially humbled by the Cross. Suddenly, the central Bible themes became alive in a new light: the living God, election, judgment, Christ's death as "the stripping from himself of all human possibilities," the Resurrection as dawn heralding something beyond, and the Last Things. Jesus here, or in the writing of other dialecticians like Bultmann (*Jesus* [1926]), or Emil Brunner (*The Mediator* [1927]), stood in the sharpest contrast to all modern individualism. We do not even know what "personality" is. Jesus left no ethical legacy of general principles that allowed mankind to decide what to do with the present and in future, since Jesus really proclaimed, showing no human compassion or kindness, absolute obedience to God and his commandments. "The real Christ is the preached Christ," as the Halle Lutheran theologian Martin Kähler (d. 1912), another seminal influence and repudiator of the Jesus of history, put it. His words became a vivid shorthand for this radical Christology uniting these reformed theologians with Lutherans like Kähler's pupil, the New Testament scholar Julius Schniewind, and like-minded pastors in an informal "Confessing Church," united as a pastoral brotherhood of mostly young confessors for the faith.

The Confessing Church was the product of Christian emergency in the opening year of Hitler's dictatorship: a shocked response to the attack on the substance of the Christian faith by the Germanized natural theology of the "German Christians," which jettisoned the Jewish and "fabulous" Old Testament, and by the phoney Nazi notion of "positive Christianity." This found expression in the first synod's inevitably controversial Barthian Christology, in the Barmen Declaration of May 1934. German Lutheran tradition has always been doctrinal rather than liturgical in emphasis. The preamble stated the belief and mission of the Church to be simply "the gospel of Jesus Christ as it is attested to us in Holy Scripture and has newly come to light in the confessions of the Reformation," and the central first thesis stated: "Jesus Christ, as he is testified to us in Holy Scripture, is the one Word of God, whom we are to hear, whom we are to trust and obey in life and in death." The catechism, in particular the imperative of the first and second commandments, thus took on existential new meaning for pastors and congregations who subscribed to Barmen. They practiced informal worship wherever it was possible under a racial dictatorship that underwent a cumulative radicalization year by year. In this way they learned daily step-by-step to respect also the visible Church in terms of the explanation of the Bible, the practice of prayer, the liturgical order of service, church organization, and a pastorate to many in need. This opened a path to the modern ecumenical movement in 1945 that Protestant German wounded pride had prevented after 1918.

The remarkable feature of Germany's Catholic Church in this Christian crisis was the way Jesus became the center of a eucharistic piety and frequent communion with active lay participation. With origins in the prewar European monastic movement, Benedictine-inspired liturgical reform, emanating from centers like the abbeys of Beuron or Maria Laach, developed in the 1920s the "dialogue mass" in which the congregation joined in the responses. It proved extremely popular as a spiritual source of resistance to Nazi persecution. In addition, the parish church became the focus for a gathered practice of Christocentric prayer, and this in turn gave a new meaning to Catholic parish worship as a people's liturgy. Published wartime Nazi secret police records show that the Nazi *Weltanschauung* (worldview) proved powerless against this popular Christian witness. The Jesus Christ of faith, it seems, could be accessed by walking either of two precipitous paths: via a revaluation of theology or the liturgy, at a time when preaching Christ alone could lead to criminal proceedings—in contrast to a century earlier, when writing on the Jesus of history was possible blasphemy. Christian worship in Germany after 1945 has as a result become more informal.

Nicholas Hope

See also: Barth, Karl; Bultmann, Rudolf; Enlightenment; Harnack, Adolf von; Kierkegaard, Søren; Kingdom of God; Luther, Martin; Paul; Reimarus, Hermann Samuel; Schweitzer, Albert; Strauss, D. F.; Troeltsch, Ernst

References

Breuning, Klaus. 1969. *Die Vision des Reiches: Deutscher Katholizismus zwischen Demokratie und Diktatur 1929–1934*. Munich: Max Hueber Verlag.

Cecil, Robert. 1972. *The Myth of the Master Race: Alfred Rosenberg and Nazi Ideology*. London: Batsford.

Ericksen, Robert P. 1985. *Theologians under Hitler: Gerhard Kittel, Paul Althaus and Emanuel Hirsch*. New Haven and London: Yale University Press.

Hope, Nicholas. 1995. *German and Scandinavian Protestantism 1700 to 1918*. Oxford: Oxford University Press.

Maas-Ewerd, Theodor. 1981. *Die Krise der Liturgischen Bewegung in Deutschland und Österreich: Zu den Auseinandersetzungen um die "liturgische Frage" in den Jahren 1939 bis 1944*. Regensburg: Pustet.
McCormack, Bruce L. 1995. *Karl Barth's Critically Realistic Dialectical Theology: Its Genesis and Development 1909–1936*. Oxford: Oxford University Press.
Meier, Kurt. 1982. *Volkskirche 1918–1945: Ekklesiologie und Zeitgeschichte*. Munich: Chr. Kaiser Verlag.
Missalla, Heinrich. 1968. *"Gott mit uns": Die deutsche katholische Kriegspredigt 1914–1918*. Munich: Kösel Verlag.
Pressel, Wilhelm. 1967. *Die Kriegspredigt 1914–1918 in der evangelischen Kirche Deutschlands*. Göttingen: Vandenhoeck and Ruprecht.
Scholder, Klaus. 1987. *The Churches and the Third Reich: The Year of Disillusionment 1934, Barmen and Rome*. Vol. 2. London: SCM.
Theissen, Gerd, and Annette Merz, eds. 1998. *The Historical Jesus: A Comprehensive Guide*. London: SCM.

Gnosticism

The words "Gnostic" and "Gnosticism" derive from the Greek *gnosis*, "knowledge," and *gnostikos*, "endowed with or claiming knowledge," and are used in many different ways. We shall here consider Gnosticism as a version of Christianity, important in the second century but generally rejected since as heretical. Marcionism originates in the same period with Marcion of Pontus, and has some similar features. There are however two other meanings of *Gnostic* that we mention and set aside:

1. In the early Church many reckoned it a high ideal to "know" God, and the second- and third-century Alexandrians Clement and Origen, and their fourth-century monastic follower Evagrius Ponticus, regarded the Gnostic as one who had overcome the flesh and lived in the light of God's presence. This spiritual light was *gnosis*, "knowledge," and went beyond the simple faith that is its foundation. We leave these mainstream writers out of account here.

2. In the early twentieth century a group of German scholars, usually called the Religious History School, put forward the idea that *Gnosis* was a world religion derived from Iranian Zoroastrianism before the time of Christ. It envisaged two opposing principles in the universe, light and darkness, good and evil, spirit and matter. Such dualism reappears in Manichaeism. On this view, a Gnostic myth was widespread: a primal fall of light from the heavenly realm, the captivity of particles of light in material things, the heavenly call and the coming of a savior-figure to collect up these scattered particles, and their final restoration to their spiritual place of origin. Such a religion spread (it was held) among baptizing sects in the Jordan valley and influenced the New Testament. There we have the preexistent divine Christ, who comes from heaven to save the prisoners of death and sin, gathers them into his body through his Spirit and sacraments, and takes them with him to heaven. The central message of the New Testament, on which the historic doctrines about Jesus are based, is of pre-Christian and non-Jewish origin. This "religious-history" view lay behind much German theology in the mid-twentieth

century. Bultmann and his followers, notably Walter Schmithals and Ernst Käsemann, found it basic to Paul and the Gospel of John: Jesus the man, the prophet and rabbi, is not what Christianity is about. Kurt Rudolph's valuable survey *Gnosis* is also written on that presupposition; for another view, see Pétrement.

Whatever the merits of the Religious History School's approach, we shall here follow the older and wider convention and begin in the second century. Then the name *Gnostic* was attached to various schools of Christian thought that came to be regarded as heretical by the main churches. Various such groups, their founders and writers, are known from orthodox critics, especially Irenaeus (c. 130–c. 200) and Hippolytus (c. 175–c. 236). (1) Some groups may have called themselves "Gnostics," claiming to perceive the deep spiritual meaning of scriptural texts. Their nicknames "Ophites," "Ophians," "Naassenes" came from the Greek and Hebrew words for "snake" *(ophis. nahash)*, perhaps because they took the snake of Gen. 3 to be introducing Eve to knowledge that her Creator wanted to prevent; though there are other explanations. (2) The Sethians saw the Gnostics as the spiritual descendants of Adam's third son Seth (though again there are other connections, with Egyptian religion). A large group of Gnostic monastic texts was discovered at Nag Hammadi in upper Egypt in 1945. They were written in Coptic about 350, but have an earlier history in Greek and Syrian Christianity (cf. the Gospel of Thomas). Many of these are Sethian-Gnostic. These and some other groups belong to what some moderns (like Bentley Layton) take as the primary manifestation of Gnosticism. (3) A fundamentally biblical and philosophical system was elaborated in Alexandria by Basilides (c. 100–c. 160), very different from the sects mentioned, and his school continued and developed after his death. (4) Valentinus (c. 100–c. 175) came from Egypt but spent a long time in Rome and produced a mystical kind of biblical *gnosis*, basically like the earlier Gnosticism. Valentinus's teachings certainly developed in various directions in the East and in Rome, with leaders known to history: in the late second century Ptolemaeus wrote a surviving pamphlet on biblical interpretation, and Heracleon wrote a commentary on the Gospel of John that Origen used. Some Nag Hammadi texts are Valentinian. (5) There is some overlap of Gnosticism with early Syriac Christianity. (6) Some early books classed as *Apocryphal New Testament* contain Gnostic (or Marcionite) ideas: they come as gospels, acts of various apostles, epistles, and revelations (apocalypses). Some survived on the fringe of the church tradition, others have been recovered from Nag Hammadi.

Gnostics use typological or allegorical interpretation of the text of Scripture: what the Bible offers is not, or not only, the literal meaning, but a deeper, spiritual truth. Most Christian exegetes of the time did this, following New Testament precedent. Already for Paul, Old Testament passages are sometimes really about current Christian issues (1 Cor. 9.8–12), and so are narratives (1 Cor. 10.1–11). Difficult laws and stories in the Old Testament may be spiritualized, so that they point to Jesus and the Church, like the priesthood and temple sacrifice in the Letter to Hebrews. Soon Christian writers would follow the Hellenized Jewish philosopher Philo (fl. A.D. 40) in distinguishing the two accounts of the creation of Man and Woman in Gen. 1.26–27 and 2.6–7, 18–24: the first happens in a spiritual order, the second in the material world.

The Gnostics found all sorts of clues to this dual world, the realm of spirit and the created order. The former is ruled over by a Primal Mind, or Spirit, who is ineffable, nameless, but can be called the Father, the Progenitor, the (Primal) Man, the Deep; in Basilides he is the "Non-existent God," because (following Plato) even to say he exists is more than we can say. This Spirit has a variety of companions, consorts, sons, emanations, together constituting his Fullness (*Pleroma*, a word from texts like Col. 1.19). They are often called *Eons* (or *Aeons*, Greek for "ages" or "worlds"). In the primary Gnostic and Valentinian stories one of these beings, usually called Wisdom, desires to know too much, and some kind of "fall" occurs (a spiritual version of the temptation of Eve). Wisdom (*Sophia* in Greek), or part of her, passes out of the Fullness, and she produces an inferior being who becomes the God of the Old Testament, or one version of him; often he is called Ialdabaoth (a Semitic name of uncertain origin), or in Valentinus "The Craftsman" (*demiurgos*, following Plato's creation myth). From him, and his manifestations and angels, Adam and Eve are made, and the whole Old Testament history is the scene of the struggle of Wisdom to implant truth and light in his unfortunate creatures, and then to keep it alive in the face of the malice, greed, or incompetence of the Creator. Finally Wisdom (or her lost junior partner Achamoth, corrupt Hebrew/Aramaic for "Wisdom") pleads with the great Spirit to save her. Then the Christ/Anointed, who is one of the beings in the Fullness, is sent from the spiritual realm to restore order. This Christ, in Sethian documents also called Seth, unites himself with Sophia/Achamoth, and together they enter Jesus, usually at his baptism. In some Valentinian traditions Christ may be a son of the fallen Sophia or the Craftsman, and the Savior sent with all the powers of the Fullness is himself called Jesus. This savior/Christ figure by his teaching and resurrection enables the spiritual sparks embedded in human beings to wake to the truth, to become identified with him, and to rise to their true destiny. This is in fact the resurrection of the faithful in *The Treatise on Resurrection* and *The Gospel of Philip*. Ialdabaoth or his equivalent learns that he is not, as he thought, the only or highest god, and repents. There is usually a final judgment: the Pleroma is restored to perfection with the return of Sophia/Achamoth, and the lower elements are given their proper status, whether destruction or an intermediate eternity. In Basilides each of four realms is stabilized, and the lower ones forget all they have known of those above.

Gnostics accept the main Gospel accounts of Jesus and interpret them spiritually. In earlier sects (Carpocrates, Cerinthus, Justin's "*Baruch*") Jesus is the son of Joseph and Mary, but superior to other men, following Judeo-Christian traditions. For others he is a son of Ialdabaoth, but prepared by Wisdom ("Achamoth," or Sophia in her lower manifestation) as a specially pure vessel by virgin birth. Into him the Christ, accompanied by Wisdom, entered when he was baptized. Basilides uses Luke's and Matthew's birth stories to depict the descent of the Spirit from on high upon Mary. For the Ophites, Mary is a virgin and Ialdabaoth is father of Jesus, a saintly man on whom the transcendent Christ, married to Sophia, descends at his baptism and empowers him. In Valentinianism similarly, the material ("psychic") man is from the Craftsman, though inspired by Wisdom, and passes through Mary "as water through a pipe"; it was the Savior from the spiritual realm who came down at his baptism. In one version (Exc. Theod. 59–61) the Savior took first the seed of Sophia, then the Christ, who is the Craftsman's Son and already "the image of the Saviour," and finally a body "woven out of invisible, psychic substance" so as to be perceptible to sense. In Luke 1.35 the "Holy Spirit" that comes upon Mary is Sophia, and the "power of the Most High" that overshadows her is the Craftsman (Hippolytus Ref. 6.35). It is his body and spirit that grew in wisdom and stature (Luke 2.52). Valentinus himself suggested (Clem. Alex., *Strom.* 3.7 [59.3]) that his divinity was such that he ate and drank in a miraculous way, without evacuating the bowel. A similar idea is found in Acts of John 89, 93, where not only does Jesus appear different to different people, but, in addition, his body sometimes is material, sometimes immaterial and weightless; this is suggested by Gospel ideas like walking on water.

The teachings of Jesus are inspired. Theodotus explains, following certain Gospel texts (Exc. Thdt. 33): "The Saviour taught the apostles, first in a figurative and mystical way, then in parables and riddles, and thirdly, clearly and directly in private." This can mean three inspirational sources, corresponding to Jesus' own makeup: some are from the Savior, some from Sophia/Achamoth, some from the Craftsman. This continues a pattern of varied inspiration that Gnostics perceive in the Old Testament too (Irenaeus *haer.* 1.7.3; Ptolemaeus, *To Flora*). To some extent Gnostics anticipate the practice, declared orthodox at Chalcedon, of reading some words of Jesus as human, others divine.

Similarly, the Church's later problems of reconciling human passions and suffering with Christ's deity appear, with a tendency to distinguish the Son of Man who suffers from the Son of God, who does not. The heavenly savior could not suffer. In some Basilidean teaching the nations of this world are under the control of angels, and the ineffable Father sent his firstborn Mind *(Nous)* to rescue the souls of human beings. He deceived the world-rulers, who crucified Simon of Cyrene by mistake (Mark 15.20–21 and parallels), while Jesus, disguised as Simon, laughs at them (cf. Ps. 2.4). For some, Jesus died (Exc. Thdt. 61–62) when the (savior-) Spirit withdrew; some place this withdrawal at his trial before Pilate. In Acts of John 97–99 Jesus comes to John on the Mount of Olives even while the physical crucifixion proceeds, and there explains the cosmic meaning of the Cross.

The Gospel accounts of the resurrection of Jesus are generally accepted by Gnostics, though the meaning of resurrection for the believer is spiritualized (see *The Treatise on the Resurrection*). In the period after the resurrection of Jesus, already a time for explaining the mysteries of Scripture in Luke 24.25–27, 44–47, mysteries are revealed. In the very popular *Secret Book of John (Apocryphon of John)* a whole Gnostic system is revealed to the apostle

John in a special manifestation on the Mount of Olives. The *Gospel of Thomas* and *The Book of Thomas the Contender* present teachings of Jesus after the resurrection; *The Sophia of Jesus Christ* frames Gnostic revelations to the apostles with the risen Jesus on a mountain in Galilee. The risen Lord may also be actively visible, spectacularly in the Acts of Thomas, where he intervenes repeatedly in his twin brother Thomas's mission to India, sometimes changing places with him. In Valentinianism the Spirit revived Jesus Christ with life: his spiritual part rejoined the Pleroma, while his psychic part rose from the dead and ascended to sit at the Craftsman's right hand, in that intermediate position that he finally attains. In Basilides, part of the unformed Sonship gathers to Jesus when he brings the light from above, taking pure form: the world ceases to groan and travail as the sons of God are revealed (Rom. 8.19, 22), and with Jesus they rise through the spheres and the firmament to the Nonexistent. In the death and rising of Jesus begins the "separation of kinds": the material body remained in the "formlessness"; his "animal" soul remained with the Ruler of the Seven, his spirit with the Ruler of the Eight, and the pure Sonship (with all those gathered to Jesus) returns to the realm above.

Gnostics generally do not question the four Gospels: they interpret them allegorically, or put them in the frame of a wider system. The *Gospel of Truth* is a sermon, probably by Valentinus himself, interpreting the whole Gospel history in spiritual terms. In *The Gospel of Philip* 71 (119) the birth from the virgin symbolizes heavenly realities: Jesus reveals the union of the original Parent with "the virgin who descended" (that is, Wisdom in her fallen condition), in order to restore peace in heaven. Heracleon continually allegorizes John's Gospel: Jesus "went down" to Capernaum and "went up" to Jerusalem (John 2.12–13) to signify his descent into matter and his ascension from it. Among Valentinians Jesus' cry from the Cross, "My God, my God, why have you forsaken me?" represents the anguish of Sophia when she was deserted by Light and excluded from the Pleroma. The twelve-year-old girl whom Jesus raised to life also represents Achamoth (the twelfth Eon), saved by Christ. In Basilides's long account there are four levels of reality, the nonexistent God (he is "beyond being") and three "Sonships" (classes of "sons") that come from his seed: one mounts up to the Nonexistent; below the firmament is the Great Ruler of the Eight Powers above the heaven, and his Son; in third place the Ruler of the Seven, the God of this world, and his Son; and at the bottom, the unformed Sonship awaiting definition, its members being trained by helping each other. There descends from the Nonexistent a light, through the Sons of the Great Ruler and of the Ruler of the Seven (astonishing their respective fathers!), finally settling on Mary and illuminating her son Jesus. Then "all that concerns the Saviour happened just as is written in the Gospels"—with no further detail, except the explanation of his death as "the separation of kinds."

All such allegorizing and speculation are alien to the version of Christianity put forward by Marcion (fl. c. A.D. 140, perhaps earlier). Marcion shares with Gnosticism only the idea that God the Creator is not the Father of Jesus Christ, who is the higher "Unknown God." Marcion regarded the whole Old Testament as written by the clumsy and violent Creator, and he rejected all the subtle allegory by which the Gnostics found their doctrines underlying the Bible, and by which mainstream Christians like Origen made sense of biblical contradictions and absurdities. The Creator is "the god of this world" of 2 Cor. 4.4. The Unknown God, says Marcion, took pity on the human race, afflicted in the name of justice and law by their Creator, and sent his Son as Jesus Christ to rescue them. The story is told in Luke's Gospel adapted for the purpose (or, just possibly, in an earlier draft than the one we know). This started with a sudden appearance in the synagogue (Luke 4.16). Marcion omits the birth stories, presumably because he held sex, marriage, and reproduction as abominations (together with mosquitoes and beasts of prey) invented by the whimsical Creator. It is likely, but not certain, that Marcion's prejudice against the body and matter meant that his Christ is "docetic"—that is, that he only appeared to have a body (cf. Ignatius). Jesus gathered and commissioned disciples, as in the Gospel, and offered his life to the Creator, the god of the Law, in exchange for the souls of the damned in Hades, so getting them liberated with believers of all nations. He himself could not be held by death. The Creator, thus tricked, countered by corrupting the Apostles with his own legalistic-Jewish errors. All the other Gospel accounts are poisoned with this corruption. The Unknown God then raised up Paul to oppose the Apostles (cf. Gal. 2.11–14), and then raised up Marcion to rescue his Church from the false doctrines they had propagated. Paul's genuine letters are the linchpin and inspiration of Marcion's system.

We do not know whether Marcion (or his mysterious predecessor Cerdon) was the first to use Paul's antithesis of Law and Gospel, Flesh and Spirit, to dethrone the Creator and generate a "God above God." He might have supplied the idea that the Gnostics all develop. More likely, primitive Gnosticism existed, and Basilides and Valentinus refined it, while Marcion repudiated all allegorical interpretation, insisting on taking the Old Testament literally. Whatever the history, the main Churches shrank back from both extremes. They insisted on one God of prophets and apostles, Supreme, Creator and Savior, and one Jesus Christ, effecting in himself the union of human and divine life, of flesh and spirit. If there is a distinct divine being or "Craftsman" other than the supreme Father, it is his own Word and Son, by whom he made all things, and that Son is enfleshed in Jesus.

In modern eyes much of what the Gnostics wrote and Marcion surmised may seem outlandish. Yet they were mostly serious Christians trying to make sense of scriptural texts that were hard to understand, before there were any general creedal guidelines, and when even the limits ("canon") of Scripture were still not fixed. For the Gnostics, Jesus Christ had reconciled or overpowered all things in heaven and earth (cf. Col. 1.15–20), and reveals divine secrets to the spiritually minded (1 Cor. 2.6–11). In exploring such thoughts they opened up questions of lasting importance: Which traditions give a reliable guide to the message of Jesus? How are the ancient Hebrew Scriptures to be understood in the light of that message? Does Jesus call people out of the world into a purely spiritual life, or does he save and heal us in our human wholeness? How is the claim that Jesus is Lord and God and creative Spirit to be reconciled with his human existence as a fleshly, growing, suffering man? The Church may have rejected the Gnostic and Marcionite answers, but it has had to return to the questions again and again.

Finally, it is pleasant to note that one of our more tangible legacies from Gnosticism is Gustav Holst's (d. 1934) setting to music, in the "Hymn of Jesus," of the dance of Jesus with his disciples in the Garden of Gethsemane before the Passion, described in the early-third-century Acts of John. It is a motif made widely popular in Sydney Carter's hymn "The Lord of the Dance."

S. G. *Hall*

See also: Alexandrian Theology; Bultmann, Rudolf; Chalcedon; Hebrew Bible; Hebrews; Ignatius of Antioch; Irenaeus; Jesus, Origins of; John, Gospel of; Manichaeism; Origen; Paul; Preexistence; Resurrection; Thomas, Gospel of

References

Elliott, J. K., ed. 1993. *The Apocryphal New Testament*. Oxford: Clarendon.

Foerster, Werner, ed. 1972–1974. *Gnosis: A Selection of Gnostic Texts*. English translation edited by R. McL. Wilson. Oxford: Clarendon.

Hennecke, E., ed. 1963–1964. *New Testament Apocrypha*. English translation edited by R. McL. Wilson. London: Lutterworth/SCM.

Layton, Bentley. 1987. *The Gnostic Scriptures*. Garden City, NY: Doubleday/London: SCM.

Robinson, James M., ed. 1977. *The Nag Hammadi Library in English*. Leiden: E. J. Brill.

Stevenson, James, ed. 1987. *A New Eusebius*. Rev. with additional documents by W. H. C. Frend. London: SPCK.

Studies:

Aland, Barbara. 1992. "Marcion/Marcioniten." Pp. 89–101 in *Theologische Realenzyklopädie* 22. Berlin/New York: Walter de Gruyter.

Blackman, E. C. 1948. *Marcion and His Influence*. London: SPCK.

Hall, Stuart G. 1985. "Knowing Your Gnostics." *Journal of Ecclesiastical History* 36: 103–108.

May, Gerhard. 1987. "Marcion in Contemporary Views." *Second Century* 6, no. 3: 129–151.

Pétrement, Simone. 1991. *A Separate God: The Christian Origins of Gnosticism*. London: Darton, Longman and Todd.

Rudolph, Kurt. 1983. *Gnosis: The Nature and History of an Ancient Religion*. Edited by Robert McLachlan Wilson. Edinburgh: T. and T. Clark.

Great War

The Great War of 1914–1918, which cost the lives of more than eight million people, most of them young men, was dominated theologically by the figure of Jesus on the Cross. How that figure was used and interpreted varied greatly between the start of the war and its end, and between the home front and the battlefronts. The two most common interpretations of the crucifixion were that it gave an example of self-sacrificial leadership, or the model of suffering humanity.

Jesus the self-sacrificing leader of men was the figure in widest circulation at the beginning of the war, and the credibility of this figure lasted longest the further it was from the fighting itself. On the Cross Jesus was held to provide the supreme example of someone giving up their life for others. Thus, he was offered as an example to young British men of how they should respond to the German invasion of Belgium, which began on 4 August 1914. The invasion was generally presented to the British public in emotionally charged accounts of the weak and helpless being overpowered by the mighty and tyrannical. When this was combined with the story of Jesus laying down his life for his friends, it formed an evocative recruiting tool. In a similar vein, appeals were made to the glory and honor attached to laying down one's life for a higher cause. Although such appeals lacked the immediacy of asking men to risk their lives for the well-being of the Belgians under occupation, they had a greater potency insofar as they were more readily susceptible to an overt kind of theologizing. For example, the Bishop of London, A. F. Winnington-Ingram, was able to assert that those who fought and died "to save the world" were martyrs, and one chaplain to the British Expeditionary Force claimed that the fallen British troops had died "for Jesus." Some concern was shown to ensure that the crucified Jesus was not portrayed as being in any way passive or weak, such traits being the opposite of what recruiting agents like to appeal to. So emphasis was placed on the courage of Jesus, the "manliness" of his self-sacrifice; one chaplain went so far as to describe him as "the Man with the iron body, and the iron will." Similar appeals to the Cross were being made in Germany, which led Karl Barth to write as early as September 1914 that such talk was "war theology . . . its Christian trimming consisting of a lot of talk about sacrifice and the like" (Dorrien, 37).

Jesus the courageous leader of men proved ill-equipped to survive the violence and enormous death toll of the front lines of the Great War. The idea that the war was being fought for some great cause was not sustainable among the men who saw hundreds and thousands die in the most awful conditions for small territorial gains that were often reversed several times in the course of the war. The poet Wilfred Owen, who was killed in action on 4 November 1918, described as "The old Lie" the Latin line "Dulce et decorum est pro patria mori" ("It is sweet and meet to die for one's country. Sweet and decorous."). However, if anything, the significance attached to the crucified Jesus by many of those actually engaged in the fighting increased. The suffering Jesus was seen as the archetype of suffering and dying man. The poet Herbert Read, who served with the Royal Howards from 1915 to 1918, wrote:

> My men, my modern Christs,
> Your bloody agony confronts the world. (Gardner, 88)

This understanding of Jesus was usually stripped of overt theological content; Jesus was a good man who died, and as such a symbol for all the other good men who were dying in the trenches. Not only was the suffering Jesus rarely portrayed in an overtly theological context, at times his suffering was held up as a challenge to any understanding of an Almighty God. This division between the suffering Jesus and God was perhaps best described by the Army chaplain Rev. G. A. Studdert Kennedy (he was best known as "Woodbine Willie" after his custom of handing out packets of Woodbine cigarettes to the troops). He described pointing to a crucifix when a wounded officer asked him what God was like. Studdert Kennedy wrote that the officer replied: "I asked you not what Jesus *was* like, but what God *is* like, God Who willed His death in agony upon the Cross, and Who apparently wills the wholesale slaughter in this war. Jesus Christ I know and admire, but what is God almighty like?" (Studdert Kennedy, xv). It seems that many of those who fought grew in empathy with the crucified Jesus, even as their belief in God was being exploded.

Studdert Kennedy claimed that it was in response to the officer's question "What is God almighty like?" that he wrote his book *The Hardest Part*. The answer that he, and some others, came to was that "God almighty" was not above or beyond the suffering of the trenches, but that in the crucifixion of Jesus we are shown that God is "in" human suffering. This response sought to make sense of human suffering, the suffering Jesus of history and the Godhead. Writing of the bodies on the battlefields, Studdert Kennedy asked the question: "Is it wrong to see in them His Body and His Blood—God's Body, God's Blood?" (ibid., 134). He was criticized for going as far as he did in asserting not only a connection between the suffering of the soldiers and the suffering of Jesus Christ, but also God's participation in that suffering. Although his books sold in large numbers and he preached all over the country, it was to be several decades before the passibilist position that he so publicly espoused (that is, that God can be, and is, "moved" or affected by the experiences of humankind) was to gain an established place in the theological mainstream.

Several "minority" responses to Jesus current during the Great War are worth noting. Some rejected Jesus as being just as redundant in the trenches as God. One anonymous soldier wrote that if Jesus was still alive he could only conclude that he had "lost interest in the welfare of men and the world" (*The Army and Religion*, 48). Some remained heartily unconvinced by the "iron Man" Jesus, and concluded that both he and his doctrines were "womanly." This may have been born of the concern shown by some in the religious and military hierarchies about the swearing and sexual conduct of the troops, which to most of the troops themselves did not seem to be the most grievous wrongs arising from the war. Lastly, there were those whose faith in Jesus as a man of peace and nonviolence led them to reject participation in the war as conscientious objectors. Even among the men who were involved in the fighting some believed that they were engaged in something that Jesus would clearly have been against. Wilfred Owen wrote:

> I dreamed kind Jesus fouled the big-gun gears . . .
> And rusted every bayonet with his tears. (Stallworthy, 69)

In the years following the war, it was this last position that was to gain ground, within the churches at least. The 1930 Lambeth Conference was to declare that "war as a method of settling international disputes is incompatible with the teaching and example of our Lord Jesus Christ."

Stuart Owen

See also: Barth, Karl; English Christianity, 1750–1940; German Christianity; Liberation Theology; Literature, English

References

Anon. 1919. *The Army and Religion: An Enquiry and Its Bearing upon the Religious Life of the Nation*. London: Macmillan.

Dorrien, Gary. 2000. *The Barthian Revolution in Modern Theology*. Louisville, KY: Westminster John Knox.

Gardner, Brian, ed. 1964. *Up the Line to Death: The War Poets 1914–1918*. London: Methuen.

Stallworthy, John, ed. 2000. *Wilfred Owen: The War Poems*. London: Chatto and Windus.

Studdert Kennedy, Geoffrey A. 1918. *The Hardest Part*. London: Hodder and Stoughton.

Wilkinson, Alan. 1996. *The Church of England and the First World War*. 2d ed. London: SCM.

H

Harnack, Adolf von (1851–1930)

Adolf von Harnack was the embodiment of liberal theology at the beginning of the twentieth century. He was a pupil of Ritschl and became his disciple. His call to Berlin in 1888, though eventually upheld by the German emperor, was opposed by the Evangelical Church. His views (for example, concerning the meaning of the Apostles' Creed and the status of the Old Testament) continued to provoke ecclesiastical hostility. His influence was nevertheless profound. He wrote prolifically, chiefly in the field of early Church history and the development of doctrine. He was the quintessential representative of *Kulturprotestantismus*.

The liberal Protestants' famous "quest of the historical Jesus" was motivated by the desire to discover Jesus "as he really was," before he was transformed by the faith of the Church into the "biblical Christ." Dogma was problematic, but the new science, history, presented them with the opportunity to establish the Christian faith on the firm basis of historical fact. But to satisfy the criteria of the modern historian, any picture of Jesus must be of a purely human figure. Harnack drew the logical conclusion and banished from history, and therefore from theology, such concepts as revelation, incarnation, miracle, and resurrection, which he considered unscientific. From now on the Jesus of history *was* the Christ of liberal faith.

Harnack's magnum opus was his *History of Dogma,* which appeared in three volumes between 1886 and 1889. *Outlines of the History of Dogma* (1889, 1893) was a more accessible presentation. His essential thesis was that dogma was "a work of the Greek spirit on the ground of the gospel." The kernel of the gospel had been overlaid by husks as alien metaphysical concepts and categories corrupted primitive Christianity into historic Catholicism. It was therefore necessary for the gospel to be emancipated. At the Reformation Luther had begun the process of emancipation; it was now the task of the historian of dogma to complete it. Harnack sought to carry out that task in *Das Wesen des Christentums* ("the essence of Christianity"), a course of popular lectures delivered in 1899–1900. (The title was a deliberate echo of the radical thinker Feuerbach's 1841 book of the same name.) The English translation's title asked a question: *What Is Christianity?* The answer that Harnack gives is often misrepresented. The familiar summary that the teaching of Jesus is about the fatherhood of God and the brotherhood and sisterhood of men and women is an oversimplification. Harnack in fact summarizes Jesus' teaching under three heads: the kingdom of God and its coming; God the Father and the infinite value of the human soul; and the higher righteousness and the command of love. But he does not contend that the kingdom is brought about by human effort. "The kingdom of God comes by coming to the individual, by entering into his soul and laying hold of it. True, the kingdom of God is the rule of God; but it is the rule of the holy God in the hearts of individuals; it is God himself in his power" (56). A key text for Harnack is Matt. 11.27: "Jesus is convinced that he knows God in a way in which no one ever knew Him before, and he knows that it is his vocation to communicate this knowledge of God to others" (128). Jesus is unique, but his uniqueness is not ontological. The Gospel "has to do with the Father only and not with the Son" (144). Jesus' own place in the Gospel is as "its personal realization and its strength" (145), but "he desired no other belief in his person and no other attachment to it than is contained in the keeping of his commandments" (125). The reality of Christianity for Harnack is the treasure that the soul possesses in Communion with God. "[It] means one thing and one thing only: Eternal life in the midst of time, by the strength and under the eyes of God" (8).

The historical work of the liberal Protestants concealed an apologetic motive. They were not disinterested enquirers. Their hidden assumption was that, if only the "real" Jesus could be recovered, he would certainly prove to be the inspiration for a renewed Christianity, capable of claiming the credence of cultured modern people. Their religious viewpoint can be read between the lines. In the much-quoted judgment of the Catholic modernist George Tyrrell: "The Christ that Harnack sees, looking back through nineteen centuries of Catholic darkness, is only the reflection of a Liberal Protestant face, seen at the bottom of a deep well" (49). Nevertheless, *What Is Christianity?* continues to attract by its humanity, and Rudolf Bultmann was surely right to say, in his introduction to a fiftieth anniversary edition, that "the popular understanding of the Christian faith . . . accords in some measure with the portrait drawn by Harnack, even if it does not achieve his earnestness and subtlety" (viii).

Brian G. Powley

See also: Bultmann, Rudolf; Christology, Modern; Enlightenment; German Christianity; Jesus as a Historical Figure; Kingdom of God

References

Glick, G. Wayne. 1967. *The Reality of Christianity: A Study of Adolf von Harnack as Historian and Theologian*. New York: Harper and Row.

Harnack, Adolf. 1957. *What Is Christianity?* New York: Harper Torchbooks.

Rumscheidt, Martin. 1991. *Adolf von Harnack: Liberal Theology at Its Height*. Minneapolis: Fortress.

Sykes, Stephen. 1984. *The Identity of Christianity: Theologians and the Essence of Christianity from Schleiermacher to Barth*. London: SPCK.

Tyrrell, George. 1963. *Christianity at the Cross-Roads*. London: George Allen and Unwin.

Harvey, A. E. (b. 1930)

An Oxford-educated classicist, Harvey was ordained in 1958 and returned to Oxford (Christ Church) in 1962, where he wrote the widely used one-volume commentary *Companion to the New Testament* (1970, 2d ed. 1979—new edition forthcoming). His major contributions to the historical study of Jesus are the 1980 Bampton lectures, *Jesus and the Constraints of History* (1982), and an equally lucid work on "the ethic of Jesus," *Strenuous Commands* (1990). An earlier study of the Fourth Gospel, *Jesus on Trial* (1976), and several articles and reviews, notably "Christ as Agent" (1987), show his concern to relate historical and Christological insights. Harvey combines the ancient historian's deep knowledge of the Hellenistic and Jewish worlds, a particular interest in ethics, and the well-tuned theological instincts of an Anglican churchman who until retirement in 1999 held several posts in Oxford, Canterbury (principal of St. Augustine's) and London (from 1982, Westminster Abbey). His writings exemplify the liberal Anglican preoccupation with history and its apologetic potential. The 1982 work is arguably the best book on Jesus by an English author, judicious in assessing the evidence and with no trace of conservative special pleading, attuned equally well to the early Jewish context and to the religious subject matter.

The strategy adopted is to allow recent advances in the study of Jesus' historical milieu to suggest what options were available to him as he aimed to communicate his religious vision within the conventions of his culture and civilization. This in turn suggests what it might mean to claim that "God was with" a historical figure in such a unique and decisive way that he could be regarded as an agent of the divine and be the object of love and worship. Harvey moves from the legal questions raised by Jesus' teaching, conduct, and crucifixion, to his attitude to the law, his eschatology, and "the intelligibility of miracle." He claims that Jesus creatively combined several strands of Jewish tradition, but is best described as an eschatological prophet. Messiahship was a relatively undefined category to which his followers gave specificity. Jewish expectations were focused more on the new age than on the divine agent who might inaugurate it. Jesus spoke not of himself but of the kingdom of God already partly present in his activity, and to be fully realized in the future. He might well have been called "anointed" during his ministry—and before the term became a formal title. The prophetic symbolism of his entering Jerusalem on an animal instead of on foot like other pilgrims is significant, but Jesus' conviction of divine authorization must be interpreted within the "constraint" of monotheism.

Bampton lectures are university sermons, and themselves subject to the double constraint of minimal time and religious genre. Both of Harvey's "historical Jesus" books, like those of Bultmann, Cadbury, and Bornkamm, are short, historically plausible, and based on strong but largely concealed academic foundations and engagement with other scholars. They have much to say to contemporary Christian reflection on ethical issues and the practice of discipleship. The later account of Jesus' "ethic" explores its relationship to other "projects of moral persuasion." Jesus' style was that of a wisdom teacher, "building up moral attitudes through particular examples, forming the will through a series of memorable maxims, challenging presuppositions through taking extreme instances" (193), not writing moral codes or community rules. People are challenged to live as if the distant ideal were actually present. This has made effective action possible, and some of its impact becomes visible in Harvey's social and political theology reflected in *By What Authority?* (2001).

Robert Morgan

See also: Bultmann, Rudolf; Cadbury, H. J.; Jesus, Miracles of; Jesus as a Historical Figure; Kingdom of God; Law; Messiah

References

Harvey, A. E. 1970, 1979. *Companion to the New Testament*. Oxford: Oxford University Press; Cambridge: Cambridge University Press.

———. 1976. *Jesus on Trial*. London: SPCK.

———. 1982. *Jesus and the Constraints of History*. London: Duckworth.

———. 1990. *Strenuous Commands*. London: SCM.

Healing

See Jesus, Miracles of

Hebrew Bible

Christians have traditionally believed that Jesus relates to the Hebrew Bible in two primary ways—first (and best known, for it is a major theme of the New Testament) as a fulfilment of its hopes and expectations, and secondly (a recurrent theme of Christian spirituality) as in some sense already present within its texts. This article will briefly survey the ways in which Jesus is understood to fulfill Israel's Scripture, and then consider a little more fully how Jesus may be understood to be present within texts written before he was born.

That Jesus "fulfills Scripture" is a recurrent theme in the New Testament, which presents his death and resurrection as being "according to the scriptures" (1 Cor. 15.3, 4, cf. Luke 24.25–27), an understanding present also in the Nicene Creed. This general theme is perhaps seen most clearly in what has become his name within Christian faith—that is, Jesus Christ. For "Christ" is a Greek translation of the Hebrew term "messiah," a term that means "anointed one" and occurs regularly in the Hebrew Bible where it is used of priests and especially kings. It is a term that is not comprehensible apart from this Jewish context. Admittedly "Christ" as a particular title and role—that is, "the Christ"—is not found within the Hebrew Bible; but it was developed as an expression of Jewish hope within early Jewish interpretation of Scripture before the time of Jesus. Thus a major issue in the Gospels is whether or not Jesus is "the Christ/Messiah" (e.g., John 1.20; 20.31), and Jesus indeed accepts the title though only as he redefines its meaning (esp. Matt. 16.13–28 and parallels Matt. 26.63–65). Within Paul's letters the title is already more or less a name, and the followers of Jesus were known as "Christians" from an early period (Acts 11.26). Thus to call Jesus "Jesus

Christ" is already in effect to claim Jesus and Christian faith as the fulfilment of Israel's hopes.

The varying uses of the Hebrew Scriptures in relation to Jesus can be seen throughout the New Testament. A good illustration is Matthew's Gospel, in which at least three distinct uses are found. First, there are Matthew's own editorial comments, whose refrain is that the story he tells took place "to fulfil the Scriptures." One difficult key question is exactly what Matthew means by "fulfil," which must be inferred from his usage (though the difficulty of finding modern categories aptly to characterize this usage are considerable). His refrain appears prima facie to envisage a straightforward pattern of prediction and realization, of which the use of the Emmanuel passage of Isa. 7.14 in relation to the birth of Jesus is the most famous example (Matt. 1.22–23); compare the citation of Isaiah's gentle and persistent servant in relation to Jesus' healing ministry (Isa. 42.1–4; Matt. 12.15–21), or Zechariah's king on a donkey (with foal?) in relation to Jesus' "Triumphal Entry" into Jerusalem (Zech. 9.9; Matt. 21.1–7). Since the texts cited are generally not predictive within their Old Testament context (or if in some sense looking to the future then to a near and not to a distant future), this usage is puzzling to readers; does it show artificial and arbitrary proof-texting, or does it display a subtle analogical imagination, or what? Opinions differ, and the answer may well be complex.

Secondly, there is Jesus' own use of Scripture (as Jesus is presented by Matthew). Jesus' use, like Matthew's own, is presented as "fulfilling" Scripture (Matt. 5.17). But Jesus' usage is characterized less by "prediction" of some kind (though this in some form is found, e.g., 26.31; 26.52–54) than by a robust engagement with the moral and religious content of Scripture. Most famously there is the summary of the law (Torah) in terms of the two love commandments (22.34–40), but there is also Jesus' extended penetration of the fundamental meaning of Torah (5.21–48) and a clear evaluative statement of priorities (23.23). It is likely also that Jesus sees his own messiahship and vocation to suffer and die in terms of fulfilling Scripture. Although no explicit reference to Scripture is made in the key episode at Caesarea Philippi (16.13–28), the "necessity" of his suffering and dying is probably related to his understanding of Scripture; at the beginning of Jesus' ministry the nature of his vocation is probed with explicit reference to Scripture (4.1–11; Jesus appeals to passages within Deuteronomy that enunciate principles whose high religious significance is uncontroversial in a Jewish context), while the transfiguration, directly following Caesarea Philippi, shows Jesus engaging with Moses and Elijah, who probably represent the content of Israel's Scripture (i.e., the law and the prophets).

Thirdly, there is an implicit and allusive use of Scripture throughout, in the sense that the substantive issues to do with life before God within the Hebrew Scriptures are constantly taken up and developed, whether or not explicit citation is made (see Moberly). Thus, for example, an important scriptural theme is God's testing Israel with a view to ascertaining and furthering Israel's faithfulness and obedience: this is the reason for the giving of the Ten Commandments (Exod. 20.20, cf. Deut. 8.2–3) and is displayed in paradigmatic form in the story of Abraham and Isaac (Gen. 22), where the divine purpose to "test" (v. 1) is answered by Abraham's appropriate responsiveness—that is, "fear of God" (v. 12). Jesus' ministry as Son of God begins with tests as to whether he will subvert this vocation to serve his own purposes (Matt. 4.1–11); his prime disciple wants him to subvert his vocation as messiah (16.21–23, wherein Jesus rebukes Peter as though he were Satan, cf. 4.10); at the end of his ministry, as Jesus dies on the Cross, the passersby and religious leaders of Israel say (Satan clearly speaking again) that he can fulfill his ministry to Israel there and then by simply coming down from the Cross (27.39–43). As Abraham is tested by God, shows faithfulness, and receives renewed blessing (Gen. 22.15–18), so too Jesus, whose faithfulness leads him into the darkness of dereliction and death (27.45–50)—but beyond that to resurrection. In all these ways one can see something of what it means in Matthew's Gospel that Jesus "has come not to abolish but to fulfil" the law and the prophets (5.17).

What, then, about our second issue, the presence of Jesus within Israel's Scripture? This idea occurs within the New Testament, a notable instance being John 12.41. The context is John's commentary on the public ministry of Jesus, that "although he [Jesus] had performed so many signs in their presence, they did not believe in him. This was to fulfil the word spoken by the prophet Isaiah," where two citations of Isaiah follow (53.1; 6.10), about the second of which John says: "Isaiah said this because he saw his glory and spoke about him"—where the subject of "his/him" is clearly Jesus. Within John's Gospel part of the underlying logic is to do with the Word *(Logos)*, divine, agent of creation, and light of the world, who becomes flesh in the person of Jesus (John 1.1–5, 14). If Jesus is the Word, and the Word has been with God as God's agent from the beginning, then it may become possible to see how John could think of Isaiah's vision of God as a vision of God's Word—who is Jesus.

This Johannine understanding was developed by the Fathers of the Church in relation to their Trinitarian understanding of God, whereby God is Father, Son, and Holy Spirit in eternity. Thus when God speaks to, appears to, or acts within Israel in the Old Testament, it must be the Trinitarian God who thus speaks, appears, or acts; in some sense therefore it was really Jesus Christ whom Israel encountered, even if Israel did not realize that this was the case.

More generally, the understanding that God is definitively known in Jesus Christ encouraged an analogical way of thinking, whereby Jesus becomes the model, or pattern, or figure, for appropriating Israel's Scripture, the particular lens through which the text is read. This ancient perspective, which took numerous forms down the years (some much better than others), and which could be called *figural* reading, is receiving fresh attention as a possibility for contemporary Christian reading (see Seitz).

In an ancient context, St. Augustine, especially in his expositions of the psalms (see Fiedrowicz, in Rotelle), is a prime exemplar of Christ-focused interpretation. Augustine continued and developed an already existing Christian instinct to read the psalms as spoken to, about, and by Christ (who represents the body of Christ, the people of God) and so to relate their content to the life of Christ (and also to the life of the Church). Ps. 22 (21 in the Septuagint, which Augustine used), whose opening words "My God, my God, why have you forsaken me?" are on the lips of Jesus as he dies (Matt. 27.46; Mark 15.34), is a good example. The psalm heading was rendered in the Septuagint "To the end, for the taking up in the morning, a psalm of David" and on this Augustine comments (Rotelle, 221): "To the end, because the Lord Jesus speaks here, praying for his own resurrection, for he was raised in the morning, on the first day of the week . . . but the words of this psalm are spoken in the person of the crucified one, for here at its beginning is the cry he uttered while he hung upon the cross. He speaks consistently in the character of our old self, whose mortality he bore and which was nailed to the cross with him."

The New Testament roots and the patristic developments led to a flowering in Christian spirituality and art (Rublev's famous icon of the Trinity, interpreting the scene in Gen. 18.1–15, is an outstanding example); and it is striking that one of the great Christian thinkers of the twentieth century, Dietrich Bonhoeffer, repristinated Augustine's conception and argued that Christians pray the psalms insofar as they are incorporated into Christ who prays the psalms (Bonhoeffer). Nonetheless most modern biblical scholarship has, unsurprisingly, been dismissive of this whole conception. Roland Murphy, an eminent Roman Catholic biblical scholar, in a recent essay (Murphy, 82) expresses the point clearly: "It is often said or implied that Jesus is in the Old Testament. The ambiguity (and even, error) of such a statement should be clear. Jesus is not there. He is to be found in the New Testament. . . . If I am not mistaken, the 'finding' of Jesus in the Old Testament is the heirloom of patristic and medieval theology."

Two things seem to characterize this dismissal. On the one hand, a clear sense of history, a sense clearer than that held by most premoderns; Jesus as a historical figure lived long after the time of all Old Testament writers, none of whom envisaged or had him in mind as they wrote (as intensive modern study of Israel's Scriptures in relation to their originating contexts within the life of ancient Israel has shown). On the other hand, a distaste for, or at least a distancing from, the characteristic outlooks of premodern theologians whose lack of the disciplines afforded by modern critical historiography led them into making unwarranted assertions about the past, which must now be eschewed. Yet even if one fully grants the differences made by a modern sense of history and the discipline of critical historiography, and one does not dispute that the figure of Jesus was in no way in the minds of the writers of the Hebrew Scriptures, nonetheless recent hermeneutical debate about the nature of texts and textual interpretation may make it appropriate in certain ways to qualify Murphy's brusque dismissal.

For recent hermeneutical debate has moved away from the rather unreflective, often positivist, understanding of language in general and religious language in particular that has tended to characterize much modern historically oriented biblical criticism (see Thiselton). Important philosophical issues about the nature of language and understanding and reality have been freshly reengaged. Insofar as patristic and medieval biblical interpreters took for granted that their interpretation was inseparable from particular philosophical understandings (often highly sophisticated, as in Augustine) of language in relation to life, it is unsurprising that the recent revival of interest in hermeneutics should make possible a more sympathetic retrieval of some premodern interpretation. This is in no way a turning back of the clock, for any retrieval must still take seriously the issues of modernity, not least those of critical historiography and a scientific understanding of humanity, and so no replication of premodern outlooks is feasible. Nonetheless the recent growth in hermeneutical sophistication tends to create a more respectful attitude toward the hermeneutics of premodern interpreters.

Two different kinds of consideration deserve mention. On the one hand, religious texts that become enduringly significant for a community can go through various recontextualizations; as context changes, so may (in some way) the meaning of the text. Modern biblical study has shown that processes of reuse and recontextualization have deeply characterized the formation and compilation of Israel's Scriptures. In, for example, the book of Isaiah (which is clearly important for both of the ways we are discussing in which Jesus may be seen to relate to the Hebrew Scriptures), the actual ministry of the prophet Isaiah in Jerusalem in the eighth century has receded into near invisibility even in those texts that are ascribed to him, never mind those other texts (the majority of the book) that now keep them company; the book appears to have become a kind of literary context of its own, shaped by moral, religious, and symbolic concerns.

How one is to read such a book well becomes a difficult issue. For several generations of biblical scholars the all-important thing was to recover from the text the generative prophetic personalities in their originating historical contexts; for this exercise some of the book of Isaiah has to be rearranged, and some of it discarded. But when one ceases to be interested primarily in what one thinks the text "ought" to have provided its readers, and one attends instead to how one might understand what the text actually does offer its readers, the interpretative task changes. Particular prophets and kings and historical contexts become one element in a kaleidoscope of oracles and images and contexts, whose purpose appears to be to sustain continuing hope among successive generations of Jews in the recognition and implementation of God's royal rule over Israel and the nations, in which the role of human kingship may be implemented in many and varied ways. At the very least, the kind of thinking that has symbolically patterned a literary compilation within the Old Testament according to criteria far removed from those concerned with the actual life and message of the prophet Isaiah may be less distant from some of the kinds of thinking present in the New Testament than has sometimes been supposed.

On the other hand, there are interrelated issues to do with what a reader brings to a text in order for that text to be meaningful. This can take many forms, and "reader-response criticism" is a lively area of contemporary debate. Here we must note the role of theological convictions that a Christian reader brings to the biblical text, not least convictions about God. Basic to Christian faith is the conviction that there is one true God, who has made himself known in many and varied ways and supremely in his son Jesus (cf. Heb. 1.1–2). If Christians believe that God is definitively known in Jesus, what difference should that make to the way they read what Israel's Scriptures, which are accepted as authoritative by the Church, say about God? The question becomes not solely "Did Israel's writers, when they spoke of God, think in terms of Jesus?" (to which the answer is undoubtedly No), but rather something along the lines of "When we as Christians read these texts which we believe truly depict God (at least generally speaking), and we know God in terms of Jesus, then insofar as these texts continue to mediate and enable an encounter with God (in, say, preaching or Bible study), does not our encounter with the God of the Old Testament when we engage with the Old Testament take the form of an encounter with God in Christ?" There is thus a certain kind of existential sense whereby one may encounter Jesus within a text that does not of itself envisage Jesus but that is used in a context in which the God of whom the text speaks is envisaged in relation to Jesus.

Such a move in relation to the interpreter here and now is independent of making a possible further move, which has already been noted to be characteristic of the Church Fathers, that is, to appeal to divine ontology in the light of the Johannine conception of the *Logos*/Word which became flesh in Jesus. This conception was much utilized in patristic thought to account for the Christian understanding of particularity and finality in Jesus in relation to pre-Christian (i.e., Israel) and non-Christian (i.e., predominantly the great classical traditions of Greece and Rome) contexts: the divine *Logos* was active in these contexts, and the *Logos* is not other than Jesus. The issues here are not dissimilar to those that have been raised in recent years in attempts to offer Christian accounts of other religions, where Karl Rahner's notion of "anonymous Christians," whatever its merits, is a clear attempt to hold together a particular and historically specific knowledge of God in Jesus with the working of God in contexts that are not those of Christian belief—a divine working that is not intrinsically other than that which Christians recognize, however much it may be perceived otherwise by those who respond to it.

Finally in this regard there are conceptions related to the general issue of Christian discernment of God in the world. Where can God be seen in the world? Everywhere and nowhere. If one looks at the world without some prior conception of God (as the Bible depicts God) then, according to a common Christian (and Jewish) perspective, one is not likely to find God there. The world is patient of many interpretations, and the would-be believer is all too likely to end up in unbelief or idolatry (treating as God that which is not God) rather than in true faith. Yet to those who already know God, and so in some sense know what they are looking for, God can be seen in principle anywhere, and the ability to see God's presence and action more and more is generally regarded as a mark of spiritual maturity. By analogy, those who do not know God through Jesus will not find Jesus in Israel's Scriptures; but those who do, will, or at least may. And what would be found would be not as such the person depicted in the Gospels, but rather the kind of moral and spiritual understanding of God and human life that for Christians is summed up and focused supremely in Jesus.

These considerations are unlikely to appeal to all readers of Israel's Scriptures. Yet they offer ways in which Christians, even while sensitive to the issues properly involved in respecting particular texts as both ancient and Jewish, may yet make sense of the notion of Jesus Christ as present in texts whose writers were unaware of him.

R. W. L. Moberly

See also: Augustine of Hippo; Bonhoeffer, Dietrich; Creeds; Icons and the Icon Tradition; Interfaith Thought and Relations; John, Gospel of; Matthew, Gospel of; Messiah; Second Person of the Trinity; Transfiguration

References

Bonhoeffer, Dietrich. 1982. *The Psalms: Prayer Book of the Bible*. Oxford: SLG.

Moberly, R. W. L. 2000. *The Bible, Theology, and Faith: A Study of Abraham and Jesus*. Cambridge: Cambridge University Press.

Murphy, Roland. 2000. "Questions Concerning Biblical Theology." *Biblical Theology Bulletin* 30, no. 3: 81–89.

Rotelle, John, ed. 2000. *The Works of Saint Augustine: Expositions of the Psalms, 1–32*. Intro. by M. Fiedrowicz; translated and notes by M. Boulding. Hyde Park, NY: New City.

Seitz, Christopher. 2001. *Figured Out*. Louisville, KY: Westminster John Knox.

Thiselton, Anthony C. 1992. *New Horizons in Hermeneutics: The Theory and Practice of Transforming Biblical Criticism*. London: HarperCollins.

Hebrews, Letter to the

The distinctive features of the presentation of Jesus in the Letter to the Hebrews are its emphasis on his continuing presence in heaven, and its use of the model of high priesthood to express the author's understanding of his work. This model is clearly drawn from the Jewish heritage of Christianity, whether from experience of Jewish practice in the Temple at Jerusalem or from a close knowledge of the Jewish Scripture. There is an uncompromising insistence on the full yet sinless humanity of Jesus, seen as an essential factor in the effecting of salvation—yet in the opening verses a suggestion that he is beginning to be thought of as in some sense divine as well as human. These two ideas—that Jesus is human, yet sinless; and fully human, yet reflecting the divine nature—are affirmed in Hebrews without argument: they will be central to later Christological controversy and definition. More peaceably, the presentation of Jesus in Hebrews has influenced Christian visual art, in the representation of Christ as "Great High Priest" in the icons of Eastern Orthodoxy.

This central image of Jesus as high priest is expounded in chapters 5 and 8–10 of the Letter, and drawn from the ritual of the Day of Atonement *(Yom Kippur)* prescribed in Lev. 16. There the high priest is directed on one day only in the year to enter the holy place, the innermost part of the tabernacle, into the presence of God, taking with him the blood of a sacrificed animal, in order to make atonement corporately and cumulatively for the sins of the people. The author of Hebrews is selective in his use of the model: he has no interest, for instance, in the role of the scapegoat in the ceremony. He argues that the intention of the Day of Atonement ritual, to provide a representative of the people and a single sacrifice for their sin, is correct: but the performance of it is flawed in three respects: the ritual is constantly repeated; the sacrifice is of an animal; and the high priest does not enter the real place of God's presence. The root cause of this inadequacy is that the high priest is identified too far with the people he represents: to the point of sharing their sin. What is needed is a high priest who is fully human so as to represent his people, yet sinless, so that he can offer himself as an unblemished sacrifice to God. Because this sacrifice will be effective, it can be presented in the true and permanent presence of God, heaven itself, and because it is effective it will never need to be repeated. This, for the author, is the need that Jesus meets: he has offered himself as a once-for-all sacrifice and has entered heaven where he now remains, offering continual intercession and opening up access there for all whom he represents (4.14–16; 7.26–27). The time between Jesus' death and the final act of God to which the author still looks forward (12.25–29) is not an interlude or only a time of waiting, but is given a real content in the experience of salvation.

The image of Jesus as priest is not the author's free creation: it is given to him by tradition, in Ps. 110, which was read by Christians, and probably by Jews before them, as prophetic of the Messiah (v. 1 appears in many of the New Testament writings). There God says to the king: "Thou art a priest for ever after the order of Melchizedek" (v. 4). The mysterious and enigmatic figure of Melchizedek, priest-king of Salem in Genesis 14.18–20, is therefore also woven into the image, in chapter 7 of the Letter. Because Melchizedek appears in Genesis with no note of any antecedents or descendants, he is seen as having an "unrepeatable" priesthood; and because he blesses Abraham and takes tithes from him, he indicates a "better" priesthood than that of Abraham's descendant Levi, founder of the levitical or Aaronic priesthood of tabernacle and Temple. In both these respects, Melchizedek therefore prefigures and is a type of Christ.

Another psalm drawn on by the author that formed part of early Christian tradition, is Ps. 2, quoted in Heb. 1.5. Here God is seen to address the messiah as "my Son" (Ps. 2.7). This idea of Jesus as "Son of God" is explored in chapters 1 and 2, with two points being made: first, that the son is greater than angels (1.4–14); and secondly, that the son is one of many brethren (2.10–18). Jesus' sonship is seen, like his priesthood, in terms of his full humanity, flesh and blood and subject to death. The glory that he has received after death is therefore a fulfillment of the destiny of humanity and a hope for all. A different note is struck in the opening verses of the letter. There the Son is the agent of God in creation, reflecting God's glory and his real being (1.1–2). The source of this language is not models of priesthood or prophecies of a king-messiah but the figure of Wisdom as described in the Wisdom of Solomon 7.22–26 (cf. Prov. 8.22–31). Scholars dispute whether "wisdom" in Jewish writings should be understood as a preexistent, heavenly, semidivine being or as a personification: a vivid way of talking about the power and rational sense of God. When wisdom language is applied to Jesus it suggests that claims are beginning to be made about him that go beyond his human character. In Hebrews, the language forms a highly rhetorical opening to the Letter, and is not integrated into the following argument (it is not argued, for instance, that as priest Jesus represents God to human beings, but only that he represents human beings to God). The full affirmation of, and relationship between, his "two natures" will be the stuff of later Christological definition.

An author who lays so much stress on the humanity of Jesus might be expected to demonstrate it with reference to the historical memory of his life, as preserved in the Gospel traditions. Hebrews frequently uses the personal name "Jesus," as well as the confessional title "Christ," and refers to his suffering and death, though without any specific indication of its means, by crucifixion. The allusions to his suffering "outside the gate" or "outside the camp" (13.11–13) are more probably drawn from the fate of the sacrificial victims of the Day of Atonement (Lev. 16.27) than from Jesus' execution at Golgotha outside the city of Jerusalem (Mark 15.20–22). Similarly, and perhaps even more strikingly, there is only one reference specifically to resurrection from the dead (13.20); the author concentrates instead on Jesus' entry into and continuing presence in heaven. It is important for the author's central argument that Jesus as high priest was without sin, and he makes it clear that this was not because of any exceptional condition of his humanity (as some patristic theologians would argue, with reference to the Virgin Birth tradition). Rather, it was a matter of sustained effort and obedience. He was "in every respect tempted as we are" (4.15; cf. 2.18), and although this claim might suggest a knowledge of the temptation narratives in Matt. 4 and Luke 4, there is again no specific reference. Even the author's choice of the Day of Atonement model seems to set him at some distance from the Gospel tradition, where it is the Passover ritual that plays a prominent part (Mark 14.12–26, cf. Luke 22.15 and John 19.31–36). One passage, however, stands out: it is difficult to read 5.7 as other than a reference to Jesus' agony in the garden of Gethsemane, maybe specifically in the Lucan tradition that emphasizes its intensity (Luke 22.39–46; cf. Mark 14.32–42). It may be that the author is aware of, and takes for granted, more of the Gospel tradition, but does not find it useful in establishing his chosen arguments.

Given that the author's distinctive presentation of Jesus is not closely linked to the Gospel tradition, it is interesting to speculate on its origins. His use of the image of high priesthood, worked out in close reference to the ritual prescriptions of the Jewish law, might naturally suggest that he and his readers came from Jewish circles close to the Jerusalem Temple: hence the Letter's traditional title: "To the Hebrews." It would be important for Christian converts coming from such a background to make sense of Jesus in their cultural and religious milieu, and to show how he satisfied and fulfilled their aspirations. On the other hand, some features of the Letter have been taken to suggest a Hellenistic context: its use of typology, with the levitical rituals seen as ineffective models of true priesthood and sacrifice; with repetition in time seen as a sign of imperfection; and with the emphasis on heaven of which the earthly tabernacle is only a "copy and shadow" (8.5). All these might reflect a Platonic metaphysic in which the material world of time, change, and imperfection shadows the world of eternal and unchanging realities. Older commentators compared the author of Hebrews with the Alexandrian Jew Philo, who sought to bring together the Jewish Scriptures and Greek philosophy. Philo also made use of the figure of Melchizedek, as representing "wisdom," and noted his absence of genealogy. In turn, the author of Hebrews could also be seen as a forerunner of the Christian Apologists of the second century, who sought to restate their Christian faith in the language of philosophy. A more recent interpretation has seen Hebrews' emphasis on Jesus passing through into the heavens in the light of Jewish mystical thought, which aimed through contemplation to transcend the material world and pass through the heavens to attain a vision of the throne of God. The author and readers of the Letter are alike unknown, so its distinctive ideas cannot be explained from its known context; rather the context can only be speculatively reconstructed from the ideas. It seems clear, however, that the author expected his readers to be making progress in their faith in intellectual as well as practical terms (5.11–6.3), and his method of detailed exegesis may be deliberately demanding on them. If they follow his argument, however, they will gain an understanding of Jesus that will give them the confidence to face whatever lies ahead.

Sophie Laws

See also: Chalcedon; Icons and the Icon Tradition; Jesus, Origins of; Scapegoat; Son of God

References

Browne, Arnold. 2004 (forthcoming). *Epistle to the Hebrews*. London: Continuum.
Dunn, James D. G. 1989. *Christology in the Making*, 2d ed. London: SCM.
Lindars, Barnabas. 1991. *The Theology of the Letter to the Hebrews*. Cambridge: Cambridge University Press.
Pfitzner, Victor C. 1997. *Hebrews*. Nashville: Abingdon.
Reumann, John. 1991. *Variety and Unity in New Testament Thought*. Oxford: Oxford University Press.

Hellenistic Religions

To raise questions about Jesus and religions contemporary to him, and to search for answers beyond Scripture and early Christian literature, is to investigate Jesus and the Hellenistic history of religions. What at first might seem simple questions about religious matters during the time of Jesus (organized religion, religious terminology employed by emperors, miracles and portents, temples, personal devotion, prayers, exorcists, magicians) turn out to be richly rewarding questions that compel our inquiry into Hellenistic religions. Whether puritan or progressive, syncretistic or conservative, philosophical or practical, of one ethnic group or another, all religions that occur in the Hellenistic period are to be considered Hellenistic religions.

This does not mean that all these religions were the same, that one temple was like another, one sacred text like another, or one association like another. It means that the establishment of Hellenistic kingdoms after Alexander the

Great and the cultural impact subsequently sustained by them altered the Mediterranean world so that Greek language and ideas became primary currency. Such currency allowed for the exchange and combining of ideas previously unknown. It also created pockets of fierce resistance to its influence, giving the globalization process of Hellenistic culture its overall shape: a drift toward standardization with many debating the merits of that drift.

Hellenization did have its limits. The influence of Greek ideas, language, and religion varied in the impact of its particular results, depending on the cultures and peoples it saturated. The later coming of Rome did not destroy Hellenistic culture, but instead accommodated new ways for that culture to express itself under its new landlord. All along the way, old kingdoms, dynasties, and tribes held themselves together, using Greek to deal with Rome from faraway places. By the time of the emperor Tiberius, the Hellenistic milieu had been remixed through its Romanization. This included building programs, tax collection, new ways of public administration, new objects of devotion, and new avenues for the reception of *gratia* and benefaction. The interlocking relationship between Rome and Hellenistic cultures persisted. It provided an opportunity for the reinvention of Hellenistic language and impulses up through and beyond that strangest of historical moments when Flavius Claudius Julianus, a Roman general installed as emperor by his army, sought a revival of Greek religion (361–363).

Within this general cultural domain were many particular religions, each with a unique relationship to the domain. When we ask questions about Jesus, and the search for answers takes us outside the Scripture and Christian sources, then it is these religions that become the focus of our inquiry. Given the sheer volume of evidence about them, we shall do well with some paths to guide investigations. Fortunately, there are three general models available to approach questions about Jesus in the context of Hellenistic religions. Each model is geared toward different goals. One goal is determination of how information about Hellenistic religions might help explain specific things reported about Jesus in early Christians' witnesses (Semantics of Jesus). A second goal is discovery of what other Hellenistic religions thought about Jesus and the traditions representing him (Reception of Jesus). A third and most difficult goal is ascertainment of how and to what extent Hellenistic religions interacted with the traditions about Jesus, either to change those traditions or be changed by them (Inculturation of Jesus).

Determination of the Semantics of Jesus involves investigation into and explication of a diverse list of items, and ultimately begins to look like the compilation of a dictionary or encyclopedia of words, people, places, things, and topics from the period of the New Testament. One item is what the term "lord" (*kurios*) might mean when applied to Jesus in the New Testament and at the same time used elsewhere for Roman emperors, Serapis, and the God of Israel. Another item is what the content of reports about the miracles of Jesus might mean in light of reports about miracles performed by others. Still another item is establishing the meaning of statements attributed to Jesus about the end of the world in light of similar statements reported elsewhere in other messianic and apocalyptic texts. The number of issues and items on the list needing investigation is large, and efforts to address the Semantics of Jesus make up a good part of New Testament studies.

Compared with investigation of the Semantics of Jesus, the goal of discovering the Reception of Jesus by Hellenistic religions is less frequently pursued. Van Voorst reviews most of the non-Christian texts that contain the earliest direct references to "Jesus" or "Christ." Most of this material stems from the Neoplatonist, Celsus, who around 175 wrote a book against Christianity to which Origen of Alexandria later responded in his *Contra Celsum*. Among his many complaints Celsus states that Jesus was a failure (1.67) who was unable to stop the violence done against him through crucifixion (6.34) and appeared after his death merely as a ghost (3.22). Celsus links Jesus to magic and its practitioners, suggesting that the exorcisms of Jesus were no different than those performed for a few pennies by Egyptian magicians (1.60). Besides this there are comments by Lucian of Samosata. In the mid-second century while writing about Peregrinus, he suggested that Jesus instituted crucifixion as a new form of religious initiation. Lucian recorded his belief that Christians considered Jesus a new lawgiver who specifically commanded his followers to deny Greek gods. These examples, along with a few others like them that make up the limited evidence we have, suggest that outsiders generally had a difficult time reporting detailed and accurate information about Christianity. Still, their reflections about Jesus show what kind of ears the Hellenistic religions had when hearing reports about the Christians' unusual savior.

Investigation of the Inculturation of traditions about Jesus, like the problem of the Semantics of Jesus, has attracted many. Those who labor toward this goal must first develop plausible methods by which to compare the Jesus traditions to elements from Hellenistic religions. Appropriate development of methods is not as easy as might first appear, since the methods are liable to the logical traps involved with the establishment of any circumstantial evidence. This liability fortunately is offset by a long history (especially among Christians) of attempts at such comparisons, so that for those interested in this goal today there are many precedents of method. The precedents reach back very early. For example, in Acts 17.16–31 there is a story about the Apostle Paul, who in the Athenian Areopagus preaches about Jesus from a Greek inscription, "To the Unknown God," and quotes Aratus, *Phaenomena* 5. Later, Justin Martyr, *Dialogue with Trypho*, 69.4, compares traditions about Jesus to those about Herakles' ascent into heaven and about the healing attributed to Asclepius. With a different eye, Athenagoras, *Supplication on Behalf of Christians*, 31.1, compares traditions about the death of Jesus to those about the virtuous deaths of Pythagoras, Heraclitus, Democritus, and especially Socrates. Clearly, these comparisons of traditions about Jesus to other traditions were done in order to support the promotion of Christian ideas and beliefs.

The goal of uncovering the Inculturation of Jesus traditions, however, involves more than apologetic comparison of Jesus to his competitors. It is really about the determination of lines of influence and causation between the traditions about Jesus and the Hellenistic religions. These kinds of comparisons produce very different results, the investigative interests of which range from literary influence to social influence. With literary concern, some have detected an inculturation of traditions about Jesus in the context of Jewish midrash or Homeric epic. With social concern, some have detected the Inculturation of Jesus traditions within Hellenistic religious organizations and society at large. Those who seek after the goal of the Inculturation of Jesus and traditions about him shall do well to spread wide their net, collect many sources and expert opinions about those sources, and then only with the most deliberate care propose statements about what influenced what.

One of the more gripping results of investigation into the Inculturation of Jesus is discovery of ways in which traditions about Jesus, outside of the early Christian churches, began to influence and change the Hellenistic context with its religions. In his 1991 Sather Lectures, Bowersock recommends the idea that Christian proclamation about resurrection effected unique thematic developments in Greek novels. Other aspects of the influence of the Jesus traditions in the context of Hellenistic religions include its emphases on suffering, healing, helping the poor and sick, and martyrdom. In the *Martyrdom of Pionius* we find a record of some who opposed Christians, claiming their success in matters of healing and exorcism was based on the fact that Christians called upon their dead Jesus in rituals of necromancy. The author disagrees, suggesting that the impact of Jesus in the Hellenistic context was just too great for that criticism to be true. And, so it would seem.

Douglas W. Geyer

See also: Homer; Jesus, Miracles of; Lord; Origen; Resurrection; Second Coming of Jesus, Origins of

References

Bowersock, Glen W. 1994. *Fiction as History: Nero to Julian*. Sather Classical Lectures 58. Berkeley: University of California Press.

Geyer, Douglas W. 2002. *Fear, Anomaly, and Uncertainty in the Gospel of Mark*. ATLA Monograph Series 47. Lanham, MD: Scarecrow.

Lane Fox, Robin. 1986. *Pagans and Christians*. London: Viking.

Perkins, Judith. 1995. *The Suffering Self: Pain and Narrative Representation in the Early Christian Era*. New York: Routledge.

Smith, Jonathan Z. 1990. *Drudgery Divine: On the Comparisons of Early Christianities and the Religions of Late Antiquity*. Chicago: University of Chicago Press.

Snyder, Graydon F. 1985. *Ante Pacem: Archaeological Evidence of Church Life before Constantine*. Macon, GA: Mercer University Press.

———. 1999. *Inculturation of the Jesus Tradition: The Impact of Jesus on Jewish and Roman Cultures*. Harrisburg, PA: Trinity.

Van Voorst, Robert. 2000. *Jesus outside the New Testament: An Introduction to the Ancient Evidence*. Grand Rapids, MI: Eerdmans.

Hengel, Martin (b. 1926)

Martin Hengel, formerly professor of New Testament and Early Christianity at the University of Tübingen, is best known for his influential work on the involvement of Greek culture in Judaism in the final centuries of the pre-Christian era. He showed this involvement to have been more varied and pervasive than had generally been recognized. He has, however, published a large number of works, often brief monographs, on New Testament matters—and in particular on the life of Jesus in its first-century setting. Much of this work has been notably traditional in tendency, reasserting unfashionable opinions about matters of authorship and the relations between the various New Testament writings.

He was, however, responsible for one of the most original and helpful models available to us for understanding the character of Jesus' person and mission in the context of his times. It comes in his short book *The Charismatic Leader and His Followers* (1968). The question is: How may Jesus best be characterized? As rabbi, or prophet, or messianic leader, or liberator? On the evidence of the Gospels' contents, none of these is an impossible candidate, understood in context. From some passages, especially in the Gospel of John, we might add: Jewish mystic. But Hengel's proposal makes us attend to some of the most striking and undeniable features of Jesus. One of its chief virtues is that while "leader" allows us to do justice to the undoubtedly political aspect of his activity, given the realities of Jewish life—and indeed, in one way or another, to the manner of his death, "charismatic" leads us to consider Jesus' striking originality. He took people by surprise and stirred them to a fresh sense of God. Above all, and it is often forgotten, his mission was unique in its surviving and its spreading, however much later developments of course aided the process.

Hengel chose to focus on Matt. 8.22: "Let the dead bury their dead," and to ask us to face the sheer cultural and religious novelty, and even immorality in conventional terms, of such a command to would-be followers. In working out such a view and claiming its historical authenticity, Hengel is firmly among those who are far from despairing of the possibility—as well as the importance—of forming a valid picture of the historical Jesus. It was Hengel's further strength that he chose to see him in terms that both appeal to modern sociological categorizing and have helpful theological resonance. Jesus was a radical challenger of conventional wisdom and morality. The summons of the Kingdom of God put into the shade the religion of day-by-day obedience, or at least gave it a refreshing new context and purpose.

When it comes to a wider study of the origins of Christology, Hengel sees Jesus himself as the most likely innovator—that is, the gist of the messianic claims that came to be made for him, as early as Paul and indeed before, are best seen as issuing in essence from Jesus himself.

Leslie Houlden

See also: Kingdom of God; Matthew, Gospel of; Messiah; Son of God

References

Hengel, M. 1968, 1981. *The Charismatic Leader and His Followers*. Edinburgh: T. and T. Clark.

———. *The Son of God*. 1976. Philadelphia: Fortress.

———. *Crucifixion*. 1977. Philadelphia: Fortress.

———. 1995. *Studies in Early Christology*. Edinburgh: T. and T. Clark.

Herod

See Jesus in Social Context

Hinduism

Less than 3 percent of Indians had become Christians by the end of the twentieth century. Christian impact has been much greater than this suggests because of its influence through institutions. A large minority of the Hindu elite have been educated in Christian schools and colleges. Here they have imbibed Christian values and learned something of Jesus. When ill, they have often been treated in the widespread network of Christian hospitals and clinics where they have experienced a link between Jesus the healer and medical work. In the renowned Vellore Christian Medical College Hospital, pictures of Jesus hang over the operating theaters, and the chapel is inundated with Hindus praying to Jesus for their relatives and making thank-offerings after the successful completion of treatment. This is felt too at the village level, where healing prayer has been deeply appreciated. Hindus may have seen something of social work done in the name of Jesus. Examples are the care of those with leprosy, a special concern of Jesus, and recent work on advocacy for the poor and excluded. Mother Teresa's ministry in Calcutta was widely, if not universally, appreciated by the Hindu community. It was work done explicitly to express the love of Christ for those who were dying.

It is not, therefore, surprising to find the name of Jesus greeted with strong affection by a far larger number of Hindus than the small percentage who have converted. Such an impact is increased through modern media, where radio and television programs and tapes of Christian songs have spread the name of Jesus widely. There have been films of the life of Jesus in vernacular languages that have had an enormous effect in villages, particularly one in which a Hindu film star played the part of Jesus. Some Hindus have responded to Jesus in art forms—for example, in a series of bronze reliefs on Jesus' life in Pandyan (Tamil) style. These are in the library of the Tamilnadu Theological Seminary in Madurai, because some from the sponsoring churches would not accept them in the chapel.

We now consider the many who have remained Hindus but who have responded to Jesus specifically. Some have become unbaptized believers; others have remained firmly Hindu but allowed the impact of Christ to affect their theology/philosophy. Through them there have also been changes within Hinduism, not least to enable it to learn from Christian mission and to defend traditional Indian religion from this "Western" import and make conversions less likely. Another group are those who have formed small communities somewhere between Hinduism and Christianity, not willing to be part of a colonial church, but who have been deeply affected by Jesus.

Hinduism is not a monolithic faith with a founder and a canon of scripture like Judaism, Christianity, and Islam, the "religions of the book." It is a way of life, around a certain worldview and family of ideas. As such, it is more easily influenced from outside, as it absorbs and adds to its possibilities. Jesus has thus been enabled to become a significant figure in the lives of many. For most, the main impact has been from the Gospels, which have had a greater impact than the Epistles of Paul. Their narrative style and direct teaching is easier to grasp. The personhood of Jesus shines through. For some Jesus becomes an avatar (incarnation) alongside Krishna, Rama, and others. Christian Scriptures can be included with the many Hindu sacred texts in a religion in which there is no restrictive canon. Jesus' teaching, as recorded in the Synoptic Gospels, makes an immediate impact on many Hindus, particularly the parables and the Sermon on the Mount. Others appreciate the meditative style of St. John's Gospel, with its apparent mysticism and symbolism, and the identification of Jesus with God in verses like "I and the Father are one," a relationship offered also to the disciples through Christ. There are obvious parallels with the *advaita* (philosophy of Sankara), with its understanding that salvation consists in the realization that the ultimate and my soul are a unity: "That art thou."

The first Christians came to southeast India in the earliest centuries after Christ. The impact of St. Thomas Christians was significant but local, and they soon adjusted to live within the Hindu world as a separate community, with little mutual interchange. With some exceptions, early Western missions from all churches were very negative to Hinduism, which was seen as a place of darkness and the demonic, and the home of all manner of social evils. Conversions happened for many different reasons, but there was little learning from each other.

It was from the early nineteenth century that wider and more positive interaction began. Hinduism itself became influenced by the person of Jesus and his teaching. A Bengali, Rammohan Roy, found himself in creative dialogue with the earliest Baptist Serampore missionaries: William Carey, and especially Dr. Joshua Marshman. Roy, who died in 1833 (his statue is in Bristol), was a rationalist, strongly Unitarian in his understanding of God. He became deeply impressed with the ethical teaching of Jesus and saw this as a basis for a reformation of Indian society and of Hinduism. But he had no sympathy with the doctrines around Jesus, particularly those of incarnation, atonement, and Trinity. He saw Jesus definitely as a creature and not creator. He separated Jesus' teaching from the history of his life. He had little time for a *bhakti* (devotional) approach to religion in either faith, and therefore was not a lover of John's Gospel or St. Paul. On a practical front, he was inspired to challenge the caste system (unsuccessfully) and the practice of suttee (widow burning) (successfully), and became acknowledged as the first significant Hindu reformer. He also founded the Brahmo Samaj to further his reformation ideas.

Keshub Chunder Sen, a Marathi, came out of the same school. Rather than rejecting *bhakti*, he embraced it as part both of the essence of Hinduism, and also of Christianity. He became devoted to Jesus, whom he saw at the center of a religion of the Spirit that could be absorbed within one universal religion. Accepting both the preexistence and incarnation of Christ, he wished to bring Hinduism into discipleship to Jesus. Jesus is the model of active surrender to God. Sen founded what he called the Church of the New Dispensation, to harmonize religions and revelations, to be firmly Asiatic and not Western. Another important figure in this movement was P. C. Mozoomdar, who, in his book *The Oriental Christ* (1883), emphasized the unbounded love and grace of God revealed in Jesus. Sen's formal movement did not last, but it was an important stimulus in encouraging the search for an Indian Jesus and indigenous Christianity, as represented, for example, in the Rethinking Christianity Group.

Sri Ramakrishna and Swami Vivekenanda dominate the end of the nineteenth century and start of the twentieth in terms of their abiding influence. Ramakrishna was a simple Bengali priest who died relatively unknown in 1886. His disciple, Vivekenanda, revealed his ideas to the wider world. This became unforgettably linked with the World Parliament of Religions in Chicago in 1893, when he introduced Hinduism to the West in a way that made an enormous impact on his hearers. Ramakrishna was a mystic and had a number of visions of Jesus, as the master yogi, in eternal union with God. He felt an identity with Christ, whom he knew as *Sri Isa,* as he had felt also with Radha and Krishna, Kali, and other Hindu gods, and indeed with Muhammad. He concluded that a separation between different religions was a thing of the past. Hinduism was the superior dharma (way) because it realized this, was inclusive of all, and stood against the idea of mission and conversion.

These two did much to mold modern-day classical Hinduism. Their followers have included Professor Radhakrishnan, the first president of Independent India, and Mahatma Gandhi. Radhakrishnan was at one time professor at Oxford University, and he wrote a major tome, *Eastern Religions and Western Thought.* He compares the Jesus of the Gospels with the complexity of the Nicene Creed's understanding of Christ. Simplicity has been replaced by dogma, a way of life by metaphysics. He argues that the mystical Jesus found in the Fourth Gospel and St. Paul was deeply influenced by Eastern thought. In his work, the Jewish Jesus has become overlaid by the Spirit of the Upanishads and of the Buddha, and so can have a universal message.

Gandhi centered much of his devotion on Jesus, and particularly on his reputed daily reading of the Sermon on the Mount. The Sermon on the Mount centers on teaching about simplicity of life, and *ahimsa* (nonviolence). Jesus' life displayed both. His death was the supreme example of someone dying for others because of faithfulness to truth. Gandhi himself was to follow the same path. The cross was of deep personal significance for him, as signified in his love of the hymn "When I survey the wondrous cross." But what was important was not the historical event but the lessons it taught. For Gandhi, whether Jesus lived at all was not the key question, but the truth of his teachings, as illustrated by his dying as innocent victim. But Gandhi could not accept the exclusivity of Jesus, or of the New Testament. Others like Krishna or the Buddha could also teach eternal lessons; the *Gita* was a sublime poem; and sacrificial deaths could be found elsewhere. Jesus was as near a perfect human being as can be found, but he was neither God nor the only-begotten Son of God. We make a mistake if we co-opt Gandhi into being a Christian without the name. He admired Jesus as a person of action: "God will ask us, and asks now, not what we label ourselves, but what we are, i.e., what we do. With God, deed is everything, belief without doing is not believing" (*Young India*, 4.9.24).

Gandhi was typical of many Hindus who made a distinction between Jesus and Christianity. Jesus is not the possession of Christians, but a universal figure. Christianity is a religion brought by missionaries from the West. It is an accompaniment of colonialism, about which Indians should be wary. This is why Gandhi abhorred interreligious conversion, if it meant, not conversion to Jesus, but baptism and joining the Church. His friendship with the missionary C. F. Andrews enabled him to express his love of Jesus; at the same time he considered the task of missionaries to make Muslims better Muslims, Christians better Christians, and Hindus better Hindus, for their mutual enrichment.

We can see the abiding influence of Hindu thinkers on the philosophy and practice of various Hindu nationalist movements that led to the present Bharathiya Janata Party (BJP) national government, and the extreme reactions to conversion in several parts of India. Rarely is there expressed any antagonism to Jesus—rather the opposite—but there is deep suspicion of any movement to follow him exclusively by becoming members of his visible Church. Gandhi would, of course, emphatically reject the violent means increasingly used to thwart such movements and to interfere with the free choice of the individual.

Reflecting on this link between Christianity and the West, a number of attempts have been made to form Hindu-Christian fellowships. These included the initiatives of Parani Andi (the National Church of Madras, 1886–1922), and of Kandiswamy Chetti (the Fellowship of the Followers of Jesus, founded in 1933 in the Bhakti tradition), and the Hindu Church of the Lord Jesus, formed in Tinnevelly in 1858. Perhaps best known is the movement around Subba Rao, who had a direct vision of Christ in what is now Andhra Pradesh in 1942. He healed in the name of Jesus, and saw the Cross as the destruction of the ego. The aim of all prayer is to realize one's unity with God and Christ. He wrote vitriolic pamphlets against baptism as a meaningless, ridiculous outward ceremony; he and his group remained Hindu unbaptized believers in Jesus, and numbers gradually declined. All these and other groups seem to glow like newly lit candles and blow themselves out. It is difficult to live on the border between two religions in the long term.

Another phenomenon has been that of individual unbaptized believers. These may be secret or open. Those who are secret fall into two categories. Some are, in fact, secretly baptized and exclusively devoted to Jesus. They remain within their families and practice the Hindu rituals, outwardly conforming. They fear the consequences of coming out into the open, with possible family disruption. A renowned example is the Secret Christians of Sivakasi, in Tamilnadu. They belong to the Nadars, a prominent business community. Some women have even passed on their faith through three generations. Others follow Jesus in an unbaptized way, and unidentified with any church. They listen to the radio, pray, and read their bibles. They may meet in small groups, but they do not wish to identify with a Western and culturally alien organization. A survey in Madras in 1981 revealed that 10 percent were Christians, but 6.4 percent were nonbaptized believers. The majority were women. One, for example, thought of Jesus as a *mahatma* (a great soul) to whom she could pray, as well as to Krishna. Jesus was a way of seeing *Brahman*, but not as Son of God. She felt Christ would have a problem with the kind of "superior" Christians she had met, who had hurt her when they had attacked Hindu gods as mere idols.

In the West, there are several Hindu reactions to Jesus. There are a small number who call themselves proudly Hindu Christians, and they tend to be of the higher castes. They have been baptized, and some have even become clergy. But at the same time, they are clear that their spirituality was molded by the religion of their home. To deny the religion of their parents would be to betray their love. So they live at home in neither place, while holding firmly to Jesus as their guide. Some postpone their baptism until after the death of their parents. They are devotees of Jesus, but also feel it a primary duty that they complete the Hindu funeral rituals for mother and father. Others get baptized, join mainline churches, but never feel at home. They may join Indian Christian fellowships, with a very conservative and exclusive understanding of Jesus, or they revert to Hinduism. Rarely do they reject Jesus, but rather the churches. A majority of Hindus reverted in Britain within two years, as calculated in a survey by Pradip Sudra in the early 1990s.

A particular understanding of Jesus has been found among Dalit communities ("untouchables"). Some have not converted but found Jesus as an inspiration to them in their quest for social justice. They are impressed by Jesus as the suffering servant, who was biased toward the poor, as shown in his teaching, ministry, and death. This understanding is very different from the response to Jesus among most of the Hindus outlined above. Jesus here becomes a challenge to Hinduism and the inequities of the caste system.

Another response is found in various *bhakti* sects. A prominent example is the Sai Baba movement. Sai Baba is seen by his numerous devotees as a revelation of God. In their meeting rooms, or prayer shrines at home, there will often be a picture of Jesus beside Hindu Gods and the long dark-haired Sai Baba. This inclusivism is seen also in the exhibitions developed by the Swaminarayan sect, in Gujarat and at their Neasden Temple in London. Quotations from Jesus are included as part of religious teaching.

A future challenge is likely to be offered from the Hindu nationalist movement upon the understanding of Jesus. Widespread admiration and devotion to Jesus found among Hindu communities as described at the beginning of this article has so far stood firm within growing antagonistic attitudes to the Church among a vociferous minority. The question is whether this can continue. Can Hindu sympathizers in this coming century still feel free to be challenged deeply by Jesus as were the outstanding thinkers discussed above in the last century? Another challenge is among expatriate communities, now large in both Europe and the Americas. How far can the freedom available there enable creative interaction and dialogue between Christians and Hindus about Jesus, and how far can Christians feel able to learn from Hindus who bring distinctive reflections from their own traditions? The challenge for Hindus remains whether they can tolerate the reality that Jesus also encouraged a mission to all people in all cultures and communities, and that this has meant, and will continue to mean, that some Indians will become his disciples and members of his visible Church.

Andrew Wingate

See also: Art; Indian Christianity; Interfaith Thought and Relations; John, Gospel of

References

Baago, K. 1968. *The Movement around Subba Rao*. Madras: CLS.
———. 1969. *Pioneers of Indigenous Christianity*. Madras: CLS.
Badrinath, Chaturvedi. 2000. *Finding Jesus in Dharma*. Delhi: SPCK.
Faivre, Daniel, et al. 1999. *Celebrating Jesus: A Multi-Faith Appreciation*. Southall: Faivre.
Johanns, P. 1996. *To Christ through Vedanta*. Bangalore: UTC.
Parrinder, Geoffrey. 1970, 1982. *Avatar and Incarnation*. New York: Oxford University Press.
Pushparajan, A. 1990. *From Conversion to Fellowship: The Hindu-Christian Encounter in the Gandhian Perspective*. Allahabad: St. Paul's.
Radhakrishnan, S. 1939, 1989. *Eastern Religions and Western Thought*. New York and Delhi: Oxford.
Robinson, J. A. T. 1979. *Truth Is Two-Eyed*. London: SCM.
Sharpe, Eric J. 1977. *Faith Meets Faith*. London: SCM.
Staffner, Hans. 1988. *Jesus Christ and the Hindu Community*. Anand: Gujarat Sahitya Prakash.
Thomas, M. M. 1976, 1991. *The Acknowledged Christ of the Indian Renaissance*. Madras: CLS.

Historical Jesus

See Bultman, Rudolf; Jesus, Origins of; Jesus, Teaching of; Jesus as a Historical Figure; Jesus in Social Context; Tillich, Paul

Holy Sepulchre

The Site

Jesus was undoubtedly buried outside the city wall at Jerusalem, but the Gospels do not tell us exactly where. They all say that he was crucified at Golgotha, the location of which is not mentioned anywhere else; and John 19.41 says that the tomb was nearby. The early Christians may be reasonably supposed to have retained a memory of where it was. Respect for the burial places of holy men was strong in contemporary Judaism, and as Jesus' own family was prominent in the leadership of the church at Jerusalem, they are unlikely to have been indifferent to so sacred a place. The destruction of the Temple in A.D. 70 and the rebuilding of Jerusalem as Aelia Capitolina in the 130s by the emperor Hadrian, which included the construction of pagan temples within the walls, raises questions whether the local church could have preserved a continued memory of the location of the tomb. It is, however, striking that about 300 Bishop Eusebius of Caesarea could tell his readers where Golgotha "was shown," and it is apparent that he thought that Hadrian's pagan holy places concealed a sacred Christian site. When Constantine took over the eastern Roman Empire in 324, excavations almost immediately began at Aelia to clear away the Roman temple buildings. Originally the area had been a quarry, and around and beneath the Hadrianic structures were a number of Jewish tombs.

In the course of the excavations, "beyond all expectation," as Eusebius says, one of these was identified as the sepulchre of Jesus. It was a two-chambered tomb, excavated like a cave into the wall of the quarry, with a rock-cut bench designed to receive a body for its initial burial. Its form is similar to that of known burial chambers of the time of Jesus. Constantine's builders cut away the quarry wall that surrounded the tomb, presumably to make it more easily accessible to pilgrims, and constructed an elegant small house, or "edicule," to shelter the cave. Representations in the following period give us a fairly accurate idea of the appearance of the Constantinian edicule. By the end of the fourth century it had been further dignified by the creation above it of a huge rotunda, supporting a dome that still exists in a restored form. To the east of the edicule Constantine created a huge and magnificent basilica, consecrated in 335. To Eastern Christians, the great buildings became known as the Church of the Resurrection; to Westerners, as the Church of the Holy Sepulchre. For more than a thousand years after Constantine, no one doubted that this Holy Sepulchre was indeed the true burial-place of Jesus. The accuracy of this tradition depends on whether a genuine memory survived in the Christian community at Jerusalem during the "tunnel period" of two centuries before Constantine. In my view, it is likely that a recollection of the location of Golgotha continued, although not all scholars would agree. As to the precise tomb, there could be no memory of that, but it is a plausible identification, and there is certainly no alternative tradition. The so-called Garden Tomb, beloved by General Gordon and still shown to visitors to Jerusalem, may well look quite like the Holy Sepulchre in its original form, but is implausible as the original site. If the traditional Holy Sepulchre is not the original place, then we simply do not know where Jesus was buried.

Pilgrimage

Travel to holy places did not stand high among the priorities of early Christians. There was, on the contrary, a strongly held view that the worship of God was open to believers, wherever they might be; it is an idea found widely in the writing of the Fathers as well as in the Gospel of John: "[T]he hour is coming when you will worship the Father neither on this mountain nor in Jerusalem" (4.21). Nevertheless, there was a tradition in contemporary Judaism of visiting holy places and the tombs of great men, and there is some ambiguous evidence, in the second and third centuries, of visits from outside Palestine to both Christian and Jewish sacred sites. The unambiguous dawn of pilgrimage there began with Constantine's building work. The first known pilgrim from the Latin West was an anonymous traveler from Bordeaux in 333, two years before the consecration of Constantine's basilica. In subsequent years, the Holy Sepulchre became a magnet to draw pilgrims from many parts of the Roman Empire. Constantine's mother, the Empress Helena, came to Jerusalem in 326. Her arrival is perhaps to be seen within the tradition of imperial visitations of the provinces, but it subsequently was understood as an example of devout pilgrimage. About 382, the devout lady Egeria arrived to spend some three years in visiting the sites of the East, and she wrote a long account of the liturgy that she found in use. Soon afterward, Jerome settled at Bethlehem, and Melania the elder, a member of one of the richest of all senatorial families, came from Rome to settle on the Mount of Olives. By 400, travel to Jerusalem had become an accepted part of Christian piety, even if the costs of the journey made it available only to members of the upper classes. Visitors from the Eastern Empire were undoubtedly much more numerous, and those who stayed helped to build up the pattern of monasteries that spread widely in the Judean wilderness. The monasteries provided hospitality and guides to travelers, and in this way the development of pilgrimage helped to build up a flourishing Christian society in Byzantine Palestine and Syria.

With the collapse of the Roman Empire, travel from the West became much more difficult, but there continued to be a tradition, thin at times, of visits to the Holy City. A few of these pilgrims wrote accounts of their journeys, including the Anonymous from Piacenza, who traveled to Jerusalem in about 570. They brought back relics: fragments of rock from the Holy Sepulchre, oil from the lamps there, vases or *ampullae* decorated with motifs from the holy places. The loss of Jerusalem to Muslim armies in 638 made Latin pilgrimage even more difficult, but it was never completely extinguished. One of the most influential accounts was written just before 700 by Adomnan of Iona and reedited by Bede. His book *On the Holy Places*, based partly on earlier accounts and partly on the description of a rather mysterious Bishop Arculf, contained a plan of the Holy Sepulchre and of other sites and was very widely circulated in Western Europe. In the eleventh century, Latin pilgrimage increased in volume, and in 1095 Pope Urban II proclaimed the First Crusade, which succeeded in 1099 in subjecting Jerusalem to the lordship of Latin Christians. From then until Saladin recovered Jerusalem in 1187 the Holy Sepulchre was the high point of Latin pilgrimage. Although the numbers of travelers cannot be calculated, they were undoubtedly very large, and the church of the Holy Sepulchre was reconstructed to provide a house for Latin canons: substantially, the building now is the one that the crusaders left. The progressive loss during the thirteenth century of the remaining Western possessions in Syria and Palestine made pilgrimage increasingly difficult.

Paradoxically, pilgrimage had a revival in the later Middle Ages. The Franciscans were allowed to establish a house on Mount Sion and to direct pilgrimages in and around Jerusalem, and Venice offered package tours including shipping, subsistence on board, and escort to the Holy City. Culturally this last flowering of the medieval Jerusalem pilgrimage was of great significance: it generated large numbers of narratives and influenced the developing piety of the West. The creation of hillside Calvaries, of "holy mountains" that reproduced the layout of Jerusalem, and of Stations of the Cross (in almost every Catholic church) drew on the experience of fifteenth-century pilgrims. By the end of the sixteenth century, the hostility of the Ottoman Turks and the criticism of pilgrimage in the West had almost brought it to an end; it did not revive until it had taken a new form with the renewed Western interest in the Holy Land about the middle of the nineteenth century.

Colin Morris

See also: Jesus, Death of; Pilgrimage; Roman Catholicism

References

Biddle, Martin. 1999. *The Tomb of Christ*. Stroud: Sutton.

Freeman-Grenville, G. S. P. 1993. *The Basilica of the Holy Sepulchre in Jerusalem*. Jerusalem: Carta.

Gibson, Shimon, and Joan E. Taylor. 1994. *Beneath the Church of the Holy Sepulchre*. London: Palestine Exploration Fund.

Graboïs, André. 1998. *Le pèlerin occidental en Terre-Sainte au Moyen Âge*. Brussels: De Boeck.

Wilkinson, John. 1977. *Jerusalem Pilgrims before the Crusades*. Warminster: Aris and Philipps.

———. 1978. *The Jerusalem Jesus Knew*. London: Thames and Hudson.

———. 1988. *Jerusalem Pilgrimage 1099–1185*. Series II, vol. 167. London: Hakluyt Society.

Holy Spirit

In developed Christian teaching, Jesus and the Holy Spirit are spoken of alongside the Father as the "persons" of the Trinity, which is the single Godhead. The three are one, yet they may be differentiated in terms of mutual relationship, and are often thought of in terms of distinct roles or functions that are, however, variously defined. But developed and relatively settled conceptualizing of this kind, especially with regard to the Holy Spirit, is scarcely to be found before the later part of the fourth century, and in order to have a chance of grasping what is being claimed, it is necessary to go back to Christian origins in the first century and indeed to their Jewish antecedents in the uses of the terms involved. It must be remembered that the philosophically minded theologians of the later period were not sensitive in anything like a modern way to the cultural and intellectual distance between themselves and their biblical predecessors, when they used their writings as authoritative (if not always mutually reconcilable—except with difficulty) texts for their own formulations. They were like men using wood to build an engine requiring metal, the triumph being that anything workable emerged at all. Or, better perhaps, like politicians using the slogans and ideas of a previous era to construct policies in later and different times, unaware that their senses had changed.

In this context, there is no more problematic term than "spirit." In both Hebrew *(ruach)* and Greek *(pneuma)*, the word signifies "wind" or "breeze" and, by metaphorical extension, the "breath" of humans and beasts. (For English readers, it is a pity that the English word does not carry this range of senses; though, like French *esprit* and German *Geist*, it has its own separate set of ambiguities.) The word comes into theological usage chiefly by way of anthropomorphic image-making in the Jewish scriptures. How, for example, does God bring about the remarkable power of great leaders or preachers? Well, by filling them with his windlike breath, which tosses and drives them into thoughts and deeds beyond ordinary human possibilities (cf. 1 Sam. 10.9–12). In this usage, "spirit" is an attribute of God, or rather a way of speaking of his power or of God-as-powerful. But it developed a second imaginative style of use, by being reified or hypostatized—that is, seen as a kind of agent or servant of God. The same thing happened to other attributes of God-as-seen-in-humanlike-terms, notably his wisdom (Prov. 8) and his speech or word (Ps. 33.6; Isa. 55.9–11). Sometimes it is plain that conscious metaphor is involved, though uncertain whether the usage is attributive or substantial; as in Ps. 33.6, where creation is credited to both God's "word" and his "breath." Here, it is at least clear that we are not dealing with hard-and-fast concepts but with imagery, and the context is poetry.

The New Testament writers are heirs to this range of usage. It is obvious, for example, that in John 1.1–18, we have a use of the idea of God's "word" that has moved, like "wisdom" elsewhere, beyond being an attribute of God, seen anthropomorphically, and become his empowered agent. But with regard to "spirit," it seems that usually we scarcely move beyond the attributive metaphor of Old Testament usage; and the literal sense of *pneuma* as "wind" can jostle happily with its metaphorical use for God's powerful activity, as in John 3.8. In 1 Cor. 2.10–16, we read Paul at his most analytic in this regard. In what we would classify as anthropomorphism, but he saw in terms of the belief that man is modeled on God (cf. Gen. 1.26), we see "spirit" as apparently the inner rational self, whereby one can reflect and consider: just as God can do the same, "using" *his* spirit. In v. 16, with what might seem to the seeker after tight concepts a piece of gratuitous carelessness, "mind" is apparently the equivalent of "spirit." Again, Paul is in the business of metaphor (and he is able to draw in the contribution of a helpful scriptural text). In Rom. 8.1–11, there is another piece of neatness-defying work, where he engages in what might later seem cavalier or at any rate exegetically challenging writing, as the Spirit of God and of Christ seem to be used interchangeably (as also, indeed, "the Spirit of life in Christ Jesus"). It is of course not easy to see these diverse expressions in terms of later Trinitarian orthodoxy—and it is anachronistic and futile: for Paul, one's "spirit" was one's powerful and effective inner driving force, and God and Christ were at one in such work in Christian believers, impelling them in their new life.

The simple anthropomorphic usage is most clearly seen in the Gospel of Luke, where, especially in the opening chapters, the episodes are spirit-induced and spirit-driven, just as they are often led by angels: 1.35, 67, 80; 2.26; 3.22; 4.1, 14. It is a way of saying that this is an unprecedentedly concentrated manifestation of God's holy and powerful work for our salvation. Of course, Luke maintains the theme, most notably in the Pentecost story in Acts 2, with its antecedent in Joel 2.28–32, but also elsewhere: see especially Jesus' quoting of Isa. 61.1 at Luke 4.18, and, in relation to the Church as a whole, Acts 9.31, and to Paul, 13.9; and to church leaders in their decision-making, 15.8, 28. For Luke, "spirit" provides the obvious language, used repeatedly, for the constant onward drive of the Church's mission—under God and on the impulse of Jesus. Sometimes, however, the Spirit becomes in effect a piece of equipment that the true Christian ought to receive and without which he or she cannot be counted as properly equipped: see Acts 8.14–24; 18.24–19.6. Here, the idea almost enters the realm of the magical, with the Christian "magic" being seen as more powerful than that of the new movement's enemies.

In such thinking, both the link with Jesus may be maintained, as his "name" accompanies the Spirit as the true Christian's endowment (19.5–6), and yet there is also differentiation. There is of course nothing surprising in this (as it may seem) confused association of identification and distinction; for in Judaism, the coming of Messiah and the outpouring of Spirit were twin testimonies or signs of the coming of the new age. Both were eschatological symbols, and in that perspective, the more fundamental idea underlying both is the fulfilment of God's great purpose for the world and for his people. At this point, the biblical manner of operating by way of images, juxtaposed and often apparently conflicting, may join hands with insistence on the oneness of God, whatever terms might be used for his relations with us and whatever logic is used to express them. As far as Christian origins go, there is no doubt of the conviction that God's work is one and is constant, whether experienced through Jesus or through the community of his people, or indeed by way of his direct intervention in speech or signs and wonders.

The Gospel of John is not out of line with the usage elsewhere, but has its own special feature in seeing the Spirit under the language of *parakletos*—that is, as counseling, strengthening, perhaps sponsoring or speaking on behalf of the Christian community (John 14–16). But, as in Paul, the Spirit is one with Jesus, not exactly as in later Trinitarian oneness, but as being his own alter ego after the crucifixion: John 14.16–18. The Spirit is the guarantee that the "departure" of Jesus results in no diminution from the highest of all possible high points experienced in Jesus, but even leads to an intensification of the divine work (14.12). This language carries the strongest possible deterrent against discouragement or religious nostalgia. At the same time, John gives no encouragement to Christians to innovate or develop what they have received and come to believe, for the Spirit will simply pass on to them "the things of Jesus" (16.12–15); and his leading of them "into all truth" (v. 13) is one with leading them "into Jesus," who is himself "the truth" (14.6). A good deal of later thought and devotion about the Spirit, perhaps especially in Orthodox Christianity, owes much to these Johannine trains of thought.

There is no doubt that in subsequent times, the difference between the attributive (God's "breath" is man's breath writ large) and the substantial was hard to handle. In the New Testament, the use of "spirit" language falls predominantly into the former category, and, as perhaps most notably in Luke, Jesus is seen after the model of great Old Testament prophets and others, and as Messiah, himself a divinely inspired and charismatic figure, one supremely imbued with God's ("holy" therefore) spirit. Where there is substantial or hypostatic usage, it remains within the kind of metaphorical language found in Judaism.

It is therefore in large measure an independent question how far the Trinitarian concept, and especially the distinctive role of the Holy Spirit as "third person," is a useful or adequate way of thinking about the divine mystery: that must depend on considerations of a philosophical kind such as the New Testament does not employ. It is open to discussion, however, how far those in the subsequent period who sought to elucidate these matters were able to free themselves with any clarity from the image-idiom of the New Testament. For those who depended more on Platonist thought, Jesus-the-Word sufficed for the mediatorial role between God and all else, and the Spirit may be seen as conceptually redundant. Yet the tradition forbade the jettisoning of such an entrenched mode of Christian speech and prayer. However, the more one emphasized the Spirit as God's creative power, the more risk there was of confusing Spirit with the Father as fount of all things. So although the Spirit's scriptural roles remained, in liturgical and other uses, prominently before the Church's mind, other lines of thought had to be followed to give substantive force to a distinctive place for the Spirit—for example, as the bond of love between Father and Son or as the fount and archetype of the will within the human personality, as the Father was the fount of memory and the Son of understanding (both in Augustine of Hippo). But however profound the thought here, it is hard not to see a measure of contrivance at work, an attempt to accommodate an embarrassment of inherited images that were never meant to form into the neat ranks of our mental organizing.

The centuries-long dispute between Eastern and Western Christians, centered on the Nicene Creed, whether the Spirit should be seen as proceeding directly from the Father or also from the Son *(filoque)*, though still alive, seems to many to be the kind of enquiry that is meaningless, whether in scriptural or conceptual terms—and indeed to be a blatant intrusion upon the divine mystery. But it neatly illustrates the difficulty of asking questions of texts that they were not designed to answer and of seeking to define the interior relationships of the divine in a way that is impossible for us. Nevertheless, however uncongenial the idiom may be, it is possible to see it as raising the important question of how far the continuing activity of God ("Spirit") is to be seen as constrained by what we have seen in Jesus ("Son") or has an unfettered independence of creative energy: real issues hidden in unlikely garments. It must, however, be admitted that the question has mostly been fought over down the centuries on the less interesting and on the whole counterproductive ground of scriptural texts that might be appealed to in support of one or the other position, with the word "anachronism" never so much as raising its voice.

The phenomenal growth of Pentecostal Christianity in the last hundred years, and especially in the last fifty, adds a new and vibrant dimension to our subject. Manifesting itself in Charismatic Renewal, and found in both Catholicism and Protestantism, as well as in Pentecostal churches themselves, it has come to flourish in many parts of the world—not just the United States and parts of Western Europe but also, and explosively, in South America as well as many parts of the Third World. It stands as a strident symbol of uncompromising religious protest against secularization and "wishy-washy" religion, often among the poor but also, in richer societies, among members of the disenchanted middle classes, longing for a disciplined and truth-assuring framework of life. The doctrinal emphasis of this brand of Christianity is on the work of the Holy Spirit, with its model in the style of religious practice described in 1 Cor. 14 (and much criticized by Paul!). The theology of these groups is normally strictly orthodox in the manner of Evangelical Christianity in general, so of course the role of Jesus is vital, but in practice the emphasis falls on the present extravagant activity of the Holy Spirit, in ecstatic experience, speaking in tongues and amazing healings. In that way, the practical effect may be said to be a shifting of religious proportion away from Jesus and onto the Spirit.

Leslie Houlden

See also: Augustine of Hippo; Creeds; John, Gospel of; Orthodox Tradition; Paul; Pentecostalism

References

Dunn, J. D. G. 1975. *Jesus and the Spirit*. London: SCM.
Lampe, G. W. H. 1977. *God as Spirit*. Oxford: Clarendon.
Martin, David. 2001. *Pentecostalism*. Oxford: Blackwell.

Homer

If one were to compile a profile of Jesus from the writings of Paul and Q, one could derive a narrative framework largely consonant with the Gospel of Mark. The earliest evangelist clearly inherited similar traditions about Jesus and his disciples that included ethical teachings, predictions of the future, and stories of healings, exorcisms, the Last Supper, Jesus' crucifixion, and resurrection, but his narrative goes far beyond this skeleton. Indeed, most of his stories find no confirmation in Paul, Q, or other independent witnesses. For example, before Mark no one ever called the Chinnerth "the Sea of Galilee"; no independent evidence exists for fishing disciples, the Gerasene demoniac, the feeding of the thousands, the transfiguration, the so-called triumphal Entry, or most details of the crucifixion. Many scholars nonetheless assume that Mark inherited these materials from antecedent tradition, while others suspect that the earliest evangelist created many of them himself after models supplied by Jewish writings or contemporary Greek biographies, histories, and novels.

Many distinctively Marcan tales, however, seem to imitate Homer's *Iliad* and *Odyssey*. These two enormous Greek epics had been composed by 700 B.C. and became the undisputed pillars of literary education throughout antiquity. A contemporary of the Gospels wrote that "from the earliest age, children beginning their studies are nursed on Homer's teaching. One might say that while we were still in swathing bands we sucked from his epics as from fresh milk. He assists the beginner and later the adult in his prime. In no stage of life, from boyhood to old age, do we ever cease to drink from him" (Ps.-Heraclitus *Quaestiones Homericae*, 1.5–6). Students often memorized long sections of the epic, performers memorized them for public performances, and artists depicted their scenes on vases, sarcophagi, gems, and coins. Grammatical handbooks and surviving school exercises illustrate the importance of *mimesis* or *imitatio* of highly regarded models, Homer above all. Students often wrote lists of epic words with more familiar equivalents and then paraphrased the original. Consequently, imitations of the epics are common in ancient literature; even Jewish poets and historians borrowed from Homer in retelling biblical tales. Because the epics were cultural inevitabilities, ancient readers could recognize allusions to them that are invisible to us.

By comparing the Gospel of Mark with the epics, one may observe the earliest evangelist adapting epic characterizations, plot devices, and entire episodes to express his faith in Jesus Christ. Like Odysseus, Jesus travels with foolish comrades unable to endure suffering, sails dangerous seas, encounters supernatural foes, confronts a monster who lives in caves, conceals his true identity lest his enemies destroy him, transforms into his actual identity before his most intimate friends, makes a picaresque entry into a city, finds his home infested with murderous rivals, predicts his own return in the third person, is anointed by a woman who recognizes him, visits the dead, and returns alive from Hades. Like the gods Aeolus, Athena, and Poseidon, Jesus calms the seas. Like Nestor, who fed 4,500 men at the shore, Jesus feeds 5,000 men and again 4,000 women and men at the shore. None of these episodes finds attestation in Christian tradition before Mark; none finds closer parallels in Jewish texts than those in the *Odyssey*.

Several other characters in Mark also have counterparts in the epic. The disciples resemble Odysseus's crew; the Jewish authorities, who "devour the houses of widows" (12.40), play roles similar to those of Penelope's suitors; James and John (the Boanerges) echo Castor and Polydeuces (the Dioscuri); the Gerasene demoniac plays the part of Polyphemus, while Jesus resembles Circe by turning the legion of demons into swine (5.1–20); the death of John the Baptist compares with the death of Agamemnon (6.14–29); Bartimaeus, a blind seer, is Mark's answer to Homer's blind seer Tiresias (10.46–52); the woman who anoints Jesus for his burial is an imitation of Eurycleia, who recognized Odysseus while washing his feet (14.3–9); Judas resembles Odysseus's traitorous servant Melanthius; Barabbas is Mark's answer to Irus the greedy buffoon; the young man who ran away naked at Jesus' arrest and reappears in Jesus' tomb is an imitation of young Elpenor who died at Circe's island, met Odysseus from Hades, and whose body the hero later buried (14.51–52 and 16.5–8).

For the death of Jesus, however, Mark borrows not from the *Odyssey* but from the *Iliad*. Like Achilles, Jesus predicts his untimely death and goes to it with courage. Like Hector, he dies alone, abandoned by his comrades and even his god. His executioner gloats over him, women watch and mourn his death from afar, and his corpse must be rescued from his executioner for a proper burial (15.16–47).

Mark was no slave to his models; on the contrary, he not only borrows, he also transforms them to portray Jesus as superior to the likes of Odysseus and Hector. Unlike Odysseus, Jesus needs no god to calm the sea for him. Instead of overcoming the Gerasene demoniac with deception and violence as Odysseus had overcome Polyphemus, Jesus exorcised him and returned him to his right mind. The woman who anointed Jesus gets the fame implied by the name of Eurycleia ("far-flung-fame"): wherever the Gospel is preached, what she had done would be remembered. Whereas Elpenor died a tragic death and remained in dank Hades, the young man in the tomb gives witness to the resurrection. Unlike Hector, Jesus rises from the dead. Whereas the *Iliad* ends as a tragedy, the Gospel ends with the victory of Jesus over death; it is indeed a Gospel, "good news." Such theologically significant contrasts characterize nearly every episode that Mark shares with the epics.

Dependence on Homer is by no means limited to the Gospel of Mark. The author of Luke-Acts repeatedly imitated the epics for narrating the exploits of the apostles in Acts. The casting of lots to replace Judas resembles the casting of lots in *Iliad* 7 to select a Greek warrior to fight Hector (1.15–26); the visions of Cornelius and Peter seem to have been modeled after the lying dream to Agamemnon and the vision of the serpent and sparrows in *Iliad* 2 (10.1–11.18); Peter's escape from jail in Acts 12 is an imitation of Priam's escape from Achilles in *Iliad* 24 (4–17); Paul's farewell to the Ephesian elders closely parallels Hector's farewell to Andromache in *Iliad* 6 (20.17–38); the death of Eutychus ("Lucky") at Troas in Acts 20, is a transformation of the death of "unfortunate" Elpenor, who was returning from the Troad (20.7–12); the so-called we-voyages in Acts may have been inspired by Odysseus' "we"-voyages in *Odyssey* 9–12; and his shipwreck finds no closer literary analogy than the shipwrecks of Odysseus (27.1–28.10).

Luke also borrowed from the *Odyssey* to narrate Jesus' postresurrection appearances in a passage that illustrates how such Homeric imitations worked. In the last book of the epic, Odysseus reveals himself to his father Laertes, who had presumed that his son had died long ago. Penelope's suitors were devouring the estate, so he, in sorrow, chose to live by himself apart from the devastation. Instead of revealing himself to his father straightaway, Odysseus pretends to be a stranger and tests him. Later, to reveal true identity, he says, "It is I" and shows him a wound on his thigh that he suffered as a boy. Laertes then recognizes him, and they dine together with the old man's joyful servants.

The parallels to the last chapter of the Gospel of Luke are uncanny. Jesus, returned from the dead, walks with two disciples, Cleopas and another unnamed, on the road to Emmaus but does not reveal himself to them. As they walk, they tell him that their lord had died and that his murderers held sway in the city. They eat with Jesus, and he suddenly departs; then they recognize that the stranger was Jesus returned from the dead. The two disciples tell this to the others, and suddenly Jesus appears to them again, this time saying, "It is I" and demonstrating his identity by showing them the wounds on his hands and feet (24.13–49). Luke seems to notify the reader of the parallels between this story and the end of the epic by his use of proper nouns. Two of the servants who recognized Odysseus on his return were Eumaeus and Eurycleia. In Greek as in English, the words "Emmaus" and "Eumaeus" are visually and phonetically similar. Eurycleia ("far-flung-fame") finds an echo in Cleopas ("glory-galore"). Other imitations of Homer in the Gospel of Luke are possible.

To grant that Mark and Luke creatively imitated Homeric epic does not necessarily exclude other interpretive interests or methods. After all, both evangelists knew traditions about Jesus, some of which may reasonably be traced to historical memory. An analogy to this combination of fiction, tradition, and history is Vergil's *Aeneid*, which not only "imitated Homer and praised Augustus" (Servius), but also retained many Roman traditions and even historical information. Even though the ascription of literary creativity to Mark and Luke calls into question how much of their narrative is historical or even traditional, it does not render historical investigations altogether invalid. On the other hand, it does mean that the Gospels of Mark and Luke must be read against the rich literary legacy of Greek antiquity if one is to understand fully their impact on their intended readers, some of whom were far more sophisticated than scholars often suppose.

Dennis Ronald MacDonald

See also: Jesus, Death of; Luke, Gospel of, and Acts of the Apostles; Mark, Gospel of; Transfiguration

References:

Hock, Ronald F. 2001. "Homer in Greco-Roman Education." In *Mimesis and Intertexuality in Antiquity and Christianity*. Edited by Dennis Ronald MacDonald. Studies in Antiquity and Christianity. Harrisburg, PA: Trinity.

MacDonald, Dennis Ronald. 1984. *Christianizing Homer: The "Odyssey," Plato, and the "Acts of Andrew."* New York: Oxford University Press.

———. 1999. "The Shipwrecks of Odysseus and Paul." *New Testament Studies* 45: 88–107.

———. 2000a. *The Homeric Epics and the Gospel of Mark*. New Haven: Yale University Press.

———. 2000b. "The Ending of Luke and the Ending of the *Odyssey*." Pp. 161–168 in *For a Later Generation: The Transformation of Tradition in Israel, Early Judaism and Early Christianity*. Edited by Randall A. Argall et al. Harrisburg, PA: Trinity.

Hymns

In a famous letter to the Emperor Trajan (c. A.D. 110–112), Pliny, governor of Bithynia, reported on the habits of Christians, and understood that one of these was to meet on a certain day before daybreak and to sing praises to Christ as a god. Later generations of Christians might express this less crudely, but over the centuries the overwhelming majority of their hymns have been centered on Jesus, and his divinity accepted as normal.

The word "hymn" can have more than one meaning even in the context of Christian worship, but for the purpose of this article, the conventional use is assumed, and with a definition offered by Erik Routley: "a strophic song on a Christian subject, capable of being sung by a congregation not in any sense made up of trained singers" (Routley 1983, 4–5).

Hymns Addressed to Jesus

We must first notice those hymns directly addressed to Jesus—songs of devotion to him. Among the most ancient are those of the twelfth century: "Jesu, the Very Thought of Thee" (*Common Praise* [henceforth designated *CP*], 485); "Jesus! the Very Thought Is Sweet" (*New English Hymnal*, 291 [Canterbury Press, Norwich, 1986]); and "Jesu, Thou Joy of Loving Hearts" (*CP*, 486). These were translated from Latin (respectively) by Edward Caswall, John Mason Neale, and Ray Palmer, so did not attain their present English form and use until the nineteenth century. They were an important part of the warm devotion to the person and name of Jesus in the twelfth century.

After the Reformation, the German pietistic movement produced hymns of devotion that were in contrast to the creedal and liturgical hymns of Luther himself. One of these, "Jesu, Priceless Treasure" (*CP*, 484), has found its way into most hymnbooks if not into the repertoire of most congregations. A century earlier "I Greet Thee, Who My Sure Redeemer Art" (*Hymns and Psalms* [henceforth *HP*], 391) came from the "school" of John Calvin, and a century later exuberant praise of Jesus flowed from the pen of Charles Wesley. One of the most famous is:

> O for a thousand tongues to sing
> My dear Redeemer's praise,
> the glories of my God and King, the triumphs of his grace!
> Jesus! the name that charms our fears, that bids our sorrows cease;
> 'tis music in the sinner's ears,
> 'tis life and health and peace. (*CP*, 534)

The ethos of such hymns does not vary too much in the course of time or the tradition of Christianity from which it springs. A hymn with the refrain:

> Jesus, my Lord I thee adore
> O make me love thee more and more (*CP*, 483)

comes from the pen of Henry Collins, an Anglican who became a Roman Catholic, and:

> Jesus, these eyes have never seen
> that radiant form of thine (*CP*, 491)

from the American Congregationalist Ray Palmer. The tradition continued in the twentieth century with hymns like Percy Dearmer's "Jesus, Good above All Other" (*CP*, 487) and is amply represented in the songbooks that proliferated in the last quarter of that century.

Hymns Celebrating Jesus

More often, hymn-writers have focused on some aspect of Jesus' life, death, and resurrection. In some hymnbooks (e.g., *CP*) these are classified according to the seasons of the Christian year—Advent, Christmas, Passiontide, and so forth, but in others (e.g., *HP*) the classification runs: Christ's birth, Christ's ministry, Christ's passion and cross, resurrection and ascension, Christ's work of salvation, Christ's coming in glory. These classifications arise from past traditions rather than present practice, since the mainstream churches all tend now to observe the Christian year. Of course, many hymns appointed for certain seasons can equally well be used in others, and editorial classification is by no means infallible.

The seasonal hymns themselves offer different and sometimes contrasting perceptions of the Gospel events. Besides the time-worn items for Christmas, often retelling Luke 2 and Matt. 2, there are the devotional "O Little One Sweet" (*HP*, 111), the more theological "Of the Father's Love/Heart Begotten" (*CP*, 65), and the interpretations of Charles Wesley in "Let Earth and Heaven Combine" (*HP*, 109) or "Glory Be to God on High" (*HP*, 101). "A Stable Lamp Is Lighted" (*CP*, 42) takes us far beyond the stable, and "Who Would Think That What Was Needed" (*Rejoice and Sing* [henceforth *RS*]), 178, ends each verse with:

> God surprises earth with heaven
> Coming here on Christmas Day.

The Passiontide section of *Rejoice and Sing*, as well as including the two famous hymns by Isaac Watts, "When I Survey the Wondrous Cross" (*RS*, 217) and "Nature with Open Volume Stands" (*RS*, 219) and the internationally sung "O Sacred Head Once/Sore Wounded" (*RS*, 220), has an unusual hymn by the contemporary writer Brian Wren:

> Here hangs a man discarded,
> a scarecrow hoisted high,
> a nonsense pointing nowhere
> to all who hurry by. (*RS*, 225)

The grim realism persists through the early verses, and the hymn ends:

> Lord, if you now are risen help all who long for light
> to hold the hand of promise and walk into the night.

Other contemporary writers have sought to supply hymns for those parts of the Passion narrative for which there has been slender provision: "Jesus in Dark Gethsemane" (*RS*, 213) for Maundy Thursday and "To Mock Your Reign" (*RS*, 221) for the events early on Good Friday.

By contrast with these examples of seasonal hymnody, provision for Christ's ministry and teaching has always been rather thin. Of course, "Blest Are the Pure in Heart" (*CP*, 391) is partly based on a Beatitude (Matt. 5.8) and "Thou Art the Way" (*CP*, 600) on John 14.6. Older and less well known hymns on Jesus' earthly life include "My Dear Redeemer and My Lord" (*RS*, 205) and "O Thou, Whom Once They Flocked to Hear" (*HP*, 150), but the contemporary "The Kingdom of God Is Justice and Joy" (*CP*, 591) offers a text on one of the main emphases of Jesus' teaching. The renewed interest in healing has produced some recent writing on that theme (e.g., *CP*, 346, 348, 349).

A few hymns take an overview of the events of the Gospel and comprehend part of what is contained in the Apostles' Creed. "O Love, How Deep, How Broad, How High!" (*CP*, 118), attributed to Thomas à Kempis, is one of the earliest of these, and the twentieth-century "We Have a Gospel to Proclaim" (*CP*, 612) has been immensely popular in the United Kingdom in recent years. "Son of the Lord Most High" (*HP*, 152) concentrates on the early life of Jesus.

Hints at the preexistent *Logos* are more common than direct references, but one nineteenth-century hymn has the verse:

Ere he raised the lofty mountains,
formed the seas, or built the sky,
Love eternal, free, and boundless,
moved the Lord of life to die
fore-ordained the Prince of princes
for the throne of Calvary. (*CP*, 409)

and a song of the twentieth century begins:

Jesus is Lord! Creation's voice proclaims it,
for by his power each tree and flower was planned and made. (*CP* 170)

There is, however, no dearth of hymnody on what is now often entitled "Christ's coming in glory." Contemporary hymnbooks do not often use the term "Second Coming," and options seem to be left open as to whether this "coming" may be expected on earth or at the end of time, or, indeed, whether the kingdom is to be on this planet or in the heavenly realm. Wesley's hymn "Lo, He Comes with Clouds Descending" (*CP*, 31) affirms "God appears on earth to reign," while "Mine Eyes Have Seen the Glory of the Coming of the Lord" (*HP*, 242) has become a song of national aspiration, even for non-American Christians. It is interesting, in this connection, that contemporary hymnbooks have tended to restore the last verse of "Rejoice! the Lord Is King," by Charles Wesley (*CP*, 563):

Rejoice in glorious hope;
Jesus the Judge shall come
and take his servants up to their eternal home:
We soon shall hear the archangel's voice,
the trump of God shall sound: rejoice!

Hymns Describing Jesus

A large proportion of hymns about Jesus are concerned with the names given to him and the characteristics that they imply. A panoramic view of these is provided in a hymn by Isaac Watts that begins:

Join all the glorious names
of wisdom, love, and power,
that ever mortals knew, that angels ever bore:
all are too mean to speak his worth,
too mean to set my Saviour forth.

The hymn is to be found in all three of the collections to which constant reference is made in this article (*CP*, 493; *HP*, 78; *RS*, 280), but none includes all twelve verses of the original. (These may be found in *A Panorama of Christian Hymnody*, 18.) The first of the "glorious names" (Savior) occurs in the verse quoted above, and in the remainder, Jesus is described as Redeemer, Prophet, Counselor, Pattern, Guide, Shepherd, High Priest, Advocate, Surety, Captain, Lord, Conqueror, King, and said to be "like an angel." The hymn has the title "The Offices of Christ from Several Scriptures," and in some modern hymnbooks, as in the original, these "offices" are italicized.

The titles provided by Watts are hardly intended to be exhaustive. The *Companion to Hymns and Psalms* has a subject index in which no less than six long columns are devoted to hymns about Jesus (pp. 477–480). Among the titles listed here are Brother, Bridegroom, Example, Friend, Head, Lamb of God, Sacrifice, Servant, and Victim. Such a list (of which those just quoted are but a small selection) again is not exhaustive, since it can refer only to the 823 hymns contained in *Hymns and Psalms*, but it suffices to indicate the variety of ways in which Jesus is portrayed in Christian hymnody. And, besides those titles for Jesus that have their origin in Scripture, there are those that arise from the experience or occupation of worshippers such as:

> Jesus, Saviour, pilot me
> Over life's tempestuous sea (*Baptist Hymn Book* 1962, Novello no. 543)

written, not surprisingly, for sailors.

Before examining the place in Christian hymnody of the most commonly used titles for Jesus, we must note those hymns that focus on the name itself. The most outstanding example is the fifteenth-century Latin hymn translated by J. M. Neale, "To the Name of Our/That Brings Salvation" of which the second verse runs:

> Jesus is the name we treasure,
> name beyond what words can tell;
> name of gladness, name of pleasure, ear and heart delighting well;
> name of sweetness passing measure,
> saving us from sin and hell. (*CP*, 610)

The remaining verses continue in the same vein. Perhaps more frequently used is Newton's

> How sweet the name of Jesus sounds
> In a believer's ear (*CP*, 467)

and hymns on this theme continue to be written—as by Timothy Dudley-Smith in "Name of All Majesty" (*CP*, 525) in which each verse ends "Jesus is Lord!"

It is not surprising that the bulk of hymns about Jesus concentrate on such titles as "Saviour," "Redeemer," and "Lamb of God." Some hymn-writers—notably Charles Wesley and Cecil Frances Alexander—have deliberately set out to teach theology through hymns, but most do not explain what is meant by redemption, and instead portray and underline what has been taught elsewhere. Nevertheless, particular interpretations of the Atonement do appear in many hymns. The more Evangelical collections tend to include "Man of Sorrows" with the verse:

> Bearing shame and scoffing rude,
> In my place condemned he stood; Sealed my pardon with his blood:
> Alleluia! What a Saviour! (*HP*, 228)

which implies a substitutionary view of the Atonement. On the other hand, we find the *Christus Victor* note struck in such ancient hymns as "Sing, My Tongue, the Glorious Battle" (*CP*, 121) or "The Royal Banners Forward Go" (*CP* 122). And a further interpretation is offered in a hymn by the twelfth-century Peter Abelard:

> Alone thou goest forth, O Lord,
> in sacrifice to die;
> is this thy sorrow naught to us
> who pass unheeding by?
>
> Our sins, not thine, thou bearest, Lord,
> make us thy sorrow feel,
> till through our pity and our shame
> love answers love's appeal. (*CP*, 102)

But, in general, worshippers who sing of Jesus as redeemer or savior are left to make what meaning they can from these august words. A simple hymn by Dora Greenwell, "I Am Not Skilled to Understand," perhaps speaks for many:

> I take God at his word and deed:
> Christ died to save me, this I read;
> And in my heart I find a need
> Of him to be my Saviour.
> And was there then no other way
> For God to take? I cannot say
> I only bless him, day by day,
> Who saved me through my Saviour. (*HP*, 221)

Our consideration of hymns on this theme must include those that see the crucifixion as a present or ongoing event. An example is Timothy Rees's "O Crucified Redeemer." A verse omitted from many recent hymnals, but included in those of a generation earlier runs:

> Wherever love is outraged,
> wherever hope is killed,
> where man still wrongs his brother man,
> thy Passion is fulfilled.
> We see thy tortured body,
> we see the wounds that bleed,

where brotherhood hangs crucified,
nailed to the cross of greed.
(*Hymns Ancient and Modern New Standard* [1983], 404)

Only second in number to those hymns that speak of Jesus as Redeemer are those in which he is portrayed as king or prince. If some hymn-writers have unwittingly given the impression that Jesus' kingship is a vastly bigger and better version of kingship experienced on earth, others have gone to great pains to establish that it is of a totally different quality and nature. "Crown Him with Many Crowns" (*CP*, 166) appears in most collections, but versions of it vary from book to book since what is offered is often an amalgam of Matthew Bridges and Geoffrey Thring. But in many of these, Jesus is crowned as "Lord of Love," "Lord of Peace," and "Lord of Years." A twentieth-century hymn by Michael Saward begins "Christ Triumphant, Ever Reigning" (*CP*, 398) but the next three verses refer to the Word incarnate, the Suffering Servant, and the Priestly King. On the same theme is Graham Kendrick's "From Heaven You Came" (*CP*, 432), often given the title "The Servant King."

In recent years, there has been criticism of the widespread use in hymnody of metaphors that are masculine, militaristic, and imperial. This is a theme in a book by a contemporary hymn-writer, Brian Wren, entitled *What Language Shall I Borrow?* (SCM, 1989). The epilogue to this book (pp. 227–235) asks what is meant by the Ascension, so often portrayed as the return of a Crown Prince to reign at his Father's side, and Wren offers a hymn (and illustrates how it is constructed) expressing what he believes to be the essential meaning of the Ascension. It is not too far removed from the concept of Jesus as the High Priest, which is also a theme of this season, reflected in a number of hymns and made specific in Watts's paraphrase of verses from Heb. 4 and 5.

With joy we meditate the grace
of our High Priest above;
his heart is made of tenderness
and ever yearns with love. (*CP*, 624)

But the question of language as well as theology will continue to exercise the minds of hymn-writers.

It is not possible, within the limits of space, to refer to all the titles and characteristics of Jesus to which reference has been made. But a few further illustrations may be added. The description of Jesus as Shepherd is frequently used in hymnody, and in "Jesus, the Good Shepherd Is" (*HP*, 263), Charles Wesley blends John 10 with Ps. 23. Many hymns, as already noted, use more than one description of Jesus. One twentieth-century example begins "Christ Be My Leader" (*HP*, 709), but in the next two verses speaks of him as Teacher and Savior. A translation of an Urdu lyric (*HP*, 137) has five verses based on the Fourth Gospel in which Jesus refers to himself as the Bread, the Door, the Light, the Shepherd, and finally as the Resurrection and the Life.

Reference has been made to the representation of the crucifixion as a contemporary event, but many hymns in recent years have drawn their inspiration from Matt. 25.31–46, including this song from the Iona Community ("Love from Below," by John L. Bell and Graham Maule, Wild Goose Publications, 1989, p. 66):

Christ's is the world in which we move,
Christ's are the folk we're summoned to love,
Christ's is the voice which calls us to care,
And Christ is the one who meets us here.

The remaining three verses are intended as an aid to intercessory prayer, and each ends with the refrain:

To the lost Christ shows his face;
To the unloved he gives his embrace;
To those who cry in pain or disgrace,
Christ makes, with his friends, a touching place.

This is one of the most modern of the hymns quoted in this article, but the present reality of Christ is hardly novel, and is vividly expressed in one of the most ancient of hymns, known as "St. Patrick's Breastplate" (*CP,* 203):

Christ be with me, Christ within me,
Christ behind me, Christ before me,
Christ beside me, Christ to win me,
Christ to comfort and restore me;
Christ beneath me, Christ above me,
Christ in quiet, Christ in danger,
Christ in hearts of all that love me,
Christ in mouth of friend and stranger.

Alan Dunstan

See also: Calvin, John; English Christianity, Medieval; Jesus, Name of; John of the Cross; Kempis, Thomas à; Liturgy; Luther, Martin; Preexistence; Spirituality; Wesley, Charles and Wesley, John

References

Common Praise: A New Edition of Hymns Ancient and Modern. 2000. Norwich: Canterbury.

Hymns and Psalms: A Methodist and Ecumenical Hymn Book. 1983. Peterborough, UK: Methodist Publishing House.

Rejoice and Sing. 1991. Oxford: Oxford University Press for the United Reformed Church.

Routley, Erik. 1979. *A Panorama of Christian Hymnody*. Collegeville, MN: Liturgical Press.

_______. 1983. *Christian Hymns Observed*. London: Mowbray.

Watson, J. R. 1997. *The English Hymn: A Critical and Historical Study*. Oxford: Clarendon.

Watson, Richard, and Kenneth Trickett, eds. 1988. *Companion to Hymns and Psalms*. Peterborough, UK: Methodist Publishing House.

I

Icons and the Icon Tradition

Jesus is portrayed in icons mainly in the Orthodox tradition of Christianity, best known through the Greek and Russian expressions of Orthodoxy. Icons of Christ are also common in the Eastern Rite Catholic tradition, and their use has spread into other Christian traditions since the mid-twentieth century. The visible icon of Jesus presents the Person of Jesus Christ as the focal point of divine revelation, the One in whom God and humanity are perfectly united; he is the Incarnate Son who accomplished the redemption of humanity through his death and resurrection and opened up to us life in communion with God; the outpouring of the Holy Spirit completed the revelation of the Trinity and brought into being the Church within which the divine life is shared and through which revelation is made known. Jesus Christ is perceived as present not only through the Holy Scriptures and the Sacraments but also through the Holy Icons.

The word *icon* (that is, "image") is used in the Greek version of the Old Testament at Gen. 1.26–27; "And God said, Let us make man according to our *icon* and likeness. . . . And God made man, according to the *icon* of God he made him, male and female he made them." In the New Testament, St. Paul says that Jesus Christ is "the *icon* of the invisible God" (Col. 1.15). This use of the word *icon* brings together revelation about the nature of human beings as created "according to the icon of God," and also revelation about the divinity of Jesus Christ. The creation of material icons of Christ, the Blessed Virgin Mary, and the saints spread widely from the fourth century onward, in such varied forms as painted wooden panels, mosaics, wall paintings, ivory, and woven fabrics. Controversies about the use of icons became acute in the eighth and ninth centuries, a period in which the defenders of the Holy Icons developed a theology of the icon that remains central to Orthodox Church life to this day. God the Son, who has united himself to our humanity in the Person of Jesus, is capable of being portrayed in icons; the icons present the Person of Jesus as the God-Man, the "One Who Is" (cf. Exod. 3.14) who has become incarnate for our salvation. To venerate or honor the material icon is not an act of idolatry, but an honoring of the person who is represented in the icon. Thus icons functions as doors or windows between heaven and earth, between the divine realm and the material world; they assist us in our spiritual growth to become more truly human "according to the *icon* and likeness" of the God-Man Jesus.

Two ancient traditions express something of the importance of icons in the Orthodox world. The first tradition is that St. Luke painted an icon of the Virgin Mary, the "Mother of God," and that she gave her blessing to his work. This is expressed in Illustration 1 (twentieth-century mosaic, Kykko Monastery, Cyprus). On the left St. Luke is seated, painting the icon; in the center he stands with an icon of the Mother of God with her Son; on the right the Mother of God raises her right hand in blessing. This tradition asserts the reality of the Incarnation and shows St. Luke as an Evangelist who after the day of Pentecost communicates the Gospel not only through the written words of his Gospel and the Acts of the Apostles but also through iconography—literally "icon writing." Thus word and image, what is heard and what is seen, become key instruments in the communication of divine revelation. The second tradition is that King Agbar of Edessa, suffering from some form of leprosy, sent his messengers to ask Jesus to come and heal him; Jesus declined but placed a cloth over his face that received the image of his face; the cloth was sent to Agbar, who was healed as he beheld the image of the face of Christ, subsequently referred to as the icon "made without hands" *(acheiropoietos)*. This tradition could almost be an illustration of the truth that St. Paul expresses in 2 Cor. 3:18: "We all, with unveiled face, beholding the glory of the Lord, are being changed into his likeness from one degree of glory to another; for this comes from the Lord, who is the Spirit." Just as the

Illustration 1: Mosaic of St. Luke painting an icon of the Mother of God. This twentieth-century mosaic carries out the ancient Orthodox tradition that shows St. Luke as an Evangelist who communicates the gospel not only through written words but also through iconography—literally "icon writing." Kykko Monastery, Cyprus. (Photo courtesy John Bagley)

leprous face of Agbar was healed when he beheld the image of Christ's face, so too our lives are healed and restored through the work of the Spirit as we behold the face of Christ. The material image of the face of Christ is central in Orthodox iconography. In Illustration 2, we have a twelfth-century Russian icon of the Holy Face of Christ—pensive, compassionate, triumphant over human passions and death, and open to the sufferings of humanity. The square panel and the cross-inscribed circular halo focus our attention on the Holy Face (see also Illustration 1 in the Art entry in this encyclopedia).

In Orthodox lands icons of Christ can be seen in churches, homes, public buildings, and wayside shrines. Such widespread and varied distribution of icons expresses the way in which sacred and secular aspects of

Illustration 2: The Holy Face: The Savior, "Acheiropoietos." Twelfth century. Tretyakov Gallery, Moscow. (Scala/Art Resource, New York)

life are interpenetrated; as the Incarnation brings together heaven and earth, so the Holy Icons express this union in the Person of Christ and in the places where the icons make his presence visible. Illustration 3 shows a sixteenth-century Russian painted panel icon of the Savior. Christ's head is surrounded by a halo on which the form of the Cross is inscribed and in which the remains of the inscription "The One Who Is" can be seen; there

Illustration 3: The Saviour. This icon communicates an attractive presence who draws the viewer in to share Christ's inner life. First half of the sixteenth century. Rublev Museum, Moscow. (Photo courtesy John Bagley)

would originally have been an inscription with the name Jesus Christ. Thus the Person depicted is identified as the Incarnate Son, the God-Man Jesus. Christ's left hand holds the open book of the Scriptures, the written manifestation of his teaching; his right hand, often shown raised to bless those who stand before the icon, is here turned inward toward the heart; the sense of inner attentiveness is increased by the contrast between the outer and inner garments of Christ. In this icon there is a strong sense of an attractive presence; we are held in the Savior's gaze; his teaching is presented to us, and we are drawn to share in his inner life, to be restored after his image and likeness (see also Illustration 2 in Art entry). In Illustration 4 we have an eighteenth-century image of Christ Pantocrator, the ruler of all, in the dome of the monastery church at Kaiseriani near Athens. This majestic figure looks down from the heights of heaven; beneath him in the upper levels of the drum all is prepared for the Last Judgment; between the windows are the prophets, sent to prepare for the Incarnation; beneath them as the drum joins the vaults of the church there would have been four figures of the Evangelists (two of whom have survived) recording the events of Christ's earthly ministry, and in the vaults of the church the main events of Christ's earthly life, which are commemorated in the festivals of the Church; on the lower walls of the church would be the saints who have shared the same earthly struggles as those who are present to celebrate the Divine Liturgy. The interior decoration of the church beneath the central figure of Christ forms a coherent context within which the faithful worship

Illustration 4: Created in the eighteenth century, the majestic figure of Christ Pantocrator (ruler of all) in the Dome of the Church at Kaiseriani, near Athens, looks down from the heights of heaven. (Photo courtesy John Bagley)

and grow in holiness. In Illustration 5, we have a small panel icon of *Christ in Glory* painted by Andrei Rublev about 1410–1415. Christ is enthroned, with the open book supported by his left hand; the right hand is raised in the gesture of blessing, but as in Illustration 3, the hand is turned inward

Illustration 5: Christ in Glory, *painted by Andrei Rublev, ca. 1410–1415. The geometrical forms and contrasting colors of the diamond, the oval, and the rectangle focus the viewer's attention on Christ, from whom light and truth radiate out to the four corners of the earth. Tretyakov Museum, Moscow. (Photo courtesy John Bagley)*

toward the heart of Christ; Christ's feet rest on a footstool behind which are wheels reminiscent of Ezekiel's vision of God (Ezek. 1). Within the mandorla behind Christ we see the seraphim. Rays of light go from Christ to the four corners of the icon, where we see the symbols of the four evangelists. The geometrical forms and contrasting colors of the diamond, the oval, and the rectangle help to focus our attention on Christ from whom light and truth radiate out to the four corners of the earth. Larger examples of this iconographic theme form the center of the *deesis* (intercession) group of figures on the *iconostasis* (icon screen) in an Orthodox church; the *deesis* group consists of Christ in the center, and on either side the Mother of God and John the Baptist, the Archangels Michael and Gabriel, St. Peter and St. Paul, and other saints according to the space available; all the attendant figures have their hands raised in a gesture of intercession toward Christ, linking the praying Church on earth with the heavenly Kingdom.

Christ is also seen in icons associated with the Festivals of the Church. The Transfiguration of Christ is illustrated in Illustration 6, a sixth-century mosaic in the apse of the church in the Monastery of St. Catherine at the foothills of Mount Sinai. This mosaic comes from a period when the theological significance of the Transfiguration was well understood, but before the

Illustration 6: Sixth-century apse mosaic of the transfiguration of Christ in St. Catherine's Monastery, Sinai. The mosaic dates from a period when the theological significance of the Transfiguration was well understood, but before the feast was widely observed. (Photo courtesy John Bagley)

feast was widely observed. Mount Sinai is associated with the gift of the Law to Moses, and the monastery at the foothills commemorates God's call to Moses from the Burning Bush (Exod. 3). In this mosaic of the Transfiguration we see details that become standard features in icons of the feast, derived as they are from the Gospel narratives (Matt. 17.1–8; Mark 9.2–8; Luke 9.28–36): the central figure of Christ is clothed in white and placed against a mandorla signifying the divine realm; Elijah and Moses appear with Christ, here as large figures on the outer edge of the conch of the apse; the apostles John, Peter, and James are shown near to the lower half of the mandorla; above Christ we see the Cross and the Lamb (not usual in icons of the feast), which link the glory of Christ in the Transfiguration to the sacrificial death he willingly accepts at Calvary; rays of light shine from the figure of Christ to the representatives of the Law, the Prophets, and the Apostolic witness.

In Illustration 7, we have a fifteenth-century Easter icon from Novgorod. Commonly referred to as *The Anastasis*, this image expresses the theological significance of Christ's Resurrection; examples of this theme survive from the early eighth century but become widespread from the ninth and tenth centuries onward after the conclusion of the Iconoclast Controversy. At the lowest level of this Novgorod icon we see the depths of Hades (the underworld) opened up; Christ treads down the broken gates of Hades, and the locks lie scattered in the darkness. The brilliant white figure of Christ stands out against a mandorla of concentric circles, and the whole icon is suffused with the light of the resurrection; in his left hand Christ holds the Cross, the triumphant symbol of his redemptive sacrifice; with his right hand he raises Adam; behind Christ Eve raises her hands in prayer. Above Adam we see David and Solomon (royal ancestors and prophets of Christ), the prophet Daniel, and St. John the Baptist (the "Forerunner" who prepared the way for Christ and before him entered Hades after a martyr's death); above Eve we see other examples of the righteous dead including Moses with the tablets of the Law, and Abel, the murdered shepherd son of Adam and Eve. In the upper part of this icon the divided rocky peaks are reminiscent of St. Matthew's statement that at the crucifixion "the earth shook and the rocks were split" (Matt. 27.51), and also of the passage of the Israelites through the Red Sea: "the waters being a wall to them on their right and on their left" (Exod. 14.29). The imagery of the Old Testament Exodus and Passover is used to interpret the significance of Christ's redemption of humanity from sin and death. The Anastasis icon is not only an image of Christ's resurrection; it is an image of humanity being raised up to share the divine life in Christ (see also Illustration 5 in the Art entry).

Illustration 8 shows a remarkable image of the dead Christ, with the inscription "The King of Glory." It forms one side of a double-sided wood panel icon from Kastoria in northern Greece and dates from the second half of the twelfth century; on the other side of the icon is an anguished figure of the Mother of God with her Son enthroned on her left arm. This icon comes from a time of increasingly intense devotion to the Passion of Christ, and the place of his Mother in the Passion. It is the earliest known example of its kind and seems to have been a prototype that led to the widespread use of

Illustration 7: Icon from Novgorod from the second half of the fifteenth century. The resurrection is represented in terms of Christ's descent into Hades (the Anastasis). The Anastasis icon is not only an image of Christ's resurrection, but one of humanity being raised up to share the divine life in Christ. Novgorod Museum. (Photo courtesy John Bagley)

Illustration 8: The Akra Tapeinosis (Man of Sorrows) icon from northern Greece dates from the second half of the twelfth century. It may have been a prototype that led to the widespread use of "The Man of Sorrows" image in the Orthodox tradition as well as the medieval Western Church. Kastoria Cathedral, Kastoria, Greece. (Photo courtesy John Bagley)

"The Man of Sorrows" image in the Orthodox tradition, and also in the medieval Western Church (see also Illustration 13 in the Art entry).

John Baggley

See also: Art; Orthodox Tradition; Resurrection; Transfiguration

References

Baggley, John S. 1987, 1995. *Doors of Perception—Icons and Their Spiritual Significance*. New York: St. Vladimir's Seminary Press.

Cavarnos, Constantine, 1977. *Orthodox Iconography*. Belmont, MA: Institute for Byzantine and Modern Greek Studies.

Cormack, Robin. 2000. *Byzantine Art*. Oxford: Oxford University Press.

Maguire, Henry. 1981. *Art and Eloquence in Byzantium*. Princeton: Princeton University Press.

Ouspensky, Leonid. 1992. *The Theology of the Icon*. New York: St. Vladimir's Seminary Press.

Ouspensky, Leonid, and Vladimir Lossky. 1982. *The Meaning of Icons*. New York: St. Vladimir's Seminary Press.

Ignatius of Antioch

Ignatius, whose writings are among those of the *Apostolic Fathers*, was an early-second-century bishop from Syrian Antioch, an important center of the Christian movement from almost the beginning. His work was produced while he traveled, under guard, through the Roman province of Asia, and it is a rich quarry for insights into the development of Christology and of church order. His often florid phrases are (for the modern reader) sometimes opaque, but still Ignatius of Antioch provides us with important first instances of Christian theological language and ideas. Two things come over clearly: (1) his wish to clarify and to promote a certain understanding of Jesus Christ (Magn. 1.2), and (2) his ardent desire, as a martyr-in-the-making, to imitate "my God's Passion" (Rom. 6.3). Ignatius was the first Christian writer we know of who repeatedly described his Lord using phrases such as "Christ our God" (Eph., Intro.); "our God in us" (Eph. 15.3, cf. Rom., Intro, 3.3 [John 20.28]; Eph. 18.2; Trall. 7.1; Smyrn. 1.1–2; Pol. 8.3).

His seven letters to Roman Asia (now western Turkey) and to Rome are usually dated before A.D. 115. The churches he was addressing were loyal to an understanding of tradition and order that led him to term them (presumably like his own in Antioch) "catholic." The phrase "the catholic church" (literally "universal" as opposed to local, but already also carrying the sense of "mainstream" or "normative") appears for the first time in Ignatius (Smyrn. 8.2). "Catholic" Christian teaching about the nature and the saving work of Jesus Christ was beginning to be sculpted, partly in response to alternative understandings that were prevalent among Christians from a variety of religious and cultural backgrounds. The discussion that follows will consider briefly the letters and the challenges they pose for the interpreter and then the Ignatian understanding of Jesus Christ.

The problem for the interpreter of Ignatius' letters is that for centuries they have been a battleground for scholars. Even in the twentieth century the date and authenticity of the seven letters were disputed (in different ways) nine times. That debate continues. A seven-letter-corpus (letters addressed to Ephesus, Magnesia, Tralles, Rome, Philadelphia, Smyrna, and to bishop Polycarp of Smyrna), known as the *Middle Recension* of Ignatius' work, was isolated as authentic in the nineteenth century. It was distinguished from a larger collection, which is now known as the *Long Recension*. I assume, with most writers, that the seven letters are authentically from the early years of the second century and these form the basis for what follows. I shall not be considering the Antiochene and Roman *Acts of Martyrdom* associated with Ignatius, for these stem from a later date and cannot be shown to reflect accurately the thought of Ignatius himself. Similarly six additional and later letters in the *Long Recension* do not figure in what follows.

There is a further difficulty, however. It arises because Ignatius is clearly writing in opposition to certain kinds of teaching of which he disapproves. The challenges for interpreters have been (1) to discern how many such "opponents" Ignatius was countering; (2) to determine of what kind they were (e.g., Were they of Gnostic type, or in one way or another "Jewish Christians"? Was their teaching perhaps akin to that of Cerinthus and his followers or were they Ebionites?), and what they were saying about Jesus Christ, the church, and so on; and (3) to know how far Ignatius' language, not least his language about Jesus Christ, was formulated in response to their teachings.

The title *Jesus Christ* and also the appellation "Christian" are significant in these letters. It had been in Antioch that the term "Christian" had first been applied to the new sect (Acts 11.26), and for Ignatius of Antioch its use, rather than its being known by any other name, was important (Magn. 4; 10.1, and cf. Trall. 6.1, where it is contrasted with "heresy"). So too was the kind of discipleship the word "Christian" implied. It should not involve "judaizing" and should involve loyalty to the kind of church order Ignatius favored.

The word *Christianity* (*christianismos*) appears in Magn. 10.3 and Rom. 3.3, and the newness of the Christian dispensation was stressed. Ignatius wrote of the dispensation (*oikonomia*) of the "new man Jesus Christ" (Eph. 20.1, cf. "the perfect man" of Smyrn. 4.2, and "new hope" of Magn. 9.1) and affirmed that the old kingdom was overcome, because God was made manifest as man for the newness (*kainoteta*) of life eternal (Eph. 19.3).

The contrast was with what he termed "Judaism," an old, sour leaven, not the "new leaven which is Jesus Christ" (Magn. 10.2, cf. Phld. 6). Ignatius stood in that line of early Christian writers that determinedly was distinguishing Christian practice from the kind of Jewish observance (or its remnants) that still pertained in some groups of Christians.

When we come to the figure of Jesus Christ in these letters, there are themes familiar from New Testament sources, but it is insistence on the reality of the events of the Lord's human existence that offers the clue to Ignatius's deepest concerns. Jesus Christ was born of a virgin (Smyrn. 1.1; Eph. 19.1). His coming had been signified by a star (Eph. 19), but in this passage, where also magic (*mageia*) is said to be overcome, there is more than a reflection of the star and Magi of Matthew's birth narrative. In Eph. 19, Ignatius was offering a carefully stylized reflection on the cosmic significance of the Incarnation, and his unusual language has many parallels, some of them in Gnostic sources: "And hidden from the prince of this world were the virginity of Mary, her birthgiving as also the death of the Lord; three 'cried out' mysteries, accomplished in the silence of God. . . . God was made manifest as man for the newness of life eternal, and what had been prepared by God had its beginning. Consequently all things were disturbed, because the destruction of death was being wrought" (ibid. 19.1, 3).

The Lord's baptism had also been to fulfill all righteousness (Matt. 3.15, cf. Smyrn. 1.1), so that here was a Syrian echoing a baptismal tradition that was incorporated only in Matthew's Syrian Gospel. Alongside Jesus Christ's coming/birth in flesh, it was his passion, his death and resurrection that were the planks on which faith rested (Phld. 8.2, cf. Magn. 11; Rom. 6.1; Phld. 9.2; Smyrn. 12.2).

In passages that seem quasi-credal Ignatius asserted important truths: "Our God, Jesus the Christ, was conceived by Mary . . . [also was] of the seed of David as of the Holy Spirit; he was born and was baptised" (Eph. 18.2).

In Smyrn. 1.1 he wrote that "truly he was of the family of David . . . God's Son . . . truly born of a virgin, baptised by John . . . truly nailed in the flesh for us, under Pontius Pilate and Herod the Tetrarch."

The word "truly," here and elsewhere, asserted the reality of these happenings for the flesh-and-blood Jesus Christ. He was a man of flesh (Eph. 1) postresurrection too, when "in the flesh" he ate and drank and then was united "in spirit" to the Father (Smyrn. 3.1).

The reason for such language was that some churches of Ignatius' day (cf. 1 John 4.1–2) were having to counter alternative Christologies. Indeed Ignatius was the first Christian writer to use the word "heresy" (Greek *hairesis*, Eph. 6.2; Trall. 6.1) in something approaching its technical Christian sense (rather than its ordinary meaning of "partisanship" or "school of thought"), and that is significant. Creedlike assertions (such as in Smyrn. 1.1, above) with the qualification "truly" suggest something about the nature of the false teaching. In Trall. 9.1 we are told that Jesus Christ "truly" was born, ate, and drank, "truly" was crucified, died, and was raised from death in sight of all in heaven, earth, and under the earth. Such language points to the existence of others in the orbit of Ignatian-type catholic churches who did not believe that the Lord Jesus Christ had "truly suffered" (Smyrn. 1.1) or had been raised in the flesh.

Rather, they maintained, "his Passion was only in semblance" (Smyrn. 2, cf. Trall. 10.1), and there was talk of a bodiless, phantasmal entity. Tartly, Ignatius observed that *they* will be bodiless and phantasmal (with promised resurrection in mind, Smyrn. 2).

The people of this tendency, which made Jesus Christ "seemingly" human, crucified, and so forth, have been labeled docetists (a term derived from the Greek verb *dokein*, "to seem/appear to be"). The term was first coined by Serapion of Antioch in the latter half of the second century. Docetism took a variety of forms and was to be found also in Gnosticism. Its substitutionary form, according to which Jesus was in fact replaced on the Cross by Simon of Cyrene or Judas Iscariot, found echoes in some Islamic interpretations of the "crucifixion" of Jesus, though there is nothing of this kind in Ignatius' account.

Ignatius reported that such people did not share in the eucharistic gatherings for catholic Christians (ibid. 7.1), where the Eucharist was being presented as "the flesh of our Saviour Jesus Christ who suffered for our sins." A Jesus Christ who suffered, and in the flesh, was not what the others affirmed. With the constant danger of divided and squabbling churches, however, Ignatius tried to convince those to whom he was writing that "the bread of God" (Eph. 5.2), in a church that was "breaking one bread" (ibid. 20.2, cf. ibid. 13.1 and Phld. 4 ["one cup for union with his blood"]; Smyrn. 7.1; 8.1), was the focus for unity and was power for the Church. The elements were real for him (Eph. 1.1; Phld. 4), so that his own desire as he moved ever closer to Rome and his death was "for the bread of God, which is Jesus Christ's flesh" and "for drink I desire his blood" (Rom. 7.3, cf. Smyrn. 7.1).

What exactly was Ignatius countering? The matter is disputed. From docetists of the sort associated with Johannine communities (1 John 4.1–3; 2 John 7) through Ebionites or Cerinthus and his followers, to the teachings of the school of the Gnostic Valentinus, all have been suggested. For Ignatius what mattered was that neither salvation for the believer, nor the unity of the Church, nor yet a Christian discipleship that would countenance persecution (as his own did) could be reality, if such an error took hold in congregations (Trall. 9–10; Phld. 3.3; Smyrn. 1.2–2.1; 3; 4.2; 5.3). Jesus Christ's very real Passion, he insisted, was the key to the believer's justification and resurrection (Trall., Intro; Phld. 8.2). It was belief in "the faith of God," for which he had been crucified that saved one from "unquenchable fire" (Eph. 16.2).

His repeated use of "Jesus Christ" or "Christ Jesus" (almost 120 times) may be a more precise clue to the kind of teaching he was countering. The single name Jesus occurs rarely in these letters, and those he opposed may have separated the human teacher Jesus from "the Christ," thought of in spiritual or angelic-being terms. Some errorists are known to have claimed (1) that "Christ" entered Jesus at baptism, (2) that possession of/by "Christ-power" lay behind the miracle-working and more, and (3) that at the time of crucifixion ("why have you forsaken me?") Jesus alone was left. This adoptionist, or possessionist, Christology, found among Ebionites, followers of Cerinthus, and other Jewish Christians, would not have allowed that "Christ" had suffered or died, though the experience of "Jesus" may have made such things a seeming reality (cf. "his suffering was only a semblance," Trall. 10.1, and. Smyrn. 4.2).

If such teaching was in mind then, by contrast, when Ignatius stressed "his suffering," it would have been the Passion of "Christ" as well as Jesus that he had in mind. He determinedly bonded together the dual name *Jesus Christ* and in describing "Jesus Christ, from eternity with the Father" (Magn. 6.1) and "Jesus Christ who came forth from the one Father" (ibid. 7.2) Ignatius may have been clarifying both the relation of the Son to the single God of Jews and Christians and the indivisibility of Jesus and the Christ.

These kinds of questions of interpretation apart, Ignatius provided a number of important descriptions of Jesus Christ. He was now God who "cannot be touched, who cannot suffer"—that is, impassible (Pol. 3.2, but contrast Smyrn. 3.2, on his being "like any natural man" after his resurrection). He had been, at different stages, flesh and spirit, born and unborn, God in man, true life in death, both of Mary and of God, first suffering and then impassible (Eph. 7.2).

He was at once "our only teacher" (Magn. 9.1–2) and as God's Word he had proceeded from silence (ibid. 8.2). Here was "the mouth . . . by which the Father has spoken truly" (Rom. 8.2).

Son, Father, and Spirit appear together in Magn. 8.1 (cf. by implication Phld., Intro.), but this does not represent a polished Trinitarian formulation. Elsewhere in the letters Ignatius was struggling to express Christological paradoxes concerning Jesus Christ's humanity, his preincarnation relation to the Father, and the relation to the divinity that was made manifest with his death and resurrection. Moreover, what he says about Jesus Christ is inseparable from what he also says about the Church. Throughout his letters he affirms the close bonding of Jesus Christ with the life of the Church and the progress of the believer. The Lord who was anointed on his head (Matt. 26.7) breathed incorruptibility on the Church. By his birth and baptism he had signified that "the water" would be purified (Eph. 17.1; 18.2), an act that his Passion had ensured. Ignatius' language would be echoed in theology and liturgy thereafter, notably in the Orthodox traditions, in which chrismation was associated with baptism and the waters of baptism were blessed and purified in exorcistic fashion. The bishop-martyr holds an especially significant position for the Antiochene Orthodox church.

His presentation of Jesus Christ as the physician-healer and as the cure of ills is particularly notable. He was the "one physician" (ibid. 7.2) and in an often-quoted phrase Ignatius described the Eucharist as the "medicine of immortality, the antidote against dying" (ibid. 20.2). In the Eucharist (again understood realistically in terms of Jesus Christ's presence) was "the flesh of our saviour who suffered for our sins." Those who denied the identification of the flesh of Christ with the Eucharist perished (Smyrn. 7.1) and whereas the poison of false teaching might destroy (Trall. 5.2), in Him was the antidote to false teaching (Eph. 7.1–2).

Ignatian Christology was forged in opposition. So whereas the Lord anointed (with sweetly smelling ointment), breathed incorruptibility over his Church (cf. "breathing" in John 20.22, where his followers receive the Holy Spirit), the teachers of error, by contrast, brought corruption (Eph. 16–17) and the anointing of Satan, "the prince of this world," was foul-smelling.

For all such language there was a broad range of literature—Jewish scriptural, early Christian (e.g., Pauline), sacred and secular Greco-Roman, medical, and other—that he might have called upon from his memory. In the final weeks before his death, and in the light of the situations in Asian churches, Ignatius molded it into something distinctive. Subsequent Christian writers, readers, and liturgists recognized it as containing important insights about the Church and Jesus Christ.

Christine Trevett

See also: Adoptianism; Creeds; Eucharist; Gnosticism; Orthodox Tradition; Pre-existence; Resurrection

References

Brent, Allen. 1991. "The Relations between Ignatius and the Didascalia." *The Second Century* 8: 129–156.

de Bhaldraithe, Eoin. 2001. "The Christology of Ignatius of Antioch." Pp. 200–206 in *Studia Patristica* 36. Edited by M. F. Wiles and E. J. Yarnold. Leuven: Peeters.

Goulder, Michael. 1994. *A Tale of Two Missions*. London: SCM.

———. 1999. "Ignatius' 'docetists.'" *Vigiliae Christianae* 53: 16–30.

Lechner, Thomas. 1999. *Ignatius adversus Valentinianos? Chronologische und theologiegeschichtliche Studien zu den Briefen des Ignatius von Antiochien*. Leiden: Brill.

Munier, Charles. 1993. "Où en est la question d'Ignace d'Antioche? Bilan d'un siècle de recherches 1870–1988." Pp. 361–484 in *Rise and Decline of the Roman World*. Berlin, New York: de Gruyter.

Pelikan, Jaroslav. 1985. *Jesus through the Ages: His Place in the History of Culture*. New Haven and London: Yale University Press.

Schoedel, William. 1985. *Ignatius of Antioch*. Hermeneia Commentary Series. Philadelphia: Fortress.

Trevett, Christine. 1992. *A Study of Ignatius of Antioch in Syria and Asia*. New York: Edwin Mellen.

Ignatius of Loyola (c. 1491–1556)

Ignatius Loyola was a man of intense personal devotion to Jesus Christ. More remarkable, however, was his ability to abstract from his own personal style of devotion. Ignatius' *Spiritual Exercises* reflect a style of ministry profoundly respectful of human individuality, and facilitate responses to Christ of indefinitely many different kinds. Ignatius also founded the Society of Jesus, a group of priests with a quite distinctive spirituality of ministry. Jesus is thus at once the chief object of Ignatius' personal love, the central figure in Ignatius' process for discerning God's will, and the true head and founder of Ignatius' society. We can appreciate Jesus' full significance for Ignatius, and Ignatius' full contribution to Christian tradition, only if we recognize that these three roles involve different, if related, spiritual dynamics.

Personal Devotion

"Crazy on the Lord Jesus" runs one apocryphal early description of Ignatius. His initial impulse following his conversion was "to remain in Jerusalem, forever visiting those holy places"; when he was forced to leave, he twice—on both occasions bribing the guards—revisited the Mount of Olives, reputedly the site of the Ascension, in order to contemplate Christ's two final footprints (*Autobiography*, nn. 45, 47). As he entered Rome in 1537—a turning point in his life—Ignatius had a vision of Christ carrying the Cross; the Father was saying to Christ, "I want you to take this person as your servant," and Jesus was agreeing (*Personal Writings* [PW], 376, fn. 153).

Ignatius' *Spiritual Diary*, the longer entries in which cover some months in 1544, contains several intense expressions of devotion to Jesus, often in a Trinitarian context, and often focusing on the Son's intercession. On 24 February 1544, for example, Ignatius felt, while preparing for Mass, that "the name of Jesus was shown me"; throughout the Mass, he felt "great love, confirmation, and an increased resolve to follow Him," and "all the devotion and feelings had Jesus as their object." He adds: "I could not turn myself to the other Persons, except in so far as the First Person was Father of such a Son; then I began to exclaim spiritually, 'How He is Father, and how He is Son!'" After Mass, he felt that a confirmation of his decision that he was expecting from the Trinity was in fact coming through Jesus: "He showed Himself to me, and gave me great interior strength and a sense of security that the confirmation was granted. I did not fear for the future. So it occurred to me . . . to pray to Jesus to obtain pardon for me from the Blessed Trinity." At the end of the day, "I so felt and saw Jesus that it seemed that nothing could happen in the future capable of separating me from Him or of making me doubt about the graces and confirmation that I had received" (PW, 85–86).

The intensity of such texts is unmistakable, and has massively influenced Ignatian hagiography. Even a critical Freudian biographer has noted that "identification with Christ . . . served multiple functions in his [Ignatius'] psychic economy," and that the values "embedded in the figure and teaching of Christ" became "the centerpiece of his revitalized and transformed spiritual identity" (Meissner, 398–400). However, it is doubtful that more than a conventional theology can be found coherently stated in such personal texts, although one should note Ignatius' fondness for referring to Christ not only as Lord but also as Creator.

The Spiritual Exercises

Fascinating though Ignatius' personal writings may be, his most significant contributions to Christian tradition lie elsewhere: in the foundation of the Society of Jesus and in the composition of the *Spiritual Exercises*. Christian tradition abounds in figures gifted with vivid experiences in prayer, or who related to Jesus Christ in a way that was somehow striking. Ignatius' special quality, however, lies in his ability to abstract from the colorful features of his personal spirituality, and to offer others no more (or rather no less) than what he calls *modo y orden para meditar y contemplar* (*Spiritual Exercises* [Exx], 2). This "method and structure for meditating and contemplating," and more broadly for exploring and deepening one's own relationship with God, may lead a person along a path biographically or psychologically similar to that of Ignatius, but it is equally likely to lead to something radically different.

Ignatius' *Spiritual Exercises* are thus deliberately dry; their expression is elliptical, and their structure disconnected. The energy is to come from the free encounter of Creator and creature (Exx, 15); each person encountering the texts is challenged to open themselves to divine grace so as themselves to shape a life-narrative that is personal and unprecedented. Through various literary strategies, the texts seek to say enough to be helpful, but not so much as to undermine their purpose by prescribing, even implicitly, the particular forms such an encounter might take. (The principle is also profoundly influential on the *Constitutions* that Ignatius wrote for the Society of Jesus, which are concerned to hold apostolic ministers open to how Christ's "supreme wisdom and goodness" carry people forward along "the path which is the divine service" [n. 134].)

Much scholarship on Jesus' role in the *Spiritual Exercises* has imitated the uncritical, conventional intensity of Ignatius' personal writings. The exceptions have been preoccupied by the discontinuity in Ignatius' rhetoric. Whereas much of the prayer centers on the figure of Christ, Ignatius' more theoretical statements—about the purpose of life, or the action of God in creation, or about the choices we should make—make relatively sparse reference to Jesus. Juan Luis Segundo has attacked Ignatius for inconsistency and for excessive rationalism; by contrast, Hugo Rahner and a number of Spanish textual scholars have articulated how there is a Christology latent in the more theoretical parts of the treatise, as reflected in how Ignatian retreat-givers normally supplement such material with Gospel texts.

Once, however, we interpret the *Spiritual Exercises* as fostering the discovery of personal vocation, this abstractness becomes readily intelligible in terms of reticence about specifying the particular way in which Jesus' centrality should be manifest in a person's life. Moreover, Ignatian Gospel contemplation—which is certainly influenced by earlier sources—is not simply an exercise in internalizing some moral ideal. It is designed to generate a response quite personal in kind. The person praying is constantly encouraged to "reflect in themselves and draw profit," to enter into imaginative conversation with the people in the scene even on the basis of what they "*might* be saying," to be "re-seeking" (often misleadingly translated as "making repetitions") in ways directed not by the Gospel text itself but by how they themselves have been responding to it. Ignatius takes up the Gospel vision of divine compassion incarnate in Jesus, and develops a mode of prayer on the implicit presupposition that each person can come to *conocimiento interior* of this Jesus—best, if controversially, translated as "knowledge from inside"—and therefore "follow" him. "Following" here does not mean identification with the historical Jesus so much as a developing of one's own discipleship in creative response. Two phrases of the Victorian Jesuit poet Hopkins point up the contrast: it is not so much that "I am all at once what Christ is, since he was what I am"; rather, the Gospel is a "masterpiece," whose effect is to make us "admire and do otherwise."

Ignatius' densest presentation of Jesus in the *Spiritual Exercises* comes in directives preparing a possible choice of lifestyle. We are encouraged to desire poverty and insults in union with Jesus "if only I can suffer them without the sin of any person, or displeasure of His Divine Majesty" (Exx, nn. 147, see 165–67). The complexity here has often been overlooked: either Ignatius' teaching here is equated with a straightforward devotion to the crucified Christ, or else the proviso is stressed, the explicit references to poverty and insults downplayed, and the whole interpreted—implausibly—as an encouragement to make choices in accord with right reason. It may be more helpful to note that the proviso as stated could never in fact be fulfilled: Ignatius is asking us to make abstractions. Without colluding with the evil that led to the Cross and with other instances of innocent suffering, we may nevertheless focus on the God-given possibility that, with Christ, good can come from horror. By remembering that fact, or more rather by prayerfully "cherishing and pondering it" in Christ's presence (*Constitutions*, n. 101), we may be freed from certain sorts of fear and defensiveness prior to making an appropriate choice.

The full thirty-day process of the Exercises leads, after the making of a decision, into sustained prayer on the Passion and the Resurrection. Ignatius says surprisingly little about what he expects here, and what he did say was ignored even in his own lifetime. However, the petitions on which the prayer in this phase centers are strikingly formulated; the prayer on the Passion asks for "grief with Christ in grief, shatteredness [*quebranto*] with Christ shattered, tears and interior pain at such great pain which Christ suffered for me" (Exx, 203), and the unitive note here is emphasized in the prayer on the resurrection, where we are encouraged to reflect not on what the resurrection might mean for us, but rather to focus selflessly on the joy experienced by the risen Christ himself.

The Society of Jesus

Ignatian spirituality is not to be identified with Jesuit spirituality. The development of the spiritual pedagogy in the Exercises and the foundation of the Society of Jesus overlapped in Ignatius' biography, and were closely associated in his mind. Nevertheless, they are conceptually separate. The Jesuit vocation can be seen as the fruit of one possible outcome of the Exercises: a decision to take as central to one's identity the image found in Matt. 10, that of Jesus calling disciples by name, implicitly separating them from family and career, and sending them out to preach the Kingdom. Other responses take other Gospel images as central: a vocation to social work might be centered on the Good Samaritan; a vocation to contemplative prayer might focus on Jesus' experiences on Tabor and in Gethsemane.

This account of the Jesuit vocation finds some corroboration in hagiographical tradition, but its primary justification is inductive: this kind of use of Matt. 10 provides an elegantly simple framework within which we can locate the values and tensions central to Jesuit life. Both in Matt. 10 and in Jesuit self-understanding we find an unclarified relationship between explicit proclamation of the Word and healing the sick. Both exhibit a tension between Jesus' call to poverty ("Jesus, the Lord of us all, chose this poverty for himself, and this was what He taught them, when He sent His apostles and beloved disciples to preach" [PW, 71]), and an impulse to carry out the mission as effectively as possible. Most important, if dispersion on mission is permanently to remain identity-defining, and not lead to the group's dissolution, those missioned must maintain a link with the sending Christ, even as they exercise freedom and creativity where they have been sent.

Ignatius' companions thus called themselves the Society of Jesus, because their sense of identity centered on the image of the disciples sent on mission by Christ; they persisted in maintaining this name even when challenged by the quite legitimate objection that such a designation could apply to the Church at large. As they grew and institutionalized they extended rather than lost this sense. They developed a strong—and at the time unusual—sense of the pope as Vicar of Christ; they developed the office of the Jesuit superior as the one sending "in place of Christ our Lord." As the Reformation split hardened in the later sixteenth century, and even more so as devotion to the Pope's person became a commonplace of Catholic devotion in the nineteenth, these ways of conceiving religious office came to acquire polemical confessional nuances, and to sound authoritarian. Originally, however, the early Jesuits paralleled other Reformation movements in an insistence that their bond with Jesus transcended all other affiliations, whether tribal, political, or ecclesiastical. Ignatius and his companions contributed to Christian spirituality a particular sense of Jesus caring for those who were like sheep without a shepherd, and out of that care sending laborers—laborers free enough from other affiliations for the Lord of the harvest to be able to send them to people and places otherwise neglected.

Philip Endean

See also: Chinese Christianity; Jesus, Name of; John of Caulibus; Spanish Christianity; Spirituality

References

Ignatius' own works are cited from the following:

- *Spiritual Exercises* (Exx): "The Literal Version," translated by Elder Mullan in 1996. *Draw Me into Your Friendship: A Literal Translation and a Contemporary Reading of the Spiritual Exercises*. Edited by David L. Fleming. St. Louis: Institute of Jesuit Sources.
- *Autobiography* and *Spiritual Diary*. In Saint Ignatius of Loyola. 1996. *Personal Writings* (PW). Translated and edited by Joseph A. Munitiz and Philip Endean. London: Penguin.
- *Constitutions: The Constitutions of the Society of Jesus*. 1970. Edited and translated by George E. Ganss. St. Louis: Institute of Jesuit Sources.

Endean, Philip. 2001. *Karl Rahner and Ignatian Spirituality*. (See esp. ch. 8.) Oxford: Clarendon.

Lonsdale, David. 2000, 1990. *Eyes to See, Ears to Hear: An Introduction to Ignatian Spirituality*. (See esp. ch. 2.) London: Darton, Longman and Todd.

Meissner, W. W. 1992. *Ignatius of Loyola: The Psychology of a Saint*. New Haven and London: Yale University Press.

O'Malley, John W. 1993. *The First Jesuits*. Cambridge and London: Harvard University Press.

Rahner, Hugo. 1968, 1962. "The Christology of the Exercises." Pp. 53–135 in *Ignatius the Theologian*. Translated by Michael Barry. London: Geoffrey Chapman.

Segundo, Juan Luis. 1987. *The Christ of the Ignatian Exercises*. Translated by John Drury. Maryknoll: Orbis.

Tellechea Idígoras, José Ignacio. 1994. *Ignatius of Loyola: The Pilgrim Saint*. Translated by Cornelius Michael Buckley. Chicago: Loyola University Press.

Incarnation

See Alexandrian Theology; Bernard of Clairvaux; Hinduism; John, Gospel of; Macquarrie, John; Pannenberg, Wolfhart

Incarnation in Contemporary Analytic Philosophy

The idea of divine incarnation in the person of Jesus of Nazareth has been analyzed and discussed by contemporary analytical philosophers who also work in philosophical theology. The majority have sought to make the idea, literally understood, intelligible, and believable in the face of its conceptual difficulties, while a minority have found this unachievable and have investigated nonliteral uses of the language of incarnation.

The traditional doctrine is that Jesus was God the Son, Second Person of the divine Trinity, incarnate, and the official philosophical understanding of this, arrived at by the Council of Chalcedon (451), was that the one person Jesus Christ united in himself two complete natures, one divine and the other human, so that he was both fully God and fully man. The philosophical problem is to make intelligible the idea of a historical individual having at the same time all the attributes without which a being is not God and all the attributes without which a being is not a member of the human race. How can an individual be both divinely infinite and humanly finite, divinely omnipotent and humanly weak, divinely omniscient and humanly ignorant, divinely immutable and humanly changing, divinely omnipresent and humanly confined to a particular region of space, divinely the creator of everything other than him/herself and humanly a creature?

One possible solution, proposed by Stephen Davis and others, is to stipulate that those divine attributes, such as omnipotence, omniscience, and so forth, which are apparently incompatible with being genuinely human, are not *essential* divine attributes. "If Jesus was God; and if Jesus was nonomnipotent; then being omnipotent is not essential to God" (Davis, 72). However, this solution has not appealed to most other philosophical defenders of the incarnation doctrine, who are unwilling to jettison the necessary modality of the divine attributes. Nor for the same reason has the kenotic (divine self-emptying) theory appealed to them. For if God has his/her attributes not contingently but necessarily, as being of the essence of the divine nature, God cannot cease to have any of these attributes, even temporarily (i.e., during the period of incarnation), as the kenotic theory requires.

Instead several of them have developed versions of the two minds theory. This has its antecedents in theological writings—its history is traced in Hanson (1984)—and is rigorously examined and defended by some contemporary analytical philosophers. Thomas Morris (1986) provides its most thorough exposition. Instead of speaking of two natures, with all the problems that this provokes, he speaks of two minds, the eternal mind of God the Son and the human mind of Jesus. These two minds exist in an asymmetrical relationship. The divine range of consciousness contains, but is not contained by, the human range of consciousness. Thus the divine mind is conscious of everything occurring in the human mind, but not vice versa. Jesus' human mind was genuinely human, developing as the child grew into the man, and was the mind of a first-century Palestinian Jew, sharing the cultural presuppositions of his time. The mind of God the Son had full access to this entire human consciousness, from birth to death, but Jesus was not likewise continuously aware of the divine mind that enclosed and monitored his own consciousness.

The theory, however, goes beyond this, because it is true of all human beings that God omnisciently knows everything, including what is going on in every human consciousness. Thus if divine incarnation consisted simply in a completely assymetrical cognitive relationship, this would not single Jesus out from the rest of humankind. God would be incarnate, in this sense, in all human beings. And so the theory has to attribute to Jesus, uniquely, "such access, on occasion, as the divine mind allowed it to have. There was thus a metaphysical and personal depth to the man Jesus lacking in every individual who is merely human" (69–70). That this access occurs occasionally and partially, rather than continuously and fully throughout Jesus' life, is intended to preserve the independent reality of his human consciousness, as depicted in the synoptic Gospels. This would thus fit those New Testament passages in which Jesus is conscious of the divine presence, but as distinct from himself, praying to God as father; though there is also a lack of fit in that here Jesus' consciousness was (apparently) a unitarian awareness of the heavenly Father, not a Trinitarian awareness of God the Son. Another possibility, however, that would fit other New Testament passages, particularly in the Fourth Gospel, would be that on occasion the divine consciousness opened itself fully to the human consciousness, so that Jesus was then aware of being the divine Son. The difficulty here, however, might be that Jesus, when not currently directly aware of being God the Son, would presumably nevertheless still know of his divine status and would accordingly not share many features of ordinary human nature, such as the anxieties arising from our finitude and vulnerability, including the fear of death.

An alternative version of the theory is proposed by Richard Swinburne (1994). He speaks not of two minds but of one divided mind, on the analogy of Freud's account of individuals with split mentalities, each side of the split holding a different set of beliefs. Thus "a divine individual could not give up his knowledge, and so his beliefs, but he could, in becoming incarnate in Christ and acquiring a human belief-acquisition system, through his choice, keep the inclinations to belief resulting therefrom to some extent separate from his divine knowledge system" (202).

It is characteristic of these theories that they are formed primarily around the cognitive relationship between the divine mind of God the Son and the human mind of Jesus of Nazareth. But they also recognize the volitional aspect of deity and humanity, and the relationship between the divine and human wills. They insist that God Incarnate was necessarily good, that it was impossible for him to sin. Jesus possessed "the divine property of being necessarily good" (Morris, 152); he was "necessarily perfectly good" (Swinburne, 195). They also, however, intend at the same time to preserve the moral freedom of the human Jesus. For the idea of the divine will making all Jesus' choices, with no autonomous human will operating, was condemned as the monothelite heresy by the sixth Ecumenical Council at Constantinople in 681–682, citing such passages as "I seek not my own will, but the will of him who sent me" (John 5.30). And the contemporary orthodox philosophical theologians, intent on defending the traditional incarnation doctrine in its purity, likewise affirm the reality of Jesus' human will as well as the absolute impossibility of his ever sinning. It is here that the main difficulty, indeed incoherence, in the theory is alleged by critics to arise.

How could Jesus be humanly free and yet necessarily good, incapable of sinning? Morris says, "Was [Jesus'] choosing rightly a free act of his own? Well, it must be admitted that from the outset he could not have chosen otherwise. His divine nature would have prevented it" (150). But he seeks to make this compatible with Jesus' genuine freedom by means of an analogy. Suppose someone, Jones, is placed in a room and told not to leave it for the next two hours. "Unknown to him, electrodes have been implanted in his brain which upon activation will prevent his deciding, or attempting, to leave the room before the two-hour mark" (151). In the event the electrodes never needed to be activated. Thus it was true both that Jones freely obeyed his order not to leave the room, and also that in fact he was not free to have done otherwise. And Morris concludes, "As Jones was unaware of the electrodes, Jesus was unaware in his earthly consciousness that he was necessarily good, unable to sin" (153). For if he had begun to initiate a sinful action, or even to form a sinful intent, the divine mind of God the Son would have blocked this so that it could never come to fruition.

A difficulty has however been pointed out (Hick). We know (according to the orthodox doctrine) that Jesus in fact never committed a sinful act. But how, on Morris's theory, can we know that he never, in his human freedom, began to form a sinful intent, which was then blocked by the controlling divine mind of God the Son? How can we know that, if the human mind had been left to its own devices, he would never have sinned? For if this has happened, we would never be aware of it since the sinful intent would have been prevented from becoming overt. The suggested criticism, then, is that Morris's theory undermines the genuine humanity of the incarnate one by circumscribing his free will, and thus fails in its object of making the fully-God/fully-man doctrine intelligible and coherent.

However, the view that the traditional doctrine, even in its new two minds form, is still not acceptably intelligible and coherent has led yet others to ask what kind of language the language of incarnation is. Divine incarnation has been accepted for centuries as a literal truth to be explained in metaphysical language about two natures or substances united in one person, or about divine identity without the omni-attributes, or now about two minds in one individual. But New Testament scholars have questioned whether the biblical passages to which the traditional doctrine appeals were originally intended in this literal mode, or were more probably in the mode of poetic expression of a Jesus-centered life. Attention has also been drawn recently to the idea of incarnation as a very familiar metaphor. We say that "great men incarnate the spirit of their age," or George Washington incarnated the spirit of

American independence, or Winston Churchill in 1940 incarnated the British will to resist Hitler, or Nelson Mandela has incarnated the ideal of reconciliation in South Africa, and so on. Used in this way incarnation does not require any metaphysical explanation. Can Jesus, then, be seen as in this metaphorical sense incarnating—that is, embodying in his life—a quality of love that reflects on the finite human level the infinite love of God, or as incarnating the ideal of a full human openness to God within the limitations of earthly life at a particular historical moment, or as doing God's will in the world so that, in this metaphorical sense, God was incarnate in his life—or indeed may it have all of these meanings at once? On this metaphorical understanding of incarnation, God wants to become incarnate in the lives of us all, but depends upon a free human response to bring this about. This would be in line with the teaching of the *Theologica Germanica* that the Christian should be able to say, "I would fain be to the Eternal Goodness what his own hand is to a man" (ch. 10). To be God's instrument in this way is the meaning of divine incarnation in its metaphorical sense. On this view, whenever anyone anywhere acts in unselfish love of neighbor, in that action God's universal presence is incarnated in human life.

The criticism of such a metaphorical understanding of the concept of incarnation is, of course, that it is clearly not the traditionally orthodox doctrine. It makes divine incarnation a matter of degree, applying to varying extents to some of the saints and to some moments in the lives of ordinary people, and thus as not restricted to one individual in all history, namely Jesus of Nazareth, or even to one religious tradition, namely Christianity. Thus while, philosophically, it has the virtue of being straightforwardly intelligible, theologically it is highly controversial in that it constitutes a radical departure from the orthodoxy that has prevailed ever since Chalcedon.

John Hick

See also: Chalcedon; Christology, Modern; Incarnation in Contemporary Analytic Philosophy; John, Gospel of; Kenoticism; Second Person of the Trinity; Son of God

References

Davis, Stephen. 1988. "Jesus Christ: Savior or Guru?" Pp. 39–59 in *Encountering Jesus*. Edited by Stephen Davis. Atlanta: John Knox.

Hanson, A. T. 1984. "Two Consciousnesses: The Modern Version of Chalcedon." *The Scottish Journal of Theology* 37, no. 4: 471–483.

Hick, John. 1993. *The Metaphor of God Incarnate*. London: SCM; Louisville, KY: Westminster John Knox.

Morris, Thomas V. 1986. *The Logic of God Incarnate*. Ithaca, NY: Cornell University Press.

Swinburne, Richard. 1994. *The Christian God*. Oxford: Clarendon.

Winkworth, Susanna, trans. 1937. *Theologica Germanica* (15th century). London: Macmillan.

Indian Christianity

The search for an Indian response to Jesus has particular importance because it has taken place in a society dominated by the Hindu view of life, where the

Muslim population is the second largest in the world, and where both Buddhist and Sikh faiths had their birth. The struggle has been to maintain the integrity of Christian belief, without that leading to a mirror image of the Western Christ. This article, which records that unfinished journey, can provide fresh ideas for those seeking to reflect on Christology in any multireligious context.

The earliest Indian response to Jesus lies soon after Christ. Legend rather than documentary evidence links this with the mission of St. Thomas, one of the original twelve disciples of Jesus. This has rightly made the Indian Church sensitive to the assumption, often made in the West, that the Europeans brought Jesus to India, with their full range of denominations. The church, at least on the Malabar coast of South East India, present-day Kerala, is not merely the product of colonial movements from the fifteenth century onward. A close relationship with the Nestorian East-Syrian Persian church from the third or fourth century led to their identification as Syrian Christians. When the Portuguese arrived in the early sixteenth century, they found four Nestorian bishops.

The existence of such ancient Christian churches did not lead to a distinctive and indigenous early Indian Christology. Churches were concerned mainly with survival in an overwhelmingly Hindu environment. Liturgy was the center of their life. There was no evangelism or theological development, and they, within society as a whole, became a high caste for whom marriage outside was anathema. As their social structure became static, so did their response to Jesus. Their disputes mirrored those of the Middle Eastern Churches. Although known as Nestorians, their predominant theological position became Jacobite (i.e., Monophysite, the very opposite of the Nestorian or Antiochene tradition). They questioned Chalcedon, and followed the Syrians in affirming the oneness of the nature of Christ. Only in recent decades have Indian Orthodox theologians begun to contribute to the search for an Indian Christology.

The Mar Thoma ("Lord Thomas") Church was formed in 1887 as a result of the sending of Church Missionary Society missionaries from the Church of England, to encourage a new sense of mission and theological development. From here came the outstanding twentieth-century lay theologian M. M. Thomas, with his understanding of Jesus Christ as the true man, "God-for-man." From here stems his theology of humanization, as Christ becomes the pattern for a new humanity, with his loving service of a struggling world. The Cross shows the power of creative love in the face of tragedy at the center of human life. The resurrection is the affirmation that love is at the heart of the universe.

In all Indian churches the struggle has increasingly been how to maintain the distinctiveness of Christianity, with Jesus at its center, while at the same time showing that this does not mean a Western religion and a Western Christ. At the popular level Jesus remains a Western import even today. The popularity of small pictures of the Catholic image of the Jesus of the Sacred Heart, seen in most Christian homes across denominations, is universal. Much of the hymnody translated from the West, and modern choruses derived from the United States or Britain, reinforce a Jesus piety that appears on the surface little different from that found in these countries of origin. But alongside this has gone the search for an Indian understanding of Jesus. I will attempt here to provide some snapshots of this, both historical and contemporary.

The Jesuit Robert de Nobili in the early seventeenth century began a radical attempt to indigenize the Madura Mission, working in what is now Tamilnadu. He adopted the culture and norms of the Brahmin community, and learned Sanskrit. He attempted to interpret the Christian faith in terms understandable within that community, calling the story of Jesus the lost Veda (holy scripture), the *Sattia Veda* (the True Veda). The Lord's Prayer he called the mantra of Jesus. Jesus is the divine guru (teacher), Peter a chief guru. Jesus is the incarnation of God, where the word "avatar" (incarnation) is used by de Nobili, but in a different way from the standard Hindu use of the word.

In the late nineteenth century, a Bengali convert to Catholicism, Brahmabandhab Upadhyaya, went much further. He translated the concept of the Trinity into Sanskrit as *Sat-cit-ananda* (Being, consciousness, and bliss). Christ is the eternal Word (*cit*) in which the fullness of God dwells; he is also the image of God (Brahman). He used Vedic language to explain Catholic orthodoxy. Christ is clearly God, but also the unique incarnation of God. There are, he asserted, other incarnations, such as Krishna, and they can be called *avatara*, but they are secondary, like "a juicy ball, compared with the sun."

In the twentieth century, understanding of Jesus followed a number of directions, depending largely on understanding of mission. Conservative evangelicals feel there needs to be an absolute break between Christ and other religions. As Lord and savior, Jesus stands supreme. Christianity may be flawed, but Christ is the answer to all the questions that Hindus ask. This Barthian approach was articulated most clearly at Tambaram in 1938, with the publication of Hendrik Kraemar's book *The Christian Message in a Non-Christian World*, the title itself revealing the content. Through close engagement with India for decades, Lesslie Newbigin came to a similar, if sensitive and more nuanced, position, in his book *The Finality of Christ*. V. Ramachandran takes a similar stance in recent writings, as does much popular evangelical writing, traditionally found in tracts and pamphlets.

Another major group are those who follow "fulfillment theology." This came to the fore in 1913, in J. N. Farquhar's book *The Crown of Hinduism*. He affirms the principle of continuity, holding that there is much good in Hinduism to be built on. But Christ is its fulfillment. Jesus provides the answer to the longing felt by the Hindu for a divine savior, who will release him from the need to complete endless sacrifices, rituals, and vows; he provides liberation from the temporal, shown to be illusion through Hinduism, and offers eternal truth. Many Indian Christians follow this tradition explicitly or implicitly. An example is the Brahmin convert Paul Sudhakar: "Hinduism is a hunger and Christ comes to satisfy it. So I emphasise Christ as 'the answer' rather than Christ 'the fulfilment.'"

Another strand centers on bhakti, devotion to Jesus, mirroring the strong bhakti tradition in Hinduism. The focus becomes, no longer a Hindu deity, but Jesus. Sadhu Sunder Singh, a Sikh convert, and now considered a saint of the Indian church, found the center of his faith in Jesus the water of life, experienced in the heart. He tells homely stories as parables of Indian life. The aim is for faith-union with Christ, to realize, as the Vedas (Hindu scriptures) put it, that "That art thou." The same spirit inspired the Tamil Christian poets, who produced devotional songs, focused usually on Jesus, and on his work in enabling personal salvation. The most famous is Krishna Pillai (1827–1900), whose lyrics are much sung to this day. Narayan Tilak, centering on God's love and grace, even calls Christ "Mother-Guru," whose deep longing is for India to come to Christ: "When shall I see my country lay her homage at the foot of Christ?"

More theological in expression is the Tamil Bishop Appaswamy. Deeply versed in the Gospel of John, he struggles with the identity of Father and Son shown in "I and the Father are one" (10.30) and with the difference between them shown in "The Father is greater than I" (14.28). He thinks that the term *avatara* is a useful one to interpret Jesus, but as an *avatara* who does leave footprints on the ground, unlike traditional Hindu *avataras*. "Christ is a towering peak," and through him we seek to understand something more of the ineffable God. Through Christ and his cross we get release from karma; identity with the suffering Christ can lead us directly to eternal life.

Another Tamil group active at the same time as Appaswamy was the *Rethinking Christianity in India* group. They were deeply conscious of their Indian-ness. Chenchiah was a convert from Hinduism. As with many converts the central fact for him was what he called "the Raw Fact of Christ" that should come before doctrines. He emphasized the humanity of Jesus, that he was *adi-purusha*, a new creation. God and man are united in Jesus, who is a new step in the evolutionary process, the origin of the species of "the Sons of God." The Hindu concept of the identity between God and man is realized in Christ. Our task is to reproduce Jesus, if we want to establish the kingdom of God.

Another in the group was V. Chakkarai, a high caste convert, who devoted his life to the national struggle and the Indianization of the Church. He affirms that we see God with the face of Jesus. Christ becomes immanent in the human soul. Jesus as *avatara* did not end with the Cross. The *avataras* of Hinduism were temporary, Jesus as *avatar* is permanent. It is the Holy Spirit who embodies that presence today. This identification is centered on the Cross, which is where our devotion, bhakti, leads us into the transforming power of his sufferings. Here the *paramatman* (the Supreme) is unified with the *atman* (individual soul), in a mystical rather than metaphysical way.

The last fifty years have seen a number of significant developments. Some have come from the dialogical movement, some from deep engagement with the context of contemporary India.

We begin first with examples from the Roman Catholic side. Raimundo Panikkar's book *The Unknown Christ of Hinduism* is subtitled *Towards an Ecumenical Christophany*. The book is a search for Christ within the texts and philosophy of classical Hinduism, in the way that Christ was found within Greek traditions as *Logos*, or as Paul unveiled the true face of the unknown God at Athens in Acts 17. He interprets Christ as the place where the human and divine meet, and likens this to Rama or Krishna, or above all, *Isvara*, the word used by the philosopher Sankara for God working within the world. This can be translated as "Lord," and described as "creator, ruler, protector, refuge." Panikkar compares Aquinas discovering the roots of truth in Plato and Aristotle with his own finding of Christ within Hindu philosophy. The result is an important but difficult book. Some Hindus may feel he reads Christ into the text in an unacceptable way.

A recent theologian, J. B. Chettimattam, uses Hindu language to describe theology as "human interiority," and Christ as "God's decisive, eschatological and soteriological presence to the individual." Emphasizing the mystical are two other priests transformed by India, Bede Griffiths and Klaus Klostermaier. Bede Griffiths sees East and West meeting in the encounter between Christianity and Hinduism, and though they are far apart doctrinally, they meet spiritually "in the heart of the lotus," which for Christians is "in Christ." Klostermaier, living in Vrindaban, the birthplace of Krishna, rediscovers Christ in "the very heart of *Brahman*," in the cave of the heart. Out of this encounter arises his beautiful and eminently readable *Hindu and Christian in Vrindaban*.

In contrast, there are the Roman Catholics who see Jesus' significance not primarily in a metaphysical sense, but in terms of his social gospel. Samuel Rayan and Sebastien Kappan are two examples. Samuel Rayan wrote: "Emphasis on the historical should be made meaningful by showing in relief the significance of Jesus for society and social change. Otherwise situating Jesus in history becomes unimportant, and history fails to enter truly into the heart of religion" (quoted in Thangaraj, 149).

We consider now some contributors from other churches. Dr. Stanley Samartha (1920–2001) is well known through his work with the World Council of Churches over several decades. His developed Christological work is best found in his book *One Christ—Many Religions* (1991). He affirmed here the Lordship of Christ, but felt that what was central was Phil. 2.5–11, where this is combined with self-emptying. "It is extraordinary that when the Church was weak and powerless, Christians could sing such hymns of victory and praise to God through Jesus Christ, without any sense of Christian triumphalism" (*Ecumenical Review* 23, no. 2 [April 1971]). He does not see such a Lord as being there to beat down other Lords. Rather the Lordship of Christ has to be lived out in concrete life situations, by those to whom this Lordship has become primary, in dialogue with those who follow other Lords, under the One God.

A recent way of interpreting Jesus is that of Thomas Thangaraj. He has developed the idea of Jesus as guru, or teacher, found elsewhere, but for him it is the fundamental paradigm. Although this concept is central in Sikhism, and links have been made there, Thangaraj has engaged in deep dialogue with Saiva Siddhanta, the major South Indian Hindu philosophy, in which the concept of guru is also central. He makes clear the distinctiveness of how he sees Jesus as guru. "It is no longer the teacher guru who dominates the scene, but the victim guru, the dying guru, the crucified guru" (Thangaraj, 101). This guru becomes universalized through the resurrection and ascension. We see the power of love and sacrifice. And just as the work of the guru is extended through his disciples, so the work of Jesus is incarnated in the ongoing community.

Recent years have seen growing Dalit self-consciousness. Known previously as "untouchables," and renamed by Gandhi "Harijans" (people blessed by God), these communities, who represent about 18 percent of India's billion people, have named themselves Dalits (oppressed, crushed, bruised peoples). Christians of Dalit background have developed Dalit understandings of Jesus. Such were found implicitly in their stories of conversion, as they sought liberation from caste oppression. They learned of a Jesus who was a liberator, standing alongside people like themselves such as the Samaritans. Moreover, he died like them "outside the camp," shamed and without dignity. Golgotha was a place of curse; to come close to him, as to them, was to become polluted. Jesus did not just become human, he became a Dalit.

A variation on this theme comes in the tribal response to Jesus. Many tribal people have become his followers all over India, and Nirmal Minz, a bishop from Ranchi, has emphasized that God's covenant in Jesus Christ is one that transcends selected nations and peoples, and that he was prepared to confront the powers that be, political and religious.

These understandings of Jesus can be seen as "post-colonial." They increasingly went alongside a rejection of those found in traditional Western theology, and in Indian Christian theology as described earlier, now termed "Brahminic," and therefore equally oppressive. The Jesus who identifies with their pain is decisively on their side of the caste divide, the fundamental sociological category for them. Since more than two-thirds of Indian Christians are from Dalit background, this understanding of Jesus is of potentially enormous importance. Dalit theologians have included James Massey, Arvind Nirmal, M. Prabhakar, and the last two bishops of Madras, M. Azariah and V. Devasayagam.

Not himself a Dalit, but writing from close identification with Dalits in his parish ministry, Sathianathan Clarke has written a powerful book on the Dalit Paraiyar community in Tamilnadu. He uses the image of Christ as the drum, as the center of his Christology, and he sees this as complementary to the concept of *Logos*. Paraiyars are characterized by this musical instrument, which they are required to play at high caste weddings and funerals. It is a sign of oppression. But it is also how they express their relationship with God: "It is a drum that invites all human beings to dismantle the respective borders that characterise their kingdoms and celebrate the borderless kingdom of God. Just as sound is available to all irrespective of boundaries, the kingdom call goes out to all people—first to the Dalits and then to the caste communities" (Clarke, 205). Jesus was like this, and Clarke calls him a "deviant."

The account so far has left out two groups of significance. The first are Indian Christian artists, poets, and musicians. To take only the example of artists, they have included such painters as Alfred Thomas, who places Jesus in Indian settings with Indian symbolism, using gestures found in the Buddha and in Indian dance. Sister Genevieve portrays Jesus as a Guru, and Jyoti Sahi, now well known in the West, as a yogi, though he also conveys a strong sense of the social gospel of Jesus, and his suffering.

The second is women. They are almost entirely absent from historical writing, though as everywhere, they form the majority in congregations. The Indian feminine response to Jesus is beginning, and this is found notably in the particular contribution of Dalit women, who feel they are thrice discriminated against, as women, as Dalits, and as Christians. A forerunner of all these women was Pandita Ramabai, who was converted to Christianity through reading the story of the Samaritan woman in John 4 and seeing Jesus' deep concern for women mirrored in the compassion shown to "fallen women" by Christians when she was in England. It was in following him that she gave her life for the uplifting of the downtrodden women of British India. It is to be hoped that there will be many more such contributions from today's Indian Christian women, offering a distinctive response to Jesus from their experience, which so often in the past has rarely had a voice.

Andrew Wingate

See also: Antiochene Theology; Art; Chalcedon; Hinduism; Holy Spirit; Interfaith Thought and Relations; Liberation Theology; Resurrection

References

Various authors, six volumes of the *History of Christianity in India*, Bangalore, Church History Association, 1984 onward.
Boyd, Robin.1969. *Indian Christian Theology*. Madras: CLS.
Clarke, Sathianathan. 1999. *Dalits and Christianity*. Delhi: Oxford University Press.
Griffiths, Bede. 1982. *The Marriage of East and West*. London: Collins.
James Massey, ed. 1994. *Indigenous People: Dalits: Dalit Issues in Today's Theological Debate*. Delhi: ISPCK.
Klostermaier, Klaus. 1969, 1993. *Hindu and Christian in Vrindaban*. London: SCM.
Panikkar, Raimundo. 1964, 1981. *The Unknown Christ of Hinduism*. London: DLT.
Samartha, Stanley J. 1991. *One Christ—Many Religions*. New York: Orbis.
Sugirtharajah, R. S. 1993. *Asian Faces of Jesus*. New York: Orbis.
Thangaraj, Thomas. 1994. *The Crucified Guru*. Nashville, TN: Abingdon.

Interfaith Thought and Relations

There are two sides to the question of how Christians interpret the figure of Jesus in the context of religious plurality, and the result depends on the balance being struck. From the side of Christian belief, a gradual development has taken place in mainstream Christian theology toward accepting that the salvific benefits of the figure of Jesus apply also to other religions. Approaching from the side of interfaith relations, the pressure on Christianity to adjust itself to assumptions that accord equal respect to differences of cultural and religious identity in society increases the demand to dismantle any reliance on Christian triumphalism, including vestiges of claims to superiority attaching to Jesus himself. Both sides have strayed away from the concept of the "uniqueness" of Jesus as the most serviceable means for negotiating the issues. This in itself is indicative of the change that the twenty-first century context of religious plurality is inaugurating. The resulting challenge has been neatly laid out by the International Theological Commission of the Vatican as follows: "How can one enter into an interreligious dialogue, respecting all religions and not considering them in advance as imperfect and inferior, if we recognize in Jesus Christ and only in him the unique and universal Saviour of mankind?" (International Theological Commission, *Christianity and the World Religions*, 15).

From the biblical perspective, the absoluteness of Jesus derives either from textual references such as John 14.6: "I am the way, the truth and the life; no one comes to the Father except by me," or from the general impression in the New Testament that Jesus is God's chosen agent for bringing about the final triumph of God's rule as the goal of history. From the point of view of later Christian orthodoxy, a similar affirmation of Jesus' absoluteness is enshrined in the doctrine of the Incarnation whereby Jesus is both divine and human in a manner that is unsurpassable and unrepeatable on the plane of history. Therefore, whether Jesus is interpreted as the final revelatory figure within a scheme of divinely ordained history or as the incarnation of the second Person of the Trinity (as in the classical metaphysics employed at the Council of Chalcedon), it has been hard to avoid the conclusion that other religions either lie outside the purposes of God or are in some sense a preparation for the greater revelation of Christ and are therefore only partially acceptable. These interpretations have, in turn, sanctioned claims for the superiority of Christianity and the Church.

However, critical approaches in Christological doctrine, which seek to interpret Jesus in the light both of an evolutionary view of creation and of the consciousness of history as a humanly shaped process of cause and effect in time, struggle to devise any formulation that is equivalent to the orthodox intention behind the concepts of "finality" and "incarnation." "Finality" translates into the language of existentialist fulfillment and "incarnation" becomes historicized as the Christian term for the way in which God relates to the whole of history through many cultural forms, while retaining a preeminence for Jesus among a number of potentially different revealers/mediators. In the context of a positive approach to interfaith relations, it remains a formidable task to demonstrate precisely how Jesus fulfills other traditions or how the preeminence attached to him outstrips other sources of revelation and transformation.

Reluctance to move away from the orthodox framework has resulted in either the arbitrary evaluation of Jesus as God's exclusive means for salvation or an ambiguity in precisely how other religions are partially (or even wholly) acceptable to the Christian understanding of God revealed in Jesus. Arbitrary here means giving full weight to the perceived qualitative difference between Jesus and other foci of revelation, so that other traditions are bound to be cast as being in error or morally inadequate in some degree. With the rise of the dialogue movement over the second half of the twentieth century, however, this arbitrary evaluation, short of its affirmation in fundamentalist circles, has generally come to be seen as unwarranted. Most theologians and official ecclesiastical pronouncements have embraced the ambiguous position whereby Jesus is "decisive" or "normative" (not unsurpassable or unrepeatable) for salvation that is operative everywhere. Most often this is based on a Trinitarian theology that distinguishes between the universal divine presence (Spirit) that is operative at the heart of many religions under different historical and cultural circumstances and the particular divine presence in Jesus (Word), which is counted as historically climactic from the perspective of Christian theology. The ambiguity of this position derives from uncertainty as to whether or not other religions as such can be vehicles for salvation apart from any explicit endorsement of Jesus as salvation's origin and goal. It is possible to soften the ambiguity by declaring religious plurality to be de facto a manifestation of God's providence in history. Yet those theologians who have endorsed this also add speculatively that members of other religious traditions will be faced by an encounter with the risen Jesus in a postmortem setting, thus reinforcing the ambiguity of the salvific status of other religions.

From the side of interfaith relations a momentum has built up that challenges any a priori claims to finality or superiority. In dialogue, religions may offer firm witness from their respective traditions, but any claim to final truth undermines the rules of mutuality and shared accountability that have shaped expectations within the practice of dialogue itself. Both the rejection and partial acceptance of other religions sit awkwardly with the philosophical recognition that religious apprehension always occurs under historical conditions and that therefore no religion, including Christianity, can reasonably claim to have grasped the whole of religious truth. Moreover, at the empirical level of spiritual and moral effects, it seems that no one religion has been overall more successful than any other. In order to accommodate these new cumulative insights some theologians have turned to a pluralist theory whereby the major world religions are vehicles of equal value for the purposes of transcendent vision and human transformation. Within this context, Christianity is one stream of religious life, and Jesus is interpreted in metaphorical, parabolic, and symbolic forms. These interpretations contend that Jesus was so transparent to the creative love of God and so embodied that love that he became the focus of Christian devotion and commitment, which in classical Christian doctrine eventually led to the God-Man formula of Chalcedon. For pluralists, it is possible to discard the Chalcedonian formula but retain the power of Jesus' transforming impact by averring that he "incarnates" metaphorically the life of God that is offered to the world through him. Symbolic or metaphorical interpretations of incarnation leave open the possibility of other powerful instances in history in which transcendent reality and human response intersect. Pluralists maintain that the cosmically affirmative world religions, theistic (e.g., Islam, Sikhism, Christianity) and transtheistic (e.g., Buddhism), arise from the impact of different symbolic instances of the transcendentally real being communicated through human or material forms.

Critics of the pluralist position resist the notion that good interfaith relations necessarily involve adjustments in the heartland of Christology. They claim that Christ can be definitive, normative, and decisive without the political overtones of superiority. Indeed, they continue, if Christ is not definitive then the practice of dialogue and interfaith relations loses its cutting edge and real interest. From another perspective, that of postmodernism, the pluralist hypothesis smacks of an Enlightenment attempt to gloss over religious differences and create a rationalist "grand narrative" that is bound to be distorting of the particularities of any of the religions. Religions, they maintain, are more or less incommensurable at the phenomenological level, and this militates against any proposals to unify them even at some higher transcendental level. The Christological position of both sets of critics is generally orthodox, arguing that these are simply the given parameters for Christian identity. What this amounts to in terms of content, however, is usually the reiteration of some version of the ancient *Logos* doctrine, borrowed from John's Gospel, whereby Jesus is the incarnate form of the creative Word of God that operates cosmically for the sake of goodness and justice. Yet this, in turn, lands us back with the problem of the logic of Chalcedonian incarnationalism in relation to interfaith dialogue and cooperation. It may be possible to maintain a firm distinction between Christian theology and dialogue for the sake of good interfaith relations, but the logic of incarnational Christology surely leads to the supremacy of Jesus as a revealer/mediator figure on the stage of world history. How to retain some sense of distinctiveness about Jesus without being drawn into the logic of Christological superiority in interfaith relations remains a problem for those who rely on Christological orthodoxy, quite apart from difficulties with its own internal intelligibility in the light of biblical, historical, and philosophical criticism.

Theological voices from the developing world have shed some light on this problem. From their perceived contexts of economic and political oppression, concern for justice and liberation combines with the realities of religious pluralism to form the starting-point for Christian praxis. Interfaith relations are not an optional dimension of Christian existence but represent a socially given context for Christian life and witness. This has led to an emphasis on the prophetic dimensions of the figure of Jesus, his announcement of the Kingdom of God, and his radical acceptance of the marginalized poor. On the whole, these theologians are content not so much to dismantle Christological orthodoxy as place the emphasis of dialogue and Christian witness elsewhere. The God who gives priority to establishing the radically egalitarian kingdom of justice and love offers a distinctive Christian voice in interfaith relations, challenging other religions and any colonialist echoes of Christian faith alike. Redirecting the focus away from preoccupation with philosophical problems centered on categories of Jesus' uniqueness or definitiveness provides a welcome rebalancing in the dialogical process—especially when this is combined with reclaiming the ethical dimensions of the servanthood of Jesus and openness to the stranger—irrespective of whatever Christological stance is adopted. This does not, however, remove those problems altogether.

There are useful distinctions from Christological discussion that can be applied in the interfaith context. Chief among these is that between Jesus as either "constitutive" or "representative" of the Christian experience of salvation. The former holds that Jesus somehow inaugurates or causes the experience of salvation that was not previously available, while the latter speaks of Jesus as the consolidated exemplar of God's boundless love that is at work universally to elicit the human response, including responses not easily recognizable from the Christian standpoint. Clearly, the "constitutive" type of Christological assessment creates difficulties if part of the ground rules of interfaith relations is that the religions approach one another with a rough sense of parity in truth and expectation of mutual enlargement in spirituality. On the other hand, the "representative" type lends itself more readily to portraying Jesus as a distinctive figure who mediates his own particular challenge and revelatory insight alongside other figures who have made their own impact stemming from the cultural circumstances of their time and place. The choice between these two approaches is not one between a strong and a weak Christian identity. But it is one between a view of Jesus that is able to make its own impact within the dialogical processes of interfaith relations as a matter of experience and one that already assumes the finality of religious truth prior to the dialogue, however nonimperialistically that finality is offered.

Alan Race

See also: Buddhism; Chalcedon; Chinese Christianity; Christology, Modern; Enlightenment; Hinduism; Incarnation in Contemporary Analytic Philosophy; Indian Christianity; Islam; John, Gospel of; Kingdom of God; Second Person of the Trinity

References

Braaten, Carl E. 1992. *No Other Gospel! Christianity among the World's Religions*. Minneapolis, MN: Augsburg Fortress.

Dupuis, Jacques. S.J. 1997. *Toward a Christian Theology of Religious Pluralism*. New York: Orbis Books.

Heim, S. Mark. 2001. *The Depths of the Riches: A Trinitarian Theology of Religious Ends*. Grand Rapids, MI, and Cambridge, UK: Eerdmans.

Hick, John. 1993. *The Metaphor of God Incarnate*. London: SCM.

Race, Alan. 2001. *Interfaith Encounter: The Twin Tracks of Theology and Dialogue*. London: SCM.

Swidler, L., and P. Mojzes. 1997. *The Uniqueness of Jesus: A Dialogue with Paul F. Knitter*. New York: Orbis Books.

Irenaeus (c. 130–c. 200)

It would be an unlikely thing to happen in the semi-integrated Europe of the twenty-first century, but in the second century, Irenaeus, brought up in Asia Minor (that is, Turkey), where he had been influenced by the famed Polycarp, bishop of Smyrna, himself a follower of the apostle John, became bishop of the church in Lyon in southern Gaul (France). Like others for some centuries after him, this Eastern Christian studied at Rome and did his main life's work in the West. His main writings show the influence of his formation in different parts of the Church and make plain his standing as a leading exponent of what was already coming to be seen (and to see itself) as mainstream or orthodox Christianity. Teaching always tends to define itself against some contrary position; in this case the rejected versions were the various types of Gnosticism, against which Irenaeus wrote his major work. He was therefore a man of the center and against innovative speculation, which tended to thrive on ideas drawn from all kinds of quarters other than the authentic Christian stream.

Irenaeus laid chief emphasis on sober scriptural teaching as interpreted by official leaders, the bishops of the leading Christian communities. His *Demonstration of the Apostolic Preaching* is a handbook of the core of Christian teaching. It brings together the main passages of Scripture on which Christians had come to rely, both from the old Jewish writings (the Old Testament), read through Christian eyes, and from the New Testament writings, notably the Gospel of John and the letters of Paul. Here too Gnostic tendencies are the implicit enemy. There is to be no giving in to any tendency to drive a wedge between God the Father and Jesus, his "word" and his anointed one. Divinity is not to be seen as diffused or diluted through the universe. It is to be truly found only in the one God who has made himself known with total authenticity in Christ, and the two are twin sides of a coin, the latter alone making the invisible God visible to us. Here Irenaeus builds on the core doctrine of the prologue of the Gospel of John.

The achievement of Jesus is expounded in terms of "recapitulation" (cf. Eph. 1.10). Taking flesh of Mary, the preexistent Word has, in Jesus, undergone the whole of our human predicament, up to death itself; but by his victory in resurrection he has undone our bondage and reversed our fall. And all this he has done as the sole and complete agent of the Father. Every part of the story expounded is seen in terms of texts drawn from the Old Testament, some by this time conventional in Christian speech and thought, but often used with great ingenuity. It is possible to speak of Irenaeus as if he were simply the reliable and worthy expositor of solid but unexciting central Christian thinking. But that is to underestimate him. It is true that there is little here in the way of philosophical or speculative framework, such as was to come on the scene soon after, notably in Alexandrian Christianity; but there is great sophistication in Irenaeus's ways of using scriptural texts in stating and expounding Christian belief, centered on the person and work of Christ, the two aspects being one. So though he can be regarded as a sober and dependable theologian of the Catholic Church whose basic faith may be seen as represented in the Apostles' Creed and its predecessors, he shows himself a man of wide-ranging intellect, so long as the center holds. His sole aim is to preserve the authentic faith, handed down in the Church from the apostles.

Leslie Houlden

See also: Alexandrian Theology; Creeds; Gnosticism; Jesus, Achievement of

References

Grant, R. M. 1997. *Irenaeus of Lyon*. London: Routledge.
Kelly, J. N. D. 1958. *Early Christian Doctrines*. London: A. and C. Black.

Lawson, J. 1948. *The Biblical Theology of Irenaeus*. London: SPCK.
Osborn, Eric. 2001. *Irenaeus of Lyons*. Cambridge: Cambridge University Press.

Irish Christianity

When Jesus is first seen in extant Irish literature, coincident with Christianity's early enculturation in Ireland, he is fitted to the form of the sacral king of the heroic age: he provides for his people (the ethos of generous hospitality); he is their protector from enemies (he rides into the world on his cross, a triumphant warrior over the powers of evil); he guides and governs his people with a wisdom that is in his case proper to his own divine status. So, in all of this, since he is always also the creator-king of "the elements" that constitute the creation, he is the paradigm for those sacral kings of the heroic age on which he is modeled, and for their long-lived dynasties. For these sacral kings secure peace and prosperity for their peoples and promote the very life-giving fruitfulness of the earth itself, precisely by receiving the truth (word) or wisdom that is in origin and nature divine. Or, to put the point in other words, precisely by the earthly king marrying and remaining faithful to Sophia (Wisdom) through whom God creates and providentially guides the cosmos—the feminist equivalent in Prov. 8:22ff. of the Prologue to the Fourth Gospel, and the cultural equivalent of the old Irish marriage and fidelity of the true king to the shape-changing goddess now in her name and form of the Sovereignty—he is the conduit of the continuously created prosperity and peace of nature and society. But Jesus is this divine Word or Wisdom incarnate, and as such he is incarnate king of the cosmos, paradigm and source of all earthly government when it is just and then source of the peace and prosperity of society, as much as his providential governance of the cosmos maintains the life-enhancing riches and beauty of the natural world. But when earthly government becomes unjust, Jesus is then judge and witness of the destructive violence that erupts in society, and simultaneously of the wasting of nature itself, the encroachment of the primeval chaos in which death, not life, is dealt (just as the Sovereignty originally turned in similar circumstances into the death-prophesying and indeed death-dealing old hag).

This picture of Jesus as the incarnate King-Hero of the cosmos and of the human race can be seen already fully developed, for instance, in the eighth-century text called *The Poems of Blathmac*. And when it is said in that text that he is "a king who was *bishop* and full sage," or more intriguingly, that "he called to him a stout band of people whose warrior qualities were renowned: twelve apostles to whom he was *abbot*" (Carney, 7–9, 27; italics added), none of this really confuses the clear picture offered above. For when one notices that Colmcille, for instance, was a prince of the O'Neill dynasty, eligible for kingship within that dynasty, and that the next eight of his successor abbots of Iona were of that same royal lineage, succeeding each other as abbots according to the same protocol used for the succession of their secular counterparts as chiefs or kings, one realizes that (as with the king-bishops of Munster, for instance) what we are seeing here is a copying on the Irish scene of the secular institutions by the ecclesiastical institutions, similar to that which obtained in the wider Church, which was busy copying the institutions of the Roman Empire (from which derived in time the primacy of the Roman papa, or "pope"). This copying, in both forms, should have facilitated the growth of that truth and well-being that allegiance to Jesus as incarnate King of the Cosmos was meant to foster, and is meant to foster to this day; for the ecclesiastical institutions, formed in this copycat fashion, could preach by example and not just with words. If however the borrowings and similarities meant that the ecclesiastical institutions imitated the worst features of the secular arrangements, instead of influencing the latter with their own best formulations of the true wisdom of Jesus, then that unfortunate outcome of the process just raises for everyone the problem of evil and sin continuing after Jesus won the battle of the Cross—a problem to which the Irish proposed a distinctive approach and, in consequence, a variation on Latin Christology.

But before coming to that variation it is well to observe the influence of another master-image of Jesus and its presence in Irish spirituality from the earliest Christian centuries to the present day. The first master-image of the Cosmic Hero-King sees and seeks, out there in the cosmos and in society, the wisdom and continuously creative power of Jesus, Creator, Providence and King; out there in the patterns of social relationships and in the constituent elements of the universe that are agents of the Supreme Arbiter of Life and Death, the sun, the winds, the mighty oceans, the patient earth beneath our feet, with its furnishings of mineral, vegetable, and animal species; so that we can even invoke these elements to maintain and protect our lives, and some of them even to guarantee our oaths; because we really invoke the Word himself (the Wisdom herself) who rules and guides in and through them all—as in the ancient eighth-century hymn known as "St. Patrick's Breastplate." In the second master-image, in apparent contrast we are directed to look inward, to meet this incarnate King and warrior savior in the innermost sanctuary of our own hearts. An early expression of this image can be found at the end of the sixth century in the writings of one of those mighty Irish abbots who was a "wanderer for Christ," Columbanus, who died in A.D. 615 in the last monastery he founded on the continent, at Bobbio in present-day Italy.

Columbanus reveals in his extant *Opera* (works), and especially in his sermons and letters, a highly sophisticated understanding of the theology of Jesus as Son of God and savior, and of the accompanying Trinitarian theology, as these had been developed by the Fathers of the Church over the first five Christian centuries. Indeed he has the confidence in his thorough grasp of this theology to complain to Pope Boniface that he suspects him of dallying with heresy. Yet Columbanus is equally adamant that it is not by means of the logical exercises and rational arguments that result in such orthodox theologies that God is known to us; but rather through the living of a good life. God is known by allowing Christ to live in and through us, so that his light may lighten up the darkness of the way we must walk while on our earthly sojourn through this world to eternal life and eternal joy beyond the grave; so that his love, which is his very Spirit, may inspire in us an all-conquering love of God and neighbor, by which we simultaneously serve the latter and know the former, as well as human mind can know the divine. Or, in the eucharistic symbolism, Jesus is known to us as our bread and wine, staff and fountain of our pilgrim lives as we journey to life eternal.

Now this severe second-rating of theoretical theology and its resulting doctrines with respect to life itself as the prime source of the salving revelation and knowledge of God means—among other things (such as, for example, that the Irish produced very few great theologians in the history of Christianity)—that the two access points to the inspiring and blessed-making knowledge of God, the inward-looking or private and the outward-looking or public, and correspondingly the two master-images of Jesus as Lord of the hearts and King of the cosmos, are really, despite the appearance of contrast, as unified as two sides of the same coin. For the continuously creative, life-giving Word/Wisdom of God incarnate in Jesus, whose power and presence is revealed in the manner in which the "elements" of the natural world as well as the human societies that inhabit it cooperate to promote the life and well-being of all; this is perceptible in our innermost hearts and minds through the very processes by which we share in the give-and-take that characterizes living and living ever more abundantly throughout the universe—the very process by which we then perceive our lives, like the lives of all creatures great and small that make up with us this world, as the gift (grace) of the one creator God who acts within all toward all. Dante puts it best in the closing lines of his *Paradiso* when he writes of "my desire and my will . . . being turned like a wheel. . . . By the love that moves the sun and the other stars." For there is not in Columbanus or in any of the other prominent practitioners and recorders of the Irish Christian tradition, any sense of the presence of that common corruption of true Platonism that sees bodily existence and indeed the natural world itself to be inherently tainted by sin (as when the flesh and the world are lumped together with the devil, in a frequently used phrase).

There is always the temptation of course—but it is a temptation of spirit—to concentrate on the most material kinds of consumerism in our quest for fulfillment in happiness, and the devil uses such temptation in order to make us collaborators in evil and sharers in the destructive ends of such evil. And it may take much painful discipline to bring us back from falling into such temptation, back to an appreciation of bodily life on earth as a real but transient earnest of the life that can be ours for eternity. As Columbanus himself puts it in his Ninth Sermon (par. 2): "[L]ife before death and, after death, life; the just and godly enjoys both, and the ungodly sinner keeps one to his woe, losing the other."

Next, then, to the further developments of the image of Jesus in Irish Christianity that emerge from accounts of his triumph over the devil and his cleansing of sin. These developments are best seen from the perspective of Mary's relationship to Jesus and to the Triune God—two sets of relationships that bring out something distinctive in the Irish image of Jesus—and they can be best illustrated from traditional bardic poetry, which remained influential as long as Gaelic lasted in Ireland and Scotland, into the nineteenth century. Briefly, Jesus on his cross gained victory over sin and Satan; and that should have been the end of both, at least in the case of those who then accepted Jesus' lordship. But even those who called him Lord continued to sin, and so to wound him over and over again, as the Irish imagery has it. Most may have cleansed these further falls and healed these further wounds by doing their own penance. But for others who had not done so, Jesus on judgment day would appear "with his cross on his reddened back" (as Blathmac puts it; Carney, 142) as their judge and accuser. On whose merits could these misfortunates then call, since the time for their own penance was over? On Mary's, is the bards' frequent answer. And on what grounds? On three grounds. On the honor-price system by which blood relatives were responsible for making recompense for kin who could not do so. On the fact that Mary was kin to humankind by nature, whereas the Word or Son of God had such kinship only through Mary's consent to conceive him as a human being. And on the fact that Mary had suffered even more on Calvary than Jesus did and did not need the ensuing merits to atone for any sin of her own. Mary then emerges as a real coredemptrix of the race throughout that long tradition of Gaelic (i.e., Irish) religious poetry.

Furthermore, in the course of that long bardic tradition that both reflected and influenced the Irish Christian imagination, and particularly perhaps in the poetry of Philip O'Huiginn of the Franciscan Order, Mary's place vis-à-vis the Trinity took a distinctive form. Mindful of the theology that said that Father, Word, and Spirit enjoyed the absolute unity of being "one in substance" or "one in being," some of the bards naturally imagined Mary, in the course of conceiving one in human form, simultaneously in a sense encompassing all three in that same process. So that Mary's Husband (the Spirit who asexually brought about the conception of the Word) together with her "Father" and her Son were together in her womb and on her knee, and she is then Mother of God in a more comprehensive image of that status than the rest of Christendom would possibly consider orthodox. Add to that the increased substance of her role as coredemptrix in the context of Irish institutions of recompense, and, although an odd bard might pray "O Four Persons," the sense received most often is that the operative Trinity in Irish Christian spirituality is composed of God the Father, Mary the Mother of God, and God the Son—Jesus. And this is in fact confirmed in popular Irish Christian spirituality to this day.

An example: on the traditional Irish model of each person as client of a chief or king who is the source of support for life, of defense of one's life, and of providential governance toward life more abundant; of petitions to the King (or to the Queen, or the courtiers—the great saints) in cases where these things are not forthcoming; and of obligatory publication of the King's goodness and greatness when he meets the client's petition; Irish provincial newspapers publish the prayer-petitions that have proved successful in order to acknowledge on each occasion the one who graciously answered. The result is an accumulative database from which one can reconstruct the active image of Jesus, still the Hero-King, in relationship to that of the other Persons of the Trinity, of Mary, and of the saints.

Two persistent features of the material in this database are relevant here. First, the Holy Spirit seldom if ever features individually and alone. In fact, in one of the most frequently appearing prayer-petitions published in recent years, the Holy Spirit is subsumed under Mary in the course of quite an elaborate petition; concrete confirmation of the view that the operative Trinity is Father, Mother, and Son, and a very Irish way of securing the feminine side of the divine nature. Second, if there are petition-prayers addressed to the Sacred Heart of Jesus, there will be an equal number of petition-prayers publicized in honor of the Sacred Heart of Mary or of Mary as Mother of the Sacred Heart; concrete evidence of the profound conviction that, on the analogy of the formidable influence of an Irish mother over her sons, the gracious creative and re-creative power of the King is more likely to come to the client's aid if moved by the more approachable and more compassionate power of the Queen Mother of heaven and earth.

Mention of the Sacred Heart is a timely reminder of the fact that, coincident with the loss of the Irish language, chief vehicle of Irish culture, from the mid-nineteenth century, certain Continental forms of prayer, liturgy, and general spirituality were brought into Ireland by reformers of Irish Christianity of Roman origin or authorization. Two of these in particular affect the image of Jesus in Irish Christianity; both of them, and especially in combination, with a potential for affecting that image for the worse.

The first was a devotion to Jesus centered on an image of Jesus that graphically foregrounded a wounded and bleeding heart. The second was a devotion to the Eucharist that equally foregrounded the idea of the "real presence" of Jesus, body, blood, soul, and divinity in each communion wafer, albeit in mysterious or miraculous manner. The first devotion inevitably propagated a kind of inner, individualist relationship ("This Tremendous Lover") based, as it was, upon the ideal of romantic love from the Romantic era in late European culture; a potentially serious decline, it must be said, from that coincidence of inner and outer relationship to Jesus the King-Creator as described above, and as encountered simultaneously within one's own consciousness of living and in one's consciousness of the shared life of the whole continuously created and creative universe. For that latter is an intimate heartfelt love relationship indeed, but a love relationship with "the love that moves the sun and the other stars"; and hence one that is now both experienced and exercised in the most practical course of the life we share (literally) with all creatures great and small; and which therefore finds in every activity in home or farm or marketplace, in every craft or profession, an occasion for prayers of praise, thanksgiving (Eucharist), and petition—as great modern collections of the traditional Gaelic prayers and hymns of the ordinary people, such as the *Carmina Gadelica*, illustrate most amply—rather than find such occasion principally in a more private heart-to-heart scenario.

The second devotion, aptly indicated by the phrase *Corpus Christi*, or Body of Christ, centered of course on the Eucharist. But since, as that phrase indicates, the focus is on the real presence of the real body of Christ (together with his soul and divinity), the aim of the Eucharist as sacrament, of the Mass itself, was easily thought to be the production by the priestly words and acts of this bodily presence in the eucharistic wafer or "host." As a further result, it is no exaggeration to say, a sea change occurred in the whole understanding and experience of the central liturgy of Christianity. Instead of the Mass being experienced as the sacrament of creation; taking bread "which earth has given and human hands have made," and wine, "fruit of the vine and work of human hands"; eating and drinking bread and wine and breaking and pouring them to be offered equally to all others; thus symbolizing and effecting what this symbolizes—namely, the grateful reception of God's continual creation of life and of all the supports and enhancements of life, together with the cocreation and sharing of that life, always at some cost to oneself, with all other things that also act as receivers and cocreators of life, with the divine Creator, in the creation; and in this way making ever more present in the whole Christian community and indeed in the whole world, the risen Jesus, the Life-giving Spirit, as Paul called him—instead of this, there developed with the *Corpus Christi* devotion a gradual shift toward a more inwardly, privately, and indeed spatially localized experience of access to the presence of the King of the Elements.

This shift is seen most clearly in the frequency with which the promised experience of access to the gracious, powerful presence of Jesus is focused upon "visits to the Blessed Sacrament." The access was localized insofar as this phrase meant either carrying consecrated wafers in procession round the town, or inviting people to visit churches or chapels in whose tabernacles consecrated wafers were reserved. Indeed Mass itself, certainly before frequent taking of communion came to be encouraged, was largely experienced as a weekly, obligatory visit to the Blessed Sacrament. And the romantic element was assiduously fostered, by reference for example to the "Prisoner in (or of) the Tabernacle," waiting, it was implied, lonely for a visit.

An issue of the newspaper *Waterford Today* (19 February 2002), after the usual collection of published prayer-petitions already referred to, advertises the setting up in a parish in Waterford city of a "Eucharistic adoration centre" and issues the following invitation to its readers: "Promise to spend just one hour each week (before Jesus in the Blessed Sacrament) silently and relaxed in his presence, opening your heart to the wonderful graces the Lord has waiting for you. The rewards for you personally, your family and your community cannot be measured" (p. 37).

In this last feature in particular the second example joins the first in romanticizing, internalizing, and, further, localizing the gracious presences of the God Christians believe to be incarnate in Jesus. Now there is nothing whatever wrong with cultivating the inward access to Jesus. Nor indeed is there anything wrong with giving this a local focus, provided all of this is kept firmly within that unity of inward/outward presence and access described above as a prominent feature of traditional Irish Christian prayer and praxis. For otherwise religion is too private an affair, and its god too small; and neither can be worthy of the spiritual depth and of the communal and cosmic breadth of the traditional image of Jesus to which Irish Christianity is heir.

James P. Mackey

See also: Eucharist; Jesus, Name of; Jesus as Emperor; John, Gospel of; Mary; Roman Catholicism

References

Bergin, Osborn. 1970. *Irish Bardic Poetry*. Dublin: Institute for Advanced Studies.

Carmichael, Alexander. 1928. *Carmina Gadelica*. Edinburgh: Oliver and Boyd.

Carney, James, ed. 1964. *The Poems of Blathmac Son of Cu Brethan*. Dublin: Irish Texts Society.

Mackey, James P. 1994. "Mary in Bardic Poetry." *Cosmos* 10, no. 1: 70–78.

———. 1996. "The Theology of Columbanus." Pp. 228–39 in *Irland und Europa im Frueheren Mittelalter*. Edited by Proinseas Ni Chathain and Michael Richter. Stuttgart: Klett-Cotta.

McKenna, Lambert. 1931. *Philip Bocht O'Huiginn*. Dublin: Talbot.

O'Donoghue, N. D. 1995. "St. Patrick's Breastplate." Pp. 45–63 in *An Introduction to Celtic Christianity*. Edited by James P. Mackey. Edinburgh: T. and T. Clark.

O'Laoghaire, Diarmuid. 1995. "Prayers and Hymns in the Vernacular." Pp. 268–304 in *An Introduction to Celtic Christianity*. Edited by James P. Mackey. Edinburgh: T. and T. Clark.

Walker, G. S. M. 1957. *Sancti Columbani Opera*. Dublin: Institute for Advanced Studies.

Isidore of Seville (d. 636)

Isidore, bishop of Seville, contributed indirectly, but influentially, to the medieval Western understanding of Jesus through (1) producing widely used textbooks and (2) a systematic hermeneutic for reading Scripture as a series of documents in which every sentence "speaks" of Jesus Christ. Isidore was one of the last writers to observe the contest between Arianism and Catholicism at first hand. He saw the Visigothic king, Leovigild, attempt to force his subjects to accept Arianism, and later saw his own brother, Leander, convert King Recared and his Arian subjects to Catholicism at the third Council of Toledo (589). He can be considered both a late-Latin patristic writer with access to a large library of pagan and Christian authors and a medieval theologian who uses "authorities" in combination to support the accepted orthodox positions. Moreover, he acted as a conduit by which patristic material was sifted and systematically arranged for later writers: when later writers quote a chain of patristic opinions on a topic, frequently their selection stems from Isidore.

Much of Isidore's work was devoted to the writing of student manuals making what he considered essential information available in easily accessible forms, yet he never compiled a tract formally dedicated to Christology. This is all the more surprising in that few theologians have been as sensitive to issues of order and structure in theology, so a handbook with a structured presentation of beliefs about Jesus would seem an obvious choice, especially since he witnessed the Arian controversy at first hand. However, in his great encyclopedic work, the *Etymologiae*, he devotes a substantial section (Bk. 7, 2) to Jesus as "the Son of God," providing an overview of how Latin theology understood his relationship to the Father (7, 1) and the Spirit (7, 3) in the light of the Christological councils. Although this is a summary of the conciliar positions, and, in effect, an exposition of the standard creeds,

Isidore is careful to present what he sees as the key scriptural proof texts for each decision—and in time these texts (e.g., John 10.30 at 7, 2, 36) became the standard scriptural bases over which various interpreters fought.

In addition to the doctrinal summary, Isidore provided etymologies and explanations of the key terms used about Jesus by Christians. Thus he explains basic terms like *soter* (savior), *christos*, and messiah both theologically and as unusual words, and explains technical theological terms such as *homoousios* ("of one substance") and *primogenitus* ("first-begotten"). However, more significantly, he also examined various scriptural and liturgical terms—so he explains, for example, "Alpha and Omega," Jesus as "Image," "the Hand of God," "Light," "Sun," alongside terms of address such as "Shepherd" and "Teacher." But he went further than the obvious examples of images for Jesus (e.g., "Lamb" at 7, 2, 42, based on John 1.29) to look at images that can stand for Jesus in particular contexts, such as "worm" (7, 2, 43), which points to the resurrection. In this range of images Isidore brings us into the sacramental world of medieval culture: his text stands behind many manuscript illuminations, wall paintings, and sculptures in which the most unlikely beasts are given semiotic value in relation to Jesus.

One reason for the absence of a manual on Christology is that the need was met, in part, by the method he employed in the exegesis of Genesis. His *In Genesim* was deliberately constructed as a sustained reflection on the person and work of Christ, to the exclusion of other matters. Moreover, when the material of the *In Genesim* is situated with the wider context of Isidore's educational works, it marks a new threshold in the development of academic systematic Christology. Read "historically," Genesis could provide information on cosmology and history—and these were to be studied in the appropriate textbooks—but when read by the Christian, who lives as a member of the Church at the optimum time (based on Gal. 4.4) for understanding the text, Genesis is to be read in terms of its fuller, providential purpose—which is what it says about Jesus (he bases this notion on Luke 24.27). This *Christ*-ian meaning was hidden from its readers until Jesus' coming, but now it is the reason why the book should be read in the liturgy and studied in its every detail.

Isidore understood Genesis to be made up of thirty-one sections each of which was centered on one event or moment of history. Although they were interconnected by sharing characters over the sequence of time, they were also distinct episodes in sacred history. As such, each event exhibited the basic truths about Christ and the Christian people, the difference between them being the nuances arising from particular situations. Isidore studies each separately, culling the patristic legacy for the best comments on each verse of Genesis. He did not have to seek a single didactic arrangement that ranged over the whole book; rather, by finding common Christian elements in each, they became collectively so many different historical lessons about the one mystery that is Christ. The result is to our eyes a continual repetition of a few themes, but to Isidore this is evidence of the unity of the whole of revelation: in all those times in the past and in all those different ways, God was speaking (Heb. 1.1), and he of whom Genesis spoke was the same yesterday, today, and forever (Heb. 13.8). The method's influence until the seventeenth century, and its most important legacy, was not in relation to Christian perceptions of Jesus but to the status it gave to the Old Testament as a quarry to be drawn upon by Christians for their self-understanding and practice—a process in which Isidore's sophisticated interpretative method, which avoided literalism, was commonly ignored.

Thomas O'Loughlin

See also: Chalcedon; Creeds; Jesus, Achievement of; Messiah

References

O'Loughlin, Thomas. 1998. "Christ as the Focus of Genesis Exegesis in Isidore of Seville." Pp. 144–62 in *Studies in Patristic Christology*. Edited by Thomas Finan and Vincent Twomey. Dublin: Four Courts.

———. 1999. *Teachers and Code-Breakers: The Latin Genesis Tradition, 430–800*. Turnhout, Belgium: Brepols.

Islam

Overview

It is not often appreciated by Christians that the New Testament is not the only scripture that discusses the meaning and significance of Jesus, for the Muslim scripture, the Qur'an, also devotes considerable space to his life and work, even if not in a particularly systematic way. Essentially what the Qur'an teaches about Jesus is firstly that he was a prophet, sent by God to proclaim a message to the Jews of his day, but secondly that he was no more than a human figure, whom it is therefore inappropriate to describe as "the Son of God" or "God the Son." As regards the chronology of his life, his conception and birth were miraculous, and he taught wisely and performed miracles, but at the end of his time on earth, rather than being crucified and resurrected before ascending to be with God, he was delivered by God from crucifixion, so that he did not die and was taken to be with God directly. On this foundation the later Islamic community has developed a number of traditions concerning Jesus that are always positive about his person, so that Muslims will always use the phrase "peace be upon him" whenever they mention the name of Jesus, whom Muslims usually call 'Isa. But combined with this positive element, Muslims will usually be bitterly critical of some of the affirmations that Christians make about Jesus, most obviously that he is "Son of God," the second person of the Trinity, and the savior or redeemer of the world.

The Qur'anic Foundation in More Detail

There are 36 references to Jesus in the Qur'an, compared with 69 for Abraham and 136 for Moses, the biblical figures most often referred to, and whom the Qur'an also affirms as prophets. The references to Jesus can be grouped under six main headings. The first of these concerns the events leading up to his birth, which the Qur'an unhesitatingly affirms to be miraculous, based on an angel appearing to Mary and announcing to her that she is to give birth to a son (Qur'an 19.16–21, in which the story is told in the greatest detail), and could easily be presented in a column on a sheet of paper with Luke 1.26–38 alongside, to make clear the similarities in structure between the two accounts. When it comes to the birth itself, however, there are rather greater differences between Qur'an 19.22–33 and the remainder of Luke 1, not least the fact that in the Qur'anic account, Jesus speaks more or less as soon as he is born, but Western scholars of Islam have suggested possible influence from some of the early apocryphal gospels, especially the Arabic Infancy Gospel, at this point, though traditional Muslim writers, for whom the Qur'an was literally dictated by God, find this suggestion both unnecessary and offensive.

Secondly, the Qur'an discusses the mission of Jesus, and on this Qur'an 5.49, for example, states that Jesus, the son of Mary, was sent by God in the footsteps of the earlier prophets such as Moses to confirm the Torah and to bring the message of the Injil (or Gospel—cf. Greek "evangel"), which contained guidance and light and basically confirmed the earlier teaching of the Torah. The emphasis here, in other words, is on the essential continuity between the message of the earlier prophets and the message of Jesus, even if he brings a scripture (the Gospel) that merits its own distinctive name; this view serves to illustrate effectively what has been called the Qur'an's cyclical view of prophecy, whereby God sends a prophet at a certain stage of history, and even if the prophet's message is accepted by some people for some time it soon becomes forgotten or corrupted, so that the sending of another prophet is necessitated; the message of the most recent prophet, however, is fundamentally the same as that of the earlier ones.

Jesus' miracles, thirdly, are discussed in the Qur'an, and 3.49 refers to a number of these: some will be very familiar to anyone who knows the New Testament, such as healing the blind, healing lepers, and bringing the dead back to life, but two will probably seem less familiar: Jesus making a bird out of clay and then breathing onto it so that it comes alive and flies away; and his knowing what people eat and what they store up in their homes, a kind of second sight. These are not referred to in the canonical Gospel accounts, but again Western scholars have suggested that precedents for these accounts may also be found in apocryphal gospels such as the Gospel of Thomas.

Fourthly, and perhaps most important, the Qur'an discusses the question of Jesus' identity, and many positive statements are made concerning it, perhaps most dramatically in 4.171, in which Jesus is described as "the messenger of God, his word which he gave to Mary, and a spirit proceeding from him." The first of these three titles is not unique to Jesus in the Qur'an, some twenty-five other individuals being named as messengers of God, but the last two are used of no one else and are the basis of the view held by some Muslims that as well as being the penultimate prophet, with only Muhammad coming after him, Jesus is also the second most important prophet in the Qur'an, again second only to Muhammad, who is described as the "seal of the prophets" (33.40), the person with whom the line of prophecy comes to an end.

Jesus is also given many other positive titles in the Qur'an: he is the servant (*'abd*) of God, the prophet (*nabi*) of God, a sign (*aya*) of God, an example (*mathal*), a witness (*shahid*), and a mercy (*rahma*), and he is also eminent (*wajih*), brought near to God (*min al-muqarrabin*), one of the upright (*min al-salihin*), and blessed (*mubarak*). The title "al-Masih" (messiah) is also used of him, but it is probable that this should be taken simply as an honorific title, a kind of nickname, rather than bearing the full weight of meaning that the term bears in the Jewish and Christian traditions.

All this is positive, then, but as hinted earlier, there is also a considerable element of qualification, and even of challenge to and denial of several traditional Christian affirmations about Jesus. This can be found in 19.35–36, immediately after the Qur'anic story of the miraculous conception and birth of Jesus, which Christians have traditionally taken as a sign or symbol of his being in some way "Son of God," on the basis of his having no human father. The Qur'an takes a very different, even diametrically opposite, view, however: "It is not for God to take a son. Glory be to Him! When He decides a matter, He simply says 'Be,' and it is." Any idea of sonship is therefore rejected, and this is repeated immediately after the positive affirmations of 4.171: "God is one! Glory be to Him, that He should have a son!" And the objection here is combined with a vigorous rebuttal of any reference to "three" in connection with God: "Say not 'three.' Stop! God is one!" so that any Christian reference to a concept such as that of there being three persons in the godhead appears to be prohibited.

On the basis of verses such as these Muslims have evolved the view that Christian concepts such as the Incarnation and the Trinity are unacceptable, and although Christian scholars have observed that, strictly speaking, what the Qur'an seems to be condemning here is adoptianism (God "taking" a son) and tritheism (the suggestion that there are three gods), Muslim opinion does not generally differentiate between these concepts on the one hand and the Incarnation and the Trinity on the other.

Christian affirmations about Jesus' identity, then, seem to be denied, or at least challenged, in the Qur'an, but even so this does nothing to undermine Muslims' fundamental respect, and even reverence, for Jesus. On this basis it is surely accurate to suggest that the Qur'an too has its Christology, so that this topic is not only of concern for Christians; even if, in Christian terms, the Qur'an's Christology is a "low" one, it still exists. Occasionally, too, it has had some remarkable consequences, most notably the coming into existence in Nigeria in the twentieth century of a group who, without any known contact with Christian missionaries, came to call themselves the 'Isawas (followers of 'Isa), on the basis of the distinguished titles uniquely given to Jesus/'Isa in the Qur'an.

The fifth aspect of the Qur'an's teaching about Jesus relates to the events at the end of his period on earth as a prophet. Here, again on the basis of one verse of the Qur'an, 4.157, a long tradition of controversy and polemic has arisen. A literal translation of the middle section of the verse reads as follows: "They did not kill him, and they did not crucify him. It appeared so to them," and this is repeated at the end of the verse: "They certainly did not kill him." Instead, according to the next verse, "God raised him up to Himself." The mainstream Muslim interpretation of these statements is that Jesus was not crucified, but was rather delivered from crucifixion and taken directly to be with God. There is therefore, it could be said, an ascension, but not, as in the

Christian view, *after* crucifixion and resurrection, but *instead of* crucifixion and resurrection, and Muslim commentators on the Qur'an add the explanation that someone was certainly crucified, but it was not Jesus. Various suggestions are given as to the identity of the substitute—Judas, a disciple who volunteered, or simply an innocent passerby—but the main body of the Muslim community is insistent that Jesus was not crucified.

For Christians, and indeed for the members of almost every other religious community, this is mysterious, as while many people are resistant to any claim by Christians that Jesus was raised from the dead, almost everyone apart from Muslims agrees that he was crucified. Some light may be shed on the mystery, however, by observing that the intention of the Muslim account seems to be fundamentally positive—based on the conviction, in other words, that God would not allow one of his prophets to die in such an appalling way—and that the context of this verse of the Qur'an is discussion between Muhammad and the Jewish communities of Arabia, who in the preceding verses are condemned for their pride, for breaking their covenant with God, for slaying God's messengers, for insulting Mary by accusing her of immorality, and then, finally, for saying, "We killed the Messiah, Jesus the son of Mary, the messenger of God"; it is against this background that the Qur'an goes on to affirm that they did not kill him or crucify him. Some modern Western scholars, using post-Enlightenment techniques of critical textual study, have therefore suggested that the denial is a rhetorical one, a denial of the Jewish argument, familiar to readers of Galatians, that because Jesus was crucified he could not have been the messiah, rather than primarily a historical one; but Muslim opinion generally remains unpersuaded.

Finally, one verse of the Qur'an refers to Jesus looking ahead to events after his own time: "Children of Israel, I am the messenger of God to you, confirming the Torah . . . and bringing the good news of a messenger who will come after me, whose name will be Ahmad" (61.6). The Muslim understanding of this verse is that it is a clear reference to Muhammad (whose name, semantically, is closely related to the name Ahmad), so that Jesus himself foretold the coming of Muhammad several centuries later. Western critical scholars, by contrast, have posited that what has happened here is that the Johannine references to the Paraclete who will come later have been misunderstood, perhaps as a result of poor translation between Greek, Syriac, and Arabic; but once again the main body of Muslim opinion is confident of the accuracy of its understanding.

Later Developments

On this scriptural foundation, the Muslim community in medieval times further developed its thinking about Jesus, and it did so in several different ways. On the one hand, as the Muslim community expanded from Arabia, where Christians had been few and far between, into the wider Middle East, where Christianity had been the established majority religion for several centuries in such places as Egypt, Palestine, and Syria, considerably greater opportunities became available for Muslims to converse with well-informed Christians, and even in some cases to develop firsthand acquaintance with the Christian scriptures, especially once they were translated into Arabic, probably in the ninth century. Some of this extra material was used to fill out the more positive statements of the Qur'an, so that fuller and more systematic accounts of Jesus' life are found in some medieval Muslim literature.

On the other hand, this extra knowledge of Christianity could also be used to reinforce the more negative aspects of the message of the Qur'an, which challenge traditional Christian affirmations about Jesus, and this line of argument became quite sophisticated in the hands of some medieval Muslim thinkers, who argued that the existence of four canonical Christian accounts of Jesus' life was clear evidence that Jesus' original message had not been authentically preserved in the Christian community, and that the credal formulations of the councils of the early Church deviated substantially from Jesus' own teaching as it was recorded in the New Testament, so that Muslim respect for Jesus was able to be combined with harsh criticism of Christian affirmations about Jesus by simply arguing that in the course of its early history the Christian community had deviated from Jesus' teaching by introducing a series of basically Hellenistic beliefs, and that Jesus' original message had therefore been corrupted during the course of Christian history.

Examples of the more positive material can be found in the various sayings of and stories about Jesus that circulated in many different kinds of Islamic literature in the medieval period, and that have been helpfully collected and edited recently by Tarif Khalidi, the Sir Thomas Adams Professor of Arabic in Cambridge. Two more particular examples are the group known as the Ikhwan al-Safa (Brethren of Purity), who lived in Iraq in the tenth and eleventh centuries, and whose forty-fourth letter (or treatise) contains a very full account of the religious situation in the time of Jesus, Jesus' own teaching and message, and even an account of Jesus' trial, crucifixion, and resurrection (see Goddard, 20–23). And the writings of the Spanish Sufi (mystical writer) Ibn 'Arabi (d. 1240) are interesting because he posits one of the highest Muslim Christologies, on the basis of the absolutely unique manner of Jesus' coming into existence, and ascribes to Jesus the title of "seal of the saints" to balance the ascription of the title "seal of the prophets" to Muhammad (see Leirvik, 89–90).

Other medieval Islamic literature, on the other hand, is much more confrontational and polemical, and although it is never disrespectful of the person of Jesus himself, it is sometimes extremely negative, even mocking, of Christian affirmations about Jesus. Thus the eleventh-century writer 'Abd al-Jabbar insists that Christ's religion was falsified over the early centuries by the adoption of Roman customs, a process in which the apostle Paul and the Roman emperor Constantine were the two most important figures (see Goddard, 26–28); and slightly later Ibn Taimiyya (d. 1328) ridicules Christian thinking about the two natures of Christ by suggesting that "the explanation of Christians on this matter is muddled, differing, and contradictory. . . . Their position is neither reasonable nor indicated by any sacred book. . . . They have divided into sects and groups on this issue, each sect declaring the others unbelievers" (see Michel, 308–12).

Discussion Today

More contemporary Muslim literature about Jesus can also be divided into two main categories. Some adopts the line of argument that however much Muslims should respect Jesus, the Christian community has, whether by accident or maliciously, deviated radically from Jesus' own original message. Two writers who come originally from South Asia, Muhammad 'Ata ur-Rahim and Ahmad Shafaat, can usefully serve to illustrate this view. Rahim, firstly, in a book that was originally entitled *Jesus, Prophet of Islam*, but which later became *Jesus, a Prophet of Islam*, argues that it is the Unitarian tradition, from Arius through to the seventeenth-century figure John Toland, that has most faithfully preserved the authentic message of Jesus, rather than the so-called mainstream Christian churches. And Shafaat, in a new approach, produced *The Gospel According to Islam*, which attempts to follow in the footsteps of the various attempts in Christian history to produce a "harmony" of the four Gospel accounts, but goes one stage further to harmonize not only those four documents but also the Qur'an. The result is a work that in form appears not unlike a Gospel account, in that it is roughly the same length as the Gospel according to Mark and is broken up into twenty-seven chapters, but which in content is very much a traditional Muslim account, especially in chapter 3. That chapter focuses on Jesus' prophecy of the coming of Muhammad; the final six chapters focus on the end of Jesus' time on earth, and in a rather telling note refer to "crucifiction" instead of crucifixion!

Two works that have come out of Egypt, however, adopt a very different point of view indeed, throughout attempting to take Christian sources seriously, and formulating a picture of Jesus that while sometimes imaginative is nevertheless always positive and sympathetic. Muhammad Kamil Hussein's *City of Wrong*, first published in 1954 and translated by Kenneth Cragg, is a highly original study of the events that took place in Jerusalem on what Christians call Good Friday, focusing particularly on the motivations of all those who participated in them. In form it is a work of fiction, and in a sense it is not a study of Jesus at all, but, given the mainstream Muslim view that Jesus was not crucified, the choice of these events as the focus of the author's meditations on human beings' mixed motives and their ability to stifle their consciences is extremely interesting. The preface to the book, in which the author sets the scene for what follows, is probably the only piece of writing by a Muslim that could profitably be included in a Christian Good Friday service.

'Abbas Mahmud al-'Aqqad's study, *The Genius of Christ*, appeared in the preceding year, but was substantially revised for a second edition that was published in 1958, and it is this which forms the basis of the recent translation by F. Peter Ford. Compared with Hussein's work, this is much more obviously a biographical study of Jesus, and the author was considerably influenced in his study by the *Life of Jesus* by the German scholar Emil Ludwig. The structure of the book is therefore more chronological, in that it begins with the religious and political background to Jesus' life and proceeds through his birth to his teaching and ministry, where al-'Aqqad manifests huge admiration for Jesus' teaching about the Kingdom of God, to the events surrounding the end of Jesus' life, where in the light of the differences between the traditional Christian and Muslim accounts al-'Aqqad simply states: "Here we leave the realm of history and enter the realm of faith." For the second edition, full account was taken of the discovery of the Dead Sea Scrolls at Wadi Qumran, and this too serves to illustrate the author's readiness to take account of new discoveries and alternative perspectives.

Hugh Goddard

See also: Adoptianism; Christology, Modern; Creeds; Dead Sea Scrolls; Interfaith Thought and Relations; Jesus, Origins of; Kingdom of God; Messiah; Nicea; Second Person of the Trinity; Son of God

References

Al-'Aqqad, 'Abbas Mahmud. 2001. *The Genius of Christ*. Translated by F. Peter Ford. Binghamton, NY: Global.

Goddard, Hugh. 1996. *Muslim Perceptions of Christianity*. London: Grey Seal.

Hussein, M. Kamel. 1959/1994. *City of Wrong: A Friday in Jerusalem*. Translated by Kenneth Cragg. Amsterdam: Djambatan; Oxford: Oneworld.

Khalidi, Tarif. 2001. *The Muslim Jesus: Sayings and Stories in Islamic Literature*. Cambridge: Harvard University Press.

Leirvik, Oddbjorn. 1999. *Images of Jesus Christ in Islam*. Uppsala: Swedish Institute of Missionary Research.

Michel, Tom. 1984. *A Muslim Theologian's Response to Christianity*. Delmar, NY: Caravan.

Parrinder, Geoffrey. 1965, 1995. *Jesus in the Qur'an*. London: Faber; Oxford: Oneworld.

Rahim, Muhammad 'Ata ur-. 1977. *Jesus, Prophet of Islam*. Norwich: Diwan; reprinted in 1979 as *Jesus, a Prophet of Islam*.

Robinson, Neal. 1991. *Christ in Islam and Christianity*. London: Macmillan.

Shafaat, Ahmad. 1979. *The Gospel According to Islam*. New York: Vantage.

J

Jesus, Absences of

As the reader surveys the range and extent of this book, the dominant impression is likely to be of the manifold presence of Jesus, rather than his absence. It is indeed extraordinary into how many aspects of human life and experience he has entered—and we are far from having exhausted them. But there are also areas of Christian reflection and statement where he might have been expected to be significant, even central, and where he is virtually or even totally absent.

The claim needs explaining. What is involved is one aspect of the familiar dichotomy between "the Jesus of history" and "the Christ of faith." This can be referred to merely to draw attention to the obvious fact that one can view Jesus (like any other figure) in different ways and under different aspects; here, as a Jewish man of first-century Palestine on the one hand, and as the object of loyalty and faith (under a variety of concepts or symbols) on the other. In itself, this dual appreciation of Jesus occasions neither conflict nor puzzle, any more than, for example, a perception of the president or prime minister as, on the one hand, the holder of a great public office and, on the other, as a family man or (for all one knows) as an enthusiast for butterflies or snails. Where the difficulty comes in the case of Jesus is when the claims of faith seem to be so elevated or of such a character that the ordinary historical perception and interest is in effect sidelined or even obliterated.

It is also a matter of the mind-set or concerns of a particular observer of Jesus. Whereas the historically or humanly minded will bring imagination or knowledge of the time of Jesus to bear, those of a philosophical or conceptual disposition will focus on patterns of ideas in which he may play a part—for example, as Second Person of the Holy Trinity. Sometimes the two may seem mutually exclusive, if not in strict theory then at least in practical attentiveness. And in discussions of the second kind, Jesus the historical figure, who taught and acted in Galilee and Jerusalem and whom we may imagine, is liable to be sidelined or excluded. That is what is meant by an absence of Jesus as a human figure.

The most obvious way to gain a sense of the figure of Jesus is to read the Gospels. Whatever the ideas that motivate them, however fragmentary they are, and however strongly they express, in narrative form, ideas and beliefs about Jesus, nevertheless they are windows giving on to him; and, apart from our historical knowledge of the land, society, and world of his day, we have no other. Imperfect they may be in showing us Jesus as a figure of history, but they are inescapable and they are very far from being negligible.

It is then surprising how little they have often been drawn upon by Christians seeking to write or think about Jesus or to relate to him. Leaving aside the small number of commentaries on the Gospels in the early centuries and turning to the work of some of the leading writers of the period, we find strikingly little appeal to or use of the Gospels. In writers such as Justin, Irenaeus, and Athanasius, there is far more use of Old Testament texts than of the Gospels: it was necessary to establish the historical credentials of the Church (in relation and opposition to Judaism and in a society that valued venerable roots) and to assert Jesus' doctrinal status, which could be best done by using conceptual patterns or by using appropriate (but decontextualized) scriptural tags, as much from the Old as from the New Testament.

The phenomenon was accentuated by that doctrinal role of Jesus itself. As God's creative Word (John 1.1), preexistent from "the beginning," he was himself active in the Old Testament story (even if covertly). Such transcendent eminence tended to divert attention from the teaching in the Gospels, even to devalue its historical realism; unless it impinged for a particular reason, such as the need to warrant a particular moral stance; and this eminence certainly tended to erase any conception of the Gospels as presenting rounded and particular portraits of Jesus, themselves conveying meaning and presenting beliefs about him.

With all necessary qualifications (e.g., the prominence of Jesus as a visualized figure in Christian art, in preaching, and in prayer), it remains true that, in many contexts, he is notable by his absence, or so strangely perceived as to be distorted: experiment by searching standard works of Christian theology down to our own day for references to his deeds or words (as distinct from his role in Christian conceptual patterns); and notice a similar omission from Christian creeds and the analogously formed eucharistic prayers, which tend to move directly from Jesus' coming to his death, leaving him unconsidered between the two. Our topic could more ominously be headed "the silences of Jesus," drawing attention to the curious distinction between what in his teaching is insisted on and what is ignored, or not even absorbed in order to be, often necessarily, reminted for new circumstances.

Leslie Houlden

See also: Irenaeus; Second Person of the Trinity

References

Houlden, Leslie. 2002. *The Strange Story of the Gospels*. London: SPCK.

Jesus, Achievement of

Most of the articles in this volume bear, in a variety of ways, on the subject of this one, but it may be useful to consider the matter in its own right. The title itself is open to criticism, and may even seem patronizing. It is meant to be a neutral word, encouraging wide coverage. Its more theological equivalent is "work," and in formal theology there has long been separate treatment of "the work of Christ" as distinct from "the person of Christ," each having its own agenda and its own biblical roots. It is however doubtful whether the New Testament writers themselves would have distinguished in this way: for them, Jesus was a unified and single phenomenon, to be spoken of under a wide range of images, most of them drawn from the old scriptural tradition of Judaism.

But the very secular word "achievement" leads us to begin at a basic historical level. In one sense, the achievement of Jesus was negative in the extreme: he died in the ignominy of crucifixion, his work apparently a flop, and even (according to the first account of his death, Mark 15.34) feeling himself abandoned by the God he had proclaimed. In another sense, of course, scarcely any other person in the whole of human history has had such spectacular success (Mohammed or the Buddha would come into discussion), with countless millions devoted to his worship and to following him, in endless different cultural and national contexts and forms. This is undeniable fact, however much one may think of the molding of his image into unlikely forms, even to the point of travesty.

In a theological context, reflection on what Jesus had in fact accomplished goes back to the very beginning of known Christian adherence to him, in the writings of the apostle Paul. That is, such adherence focused not simply on Jesus' status (e.g., as Messiah) but on what had changed as a result of his being in the world. We should think that behind all the ways in which this was articulated lay inner experience, seen as resulting in some way from Jesus, of a fresh standing with God, fresh community life, and fresh sense of one's inner status and prospects. Paul expressed it in a number of different ways, many derived (as we should expect) from his Jewish formation: he felt himself to be "reconciled" (as indeed also "the world," 2 Cor. 5.19), led and indwelt by God's powerful creative "Spirit" (Rom. 8.14), even "having" Christ's "mind" (1 Cor. 2.16), and certainly incorporated into a new community, which he could designate not only by the relatively colorless word "church" but also as "the body of Christ" (1 Cor. 12.27); for it had no life apart from him. More explosively still, there was a new creation (2 Cor. 5.17; Gal. 6.15). *Everything* had changed.

The new status merges into comparable understandings of the actual "work" of Jesus, which brought about the results just described. These tended to focus, for Paul, on his death and then on his present heavenly status and future role. Old Testament and Jewish religious practice drew his attention: one knew oneself reconciled and forgiven, so Jesus' death could be interpreted under the heading of an atoning sacrifice for sin—an image, with special attention to the Day of Atonement ritual, taken up with great rigor and detail by the writer of the Letter to the Hebrews (but for Paul, see Rom. 3.25). There has been much discussion of the precise bearing of the imagery here, but the main point is sufficiently clear: as a result of Jesus' death, one knew oneself no more estranged from God, no more like fallen Adam with all "glory" gone, but, by sheer faith, accepted by God. Not only accepted but also "redeemed"—the image perhaps of the slave-market, perhaps of the liberation of a subject people, like Israel from Egypt or Babylon. But Paul also had in mind the ever-present dimension of the unseen world, of angels and demons, where, in a more dramatic and crucial way, earth's conflicts were fought out—and had now, as a result of Jesus, reached a decisive moment: he had defeated the evil powers and, linger on though they did, their force had come to its end. How precisely Paul saw this as having been done remains unclear, but, in his thought-world, his experience of forgiveness and healing made this kind of language almost inevitable to account for it (Col. 2.15; Rom. 8.37–39). These images of (1) sacrifice and (2) victory, which in Paul simply lie side by side without any attempt to relate them conceptually (they were more like poetic images than logical ideas), had a great future ahead of them, each fostering both its own mythology and its own rational schemes. The same is true of Paul's conviction of Jesus' long-term role. Because of who he was and what he had done, undeniable in Paul's experience (and of course not Paul's alone, as he is a member and leader of a community), Jesus' return is assured together with his final triumphant concluding the work already so palpably begun (1 Thess. 4.13–17; 1 Cor. 15).

But to continue to focus on Jesus' death: in a few New Testament passages (e.g., Acts 8.32–33, and perhaps in the silence of Jesus in Mark 15.5), we have the beginnings of attention to Isa. 53 as illuminating the meaning of Jesus' death (see entry on Irenaeus). In due course it became a standard extended metaphor for the understanding of the passion; cf. also Ps. 22, much more obvious in affecting the story of the passion in the Gospels. What Jews mostly took to be about Israel as a people, Christians saw as foreseeing and making sense of the dying of Jesus.

Other early Christians had different ways of expressing a comparable conviction of Jesus' decisive achievement: he had, they believed, changed everything; or rather, to put the matter with greater precision, God had changed everything, with him as his agent. The Gospel of John, for example, gives a picture of what Jesus had achieved that is even more far-reaching than (though in some ways not unlike) that of Paul. For him, as John 17 describes most vividly, "his own" are one with Jesus and so with the Father, and Jesus is as devoted to them as a good shepherd to his precious flock (John 10). Although the picture seems in a way more abstract and more general, here too there is a focus on Jesus' death as the crucial episode that epitomizes and, as it were, enacts, his saving purpose—like a lamb dying in sacrifice (1.29) or a shepherd dying for his sheep (10.11). The outcome is the gift of the life of the coming age, already given now to those who believe (5.24).

Jesus is also "savior" (Luke 2.11; John 4.42; 1 Tim. 1.15). It is the dramatic image of rescue—again, with the God of Israel as prototype (e.g., 1 Sam. 2.1); and in the background is the crucial rescue of Israel's whole history, that from slavery in Egypt. Thus "freedom" (understood in this context) comes to be seen as a central part of Jesus' achievement, one recently much accentuated in liberation theology and comparable movements.

As has been suggested, these varied images, which meld and converge in the earliest Christian writings like (as has been suggested) images in a poem, have had their place in Christian thought as it has developed, and some have been taken into paths of rational construction, which they could not properly sustain, with metaphors taken as if they were capable of turning helpfully into full-blown stories (e.g., the fourth-century Gregory of Nyssa's use of the idea of ransom and redemption, with Jesus "paid" at death temporarily to the devil, who lost him again and was ruined for his unjust usurpation). Especially in Protestantism, massively, down to the present, Jesus' death has been seen—and "felt"—chiefly as the all-sufficient atoning sacrifice for "my" sins, revolutionizing one's whole existence, often individualistically perceived, separating one from "the rest." It may be most helpful to go behind the images, inevitably bound to time and culture, to the experience that brought them to mind—which relates to the difference made by Jesus, in cases beyond number, to human awareness of God and relationship with him.

It is fair to say that, especially in recent times, Jesus has been seen as at the root of less desirable tendencies in human thought and culture: such as otherworldliness, leading to the neglect of social ills (but Christians have often been in the forefront in healing and works of charity); or morbidity and fear about even peccadilloes (yet Jesus was the giver of free forgiveness); or fear of a threatening and censorious God (yet Jesus gave us a most open picture of God's love). This last charge is perhaps the most serious, and we should recognize that a strong sense of God's moral justice was inescapable in contemporary Jewish faith and piety, though it was joined to a sense of his ready forgiveness; at the same time, we may reflect that much the most vengeful or retributive picture of God is in the one Gospel of Matthew, most Jewish of all the four: it may have seemed to him in particular to be essential to true religion, or the cosmic structure would collapse. And he too knows God's tenderness—for example, 11.15–30. More broadly, it is of course the case that much of Jesus' vision, as seen in the Gospels, has been found too generous and free for some of his followers to stomach!

Leslie Houlden

See also: Anselm; Hebrews, Letter to the; Jesus as Servant; Jesus, Death of; Liberation Theology; Paul; Second Coming of Jesus, in Current Belief; Second Coming of Jesus, Origins of. See also Glossary: *Atonement*

References

Aulén, G. 1931. *Christus Victor*. London: Macmillan.
Fiddes, P. S. 1989. *Past Event and Present Salvation*. London: DLT.
Gunton, C. E. 1988. *The Actuality of Atonement*. Edinburgh: T. and T. Clark.
Hengel, M. 1982. *The Atonement*. London: SCM.
Lampe, G. W. H. 1962. "The Atonement." Pp. 173–191 in *Soundings*. Edited by A. R. Vidler. Cambridge: Cambridge University Press.

Jesus, Death of

There are three chief areas of interest, as far as this article is concerned: historical, literary, and theological. (For the important artistic and musical reflections on Jesus' death, see the relevant articles.) In effect, it is a matter of these questions: What happened and how did it come about? How and with what meaning was it recounted? and What significance may be given to it in relation to God? The earliest material on the subject of Jesus' death, Paul's letters and, most obviously, the Gospels, straddles all three questions, so, for the sake of clarity, we begin with this material, working first on the surface, and then going deeper.

The Story

It is the Gospels that tell the story—in considerable detail. Very broadly, it is the same in all four accounts: after a largely Galilean ministry, Jesus comes to Jerusalem for Passover and is acclaimed as "king" (surely with messianic significance). He is the agent of a violent incident of protest in the Temple (though not in John at this point, see John 2.1–11), provoking hostility among leading Jews. There is controversy on various issues, and then a plot is hatched by the Jewish authorities to arrest Jesus. This is achieved with the help of Judas, one of Jesus' close followers, and, on the very night of the Passover meal (a day earlier in John, however), there is a kind of trial before Jewish leaders. As they possess no final authority in such a case, where a death penalty is sought, he is sent on to Pontius Pilate, the Roman governor, who is in Jerusalem for the feast—when the city was thronged and public order was in jeopardy. Apparently with some reluctance and under popular pressure, Pilate agrees to condemn Jesus to death, and, alongside two brigands or terrorists, he is speedily crucified, in line with Roman practice in such cases. Jesus quickly dies and is buried in a rock tomb that is found empty thirty-six hours later, and (though not in Mark) he appears, alive, to various of his followers. Such is the tale, told plain.

The History

The stories have been subjected to the most intense scrutiny, both for inner differences, contradictions, and implausibilities, and in the light of what is known or thought likely, given the circumstances and practices of the time. Scarcely any item in the story goes undisputed, quite apart from the historical interpretation of the event as a whole.

Symptomatic, in terms of the considerations that arise, is the question of date. As already noted, the Gospel of John places the whole event one day earlier in relation to Passover than the first three Gospels: for the latter, the last supper is the Passover meal and the death occurs the following day, while for John the death coincides with the ritual slaughter of countless beasts in the Temple, for consumption by households that same evening (and it is possible, from 1 Cor. 5.7, that Paul had the same view). Reconciling suggestions have been made: perhaps the group around Jesus worked with a sectarian calendar, which may have been kept by the Qumran community, whereby the feast was celebrated a day before the rest of the population. But, leaving aside the possibility of sheer ignorance or confusion (a last resort and sign of defeat in historical research), it may be more likely, despite some difficulties over wording, that John wishes us to see the irony in the true Lamb of God's death (1.29), unrecognized, coinciding with the now superseded and futile killing of lambs being carried out on a massive scale by the alleged people of God in the Temple. John manifests such irony on so many occasions that it need cause no surprise here. Its basis is that the truth, identified with Jesus (John 14.6), is visible to those in the light, while to those outside its range all is darkness and the truth is invisible.

It is not possible here to discuss every element in the story in detail, but little goes without question or discussion. For example, for many historians, the key happening leading to Jesus' condemnation was the so-called "cleansing of the Temple" (Mark 11.15–17 and parallels); but it can plausibly be held that, given the great size of the crowds thronging the vast Temple court at this time, it was so minor an incident that it would scarcely have been noticed—it was no more than a minor scuffle. Similarly, the "triumphal entry" (Mark 11.1–10 and parallels), with its apparent political overtones, may be put forward as the vital trigger, helping to explain the "king of the Jews" placard put on Jesus' cross; or else as (again) a minor event, or even as a fictional story created out of prophecy here seen as fulfilled. And the so-called Jewish trial (Mark 14.53–65 and parallels) may be seen as having had a major or (as indeed in John) minor role in the process as a whole. After all, the assembling of an officially constituted body late on Passover night is pretty implausible, and the unlikelihood of the emergence of details from a private meeting and of their reaching the hands of Jesus' adherents casts doubt on the accuracy of the account, only known in writings composed several decades later. May the account of the "Jewish trial" not reflect Jewish-Christian relations at that later time?

Where there is more general agreement is on the probable reason for the speedy elimination of Jesus. There is ample evidence for the jumpiness of the Roman and high priestly authorities, who shared an interest in good order and were nervous of all signs of sedition at the time of the great pilgrim festivals in Jerusalem. For whatever precise reason (previous record? the "triumphal entry"? the Temple disturbance? crowd rumors?), Jesus was perceived as a possible threat to good order, meriting elimination by way of precaution rather than punishment. It was then done out of policing motives. On this view, it was left to his followers to introduce theology and God-given destiny. They did this, it seems, without long delay. How far these thoughts were already rooted in Jesus' mind, so that, in that way, he "managed," or at least was ready for, his fate is, unsurprisingly, disputed: but the Gospels are clear that it was his destiny and his goal all along (e.g., Mark 8.31; 10.32–34).

There is, however, nothing surprising about death by crucifixion in such a case, nor in some of the surrounding torture and ill-treatment. Of course the Gospels give a prominence to these events, for example in the life of Pilate (it is one of two or three matters that make him at all memorable in the annals of the time), that they would scarcely have had at the time—and would never have had without the resurrection and the subsequent Christian movement. And Pilate's reluctance to condemn Jesus, so that the blame falls much more heavily on the Jewish authorities (and increasingly so as the Gospel tradition develops), is improbable, given the general situation and what is otherwise known of Pilate's character. Rather, it is likely to reflect the circumstances and biases of the later first century, when the Gospels were being written, with the Church in controversy with Judaism, from which it was increasingly differentiated. In reality, Pilate was surely the decisive agent, though the priestly aristocrats would not have been averse to the removal of a "trouble-maker."

The Literature

All through the previous section, surveying the history, the Gospels have appeared as our basic source, but in a kind of dialogue with what can be known from the history and practice of the time. Moreover, it has already become apparent that the Gospels themselves are far from being mere chronicles, written on the basis of a body of static traditions and content somehow "to tell it how it was." Rather, they exhibit lively religious, theological, even church-political beliefs on the matters they relate; also, each of them comes from its own distinct early Christian style of response to Jesus. More precisely, it reflects the creative mind of a particular early Christian writer, who brings his creativity to bear on what he has inherited.

Certain things, however, they share: the general outline; the conviction that what happens is "meant" by God, a sense conveyed by the demonstration that, in principle and in detail, it fulfils prophecy, God's ancient communication with his people; also, the conviction that this act is decisive for both a grasp of God's character and purpose and for the restoration of true relationship with him—it is redemptive or salvific. But for Mark, the death of Jesus is an act of awesome, dreadful solemnity, whereby Jesus dies "as a ransom for many" (10.45), and its story is scarcely capable of any but the most black and terrifying telling. So the darkness covers the land and is unrelieved (15.33); and Jesus' one saying from the Cross is his cry of abandonment by God (15.34); and he is totally without support (14.50; 15.40). It is the bravest of narratives, and no easy following cheerfulness relieves it: the message of the lad at the tomb is obscure in its results (16.8), and the death itself retains its hold as the impulse for the very executioner's conversion (15.39). If this is how salvation comes, it is indeed by the skin of the teeth.

Matthew retains most of Mark, but explains obscurities (how Pilate came to act as he did, 27.19, 24; how Judas, the really guilty one, met his reward, 27.3–10; how the centurion came to be so impressed, 27.54); and so, to a degree, he obscures (or lightens) Mark's starkness of doctrine. Luke, by contrast, humanizes the story and steers it for our edification, as Jesus himself shows compassion to his persecutors (23.34), converts one of the brigands crucified alongside him (23.39–43), and surrenders himself to God with calm devotion (23.46). And earlier, Luke's Jesus had lightened the burden of guilt on the disciples (the Church's future leaders and saints, after all): it was Satan who suborned Judas (22.3) and sought to get at Peter too (22.31), and it was exhausted grief and not callousness that led the disciples to fall asleep in Gethsemane (22.45). Jesus even performed his last act of healing in the extremity of his arrest (22.51), his graciousness and love being inextinguishable. For John, Jesus' death is the supreme act of Jesus' identity (of life, purpose, and meaning) with God himself. So it is his supreme disclosure of glory (13.31), to be seen by those who have been received into the light and the truth. So his apparent defeat is, without doubt, his triumph: 16.33; 19.30.

The Theology

Theological ideas and emphases are present in the Gospels by way of narrative. Already, however, Paul had used in his letters many theological symbols, images, and ideas to express his conviction of the crucial salvific role of Jesus' death, some of them presaging ideas to be found in the Gospels. Many of the ideas and images we find in Paul, mostly Jewish in origin and association, were to undergo adoption and development in very different intellectual climates in the Church's later history—sometimes being made unhelpfully rigid or abstract in the process.

So, for Paul, Jesus' death was a kind of offering for God, comparable to the willingness to sacrifice himself (as believed by the first century) of Isaac in Gen. 22 (cf. Rom. 8.32). Or it was a kind of sin-offering, as in the Levitical system (Rom. 3.25). Or it was like the triumph of a victorious general who displays his captives, formerly threats to his people's well-being (Col. 2.15). The hostile forces were those associated malign evils in human life—Satan, sin, and death, seen sometimes as linked with the Jewish law—a major reversal in the former Pharisee's scale of things (Gal. 2.16ff.; Rom. 7.4–6; Phil. 3.2–11). All these were ways, relevant to Paul's setting in life, of expressing his conviction of the root-and-branch value and effectiveness resulting from Christ; and it seemed to him compelling to link it to his death—this was where the images came home and fitted in: here was the point of sharpest focus where the conviction came to rest. Clearly, for other Christians, such as the evangelists, there was scope to look also elsewhere—to Jesus' teaching or his deeds of love and healing; or else to his exaltation to heaven, the end of his sacrificial act and journey, as perceived in, for example, the letter to the Hebrews; and for many, to the hope and assurance of his ultimate return, when salvation would be complete and unending (see the Revelation of John most vividly).

Many of these images, in Paul and elsewhere, became in later times the seeds of full-blown theories—with a strong tendency for imagery to move in the direction of mechanism (poetry in the direction of prose), and with questions that never occurred to Paul and other originators now being forced to an answer. So they became "doctrines of atonement," each with its own logic and its own appeal within different Christian groups and traditions. Over the centuries, each had its own period of favor, as in the case of the "Christus victor" symbol, under the inspiration of Gustav Aulén's book of that name (1931), reviving and fortifying (while modifying) a particular patristic emphasis going back to Gregory of Nyssa; or, in the early Middle Ages, a version of the idea of Christ "satisfying" God's legitimate requirement of human service, now put in "feudalized" dress (cf. Anselm's *Cur Deus Homo*). In the same period, Abelard (in addition to more traditional ideas) saw the saving benefit of Christ's death as lying in its moral character—a thought that we can see implicit in the Gospels and especially (see above) in Luke's Passion narrative. His "exemplary theory" has many modern resonances, in a time when the mythical character of some other theories makes them seem far-fetched or obscure. Christ died in such a manner that may attract us to generosity and self-giving, and so unite us to God. It is unfair to dismiss this as a weakly inspirational theory rather than one that "does something" for us by divine *action*. In the latter case, of course, there is the difficulty that God "changed" in disposition or attitude as a result of Jesus' death, and how could God do that? The death of Jesus was certainly an event; and if believers enter into fellowship with God in its light, its religious and existential point is achieved. None of the traditional "theories" does more to underline the existential sense of Jesus' death as an essential and unrepeatable event than the pervasive tradition of that death as the sacrifice to end all sacrifices, which Paul and then the Letter to the Hebrews, with its imagery from the Day of Atonement ritual and its insistence on Jesus' act as "once for all" (7.27; 9.12), impressed upon the Christian consciousness and which Protestant thought and preaching have particularly held to with tenacity. At the same time, the Gospels encourage us not to concentrate wholly on Jesus' death, crucial though it was as the climax of his earthly career as the representative and agent of God and however profound the degree to which it moves us and determines people's lives.

Leslie Houlden

See also: Anselm; Jesus, Achievement of; John, Gospel of; Kingdom of God; Luke, Gospel of, and Acts of the Apostles; Mark, Gospel of; Matthew, Gospel of; Messiah; Paul

References

Bammel, E., and C. F. D. Moule, eds. 1984. *Jesus and the Politics of His Day*. Cambridge: Cambridge University Press.

Brown, R. E. 1993. *The Death of the Messiah*. 2 vols. New York: Doubleday.

Houlden, J. L. 1987. *Backward into Light*. London: SCM.

Knox, J. 1959. *The Death of Christ*. London: Collins.

Lampe, G. W. H. 1962. "The Atonement." In *Soundings*. Edited by A. R. Vidler. Cambridge: Cambridge University Press.

Rivkin, E. 1984. *What Crucified Jesus?* London: SCM.

Jesus, Family of

The family of Jesus referred to in early sources (i.e., the Letters of Paul and the Gospels) is made up of Mary and Joseph as parents, and four brothers, James, Joses, Judas, and Simon (Mark 6.1–6; with Joses becoming Joseph in Matthew's parallel passage, 13.55). Apart from possible references to Joses at Mark 15.40, 47, only James among the brothers receives further notice in the documents. In Luke 1.36, and there alone, we learn that John the Baptist's parents were kinsfolk of Mary; and there must be a suspicion that this relates to a general Lucan tendency to bring the work and inheritance of John and Jesus into proximity. In addition, in medieval stained-glass windows (e.g., in the cathedral at Chartres in northern France), in Christian paintings of the Renaissance and other periods, and in the traditional devotion and observance of, chiefly, the Roman Catholic Church, we learn of Mary's parents, Joachim and Anne. But the earliest mention of them comes in the Gospel or Protevangelium of James, which dates from the second century and is generally thought to be a largely legendary development, ascribed pseudonymously to the brother of Jesus.

In fact, from the early period, only Mary and James come before us with any clarity. No father for Jesus is either named or even implied in the Gospel of Mark, or indeed in Paul, where the only reference to parentage is the minimal "born of a woman" at Gal. 4.4. Only in the Gospels of Matthew and Luke do we have stories that give substance to both Joseph and Mary. This happens chiefly in the first two chapters of each Gospel, but we learn from Matt. 13.55 that Jesus' father (rather than Jesus himself, as in Mark 6.3) was a "carpenter." There is discussion about the exact social position (high or low?) implied by the term; discussion too whether the transference of the description from Jesus to Joseph in the later Gospel is a minor sign of deference to Jesus the Messiah, who should not be linked to humble toil.

It is certainly the case that neither Matthew nor Luke, despite their both implying Jesus' virginal conception by Mary, is reluctant to see Joseph and Mary as his two parents: cf. Luke 2.41, 48. This may refer to legal and practical rather than physical parentage, but it is not wholly easy to know what either evangelist exactly meant by the stories of the circumstances of Jesus' conception. Mary alone makes other appearances: clearly at Acts 1.14, implicitly at Luke 11.28, and perhaps at Mark 15.40, 47 and 16.1. Unnamed, she appears in John 2.1–11 and 19.25–27 simply as "the mother of Jesus." Mark's two references (again, not by name), at 3.21–22 and 3.31–35, are usually understood not to be particularly positive and are often taken to be part of Mark's doctrine that Jesus, like those who follow him, renounces family (10.28–31); or may it be that Mark had dramatic or ecclesiastico-political reasons for underplaying the role of Jesus' family?

This possibility leads to a consideration of the figure of James (often called "the Just"), the brother of Jesus, who is in many ways more prominent and perhaps clearer to our sight than the other members of Jesus' family. Earliest of all and probably most reliably, he appears in Gal. 1–2 as one of three apostolic "pillars" of the church in Jerusalem in the years after the crucifixion. By the later forties, it appears that he was indeed the leading figure in that community. This is borne out in the narrative of Acts: anonymously (and with the other brothers) at 1.14; by name at 12.17 and then at the crucial episode of the council at 15.13; and then at 21.17. Reading somewhat between the lines in both Galatians and Acts, it seems that possibly James took over the leading role from Peter, perhaps when the latter engaged more in missionary activity elsewhere (cf. Gal. 2.9; 1 Cor. 9.5; and his later association with Rome).

The evidence points to James, whose death at opposing Jewish hands in A.D. 62 is recorded by Josephus and the second-century Christian writer Hegesippus, being in truth the most clear and direct inheritor of the mantle of Jesus, carrying on his mission among Jews and teaching and acting as leader of his immediate followers. The effect of his work is so often not recognized largely because (1) the Jerusalem community was dispersed after the fall of the city to the Romans in A.D. 70, and (2) other tendencies in the Christian movement came to the fore and have left a much stronger mark on the written sources and indeed on the subsequent history of the Church. Only "the Twelve" really thrive in Christian memory. It is as if, even without a deliberate conspiracy, the work of James found itself muted (though not obliterated)—sometimes in surprising ways.

The main thrust of the successful mission turned out to be that which centered on the apostle Paul, carrying belief in Jesus out into the wider world of the Roman Empire, on terms that made it easier for gentiles to become full parts of the Church, free from the alien requirements of the Jewish law—and in accordance with a way of seeing Jesus (even as universal savior) that seems removed from his own probable perception of himself. After his death, however, it is evident that, as was surely to be expected, a more rule-and-organization-minded outlook developed, even among the followers of Paul: we find it in the letters to Timothy and Titus and, with an irenic slant (in relation to Jewish Christians), in Acts. This natural trend made it easier for other elements in early Christianity, including those keen to retain the Jewish inheritance more fully, to make headway. In the soon highly successful Gospel of Matthew we find adherence to the Jewish law enjoined by Jesus (5.17–20; 23.3, 23): it is remarkable how rarely those texts have been read in what is surely their intended rigor, but rather as simply commanding Christians to moral firmness and strict observance of the rules (whatever they might be seen to be). This tendency then established itself in church life against more liberal, lax, or "inspirational" tendencies.

In line with such a reaction, the Letter ascribed to James (and his role in its message gains more acceptance) takes its place, and the document gradually won its way into the writings accepted by the churches, to make up the New Testament. Like the Gospel of Matthew, it simply assumes that the Jewish law remains in force for the followers of Jesus. Unlike Matthew (which thus seems to occupy a middle ground and to center on Peter [see 16.17–19] rather than James), it gives little space to the thought that doctrinal prominence is to be accorded to Jesus: he is the Lord and his teaching is revered by frequent echoes, but there is little evidence of the Christians associated with James seeing him as anything approaching divine in status, receiving worship, or being taken as universal savior. For the Letter of James, the Christian movement, centering on Jesus, is a reform movement in Judaism, and the age-old heritage, given by God, is in no way abrogated or superseded. The Letter "got through" into general Christian acceptance because its moral emphasis reverberated sufficiently in the Church of the later first century. It was a time when there was a gathering of appropriate resources from a range of quarters; and once established in the Christian canon, the Letter proved to have sufficiently strong echoes of support in the ethos of the Church for it to survive in (somewhat marginal, it must be admitted) use to this day; challenged by Luther in the sixteenth century, enthusiast for the purity of Paul's quite different message on behalf of "faith alone" and disposer of the essence of what he saw "the law" as standing for to the rubbish-heap where salvation is concerned. In general, however, apart of course from Mary herself (and Joseph as her consort), it has to be said that the family of Jesus, while not ignored, have not played a major role in Christian faith or devotion. The causes they were chiefly associated with ceased to be central to the Church's doctrinal understanding of Jesus.

There is, however, an exception. In the second century, legends developed about Jesus' (unsubstantiated) grandparents, Joachim and Anne, parents of Mary. In medieval piety, these characters, together with their other children, came to play a part in what amounted to a picture of a domestic (and so more "normal") Jesus, at any rate in his childhood. It was one aspect of the emotive devotion to "sweet Jesus" so prominent in the period. The Reformation swept this away, in the interests of a return to the savior Jesus of orthodox doctrine, less easy for ordinary humans to identify with, even though they owed him all.

Leslie Houlden

See also: English Christianity, Medieval; Jesus, Origins of; Jesus in Social Context; Luke, Gospel of, and Acts of the Apostles; Mary; Paul; Work

References

Bauckham, R. 1990. *Jude and the Relatives of Jesus in the Early Church*. Edinburgh: T. and T. Clark.

Brown, R. E. 1993. *The Birth of the Messiah*. London: Geoffrey Chapman.

Chilton, Bruce, and Jacob Neusner, eds. 2001. *The Brother of Jesus*. Louisville, KY: Westminster John Knox.

Painter, J. 1997. *Just James: The Brother of Jesus in History and Tradition*. Columbia: University of South Carolina Press.

Jesus, Miracles of

It has become customary to think of the miracles associated with Jesus as falling into three categories: (1) those remarkable events that have strong theological significance, chiefly his virginal conception and resurrection, but also transfiguration and ascension; (2) deeds performed by (rather than to) Jesus involving "nature" in one form or another: the feeding of large crowds with small amounts of food; the calming of a storm and walking on water; the changing of water into wine; and (3) acts of healing, including exorcisms, performed by Jesus on people suffering from a wide range of disabilities and even death itself.

This classification stems largely from the legacy of the thought-forms of the Enlightenment of the seventeenth and eighteenth centuries, and it would not be intelligible in first-century terms. In the time of Jesus and of the evangelists, when there was no watertight doctrine of natural causation and natural laws to determine events, when personal powers of evil and God fought it out on the world's stage, and when divine intervention in the world was to be expected and either feared or welcomed, happenings such as these were regarded as "wonders" rather than as "problems," amazing manifestations of God rather than, for most, as occasions of instinctive skepticism or challenges to our explanatory powers. (The word "miracle" itself began by meaning something to be wondered at, and only in recent centuries came to signify an event contrary to nature.) This was true of Jews and pagans alike (see the work of Robin Lane Fox, listed below). Hence, the use in the Gospels and elsewhere of the word "wonders" to describe such events (e.g., Mark 13.22; John 4.28; Rom. 15.29).

The other word that is commonly used (as in the texts just referred to) is "signs." This points to the fact that they were not seen as simply occasions for gaping: they pointed to accessible meaning. Divine intervention was intelligible not just because of belief in the power of God to intervene in his creation but also because of prophecy. It was this, whether specific or thematic, that gave intelligibility to the events in question and warranted their role as deeds done to or by the Messiah, the agent of God and his purposes: see Isa. 35.5–end; 61.1–3; 2 Kings 4.42–44; Isa. 7.14; all passages quoted or referred to implicitly in the Gospels. "Signs" could of course be regrettable: people might seek them not out of faith but out of curiosity or as a kind of dare—"convince me if you can." So in the Gospels, it is both a good and a bad word: see, for example, Mark 8.11 and John 2.11.

Our tendency to assign these happenings to a number of different categories arises, in truth, from a wish to deal appropriately with the different degrees of difficulty that have been widely felt over the credibility of what is claimed. Thus, because of modern cases of "faith-healing" and familiarity with gifted "healers," for which it is felt there may be some "respectable" (if arcane) explanation, people can feel relatively accommodating to the cures ascribed to Jesus, and even assign some of them to "natural" processes—for example, Jairus' daughter had not died but was in a coma (not so easy with the story of Lazarus in John 11, as there told). The same allegedly helpful procedure used to be applied to the feeding miracles: in truth, they had all brought packed lunches. It was a common post-Enlightenment ploy. When it came to the virginal conception of Jesus, modern people might be faced with a starker choice: either to disbelieve because "such things do not and cannot occur" or to believe by an act of faith, perhaps with difficulty in seeing why such a thing might be thought helpful to the Christian cause.

The fact of the matter is that none of this categorizing or explaining gets us anywhere near the world of Jesus or the evangelists. That has to be our starting point, and our task is then to enter into that "world" of understanding. We may then be compelled to recognize the culture-conditioned character of our own quasi-scientific instincts. But we must also realize that "what actually happened" has to remain more elusive.

As far as the "theological miracles" (first category) are concerned, there are separate articles in this book on the Origins of Jesus and the resurrection. In both cases, we have the force of scripturally based understanding, enabling the reader and believer to understand the role of Jesus. They are not simply there to inform or to dazzle, but to bring out the meaning of Jesus, who is at their center. It is apparent indeed that the way they are described by the evangelists (and, for the resurrection, Paul) already shows the marks of the general theological standpoint of the author concerned. They are integrated into larger patterns of thought, as we might expect and indeed might hope.

Some of the same considerations apply, as we have already seen, when it comes to the second and third categories of miracle: chiefly, there are prophetic texts that give them both backing and meaning—they are not random events, without context or without sense that goes deeper than the surface.

It is worth recognizing that though superficially the miracles of Jesus spread across the four Gospels with much the same range and sense in all of them, in fact each evangelist has his own way of seeing them in the context of his whole perception of Jesus' significance. Thus, common understandings of them—for example, as vivid "samples" of the Kingdom of God's arrival, being enacted in deed to go alongside Jesus' words, may seem not false but too general. Such a way of interpreting the meaning of Jesus' deeds does indeed do a good measure of justice to Jesus' mission as a whole, as summarized, for example, at Mark 1.14–15, and it is virtually stated in a saying of Jesus concerning his exorcisms, found in both Matthew (12.28) and Luke (11.20): his antidiabolical acts are themselves no less than the irruption of the kingdom. But we can also look for nuances of understanding.

It is Mark who perhaps comes closest to the "kingdom" proposal. Jesus performs, for the most part, one instance of all the main kinds of healing. But the fact that, for example, there is a healing of a blind man at each end of the journey to Jerusalem (8.22–26; 10.46–52) might prompt us to see that a healing may also carry a deeper meaning in the evangelist's use of it (and perhaps the Church's use too): to "see" is to share in Jesus' Passion and its meaning in the purposes of God. To be blind is to fail or refuse to see, like the disciples at 8.31–33; 9.30–32. Such deeds are far indeed from being merely impressive actions to induce attachment to the cause. In fact that is what those who oppose Jesus try to extort from him: 8.11–12.

Matthew takes over most of Jesus' deeds of power, but adds some and curtails others. For example, he seems unhappy with the (perhaps to him crude) story of the Gadarene swine and gives it less than half its Marcan space. Similarly perhaps, one of his rare omissions from Mark is the story of the healing of the deaf and dumb man in 7.31–37, possibly again because of the crudity of Jesus' technique; but as a result he misses what may be one of Mark's best "tricks." The term for the man's condition (he is *mogilalos*) that occurs only here in the Gospels also has only one occurrence in the old Scriptures: Isa. 35.6. Did Mark perhaps hope or even trust that those who heard his book would know the passage and pick up the allusion?

Like the others, Luke can use healings to prove a point of a different kind, for example about the observance of the Sabbath (Mark 3.1–6; Luke 13.10–17). He also has healings that are gratuitous acts of mercy, as in the case of the man whom Peter attacked at Jesus' arrest (22.51). In John, healings come into their own as "signs" alongside other signs of different kinds, intensifying in weight as the book proceeds: from water into wine in chapter 2 to the raising of Lazarus in chapter 11. Their role is to demonstrate, for those who can "see," the glory of God revealed in Jesus; in that perspective, the death of Jesus, apparent failure, is glory in its purest and supreme form.

In one sense there is "nothing special" about Jesus as miracle-worker. The ancient world was accustomed to such men and wondered at them. (Apollonius of Tyana is the best known, from his "life" by Philostratus.) So, as we have seen, it was to the meaning he and his followers gave to them, the purpose for which they were done, that we have to look. And the same is true of his followers: in Acts, Luke seems deliberately to show the disciples carrying out acts of power that recall closely those of Jesus as recorded in the Gospel (e.g., 3.1–10; 9.36–43). Thus they help to authenticate the mission of the apostles who perform them. Paul too in his letters refers to the carrying out of such acts as one of the Spirit's gifts (1 Cor. 12.9), but he gives it no special weight. Certainly, he did not expect any kind of magic to make him immune to suffering—quite the contrary, to suffer like Christ was his "glory," his ground for boasting (2 Cor. 12.5–10). Neither in Jesus himself nor in his followers did the performing of miracles serve as a "proof" or even, quite, as a drawer of people's attention, like a trick by a man at the entrance to a circus, though they surely gave rise to a reputation. Nor were the healings primarily presented as acts of compassion (though the word occurs, rarely: in Mark four times, in Matthew five, in Luke three). They were neither more nor less than acted parables of the message that Jesus proclaimed, which centered on God and of which he himself was the key demonstration.

In recent years, and partly as a result of study of more accessible periods and situations, other kinds of interpretations or explanations of some kinds of miracles have been presented. They work less with how they were understood in the time of their happening or reporting than with perspectives only recently available. Thus, seasonal blindness, resulting from seasonal dietary shortages, may explain how "healing" can occur if it happens to be carried out at the time when fresh fruit is available again. And miracles can have sociological or even political overtones at some level, not made explicit in the text; note, for example, the obscure use of the name "legion" in the story of the Gadarene swine in Mark 5.1–20—in an occupied land. Or stories of healings and exorcisms may testify to unbearable social pains bursting out in demands for betterment or, as we now say, liberation.

There is one more aspect of our subject, in a way foreshadowed by the miracles done in Jesus' name by Paul and by apostles as recorded in Acts. This is what might be seen as the posthumous miraculous activity associated with Jesus by way of objects related to his life and death. Here, we are in the world of devotion whereby physical objects, including body parts ("relics"), linked to a heroic religious figure (saint or martyr), whether local or widely known, and all the more Jesus himself, have long been perceived as if they were the person him/herself. So in the case of Jesus, raised bodily from the dead, we have devotion to far-flung fragments of the true Cross after its alleged "finding" by Helena in the fourth century, to the crown of thorns from the fifth, and much later to the shroud of Jesus—among numerous other objects. There was a surge of such devotion (similarly to objects associated with Mary) in the Middle Ages, but it remains alive and well, especially in Roman Catholic countries.

In terms of devotional psychology (though perhaps from no other point of view), the sacrament of the Eucharist, the sacred host (consecrated bread), especially as kept permanently in churches (like relics of saints, for devotion to the saint via the physical presence), has long played a comparable role and has itself been associated with miraculous happenings. We may see the viaticum (the eucharist given to the dying) as either a final act of grace given to the faithful, Jesus himself, present in the sacrament, or perhaps as a wondrous deed (miracle?) provided for the great transition. Whatever the formal definitions, in religious terms, the line can be fine, especially as far as the worshipper is concerned. In such a context, the wonderful activity of Jesus continues unabated.

Leslie Houlden

See also: Enlightenment; Jesus, Origins of; Jesus in Social Context; John, Gospel of; Kingdom of God; Luke, Gospel of, and Acts of the Apostles; Mark, Gospel of; Matthew, Gospel of; Meier, J. P.; Messiah; Resurrection; Transfiguration

References

Brown, P. R. L. 1981. *The Cult of the Saints*. Chicago: University of Chicago Press.

Fox, Robin Lane. 1986. *Pagans and Christians*. Harmondsworth: Viking.

Hull, J. H. 1974. *Hellenistic Magic and the Synoptic Tradition*. London: SCM.

Kee, H. C. 1983. *Miracle in the Early Christian World*. New Haven and London: Yale University Press.

———. 1986. *Medicine, Miracle and Magic*. Cambridge: Cambridge University Press.

Philostratus. 1969. *The Life of Apollonius of Tyana*. Loeb Classical Library. Cambridge: Harvard University Press.

Theissen, G. 1983. *Miracle Stories of the Early Christian Tradition*. London: SCM.

Jesus, Name of

Jesus is the English form of the Latin "Iesus," the letter "J" being a late (seventeenth-century) development. The Latin is itself adapted from the Greek "Iesous," as found in the Greek of the New Testament; and that is the standard rendering of the Hebrew name "Joshua," most famously the name of the inheritor of Moses' mantle and leader of the entry into the Promised Land (see the Book of Joshua). As was customary, it is a name with a meaning: "Yahweh is salvation." As was also common, the name's meaning is appropriate to the life. By his very name, the Jesus of Christianity is the bringer of God's salvation (Matt. 1.21). The name (and so the work) was seen as having been bestowed before his birth, even from his conception, by divine authority (Luke 1.31; Matt. 1.21).

But Jesus goes by other designations—for example, he is "Jesus of Nazareth" (Mark 1.9, 24). To explain it, there is Matthew 2.23. It was reckoned as his place of origin and distinguishes him. He is, more importantly, "Jesus Christ" or "Christ Jesus." This amplifies the meaning of his name itself by referring to a specific role: he is "Jesus Messiah." The two terms go together as early as we can trace, being very frequent indeed in Paul's letters. What is remarkable is that, for all we can tell, and despite its clear importance, "Christ" has already largely lost its technical sense: "King Charles," we may say, has turned into "Charles King." Of course this may not be so: Paul may be "hearing" Messiah every time he calls Jesus by the twin name; but the times when he makes anything of it in this way are few, Rom. 9.5 being by far the clearest. Jesus is also called "Lord Jesus," and is prayed to by this address in Rev. 22.20. Paul too saw Christians as those who "call on the name of our Lord Jesus Christ" (1 Cor. 1.2). In the light of his being seen as fulfilling Ps. 110.1, this term is especially associated with his heavenly and exalted state.

In Israel, as elsewhere, names might not only have meanings but also carried power. The Book of Deuteronomy is much concerned with the place (= sanctuary) where God wishes to make his name dwell, where he could be encountered in worship and depended on (e.g., 12.5). It would be the place of his (sacramental?) presence. So early Christians saw the name of Jesus as carrying (and perpetuating among his followers) the power he showed in his time on earth—especially to heal: Acts 3.6, 16. Similarly, one could be baptized "into the name of Jesus," so, probably, being transferred into his ownership: Acts 8.16; 9.5; 22.16. It is a favorite Lucan expression. Matthew 28.19 uses a different, ampler form; and Paul thought of baptism as "into Christ Jesus," Rom. 6.3; though see 1 Cor. 1.13. For John, Jesus' acting in God's name is an important way of speaking of his authority: 5.43; 15.16. One should believe on Jesus' name (1.12), and one may pray in his name (= authority) (14.14). His followers are "sent" in his name (14.26).

We can tell from the earliest manuscripts of the New Testament writings, even from the later second century, that the name of Jesus was seen as holy, along with other "holy names" *(nomina sacra)* such as "God," "Lord," "Son." These were marked by abbreviation (first and final letters only) and perhaps by a space to indicate formal reverence when reading out. So the special holiness of "Jesus" found constant practical expression.

In due course, especially in Eastern Orthodox Christianity, from at least the sixth century, the repetition of the name of Jesus, mantralike, became a common form of prayer (the Jesus Prayer), often associated with discipline of posture and breathing.

In both Eastern and Western Christianity, there developed observance of the Holy Name of Jesus as a liturgical feast (with varied date). It was particularly associated with the development of devotion to the sacred humanity of Jesus, expressed with almost erotic fervor, in the medieval West, from the eleventh and especially the twelfth centuries, continuing throughout the Middle Ages, and, with variations, to the present. It was particularly associated with the early Cistercian monastic reform, and expressed in hymns still in use—for example, "Jesus!—the Very Thought Is Sweet! In that dear name all heart-joys meet." And the Evangelical John Newton's "How Sweet the Name of Jesus Sounds" shows it bridging the Reformation divide in the eighteenth century. Pentecostal fervor gives to this devotion a fresh impulse. The use of the name in profane oaths, down to the present, is a dark side of the same phenomenon. By contrast, in English schools at any rate down to the 1960s, children might be taught to bow at every mention of the name of Jesus, linking them perhaps with the practice of the earliest reading of the New Testament writings in Christian gatherings for worship in the second century.

Leslie Houlden

See also: Baptism; Bernard of Clairvaux; English Christianity, Medieval; Franciscan Thought and Piety; Hymns; Lord; Messiah; Orthodox Tradition; Paul; Pentecostalism; Roman Catholicism; Textual Criticism

References

Duffy, Eamon. 1992. *The Stripping of the Altars*. New Haven and London: Yale University Press.

Roberts, Colin H. 1979. *Manuscript, Society and Belief in Early Christian Egypt*. London: Oxford University Press.

Jesus, Origins of

The question of where Jesus came from and how his coming occurred finds answers in most of the major strands in early Christian thought. The answers differ according to the way the question was asked by the writer concerned; and that depended on the interests and "shape" of his mind. We take the writers in turn.

Paul: our question cannot be said to have been a major preoccupation with Paul, the earliest Christian writer known to us. He is more interested in the nature and outcome of Jesus' work as a whole. All the same, it is interesting to see how it figures in his letters, even in apparently throwaway statements. At Gal. 4.4, we read that "God sent his son, born of a woman." This meager reference, in effect simply to Jesus' humanness, is the nearest we get to any interest whatsoever in Jesus' family background. It can hardly be said to be vivid. There is a question whether Paul had in mind a heavenly base from which God "sent" him into the world. But we may think that this is no more worth raising than it would be, for example, in the case of the prophets: when we read of God "sending" them, we take it to mean simply that they were called and that their mission began. But it is possible (no more) that in the case of Jesus, his "pre-existence" was already in mind. In 1 Cor., Paul three times implies, perhaps even states, such a belief: at 1.24, 31, he identifies Christ with the figure, prominent in Jewish speculative thought and devotion, of God's "wisdom," his companion from the beginning and his agent in the world's creation. This latter aspect is clearer still at 8.6—and harder to dismiss as bearing any other sense. We may feel inclined to categorize it as "poetic" or "mythological"; but in Paul's thought-world, before such distinctions were likely to be available to him, it seems like a claim for Christ's universal effectiveness, not only for our salvation in present and future but also for the fulfilling of the deepest intentions and deeds of God: whatever God has done and now does for good, involves Jesus. In Judaism (see, for example, Prov. 8.22–31), the idea of "wisdom" was surely a way of witnessing to the essential rationality and orderliness of God's creative and world-sustaining work: it was and is not chaotic or haphazard (despite appearances). How far this thought was prominent for Paul is not clear, though it may play a part in his thinking about a kind of "natural law" in the final section of Rom. 1.

Mark: the first of the Gospels to see the light of day shows little interest in Jesus' antecedents. We read of his family background, with the names of his mother and four brothers. But they are not given as useful information, but incidentally (almost as if "everybody knows"), in connection with the story of Jesus' ill-starred visit to his hometown of Nazareth. What is more, we have already read (3.21–22, 31–35) of their dismissal of Jesus as mad and their peremptory treatment of him, to which Jesus responds with equal dismissiveness. Mark is no source whatsoever for either information about Jesus' origins (in this world or before it) or any sort of even incipient devotion to, for example, Mary his mother. If anything, the reverse. As for a basis for formal doctrines concerning the manner of Jesus' birth, we read Mark in vain. For him, Jesus' origin is in his appearance for his mission and ministry, with John the Baptist for his herald: he leaps onto the stage, as if from nowhere (except that prophecy helps to foretell him and then God gives him plenary authority, 1.11). All the same, we do read, in passing, that he "came out" (1.38): was this from Nazareth (as 1.9 says) or, in some unstated way, from God?

The explanation for Mark's almost gratuitous hostility to Jesus' family is unclear: perhaps it was church-political (they were too closely associated with narrow Jewish-Christianity, which Mark abhorred); perhaps it was semi-devotional (like the disciples and the scribes, they serve as a warning to certain tendencies in Christian circles close to Mark, and the passages say: Do not be like them, stupid and overfamiliar). As far as the lack of seeds of doctrinal development goes, we can point to the similarity to Paul. Here, as so often, Mark is not distant from the proportions of faith found in Paul. Anyway, we must not for an instant be anachronistic.

Matthew: it is not in the least surprising that questions came to be asked about the circumstances of Jesus' birth, or that a "tidy-minded" evangelist like Matthew saw fit to develop the Gospel of Mark in this particular direction, among others. But it is not a matter of sheer curiosity on his part or even on the part of his readers, to be dealt with after the manner of a journalist or interviewer. Rather it is a question of rooting Jesus in Jewish antecedents and "proving," from as many scriptural passages as can properly be brought together, that he truly was and is the Messiah of Israel's hope. So in Matt. 1–2 we have first the genealogy, then the stories, each backed by Scripture. The birth is remarkable. We read it with biological or medical incredulity, and it becomes for us a crucial miracle. It is doubtful whether Matthew saw it in quite that way. It was a wonder, wrought by God, like the births of earlier heroes of God's purposes, such as Isaac (Gen. 18; 21), Samson (Judg. 13), and Samuel (1 Sam. 1–2). There is argument about the amount of early story that was available to Matthew as source-material: perhaps information of some kind from Joseph, who at last receives a name.

Luke: in his own different (but not wholly unrelated) way, Luke develops the subject along scriptural lines that are "atmospheric" rather than simply a matter of literal "fulfilments." He writes here, in chs. 1–2, as one soaked in the style and language of the Greek old Scriptures. And his characters recall those of former days—for example, Mary speaks as the Hannah of 1 Sam. 2; while Simeon speaks the language of Second Isaiah (40–55). More than Matthew, Luke is the originator and inspirer of Marian devotion; and indeed of the calendar—the feasts of Annunciation, Visitation, Circumcision, and Purification, not to speak of much of Christmas, come straight from Luke and without him would not exist. He also gives us a family tie-up between Jesus and John the Baptist: and we may compare Luke's special interest (right through to Acts 18.24–19.6) in connections between the movements issuing from the two. Once more, interest of a modern kind in the alleged strangeness of Jesus' birth is subsumed without question in the scriptural ethos: Jesus is like Samuel, an unexpected God-given birth for a great work, just as Mary is like Hannah. So authority is bestowed or fortified.

John: this Gospel shows an almost willful lack of interest in Jesus' human antecedents. His mother appears twice (unnamed): at 2.1–11 and 19.25–27. In both cases there is a legitimate suspicion that she is, at least in part, a symbolic figure, probably representing the old Israel to whom Jesus brings fulfilment and from which the Church springs, standing for an ampler salvation. Otherwise, we have only confused references to Jesus' place of origin: Nazareth, 1.45–46, where, with no hint of qualification, we read of Joseph as Jesus' father (cf. 6.42, where there is heavy irony and where we, being "in the light," may know better); and Bethlehem, 7.42, where readers are taken to know what muddled Jews do not; plus a passing (and undiscussed) reference to Jesus' brothers at 7.3–5, though here, as in Mark, family are said not to "believe in him." All these matters pass unremarked in John as far as theology is concerned. There is no hint at any point of his human life, including his birth, having any unusual features, except perhaps at 6.42: he seems to be taking at face value his overarching doctrine that "the Word was made flesh"—that is, truly human (1.14). In other words, what was special about Jesus related to other matters than his biological beginnings: his deeper "origins" and his real significance in the light of God and his purposes. So though at the ordinary earthly level he was indeed "the son of Joseph," this is told in passing; at the much more important level of divine truth, he is the "son of God," source of all good (and indeed of scandal, 10.30–36; 19.7), and the Father-Son relationship is the axis on which the Johannine view of things chiefly rests. At the same time, human parentage is not his most basic understanding of Jesus' origins. Here, in effect, though probably independently, he builds, right at the start of his book, on the undeveloped hints in Paul. In the Prologue, 1.1–18, the term "word" is the alternate, in Jewish thought, to "wisdom," as a way of speaking of God's creative and universal activity. So using this image for him is the most comprehensive way in which Jesus could possibly be thought of. It transcends mere speculation about the manner of his birth, and John reduces such matters to mere gossip among unbelieving or half-believing Jews. Jesus' "origin" is in God, at "the beginning" (1.1; 17.24): he is "pre-existent."

Hebrews: at 1.1–3, this writer follows, by a different route, the same thought as John: Jesus takes the role of "wisdom" as God's agent in creation, as now for salvation (cf. Wisdom of Solomon 7.26). But nowhere else does this writer attend to Jesus' origins at any level. His eyes are on his death, his entry to heaven, and his eternal triumph. It is a final reminder of the dominant perspective and sense of proportion in the theology and devotion of these first Christian years.

Both poetry and doctrine were not slow to develop. In Ignatius of Antioch's Ephesians (ch. 19), for example, we read: "Mary's virginity was hidden from the prince of this world; so was her child-bearing, and so was the death of the Lord. All these three trumpet-tongued secrets were brought to pass in the deep silence of God." And the Old Roman Creed, the ancestor of later creeds, listed Jesus' virginal conception among its tenets, a fact among others.

As to modern questions about the manner of Jesus' birth, historical enquiry will get us no further than we have gone, and there is no more evidence. Therefore, we are thrown back (if we are interested) upon the biology of human procreation (a subject of which first-century people—and their successors for centuries—knew little that was in the least accurate), and upon our general philosophical or instinctive beliefs about miraculous happenings. But the New Testament writers, notably Paul, Mark, and John, give us little encouragement to think that much depends on such things, least of all true Christian faith. Perhaps doctrinal authorities over many centuries have not done us a favor in creating the impression that matters relating to Christ's birth (e.g., virginal conception, Mary's perpetual virginity) had a vital factual nature on a par with his death, where they might figure without comment in a single list.

Leslie Houlden

See also: Ignatius of Antioch; Jesus, Family of; John, Gospel of; Luke, Gospel of, and Acts of the Apostles; Mark, Gospel of; Mary; Matthew, Gospel of; Messiah; Preexistence; Son of God

References

Brown, Raymond E. 1993. *The Birth of the Messiah*. New York: Doubleday; and London: Geoffrey Chapman.

Dunn, J. D. G. 1996. *Christology in the Making*. London and Grand Rapids, MI: Eerdmans.

Hoffmann, R. Joseph, ed. 1996. *The Secret Gospels*. New York: Prometheus.

Jesus, Parables of

Our earliest witness to Jesus' teaching could not be more explicit: "With many such parables, he spoke the word to them, as they were able to hear it; he did not speak to them without a parable, but privately to his own disciples he explained everything" (4.33–34). If then Jesus spoke exclusively in parables, when engaged with "the word" (= presumably, the proclamation of the kingdom of God, 1.14–15), it is necessary to have a picture of what "parable" meant. In our ordinary usage, so far as the word has a place, it tends to mean a story that carries a message, attractively and forcefully; and somewhere in the background there probably lie vivid Gospel stories, strong in narrative power, like those of the Prodigal Son (as it is, rather meanly, called in English: in German, it is "the *lost* son," but in truth it is the story of "the loving father") and the Good Samaritan. These are both found in Luke alone and, as we shall see, are admirably typical of Luke's writing. But Mark is where, as far as visible evidence goes, the process begins, and the "parables" in Mark, which, if he is to be believed, represent the whole of Jesus' teaching or preaching, are not quite of that character. If we had Mark's evidence alone, we should have to say that "parable" is a very general word, covering all kinds of statements that involve images or comparisons (the word's basic sense) of one kind or another.

There is also another key feature, which is evident in Mark 4.10–12. Here, by contrast with 4.33–34, we find to our surprise that "parables" are for outsiders, apparently with the aim of befogging rather than enlightening them. It is surely right to see here the key to the meaning of the phenomenon that Wrede called "the messianic secret"—that is, Mark's deliberate explaining of the puzzling, even embarrassing fact that Jesus had brought a message crucial and life-giving for everybody, but had been ignored or rejected by most. How could such a thing be? Mark's answer: he concealed his true identity as Messiah, and, here, he actually preached with a view to nonperception on the part of "those outside." To us (and indeed to Mark's successors: Matthew made it a simple explanation of what had happened—cf. "because" in 13.13—rather than Jesus' deliberate intent) it may seem a strange doctrine for Jesus (or any preacher) to hold. But for Mark, "parable" means riddle, hidden, puzzling saying, whose "secret" ("mystery") only the inner group of disciples is "given." "To those outside, all is enigma, riddlesome." (Matthew avoids the word as bearing this sense; compare 13.11 with Mark 4.11.) The observable outcome must be what was "meant" from the start: otherwise, how could one continue to trust?

This draws attention, not only to Mark's picture of Jesus' preaching—that it was divisive and, for many, unacceptable—but also to the wide range of meaning that the word "parable" can carry, notably against the Old Testament Hebrew background of the word *mashal*, rendered in the Greek version by *parabole*. The word can carry such a wide variety of senses, most of them, evidently, within Mark's repertoire—from pithy saying (such as those in the Book of Proverbs, cf. Mark 2.21–22), to enigmatic remarks, like our present passage, and full-blown stories, often with allegorical content, such as the Sower in 4.1–20 and the Vineyard in 12.1–12.

The question then arises how far this facet of his book is in effect simply Mark's way of accounting for the discouraging situation faced by the Christian communities of his own day, for whom the doctrine of 4.10–12 is then some comfort. The parables' message was explosive, full of apparent attraction for anyone (those "with ears to hear," 4.9), and indeed its ultimate success is assured (4.8, 20, 26–29, 30–32); but for the time being, it seems to be struggling. If so, then the Sower story, and especially vv. 10–12, is less a genuine parable of Jesus than a key to Mark's idea of reality and of Christian strategy. Of course it is true that many of Mark's parables, especially in chapter 4, are broadly of a kind well known from the scriptural past, being drawn from nature, cf. Judges 9.7–15; Ezekiel 17.22–24; but we cannot tell how far he bases himself on actual knowledge of Jesus or of how (or perhaps, more, what) Jesus actually taught, because response to the pressing circumstances of his own day seems so obvious as helping to determine the manner of his writing.

Matthew is content to take over Mark's parables, though (as we saw) he can slant them differently and, more obviously, he supplements them with sharp-edged stories about "the kingdom" and the terms of its life (e.g., 18.23–35). Their sense is not usually enigmatic at all: we note that Mark's singular *musterion* in 4.10 (secret, enigma—a word suggesting profundity and mysteriousness, a quality esteemed in the Dead Sea Scrolls as well as some Christian circles, cf. Paul, 2 Cor. 12.1–4; 1 Cor. 2.1, 7; 4.1; 15.51; Col. 1.26) is turned into the plural (13.11): does Matthew mean something more concrete, such as the listable doctrines or precepts that, for him, constitute the Christian message, and that his Christians know perfectly well?

Especially, Matthew amplifies Mark's collection of parables in chapter 13 (= Mark 4), adding some that illustrate the progress of Christian mission, as provided for in the instructions in chapter 10—that is, those of the Treasure and the Pearl, others that link up with the eschatological teaching in chapter 24—that is, the Tares and the Drag-net. So they fortify, in parabolic mode, some of Matthew's main concerns. And as far as the latter theme is concerned, Matthew goes further still in adding the sequence of parables in chapter 25, with their stark cautionary (even terrifying) message.

The Gospel of Luke contains, as has been said, what many regard as Jesus' quintessential parables. But these too are typical of the evangelist, with his open and literary narrative style, personal in tone and generous in morality, encouraging a loving and welcoming spirit (e.g., 14.15–24) and condemning tendencies to meanness, whether in attitude (like the brother of the wanderer-son, 15.25–32) or with money (like the rich man in 16.19–31). Luke is keen to include other stories not found elsewhere, such as those in 11.1–5 and 18.1–5, urging, with vivid and amusing force, persistence in prayer—qualities that may (it may be hoped) truly reflect Jesus' teaching. One of Luke's parables, that of the Unjust Steward, defies clear interpretation (is the steward commended by Jesus—"the Lord" in v. 8—or by "the lord" in the story, and why, precisely? And are the following sayings, some paralleled in Matthew, haphazardly or logically connected with the story and/or with each other?). If we take "parable" in its widest sense—for example, on the basis of scriptural precedent, then Luke is full of images and vivid sayings (John Drury lists no fewer than fifty-three parabolic items!), even though (unlike Matthew, 13.34) he does not reproduce Mark's bold statement that Jesus taught exclusively in parables.

As is well known, John's Gospel is notably different in its dearth of parables, and even the word itself fails to appear, though a synonym comes in 10.6; 16.25, 29. But the picture of the Shepherd in chapter 10 and that of the Vine in chapter 15, though "Johannized" in style, like everything else in the book, are recognizably of the parabolic genre, as are a few brief images such as the dying and rising grain (12.24) and the childbearing woman (16.21).

The parables, as a body of material, are notable, in almost all cases, for their relative simplicity and directness: they have a luminous directness not always found in (later) rabbinic examples. Is this a sign that, whatever the twists they have been given by a particular evangelist (a matter now clearer than it used to be), they are, as of course they are presented, close to the Master's voice? That must remain speculative, but both the directness and the "twists" are undeniable.

Much ink has been spilt in the past on the question of allegory in the parables. It arose in the first place as a questioning of the high degree of allegorizing interpretation, giving "meaning" to each item in a story, that was popular from the Church's early centuries. Viewing them in the context of their times (they do bespeak a Palestinian, largely rural, world, notably in the case of Mark, their first provider), it is hard now to deny substantial elements of allegory—for example, in the Vineyard story in Mark 12.1–12, and indeed explicitly in the Sower, which seems meant to be read as a parable-about-the-parables, as well as containing pointers to later episodes in Mark (for "rocky" ground, see Peter [= the Rock], 8.27–33, and for thorny ground, see the man who resists surrendering riches in 10.17–22).

Leslie Houlden

See also: Jesus, Teaching of; John, Gospel of; Kingdom of God; Luke, Gospel of, and Acts of the Apostles; Mark, Gospel of; Matthew, Gospel of

References

Dodd, C. H. 1961. *The Parables of the Kingdom*. London: Nisbet.
Drury, J. 1985. *The Parables in the Gospels*. London: SPCK.
Jeremias, J. 1963. *The Parables of Jesus*. London: SCM.
Parker, A. 1996. *Painfully Clear*. Sheffield Academic.

Jesus, Teaching of

There can be no reasonable doubt that Jesus was celebrated in his lifetime as a teacher and that afterward both this reputation and some at least of the content of his teaching were remembered, handed on, and probably developed as new needs appeared. We also see him as a preacher and a prophet, and these terms refer surely to the force of his words and to the eschatological dimension of his message. But "teacher," "teach," and "teaching" are frequent words, especially in the first three Gospels. So what does the role of teacher imply in Jesus' world? In his Jewish context, it would certainly center on devotion to the law, its meaning and application.

In a passage like Matt. 5.17–48, we see Jesus in this role, stringently and uncompromisingly so; though in Mark 12.28–34, we find what seems to be a more discriminating attitude, apparently highlighting the commands to love God and one's neighbor above the rest. Paul seems to confirm this doctrine (Rom. 13.10), and Matthew reverses it (22.34–40)—the law is one and, when it comes to observance, all is on the same footing (v. 40). We are therefore left uncertain, which is truly the voice of Jesus on this central matter. It is a warning when it comes to deciding how Jesus actually exercised his teaching role.

At the pre-A.D. 70 date, it may be anachronistic to give to Jesus the mantle of a trained rabbi, as found later. The role seems to have developed its formal identity only after Jerusalem's fall. Nor, despite some claims, was he a Pharisee, with that sect's style of devotion to the law. It is not possible, surely, to attribute everything that the Gospels allege about his assertion of a different point of view from theirs on common problems to the attitudes of the subsequent Christian communities.

So it is reasonable to suggest that Jesus' accent and style were other. F. G. Downing and J. D. Crossan especially suggest the influence of Cynic teachers, with a message for the conduct of life in the here and now; but their presence in or near Galilee in the period is not confirmed. More plausibly, the Jewish tradition of "wisdom" teaching, as found in Proverbs, Ecclesiasticus, and (closer to Jesus' time) both at Qumran and in the Wisdom of Solomon, comes forward as a model that seems to have formed much of the agenda for Jesus. Subjects such as the proper use of possessions, the favoring of the poor above the rich, the reversal of conventional ideas of precedence and power, the need for modest and prudent speech, a stress on generosity of heart and deed, a radicalizing of one's attitude to conventional moral commands—all these figure in the wisdom tradition and in the teaching of Jesus. (They also figure in the Letter of James, lending support to the view that it may owe more to the brother of Jesus than has often been supposed and that he—or the one who wrote in his name—was continuing the tradition of his messianic brother's teaching.) What is more, by this time, wisdom thought had come to embrace a concern with the future fulfillment of God's purposes, as the context of present ethics—and that is certainly the case with the teaching of Jesus.

Most of the topics just listed figure chiefly (and not always in quite the same form) in the Gospels of Matthew and Luke. They form main features of the Q material (i.e., that which these two Gospels share but do not derive from Mark). This means that the question is raised how far we can be sure that this teaching, in its actual content, goes back to Jesus himself and how far we are to suspect that it might derive (in part at least) from the ethical needs of the various early Christian churches. At the same time, all three of the synoptic Gospels agree that the center of Jesus' teaching-preaching was "the kingdom of God" and was concerned with the fulfilment of God's salvation for his people. It would be surprising if such preaching were not accompanied by a message of what Jesus believed to be appropriate conduct; surprising too if that message were not strong on the abandonment of wealth and family, a readiness to "follow" regardless of the cost, and if it did not involve a radicalizing of current morals along the lines of Matt. 5.21–48 and a reversal of "the world's" social conventions and structures.

Opinions vary, from one end of the spectrum to the other, on how far the Gospels' presentations of Jesus, including his teaching and differing somewhat (and sometimes, as we saw, strongly) from one to another, reflect Jesus himself with reasonable accuracy, and how far they represent the ways of thinking, derived from him but also differing, of the various evangelists. Sometimes their differences are plain—for example, on divorce (Mark 10.2ff.; Matt. 19.2–11), presumably a practical issue for the churches. There is no certainty what (if anything) Jesus actually taught on the subject (though Paul, in 1 Cor. 7.10, is on the side of Mark).

In any case, the form of much of Jesus' teaching is in parables, and indeed Mark holds that this was his only form of teaching (4.33–34): rather different from the books of wisdom! Are we to suppose that Jesus' teaching had a quality of imaginative appeal, rather than perhaps a "laying down of the law," a concern to win hearts for the cause of God rather than to dragoon into a standard form of obedience? It is perhaps not surprising that this latter element comes under pressure in what may be somewhat later aspects of the contents of the Gospels (e.g., the punitive slant given in Matthew to some of the parables themselves). Whatever we may wish to think, we cannot be certain where the Master's voice exactly sounds. But there is enough agreement for us to be foolish to doubt that Jesus' teaching had a radical and startling character that caused a stir at the time and has continued to disturb all the attempts of later generations to tone it down or domesticate it to human convenience. The End-time's nonappearance naturally caused the most drastic rethink. And it is not surprising (indeed, it is salvation) that the Gospel of John was able to internalize Jesus' teaching in terms of the mutual love that must be found within the Christian community itself in the present, so that the command to love one another (13.34) becomes the whole content of the book's ethical teaching. It draws the rest into itself and yet necessitates a constant process of application to the constantly shifting present. "Jesus as teacher" cannot, it seems, bear the whole burden of Christian ethics; perhaps he never has since his lifetime's ministry.

Leslie Houlden

See also: Crossan, J. D.; Jesus, Parables of; Jesus as Prophet; Law

References

Bauckham, Richard. 2001. "James and Jesus." Pp. 100–137 in *The Brother of Jesus*. Edited by B. Chilton and J. Neusner. Louisville, KY: Westminster John Knox.

Crossan, J. D. 1993. *The Historical Jesus*. 1993. San Francisco: Harper.

Houlden, J. L. 1973. *Ethics and the New Testament*. Edinburgh: T. and T. Clark.

Meier, J. P. 1994. *A Marginal Jew*. Vol. 2. New York: Doubleday.

Jesus as a Historical Figure

For the greater part of the history of Christianity, Jesus as a Historical Figure could hardly have been the title of a serious enquiry. Until the Renaissance, no one doubted that Jesus had existed, or that he belonged to the relatively distant past; and access to knowledge of such a person, as to all major events and personalities of the ancient world, was through the work of the great historians—Thucydides in the case of the Peloponnesian War, Tacitus for imperial Rome, the Gospels for Jesus. In the case of the Gospels there was the particular circumstance that these writings were inspired by the Holy Spirit and consequently (for all who believed) enjoyed exceptional authority. What they said about Jesus could be relied upon as being true. But in modern times these same Gospels have come to be regarded by scholars as biased, tendentious, and in many respects unreliable, with the result that "Jesus as a historical figure" has become the object of a "quest" for knowledge about him independent of, and more reliable than, what is offered by any of the Gospels. How has this happened? And what are the prospects for the success of the enquiry?

A radical change took place in historical studies around the later part of the seventeenth century that was by no means confined to "sacred history." The Renaissance urge to challenge received truth, epitomized by Descartes's systematic. philosophical skepticism, called into question the reliability even of the classic historians and subjected their accounts to cross-examination. The main tool of this "historical Pyrrhonism" (as the skeptical approach was called) was the rapidly growing study of ancient monuments and inscriptions, which provided an alternative source of knowledge of the past and arguably possessed an objectivity, and therefore reliability, far superior to that of any literary chronicles. In the light of these it seemed that it might be possible to establish a record of past history that would correct the philosophical or religious bias of individual historians. So began a search for the "facts" of history, lying behind and independent of all literary accounts, which continued into the nineteenth century and resulted in the short-lived claims of Lord Acton and others (notably in the *Cambridge Modern History*) to provide an authoritative, objective, and enduring account of the past.

But when subjected to this skeptical scrutiny, the New Testament was found to be a special case. The persons and events that it records left for the most part no physical traces on their environment that could be recovered by archaeologists or numismatists. The story of Jesus belonged to a culture that was singularly isolated and exclusive within the Hellenistic and Roman world, and barely aroused any attention from the classical historians. There was virtually no hard evidence outside the New Testament that could be brought to bear on the question of its reliability. The question therefore had to be examined in other terms—namely, those of the degree to which these isolated witnesses to the Gospel story could be trusted to be telling the truth. And the tools for this enquiry were not provided by antiquaries who collected physical data so much as by lawyers, whose whole profession was devoted to establishing the credibility of personal testimony. Could the Gospel writers be trusted? A miracle similar to the raising from death of the son of the widow of Nain is attributed (somewhat skeptically) by the early-third-century writer Philostratus to a traveling philosopher almost contemporary with Jesus, Apollonius of Tyana. On what grounds should we be prepared to accept the word of Luke's Gospel for such an improbable event any more than that of Philostratus? Such were the terms on which some notable debates on the veracity of the Gospel accounts of miracles were conducted at the beginning of the eighteenth century.

Skepticism could of course go further than this. The eccentric and perhaps psychopathically suspicious Jesuit Père Hardouin at the end of the seventeenth century believed that he could show (on the basis of "hard" physical evidence) virtually the whole of classical literature (as well as Dante) to be the work of a gang of Italian forgers, and his arguments were taken seriously enough to elicit a number of learned refutations. Similarly, it was possible to cast doubt on virtually any fact recorded in the Gospels, and before the end of the nineteenth century there were those who were prepared to argue that Jesus never existed at all (a thesis still occasionally defended today). But closer to the center of serious critical and theological enquiry was the question raised more generally by the new historical methods. If ancient history could be rewritten in the light of more "objective" evidence, could the same be true of the records of Jesus? Even if no independent evidence existed by which to check the Gospel accounts, could their evidence be put to the same kind of tests as would be used on living witnesses and a version of their story be arrived at that could claim to be truly "historical"? So began the successive "quests" of the "historical Jesus."

But the evidence for any such quest remained stubbornly within the covers of the New Testament. Even in modern times the possibility of checking its information against any external sources remains extremely limited. The only possible procedure is one that can best be likened to minute cross-examination. And to this the four Gospels, and the first three in particular, lay themselves open to a remarkable degree. Although in outline they tell the same story, in detail they exhibit striking differences. Many preachers, and even some scholars, have been quick to make apologetic capital out of this: independent witnesses of any series of events will always differ from one another; the fact that the Gospel writers do so surely adds to their credibility as witnesses; if they did not do so we would know that they had connived outside the courtroom, and we would be justified in doubting their evidence. But this facile explanation fails to do justice to the immensely complex relationship between them. In some cases their accounts run so closely in parallel that they have certainly connived—or rather, to replace legal by literary terms, they have either copied each other or used a common source; in other cases they diverge so sharply that they must either have had access to independent information or else be allowing themselves considerable creative freedom. To unravel this complexity it has been necessary to make certain assumptions by way of working hypotheses.

It is assumed, first, that some "conniving" must have taken place—that is, that at least one Gospel writer had access to the work of another; in that case, a decision has to be made which was written first—a competition that has been won by Mark for at least the last century and a half, though not without lingering opposition from others.

Added to this is an empirical observation that any reader can make: small items, such as sayings or episodes, occur in different contexts in different Gospels, and appear to have existed independently before they were incorporated in a continuous narrative. It may therefore be assumed that the first Gospel writer must be seen, not so much as an inspired historian, but rather as an editor doing his best (not always successfully) to make a connected sequence out of a mass of disparate material, of which the selection and transmission may well have been due, not to his own choices, but to the needs and interests of the churches that had preserved them.

These assumptions dominated critical study of the Gospels for nearly a century. But then a further procedure was introduced. By systematically comparing parallel accounts of the same sayings and episodes and noting the variations introduced by each writer, it is possible to build up a kind of profile of the personality and interests of each. Instead of dissecting the Gospels in order to study the units out of which they are composed, scholars began to read them as literary creations in their own right. As a result, the evangelists ceased to be seen as mere editors; by virtue of their sophisticated treatment of their sources and the subtle theological nuances they give to their narratives, they began to receive the highest accolade that professional students of sacred writings could give them: they were *theologians!*

The widespread adoption of these assumptions and procedures had consequences both for theologians and for Gospel criticism. Theologically, the demonstration that the Gospel writers were either fallible editors or creative "redactors" (or interpreters) made it impossible to accept their evidence at face value; in that case, what became of their credibility as allegedly inspired writers and privileged witnesses? And if that were questioned, what became of the authority that for centuries had been ascribed to Holy Scripture and on which the claims of the Christian religion rested? Would it now be necessary to find other foundations for Christian belief? Must the Christ of faith be separated from the Jesus who could be at best partially and imperfectly known from the Gospel accounts? The theological problem was apparent to Spinoza in the seventeenth century (who had the radical solution that faith must be totally divorced from "history") and has continued to exercise some of the most acute theological minds to the present day. In the light of it, many have come to regard the whole critical enterprise, not without justice, as a threat to faith, and have taken refuge in a simplistic "literal" reading of the sacred texts.

The consequence for Gospel criticism and Jesus research was perhaps more unexpected. Increasingly minute examination of the variations introduced by each evangelist to the material assumed to be available to him, combined with an immense, now computer-assisted, effort to reconstruct the hypothetical source ("Q") lying behind at least two of the synoptic Gospels, has resulted in a striking diversion of attention away from the figure of Jesus toward the personalities and interests of individual evangelists and the milieus in which the traditions they made use of may have been formed. Modern students of the Gospels may easily find that they are learning much about the "theology" of Luke or the compositional methods of Mark (or indeed about the character of the nonexistent source "Q") but very little about Jesus (whose name may barely occur in the indexes of specialist monographs). The original aim of testing the witnesses for their veracity and reliability has been largely lost from view and given place to a technical enterprise concerned, not with the recovery of a historical person, but with the critical study of documents, real or hypothetical.

On these terms, the enterprise was inevitably subject to the law of diminishing returns. The evidence available for study being almost confined to the Gospels, there is a limit to the results that can be yielded by minute scrutiny of such a small range of texts. The subject was saved from an almost obsessive preoccupation with small textual details only by the introduction of new techniques derived from sociology and literary criticism and by a shift in interpretative priorities under the impact of liberation, black and feminist theology. But these new techniques and interests, though they brought welcome refreshment to the somewhat fetid air of Gospel studies, tended only to reinforce the tendency to concentrate on the witnesses rather than on the person to whom they witness. Sociological analysis (based on a perilously narrow range of evidence), though it threw some light on Jesus' environment, had more to say about the world as it was when the Gospels were written than about conditions in Jesus' time some fifty years earlier. Literary criticism directed attention to the techniques of the writers rather than to the story they were telling. Feminism castigated the evangelists rather than Jesus for their patriarchal assumptions. Liberation and other "theologies" seized on traits in particular Gospel accounts that could be said to imply the priorities they had at heart. Even when, somewhat exceptionally, these disciplines were applied to the figure of Jesus they failed to bring any new degree of objectivity into the "quest"—witness the repeated appearance in recent Jesus-research of the sociological category of "peasant," misleadingly applied to Jesus, the son of a possibly quite prosperous artisan.

But if these studies directed to understanding written texts have yielded little to the purpose, the same is not true of more strictly historical research. We have already noted the absence of physical evidence that could provide an objective criterion by which to judge the written accounts; but the more that can be learned about the historical context and environment in which Jesus lived the greater the possibility, it might seem, of checking the plausibility (which is not of course the same as the veracity) of the Gospels. A great deal of solid historical work of this kind was done on both the Hellenistic and the Jewish environment in the nineteenth century and in the first half of the twentieth, and this work still continues. But more recently new impetus has been given by the readiness of Jewish scholars to see Jesus, not as a total renegade from, but as a significant part of, Jewish religious and cultural history. Whereas previously the genius of Jesus had often been seen by Christian scholars as consisting in his fundamental rejection and transcending of Jewish religious and cultural priorities, now it was claimed that a convincing category could be found for him *within* the Jewish environment. The Dead Sea Scrolls had demonstrated a previously unsuspected diversity in Palestinian Judaism—indeed, it was becoming fashionable to speak not of Judaism but of *Judaisms*. And in this more varied scene it seemed possible to find an already existing profile (such as "charismatic teacher") that gave historical plausibility to many aspects of the Gospel portraits of Jesus. Indeed, Jewish scholars might even go so far as to claim that, free of the inevitable anti-Jewish bias of Christian researchers, they could bring a new degree of objectivity to the search for the "historical Jesus."

These contributions from historical and Jewish studies once again brought welcome reinvigoration to mainstream Gospel criticism. But their claims to bring us closer to the Jesus "behind" the Gospels were open to a formidable objection. The more it could be shown that Jesus "fitted in" to his environment or was "characteristic" of a particular movement or tradition, the harder it became to explain why his influence has been immeasurably greater than that of any of his contemporaries. To put it another way: research into the extent to which Jesus conformed to an existing social and religious category has to be balanced by a recognition that he must also have radically departed from it or transcended it if we are to explain the rise of the Christian religion. Study of Jesus' historical environment may continue to throw new light on many details of his activity and teaching; but it cannot settle the question of the veracity and reliability of the Gospel accounts if the person they portray was both (as we are learning more and more) a man of his time and also a religious innovator unprecedented in his own culture.

It has come to be accepted by most historians that the writing of history implies an effort to enter imaginatively into the culture of a previous century. It is necessary to get inside the mind and attitudes of a historical figure, to recreate the atmosphere of the epoch, if we are to do justice to any person or event of the past. But in the case of Jesus, this is a task made particularly difficult by the conventions within which the evangelists worked.

Jesus spoke Aramaic (though possibly not exclusively), but all the records of his teaching are in Greek. Occasionally it is possible to find an Aramaic phrase that would explain an unnatural Greek expression in the Gospels, and this has encouraged a search for the *ipsissima verba* of Jesus: if these can be recovered, an important step will have been taken in the reconstruction of the "real" Jesus. Yet translation back into an ancient language is a problematic enterprise, and those who have pursued it have failed to establish an agreed gamut of Jesus' characteristic forms of self-expression; the search for *ipsissima verba* has yielded less fruit than was first hoped.

The Gospels belong to a culture that had a distinctive approach to the recording of the past. If they were to have meaning, recent events needed to be set in, and if necessary adapted to, a pattern that was set by scriptural precedent, such that ancient prophecies and declarations could now be said to have been definitively "fulfilled"—indeed, a precedent found in the ancient scriptures appears sometimes to have been regarded as a prime source of information about a quite recent event. A large number of sayings or events in the Gospels may be suspected of having been recast, or even created, in response to a precedent laid down centuries before by Scripture.

Distinctions such as we instinctively draw between myth and history, or between literal and figurative description, were largely ignored. The creation narrative in Genesis, which we would now classify as myth, runs forward through the patriarchs and eventually arrives, without any apparent change of intention or idiom, at a period of "kings" when the chronicle of events can justifiably be called "historical." There is no point at which we can say that the narrator has consciously moved from myth to history. Or again: when the Gospel writer places next to each other two sentences, one recording the moment of Jesus' death, the next reporting that the curtain of the temple was torn, the first is clearly a factual statement, the second (in the opinion of most scholars) is metaphorical. But the writer shows no consciousness of any need to indicate a change of idiom. Where a modern writer would say that "it was as if" the curtain was torn, the evangelist reports it as a fact—and who knows how often we ought to insert the words "it was as if" into the Gospel narratives if we are to understand them as the authors intended? It is amid such culturally alien ambiguities that modern interpreters of the Gospels have to attempt some imaginative identification with their subject.

In the face of such differences of culture and mind-set, some have been led to conclude that to recover substantial traces of the "real" Jesus from the culturally conditioned interpretations of him offered by the Gospels is now impossible, and that even if we could do so the resultant figure would be so alien that he could hardly be integrated into the religion of people of today. But this extreme skepticism is not shared by the majority of those who still faithfully continue to pursue a "quest." Attention is drawn to certain features of the Gospel records—such as Jesus' readiness to consort with persons regarded as disreputable, his entry into Jerusalem, even the crucifixion itself—that are so well attested that it would be unreasonable to doubt their historicity. Given our knowledge of how such events are likely to have been caused, and what their consequences are likely to have been, we can arguably build up a framework of knowledge relating to Jesus that is immune from suspicion of bias or distortion.

But at this point we have to ask a more fundamental question. What is the nature of the historical reality we are trying to reconstruct? It is one thing to assemble facts that may be beyond suspicion; but facts are not history. It is only when they are subjected to arrangement, presentation, and interpretation that they can assist us to know a person of the past. Archival material remains uninformative until it is marshaled to answer the questions that the researcher wishes to put to it. A data bank that can be stored in a computer becomes material for history only when it is used and interpreted; indeed, despite its apparent objectivity, it owes its existence to subjective decisions taken at an earlier stage regarding the selection of material and the scheme by which it is to be classified. Even if, *per impossibile*, researchers were to come up with allegedly "hard" evidence, such as a contemporary inscription recording one of Jesus' miracles, there would still be the task of evaluating its authenticity, establishing the motivation for its creation, and assessing its significance for understanding the impact made by Jesus' alleged miracles. Those who lament that the objective facts of the story of Jesus are forever concealed behind the thick veil of interpretation placed on them by the Gospels are liable to forget that (as every historian knows) there is no such thing as pure, unadorned history. A haphazard row of allegedly objective "facts" can make little contribution to a real understanding of the past. No "historical figure" can be dragged into the present by means only of uninterpreted data.

For the historian, this conclusion may be easier to accept now than in the past. We are today much more conscious than were our predecessors of the extent to which we are conditioned by our cultural environment and bring our own assumptions and prejudices into every form of human enquiry. It is true that for the theologian this continues to present acute problems. Religion likes to deal in eternal truths: how is it to relate to a continually shifting historical portrayal of one whose existence, character, and destiny are foundational for faith? But for students of the Gospels the persistent elusiveness of the historical figure of Jesus need not seem so threatening; for they may learn from historians that the goal of historical study can never be a single and enduring account of the past. Every new generation brings new assumptions, new techniques, and new questions to the study of history. To make sense of the past is not a matter of establishing a historical databank but of entering a continuing debate conducted on the basis of the best available evidence. As Sir George Clark memorably expressed the matter in his introduction to *The New Cambridge Modern History*, the aim of the historian is to assemble "a coherent body of judgments true to the facts" (p. xxxiv). A "quest of the historical Jesus" that aspired to reach total objectivity would be a dangerous delusion; but so long as it is the subject of informed and imaginative debate it can properly claim the status of serious historical research and will continue to enrich Christian understanding and faith.

A. E. Harvey

See also: Christology, Modern; Dead Sea Scrolls; Enlightenment; Feminist Theology; Hengel, Martin; Jesus in Social Context; Jewish Scholarship; Liberation Theology; Luke, Gospel of, and Acts of the Apostles; Mark, Gospel of; Matthew, Gospel of; Nonexistence Hypothesis; Schweitzer, Albert

References

Bockmuehl, Markus, ed. 2001. *The Cambridge Companion to Jesus*. Cambridge: Cambridge University Press.

Bultmann, Rudolf. 1964. "The New Testament and Mythology." In *Kerygma and Myth: A Theological Debate*. 2d ed. Edited by Hans Werner Bartsch. Translated by Reginald H. Fuller. London: SPCK.

Clark, Sir George. 1957. *The New Cambridge Modern History*. Vol. 1, *History and the Modern Historian*. Cambridge: Cambridge University Press.

Dawes, Gregory. 2001. *The Historical Jesus Question: The Challenge of History to Religious Authority*. Louisville, KY: Westminster John Knox.

Keck, Leander E. 2000. *Who Is Jesus? History in Perfect Tense*. Edinburgh: T. and T. Clark.

Sanders, E. P. 1993. *The Historical Figure of Jesus*. London: Allen Lane and Penguin.

Schweitzer, Albert. 1906, 2000. *The Quest of the Historical Jesus*. Translated by J. Bowden. London: SCM.

Stanford, Michael. 1998. *An Introduction to the Philosophy of History*. Oxford: Blackwell.

Theissen, Gerd, and Annette Merz. 1998. *The Historical Jesus: A Comprehensive Guide*. Translated by J. Bowden. London: SCM.

Vermes, Geza. 1973, 1983. *Jesus the Jew*. London: SCM.

Jesus as Emperor

To be accurate one ought to distinguish between Jesus as emperor and Jesus as king, but in common parlance the term "king" (Latin: *rex*, or Greek: *basileus*) served for both, and they are treated as one here. Right from the start the idea of a spiritual kingship of Jesus was a source of confusion. Matthew's Gospel opens with a strong claim for Christ's royal Davidic ancestry, and in John 18–19 Pilate's interrogation of Jesus turns on the allegation that his kingship represented some sort of challenge to the rule of the Roman emperor; "King of the Jews" was the charge written over his head at his execution. In spite of the fact that Christ taught his followers to "render to Caesar the things that are Caesar's" (Matt. 22.21), and Paul urged them to obey their secular authorities (Rom. 13.1–7), a sense that Christians were subversive and disloyal to their earthly lords underlay their persecution in the early centuries. One may legitimately ask to what extent the liturgical language that called Christ "Lord of lords and King of kings" (Rev. 17.14) confused the Christians themselves about the imperial character of Jesus. Saint Anthony asserted that Jesus was the only true king.

On the secular side, kingship in Christian Europe was founded on belief in its divine institution. This developed somewhat differently in the East and the West, and the results were a little different. In the Byzantine Empire rulership was continuous from the ancient Roman Empire; although the capital had been moved from Rome to Constantinople, the same civil law and the same apparatus of government remained in place. The emperor was known as Augustus, "Autokrator Romaion"—that is, the emperor of the Romans, and in court ceremonial he received quasi-divine honors. With the Christianization of the empire the emperor's rulership acquired a Christian overlay: emperors from Constantine on assumed the right to convoke the Church's ecumenical councils and took a prominent role in church ritual; from the fifth century on, the patriarch participated in the coronation, and the ceremony was moved to the cathedral. Still, the patriarch's role does not seem to have been interpreted in a constitutional sense, as if the patriarch were the source of the emperor's authority, but simply as a manifestation of his political stature.

In Western Europe, on the other hand, after the Roman Empire disintegrated in the fifth century, kings were many and the title of emperor was not employed, until in 800 Pope Leo III conferred the title on Charlemagne, the king of the Franks, in return for his alliance. Defiance of Constantinople, which was then under the rule of an empress, gave impetus to this innovation. The Carolingian concept of emperor was revived in the late tenth century by the Saxon Ottonian kings, who even called themselves expressly "Augustus, emperor of the Romans." The Pope's free authority to confer the title was clouded by the emperor's control of papal elections. The reciprocal limits of papal and royal power were better defined in the course of the Investiture Controversy of the late eleventh century, but an aura of sacredness always clung to the person of emperors and kings; royal properties and prerogatives were always termed "sacred."

In the properly religious sphere, invocations of Jesus' kingship were commonplace, from Isaiah's (9.6) "the government *[imperium]* will be upon his shoulders" in the Christmas liturgy to Palm Sunday's "Hosanna to the Son of David, Oh King of Israel." Theologians, however, insisted on the otherworldliness of this kingship, emphasizing the humility of Jesus' transport into Jerusalem on a donkey and the spiritual means of his conquests. Jesus' reign was the transcendent rule of God the Father, whose nature and attributes he shared in the Nicene creed.

How the man on the street understood this can best be judged not from written sources, since literacy was rare, but from works of art, which presented Jesus to the believer in thousands of public contexts in every city and hamlet. Entering the grand portals of the Gothic cathedral, the visitor discovered the solemn ancestors of Christ crowding in on either side. Crowns and scepters and elegant dress made their status easily recognizable, even to the revolutionary rabble of the French Revolution who mistook them for the royalty of France and attacked them with pick and axe. Mary, the Mother of Jesus, as last in the line of ancestors was also commonly shown with a crown in medieval art in the West, even though Byzantine art clung to the early Christian tradition of representing her as a Roman matron with only a veil or *maphorion* over her head.

The figure of Jesus was the climax of medieval iconography, and he commonly occupied the tympanum, or great arch, above the principal entrance of the Gothic church, as he had occupied the apse of Early Christian and Romanesque churches. The composition is imposing. Jesus is seated on an arc of heaven within a mandorla—that is, a great oval of light, and the four marvelous beasts of Ezekiel's vision (or of Revelation) fly about him. But the surprise is that this scion of Davidic ancestry wears no emblems of royalty. The common insignia of king or emperor are all missing: the crown, the *chlamys*, or military mantle (or the Byzantine *loros*, or scarf), the scepter, and the orb or globe that signified world dominion. Modern art historians have labeled this grand composition of Christ amid the four beasts the *Maiestas Domini*, or the Lord in Majesty, and they have alleged a derivation from Roman imperial iconography. But on closer inspection it becomes clear that Roman iconography had no imperial image of this sort. The oval of light that surrounds him is traceable not to imperial prototypes but to early images of the Buddha. Instead of imperial dress, Jesus wears the teacher's tunic and cloak that were assigned to him in the earliest images of the catacombs. With his right hand he makes a gesture of blessing or teaching and in his left he holds the gospel of his teaching—a book either closed or open. When open it commonly carries the inscription, "I am the way, the truth and the life" (John 14.6).

This teacher iconography is canonical for Jesus, so that even in narrative scenes of his miracles he carries the book (or scroll) of his teaching. Exceptions are few and far apart. Significantly the only images in which Jesus is commonly crowned are from the story of his Passion and Death, where the crown is the crown of thorns. The purpose must have been to distinguish very clearly the rule of Christ from any terrestrial ruler's authority. The kingship of Christ was meant to be understood as metaphorical and spiritual. The canonical iconography breaks down only at the end of the Middle Ages when indeed the medieval empires had also broken down and danger of confusion was less. At this point a new conglomerate iconography was created dressing Jesus simultaneously as emperor and high priest. The Catholic Church did not introduce a Feast of Christ the King until 1925, when Pope Pius XI felt the need to counteract the secularism and atheism of Europe in the era after the Great War. Significantly, it was at this point too that modern historians started assigning an imperial terminology to Jesus.

Thomas F. Mathews

See also: Art; Icons and the Icon Tradition; Irish Christianity; Kingdom of God; Messiah

References

Grabar, André. 1936. *L'Empereur dans l'art byzantin*. Paris: Les Belles Lettres.

Mathews, Thomas F. 1998. *The Clash of Gods: A Re-interpretation of Early Christian Art*. Princeton: Princeton University Press.

Schiller, Gertrud. 1971. *The Iconography of Christian Art*. Translated by J. Seligman. Greenwich, CT: New York Graphic Society.

Twining, Lord. 1967. *European Regalia*. London: B. T. Batsford.

Jesus as Prophet

There is nothing surprising in the fact that in the Gospels Jesus is quite often referred to as a prophet. For readers of the modern world it often seems the most natural basic term that can be applied to him, and it makes minimal theological demands or claims. He conforms to most of the ordinary expectations of the role: he utters profound thoughts and gives simple yet striking teaching; he speaks courageously and holds fast in the face of opposition that in the end brings about his death; he stands for a great cause and sticks to it; he has a passionate care for the downtrodden and attacks the well-heeled and complacent in society. All these are qualities that attract the label "prophet." And of course that fact itself, despite its wider and secular use in modern times, comes from biblical roots. The Old Testament prophets, such as Elijah, Amos, and Jeremiah, are men of that stamp, and Jesus seems to be of their lineage, as was his immediate forerunner, John the Baptist—who also suffered for his brave candor.

But, in the case of Jesus, the Gospels use the word largely as a minimal term that outsiders, observers from the touch-line, use of him, signifying that his being God's agent or spokesman is recognized (Mark 8.28; John 4.19). In the Judaism of Jesus' day, prophets were in fact more figures of the past, whose writings were read, or of the messianic future, than of the familiar present. For Jesus, the word is not false, but it is not sufficient. The "insider" has other, more specific or more far-reaching terms, such as "Messiah" (Mark 8.27–30) or "Son of God" (Mark 1.11; Matt. 14.33). Even John the Baptist was, in Jesus' eyes, yes, a prophet, but more than a prophet (Matt. 11.9). All the same, Jesus is like a prophet in, for example, being rejected (Mark 6.4; Matt. 23.37).

There is however one particular prophet whose mantle Jesus does especially wear. In Deut. 18.15, there is an assurance that a prophet like Moses will come, who must be heeded. This figure had an influence on the reception of Jesus. For example, the heavenly words at the Transfiguration (Mark 9.7), "Hear him," may echo those of the Deuteronomy text. More clearly, there are references to "that prophet" in John 1.21, 25; 6.14; 7.40: cf. Acts 3.22f.; 7.37. This ascription is virtually confined to Luke (in Acts) and John; and the suggestion is made that its naturalness relates to the links that both writers surely had with Samaritans. Both are friendly to these despised half-Jews, and perhaps both writers had been involved in evangelizing them, drawing some into the Christian fold (John 4; Acts 8). And the Samaritans, whose scriptural canon was confined to the Pentateuch, saw God's "coming One" in terms of the prophet assured in Deuteronomy 18. In this way, "prophet" takes its place among the messianic titles given to Jesus in early Christianity, at any rate for a time.

In recent times, however, especially since the Enlightenment, "prophet" has become, as was suggested above, a kind of "lowest-common-denominator" term for Jesus: we can all agree, whether we are Christians or not, that Jesus was a prophet, one who stood bravely and at cost for noble causes. Such a sense is of course some way from the biblical world. The word remains, however, to evoke Jesus as a model for Christians concerned with justice and the common good.

Leslie Houlden

See also: Jesus in Social Context; Jewish Perspective; John the Baptist; Literature, English; Messiah; Son of God

Reference

Hooker, M. D. 1997. *The Signs of a Prophet*. London: SCM.

Jesus as Servant

Among the many images for Jesus, none is so persistent in Christian history as that of "servant." Often it has vied with others more prominent, such as "king," but it has had the capacity constantly, or at any rate periodically, to revive. Perhaps this has rarely been more true than in our own day, especially in societies in which the poor dominate the social scene and where Christian power carries less weight than in other and former times. The theme raises acutely the question of Christianity's capacity to adapt to the moral demands of the situation in which it is placed. But this image is more than an example of a chameleonlike quality in the way Jesus is perceived.

However, the earliest use of such language about Jesus (in Phil. 2.6–8) was not social or ethical at all. Rather, it was theological and describes the act of incarnation: instead of holding on to his heavenly status, he "emptied himself and took the form of a slave"—that is, he became human, at the furthest pole from his previous being. It is unclear whether, in such a case, becoming human was itself in effect "slavish," on earth by contrast with in heaven, or whether it is being claimed that Jesus experienced human life at the bottom of the social heap—which may not be unambiguously true in the Galilee of his day: but it is probably the sheer contrast that is chiefly in view. True, in the context of the whole chapter, Paul uses the picture of Christ's abasement to encourage the virtue of humility (not, however, specifically slave-status), but it is almost certain that vv. 5–11, with their theological character, were originally an independent hymnic composition, summing up Christian belief.

The context is the society of the cities of the Greco-Roman world, where one is, for preference, a citizen—that is, whether rich or poor, one has legal rights and social standing. To be a slave is not necessarily to be in abject poverty at all, but it is to be without rights or claims upon the society. So Jesus' coming to the world was seen in Phil. 2 as an act of the most extreme self-loss and renunciation. The passage is then comparable to Paul's statement, working now with the image of wealth and poverty, in 2 Cor. 8.9: "[T]hough he was rich, yet for your sake he became poor, so that by his poverty you might become rich." Here again, it is a matter of our standing before God, which is seen to be transformed by Christ's mission: that was the object of the exercise.

So Jesus' self-abasement has a purpose beyond itself: the elevation or "enrichment" of his own people, perhaps of humankind. For Paul, the "enslavement" is not an end in itself. There is no hint, however, that the language of either poverty or riches is other than theological in its bearing, expressed in this imagery. That is, even though Jesus may have lived as a relatively poor man in Galilean society, that is not in Paul's mind: his coming among us is the point. The heavenly one became the earthly one—for us. The social setting of his earthly life is not of interest. Nor, in Paul's letters, is there any open criticism of the "comfortable" social status of at least some of the Christians in cities like Corinth. Such people were indeed welcome if only because they were in a position to host the meetings of the socially diverse members of the Christian communities (see 1 Cor. 11). We read Paul in vain for any serious critique of the social range in the churches, even though aspects of the behavior of the better-off, especially at the eucharistic assembly, come in for condemnation (1 Cor. 11.17ff.). The nearest we get is purely conventional exhortation to almsgiving (Rom. 12.13). Even that is rare, apart from the doctrinally motivated collection for the impoverished mother-church in Jerusalem (Gal. 2.10; Rom. 15.26–27).

It is only when we turn to the Gospels (written after Paul's death) that we find, alongside doctrinal elements, a moral or social dimension to the idea of Jesus as servant; and it is (in our terms) more moral than social—except that there are echoes of the Old Testament prophets' denunciation of wealth and the blessing of poverty as itself propitious for a disposition toward God.

Luke is the writer who chiefly highlights this way of seeing the life and teaching of Jesus. For him, Jesus is against wealth, almost in principle: it is spiritually crippling, cutting us off from God. So we find numerous passages that exhibit (in modern terms) a "bias to the poor"—a feature of today's Christian self-awareness that owes much to Luke and fosters special attention to his book. We think of: Mary's song (*Magnificat*), even before Jesus' birth; Jesus' "key-note speech" coming at the start of his ministry in Luke's order of events, where the poor are singled out to receive the saving message (4.18); the first beatitude by which the poor are to receive God's blessing and then the rich are cursed (6.20); parables such as that of the rich man and Lazarus (16.19–31); and acts of rescue that involve coming to terms with wealth (19.1–10). True, Luke does not maintain this angle in the story of the early Church's life and mission in Acts: it turns into provision for the poor within the Christian community itself (Acts 6.1; and hostility is reserved for those whose retention of wealth is an expression not just of greed but also of disloyalty to the Christian community, 4.32–5.11). In any case, there is no trace here of Jesus himself as "servant" or low in status. And this is notable, as in his Gospel Luke had shown Jesus emphasizing precisely this role at the Last Supper (22.27).

The servant role is even more plainly exemplified, again in the Supper context, in John 13, in which Jesus performs, in the face of protest, the menial task of washing the feet of his disciples. But here there is (as in Paul) a theological (rather than moral or social) motivation. He performs this act in furtherance of his being "the Word become flesh." God sent him as the prime expression of the love that is now to be the bond of the Jesus-community (John 13.15, 34).

Already in Mark (and Matthew by derivation), the point of servanthood had been made, less fully and schematically, in relation to the question of power and gradation as a consideration within the body of Jesus' followers. This factor is ruled out—firmly, for to serve, rather than to be served by others, is to mark their life. This is because "the Son of man came not to be served but to serve, and to give his life as a ransom for many" (Mark 10.35–45; 9.35; Matt. 23.5–12). Here, the term "servant" (*diakonos*), more general than "slave" (*doulos*), and signifying role rather than status, is introduced to describe the heart of Jesus' selfhood, and his death is seen as its chief manifestation: it is what he does that counts. In fact, in Mark 10.35–45, both words appear, with no apparent distinction of sense. In Mark, this is the single, but normative, statement of Jesus' role as servant. And (like "slave" in Phil. 2.5–11) its prime manifestation is in his dying. But here (in distinction from the Philippians passage), the dying has a stated purpose—to be "a ransom for many," probably to be understood as a way to freedom, a means of release. The idea is not elaborated, but, though the term "servant" does not recur, Jesus in Mark is indeed the means of release from all kinds of ills—for example, diabolical possession (1.21–28), leprosy (1.40–45), deafness (7.31–37), and blindness (8.22–26; 10.46–52). (In Mark 15.41, we learn that Jesus himself had been accompanied by women who "served" him.)

But what gave being a servant who surrendered his life a connection with such acts of release? There is, after, all no logical link between the two. To move toward an answer, we may ask how much of what we see in the Gospels about his role was in the consciousness of Jesus himself, and how much comes from his followers reflecting on his significance. The answer remains unsure; but it was not long before this significance was seen chiefly in relation to images and ideas derived from the old Scriptures—what other source could there be? "Messiah" ("Christ") was surely dominant among them, together with related terms like "Son of God," "king," "lord." All these are images of power and authority, and they chiefly relate to a status whose full manifestation is eschatological in character—that is, it will be ultimately made plain when God's kingdom or rule comes to its full realization. As things stood, Jesus was an unlikely or at any rate paradoxical candidate for such a role—in terms of the usual connotations of those terms and images. But these Old Testament images do not stand alone. So, Jesus also exemplifies the role of prophet, both generally in the character of much of his preaching and with specific reference to the coming prophet like Moses referred to in Deut. 18.15, a passage that probably comes into play in John 1.21; 6.14, and more clearly in Acts 3.22; 7.37.

None of these images accords well, however, with the fact of Jesus' humiliating death, whether it be seen as "meant" or as a cruel frustration of his true purpose. There was in early Christianity, probably in the mind of Jesus himself (assuming that he saw the likely character of his future), a need for images to give warrant to the God-given character of his suffering and death—as redemptive and the means to great and necessary good. There were scriptural passages to aid this purpose, notably the figure of a suffering prophet like Elijah or Jeremiah (cf. Matt. 16.14)—and, more immediately to our purpose, that of God's "servant" depicted in certain passages in Isa. 40–55. Since the later nineteenth century, these passages have been identified as the "Servant Songs," and so picked out from their context (42.1–4; 49.1–6; 50.4–11, which does not actually refer to the figure who is depicted as "servant"; and 52.13–53.12). It is, however, false to suppose that they were seen as a group, standing out from all else, in the time of Jesus or the early Church. All the same, these passages lent themselves to the illumination of Jesus' career in a number of ways, and words from them are quoted or alluded to in the Gospels and elsewhere (e.g., the first "Song" appears in Matt. 12.18–21, but only to point to Jesus' humility of bearing; 49.6 features in Simeon's Song, Luke 2.29–32; perhaps the rare word for "blows" in Mark 14.65 comes from its use in the Greek version of Isa. 50.6; and the fourth "Song," though never referred to as a whole, except perhaps in Acts 8.32–33, is quoted briefly in Matt. 8.17, though simply to "back" Jesus' healing activity, and, for example, in 1 Peter 2.24–25). It is natural now to see in the figure of "the servant," especially in the Fourth Song, a "gift" of a passage for the understanding of Jesus, but its use in the early decades is, as we have seen, patchy; though, despite academic controversy on the matter, it can be said that the idea of the "suffering servant" was probably beginning to be taken as illuminating the significance of Jesus' Passion. Near the end of the second century, in Irenaeus's *The Demonstration of the Apostolic Preaching*, we do at last find (in ch. 68) an exposition of a substantial part of the passage in Christological terms. As far as our subject of Jesus as "servant" is concerned, the matter is not helped by the fact that yet another Greek word is used in the Isaiah "Songs" to convey the sense: *pais*. Apart from being quoted in Matt. 12.18 and used, though without allusion to any Old Testament passage, four times in a couple of Acts speeches (3.13, 26; 4.27, 30), it is not the word employed in the New Testament to speak of Jesus in "servant" terms (the word is in fact more commonly used to mean "child," and it may indeed carry this sense in the Acts passages).

It is apparent that the image of Jesus as servant or slave covers a wide range of ideas—from pure theological statement, as in Philippians, to moral example, as in Luke 22.27, with mixed instances such as the footwashing in John 13. Predominantly, when Jesus acts in the Gospels, without the term being used, in what we might see as a servantlike way (in deeds of compassion and generosity), there is always a theological aspect: he acts thus as God's agent on the path of the kingdom, whose "bringer in" and focus he is. There is a disjunction between this picture and some modern tendencies to see "Jesus as servant" as a congenial icon for a much less theological sense of "Jesus as carer" and in relation to the Church as a "servant-Church."

The latter indeed often seems to the cynical to be an attempt (worthy, no doubt) to make something good out of the Church's loss of power in many modern societies. Down the centuries, the model of Jesus as "servant" has typically been witnessed to by particular Christians, often founders of new religious orders and movements (e.g., Francis of Assisi, Vincent de Paul, and countless others), who have given themselves, as witnesses to Christ and followers of his example, to the care of the poor and wretched. The Church as an institution has tended instead, often perforce, to act as a prosperous wielder of power and authority, following Jesus as king rather than Jesus as servant. It is the former who dominates the stained glass windows of the churches. But "servant" has from the start served as one symbol to give sense to the fact that Jesus, ruler of all, raised to God's right hand, once lived on earth in obscurity and died in ignominy, and that this is vital to the Christian perception not only of Jesus and of humanity but also of God himself. The integration of divergent images has not always been perfect: we lack icons—and prominent institutions—that really do justice to the paradox of rule-through-service.

Leslie Houlden

See also: Francis of Assisi; Irenaeus; Jesus as Emperor; Jesus as Prophet; Jesus in Social Context; Julian of Norwich; Kenoticism; Kingdom of God; Liberation Theology; Luke, Gospel of, and Acts of the Apostles; Messiah; Wealth

References

Alexander, T. D. 1998. *The Servant King*. Leicester: Publisher unknown.
Hooker, M. D. 1959. *Jesus and the Servant*. London: SPCK.
Jeremias, J., and W. Zimmerli. 1965. *The Servant of God*. London: SCM.
Juel, D. 1988. *Messianic Exegesis*. Philadelphia: Fortress.
Mathews, T. F. 1993. *The Clash of Gods*. Princeton: Princeton University Press.

Jesus in Social Context

The relationship Jesus had with his own social, political, and religious context—how it impacted on him and how he influenced it—constitutes the first and defining moment of his role in history, culture, and thought that now stretches through two thousand years. There were many dimensions to the context in which Jesus lived—all of them likely to be in play at any moment in his career but that can be separated for analytic purposes by proceeding from the general to the particular. At the most fundamental level are geography and climate, which came together in patterns of agricultural production and exploitation (especially in relations between city and country) that were typical of the Mediterranean littoral, in spite of its marked ecological and regional diversity. The next dimension is that of the distinctive nonmaterial culture of the Mediterranean lands of the first century A.D. This encompassed elements such as the dominance of kinship as the primary social domain and honor as the pivotal social value, attitudes to the human self that were group-oriented rather than individualistic—the notion that all goods existed in finite quantities, the importance of patron-client relations, and concerns with purity. These elements appear everywhere, although subject to significant local variation. The third dimension is the history of political rule in Palestine, which covers the cultural impacts on the country of foreign and indigenous powers, usually representing distinct ethnic groups, and is concerned with the processes of dominance by Hellenistic rulers (332–164 B.C.), Judean high priests and kings of the Maccabean/Hasmonaean dynasty (142–63 B.C.), and finally Rome, often through the agency of client kings (63 B.C. onward). The fourth dimension consists of the unique characteristics of Judea as a state that was centered on its capital Jerusalem (containing its magnificent temple to a God aniconically worshipped—that is, without any image or statue of a deity—and the focus of a developed literary tradition) and that had loyal subjects both in Judea itself but also in Galilee, Idumea, and other parts of the Mediterranean area but that also generated a variety of socioreligious groups. The fifth and final dimension is that of Galilee under the rule of Herod Antipas in the period 4 B.C.–A.D. 39, during which time the city of Sepphoris was refurbished and Tiberias founded, processes that placed considerable strains on the Galilean peasantry. The relationship of Jesus with each of these contextual dimensions will now be assessed, taking a broad rather than a narrow view of traditions reliably connected with him.

There are numerous ways of understanding the historical Jesus. He has been viewed, for example, as an "eschatological prophet"—someone advocating a present or imminent radical transformation of the world and human existence (J. Weiss, A. Schweitzer, E. P. Sanders, D. C. Allison, B. D. Ehrman), a "Jewish" peasant cynic (J. D. Crossan and F. G. Downing), an aphoristic sage (M. Borg), a magician (M. Smith), a Zealot sympathizer (S. G. F. Brandon), a socially radical Wisdom sage (S. Patterson), a rabbi (B. Chilton), a healer affected by altered states of consciousness (S. L. Davies), and so on. Although adjudicating among these options is beyond the scope of this essay, a consideration of the context in which Jesus lived and died does make some of them seem more plausible than others, as we will suggest at the end.

Geography, Climate, Agriculture, Urbanization

The Mediterranean Sea runs some 3,730 kilometers from the Straits of Gibraltar to Lebanon and is enclosed by three continents to the north, east, and south: Europe, Asia, and Africa. Throughout the region there occur narrow coastal plains, while further inland deep valleys separate the folds of mountains or intersperse old plateaus that survive recent periods of mountain-building. Extensive flat areas suitable for cultivation are not common (Esler). There is considerable regional and ecological variation (Horden and Purcell). In Palestine there are four principal geological features that run roughly parallel from north to south: the maritime plain, the central mountain range, the Jordan valley (running down to the Dead Sea), and the eastern range. In the north the Plain of Esdraelon connects the maritime plain with the Jordan valley.

The characteristic pattern of climate is that of winter rains and summer droughts. In summer hot and dry northeast trade winds are common, while in winter westerly winds sweep in across the sea bringing precipitation, especially when they meet mountains, such as those of Palestine. In Palestine rainfall increases dramatically as one moves from south to north, with as little as 1.2 inches of rainfall per annum falling in the desert regions of the south, compared with 44 inches in the mountains of upper Galilee. High levels of rainfall make Galilee agriculturally productive.

In the first century of our era the main food across the region was bread baked from wheat or barley, crops that were generally sown in autumn when the rains arrived and harvested in early summer. Also important were fruit, especially the ubiquitous olive, which supplied edible fruit but also oil for illumination and cooking, figs (a highly nutritious food source that ripens in late summer), grapes, and various types of vegetables. The region provided reasonable pasturage for sheep and goats, who were often tended by single shepherds in fairly remote locations, but it was not as suitable for cattle. Fish, caught in the Mediterranean itself, or in lakes (like the Sea of Galilee) and rivers, were also significant in the diet.

These basic agricultural processes and products form the context of many aspects of the Jesus tradition. Jesus explained something as fundamental to his message as the Kingdom of God in relation to the vagaries and mystery of plant growth in the Parables of the Sower, the Growing Seed, the Mustard Seed (Mark 4.3–9, 26–29, and 30–32) and the Weeds among the Wheat (Matt. 13.24–30). He was aware of men clearing the threshing floor (Matt. 3.12 and Luke 3.17) and of women milling grain (Matt. 24.41 and Luke 17.35). He cursed a fig tree that had no fruit to make a point about the power of prayer (Mark 11.12–14 and 20–24). He likened himself as shepherd to a flock that lacked one (Mark 6.34) and as a shepherd who would go off after the one sheep that was lost (Matt. 18.10–14/Luke 15.3–7). Loaves and fish were an appropriate meal for a hungry crowd (Mark 6.35–44).

Agricultural production was also central to patterns of political and economic dominance across the region. This was a society that sociologists Gerhard and Jean Lenski have termed "advanced agrarian." The use of steel-tipped plows in the production of cereal crops led to the production of surpluses beyond what a peasant family needed for its own subsistence, and in many places powerful local elites (representing as little as 2 percent of the population) arose to take control of this surplus, characteristically by basing themselves in cities and using military force to exact onerous levels of tax and tithe from the local peasantry. In the cities the elite lived a luxurious lifestyle, supported by their retainers (scribes, soldiers, and artisans), merchants, and traders who kept the system working and provided for their needs. Families easily fell into debt and were forced off their land, leaving day labor, banditry, or beggary as the main survival options available, while the elites turned their land over to the production of cash crops such as grapes, olives, or cattle. This heavily stratified pattern typified the temple states of Mesopotamia, with religious observance being used to legitimate the movement of produce from countryside to city. It had been present in the northern kingdom of Israel in the eighth century B.C. (as can be seen in the writings of Amos, Isaiah, Hosea, and Micah), and it was also represented in Judea and Galilee in the first century A.D. (below). Such a city has been described as the "consumer city," since given the primacy of agriculture and the prohibitive cost of overland transport, it tended to consume what its hinterland produced and strove for self-sufficiency. This resulted in pressures to fuse small peasant plots used for cereal-based subsistence into larger holdings, for growing crops like olives (whose oil could also be exported for cash) or for grazing, and to monetarize the local economies previously operating on a barter system (Reed, 66–68).

Under such circumstances, arenas of social life that we distinguish as economics, politics, kinship, and religion tended to be embedded in one another (Hanson and Oakman, 20–21, 69). To speak of "Judaism" solely as a religion in relation to the first century A.D. represents an anachronistic retrojection of modern understandings. It is more useful to think of a pronounced distinction existing between "political religion," the religion of the secular and priestly aristocrats controlling city and temple and embodied in cult and a "Great Tradition," the high and learned culture of the elite, and "domestic religion," which used the roles, values, and aspirations of the household in the articulation and expression of religion and was legitimated in "the Little Tradition," the low folk-culture of the nonelite, peasants especially (Redfield). In some places, including Judea and Galilee (below), the Little Tradition interacted with the Great Tradition in various ways.

Jesus frequently responded to these aspects of context. He was aware of the heavily stratified and debt-ridden nature of this world (Matt. 18.23–35), of the sight of men forced to hire themselves one day at a time (Matt. 20.1–16), of life as a daily battle to stave off hunger (Matt. 6.11 and Luke 11.3), of land pushed into cash crop production (Matt. 21.33–41), of the tensions that could arise among peasant families (Luke 15.11–16), of the vicious meanness of the rich toward the destitute among them (Luke 16.19–31) and of their instinctive lack of interest in the plight of the poor, such as widows (Luke 18.1–8), of the wickedness of tax collectors (Matt. 5.46), and even of the occasionally ambiguous relationships between the elite and their retainers (Luke 16.1–13).

Mediterranean Culture

There is a cultural gap between Jesus and people in modern Northern European and North American countries at least as great as that between such people and those who dwell in the Middle East today. Understanding Jesus in his original social and political context necessitates taking conscious steps to interpret the evidence concerning him in a manner that tries to eschew modern North Atlantic values and worldviews and that is sensitive to his ancient Mediterranean culture. The best way to do this is by utilizing insights from recent anthropological research conducted in the Mediterranean region to formulate alternative scenarios for interpreting the biblical material (Malina; Rohrbaugh). This process does not mean ignoring local variation or forgetting that these scenarios are heuristic, not nomistic, constructs (i.e., they aid us as we make our enquiry, but are not to be rigidly applied). Features of the Jesus tradition will now be briefly related to some of the key dimensions of this research.

Ancient Mediterranean persons were group-oriented rather than individualistic (which is not to deny that there were prominent individuals), and the family was the most important group; kinship was the primary social domain. The identity of people was closely linked to the family and village from which they came. Breaking away from one's origins was difficult in a setting of low social and physical mobility and caused tensions when it occurred. The inhabitants of Jesus' own village, having heard him teaching in their synagogue, asked, "Is not this the carpenter, the son of Mary and brother of James and Joses and Judas and Simon, and are not his sisters here with us?" (Mark 6.3) and took offense at him. His own family thought he was mad (Mark 3.21, 31). People were judged by the role they filled, not by the inner qualities that feature in modern methods of personal assessment in our post-Romantic and post-Freudian era. When Jesus asked his disciples, "Who do people say that I am?" (Mark 8.27), they did not reply in relation to his personal qualities or psychological characteristics but solely in terms of established personalities and social roles: John the Baptist, Elijah, one of the prophets, the Christ (Mark 8.28–30).

The primary measure by which the worth of individuals and groups was measured was honor, meaning the value they had in their own eyes and the fact that such assessment was agreed to by the local population. Honor was either ascribed, something one got just by being a person of a particular honorable family or group, or was acquired, actively gained in jousting with social competitors. The controversies that Jesus has with opponents throughout the Gospels can be appropriately analyzed as just such competitions over honor, although at times countercultural attitudes to honor emerge. Similarly, the various Passion narratives in the Gospels make much of the extent to which Jesus' tormenters sought to dishonor him, subjecting him ultimately to crucifixion, the most shameful death of all, but there is very little mention of the pain he must have suffered. The whole process was a status degradation ritual. On the other hand, the Gospels also make clear that through his resurrection Jesus experienced a process of status elevation, to the right hand of the Father, thus reversing the dishonorable status the wider society would have imputed to him because of the apparently shameful way in which he had died.

This was a culture characterized by the notion of limited good; all goods, material and immaterial, were thought to exist in finite quantities, and those who increased their store did so at the expense of someone else. This is a common outlook among peasants living in an advanced agrarian culture and constitutes a powerful disincentive to upward mobility, even though such movement occasionally happens. One way to ameliorate the effects of such a system was to enter into a relationship with someone socially superior—that is, become a client to a patron. Patronage was a relationship asymmetrical in its distribution of power in which the patron provided material benefits and the clients responded by honoring the patron and doing him (or her) services when required. Often there would be an intermediary, a broker, between patron and client when the social distance was large. The pattern of patron-broker-client is brilliantly revealed in the Old Testament in the relationship between God, Nathan the prophet, and King David (2 Sam. 11), and it crops up in the New Testament in various places, such as the story of the centurion depicted as a patron in Luke 7.2–10. It also offers a useful way of understanding the relationship between God (patron), Jesus (broker), and his followers (clients), in the Synoptic Gospels, John, and Hebrews especially.

Patterns of Political Rule and Influence

In 539 B.C. the Persian king Cyrus defeated the Babylonians, and in 538 he allowed the people from Jerusalem who had been exiled to Babylon after the Babylonian conquest of the city in 587 B.C. to return home. Later he even permitted them to begin rebuilding the Temple. Josephus tells the story in Book 11 of his *Judean Antiquities*, thereafter regularly referring to the people as *Ioudaioi* ("Judeans"), since Cyrus had sent them back to their homeland, Judea. From this time onward (at least until A.D. 70), the Judeans were an ethnic group, just like almost all others in the Mediterranean region, occupying a particular land from which they were named—a land containing in their case, however, Jerusalem as capital city with its Temple (recommissioned in 520 B.C.), in which they worshipped their one God aniconically. In 332 B.C. Alexander the Great conquered Palestine, including Judea, and for almost the next two centuries the land was under the control either of the Seleucid kings (ruling from Syrian Antioch) or the Ptolemaic kings (ruling from Egypt), the dynasties being named after two of his Macedonian generals—Seleucus and Ptolemy. This situation led to the pronounced Hellenization of the region, since Seleucid and Ptolemaic administration was conducted in Greek. The Hellenization of Palestine reached its zenith with the attempt by the Seleucid king Antiochus IV Epiphanes to crush Judean religion and to profane the Temple in 167 B.C. (1 Macc. 1). The result was rebellion, initially led by Judas Mattathias and his five sons. One of his sons, Judas Maccabaeus, took over as general on the death of Mattathias in 166 B.C., and his successes led to the rededication of the Temple in 164 B.C. The campaign lasted more than twenty years, with Jonathan, oldest son of Judas Mattathias, taking over on the death of Judas Maccabaeus in 160 B.C., and later Simon from him. The family were called Maccabees, or Hasmonaeans (from a distant ancestor). By 142 B.C. Seleucid rule in Judea was effectively over, and in that year Simon became high priest and ethnarch of the Judeans (1 Macc. 15.1). Simon was murdered in 135 B.C., and his place was taken by his son, John Hyrcanus I, who ruled to 104 B.C. and issued coinage bearing the subscription "Yehohanan the High Priest and the *Hever* ["council" or "Sanhedrin"] of the *Jehudim* ["Judeans"]." He was followed by his son Judah Aristobulus (104–103 B.C.).

Of fundamental importance to understanding Jesus in his context is the expansion by the Hasmonaeans into Galilee, which began late in the reign of John Hyrcanus and continued in that of his son Judah Aristobulus. Archaeological research at present suggests that Galilee was thinly populated after the Assyrian conquest and deportation of much of its population in the eighth century B.C., although more work needs to be done on that subject. Initial Hasmonaean control of Galilee can be seen in their erection of hill forts. Thereafter Judean colonizers from a possibly overpopulated Judea seem to have moved into the area in considerable numbers. The cultural identity of Galilean Judeans and Judea-born Judeans can be seen in their common use of the same style of stone vessels, *miqwaoth* (ritual bathing pools), secondary burial with ossuaries (i.e., of bones, once the flesh has decayed) in *kokkim* (small recesses cut in rock), and abstinence from pork, as shown by the lack of pig bones where collections of bones from consumption of domestic animals have been found (Reed).

There is no doubt that the Judeans of Galilee continued to look to Jerusalem and its Temple as the center of their national and religious life, as seen in the pilgrimages they made to the city and the tithes and respect paid to the priests of the Temple. Even by the time of Jesus in the early first century A.D. some Galilean Judeans must still have had relatives living in Judea. They would have been familiar with Judean writings, such as those containing the law of Moses, prophecy, psalms, proverbs, and so on, from their being read in local assemblies or synagogues. On the other hand, their physical separation from Judea inevitably meant the development of some distinctive traits, such as a Galilean accent of Aramaic, like that attributed to Peter (Matt. 26.73).

Hasmonaean rule over Judea and Galilee continued with Alexander Jannaeus (103–76 B.C.), Alexandra Salome (76–67 B.C.), and Aristobulus II (67–63 B.C.). The disputes of the latter with his brother, John Hyrcanus II, however, led to intervention by Pompey, who was let into the city by the Hyrcanus faction in 63 B.C. and took the Temple from the Aristobulus faction with great bloodshed a few months later. Henceforward Judea and Galilee would be under Roman control, either through the agency of client kings, such as Herod the Great, who ruled much of Palestine in the years 37–34 B.C., or his son Herod Antipas, who ruled Galilee and Perea from 4 B.C. to A.D. 39, or through direct rule under a prefect, as for most of the time from A.D. 6 to 66. Pontius Pilate was prefect from 26 to 36. Under either style of rule, Rome took tribute. Nevertheless, there were some differences. The poll tax (mentioned in Mark 12.13–17) was levied in the Roman province of Judea but not in the tetrarchy of Galilee and Perea.

Whether under Roman governors or Herodian client kings, the processes of Hellenization and Romanization proceeded apace. Apart from the common use of Greek for administrative purposes, building work undertaken by Herod the Great and, to a lesser extent, by Herod Antipas (below) was a powerful stimulus to the advance of Greek and Roman culture. Although Herod rebuilt the Temple in Jerusalem and thus facilitated Judean cultic practice (together with its economic aspects), his main project was the construction of the major new city Caesarea Maritima and its superb port Sebastos on the Palestinian coast. The city contained a significant non-Judean population and was characterized by a mixture of Greek and Roman city layout and architectural features. It was the site, for example, of a massive temple dedicated to the goddess Roma and Caesar Augustus, a theater, and an amphitheater, and it received its water from a magnificent aqueduct, parts of which survive to this day. It opened up Palestine to seaborne trade and to Greek cultural influences (possibly including the wandering ascetics called the Cynics), and facilitated payment of Roman tribute. Caesarea Maritima is a good case of a "heterogenetic city," one where novel modes of thought come into conflict with old traditions and civilizations. Herod Antipas followed his father, admittedly in a much smaller way, by rebuilding the Galilean town of Sepphoris and building a new city Tiberias, in Hellenistic style, and the effects of that work are considered below.

Judea, Its Temple and Great Tradition

For much of the first century, including the years A.D. 6–40, Judea was a Roman province ruled by a prefect who was subordinate to the governor of the more important province of Syria. The Roman administrative center was the port city of Caesarea Maritima, just mentioned. On the other hand, Jerusalem was the heart of Judea's political religion and the main site of its

Aqueduct at Caesarea Maritima (B. Matlock)

Great Tradition. The city was dominated by its Temple, controlled by the high priests. The building itself had been constructed by Herod the Great on a greatly enlarged hill (of which the still extant Western Wall is one of the Herodian retaining walls) to replace the structure erected by those who had returned from exile in the late sixth century B.C. Herod's rebuilding began in 20 B.C. and was largely completed in twenty months, although some work dragged on for another seventy years. It was one of the finest buildings of the ancient world, with superlative masonry and huge quantities of cedar, marble, and gold in its ornamentation—the latter two materials causing such blinding reflections that those journeying to the city had to avert their gaze. The principal function of the Temple was to house the cult, the daily round of sacrifice and praise by which the relationship was maintained between God and his people—a round punctuated by occasional festivals (such as Passover and Pentecost).

Jerusalem was also home for the scribes who maintained the noncultic, literary dimension of the Great Tradition of Judea, by copying manuscripts of the Mosaic law (much of it relevant to the Temple cult), of the Prophets, and of Psalms, Proverbs, and other writings, and, at times, producing new works, such as the so-called Psalms of Solomon, which were probably composed in Hebrew in Jerusalem in the second half of the first century B.C.

Scribes were also found elsewhere, in the towns and even villages of Judea and Galilee (Schams). Their role extended from drafting letters and other documents for the largely illiterate peasantry to teaching and interpreting Judean legal and religious traditions, which they no doubt defended against perceived challenges, especially since others claiming expertise in such matters posed a threat to their local status in this culture of honor and limited good. Accordingly, Gospel descriptions of scribes in conflict with Jesus over the meaning of the law of Moses or other matters (e.g., Mark 2.1–11; 3.20–29; 7.1–13) are historically credible at a general level, even if the historicity of particular confrontations needs to be carefully assessed.

Judeans in general felt strong attachment to Jerusalem and its Temple. Its festivals attracted them in their thousands from Judea itself, from Galilee and all over the Mediterranean. They gave tithes to the priests. Many of them paid the annual Temple tax. They listened to the texts of the Judean Great Tradition being read in their synagogues, even if they heard them in Aramaic or Greek translation. Good evidence exists that in the period before A.D. 70 there were synagogues in Judea (for example, in Jerusalem, Masada, and Herodium) and in Galilee (for example, in Gamla and Capernaum) and that the Judeans who gathered in them were aware of a relationship they had with the Temple and its cult—for example, in relation to the fact that the synagogues were the places for the collection and dispatch of the Temple tax (Binder). It is thus possible to view Jerusalem as an "orthogenetic city," meaning one that carries forward systematic and reflective dimensions of an old, or ancestral, culture often embodied in a Great Tradition and that has a relationship with the peasantry based on a common loyalty to a shared worldview and tradition. This type is distinguished from a "heterogenetic city," meaning one that creates novel modes of thought that have authority over or are in conflict with old civilizations and cultures—for example, Caesarea Maritima or Scythopolis with their Hellenistic culture (Freyne, 46).

Jesus seems to have had at least some positive attitudes to the Great Tradition in its cultic and literary forms, typical of other Judeans. He reportedly told a leper he had cured to show himself to a priest in accordance with the law of Moses (Mark 1.40–45). He admired the Mosaic ethical code (Mark 10.17–22). He journeyed to Jerusalem for the Passover festival and ate the Passover meal (Mark 11; 14). He was zealous for the Temple (Mark 11.15–19). At the same time, there is good evidence that he saw himself and his mission (or was seen by others) in relation to strands of Judean tradition (represented, for example, in Daniel 7–12 and Psalm of Solomon 17), commonly (but unhelpfully) referred to as "eschatological," which spoke of a coming incursion by God into the world that would radically transform it (Allison 1998).

But there was another side to the Temple. It was also the source of wealth and power for the high priests, the extent of which was revealed in N. Avigad's excavations of their magnificent houses, which were destroyed by the Romans when they took the city and burned the Temple in A.D. 70. Some of this wealth originated in the tithe they were due, but they probably also benefited from monopolistic control over the sale of sacrificial animals and money-changing for payment of the Temple tax. There is considerable evidence that the high priestly families in the first century corruptly and violently exercised their powers to maintain their position, just like elites across the Mediterranean world. The Temple was also a repository for debt records. Finally, the Romans even maintained a garrison in the Temple—in the fortress Antonia, located on the northwest corner of the temple mount. It is likely that, during the lifetime of Jesus especially, the high priests worked closely with the Romans. The long prefecture of Pontius Pilate (26–36) was almost matched by that of his predecessor, Valerius Gratus (15–26), whereas all other Roman governors in Judea in the first century lasted no more than five years. Joseph the son of Caiaphas was high priest from 18–36, a period of tenure unmatched in the period 40 B.C. to A.D. 70. In spite of occasional complaints about the insensitivity of Roman governors to Judean socioreligious feelings, the long period of coexistence, first between Caiaphas and Valerius, and then between himself and Pilate, suggests that their political and economic interests were closely aligned.

Yet there were countervailing influences to those who controlled the Temple. The literary side of the Judean Great Tradition, for example, was not monolithic, but contained a variety of views and was subject to diverse interpretation (below), thus allowing various religious and political positions to be legitimated or subverted. Psalm of Solomon 17, for example, proclaiming the coming Kingdom of God and the arrival of a messiah who would purge Jerusalem of its sinners, represented bad news for all existing authorities in the city, and they would have been very wary of anyone who seemed similar to the messiah in this text. At the same time, the Great Tradition was inevitably modified as it found its way to the nonelite who were busy generating their own Little Tradition from its resources but also on the basis of their own particular social and economic situation.

Jesus appears to have challenged current interpretations of the Mosaic law in numerous ways, which, even if acceptable in any given case, must—when considered en masse—have caused high priests and their scribal retainers to view him with grave suspicion. But he went much further than that, by articulating highly negative views of the way the Temple was being administered. He interfered with the trade in sacrificial animals and rightly claimed the place had become a den of robbers, since it was where the high priests accumulated the fruits of their exploitation (Mark 11.15–17). He probably made a prediction that he would destroy the Temple and in three days build another (Mark 14.58). His proclamation of the coming Kingdom of God could easily have been taken to mean the replacement of the rule by the Romans and the high priests and thus to constitute a threat to both. The fact that he was crucified by the Romans, probably at the urging of the high priests, showed that they took the threat with some seriousness, even if the fact that they only executed Jesus and none of his followers suggests that they did not see him as the head of a dangerous, revolutionary movement. His impact was real but limited.

Judean life of the first century A.D. also revealed other socioreligious phenomena with some bearing on Jesus. Groups developed distinct identities in relation to their attitude to the Mosaic law and the Temple (Saldarini). These groups are sometimes called "sects," but this is a word that is best used of a socioreligious group that has broken way from another group so that joint membership is no longer possible. "Reform movements" or "factions" is more appropriate nomenclature.

Thus the Pharisees were a group who ascribed authority to a body of oral tradition in addition to the Mosaic law, much of it related to a heightened concern with purity. They also believed in resurrection. The use of "reform movement" seems appropriate to them, although Saldarini (1989) is correct in seeking to set them with the larger social system of Judea and Galilee as retainers to the elite. There seems a strong likelihood that the independent and innovative attitude to the Mosaic law exhibited by Jesus brought him into conflict with them.

The Sadducees are appropriately seen as a faction within the Judean socioreligious system, certainly embracing some members of the priestly and nonpriestly elite. They rejected oral additions to the Mosaic law (which they had a reputation for strictly enforcing) and did not believe in the resurrection.

The Essenes were a movement that encompassed a strict (indeed sectarian) wing living at Qumran, overlooking the Dead Sea and quite isolated from the Jerusalem cult, and a less extreme wing that lived throughout the towns and villages of Judea and had some continuing connection with the Temple. Documents characteristic of the group, as well as biblical and extrabiblical Judean literature, were discovered in eleven caves near Qumran in the 1940s and 1950s (Vanderkam). The documents belonging to the group reveal an identity built on a perfectionist seclusion from Judean life and a belief that they were living in the beginning of the final days, as allegedly predicted in biblical prophecies. Efforts to prove any direct link between Jesus or his followers and the sectarians of Qumran have proved unsuccessful, although their common Judean traditions and broad sociopolitical context occasionally produce similarities of language or outlook.

Galilee

Although his exact dates are uncertain, we can be fairly confident that Jesus lived and died during the time when Herod Antipas was tetrarch of Galilee and Perea (4 B.C. to A.D. 39). The context for his activity was the advanced agrarian lifestyle (described above), by which peasants labored to provide a subsistence for their families while paying taxes to the local elite, in this case Herod Antipas and, ultimately, to Rome. Much of the population lived in very modest villages, going out to work the fields during the day. These villages were humble affairs, characterized by the Judean material culture mentioned above, with low levels of literacy and virtually no penetration by Hellenism. In Jesus' time Nazareth, his own village, had a population of only about 400, and Caphernaum, the larger fishing village that he made his base, about 1,700 (Reed). Herod Antipas began to rebuild Sepphoris in 4 B.C., upon his accession. The town was only four miles from Nazareth. By the 30s it probably had a population of 8,000 to 12,000 (ibid.). The famous theater excavated there was probably built in the second half of the century, after Jesus' time. Much later, in A.D. 19, Herod Antipas founded Tiberias on the Sea of Galilee. When built, it probably had a population similar to that of Sepphoris. Like his father, he aimed to build a city and a port in Greek and Roman style named in honor of the reigning emperor, by this time Tiberius.

Many scholars (for example, Sean Freyne, Jonathan Reed, and William Arnal) have pointed out that the rebuilding of Sepphoris and the foundation of Tiberias would have imposed considerable strains on the Galilean peasantry. They must have been the source of most of the resources required, and the work carried out would have allowed Herod Antipas and his retainers to tax them more effectively. Under such circumstances we would expect many peasants to be forced off their land, to become day laborers, beggars, or even bandits. In addition, the Galilean economy was more consistently monetarized in the wake of these projects, and peasants are always at greater risk of being exploited when they must move from a barter to a cash economy (Hanson and Oakman, 120–25). Local village scribes may even have been displaced by Herodian retainers (Arnal). In a very conservative peasant culture, traditional modes of production and exchange were being transformed and old lifestyles were being disrupted. Sepphoris and Tiberias constitute two further examples of the "heterogenetic city," one in which novel modes of thought come into conflict with old civilizations.

Much Jesus material makes good sense in such a context (Herzog; Hanson and Oakman). Many signs of distress, some stemming from the basic harshness of peasant subsistence agriculture but others also attributable to the Herodian reorganization of Galilee, are visible, even if some of the passages in question have been domesticated in the Gospel tradition. Although Jesus is frequently described as entering Galilean villages, he never goes into Sepphoris or Tiberias, probably because he opposed the political and economic domination they represented. Such feelings were reciprocated by the

"Herodians," the elite and their retainers who were allied with Herod Antipas and maintained his rule, since they reportedly plotted against him (Mark 3.6), while Herod himself also had John the Baptist executed. Hunger was a common experience, so some people can go to bed with literally nothing in their house left to eat (Luke 11.5–6), and Jesus can advocate a prayer with the words of literal and not metaphorical import: "Give us each day our daily bread" (Luke 11.3). Tax collectors take more than they ought (Luke 19.1–10). Wealthy men are turning land suitable for subsistence agriculture into cash crop production, such as vineyards (Matt. 21.33–44), and there is a population of men needing day labor in such work (Matt. 20.1–16). Money is in circulation, and the elite expect it to be used productively (Matt. 25.14–30). Debts can be owed in money and are likely to be ruthlessly enforced (Matt. 18.23–35). Jesus links divine forgiveness to human willingness to forgive debts (Luke 11.4).

His preaching of the Kingdom of God, which was firmly rooted in Mediterranean, Judean, and Galilean contexts (Malina; Theissen), provided a promise of relief to this kind of distress, while also connecting with End-time and messianic traditions of the Judean Great Tradition mentioned above. At the same time, while he and his followers may have been aware of Cynic ideas and practices, even to the extent of their providing useful models for certain countercultural attitudes and behavior, it is unhelpful to construe Jesus too much in Cynic terms given that this would push him in the direction of values possibly to be found in Sepphoris and Tiberias but probably quite alien to the humble and largely illiterate villages of Galilee.

Jesus in Context

To understand Jesus in his context, then, means assessing his words and actions in relation to the complex social and religious realities of both Hellenized and Romanized Judea and Galilee. He shows clear connections with the plight of the peasantry in Herodian Galilee yet also relates closely to the Great Tradition of Judea, traveling ultimately to its capital and Temple, and to his death. Both dimensions to his career must be kept together. His attitude and behavior set him at odds with Herodians, with the scribal interpreters of Judean law, with the Jerusalem high priests, and with the Roman prefect.

The extent to which he envisaged a coming transformation of the world (Allison) was based on his own experience in Galilee, yet also drew upon the resources provided by Judean eschatological and messianic expectations as seen in works like Dan. 7–12 and Psalms of Solomon 17. Explanations that construe him as a Cynic or an aphoristic sage of some sort, or as a healer or a magician, seem to underplay this combination at the heart of his message of Galilean social criticism and a critique of Judean traditions that ultimately led to his being killed. Only this sort of explanation, as A. Schweitzer pointed out a century ago, leaves us with a Jesus sufficiently strange to his own time *and to ours* as to fit the evidence we have of him.

Soon after his crucifixion, however, the movement started by Jesus underwent a major transformation, as its missionaries moved out of Judea and into other parts of the Mediterranean world, reaching out to Greeks and Romans as well as Judeans. Ironically, this meant that the context in which Christianity laid the foundations for its growth in the first century—for example, producing works as central to its identity as the letters of Paul and the Gospel tellings of Jesus' life—by and large lay outside the Galilean and Judean settings of the life, ministry, and death of Jesus with which we have been concerned here. It is the realities of Greco-Roman life and culture in the first century A.D. (and beyond) that constitute the primary context for understanding Christianity after Jesus.

Philip F. Esler

See also: Borg, J. M.; Crossan, J. D.; Dead Sea Scrolls; Jesus, Parables of; Jesus as a Historical Figure; John the Baptist; Josephus; Kingdom of God; Resurrection; Sanders, E. P.; Schweitzer, Albert

References

Allison, Dale C. 1998. *Jesus of Nazareth: Millenarian Prophet*. Minneapolis: Fortress.

Arnal, William E. 2001. *Jesus and the Village Scribes: Galilean Conflicts and the Setting of Q*. Minneapolis: Fortress.

Binder, Donald D. 1999. *Into the Temple Courts: The Place of the Synagogues in the Second Temple Period*. SBL Diss. Series 169. Atlanta: Society of Biblical Literature.

Esler, Philip F. 2000. "The Mediterranean Context of Early Christianity." Pp. 3–25 in *The Early Christian World*. Edited by Philip F. Esler. London and New York: Routledge.

Freyne, Sean. 2000. *Galilee and Gospel*. Wissenschaftliche Untersuchungen zum Neuen Testament 125. Tübingen: Mohr Siebeck.

Hanson, K. C., and Douglas E. Oakman. 1998. *Palestine in the Time of Jesus: Social Structures and Social Conflicts*. Minneapolis: Fortress.

Herzog, William, II. 1994. *Parables as Subversive Speech: Jesus as Pedagogue of the Oppressed*. Atlanta: Westminster John Knox.

Horden, Peregrine, and Nicholas Purcell. 2000. *The Corrupting Sea: A Study of Mediterranean History*. Oxford: Blackwell.

Malina, Bruce J. 2001a. *The New Testament World: Insights from Cultural Anthropology*. 3d ed. Louisville, KY: Westminster John Knox.

———. 2001b. *The Social Gospel of Jesus: The Kingdom of God in Mediterranean Perspective*. Minneapolis: Fortress.

Redfield, R. 1956. *Peasant Society and Culture*. Chicago: University of Chicago Press.

Reed, Jonathan L. 2000. *Archaeology and the Galilean Jesus: A Re-examination of the Evidence*. Harrisburg, PA.: Trinity.

Rohrbaugh, Richard L., ed. 1996. *The Social Sciences and New Testament Interpretation*. Peabody, MA: Hendrickson.

Saldarini, Anthony J. 1989. *Pharisees, Scribes and Sadducees in Palestinian Society: A Sociological Approach*. Wilmington, DE: Michael Glazier.

Sanders, E. P. 1985. *Jesus and Judaism*. London: SCM.

Schams, Christine. 1998. *Jewish Scribes in the Second-Temple Period*. JSOT Supp. Series 291. Sheffield: Sheffield Academic.

Theissen, Gerd. 1991. *The Gospels in Context: Social and Political History in the Synoptic Tradition*. Minneapolis: Fortress.

Vanderkam, James C. 1994. *The Dead Sea Scrolls Today*. Grand Rapids, MI: William B. Eerdmans.

Jesus Letters

The canonical Christian Scriptures never claim Jesus as a writer, yet several extant documents purport to be letters by him; but if most Christians today, and many in the past, reject these as apocryphal pseudepigraphs, they have been accepted by others as genuine, influencing both perceptions of Jesus and Christian practice. Moreover, even when their authorial claims were rejected, the notion that Jesus continues to send detailed instructions by miraculous means has been widely accepted.

Two instances of this phenomenon stand out:

The Letter of Jesus to Abgar

The story of this letter's origins and text are found in Eusebius's *History* I.xiii (and see II.i.6–8). It claims to be a petition to Jesus sent in A.D. 28/29 by King Abgar V Ukkama (reign A.D. 9–46) of Edessa (now Sanliurfa, Turkey) acknowledging Jesus as Son of God and a great healer, asking for healing for himself and offering Jesus a refuge from the Jews. Jesus replies that his mission precludes traveling there, but, because of the king's faith, he will send a disciple after his Ascension to heal the king. That disciple duly went and healed the king, and the letters and account were placed in the city archive.

The letter probably originated in Edessa (Christianity is first recorded there during the reign of Abgar IX, A.D. 179–214) shortly before Eusebius wrote (c. 313) to show that the orthodox party were the city's original Christians. The legend's fame spread rapidly, so that it was known in Spain by the 380s, where it was believed that a copy of the letter held in Jerusalem had healing powers. By the early fifth century its fame was such that both Jerome and Augustine felt the need to note that Jesus had not left writings, while by the sixth century a Roman list of accepted and rejected writings (the *Decretum Gelasianum*) rejected it as apocryphal. Despite such doubts, vernacular copies survive from across Christendom. Its fame as a healing talisman and a protection for travelers became a part of popular belief, while the authority of Eusebius ensured it retained some credibility for scholars.

The Letter of Jesus Regarding Sunday

The Abgar letter's fame inspired imitations, most famously the *Carta Dominica* (sometimes called *Epistola Iesu*), on observing Sunday as "the Sabbath." It originated in Latin prior to 602 probably in Spain and was widespread in Western Europe within a century; its survival in many vernaculars testifies to its popularity. Its claim is that Jesus wrote the letter and then dropped it from heaven to land on the altar of the cathedral in Rome, Jerusalem, or Bethlehem (different variants of the story), to express his dismay at the way that Sunday was not being observed. The letter equates Sunday with the Sabbath and thus wishes to transfer to it—something Christians had not done previously—the prescriptions on work and travel found in Lev. 17–26. If these rules were broken, then Jesus who "punishes evil" threatens his judgment of lightning and disease upon the transgressors. The letter arose at a time when Christians were searching their Old Testament to provide sources for law while failing to notice that their Sunday was in origin a deliberate departure from the Sabbath, and in the process they altered their image of Jesus (a healer in the Abgar letter) to that of a law-enforcer and a constantly observing judge who required his law to be fulfilled in explicit detail. The *Carta* was used widely in preaching, and later Christian views of Sunday as "the Christian Sabbath" owe much to its influence on popular culture.

Although messages from Jesus have always attracted criticism from bishops, councils, and theologians, they often gain an indirect authority in that they later appear to fit so well with the popular sentiments they help generate or reflect: for example, Margaret Mary Alacoque (1647–1690) received messages from Jesus about his "Sacred Heart" that she passed on to others. These fed the developing cult, and eventually became semiofficial teaching in the Roman Catholic Church in that they have been widely used in sermons and devotional images, while the recipient was eventually canonized a saint (1920). Moreover, they have had great influence on popular perceptions of Jesus and the religious observance demanded from his followers.

Thomas O'Loughlin

See also: Hebrew Bible; Jesus, Teaching of; Paul; Roman Catholicism

References

Hennecke, Edgar, and Wilhelm Schneemelcher. 1963. *New Testament Apocrypha*. Vol. 1. London: SCM.

O'Loughlin, Thomas. 1990. "The Significance of Sunday: Three Ninth-Century Catecheses." *Worship* 64: 533–544.

Williamson, G. A. 1965. *Eusebius*. London: Penguin.

Jesus Seminar

The Jesus Seminar is a colloquy of mostly American scholars whose work aroused an uprecedented interest in the historical person of Jesus in the last decade of the twentieth century. In European circles, their studies were often dismissed or ignored, but in the United States they dominated discussions about the historical figure of Jesus for more than a decade. The group challenged the authenticity of the bulk of the New Testament Gospels, deeming most of what the Bible reports about Jesus as "historically unauthentic." Several Seminar members (including Marcus Borg, John Dominic Crossan, and Robert Funk) produced independent studies of Jesus that try to build on the Seminar's work.

The Jesus Seminar was founded in 1985 by Funk and is officially sponsored by the Westar Institute, which Funk directs. The Seminar is an ecumenical group of scholars, all of whom possess earned doctorates and recognized credentials for conducting historical research. The group has striven for theological neutrality, maintaining that all decisions are to be made on the basis of historical evidence alone, putting aside the influence of religious faith. Over two hundred scholars have been involved with the group at one time or another, though their published membership was seventy-four in 1993 and seventy-nine in 1998. Most of the work has been conducted at biannual conferences that have typically been attended by thirty to forty persons.

The foundational goal of the Jesus Seminar was to assess the historical authenticity of every tradition regarding Jesus from the first three centuries. A novel aspect of the group was that the scholars actually voted on whether they believed particular traditions were authentic. A color scheme was devised for conveying the results of these votes: every tradition was labeled red, pink, gray, or black in accord with the degree of authenticity accorded it, red being most authentic and black, least.

The bulk of the Seminar's work took place in two phases. In Phase One, the group devised an index of everything Jesus is ever reported to have said in any document prior to A.D. 313. Over a seven-year period, the group met to debate the authenticity of these sayings and to record their ultimate votes. The results tended to be negative, fueling sensational newspaper headlines such as "Bible Scholars Determine Jesus Did Not Teach the Lord's Prayer." When the group completed its survey of the "sayings" material, it published its results in a book called *The Five Gospels*, so-named because the four canonical Gospels and the apocryphal Gospel of Thomas had been the only writings found to contain any red or pink sayings. The Gospel of John just barely made the cut, with no red and only one pink saying (John 4.44). Likewise, Mark had only one red saying (Mark 2.17), though eighteen qualified as "possibly authentic" pink traditions. Analysts noted that the bulk of the sayings that were deemed authentic came from the material common to Matthew and Luke that is usually ascribed to the Q source. Most of the authentic sayings are of an ethical or proverbial nature, presenting Jesus as a moral teacher who draws upon the wisdom traditions of Jewish sages and Greek philosophers. Sayings in which Jesus speaks of the end times or identifies his own significance were invariably found unauthentic.

The second phase of the Jesus Seminar's work involved a similar study of deeds attributed to Jesus. *The Acts of Jesus* revealed that all actions involving "supernatural" occurrences were deemed unauthentic (nature miracles, the Virgin Birth, the bodily resurrection), though it was granted that Jesus cured some sick people and exorcized people of what were thought to be demons. His practice of eating with social outcasts, his Galilean ministry proclaiming an egalitarian (but present-day) "kingdom of God," and his death by crucifixion were also deemed to be authentic aspects of the tradition. The Jesus Seminar itself did not produce a sustained biography of Jesus, but Robert Funk would include a description of Jesus based on the Seminar's findings in his book *Honest to Jesus*.

The Seminar had a penchant for communicating its work through popular media and proved adept at bringing the results of "ivory tower scholarship" into the homes of average men and women. Every major newsmagazine in America did at least one cover story on the Jesus Seminar at some point during the nineties, and members of the group were prominently featured on popular television talk shows. Because of its high profile and controversial findings, the Jesus Seminar often became the target of polemical attacks by conservative scholars and various church groups.

Critique of the Seminar's work focused on a number of points. Methodologically, the question was raised as to whether individual traditions can be legitimately evaluated in piecemeal fashion apart from an overall hypothesis.

The Seminar's supposed neutrality was also challenged, insofar as "lack of commitment to a faith perspective" can be construed as constituting an ideological orientation in its own right. In terms of analysis of the group's findings, it was often alleged that the large body of material deemed "gray" should not be labeled "probably unauthentic" (the Seminar's own interpretation) but should be regarded as controversial material on which the Seminar remained divided (pink and black votes would often "average out" to produce a final gray result). Finally, there appears to have been some discrepancy among the scholars involved as to whether a negative vote meant "This did not happen" or merely "This is not historically verifiable."

Mark A. Powell

See also: Borg, J. M.; Crossan, J. D.; Funk, Robert; Jesus, Miracles of; Jesus, Parables of; John, Gospel of; Kingdom of God; Luke, Gospel of, and Acts of the Apostles; Mark, Gospel of; Matthew, Gospel of; Resurrection; Thomas, Gospel of

References

Funk, Robert W. 1996. *Honest to Jesus: Jesus for a New Millennium*. San Francisco: HarperSanFrancisco.

Funk, Robert W., Roy W. Hoover, and the Jesus Seminar. 1993. *The Five Gospels: The Search for the Authentic Words of Jesus*. New York: Macmillan.

Funk, Robert W., and the Jesus Seminar. 1998. *The Acts of Jesus: The Search for the Authentic Deeds of Jesus*. San Francisco: HarperSanFrancisco.

Miller, Robert J. 1999. *The Jesus Seminar and Its Critics*. Sonoma, CA: Polebridge.

Jewish Perspective

One of the certain facts about Jesus is that he was a Jew. He was a child of Jewish parents, brought up in a Jewish home, and reared among Jewish traditions. Throughout his life, Jesus lived among Jews and his early followers were Jews.

No other Jew in history has rivaled Jesus in the exalted magnitude of his influence. The words and deeds of Jesus the Jew have been, and are, an inspiration to countless millions of men and women. His death marked a turning point in the history of the world. In his name a great religion was founded and Christians have gone forth carrying his message to the remotest corners of the earth.

Strange, is it not, that Jews have given little attention to the life and teaching of this outstanding Jew. Yet this is true. For almost two thousand years, Jesus has been ignored by the Jews. Because the Christian followers of Jesus came to cherish beliefs about his life and personality that no Jew could hold, Jesus was taken right out of the realm of the Jewish tradition. When the Church persecuted Jews in an effort to convert them, the Jews' indifference to Jesus turned to hostility. It is a sad fact of history that the followers of this great Jew have brought much suffering upon the Jewish people, so that for centuries it was very hard for any Jew even to think of Jesus without difficulty. Up until very recently, most Jews have chosen not to think of him at all.

For example, in the rabbinic Jewish writings there are very few statements that refer to Jesus, and those that exist are confused and conflicting.

Their depiction of Jesus adds nothing to our knowledge about the historical Jesus but tells us something about early arguments with the Jewish-Christians. References to and stories about Jesus and the Gospel traditions indicate from the Jewish perspective the bitterness that was developing between the two communities in the early centuries of the Common Era.

Accusations against Jesus included the charge that he knew magical spells and possessed magical powers. Jesus is described as having learned his magical craft in Egypt, from where he brought these spells on his flesh—in other words, through tattoos. Egypt was well known in ancient times as a place of magic, and it is possible that the rabbis were aware of the Matthean tradition, which describes how Jesus, as a baby, was taken from Bethlehem to Egypt to avoid being killed by Herod (2.13–14).

Perhaps the most important charge against Jesus was that he had "deceived Israel" because Christianity had not only resulted in some Jews "going astray" (in other words, being converted) but also, as Christianity became more powerful, it came to threaten the very existence of Judaism. Overall, the rabbinic writings have preserved only a very vague and confused recollection of Jesus, and although his name was held as that of a dangerous heretic and deceiver, extremely little was known of him.

In more recent times there has been a dramatic change. Jewish as well as Christian scholars have come to study the teaching of Jesus and have striven to appreciate the nobility of his life. A re-evaluation has gradually taken place, and although the hostility of centuries cannot be eliminated in the twinkling of an eye—and the traditional Jewish attitude of indifference to Jesus, to all that he was and all that he taught, has not by any means disappeared—the signs are encouraging.

Christian scholars also, who have studied the Jewish background of the life of Jesus, have come to admire the true greatness of Judaism and have ceased to affront the Jew with the oft-repeated slander that Judaism is nothing but a mere set of empty formalistic rules. Christians have begun to realize the immense debt Christianity owes to Judaism and to the Jews.

Unlike some of his contemporaries, such as Philip and Andrew, Jesus bore a Jewish name: Yeshua. Family names indicate a strong commitment to Judaism, and it is worth pointing out the names of Jesus' brothers: James (Jacob), Joseph (Joses), Judas or Jude (Judah), Simon, and his father, Joseph and mother, Mary (Miriam).

Jesus and his family would have been observant of Torah, paid tithes, kept the Sabbath, circumcised their males, attended the synagogue, observed relevant purity laws concerning foods, upheld days of purification in relation to childbirth and menstruation, kept the dietary code—one could go on to all the other elements of the Torah that applied to daily life. Although the Christian Gospels record disputes about Jesus' interpretation of a few of these, the notion of a Christian Jesus, who did not live by Torah or only by its ethical values, does not fit historical realities. Jesus was a Jew.

There is no official Jewish view of Jesus, nor is there any view that is generally held by Jews. In one respect, however, but one respect only, it can be said that all Jews are agreed in their attitude toward Jesus. Every Jew who is faithful to Jewish teaching has to reject the tremendous claim that is made for Jesus by his Christian followers—that Jesus is the Lord Christ, God Incarnate, the very Son of God the Father. Moreover, it is almost impossible for a Jew to believe that Jesus, having been brought up amid Jewish traditions, could ever have claimed to be God Incarnate. Such a claim would have been in fundamental conflict with the profoundest teaching of the Judaism of his time as it is in conflict with the fundamental teachings of Judaism today—that the One God, Creator and Ruler of the whole Universe, is a Being invisible and unique, whose nature is incomparable in perfection and power, in goodness and love, in majesty and excellence. Indeed, when the rich man called Jesus good he replies: "[W]hy do you call me good? None is good save one, that is God" (Mark 10.18).

Nevertheless, although the belief was expounded with great subtlety, Christians believe that Jesus was, and knew himself to be, God Incarnate. On that belief, Jews and Christians must continue to respectfully differ. Jews believe that all share the divine spirit and are stamped with the divine image but no person—not even the greatest of all people—can possess the perfection of God, the splendor of the divine excellence, the fullness of God's glory. No one can be God's equal.

The belief that Jesus was God is an impossibility for Jewish thought. But not so the belief that Jesus claimed to be the messiah. Several Jews have in the course of 2000 years claimed to be the messiah—sent by God to inaugurate God's kingdom on earth. Simon Bar Kochba in A.D. 132 and Shabbetai Zvi in A.D. 1665 were two among many who claimed such a position, though none have been endorsed by Judaism at large.

Jesus was put to death by the Romans on the charge that he claimed to be the messiah, and it was a charge that, at least, he did not deny. According to Mark, Jesus made it clear to Peter that he regarded himself as the messiah (8.29) and asserted before the high priest that he was the messiah (14.62). Some of the Jews of his time undoubtedly accepted Jesus to be the messiah, believing that he would redeem them from the bitter yoke of Rome and would, after a time of judgment, bring in the messianic age. According to Mark 11.10, when Jesus rode into Jerusalem he was acclaimed by the crowds, "blessed is the kingdom that comes, the kingdom of our father David." Other Jews certainly rejected the claim.

The charge against Jesus on the Cross and his mockery as "King of the Jews," his execution between two brigands, the tradition about swapping Jesus for the brigand, Barabbas, the appearance of the royal messianic motifs—these all suggest that Pilate faced a man charged with sedition in general terms. Jesus was not crucified because he denied his Jewishness, abandoned the Scriptures, or disowned his people. He remained a Jew, Jesus of Nazareth, the Jew from Galilee, and was executed for what we should see as political rather than religious reasons.

To claim to be the messiah, if it was an offense against Judaism at all, was certainly not (as the Gospels contend) an offense against Jewish law for which Jesus could have been put to death. The Gospels say that Jesus' claim to be the messiah was blasphemy, but in Jewish law, blasphemy was to revile and curse God using God's sacred name. Jesus did nothing of the sort. There were others who claimed to be a messiah, and Josephus mentions some of them. But they were not tried by a Jewish court nor sought out by any Jewish authority. The religious rulers were not disturbed by them; but the political rulers were. The Romans sought out and executed these "messiahs" as rebels or potential rebels. The Romans had reason to fear anyone who was, or might be, looked at as the Christ (= Messiah). To the Jews of Jesus' time, "Christ" referred to the king of the Jews who would deliver them from Rome.

For Jews, history has proved that Jesus was not the long-awaited messiah, for Jesus did not deliver them from the yoke of Roman bondage and the Golden Age most certainly did not come. However, some Jews have suggested that Jesus was following in the footsteps of the biblical prophets. We know that some of his followers viewed him as a prophet (e.g., Mark 6.15; Matt 21.11 during his entry to Jerusalem).

"What commandment is the first of all?" he was asked. Jesus answered as any good Jew would have answered: "[T]he first is: Hear O Israel the Lord our God, the Lord is One. And you shall love the Lord your God with all your heart, with all your soul and with all your might. The second is this: You shall love your neighbour as yourself. There is no other commandment greater than these" (Mark 12.28–31).

Every Jew will recognize in Jesus' answer the Shema, a Jewish declaration of faith that is recited at every Jewish service, day and night. The famous command of Lev. 19.18 is also a fundamental precept of Judaism. This illustrates the view that Jesus cannot be viewed outside his Jewish context. The same Jewishness might be claimed for the New Testament as a whole, which, it might be argued, is part of Jewish literature.

It was in his attitude toward the Torah that Jesus seems to have departed from the Judaism of his time. In all their teaching, the rabbis would state: "[T]hus says the Torah." Jesus showed striking originality and amazing independence by standing above the Torah and speaking as one "having authority" (Mark 1.22). He dared to base his teachings on "I say to you," rather than on "thus says the Torah." It was this courage and daring that brought him into conflict with contemporary Judaism.

However, it is highly improbable that Jesus told his followers to ignore the Torah altogether (Matt. 5.17), but rather more probably he emphasized that "the kingdom of God is within you" (Luke 17.21)—that is, follow the deepest instinct for truth and love in your heart, for therein, not through obedience to the law, lies salvation. This was a courageous message, one that made some Jews unbounded in their devotion to him and others to regard him as a heretic.

The death of Jesus cannot have for the Jew the same significance as for the Christian. For the Christian the death of Jesus is the supreme example of self-sacrifice: the willing sacrifice of his life by the Son of God that the world might be redeemed from sin. For the Jew, the significance of Jesus must be in his life rather than his death. It was a life of exalted faith in God, a life filled with nobility of thought and teaching, magnificent in its courage and tremendous in its grandeur. His was a personality that expressed itself in simple yet moving deeds of goodness. He was a great Jew who knew that he was always in the presence of God and who defied great suffering.

For the Jew, Jesus can never be what he is to Christian hearts. For Jews, not Jesus but God alone is the Divine Master. Yet an increasing number of Jews are proud that Jesus was reared in the Jewish tradition; that indeed he was born, lived, and died a Jew.

Edward Kessler

See also: Interfaith Thought and Relations; Jesus, Death of; Jesus as Prophet; Jesus in Social Context; Jewish Scholarship; John, Gospel of; Josephus; Kingdom of God; Matthew, Gospel of; Messiah; Paul; Vermes, Geza

References

Flusser, D. 1997. *Jesus*. Jerusalem: Magnes.
Sandmel, S. 1965. *We Jews and Jesu*. New York: Oxford University Press.
Zannoni, A. E., ed. 1994. *Jews and Christians Speak of Jesus*. Minneapolis: Fortress.

Jewish Scholarship

In recent times, Jews have begun to read the New Testament in a more positive light. There is of course no reason intrinsic to their faith why they should do so, since it is not sacred scripture for them. Indeed, there is every reason why they should ignore it, since it has been used to justify, and may even be the source of, anti-Semitic actions by Christians. Yet an increasing number of Jewish scholars have turned their attention to studies of Jesus. The pioneers in this field in the early twentieth century include Abraham Geiger, Joseph Klausner, and Claude Montefiore. In more recent years, the most significant studies have been produced by Geza Vermes and David Flusser.

Abraham Geiger, leader of German Reform Judaism in Germany in the nineteenth century, dealt with Jesus in several large sections of his *Judaism and Its History* (1866). He concluded that Jesus was a Pharisee, who walked in the ways of Hillel (the foremost teacher in Palestine in the first century B.C.) but expressed no new ideas. According to Susannah Heschel's biography (*Abraham Geiger and the Jewish Jesus*, 1998), Geiger wanted to find the place of Jesus in Jewish history. Judaism could therefore claim Jesus as one of its own, a Pharisee who lost his bearings. But what Jesus did himself was not nearly as pernicious, Geiger says, as what his followers did with their understanding of Jesus. Many of the themes that have emerged repeatedly in modern Jewish-Christian discussions and in the debate about the Jewishness of Jesus were first broached by Geiger.

One of the first modern studies by a Jewish scholar, Joseph Klausner, was entitled *Jesus of Nazareth*, published in English in 1925 (Hebrew original 1921). Klausner observed that "in his [Jesus'] ethical code there is a sublimity, distinctiveness and originality in form unparalleled in any other Hebrew ethical code; neither is there any parallel to the remarkable art of his parables. The shrewdness and sharpness of his proverbs and his forceful epigrams serve, in an exceptional degree, to make ethical ideas a popular possession. If ever the day should come and this ethical code be stripped of its wrappings of miracle and mysticism, the Book of the Ethics of Jesus will be one of the choicest treasures in the literature of Israel for all time" (Klausner 414).

Klausner suggests that Jesus surpassed Hillel in his ethical ideals, by changing the Golden Rule from a negative form ("What thou thyself hatest do not unto thy neighbour") to the positive form ("What thou thyself wouldest that men should do unto thee, so do thou also unto them"). Even so, Klausner observes that Jesus' ethical teaching has not proved possible in practice. One can notice an apologetic strand running through Klausner's work, for he argued, like a number of other Jewish writers, that Paul distorted the message of Jesus by Hellenizing it, and that Judaism is more fitted to be the bearer of monotheism to a needy world. For example, Montefiore called Paul "no rabbinic Jew."

For his part, Claude Montefiore expressed the view that it was time for Jews to abandon a negative attitude toward Christianity. The appropriate moment had arrived for a Jewish reappraisal of Christianity and a Christian reappraisal of Judaism. It was time for these two religions to stop judging each other from their defects; instead they should examine the positive qualities. Previously, it was the norm for Jews to look for defects in Christian works or for parallels in rabbinic writings: "What was true could not be new and what was new could not be true." This phrase summarized many Jewish attitudes toward Christianity. Montefiore took a more balanced approach. As far as Christians were concerned, he did not feel that he must assume that Jesus was always right; with Jews he did not feel obligated to defend the ancient rabbis. As a result, Christian scholars attacked him for being too Jewish and Jewish scholars for being too Christian.

Montefiore admired enormously the figure of Jesus, and in *The Synoptic Gospels* (1909) suggested that his teaching was a revival of prophetic Judaism and in some respects pointed forward to Liberal Judaism. Jesus emphasized precisely those values that Liberal Judaism wanted to bring out. For example, he emphasized inward goodness at the expense of outward forms. Jesus, Montefiore argued, should be viewed as a great and wise teacher, but in no sense God. Part of the significance of Jesus lay in the fact that "he started the movement which broke down the old barriers and brought about the translation of Judaism into the Gentile world—the translation of Judaism with many modifications, curtailments, additions both for the better and worse, good and evil" ("The Significance of Jesus for His Own Age," *Hibbert Journal* 10 [1911–1912]: 773).

Among more recent Jewish writings on the New Testament, one of the most interesting, from a Christian perspective, is Pinchas Lapide's *The Resurrection of Jesus* (1983). He believes that the resurrection actually happened, though he is a practicing Orthodox Jew. He is unconvinced by the "strange paraphrases" of many modern Christian theologians about the resurrection. He believes them "all too abstract and scholarly to explain the fact that the solid hillbillies from Galilee who, for the very real reason of the crucifixion of their master, were saddened to death, were changed within a short period of time into a jubilant community of believers." Only resurrection could have accomplished that.

Lapide, building on the thought of Franz Rosenzweig, suggested that Christianity is the "Judaizing" of the pagans. Lapide refers approvingly to Clemens Thoma, a Catholic theologian, who argued that through the resurrection of Jesus, an access to faith in the one, until then unknown, God of Israel was opened to the Gentiles. In other words, Jesus is the way for the Gentiles, but the Jews, who already know God, do not need Jesus. This conviction has not gained wide acceptance among either Jews or Christians, though it is an intriguing one.

The Jew Martin Buber, who in *I and Thou* (1937) interpreted the Bible and relations with God in a personal and existential fashion, has had a huge impact on modern Protestant theology, though he has been rather less influential in Jewish circles. He argued that Jewish faith, *emunah*, is in the history of a nation, whereas Christian faith, *pistis*, is in that of an individual. Buber wrote that "from my youth onwards I have found in Jesus my great brother. That Christianity has regarded and does regard him as God and Saviour has always appeared to me a fact of the highest importance which, for his sake and for my own, I must endeavour to understand. . . . I am more than ever certain that a great place belongs to [Jesus] in Israel's history of faith."

The most significant Jewish scholars of the New Testament in the latter part of the twentieth century are Geza Vermes and David Flusser. In *Jesus the Jew* (1973), Vermes opened the eyes of many to the Jewishness of Jesus, whom he depicted as a Galilean Hasid, holy man. In his careful examination of titles claimed for Jesus (such as prophet, lord, messiah, Son of Man, and Son of God) he concluded, controversially, that none of the claims and aspirations of Jesus link him with the messiah, that no titular use of "Son of Man" is attested in Jewish literature, and that "prophet," "lord," or even, figuratively, "Son of God" could be easily applied to holy men in the Judaism of Jesus' day. As far as Vermes is concerned, Jesus was a charismatic teacher, healer, and prophet.

He compares Jesus to his contemporary, Hanina ben Dosa, another charismatic leader and healer. He concludes:

> The main finding of this exploration of the historical and linguistic elements of the Gospels . . . is that whereas none of the claims and aspirations of Jesus can be said definitely to associate him with the role of the Messiah . . . everything combines . . . to place him in the venerable company of the Devout, the ancient *Hasidim*. . . . [This] means that any new enquiry may accept as its point of departure the safe assumption that Jesus did not belong among the Pharisees, Essenes, Zealots or Gnostics, but among the holy miracle workers of Galilee. (Vermes 1973, 223)

Jesus died, said Vermes, because he was perceived as a potential threat to the authorities. The real Jesus, Jesus the Jew, challenges traditional Christianity as well as traditional Judaism. In his view Jesus cannot be viewed as the founder of Christianity. The significance of Vermes's work can be illustrated by the fact that the title of his first book, *Jesus the Jew*, seemed revolutionary. Now it is almost taken for granted in New Testament scholarship. A synthesis of his writings on Jesus can be found in *The Changing Faces of Jesus* (2000).

Since the late 1960s, one other Jewish scholar of the study of Jesus stands out—David Flusser. In his biography, *Jesus* (1969), Flusser accepts Jesus fundamentally as he is portrayed in the Gospels (with some preference for Luke), recognizes him as a charismatic figure, and respects his teaching and his extraordinary sense of mission. He invites his readers to listen to Jesus himself and wonders out loud whether the responses that Jesus gave in connection with human conflict may not still be the best that anyone has proposed. Flusser commends Jesus for remaining aloof from the zealotism that destroyed the temple and Jerusalem. Jesus instructed his disciples not to resist authority; it would only make the civil authorities worse; they would very soon put you in prison.

The recognition that Jesus was a Jew and has to be understood in his Jewish context represents the most important contributions made by modern Jewish scholars in the study of Jesus. Not all New Testament scholars take this point seriously, and many of those who do are unable to master first-century Judaism. Others, unfortunately, prefer to ignore and others even to minimize the Jewishness of Jesus by categorizing Jesus as a "peasant" or as a "Cynic."

The work of Flusser and Vermes, which has built on the work of other scholarly Jewish studies of Jesus, should encourage everyone to take the Jewishness of Jesus seriously. It is time to recognize fully the work of Jewish scholars in the same way as Christianity has reawakened to the fact that Judaism nurtured Jesus the Jew.

Edward Kessler

See also: Jesus, Teaching of; Jewish Perspective; Messiah; Paul; Rabbis; Resurrection; Son of God; Son of Man; Vermes, Geza

References

Flusser, David. 1969. *Jesus*. Jerusalem: Magnes.
Forward, M. 1998. *Jesus: A Short Biography*. Oxford: Oneworld.
Klassen, W. 1999. *The Contribution of Jewish Scholars to the Quest for the Historical Jesus*. Cambridge: CJCR.
Klausner, Joseph. 1925. *Jesus of Nazareth*. London: George Allen.
Vermes, Geza. 1973, 1983. *Jesus the Jew*. London: SCM.
———. 2000. *The Changing Faces of Jesus*. London: SCM.

John, Gospel of

Anyone turning from the other Gospels to that of John ("the Fourth Gospel") is bound to feel that Jesus is depicted there differently in a number of ways. He seems more otherworldly, and he speaks at length, in a hieratic style, using repeatedly a number of words not much found elsewhere. Explaining the difference is another matter. Some (e.g., J. A. T. Robinson) have seen it as relaying the teaching of Jesus in contexts and moods (e.g., the private and more esoteric instruction of his disciples) that are particularly applicable here. But as the individuality of the voices of the other three evangelists has come to be more understood and appreciated (despite their sharing of much basic material), the specialness of John is seen more clearly and candidly as simply one more, rather more distinctive variant. Yet not wholly distinctive: compared with, say, the Gospel of Thomas or the other, later, apocryphal Gospels, there is much that is familiar. Like the other three canonical Gospels, that of John moves from Jesus' origins, through a ministry of deeds and teaching in Galilee and Judea, to his arrest, trial, and death, and finally resurrection. That is to say, they are all recognizably at one in their broad "life-story" approach to their subject.

So how are we to identify the Jesus of the Gospel of John, and how does its writer see and understand him? Fortunately, he tells us in a succinct final sentence (taking chapter 21 as an appendix) that gives his aim in writing the book: "[T]hese things are written that you may believe that Jesus is the Christ, the Son of God, and that believing you may have life in his name." Put like that, John's aim could have been shared by the other three. For almost all early Christian writers, "Christ" (= Messiah) and "Son of God" were almost synonymous, basic defining terms for Jesus, both drawn from relevant Jewish terminology, signifying his role as the decisive agent of God's purposes. John also calls Jesus "son of man" (e.g., 1.51; 5.27) and "lord" (e.g., 20.13, 28), again like the others, in the latter case similarly to Luke. For all the attempts in the past to see John as a more Hellenistic Gospel in its forms of thought, there is nothing in the picture so far that moves at all beyond styles of Jewish culture—despite the undoubtedly different "feel" of the book in so much of its structure and use of vocabulary. This comes out most notably in its consisting of only a few episodes, chiefly much longer and more amply explored in speech and dialogue than the much greater number included in the other Gospels, and in its focusing on a few key words or images (e.g., light, life, glory, love).

Moreover, the Jesus of the Fourth Gospel, with his lengthy orations that comment on his various deeds, and then finally and supremely to his disciples at the Last Supper (chs. 13–17), elaborates a doctrine of his relationship with his Father, and then with his "own," that is so intricately and relentlessly explored, and yet with extreme economy of vocabulary, that we feel we are reading of a Jesus who, if not in essence different, is then very differently presented and is differently, more intensely perceived and explored than the Jesus of the other Gospels.

We can penetrate this achievement by saying that John seems to have brought about a concentration and comprehensiveness in his perception of Jesus' significance that go beyond what we find elsewhere—at least as far as Gospels are concerned; most of his leading thoughts are already in Paul, but expressed allusively, diffusely, or unsystematically, in letters addressed to specific church situations. John's conception of Jesus tends to explore one angle at a time, tending to focus on a single word or theme (e.g., bread in John 6, shepherd in John 10), even though there are constant overlaps, creating a spiraling effect as new levels are reached while others are not wholly left behind.

We may also see John's conception of Jesus as consisting of a series of circles, each narrower than what precedes it, and together amounting to an affirmation of Jesus' universal and comprehensive significance.

Thus, to begin with the deepest level or widest dimension of all, John sees Jesus as decisive for the existence and meaning of the entire created order, from "the beginning." Already put forward in Pauline passages like 1 Cor. 8.6 and Col. 1.15–20, the doctrine appears in the opening of the Gospel, 1.1–18, where Jesus' significance is stated under the established Jewish image of God's "word"—the powerful utterance, whereby he, in his great might, brought everything into being; cf. Ps. 33.6; Isa. 55.10–11; Wisdom of Solomon 9.1; and Gen. 1, in which God creates by speaking (e.g., "Let there be light")—a passage that is surely a model for the flow of themes in John's prologue, culminating in the forming of Adam that is paralleled in the Word-become-flesh of 1.14. The image of a word that cannot but achieve its aim is parallel in Jewish thinking to that of God's "wisdom," which speaks of the rational orderliness (rather than chaotic randomness) that is held to mark the universe (Prov. 8.22–31). So Jesus' significance and "existence" go back beyond Abraham (Matt. 1.2) and Adam (Luke 3.38) to "the beginning" itself (John 1.1).

Modern readers unaccustomed to this idea are likely to find it perhaps lyrically poetic, but, in anything approaching "literal" terms, strange and extravagant beyond reasonable sense. The difficulty may be relieved by seeing that, once one was convinced of the comprehensiveness of Jesus' role as mediator of God to the world, it was impossible to exclude him from the universal dimension, the widest and deepest of all—that is, that of the forming of the created order itself. So, as he was to slot (more readily perhaps) into other mediatorial roles, so it would be grossly to reduce his significance to exclude him at this fundamental point. Therefore Jesus wears the mantle, among others, of the "word" of God "through whom all things were made" (1.3). In addition, some of the distinctively Johannine sayings of Jesus that take the form "I am"—for example, "bread of life," "the way, the truth and the life" (6.35; 14.6)—involve symbols that Jewish writings had used for "wisdom" or "word" (Prov. 9.5; Ps. 119.105).

Within creation, there is the human race as a whole, the climax of God's work in the eyes of Gen. 1 and the final expression of his decisive "word": "[L]et us make man in our own image" (Gen. 1.26; cf. John 19.5, and perhaps 20.15, where the risen Jesus is seen in the Adamic role of gardener). Paul had already used such an idea in 1 Cor. 15.22, 45 and Rom. 5.12ff.; and in the Third Evangelist's less far-reaching idiom, we find it perhaps in the collocation of Luke 3.22 and 38 and in the symbolism of Mark 1.13 (beasts and angels, as in Eden, now in harmony again under the new Adam).

Within the world as a whole, there is, for any biblically and Jewishly formed Christian, the people of Israel, with their messianic focus. So Jesus fulfills roles and images that demonstrate his place: 1.51 echoes Jacob (= Israel) in Gen. 28.10–17; with irony, we readers are to hear of his Davidic birth in Bethlehem (7.42); and that he is messiah is the Gospel's leading claim (20.30–31).

Narrowing his view, John also sees Jesus as assuming the mantle of the Jewish law itself, and intensifying its gift: the former came through Moses, but Jesus brings "grace and truth" (1.17). Moreover, most of the symbols that figure in the "I am" sayings referred to above were regularly applied to the law, itself seen, notably in the Jewish "wisdom" writings, as a climactic and normative expression of the divine "wisdom" or "word"; see notably Ecclus. 24 and Ps. 119, itself a mosaic of "law" symbols and themes. The law was for Judaism the light, the truth, the way, the bread of life, and so forth.

In a further step, John depicts Jesus as fulfilling the role and meaning both of the Jerusalem Temple (2.21) and of the great festivals celebrated there as provided within the law; chiefly Passover, which marks John 2, 6 and, above all, the Passion (13–19). Then, in this Gospel, Jesus dies at the time of the slaughter of the Passover lambs, fulfilling and superseding their commemoration of the redemption of God's people from Egypt in the Exodus (cf. 19.36 and 12.46). And Tabernacles is the scene for John 7–9.

There is one more—and crucial—claim that John, uniquely in the Gospels and with special clarity in the whole New Testament, makes for Jesus: he equates him with God (1.1, 18; 20.28). In the light of later Christian formulations and statements of faith (e.g., the fourth-century creeds), it is possible to see John as foreshadowing, and indeed authorizing, this claim (as he certainly contributed to its emergence). But if we are aware of the danger of anachronism, we are bound to feel that it is highly improbable that a late-first-century writer, undoubtedly formed intellectually in Judaism before his Christian allegiance, would have thought in the conceptual terms, Greek in provenance, that were current among Christians in the later centuries. Yet so insistent was Jewish mentality on monotheism and so hostile to any whiff of idolatry, that it is hard to see how such a one as our writer can have proposed such statements as "the Word was God" (1.1) or "my Lord and my God" (20.28)—unless perhaps in some act of pure ecstatic faith transcending all conscious cogitation.

It has to be said, however, that, for all its determined monotheism, there were in Judaism modifications whereby God was not seen as, one may say, lonely and unaccompanied or without mediatorial agents (angels most obviously) linking him with human beings (see Hurtado). And in any case, we should also note that in all three cases where John expresses the intimacy of this image, seeming to equate Jesus with God, he is also careful to differentiate between them. In 1.1, note the "with" as well as the "was" in the following clause. In 1.18, taking the manuscripts that read "only-begotten God" (rather than those that read "Son"), we must note that the adjective has the effect of making a distinction between Father and Son. And in the case of 20.28, we see a few verses earlier, in 20.17, Jesus clearly placing himself alongside his followers in relation to the Father. Distinction and oneness (cf. 10.30) are juxtaposed, inviting both care and explanation.

It has most helpfully been suggested in recent years that the Evangelist, far from being a fourth-century Platonist Christian before the time, was working with a down-to-earth image, drawn from Jewish legal and commercial practice: the institution of agency. In an era of slow communication, it was desirable for traders' agents to have full authority to conclude agreements on behalf of their superiors that would be binding on all parties: a man's agent must be as the man himself. John 13.16 virtually quotes the maxim. Moreover, in a society in which a son had the biggest stake in and expectation from his father's business, he was the best and most reliable of all agents. So with Jesus as he undertakes the crucial saving work as Son of the divine Father (see A. E. Harvey).

There is one more feature of this Gospel, related to what has just been discussed. In addition to his use on Jesus' lips of the first person singular, "I am," followed by a well-established, often messianic term, we find a number of uses of the words "I am" alone, used absolutely (and translated "I am he" in 8.28). "Before Abraham was, I am" (8.58) is the best known and most awesome example. It has been commonly believed that this is Jesus' adoption (audacious, blasphemous, or plainly factual, according to one's assumptions) of the divine name, revealed to Moses in the crucial episode of the burning bush, Exod. 3.14. In fact, in the eventually standard Greek version of the passage, the wording was different from the "I am" (*ego eimi*) of John. It is perhaps more likely that his model was the frequent self-affirmation of God in a number of passages in Isaiah (e.g., 43.10, 13, 23; 45.19; 51.12; where sometimes the Septuagint solemnly repeats the crucial words "I am, I am"). The expression then fortifies the "agency" theory, showing Jesus as taking on the role and standing of God—just as he may be seen to do in John 10, with regard to the image of shepherd (cf. Ps. 23.1; Ezek. 34); just as he personifies (and fulfills the role of) Israel in taking on the image of the vine, himself with his own (John 15; cf. Isa. 5; Ps. 81).

In a seemingly endless series of scriptural allusions and references, what the writer has brought about is a concentration, unparalleled in early Christian writing (though many of its elements are found elsewhere), of words, images, and symbols that make plain the all-embracing role of Jesus as God's fully empowered agent to demonstrate his character and achieve his saving and regenerating purpose.

Leslie Houlden

See also: Church; Creeds; Jesus, Death of; Jesus, Miracles of; Jesus, Origins of; Jesus, Parables of; Kingdom of God; Law; Lord; Messiah; Preexistence; Son of God; Son of Man

References

Ashton, J. 1991. *Understanding the Fourth Gospel*. Cambridge: Cambridge University Press.

Brown, R. E. 1966. *Gospel According to St. John*. 2 vols. New York: Doubleday.

De Jonge, M. 1977. *Stranger from Heaven and Son of God*. Missoula, MT: Scholars.

Harvey, A. E. 1987. *The Glory of Christ in the New Testament*. Edited by L. D. Hurst and N. T. Wright. Oxford: Oxford University Press.

Hurtado, L. W. 1998. *One God, One Lord*. Edinburgh: T. and T. Clark.

Meeks, W. A. 1967. *The Prophet-King*. Leiden: Brill.

John, Revelation of

John reveals the hidden significance of Jesus' victory and lordship over the idolatrous Roman world, to encourage the churches and prepare them for his coming. John was soon taken to be the Apostle and author of the Gospel of

John, but the text implies only that he is a "prophet" and brother Christian. He tells how Jesus appeared to him as the exalted Son of Man on the island of Patmos in the Roman province of Asia, toward the end (probably) of the first century A.D. He gave John messages for "the seven churches of Asia" (representing all the churches) at a time when faithful discipleship was challenged both by local persecution and by compromise with pagan society (chs. 2 and 3). A voice then summoned him up to heaven (4.1) to see the catastrophic effects of Jesus' victory on the idolatrous world (chs. 6–20), and the reward for fidelity to Jesus in the renewal of heaven and earth and paradise restored (chs. 21 and 22). The vision was "on the Lord's Day," in the context of the Eucharist in which Christians joined with the worship of heaven, celebrating the presence of Jesus, soon to come in final triumph. He appears under a variety of titles and images—Son of Man, Son of God, Lamb, Bridegroom—which declare the effects of his death and exaltation, his oneness both with God and with his people, and his role in God's plan for the world. The vision has particular force at times of affluence and worldly success for Christian churches, as well as at times of oppression and persecution because of faithful witness to Christ; "apocalyptic" takes one behind worldly appearances both to comfort the afflicted and to afflict the comfortable.

John's opening greeting to the churches sets out in pregnant phrases the view of Jesus he shared with them: " from Jesus Christ (or Messiah), the faithful witness, the firstborn of the dead, and the ruler of the kings of the earth," words taken from the messianic Ps. 89.27, 37. "Witness" to God, the role Israel had been chosen for, is a central theme of the Gospel of John; "first born of the dead": Jesus' resurrection was the beginning of the general resurrection, which for Jews marked the Last Day, an echo of Paul's letter to Colossae (1.18), a daughter church of Laodicea; "ruler of the kings of the earth": the king messiah, not the Roman emperor.

An ascription to Jesus then sets out what he has achieved (1.5–7): "To him who loves us, and freed us from our sins by his blood"—his sacrificial death as the Passover Lamb; "and made us a kingdom and priests"—what God rescued Israel from Egypt to be (Exod. 19.6); "See, he is coming with the clouds"—and every eye will see him, in anguished recognition, an allusion to Dan. 7.13.

Son of Man

The book of Daniel is one of the chief scriptural influences on John, and in his opening vision he sees "one like a son of man" (1.13); at Dan. 7.13 such a figure, representing the persecuted people of God, appears with the clouds of heaven before the "Ancient of Days" and is invested with sovereignty. John describes him as clothed in priestly garments and with the attributes of the angel of Dan. 10.6; again in 14:6ff. he sees seated on a white cloud "one like a son of man," associated with other angels. But this is more than an agent of God's will: he has "hair like white wool" (1.14), like the Ancient of Days himself; there are echoes of the enthroned glory, in human form, of Ezekiel's opening vision (Ezek. 1.25); and he says to John, "I am the first and the last," God's self-description at Isa. 44.6, equivalent to "Alpha and

Omega" at Rev. 1.8. John's greeting to the churches from God, the sevenfold Spirit and Jesus Christ echoes the greetings in Paul's letters, wherein Jesus appears on a level with God himself, and as in the other New Testament epistles scriptural attributes of God are attached to Jesus. Nowhere in the New Testament is Jesus more closely associated with God, sharing his throne and his glory, yet still within Jewish monotheism: in the final vision of the New Jerusalem (22.3), "the throne of God and the Lamb will be in it, and *his* servants will worship *him*."

But if "son of man" evokes, as surely it must, Jesus' self-reference in the Gospels, then there is no denial of his humanity and his oneness with his people. He appears "in the midst of the lampstands," which represent the churches, and holds in his right hand seven stars, which are "the angels of the churches" (that is, the spiritual counterpart of each church). Roman coins depict the imperial child playing with the seven stars (sun, moon, and five planets) that control the world. John's imagery depicts Jesus as God both intimately with us and above us, as Lord and Judge, and in contrast to imperial propaganda as the true controller of human destiny.

All John's imagery is open to such unwrapping. Each message in chapters 2 and 3 ends: "[L]et anyone who has an ear listen to what the spirit is saying to the churches," echoing the parables of Jesus (Mark 4.9, etc.). In each Jesus introduces himself with titles and motifs drawn from the opening greeting and vision, for example as "the first and the last" (2.8), a title of God, and as "the Son of God" (2.18). Finally to lukewarm Laodicea he is "the Amen, the faithful and true witness, the beginning of God's creation" (3.14). "Amen" is from the same Hebrew root as "faithful and true," and echoes the "God of Amen" (or truth) in Isa. 65.16. Jesus is the spokesman in word and deed, as Israel (now the Church) is intended to be, for the true God over against the idols of the nations (Isa. 44.8, 9). "The beginning of God's creation" identifies him as the divine Wisdom of Prov. 8.22–31 and Paul's letter to Colossae, Laodicea's neighbor (Col. 1.15; 4.16); he is the true wisdom, "the bright morning star" (22.16) over against pagan astrology and magic. His sharing God's throne as conqueror at the end of this message (3.21) leads into the vision of the Enthroned One in heaven (ch. 4) and the slaughtered Lamb who is worshipped with him (ch. 5).

Lion and Lamb

John, summoned up to heaven, sees in the hand of the one on the throne a sealed scroll, which, to his distress, no one can open. A heavenly elder reassures him: "[T]he Lion of the tribe of Judah, the Root of David, has conquered to open the scroll." "Lion" and "Root" refer to the famous messianic prophecies of Gen. 49.9–11 and Isa. 11.1–10: Jesus fulfills traditional Jewish hopes of a messiah (Christ) who bears God's Spirit to strike down the wicked and bring a just new world, paradise restored.

But what Jesus hears from the elder is qualified by what he sees: a Lamb bearing the marks of slaughter standing before the throne. The crucial question of interpretation is how drastically does "Lamb" qualify "Lion"? From chapter 6 on, we are shown nothing but violent destruction of the idolatrous

And There Was War in Heaven, *Albrecht Durer's woodcut design of the Apocalypse, 1498 (Art Archive Museo Correr Venice/Dagli Orti)*

nations. All people great and small cower before the face of God and "the wrath of the Lamb" (6.16). In chapter 12 a heavenly woman gives birth to a son who is to "shepherd all the nations with a rod of iron" (an echo of Ps. 2.9). In chapter 14 the Lamb stands on Mount Zion with the 144,000 who represent the twelve tribes of redeemed Israel, over against those who bear "the mark of the Beast" (symbolizing the Roman emperor); he will conquer the Beast and his allies because he is "Lord of Lords and King of Kings" (17.14), as is indeed seen in the final battle with its ghastly picture of slaughter (19.11–21). He appears as the violent avenging executor of God's wrath, and "Lamb" could evoke the militant young ram of the first book of Enoch, well known to Christians, who leads the faithful in Israel against wild beasts, which represent the nations.

For some readers, such as D. H. Lawrence (*Apocalypse* [1931, 1974]), this *is* the Jesus of Revelation. For others the Lamb's "slaughter" evokes sacrificial death. There are closer scriptural models than Enoch's, like the Passover: the heavenly hosts hymn the Lamb's worthiness to take the scroll because by his death he has ransomed for God saints from every nation, and made them to be a kingdom and priests (5.9, 10 as at 1.16), a reference to Israel's Passover deliverance (Exod. 19.6). Then there is the defenseless lamb of Jeremiah (11.19) and of Isaiah, who bore the sins of many (53.7–12), and the lamb of the Temple sin-offering. On this view there is a "rebirth of images": the traditional messianic images of violent conquest (what Jesus hears) are transposed in the light of Jesus' death (what he sees) to free us from our sins (1.15); the "wrath of the Lamb" is an ironic reversal of human values like the "glorification" of Jesus in the Gospel of John, which is his being "lifted up" on the Cross. There is a similar irony in the Son who "shepherds the nations with an iron rod" (2.27; 12.5; 19.15) and the Lamb who is shepherd to the redeemed faithful (7.17).

The key to interpretation is to recognize that Hebrew imagery is open-ended; one does not have to choose between possible models; all are there for those who have ears; all may contribute to the truth. The gentle Jesus who gives his life in love is also the terrible Christ, who wields the "sharp two-edged sword" (1.16; 2.12, 16; 19.15, 21). But the sword represents truth, like the "rod of his mouth" (Isa. 11:4) and the piercing word of God (Heb. 4.12), which is torture to people who are in the grip of delusion and lies, but their only source of healing—the iron rod of the shepherd who lays down his life for the sheep (John 10.11). One view of the millennial reign of Christ and his saints (20.4–6) is that it is to prepare for the direct vision of God, which would otherwise be lethal.

Bridegroom

John sends his vision of a world destroyed by idolatry, injustice, and arrogant wealth to Christian churches, which, on the evidence of chapters 2 and 3, are in danger of slipping into compromise with this world instead of reproducing Jesus' costly witness to the truth of God, which alone can save it. They are in danger of sharing the world's fate. But for them Jesus is the Bridegroom. The closing visions are of "the marriage supper" ("supper" is Paul's word for the Eucharist) of the Lamb (19.7–9), and of "the Bride, the wife of the Lamb," which is the new Jerusalem coming down from heaven (21.2, 9, 10). Behind this image stands the scriptural picture of God's love for Israel, the errant bride whom he has to discipline because of love (Hos. 1–3; Jer. 2.2ff.). In the severe message to the complacent church of Laodicea Jesus says, "Those whom I love I reprove and discipline" (3.19), and in the next verse the words "Behold, I stand at the gate and knock" echo the returning Bridegroom not only of Jesus' parable (Luke 12.35) but also of the Song of Songs (5.2), coming to awaken his sleeping bride. John's opening ascription is "to him who loves us and freed us from our sins by his blood." The final words are: "Yes, I am coming soon." "Amen, come Lord Jesus."

John P. M. Sweet

See also: Eucharist; Holy Spirit; Jesus, Achievement of; Kingdom of God; Messiah; Paul; Second Coming of Jesus, Origins of; Son of God; Son of Man

References

Aune, D. E. 1997–1998. *Revelation*. 3 vols. Dallas: Word Book.

Bauckham, Richard. 1993a. *The Theology of the Book of Revelation*. Cambridge: Cambridge University Press.

———. 1993b. *The Climax of Prophecy*. Edinburgh: T. and T. Clark.

Caird, G. B. 1966. *A Commentary on the Revelation of St. John the Divine*. London: A. and C. Black.

Prevost, J-P. 1993. *How to Read the Apocalypse*. London: SCM.

Rowland, Christopher. 1993. *Revelation*. London: Epworth.

John of Caulibus

An unquestionably intriguing and immensely popular Franciscan spiritual work of the fourteenth century, the *Meditations on the Life of Christ* (*Meditaciones vite Christi* [MVC]) is a synthesis and culmination of the new religious spirit, begun in the eleventh century and finding its ultimate expression in the person of St. Francis of Assisi.

The MVC was for centuries attributed to St. Bonaventure (d. 1274). Although Bartholomew of Pisa, a contemporary fellow Franciscan of John of Caulibus, stated in 1385 that Caulibus was the author of a tract of meditations on the Gospels, it was not until 1767 that Benedict Bonelli identified Caulibus's *Meditations* as the MVC. Although there have been attempts to discount a Caulibus authorship (no other works of Caulibus survive), serious scholars have subsequently concluded that the probabilities are in favor of the friar John de Caulibus of San Gimignano. Not only did Bartholomew of Pisa use the same terms to describe the meditations as did the MVC author, but he also identified the author as Tuscan, of the fourteenth century, and a Franciscan who was a great preacher. These identifying characteristics surface repeatedly in the MVC.

The first critical text of the MVC (*Corpus Christianorum*, 1997), brings to light in the original Italianized Latin the author's intent to introduce a Poor Clare nun to a way of meditation, centered initially on the humanity of Jesus but designed to arrive at a contemplative state, centered on his divinity. She, like Caulibus, is an Italian Franciscan from Tuscany, literate enough to read the author's rudimentary instruction. What he lacks as a scholastic theologian, however, Caulibus supplies in his skill as an extraordinary narrator, a man who is gentle and above all a man of profound simplicity and humility.

Sweeping aside a rigidly distant Byzantine Madonna, an implacable Jesus, and severely judgmental God the Father, St. Francis of Assisi expressed a longing for a spirit of love, of joy, of the world as a potential good. His spiritual vision, rooted in devotion to Jesus, was a culmination of the rising new religious spirit begun as early as the eleventh century and fostered by the Cistercians in the twelfth. Caulibus captured the defining characteristics of this movement, but importantly he brought this new spirit to the man on the street, stimulating as well—and remarkably—the enthusiasm and support of the monastic clergy. In place of dogmatic discourses and cold doctrine, he offers the spiritual athlete a personal, intense human experience.

Perhaps precisely because Caulibus's aim was limited to the instruction of his "beloved daughter" (avoiding for example the Franciscan polemics over the question of poverty of the fourteenth century), he achieved more than he could have imagined or intended. Caulibus directed the Poor Clare to divide the Gospel events of Jesus' life into a week's time, then each day to choose one episode within each time frame for meditation and contemplation. He invites her to enter into the scene with all the forces of her imagination, born of her life experience, and to expand and elaborate as the Lord Jesus inspires her. In effect, he legitimizes imagination and imaginary familial scenes by wedding them to the events of Jesus' life and that of his mother, Mary. Caulibus sets the meditations within the framework of the Church's liturgical year in Franciscan devotions and in the practice of Franciscan virtues (poverty, humility, charity, prayer), all virtues that Jesus exemplifies.

Although Caulibus disclaims theological expertise, he treads an orthodox path in his depiction of a Chalcedonian Jesus: a Jesus who is one person having two natures, divine and human. He invites his spiritual daughter to imagine Jesus as human, having human needs that she can minister to; and as one who has good days and bitter days just like the rest of humanity. This Jesus will experience both human frustrations, vivid and earthy, as well as tender, joyful moments. Jesus, the searcher of hearts, knew how to thwart the hypocritical Pharisees, and refused to be caught in their traps. Caulibus often crafts his narrative in legal and judicial terminology, leading the reader with a deft verbal picture at the same time to see the frustration of religious leaders, who learn not to spar with Jesus, and whose frustration becomes murderous hatred. Concomitantly Caulibus speaks of Jesus as ever willing to receive the reluctant unbelievers.

Especially poignant and tender is the conversation of Jesus and his mother Mary after the death of St. John the Baptist. Mary asked him why he had not prevented John's death. Jesus' reply, that it was the will of his Father, points to his divinity, but the scene emphasizes his gentle sensitivity toward his mother, a moment devoid of judgmental rancor.

Caulibus intends to lead his spiritual daughter beyond an imaginary experience, via the imitation of the virtues of Jesus to the contemplation of the divinity of Jesus, a state he admits is difficult to achieve. Aware of his own inadequacy to plumb the mystical, Caulibus depends on St. Bernard for direction at this level. Chapters 45 to 58 are almost entirely a series of excerpts from St. Bernard.

The author is, however, most comfortable and at once more original in painting the warm, moving, and lively scenes of Jesus in his humanity, drawn from Scripture, but often enlarged upon by his own remarkable insights. Jesus, for example, practices an abject poverty that is despised, in contrast to the (more formal) poverty of professional religious, who are honored for their poverty. The strong emphasis on personal relationships and humble interaction with the poor is reflected in Caulibus's observation that rather than reserve his discourse for crowds of thousands, Jesus did not disdain to speak to an audience of one. The Passion comes alive as if seen by an eyewitness: horrible and wrenching in detail, and Caulibus urges the nun to translate imagination into compassion for Jesus.

Caulibus's devotion to the Incarnation and to the sufferings of Jesus' Passion, Franciscan in origin, became popular in subsequent centuries, influencing the plastic arts, literature, the theater, and music. The chapters devoted to salvation history (the Canticle chapters) and to Jesus in his glory, the Ascension, are significant and powerful but do not figure in the influence of the MVC. They are nonetheless an important facet of Caulibus's vision.

Unforeseen by Caulibus, his MVC quickly gained far-reaching popularity. Translations appeared in Italian, French, Provençal, English, Flemish, Irish, Bulgarian, Swedish, German, Catalan, Spanish, and Hungarian, and multiplied throughout Europe. Apart from its inclusion in every edition of the works of St. Bonaventure (excluding the Quaracchi edition of 1882–1901), more than 250 MVC manuscripts survive in Latin, Italian, English, French, and Irish. The printing press gave further impetus, the *editio princeps* appearing in Augsburg (1468).

Of the early English translations, the most popular was that of Nicholas Love's *The Mirror of the Blessed Life of Jesus Christ*. This fifteenth-century translation was an abridged adaptation of the MVC, which Love directed to the needs of his Carthusian confrères, and to the combating of the Lollard heresy.

Of the literature inspired by the MVC, the most remarkable is that of Ludolf of Saxony (d. 1378), who in his *Vita Jesu Christi* throughout borrows entire verbatim passages as well as the structure from the MVC, albeit in a humanistic Latin, replete with a Germanic and monastic coloration. It was this version that influenced St. Ignatius of Loyola in formulating his *Spiritual Exercises*. In the nineteenth and twentieth centuries five MVC translations have appeared in French. The appearance in 1997 of the first critical text of the original Latin MVC made possible the first complete and accurate translation (2001) in English.

From the time of the MVC on, paintings of the Virgin and Child became one of the most popular subjects, with changes reflecting MVC influences. Mary is now represented as kneeling rather than, as formerly, standing at the time of the Annunciation, and St. Joseph is pictured at a modest distance from the birth scene. Raphael, Murillo, and Van Dyck are the most renowned artists whose subjects reflect influence, and the Italian, French, and German paintings draw as well from the wonderfully human elements of mother and child. Other scenes popularized by the MVC include the women surrounding Jesus on the Cross, St. John the Baptist with the child Jesus in the desert, Mary's encounter with Jesus as he carries his Cross, her pleading with the soldiers not to break Jesus' legs, and the removal of Jesus' body from the Cross.

Musical art bore an imprint of the MVC as well. The eighteenth-century Johann Sebastian Bach's Passions and Alphonsus Ligouri's *Dialogue of the Soul with Jesus* reflect the imagery of Caulibus.

The MVC was the product of the influences of its era. Although such attitudes and scenes are not completely original, the MVC certainly did greatly encourage their depiction. The itinerant Franciscans had in the MVC a text that was convenient and essentially complete to convey the vision of Francis. Its major emphases became and remained the basic teachings of religious schools well into the twentieth century.

C. Mary Stallings-Taney

See also: Art; Bernard of Clairvaux; Bonaventure; Chalcedon; English Christianity, Medieval; Francis of Assisi; Franciscan Thought and Piety; Ignatius of Loyola; Mary

References

Mooney, Canisius. 1944. "English Appendix." Pp. 323–366 in *Smaointe Beatha Chríost*. Dublin: Dublin Institute for Advanced Studies.

Stallings-Taney, C. Mary. 1997. *Iohannis de Caulibus Meditaciones vite Christi olim S. Bonaventurae attributae*. Corpus Christianorum CM 153. Turnhout: Brepols.

Taney, Francis X., Anne Miller, and C. Mary Stallings-Taney. 2001. *Meditations on the Life of Christ. Translated from the Original Latin and Edited*. Asheville, NC: Pegasus.

John of the Cross (1542–1591)

St. John of the Cross was a Spanish Carmelite friar and mystic in the period of Catholic reform that centered on the Council of Trent. A journey into night, away from familiar lights, to one who waits, in the darkness, ready to embrace and transform: this is his language about Jesus. Hence the emphases of the Christology of St. John of the Cross: the vitality of the risen Jesus; Christ's power to transform; Jesus' paschal mystery as a perennial power shaping lives. Doctrinally, his Jesus is one of the Trinity come to rescue his bride-Church; the permanently valid Word who in flesh says all the Father has to say. Historically, John's experience offers a window back onto the Gospels: John's "night" interpreting Jesus' forsakenness; contemplative stillness opening up the dimensions of Jesus' prayer.

Nonetheless, the name "Jesus" occurs rarely in the sanjuanist (i.e., St. John's) corpus. It has been asked whether Jesus is integral to John's spirituality at all. To respond, his Christology must be set within the dynamic of his work.

Pattern of John's Writing

This Castilian mystic was preeminently poet and pastor: verses decanting his experience of God; letters and sayings leading others to their own. His mature poems issued from life at its most vulnerable, his imprisonment in Toledo

(1577–1578) for his part in Teresa of Avila's reform of the Carmelite Order. The poems distill his encounter with the Trinity, despite and within such darkness. His longer works are all commentaries on their respective poems: *Spiritual Canticle; Ascent of Mount Carmel* and *Dark Night; Living Flame*.

There is then an order to John's writing: experience—poetry—prose. There is, too, a dynamic: a God who gives all (*todo*), in emptiness (*nada*); encounter, at night. Faith, hope, love sustain both gift and emptying. All his works convey this dynamic, though with emphases. Broadly: God is communicating himself (especially *Flame* and *Canticle*); therefore make space for the gift (*Ascent*); God himself makes the space through darkness (*Night*); this is a lifelong journey of love (*Canticle*).

John's writing does not detail everything that mattered to him. To discern his Christology, the question is not how often Jesus is named or how much doctrine rehearsed, but how Jesus relates to the order of writing (experience, verse, commentary); and what Jesus' role is in the sanjuanist dynamic (*todo* and *nada*, contemplative bestowal in purifying night).

Jesus and the Genesis of John's Writing

Contemporary witnesses attest to John's feeling for the Infant, for Mary, for Eucharist. His empathy for the weak—nursing syphilis patients in his teens; coaxing disaffected members of religious orders—speaks to the fleshliness of his faith. This informs his sketch of the Crucified inclining over a festering world. Hence his letters typically begin wishing the human Son to be most intimate to the reader: "Jesus be in your soul." In life, John was incarnational.

This grounds his poetry. The confidence with which he, herald of divine otherness, could trust the ineffable to sensuous language bespeaks a Word-flesh universe.

The process of voicing the divine came to a head when John's imprisonment had pushed him beyond his resources. His poverty released a raw cry, the first line of his *Canticle* poem, "Where have you hidden, Beloved . . . ?" And poverty permitted unprecedented giftedness, "My Beloved, the mountains / lonely wooded valleys / rare islands / thundering rivers / the whisper of love carried by the breeze" (*Canticle*, stanza 14).

These are John's first words about Christ: the one he most radically needs; the one whose beauty overwhelms him. Thirst for the "absent" Christ (so *Night*) declares how much Christ matters. John's protesting the inadequacy of language to convey his wonder (*Canticle, Flame*) is inverse witness to a surplus of meaning experienced in Christ.

If the *Canticle* verses communicate the energy of sanjuanist Christology, the three other prison poems explore its content. Each finds its resolution in the Son made flesh: Christ the rock, protecting those in exile (*Ballad on Psalm*, 137); eucharist-Christ, cupping and offering divine water (*Fountain*); and infant-Christ, wedding God to the universe (the nine *Ballads on Trinity and Incarnation*). These nine scenes (at least initiated in Toledo) are John's *lectio divina* of salvation history. Conceived in circumstances that were most alienating, the *Ballads* balance history on a mystery of infinite welcome: the love of Father for Son; of Son for Father; love, which is Spirit, and which shares joy in creating the world (*Romances*, 1–4). Humanity is created for a love unbearably beyond her (5–6) but made accessible in the Son's coming to her (7). The drama comes home in Mary, at Nazareth and Bethlehem (8–9), as she consents to welcome "God in the feeding-trough." The *admirabile commercium* becomes an exchange of wedding gifts: humanity finds God's joy, the baby cries our tears. Divinization, known at white heat in *Canticle* and *Flame*, is rooted here in Incarnation and given cosmic proportions.

John's Christ transforms, by accompanying. The *Ballads* present a Son who wishes to come alongside his bride, to share her experience, suffering included. As the Trinity plans Incarnation, the focus (contrast Aquinas, Ignatius Loyola) is fellowship in pain.

Where is Jesus in John's generative experience? Jesus is the one who in faith he perceives at his side, healing, by sharing.

Jesus and the Gift

John's awareness of God's self-gift governs the dynamic of his writing. Turning to this, what is Jesus' place? His role might appear tangential, given John's emphasis on the otherness of divine bestowal. Contemplation, "an inflow of God" (*Night*, bk. two, ch. 5), is so total and proximate as to transcend the specifics of word and image. What place could the highly specific Nazarene have in a communion whose supereminence darkens the faculties of the soul?

Ascent provides an answer without resolving the tension. The work insists relentlessly on theological virtue as the only proximate means to union with God. Only faith, not pet insights or supernatural phenomena, is diaphanous enough to welcome the divine. Why so, the reader asks? What now is this *todo*, "totality," for which anything less must be surrendered?

A hinge chapter of *Ascent* answers: Christ, the Son *humanado* (bk. two, ch. 22). Jesus constitutes a new economy of communication. "God is as it were speechless: he has no more to say, because what he once said piecemeal to the prophets, he has now said totally in him, giving us the All, who is his Son" (22.4). He is the *todo* making emptiness worthwhile.

Christ is thus proposed as the only particular historical locus of God's total self-communication: historical, since given; but permanently valid, and therefore risen. John has the Father declare, "He is my total message, my answer, my entire vision and revelation. This I have already spoken to you, answered, manifested, revealed, in giving him to you as brother, companion and master, ransom and reward" (22.5). For this writer, "faith" is faith in him.

Historical, risen, and indeed ecclesial, since Incarnation has canonized human connectedness (22.7–19). As *Ascent* proceeds, converging terms mark the space of encounter: Christ, Spirit, faith, Church, spirit, contemplation, night. To messages or insights, we are to prefer the "abyss of faith," with the "simplicity" proposed by "the Church"; here is found the "recollection" where the "Holy Spirit" communicates "the entire Wisdom of God in an all-embracing way, who is the Son of God, who is communicated to the soul in faith" (2A 29.6, 12).

Still there is a tension. Christ, historical and risen, is the content of the gift; yet no image, even of Christ, can ultimately effect union (2A 12). *Canticle* points a way forward here.

John's nomenclature can be loose: God, Word, Wisdom, Son, Jesus—each can point to Christ in the totality of his mystery. John can be specific ("according to the Humanity"), but his focus is Christ's person more than his human or divine natures. Hence John's preference for spousal language: "Bridegroom," "Beloved," the Son who comes and is sought. This personal focus prioritizes love, encounter, and so prayer; it also secures a center, which permits extremes: "this great God of ours, humiliated and crucified."

Turning to *Canticle*, the journey to union means progressive entry into the Gospel mysteries. *Ascent's* recipe for freedom from the dominion of sensuality was "a habitual desire to imitate Christ in all things, so that one's life takes on the form of his." The way to this was a loving assimilation of the scriptural text (1A 13.3). Accordingly *Canticle* calls for a "handling" of Christ's mysteries, so that "love disclose" what "faith contains, the Bridegroom" (SC 1.11).

As *Canticle* proceeds, the Gospel Christ is rediscovered, increasingly from the inside. In the final stanzas, anticipating eternity, bride and Bridegroom enter the "caverns of the rock," Christ's "mysteries," the theater of encounter where union may be total. The commentary on *las cavernas* (stanza 37) highlights with rare Chalcedonian precision the "correspondence" between the "hypostatic union of the human nature with the divine Word" and the soul's union with God. The correspondence is organic. By entering the caverns, assuming the mysteries of Christ's earthly existence, the person is embraced by the person of the Son—"hiding in the heart of her Beloved"—and shares, from a common wedding cup, the "liquor of the Holy Spirit." From there, from the interior of Christ, she can gaze upon "the Father."

Canticle's personal focus illuminates John's willingness, where appropriate, to surrender Gospel images in prayer (2 *Ascent* 12). Union means persons, not images of persons. The one who comes is the risen Son, exalted to "fill all things" (Eph. 4.10). If prayer becomes imageless, wordless, that would herald, not a dismissal of Christ, but a communion too total for commentary. Being personal, contemplation is assimilative. The *Canticle* Christ shapes the believer to his contours. Union means gospel living, sharing Jesus' virtues (stanza 24). More, it means transformation into filial divine knowing and loving (stanzas 38–39). This participation in the Son's Trinitarian life stands most revealed in the *Living Flame*.

The protagonist in *Flame* is the Spirit, "the Spirit of the Bridegroom"; the Spirit, then, of Christ. What the Spirit communicates is the vitality of Christ. The text displays Paul's "Christ lives in me" in action (Gal. 2.20; LF 2.34). It is a testimony to the risen Christ's vivifying power; a Pentecost hymn, declaring a cosmos where Jesus is Lord.

When the Word awakes, creation comes home (*Flame* 4). Far from isolating the mystic, his surrender to the risen Christ lays bare the world's connectedness.

Mine are the heavens, and mine is the earth; mine are the peoples, the just are mine, and mine the sinners; the angels are mine, and the Mother of

God, and all things are mine, and God himself is mine and for me, because Christ is mine, and all for me (*Sayings of Light and Love*, 26).

Jesus and Emptiness

The book *Night* portrays spiritual pain. Christ's love is impetus and goal in the journey; but he is not explicitly model. Where is Jesus, then, in the second coordinate in John's system: poverty, space for the gift, *nada?* An answer comes from the wider context, and from another hinge chapter of *Ascent* (2A 7).

The context is John's life, with his empathy for the disfigured Christ; his poetry, a Jesus who accompanies (*Ballads*); the systematic call to "imitation" (2A 29) of the one who was "born in obscurity, lived poor, and died destitute" (2A 19); and the emphasis on assimilation: Christ's mysteries shaping the disciple. Entry into "wisdom" comes by entry into "suffering," "cross" (*Canticle*, 36). Assimilation means being shaped to Christ's pasch.

This is made explicit in 2 *Ascent* 7. The chapter validates the diptych *Ascent-Night* by showing its message rooted in Jesus' teaching and example. Discipleship is all-embracing: a purification of "sense and spirit," "utter nakedness and emptiness," "annihilation in all things." But John has confidence to lead people into night, because Jesus has been there first. The chapter shows the dying Jesus "annihilated in soul, without any comfort or relief," his *Eloi* cry the "most extreme forsakenness" felt in his life (cf. Mark 15.34). This nadir constituted Jesus' "greatest work," uniting humankind with God.

Noteworthy, first, is the focus on passivity, on what is done *to* Jesus: mocked; physically destroyed; spiritually abandoned. The context, *Ascent*, concerns active endeavor; Jesus' example goes further, embracing the passive night.

Second, the gravamen is "spiritual consolation from his Father." The Salamanca syllabus while John was a student (1567–1568) included Thomist Christology. Appreciation of Christ's luminosity restrained Aquinas from ascribing spiritual suffering to Jesus (ST III Q 46, art 5). For the Carmelite, that is precisely the key: that Jesus knows abandonment even by his Father (2 *Ascent* 7 speaks of Jesus' dryness "according to the lower part": a relic of Thomist terminology that, like Tauler, Suso, or Melchor Cano, John preserves while exceeding its dynamic. The terminology safeguards a fundamental union with the Father, however far-reaching the desolation).

Third, a difference between the reader and the forsaken Jesus. Night is a process; but the Cross is a still point, at the world's alienated core. Jesus' darkness in *Ascent* offers not just a parallel but also an archetype. The Son's "Why . . . ?" opens a space wide enough for every human anguish.

Fourth, the key to restoration is love. John's spirituality seeks *unión de amor*, and sees "pure love" as more fruitful for the Church than all other activities (*Canticle*, 29). Similarly, Jesus' suffering "unites" humanity with God, "a greater work than any he had done." But John's Jesus redefines love's radiance. He achieved universal reconciliation at "the very moment, when in all things this Lord was most reduced to nothing" (2A 7.11).

If Jesus is a model of passive, spiritual emptying in *Ascent*, why the silence in *Night?* Admittedly Old Testament lament (prominent in *Night)*, not New Testament proclamation, is best suited to articulate desolation. More significantly, in the core chapters (2 *Night* 5–10), the author's aim is not only to explain but also to convey feeling. What night feels like is lonely; the Beloved is not there. If Jesus were named, that would suggest a *sense* of purposefulness that the experience does not enjoy. Instead, so far as literature can, *Night* simulates night darkness, a portrayal graphic enough for any reader to find a home. The doctrinal explanation came already in *Ascent*.

In fact, Jesus is not so distant from *Night* as might appear. John's Christ shapes the believer to his mysteries. *Night's* sense of spiritual disintegration relives the sign of Jonah, an entry into the "tomb of dark death" for the sake of "resurrection" (2N 6). The *dark night* poem itself drew intimately upon the Easter *Exsultet*. The archetype for the journey into darkness where the Beloved waits is Jesus' surrender through death to the embrace of the Father. Closeness to Christ makes him less over-against, more shaping from within. *Flame* conveyed resurrection from the inside. *Night* too is contoured by Jesus.

Mystical Christology

John's experience is therefore a privileged witness to Jesus' interiority. The mystic provides a theological source for interpreting Jesus' journey in Spirit and pain. He sustains the meaningfulness of the indescribable, and helps us not to banalize what may exceed our measurements.

Thus, John's testimony to human depth, *capacidad infinita*, keeps possibilities open when we assess the limits of humanity in Jesus' case. John's experience of transformation in the Trinity supports the exegete's pointing to Jesus' *Abba* relationship (that with God as "father") as source of Jesus' authority. For John, contemplation as silent communion, "pure spirit to pure spirit" (2N 17), God's loving light met by "loving attentiveness" (LF 3), suggests an access to Jesus' prayer. John's experience, of night and glory, rests within that of Jesus, and offers a horizon beyond which that of the human Son of God may be sought.

Iain Matthew

See also: Aquinas, Thomas; Chalcedon; Holy Spirit; Ignatius of Loyola; Paul; Son of God; Teresa of Avila

References

Castro, Secundino. 1990. "La experiencia de Cristo, foco central de la mística." Pp. 169–193 in *Experiencia y Pensamiento en San Juan de la Cruz*. Edited by Federico Ruiz. Madrid: Editorial de Espiritualidad.

Collings, Ross. 1990. *John of the Cross*. Collegeville, MN: Michael Glazier.

De Goedt, Michel. 1993. *Le Christ de Jean de la Croix*. Paris: Desclée.

Matthew, Iain. 1995. *The Impact of God*. London: Hodder & Stoughton.

McIntosh, Mark A. 1998. *Mystical Theology*. Oxford: Blackwells.

Von Balthasar, Hans Urs. 1986. "St. John of the Cross." Pp. 105–171 in *The Glory of the Lord: A Theological Aesthetics*. Vol. 3, *Studies in Theological Style: Lay Styles*. Edinburgh: T. and T. Clark.

John the Baptist

No person is more important for understanding the historical figure of Jesus than John the Baptist. In the Gospels and Acts of the Apostles, John is the herald who announces the arrival of Jesus, and it is his baptism of Jesus that reveals Jesus' divine identity and marks the beginning of his public ministry. John's preaching, actions, and death also presage those of Jesus. In the New Testament, John the Baptist is subordinate to Jesus but indispensable for his revelation. The actual historical relationship between the two is harder to determine. The only non-Christian account of John, provided by the Jewish historian Josephus (*Antiquities*, 18.116–19), presents a very different picture of the Baptist and makes no reference to him proclaiming anything about Jesus. However, even if Josephus accurately reflects the historical John's lack of knowledge of Jesus, it seems likely that the Baptist had a determinative influence upon the historical Jesus, and is consequently indispensable for his interpretation.

In the New Testament

John is not of interest to the authors of the New Testament for his own sake. Although Mark (and to a lesser extent Matthew) give us a relatively lengthy account of events surrounding his death (Mark 6.17–29; Matt. 14.3–12), and Luke likewise gives us an extensive description of those surrounding his birth (Luke 1), the authors are only concerned with John insofar as he relates to the figure of Jesus.

Their primary interest in John is in his role as a forerunner of Jesus. For the Gospel writers, John proclaimed the imminence of the day of the Lord (Matt. 3.3; Mark 1.3; Luke 3.4–6; John 1.23; Isa. 40.3) and the arrival of one greater than him (Matt. 3.11; Mark 1.7; Luke 3.16; John 1.15, 27; 3.30; Acts 13.25; 19.4) who would baptize with the Holy Spirit (Mark 1.8; John 1.33; Acts 1.5; and fire Matt. 3.11; Luke 3.16). His role as forerunner is confirmed directly by Jesus himself (Matt. 11.10; Luke 5.27). Indeed, the synoptic Gospels all agree that Jesus began his ministry only *after* John had been arrested (Matt. 4.12; Mark 1.14; Luke 3.20)—although the Fourth Gospel differs in this respect, having the two engaging briefly in simultaneous missions (John 3.22–24).

There is, however, some disagreement between the New Testament sources as to exactly what kind of forerunner John was. Although the synoptic Gospels present him as a prophetlike figure (Matt. 11.9; Luke 7.26; Matt. 21.26; Mark 11.32; Luke 20.6), and Matthew and Mark identify him, to varying degrees, with Elijah (Matt. 3.4; Mark 1.6; 2 Kings 1.8; Matt. 11.14; Matt. 17.9–13; Mark 9.9–13) whose return was expected to inaugurate the arrival of the day of the Lord (Mal. 4.5; Sirach 48.10), Luke downplays this association (see only Luke 1.17) and in the Fourth Gospel this identification is explicitly denied (John 1.21). However, they are all united in showing that he was subordinate to Jesus. Indeed, Luke and the Fourth Gospel are adamant that he explicitly denied that he was Christ (Luke 3.15; John 1.20).

John's baptism of Jesus is also a significant concern of the Gospels and Acts (Matt. 3.13–17; Mark 1.9–11; Luke 3.21–22; John 1.31; cf. also Acts

1.22; 10.37). It is at the baptism that Jesus' identity as the Son of God is confirmed from heaven (Matt. 3.17; Mark 1.11; Luke 3.22; John 1.33–34), and the Holy Spirit descends upon him (Matt. 3.16; Mark 1.10; Luke 3.22; John 1.33). The baptism marks the beginning of Jesus' public ministry (Acts 1.22; 10.37).

Here, again, there are significant differences between the New Testament authors. Although dependent upon Mark, Matthew and Luke depart noticeably from his account. In Matthew, John initially declares himself unworthy to baptize Jesus (3.14). In Luke, the baptism takes place *after* John has been incarcerated (Luke 3.20), the descent of the Spirit and the heavenly declaration of Jesus' identity occur only subsequently, as Jesus prays (Luke 3.21). In the Fourth Gospel the baptismal events are recounted by John *after* they have taken place. These variations may have come about because the Gospel writers (apart from Mark) were uncomfortable with the implications for their Christology of the fact that Jesus underwent a "baptism of repentance for the forgiveness of sins" (Matt. 3.6; Mark 1.4; Luke 3.3; Acts 13.24; 19.4): something that we can also see disturbed second-century Christian authors (Ignatius, *Ephesians*, 18.2; Justin, *Dialogue with Trypho*, 88). They may also have been concerned that the act of baptism by John could have been interpreted as indicating that the one baptized was in fact inferior to the one doing the baptism.

The relationship between the preaching, activity, and fate of John and of Jesus is a prominent preoccupation of the New Testament. Both are depicted as preaching similar eschatological messages of judgment and repentance (Matt. 3.7–10, 12; Luke 3.7–9; Matt. 10.15; Luke 10.12; Matt. 11.20–24; Luke 10.13–15; see especially Matt. 3.2; 4.17) and as demanding similarly high standards of righteousness (Luke 3.10–14; Mark 6.18 and parallels; Mark 10.17–31 and parallels); in the last days of his life, Jesus is shown as justifying his dramatic action in the Temple by reference to John's authority to initiate his baptism (Mark 11.27–33 and parallels), having previously predicted that John's fate presaged his own (Matt. 17.9–13; Mark 9.9–13). Although the New Testament is keen to emphasize that the two did not resemble each other in some ways (Matt. 11.18–19; Luke 7.33–34), it is perhaps unsurprising that Jesus is mistaken for John *redivivus* on a number of occasions in the Gospel narratives (Matt. 14.2; Mark 6.14; Luke 9.7; Matt. 16.14; Mark 8.28; Luke 9.19). Nor is it surprising that the Fourth Gospel includes the tradition that some of Jesus' disciples may well have come from among John's followers (John 1.40; cf. also Acts 18.25; 19.1–7).

The distinctive treatments of the relationship of John and Jesus by individual New Testament sources are also worthy of comment. Most of the variations can be ascribed to familiar redactional concerns of the authors. For example, in Mark's Gospel, John is presented as an unrecognized Elijah who heralds a hidden messiah (Mark 9.9–13), and thus contributes to the "messianic secret" motif found in that work. However, the ways of handling the relationship between John and Jesus by the double tradition (material common to Matthew and Luke but not found in Mark, often termed "Q") and by the author of Luke are especially striking. Although John's status as the harbinger of the new age is emphasized (Matt. 11.12–14; Luke 16.16), the double tradition presents a far more equivocal portrayal of John. In his question from prison he appears perplexed by Jesus' ministry and uncertain of his identity (Matt. 11.2–6; Luke 7.18–23). Despite being revered, he is inferior not just to Jesus but also to the "least in the kingdom of God" (Matt. 11.11; Luke 5.28; cf. also Gospel of Thomas 46). In Luke's unique account of the births of John and Jesus the degree of association between the two characters is intensified: not only are we informed that they are related (1.36) but also that their respective births are the result of a similar series of extraordinary events (for example, both involve angelic annunciations and miraculous conceptions). John's role as a forerunner is considerably emphasized (he recognizes Jesus' identity *before* either of them is born [1.41, 44]), as is his subordinate status. While John is declared a prophet (1.76), it is Jesus who is the Son of God (1.32–35).

Finally, it should be noted that despite John the Baptist's importance in the Gospels and Acts, he is not significant for all New Testament authors. Paul, for example, makes no reference to him.

In History

The historical relationship between Jesus and John the Baptist is not something that can easily be determined. Not only are there significant differences between the various New Testament sources but, more important, Josephus's account of John does not mention any such relationship at all. Indeed, in Josephus, John does not preach an eschatological message and makes no prediction of one who would come after him who would baptize with the Spirit. Instead John resembles a Hellenistic teacher of virtue. Although it is possible, as many have argued, that Josephus may have deliberately suppressed details of John's preaching in order to present a less threatening picture of Judaism, in the light of the disaster of the Romano-Jewish war, this is by no means certain. Indeed, according to the tradition found in Acts 19.1–7, Paul discovered disciples of John at Ephesus who were ignorant of the Holy Spirit and seemed unaware that John proclaimed anything about a successor (though cf. Acts 18.24–28); and so it seems likely that Josephus may not have been so wide of the mark in his description of John. It is quite possible that John the Baptist did not perceive of himself as a forerunner to Jesus or anyone else, or that if he did, he was not consistent or coherent in his understanding of this role (see Mason).

However, even if Jesus was not significant for John, the reverse is unlikely to be true. The historical John was probably important for the historical Jesus' understanding of his identity, authority, and, perhaps most important, his death.

Given the prominence the awkward story of Jesus' baptism by John has in all the Gospel traditions, it is probable that it is in some sense authentic and likely that it was formative for the historical Jesus, perhaps the crucial event in the development of his self-consciousness (see Taylor). John's ability to initiate an unprecedented rite within Judaism was also significant for the historical Jesus and something that he evidently saw legitimizing his own pious but maverick actions. (The nature of John's baptism is difficult to ascertain, as Josephus maintains that it was not a baptism of forgiveness but of purification. Whatever the case, despite some resemblances [see Webb], it was an innovation without close analogy among Jewish practices of the day.) To Jesus, both he and John were independent, righteous innovators within Judaism (Josephus, *Life*, 11).

John the Baptist's death almost certainly affected the historical Jesus and may explain the striking interest in his own death that dominated his ministry (and, to a large extent, explains the genesis of Christianity). The fate of John was clearly well known and something that the historical Jesus appears to have referred to on a number of occasions (perhaps in the Elijah reference in Matt. 17.12; Mark 9.13; Matt. 11.12b; Luke 16.16b; Mark 12.4). Although Josephus and the Gospels give different explanations of its cause (in Josephus, Herod Antipas executed John as a preemptive measure, fearful of his influence, whereas in the synoptic Gospels, his execution was the consequence of his criticism of Herod Antipas's marriage to his brother's wife, Herodias [Matt. 14.4; Mark 6.18; Luke 3.19; although cf. also Luke 3.19b and John 3.24], in violation of the law [Lev. 18.16; 20.21]), both agree that John was a popular figure who had not directly challenged the political authority of Antipas, who had him put to death. As a similarly outspoken and popular figure, the historical Jesus would have good cause to expect a similar fate to that of John and to speculate on its significance (see, for example, Luke 13.31–33). Indeed, with hindsight, the historical similarity between the two figures appears all the greater: in both cases, only the charismatic leader was initially put to death and not any of his disciples.

Justin Meggitt

See also: Jesus, Death of; Jesus, Family of; John, Gospel of; Luke, Gospel of, and Acts of the Apostles; Mark, Gospel of; Matthew, Gospel of

References

Mason, S. N. 1992. "Fire, Water and Spirit: John the Baptist and the Tyranny of Canon." *Studies in Religion* 21, no. 2.
Scobie, Charles H. 1964. *John the Baptist*. London: SCM Press.
Tatum, W. Barnes. 1994. *John the Baptist and Jesus: A Report of the Jesus Seminar*. Sonoma, CA: Polebridge.
Taylor, Joan. 1997. *John the Baptist within Second Temple Judaism*. London: SPCK.
Webb, Robert L. 1991. *John the Baptizer and Prophet: A Socio-Historical Study*. Sheffield, UK: JSOT.
Wink, Walter. 1968. *John the Baptist in the Gospel Tradition*. Cambridge: Cambridge University Press.

Josephus

The ancient Jewish historian Josephus provides important information about the life and death of Jesus. Although his two references to Jesus have been hotly debated since the sixteenth century, most scholars accept them in some reconstructed form as valid and important references to Jesus. Josephus's information aligns with the New Testament outline of the story of Jesus and his followers, and may be fairly said to corroborate it. Josephus has given us in two passages something unique among all ancient non-Christian witnesses to Jesus: a carefully neutral, mostly accurate and perhaps independent witness to Jesus, a wise man whom his persistent followers called "the Christ."

Flavius Josephus (A.D. 37–ca. 100) was born of Jewish descent but went over to the Roman side during the Jewish revolt against Rome. He wrote several works, including *Jewish War* and *Jewish Antiquities*, designed to explain and justify Rome and the Jews to each other. Although Josephus saw himself as a lifelong loyal Jew, other Jews viewed him as a self-serving traitor. Therefore, his works were not read or copied by Jews or cited by other ancient Jewish writers. Christians copied Josephus's works for (among other reasons) their rich information on a few figures in the New Testament, especially John the Baptizer, James the leader of the early Jerusalem church, and Jesus.

Josephus's smaller statement about Jesus comes in *Antiquities* 20.9.1 § 200: "He [Ananus the high priest] assembled the Sanhedrin of the judges, and brought before it the brother of Jesus called Christ, whose name was James, and some others." The overwhelming majority of scholars hold that the words "the brother of Jesus called Christ," as well as the whole passage in which it is found, are authentic.

Josephus's main statement about Jesus, traditionally known as the *Testimonium Flavianum*, the "Witness of Flavius (Josephus)" to Jesus, is found in *Antiquities* 18.3.3 §63–64. (A much fuller form of this passage in a later Slavonic version is discounted by all scholars.) The present text reads:

> Around this time lived Jesus, a wise man, if indeed it is right to call him a man. For he was a worker of amazing deeds and was a teacher of people who accept the truth with pleasure. He won over both many Jews and many Greeks. He was the Messiah. Pilate, when he heard him accused by the leading men among us, condemned him to the cross, [but] those who had first loved him did not cease [doing so]. For on the third day he appeared to them alive again, because the divine prophets had prophesied these and myriad other things about him. To this time the tribe of Christians named after him has not disappeared.

Until the rise of historical criticism in early modern times, most scholars believed this passage to be authentic. Their evidence for its authenticity is based on the wording of the passage, which points away from Christian interpolation at several key points. Moreover, if it were a Christian interpolation, we should expect more laudatory language about Jesus. However, other scholars deny the authenticity of the entire passage. Their argument is based on the context of the passage in the *Antiquities*, the arguably Christian wording of the passage, and Josephus's belief that the Roman general Vespasian was the messiah (*Jewish War* 6.6.4 §310–13; cf. 3.8.9 §392–408).

This debate over the authenticity of this passage has continued for hundreds of years, partly because the evidence can be—and has been—argued both ways. Although a few scholars still reject it fully and even fewer accept it fully, most now prefer one of two middle positions involving a conjectural reconstruction of this passage. The first middle position reconstructs an authentic Josephan passage *negative* to Jesus, and the second reconstructs an authentic passage *neutral* toward Jesus. The negative reconstruction reads, according to F. F. Bruce:

> Now there arose about this time a source of further trouble in one Jesus, a wise man who performed surprising works, a teacher of men who gladly welcome strange things. He led away many Jews, and many Gentiles. He was the so-called Christ. When Pilate, acting on information supplied by the chief men among us, condemned him to the cross, those who had attached themselves to him at first did not cease to cause trouble. The tribe of Christians, which has taken its name from him, is not extinct even today. (Bruce, 39)

The neutral reconstruction reads, according to John P. Meier:

> Around this time lived Jesus, a wise man. For he was a worker of amazing deeds and was a teacher of people who gladly accept the truth. He won over both many Jews and many Greeks. Pilate, when he heard him accused by the leading men among us, condemned him to the cross, [but] those who had first loved him did not cease [doing so]. To this time the tribe of Christians named after him has not disappeared. (Meier, 61)

Although certainty is not possible, the neutral reconstruction is the better explanation of this difficult passage. Most scholars favor it, adducing seven main reasons among them. First, the neutral reconstruction explains why we still have any mention of Jesus in Josephus at all. At the end of antiquity only Christians copied Josephus's books, to a significant degree because of their value to the Christians. If Christian copyists had found in Josephus's writings a negative passage about Jesus, it is more likely that they would have deleted it as an embarrassment rather than rewrite it. Second is an argument from style: the neutral reconstruction reads just as smoothly as the negative reconstruction. Third, the neutral reconstruction accords better than the negative reconstruction (note its hostile "so-called") with the more certain reference to Jesus in the *Antiquities*: "Jesus who is called the Christ." Fourth, the neutral reconstruction with its later pro-Christian interpolations makes good sense of the pattern of ancient Christian references to Josephus. In about 250, Origen does not know these interpolations (*Against Celsus*, 1.45; *Commentary on Matthew*, 10.17), while Eusebius several decades later does (*Ecclesiastical History*, 1.1.7–8). The fifth reason for favoring the neutral over the negative reconstruction is based on a recent "discovery" that tends to corroborate the neutral reconstruction. In 1971, an Arabic version of the *Testimonium* was found in Agapius's tenth-century *Universal History*, in a form that resembles the neutral reconstruction more than the negative reconstruction. Sixth, the neutral presentation of Jesus is supported by a roughly parallel presentation, held undoubtedly genuine by most interpreters, of John the Baptizer (*Antiquities* 18.5.2 §116–19). That Josephus can write sympathetically about a controversial figure like John the Baptizer indicates that he could write a neutral description about Jesus as well. Finally, this neutral reconstruction has much to commend it by two important scholarly conventions of reasoning from evidence, on explanation and simplicity. It explains well the passage as we have it now, with its mixture of authentic and interpolated content, and it is the simplest theory to account for most of the facts, internal and external, in the interpretation of the *Testimonium*. It involves significantly less conjectural wording than the negative reconstruction, while proposing a solution that is as fully explanatory. Thus, while certainty is not possible, and the negative reconstruction has strengths that commend it to several leading researchers, we may conclude that the neutral reconstruction is more likely, and correctly supported by a majority of scholars today.

By employing the neutral reconstruction of the *Testimonium Flavianum* and the other reference to Jesus, significant information about the life, ministry, and death of Jesus emerges. Josephus corroborates the New Testament's dating of Jesus' life and ministry. He confirms Jesus' reputation as a teacher and miracle-worker. He corroborates that both the Jewish Sanhedrin and Pontius Pilate acted to condemn Jesus to death. Finally, he states that Jesus "the Christ" was the founder of a continuing movement that bears this name.

Robert E. Van Voorst

See also: Jesus, Family of; Jesus, Miracles of; Jesus in Social Context; Jewish Perspective; John the Baptist; Messiah

References

Bruce, F. F. 1974. *Jesus and Christian Origins outside the New Testament*. London: Hodder and Stoughton.

Feldman, Louis. 1984. *Josephus and Modern Scholarship*. Berlin: de Gruyter.

Meier, John P. 1991. *A Marginal Jew: Rethinking the Historical Jesus*. Vol. 1. New York: Doubleday.

Van Voorst, Robert E. 2000. *Jesus outside the New Testament: An Introduction to the Ancient Evidence*. Grand Rapids, MI; Cambridge, UK: Eerdmans.

Julian of Norwich (c. 1342–1416 or later)

Julian may or may not already have been an anchoress when in May 1373 she received her *Revelations of Divine Love*. These were granted in answer to her prayer for recollection of the Passion of Christ, so that she might suffer with him; for remembrance of bodily sickness in her youth (to the same end); and for the three "wounds" of contrition, compassion, and desire for God. As she lay close to death, as it seemed, receiving the last sacraments, with the crucifix before her eyes, her desire for "com-passion" with Christ was realized, with the sixteen *Revelations*. Her account has many biblical resonances; but particularly there are suggestions of the iconography and the liturgical (and paraliturgical) observances of the contemporary Church.

The *Short Text* (ST), written soon after the event, is relatively straightforward, though containing the roots of her characteristic theological interpretation; the *Long Text* (LT), on which she may still have been working in old age, contains a more sophisticated exploration.

Consideration of the Passion is central to the whole, but the *Revelations* embrace the mysteries of Christ's life, beginning with the Annunciation to Mary (LT ch. 4; ST ch. 4), who has an important secondary place (e.g., LT ch. 25), and seeing the Passion always in the light of the Resurrection (LT ch. 23). The revelations of Jesus, God, and man embody the love of the Trinity (LT ch. 23; ST ch. 12). Julian constantly echoes the traditional Augustinian appropriations of Power, Wisdom, and Goodness (or Love) to the three Persons. She speaks of God's loving condescension in Jesus: "the marvellous courtesy and homeliness of our Father, that is our Maker, in our Lord Jesus Christ that is our Brother and our Saviour" (LT ch. 7).

Julian does not speak of the Passion as satisfying the needs of justice; rather, she sees it as the instrument of God's victory over the Devil: "I saw our Lord scorn his malice and despise his powerlessness" (LT ch. 13). Jesus' thirst on the Cross is not only physical but also spiritual, for the restoration of the "members" of his Body, who are his joy and his crown (LT chs. 17, 31). There is a mutual compassion between Jesus and his members. When he suffers, not only Mary and his disciples suffer but also the firmament and the earth that he created and sustains (LT ch. 18). The union of his humanity with the godhead strengthens him to suffer more than all men could; he suffers for every man's sin and sorrow (LT ch. 20; ST ch. 11). His love incomparably exceeds the pain of the Passion, and he would gladly suffer more for us (LT ch. 22; ST ch. 12). The wound in his side displays his riven heart (LT ch. 24; ST ch. 13).

Already in ST, Julian wrestles with the reality of evil in the face of God's victorious love in Christ. Jesus addresses her: "Sin is necessary, but . . . all manner of thing shall be well" (LT ch. 27; ST ch. 13). Among various background sources, Julian's optimism recalls the Paschal Proclamation: "O truly necessary sin of Adam, which merited to have such a Redeemer." Jesus "keeps" us and bears with us while we are in sin, and shows us our sin by the light of mercy and grace (LT ch. 40).

In the life of prayer, Christ is the "ground of [our] beseeching" (LT ch. 41; ST ch. 19). Here, as elsewhere, Julian echoes the Augustinian theology of prevenient grace. Prayer is the act of the will drawn by God to conformity with his will in Christ, and conformity to God's will is the ground of confidence that such prayer is granted.

A particular development in LT is the exposition of the vision of the Lord and the Servant (LT ch. 51). The Lord, representing God the Father, sends his servant to do his bidding; in his eagerness to do the Lord's will, the servant, entering a deep valley, stumbles and falls, lying helpless. The Lord has pity on his servant, seeing that it was eagerness to do his will that occasioned the Fall, and so raises him to greater dignity than he had before. The servant represents simultaneously Adam (All men) and Christ, who are both one in the Father's sight. Adam's fall from Paradise is matched and balanced by Christ's saving fall into Mary's womb, followed by the Passion. LT takes up what ST already states, that "the Passion was a deed done in time by the working of love, but love was without beginning" (ST ch. 11). The image of the servant recalls especially Phil. 2.6–7, and the whole context is a development from Augustine, *De Trinitate*, 2.5.9 (which recalls Philippians, among other texts), on the sending (mission) of the eternal Second Person of the Trinity into the world in time.

Already in ST Julian speaks tenderly of Christ as "our clothing . . . that love which wraps and enfolds us" (ST ch. 4). In LT this is developed much further in terms of the "motherhood" of God in Christ. The image of God's "motherhood" is not a novelty in the Christian tradition, but Julian develops this in an original manner in the setting of a profoundly Christocentric and Trinitarian theology. LT attributes God's Mercy to God's Motherhood, and God's Grace to God's Lordship (ascribed to the Holy Spirit) (LT ch. 48). Julian builds further on the conventional Augustinian Trinitarian appropriations, referring to the Truth of the Father, the Wisdom of our Mother (the Second Person), and the Goodness of our Lord (here the Third Person, the Holy Spirit) (LT ch. 54). Within this Trinitarian setting, here and elsewhere in LT, it is consistently to Jesus, as the incarnate Second Person of the Trinity, that Motherhood is appropriated. Apart from Julian's womanly perception, a theological basis can be found for this in the feminine gender of Latin *Sapientia*, Wisdom, as also in the various references to Wisdom as a female figure in the Bible, a tradition of which Julian was not unaware.

John P. H. Clark

See also: Augustine of Hippo; English Christianity, Medieval; Jesus as Servant; Mary; Second Person of the Trinity

References

Primary Sources

Colledge, E., and J. Walsh, eds. 1978a. *A Book of Showings to the Anchoress Julian of Norwich*. Pontifical Institute of Mediaeval Studies, Studies and Texts 35. Toronto: Paulist.

Glasscoe, Marion. 1993. *Julian of Norwich: A Revelation of Love*. Exeter: University of Exeter Press.

Spearing, Elizabeth, trans. 1998. *Julian of Norwich: Revelations of Divine Love*. Harmondsworth: Penguin.

Secondary Sources

Baker, Denise N. 1994. *Julian of Norwich's "Showings": From Vision to Book*. Princeton: Princeton University Press.

Bradley, Ritamary. 1992. *Julian's Way: A Practical Commentary on Julian of Norwich*. London: Twenty-Third.

Clark, J. P. H. 1982a. "*Fiducia* in Julian of Norwich." *Downside Review* 99: 97–108, 214–229.

———. 1982b. "Nature, Grace and the Trinity in Julian of Norwich." *Downside Review* 99: 203–220.

———. 1991. "Time and Eternity in Julian of Norwich." *Downside Review* 99: 259–276.

Nuth, Joan M. 1991. *Wisdom's Daughter: The Theology of Julian of Norwich*. New York: Crossroad.

Palliser, Margaret Ann. 1992. *Christ, Our Mother of Mercy: Divine Mercy and Compassion in the Theology of the "Shewings" of Julian of Norwich*. New York: Walter de Gruyter.

K

Kant, Immanuel

See Christology, Modern; Enlightenment

Keck, Leander E. (b. 1928)

From working in the 1950s on his Yale dissertation on the gnostic use of the life of Jesus, through a career in teaching at Wellesley College, Vanderbilt, Emory, and Yale (including ten years as dean), to the publication of *Who Is Jesus? History in Perfect Tense* (2000) around the time of his retirement, Keck has probed the theological significance of Jesus research as well as contributing to that research with a profundity rarely matched in current writing. Landmarks include *A Future for the Historical Jesus* (1981 [1971]), perhaps the best American contribution to the debate between Rudolf Bultmann and his pupils, which pointed to the later American discussion of the "historical," that is, the historian's, Jesus. Exhibiting a deep knowledge of and sympathy for the German tradition and boldness in pioneering new emphases for a new and more secular world, it included a rethinking of the concept of faith, emphasizing the Old Testament dimension of trust and the character of God. In the 1970s, Keck edited the Fortress Press Lives of Jesus series, including in it his own translation, with substantial introduction and notes, of D. F. Strauss's *The Christ of Faith and the Jesus of History* (1977 [1865]). Also indicative of his reflection on the German tradition was his critique of Günther Bornkamm's *Jesus of Nazareth* (1956), the flagship of the Bultmannian "new quest" of the 1950s and early 1960s, in the *Journal of Religion* 49 (1969), 1–17. Although sympathetic to the theological aims of this revival of interest in the historical figure, Keck identified weaknesses that would surface again in writing on Jesus in North America in the 1980s and 1990s. Chief among these was a failure to do full justice to the Jewishness of Jesus. The so-called criterion of dissimilarity used in identifying authentic Jesus material in the Gospels minimized what Jesus shared with his people. The new surge of twentieth-century research into Second Temple Judaism made most earlier work on Jesus seem dated. Keck's own historical Jesus book (2000) discusses Jewish research in its account of "Jesus the Jew" and also reflects theologically on Gentile Christianity's stake in Jesus' Jewishness.

Jesus the teacher represents the kingdom of God as "rectifying power," and the fatherhood of God is elucidated with due appreciation of Adolf von Harnack but combined with the twentieth-century rediscovery of the apocalyptic horizon of Jesus' mission. He probably saw himself as God's obedient Son, and the Christological implications of his activity are neither exaggerated nor evaded by Keck. "The living God Jesus trusted," learned from the Jewish Scriptures' assertions about God's holiness and love, is the ultimate focus of all Keck's reflections on Jesus because "call him what one will—prophet, peasant, protester, insurrectionist, patriot, holy man, charismatic healer-teacher, apocalyptic preacher, anti-apocalyptic sage, Jewish cynic—Jesus was about God and God's reign in human affairs" (Keck 2000, 127). Whereas most Jesus research since the Enlightenment has emphasized his teaching, Keck's fundamentally Pauline understanding of the gospel means that the Cross is finally the prism—the fractured prism—through which "Christian Gentiles" must understand both God and themselves. Validated by the resurrection and symbolized by the Cross, Jesus' death generates and nourishes a distinct way of interpreting the world again and again in fresh acts of discernment. The silence of God at Golgotha is incorporated into a story told by the evangelists from the perspective of belief in the resurrection—and it is this fact that demands its retelling. Finally, Jesus' significance for the moral life of Christians (and of others influenced by him) features prominently in Keck's writings and concludes a work that can be expected to influence those scholars, students, and lay readers who are willing to engage with it at the level demanded by its subject matter.

R. Morgan

See also: Bultmann, Rudolf; Enlightenment; Harnack, Adolf von; Jesus as a Historical Figure; Kingdom of God; Resurrection; Strauss, D. F.

References

Keck, L. E. 1981 [1971]. *A Future for the Historical Jesus*. Philadelphia: Fortress.

———. 2000. *Who Is Jesus? History in Perfect Tense*. University of South Carolina Press.

Strauss, D. F. 1997 [1865]. *The Christ of Faith and the Jesus of History*. Translated by L. E. Keck. Philadelphia: Fortress.

Kempis, Thomas à (1380–1471)

Thomas à Kempis was born in Kempen, near Köln (Cologne), and educated by the Brethren of the Common Life, who imbued him with their austere spirituality focused on a life of dedicated work and individual prayer, with a strong emphasis on mortification for sins that well fitted the European religious climate after the Black Death (1347–1350). He later joined a community of Canons Regular at Zwolle (Netherlands) and was ordained as a priest (1413). He spent his entire life there preaching and writing—most famously *De imitatione Christi* (The Imitation of Christ), published anonymously in 1418.

De imitatione (the title's inspiration is 1 Cor. 11.1: "Imitate me, as I imitate Christ") is widely considered a classic work of spirituality. By the end of the nineteenth century, it was second only to the Bible in the number of editions, and it has had a profound effect on how both Roman Catholic and Reformed traditions perceive Jesus and a Christian's relationship with him. Published in umpteen small pocket editions, the work affected virtually every religious figure until well into the twentieth century, many of them using it for meditation throughout their lives. Although its popularity has declined, it is still widely appreciated as spiritual reading and receives much scholarly attention, while excerpts, especially prayers, ensure it has a continuing influence.

The *De imitatione* theme is that perfection, and thus the ultimate end of the human being, which is eternal life with God entered through being cleansed of sin (see Book 3,9), is found through fixing attention on Christ and developing the inner attitudes of perfect discipleship. The work's two opening sections (Books 1 and 2) are devoted to general counsels on the correct dispositions of Christians, such as controlling desires (1,6), being peaceable (1,16), having self-knowledge (2,5), and other qualities and activities traditionally associated with the religious lives of those in monasteries (e.g., 1,17–19). This focus is not surprising, for although the book has been used by countless people not in the least interested in a "monkish" life, à Kempis lived in a monastic-style community assuming that a perfect follower of Christ would join such a vowed religious group. We also see the particular flavor of Thomas, his time and spiritual milieu: the work is suspicious of the intellect (famously at 1,2) and sees material engagements as distractions and vanity, while stressing humility, mortification, and self-abnegation: "[T]his is the high-point of wisdom: to strain towards the heavenly realms through contempt for the material universe" (1,1). On this path the key steps are having a close friendship with (2,8) and love for Jesus (2,7), reflecting on his Cross—"the royal road"—(2,11–12), and meditating on one's own mortality and sinfulness (1,23–24).

Books 3 and 4 take the form of a dialogue between Jesus and the disciple, where Jesus (the master to be imitated) addresses the reader as *Fili:* "my son." Here the individualism of the relationship between the devotee and Christ becomes most obvious, to the point where the community of disciples—the Church—is invisible: Jesus speaks inwardly to each soul (e.g., 3,1). The individual places complete trust in Jesus—without thought of others except as a moral demand—and acknowledges total dependence (e.g., 3,46). Alone, sinful, and aware of his nothingness, the Christian begs undeservedly for mercy. The final book is devoted to Holy Communion (the Eucharist) within the late medieval understanding as the presence of Jesus available to Christians for their individual sanctification; consequently, many older editions omitted it as incompatible with a Reformation view of the Eucharist, especially because of phrases such as "[T]he priest wearing sacred vestments acts in lieu of Christ" (4,5). It stresses the need for purity to enter this presence, and the condescension of Jesus in becoming present to, and taking up abode within, such sinners as are seeking to be disciples. The Christian, who, after careful preparation (e.g., 4,6 and 12), frequently (4,3 and 10) "receives" Jesus in Holy Communion, gains many blessings (4,4), is united with Christ's offering on the Cross (4,8), is brought into union with him as the Son of God (4,13), and is prepared for eternal bliss (e.g., 4,18).

Modern readers of *The Imitation* may be surprised how little direct reference it makes to the words of Jesus' teaching found in the Gospels. The work antedates preoccupation with history in its own right.

Thomas O'Loughlin

See also: English Christianity, Medieval; Eucharist; Spirituality

References

Geest, Paul van. 1996. *Thomas à Kempis (1379/80–1471), een studie van zijn mens- en godsbeeld*. Kampen: Kok.

Kempis, Thomas à. 1418 [1984]. *The Imitation of Christ*. Translated by J. N. Tylenda. New York: Vintage.

Kenoticism

Kenoticism is the idea or thought about "emptying" (Greek *kenosis*) as employed in Christology and, by extension, theology. The term derives from Paul's use of the Greek verb *kenoo*, "to empty," in the so-called "kenotic hymn," Phil. 2.6–11, at v. 7: "[Christ Jesus] emptied himself, taking the form of a slave, being born in human likeness." Like its New Testament context, the hymn intertwines doctrine and ethics, and so the understanding of the text is susceptible to two principal emphases: incarnational (kenosis as an explanation of how God's Incarnation in Christ occurred) and ethical (kenosis as a value seen in Christ for imitation by his followers). Both these strands have featured in the various applications of kenosis in the course of its interpretative history.

In the patristic period, the passage was interpreted according to the growing acceptance of Christ's preexistence: as the person of Jesus was made to be continuous with God's coeternal Logos (Word), so the self-emptying of Christ Jesus, who was equal with God, was made to be the means by which that Logos came to be found on earth as a human being. In other words, kenosis came to be understood as the mechanism of the Incarnation. For Cyril of Alexandria, whose doctrine posthumously dominated the orthodoxy formulated at Chalcedon, the Godhead could not be subject to change or loss, and so kenosis, ironically, was not so much a "letting go" for the Logos as a taking on of flesh.

The ethical understanding can stand independently of the concept of Christ's preexistence if one reads Philippians in terms of the "Adam Christology" found elsewhere in the Pauline corpus: according to this exegesis, advanced by James Dunn, the "form" of God possessed by Christ Jesus was not a coexistence with God before the Incarnation but the "image" of God held in common with Adam and all humanity. Where Adam exploited that image, Christ, by contrast, lived humbly, and for this reason was glorified. Kenosis, on this view, is not the way the second person of the Trinity travels to earth from heaven, but the servant-like way of human living, which leads to exaltation.

Although the Christological debates of the patristic period accentuated the incarnational more than the ethical side of kenosis, Cyrilline orthodoxy had not provided a sufficiently convincing interpretation to satisfy later generations. Christ seemed in the hymn actually to put off something of his divinity, and so the incarnational aspect of kenosis was bound to be revisited, especially as it raised the question of whether or not God was changed or limited by the process. The sixteenth-century Lutheran school at Giessen began modern treatment of the question by suggesting that the emptying was of divine attributes by Christ's human nature, although these qualities remained available to him through his divine nature. The school's rivals at Tübingen argued that Christ's human nature did in fact possess the attributes but simply concealed them from view (more a "krypsis" or concealment than a "kenosis").

This attention to Christ's divine attributes paved the way for discussion in the wake of the Enlightenment, with its pressure to reconceive Christology "from below," that is, from the human side. The nineteenth-century German Gottfried Thomasius distinguished between "essential" divine powers (such as mercy, justice, and love), and "relational" divine powers (such as omniscience, omnipotence, and omnipresence) and held that Christ became incarnate by emptying himself of the latter while retaining the former. This type of incarnational approach to kenosis, ready for the first time to predicate limitations of the divine nature, was developed at the turn of the century by a host of early British kenoticists (most famously, Charles Gore, as well as Andrew Fairbairn, Frank Weston, Peter Forsyth, Hugh Ross Mackintosh, and Oliver Quick). For them, kenosis was a scriptural response to the problem of Christ's ignorance (in other words, though so, one would think, omniscient, he said he did not know when the End of things would be, Mark 13.22, and surely did not know, for example, modern science) thrown up by biblical criticism, and their stance became the classic view of kenosis of the modern era.

It was not long, however, before the pressure to "de-supernaturalize" doctrine reached its logical conclusion and the Incarnation was interpreted *entirely* on the basis of Jesus' humanity. In terms of kenosis, the incarnational strand became dependent on the ethical strand. This view was exegetically justified by Charles Moule, who *identified* Christ's emptying behavior in Philippians with the nature of God, which Christ was said in the hymn to have: kenosis, rather than a climb-down from divine fullness of being, was a general climb-down in behavior, and this humility was, itself, fullness; kenosis is "plerosis." Incarnation, on this view, was the revelation by Jesus in human life of what God is always like; kenosis was a human ethic applied back to the nature of God. This position was advocated by John Robinson, Piet Schoonenberg, John Macquarrie, Geddes MacGregor, Ray Anderson, William Vanstone, Lucien Richard, Donald MacKinnon, John Taylor, Richard Holloway, and Keith Ward and carried to extremes by Thomas Altizer. John Macquarrie hailed it "new-style kenoticism," but it is better called "radical kenoticism" to distinguish it from the classic modern (and more "traditional" incarnational) kenoticism, which still finds "new" expression in the work of Stephen Davis, David Brown, Brian Hebblethwaite, and Ronald Feenstra.

Radical kenoticism represented a fundamental shift in the application of kenosis, from the Logos, or Christ, to God (with Christ as the revelation or example of God's nature). Kenosis thus became a way of describing God's work of creation (John Polkinghorne) or the interrelationships of the Trinity (Hans Urs von Balthasar and Jürgen Moltmann). In the 1980s and 1990s, the concept was drawn into the contextualization of theology and applied to Judaism (Emmanuel Levinas), interfaith dialogue (Masao Abe), feminism (Sarah Coakley), and postmodernism (Graham Ward).

The fiercest criticisms of the concept in both its classic modern and radical forms have come from feminism. Daphne Hampson has argued that kenosis is a masculine construct that attempts to counterbalance a history of patriarchy; it is men's misguided ethical attempt to correct their own oppression, writ large in terms of doctrine—misguided, because it perpetuates a cycle of mastery and slavery, domination and abasement. This critique of powerfulness and powerlessness is illuminated when translated into sexual theology, as by Beverly Harrison and Carter Heyward. Such dualism, however, may not simply be masculine but intrinsic to reality, which misses the target of the ideal. The feminist emphasis on mutual empowerment (an ethic suitable for both genders) may in practice always result in both men and women occasionally having "over-power," which then requires kenosis: kenosis would then be as necessary as liberation to achieving mutual empowerment.

Kenosis, therefore, retaining its place in ethics, can continue to be a constructive element in both Christology and the doctrine of God. The connection of the doctrine to such fundamental issues for human identity as sexuality and power ensures what Stephen Sykes has called its "strange persistence" and Graham James its "enduring appeal." Even if, after the twentieth century, the doctrine of God rather than Christology is the primary location of its application, the roots of the concept in Scripture and Christology mean that kenosis and Jesus can never be entirely divorced.

Michael Brierley

See also: Alexandrian Theology; Balthasar, Hans Urs von; Chalcedon; Enlightenment; Interfaith Thought and Relations; Macquarrie, John; Paul; Preexistence

References

Coakley, Sarah. 1996. "*Kenosis* and Subversion: On the Repression of 'Vulnerability' in *Christian Feminist Writing*', and "Afterword." Pp. 82–111 and 168–170 in *Swallowing a Fishbone? Feminist Theologians Debate Christianity*. Edited by M. Daphne Hampson. London: SPCK.

———. 2002. *Powers and Submissions: Spirituality, Philosophy and Gender*. Oxford: Blackwell.

Martin, Ralph p., 1997 (2nd ed.). *A Hymn of Christ: Philippians 2:5–11 in Recent Interpretation and in the Setting of Early Christian Worship*. Downers Grove, IL: Intervarsity Press.

Kierkegaard, Søren (1813–1855)

Kierkegaard, the Danish theologian, is sometimes described as "the father of existentialism," but he was a committed Christian whose prime anxiety was to bring home to individuals the challenge that Christianity represented in a world where everyone considered themselves to be a Christian merely because of the accident of birth. He wanted to force individuals to an either/or decision— either God exists or God does not, either Jesus is God or Jesus is not. There is no proof of these statements, but that does not mean that they are neither true nor false—each individual has to decide on this issue of truth and stake his or her life by living out this decision. Neutrality is not an option; nor is indifference. There is a forced choice to be made, and individuals will give their answers not by the words they say but in terms of how their lives are lived.

Philosophic Fragments (1992 [1843]), written in the early years of his authorship, is Kierkegaard's attempt to explore the significance of Jesus. He did not, as more conventional writers of the time did, set out what he considered Jesus to be or what traditional Christian doctrine said about Jesus. Instead he confronted his reader with a "what if" choice: What if Jesus is ontologically different from Socrates? It is easy to assume that Jesus was just one more good man—many philosophers and not a few theologians have talked in these terms. Jesus has often been considered to be on a par with the Buddha, Socrates, and Gandhi—an extraordinary individual who showed human beings how life should be lived. Kierkegaard considered that if Jesus was simply one more teacher like other great human teachers, then Christianity is false and deserves to be opposed and suppressed. His book explored what it would mean to claim that Jesus was not like this, that he was unique and in a completely different category. If, and Kierkegaard recognized that there was an "if" here, Jesus is not just another human being but God, then everything changes. Instead of being one more human teacher who brings to humanity insights into the human condition, Jesus can convey Truth (with a capital "T") that would not otherwise be available, Eternal Truth about the purpose and destiny of human beings. Jesus could also change individuals so that they were no longer locked into the power of the past, so that reason no longer held them captive within narrow constraints.

Reason will say that the claim that a human being is God, that the infinite became finite, or that Jesus was dead and is now alive is nonsense—reason will proclaim these statements to be paradoxical. They are apparent contradictions that reason will reject. Kierkegaard nevertheless considered, as a philosophic realist who stands in the Aristotelian tradition, that these statements are either true or they are false. However, they cannot be proved to be true—even if one was a disciple of Jesus and was present with him during his ministry, there would be no proof. Each person has to make a decision for him or herself and must then stake his or her life on this decision. Kierkegaard, therefore, considered that there were two possible responses to the paradox of the Incarnation. The first is faith when reason is set aside and the individual assents in faith to the truth claim that Jesus is both God and man and stakes his or her life on this claim. The alternative is offense, which occurs when reason is put in first place and when reason rejects the paradox precisely because of its paradoxical nature.

Kierkegaard saw his task to awaken individuals from their slumbers and to confront themselves with the choice—faith or offense—and then to help them think through the consequences of this decision. This is the purpose of all his writings.

Peter Vardy

References

Gouwens, David J. 1996. *Kierkegaard as a Religious Thinker.* Cambridge: Cambridge University Press.

Hannay, A. 2001. *Kierkegaard: A Biography*. Cambridge: Cambridge University Press.

Kierkegaard, S. 1992 [1843]. *Philosophic Fragments*. In *Kierkegaard's Writings, Vol. 7*. Edited by J. Climacus. Princeton: Princeton University Press.

Pattison, George. 1997. *Kierkegaard and the Crisis of Faith*. London: SPCK.

King, Jesus as

See Jesus as Emperor; Kingdom of God; Messiah

Kingdom of God

For visitors to churches and singers of hymns, the image of Jesus as "king" is as prominent as any. It dominates so many east windows, showing him crowned and enthroned in a stylized and rather medievalized version of a modern English coronation ceremony, and it is of course closely related to the history of ideology from medieval times. The origins and early formation of such ideas are, however, both different from all that and a good deal more complex than the apparently simple images in the windows suggest.

The "kingdom of God" is generally seen as the core and sum of Jesus' message—his defining doctrine. A summary statement like that near the start of Mark's Gospel (1.14–15) leaves little room for doubt: "The time is fulfilled, and the kingdom of God has drawn near." Few would contest its centrality, but there is less agreement about its sense or content and about its "journey" through the various phases of early Christianity, discernible in the NT writings, not to speak of its use in later Christianity down to the present.

Some matters, however, are reasonably clear. The expression's roots lie in Judaism, fundamentally the long-established use of the image "king" for God in relation to Israel and indeed the world. Interestingly (and the fact inspires caution), the expression "the kingdom of God" itself never occurs in the Jewish Scriptures or indeed in other pre-Christian Jewish writings, except once in Psalms of Solomon 17.3 (first century B.C.), though it almost does in late scriptural books (1 Chron. 28.5; 2 Chron. 13.8). Rather, we look to passages such as the opening of Psalms 93 and 99, "The Lord is king," and to numerous other places, including the Dead Sea Scrolls, where references to the idea of Yahweh as the universe's or Israel's king (often with an earthly king as his deputy and representative) are abundant. Often, especially in later works, the context is apocalyptic and visionary: such kingship will be restored or manifested. (Historically, Jewish monarchy effectively ceased in 587 B.C.) The rarity of the actual phrase may suggest that the emphasis upon it in the first three Gospels indicates that it was indeed a feature of Jesus' teaching, to the extent of its being a kind of slogan, almost his logo; though, as we shall see, even if that were true, it would not tell all.

It seems that behind the Greek *basileia* ("kingdom") lies the Hebrew *malkuth*, which means more properly "sovereignty" or "kingship" and gives the expression a dynamic (or abstract?) edge. So "kingdom" is not so much a recognizable sphere, still less a territory, but more a matter of power and authority. This distinction is all very well, but it is undeniable that this supposed abstraction always had a tendency to turn concrete—naturally so, when Yahweh was traditionally seen as having a definable (minimum) sphere within which his rule was, or ought to be, exercised, that is, the land of Israel, with the very physical Jerusalem temple as its cultic center. In the New Testament, there is, in any case, an easy flow between the one emphasis and the other.

In the earliest Christian uses of it, in the letters of Paul, the term is often somewhat colorless, and it is by no means central to his thought. Sometimes it is even banal: "[T]he kingdom of God is not food and drink" (Rom. 14.17); and it is not a great deal more illuminating when we read what follows: "but righteousness and peace and joy in the Holy Spirit." Is Paul referring simply to the proportions of the Christian way of life, or to the coming dispensation? It is much the same with 1 Corinthians 4.20. But in another use the eye is chiefly on the future completion of things: various listed categories of wicked persons "will not inherit the kingdom of God" (1 Cor. 6.9, 10; Gal. 5.21); and the same is said of "flesh and blood," that is, our ordinary present state, as contrasted with "spiritual bodies" created by God's transforming act (1 Cor. 15.50). The one place of extended, considered treatment (1 Cor. 15.24–28) will be examined later, in another context.

If the Gospels are right in showing "the kingdom of God" as central in the ministry of Jesus, then here we have a prime example of Paul's lack of interest in (or ignorance of) the actual teaching and activity of Jesus of Nazareth. Is he so far sure in seeing himself as apostle of the risen, exalted Jesus that he has no spare energy or attention to give to the historical figure, except in the most meager way (if perhaps just sufficient to suggest the opposite)? At all events, the term appears a mere six times in the undoubted letters.

Most but not quite all of these Pauline instances clearly bear out the dominant eschatological character of this kind of language and idea in contemporary Judaism. That is, "the kingdom" speaks (as one image or idiom among many) of the "day"—perhaps imminent and longed for, perhaps dreaded—when God will indeed establish direct rule over his own, replacing the Romans for sure and perhaps the existing puppet Jewish authorities (the Herods and the Jerusalem high-priesthood), and probably doing it in the setting of a renewed world ("a new heaven and a new earth," Rev. 21.1—incidentally, a work in which the expression "kingdom of God" does not appear, despite every cue, though we read of God as "king of kings," 19.16).

There is no such sparseness of reference in the Gospels, which represent, with whatever degree of indirectness, the tradition, even the memory, of what Jesus did and stood for. In Mark, the earliest Gospel, the opening summary, as we saw, centers on "the kingdom of God," apparently without there being need to explain or elaborate. Moreover, in Jesus' parables (his whole teaching, 4.34), it is the single and exclusive theme. The message seems to be that "the kingdom" is both utterly assured and yet hidden, both imminent and yet already present in its subterranean workings (4.26–29), both unmistakable to those given the "secret" of it (4.11) and yet diverse in its effects on those who experience it (4.1–20). For Mark, these people include, it seems, those healed or fed by Jesus as well as those who hear his words: to eat at his hand or to see because he makes it possible is a vivid way into the sphere of the kingdom. So it is right to speak of "realized eschatology": here and here and here, in these words and acts, the regime of God, the things of the new world or age, are palpably with us.

Richard A. Horsley and others have drawn attention to the actual human dimension underlying and even forming this preaching and action. Galilee, along with the rest of Palestine, was burdened with alien (Roman) or semialien (Herodian) rule, with taxation to match, and the folk-memory of a past of independence, won by Moses, fought for by the prophetic power of Elijah, was far from dead. In this context, the ministry of Jesus was more than, in our sense, religious: it had to do with "real life" and what we would see as sociopolitical realities. It meant no mere "spiritual" kingdom, a matter of interior piety. This is, of course, a dimension long absent in ordinary Christian use of Mark, perhaps from within a few years of its writing. There is a question: even if Mark depicted this institutional reality or the memory of it, did he, by his time of writing, still see the world in its terms, or was he, writing some forty years after the time of Jesus, bound to see him within the Church, and was he not perhaps formed significantly by the theology of Paul?

In any case, it is far from clear, in Mark, where Jesus himself actually stands in relation to the kingdom that he brings to bear on those around him. Is he the king (as temporary deputy for God) in the kingdom, as Paul thought, in his most considered "kingdom" passage (1 Cor. 15.24–28), or is he merely its agent and spokesman, a more vital and greater John the Baptist ("God's son"), as Mark 1.7 and 11 imply? Mark certainly used a large measure of irony, even ambiguity, in depicting Jesus' place in the kingdom (as Messiah-king, for example): Mark's Jesus says he indeed has this role—or perhaps he does not, or is at least teasingly reluctant to claim it plainly (12.35–37). Only when the high priest asks him directly at the trial does he admit it in so many words (14.62); and then he dies, renewing our sense of bewilderment and mystification about him—a sense that Mark never resolves. If Jesus is king (cf. Mark 11.1–10) in some kind of "real sense" (and this passage by Mark never quite says so openly), his "reign" never gets anywhere at all, it seems. He is certainly a king-with-a-difference: though the kingdom of God is surely what his followers must still stand for (though even that is never quite said, unless the mission of the twelve in 6.7–13 is meant as a paradigm; but in Mark that passage never uses "kingdom" language). And all other rules are shortly to be done away with (chapter 13), so the point is in a sense "academic."

In Matthew's use of this language, as in so many matters where perhaps Mark's obscurity was found too much to tolerate, there is much more clarity. It is of no significance (it is purely reverentially synonymous) that in all but four places, he prefers "kingdom of heaven" to "kingdom of God," and more interesting that he seeks to give more definition to the kingdom. He is surer than Mark that it is present already, especially in Jesus' defeating of the devil, the kingdom's (and God's) great adversary (12.28). He is also more inclined than Mark to see the kingdom as an identifiable sphere, no doubt in effect and in part the Church, which one can enter and "stray" from (18.12–14) and where discipline, including expulsion, can be exercised (22.1–14), though Mark too could speak of "entering" the kingdom of God (10.23), equating it explicitly with "eternal life" (10.17). Already for him, the kingdom was both eschatological yet also had at least the makings of being an identifiable entity.

Moreover, like Paul in 1 Cor. 15.24–28, Matthew sees Jesus himself as the king (indeed, a "meek" or modest king, in accordance with contemporary ideals, 21.5), perhaps at least for the first stages of the kingdom's final manifestation (25.31–46). And Matthew can personalize the kingdom, removing any vagueness by replacing Mark's "the kingdom of God" with reference to Jesus as king (compare Mark 9.1 with Matt. 16.28; and Mark 11.10 with Matt. 21.9, cf. v. 5). It is in fact not said in Matthew how long Jesus' kingship of heaven will last. Maybe, in view of Psalm 110.1, which Mark seems to have seen as inconclusive (12.35–37), though others plainly did not, he will reign forever, as God's partner (at his right hand). That text has a good claim to being the earliest to be used by Christians to back Jesus' title to allegiance. Finally, in Matthew it seems that the term "the kingdom" was indeed moving away from sociopolitical associations alive in Jesus' lifetime (the fall of Jerusalem was almost twenty years before Matthew wrote) and moving toward ecclesiastical awareness: the Church was all one now had if one belonged to the people of Christ; it was the new ark of salvation.

Luke certainly believed that Jesus was king forever: at 1.33 ("of his kingdom there will be no end") he differs from Paul's speculation (1 Cor. 15.24–28) that Christ's rule would be only until "the end," when he would hand it over to God. In the fourth century, although Marcellus of Ancyra favored Paul's opinion, Luke was generally preferred, and his opinion was included in the Creed of Constantinople in the year 381, in other words the permanent form of the Nicene Creed, which has the wording "of whose kingdom there will be no end." But Luke had a more important and immediate decision to make in relation to "the kingdom of God." If he was going to write the story of the early missions (the Acts of the Apostles), how would talk of "the kingdom" fit in, if at all? He seems to have decided, in his rather visually "solid" way of looking at things, that "the kingdom of God" could serve, in Acts, as a sort of shorthand for the package of events surrounding the final consummation (as laid out by him in Luke 17 and 21). In other words, for Acts, he opted for its eschatological associations. There, "Christianity" (and we can begin to think in such a formal way) is seen to consist of two aspects: "the things concerning Jesus" and "the kingdom of God"—

that is, in effect, the story told in his Gospel, centering on Jesus throughout, and then the coming end-time (8.12; 28.23, 31).There is that which has already happened (the Gospel) and that which is still to come, so that Acts represents the story and conditions of the interim. Putting it another way, it is as if "the kingdom" were like a pool of light surrounding Jesus as he walks the stage of this world (where he is, the kingdom is, 11.20; 17.21); it is therefore removed at his ascension; but it will later return, and the mistaken (Jewish) hopes (19.11; cf. Acts 1.6 for their persistence among Christians) will then finally be fulfilled. (Unlike Paul, Luke never tells us how the unending kingdom of Jesus and the kingdom of God relate to each other: speculative theology is not his interest.) As far as it goes and in its own rather concrete terms, Luke's picture is comprehensible—but it is far indeed from the brave elusiveness of Mark.

It is also far from the Gospel of John, where the term itself barely appears—it is confined to the very Jewish discussion of Jesus with Nicodemus, the half-believer, in John 3 (vv. 3, 5). It is language the latter understands but fails to see in its true sense. In the rest of the book, we have not "the kingdom of God" but "Jesus the king"—here and now. It forms the backbone of the account of Jesus' appearance before Pilate, in the lengthy discussion in 18.33–19.16, which turns on the place of "true" kingship, in this world or in God—or rather in Jesus, his representative, one with him, whose "kingdom" is not "of this world," that is, not based here (18.36). So "king" takes its place alongside all the other Jewish images that Jesus unites in himself in this Gospel. Because he is God's plenary agent (the Word made flesh), there is no problem with his being himself "king" (cf. also 12.15), and his rule, unlike Pilate's, is not rooted here, but in God.

The King Jesus of the church windows may indeed have his origins here, remotely; but the image lies more immediately in the medieval union (or rather tumultuous partnership) of Church and Empire, whereby his supreme kingship might be a reassuring backing or foundation for its earthly and local counterparts. But the idea could then also prove a base for the disputing of territory or primacy between Church and State, twin kingships, both Christian in allegiance, with Jesus as the Church's ace and supreme "weapon," with biblical texts brought anachronistically to bear. But if Jesus was depicted wearing a king's crown, like that of a king in France or England or the German emperor, where did that leave the power of the Church (so the pope dons a *triple* crown)? It is a sign of growing secularism that the frontispiece of Thomas Hobbes's *Leviathan*, in the mid-seventeenth century, showed a crowned figure, looking for all the world like the Jesus of the windows, but in fact representing the secular state, who has both sacred and secular authority in his own hands. In England, Henry VIII had made explicit over a century before what had long lain half-concealed or been fiercely disputed. But the image of God's kingdom continued to have its own resources: "the kingdom of God" has come to be a slogan and aspiration for Christian efforts and hopes for the improvement of society along Christian lines, however those might precisely be conceived. It is to be done in the here and now, and the old eschatological associations of "the kingdom" tend to fade still more.

Leslie Houlden

See also: Art; Christology, Modern; Church; Creeds; Hymns; Jesus, Miracles of; Jesus, Parables of; Jesus as Emperor; John, Gospel of; Luke, Gospel of, and Acts of the Apostles; Mark, Gospel of; Matthew, Gospel of; Messiah; Paul; Son of God

References

Good, D. J. 1999. *Jesus, the Meek King*. Harrisburg, PA: TPI.

Horsley, Richard A. 2001. *Hearing a Whole Story*. Louisville and London: Westminster John Knox.

Kingsbury, J. D. 1975. *Matthew: Structure, Christology, Kingdom*. Philadelphia: Fortress.

Morris, Colin. 1989. *The Papal Monarchy*. Oxford: Clarendon.

Perrin, N. 1976. *Jesus and the Language of the Kingdom*. Philadelphia: Fortress.

Sanders, E. P. 1985. *Jesus and Judaism*. Philadelphia: Fortress.

Willis, W. 1987. *The Kingdom of God in Twentieth-Century Interpretation*. Peabody, MA: Hendrickson.

Küng, Hans (b. 1928)

Like his older contemporary Edward Schillebeeckx, Hans Küng came to focus his attention on the historical Jesus as a result of the Second Vatican Council, after which he found himself facing a wide international audience of both Christians and non-Christians. His earlier works, even his postdoctoral thesis, *The Incarnation of God*, begun well before the council but not completed until 1970 (English translation 1987), had been very much in the tradition of Roman Catholic dogmatic theology, though always with marked openness to other traditions. The first signs of the focus on Jesus appeared in *The Church* (1967), the second section of which begins with a discussion of Jesus' preaching of the kingdom of God (ibid., 47–79), culminating in the statement that during his lifetime Jesus did not found a church (ibid., 72). Here, as with Schillebeeckx, there are signs of familiarity with current exegetical work by biblical scholars. Küng's major treatment of Jesus, though, appeared in *On Being a Christian* (1977), where he introduced themes that have dominated his work ever since (1977, 119–396). These themes reappeared and were endorsed almost twenty years later in *Christianity* (1995) and in the shorter *Credo* (1993, 33–121). According to Küng, Jesus Christ is the constant center and abiding substance of Christian faith and life (1995, 25–27), the element in Christianity that is abidingly valid, its criterion. His message is contained in the Sermon on the Mount (ibid., 52–55), and the Christian life is discipleship of Jesus (ibid., 33–36). Jesus' cause is God's cause, which he embodies, and the special relationship between Jesus and his God is the germ from which Christianity begins, the nucleus around which it crystallizes.

Although *On Being a Christian* discusses the life, death, and resurrection in some detail, Küng's picture is essentially a generalized one. He is aware of exegetical controversies, say, over the titles of Jesus, but his footnotes show little recourse to specialist studies on specific points; they either refer directly to the Gospel texts or list a wide range of works of synthesis. This reluctance to go into detail that might entangle him in controversy is also evident in his references to the doctrine of the person of Christ, though their very openness makes them provocative. Concentration on Jesus, he argues, must not lead to any Christocentric narrowness (1995, 21). He is very restrained about any kind of developed Christology. The heart of Christian faith, he argues, is not a theological theory but belief that God the Father works in a revealing, redeeming, and liberating way through his Son Jesus Christ in the Spirit. This basis leads him to make some extremely open statements about the classical doctrines: they (and here he particularly has the doctrine of the Trinity in mind) must not be dismissed unthinkingly, but they must not be repeated unthinkingly either. After all, he asks, what would Jesus and his disciples have understood by them? Christians are to believe in Father, Son, and Spirit, but they need not believe in Trinitarian speculation (ibid., 305). Similarly, the Incarnation seems almost to become a metaphor: for Küng, it can be said that Jesus, in whom word and deed, teaching and life, being and action, completely coincide, is the embodiment of God's word and will—God's word and will in human form.

Küng's minimalist approach here, only hinting at the complexities of New Testament exegesis and Christological definition, is the result not so much of cautiousness about possible censure from the authorities as of his constant awareness of his wide circle of readers. This sense of audience is always evident and governs the whole presentation. Time and again he seems to be voicing the thoughts and possible objections of readers or trying to make contact with their experiences. Thus, Jesus is regularly compared with Buddha Gautama to bring out his specific characteristics (e.g., 1993, 49–54), or described to readers in terms of what they might have thought that he was but is not: neither priest nor theologian, neither with the rulers nor a social revolutionary, not an ascetic or monk, not a religious, not a pious legalist (1977, 179–213).

At the end of the day, Küng's view of Jesus is a very simple and straightforward one, not centered, like traditional doctrine, on who Jesus was and how he brought about salvation, but on who Jesus is and what people must do in order to become his disciples. It is summed up in a formula that is used, word for word, at the conclusion of both *On Being a Christian* and *Credo:* "By following Jesus Christ people in the world of today can live, act, suffer and die in a truly human way; in happiness and unhappiness, life and death, sustained by God and helpful to fellow men and women" (1977, 602; 1993, 190).

John Bowden

See also: Buddhism; Christology, Modern; Church; Jesus, Death of; Kingdom of God; Resurrection; Schillebeeckx, Edward; Second Person of the Trinity

References

Küng, Hans. 1967. *The Church*. London: Collins.
———. 1977. *On Being a Christian*. London: Collins.
———. 1993. *Credo*. London: SCM.
———. 1995. *Christianity*. London: SCM.

L

Law

The question of how Jesus viewed the place of "law" takes a number of different forms. There is first the historical question of his attitude, not so much to law in general as a principle or feature in human society, as to Judaism, "the Law," the Torah, which was the basis of Judaism. There is also the more general question, perhaps of special interest in times and places where emphasis is placed on human "freedom" and the exercise of human choice, of whether, in the face of social conventions and traditions or of more formal enactments, Jesus can (without too much anachronism) be claimed as a hero for what we may loosely describe as "modern Western culture," especially seen as a youth culture, with its dislike of constraint. After all, he did not survive to be more than a young man. (At the same time, we have plenty of modern examples—in Islam, Judaism, and some forms of Christianity—of extreme attachment to rules and structures among some of the young.) This more general question is open to anachronistic hunches, a failure to focus on the possibilities of his time and place. For this reason, it is sensible to go first to the historical question.

This question, too, has its difficulties. The most detailed and only immediate evidence of Jesus' attitude toward law is in the Gospels, but it soon becomes clear that their not inconsiderable quantity of material bearing on the matter is not homogeneous, nor is it plain, unadorned historical reminiscence. Other forces, subsequent to Jesus himself, have intervened to shape the way his teaching and attitudes are presented, and the picture varies from one Gospel to another. There can be little doubt that both different attitudes among the evangelists themselves and different situations and needs among the various Christian communities of the later first century influenced, even determined, the way Jesus was presented in relation to this central question of his own position; which is not to say that the whole matter was a free-for-all in early Christianity, with Jesus pushed into the role of supporting whatever various groups of his followers happened to think. Still, as we shall see, life at ground level in one Christian community must have been very different in various relevant respects from life in another: for example, what did one do on Saturdays, or what, if any, dietary rules did one observe? And behind such matters of detailed practice, there would have been differences of ethical ethos.

A major factor in interpreting the Gospels with regard to this subject is the simple truth that all of them were written after the dominant work of Paul, who had seen attitudes toward the Torah as crucial to Christian definition, to the extent that "Torah" and "Christ" were mutually exclusive as bases for attaining salvation and entering into relationship with God (e.g., Rom. 10.4; Gal. 3–4). It is not, however, remotely true that he was antinomian, looking for a morally anarchic universe, and in a way the question is not best seen in ethical terms: it was rather a matter of the basis and means of salvation. And the divergence has its roots in the dual role of the Torah not just as a code for conduct but also as the rock on which the relationship of God with his people rested. Indeed, the books of the Law contained not just laws but also the foundation-story of Israel, and early Christians had to reinterpret that story as well as adopt a position toward the laws themselves. When it comes to ethical teaching, though Paul certainly had original things to say, determined largely by his having to provide for mixed Jewish and Gentile Christian communities, when he is simply "laying down the law" (as we say), his lists of vices and virtues are such that nobody, then or now, would take exception (apart from one or two details, largely arising from their seeming to harp on sexual sins), and his firmness about them certainly invites no challenge (e.g., Gal. 5.19–23).

But to return to Jesus himself. As many articles in this volume illustrate, the life of Jesus has recently come under the most intense and detailed scrutiny in the light of what is felt to be an ever more realistic appreciation of the society in which he lived, and so of the human possibilities for his outlook on matters such as concern us here. There has come to be broad agreement that it is highly unlikely (to take one extreme possibility) that he was a radical critic or rejecter of the Law of Moses and therefore pushed aside Sabbath observance or food laws—which were matters of the basic social fabric. (Interestingly, nothing is said in the Gospels about his attitude toward circumcision, which, in the setting of Paul's Gentile mission, became a major topic; in fact, the apostle's "liberal"—as we might categorize it—policy made it central in his theological argumentation in, for example, Romans 4 and in Galatians. In Paul's setting, this, along with Sabbath observance and dietary rules, was a matter less of "ethics" as we would see it than of social or communal identity.) It follows that stories suggesting such radicalism need to be seen in terms other than those of at least some of the evangelists. Take, for example, Mark 2.23–28, the disciples' apparently wanton breaking of Sabbath rules in a cornfield. Whatever Mark may have meant by it, if we take it as a genuine historical reminiscence, we should see that Jesus' direction is far from being outside current Jewish discussion, perhaps all the more in Galilee where there was distance from the more professional scribal discussions of Jerusalem. Even what seems to us (and to Mark?) the striking judgment, "the Sabbath was made for man, not man for the Sabbath" (v. 27), can bear a Jewishly acceptable sense: Sabbath is a gift of God for human good, not an instrument of oppression (and the disciples' conduct was not outside the bounds of justifiable decision). If that is so, it is true that both Matthew and Luke still saw fit to drop the saying: perhaps, from their different standpoints, they saw—and rejected—the more dismissive sense in which Mark had meant it. Similarly, in Mark 7.19, we have a rejection (in the manner of Paul) of food laws, but the words are a palpable Marcan comment, and the main text of the passage is understandable as another case of Jesus pointing people to the true purpose of the Law and away from casuistic frauds. With regard to the primacy given to the command of love (12.28–34), though the strength and directness of the formulation stands out, there is even less reason than in the other cases to suppose that Jesus was out of line with current rabbinic teaching (all the more if we see him in the role of a "charismatic man"). And when Jesus comes to be tried and condemned in Jerusalem, nothing is said (except just possibly in Luke 23.2, "perverting our nation") about his views on Torah. His offense lay elsewhere. If he was critical of Torah, it was with regard to evasions and fudges of its generous provisions. No rabbi on later models indeed, he was a charismatic preacher of the kingdom of God and a bringer-in of its life, but this did not lead him to dismiss or contravene the Law. Even if he was influenced by Greek Cynic–like moral teaching, as J. D. Crossan claims, he would be not so much against Torah as working in other directions: for example, the spiritual good derived from eating together and finding new bases for human fulfillment under God.

In any case, it remains that, whatever the probabilities of history, our picture of Jesus in this matter comes through the evangelists, who did indeed differ on this very question. As we have seen, though we may look behind him to a rather different historical basis, Mark presents Jesus as distinctly radical about the Law, and this is but one symptom of his very possible formation (partially at least) by Pauline teaching; he even uses some distinctive Pauline vocabulary (e.g., his use of "gospel"). The whole spirit of Mark is to show the unique centrality of Jesus, leaving no room for other authorities.

Plainly, in the last two decades of the first century, there were Christian groups that saw the situation in a quite different way. Jewish Christians, for example, saw in Jesus no reason to dethrone the Law and presented his teaching (authentically or not) as positively enjoining the opposite. Matthew is the leading example: for him, Jesus indeed intensified the Law along the lines that the Law itself set down (5.17–48; 23.3, 23). Of course, Matthew has been read in a quite different sense by later Christians who valued simply his strong ethical clarity and fullness of teaching (and popular approval of "the Sermon on the Mount" has rarely reckoned with its original sense and orientation); he himself meant Christians to continue to obey the full Mosaic Law, indeed with extra strictness. There is, of course, as has already been indicated, a case for saying that this view carries further a probable tendency in the teaching of Jesus himself favoring the removal of fudge and slackness. Despite this adherence to the Law, the chief preoccupation for Matthew, as for Mark, is following Jesus himself, not an impersonal code, and it is Jesus' voice that now chiefly gives the Law its authority for Christians ("I say to you," 5.22ff.; but see 23.3). What we must then say is that Mark moved along a quite different line of reasoning: he was not so much concerned to answer the question, How shall we behave under God? as the question, How should human beings enter into relationship with God? This was less a rabbinic than a Pauline order of priority.

At first sight, Luke seems to present a Jesus who is midway between the Paulineness of Mark's portrait and the Jewishness of Matthew's. The reason may well be that this is precisely close to the center of his concern: to help the churches of his day to heal their divisions and end their controversies, precisely over issues such as this one. In Acts, Luke is at pains to depict the two sides on the crucial struggle over Torah-observance as capable of unity: in Acts 15, he makes the most of pacific straws in the wind and unitive strands in the past (as indicated, for example, in the irenic "moment" in Galatians 2.1–10, so rudely upset in what Paul tells us happened next) to depict the grounds for unity and reconciliation. He does it partly on grounds of quasi-doctrine that might apply to Gentiles now within "the people of God" (the Law itself was generous to the stranger within the gates, the resident alien, requiring only minimum conformity) and partly on grounds of an ethic where generosity of both spirit and pocket were central. It was an ethic of which Jesus himself was the preacher, a true ethics of the kingdom, and it might move stony hearts (e.g., 6.20–23; 4.16–21). It was nevertheless stringent in the choices for allegiance that lay beneath it (see 14.15–33).

In John, the case is both simpler and stranger. We no longer have a sense of the Law as a body of provisions to which one might discuss one's attitude in detail as well as in principle. Rather, the Law is among those great entities in Judaism that Jesus, as God's Word made flesh, replaces. It stands alongside the temple (where indeed some of its central provisions had been carried out) and prophetic "words" of old, indeed the whole mediatorial apparatus of Israel. In relation to all of them, Jesus is all-sufficient. That is all very well, but where did this writer suppose his Christians were to turn for moral guidance? Did he simply take for granted (as surely Paul did) that when it came to everyday ethics the Law stood in place? Or are we to take him at his word, where he depicts Jesus as giving only one command (13.34): that his followers "love one another"? It is true that once or twice we read of Jesus' "commandments" in the plural (e.g., 15.10); but we never learn what they might be. In 1 John 3.15–17, we have an assumption of practical care for the needy brother, the nearest we get in the Johannine writings to a practical ethical situation, so illustrating one outcome of "loving one another." Otherwise we draw a blank. Was the whole matter of behavior simply not on the evangelist's agenda for this book, whose subject was intended to be different, or was the level of commitment and spirituality in this community seen as so high that such mundane instruction was not required? In the latter case, the Johannine epistles demonstrate, alas, that such trust was misplaced, for hatred and narrowness were just below the surface and soon erupted (1 John 2.18f.).

What is certainly true is that in the religion that stems from Jesus, the centrality of "salvation" and of relationship with him to that end has meant a quite different approach to "law" from that in, for example, Judaism. Despite the later development of both moral stringency and inflexibility in most branches of Christianity (with some exceptions in, for example, the English seventeenth century and more widely in recent years), and despite the elaboration of ethics as a rational "science," especially in Western Christianity, even since medieval times, there has never been the tendency to highly detailed textual legalism that strict rabbinic interpretation of the Torah often strikes others as pursuing. In Christian lands, "law" has characteristically been largely seen as a matter of what we would now call secular administration, even in Christian states and in times of Christian dominance, even though Church law has concerned itself not just with ecclesiastical arrangements but with some aspects of morality, notably in relation to marriage and other family affairs. And Christian thought has generally come to be a matter of furthering Christian moral principles, largely in a general, even if forceful way (e.g., with regard to war and issues of social justice), with smaller detail being confined in recent times largely to sexual matters, Christianity being seen implicitly as now specially relating, ethically, to matters of intimate human relations. That is a far cry from the broad canvas and large-scale force of the preaching of the kingdom in the mission of Jesus. But it is perhaps a legacy of the force of that preaching that there has never quite been a Christian rabbinism, despite recurring tendencies in that direction.

Leslie Houlden

See also: Crossan, J. D.; Hengel, Martin; Jesus in Social Context; John, Gospel of; Luke, Gospel of, and Acts of the Apostles; Mark, Gospel of; Matthew, Gospel of; Paul; Sanders, E. P.

References

Houlden, J. L. 1992. *Ethics and the New Testament*. Edinburgh: T. & T. Clark.

Meier, J. P. 1991. A *Marginal Jew*. New York and London: Doubleday.

Sanders, E. P. 1983. *Paul, the Law and the Jewish People*. London: SCM Press.

———. 1990. *Jewish Law from Jesus to the Rabbis*. London: SCM-TPI.

Liberation Theology

Liberation theology is theology not *for* the poor but *of* the poor. It is a second-order activity that gives primacy to the praxis of the Church of the poor manifest in Base Ecclesial Communities. As a consequence, liberation theologians do not speak *of* Jesus but *with* Jesus, who himself was poor and is the liberator and the anticipation of the reign (or kingdom) of God, the new humanity liberated from poverty and oppression. In the context of liberation theology, the praxis of Jesus cannot be understood apart from his own sociopolitical context as well as that of those doing liberation theology. This theology entails a strong commitment to disrupting the cycle of domination and oppression that shape this context. The praxis of Jesus the Liberator is the motive and the stimulus for the cause of liberation: "He liberates from the destructiveness of social structures by offering himself as a focal point of commitment more enduring and fulfilling than commitment to any social structure could ever be; he liberates from fate by demonstrating that new things are always possible and that the dignity of human choice is not to be surrendered but to be enhanced; and he liberates from personal sin and guilt by the nature of his forgiving love, a love channelled through him by God" (Sobrino 1993, 63).

In writing the history of Jesus, the authors of the Gospels produced a theology of Jesus. This mutual relationship of doing theology by writing history and writing history by doing theology is what Latin American Christology tries to introduce into its own method in order to be faithful to its object, Jesus Christ, who has been given to it in "gospels": the life of Jesus is *gospel* and gospel is the *life* of Jesus.

Liberation theology advocates a *Christology from below* in contrast to the *Christology from above* that has in the past served as a means of oppression and justification of unjust social structures: its focus is no longer the Church but the human being in need of liberation. Jesus manifests God's fundamental "bias toward the poor," who in turn have an epistemological privilege of recognizing his praxis as liberation. Although his suffering and death are repeated in the suffering and the violent deaths of many in Latin America, he inspires those who suffer poverty and various other forces of oppression and slavery to become agents of their own liberation.

Speaking of Jesus in the context of liberation theology means moving beyond the Christological dogmas of Nicea and Chalcedon in order to develop a "historical Christology," a theological reflection on the life and development of Jesus of Nazareth as a person of faith in the particular historical situation of first-century Palestine. Systematic Christology needs to be reformulated in the light of the history of Jesus of Nazareth in order to overcome its involvement in the history of power and oppression. As most liberation theologians were, however, trained in the theological academies of Europe, and liberation theology regards itself as a contribution to doing theology of the whole Christian Church, traditional systematic theology remains an inevitable dialogue partner for reflection on Jesus in a liberation theological paradigm. An example is the distinction between the Christ of faith and the historical Jesus. For liberation theologians, the Christ of faith has been the ally of institutional and cultic religion that sides with the powers of oppression and perpetuates their sway. Access to the Christ of faith is only possible through radical discipleship following the praxis of the historical Jesus.

Jesus is not an object of academic theological investigation and reflection, but his life and death act as a "criterion of discipleship" in Latin America today. Liberation theology strives not to establish correct doctrine on the life and saving work of Jesus but rather *Christopraxis*, a following in the footsteps of Jesus even unto death and toward liberation. Christopraxis is the realization of the reign of God, which by necessity enters into situations of conflict in order to eradicate the evil of sinful structures that permeate society. In the context of a liberation theological paradigm, it is not possible to reflect on the person of Jesus without an active, radical discipleship. Such discipleship is, however, not a mere imitation of Christ but a radical openness to a new history of humanity in which the values of God's reign can be realized, founded in the "dangerous memory" of the history of Jesus.

Leonardo Boff (1980) outlined some of the main characteristics of a new Christological hermeneutic. These are the primacy of the human being over the Church as an institution; of the utopian future of liberation over the past history of dogmatics and hermeneutics in building and anticipating the world promised and demonstrated as possible by Jesus himself; of a critical approach over a dogmatic one, which enables the Christian experience to become incarnate within the historical experience of the people of Latin America; of the social over the individual dimension of life; and of orthopraxis over orthodoxy, since for Christ and for the earliest Christians the essential did not consist in the reduction of the message of Christ to systematic categories of intellectual comprehension but in creating new habits of acting and living in the world. This transfiguration of this world is the reign of God, which Jesus came to proclaim and anticipate in his own life, death, and resurrection and in the life and history of the suffering people.

According to Jon Sobrino, the reign of God, which Jesus proclaimed and anticipated in his own life, death, and resurrection, is "a utopian symbol for a wholly new and definitive way of living" (Sobrino 1978, 119). The fundamental value at the heart of the reign of God is to do justice. This involves overcoming the will to power that forces people to oppress others. The ultimate aim is reconciliation and fellowship. Justice cannot be done in the abstract but is always rooted in the concrete situation of the lives of the poor. Jesus himself experienced poverty in his own life. Such a concretization of justice is essentially a reinterpretation of the concept of the Incarnation, the first principle of classical Christologies.

According to Boff, Jesus is in his own person God's answer to the human condition: "Jesus affected human beings at their very roots, activating their hope-principle and making them dream of the kingdom, which is not an entirely different world but this world completely new and renewed" (Boff, 79).

Jesus is the archetype of humanity in the image of God, the archetypal person of faith. He is a person with a particularly deep experience of God and a particularly close relationship with God the Father. For Jesus, God existed in the dialectic tension of being absolute in intimacy and absolute otherness at the same time. Jesus, according to liberation theologians, regarded God as the personal ultimate with whom he had a relationship of trust-availability. Here we find reminiscences of Friedrich Schleiermacher's Jesus as a person of a high level of "God-consciousness" who is, however, not himself divine. Unlike in classical Christologies, Jesus is not seen as being the Son of God from eternity, "of one being with the Father," but he *becomes* the Son of God through his history of faith in God the Father. Sobrino has argued that Jesus did not reveal God the Father, but rather revealed how one as a person of faith becomes a Son of God (Sobrino 1978, 106).

The whole story of Jesus is read in the light of his proclamation as the one who brings the good news to the poor and liberty to the captives. His praxis is announced and summarized in Luke 4.16–21: "The spirit of the Lord has been given to me, for he has anointed me. He has sent me to bring the good news to the poor, to proclaim liberty to the captives and to the blind new sight, to set the downtrodden free, to proclaim the Lord's year of favour. . . . This text is being fulfilled today even as you listen." Speaking about Jesus remains essentially good news, as it was for the first Christian communities. The good news that Jesus proclaimed through his life and message, which is essentially also the life and message of the church of the poor, is that of the reign of God. Following Adolf von Harnack, liberation theologians assert that Jesus did not make himself the focus of his preaching and mission. At the heart of the mission of Jesus was not merely God, but the reign of God as the final reality. The reign of God, however, is not a transcendent "kingdom of heaven," but God's sovereignty in creating justice for and with the poor. Jesus was both proclaimer and initiator of the reign of God: "[I]t entails hope in people's filiation with the Father and in brotherhood between human beings" (Sobrino 1978, 91).

Jesus' violent death on the cross is seen as being in solidarity with the suffering poor and marginalized people. The experience of crucifixion is essentially connected with the hope of liberation. Its focus is not on the resurrection as an otherworldly event; rather, resurrection of both Jesus and the poor means liberation from structures of oppression and new life. Jesus is an ally of those who fight for their liberation, not of their oppressors. His violent death correlates with and is re-embodied in the life of the crucified peoples of Latin America and their experience of suffering violence. Sobrino spoke of Jesus' acceptance of his own violent death as Jesus' surrender of his own ideas and his own person. It was the "power of love in suffering," which alone conquers the reality of sin (Sobrino 1978, 94f.). Liberation theologians reject the concept of substitutionary atonement. The death of Jesus is not an act of redemption to be received passively, but an example of surrender and active radical discipleship, which initiates and anticipates the reign of God and the liberation of humanity in concrete historical situations. "The issue at stake is not just how God can *pardon* an 'offense' against him insofar as it is an internal human act; it is how God can *take away* an external sin that leads to the cross of his Son and to all the crosses of history" (Sobrino 1978, 190). Suffering is essentially a mode of being of God as it is of humanity. Although Western theology has been concerned with the "death of God," liberation theology cannot reflect on the cross without reflecting on the death of the other human being.

The cross and the resurrection of Jesus essentially belong together. Without the cross, the resurrection of Jesus becomes idealistic. The cross needs to be seen in all of its scandalous reality without an immediate soteriological or spiritual escape. Following Jürgen Moltmann's concept of the "crucified God," Sobrino and others have called for a reflection on the presence of God who abandoned Jesus on the cross at the crucifixion. On the cross, God was absent to Jesus but present to humanity. The cross is the contradiction of humanity but also the ultimate act of solidarity with it and love for it. Jesus' resurrection is the realization of his announcement of liberation. It signifies a concretization of the reign of God in Jesus' own life and thereby the concrete liberation of all people from the reign of death and from all forms of oppression. This is a fundamental act of solidarity with humanity.

Jesus did not allow himself to be determined by his situation, but loved us to the end. He took on himself this perverted condition and identified with humanity. He died alone so that no one else in the world would have to die alone; he is with each person so that all might partake of the life that manifested itself in the resurrection: eternal life in communion with God, with others, and with the cosmos (Boff, 133).

Natalie K. Watson

See also: American (South) Christianity; Chalcedon; Christology, Modern; Harnack, Adolf von; Jesus, Death of; Jesus in Social Context; Kingdom of God; Macquarrie, John; Nicea; Resurrection; Schleiermacher, F. D. E.; Son of God

References

Assmann, Hugo. 1980. "The Power of Christ in History." Pp. 133–150 in *Frontiers of Theology in Latin America*. Edited by Rosino Gibellini. London: SCM.

Boff, Leonardo. 1980. *Jesus Christ Liberator: A Critical Christology of Our Time*. London: SPCK.

Brown, Robert McAfee. 1993. *Liberation Theology: An Introductory Guide*. Westminster: John Knox.

Sobrino, Jon. 1978. *Christology at the Crossroads*. Maryknoll, NY: Orbis.

———. 1993. *Jesus the Liberator*. Maryknoll, NY: Orbis.

Lightfoot, J. B.

See Westcott, B. F., Lightfoot, J. B., and Hort, F. J. A.

Lightfoot, R. H. (1883–1953)

Robert Henry Lightfoot (no relation to Bishop J. B. Lightfoot, 1828–1889) spent the greater part of his working life in Oxford as a fellow of Lincoln College (1919–1921) and New College (1921–1950); and in his later years, he was the Dean Ireland Professor of Exegesis of Holy Scripture (1934–1949). His publications include *History and Interpretation in the Gospels* (the Bampton Lectures for 1934, published in 1935), *Locality and Doctrine in the Gospels* (1938), *The Gospel Message of St. Mark* (1950), and *St. John's Gospel* (edited by C. F. Evans, 1956). He was thus fifty-two when his first book was published, and this was no doubt partly because, in those days, scholars were not expected to rush into print, but also, in the case of Lightfoot, because, before 1931 (when he was forty-eight years old), he had, apparently, nothing new to say.

In that year, however, he went to Germany, met Rudolf Bultmann and Martin Dibelius, and was introduced to form criticism, and this opened up for him new ways of studying and understanding the Gospels. Before this, he had followed the methods of the source critics (e.g., B. H. Streeter) and had adopted the Marcan Hypothesis, according to which Mark's Gospel was not only the earliest of the four but also provided a historical account of the ministry of Jesus as remembered by Peter, who passed it on to Mark. Lightfoot was not convinced of this theory, however, and found that the methods and assumptions of the source critics failed to answer many questions. He described how he had been puzzled by the apparent lack of connection between the end of the first chapter of Mark and the beginning of the second chapter: "Jesus could no longer show himself in any town. . . . After some days he returned to Capernaum." He went for a walk on Otmoor and the truth dawned: Mark's stories were not linked by chronology but by theology.

Among other scholars who influenced him were William Wrede, whose book on *The Messianic Secret in the Gospels* had been published in 1901 in Germany (the first English translation was not made until 1971; in England it had to face the uphill task of overcoming Dr. William Sanday's judgment that it was "not only very wrong, but distinctly wrong-headed"), H. J. Cadbury, and J. H. Ropes (to whose book *The Synoptic Gospels* [1934] Lightfoot declared his indebtedness in *The Gospel Message of St. Mark:* "a book which, unless I am mistaken, is too little known in this country," p. 37 footnote).

In his Bampton Lectures, he spoke of "the excessive historical value assigned in the last two generations to St. Mark's Gospel, and this, we are now beginning to see, was mistaken" (Lightfoot 1935, 220). One wonders how many people in England, in 1934, would have accepted representation in the first person plural in this sentence. The lectures ended with a paragraph that was to become famous—or infamous according to the majority at that time:

> It seems, then, that the form of the earthly no less than of the heavenly Christ is for the most part hidden from us. For all the inestimable value of the gospels, they yield us little more than a whisper of his voice; we trace in them but the outskirts of his ways. Only when we see him hereafter in his fullness shall we know him also as he was on earth. And perhaps the more we ponder the matter, the more clearly we shall understand the reason for it, and therefore shall not wish it otherwise. For probably we are at present as little prepared for the one as for the other (ibid., 225).

The allusion to Job 26.14 was frequently missed; the possible parallel to the conclusion to Albert Schweitzer's *Quest of the Historical Jesus* (1910)—"He comes to us as one unknown, without a name, as of old, by the lakeside, he came to those men who did not know who he was . . . "—would, if it had been recognized, have done nothing to commend Lightfoot to his contemporary audience in Oxford or to the first generation of readers of his book. The then Warden of New College (Dr. H. A. L. Fisher) introduced Lightfoot to a guest at the time of the Bamptons as "Professor Lightfoot, who is currently making out a case for the Roman Catholic Church."

In his next two books, *Locality and Doctrine in the Gospels* and *The Gospel Message of St. Mark*, he argued repeatedly for the authenticity of the ending of Mark's Gospel at 16.8: "And they said nothing to anyone; for they were afraid." When he was criticized on the grounds that the resurrection was the most important event in the life of Jesus, so how could Mark have failed to record it, his reply was that a Gospel is not a biography; you must read a Gospel in order to find out what it is, and not ask questions that it was not intended to answer. He might justly be described as the father of redaction criticism in the English-speaking world.

Lightfoot was a man of deep personal piety, which he did everything he could to conceal. It shines out, however, from nearly every page he wrote. What was important to him was the evangelists and their several portraits of the Lord, not the most recent reconstruction of the historical Jesus: "There does not seem ever to have been a desire to bequeath to the church what we should call a purely historical picture of Jesus" (Lightfoot 1935, 209). He did not think there was any need for one now.

Both in his writing, and, even more, in his teaching and conversation, his personal faith came through to readers, students, and others who knew him. One of his former students, who returned to Oxford to consult him on his vocation, said afterward: "There could be no doubt one was in the presence of a priest."

If the question were asked, "What is to be said about Jesus in the work of R. H. Lightfoot?" part at least of the answer must be that Lightfoot belonged to a generation that did not employ familiarity when speaking or writing on this subject. He continued to refer to Jesus as "The Lord" or "The Master" and to use capital letters for the relevant pronouns, at least in *The Gospel Message of St. Mark*. He quoted his much admired guide, C. C. J. Webb: "Perfect love casts out fear (1 John 4.18) but the fear must be there; it is, as we know, the beginning of wisdom (Ps. 111.10)" (Lightfoot 1950, 91). As long as we are *in via*, a certain distance between him and us is both necessary and inevitable.

John Fenton

See also: Bultmann, Rudolf; Cadbury, H. J.; Mark, Gospel of

References

Lightfoot, R. H. 1935. *History and Interpretation in the Gospels*. London: Hodder and Stoughton.

———. 1950. *The Gospel Message of St. Mark*. Oxford: Clarendon.

Literature, English

Early English Literature

Old English literature is dominated by two great "Jesus" poems. The first is by the eighth- or ninth-century Northumbrian or Mercian poet Cynewulf and constitutes the second part of a three-part poem in the Exeter Book, a manuscript of poetry copied c. 940 and given by Bishop Leofric to Exeter Cathedral, where it remains. The poem focuses on the Incarnation, the Ascension (usually known as *Christ II*), and the Last Judgment. Numerous other works have been attributed to Cynewulf, most notably, and almost certainly wrongly, the greatest of Old English poems, *The Dream of the Rood* of the early ninth century or even earlier, which has a fascinating history linked to the obsession with finding the true cross of Jesus. The earliest evidence of *The Dream* is to be found in runic characters inscribed on a stone cross (or "rood") in the church at Ruthwell in Dumfriesshire, Scotland. The other early copy of the poem, about ninety years later than the Ruthwell Cross, is in the *Codice Vercellese*, which remains in the cathedral library at Vercelli on the pilgrim route from England to Rome. Other fragments of the poem indicate its remarkably wide, international circulation. The first seventy-eight lines are probably the oldest and describe how the poet, in a dream, saw the Cross of Jesus, which spoke to him and described how as a forest tree it was cut down and fashioned into a gallows for the "High King of Heaven." The events of the Passion and the suffering of the Cross itself are vividly described, until later "friends" of Jesus dig it out of the pit in which it was buried and cover it in glorious gold and jewels—the Cross itself follows the resurrection of the King. Told in the literary form of the riddle, the poem is closely linked with the Passiontide liturgy.

The Medieval Period

Medieval English literature is saturated with the language and images of the Church's liturgy and the learned as well as the folkloric traditions of Christendom. The thousands of popular songs and lyrics that survive work from within the theology of their time and often with great originality. For example, the tendency to interpret the Bible typologically and allegorically provided a vast resource of imagery from the Old Testament to describe Christian themes, and particularly poems about Jesus and the Blessed Virgin Mary. Thus the early fifteenth-century lyric about Mary, "I Sing of a Maiden," draws on the dew that falls on Gideon's fleece in Judges 6 as an image for the Spirit coming to Mary before the birth of Jesus. In such popular poetry, Jesus takes on a dramatic dynamism as the imagery frees itself from the restraints of the Church and its worship. A favorite theme is the "harrowing of hell," which is the subject of a semidramatic poem dating from about 1250. Deriving ultimately from the apocryphal Gospel of Nicodemus (second or third century A.D.), it describes the three days of Jesus in hell after the crucifixion when he rescues the souls lost to Satan since the Fall of Adam. This dramatic moment finds its most popular expression in the art and drama of the great cycles of mystery plays and also in the work of poets such as the Scottish court poet William Dunbar (c. 1456–c. 1513), whose great poem "Done Is a Battell on the Dragoun Blak" portrays Jesus as a medieval knight jousting with Satan for the souls of the lost.

Medieval lyrics on Jesus fall into three broad categories—the poems of the Nativity, poems of the Passion, and poems of adoration, many of them focusing as much on Mary as on Jesus himself. There are relatively few poems on the ministry or teachings of Jesus. Some of these works connect the liturgical year with folklore; for example, the well-known "Corpus Christi Carol" (early sixteenth century), which is linked with the popular grail legends and medieval chivalry. But by far the greatest source for medieval literature about Jesus is the liturgy and the Mass, and it is the dramatic fragment from the tenth century known as the *Quem Quaeritis* ("Whom seek ye in the tomb . . ." —a rough paraphrase of Luke 24.5) in the Easter liturgy, which eventually takes the Passion narrative out of the sanctuary of the church into the marketplace in the great mystery cycles popular in the thirteenth through the early sixteenth centuries. The greatest flowering of these plays appeared in the early fifteenth century in the work of the Wakefield Master, whose six pageants in the Towneley Cycle included three plays on the Nativity and the "Coliphizacio," a play of the crucifixion. The finest of these, the so-called "Second Shepherds' Play," combines a farcical pastiche of the Nativity in which the infant Jesus is replaced by a stolen lamb that is hidden in a manger with a beautiful final scene in the "real" Bethlehem stable and features the shepherds offering gifts of cherries and a bird to the infant Jesus. In these mystery plays (performed by the tradespeople of the town, and thus named from the *mestier*—métier or trade—of the different guilds), characters like Herod took on popular stock forms such as the buffoon, and Jesus was portrayed almost entirely from Gospel material, speaking words only from the Bible except in the great drama of the Harrowing of Hell and the Last Judgment.

At the other end of the learned spectrum is William Langland's (c. 1330–c. 1386) great poem *Piers Plowman*, which was written for a highly literate and theologically educated readership. In this great poem, the Passion and Jesus on the Cross are central but rarely presented directly except in hints. There is no place for the Virgin Mary or the disciples. Langland's Jesus is a theological figure in a Christocentric vision (or dream) that focuses on his *humanitas* as the sublime expression of God's love for humanity.

Middle English also has a number of prose lives of Jesus, of which the best known is *The Mirrour of the Blessed Lyf of Iesu Christ* (c. 1400) by Nicholas Love, prior of the Carthusian House of Mount Grace near York. This work is an elegant translation and adaptation of a Latin life of Jesus thought to be by St. Bonaventure.

The Sixteenth and Seventeenth Centuries

The tradition of Lives of Jesus found its greatest flowering in the work of Bishop Jeremy Taylor, who wrote the first true English work on this subject in his massive *Great Exemplar of Sanctity and Holy Life: Described in the History of the Life and Death of the Ever Blessed Jesus Christ, the Saviour of the World* (1649). Drawn initially from his sermons, it was described by Edmund Gosse (*Jeremy Taylor* [1904]) as "a celebration of the beauty of the Lord Jesus—God and Man." Taylor mingled biblical material with later legends and imaginative material, such as the worship offered by the Egyptian deities when the infant Jesus fled into Egypt. ("And they made their first abode in Hermopolis in the country of Thebais, whither when they first arrived, the child Jesus being by design or providence carried into a Temple, all the statues of the Idol gods fell down, like Dagon at the presence of the Ark, and suffered their timely dissolution and dishonour." The legend was attributed by the learned Taylor to St. Palladius.) Taylor's purpose was devotional, and he made no attempt to acknowledge the biblical criticism of his day. Other lives of Jesus include Abraham Woodhead's *Historical Narrative of Our Lord* (1685).

Following the tradition of the medieval lyrics, much devotional verse of the sixteenth and seventeenth centuries focused on the life of Jesus, and in particular the Incarnation and the Passion. In Edmund Spenser's (c. 1552–1599) sequence of eighty-eight sonnets, *Amoretti* (1595), the resurrection is celebrated in the poem "Most Glorious Lord of Life!" which looks back to the medieval tradition of the harrowing of hell and uses the example of Christ's love for us in his Passion to illustrate the nature of the poet's own love for his future wife Elizabeth Boyle ("Love is the lesson which the Lord us taught"). Another Easter poem is George Herbert's (1593–1633) "Rise Heart, Thy Lord Is Risen," which celebrates Herbert's "art" in its singing of Christ's praises and links Easter Day with Palm Sunday as the poet "Got me flowers to straw thy way." In a charming anonymous sixteenth-century lyric known as "The Holy Well," Jesus is seen as a child asking permission from his mother to go out to play. Permission is granted on the understanding that he come back in the evening without complaining. But the children whom he meets will not play with him because he is "meaner [i.e., poorer] than us all," having been born in an ox's stall, and he returns to his mother in tears. The poem concludes with Gabriel reminding Jesus that he may have been born humbly, but he yet is "the King of Heaven." In Robert Southwell's (1561–1595) poem "The Burning Babe," Jesus appears to the poet as a "pretty Babe all burning bright," whose burning, fueled by Justice and Mercy, will melt human souls into a bath "to wash them in my blood." When the vision vanishes, the poet recalls that it is Christmas Day.

The greatest of the English Renaissance poets who took the life of Jesus as the basis for devotional verse was John Donne (1572–1631), consummately in the sequence of seven sonnets, *La Corona,* in which he likened his offering as a poet to the offering of the Eucharist. The sonnets are linked to the liturgical cycle through the Christian year from the Annunciation to the Nativity, the incident at the temple, the Crucifixion, the Resurrection, and finally the Ascension. The last line of each poem is also the first of the one that follows. In *La Corona,* Jesus is closely connected to the piety and theology of the Catholic Mass, although Donne was himself a Protestant (though raised as a Catholic), and at the same time with the humanistic ideals of the Renaissance. As a boy in the temple (Luke 2.41–51), Jesus sits "blowing out those sparks of wit"—characteristic of the "wit" of the metaphysical poets themselves—and Christ's Holy Spirit is the inspiration for Donne's own Muse. Donne used and expanded biblical imagery: Jesus is the lamb that becomes the "strong ram, which has battered heaven for me."

Beside the Anglican Donne, the Puritan John Milton (1608–1674) stands as perhaps the greatest of all English poetic contributors to literature on Jesus Christ. A major and too little recognized influence on Milton's epic *Paradise Lost* (published in 1667) is Giles Fletcher's (c. 1585–1623) *Christ's Victory and Triumph in Heaven and Earth, over and after Death* (1610), which emphasizes both Christ's humility in his Incarnation and his eternal nature as the creative Word: "A child he was, and had not learnt to speak, / That with his word the world before did make." In Book VII of *Paradise Lost,* Raphael recounts to Adam how it was God's pleasure to create a new world after the expulsion of Satan from heaven, and accordingly he sent his Son with angels to perform the work of creation in six days out of the unformed matter that had originated in the Father. Milton thus linked the Genesis story with the first chapter of the Fourth Gospel. In Book III, the Father accepts the free offer of the Son to be a ransom for mankind and ordains his Incarnation ("Thou therefore, whom thou only canst redeem, / Their nature also to thy nature join; / And be thyself man among men on earth, / Made flesh . . ."). In *Paradise Regained* (published in 1671), Jesus is given the role of epic hero in a poem that concentrates on the biblical accounts of his baptism and temptations by Satan in the wilderness. At the end of his epic encounter in four books, Jesus returns privately and meekly to his mother's home in Nazareth.

The Eighteenth and Nineteenth Centuries

Jesus is not a notable presence in English literature and poetry of the eighteenth century. In 1701, Sir Richard Steele published *The Christian Hero*, a guide to ethics, in which Jesus and the Bible generally were offered as moral teachers and examples in place of Stoic and classical philosophy. Alexander Pope wrote his poem *Messiah* (1712) more to render the great prophetic poem in Isaiah 53 as a classical Virgilian eclogue than from any interest in Christian theology. More pious is the text of Handel's great oratorio *The Messiah* (1742), which was compiled by Jennens from biblical texts and the Psalter of the Book of Common Prayer. Following roughly the chronology of the Gospel narratives, *The Messiah* nevertheless has little interest in the actual life of Jesus. Christopher Smart (1722–1771) versified at tedious length some of the Gospel parables, and in his best-known poem, *A Song to David* (1763), celebrated the Creation and the Incarnation, building his verse on mathematical principles and without much reference to Jesus. For Smart, for all his extravagant piety, Jesus was primarily a moral teacher on Enlightenment principles.

In eighteenth-century poetry, Jesus emerged most dramatically from the poets of nonconformity and religious revival, notably Isaac Watts (1674–1748), Philip Doddridge (1702–1751), and Charles Wesley (1707–1788). Such poets fervently reminded their readers of the personal encounter between the individual and Jesus. Thus, in Watts's hymn "Crucifixion to the World by the Cross of Christ," still sung at Passiontide today, we are called to "survey" the figure on the cross from head to toe in a meditation that is the more powerful for being starkly physical. In Wesley's hymn "The Incarnation," a call to contemplate Jesus in the manger concludes with the claim that "Jesus is our Brother now." In these poems, an essentially simple evangelical piety makes full use of the physical presence of the Incarnation to fix our attention on Jesus and his work in salvation.

Within the poetry of English Romanticism, one writer stands out for whom Jesus is central: William Blake (1757–1827). In his poetry, Jesus becomes one with the Romantic poet-genius within his apocalyptic vision. In the prose preface to *Jerusalem* (1804–1820), Blake wrote that "the Spirit of Jesus is continual forgiveness of Sin" and quoted (in Greek) Jesus' last words from Matthew's Gospel (28.18): "all authority in heaven and on earth has been given to me." Yet it is the Johannine Jesus who predominates in Blake's mythology, as in the writings of other Romantic poets, such as Samuel Taylor Coleridge. In Plate 62 of Blake's *Jerusalem*, Jesus replies to the "outcast" Jerusalem, "I am the Resurrection & the Life. / I Die & pass the limits of possibility as it appears / To individual perception." But at other moments in his poem, Blake stressed the humanity of Jesus brought up in the house of a carpenter in Nazareth (Plate 61), or Jesus as the Good Shepherd (Plate 98). For Blake, Jesus was an iconoclastic figure set against the Church and the Christian institutions that the poet so despised. Thus the "humble" Jesus of *The*

Everlasting Gospel (c. 1818)—"His Seventy Disciples sent / Against Religion & Government"—contrasts with the great hook-nosed vision of Christ of the Church's tradition, who is his "Vision's Greatest Enemy."

On the whole, however, the Romantic movement in English literature gave scant attention to the figure of Jesus. But the rise of historical biblical criticism in Germany and later England in the eighteenth and nineteenth centuries paved the way for a new wave of lives of Jesus in English, following earlier German lives by writers such as Johann Jakob Hess (1768) and, much more important, Hermann Samuel Reimarus (1778). "Before Reimarus," Albert Schweitzer remarked in his hugely influential *The Quest of the Historical Jesus*, "no one had attempted to form a historical conception of the life of Jesus." Perhaps the most important and notorious of these German lives was *Das Leben Jesu* (1835) by David Friedrich Strauss, which found a significant role in English literature through its magnificent translation (1846) by the young Mary Ann Evans, later to become the novelist George Eliot. Written under the influence of Hegelian philosophy, this work asserts that in our reading of Jesus in the Gospels "we stand . . . upon purely mythical-poetical ground" with little hold, if any, on historical reality. Very similar to the thought of Strauss (though without the Hegelianism) is the work of the American Transcendentalist Ralph Waldo Emerson (1803–1882), who in his celebrated "Divinity School Address" (1838) denied that Jesus is God any more than every other person is God, but saw him instead as a prophet.

But alongside this academic writing, popular piety in Victorian England continued to produce "lives of Jesus," one of the most influential being that by Frederic William Farrar (1831–1903), dean of Canterbury Cathedral. Rejecting in the Preface to his *Life of Christ* (1874) others who "have impugned the authority of the Gospels," among them Strauss, Ernest Renan, Sir R. Hanson, and Thomas Scott, Farrar offered a highly readable narrative in the tradition of Jeremy Taylor, at once literal and learned, mentioning, like Taylor, the idols in Egypt who "fell from their pedestals with a sudden crash" before the infant Jesus. Almost as popular was Sir John Seeley's *Ecce Homo* ("Behold the Man"; 1865, published anonymously), which presented Jesus as a moral reformer and earned the criticism of more orthodox opponents as different as Cardinal Newman and W. E. Gladstone for its failure to acknowledge the Christ of the Christian creeds.

Despite this opposition from churchmen, Victorian fiction eagerly took up the Jesus of Christian socialism in such novels as Eliza Lynn Linton's *The True History of Joshua Davidson* (1872), Elizabeth Phelps's *A Singular Life* (1895), and Hall Caine's *The Christian* (1897). In Linton's crude but readable novel, Joshua, son of David, is a carpenter's son from a provincial Cornish village who is eventually killed in London while attempting to preach that Christ and his followers were actually communists. This modern Jesus is presented as a working-class man opposed to the world of nineteenth-century capitalism and institutionalized churches. Similarly, Phelps's contemporary Jesus is an idealistic young clergyman who ministers to the poor, scandalously befriends a prostitute, and dies young. Caine's latter-day Jesus represents the "new social application" of Christianity; he dies with the Gospel words "Father, forgive them, for they know not what they do" on his lips. But the most substantial of all such Victorian "Christs" is found in Mrs. Humphrey Ward's *Robert Elsmere* (1888); this character's intellectual honesty compels him to renounce his Anglican orders and end his life ministering to the working-class men of London's East End. Elsmere was Mrs. Ward's attempt to "reconceive the Christ" for the nineteenth century. This highly academic novel earned her the approbation of W. E. Gladstone but spawned a literature of "reconstruction," notably W. H. Mallock's *The Reconstruction of Belief* (1905), which is prefaced by the poem "The Veil of the Temple," asking, "How wilt thou bear the creeds that bleat / Like starving sheep from frozen downs?"

Apart from the socialist Jesus, Victorian fiction produced other, sometimes bizarre versions of the Christ figure. Marie Corelli's melodramas, in which Jesus often appeared in lush and exotic forms or settings, were hugely popular. In *Barabbas* (1893), Jesus on the Cross was surrounded by angels, whirlwinds, and visions; the scene ended in the conversion of Barabbas himself, who dies after seeing a vision of Jesus in prison, and then his soul is lifted to heaven. More sober, though deeply romantic, was the portrayal of Jesus in the American Lew Wallace's *Ben-Hur: A Tale of the Christ* (1880), which was followed in 1888 with his novel *The Boyhood of Christ*.

Perhaps surprisingly, Jesus did not appear particularly frequently in nineteenth-century poetry except in the work of hymn writers. Indeed, it is notable that major Christian poets, such as Gerard Manley Hopkins and Alice Meynell, made relatively few direct references to Jesus in their work, though the Incarnate Christ is the undercurrent in the former's "Wreck of the Deutschland." A few poems have survived in hymnaries, such as lines from the American Quaker John Greenleaf Whittier (1807–1892) in his work *The Brewing of Soma*, which paint a sentimental portrait of Galilee, "Where Jesus knelt to share with thee / The silence of Eternity." It was of this romantic Jesus that D. H. Lawrence, having abandoned the Christian faith, wrote in his 1928 essay "Hymns in a Man's Life": "The Lake of Galilee! I don't want to know where it is. I never want to go to Palestine. Galilee is one of those lovely, glamorous worlds, not places, that exist in the golden haze of child's half-formed imagination." The child's Jesus is also recalled in Christina Rossetti's (1830–1894) familiar "A Christmas Carol" ("In the bleak mid winter"), which paints a picture of the Victorian nativity scene contrasting human simplicity with the infant Jesus as "Lord God Almighty." But alongside the Jesus of the pious, there is also the Jesus of the honest and tortured Victorian doubter, as in Arthur Hugh Clough's (1819–1861) "Easter Day: Naples, 1849," which is a kind of anti-gospel denying the resurrection: "Christ is not risen, no, / He lies and moulders low."

The Twentieth Century

The modern period sees a revival of Jesus in drama. A law in England forbidding the representation of Jesus on stage or film did not prevent Dorothy L. Sayers from writing her 1941–1942 play-cycle *The Man Born to Be King* for radio broadcast, a work at once highly theological and contemporary—

although Jesus tends to call his disciples familiarly "my lads," the story remains close to the incidents of the Gospel narratives. The relaxing of the law made Jesus available for television and film, notably in Dennis Potter's television play *Son of Man* (1969), in which a skeptical Potter has Jesus as a "brave, witty, sometimes oddly petulant, man striding around in an occupied territory knowing and then not wanting to know that he's bound to die." More straightforward is Anthony Burgess's *Jesus of Nazareth* (1977), which Franco Zeffirelli made into a hugely successful film. Edwin Morgan, the "poet laureate" of Glasgow, has written *A.D.: A Trilogy of Plays on the Life of Jesus* (2000), a minor classic that is only loosely based on the Gospels and portrays Jesus as "a human figure in an inhuman time."

Fictional lives of Jesus, or portraits of Jesus seen through the eyes of another character, continue to be written, from George Moore's *The Brook Kerith: A Syrian Story* (1916) to Lloyd C. Douglas's *The Big Fisherman* (1948) and Taylor Caldwell's *Great Lion of God* (1970). A more recent contribution, born of piety, is Moelwyn Merchant's *Jeshua: Nazareth to Jerusalem* (1987). Few of these novels have much literary merit, though an exception is Robert Graves's *King Jesus* (1946), a scholarly work. Graves took, in his own words, "more than ordinary pains to verify the historical background" and adopted an "analeptic method," putting the narrative into the words of a Hellenistic historian writing about A.D. 93. In the end, "Jesus by his defeat of death remains alive, an earth-bound Power, excused incarceration in Sheol but not yet risen to Heaven." Other novels introduce Jesus as a character in narratives that focus primarily on other individuals, biblical or otherwise. Michèle Roberts's *The Wild Girl* (1984) is a first-person narrative life of Mary Magdalene, written from a feminist perspective, with a rather pallid Jesus as her lover. One of the most fascinating of recent Jesus novels is Jim Crace's *Quarantine* (1997), a retelling of the forty days of temptation; a miscellaneous group of pilgrims, dominated over by the evil merchant Musa, joins Jesus, an adolescent, idealistic figure who, it would appear, actually dies in the wilderness, though through him his fellow travelers variously receive some kind of redemption.

Frequently, Jesus is presented in fiction in modern guise, as in William Faulkner's *A Fable* (1954), in which he appears as Stephan: born at Christmastime in a Middle Eastern stable, he becomes a corporal leading a squadron of twelve men and is executed at the age of thirty-three, after which his body is claimed by two women, Marthe and Marye. In an earlier novel, Upton Sinclair's *They Call Me Carpenter* (1922), the narrator dreams that Jesus steps down from a stained-glass window and assumes the name of Mr. Carpenter. In the tradition of the socialist Jesus, he supports a trade union strike while befriending a film star called Mary Magna. Other novels have a less direct relationship with the traditional Jesus. As Theodore Ziolkowski has written, "The modern hero whose life is prefigured by the life of Jesus may occasionally be a good or even a Christlike man, but . . . he may also be an obsessed paranoid, a Nietzschean élitist, an atheistic Party functionary, or a scheming opportunist"(Ziolkowski, 1972). In John Steinbeck's *The Grapes of Wrath* (1939), in a mixture of Old Testament and New Testament references,

Jim Casy (JC) and the twelve members of the Joad family set out from Oklahoma to the promised land of California. At his violent death, Jim echoes Jesus' words from the Cross, "You don't know what you're a-doin." Graham Greene's whiskey priest in *The Power and the Glory* (1940) chaotically follows the pattern of Jesus' ministry until he is finally executed by the state for the sake of the criminal James Calver (he meets, it might be said, his calvary).

A persistent subcategory of such fiction has been the novel that parodies the life of Jesus. Gore Vidal's *Messiah* (1954) "reinvents" Christianity in modern America through the life of John Cave (JC) and the publicity agents who promote the religion of Cavesword or Cavesway. John Barth's hugely complex *Giles Goat-Boy, or The Revised New Syllabus* (1966), a debunking of American university life, mercilessly caricatures Jesus (in the figure of Enos Enoch, the Shepherd Emeritus, and the "goat-boy"—born in a stable—Giles), Mary Magdalene, John the Baptist, and other Gospel characters. Christianity here meets an emergent postmodernism.

In the poetry of the twentieth century, Jesus has found a new and creative environment after the somewhat sterile doubts and pieties of the nineteenth century. The Parousia, or "Second Coming," is terrifyingly presented in W. B. Yeats's 1921 poem of that title, which ends with the question, "And what rough beast, its hour come round at last, slouches towards Bethlehem to be born?"—a Jesus reborn, or perhaps usurped by the violence of the new century. A more conventional Nativity scene is presented in T. S. Eliot's "Journey of the Magi" (1927), a meditation on birth and death. The wars of modern time have given a place to Jesus, as in Wilfred Owen's "Soldier's Dream" (1917), in which the young English officer in the trenches "dreamed kind Jesus fouled the big-gun gears" but wakes to find that, instead, "God was vexed" and had made sure that all the guns were in working order. Owen's "At a Calvary near the Ancre" (1918) reflects on a wayside calvary in France that has been damaged in the war. In the poem's final verse, by implication, the soldiers fighting at the front follow Christ in the laying down of their lives, though not for the state or for political reasons. From the Second World War, Edith Sitwell's "Still Falls the Rain" (1941) links the 1940 air raids on London with the Passion and Crucifixion, and as the bombs fall the poet asks for mercy from "the Starved Man hung upon the Cross." A later crucifixion poem is Geoffrey Hill's "Canticle for Good Friday" (1956), in which Calvary is seen from the perspective of doubting Thomas in verse of stark, physical power that struggles toward some kind of theological resolution of the mystery of suffering.

In a different vein, the joyful Jesus is represented by Stevie Smith's (1902–1971) "The Airy Christ," a poem written to celebrate E. V. Rieu's modern translation of Mark's Gospel. This poem looks back to the medieval "question" poems that sought Jesus' identity. "Who is this that comes in splendour, coming from the blazing East?" the poet asks, as Jesus appears afresh in the garments of modern English in a manner "we had not thought of." Her poem "Was He Married?" asks a long series of searching Christological questions. In David Jones's epic *Anathemata* (1952), modern poetry returns to the worlds of *The Dream of the Rood* and *Piers Plowman* in a vision of the Passion that is spare, learned, immersed in the Church's liturgy and theology. But in it, theology is liberated from the formulaic and plays its part in the history of human suffering and hope.

The twentieth century has given Jesus the possibility of appearing on film, and the cinema has not been slow to undertake lives of Jesus that are epic (the 1965 *The Greatest Story Ever Told*), parodic (the 1979 *Monty Python's Life of Brian*), and controversial (the 1988 *Last Temptation of Christ*, based on the novel by Nikos Kazantzakis). Although these works lie outside the strictly literary concerns of this article, they cannot easily be dissociated from the literary traditions that have been traced here—for example, there is renewed interest in the medieval popular dramas of the mystery plays, which have also frequently been revived on the stage and in more "authentic" settings in various ancient cities. The cinema has also been particularly sensitive to the ability of the figure Jesus to adapt to changing cultural surroundings. Just as the nineteenth-century novel gave rise to the "socialist" Christ, so the cinema has given us the "flower-power" musical Jesus of *Godspell* (1973) and the "rock" Jesus of *Jesus Christ, Superstar* (1973).

Of necessity, this article has omitted much literature that could legitimately have claimed a place here, and its purpose has been indicative rather than exhaustive. But one poem in particular, David Gascoigne's (b. 1916) powerful "Ecce Homo," encapsulates, in its version of the crucifixion, the Jesus of the twentieth century: anticlerical, suffering with the political and social victims of modern society, the subversive Jesus that literature has always embraced, the "Christ of Revolution and of Poetry."

David Jasper

See also: Auden, W. H.; Celtic and Early English Christianity; Eliot, T. S.; Eucharist; Film; Great War; Holy Sepulchre; Hymns; Literature, World; Mary; Milton, John; Music; Preexistence; Reimarus, Hermann Samuel; Schweitzer, Albert; Strauss, D. F.; Wesley, Charles, and Wesley, John

References

Atwan, Robert, George Dardess, and Peggy Rosenthal, eds. 1998. *Divine Inspiration: The Life of Jesus in World Poetry*. New York: Oxford University Press.

Bennett, J. A. W. 1982. *Poetry of the Passion: Studies in Twelve Centuries of English Verse*. Oxford: Clarendon.

Birney, A. 1989. *The Literary Lives of Jesus: An International Bibliography*. New York: Oxford University Press.

Detweiler, Robert. 1964. "Christ and the Christ Figure in American Fiction." Pp. 111–124 in *The Christian Scholar* 47.

Eastman, F. 1947. *Christ in the Drama: A Study of the Influence of Christ on the Drama of England and America*. New York: Macmillan.

Jeffrey, David Lyle, ed. 1992. *A Dictionary of Biblical Tradition in English Literature*. Grand Rapids, MI: William B. Eerdmans.

Kinnard, Roy, and Tim Davis. 1992. *Divine Images: The History of Jesus on the Screen*. New York: Citadel Press.

Rosenthal, Peggy. 2000. *The Poets' Jesus: Representations at the End of a Millennium*. New York: Oxford University Press.

Schweitzer, Albert. 1910. *The Quest of the Historical Jesus*. First edition. Translated by W. Montgomery. London: A. & C. Black.

Ziolkowski, Theodore. 1972. *Fictional Transfigurations of Jesus*. Princeton: Princeton University Press.

Literature, World

Introduction

Despite what may be perceived as a growing "anglicization" of the figure of Jesus throughout the contemporary world—a result, in large part, of the increasing dominance of North American technology in media and communications—the non-English-speaking world has maintained a rich and divergent tradition of Jesus throughout its imaginative literature. We might distinguish four categories within this tradition, according to chronological emergence: Semitic, European, colonial, and global.

Semitic

"Semitic" refers to the literature that has arisen within the Semitic cultures, beginning with the New Testament Scriptures themselves, the original literary source of Jesus. Indeed, the New Testament must be considered literature as much as a sacred text, and Jesus at his very origin a literary figure, whose portrayals in the four Gospels provide the exempla of future depictions. The Gospels give credence not only to Jesus as a literary subject, but to the heterogeneous nature of portraying that subject, as later manifested in the numerous apocryphal gospels or the Nag Hammadi texts that followed in the early Christian era. In the apocryphal gospels, Jesus' birth and death are often retold in different or greater detail: in Pseudo-Matthew, for example, the infant Jesus commands palm trees to bend down and offer their fruit to his hungry mother, while the *Infancy Gospel of Thomas* recounts miracles performed by Jesus between the ages of five and twelve, such as stretching beam sizes to perfect fit within his father's carpentry shop; in the *Gospel of Peter,* Jesus' resurrection is witnessed by the guards themselves; and in the *Gospel of Nicodemus (Acts of Pilate)*, ten chapters are devoted to Jesus' descent to the underworld. In the more sectarian Nag Hammadi gospels, Jesus' sayings more than his life's deeds are recast, especially within Gnostic terms: the Coptic *Gospel of Thomas*, for example, offers several new parables spoken by Jesus. This early tradition of gospel portrayal, often Jewish-Christian in nature, continues well into the present times, as represented perhaps best by Yiddish novelist Sholem Asch's *The Nazarene* (1939), a story involving the discovery of the supposed lost Fifth Gospel, a portrayal of Jesus' life according to Judas Iscariot.

European

"European" refers to literature arising within a strictly European context of the last two millennia. Certainly, Continental Europe has had a long history of Christendom to develop a wealth of literary works in which the portrayal of Jesus figures directly. Medieval depictions were predominantly visual or iconographic, but there were no doubt stories of Jesus transmitted orally in which the colorations of his life and deeds reached imaginative heights. With illiteracy so prevalent, very few survived in written form, though the early *The Dream of the Rood* (seventh to tenth century), in which an unknown narrator visits the crucifixion scene in a vivid dream, is one notable exception. What has survived from this period comes to us more often in the form of Passion and mystery plays, lyrics, and devotional poetry. The Passion plays, rife throughout Europe, reenacted the story of Jesus' final days leading to crucifixion and resurrection, frequently in outdoor settings, and with much dramatic variance. Medieval lyrics, chiefly in Latin, served the early musical traditions of the monasteries and cathedrals and furnished some remarkable poetry concerning Jesus in the form of liturgical chants and Masses, motets, or, later, festive carols. Devotional poetry developed the lyric even further and was used to cultivate an imaginative spirituality within a believer's meditative and prayer life. St. Anselm's "Prayer to St. Mary Magdalen" of the late eleventh century is a fine example of such Latin verse; in this poem, Jesus is called upon to comfort both a lamenting Mary Magdalen and, by extension, the devout reader. Other such examples can be found within the aesthetically fertile mystical tradition of this period. The great religious masterpiece of medieval literature, Dante's fourteenth-century *Divine Comedy*, is of course filled with references to Christ; yet it is not until the final canto of the *Paradiso* that the exalted divine figure makes a significant entry into the poetic narrative, and then only as an ecstatic and numinous culmination of the poet's journey, an ethereal vision of Eternal Light *"maggio / che 'l parlar mostra"* ("greater / than what speech can show").

The Renaissance, and more particularly the Reformation, with its technical invention of the printing press and the Lutheran injunction of *sola scriptura* ("scripture alone," in other words, leaving tradition aside as a source of belief), brought a new understanding of "the text." Here, a text, like the soul of the individual, could develop on its own terms rather than being governed by the preconditions of ecclesiastical doctrine. The rise of the novel in the seventeenth century correlated with this new freedom and provided a new way to narrativize story. Despite Protestant piety centered upon the Word, or perhaps, indeed, because of it, the life and character of Jesus began to emerge in these novel forms as early as the eighteenth century. Poetry, too, freed itself from general ecclesiastical control during this period to explore some of the more individual and lyrical sides of Jesus. With the eventual retreat of the Church, Catholic or Protestant, from the center of European intellectual culture from the eighteenth to the twentieth centuries, the figure of Jesus has been pursued from much more unorthodox or secular positions, though always with the rich heritage of Christendom unmistakable in the backdrop.

Colonial

"Colonial" refers, generically, to literature arising as a result of Europe's expansion beyond its own borders, particularly from the sixteenth century onwards. During this age of discovery, the figure of Jesus was exported under two often connected thrusts: exploration and missionary activity, the one usually following upon the other, especially where colonization developed. An exception to this rule might be the Far East, and especially the Jesuits in Japan under the missionary zeal of Francis Xavier in the 1500s, where spiritual concerns preceded economic or political motivation. In the West, conversion almost always followed upon conquest, as evidenced best in the non-English-speaking regions of Central and South America, particularly under Spanish colonization. Here, and in the subsequent colonization of the African continent, the introduction of Jesus into a culture where Christianity was not indigenous meant certain adaptations. These included, on the aboriginal side, the requirement (to at least some degree) of literacy, and on the colonizer's side, the requirement of translating stories that were centuries if not millennia old into extremely foreign contexts. In this process, and over the succeeding centuries, the figure of Jesus became localized or naturalized into specific non-Western cultures, each with their particular language, customs, and systems of values, and no more vividly is this naturalization seen than in the imaginative literature these cultures in time produced. An African, Asian, or Hispanic Jesus emerges, if only well after literacy has been established, who shows a definite European bloodline, but in the distinct dress of local tradition. This cross-fertilization is especially clear in the growing literature of colonial and postcolonial Africa, where the adoption of the "European" forms of poetry, novels, and other literature was coupled with writing in indigenous languages well outside Indo-European genealogy.

Global

Global refers both to literature from the remaining parts of the world, especially Asia, where European expansion was less a force, and, more recently, to literature affected by the recent trends of globalization. Here, the figure of Jesus is presented less under the legacy of a once ruling power, with its accompanying ecclesiastical auspices, and more and more by ready access made possible through a burgeoning technology of media and communications. This current phenomenon tends to produce a literary Jesus of greater cosmopolitanism who can converse with a variety of non-Western traditions and cultural references. This type of Jesus figure is perhaps no better exemplified than by the Chinese playwright Sha Yexin's (b. 1939) 1988 play *Jesus, Confucius and John Lennon*, which "tells of the absurdities Christ, Confucius and Lennon encounter during their travels together on the moon and in the world as representatives of God" (see http://www.sh.com/culture/drama/drama.htm). Such a globalized Jesus also tends toward greater commodification as he is taken from his own traditional context and treated as one more literary reference among a myriad, now disseminated through such globally instant means as the World Wide Web. The nature of such a thoroughly contemporized Jesus, and his future evolution within the imaginative possibilities of a postmodern world where references, however sacred once, are decontextualized and made "virtual" by largely unregulated websites, await to be fully seen.

Novels

The novel form, though comparatively late in its emergence, has had the widest development in depicting the person and character of Jesus. This is no doubt because of the novel's similarity of form to the original Gospel narratives, which not only detailed the life and ministry of Jesus sequentially from birth to death, albeit with a definite theological intention and with selective chronology, but also seemed to reveal a certain interior development of Jesus' character as he resisted the Devil's temptations in the desert, wept over the loss of friends at Bethany, and grappled with the weight of his impending death in the Garden of Gethsemane. Psychological development within a linear historical framework, through which the self unfolds as the continuum of internal processes in confrontation with the external world, is precisely what the novelistic form excels in.

It is no surprise then that the earliest manifestations of this form, in representing Jesus, were attempts to understand and reimagine the historical reality of Jesus' life. Albert Schweitzer, in his seminal book *The Quest of the Historical Jesus* (1910), traced the emerging efforts by predominantly Protestant German scholars of the late 1700s to represent Jesus from outside the prevailing myths and supernaturalism passed down by an "unenlightened" tradition. Among the works of eighteenth-century scholars such as Hermann Reimarus and Karl Barhdt, the quasi-novel of Karl Heinrich Venturini (1768–1849), translated as *A Non-supernatural History of the Great Prophet of Nazareth*, was perhaps foremost among the ambitious fictional accounts of Jesus' life. Written around 1800, it endeavored, as Schweitzer wrote, "to grasp the inner connexion of cause and effect in the events and experiences of the life of Jesus" (Schweitzer, 38). On the one hand, the author demythologized the miracles of Jesus in a thoroughly rational account of the "cause and effect"; on the other hand, since little if any "inner connexion" was indicated in the Gospels themselves, the author was pressed upon to fill in the gaps creatively, leaving a portraiture "at once crude and fantastic"—crude by the standards Schweitzer would have understood for historical-critical theology in the early twentieth century, but fantastic insofar as such works were highly imaginative fictions that included dramatic dialogue and scenic descriptions typical of many novels of its day.

Such reconstructions of Jesus have continued under the auspices of scholarship to this day, but these early examples in Germany also gave impetus to imaginative works outside of the historicism and rationalism of the academy. By the late 1800s, the figure of Jesus was able to leave his historical context altogether and appear in contemporary works not bound in any way by the strictures of historical reconstruction. One of most striking and, still to this day, most famous of such appearances is in *The Brothers Karamazov* (1880) by Russian novelist Fyodor Dostoyevsky (1821–1881). In a chapter that has taken on a life of its own, "The Grand Inquisitor," the figure of Jesus appears in a prose "poem" by one of the titular brothers, Ivan. Unlike previous authors who engaged in the quest for the historical Jesus, Dostoyevsky had little concern here with filling in the gaps left by the Gospels. In fact, he deliberately and completely avoided the original biblical context. Rather, he recast Jesus into a new setting, in sixteenth-century Spain, at the height of the Spanish Inquisition, so that the radical, antiestablishment nature of Jesus' life and message might be placed in its greatest relief. Jesus appears a day after a major auto-da-fé, a mass burning of heretics, and is instantly recognized by the people. On the steps of the cathedral, he raises a young child from the dead, just as the Cardinal, the Grand Inquisitor, is passing by. Jesus is seized and taken away to prison, where he is later visited by the Cardinal. In the ensuing private discussion—a monologue, for Jesus himself never speaks—the Cardinal reveals to Jesus what "he has been thinking in silence for ninety years," that humans are essentially weak and rebellious, and religion offers them the happiness they seek by providing the very three things Jesus denied in the temptation of the desert: miracle, mystery, and authority. Jesus' problem is that he overestimated humans. They do not want, nor can they endure, the freedom from miracle, mystery, and authority he promised. The Church—and specifically here, the Roman Catholic Church—by giving the people exactly what they want and can endure, corrects, in the name of Jesus, Jesus' own work. Jesus' return is not only meddlesome but perilous to the Church and its mission, and thus warrants the same fate as that of the heretics a day earlier. Jesus' only response is to rise and kiss the Cardinal on his "bloodless, aged lips," upon which the Cardinal opens the prison door with the stern words "Go, and come no more—don't come at all—never, never!" (ibid., 308).

This story may be seen not so much as a departure from the historical "quests" as a new development: rather than seeking the "essence" of Jesus' life and message through a rational historicizing of the original context, its seeks the "essence" through an imaginative displacement of the original in a hypothetical, and perhaps more relevant, scenario. It is also significant for the way it exposes the difficult relationship between freedom and authority at the heart of any reinterpretation or representation of Jesus: Ivan the atheist, like Dostoyevsky the novelist, is free to recast Jesus, yet he does so only to his piously religious brother, who is keen enough to respond, "Your poem is in praise of Jesus, and not in his disparagement" (ibid., 305). The brother then kisses Ivan on the lips, in deliberate imitation of Ivan's Jesus, and in a complex move that suggests traditional authority, he embraces a new freedom.

Such a freedom is taken further by Dostoyevsky's compatriot Mikhail Bulgakov (1891–1940). In his novel *The Master and Margarita* (1938), the hermeneutical layers involving freedom and authority are complicated well beyond any kind of orthodoxy. Two narratives are interwoven in the novel. One takes place in contemporary Moscow and involves the prankish exploits of the Devil (called Woland) and his strange entourage, who play havoc with various personages of Muscovite society. The other narrative—four interspersed chapters—takes place in ancient Jerusalem and involves a confrontation between Pontius Pilate and Jesus, here called by his Hebrew name Yeshua Ha-Nostri. The former narrative is presented in scandalous and sharply satirical terms, the latter with the relative sobriety of a historical document. But the "history" of Jesus before Pilate is completely reworked. Pilate questions Jesus, and in the course of his interrogation finds him both fey and compelling. Jesus, for his part, appears both knowing and naïve. He admits to meeting Judas of Karioth yet claims to have only one follower, Matthew, a former tax collector who has pursued Jesus on his own accord. In the most unconventional passage of the narrative, Jesus speaks of Matthew to Pilate: "This man follows me everywhere with nothing but his goatskin parchment and writes incessantly. But I once caught a glimpse of that parchment and I was horrified. I had not said a word of what was written there. I begged him—please burn that parchment of yours! But he tore it out of my hands and ran away" (translated by Michael Glenny, p. 31). We must believe, then, that Bulgakov was not in the least interested in the history of Jesus, nor in adherence to tradition, a fact borne out as the narrative continues: Pilate reluctantly sentences his prisoner to death for treason, Judas is murdered in a conspiracy of which Pilate is a part, and Matthew, sole witness to the execution, is subsequently offered a job in Pilate's library, where he is encouraged to continue writing his manuscript.

The freedom to reinterpret the story of Jesus is taken far beyond Dostoyevsky here. Like *Karamazov,* the larger narrative plays an important role in granting the story a new "authority." But in Bulgakov, the "authority" is completely outside the sphere of anything one could call traditional. For in the course of the novel, the story of Jesus and Pilate is in fact subsumed into the story of the Devil in Moscow; the "biblical" story becomes an unfinished novel written by the Master of the title, who, with many allusions to Faust, has struggled against the literati of Moscow to publish his crowning achievement. The work instead comes to life: the entire novel concludes as the Master, guided by Woland, grants a living Pontius Pilate his freedom to join Yeshua in the sky's abyss "on the night of Sunday, the day of the Resurrection" (ibid., 432). In this complicated hermeneutics, Jesus is reconfigured both by Matthew and by the Master, and the question of truth, asked famously by Pilate earlier (John 18.32)—"What is truth?"—becomes now a question of creation amid the freedom of the artist, as supported by both the Devil and God. In Bulgakov's radical world, there is no "essence" of Jesus, but only an ongoing interpretation mediated through what may be seen as a theatrical or aesthetic authority and truth.

These two early Russian works in many ways represent the extreme of novelistic interpretations of Jesus, and certainly, with Bulgakov, and his Faustian references, the most daring. This radical approach is seen again in the aforementioned Yiddish novel by Sholem Asch (1880–1957), *The Nazarene*, which appeared only a year after *The Master and Margarita*. Like its predecessor, Asch's novel presents a new gospel narrative within a larger contemporary one. The new gospel is supposedly written in this case by Judah Ish Kiriot (Judas Iscariot) and is discovered in an old bookshop by an anti-Semitic Polish scholar, who divulges its generally orthodox contents to the narrator. But this eccentric scholar believes he is reincarnated and that in an earlier life he was himself a Roman governor during Christ's time. The first third of the novel is his own story of Jesus; as in Bulgakov's work, this story fuses with the later discovered gospel narrative to give a rendering of Jesus the Nazarene through multivalent voices and histories. The common feature here with the Russian works is a dehistoricizing of the original Gospels and an emphasis on the open-ended, transhistorical nature of their message as it is forever reconceived and existentially appropriated by the individual. As Asch's main character concludes: "What happened to me? I am here today, as I was yesterday, as I shall be forever. I am here, and I cannot stop being. . . . He [the Messiah of Nazareth] laid upon me the curse of being" (ibid.).

Later novels of the twentieth century fall generally into two categories: those that return Jesus to first-century Palestine, and those that present him typologically, through the aesthetic lineaments of another character. Of the former, the controversial novel *The Last Temptation* (1953) by Greek writer Nikos Kazantzakis (1885–1957) is perhaps the most notable. Informed by the philosophies of Friedrich Nietzsche and Henri-Louis Bergson, and placed on the Roman Catholic Index of Forbidden Books by the Pope in 1954, the novel tests the extent of Jesus' humanity, without ever denying his dual nature as both man and God. Though, like the other novelists, Kazantzakis takes up existential themes, especially that of freedom, he never leaves the realm of first-century Palestine. Yet he boldly reinterprets Jesus' life as one of profound struggle between the two warring factions of spirit and flesh, in effect lifting Jesus out of the doctrinal tradition of the Church to depict him as one who must choose, out of freedom, against the very real temptations of family life, bodily pleasures—the love of Mary Magdalene in particular—and the avoidance of pain and suffering. This story becomes "not a biography," and not a Passion narrative, but a narrative of passion, of human passion and its wrenching struggle, in the face of death, to take an easier, and more human, way out.

A later retelling of Jesus' life by the Portuguese Nobel Prize winner José Saramago (b. 1922), in his provocative *The Gospel According to Jesus Christ* (1991), also explores the psychology of Jesus from an earthly and human point of view. But unlike Kazantzakis's work, this novel tends more toward a magic realism, where new miracles and prophecies add to Jesus' reputation, where the Devil and God discuss the nature of evil, and where irony and irreverence are more explicitly prevalent throughout. This novel is indebted to the tradition of fantastic literature as represented by Saramago's own countryman Eça de Quieroz (1845–1900), whose picaresque novel *The Relic* (1887) follows its antihero to the Holy Land, where, with satiric flair, he encounters in a dream Jesus himself.

Two novels are worth mentioning because of their indirect approach to the life of Jesus: *Barabbas* (1951) by the Swedish writer Pär Lagerkvist (1891–1974—also a Nobel Prize winner for literature) and *The Four Wise Men* (1980) by French writer Michel Tournier (b. 1924). Both deal with famous characters associated with Jesus, but whose contact with Jesus in the narrative is largely through historical implication. Barabbas in the first novel struggles to come to terms with the question of belief, as "Christos Iesus" is carved on a plaque around his neck. In the second novel, a fourth wise man, Taor, never reaches Bethlehem in time for the sacred birth but instead rescues children from the Massacre of the Innocent, learning of the meaning of the Christ-child in the process.

In the second category, where Christ figures are presented instead of Christ himself, reinterpretations of Jesus are pressed further. Without the controversy of redefining the historical Jesus, but with the freedom of exploring certain aspects of his words and actions, and their continuing relevance to later times, such novels displace Jesus in the manifold, extraordinary human contexts that history continues to furnish. The nature of this typological approach makes it difficult to enumerate and summarize all the instances where Christ figures may emerge—subtlety and obliquity are often this approach's greatest strengths. But some of the more noteworthy and poignant examples from around the globe include Spanish writer Benito Peréz Galdós's *Nazarín* (1895), Japanese writer Shusaku Endo's *Wonderful Fool* (1959—deliberately reminiscent of Prince Myshkin in Dostoyevsky's *The Idiot*), and Kenyan writer Ngugi Wa Thiong'o's *Matigari* (1986).

Poetry

If the novel form has allowed for wide reinterpretations of Jesus through an ongoing reproduction of the Gospel narrative itself, with its concomitant questions of authority and historical truth, the poetic form, as a narrative, is more selective and focusing. It is on the whole less concerned with distilling an "essence" through historical reconstruction or displacement, or with exploring psychological development through time, and more concerned with distilling a moment of insight or inspiration that transcends the linear progression of history. The poetic Jesus arises from the questions of divine inspiration, where the relationship between the human and the divine inspires some kind of poetic annunciation. For this reason, the poetic Jesus is much harder to categorize, since poetic inspiration may come from many places and lead in many directions. If we return to our initial fourfold division of world literature into Semitic, European, colonial, and global, but now deemphasize its historical elements, we can focus on more recent poetry where the figure of Jesus is annunciated anew.

Semitic Poetry

Semitic traditions have produced poetry about Jesus reflective of their ethnic and geopolitical situations. Many modern poets of the Middle East write in Arabic, the sacred language of the Qur'an. But Syrian-born poet Taufīq Sāyigh (1923–1971) wrote in Arabic free verse as a Christian; his poem "The Sermon on the Mount" elicits Jesus in a context of modern Palestinian strife, where the poem's narrator is "a pilgrim in my native land" (Atwan et al., 295). Such use of Jesus as a figure of protest against foreign occupation and of suffering for the sake of the people is common among twentieth-century Arabic poets, whether within the Christian tradition, as with Lebanese poet Yūsuf al-Khāl (1917–1987) and his poem "Repentance" (with its refrain "Father, when will my cup pass," ibid., 514), or within the Muslim tradition, as in Iraqi poet Badr Shākir al-Sayyāb (1926–1964), whose famous poem "The Messiah after the Crucifixion" uses Jesus and Judas as images of suffering and tyranny, respectively. Jesus figures directly as a means of protest in a poem by female Palestinian poet Fadwā Tūquān (b. 1917), "To Christ," and indirectly in the politically charged poem "The Magi in Europe" by Khalīl Hāwī (1925–1982), who committed suicide in protest of Israel's 1982 invasion of Beirut. The poem of Palestinian-born Jabrā Ibrāhīm Jabrā (b. 1919) entitled "A Stranger at the Fountain" uses the resurrection of Christ metaphorically to bring hope to Arab people. Thus, modern Arab poets have found a transferable richness in the figure of Jesus that has great historical resonance for their specific regional and political situation.

European Poetry

European poetry of Jesus is vast. We have already seen its history in medieval devotional writings and lyrics and its eventual freedom from ecclesiastical control in modernity. More recent works in the past two centuries have struggled for a spirituality within the prevalence of a secularizing culture. German poet Rainer Maria Rilke (1875–1926), who understood the deeply spiritual side of humanity even after rejecting his mother's Roman Catholicism, furnished many such works. His contemplative *Book of Hours*, for example, is a collection of poetry that borrows heavily from the Christian tradition. In pieces such as "Du Bist der Erbe," it evokes images of Christ introspectively: "So God, you are the one / who comes after. / It is sons who inherit / while fathers die. / Sons stand and bloom. / You are my heir." (Barrows and Macy, 107). Other poems, such as the "The Marriage at Cana," "The Last Supper," and "The Arisen," evoke the Jesus of the Gospels more directly, but always with great subtlety and nonconforming reflection. Rilke's contemporary in France, Charles Péguy (1873–1914), is more orthodox in his Catholicism yet equally probing of the mysteries of faith. His poetry often uses God as the narrative voice, as seen in the title "I Am Their Father, Says God," which repeats the refrain "Our Father who art in Heaven" in a manner suggesting the unavoidable connection of the Father with the Son. In Spain, Miguel de Unamuno (1846–1936), in his great work *The Christ of Velazquez* (1920), eighty-nine poems on Velazquez's painting of Christ, also reflected from a committed yet troubled Catholic position. The Spanish fixation with crucifixion imagery is in vivid evidence in this collection. The poem "Crucifixion," by countryman Frederico García Lorca (1899–1936), is another graphic example of such fascination.

Modern European artists have experienced two devastating world wars that have forced religion and its place in society to be thought anew. The figure of Jesus has especially undergone a major change as modern warfare and politics have altered his role in poetry. "Jesus and the Carrion Path," for example, by German poet Franz Werfel (1890–1945), juxtaposes the high ideals of Jesus with the carnage of the Russian front as experienced by the poet in World War I. In Russia, Boris Pasternak (1890–1960) wrote, in his poem "The Miracle," of Jesus' cursing the fig tree, with sympathy for the fig tree itself. The poem ends in reflection on such a "miracle": "When we're in confusion, in the midst of disorder, / It overtakes us instantly, by surprise"

(Atwan et al., 368). Russian poet Anna Akhmatova (1889–1966) wrote frequently of her country's suffering using the figure of Christ (e.g., "The One People Once Called"). Her husband Nikolai Gumilyov (1886–1921), whose poem "Words," while invoking Christ as the Word, ends with the provocative line "Dead words smell foul," fell victim to his country's upheavals when he was executed by a Bolshevik firing squad for conspiracy.

World War II and its aftermath continued such reappraisals and reappropriations of Jesus. György Ronay (1913–1978) from Hungary set the poem "The Destruction of Jerusalem" during the siege of Budapest in 1945 as Russian and German forces fought for the city; the poem elicits Jesus' prophecy against Jerusalem using striking and relevant images of a city being dismantled by war. The work of Polish poet Czeslaw Milosz (1911–2004) and Lithuanian/Polish writer Tadeusz Rózewicz (b. 1921), both of whom fought against Nazi occupation, also offer views of Jesus within the devastating specter of war. In "Love of One's Neighbor," French poet Max Jacob (1876–1944), a Jew who converted to Catholicism, claims a sickly toad is happier than one who must wear a "yellow star": Jacob was later to die in a Nazi concentration camp having worn such a star. Primo Levi (1919–1987), the renowned Italian concentration camp survivor, projects his Holocaust experience through the poem "Annunciation," where the Annunciation of Christ in Luke's Gospel takes on apocalyptic grimness. And Swiss poet Thomas Immoos (b. 1919), priest and resident of Japan, responds to the horrors of the atomic bomb in his poem "Kyrie Eleison I (Nagasaki 1961)."

The Cold War aftermath also produced its own references to Jesus. Several poets referred or alluded to Jesus in support of socialist or Marxist politics: Elmer Diktonius (1896–1961) from Finland, Kóstas Várnalis (1884–1974) from Greece, and Italians Franco Fortini (b. 1917) and filmmaker/poet Pier Paolo Pasolini (1922–1975), for example. Conversely, Béla Csendes (1921–1996) from Hungary struggled against Soviet communism in his poetic use of Gospel imagery ("Peter," for example), and Yuliya Drunina (1924–1991), a female poet from Russia who was a national deputy during Perestroika, wrote of Judas' betrayal in her poem "In All Ages." So as the European poetic landscape has been reshaped by the political and military machinery of the twentieth century, the figure of Jesus, too, has been reshaped as it has been forced to traverse a landscape torn up by war and its harsh consequences.

Of course, not all European poets respond to war. In the more Protestant Scandinavia, Anders Johan Österling (1884–1979) of Sweden asked in his poem "Unemployed" where Jesus was amid the severe economic realities of his day, and from a brighter side, Nis Petersen (1897–1940) of Denmark showed great compassion in "Gipsy Privilege," applying the charity of Jesus to the disenfranchised. And we should not overlook the poetry of Karol Wojtyla (b. 1920) of Poland, better known now as Pope John Paul II. In his two pieces "The Samaritan Woman" and "John Beseeches Her," Jesus reaches out to extend his mysterious, divine love to women, transcending the pedestrian realities of this world.

Colonial Poetry

The colonial Jesus is certainly as broad, as Europe spread its faith to many and varied distant shores. In the Americas, Catholicism still dominates, but the sociopolitical conditions that can make for desperate living standards, combined with a penchant for spectacle and iconic display, have produced unique poetic portrayals of Jesus at once revolutionary and exotic. In Peru, for example, César Vallejo (1892–1938) wrote under the influence of surrealism as he painted a stark picture of poverty in his poem "Stumble between Two Stars" (1936), where the blessed in Christ's beatitudes become "he who has bedbugs, / he who wears a torn shoe in the rain, / the simply miserable, the poor poor!" Chilean poet Gabriela Mistral (1889–1957), who won the Nobel Prize for literature in 1945, began her poem "Nocturne" with a similar adapting of Christ's words: "Our Father in Heaven, / Why hast thou forsaken me?" Puerto Rican poet Hjalmar Flax (b. 1942) went even further in an anticapitalist parody of the Lord's Prayer in his more contemporary poem "Our Father."

The revolutionary spirit that arises from destitute conditions can be seen in Latin America especially. Rubén Darío (1867–1916) from Nicaragua featured Jesus from a Modernist perspective where the transcendent qualities of his divinity give way to the material struggles against oppression, while there remains, as his poem "Spes" suggests, a yearning for some kind of spiritual hope. The "Cosmic Canticle" of his compatriot Ernesto Cardenal (b. 1925) invokes Jesus within the cries of liberation theology, where the people, the "proletariat," become king. An even more explicitly Marxist Jesus can be found in the work of Caribbean poet René Depestre (b. 1926) of Haiti, who often combines local pagan religions (such as voodoo) with his politics and Christianity. And local color figures widely in the Christ imagery of Cuban poet José Sánchez-Boudy (b. 1928), especially from an Afro-Cuban perspective. Thus, the non-English Americas offer visions of a Jesus never far from the immediate circumstances of a people in perpetual struggle, while darkness and color merge with powerful contrast. The exception to such locality is arguably found in the work of the most famous of South American writers: Jorge Luis Borges (1899–1986) from Argentina. His learned and cosmopolitan writings—for example, the unconventional story "The Gospel According to Mark"—also include poetry on the Gospels. "Matthew XXV: 30" is a poem that takes the reader well outside biblical boundaries, and well beyond the weeping and gnashing of teeth of Jesus' words, with a style typically Borgesian—cryptic yet ever-intriguing.

In Africa, colonialism is far more evident and categorical in its effect on the literary portrayal of Jesus. Europe is forever present in the picture, yet often ambivalently. In the work of Gérard Félix Tchicaya U Tam'si (1931–1988) from Congo, who lived most of his life self-exiled in France, cultural tensions are always on the surface, as seen vividly in "The Scorner," a sequence of six poems in French addressed to Christ. Here the narrator takes on the title role in directing scorn both to the internal ravages of his country and to the Christianity and Jesus that have helped shape it, while at the same time betraying his attraction to the power of Christ imagery. Léopold Sédar Senghor (b. 1906) of Senegal, also educated in France, where he was trained as a Catholic priest, wrote poetry celebrating his native culture amid the colonial realities of his land: "Snow in Paris," also addressed to Christ, captures the feeling of being caught between two lands as the poet's heart "melts like snow in the sun." Senghor became president of Senegal after its independence in 1960 and continued to write poetry throughout his career. Nigerian Nobel Prize winner Chinua Achebe (b. 1930) offers poetry in similar tension with the Christian West, and though he wrote in English, his Igbo culture and language figure largely in all his works. The same could be said for South African Oswald Mbuyoseni Mtshali (b. 1940) and his culture of Soweto. In his poem "Ride upon the Death Chariot," Jesus' march to Golgotha is equated with three black prisoners whose visa papers are not in order. The figure of Jesus has become an important postcolonial marker in Africa as the struggles to emerge from colonial rule were complicated by the indelible Christian imprint left on modern independent African nations.

In India, and from its colonial legacy, Christ can be explicitly found in the work of two poets in particular. Rabindranath Tagore (1861–1941), awarded the Nobel Prize for literature in 1913, portrayed in his "The Son of Man" a Jesus with universal appeal, while Nirendra Nath Chakrabarti (b. 1924), in his "Christ of Calcutta," has depicted a Jesus transplanted into the realities of Indian culture, and more specifically, in the character of the child of a begging mother.

Global Poetry

Globally, Jesus has emerged poetically in two Asian countries, though less through the forces of media globalization and more through missionary activity. In China, the Jesuit presence in the sixteenth century led to many converts. Among them, the early poet Zhang Xingyao (1633–1715) wrote of Christianity as fused with Confucianism. But the contemporary Simon Zhao (b. 1925) has written as a poet who has spent much of his life imprisoned for his Christian beliefs. In "Explanation Without Words" he responded to his wife's death in prison as a Christ-like sacrifice. In Korea, Ku Sang (b. 1919), like Xingyao, brings Eastern religion to bear on the figure of Christ, but in more subtle ways that maintain Christian orthodoxy. In "Easter Hymn," he wrote, "since there is your Resurrection and ours, / our lives are not an empty abyss." Hae-in Lee (b. 1945), a Benedictine nun, has written poems, such as "Like the Samaritan Woman by the Well" and "Magdalene's Song," offering contemplative portrayals of biblical women who appeal directly and intimately to Jesus, showing sensitivity to a world where women seek a greater voice amid a still predominant patriarchy.

Even this limited transcontinental selection demonstrates that world poetry has kept Jesus a malleable figure, whose adaption to the specific needs of different regions is born out in the various annunciations of distinct times and places. More than the novel, poetry has shown that Jesus continues to cross all cultural and political boundaries, and that translation does not appear to be an impediment to his world-changing language.

Drama

The conspicuous paucity of references to Jesus in dramatic literature, and indeed of examples where Jesus takes a central dramatic role (other than for liturgical and evangelical purposes), suggests that there may be a general incompatibility between Jesus and the stage. Jesus is occasionally referenced in the plays of German playwright Bertold Brecht (1898–1956)—the song sung by the priest in *Mother Courage and Her Children* (1938), for example—but the references and allusions are not central. Jesus figures far more strikingly in several plays of 1997 Nobel Prize winner Dario Fo (b. 1926) from Italy. His play *Mistero Buffo* (or *The Comic Mysteries*) is a tour de force of antiestablishment farce in the medieval tradition of the jester, or *jongleur*, where, in short sketches woven together, Jesus is seen from the vantage point of an unruly, bawdy, and caustically anticlerical crowd. In one scene, "Marriage at Cana," Jesus, having turned water into wine, exhorts the guests present to indulge to the point of thorough inebriation, his own mother first and foremost. Such sardonic portrayal also figures in Fo's short Passion Plays and in the vignette *The First Miracle of the Infant Jesus*. But Fo's extremes are no doubt an exception—one that returns to the Middle Ages for its material and approach—and their parodic nature may in fact rely on the suggested incompatibility. (Sha Yexin's previously mentioned *Jesus, Confucius and John Lennon* is in similar parodic vein, though drawing from present-day popular culture.) Serious modern drama has largely steered clear of Jesus as a main dramatic character. Perhaps this is in part because the role of Jesus must be assumed by a live actor, and, as the success of novels and poetry has shown, and indeed the Gospels themselves, Jesus is more alive when he is narrativized and renarrativized in the imaginative constructs of the text. This is to say, the stage would demand a Jesus even more human than that which film presents; moreover, all previous literary examples notwithstanding, the artistic community, writers and audience alike, is still reluctant to diminish or restrain the mysterious possibility of a divine nature inherent in the Word made flesh.

Andrew W. Hass

See also: American (South) Christianity; Chinese Christianity; Dantē Alighieri; Film; Great War; Indian Christianity; Julian of Norwich; Liberation Theology; Literature, English; Luther, Martin; The Media; Nietzsche, Friedrich von; Schweitzer, Albert

References

Atwan, Robert, George Dardess, and Peggy Rosenthal, eds. 1998. *Divine Inspiration: The Life of Jesus in World Poetry*. New York: Oxford University Press.

Bulgakov, Mikhail. 2000 [1938]. *The Master and Margarita*. London: Penguin.

Celada, Carro, and José Antonio. 1997. *Jesu Cristo en la Literatura Española e Hispano Americana del Siglo XX*. Madrid: Biblioteca de Autores Cristianos.

Ditsky, John. 1980. *The Onstage Christ: Studies in the Persistence of a Theme*. Lanham, MD: Rowman & Littlefield.

Dostoyevsky, Fyodor. 1958 [1879–1880]. *The Brothers Karamazov*. London: Penguin.
Hass, Andrew. 2002. *Poetics of Critique: Interdisciplinarity and Textuality within Contemporary Thought*. Aldershot: Ashgate.
Jasper, David, and Stephen Prickett, eds. 1999. *The Bible and Literature: A Reader*. Oxford: Blackwell.
Kuschel, Karl-Josef. 1978. *Jesus in der deutschsprachigen Gegenwartsliteratur*. Zürich: Benziger Verlag.
Middleton, Darren, and Peter Bien, eds. 1996. *God's Struggler: Religion in the Writings of Nikos Kazantzakis*. Macon, GA: Mercer University Press.
Moseley, Edwin M. 1962. *Pseudonyms of Christ in the Modern Novel*. Pittsburgh: University of Pittsburgh Press.
Rosenthal, Peggy. 2000. *The Poet's Jesus: Representations at the End of the Millennium*. New York: Oxford University Press.
Schweitzer, Albert. 1910. *The Quest of the Historical Jesus: A Critical Study of its Progress from Reimarus to Wrede*. Translated by W. Montgomery. London: A. & C. Black.
Terras, Victor. 1981. *A Karamazov Companion*. Madison: University of Wisconsin Press.
Wagenknecht, Edward, ed. 1946. *The Story of Jesus in the World's Literature*. New York: Creative Age Press.
Weeks, Laura, ed. 1995. The Master and Margarita: *A Critical Companion*. Evanston: Northwestern University Press.
Ziolkowski, Theodore. 1972. *Fictional Transfigurations of Christ*. Princeton: Princeton University Press.

Liturgy

Christian worship by its very character gives Jesus a central focus. This key position has been expressed in many ways, whether in the different kinds of worship that accompany occasions in people's life experiences, such as at birth and death, or in the days and seasons of the year; the way a Christian community is ordered through its leadership; or in the two principal sacraments, Baptism and the Eucharist. But there are also other factors, such as how Christ is expressed in prayer, whether prayer should be addressed to him or to God the Father, and the relationship between public liturgy and private prayer itself, of which the Lord's Prayer is a symptom; this tension has often been marked by mutual influence as well as the understandable tendency for the former to adopt a more disciplined style than the latter. Language is also part of the picture: Jesus is usually referred to as "Christ" and "Lord," but there are occasions when other titles become appropriate, whether "Savior" in Holy Week and Passiontide prayers or "Shepherd" at the consecration of a bishop. Christian liturgy develops through acting as a repertory of words, symbols, and actions that have to become manageable in the confines of different traditions.

Lord's Prayer

Of the two versions of the Lord's Prayer in the New Testament (Matt. 6.9–13 and Luke 11.2–4), the longer text in Matthew is the one that seems to have been adopted at an early stage (see, for example, the Didache, or *The Teach-*

ing of the Twelve Apostles, a very early Christian text rediscovered in the nineteenth century, exact date unknown); we possess no evidence for the actual use of the Lucan version in worship in the early centuries, or indeed since. Some late manuscripts of the Gospels add the doxology at the end; this was used exclusively in the Byzantine rite until the sixteenth century in the West, when it came to be used by the Reformers. The Lord's Prayer has a central place in Christian liturgy because it was delivered to the disciples on two occasions in the Gospels, both in the Sermon on the Mount (Matt. 6.9–13) and when the disciples ask Jesus to teach them to pray (Luke 11.1). In the former context, Jesus is criticizing formality of religious expression, whereas in the latter he goes on to exhort his followers to put the prayer into practice. Christian liturgy walks that tightrope—at least theoretically—since it is based on a critique of human motive and action. The Lord's Prayer can claim to be a summary of the Gospel itself, as indeed Tertullian (c. 160–c. 225) described it, and if we look at Matthew's version, we find echoes of the text elsewhere: for example, the Father is heavenly (Matt. 6.19–20; 6.25, 28; 16.19; 18.18; 28.18), and doing his will is a priority (Matt. 7.21; 12.50; 18.14; 26.42). In addition, forgiveness is taken up immediately after the giving of the prayer (Matt. 6.14, 15; cf. Matt. 9.2; 12.31; 18.21); the giving of bread recalls the feedings (Matt. 14.13–21; 15.32–39); and deliverance from evil is mentioned by Matthew more frequently than in any of the other Gospels, and the term "the evil one" is particularly used of the Devil (Matt. 13.19; 38).

The Lord's Prayer is arguably one of the earliest, if not the earliest, known prayers of the Christian Church. The Didache directs believers to say it (with a doxology) three times each day (8.3), though whether this teaching refers to regular public or private prayer is unclear. What is remarkable about the prayer is the care with which many writers of all traditions have used it as a basis of catechesis for those preparing for baptism (e.g., Cyril of Jerusalem, c. 315–387); when infant baptism became the norm, parents and sponsors were urged to teach the children this prayer, which in turn often made it a prerequisite for confirmation. The prayer's uniqueness is signaled by the way in which it has been formally introduced by the priest in the Roman Mass since at least the sixth century with words recalling the fact that Jesus *taught* his disciples to say it. Two other factors may explain the need for such an introduction: the need for the whole congregation to come in with the opening words (by which it came to be called in Latin Christianity—"Pater Noster"), as a way of uniting them all with Christ; and the fact that this prayer was one of the few "corporate" prayers of Christianity in public liturgy, said together by all.

But at the Reformation there were those, like the early Puritans John Smyth (c. 1570–1612) and John Robinson (c. 1575–1625), who so rebelled against set forms of prayer that they interpreted Christ's critique as aimed at any liturgy; "vain repetitions" came to be the favored translation of Matt. 6.7 (Geneva Bible and authorized version), whereas "babbling" like a baby, or someone talking nonsense, is the more accurate translation (it appears in the sixteenth-century translations by William Tyndale and Myles Coverdale and is the view adopted in many modern versions). More to the point, Smyth and

Robinson and those like them interpreted Jesus as giving the disciples a basis for prayer, rather than a set form, which is the interpretation of John Calvin (1509–1564), whose Genevan Service Book provided forms of intercession inspired by the structure and themes of the Lord's Prayer. Such a tendency found both baffling and unacceptable the frequent use of the prayer in the offices of the medieval Catholic Church (where, as in the Anglican Prayer Book, it often appeared more than once in the same service) as well as in private devotion (e.g., in the use of the rosary). When Protestants of this persuasion did use it, their adoption of the late text with the doxology was for theological reasons: only God—and not the saints, and certainly not the Church—must have the kingdom, the power, and the glory. The "words of Christ" evidently give rise to many interpretations and uses.

Prayer to Christ

Should prayer be addressed directly to Christ? History gives no clear answer to this question. The New Testament gives incontrovertible evidence, both in the drama of Paul's conversion (Acts 9.5) and in the account of Stephen at his death, when he not only commends his spirit to Jesus but prays that those who are stoning him might be forgiven (Acts 7.59f.). And yet, when we come to the Council of Carthage in 397, we read in its twenty-first canon that public prayer should always be offered to the Father, and not to the Son. Such a view has often been followed to the point of trying to exclude liturgical prayer to Christ, which is regarded as devotionally justifiable but belonging to a later stage in the tradition of public prayer. This view has been questioned by others, who take into account not only the New Testament itself (e.g., 1 Cor. 16.23) but also the variations in early eucharistic prayers. For example, the East Syrian prayer of Addai and Mari vacillates between addressing the Father and the Son, a prayer now taken seriously for its antiquity (it may well be third century). There is also the prayer of Gregory Nazianzus in the Coptic Church, which can no longer be dismissed as "late." Coupled with this, we have to take into account one of the oldest hymns of the Eastern Church, "Hail Gladdening Light," sung in the Byzantine rite during the lighting of the lamps at vespers and known as already well-established by Basil of Caesarea (c. 330–379), where the "light" is clearly Christ himself.

There is no doubt that the place of Christ in liturgical prayer was affected by the doctrinal controversies of the early centuries. For example, the convention in the West of concluding prayer with the words "through Christ our Lord" was elaborated into a Trinitarian ending in the atmosphere of anti-Arian polemic for fear of relegating Christ to a subordinate quasi-human position. Prayers that mention the Holy Spirit at the end also reflect the move toward accepting the full divinity of the third person of the Trinity in the later fourth century. A difference can be discerned between the East, where prayer frequently ends with a full doxology, and the Latin West, where liturgical prayer is usually "through Christ," and "in the unity of the Spirit." These disputes can seem overdetailed, but they are fundamentally about where Christ belongs in prayer, which is to a certain extent illuminated, if not partially explained, by the image of Christ interceding for us at the Father's right hand in Hebrews 7.23–25, a text that has been taken to mean that *if* we are to pray to Christ, then we are assuming that the prayer is ultimately addressed to God the Father. Nonetheless, the liturgical tradition provides a mixed legacy; although the classical prayers of the Roman Sacramentaries are all addressed to the Father, the more devotional prayers subsequently inserted into various parts of the Roman Mass are often addressed to Christ, an example being the prayer immediately before the Peace in the Roman rite, a prayer still in use today. Hymnody also provides interesting parallels, with a more intimate style apparent in such examples as "Adoro te devote latens deitas" ("Thee we adore, O hidden Savior thee"), a eucharistic hymn attributed to Thomas Aquinas (c. 1225–1274). The repertoire of hymns to Christ is vast and includes modern compositions such as "We Hail Thy Presence Glorious, O Christ Our Great High Priest" by Richard Godfrey Parsons (1882–1948) and "Shine, Jesus, Shine!" by Graham Kendrick (b. 1950).

Liturgical prayer is still usually addressed to the Father, although the less formal worship of the Free and Evangelical traditions has always had a Christocentric piety that has embraced prayer, often extempore or spontaneous, to Jesus himself. In comparative terms, this approach acts as a contrast, if not also a mild protest, against the official service books of recent decades, which have been marked by the more traditional style. And the devotional prayer tradition cannot exclude the "Jesus" alternative: the famous late medieval "Anima Christi" ("Soul of My Savior") came out of an important tradition of devotion to the person of Christ. But prayer to Christ has never quite won a place center stage because it has either downplayed the Trinity in general or ousted the Holy Spirit in particular. The popularity in the later twentieth century of Eastern iconography, particularly Trinitarian (e.g., Rublev's Old Testament Trinity), has had a devotional and theological influence that has redressed the Western balance, enabling many to see prayer to the Father as a fully Trinitarian experience, redolent of the warmth often associated with prayer to Christ in the past.

Rites of Passage

Childbirth and its aftermath is seen in the New Testament, in liturgy, in iconography, and in the festival celebrated on February 2 in many Churches. It relates to a complex drama only recounted in Luke's Gospel, when Mary and Joseph bring the infant Jesus to the Temple in Jerusalem (Luke 2.22–40). Indeed, the narrative itself betrays some of the contradictions of the Christian tradition that surround rites of thanksgiving after childbirth: is it a thanksgiving for the birth of the child by "presenting" him (Exod. 13.2, 12), or is it a "purification" of the mother (Lev. 12.2–8)? Both these titles are used, occasionally together, in the service books of the Western Churches, in spite of the popularity of the old medieval title, "Candlemas," from the candles traditionally lit on this day. In many rites after childbirth this contradiction lingered on, even, for example, in the Anglican Prayer Book of 1662, where the service is clearly entitled "thanksgiving after childbirth," but where the popular understanding as a rite of purification has remained in some places down to the present day.

Confirmation, however, has a different kind of ambiguous history. Starting as the latter part of the baptismal liturgy, detached from it when a presbyter has carried out the baptizing so that a bishop could ratify fully the sacramental initiation of the new member, it then developed its own life through the medieval period, searching for a theology. This the Anglican Prayer Book tradition provided, with its characteristically Reformation emphasis on teaching and on conscious and intelligent faith. But unlike childbirth, where Christ could be seen as somehow the archetype, if not the vicarious agent, and baptism, where the Christological focus is fully present in the liturgy, confirmation lacks such a focus, a problem compounded by the continued use there of the prayer for the gifts of the Spirit (Isa. 11.1–2), which can be traced back to the fourth century in the West, but at baptism.

With marriage, the New Testament provides a firm foundation based on two different passages. One is the presence of Jesus at Cana, when he turned the water into wine at the wedding of an unknown couple (John 2.1–11). The other is when Jesus teaches about the lifelong commitment that marriage involves (Matt. 19.1–6). It is interesting to note how the use of either one of these passages as an exclusive resource for the Gospel reading at a marriage or for the composition of nuptial prayers has an influence on how marriage is celebrated and perceived. The passage in Ephesians, in which the relationship between Christ and the Church is likened to that of a husband and his wife (Eph. 5.21–33), inspired part of the old Roman nuptial blessing, but it has become problematic in a society that is more sensitized to the equality of the married pair. The use of the nuptial veil for the bride alone in the West contrasts with the more egalitarian crowning of both partners in the East—where, moreover, the Cana scene inspires many of the prayers and is invariably used as the Gospel reading in the Byzantine rite.

Reconciliation and healing were so much a part of the ministry of Jesus in the Gospels that rites of forgiveness and laying-on of hands (with or without anointing) are easily seen in Christological terms. A similar tension to that which we saw over the Lord's Prayer between public and private surfaces with reconciliation, however. In the Church of the early centuries, reconciliation was a once-and-for-all public series of rites, under the bishop, with the extrusion and final readmission of the penitent after grievous sin; but it gradually became a frequently repeatable and private rite conducted by a priest. Such a development demonstrates the ambiguity of a gospel that is about affection as well as demand, accessibility as well as mystery, invitation as well as challenge. But however undertaken, reconciliation frequently has to do battle with the human condition of slavery or addiction (John 8.34–36), whereas healing has to address the fatalistic view that illness is a form of punishment (John 9.3).

Whereas reconciliation and healing may rely on human desire or need, there is with funerals the sheer necessity of removing to a place of burial for disposal of the body of the dead person. Current practice is as varied as it has been in the past, from a quick twenty minutes in the crematorium to a whole series of rites that may start at the place of death, go to the church for a time of vigil the evening before the funeral liturgy, and proceed from there to the final resting place. The New Testament images of Jesus' own burial (Matt. 27.57–61) are complemented by the promise of heavenly welcome (Matt. 25.34), as well as by Jesus' own presence at the death—and resurrection—of Lazarus his friend (John 11.17–44); indeed, Jesus' weeping at Lazarus's grave has inspired at least one prayer for those who mourn. Prayer for the dead—or not—underlines a long-running controversy in Christian liturgy, which some deal with by having recourse to the more neutral-sounding practice of "commending" the departed one to God. But once again, it is the more intimate prayers, chants, and hymns addressed to Christ in the liturgical repertoire that provide an important opportunity for mourners to relate the experience of deep personal loss to the reality of God, whether this is expressed by images of Lazarus, of transition through judgment to the kingdom of God, or of thanksgiving for the mercies of Christ manifested in the loved one's life.

Days, Times, and Seasons

The custom of holding morning and evening prayers can be traced back to the Jewish temple, but the way in which Christians have celebrated such offices has varied, and the variation has included whether there is any particular "theology" to the time and occasion or not. The Eastern Churches have tended, as a result of their conservatism, to retain such ideas more fully than the West, whether Catholic or Reformed: morning prayer rejoices in thanksgiving for the night that has past, asking for the grace of Christ in the day that lies open, whereas evening prayer gives thanks for the day that is past, seeking forgiveness for what has gone wrong, as the darkness falls and Christ the light shines in the hearts of worshipers. Both of these insights are to be found tucked away in the "Third Collect" that is directed to be said in each case in the Anglican Prayer Book Mattins and Evensong. Compline, the late-night service, sometimes includes a collect that refers to the burial of Christ in a context likening our own sleep and awakening the next day to death and resurrection. Psalmody has long been the backbone of daily prayer, sometimes "Christologized" by the use of psalm collects, just as antiphons both with the psalms and the biblical canticles often refer directly to the liturgical occasion.

As with the day, so with the week. Sunday, as the first day of the week, is the day of the resurrection of Christ. This led to the custom of associating Saturday with the burial and Friday with the crucifixion. Symbolisms for the other days are often arbitrary, though there is ancient precedent for associating Wednesday with the betrayal. But when it comes to the year, the opportunities that open up are vast. The two "cycles" of Easter and Christmas, for obvious reasons, concentrate on the atonement and the Incarnation, respectively, with periods of preparation (Advent and Lent) beforehand and seasons of celebration afterward. The provisions in the ecumenical Revised Common Lectionary (1992) give two significant occasions of transition, with the Transfiguration being set for reading and reflection on the Sunday before Lent and the Feast of Christ the King coming on the Sunday before Advent.

In addition to this elaborate scheme, whose roots go back to the fourth century, there are also significant rites on special occasions, notably during Holy Week, with the Palm procession the Sunday before Easter, the washing of the feet on Maundy Thursday, and the veneration of the cross on Good Friday, to say nothing of the archaic Easter Vigil, especially if there are baptisms, a practice drawing together the dying and rising of Christ with the spiritual dying and rising of the new Christian (Rom. 6.3–11). A liturgical year runs the risk of becoming too episodic, ironing out anomalies. Sometimes art provides an important corrective; the reredos by the Lübeck craftsman Bernt Notke, in Aarhus Cathedral, Denmark (1479), has a series of movable panels but the whole scheme of redemption is held together by the way in which the Passiontide scenes are given miniatures of the Christmas cycle between them, and the same is true of the Christmas scenes, which have miniatures of the Passiontide drama.

The liturgical pattern that developed at Jerusalem in the Emperor Constantine's time became an important driving force in the development of Holy Week traditions. Pilgrims began to flock to the holy city when the "true cross" was supposedly found there and a church built on the site in 335, and they took home many of the liturgical practices they found there. For example, Constantine had a tomb, or Holy Sepulchre, built over the site, modeled (ironically) on what would have been provided for a Roman emperor. Similar tombs were thereafter built in the West, sometimes for the relics of saints. In late medieval Northern Europe, painted wooden life-sized sarcophagi were made in which a painted figure of the dead Christ was buried on Good Friday, only to be opened and emptied on Easter Day, and a figure of Christ the Man of Sorrows was placed beside it. Such dramas, in contrast with the more symbolic liturgies of antiquity, enabled worshipers to identify pictorially with the events being celebrated. Similarly, the "Procession of Witness" on Good Friday through the streets of a village, town, or city in modern times has become a way of drawing together Christians of different traditions on the ecclesiastically neutral but missiological central terrain of the open air.

Holy Order

How Christians order their local communities is a matter of constant debate, but history provides three distinct orders that have stood the test of time, even if they have not been worked out in practice in as satisfactory a manner as could be possible. Bishop, presbyter, and deacon emerged in the early centuries as three ministries among local communities through oversight, eldership, and service, respectively. Interestingly, while the precise relationship between bishop and presbyter has varied considerably, and the ministry of the deacon has survived in many places only as a relic awaiting new opportunities, it is the diaconate that can claim to be the order that links most closely with Jesus' own self-description (e.g., Mark 10.43–45). In fact, the term "servant," that is, *diakonos* and related words, occurs no fewer than twenty-eight times in the Gospels. Down the ages, certain tasks in the Catholic tradition, such as reading the liturgical Gospel, leading the prayers of intercession, and preparing the holy table, have been given to the deacon, whereas the deacon as recently revived in many Lutheran Churches concentrates on the social work of the local community, with the liturgical expression coming in second place; perhaps this role is ripe for development, whether the "seven" who served in Jerusalem were the original deacons or not (Acts 6.5ff.).

But what of bishop and presbyter? Episcopal ordination prayers have often concentrated on the image of the shepherd (John 10.11), to the extent that when new bishops are given their shepherd's crosier, in some Anglican rites they are told to keep watch over the flock of Christ, a theme that occurs in the ordination prayer and is also inspired by the Gospel reading (John 10.15–17). The custom of holding the Gospel Book over the head of the person being made a bishop dates back to ancient times and is itself an expression of the bishop as the mouthpiece of the Church, speaking for Christ himself, often an ambiguous responsibility. The office of presbyter, in contrast, started life with no exclusive Christological image, and the term "priest" was used, at first reluctantly, of the bishop only. However, as the presbyter (elder) began to become a far more frequent figure, taking over from the bishop the two duties often restricted to him, namely preaching and presiding at the Eucharist, the word came to be used more extensively for him instead. And it is clear from many ordination rites, whether they are elaborate and include anointing and the giving of the eucharistic vessels, or simple and consist of prayer and commissioning, that the presbyter's function has in effect come to be that of the local leader of the Church, which probably explains why the imitation of Christ is so central to many presbyteral ordination liturgies.

Kenneth Stevenson

See also: Aquinas, Thomas; Baptism; Calvin, John; Coptic Christianity; *Didache*; Eucharist; Holy Sepulchre; Holy Spirit; Hymns; Icons and the Icon Tradition; Jesus, Achievement of; Jesus, Name of; Jesus as Servant; Lord's Prayer; Nicea; Pilgrimage; Prayer; Spirituality; Textual Criticism; Transfiguration

References

Bradshaw, Paul F. 1990. *Ordination Rites of the Ancient Churches of East and West*. New York: Pueblo.

———. 1992. *The Search for the Origins of Christian Worship*. London: SPCK.

Evans, C. F. 1997. *The Lord's Prayer*. London: SCM.

General Synod of the Church of England. 1997. *Eucharistic Presidency: A Theological Statement by the House of Bishops of the General Synod*. London: Church House.

Jungmann, Josef. 1989. *The Place of Christ in Liturgical Prayer*. Foreword by Balthasar Fischer. London: Chapman.

Lang, Bernhard. 1997. *Sacred Games: A History of Christian Worship*. New Haven and London: Yale University Press.

Senn, Frank C. 1997. *Christian Liturgy: Catholic and Evangelical*. Minneapolis: Fortress.

Stevenson, Kenneth. 1998. *All the Company of Heaven: A Companion to the Principal Festivals of the Church Year*. Norwich: Canterbury.

———. 2000. *Abba Father: Understanding and Using the Lord's Prayer*. Norwich: Canterbury.

Taft, Robert F. S. J. 1985. *The Liturgy of the Hours in the East and West: The Origins of the Divine Office and Its Meaning for Today*. Collegeville, MN: Liturgical Press.

Logos

See Alexandrian Theology; Holy Spirit; John, Gospel of; Origen

Lord

A good place to begin a study of "lord" as a term applied to Jesus is Psalm 110.1, the most often quoted (or alluded to) scriptural (that is, Old Testament) passage in the New Testament, and spread across a wide range of writers—it must have been an early Christian commonplace: "The Lord says to my lord, Sit at my right hand until I make your enemies your footstool" (see Mark 12.36; Acts 2.34; 1 Cor. 15.25; Eph. 1.20; Heb. 1.3, 13). It appears directly in the Gospel and Acts passages, more obliquely in 1 Corinthians and Ephesians. If we have in mind that the first Christians found their theological bearings in the authoritative (Jewish) Scriptures, then it was of prime importance for them to draw on passages that would endorse—and then give content to—their conviction of Jesus' role as God's decisive agent for human salvation. The first verse of Psalm 110 fulfilled this role admirably; for it spoke (so it seemed) of God's exaltation of Jesus and his guarantee of Jesus' future triumph over his opponents. We need to realize that "the Lord" *(kurios)* was the term used to voice the divine name, Yahweh, in the Greek version of the Scriptures, the Septuagint, and the second "lord," taken as referring to Jesus, meaning "master," was plainly an appropriate term for him on the lips of his adherents. It is likely that the early Christians already used this term for him in its ordinary sense before it acquired theological body and spiritual force, probably after his death as they sought to give definition to their conviction of Jesus' continued powerful place in the purposes of God. There is room for difference on whether this conviction centered first on what we may see as heavenly exaltation or on resurrection from death. Soon, both formed integral parts of Christian faith, and Psalm 110.1 played a central part in stabilizing the former aspect of that faith in particular.

This theologically robust sense of "lord" as applied to Jesus was not long in taking what may be a different track. In 1 Corinthians 12.3 and Romans 10.9 (and perhaps in 1 Corinthians 16.22, where an Aramaic prayer points to an origin in the early days), Paul implies that "Jesus is lord" was in effect a slogan or even an ecstatic cry in congregations that he had founded. We cannot be sure what it implied by way of ideas or convictions—and perhaps it expresses no more than the conviction that "Jesus is great." But its use in Philippians 2.11, in a quasi-liturgical piece (vv. 5–11) that may well antedate Paul's inclusion of it in his letter and spring from other hands than his, goes far to link this ecstatic use of "Jesus is lord" to the theological sense described above.

There have, however, been those, especially in the twentieth-century History of Religions School (chiefly in Germany), who have held that the slogan-like use of "lord" in these Pauline passages reflected a type of ecstatic piety that was reminiscent of mystery religions and other cults of the Hellenistic world of the time. If this were so, it indicated that, within a very few years of its Palestinian beginnings, the Christian movement was, in blunt terms, turning into a Jesus cult, alongside other comparable cults of the time. The paucity of references in Paul's writings to actual deeds and words of Jesus the historical figure seems to support the view that he himself, Pharisee though he said he was by training (Phil. 3.5), was inclined to this style of theology, or at any rate, this style of religious devotion. Yet this view may do injustice both to Paul, for whom Jesus' existence, death by crucifixion, burial, and resurrection were undoubted realities to be faced (1 Cor. 15.3–5, no "pure" other-worldliness here), and to tendencies within the very varied Judaism of the period to embrace styles of devotion that were more "mystical" than the Torah-based rabbinic piety of dominant Judaism in the next period.

In the light of this evidence centered on the use of Psalm 110.1 in the early Church, we turn to the uses of "lord" as a term of address or statement in relation to Jesus in the Gospels. Much depends on how literal a record they are taken to be. Undoubtedly, Jesus is often addressed as "lord" (vocative, *kurie*); see, for example, Mark 7.28, 10.51, and Luke 11.1. But first, supposing the Gospels to be a historically correct record simply put from Aramaic into Greek, then the theological significance of the term may well be nil: it is simply "sir," with perhaps an element of reverence for Jesus' religious repute (cf. French *monsieur* is, literally, "my lord"—but heavily democratized!). But in any case, there are instances where the earliest version of a story, in Mark, has "teacher" or "rabbi," to be replaced in Matthew or Luke by "lord," surely the result, not of more accurate knowledge of what had occurred in those instances, but of developing reverence for Jesus in the churches and the growing use of "lord" as a religiously and theologically charged term for him: he was "lord" when you prayed (see 1 Cor. 16.22; Phil. 2.11), so let him be "lord" when you told of his life. He was "lord" from start to finish (cf. Luke 2.11). Compare, for instance, Mark 10.48 with Matthew 20.31. It is impossible to be entirely sure, in any given case, how much theological weight was being given to the word and how far it was uttered, in the evangelist's inner mind, in reverential rather than intellectually weighty tones. We may note that only in the later Gospels, Luke and John, is Jesus referred to by the words "the Lord," as, it seems, a way of naming him (Luke 10.1; John 20.13, 18, 20).

So the conviction that "Jesus is lord" entered Christian usage. However, it carried the seeds of one further step. *Kurios*, as we saw, was the Septuagint's term for Yahweh. So what would be the implication if one were to use Jesus' statements in the old Scriptures that referred to Yahweh? Romans 10.9 seems to be just such a case as one reads on to the quotation from Joel 2.32 in v. 13. Is such usage then an early sign of the belief in Jesus as fully divine, one with God, which came, by way of much controversy, to carefully articulated expression in the fourth century, with its creeds and councils? Surely that can scarcely be the case; the words "to the glory of God the Father" in Philippians 2.11 seem to rule it out, whether expressly or not, in a passage that speaks of Jesus in what are surely lofty but still subordinate terms. And in 1 Corinthians 8.6, an important formulaic statement, "God" and "lord" are formally distinguished, with the latter describing Jesus in high terms as, like "wisdom" in Proverbs 8.22ff., the agent of God in creation (cf. 1 Cor. 1.24).

A passage like Romans 10.9–13 may likewise be an expression of the growing early Christian conviction, so fully developed in the Gospel of John, that Jesus was God's plenipotentiary or fully accredited agent: what he did or said was as good as the deed or word of God who had "sent" him (Gal. 4.4), and this was implicit in the deepening reflection on him as his Father's Son, again most fully worked out in the Gospel of John. This is understandably, with hindsight, the high point of the New Testament use of "lord" as a theologically charged term for Jesus. So it plays its part alongside other titles and metaphors in the rich accumulation of terms that expressed faith in him.

The heyday of "lord" as a theological-cum-religious term for Jesus was this early period. Since then, it has of course been prominent in personal prayer and Christian liturgy: it expresses Christians' sense of devotion, service, and self-giving to Christ—and this it has willingly taken from the New Testament. It has not, however, figured prominently in later theological development: it came from Jewish sources and it could find a place in the Christian heart, but theologically and conceptually, it was not fertile. Its living role lay in Christian devotion.

Leslie Houlden

See also: Paul

Lord's Prayer

See Liturgy; Prayer

Lover

See Bernard of Clairvaux; Jesus, Name of; John of the Cross; Sexuality; Teresa of Avila

Luke, Gospel of, and Acts of the Apostles

The Gospel of Luke draws substantially upon that of Mark but also upon other sources, perhaps including Matthew (but most critics think not, explaining the numerous similarities by means of a lost shared source, Q). Luke seems not to have been reluctant to adjust what he inherited, for he had his own picture to paint. That picture is our concern. In terms of later Christian doctrine, his view of Jesus was not "advanced," not speculative in abstract terms, though he was wholly convinced of his centrality in carrying forward God's purposes. One reason his view was not advanced was that, of course, certain ideas were not available to him or not current in his circles, but largely it was because his mind did not move primarily along abstract lines. Rather, he thought pictorially and was interested in people and places, time and space. In such ways, he sometimes seems definite and concrete to the point of implausibility: at the end of Jesus' earthly life, he must make sure his resurrection is "real" to the extent of describing Jesus eating cooked fish, and we want to ask him what happened to it when Jesus then disappeared from sight (24.41–43). But, of course, that is to show oneself as "factual" as Luke was, but in ways that, presumably, never occurred to him. And when Jesus finally "ascends" to heaven (Acts 1.1–11), we cannot be blamed for seeing his feet disappear into the clouds, after the manner of countless later painters of the scene, and wondering about their subsequent location. These awkwardnesses worried Luke not in the least: solid places (including heaven and paradise) and solid persons (including angels) were part of his world.

If his doctrine of Jesus was not advanced in the sense of later theologies, it was certainly not absent: he was not simply an innocent and plain teller of tales. But he expressed his beliefs most aptly in his own pictorial way, and we may feel they incline to the concrete and straightforward. We must not look to him to answer our reasonable but sophisticated questions.

Luke's Jesus springs from secure roots in the Jewish Scriptures and never really transcends that world. He is God's promised agent for salvation, and in him God has "visited his people" (1.68); with the crucial preliminary of that visit achieved, Jesus will in due time return in undoubted and permanent triumph (19.15; 21.27). So Jesus is Messiah (Christ), 2.11, but the open reality of his messiahship will not be achieved, in rule and judgment, until the great day of God (22.28–30). In the meantime, he has left us with the memory, vivid through Luke's words, of his warm and encouraging (though sometimes extremely demanding, 14.26; 18.29) teaching and manner of life, and by it we are edified. Luke wrote not only his book about Jesus but also, surely in a single design that he alone attempted, its sequel, the Acts of the Apostles. That gives us an encouraging and warming version—again in largely concrete terms, despite a number of speeches, of Christian life and mission, perhaps with one eye on his own day when in some respects things were beginning to slip (Acts 20.28–31). It is life perforce in the absence of Jesus (for he "ascended" to another place in Acts 1), but in the ample power of the Holy Spirit (Acts 2)—which had also empowered Jesus from his very conception (Luke 1.35), thus making a divine bond between what the two volumes record. And, at a few crucial points, Jesus (whose heaven is not far distant—the first-century universe was not huge by our standards) can still make contact: for example, in the visions to Stephen, first martyr and model to all others (Acts 7.56–60), and to Saul, who must be turned round and called to service (9.4–6). Luke's inclusion of such happenings without missing a beat baffles our imagination, for he shows no signs of moving into a different gear in order to write of these things, any more than with the tongues of fire in Acts 2.3. If we are inclined to dismiss such an old-style theatrical picture of the world, we have only to read Paul and John to see that contemporaries of a less concrete turn of mind, though sharing Luke's essential picture of things, were capable of combining it with a more mystical sense of Jesus and his followers living, intensely, in a state of mutual indwelling (Gal. 2.20; John 17.23).

At the beginning of Luke, the arrival of Jesus on the scene is put in wholly Septuagintal (i.e., Jewish Scriptures, the Old Testament, in Greek) terms: it is an event of providential intent and high holiness, and all the characters wear the manners and speak the language of patriarchs and prophets of old—Zechariah and Elizabeth, Joseph and Mary, Simeon and

Anna, with angels and shepherds for a chorus (Luke 1–2). So Jesus receives the most authoritative and auspicious beginning that could be imagined in Luke's world.

From that start, Jesus grows up as a model servant of God—obedient and devout, yet transcending, in degree at least, the inherited models. He is shown at prayer far more than in the Gospels that were Luke's antecedents (seven times as against three in Mark and Matthew), and he learns from ancient wisdom (2.42–52) before he embarks in due time on his own version of God's message (4.16–21), itself, however, drawn from Scripture, though reflecting his own fresh (and alarming, 4.28–29) priorities. In word and deed, he is forceful, stern, but, above all, compassionate and gentle, wooing for God and the kingdom. Nowhere is this portrayal more forcibly seen than in the Passion, where, in Luke (in contrast to Mark and Matthew), Jesus acts with generosity toward his feeble disciples—it is Satan who has suborned them (22.3, 31–32)—and toward those who put him to death (22.51; 23.28–31, 34). This readiness to exonerate is maintained in Acts (3.17; 13.27), though it does not obliterate God's judgment (Luke 19.41–44; Acts 28.25–29). Moreover, in dying, Jesus makes his last convert (23.39–43) and gives himself devoutly to God, his Father (23.46). It could scarcely be a greater contrast to Mark's bleak "My God, my God, why hast thou forsaken me?" What is more, although Jesus certainly attracts hostility, in Luke he also receives pity and support in his agonies (23.28–31, 48).

In presenting Jesus the teacher, Luke starts from his inheriting a prophet's mantle. He brings forward his public appearance at Nazareth from its position in Mark (6.1–6) to the very start of the ministry (4.16–30), so that it becomes a defining moment, and the speech that Luke adds to the episode is nothing but the reading of crucial words from Isaiah; and with the words, "Today this scripture has been fulfilled in your hearing" (v. 21), the speech becomes an utterance defining all that Jesus subsequently teaches and proclaims. So the picture of the kingdom of God, which, as in Mark and Matthew, remains the shorthand for the message of Jesus, is filled out in terms of the restoration of outcasts and sufferers (and so, to a degree, "de-apocalypticized"): 9.1–6; 10.8–11; 12.29–34. We may think, for example, of the sinful woman in 7.36–50 and Zacchaeus in 19.1–10 and of the parables in chapter 15. This characteristic is also the key to his conduct in the Passion, as we have seen.

Yet the prophet's role, with its social dimension, especially its war on the pitiless and complacent rich (1.53; 6.20; 16.19–31: they are Luke's antifavorites), is modified by his depiction of Jesus in terms reminiscent of a Greek philosopher in the Socratic (or perhaps Cynic) tradition. Thus, a great deal of Jesus' teaching in this Gospel is given in the context of meals, at which Jesus, though a guest, quizzes, teases, and shames his hosts (15.1–2; 15.3–32; 7.36–50), or, in the case of his own disciples at the Last Supper, buoys them up with hope (22.15–38). These symposium scenes, which culminate in the Emmaus story and the final meeting with the disciples in Jerusalem (24.13–49), continue in a new form in Acts (2.42; 20.7–12). They surely owe much to Luke's urban and Hellenistic background alongside his Jewish and scriptural formation and reflect church life as he knew it in the cities of the Gentile world, where the mission of Paul and others had borne fruit.

Jesus the apocalyptic prophet is, however, far from absent. Only, in adapting Mark's material, Luke modified it to accommodate his more schematic and drawn-out view of the future. Though probably Luke did not see it as lasting all that long, the time of the Church's mission had its own validity, and Acts shows it at its best in its first years—a model for Luke's own, perhaps less satisfactory time toward the end of the first century (see 20.18–35, Paul's only sermon to a Christian audience). Then, the end comes, attended by the conventional wonders and horrors (Luke 21).

The titles of Jesus, helping to define his role, are mostly those also found in the other Gospels, but Luke had his own emphases: the quoting of Isaiah 61 in 4.18 ("anointed me" means, in effect, "made me *christos*") may indicate that, for Luke, Jesus' messiahship carried this prophet's role along with its kingly Davidic associations (e.g., 2.11); and in Acts, he is seen to fulfill the prophecy of a coming Moses-like prophet foretold in Deuteronomy 18.15 (Acts 7.37). Moreover, Luke did not reserve the title "the Lord" for Jesus in his exalted state after the resurrection (fulfilling Psalm 110.1) but employed it a number of times in his lifetime: Jesus is "the Lord" (2.11; 10.1)—it is scarcely possible to see it as meaning no more than "master."

Though Jesus is, in the sense already discussed, "absent" from Acts, he is constantly "present" as the whole subject of the preaching of the apostles and others, and of the mission whose agents they are. He is the monarch, available through these agents, though temporarily removed from sight and immediate presence. So their preaching task can be summed up in terms of "the things concerning Jesus" (that is, in effect, the contents of Luke's Gospel) and "the kingdom of God" (that is, the coming triumph foretold in detail in Luke 17.22–37; 21.7–36, some of it already fulfilled in the disaster that came upon Jerusalem in A.D. 70, see 21.20). The future consummation of his reign is assured and the destiny of both Israel and the nations will be fulfilled (Luke 2.29–32; 3.6). (See Acts 28.23, 31.)

An important clue to Luke's understanding of Jesus appears in his genealogy (3.23–38), which differs notably from that in Matthew 1.1–17 in tracing the ancestry of Jesus back beyond Abraham to Adam, thereby linking him explicitly to the human race as a whole and not simply to Israel. This is a symptom of Luke's sense of Jesus' universal significance and the worldwide (in Luke's terms) mission that will ensue—as Acts demonstrates in extended narrative mode. It is typical of Luke's mental workings to see this universality of Jesus by way of human connections rather than, for example, in the more abstract terms of John or the symbolic terms of Paul, who also makes use of the figure of Adam. For Paul, Adam is more a symbol of the human race than one who lived "way back" at the start of an identifiable (in Luke's view) succession of persons. The reference to Adam also throws light on the way Luke sees Jesus as God's "Son," for the term is used of Adam in 3.38, just as it had, shortly before, been used of Jesus in the baptism story that he drew from Mark (3.21–22, cf. Mark 1.11). So Jesus is "Son of God" both vertically and, as it were, horizontally: both by God's choice and by his membership in the human race. It is true that the latter idea is not exploited formally by Luke, but he does tend to bring out the human qualities of Jesus, such as compassion and tenderness, sometimes amending Mark's dark mysteriousness to this end: see, for example, the healing of the ear at the arrest (22.51), and, as we saw, his attitude toward the disciples and the thief at the time of the Passion, not to mention the loving and scandal-causing treatment of the woman who anoints him (7.36–50, transferred from its Marcan place and atmosphere at the start of the Passion, 14.3–12).

But Jesus' "sonship" had been established earlier, in the heartland of Luke's statement about Jesus—the birth and infancy narratives of chapters 1 and 2. There, as elsewhere, "Son of God" is a statement of chosenness, a special role in God's purpose, rather than of a biological freak. The announcement by the angel (1.35) puts us on the track of Luke's model for this crucial episode: the old Jewish Scriptures included a number of such awesome promises of crucial births, often involving surprising features, such as the old age or barrenness of the mother (see, notably, Gen. 21; Judg. 13; and 1 Sam. 1–2, where Hannah's song is a rehearsal for the Magnificat of Luke 1.46–55). And John the Baptist was born, equally impressively, to a mother past childbearing age (1.18), just as Jesus may be seen as born to a mother disqualified by youth. More broadly, Luke wrote these two chapters, deliberately, in the style of the Greek version of the Scriptures, the Septuagint (that is, his Bible). His motive was, however, more than literary. It was to establish Jesus as springing from, and, in a way, summing up, the divine purpose revealed in Israel's writings, a claim made explicitly later in 24.32 and 44. Of course, this was common ground in early Christianity, but no other writer expressed it with either such beauty or such formal literary demonstration. Luke is an expert in theology-by-writing, in the very texture.

This picture of things is symbolized in his concentration on the Temple at Jerusalem throughout chapters 1 and 2 as the place of Jesus' roots, just as it will still be the place of his followers' worship at the end (24.51; cf. Acts 2–5; 21.26). Jesus, and the movement that springs from him, is no strange novelty, appearing from nowhere, but is in God-given continuity with God's whole purpose hitherto. We can see here Luke's intense feel for time and place, shown in his writing of Acts and in notices such as that in Luke 3.1–2. He really does see "salvation" as rooted in and worked out in the process of history, in all its human diversity and flux, but under God's overmastering hand.

Yet Jesus is not a magical boy, somehow transcending the process from which he comes: he is shown receiving the wisdom of Israel in 2.42–52 (contrast John's sense of Jesus' all-knowing power: 2.25; 4.1; 16.19). His destiny is already foreseen, by Simeon at the Temple—both his death and the universality of the divine purpose to be fulfilled through him (2.29–35). As we have seen, Luke is not a writer for abstract thought, and this, we may feel, limits his capacity as a conveyor of doctrine (it has indeed until recently put his readers off the scent of it altogether), but he makes the essential points about Jesus in the recognizable terms of human experience, in the varied life of Palestine, and then, in Acts, in the wider Mediterranean world of the Roman peace of the first century. "Essential points," for Luke, cannot include concepts such as "Jesus as divine": for him, Jesus as "Son" is the devout intimate of God as "Father" (e.g., 11.2; 23.34, 46): Luke prefers the direct address of the single word to Matthew's "my," "our," and "your" Father (e.g., Matthew 6.9, 32; 26.29, cf. Mark 14.25). And the devotedness of Luke's Jesus to prayer is unmistakable (see, for example, 3.21; 5.16; compared with the parallels in Matthew and Mark). He carries out his God-given role, for which Luke, unusually (but see also the Pastoral Epistles), uses the word "savior" (Luke 2.11; Acts 5.31; 13.23) with its scriptural but also Hellenistic (and even Roman imperial) associations. All of these themes point to an underlying assumption that guided Luke's faith and writings: that there were no limits to the significance of Jesus' coming among us.

Leslie Houlden

See also: Church; Holy Spirit; Jesus, Death of; Jesus, Miracles of; Jesus, Origins of; Jesus, Parables of; Law; Lord; Prayer; Son of God; Wealth

References

Drury, J. 1976. *Tradition and Design in Luke's Gospel*. London: Darton, Longman & Todd.

Franklin, E. 1975. *Christ the Lord*. London: SCM.

Keck, L. E., and J. L. Martyn. 1968. *Studies in Luke-Acts*. London: SPCK.

Maddox, R. 1982. *The Purpose of Luke-Acts*. Edinburgh: T. & T. Clark.

Luther, Martin (1483–1546)

Martin Luther, prime mover and theologian of the sixteenth-century Reformation in Germany, nowhere gives a systematic doctrinal treatise on Jesus Christ. He tended to avoid univocal definitions of Christological terms and their relationships, yet he clearly intended to be faithful to the traditional Christological teaching of the Church. One can gather the substance of Luther's faith in this regard from his Bible commentaries, sermons, treatises on topics of the day, disputations, and polemical tracts. In these works, his terminology varies markedly with the subject matter at hand. He typically formulated his thinking in faith-language that related closely to the people and situations at hand. Soteriology is the usual point of entry: Luther began with, and constantly returned to, the saving work accomplished by Jesus Christ for human beings enslaved to sin, the law, and death.

Luther's Christology also rests transparently upon biblical terminology. He consistently judged Bible texts, not in anticipation of the findings of modern historical criticism, but by how directly they point to Christ as Redeemer. The Reformer's richest Old Testament sources were Genesis, Psalms, and Isaiah 53. In the New Testament, although he clearly rested his case for justification by faith alone on Paul, Luther also made copious use of the Fourth Gospel, especially in argumentation concerning the Eucharist, a subject obviously connected with Christology. The Synoptic Gospels, if not so fruitful doctrinally, provided him with a rich source of homiletic illustrations.

But Luther also read Scripture, as all theologians do, with prior understandings characteristic of his time and place in history. One does not ordinarily approach so practical a thinker as this one by invoking philosophical

Martin Luther (Library of Congress)

categories. But Luther's university training at Erfurt had exposed him to a "nominalism" of the sort taught by William of Ockham. Such "modern" views were in the air at the time, and apparently remained in the back of the Reformer's mind throughout his life. Nominalism is the philosophical doctrine that there are no "universals" (either Platonic or Aristotelian or otherwise) but only the names we give things, which constitute working categories for thought. Simply put, only particulars are real. Nominalism claims that our categories are subjective, in the sense that they flow from naming processes, and it also contextualizes them in that in the activity of naming, we adopt vocabularies suitable to the matter or disputation at hand. What appear to be abstract entities, or "universals" (that is, substance, essence, or personhood as such), thus depend on things being described in certain contextual, that is, situationally purposeful, ways.

One can easily trace the impact of nominalism upon Luther's methods and views. He famously wrote, "God does not trifle with empty names" (Siggins, 2). Luther's avoidance of univocal Christological categories reflects a nominalist attitude of mind, if not worked-out nominalist arguments. And nominalism certainly opens the door to an interest in what we make of the world in our naming of it. This is one way to see the fundamental change in perspective sweeping over Europe in Luther's day. An observer put it, memorably: "In a world of great social, cultural, economic and other upheavals, the religious experience itself occupies a central place, while the well-established cosmological and theological conceptions collapse and human beings are left, in some sense, alone with themselves" (Lienhard, 389). In such a context, it is understandable that Luther approached Jesus Christ first of all from the standpoint of life-experience: first Luther's own, and then that of the believer.

The Reformer wrestled in early adulthood with a searing sense of the wrath of God and with the threatening uncertainties of predestination and damnation. He learned to see Christ more as a righteous judge than as a loving savior. In the monastery, as he read the Epistle to the Romans, he came to the conviction that salvation comes by faith in Jesus Christ, who brings us God's mercies, if we will receive them, entirely apart from our merit. Romans 1.17 is the key verse: "The just shall live by faith." Luther added the word "alone." Jesus himself, Luther realized, experienced the solitary anguish of separation from God and yet did not abandon trust. Faith in him is not mere intellectual assent, but the thankful, confident, trusting response of one's whole self to God's love in the midst of our own estrangement and pain.

It is difficult to trace the exact relationship between this central affirmation and the details of Luther's Christology. But many passages affirm that Luther believed that we know Christ only as we know what he has done for us, and hence the "work" is key to understanding the "person." Philipp Melanchthon, Luther's collaborator and subsequently author of the Augsburg Confession (1531), later summed it up in a famous phrase, "To know Christ is to know his benefits."

How does Jesus Christ bring us these benefits? One sees the strong influence of Anselm's *Cur Deus Homo* (1098) in Luther's formulas. The Son offers himself to the Father to bear the justly deserved punishment, to make satisfaction, on behalf of sinful human beings. But, in contrast to Anselm, who stressed the logical necessity of the Incarnation, Luther stressed that God comes to us as an act of his sheer freedom. In Luther there is also less emphasis on the need to uphold God's honor (a feudal idea) and more an emphasis on appeasing God's righteous wrath. The Anselmian formula, in any case, offers a soteriological framework for understanding both Christ's divinity and his humanity. The satisfaction that was needed had to be accomplished by man, whose sin is the presenting problem, but *can* only be made by God, for the satisfaction must be greater than anything in the universe *but* God. Hence the need for one who is both God *and* man.

But Luther also preaches the atonement in homely ways that little resemble Anselm's logic. One thinks of the famous image from the *Table Talk* in which God (in a similitude drawn from Job) baits a fishhook with Christ's vulnerable humanity (Kerr, 55). The Devil snaps at this human bait and gets caught upon the divine hook, chokes on the latter, and falls to the ground. Other graphic images abound. Christ's blessings are like the wagons (accompanied by provisions likened to wisdom, righteousness, sanctification, and redemption) that Joseph has sent from Egypt for his wayward brothers (Gen. 45). We, too, may safely ride in them (Kerr, 55).

The question of Christ's divinity as such was never at issue for Luther. The Reformer fully accepted the teaching of the Church in this regard. It is, for him, as we have seen, an implication of the gospel of grace. Luther sought a gracious God, and therefore, if there was to be access to salvation, it was God, Godself, that he must find in Jesus Christ. Here he found the love of God beyond God's wrath. In Luther's mind, any emphasis on Christ's humanity that might shortchange his divinity was associated not with ethical humanism in the style of Erasmus, but with a Christology of imitation in which Jesus is simply to be followed in the manner of a disciple (as sometimes in the sects), or with a theology in which one can find God apart from Jesus (as in many forms of mysticism).

Luther's emphasis on Christ's full humanity avoided such (to him) questionable formulations. His conviction in this regard came out especially in his preaching. Luther assumed that the Gospels provide us biographical details of Jesus' life that are there to be used for polemical and homiletical purposes. Luther was opposed to those who made Jesus less human by making him more than human in human terms: that is, picturing him as someone extraordinary who did not need to experience life as it is lived by ordinary men and women. Furthermore, Luther's nominalist perspective opened for him the heretofore little-used notion of Christ's human consciousness, in which he suffered and in which he felt the God-forsakenness of the Cross. There can thus be no alienation between Christ's Spirit and his bodily nature. That of which Christ was conscious was bodily solidarity with the human condition.

Jesus Christ, then, is fully God and fully man, and the two natures are indissolubly united in one Person. Luther, above all, stressed the latter point. It is neither the divine nor the human nature but the one Person of Jesus Christ in whom he encountered the God of his salvation. Especially in and after the eucharistic controversy, Luther felt the more constrained to emphasize the unity of the two natures. He had argued, at the Marburg Colloquy of 1529 and elsewhere, that his adversaries in effect separated the two natures by declaring Christ present in the elements (bread and wine) only in his divine nature, or only in the presence of his Spirit. Luther became fierce in his rejection of such views. He traced the words "*Hoc est corpus meum*" ("This is my body") on the table in the great hall of Marburg Castle. God suffers for us in, with, and under the tangible body of the man Jesus Christ.

The unity of the Person of Jesus Christ was early described by Luther in eschatological terms: that is, as a mystery to be revealed at the last day. But in his mature thought he made much use of the patristic conception of *communicatio idiomatum*, or "communication of attributes," whereby certain properties in Jesus, human and divine, can be attributed either to the whole person or to the other nature. In this perspective, one can envisage the divine nature participating in the suffering of humanity (a position developed by later Lutheran theologians in terms of *kenosis*, or self-emptying) or, more awkwardly, argue for a sharing of the property of ubiquity ("being simultaneously everywhere") with Jesus in his human nature.

Luther thus emphasized the role of the human nature of Christ in our salvation, but not as a separate entity or will needing to be harmonized with that of the second person of the Trinity. The humanity of Jesus Christ permits God, in God's very being, to participate in the historical realm of human life. Christ cannot win his victory over sin, death, and the Devil without being both divine and human in one single Person.

One finds no trace in Luther of the doctrine known after Calvin as the *extra calvinisticum* ("that Calvinistic extra"), according to which the divine Word exists both in union with Christ's humanity and also apart from that union. Such a doctrine would for Luther once again put the integrity of the union in question. Critics have found here a form of modalism that, failing to say sufficiently clearly that it is only God the Son who becomes incarnate in Jesus Christ, compromises the integrity of the Trinity. Yet other passages in Luther make the needed point. Only the second person of the Trinity becomes human. Human salvation, indeed, calls for a dialectic within the Trinity itself as the Son distances himself from the Father in order to enter into solidarity with the human condition.

Thus it is plain that although Luther employed much fresh Christological language, he by no means left behind the Christological *concerns* of the early Church (see his *Treatise on the Councils and the Churches* [1539]). One can, for example, discern a certain Alexandrian tendency—so concerned was he to maintain the unity of the divine and human natures in the doctrine of *communicatio*—that contrasts with Calvin's seeming preference for Antiochene perspectives. But, as biographers have observed, Luther lived in a time of cultural change that led him to see the terminology of essence and substance in a new light. His nominalism helped to open the way for a discovery of history and of the self. The humanists, such as Erasmus, had a powerful influence. Even the transition from Latin to German as the language of theological discourse played its part. But a revolution in Christian thought began in Luther's work, the end of which is not yet in sight.

Lewis S. Mudge

See also: Alexandrian Theology; Anselm; Antiochene Theology; Calvin, John; Christology, Modern; Eucharist; John, Gospel of; Kenoticism; Paul

References

Bainton, Roland H. 1950. *Here I Stand: A Life of Martin Luther*. New York: Abingdon-Cokesbury.

Hagen, Kenneth, Franz Possett, and Terry Thomas. 1984–1989. *Annotated Bibliography of Luther Studies*. St. Louis: Center for Reformation Research.

Kerr, Hugh Thompson. 1943. *A Compend of Luther's Theology*. Philadelphia: Westminster Press.

Lienhard, Marc. 1982. *Luther: Witness to Jesus Christ*. Minneapolis: Augsburg.

Luther, Martin. 1957–1966. *Three Treatises: To the Christian Nobility of the German Nation; The Babylonian Captivity of the Church; The Freedom of a Christian*. Philadelphia: Fortress.

Pelikan, Jaroslav, and Helmut T. Lehmann, eds. 1955–1986. *Luther's Works*. American ed., 55 vol. St. Louis: Concordia; Philadelphia: Fortress.

Siggins, Jan D. Kingston. 1970. *Martin Luther's Doctrine of Christ*. New Haven: Yale University Press.

M

Macquarrie, John (b. 1919)

John Macquarrie is the emeritus Lady Margaret Professor of Divinity at the University of Oxford. He also taught at Union Theological Seminary in New York City. His work played a leading role in interpreting Christianity in terms of existentialism in the twentieth century.

For Macquarrie, Jesus Christ is "the decisive or paradigmatic revelation of God" (1966, 249) whose significance lies in the context of God's wider action in creation, reconciliation, and consummation. Although God's activity can be found everywhere, Jesus is its special focus. He is a specific historical revelation of God, the place where the mystery of God is particularly made known. Macquarrie claims that Jesus is both a human figure and a divine being. Jesus was a real historical figure who lived a real human life and was limited by natural human constraints. But he is also a divine figure, the second person of the Trinity, and the Word made flesh of John 1.14. Although human, Jesus was born of a virgin, worked miracles, and was sinless. However, Jesus is not simply a figure of the past; he is also present in contemporary Christian experience.

Macquarrie's understanding of Jesus draws on classical, medieval, and modern theological and philosophical traditions. On the classical and medieval side, he draws on biblical texts, most notably the Gospels, the Councils, and the Fathers of the Church. From these he concludes that Jesus is ultimately an "absolute paradox" (1998, 9f.) who can be seen in terms of the Christology of the Council of Chalcedon in A.D. 451. On the modern side, Macquarrie's Christology has been influenced mostly by the existentialist philosophy of Martin Heidegger, for whom Being *(Dasein)* was the fundamental category of existence. For Heidegger, human experience and awareness of death orients lives toward authentic being. Within this conceptual scheme, Macquarrie sees Jesus as the one who reveals Being itself, especially in his death on the cross.

Macquarrie's understanding of Jesus involves both existential and ontological dimensions. The existential dimension includes the historical aspects of the life of Jesus. Macquarrie takes seriously the "quest for the historical Jesus," emphasizing Jesus as a historical rather than a mythical figure. He sees the quest and the history as important dimensions of the wider incarnational Christology drawn up at Chalcedon. For Macquarrie, the quest for the historical Jesus is naturally rooted in a critical reading of the New Testament, especially the Gospels. Macquarrie identifies seven specific "moments" or "mysteries" in the life of Jesus that are central to Jesus' historical revelation of God: the Nativity; the Baptism; the Temptations; the Transfiguration; the Passion and Cross; the Resurrection; and the Ascension. In all of these, Jesus reveals God in a specific way, but the crucifixion is central. These human, historical, and existential dimensions of Jesus' life and significance lead Christians to call him "Lord." In all these aspects, Macquarrie's Christology proceeds distinctly "from below," that is, from the human, historical Jesus.

But there is more to Jesus than this. The ontological dimension concerns Jesus' divinity. Although Macquarrie's understanding of Jesus Christ begins with his humanity, he aims to avoid adoptionist tendencies that imply that Jesus was merely "adopted" by God as his Son at a particular moment in his ministry. On the contrary, Macquarrie asserts Jesus' full divinity, using the classical concepts of Incarnation and Trinity: the Word that was made flesh in Jesus of Nazareth is the coeternal Logos ("Word"), the second person of the Trinity. Macquarrie also works with the classical notions of *anhypostasia* and *enhypostasia*. The notion that in Jesus, God took on impersonal humanity or humanity per se *(anhypostasia)* undermines Jesus' full humanity, for Macquarrie, who prefers the idea that in Jesus, God took on a specific human life whose humanity was fulfilled and perfected in its relation to God *(enhypostasia)*. The Incarnation of the Logos in Jesus involved not just general humanity but a particular individual human person. The distinctive natures of the human Jesus and of the divine Logos came together in one "hypostasis," or person. Macquarrie also claims that Jesus was sinless, maintaining that this does not detract from his real humanity. On the contrary, he says, real humanity is sinless humanity, and perfect humanity is humanity without sin.

For Macquarrie, the person of Jesus cannot be separated from his work and significance, and the crucifixion is the central event. Jesus' obedience and self-giving in the crucifixion reveal that God was acting in him. Macquarrie sees Jesus' death as the place where atonement and reconciliation between God and humanity was acted out. His view of the atonement attempts to bring together two major strands in medieval atonement theology: the "subjective" view (typified in the work of Peter Abelard) and the "objective" view (typified in the work of Anselm). In drawing these views together, Macquarrie follows the model laid out in Gustav Aulén's *Christus Victor* (1931), which sees the death of Christ as a defeat of demonic forces. For Macquarrie, the death of Jesus is also a revelation of Being itself.

Finally, the crucifixion of Jesus is also an eschatological event that constitutes the community of Christians, the Church. The Christ-event of history involves not only the historical Jesus but also the social reality that has gathered in his name down the ages. Jesus is known to Christians primarily not as someone from the past but as a real person in present experience. For Macquarrie, knowing Jesus today is a mystical or spiritual experience. The Incarnation is not just about Jesus but also about God creating a new humanity in him. Jesus mediates between God and nature, and in this sense the Christ-event is a cosmic event that transcends all events. Ultimately, for Macquarrie, Jesus Christ is the center of human existence and of history.

In addition to patristic, medieval, and existentialist influences, Macquarrie's Christology has also drawn upon the work of Pierre Teilhard de Chardin, Blaise Pascal, Dietrich Bonhoeffer, and Karl Rahner, among others.

Stephen W. Need

See also: Adoptianism; Anselm; Barth, Karl; Bonhoeffer, Dietrich; Chalcedon; Jesus, Achievement of; Jesus, Death of; John, Gospel of; Lord; Rahner, Karl; Resurrection; Second Person of the Trinity; Son of God; Transfiguration

References

Macquarrie, John. 1966. *Principles of Christian Theology*. London: SCM.
———. 1990. *Jesus Christ in Modern Thought*. London: SCM.
———. 1998. *Christology Revisited*. London: SCM.
———. 2003. *Stubborn Theological Questions*. London: SCM.

Manichaeism

Mani lived c. 216–276, mainly in Persia, and Manichaeism is the powerful religious movement that stemmed from him. Gnostic in pedigree and style, it attracted many in the East and in North Africa, including, famously, Augustine in his early life. The person of Jesus is a very complex figure of immense importance to Mani and the Manichaeans. In the Manichaean texts, Jesus is the revealing, saving, and transcendent god, the compassionate one who suffers for his followers.

The current general scholarly consensus is that Manichaeism had its origin in one stream of early Jewish Christianity, and, no matter to what extent Iranian elements influenced its further development, the figure of Jesus is of great significance to the Manichaean system. Within the *Cologne Mani Codex*, Mani's apparent self-designations as Apostle of Jesus Christ and Paraclete, his use of sayings and commandments attributed to Jesus, and his imitation of Jesus' style of teaching, such as his use of parables, are clear witnesses to his appreciation of that significance. Jesus' importance for Mani can also be found in Mani's use of the Jesus figure to explain the processes of salvation in the eschatological sections of the Shãbuhragãn, a text addressed to the non-Christian Persian ruler Shapur I. Most of all, Mani understood Jesus as his "Heavenly Twin," the instigator of two life-changing visions that he experienced that helped to shape him and set an indelible mark upon his career as an Apostle of Light. That the early Manichaean community was influenced to a great degree by Mani's appreciation and imitation of Jesus is borne out by their descriptions of his death as an *imitatio Christi* ("imitation of Christ").

Jesus takes several forms in Mani's cosmogony. Scholars' totals for the number of Jesus figures present in Manichaean texts range from three to six. More recent studies deal with six figures—Jesus the Splendor, Jesus Patibilis, Jesus the Apostle of Light (sometimes referred to as the historical Jesus), Jesus the Judge, Jesus the Youth (or Jesus the Child), and Jesus the Moon.

Within the Manichaean texts, the major focus is on Jesus the Splendor, Jesus the Apostle, and Jesus the Judge. These three are strongly linked through their saving descent into the world to bring knowledge and to rescue the fragments of light from the world: Jesus the Splendor comes to Adam and Eve; Jesus the Apostle comes to form a church and to save the righteous; and Jesus the Judge comes to make a judgment between the righteous and sinners at the end of the world.

Jesus the Splendor has a divine origin and nature from the Father and is himself the origin for further divine beings. Light is his place of habitation, an essential aspect of his nature, and his gift. He is, above all, a revealer and life-giver. As revealer, he has made multiple descents from the heavenly realm, including to Adam, to Mani, and to individual believers who seek him and his wisdom. As life-giver, he is especially protective of those in the throes of death, guiding them on the right path to the light, giving life, judging, and resurrecting them. Named as the God Xradeshahr in the Shãbuhragãn, he judges all nations at the end of the world. He is a cosmic warrior, struggling with and overcoming cosmic foes in order to bring his revelation. As the wise shepherd, he seeks out and liberates the Living Soul trapped in the world. For believers, he is a revealer, friend, and kinsman, and for the inner elect, he is the bridegroom of the light.

Jesus the Apostle of Light is a heavenly being, Son of the Father, his nature associated with light. He descends to the world for the purpose of revelation and to found a church. As a result of coming into the world, he is confronted by enemies, both cosmic and earthly forces, under whom he appears to suffer and be crucified. Because he combines in himself both a divine and human nature, he suffers and at the same time does not suffer. In the end he is victorious over his enemies and shatters their power on the earth, in the heavens, and in the underworld, liberating others to follow him in his return to the Father and the realm of light. From this heavenly position, he continues to guide and defend souls at the hour of death.

Jesus the Judge is a heavenly figure who comes to judge all nations and renew the world at the end of time. His enemies and the enemies of the righteous are completely overwhelmed by his appearing, and the frequent use of the title "King" for the Judge adds to this picture of might. Although the righteous are rewarded in the judgment, more is implied by texts suggesting that the Judge is so compassionate that he suffered with those who suffered because they are righteous. The connection in love and compassion made between the Judge and the righteous is further emphasized by the use of the image of bridegroom for the Judge.

The title Jesus Patibilis ("the mortal Jesus") is taken from a reference in the dialogue of Augustine with Faustus the Manichaean bishop (*Contra Faustum Manichaeum* XX, 2). Most studies of this figure focus on his suffering, although Manichaean texts also emphasize his rising and saving activity and his role as the source of joy and life for believers. As the immanent and mortal Jesus in the world, he stands as a type of the Living Soul, the light entrapped, enfleshed, put to sleep, and made unconscious within the world, and needing redemption. Jesus Patibilis takes on various extra aspects of the Living Soul—immanence within the world, the light substance within the elements of the sacred meal of the Manichaeans, and the role of liberated and redeemed savior.

The Western Manichaean text of the Kephalaia contains the strongest sources for Jesus the Youth, although the figure is vague and poorly developed. Eastern texts do not explicitly mention, nor do they seem to imply, such a figure. As with Jesus Patibilis, the figure acts as one of many possible ways of describing what happens to the Living Soul or an aspect of the Living Soul. Jesus the Youth is equivalent to the Summons and Obedience (the Counsel of Life) set within the Living Soul, which represent the desire that the Living Soul has for salvation.

Jesus the Moon appears (rarely) only in Central Asian Manichaean texts and is most probably the concrete expression of a close association between Jesus the Splendor and the moon—Jesus the Splendor's throne, vehicle, or ship is the moon, and the moon is used as an image and metaphor to describe his light and splendor.

Either the cosmological figure of Jesus the Splendor or the historical Jesus is generally considered to stand at the heart of Manichaean Christology. Scholarly consensus is moving toward seeing a unity in the figures—one Manichaean Jesus under many guises and within many different situations. Although the argument for unity may be slightly hampered by the little material available on Jesus the Youth, enough material exists in the Eastern and Western texts to make the argument highly probable. There also seems little reason to doubt Faustus's rather complicated statement of Manichaean belief in the one Christ who has a twofold nature, understood in two ways—as the power and wisdom of God, and as the Son of God and the mortal Jesus (*Contra Faustum Manichaeum* XX, 2).

The concept of a twofold nature for Jesus solves the problem of accommodating the idea of divinity or transcendence merging with what is material, and the idea that divinity can be so affected by this contact that it suffers or is at least capable of suffering. The Manichaeans chose to live with seeming contradiction and complexity in their figure of Jesus, who was both redeemer and redeemed.

As Werner Sundermann (1992, 536) wrote, most of the aspects of Jesus could be replaced by more exact mythological entities: Jesus the Splendor by the Great Nous, Jesus Patibilis by the Living Soul, Jesus the Child by the Enthymesis of Life, Jesus the Moon by the moon.

Majella Franzmann

See also: Augustine of Hippo; Gnosticism

References

Franzmann, Majella. 2000. "Jesus in the Manichaean Writings: Work in Progress." Pp. 220–246 in *Studia Manichaica: IV. Internationaler Kongreß zum Manichäismus, Berlin, 14.–18. Juli 1997*. Edited by Ronald E. Emmerick, Werner Sundermann, and Peter Zieme. Berlin: Akademie Verlag.

Richter, Siegfried. 1996. "Christology in the Coptic Manichaean Sources." *Bulletin de la Société d'Archéologie Copte* 35: 117–128.

Rose, Eugene. 1979. *Die Manichäische Christologie*. Wiesbaden: Harrassowitz.

Sundermann, Werner. 1992. "Christ in Manicheism." Pp. 535b–539a in *Encyclopaedia Iranica*. Vol. 5. Edited by E. Yarshater. London: Routledge and Kegan Paul.

Marcion

See Gnosticism

Mark, Gospel of

The Gospel of Mark is about Jesus and it is about nothing else, but it is necessary to understand the sense in which this is so. The Gospel is not, for example, to be regarded as an amenity for the modern "objective" biographer. That does not at all mean that it is devoid of worthwhile historical content. It does mean that its purpose was religious or *kerygmatic* (i.e., to do with the preaching of the gospel; see 1.1, stating its purpose), not to be informative about "Jesus in his setting." As the first Gospel book to be written, about A.D. 70, some forty years after the events it describes and the beginning of the Christian movement, its originality lay in setting out the Christian message for the first time in terms of the story of Jesus (rather than, for example, in terms of "straight" doctrine).

This aim, as seen by Mark, determines what is and is not said in the story. Thus, Mark tells scarcely anything about Jesus' family (3.21, 31–35; 6.1–6, none of it complimentary) and nothing about his birth. His picture of Judaism in Galilee and Jerusalem, although in general true to the times (i.e., there were scribes and there were Pharisees and priests), subserves the depiction of Jesus as the radical teacher (e.g., 2.23–3.6) and healer (e.g., 5.1–20; 8.22–26), and then as the victim of wicked conspiracy (3.6; 14–15). Parables are not false to agriculture as then practiced, but it is not their purpose to instruct us in the subject (4; 12.1–12) but to show the character of the "kingdom of God," which it is Jesus' purpose to proclaim. Experts in the period are not prepared to see Jesus as "unique" in his teaching or as up against the powerful because of it, especially in aspects of Jewish law, as Mark leads us to think; rather, he was surely more of a recognizable conversation-partner in the pluralistic Judaism of the day. Thus, on the mitigation of Sabbath observance (2.23–3.6), he takes one view among others, and the conclusion Mark gives in 7.19 (that all foods are ritually clean) flows more from the Church's making of Gentile converts during the mission of Paul, which doubtless Mark knew and approved of, than it owes to the actual discussion reported in the passage, which entails no such radical conclusion.

So it may be. But Mark's Jesus has a single goal and everything is written to serve its purpose: he goes the "way" (1.2f.) that leads to Jerusalem (8.32–34; 10.52) and so to the Cross. Though he is accompanied by "followers" (1.16–20; 10.52), these consistently fail to grasp his purpose (6.52; 8.14–17, 27–33) and ultimately forsake him (14.50). They are therefore depicted as pupils ("disciples") who fail to learn and followers who abandon their leader at the crisis. The narrative of the Passion (14–15) only intensifies what has been true throughout—the aloneness and uniqueness of Jesus as the agent of God's mysterious purpose (see 10.45): the coming of the kingdom, that is, God's sovereignty, whatever that may mean precisely (10.1–12 suggests that it involves the restoration of Eden; 14.62 thinks in other but not unrelated images).

How does Mark then see the figure of Jesus? He depicts him first in his God-given launch (1.1–15) and his first gathering of followers (1.16–20); then in a sequence of healings, teachings, and feedings involving numerous people in many situations, but all seen under images (such as blindness, deafness, and hunger) familiar to the God-vocabulary of the old Scriptures (e.g., Isa. 35.5ff.; 61.1ff.) that make possible the grasp of restoration and new life in samples that betoken future possibilities. But, to pinpoint Jesus, we can notice the terms Mark uses to describe him. In 1.1, he is "Messiah, Son of God." Both are reiterated (the former notably in 8.29 and 14.62; the latter in 1.11; 3.11; and 15.39, echoing the baptism as the story closes). But both are pushed in a single direction, on from their Jewish associations: it is the death of Jesus that gives them their meaning, rather than any of their (diverse) existing senses. In 8.27–33, indeed, we see that "Messiah" must now be understood in terms of suffering and death, and it is otherwise vetoed. Jesus is also "Son of Man," and whatever its background in Jewish idiom and in the texts (and however much of that usage Mark knows of), here it again becomes the tool to speak of Jesus' necessary (8.31: "must") death (see also 9.31; 10.32–34). Only by that route does it resume its Danielic (7.13) inheritance as signaling ultimate triumph (14.62). That end for Jesus Mark only allows modestly and perhaps hesitatingly (note the shadowy though real resurrection of 16.1–8), as if it runs the risk of obliterating the centrality and the necessity of the death. If Mark sensed such a triumphalist danger, we can applaud his prescience.

If, then, we shift the subject more firmly to "the Christology of Mark," it is not surprising that, despite the Christological titles, some even hold that his Christology is curiously negative, even nonexistent, as open speech is finally discouraged (16.8): how can one be a Messiah who dies, and then there is silence, as in that last verse? True, there are foreshadowings that look more positive (9.2–8; 14.62; finally, 16.7). (Note that the Gospel ended at 16.8, and the further "endings" come because second-century readers found verse 8 so unsatisfactory as to be intolerable for the go-getting Christian movement.) But nothing must detract from the strange but potent negativity of Jesus and of what "following" him truly involves (8.34–37; 10.35–45). Mark's picture and doctrine of Jesus is both his strength (for those who have ears to hear and eyes to see, 4.11–12) and his point of vulnerability. Matthew and Luke both thought the message needed more backbone, and down the centuries this book has been largely neglected, in both liturgy and study.

What has been said above is what might be called a standard account of how the Marcan picture and idea of Jesus may now reasonably be seen. Certainly it assumes that, contrary to earlier views of Mark as having no very strong overview but merely bringing together a collection of stories about Jesus, the author had a consistent idea of Jesus to communicate. It also assumes that this "idea" was theological in character: it involved the significance of Jesus in the light of God and his purposes ("the kingdom of God"). Therefore the term "Christology" came into the discussion. Conventionally, a discussion of Mark's Christology involves a treatment of how he uses terms such as Son of Man, Messiah (or Christ), and Son of God; but, as has already emerged, it also (and more importantly) involves a consideration of the flow and content of his whole narrative—his portrait of Jesus.

It may be, however, that this treatment has been set at too exalted or abstract a level. Mark did not write in an academy, away from the daily concerns of the Christian movement in which he was involved, nor was his story of Jesus removed from the realities of Jesus' own setting, however much he may have organized and directed his account of them. Richard Horsley (2001) has "placed" Mark's Jesus much closer to the latter's Galilean setting. The Gospel shows him as a prophetic figure of protest, of a kind well known in the history of Israel, both before and after Jesus, standing for the rights and fortunes of peasant villagers, with their conservative traditions (e.g., on divorce, 10.1–12), over and against tax-levying powerful authorities (landlords, 12.1–12, and city-building Herods, 6.14–29). He was therefore contemptuous of the clever, evasive, and acquisitive (7.6–13) tactics of sophisticated Jerusalem scribes and Pharisees, who had for a century sought to bring rural Galilee into line with the authority and ways of the temple (11.15–17; 12.41–44; 13.1–4). To our eyes, this depiction makes Jesus seem like a social reformer, pure and simple. In Israelite tradition, such figures were upholders of the purposes of God for his people and acted in his name: Jesus preaches the kingdom of God (1.14–15), and all his deeds and teaching further its realization. In his acts he carries on the tradition of Moses, and especially Elijah, and the transfiguration (9.2–9) makes plain even his superiority to both of them. He is therefore a renewer of the traditional covenant between God and his people, and the Last Supper seals his purpose (14.22–25). For this notably Galilean cause, he came to his death at the hands of the Roman and temple authorities.

Such a picture, accounting for a great deal of Mark's depiction of Jesus, of course raises questions that go beyond Mark's Gospel: for example, how did Mark (literate and in his way literary, as opposed to a possibly largely illiterate Galilean Jesus) relate so directly to the memory of "Jesus as he was" yet write about him with such sophistication and from the standpoint of the later Christian movement, some decades after the events he describes? And it raises a more difficult question: how did it happen that one so closely attached to such local Galilean realities, as this Jesus surely was, so quickly came to be preached in the cities of the Greco-Roman world? The more we follow this line of thought, the more crucial does the Jesus of Paul appear to be. In any case, the Jesus of Mark himself already shows many signs of having a more universal significance than this Galilean picture might suggest: he returns us to Eden in his divorce teaching, and in the temptation story (1.13), where the angels who barred Adam's way now serve him. And the God of Mark is no merely local deity. What's more, Mark wrote in Greek, the lingua franca of his day, itself a way of exit from the merely local.

Leslie Houlden

See also: Church; Jesus, Death of; Jesus, Family of; Jesus, Miracles of; Jesus, Origins of; Jesus, Parables of; Kingdom of God; Law; Lightfoot, R. H.; Messiah; Son of God; Son of Man; Transfiguration

References

Fenton, John. 2001. *More About Mark*. London: SPCK.
Hooker, M. D. 1983. *The Message of Mark*. London: Epworth.
Horsley, Richard A. 2001. *Hearing the Whole Story*. Louisville and London: WJK.
Houlden, Leslie. 2002. *The Strange Story of the Gospels*. London: SPCK.
Kee, H. C. 1977. *Community of the New Age*. London: SCM.
Telford, W. R. 1995. *The Interpretation of Mark*. Edinburgh: T. & T. Clark.

Marxism

Karl Marx (1818–1883) himself had little to say about Christianity, and what he did have to say was uniformly negative. In general, his view was that "the social principles of Christianity preach cowardice, self-contempt, abasement, submission, dejection, in a word all the qualities of the *canaille;* and the proletariat, not wishing to be treated as *canaille*, needs its courage, its self-feeling, its pride and its sense of independence more than its bread" (Marx and Engels 1957, 83). This view was partly a reaction against the tendency of many early socialists to preach a facile amalgam of socialism and Christianity.

When, in 1843, Marx arrived in Paris, then the center of socialist thought, he was dismayed to find, as he traipsed from one socialist salon to another, that his and Friedrich Engels's intended crusaders-in-arms agreed with most of their ideas but that the one thing they could not stomach was the apparent atheism of the new arrivals. Félicité Lammenais, Louis Blanc, and Etienne Cabet were all believers and held to Robespierre's anathema of godless philosophy. The dominant, if rather simple, view was that communism was just Christianity in practice and that Jesus Christ was the first Communist. By contrast, Marx's view was that the various forms of Christianity were "brought about by wholly empirical causes and in no way dependent on any influence of the religious spirit" (ibid., 154).

However, this very reductionist approach (continued by, for example, Engels and Karl Kautsky) contrasts with the view to which the more Hegelian aspects of his thought inclined him: that in some way socialism was the inheritor of the aspirations of Christianity. In his early writings, in particular, Marx claimed that "religion is precisely the recognition of man by detour through an intermediary. As Christ is the intermediary unto whom man unburdens all his divinity, all his religious bonds, so the state is the mediator unto which he transfers all his Godlessness, all his human liberty" (Marx 1977, 45).

This approach finds support in Marx's early description of the proletariat as "a sphere that cannot emancipate itself without emancipating itself from all other spheres of society and thereby emancipating these other spheres themselves. In a word, it is the complete loss of humanity and thus can only recover itself by a complete redemption of humanity. This dissolution of society, as a particular class, is the proletariat" (Marx and Engels 1957, 72).

This passage is the main source for those who have sought to find a religious inspiration in Marx's work. It is, of course, true that there are echoes of both the Old and the New Testaments in such a passage, particularly the suffering servant passages from Isaiah. But claims such as that "the universality of the proletariat echoes the claims of the universal Christ," supposedly confirmed by Marx's insistence that the proletariat will exist, precisely at the point when it becomes universal, in a scourged and emptied condition—and that this, of course, is "Marx's variant of the divine *kenosis*" (Olssen, 136)—surely overstate the case. These ideas come from Marx's pre-Marxist days: his later view was that the task of Marxist theory was "to develop from the actual, given relations of life the forms in which these have been apotheosized" (Marx 1977, 494). In this context, Marx's early view of Jesus was simple: his daughter Eleanor remembered "his telling me the story—I do not think it could ever have been so told before or since—of the carpenter whom the rich men killed, and many and many a time saying, 'After all, we can forgive Christianity much, because it taught us the worship of the child'" (Marx, see D. McLellan 1981, 81f.). Marx's legacy was, therefore, largely negative.

In contrast to Marx, whose liberal Jewish upbringing had meant little contact with any strong form of Christianity, Engels (1820–1895) came from a family from whose pietistic Protestant Christianity it took him years to escape. In this emancipation he was greatly helped by Friedrich Strauss's *Life of Jesus* published in 1835 and by the biblical criticism of his and Marx's early mentor Bruno Bauer. Engels returned to a discussion of early Christianity in several articles published in the last decade of his life. It is surprising that he devoted so much space to analyzing Christian doctrines and their intellectual sources and relatively little to any recognizably materialist account of their origin and growth. Engels insisted that the Christian religion fitted "the economic, political and ideological conditions" of the Roman Empire. And he gave us terse and insightful summations of the social structure of the time in terms of the rich, the propertyless free, and the slaves. But he was more interested in the ideological content of early Christianity. In particular, following Bauer, he paid great attention to the book of Revelation (which he believed to be the oldest in the New Testament), where he found evidence that Philo was the father of Christianity and Seneca its uncle. Given this approach, Engels was not much interested in the person of Jesus. Although for him the "keystone" of Christianity was "the incarnation of the Word become man in a definite person and his sacrifice on the cross for the redemption of sinful mankind" (Marx and Engels 1957, 195), how and why this idea arose, he said, was "completely indefinable."

Engels's contemporaries and immediate successors were more ready to give an account of the role of Jesus in the rise of Christianity. Marx's biographer Franz Mehring, for example, had some very pertinent comments on how Adolf von Harnack constructed from Jesus' sayings a doctrine remarkably similar to the then fashionable social liberalism. But it was Karl Kautsky (1854–1938) who provided the most magisterial account of early Christianity. Building on Ferdinand August Bebel's rather simplistic picture of Jesus as an anarchist agitator, Kautsky viewed him as a proletarian Messiah. According to Kautsky, Jesus' proclamation of the imminence of the kingdom of God was in keeping with the general Jewish expectation of the arrival of the Messiah within a generation. And, in contrast to Engels, he believed that the original Christian message involved the establishment of a material kingdom. Kautsky therefore portrayed Jesus as a rebel: Christianity had its origin in the Jerusalem proletariat and the roving band of Galilee, and "we must therefore assume at the outset that Christianity was characterized by violence in its beginnings" (Kautsky, 364). Of course, there is little evidence in the New Testament of this, but Kautsky made the most of the sparse references to swords. The accounts of the arrest of Jesus do seem to deny Kautsky's interpretation of the events as a failed coup d'état, and he could only take refuge in his view that Christianity was the most contradictory of religions.

Among the post–World War I Marxists, Antonio Gramsci (1891–1937) undoubtedly had the most insightful views about Christianity. But these were almost exclusively sociological: he was interested in the reasons for the success of the Catholic Church and wished to draw lessons for the future of its successor, the Communist Party. Thus, his interest in early Christianity was sparse and confined to seeing it as an example of successful revolutionary practice. This success depended on the production of appropriate intellectuals who could transform the religious impulses of primitive Christianity into practical and effective activity. It is in this context that Gramsci drew a parallel between the relationship of Lenin to Marx and that of Paul to Jesus. It was Paul who organized the expansion of Christianity and its revolutionary strategy, and therefore "historically Christianity could be called Christo-Paulinism and this expression would be more exact (only belief in the divinity of Christ prevented this happening but this belief is itself an historical element, not a theoretical one)" (Gramsci, 882).

Gramsci's contemporary Ernst Bloch (1871–1936), the patron, as it were, of later Christian-Marxist dialogue, had more to say about the person of Jesus. It would be difficult to overestimate the importance of eschatology for Bloch. He was particularly critical of liberal theology that banished eschatology from the gospel, emphasized above all purity of heart, and made the kingdom of God into an ethical phenomenon, as in Rudolf Bultmann' s existential hermeneutics. On the contrary, according to Bloch, that classical text of Christian morality, the Sermon on the Mount (Matt. 5–7), was not intended to be an ethical system of long duration: it only made sense in the context of an expectation of an imminent end to the world. Thus, "[T]he gospel is from this viewpoint not social nor primarily moral. It is a gospel of eschatological salvation" (Bloch, 112), and the Son of Man did not therefore present himself as a militant savior or romantic restorer of David's kingdom. He presented himself rather as completely new—the leader of an eschatologically revolutionary Exodus.

The Christian-Marxist dialogue inspired by Bloch was of particular interest to dissident Marxists in Soviet-dominated postwar Eastern Europe. The Czech philosopher Vitrslav Gardavsky, in his *God Is Not Yet Dead,* was struck by the emphasis in early Christianity on eschatology, even apocalypse, and the present necessity for collective choice. On this view, he wrote,

"[M]an is a creature who evolves by fighting and by answering the call of the present with a free decision" (67). Gardavsky was evidently overimpressed by Bultmann's existentialist interpretation of the Gospels. Another Czech philosopher, Milan Machovec, offered a more precise account of Jesus in his *A Marxist Looks at Jesus* (1976). His book is that of a wide-ranging philosopher—a sort of contemporary replacement for Kautsky's *Foundations of Christianity*. But whereas Kautsky's aim was to undermine and demolish, Machovec's intentions were constructive. With their view that "Christianity began with a dreamer and ended with a well-fed clergy," Engels and Kautsky had concentrated too much on "explaining away" by reference to economic forces. Like Gardavsky, Machovec took Bultmann as preeminent in his critique of religious matters. Although he rejected the manner in which Kautsky "reduced the entire content of Christianity to social interests" and portrayed Jesus as a "politically active dissident and a social revolutionary," Machovec did insist on a rigid distinction between the Jesus of history and the picture of Christ constructed in later preaching, and on the reduction of the latter to the former.

Finally, it is worth noting that Christians themselves have sometimes borrowed from Marxist thought, particularly in liberation theology during the late 1970s. Flourishing most strongly in Latin America, liberation theology, through its interpretation of the Gospel narratives, has been concerned to discover themes that find in Jesus' political messianism suggestive symbols and signposts rather than specific examples to imitate. Unlike such commentators as Engels or Kautsky, they are not concerned to link Jesus directly with the contemporary Jewish revolutionary movement of the Zealots. The picture of Jesus as an armed guerrilla fighter is not essential for liberation theology. It is clear that Jesus was engaged in active opposition to political authority. But the main point is that, for Jesus, the liberation of the Jewish people was only part of a universal revolution with more profound and permanent consequences than could be encompassed by the political liberation of a single people.

The concerns for the poor in the teachings of Jesus thus overlap with those of Marxism and show that there are more connections between Jesus and Marxism than many adherents of the latter have supposed.

David McLellan

See also: Bultmann, Rudolf; Harnack, Adolf von; Kenoticism; Kingdom of God; Liberation Theology; Messiah; Power; Son of Man; Strauss, D. F.; Wealth

References

Bentley, J. 1982. *Between Marx and Christ*. London: Verso.
Bloch, E. 1972. *Atheism in Christianity*. New York: Herder.
Fierro, A. 1977. *The Militant Gospel*. Maryknoll: Orbis.
Gramsci, A. 1975. *Quaderni del Carcere*. Vol. 2. Turin: Einaudi.
Kautsky, K. N.d. *Foundations of Christianity*. London: Orbach and Chambers.
Machovec, M. 1976. *A Marxist Looks at Jesus*. London: Darton, Longman and Todd.
Marx, K. 1977. *Selected Writings*. Edited by D. McLellan. Oxford: Oxford University Press.

Marx, K., and F. Engels. 1957. *On Religion*. Moscow: State Publishing House.
———. 1975. *Collected Works*. London: Lawrence and Wishart.
McLellan, D. 1986. *Marxism and Religion: A Description and Assessment of the Marxist Critique of Christianity*. New York: Harper and Row.
———, ed. 1981. *Karl Marx: Interviews and Recollections*. London: Macmillan.
Olssen, E. 1968. "Marx and the Resurrection." *Journal of the History of Ideas* 29, no. 1 (January–March): 131–140.

Mary

According to *Lumen gentium* (the Dogmatic Constitution on the Church, 1962), promulgated by the Second Vatican Council, Mary both embodies and reflects the greatest doctrines of Christian faith. For most of the Christian era, divine maternity (as "mother of God") has been the fundamental principle of Mariology, and everything that can be theologically predicated of Mary derives from that principle. The central issue today has shifted to discussion of her importance as an exemplar for all Christians. The fact that Jesus was "born of a woman" (Gal. 4.4) was from the beginning the guarantee of his true humanity, a safeguard against docetism. Mary's name probably appears in the creeds as a reminder of Christ's humanity. But the scriptural fact of the virginal conception led to a glorification of Mary for qualities that set her apart from humanity rather than identifying her with it and has led to an extraordinary diversity of devotional practice and theological debate. Debate continues in the fields of exegesis and doctrine, and with the persistence of cultus at sites of Marian apparitions.

The specific biblical evidence about Mary is sparse. Only Matthew and Luke mention a virginal conception; only Luke (1–2) relates the early life of Jesus and makes Mary a central figure in the salvation story, giving us the Annunciation, the Visitation, the Magnificat, the Presentation in the Temple, and Simeon's prophecy to Mary. The Visitation (of Mary to Elizabeth, mother of John the Baptist) is a key moment in the development of Mary's unique theological status. When Elizabeth addresses Mary as "mother of my Lord," she may be ascribing a divine title to the child in Mary's womb. There is a hint here of incarnational theology, which points the way to the Johannine prologue (Mary is not mentioned there, nor is she actually named in the Fourth Gospel). Luke uses the birth and childhood of Jesus to prefigure later events, but he gives no depiction of a full and unique personality for either Jesus or Mary. Mary's response to the Annunciation is grammatically passive ("Let it be to me as you have said," Luke 1.38). It has been interpreted as spiritually passive, too, with Mary the vessel of grace rather than an agent in the divine plan of salvation. According to both the Gospel genealogies, Joseph is of David's line, and Jesus was assumed to be Joseph's son (Luke 3.23). Davidic ancestry through a foster-father being inadequate for messianic purposes, a Davidic ancestry for Mary also developed later.

Mary appears unnamed at the wedding in Cana and at the foot of the Cross (John 2.1–11; 19.26–27: she is simply "the mother of Jesus"). There is no indication in these appearances of a unique grace accruing to her as mother of the Messiah. Mary at the foot of the Cross became a significant moment in the crucifixion story and was interpreted as a type of Jesus leaving Christians in care of their mother the Church, but in other passages (Matt. 12.48–50; Luke 11.27–28) Jesus seems to deny that her status is unique. Revelation 12.1–6 is a source for Mary's cultus as queen of heaven. She came to be identified with the "woman clothed with the sun," having the moon under her feet and a crown of twelve stars about her head. There is a web of allusion in this passage, but central is Genesis 3, for the woman (whether imaging Mary or faithful Israel) has reversed the serpent's defeat of Eve. Her trampling of the serpent (sin) paves the way for a doctrine of Mary's sinless conception. This is only one of a plethora of eisegeses by which images of Mary were detected in the OT. There is Miriam, Mary's namesake (Exod. 15.21), and the star from Jacob (Num. 24.17). To the personification of divine Wisdom (Prov. 8.22–36) and the woman of virtue (Prov. 31) must be added the bride in the Song of Songs, who is "black and comely" (1.5), a "locked garden," a "sealed fountain" (4.12, evoking perpetual virginity), "altogether lovely and without blemish" (4.7, evoking Immaculate Conception). There is also the prophecy of a young woman in Isaiah 7.14, traditionally translated "behold a virgin shall conceive and bear a son" (cf. Matt. 1.23).

The problem for Mariology, therefore, is how to determine what is theologically normative. The primacy of Scripture as a source for doctrine had been firmly established by the Reformation, but the pronouncement of Mary's Immaculate Conception in 1854 seemed to undermine that primacy, relying instead on oral tradition and transmission of belief and scriptural eisegesis. In 1950, Pius XII's papal bull *Munificentissimus Deus* made the popular devotion of Mary's "Assumption" binding on the faithful—she was now officially deemed to have been assumed body and soul into heaven at the close of her earthly life. The status of the dogma (now put on a par with the Trinity) proved divisive at a time of budding ecumenical initiatives. The feast of the Assumption, celebrated on 15 August, appropriated a date previously associated with another Marian festival (and in the Eastern Church from the sixth century with the dormition ["falling asleep"] of Mary). Did Mary die? Pius XII did not give an answer. But it was argued that because of her unique holiness she was not obliged to wait until the end of time for physical redemption. In the Eastern tradition, her soul is in heaven, her body in Paradise until the end of time; but both traditions insist upon the incorruption of her body.

In *Antwort auf Hiob* (1952), C. G. Jung responded to *Munificentissimus Deus* as the ultimate affirmation of the accessibility of God via Mary. He delineated Mary as an archetype of the feminine, suggesting that the drive behind the 1950 declaration was the psychological need of the collective unconscious. Feeling no obligation to harmonize his argument with orthodoxy, Jung claimed that the sinless and virginal conception of Christ rendered his humanity incomplete and the Incarnation only partial. Feminist theologians have supported Jung's perception that the dogma of the Assumption rounded off the problematically male Trinitarian symbol, an attempt (psychological not theological) by the collective psyche to overcome shallow dichotomizing of good and evil, which projects goodness onto maleness and associates the female with matter and evil. Though God is not theologically gendered, in practice, Scripture, liturgy, and culture (and the grammatical and narrative gender of the Trinity) show God as male, which adds some force to the view that Mary takes the role of counterpart.

Matthew and Luke (cf. John 1.1 with Gen. 1.1) associate the birth of Jesus with a new creation. Matthew evokes the title of Genesis with his opening phrase (perhaps also intended as a title): "The book of the genesis [perhaps 'genealogy'] of Jesus Christ" (cf. LXX Gen 2.4; 5.1). Luke's phrase, "The Holy Spirit will come upon you and the power of the Most High will overshadow you" (1.35) parallels Genesis 1.2. The idea of a new creation in Jesus was important to Paul (Rom. 8.21–22; 2 Cor. 5.17; Gal. 6.15). Luke is clear that the holiness and sonship of Christ were *because of* Mary's overshadowing by the Most High—the uniqueness of Christ depends upon the virginal nature of his conception. The Eve/Mary typology that makes Mary a second "mother of all living" (Gen. 3.20) is found only in texts later than the NT, but it parallels Paul's Adam/Christ typology (Rom. 5.19; 1 Cor. 15.22). The first extant mention, in Justin's *Dialogue with Trypho* (ch. 100) from the mid-second century A.D., contrasts the obedient and disobedient virgins (ascribing virginity to Eve before the Fall). Tertullian and Irenaeus developed the idea, Irenaeus paralleling Paul's comparison of Adam to Jesus in describing Eve, through whom death came into the world, and Mary, who became the cause of its salvation (*Against Heresy*, 5, c. A.D. 180). He pointed the way toward the universal motherhood of Mary and her cooperation in Christ's salvific work, paralleling the gardens of Gethsemane and Eden, and the tree in Eden with the cross. Eve succumbed to the serpent, but Mary crushed its head (a fulfillment of Gen. 3.15, according to a criticized but persistent manuscript reading). One met an angel and failed the test, the other did so and triumphed. In the Latin-speaking world, the symbolism of the first woman's name in Latin reversed by the angelic salutation (Eva/Ave) did not go unremarked (*Ave* means "hail," Luke 1.28).

The Eve/Mary typology is not mentioned in the apocryphal Protevangelium of James probably dating from the second century), the most important early source for Mariology. Rather, it focuses on her miraculous birth to Joachim and Anna, her wonderful childhood in the temple, and, with Origen (in contrast to Tertullian), her virginity remaining intact after giving birth to Jesus. Mary's perpetual virginity *(aeiparthenos)*, defended by Jerome, came to be universally accepted among the devout, while the response of Mary and Joseph to the Annunciation—abstention from sexual relations—set an example for the Christian ideals of virginity and celibacy. This apocryphal text attests to early interest in the precise nature of Mary's virginity. But the undamaged hymen, the unbelieving midwife whose hand was shriveled for checking, and the lack of labor pains (cf. Gen. 3.16) might all be thought to have undermined her true humanity and hence (more importantly) that of Jesus, too. In the twentieth century, the trend among Roman Catholic Mariologists was to spiritualize and rationalize this lack of pain and damage from labor, but the problem of undermined humanity remains. In the Greek view, Mary was completely human in origin, but, because she was chosen by God as vessel of grace to be the mother of Jesus, her human nature is transfigured; she becomes the supreme example of the characteristic Eastern understanding of salvation as a raising of believers to the divine *(theosis)*.

The title *theotokos* ("bearer of God"; in Latin *mater Dei* or, in a more precise but less popular rendering, *deipara*) provoked particular theological controversy about Mary. The emphasis of Antiochene theology on distinguishing the two natures of Christ and on not underplaying Jesus' humanity led to a preference for the title "mother of Christ," but the Alexandrian emphasis on the unity of the two natures prevailed, and in 431 the Council of Ephesus declared Mary to be *theotokos*. The point of the title was to clarify the theology of Christ's person and work rather than to honor Mary. But it enhanced her status at a time when she was herself beginning to be invoked in prayer. Mary reflects the glory of Christ, but that glory was easily mistaken for glory of her own.

The declaration of Mary's Immaculate (i.e., sinless) Conception by Pius IX in 1854 was driven by theological forces and devotional enthusiasm but brought up logical and doctrinal difficulties. The Immaculate Conception pointed, controversially, to a high doctrine of the potential goodness of creation. From the twelfth century the feast of her conception was celebrated, though unlike John the Baptist (Luke 1.41; the only other saint to have a Nativity feast), she had no scriptural attestation of prenatal sinlessness. This drawback provoked Bernard of Clairvaux, a principal opponent of the doctrine, to protest. All agreed that Mary was saved by Jesus, as was the rest of humankind, but the moment when this happened was unclear; the Immaculate Conception seemed to make Mary a unique exception to the universality of original sin. The greatest obstacle to the doctrine was the united view of Aquinas and Bernard that if Mary was conceived without original sin, she could not need to be redeemed by Christ (who could not therefore be the universal savior of humankind). The solution, first explored by Duns Scotus, was that her redemption was by means of preservation from, rather than rescue from, original sin—Jesus' preserving of Mary from contracting original sin was his most perfectly redemptive action. So she was born in grace, and her difference from Christ consisted in the fact that her freedom from sin was due to him. The pronouncement of Mary's Immaculate Conception alienated some Protestant and Eastern Orthodox Churches, either because it denied that all have sinned, or because a different understanding of sin obviated the need to protect Mary from the taint of guilt. The belief that she was "full of grace" rested on a Latin translation of Luke 1.28, which the Greek cannot bear and is no longer current in the Church. But the edifice of theological interpretation resting upon this fullness of grace has not been dismantled along with the translation that generated it.

In 1974 Pope Paul VI called for an updating of Mariology and Marian piety alike. His words hinted at reservations about the more extreme excrescences of devotion. In the fifth century, Augustine had distinguished worship of God as uniquely different from other types of veneration (not specifically with reference to Mary). Partly as a response to veneration of Mary, a system of distinctions of worship developed. Adoration *(latreia)* belonged to God alone. Anything else was reverence, *douleia*, and therefore not a violation of the first commandment. Aquinas used the term *hyperdulia* for Mary to mark her unique status. This distinction became important when Protestant Reformers accused Roman Catholics of Mariolatry, or worship of Mary. For the Catholics, she is to be honored because God honored her, whereas for the Reformers (and later Protestants), any honoring of created beings is idolatry.

The title *mediatrix* for Mary, found as early as the eighth century, expresses the belief that Mary sits at Christ's right hand, interceding for the faithful. Since the Second Vatican Council, this role has been played down in favor of a direct intercessory relationship with Christ for all. More controversial (as a possible encroachment on her son's role) is the title *co-redemptrix*. If Christ is the only Redeemer, then this is an exaggeration of devotion to be avoided. The liturgies of Eastern and Western Christianity alike invoke Mary's intercessions; her power and appeal consist in the help she offers to those undergoing childbirth and the vision she provides of what humankind can be in its redeemed state. In the West, two nonliturgical devotions associated with Mary reinforce her centrality—the rosary, a system of meditation on Jesus and Mary using repeated prayers counted upon a string of beads (associated in origin with the Dominicans, and popular in Europe from the fifteenth century on), and the Angelus, a daily commemoration of the Incarnation (associated with the Franciscans). In both devotions, the "Hail Mary" is the principal prayer used. A litany of the blessed virgin Mary was published in 1589 celebrating her motherhood and virginity, her fulfillment of OT prophecy, and her role as queen of heaven. Modern theology shows unease at some overlap of titles and roles (mediator, advocate, monarch) between Mary and Jesus, but in fact the difference is not one of rank, it is ontological.

Mariology took a new turn in the nineteenth century with a proliferation of apparitions and papal pronouncements on the value of the rosary and the intercessory power of Mary. In 1946, Pius XII consecrated the world to Mary's immaculate heart. A series of Marian congresses began. In the year of the first congress in Rome (1950), Pius XII defined the dogma of the Assumption. In 1954, a second congress proclaimed Mary as Queen. Principal sites of Marian apparition are Guadalupe (Mexico, 1531), Lourdes (France, 1858), and Fatima (Portugal, 1917). Others worthy of pious belief include Paris (1830, to St. Catherine Labouré), La Salette (1846), and Pontmain (1871). Such apparitions follow a regular pattern—Mary appears to a humble, simple person alone or with others; the reaction is initially skeptical, but miraculous cures follow, so the Church establishes a regulated cult. At Lourdes, Bernadette confirmed the validity of the 1854 pronouncement by reporting that Mary told her, "I am the Immaculate Conception." Her messages tend to be conservative and quietist, in contrast with a trend in recent years to associate her with liberation theology and a call to radical social justice (looking to Luke 1.46–56).

Mary's example encouraged Christians to see virginity and celibacy as superior to marriage. Paul also played his part in the development of a metaphysical dualism denigrating the physical and lauding the spiritual. Ambrose of Milan (fourth century) reinforced the perception of the superiority of chastity over marriage by underlining the connection between the virginal conception and the sinlessness of Christ. Augustine's theory of original sin, which eventually became normative, gave rise to a nexus of negativity surrounding female sexuality in particular. The childbearing of Mary contrasted with every other experience of labor, and women learned that their suffering was the consequence of their own sinfulness. This attitude to female sexuality was chiefly generated and disseminated by single men; only in the last 150 years has the edifice of male theologizing about women begun to be dismantled, and almost exclusively by women. The myth and cult of Mary have been argued as undermining and devaluing women, so that Mary's value as a role model for women is now at an end. Many feminist writers detect in her a confidence trick, a standard impossible to emulate because of her unique position. Whether people are attracted by religious symbols as mirrors of reality, or visions of what could be, is another matter. But the gap has widened (as Paul VI observed in 1974) between what the modern world offers women and what traditional Marian devotion offers them. Is her virtual deification the ultimate reinforcement of Christian patriarchy, or the ultimate challenge to it? It partly depends on whether the focus is on her uniqueness (divine maternity) or her potential typicality (obedience). Her virginal conception and perpetual virginity have been seen as depreciating the holiness of sex within marriage, and the Annunciation can even be interpreted as a male projection of fantasy, with Mary a willing, grateful victim.

In art, the Annunciation is a visual counterpart to the Incarnation in theology. The depiction of the Mother and Child and the *Pietà*, both showing a mother with her son on her lap, balance the joys and sorrows of Mary. A medieval Mary was likely to be a virgin in majesty; an early modern Mary to be depicted holding the infant Jesus to her breast. Now she is likely to appear as a humble girl with a firm custody of the eyes, never challenging the onlooker with a direct gaze, nor needing the completeness provided by the presence of her child. In the image known as the *Deesis* (from the Eastern Church), she appears in her role as intercessor for humankind; on the other side is John the Baptist. Both are interstitial figures on the cusp of OT and NT, and of ordinary and extraordinary humanity. The medieval period has been seen as the age of the virgin, a time when references and devotion in art, literature, and music proliferated. For Dante, Mary was the archetype of all the saved (different in degree but not in kind). There is Marian mysticism in William Wordsworth and Gerard Manley Hopkins, and in Goethe, whose scene of adoration at the end of *Faust* is given unforgettable musical expression by Mahler (Symphony 8), at the end of which Mary is called *das Ewig-Weibliche* ("eternal feminine"), a *mater gloriosa* acclaimed by a worshiper as *Jungfrau, Mutter, Königin, Göttin*. Her celebration in music is at least as rich and brilliant as in art, beginning with the simplest of plainsong hymns and settings of the *Ave Maria*. Texts such as the antiphon *Salve Regina* were part of the medieval devotional world, with (like the rosary) guilds dedicated to praying it daily. The Franciscan hymn Stabat Mater (set to music by most of the major European composers) provided a musical counterpart to the *Pietà;*

richer still are the votive antiphons in their veneration for her unique place in the history of the faith.

Carolyn Hammond

See also: Alexandrian Theology; Antiochene Theology; Aquinas, Thomas; Art; Augustine of Hippo; Bernard of Clairvaux; Chalcedon; Creeds; Dante Alighieri; Franciscan Thought and Piety; Gnosticism; Jesus, Origins of; John, Gospel of; John the Baptist; Liberation Theology; Luke, Gospel of and Acts of the Apostles; Orthodox Tradition; Paul; Sexuality

References

Balasuriya, Fr. Tissa. 1997. *Mary and Human Liberation: The Story and the Text*. Edited by Helen Stanton. London: Mowbray.

Boss, Sarah Jane. 2000. *Empress and Handmaid: On Nature and Gender in the Cult of the Virgin Mary*. London: Cassell.

Brown, Raymond, Karl Donfried, Joseph Fitzmyer, and John Reumann. 1978. *Mary in the New Testament*. London: Geoffrey Chapman.

Gaventa, Beverley Roberts. 1995. *Mary: Glimpses of the Mother of Jesus*. Edinburgh: T. & T. Clark.

Jameson, Anna Bronwell. 1864. *Legends of the Madonna: As Represented in the Fine Arts*. London: Longman, Green and Co.

Jung, C. G. 1984 [1952]. *Answer to Job*. London: Ark Paperbacks.

Laurentin, René. 1990. *The Apparitions of the Blessed Virgin Mary Today*. Dublin: Veritas Publications.

Macquarrie, John. 1991. *Mary for All Christians*. London: Collins.

Pelikan, Jaroslav. 1996. *Mary Through the Centuries: Her Place in the History of Culture*. New Haven and London: Yale University Press.

Rahner, Karl. 1963. *Mary, Mother of the Lord: Theological Meditations*. Translated from the German by W. J. O'Hara. Freiburg: Herder.

Ruether, Rosemary Radford. 1979. *Mary: The Feminine Face of the Church*. London: SCM.

Schillebeeckx, Edward. 1964. *Mary Mother of the Redemption*. London: Sheed and Ward.

Warner, Marina. 1976. *Alone of All Her Sex: The Myth and the Cult of the Virgin Mary*. London: Weidenfeld and Nicholson.

Masculinity

The psychological, physical, sexual, and social qualities and conditions accorded to Jesus, consciously or otherwise, are attributed to him as a member of the male sex. As such, the representation of Jesus as a human being in relationship with others is always *gendered:* Jesus' masculinity is configured by the changing power relations between women and men in society and culture.

Ideological feminism, black consciousness, and gay identity have challenged the notion of male experience as universal and undifferentiated. From this critical perspective it is possible to identify the *masculinities* of Jesus—to deconstruct the variety of ways in which the maleness of Jesus has been portrayed, and so to analyze the models of male identity and social practice that the man Jesus is held to represent. Thus the figure of Jesus identified as, for example, supreme Pantocrator or vulnerable Man of Sufferings, as a physical body depicted naked or clothed, as a person in mutual relationship or as self-sufficient, has an iconic role that may be understood as relating to a construct of men's social and sexual relations, both within the particular historical context of production and also of subsequent interpretation. This analysis of the masculinities of Jesus as he is variously depicted in the arts, cinema, literature, popular piety, spiritualities, and more formal religious doctrinal systems reveals the representational theology of Jesus to be both formed by and also formative within the gendered nature of social culture.

In *The Manliness of Christ* (1879), Thomas Hughes presented Jesus as the model man who typified ideal masculine qualities of energy, strength, and spirited courage. With other writers and social philosophers such as Charles Kingsley, Hughes developed a Victorian ideal of Christian manliness that found practical expression in the "muscular Christianity" of public schools, boys' clubs, and uniformed organizations such as the Boys' Brigade. This was a shift from earlier ideals of masculinity developed by Samuel Taylor Coleridge and Matthew Arnold, partly described in Coleridge's *Aids to Reflection in the Formation of a Manly Character* (1825), where true manhood modeled on Christ-like values was to be found in moral and intellectual character expressed in the service of others—a maturity, as opposed to childishness. By the late nineteenth century, some Protestant devotion was so integrally associated with the gender politics surrounding conventional masculinity that John Henry Newman's ritualism and embrace of the Roman Catholic faith were dismissed as unmanly and effeminate.

In the twentieth century, massive social changes, such as the decline of industrial manufacturing and associated patterns of working, the trauma of two world wars, and the impact of the women's movement, brought shifts in the relations between men and women and a reconsideration of male identity. Tackling what was perceived to be a crisis in masculinity, social philosophers brought a variety of critiques to the masculinities Jesus seemed to be modeling. The American poet Robert Bly, whose popular book *Iron John* (1990) pursued a Jungian sociopsycho analysis of Western manhood, argued that men were in need of ways to reconnect with the essential masculine subconscious deep within themselves. For Bly, Christianity has presented in Jesus meek and mild an emasculated savior figure drained of sexual energy and male spiritual power. Others, taking the same broadly "essentialist" approach, found the man Jesus to be an inspiration for a renewed masculinity. Sam Keen, for example, in his book *Fire in the Belly* (1991) saw in Jesus the obedient, compassionate man of prayer who lays down his life for others, the opportunity for men to discover that selfhood can be fully realized through self-surrender and that true virility implies life in communion. A range of masculine spiritualities, such as those developed by Patrick Arnold and Richard Rohr, have found in Jesus a mode of being a man that offers the ideals of personal integration and spiritual wholeness, God's intention for all men.

Jesus' masculinity also serves as a model for those thinkers who regard masculinity as a construction of social practice and for whom radical change toward equality and mutual respect in gender relations is a prerequisite for social justice and personal well-being. Roy McCloughry found in Jesus the "ultimate hero" who embodies a movement from power to love, a pattern of self-emptying in which individual men and the Church as a whole can find renewal when they set aside patriarchal domination. The stories of Jesus' relationship with women in the Gospels, for example, reveal to McCloughry the grounds of hope for a fully human masculinity and for a redeemed community in which women and men are at peace with one another. Similarly, James B. Nelson, in his influential book *The Intimate Connection* (1992), identified in Jesus a perfect manhood in which his sexuality and his spirituality, body and soul, are fully integrated: "a compelling picture of male sexual wholeness." Nelson found in Jesus' masculinity the inspiration to move beyond the homophobia, misogyny, and disconnectedness that conventional masculinities inculcate. Mark Pryce (1996) has suggested that the pattern of Jesus' masculinity, through his relationships with God and his fellow men and women, encourages men to embrace the challenges of feminism as an opportunity for their own imaginative self-discovery and for an embodied spirituality that is inclusive of difference and ambiguity.

Among conservative evangelicals, most notably the all-male Promise Keepers movement in the United States, there has been a move to reassert more traditional power relationships between women and men. Within these schemes, man's role of headship is divinely ordained and exemplified in Jesus Christ. In the social teaching of the Roman Catholic Church, a theology of sexual complementarity has sought to maintain difference between women and men that is divinely ordered and rooted in natural law. The role of motherhood for women is celebrated as a ministry of passive reception and loving care, retaining for an exclusively male priesthood, modeled on Jesus, the authoritative, teaching, and sacramental roles within the Church.

For some feminist theologians, the maleness of Jesus is a crucial issue, insofar as it exemplifies the andocentric, dualist nature of Christianity as a religion of male domination; Mary Daly has asserted that "if God is male, male is God" (1986). Given women's experience of the oppressiveness of male power under patriarchy, the masculinity of Jesus poses the question, Can a male savior save women? Theologians such as Daphne Hampson (1996) have argued that Christianity is intrinsically patriarchal and therefore irredeemably destructive and inhibiting for women. But others have put forward Christologies in which it is the humanity of Jesus rather than his sexual biology that is foremost. Jesus reveals "true humanness" and so opens the way for new social relationships between women and men characterized by the mutuality and justice he models. These schemes are criticized for presenting Jesus as a human being who is genderless and historical. Rosemary Radford Ruether (1983) reasserted that the community of faith should encounter Jesus in his particularity as a first-century Galilean Jewish male, yet embody the message of redemption, which he lived out as one who is "paradigmatic" of redemption for all people, of all cultures and ethnicities, both male and female. Angela West (1983), while recognizing the particular problems to which the maleness of Jesus gives rise for women seeking a theology that liberates them from male domination, saw in the helplessness of Jesus' Incarnation and crucifixion the self-revelation of God as one who lays aside power in a denial of patriarchal domination.

Mark Pryce

See also: Feminist Theology; Jesus as Servant; Kenoticism; Psychotherapy; Sexuality

References

Bly, Robert. 1990. *Iron John*. New York: Addison-Wesley.

Daly, Mary. 1986. *Beyond God the Father: Towards a Philosophy of Women's Liberalism*. London: Women's Press.

Hampson, Daphne. 1996. *After God*. London: SCM.

Isherwood, Lisa. 2001. *Introducing Feminist Christologies*. Sheffield: Continuum.

Keen, Sam. 1991. *Fire in the Belly: On Being a Man*. New York: Bantam.

McCloughry, Roy. 1992. *Men and Masculinity: From Power to Love*. London: Hodder & Stoughton.

Nelson, James B. 1992. *The Intimate Connection: Male Sexuality, Masculine Spirituality*. London: SPCK.

Newsome, David. 1961. *Godliness and Good Learning*. London: John Murray.

Pryce, Mark. 1996. *Finding a Voice: Men, Women and the Community of the Church*. London: SCM.

Ruether, Rosemary Radford. 1983. *Sexism and God-Talk*. London: SCM.

———. 1998. *Introducing Redemption in Christian Feminism*. Sheffield: Sheffield Academic Press.

West, Angela. 1983. "A Faith for Feminists." In *Walking on the Water*. Edited by J. Garcia and S. Maitland. London: Virago.

Matthew, Gospel of

The Gospel of Matthew is, in strict literary terms, a revision of Mark. That is, Matthew used Mark as his basis, altered the earlier work, sometimes subtly, sometimes drastically, while maintaining Mark's basic structure, and added to it to a considerable extent. We do not know the circumstances that led to the new book, but it seems that it cannot be explained simply by saying that Matthew had acquired information that Mark had lacked, so that he was out to provide a fuller account of Jesus' life and teaching—and that was all there was to it. It was also a matter of his having a different point of view from Mark. He disagreed with him acutely on some matters—for example, the status of the Jewish law for Christians and the character of Jesus' first disciples—and in general had what may be described as a robust and concrete attitude to the task in hand. It may partly be the case that interest had arisen in matters that had seemed of no concern to Mark—for example, the circumstances of Jesus' birth—and that Matthew sought to answer these questions. But Mark and Matthew are alike (as, indeed, are Luke and John also) in bringing a theological and religious point of view to bear on whatever material they had before them and so in being more than neutral chroniclers of Jesus' life. Opinions differ on the extent of the new material that Matthew had available to him and so on the extent of his own adaptive skills and even inventiveness as he expanded Mark. As we accustom ourselves to his distinctive features of mind, we can often make shrewd guesses about his own deliberate contributions.

In the first place, Matthew does much more than Mark to root Jesus in the actual history of Israel, seen in terms of persons and inheritance, and so to give factual answers to factual questions. What were the circumstances of Jesus' birth and from whom was he descended? Matthew 1–2 gives answers. So, was his pedigree such as to back the Christian claim to his messiahship? Indeed it was: he was of Davidic stock—and, moreover, he fulfills key prophetic texts that bear on the subject. The fulfillment of scriptural texts is, for Matthew, the most powerful of arguments to validate his story and his case; they appear at every turn, in relation to all major facets of Jesus' life and activity, like a barrister's knock-down arguments for his case (e.g., 8.17 in relation to healings; 13.35 to telling parables; 12.18–21 to the modesty of Jesus' demeanor). Matthew leaves nothing to chance or to the general impression.

Moreover, Mark's stress on Jesus' death, while in no way abandoned, is qualified in Matthew: first, by the very definite circumstantial treatment of the resurrection and its triumphal sequel, even to the point of countering a Jewish canard on the subject, to the effect that the disciples had stolen Jesus' body (27.62–66; 28.11–15); and second, by an emphasis on the kingly, powerful associations of messiahship. This point is sometimes set forth in subtle alterations of Mark: compare Mark 9.1 and Matthew 16.28, the latter centering on Jesus himself as king (and on that claim see 21.1–11; 25.31–46; and 26.53, indicating Jesus' masterful restraint). Jesus may indeed suffer and die, but his total vindication is assured, and we read of it, in a final episode that could not be in greater contrast to Mark's ending at 16.1–8, in the trumpet-blast of 28.16–20.

Matthew's Jesus is also a more determined and useful provider of guidance for his followers than Mark's: above all, in the five great speeches. He equips them for mission (10), for the problems of Church life (18), and for Christian life in its essential character (5–7). So Matthew emphasizes that to be Jesus' disciple (i.e., pupil) is indeed to learn, to undergo instruction (11.27–30—a passage where we read, beautifully, of the great reward for Christian obedience to Jesus, who is both strict and gentle; 13.52, surely revealing our author himself; and 28.20, where, as in 18.20, Jesus' own presence with his own is assured). It is a structured account of what is required—along similar lines to the Jewish law (5.17–19), but more perfectly (5.20, 21–48, and 6.1–7.12). Everything points to the author being a Jewish Christian (probably with scribal training, 13.52, which taught him how to interpret the Scriptures with such magisterial skill) of the late first century, for whom the older way had been marvelously transcended (though not thrown aside) by a new way now centered in Jesus the exalted Messiah of God (28.16f.)—a God who is himself seen confidently as "our Father" (6.9), just as Jesus knew him as "my Father" (11.25; 26.29).

It is a picture that some will see as triumphalist and sometimes cruelly grandiose (e.g., in its stress on Jesus as ultimate—and severe—judge, 16.27; 25.31–46; and see parables such as 25.1–30). It certainly speaks volumes for the confidence of a Christian community in (probably) Syria of c. 85, and no doubt it reflects facets of Jesus' own teaching, given in Matthew's distinctive accents, surely to safeguard his own Jewish and scribal inheritance and to meet the needs of his community as he saw them.

Leslie Houlden

See also: Church; Creeds; Jesus, Death of; Jesus, Miracles of; Jesus, Origins of; Jesus, Parables of; Law; Lord; Mark, Gospel of; Son of God; Son of Man

References

Kingsbury, J. D. 1986. *Matthew as Story*. Philadelphia: Fortress.

Luz, U. 1995. *The Theology of the Gospel of Matthew*. Cambridge: Cambridge University Press.

Stanton, G. N. 1992. *A Gospel for a New People*. Edinburgh: T. & T. Clark.

———. 1995. *The Interpretation of Matthew*. Edinburgh: T. & T. Clark.

The Media

Depictions of Jesus in the media today conform to two main types: the mainstream and the specialist. In the mainstream media he is often presented as a figure belonging to history. In the specialist media, in contrast, we encounter a Jesus who belongs primarily to faith. In each type, the version of Jesus depicted and reflected is a Jesus intelligible to those who produce it but not always to those for whom it is intended.

The media, in its Enlightenment origins and in its present purposes, may be broadly characterized as skeptical and mercenary, which creates conditions of some tension for broadcasters and journalists working in the field of religion. Compromises have to be struck between confessional preferences, theological and historical expertise, and the demands of a broadcast culture that is uneasy about faith claims and religious exclusivity, and, not least, that is obliged to find an audience. Consequently, the Jesus encountered in mainstream newspapers and later on radio and television and other media has differed, often sharply, from the Jesus of faith, with a strong emphasis falling on Jesus as a figure in history rather than piety. But the media's appropriation of the Jesus of history is a highly selective one. Its tendency has been to interpret the figure of Jesus as a political animal, a revolutionary opposing the twin oppressions of Roman rule and Jewish orthodoxy.

In the 1990s, independent television in Britain marked Holy Week by broadcasting a series of programs reporting on the events of Easter as if it were happening now, deploying the techniques of news coverage to "tell the story." Correspondents gave eyewitness reports of Jesus' arrival in Jerusalem, analysts assessed the mounting tensions in the region, and representatives of the Jewish temple and Roman authorities were interviewed, their views "balanced" by interviews with Jesus' followers. The advantages of such a portrayal are to make Jesus seem and feel contemporary, allowing modern, secular audiences to connect with the story when they otherwise might not. This approach also solved a problem for modern, secular broadcasters, obliged by public service considerations to make religious programming when most would prefer not to, thereby freeing more room in the schedule for output with wider appeal. In fact, television's traditional religious programming, including broadcasts of Church services, sing-along hymn sessions, and interviews with Christians talking about "My Faith" have found (and continue to find) large audiences, but as the market becomes more crowded and more competitive, and fragmenting audiences become more elusive, networks are under growing pressure to screen more quiz shows and cookery, gardening, or consumer programs. Not only do these produce high ratings, by extension they become the fields where reputations and careers are made; consequently, as priorities shift away from public service output further in the direction of popular programming, the center of gravity of the network as a whole shifts. Departments responsible for producing religious programming come under pressure to produce more accessible output; hence Jesus the Freedom Fighter.

This network-friendly portrayal of Jesus, however, has serious deficiencies, for the picture that emerges can only be as sophisticated as the interpretative means allow. In this particular version we encounter a figure somewhere between Che Guevara and Yasser Arafat, which may grab a viewer's attention but makes it harder to think with any sophistication about the historical Jesus. Little effort is spent on making the motivations of such a figure intelligible, so, for example, Jesus the first-century Jew, seen in the context of Jewish thought and practice, is all but invisible in this configuration.

Another attempt was made by the BBC in the Easter week of 2001, this time to explore ideas about the Jesus of history using state-of-the-art television techniques. A reporter was sent to the Holy Land to visit archaeological sites that were digitally filled in as he walked around them. Colonnades, fortifications, temples, and harbors sprang from the ruins, thronged by tiny digitized Palestinians going about their business, and, fittingly in a week concerned with the resurrection, first-century Palestine was "brought to life" in front of our very eyes. But it's one thing to raise a temple, another to raise a man. The climax of the series was reached with a quasi-forensic reconstruction of the face of an actual person using the skull of an adult male of the period and historical evidence concerning the appearance of first-century Palestinian men. Several newspapers ran the story, printing the likeness of an olive-skinned, thick-necked, bearded man, about thirty, looking bewildered, as if taken aback by all this unexpected attention, over the headline "Is This the Face of Jesus?" Highly unlikely—certainly no more likely than reconstructing from a seventeenth-century skull dug up in an English churchyard the likeness of, say, William Shakespeare.

It is striking that these kinds of approaches claim, directly or indirectly, a breakthrough in perceptions of Jesus, which goes against the traditional perceptions of the Jesus of faith. But there's nothing new here for theologians and Church historians who have been thinking about Jesus as a historical figure for more than 150 years, which makes it all the more surprising to see distinguished figures in those fields, their names familiar from a thousand footnotes, appearing so frequently on such programs. It can be quite startling to watch one of the world's leading New Testament scholars point awkwardly at a heap of rubble and say, "Here Salome danced for Herod," or to describe in voice-over where frankincense may have been obtained on the trade routes between Persia and Palestine, as the camera pans across a wrinkled map of the Ancient Near East. It's a measure, first, of the media's distance from the life of the Church, and, second, of its extraordinarily seductive power: no wonder the Church is so suspicious of it.

Jesus does rather better on radio, partly because of the nature of the form, partly because radio is less susceptible to the competitive pressures that afflict television. Radio has a more intimate relationship with listeners than television with viewers. A voice in the ear is better able to articulate subtleties and inflections than a parade of brightly lit images on a screen, roughly paralleling the difference between Jesus in the Gospels and Jesus on an iconostasis. By the same token, however, there are deficiencies; the voice often insists on using the language of the Authorized Version, it often sounds like a vicar, and one is left with a mental picture of a Jesus somewhere between George Herbert and the incumbent of the parish church of Ambridge. Television, by showing a succession of images of Jesus from around the Christian world and throughout Christian history, does a better job of showing him in different cultural contexts from our own Western, anglophone tradition.

Jesus' worst mainstream showing is in the print media, particularly newspapers. In the past, on grounds of propriety, he was unmentionable, like the king's mistress; more recently, particularly with the rise of the tabloid, he has become incomprehensible. Popular journalists today, like the scribes and Pharisees in the Gospels, are unsettled by an honest man—who enjoys being reminded of one's own hypocrisy?—so Jesus and his strange and difficult teaching don't figure much in their columns. Besides, it's much easier to fill them with reports of the sins of his followers, for peccadilloes, not parables, sell papers. Jesus does a little better in the broadsheets, particularly (and ironically) in the slow-news and no-news periods of Easter and Christmas. With politicians in recess, statutory holidays, and short-staffed newsrooms, print-hungry papers fill up with seasonal features. Jesus might appear in a piece about the star that led the Magi to his manger—a popular astronomer might be quoted, Babylonian astrological evidence cited, astronomical maps printed—but no connection will be made between Matthew 2.9 and Numbers 24.17, which would have saved the journalist, and the reader, some effort.

Richer, if sometimes crazier, pictures of Jesus emerge in the specialist media. This category, too, can be divided into two: the orthodox and the heterodox. The orthodox specialist media, representing conservative Protestant and Catholic traditions, tend to present Jesus in their own images, or idealized ones. In American evangelical material—newspapers, pamphlets, websites—Jesus is often blonde, bearded but barbered, square-jawed, handsome, strong, even virile. These images recall depictions of film stars in Hollywood publicity material of the 1940s and 1950s or superheroes in teenage comics. He is clean-cut, wholesome, outdoorsy, healthy, and faintly, innocently, erotic. He is often accompanied by children, which is perhaps intended to give him the appearance of benign authority, but sometimes this picture sug-

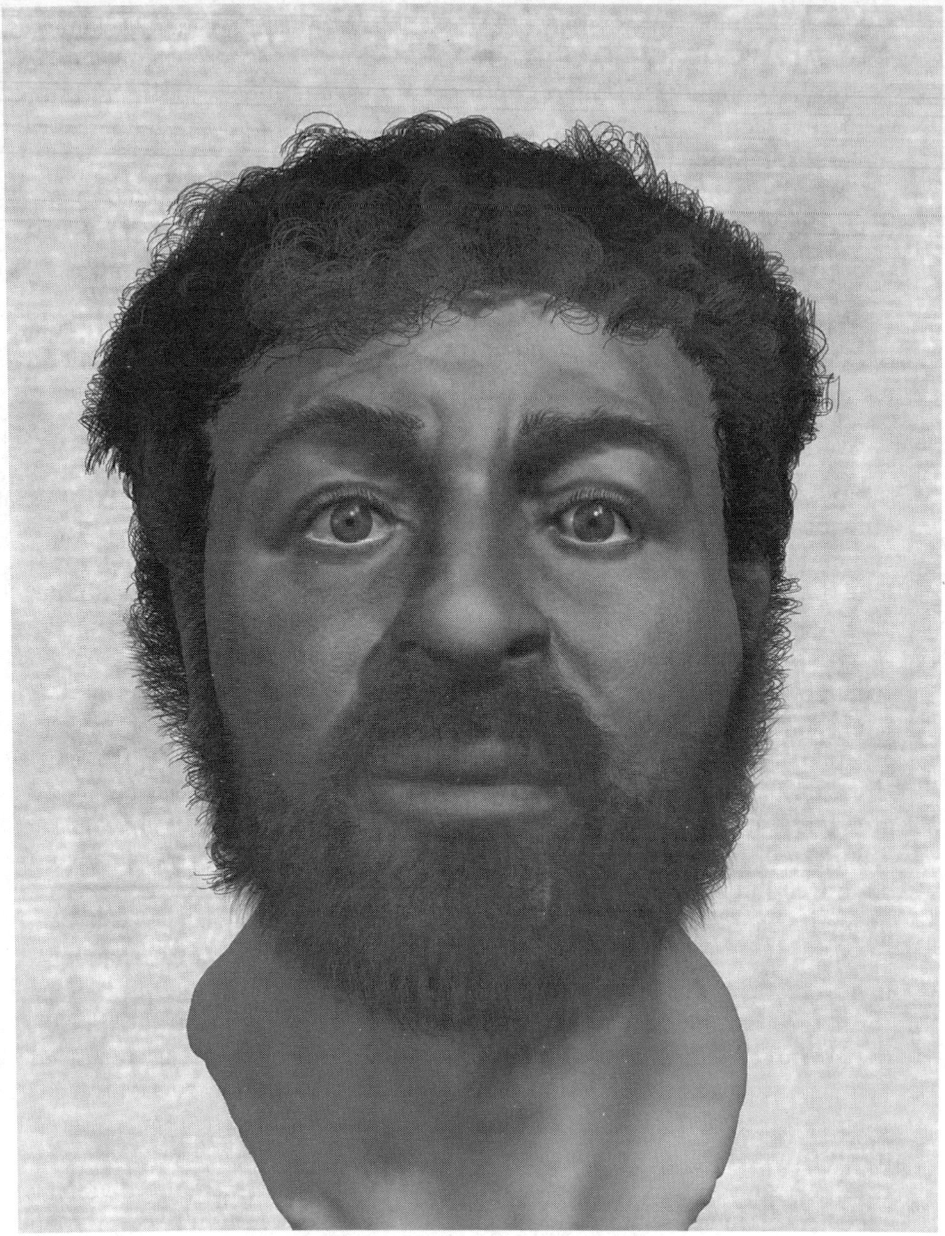

A proposed portrait of Jesus based on a digital reconstruction of a first-century Palestinian head. (BBC Photo Library)

gests a figure closer to a football coach than the Good Shepherd. His speech is often at odds with his image, the words of the Authorized Version and the New International Version out of sync with a figure who looks like a cross between Tab Hunter and Captain America. In the more conservative Catholic media, Jesus is often represented in the version familiar from popular nineteenth-century piety: the Light of the World, the Sacred Heart. He is tender, tragic, slightly feminized, slightly earnest, like a nineteenth-century French aesthete.

In the more liberal wings of both the Protestant and Catholic traditions a different picture of Jesus emerges; it is, however, strikingly similar across the traditions. Informed by historical scholarship, contemporary trends in theology and the ecumenical efforts of the postwar period, Jesus is often depicted in faux-naif line drawings, as if scratched on a catacomb wall, or, in a version aimed at younger people, as a kind of politically correct cartoon character, strong, brave, kind, and brown, like Disney's Aladdin.

The proliferation of new media in the 1990s, the Internet in particular, has democratized depictions of Jesus. Alongside mainstream and orthodox representations we now find a wealth of less familiar representations, given equal weight in quality if not quantity by the search engines employed to seek out and locate them. A search engine discriminates between words, not meanings or traditions, so if you type in "depictions of Jesus" it will return not only the mainstream Jesuses but Polynesian Jesuses, Messianic Jewish Jesuses, and extraterrestrial Jesuses. Among the less eccentric examples I found is a Jesus aimed at a Native American audience. The website, evangelical in purpose, builds a picture of Jesus from elements of Native American creation narratives. In the text, God is referred to as the Creator, and his Son as a "young warrior." The cross is a tree, and his followers seek to make the Creator's Son their "chief." Most arresting is a visual representation of Jesus. He appears, highly stylized, in a round device, like a medallion, representing the Creation. It is divided into four by his body on the cross. His head is huge and square, crowned with thorns and with a tear falling from his cheek. Over each shoulder the heads of the robbers crucified with him appear. His hands are huge, and beneath them on the left two figures reject his sacrifice and pierce his side with a spear. On the right, two figures accept his sacrifice and appear to be catching the blood that flows from his body in their cupped hands. If you didn't know what it was, your eye might pass over it, seeing a "primitive" art object; it is only when you see the details, the crown of thorns, the outstretched and pierced hands, the spear in his side, that it comes suddenly into focus as a representation of Jesus. It's a useful reminder of the persistence of highly particularized images of Jesus in contemporary Western imaginations, or at least in *this* one. Perhaps some value is to be derived from the sheer range and diversity of images of Jesus in the media. Individually they may all have serious deficiencies, but surveyed as an unruly crowd, they begin to reveal a picture—not of the "real" Jesus of Nazareth, but of his followers and observers trying to make sense, in one way or another, of this enigmatic and compelling figure.

Richard Coles

See also: Art; English Popular Culture, Modern; Enlightenment; Film; Literature, English; Literature, World; Resurrection

Reference

Marriage, Sophia, and Jolyon Mitchell, eds. 2003. *Studies in Media, Religion and Culture*. London: T. & T. Clark/Continuum.

Meier, J. P. (b. 1942)

John Meier, professor of New Testament at Notre Dame University, produced a turn-of-the-millennium study of the historical Jesus that promised to be the most comprehensive work on the subject ever published. By the beginning of 2002, the prodigious author had two large volumes in print (1991, 1994), with another slated for release and at least one more projected for the future. A Roman Catholic priest educated and ordained in Rome, Meier strives for objective neutrality in his work, examining every saying and deed attributed to Jesus from the perspective of rigorous historical science; he aims to determine which items can be regarded as established facts apart from the imposition of any faith perspective. His overarching label for Jesus has been "a marginal Jew," by which he means to affirm Jesus' Jewish identity while also recognizing that, as a Galilean peasant and as a crucified criminal, Jesus can be distinguished from the Jewish establishment of his day.

Meier's first volume includes an in-depth analysis of methodological principles for historical study. He favors four criteria for determining authenticity of traditions that are widely respected within historical Jesus studies (embarrassment, discontinuity, multiple attestation, and coherence) and proposes a fifth: the "criterion of Jesus' rejection and execution." By this, he means to indicate that a tradition is more likely to be authentic if it explains why Jesus was regarded as dangerous enough to be crucified. With regard to sources, Meier is less dismissive of the Gospel of John than many scholars, but he puts little value on such apocryphal writings as the Gospel of Thomas.

Meier regards the early years of Jesus' life as unremarkable, save for the note that Jesus apparently made the unusual decision at an early age to remain celibate (probably for religious reasons). As an adult, Jesus was baptized by John and probably joined the latter's circle of disciples. Jesus took John as a mentor in many ways, accepting his eschatological message of an impending judgment. Eventually he began his own ministry, which was similar to John's in many respects, but was itinerant rather than local and placed greater emphasis on God's mercy, as evidenced through performance of healing miracles and through the practice of open table fellowship with sinners and outcasts. Jesus also moved away from John's asceticism but continued to proclaim a message of judgment and to baptize those who repented.

Meier agrees with most scholars in affirming that the central component of Jesus' message concerned the advent of "the kingdom of God." Unlike some scholars, however, he insists that this proclamation included the announcement of a definitive act of God that would bring salvation to Israel in the near future. Meier also breaks with much Jesus scholarship by maintaining that Jesus' miracles are a well-supported and important part of the Jesus tradition. Meier insists that the historical evidence establishes that Jesus did in fact do extraordinary deeds that were regarded as miracles by the people of his day; the things he did were so regarded by himself, by his supporters, by his enemies, and even by neutral observers.

Overall, Meier views Jesus as a complex figure in whom the convergence of numerous Israelite traditions were thought to find fulfillment. He acted as a prophet of the last days, a gatherer of the twelve tribes of Israel, a teacher who was authorized by God to reinterpret Mosaic law, and a healer and exorcist on the order of Elijah or Elisha. He was probably held to be the Messiah within his own lifetime. Meier holds that it is the convergence of so many distinct attributes that marks Jesus as unique.

Meier's third volume (forthcoming at the time of this publication) deals with historical issues concerning the disciples of Jesus and the various Jewish groups (Pharisees, Sadducees, etc.) with whom he interacted. The announced fourth volume will deal with Jesus' approach to the Law, with parables, with titles attributed to Jesus, and with the circumstances of Jesus' death.

Mark A. Powell

See also: Jesus, Miracles of; John, Gospel of; John the Baptist; Kingdom of God; Messiah; Thomas, Gospel of

References

Meier, John P. 1991. *The Roots of the Problem and the Person*. Vol. 1 of *A Marginal Jew: Rethinking the Historical Jesus*. New York: Doubleday.

———. 1994. *Mentor, Message, and Miracles*. Vol. 2 of *A Marginal Jew: Rethinking the Historical Jesus*. New York: Doubleday.

———. Forthcoming. *Companions and Competitors*. Vol. 3 of *A Marginal Jew: Rethinking the Historical Jesus*. New York: Doubleday.

Messiah

The writers of the New Testament routinely referred to Jesus as *christos*, that is, "the anointed one." The term is the Greek translation of the Hebrew *māshiah*, which, in turn, is translated by the English as "Messiah" (see John 1.41). It is a matter of no little significance and debate how and why this term came to be applied to Jesus so universally among the earliest Christians.

The roots of the term lie in the OT, where it is used of certain "anointed" persons, especially kings (e.g., 2 Sam. 2.4–7; 1 Kings 1.34, 54), but also priests (e.g., Exod. 29.7; Lev. 7.36) and prophets (e.g., 1 Kings 19.16; Isa. 61.1). The ceremonial anointing of such individuals with oil denoted divine empowerment and appointment to a specific office or role. As such it also indicated a special intimacy between God and the one so anointed. The Royal Psalms (Pss. 2, 18, 20, 21, 45, 72, 89, 101, 110, 132, and 144) reflect the identification of the Davidic kings, in particular, as "the Lord's anointed." Qualities such as justice, piety, and faithfulness, along with perpetual rule, were ascribed to such kings. In these Psalms, the Davidic kings were also frequently referred to as God's "son" (e.g., Pss. 2.7; 89.26). In the book of Isaiah, the prophet looks forward to a time when God will appoint an ideal Davidic king who will be God's own representative on earth: "For a child has been born for us, a son given to us; authority rests upon his shoulders; and he is named Wonderful Counsellor, Mighty God, Everlasting Father, Prince of Peace. His authority shall grow continually, and there shall be endless peace for the throne of David and his kingdom. He will establish and uphold it with justice and with righteousness from this time onward and forevermore" (Isa.

9.6–7). Similarly, the prophet Jeremiah wrote: "The days are surely coming, says the LORD, when I will raise up for David a righteous Branch, and he shall reign as king and deal wisely, and shall execute justice and righteousness in the land. In his days Judah will be saved and Israel will live in safety" (Jer. 23.5–6). After the decline of the royal line of David in the sixth century B.C., passages such as these came to be regarded as divine promises of the reestablishment of Davidic rule by a king intimately related to God. In the postexilic period, Zerubbabel seems to have been regarded as just such a person by the prophets Haggai (Hag. 2.20–23) and Zechariah (Zech. 4.1–14).

In the two or three centuries immediately preceding the birth of Jesus, there developed within Judaism a wide range of expectations and hopes relating to, among other things, the defeat of the Gentiles, the purification of the Jewish religion, and the glorification of Jerusalem and its temple. The fulfillment of these expectations was in some, though by no means all, cases closely attached to hopes for a "Messiah" or even "Messiahs" variously defined. In texts such as *Psalms of Solomon* 17 (first century B.C.) and the *War Rule* from Qumran (late first century B.C.), a great war was envisioned in which the people of God would be delivered from their enemies and righteous rule established. In the former of these texts, God acts through the agency of his "Messiah"; in the latter, no Messiah is mentioned. Several accounts given by the Jewish historian Josephus (A.D. 37–c. 100) suggest that the expectation of God's military intervention on behalf of the Jews persisted throughout the latter part of the Second Temple period and continued to animate a substratum of anti-Roman feeling during this time.

In the New Testament, all four of the Gospels assert that Jesus is the Messiah and apparently take it for granted that this involves descent from David. The genealogies of Jesus in Matthew and Luke take pains to establish (by different means) his Davidic lineage (Matt. 1.1ff.; Luke 3.23ff.), and various characters in all three Synoptic Gospels address Jesus as the "son of David." The Gospel of John ironically portrays the crowds debating Jesus' messianic credentials in light of the fact that "the scripture said that the Messiah is descended from David" (John 7.42). However, this should not lead us to the conclusion that notions of Davidic descent were always regarded as entirely adequate for describing Jesus' identity. In Mark 12.35–37 and parallels, Jesus asserts that the Messiah is to be understood as the "Lord" of David, rather than as his son. Indeed, the term "Lord" *(kyrios)* came to have particular significance for early Christian convictions about Jesus (see further below). Nevertheless, in the story of Jesus' triumphal entry into Jerusalem, Matthew and Mark represent the crowds as hailing Jesus as the son of David and anticipating "the kingdom of our father David that is coming" (Matt. 21.9; Mark 11.10); Luke and John have the crowds referring to Jesus as the "king" and "the king of Israel" (Luke 19.38; John 12.13). The designation of Jesus as "king" later becomes a matter of irony, both in the inscription "King of the Jews" placed above Jesus' head on the cross, and in the mouths of his enemies, who taunt him with the words, "Let the Messiah, the King of Israel, come down from the cross now, so that we may see and believe" (Mark 15.32). Before that, the question of Jesus' messiahship was raised explicitly by the high priest in the trial scene when he asked Jesus, "Are you the Messiah, the Son of the Blessed One?" to which Jesus responds unambiguously in Mark, "I am" (Mark 14.62; see also Matt. 26.63–64; Luke 22.67–69).

What is surprising in the Gospels, though, is that the defining act of Jesus' messiahship is not a call to arms (despite his preaching of "the kingdom of God") but his crucifixion at the hands of the Romans. Despite Luke's assertion that "Moses and all the prophets" had already made it clear that it was "necessary that the Messiah should suffer these things and then enter into his glory" (Luke 24.25), the identification of Jesus' violent death as his central messianic task appears to be a peculiarly Christian interpretation of the role of the Messiah. In all three Synoptic Gospels, Peter's declaration that Jesus is the Messiah is immediately followed by Jesus' prediction of his own suffering and death in Jerusalem (Matt. 16.21; Mark 8.31; Luke 9.22). A possible allusion to the book of Isaiah in Mark 10.45 and a quotation from that book in Luke 22.37 may suggest that the earliest Christians redefined the role of Messiah in the light of the "servant of the Lord" in Isaiah 52.13–53.12 who suffers for the benefit of the people (see also John 11.50–52). In Acts 8.27–35, the evangelist Philip proclaimed "the good news about Jesus" to an Ethiopian traveler on the basis of this very passage in Isaiah. For the author of Acts, though, it was the resurrection and exaltation of Jesus to the right hand of God that confirmed his status as Messiah (Acts 2.22–36).

The apostle Paul used the term *christos* for Jesus more than any other writer in the New Testament. But it is striking that even though Paul wrote for Gentile audiences, who presumably would not have known much of the Old Testament background for the term, we never find Paul explaining why Jesus is called *christos*. This raises the likelihood that the designation of Jesus as "Christ" had become so well established by the time Paul began to write in the early 50s of the first century that the term was already being used as a second name for Jesus, rather than as a title (hence Paul uses the names "Christ Jesus," "Christ," "Jesus Christ," and "the Lord Jesus Christ"), though the understanding of Jesus as "the Messiah" persists as well (e.g., Rom. 9.5).

As in the Gospels, we find an assertion of Jesus' Davidic descent (Rom. 1.3; see also 2 Tim. 2.8), but it is Jesus' death more than anything else that shapes Paul's understanding of Jesus' identity as the Messiah. Indeed, Paul could summarize his own preaching under the title: "Christ crucified" (1 Cor. 1.23). Paul defined Jesus' role as the eschatological opposite of the first man Adam. Adam, by sinning, brought sin and death into the world. In contrast, Jesus Christ, by his faith and obedience to the point of death, brought grace and life into the world (Rom. 5.12–21). Those who trust in the Christ's act of self-sacrifice (Rom. 3.24–25) are joined to him (Paul says they are "in Christ"), are rescued from God's wrath (Rom. 5.9), and are empowered to live a new kind of life (Rom. 6.4) by the Holy Spirit (Rom. 8.4). How Paul came to understand the role of the Messiah in this way is a matter of debate. Presumably, Paul's own encounter with the risen Christ (reported in Acts 9; see also Gal. 1.15–16) forced him to find a way to reconcile the notions of Messiah and the purposes of God with the death of Jesus. Further, for Paul the term *christos* also had associations with the resurrection of Jesus and the designation of Jesus as *kyrios*, "Lord" (e.g., Rom. 10.9; 1 Cor. 12.3). A possibly pre-Pauline hymn in Philippians celebrates Jesus' resurrection by proclaiming that "at the name of Jesus every knee should bend, in heaven and on earth and under the earth, and every tongue should confess that Jesus Christ is Lord" (Phil. 2.10–11). In the later Pauline letters (of disputed authenticity), the term "Christ" takes on cosmic dimensions. In the letter to the Colossians, the readers are told that in Christ "the whole fullness of deity dwells bodily." In the same context, Christ's death is described as a victory over cosmic "rulers and authorities" (Col. 2.9–15).

In the letter to the Hebrews we find yet more innovation in the way the term *christos* is applied to Jesus. As in Paul and the Gospels, there is still the characteristic understanding of Jesus' death as a sacrifice (Heb. 9.26), but this concept is supplemented by the notion that Jesus is himself also the High Priest who offers the sacrifice to God (Heb. 9.11–14). Jesus Christ is designated God's Son, who, moreover, is "a priest forever according to the order of Melchizedek" (Heb. 5.6) and "the same yesterday and today and forever" (Heb. 13.8). In 1 Peter, Christ's death is presented as a basis for Christian morality: "For to this you have been called, because Christ also suffered for you, leaving you an example, so that you should follow in his steps" (1 Pet. 2.21). This letter also links Christ's death to the Passover lamb of the book of Exodus: "You know that you were ransomed from the futile ways you inherited from your ancestors . . . with the precious blood of Christ, like that of a lamb without defect or blemish" (1 Pet. 1.18–19). The connection between Jesus' death and the Passover was undoubtedly mediated to the earliest Christians through the prophet Isaiah (see, e.g., Isa. 53) and the historical circumstances of Jesus' death.

In the book of Revelation, *christos* is used both as a name and as a title for Jesus. When used as a title, the term has close associations with the idea of "the kingdom of God" (Rev. 11.15; 12.10). However, the use of a slaughtered lamb as the predominant image for Jesus in this book significantly modifies any notion of militaristic messiahship. The Messiah's victory is achieved through suffering, and those who follow him share his glory only to the extent that they embrace his example of sacrificial witness to the One who sits on the throne.

Paul Spilsbury

See also: Hebrew Bible; Josephus; Kingdom of God; Lord; Son of God

References

de Jonge, Marinus. 1988. *Christology in Context: The Earliest Christian Response to Jesus*. Philadelphia: Westminster.

Hengel, Martin. 1983. *Between Jesus and Paul*. Philadelphia: Fortress.

Horbury, William. 1998. *Jewish Messianism and the Cult of Christ*. London: SCM.

Marshall, I. Howard. 1990. *The Origins of New Testament Christology*. Rev. ed. Downers Grove, IL: InterVarsity Press.

Sanders, E. P. 1992. *Judaism: Practice and Belief 63 BCE–66 CE*. London: SCM/Philadelphia: Trinity Press International.

Watts, Rikki E. 1997. *Isaiah's New Exodus and Mark*. Tübingen: Mohr Siebeck.

Methodism

See Wesley, Charles, and Wesley, John

Milton, John (1608–1674)

It is a curious fact that the standard work of reference on the writings of the greatest Christian poet in English, the nine-volume *Milton Encyclopedia* (Hunter 1978–1982), has no entry for "Jesus." Odder still, it might be thought, is the decidedly rare occurrence of the name in the writings themselves, where it is found only eight times in some 20,000 lines of verse: once in an early Latin elegy, once in *Paradise Lost,* in a typological reference to Joshua "whom the gentiles [i.e., Greeks] Jesus call" (XII, 310), and six times in a single poem, the short epic *Paradise Regained*. Elsewhere, Milton employed more formal designations: Lord, Son of God, Messiah, Redeemer, and of course Christ—theological titles or periphrases that emphasize doctrinal function over human individuality.

Milton's early intellectual and religious milieu was Protestant and humanist. C. A. Patrides (whose study of *Milton and the Christian Tradition* itself has index entries for "Christ" and "Son of God" but not for "Jesus") observed that "while the Catholic and Orthodox Churches have usually shown preference for the Passion and Easter . . . Protestantism has in practice shown preference for the Nativity and Christmas" (Patrides, 78), and it is true that the earliest poem Milton included in his 1645 *Poems* was a hymn, written in 1629 when the poet was twenty-one, "On the Morning of Christ's Nativity." Here, in a genre traditionally associated with the intimate, domestic aspects of the Gospel narratives, we might expect to find a Jesus recognizably, even vulnerably, human. In fact, whether approached via the English carol tradition, the devotional verse of contemporaries such as George Herbert, Henry Vaughan, and Thomas Traherne, or the sentimentally personalized away-in-a-manger idiom of the Victorian hymnal, this celebration of a Herculean infant already strangling the serpent of satanic error in his cradle and scattering the pagan deities in terrified abjection seems perversely indifferent to the familial piety and pathos of the Nativity scene. Not only is the newborn child unnamed; so, too, is his mother, his stepfather (absent entirely), and his birthplace; the Nativity itself, orchestrated with a baroque syncretism that conflates the infant Jesus with "the mighty Pan," is proleptically overshadowed by the apocalyptic narrative of the "bitter cross" and the "wakeful trump of doom" when "the dreadful judge in middle air shall spread his throne" (xvi–xvii). Even the closing tableau, while alluding to a humble iconography of ox and ass, overwrites it with something altogether more regal and military:

> But see the virgin blest,
> Hath laid her babe to rest.
> Time is our tedious song should here have ending:
> Heaven's youngest teemed star,
> Hath fixed her polished car,
> Her sleeping Lord with handmaid lamp attending:
> And all about the courtly stable,
> Bright-harnessed angels sit in order serviceable.
> (xxvii)

Milton seems to have intended a sequence of poems on the feasts of the Christian calendar, since the Nativity poem was followed soon after by a shorter ode, "Upon the Circumcision," which reads the "wounding smart" of that occasion as a rehearsal for the "huge pangs and strong" of crucifixion that "ere long . . . / Will pierce more near his heart" (27–28), and another on "The Passion" that addresses its subject in the accents of neoclassical elegy and loses its way after eight stanzas. Sometime in the 1630s or early 1640s, Milton sketched out a number of "Plans for Biblical Tragedies," sixty-seven scriptural narratives, including a sequence on the life of Christ. For most of these, only a title is recorded, but the last, "Christus Patiens," expands into a brief scenario:

> The Scene in ye garden beginning fro[m] ye comming thither till Judas betraies & ye officers lead him away ye rest by message & chorus. his agony may receav noble expressions (*CPW* VIII, 560).

Only one of those youthful jottings survived into print: an Aeschylean tragedy called "Adam Unparadiz'd," which, thirty years later, in another genre and on an altogether different scale, resurfaced as *Paradise Lost*. As for the abortive Passion play, one Milton scholar has conjectured that "if Milton had actually undertaken this drama as outlined, he would have found himself as much inhibited as he had been in the ode [on the Passion]," adding that "nowhere in his poetry does he respond emotionally and artistically to the suffering Christ" (J. H. Hanford in *CPW* VIII, 594).

For a Christian poet who emulated the authors of *Job* and *Psalms* no less than those of the *Iliad* and the *Aeneid*, and who aspired "to justify the ways of God to men" (*PL* I, 26), this lack might seem a severe expressive disability. Certainly most modern readers will find the account of Jesus' life given by the archangel Michael to the repentant Adam in the last book of *Paradise Lost* an oddly cerebral and diagrammatic affair, substituting doctrinal symmetries and anonymities for the vivid, violent story that has excited and disturbed the imaginations of artists from Bach and Caravaggio to Bulgakov, Pasolini, and Kazantzakis:

> The law of God exact he shall fulfil
> Both by obedience and by love, though love
> Alone fulfil the law; thy punishment
> He shall endure by coming in the flesh
> To a reproachful life and cursèd death,
> Proclaiming life to all who shall believe
> In his redemption. . . .
> . . .
> For this he shall live hated, be blasphemed,
> Seized on by force, judged, and to death condemned
> A shameful and accurst, nailed to the cross
> By his own nation, slain for bringing life;
> But to the cross he nails thy enemies . . .
> (*PL* XII, 402–415)

Michael's discourse to Adam, like Milton's to his "fit audience . . . though few" (*PL* VII, 31), is ascetically didactic, and this (unnamed) Jesus is a theological diagram from which all human idiosyncrasy and cathartic emotion has been severely abstracted. But it nonetheless marks a highly significant shift, for the rigorous logic of atonement that underlies the passage demands a point-by-point correspondence between the first man and the last—a correspondence that requires the latter to be as fully human as the former. Where the earlier poetry (and prose) had been securely orthodox on the status of "the infant God," who "to show his Godhead true, Can in his swaddling bands control the damnèd crew" (Nativity, xxv), by the time he wrote *Paradise Lost* it is clear that Milton's thinking on the question of Christ's divinity and/or humanity had moved into more controversial territory. Precisely how far is not easy to say. These were not matters that could be openly debated in Milton's time. As late as 1612, when the poet-to-be was three, two men, Edward Wightman and Bartholomew Legate, were burned at the stake in London for the heresy of proclaiming the full humanity of Jesus. Even wholesale political and ecclesiastical revolution made little difference on this score. Only weeks before the execution of Charles I and the abolition of the Church of England, the Puritan Long Parliament passed an ordinance confirming anti-trinitarianism as a capital crime; even in the relatively free-thinking 1650s, while Milton was working as a civil servant for the Cromwellian Council of State, the Socinian (unitarian) John Bidle was jailed and exiled (only to the Scilly Isles, to be sure) for publishing an English translation of the Polish *Catechism of Raków* (1605), with its declaration that "no other than the Father of our Lord Jesus Christ is the only God of Israel; and the man Jesus of Nazareth, who was born of a virgin, and no other besides him, is the only-begotten son of God."

A year earlier, as it happens, Milton, whose duties included licensing books for publication, had approved the printing of a Latin version of that very book, and his own *De Doctrina Christiana*, unpublished in his lifetime and unknown to the world until its chance discovery in the Old State Paper Office in Whitehall in 1823, draws comparable conclusions from the same strict monotheism:

> What can this [Heb.1.2–3] imply but that God imparted to the Son as much as he wished of the divine nature, and indeed of the divine substance also? But do not take *substance* to mean total essence. If it did, it would mean that the Father gave his essence to the Son and at the same time retained it, numerically unaltered, himself. That is not a means of generation but a contradiction of terms. It is quite clear that the Father alone is a self-existent God: clear, too, that a being who is not self-existent cannot be a God (*CPW* VIII, 211–212).

This is Milton the theologian and logician. Milton the great dramatic poet finally engaged imaginatively with this humanized Jesus in his last poem, the four-book narrative of the temptation in the desert that he called, perhaps at the instigation of his Quaker friend Thomas Elwood, *Paradise Regained* (1671). It has already been noted that six of Milton's eight poetic uses of the personal name are found in this poem, five of them in the second book, the account of the temptation by hunger. Here the serious-minded young Jew ponders the nature of his mysterious calling in terms reminiscent of the poet's own accounts of his youthful sense of vocation:

> When I was yet a child, no childish play
> To me was pleasing, all my mind was set
> Serious to learn and know, and thence to do
> What might be public good.
> (*PR* I, 201–204)

Here the Gospel narrative of the birth and early life is put into the mouth of his anxious mother in language of unadorned simplicity:

> In such a season born when scarce a bed
> Could be obtained to shelter him or me
> From the bleak air; a stable was our warmth,
> A manger his . . .
> . . .
> From Egypt home returned, in Nazareth
> Hath been our dwelling many years, his life
> Private, unactive, calm, contemplative . . .
> (*PR* II, 72–81)

Here Satan mocks him for that very ordinariness:

> Great acts require great means of enterprise,
> Thou art unknown, unfriended, low of birth,
> A carpenter thy father known, thyself
> Bred up in poverty and straights at home:
> Lost in a desert here and hunger-bit:
> Which way or from what hope dost thou aspire
> To greatness?
> (*PR* II, 412–418)

And the climax, on the highest pinnacle of the Temple, has an austere, enigmatic grandeur, and a brief reversion to the classical parallelisms of the Nativity poem:

> To whom thus Jesus: Also it is written,
> Tempt not the Lord thy *God*, he said and stood,
> But Satan smitten with amazement fell
> As when Earth's son Antaeus (to compare
> Small things with greatest) in Irassa strove
> With Jove's Alcides . . .
> (*PR* IV, 560–565)

The poem ends not with the world-shattering exploits of an indestructible Herculean superhero, but with an obscure, modest, scholarly young rabbi making his solitary way homeward along a dusty road:

Thus they the Son of God our saviour meek
Sung victor, and from heavenly feast refreshed
Brought on his way with joy; he unobserved
Home to his mother's house private returned.
(*PR* IV, 636–639)

In this, as in so much else, Milton's writing straddles the threshold of intellectual modernity. The all-suffering, all-conquering, imperial Christ of the early poetry and prose belongs, like the Apollonian god in judgment of Michelangelo's Sistine ceiling, to the late Renaissance. The unassuming plebeian hero of Milton's last poem looks forward to the humanistic Jesus of D. F. Strauss, Ernest Renan, and the secular Christology of modern times.

Tony Davies

See also: Christology, Modern; Jesus as a Historical Figure; Literature, English; Lord; Messiah; Son of God; Strauss, D. F.

References
Hunter, William B. 1978–1983. *The Milton Encyclopedia.* Lewisburg, PA: Bucknell University Press.
Orgel, Stephen, and Jonathan Goldberg, eds. 1991. *The Oxford Authors: John Milton*. Oxford: Oxford University Press.
Patrides, C. A. 1966. *Milton and the Christian Tradition*. Oxford: Oxford University Press.
Wolfe, Don M., et al., eds. 1953–1982. *Complete Prose Works*. New Haven: Yale University Press.

Monophysitism
See Chalcedon

Montefiore, C.
See Jewish Scholarship

Music
Jesus has appeared in Western music in different ways. First, his words have served as texts for polyphonic motets and as part of musical settings of the Passion story. In addition, his final words on the cross have inspired several treatments, as have his teachings (such as the Beatitudes and the Lord's Prayer). Second, Jesus is the focus of a number of works in which he is mostly silent, such as those concerned with the Nativity, Handel's *Messiah*, or the Passion settings of such German composers as Georg Philipp Telemann, in which Old Testament characters and events are used as Christ-like parallels. Third, a number of works have seen Jesus through others' eyes, notably the meditation of the Virgin Mary on the crucified Christ in the medieval hymn, the Stabat Mater. Fourth, some purely instrumental works are also centered on Christ, such as Olivier Messiaen's *Vingt Regards sur l'Enfant Jésus* (1944).

Jesus in His Own Words

As Jesus was the eponymous focus of the Christian Church and its preeminent teacher, it was inevitable that his words should form a central part of the emerging liturgies of the Christian Church. Evidence shows that much of the liturgy, from the very earliest days, was sung; consequently, Christ's words were first performed musically in monophonic style derived mostly, it is argued, from the responsorial chanting of Jewish liturgy. For much of the first millennium, liturgical music was solely monophonic plainchant, with a number of repertories emerging in different parts of the Christian world. In these pieces, no attempt was made to interpret Christ's words through the music. Indeed, the purpose of music was seldom considered expressive in any modern sense, and theories about its function have veered between the functional (sung notes carry further in large buildings than spoken words) and the celebrational (music differentiates liturgy from ordinary discourse). Music was, however, also considered either a heavenly property or a means of revealing the nature of the heavens. The best exposition of this view is in the visions of Abbess Hildegard of Bingen (1098–1179).

Plainchant in the main may have been intended as a vehicle for the exposition of Christ's words, but early manuscript evidence shows that in the settings of the Passion story its performance went a stage further. After Pope Leo the Great's decree in the fifth century that the *St. Matthew Passion* (Matt. 26–27) should be chanted on Palm Sunday and the *St. John Passion* (John 18–19) on Good Friday (with the *St. Luke Passion* [Luke 22–23] replacing the Holy Wednesday repeat of the *St. Matthew Passion* 200 years later), it was inevitable that the chanting of this dramatic story should eventually move away from the emotionally neutral recitation of the words. Despite there being no conclusive evidence until the thirteenth century that the chanting of the Passion story was divided between several characters (most commonly three: Evangelist, Christ, and all other parts), there is earlier evidence that the performance of different roles required different styles. The word *tenere*, or its abbreviation "*t*," appeared above the words of Christ, indicating these should be sung more solemnly, and sometimes the pitch-range of Christ's part was lower than that of the other parts, again showing an early attempt to set apart Christ's identity through the music.

The arrival of polyphony in Western music in the tenth century affected the setting of Christ's words just as it did all other liturgical music. Christ's own words form a relatively small part of the corpus of sung liturgical texts, and though significant on account of their theological importance, they tended not to be set polyphonically but left as monodic chants. The arrival of motet in the thirteenth century, with its subsequent simultaneous settings of several texts, did not change matters. A motet might use a chant-melody associated with Christ's words, but no example can really be described as a setting or a musical interpretation of Christ's words.

The fifteenth and, in particular, sixteenth centuries saw the great flowering of the single-text motet. Even here, the number of texts taken from Christ's words is smaller than those from other sources, but some particular texts, such as *Ego sum panis vivus* ("I am the bread of life," John 6.35ff.), *Tris-*

tis est anima mea ("My soul is sad, even unto death," Matt. 26.38–39), and *Tu es Petrus* ("Thou art Peter," Matt. 16.18), inspired some celebrated compositions by such great and prolific composers as Palestrina (c. 1525–1594), Lassus (1532–1594), and William Byrd (1543–1623). Reformed liturgies resembled Catholic ones in the sparing use of Christ's words for musical settings, though in the Anglican liturgy one of the earliest celebrated examples was Thomas Tallis's (c. 1505–1585) *If Ye Love Me* (John 14.15).

The most striking settings of Christ's words are contained in the various forms of Passion narration for Holy Week. During the sixteenth century, the telling of the Passion story had, on occasions, moved from being just an expository recitation of the text to a more dramatic style. The division of solo voices had for some time been embellished by polyphonic settings of the crowd's parts, of which a notable early (though not quite the first) example from the later fifteenth century, contained in the Eton Choirbook, is by Richard Davy. In this piece, the four-part choir sings all the words, other than those of the Evangelist or Christ, blossoming into a wonderful melisma on the centurion's assertion, "Truly this was the Son of God." This is an early example of music altering reality to underline a Christological point, and it set a tradition that was to find its most famous utterance in Bach's *St. Matthew Passion* some 300 years later.

Polyphony invaded the Passion story even more in the sixteenth century when even Christ's words were occasionally set in this manner. From about 1507 on, some Passion settings were entirely polyphonic, marking a stage in which the composer increasingly used his art to color and interpret the words. It is no accident that the arrival of these more elaborate settings coincided with the development in secular music in Italy of the madrigal and its developing exploration and expression of human passions. As early as 1420 or so, a Passion setting appeared that did not draw its text from only one Gospel but from all four (the Longueval Passion). As such it cannot have been part of the liturgy and may have been intended as a private meditation for Pope Julius II. This innovation began a tradition that lasted for several more centuries.

The various ways of spreading the Passion narration among different solo voices, and possibly a choir, as known as the Responsorial Passion. In the sixteenth century, it flourished most in Italy, and the most frequent settings were from Matthew and John. Significant settings of the Passion appeared in other Catholic places, such as the Hofkapelle in Munich (by Lassus), Catholic Germany, and Mexico. In Spain, in some settings the crowd parts remained monodically chanted but the words of the Evangelist and some of Christ appeared in polyphony. Once again, this shows the developing attempts of composers to highlight and interpret Christ's words through musical differentiation. In many settings throughout the Catholic world, there are examples of particular texts being treated specially in polyphony, notably *flevit amare* (Peter weeping bitterly after his denial of Christ) and *emisit spiritum* (the moment of Christ's death—"he gave up the spirit").

Despite there being Passion settings in Catholic Europe, it was Protestant Germany that witnessed the greatest development and variety of ways of telling the Passion story through music. Luther was nominally opposed to Passion settings, stating that the Passion narrative should be reenacted in life, not in pretense. Nevertheless, from the outset of the Reformation his penchant for music overrode this ascetic stance, and Passion settings by his ardent supporters Johannes Walther (1496–1570) and Johann Bugenhagen (1485–1558) followed. Eventually, even Luther's intention that Christ's words should be audible, in German, and monodically recited was abandoned, and gradually music gained the upper hand. By the early seventeenth century, Christ's words were being set polyphonically—for instance, in Ambrosius Beber's *Mark Passion* (1610). The later seventeenth century saw even more developments, including a setting of the Passion story by Christoph Demantius (1567–1643) in 1631 for Freiburg that is wholly polyphonic like a motet. Demantius's *John Passion* is for six-part choir and typically opens with an *exordio* announcing the ensuing setting of the Passion story. Christ's words are differentiated from the others by being set for three or four voices in their lower registers. This feature is most dramatically evident in the dialogue between Pilate, represented by three upper voices, asking "Are you the King of the Jews?"; Christ answers on three lower voices "My kingdom is not of this world." The end of the first part of Demantius's Passion highlights the words Christ speaks to the high priest's officer who strikes him: "Why smitest thou me?" This question begins in the lower voices associated with Christ, but then spreads across the whole ensemble, being repeated five or six times in each voice as though Jesus' question was being asked more generally of humanity, not just of the offending officer.

Alternative to Demantius's motet-style of Passion setting ran a parallel development of Johann Walther's early Reformation style. The crowd scenes and opening exordio are choral, whereas the Evangelist, Christ, and other parts are recited in plainchant style. In the seventeenth century, the most prominent exponent of this style was Heinrich Schütz (1585–1672), who composed a *John Passion* in 1665 for performance in Dresden and in 1666 added a *Matthew* and *Luke Passion*. These use Schütz's own expressive recitative for Christ, the Evangelist, and other smaller parts and short polyphonic settings for the various ensembles of high priests, elders, disciples, and others. However, in the *Matthew Passion*, Schütz underlined the universality of the centurion's assertion by assigning his "truly this was the Son of God" to the choir and slightly embellishing the word *wahrlich* ("truly"). Both the *Matthew Passion* and the *John Passion* have an additional *conclusio* in which soteriological requests and promises are made.

Though the Waltherian style of Passion represented by Schütz and the motet style represented by Demantius were not unique, the majority of Passion settings became affected by Italian opera and began to include instruments and some nonbiblical solo numbers in addition to the nonbiblical *exordio* and *conclusio*. Thomas Selle (1599–1663) of Hamburg wrote two Passion settings, *St. John* (1641) and *St. Matthew* (1642). He employed an instrumental ensemble of two violins, two bassoons, and continuo (cello, bass, and organ) throughout the *St. John Passion*, in particular to differentiate

Christ's words from the Evangelist's, the former being accompanied by the two violins and continuo, the latter by the two bassoons. Thomas Selle's music is indebted to Venetian models, and he interpolated the biblical narrative with three *intermedii*. The second is an elaborate polychoral setting of Christ's words "My God, my God, why hast thou forsaken me?" which are made very dramatic, even poignant, by being antiphonally exchanged between the divided choirs. This large-scale manner is in telling contrast to the austerely simple setting of Christ's last words, such as the four ascending notes for "It is finished."

In the eighteenth century, the most important Protestant developments of the Passion were those that used the biblical texts with additions and were set in a hybrid style that used recitative, formal arias, crowd choruses, and choral numbers of new texts. The most celebrated of these were J. S. Bach's (1685–1750) settings of the *John Passion* (1723/1724) and the *Matthew Passion* (first performed in 1727 and revised at least once for 1736). Bach's *John Passion* is very dramatic and was possibly intended to demonstrate Bach's operatic leanings and to show his talents as a kapellmeister (in charge of court music) rather than his cantorship abilities (as head of church music). His *Matthew* is longer and more contemplative, and because his substantial enlargement and revision for 1736 included so many aspects of seventeenth-century Protestant musical practices and religious views, it is an excellent vantage point from which to view the development of Christology in the oratorio Passions of Germany in the first half of the eighteenth century.

For the 1736 revision, Bach divided the choirs, soloists, and orchestra into two and, new research reveals, separated them physically. The first choir represented the immediate witnesses of the Passion story, the second Christian people at large. Thus, the question and answer parts of the opening chorus were a dramatic enactment of Christianity at large asking the immediate witnesses about what they were now to learn. Over the top of this (physically, from a high gallery in St. Thomas's Leipzig, and musically), a choir of trebles sang a chorale stating a Christological truth: *O Lamm Gottes unschuldig* ("O Lamb of God unblemished"). This same division between Christ's contemporaries and Christianity at large is further evident when the disciples ask Christ at the Last Supper which of them will betray him. To their eleven inquiries, "Is it I?" a chorale sung by both choirs replies, "Tis I." Christ is betrayed then and now—and by his own.

There is much evidence that Bach's revisions for 1736 were inspired by his reading of Martin Luther, and in particular Luther's teaching on the will and on soteriology. Bach's *Matthew Passion* is an exploration through music of the redemptive aspects of the Passion story, and Bach used, amongst other things, different musical styles to articulate this. A good example appears in the aria *Komm süßes Kreuz*, with its *viola da gamba obbligato* and the quotation of a French *tombeau* (that is, a work commemorating a death, here Marin Marais's *Le Tombeau de M. Méliton*) as the main melodic idea of the first movement. Bach also continued the tradition of highlighting Christ's words with different musical accompaniment, in this case strings, and of setting the centurion's assertion for chorus. Bach's *Matthew Passion* deliberately used or invoked past Passion settings (for example, Reinhard Keiser's [1674–1739] *St. Mark Passion* [1717]), French and Italian musical styles, Lutheran chorales, and the intermingling of biblical texts and nonbiblical meditations. Even the penultimate number, with its statements by individual soloists interpolating the chorale, resembles the responsorial litany at a Lutheran funeral. Bach's *Matthew* resonates at so many levels it is difficult to argue against its being his theological summa in music, and given the fact that he was expressing not so much his own views but representing the views of his Lutheran congregation, it is a magnificent summary in music of the Christology of his time and place. Its revival (though not necessarily its third, fourth, or even fifth performance) by Mendelssohn in 1829 gave it another meaning and a different significance.

One striking feature of both Bach's Passions is the use of nonbiblical meditations. Possibly conceived as Lutheran concession to the personalized theology of Pietism, these texts allowed composers much scope for observing Christ and meditating quite often on the tragedy of the unfolding scene. The most frequently set text typifying this development was Heinrich Brockes's *Der für die Sünden der Welt gemarterte und sterbende Jesus* (1712). Keiser (1712), Telemann (1716), Handel (1717), Mattheson (1718), and many others set the text. Brockes's Passion is a hybrid that, unlike Bach's, dramatizes Christ by allowing (1) a paraphrase of some of his biblical words to be set as arias, for instance *Mein Vater! Schau, wie ich mich quäle* ("My father! look upon my torment"), and (2) eventually his singing of a nonbiblical duet with his mother, Mary. She inquires of Christ whether he, her Son, must die, to which he replies, "Yes, I die for you, to win Heaven for you." This greater involvement of Christ in the drama of the story removes him from the framed distance Bach gave him and makes him more directly part of the drama. This development of Christ as an operatic character may well have been why Bach did not use Brockes's libretto in its entirety, though parts of it appear in his *John Passion*.

The nineteenth century saw few remarkable Passion narrations or settings, but in the twentieth century there have been some outstanding examples. Among them are the Polish composer Krzysztof Penderecki's (b. 1933) *St. Luke Passion* (1963–1966) and the Swiss composer Frank Martin's (1890–1974) *Golgotha* (1948), which intersperses Christ's words with quotations from St. Augustine's *Confessions* (c. 398–400).

The numbers of works other than small motets in which Christ's words are used as text, but which do not deal with the Passion story, are much fewer. There are several outstanding settings of the Beatitudes from the Sermon on the Mount (Matt. 5.1–12), notable examples being *Les Béatitudes* (1869–1879), an oratorio by César Franck (1822–1890), and Sir Arthur Bliss's (1891–1975) cantata *The Beatitudes* (1962), in which the biblical text is interspersed by narrated poems. Words from the Sermon on the Mount are also used in Dave Brubeck's (b. 1920) *The Light in the Wilderness* (first performed in 1968) and Franz Liszt's (1811–1886) *Christus* (1862–1866), in which eight beatitudes are exchanged between a baritone and the chorus.

Liszt's panoramic picture of Christ in his *Christus* also contains a beautiful setting of the Lord's Prayer (*Pater noster,* Matt. 6.9–13) that alternates plainsong-type melodies with richer choral writing. The Lord's Prayer enjoys a number of settings, including a number from the Tudor period, that are often heard in Anglican services as part of choral evensong.

Another setting of the Beatitudes is to be found in the second part of Sir Edward Elgar's (1857–1934)*The Apostles* (1902–1903), the first of a projected trilogy of oratorios about the recruitment, teaching, and achievement of Christ's disciples. Jesus (bass) does not have a big role and appears only in scenes from the Sermon on the Mount, the walking on the water or Lake Galilee, his identifying of Jesus as the Messiah and Jesus' naming of Peter as the "rock" on which the Church will be built, and a very brief account of his forsaking in the garden of Gethsemane. The crucifixion is highly compressed. Tellingly, Christ's words *Eli, eli lama sabachthani* are left unsung, only alluded to by muted strings followed by an awestruck choral proclamation, "Truly this was the Son of God." This less assertive treatment showed Elgar more as the horrified onlooker than the pagan suddenly converted.

In the succeeding oratorio, *The Kingdom* (1906), Christ's "Lord's Prayer" is used by the participants in "The Breaking of Bread," in effect a celebration of the Eucharist. The reciting of the prayer has now been transformed from a didactic recital by Jesus to a uniting reiteration of the prayer Christ gave to his disciples and, through them, to the Christian Church. Elgar's setting is intended as a symbolic compression of Christian belief. Earlier in his life, Elgar had cast Christ in his *Light of Life* (1896).

One last group of works needs to be mentioned, settings of Christ's last words on the cross (some being quotations from the Old Testament). To composers from Schütz in the seventeenth century to Charles Gounod's (1818–1893) *Les Sept Paroles de N.S. Jésus Christ* (1858) and Frank Martin's *In Terra Pax* (1945), which mixes Christ's short utterances with a more apocalyptic vision, these words have proved stimulating. All composers adopt a suitably serious and mournful tone, none using the words ironically or in a way different from their accepted meaning. One more unusual setting of the words *(Die sieben letzten Worte des Erlösers am Kreuz)* was a musical meditation on them by Joseph Haydn (1732–1809). Originally commissioned in 1785 as a series of orchestral meditations in between sermons for Good Friday, they were later published in Vienna as *Seven Sonatas with an Introduction and at the End an Earthquake*. In 1787, Haydn arranged them for string quartet (op. 51 no. 1–7), and in about 1796 he rearranged them as a choral work. Haydn set out to be not a theologian but a dramatist. Each "word" is couched in a suitably lachrymose garb; the attitude is perhaps less Christ's than a tear-stained onlooker's. Nonetheless, in developing the music and shading each "word" through different keys, a richer vision of Christ's suffering is obtained—for example, the sweet vision created when the music moves into a radiant major key in the meditation on "Today thou shalt be with me in Paradise."

Jesus, the Mostly Silent Focus

In a sense all Christian musical works are about Christ, but there have been a large number of works in which the central character does not appear.

Contemporary with the biblical and semibiblical narrations of the Passion story discussed above there are a number of contemplations of the Passion and of the soteriological significance of Christ in which onlookers describe events they have witnessed. Notable amongst these in Protestant Germany were Telemann's and Carl Heinrich Graun's (1704–1757) *Der Tod Jesu* (1755), which used a newly written text by Karl Wilhelm Ramler (1725–1798) commissioned for performance in Berlin by Princess Anna Amalia of Prussia, Frederick the Great's younger sister. It is a still a mystery how Telemann's setting managed to be premiered in Hamburg one week before the much heralded Berlin performance of Graun's setting in Berlin. Neither performance was liturgical, which indicates the text and its settings were intended as a meditation on the drama and meaning of the Passion rather than as a reenactment of it. As such, they clearly indicate that a much more personalized and gory version of the Passion story had come to the fore that was quite unlike the austerity of the seventeenth-century Passions or earlier. The searing grief of the witnesses of the Passion and the sufferings of Christ are more apparent than its redemptive purpose or any theological or Christological teachings. Ironically, this new mode made the narrations both more operatic and less universal, with the result that only the Graun has survived to the present day in regular performance, and even then only in Germany.

The Protestant Passions shared this concentration on the grief and suffering of Christ's death with a number of Catholic quasi-Passions of the day. Liturgical Passions continued to be used, but so strong was the pull of opera that during Lent, when the opera-houses were closed, Passion oratorios emerged that were in fact opera in all but name. In Vienna, for instance, a favorite musical genre was the *oratorio al sanctissimo sepolcro,* of which a typical and celebrated example was *La Deposizione dalla Croce* (1728) by the chief court composer, Johann Joseph Fux (c. 1660–1741). Christ does not appear. The cast consists of the Virgin Mary, Mary Magdalene, St. John the Apostle, Joseph of Arimathea, Nicodemus, and a chorus of sinners. Like an opera, it is a succession of recitatives and arias, though unlike an opera, the drama is more psychological than physical (though in fact many contemporary Italian operas were concerned with thoughts more than actions). The purpose of the piece is both emotive and didactic. The most often set opera librettist of the mid-eighteenth century, who worked most of his life in Vienna, was Pietro Metastasio, who had written his *La Passione di Nostro Signore Gesu Christo* in Rome in 1730. Set many times, it typically has no part for Christ but includes St. Peter, St. John, Joseph of Arimathea, and Mary Magdalene. At one point, John gives Peter a graphic, but only loosely biblical picture of Christ's suffering before the crucifixion, describing how Christ's clothes stuck to his sores, how bent nails were straightened out to drive into his hands and feet, and how one of the soldiers "bent over his treacherous and stupid work, covering His face with his filthy sweat." Beethoven (1770–1827) continued this style of making the Passion story more human and passionate in his *Christus am Oelberge* (1803, revised 1804).

For obvious reasons, one of the largest bodies of music about Christ in which he does not speak deals with the Nativity. A vast amount of liturgical music exists describing and extolling the birth of Christ, as does an equally great number of para-liturgical texts, such as folk dramas. Carols, originally not exclusively about Christmas, have come to represent a kind of atavistic folk memorial in many people's minds. One of the richest early collections of carols originated in Britain in the fourteenth and fifteenth centuries (and perhaps earlier). The memorable tunes often accompany strings of strophes in which Christ is portrayed in many very unbiblical ways.

On a grander scale, the Christmas story has been told in music in oratorios, cantatas, and even in operas such as Gian Carlo Menotti's (b. 1911) television opera *Amahl and the Night Visitors* (1951). Most musical Nativity narrations are not biblical, so they did not come to fruition until the assimilation of opera by church music in the seventeenth century. Then there was an avalanche. Notable amongst the earliest was Heinrich Schütz's *Die Weihnachtshistorien* (The Christmas Story, 1660), and in the eighteenth century Bach's series of cantatas for three days of Christmas and the following feasts of the Circumcision, New Year, and Epiphany, collectively called *Weihnachts-Oratorium* (Christmas Oratorio, 1734–1735). Bach's work is a mixture of narrative, reflection, and Christology; for instance, on the feast of Circumcision, Jesus is named Emmanuel and several numbers reflect on his death and his and others' suffering to follow, but also express a desire to rejoice in the salvation offered by these events. The final chorale is a series of imprecations, "Jesus direct my beginning, remain ever near me, curb my senses, be my sole desire, be ever in my thoughts, let me never falter!" The work is, like all Bach's sacred cantatas, a sermon told through music. The role of the music is to conjure a suitable emotional attitude to each perspective; for the most part, the story is seen in retrospection, though Bach does allow himself some charming evocations of the legendary simplicity of Christ's birth attended by animals, angels, and shepherds. Amongst the most delightful, and iconic, of these is the celebrated introduction to the second part, the "Pastoral Symphony," set in the typically lilting rhythm required for eighteenth-century pastoral scenes.

Nineteenth-century and early twentieth-century composers of Christmas narrations have usually avoided Bach's Lutheran didacticism, partly because few of their works were intended liturgically as Bach's were. Frequently composers resorted to deliberately archaic echoes—whether instrumentation, harmony, or contrapuntal style. Typical of these is Hector Berlioz's (1803–1869) *L'Enfance du Christ* (1850–1854) and Mendelssohn's (1809–1847) fragmentary *Christus* (1847), as is Joseph Rheinberger's (1839–1901) deeply affectionate *Die Stern von Bethlehem* (1890) and Gabriel Pierné's (1863–1967) *Les Enfants à Bethléhem* (1907). The latter is more like a Nativity play, with its quaint blend of modern and archaic harmony and its story about children visiting the infant Jesus and being addressed by, amongst others, personifications of the donkey and the ox; a star exudes a charm that is not unlike that of *Amahl and the Night Visitors*. Both these works emphasize the simplicity and innocence around Christ's birth, as well as its hope. And even when later events are referred to, the image of Christ that remains is the same as that of countless medieval and renaissance pictures, a thousand Nativity plays, and countless carol services.

The Nativity sections of Liszt's *Christus* use a deliberately archaic counterpoint reminiscent of the sixteenth century to create a sense of stillness and contemplation. This is in marked contrast to two much more strongly robust settings: Sir John McEwan's (1868–1948) of Milton's magnificent 1629 poem *Ode on the Morning of Christ's Nativity* (1901–1905) and Sir Hubert Parry's (1848–1918) of William Dunbar's *Ode on the Nativity* (1912). Both emphasize, through powerful harmonic language, strident choral writing, and moments of luminous reflection, the cosmic transcendence of Christ's Nativity rather than its immanent charm. Ralph Vaughan Williams (1872–1958), in contrast, both in *Fantasia on Christmas Carols* and *Hodie* (1953–1954), more closely recalls the innocent charm typical of Berlioz and Pierné, as does the exquisite *Christmas Cantata* (1947) by Geoffrey Bush (1920–1998) and the masterful series of choral settings by Benjamin Britten (1913–1976), *A Boy Was Born* (1933).

One narration of Christ's life and posthumous life, but in particular his Nativity, stands out, not only for its ability to encase words so memorably that some are almost unreadable without hearing the composer's music, but also because it is so often performed in part at Christmas: Handel's (1685–1759) *Messiah* (1742). This great picture of Christ in music encompasses both the charmingly immanent in the Pastoral Symphony and the grandly transcendent in such choruses as "Hallelujah" and "Worthy Is the Lamb." Handel's, like Bach's, is not really personal music, though it may reflect much personal feeling. Both composers set out to articulate either doctrine or the received attitude of their age. In their great works they achieved through music perhaps more than anywhere else a summation not only of contemporary Christology but the more subtle, unconscious contemporary feelings about such things as the infancy of Christ, the triumph of the resurrection and the ascension, the cosmic significance of the crucifixion, the harrowing of hell, and the final judgment. Their music interpreted the words.

One significant group of works that see Christ through another's eyes is the settings of the Stabat Mater. This poem was a devotional work supposedly written by Jacopone da Todi (c. 1228–1306) and became a Lenten sequence for liturgical use. It was banned by the counter-Reformation, but not before its most celebrated setting by Palestrina. Reinstated in the eighteenth century, it has witnessed a steady flow of settings since that time. Almost the first, and the one that became the model for many subsequent settings, was by Giovanni Pergolesi (1710–1736) in 1729. Haydn's setting in 1767 established its reputation. Neither he nor Pergolesi, though writing moving works, sought to escape suitable sadness and pathos. In the nineteenth century, along with the more general move toward composers expressing themselves and engaging audiences in a different manner, settings of the Stabat Mater tended more to express a unique understanding by each composer, in most cases partly reflecting his religious upbringing or beliefs. The settings thus became both manifestations of grief and more individualized pictures of mourning. This contrast is tellingly evident in the two great Italian settings by Gioacchino Rossini (1792–1868) in 1842 and Giuseppe Verdi (1813–1901) in 1895–1897. Rossini's cheerfully, overtly operatic settings picture the Virgin Mary as a dramatic heroine, even in the choral numbers, distraught (but not too much) over the death of her son. Verdi's chorus-only setting is much more broodingly angry, suggesting a very different attitude by the Virgin to her son. There is even a hint of Job-like cursing of God for the imposition of this tragedy on the Virgin, in contrast to the agony of Christ, with its eventual "happy" ending "earned" by his death. In this thinking Verdi was much more akin (though unconsciously) to later existential Christology than to Rossini. The work is less sad than desperate. Similarly contrasting attitudes can be detected in the settings of the Stabat Mater by such diverse composers as Antonín Dvořák (1841–1904) in 1875, Sir Charles Stanford (1852–1924) in 1907, Franz Liszt in *Christus* (1862–1866), and Krzysztof Penderecki in 1963.

Christ the Focus in Instrumental Music

Apart from the isolated numbers in longer pieces, there are very few pieces devoted to contemplations and interpretations of Christ in instrumental music. One of the first and most remarkable is the so-called Rosary Sonatas by Heinrich von Biber (1644–1704). Though these sonatas are subtitled "15 mysteries in the Life of Virgin Mary," at least ten of them deal with events in Christ's life. They make little attempt to penetrate and interpret, however, and are not illustrative so much as reflective on the events they depict (the birth, the Presentation in the Temple, the agony in the Garden of Gethsemane on the Mount of Olives, the scourging, the crowning with thorns, Christ on the journey to Calvary, the Crucifixion, the Resurrection, and the Ascension). Set for a small ensemble of violin and continuo, they are obviously not intended as "public" statements and they make little attempt to penetrate and interpret the events they depict. Nevertheless, they are a good indication not only of what it was considered instrumental music could achieve at the time, but also of what a composer felt appropriate to express in abstract music.

They are thus very different from Olivier Messiaen's (1908–1992) *Vingt Regards sur L'Enfant Jésus* (1944). This series of twenty solo piano pieces lasting over two hours was inspired by the writings of Dom Columba Marmion, Maurice Toesca, St. Thomas Aquinas, St. John of the Cross, and many paintings depicting Christ both with his mother and as the Word of God. Messiaen did not regard himself as an interpreter of the religious truths he believed in but as a revealer of their deeper truths through music—the wordless expressing the ineffable. His work is saturated by symbols and recurring musical ideas representing theological phenomena. However dispassionate Messiaen may have considered himself, every note betrays an attitude and an interpretation, and the work is remarkable not only for the power of his vision but for his desire and ability to translate this into music. He maintained that it was not possible in a single movement to show at once the extent of the transcendence of Christ. He was not content to portray Christ's birth merely as a pastoral or his death as a tragedy. He aimed to view Christ from twenty different perspectives, some as abstract as the "spirit of joy," some as anthropomorphic as the Cross, and some as traditional as the Virgin Mary or her husband Joseph. Sometimes the work views Christ with almost sentimental affection, as *Le baiser de l'Enfant Jésus* and *Regard du Père*, or with frightening grandeur and intensity, as in *Regard de l'Esprit de joie* and *Regard de l'Onction terrible*. Messiaen's picture of Christ is as comprehensive as Liszt's in his *Christus*, but its intention is much more theological. Its ambition is to use music to penetrate the meanings implicit in the birth and death of Christ and, as such, to move beyond the physical events of Christ's life to express the central core of his significance for Christianity. This aim had been the property of word-based theological and philosophical works, but Messiaen pushed it further in using music. Some might argue that he aimed for the impossible and that music is not capable, as Igor Stravinsky said, of expressing anything outside itself. But Messiaen did not agree, and by aiming to reveal through sounds the full meaning of Jesus, he took music as far as it has ever gone in the representation and interpretation of Jesus in music.

Roderick Swanston

See also: Eucharist; Jesus, Death of; Jesus, Origins of; Luther, Martin; Milton, John

References

Barzun, Jacques. 1985. *Berlioz and the Romantic Century*, vol. 2. New York: Columbia University Press.

Haydon, Geoffrey. 1995. *John Tavener: Glimpses of Paradise*. London: Gollancz.

Keys, Ivor. 1993. "The Apostles: Elgar and Bach as Preachers." In *Edward Elgar: Music and Literature*. Edited by Raymond Monk. London: Scolar Press.

Johnson, Robert Sherlaw. 1975. *Messiaen*. London: University of California Press.

Smallman, Basil. 1970. *The Background of Passion Music: JS Bach and His Predecessors*. London: Dover.

Stiller, Günther. 1984. *Bach and Liturgical Life in Leipzig*. St. Louis: Concordia.

N

Nestorianism

Nestorianism is the heresy that teaches two Sons or two persons in Jesus Christ. In other words, it so stresses the division between the humanity and the divinity that it ends up with two separate realities, two independently functioning subjects, which together are somehow meant to constitute the one Christ. "Nestorianism" is, then, a traditional label for one of the dangers that beset all reflection about the person of Jesus.

The key questions are whether there ever have, in fact, been any Nestorians (at least until modern times), and how one would go about deciding whether there had been. The prime candidate for being considered a Nestorian would seem to be Nestorius himself. In the year 428, Nestorius was brought from the great city of Antioch in Syria to become bishop of the imperial capital, Constantinople. He found—as he often complained—a bitterly divided Church. One faction rallied around the slogan that Mary could be called *theotokos*—bearer of God or Mother of God; the other, around the reductionist slogan that she was only *anthropotokos*—bearer of a human being (Loofs 1914, 185, 251). Years later, Nestorius reminisced about the warring factions that came en masse to the episcopal palace in urgent need of a solution to their problems. He had, he said, restored peace by proposing, to the delight of all, that Mary should be called *Christotokos*—bearer of Christ or Mother of Christ—a title that encompassed the other two (Nestorius, 91–92).

The peace—if there ever had been peace—was short-lived. Nestorius had quickly fallen foul of Cyril, the enormously powerful patriarch of Alexandria. Cyril's agents in Constantinople, Nestorius complained, fomented trouble by campaigning against his Christotokos formula. Nestorius had bitten off more than he could chew: he was outgunned politically and theologically by Cyril. A great deal of money changed hands in the interests of Alexandrian orthodoxy, and Nestorius's support in the palace began to melt away.

A council eventually met in Ephesus in June 431 that became known as the Third Ecumenical Council of the Church. Its proceedings were messy, and there was an appeal to the emperor. But the upshot was that Nestorius was deposed and condemned. He returned to Antioch, hoping to be left in peace in his monastery. But neither his friends nor his enemies forgot about him, and he remained a focus of conflict. In 436, the emperor sent him into exile. Nestorius lived for another fifteen years or so, almost all of them spent in the inhospitable confines of the Great Oasis in the Sahara.

Both in Antioch and in the Oasis, Nestorius spent the years after his deposition refining his Christology and writing a series of works of rather prickly self-justification in which he firmly but sadly defended his beliefs and his conduct. An untidy collection of this material, known as the *Book of Heraclides*, survived in a Syriac translation among the Christians of Persia who honored the memory and the theology of Nestorius. Its publication in 1910 helped reopen debate on his orthodoxy. (The more colorful title by which it is sometimes known, the *Bazaar of Heraclides*, is unfortunately a misnomer: the original Greek word translated as "Bazaar" means "dealing" with something and can refer to a treatise [as it does here] or to a business venture.)

At the end of the seventeenth century, scholars began to ask whether Nestorius had indeed been a Nestorian. The discussion was given new point and poignancy just under a century ago by three important publications. Fragments of the works of Nestorius—preserved for the most part by his enemies, who used them against him—were published in 1905 by the great German historian of dogma Friedrich Loofs. And in 1910, the Syriac text of the *Book of Heraclides* was published by Paul Bedjan, followed in the same year by a scholarly French translation by F. Nau (Nestorius).

Was Nestorius, then, a Nestorian? In terms of formulae—that is, in terms of the expressions he used—clearly not. He said over and over again, throughout his career, that he believed in one Son and that Christ is one person. Thus, in a sermon preached in Constantinople, he said of the humanity and divinity, "That which is seen and which cannot be seen is one Son . . . the natures are twofold, but the Son is unique" (Loofs 1914, 229). Or, again, "God the Word and the human being in whom the Word was were not one and another, but there was one person of both" (ibid., 224), "a single person in two natures and two natures in a single person" (Nestorius, 209).

But at other times, Nestorius's use of the word "person"—*prosopon* in his Greek—sounds distinctly odd. Thus, he could say that two persons/*prosopa* came together to make one. The two natures—divinity and humanity—"are united in a single person [prosopon], which belongs to the natures and to the persons [prosopa in the plural]" (Nestorius, 218); "the natures subsist in their persons [prosopa] and in their natures and in the person [prosopon in the singular] of union" (Nestorius, 194).

What does that mean? Nestorius was working with an idea of what it means to be an individual—what it means to be a particular cat or a particular camel or a particular human being—that he had borrowed from the Cappadocian Fathers of the late fourth century—Basil the Great, Gregory of Nazianzus, and Gregory of Nyssa—and which they had in turn inherited from the Stoic philosophers of the Hellenistic period. In that way of thinking, the individual is made up of layers, as it were. One starts with undifferentiated being, an existence that is nothing in particular. General characteristics or common qualities are added on, which make some specific kind of thing—cat or camel or human being. And then a layer of particular characteristics or individual qualities is added on, and the undifferentiated cat template becomes the unique, identifiable cat Rudi, or the undifferentiated human being template becomes the unique, identifiable man Fred. Nestorius had a word for the separate, individual thing that comes about when the individual qualities are factored in: he called it a *hypostasis*. Rudi is a hypostasis because she is a separate, individual cat type of thing, and Fred is a hypostasis because he is a separate, individual human type of thing.

But more often, what Nestorius was thinking about was what the separate, individual thing looked like from the outside. He talked about the front it presented to the world, or its mode of appearing. And his word for that was prosopon (literally, "face"). A birthday cake provides a very crude analogy. When Nestorius thought about Rudi or Fred, his thought moved from undifferentiated being (stage 1), to a specific kind of thing (stage 2), and then on to the particular individual (stage 3). In the case of the cake, stage 1 could be thought of as an undifferentiated mixture of the basic ingredients that go into any cake. At stage 2, one thinks in the chocolate or coconut that makes it a specific kind of cake. Finally, when it is baked, it becomes a particular chocolate cake or a particular coconut cake. It has a shape and a texture and a color that mark it off as something separate, distinct from all other cakes in the world. In other words, it has become a hypostasis. But when one looks at it, what one sees is its surface appearance, its prosopon: it is covered in white icing and birthday candles and says "Happy Birthday Fred."

Now, it would be impossible to have a cake without a surface appearance of *some* sort. If it had no prosopon, it would not be a real cake but only an abstract idea—a recipe in a book. So, too, in the case of Christ, Nestorius thought that the divinity and the humanity, if they are real, must each be a hypostasis and must each have a prosopon. But what the Incarnation means is that in Jesus the divinity and humanity each share the surface appearance of the other. The Word of God is clothed in the appearance of a weak and suffering man, and the man, seated at the right hand of the Father, now receives the glory and honor and adoration that belong to the Son to whom he is joined. "The *prosopon* of the divinity and that of the humanity form one *prosopon*, the one through a lowering, the other through a raising up" (Nestorius, 218).

In Nestorius's scheme of things, the individual characteristics that go to make up the surface appearance—the prosopon—of an ordinary human being include things that, to us, operating from within quite a different framework, look rather external and transient. The features of the prosopon would include things such as age, weight, and hair color. They would also include family and class. And they would include relational elements—how the individual was regarded by others and how they treated him. But all these things enable one individual to be distinguished from another. Indeed, it is the sum total of all these things that *makes* one individual distinct from another. And, conversely, the sharing of such properties establishes a real bond between two individuals.

When Nestorius said there was "one person [prosopon]" of both "God the Word" and "the human being in whom the Word was," he went on to specify that he meant "one person in dignity and honour, worshipped by the whole creation, in no way and at no time divided by difference of purpose and will" (Loofs 1914, 224). For Nestorius, such things as shared honor and worship and a unity of will are threads in the fabric that *is* the conjunction of two natures, two hypostases, two prosopa in the one person of Jesus Christ.

It can be seen from this that "person" is not really a good translation of prosopon as Nestorius used it. In ordinary, everyday Greek, prosopon meant, among other things, the mask an actor always wore, and so the role an actor played—a character in a drama. It entered Christian theology as one of the words for what there were three of in the Trinity, but it was often used when what was especially in mind were the roles Father, Son, and Holy Spirit played—their parts in the drama of salvation.

So prosopon meant "person" in the sense of persons of the Trinity. And at the Council of Chalcedon in 451, both hypostasis and prosopon were to be used for what there was one of in Christ. It was Nestorius's misfortune that when he was writing, the concept of "person" was still being hammered out, philosophically and theologically. He was trying to use tools forged by the Stoics and the Cappadocians to answer questions they had not faced. And he seems never to have realized that those tools were not up to the job.

It would, however, be a cardinal error to think that Cyril and Nestorius were fighting about philosophical terminology. For both of them, what was at stake was nothing less than the reality of human salvation. That can be seen from the dispute over the title theotokos—bearer of God—which was the catalyst of the whole controversy. When Nestorius's compromise formula Christotokos failed to make headway, he tried to persuade the squabbling factions to say both theototokos and anthropotokós—both God-bearer and human-bearer: "You refuse to use one expression that says both—I mean both God and human. All right, then, don't say *Christokos* . . . but when you call her *theotokos*, remember to call her also *anthropotokos*, lest you eradicate the divine plan, which is the outline of our salvation" (Loofs 1914, 309).

For Nestorius, "Christ" was a sort of basket term that referred to the divine and the human in Jesus together. It was a name for the joint front they presented to the world—the common appearance they shared. Nestorius's Christology was a symmetrical one. Behind the common front—the one prosopon of Christ—nestling side by side, were the two natures with their two hypostases, each intact.

Indeed, salvation depended on their being intact. The basic human problem was sin, epitomized in the disobedience of Adam. The way back had to involve the voluntary obedience of a sinless human being. So the man Jesus had to be a center of moral action and a subject of moral choice. It is not that Jesus' human obedience in any crude sense *earned* salvation, either for him or for us (though Nestorius's enemies accused him of saying just that). It is, rather, that what had gone wrong had to be put right. A new humanity had to be called into being. Nestorius liked to think of the temptations of Jesus as a focal moment—indeed, *the* focal moment—in the history of human salvation. The desert, he said, was the ring (ancient wrestlers wrestled in a sandpit) in which Jesus—the human Jesus—had gone three falls with the Devil and defeated him (Nestorius, 338–343).

Nestorius drew heavily on the Pauline contrast between the first Adam and the second Adam—that is, Christ. He quoted Paul as saying, "Since death was through a human being, through a human being is also the resurrection of the dead" (1 Cor. 15.21). "That is why there was need of a complete human being for the Incarnation of God the Word—complete in body and in soul, to live in the nature of human beings and to observe obedience and the actions that belong to human nature" (Nestorius, 162–163). "It is for that reason that God made the second Adam worthy of all that honour—because he practiced all obedience" and sought "to conform himself to the will of God, to be as God wished him to be" (ibid., 66, a passage that Luise Abramowski thought was written by one of Nestorius's followers rather than by Nestorius himself).

That was why it was essential for Nestorius to say, not just that Christ was human, but that he was *a* human capable of moral action and moral choice—that there was a human hypostasis and a human prosopon there, hidden beneath the one prosopon that concretely presented the humanity and the divinity conjointly. That was why it was essential for Nestorius to say that Mary was anthropotokos—human-bearer—as well as theotokos—God-bearer.

That was blasphemy for Cyril, for whom the second Adam, the obedient man, no matter how virtuous he was, could never be other than a friend of God. And we cannot be saved by a friend of God, but only by God himself, taking our flesh. So Cyril's picture of Jesus is emphatically *not* symmetrical in the way that Nestorius's is. For Cyril, the divinity and the humanity do not sit comfortably side by side in Christ. Instead, Christ is and always has been the Word of God. That is the only "he"—the only acting subject—in the Incarnate. But at a point in time—at the moment of his conception in Mary's body—that "he" acquired a new mode of being. He was now God *and* man in the sense that the one "he" now acted in a divine mode, as he always had, and also in a fully human mode, doing and experiencing and suffering the things that every other human being did and experienced and suffered. (But, his critics say, was this not a kind of playacting?)

If Nestorius had been asked *who* was born of Mary, his first answer would have been "the human being who was conjoined with God" (Loofs 1914, 335). If Cyril were asked the same question, he would have said that the only possible answer was the Son or Word of God: that is the only "who" in the Incarnation. *What* was born was his human body. *How* he was born was "humanly" or "as a man." But *who* was born was the Word of God. And so Cyril could say, "If anyone does not confess that . . . the holy Virgin is *theotokos*—for she gave birth in fleshly mode to the Word made flesh—let him be anathema" (First Anathema, August 430).

For each of them, to give in would have been to throw away the hope of our salvation.

If it is far from clear that Nestorius was a Nestorian, that is even more true in the case of those Syrian Christians commonly known as Nestorians. Though the views of Nestorius were condemned within the empire, they flourished outside its confines among the half-tolerated, intermittently persecuted Christian communities of Persia and as far away as South India. Their enemies called them Nestorians, and the label was sometimes adopted by the East Syrians themselves (as by Shahdost of Tehran in the eighth century). The theology of this "Nestorian" Church was defined in the early seventh century in a confession of faith presented to the Great King Kosroes in 612 and in the writings of the monk theologian Babai the Great. This theology again affirmed one Son and one prosopon: as Babai said, "one is the person of Christ, Son of God, in his divinity and humanity" (Babai, 139). Nestorius's rather confused talk of two prosopa occasionally appears but is as often explicitly rejected. But there is the same emphasis on the necessity of the integrity of the humanity of Christ for our salvation (see the confession of 612 in Abramowski and Goodman, II, 91). The terminology is more precise and less open to misunderstanding than is that of Nestorius, but the theological scheme is essentially the same.

So, was Nestorius a Nestorian? Were the "Nestorians" of East Syria who followed him? At the beginning of this article I suggested two commonly-accepted definitions of Nestorianism. They are, in fact, complementary and imply a third. The first is in terms of formulae—the expressions that are actually used ("two Sons," "two persons"). The second is in terms of the way the system works—what Jesus does ("two independently functioning subjects"). And the third, implicit definition involves a value judgment: labeling someone a Nestorian implies that his Christology is *overly* divisive, that he keeps the divinity and the humanity of Christ *too* far apart.

In terms of formulae, the answer is certainly no. Nestorius, and even more unambiguously, the Nestorians of Persia, were committed to the belief that Christ is one person. But words change meanings, and it is more instructive to look at how Nestorius's system worked—to look at what his Jesus did. Nestorius certainly did accord a measure of independence to the humanity of Christ that Cyril and the tradition that descended from him were to find unacceptable. Nestorius had to do so because his model of salvation depended on it.

Was Nestorius's system *overly* divisive, and did he in the end keep the humanity and the divinity *too* far apart? Perhaps all we can say is that, for the most part, the men and women of the immediately subsequent centuries thought so. For most of Christendom, it was to be Cyril's theology of the irruption of the divine into our corruptible world—his affirmation that God had been born and died in human mode—that was to fill an intellectual and devotional hunger. To reopen the question, today, of whether Nestorius's theology was too divisive is in effect to ask what sort of Christ we think our world needs.

Paul Parvis

See also: Alexandrian Theology; Antiochene Theology; Chalcedon; Chinese Christianity; Indian Christianity; Mary

References

Primary

Abramowski, Luise, and Alan E. Goodman, eds. and trans. 1972. *A Nestorian Collection of Christological Texts, Cambridge University Library MS. Oriental 1319*. Cambridge: Cambridge University Press.

Babai, Magnus. 1953 [1915]. *Liber de Unione*. Edited and translated by A. Vaschalde. Corpus Scriptorum Christianorum Orientalium 79–80, Scriptores syri 34–35. Louvain: Imprimerie Orientaliste L. Durbecq.

Loofs, Friedrich. 1914. *Nestorius and His Place in the History of Christian Doctrine*. Cambridge: Cambridge University Press.

Nestorius. 1910. *Le Livre d'Héraclide de Damas*. Translated by F. Nau. Paris: Letouzey et Ané.

Secondary

Abramowski, Luise. 1963. *Untersuchungen zum Liber Heraclidis des Nestorius*. Corpus Scriptorum Christianorum Orientalium, Subsidia 22. Louvain: Secrétariat du Corpus SCO.

———. 1974. "Die Christologie des Babais des Grossen." Pp. 219–245 in *Symposium Syriacum 1972*, Orientalia Christiana Analecta 197. Rome: Pont Institutum Orientalium Studiorum.

Grillmeier, Aloys. 1975. *From the Apostolic Age to Chalcedon (451)*. Vol. 1 of *Christ in Christian Tradition*. Translated by John Bowden. London: Mowbrays.

Loofs, Friedrich, ed. 1905. *Nestoriana: Die Fragmente des Nestorius*. Halle a. S.: Max Niemeyer.

Wickham, Lionel R. 1994. "Nestorius/Nestorianische Streit." Pp. 276–286 in *Theologische Realeuzyklopädie*.

Nestorius

See Antiochene Theology; Nestorianism

New Testament as a Whole

There are many articles in this book concerned with Jesus in relation to the NT: those dealing with the way he is seen by the leading writers represented in the NT; those seeking to identify the sense of the various terms used in the NT to describe Jesus; and those discussing leading concepts or images associated with Jesus in the NT. But there is also scope for considering Jesus in relation to the NT as a whole, that is, in relation to the more or less settled collection, from perhaps as early as the second century, of accepted (or "canonical") Christian writings.

The tendency in modern historical criticism has been, understandably, to examine the NT by a process of dividing it up along a number of different lines. We may view, for example, the different writings that came to be included within it, both as whole books and in terms of the smaller units out of which they may have been formed. Or we may consider the ideas and symbols that are found there, sometimes in a variety of different senses; or the historical possibilities, probabilities, or fictions that may be represented in various passages; or else the probable story of the manuscript tradition that is represented in the various books and in the detailed writing of the text; or the precise sense of the language employed, as it may be illuminated by knowledge of the usage of the Greek and Jewish world of the period. Each type of study may be conducted independently of the others.

But though some of these analytical studies have an ancestry going back even to the early period of Christianity, most of them—certainly in terms of sophistication, rigor, and historical sensitivity—have developed in the past two or three centuries, yielding an academic "industry" of remarkable vigor and achievement (though not always of perceived usefulness outside its own enclosed purposes). However, for most of the Christian era, the NT has been overwhelmingly seen as a whole, as the culmination of the Church's two-part canon—the Old Testament and then the New. There have, it is true, been recognized divisions within it, probably from the time of its first being assembled: the four Gospels, the Pauline corpus of letters, Acts plus the "general" epistles, and the Revelation (Apocalypse) of John. Both the convenience of manuscript making and liturgical usefulness have been served by working with some of these categories. But still, all the more since the advent of printing, the NT is viewed as a single entity, given by God, held by the Church, which lives under its authority and yet is its interpreter. It is inevitable that in such a picture, there will be strong pressure to discern and communicate a single Jesus, to underplay differences between one source and another, one kind of imagery or vocabulary and another, and to subsume all that is given under one banner of meaning. Indeed, it is likely that behind the bringing together of, for example, the four Gospels into a single accepted collection in the second century lay the desire to smooth away the earlier conflicts in the Church (for example, over the relation of the new faith to Judaism and its Law) in which leading Christians and the various Gospels took different and contrary views.

That banner of meaning had long been among the Church's central resources—in the shape of succinct formulas, not necessarily agreed upon by all but at least held by influential groups. It is crystallized in statements such as baptismal creeds, eucharistic prayers, patterns of basic teaching, and eventually, from the fourth century, conciliar creeds and some aspects of formal catechisms. We should probably trace this crystallizing process back almost to the beginning—for example, in the shape of summaries of faith (e.g., 1 Cor. 15.3–5, which Paul himself had "received"), of forms used in worship (e.g., the "hymn" in Phil. 2.6–11), or of outlines of basic teaching, available for Christian preachers and evangelists, so that they might know what must be covered (as perhaps exemplified in the speeches or sermons found in the Acts of the Apostles). This distillation of the NT, which itself antedated the formation of the NT as an authoritative corpus and indeed the writing of many of its constituent parts, presents us with a Jesus who is in some ways different from the Jesus found in the NT itself when it is looked at with historical realism. It is a Jesus who is much less rich a figure than the vivid portraits revealed to us by, especially, modern studies of the Gospels. For one thing, he is homogeneous—there is no variety of view, no light or shade; for another, he is more passive than active—he is sent to the world, is put to death, is buried, is raised; that is to say, he is simply the willing agent of God. There is little color or character, no teaching or healing; much solemn grandeur, no human or even divinely human coloring; much offering of salvation, conceptually (though briefly) presented; no winning, attractive poetry in a portrait that may win the heart. In other words, this pattern of development, with the formulaic tendency gradually gaining the whip-hand (for it is the way of authority and of boundary-forming), yields us a "total Jesus." He emerges, single and entire, from the NT as a whole, inside its two authoritative covers. He is a vital part of the armory of the Christian cause. And he simply must be, not only without sin, flaw, or blemish, but without hint of difference within the impression we receive of him.

Modern historical scholarship has of course not only revealed the process of homogenizing, of which the forming of the NT was itself one important element, but also brought before us the diversity of understanding that the various parts of the NT, viewed in their own right, actually contain. A good example of the contrast between these beginnings and the eventual unified outcome is provided by the so-called Seven Words from the Cross, the seven sayings ascribed to the dying Jesus in the various Gospels. Since the sixteenth century, they have formed the basis for much of the formal preaching on Good Friday. In that traditional approach, based upon a homogenized view of the four Gospels, it is assumed that Jesus uttered all seven sentences at various points in his agony (and a conventional order was arrived at), only they happened to have been recorded by different inspired authors: one in Mark (15.34; and it is repeated in Matthew—traditionally, the order would have been taken to be the other way round); three (different) ones in Luke (23.34, 43, 46); and a further three in John (19.26–27, 28, 30). Now, however, it is commonly seen that in each case the sayings make theological and religious sense within the outlook of the author who recorded them—Mark, Luke, and John. In particular, it is not hard to see how Mark's inscrutable and brutal saying ("My God, my God, why hast thou forsaken me?") was found intolerable by Luke and in need of replacement to accord with his sense of Jesus as the model of piety and compassion.

Of course, the more subtle, differentiated Jesus revealed by the analytic candor of modern scholarship (see, especially, the articles on the Gospels of Mark, Matthew, Luke, and John) has frequently had ways of breaking through, though not generally with recognition of the implications of the variety of his qualities and colors—for example, in the standard favored subjects of Christian art, to which, as a matter of fact, affection-stirring Luke came to contribute disproportionately by late-medieval and Renaissance times with Annunciations, the Nativities, sinners healed and forgiven, and the way the Last Supper and the crucifixion were often depicted.

There have also been rebellions against the homogeneity imposed by the normatively viewed total NT—famously in Luther's antagonism to the letter of James as "not belonging" to a properly gospel-preaching collection of writings (as exemplified, especially, in the central letters of Paul). But this subversion of the inspired unity of divine provision as lying between the long-agreed limits of Scripture has not proved a favorite with the churches in general, and the NT stands as a solid whole, with its Jesus single and entire, wherever it is used, from church lecterns and pulpits to hotel bedrooms and law-courts.

In a way, the contrast between the two kinds of Jesus (the one divine-human, single and homogeneous, the other subtle, imagination-kindling, diverse in voice and direction of mind) can be overdone. And the second, inclined-to-be-multiple Jesus can be a threatening figure: whom then can we trust, and where can he truly be found and where his authentic voice heard? But there is a sense in which, whatever the formulas of faith say, every believer forms his or her own Jesus, responding, picturing as only he or she can; not necessarily with wild eccentricity, but, as in any relationship, in accordance with personal perception, and this simply indicates the inevitability of variety in understandings of Jesus, whether formal or informal. Did he himself not implicitly intensify and even endorse such variety by leaving no written self-definition, but only deeds and words uttered into the wind for followers to remember, select, and thereby interpret as they were impelled, by voice or pen, being themselves?

The "Jesus of the New Testament" is thus, from this point of view, a hodgepodge, though of course sufficiently single and unified for many purposes, especially for succinct statements of faith—but then forfeiting his sharp power to amaze, attract, and infuriate, as he differs among various manifestations of himself in significant matters of direction and teaching. Believers and students alike may rejoice in this and enjoy the challenge he offers to their minds and hearts, or else be baffled by it, and then welcome the relative clarity of the Jesus of agreed summations of doctrine and ethics, who does not even raise many of those matters at all.

Leslie Houlden

See also: Creeds; Hebrew Bible; Jesus as a Historical Figure; Music

References

Campenhausen, H. von. 1972. *The Formation of the Christian Bible*. London: A. & C. Black.

Houlden, J. L. 1986. *Connections*. London: SCM.

———. 1991. *Bible and Belief*. London: SPCK.

———. 1992. *Jesus: A Question of Identity*. London: SPCK.

Trobisch, D. 2000. *The First Edition of the New Testament*. Oxford: Oxford University Press.

Newman, John Henry (1801–1890)

John Henry Newman never composed a systematic Christology, but Christological questions permeated his writings: they were argued in his academic work, explained in his sermons, and discussed in his letters. The treatment was remarkable for its consistency. At times he wrote in response to certain evangelical or liberal views, which in his judgment lacked a firm dogmatic foundation, but his consistency was derived from his patristic studies. Throughout his life, from his first major publication, *The Arians of the Fourth Century* (1832), to his last significant work, a revision of his *Athanasian Treatises* (1887), he was fascinated by the Arian controversy and found his own sympathies engaged by the Alexandrian school, whose approach shaped his account. The influence is particularly clear when the origins of a point preached can be traced back from the sermon through the detailed critical notes he composed on Athanasius's work for his own translation of the original text. He had no desire to be original himself. He wished simply to expound the traditional Chalcedonian position, but he sought to do so from the standpoint of Alexandrian Christology, which was characterized by its emphasis on the unity of Christ. There was little development in this aspect of his work. Development can be found, however, in his understanding of the person of Jesus as savior. As the years passed, his position on that question gathered deeper and richer themes that corresponded to his own personal development.

Newman's teaching on Christ resembles a mosaic. He paid attention at times to Christ as divine, then to Christ as human, and then again to Christ as one. The method is intentional. He used it elsewhere. By concentrating on different aspects of the mystery at different times, he hoped to make it possible for people to grasp more personally what the mystery actually meant, instead of having a merely intellectual understanding of it.

A key statement can be found in an unpublished sermon from 1836 that was part of a series of four sermons he preached that spring on Christ. They form the single longest account of Christological teaching to be found in his writings. He declared: "Most men at this day will devoutly say that Christ is God, but there they stop, in those few words they neglect, or are ignorant of, the revealed circumstances, particulars, and details of this doctrine. They do not know the doctrine of the *Incarnation*. Great numbers so enlarge on our Lord's divine perfection as to forget that He was also a man exposed to temptation and infirmity" (see Birmingham Oratory Archives, MS. Sermon no. 405, 6–7; 1836). The doctrine of the Incarnation itself was the crucial issue. "What do we gain from words," he once asked, "however correct and abundant, if they end with themselves, instead of lighting up the image of the Incarnate Son in our hearts?" (Newman 1966 [1836], *Parochial and Plain Sermons*, vol. 3, 169–170). In his *Essay on Development* he used the Incarnation as the central truth of the gospel (Newman 1968 [1845], 324).

No one would suggest that Newman's intentions were ever anything other than orthodox. He affirmed that Christ was as simply God as if he were not man, as simply man as if he were not God. The equation speaks for itself. Nevertheless, his advocacy of Alexandria has attracted criticism. The Alexandrians' emphasis on the unity of Christ has been seen as monophysitism in disguise, securing the divinity of Christ at the expense of his humanity. Newman has been thought to have fallen into the same trap. In his *Athanasian Treatises*, he remarked that "the Word was 'made man,' not was made a man" (Newman 1966 [1897], *Select Treatises of St. Athanasius*, vol. 2, 427), and in a sermon he observed, "Though man, He was not, strictly speaking, in the English sense of the word, *a* man" (Newman 1967 [1842], *Parochial and Plain Sermons*, vol. 6, 62). Such statements jar on modern ears. In the modern English sense of the word, Jesus was precisely "a man."

The passage is instructive. The context shows that Newman was in fact trying to explain the Chalcedonian teaching that the *person* of the Christ was divine, not human: "His Person is not human like ours, but divine"; his account is hedged round with all kinds of qualifications to safeguard Christ's humanity, but Newman did not have at his disposal the kind of distinction that is made so readily today between "personality" in the common sense and "person" in the technical Christological sense. Elements in his text suffer from that handicap. Moreover, ironically, the absence of the indefinite article, the stress on Christ as "man, not a man," may be said to display sensitivity to the inclusive character of Christ's humanity. Modern neologisms were not available to Newman. "Christ as man" was a way of saying that he was not simply that particular individual; his humanity was also representative of the human race at large.

Newman's preoccupation with Alexandrian Christology was illustrated most plainly in 1858 when he published an article called "On St. Cyril's Formula φύσις σεσαρκωμένη" (Newman 1965–1968 [1895], *Tracts Theological and Ecclesiastical*, 329–382). He undertook a detailed examination of patristic terms and concluded that in the sense used by Cyril, *phusis* ("nature") could not be predicated of the humanity of Christ, so that to speak of two "natures" would be mistaken. His overriding concern was to make clear the unity of Christ. In a unity there could not be two sovereign principles: either the human or the divine would have to give way; humanity was not parallel to divinity but best expressed by an adjective or participle, "enfleshed," echoing the Johannine statement "The Word was made flesh." For Newman, Cyril was just one example among many of those who had sought to secure the unity of Christ; he was exceptional for his distinctive way of using the term "nature."

Newman did not adopt this way of speaking himself, but under the influence of Alexandria he was ready enough to describe Christ's humanity as an "instrument." He acknowledged that this usage could be abused but had no qualms himself about referring to the humanity of Christ in that way and affirming its intimate union with the Son (Newman 1967 [1842], *Parochial and Plain Sermons*, vol. 6, 64–65). He expounded these views into his old age.

A particular flaw in Athanasian Christology was its failure to allow proper significance to the soul of Christ as the created subject of his suffering, fear, and sorrow, and the limitations to his knowledge. On this point, however, Newman was unambiguous. Without a soul, Christ would not have been fully human. And he illustrated its presence by referring specifically to his fearing, sorrowing, and being in agony, the very points that had been wanting in Athanasius's writing. Nor did his care for the unity of Christ lead him to underestimate the Passion. His account of the physical sufferings of Jesus was not monophysite, but Chalcedonian. It was memorable for the way he identified Jesus' ordeal as the ordeal of God: as truly human and truly divine, the suffering humanity of Jesus was the suffering humanity of God. And he drew out the mental sufferings of Jesus to indicate that his divine nature was not a shield protecting him from their force. In spite of the Alexandrian influence, his presentation at this point is more reminiscent of the letter to the Hebrews.

His account of Christ as savior developed throughout his life and reflected his own development. Newman passed from youthful evangelicalism through rationalism to mainstream, patristic Anglicanism and on to Catholicism. His early evangelical conversion, though lacking the intense emotional character often typical of those experiences, led him to appeal in a direct, simple way to the cross of Christ. As a fellow of Oriel College, Oxford, he came at first under the influence of Richard Whately and for a while adopted the cerebral approach for which Whately was renowned. Later, however, his friendships changed, and he came close to Hurrell Froude, Edward Pusey, and John Keble. Through them he became absorbed in his studies of the Fathers, and his writings display all the common themes of patristic thinking about the atonement: Christ saves us as our pattern, we follow his example; he is the victor over sin and death, who overcame Satan on the tree of the Cross; he is himself our atoning sacrifice; he came to share our humanity that we might share his divinity. He also gained from the Fathers an appreciation of the doctrine of reserve. In his later Anglican years, instead of using the atonement as an instrument for conversion, which was the evangelical strategy, he argued that it should be kept back, reserved, until people felt the need for it. Later still, however, as a Catholic, he thought his earlier reluctance might have been tinged with semi-Pelagianism and he had fewer scruples about its use in the process of conversion. And finally, also as a Catholic, he indicated his preference for the Scotist view (thirteenth century) that the Incarnation was independent of the Fall and would have taken place without it, as an act of God's sheer love of humanity.

Roderick Strange

See also: Alexandrian Theology; Apollinarianism; Chalcedon; Hebrews, Letter to the; Nicea

References

[*Editor's note:* Writing by Newman referred to in this article can be found in *The Works of Cardinal Newman* (Westminster, MD: Christian Classics Inc.), 1965–1968. This is a facsimile reproduction of the edition published in London in the 1890s by Longmans, Green.]

Strange, Roderick. 1981. *Newman and the Gospel of Christ*. Oxford: Oxford University Press.

———. 1990. "Newman and the Mystery of Christ." Pp. 323–336 in *Newman after a Hundred Years*. Edited by Ian Ker and Alan G. Hill. Oxford: Clarendon.

Nicea

Early in the fourth century, as the Church emerged from the Great Persecution into the new freedom of a Christian emperor, Constantine I, its most famous heresy arose over the question, "Who is Jesus?," particularly, "In what sense is he God?" The heresy is called "Arianism," after its originator Arius (c. 260–336). "Arianism" soon became a term of abuse, freely bestowed on Church opponents by members of the theological party that ultimately prevailed.

The first phase of Arianism concerned a dispute between Alexander, bishop of Alexandria (c. 250–328), bishop from about 312 until his death, and the presbyter in charge of one of his great churches, Arius. Who launched the question and answer that led to recrimination and condemnation is uncertain, but early testimony suggests an interrogation of the presbyter by the bishop (Constantine, in Eusebius's *Life of Constantine* II.69). Alexander reported to other leading bishops that five presbyters and six deacons had been excommunicated with Arius. These dissident clergy at once sought and obtained support from other leading churchmen. According to

Alexander, they asserted that the Father was not always father, since his Son once did not exist but came from nothing; the Son is a creature and a work of God; he is only by a misuse of language called God's Wisdom and Word *(Logos)*, since those aspects of God's being are eternal, and by them the Son himself came to be. There are therefore limits to the Son's knowledge, he is distinct from the being (substance/essence) of the Father, and technically he is liable to change (and hence sin) like any other created, rational being.

Most of these allegations against the clergymen were true, but another picture emerges when one reads the surviving texts from Arius's side. Arius's verses, the *Thalia*, begin with the ineffable God, incomparable, without source or beginning, whom we know through the one who is begotten, who has a beginning, who was born in time, that is, Jesus Christ. Nevertheless, the Son is the greatest conceivable being the Father could produce and is the beginning of all created things, comprehending everything except the incomprehensible Father. He is vastly superior to all other beings, which are created through him. His own begetting and beginning, however, indicate a radical distinction between the Father and the Son. In a conciliatory letter to Alexander, Arius revealed the negative concerns that went with his view. He was not a Valentinian (Gnostic), holding that the Son issued involuntarily from the Father, or a Manichee, holding the Son to be part of the Father or the same in being *(homoousios)*, or a Sabellian, following the heretic who saw Father and Son as a single being adopting different roles; nor—and here he seemed to attack Marcellus of Ancyra (c. 280–374)—did he see the Word as coexisting with the Father eternally in one state, and then emerging as Son at the Incarnation in Jesus. Rather, there is a Trinity of distinct entities *(hupostaseis)*, in which the Father is the eternal Source, and the Son is begotten (Arius insisted) apart from time and before all things, while not being coeternal with the Father. This last point is apparently a contradiction: the loophole was exploited by Arius's arch-enemy Athanasius (c. 296–373), bishop of Alexandria from 328 to his death, who attributed to the Arians the doctrine that "there was when he [the Son] was not." It can hardly be emphasized too strongly that Arius and his associates never thought, as others since have done, that Jesus was only a man and not God. They held the Son of God to be the Creator and Savior of the world, who took flesh and suffered as Jesus; because of the suffering, he could not be eternal and immutable in the way the Father is and must be distinct from the one he reveals.

The Eastern Churches were divided over the case. Constantine, when he finally conquered the Eastern empire in 324, tried to heal the breach. The opponents of Arius won the powerful see of Antioch with the appointment in 325 of Eustathius and excommunicated leading Arian supporters. The emperor had, however, already called a council of bishops to resolve this and other issues; it met at Nicea, near his capital of Nicomedia, in the summer of 325. No formal minutes survive, and the partisan accounts of proceedings are hard to disentangle. But it is certain that the excommunicated bishops were reinstated, Arius and a few others were condemned, and a creed was agreed upon that would become momentous. Usually known as "N" (for "Nicea"), it runs:

> We believe in one God, the Father Almighty, Maker of all visible and invisible things. And in one Lord, Jesus Christ, the Son of God, begotten from his Father as Only-begotten, that is, from the being *[ousia]* of the Father, God from God, Light from Light, true God from true God, begotten not made, the same in being *[homoousios]* as the Father; through whom all things were made, those in heaven and those on earth; who for us men and for our salvation descended and was enfleshed, became man, suffered and rose on the third day, and is coming to judge the living and the dead. And in the Holy Spirit. But those who say, "There was when he was not," and, "Before he was begotten he was not," and that "He came to be from nothing," or who allege that the Son of God is of another being *[ousia]* or entity *[hupostasis]*, or changeable or alterable, these the Catholic and Apostolic Church condemns.

Clarifications are needed:

1. The formula is based on the tradition of creeds taught and recited at baptism and goes back to 1 Corinthians 8.6, "One God the Father, from whom are all things, and we for him, and one Lord, Jesus Christ, through whom are all things, and we through him."

2. The final sentence, "But those who say . . .," shows how Arius's teaching was perceived by its critics and was new. Arius would regard it as a misrepresentation, since he, too, held the Son to be unalterable, though not in the same way the Father was: the Son never deviated from perfection in practice, whereas the Father as God is by nature unchangeable.

3. In "for us men," and "became man," "man" is used (cf. the Greek *anthropos*) in its inclusive sense, that is, it means "human," not "male," and the parallel is deliberate: he became human to match our fallen humanity. The Gospel verse, "the Word became flesh" (John 1.14), is reflected in "was enfleshed" but has to be taken in a fuller sense: not just material, but human. The incarnate Lord identifies with the full humanity of male and female alike.

4. "Being" *(ousia)* has the same ambiguity in Greek as in English, either meaning "existence" or "an existing thing/person." The text interprets the biblical "begotten" (Ps. 2.7) and "Only-begotten" (*monogenes;* John 1.18ff.) as meaning "from the being of the Father." In the light of the condemnation of "another being or entity," it seems to be in the concrete sense: Father and Son are one Being. The idea that the Son was created, or came from nothing, or from some other entity, is emphatically denied. The (almost) new word "the same in being [*homoousios;* traditionally rendered 'consubstantial' or 'of the same substance'] as the Father" was perhaps intended in that sense. When the creed was accepted by many of those present, they took it differently: "same in being" meant for Eusebius of Caesarea "exactly like," and "from the being of the Father" meant only that the Son had no other origin than the Father.

Given N's novelties and ambiguities, it is not surprising that attempts were made to improve upon it. Some who signed up tried to make another credal formula that was less polemical and more in tune with their thinking. The doctrine of N is near to that of Marcellus of Ancyra and Eustathius of Antioch, who were shortly to be condemned for heresy or other crimes. According to Marcellus, God and his Son/Logos are a single Being, and passages of Scripture that refer to the birth of Christ as a distinct being (Ps. 2.7; Prov. 8.22) are interpreted of his conception and birth from Mary. This kind of exegesis is taken up by the great champion of the doctrine of Nicea, Athanasius. Athanasius constantly emphasized that the Son's being is the Father's own, that he is the Father's own personal Wisdom and Logos (that is, innermost Thought as well as spoken Word), and that the Son is exactly like the Father in his eternity and deity without distinction or inferiority. For his enemies, all this was intolerable. The creeds they tried to substitute as fundamental (such as the second Creed of Antioch, 341) would emphasize three things in particular: (1) that the Son was begotten from the Father before time began; (2) that the Son is consequently a being, subsistence, or entity distinct from the Father (for only so could his true deity be affirmed), as is also the Holy Spirit; and (3) that the relation of Son to Father was one of exact likeness (as in Heb. 1.3) or image (2 Cor. 4.4; Col. 1.15).

In the tortuous Church politics of the mid-fourth century, the West generally attached itself to N, interpreted (as at Sardica in 342/343) in a Marcellian way, while the Eastern Christians were divided: (1) there were Nicenes, represented by Athanasius, and followers of the exiled Marcellus and Eustathius; (2) there were those usually labeled Arians, or "Homeans" (meaning "Alikers"), for a long time the governing party, who sought reconciliation in the view that the Son is "like" the Father, thus avoiding nonscriptural terms such as "same in being"; (3) there was the new school, often called "Neo-Arians," chiefly Aetius (c. 300–370) and Eunomius (c. 325–c. 395), who held the essence of God to be that he is "Unbegotten," and therefore that he is infinitely superior to his Son, who is essentially "Begotten"; (4) there were those who tried to reach an accommodation with the West, and who represented the broad consensus, at different times labeled "Semi-Arians" or "Homeousians" (advocates of "Like-in-being"), who preferred, proposed, and defended alternative formulae to N's "same in being," such as "like in being" or "like in all things"; (5) there were those who accepted the Nicene "same in being" of the Son of God but adopted other views deemed heretical, especially the "Spirit-fighters," who held the Holy Spirit to be a created being inferior to God, and the Apollinarians; and (6) from some of these groups eventually emerged the "Neo-Nicenes," led by Basil of Caesarea (330–379) and the other "Cappadocian Fathers," Gregory of Nazianzus (c. 329–390) and Gregory of Nyssa (331/340–c. 395), who came to favor *homoousios* itself, interpreted as meaning "exactly like in being." It was this last view that was to prevail when the problems originating with Arianism were settled for the Church by the Council of Constantinople in 381 and associated councils in the West at Aquileia and Rome.

The Creed of Constantinople from 381 ("C" for short) became established as an interpretation of N at the Council of Chalcedon in 451, and it is the standard of doctrine for most Churches to this day, though misleadingly labeled "The Nicene Creed." How it originated and how it is related to the Council of Constantinople is still debated. It says:

> We believe in one God, the Father Almighty, Maker of heaven and earth, of all things visible and invisible. And in one Lord, Jesus Christ, the Son of God, the Only-begotten, begotten from the Father before all the ages, Light from Light, true God from true God, begotten not made, the same in being *[homoousios]* as the Father; through whom all things were made; who for us men and for our salvation descended from heaven and was enfleshed from the Holy Spirit and Mary the Virgin, and became man; he was crucified for us under Pontius Pilate, and suffered and was buried and rose on the third day in accordance with the scriptures, and is coming again with glory to judge the living and the dead; of whose reign there will be no end. And in the Holy Spirit, the Lord and Lifegiver, who proceeds from the Father, who with the Father and the Son is worshipped and glorified together, who spoke through the prophets. In one holy catholic and apostolic Church. We confess one baptism for remission of sins, we expect the resurrection of the dead, and the life of the coming age. Amen.

The final part relates to the question, then in debate, about the deity of the Holy Spirit, and to other basic Christian doctrines suitable in a baptismal creed, and it replaces the anti-Arian anathemas of N. In other respects, C varies in inessential matters from N and is plainly based on a different traditional creed. For our purposes, we note:

1. Although "the same in being *(homoousios)* as the Father" is retained, the clauses that implied the meaning that God is one Being of Father and Son have gone. The term is thus open to the "exactly-the- same" interpretation.

2. Specifically, where N interpreted "Only-begotten" as "that is, from the Being *[ousia]* of the Father," we now have, "begotten from the Father *before all the ages*" (italics added). This addition restores an idea rejected at Nicea but dear to the Eastern theologians and held by Arius, that the "begetting" or "birth" of the Son of God happens before time exists. So the Son is a divine being, distinct from the Father, who mediates between the transcendent Father and the created order. He is not a part, function, or attribute of the Father, such as an impersonal Wisdom or Power, which somehow indwells the man Jesus. The person of Jesus is the person of the divine Son. This shift from N was agreed upon by Damasus (c. 304–384), bishop of Rome from 366 to 384, in advance of the council.

3. Another development is to include the words of the angel from Luke 1.33, "of whose reign there will be no end." Marcellus appears to have held that, just as the Son of God began his distinct personal existence with his conception in Mary, so at the end of time he would surrender his kingdom to the Father, so that God might be all in all (cf. 1 Cor. 15.28). Christ's eternal existence beside the Father is thus asserted.

4. Other changes seem to be either accidental or rhetorical improvements rather than theologically significant.

One issue raised by Arianism is not apparent in C. The Arians derived important arguments from Scripture texts that ascribe weakness, suffering, mental pain, doubt, ignorance, and finally death to Jesus. If Jesus is the preexistent Son of God who comes to earth and experiences these things, he cannot have the characteristics of true deity, since God is without body, parts, or passions and is infinite and all-knowing. Athanasius would reply that these signs of weakness belong to the flesh or humanity that the Word took, not to his own being: he made them his own voluntarily in the Incarnation, as God restoring man's lost likeness to God, and as man paying the price of human sin by his death. In Antiochene Christology, the followers of Eustathius (bishop of Antioch, c. 324–327) went further and emphasized that Jesus is a man with a human soul, vulnerable and passionate as any other, while Diodore of Tarsus (died c. 390) emphasized the twofold character of Christ, two "beings" *(ousiai)*, divine and human. A great Arian (Homean) leader, Eudoxius (c. 300–370), who went in 360 from the see of Antioch to that of Constantinople, denounced such ideas, saying Jesus was "one Lord the Son, . . . made flesh, *not* made man, for he has not taken a human soul, but has become flesh, so that through the flesh, as through a veil [cf. Heb. 10.20], he might deal with us men as God; not two natures, since he was not a complete man, but, instead of the soul, God in the flesh; . . . for he could not save the world by a soul or a body suffering." So the divine person of the Son himself suffers in Jesus. The Arian conclusion follows: "Let them tell us, then, how the suffering and dying one can be the same in being *(homoousios)* as the God who is superior to these things, transcending suffering and death!"

The Nicenes and other opponents of Arius and Eunomius had to find a way of thinking about Jesus as God and Man that did not lead to this Arian conclusion. Apollinarianism was one way, and that was directly condemned in its canons by the Council of Constantinople; the human soul of Jesus has been universally acknowledged orthodoxy ever since. The "two natures" formula was established at Chalcedon but not universally accepted, though all ancient traditions hold that Jesus was complete in his godhead, contrary to Arius and his followers.

Down the centuries, "Arianism" has been a term of abuse for those who deny the deity of Christ, such as the Socinians and Unitarians of the Reformation period, and various German and English Protestant thinkers after the Enlightenment. It is also applied to various modern scholars who reject patristic formulae and pursue a Christology "from below," such as Norman Pittenger and Maurice Wiles. It should be said, however, that Arianism was never a "Christology from below." It always began with the divine Son of God, generated from his Father as a unique being before time and ages, whose direct intervention as Jesus Christ brought illumination and salvation by his life and death. If it is right to affirm that Jesus Christ is God enfleshed, then to call many modern thinkers "Arians" makes them more orthodox than they really are.

A serious difficulty for many modern Christians with the way the Church Fathers thought and taught is their apparent concern with metaphysical matters about the Incarnation, with little reference to the historical Jesus or the primitive gospel as we understand it. These matters are discussed at the end of the article on the Council of Chalcedon.

Stuart G. Hall

See also: Alexandrian Theology; Antiochene Theology; Apollinarianism; Chalcedon; Creeds; Enlightenment; Feminist Theology; Gnosticism; Manichaeism; Wiles, Maurice

References

Grillmeier, Aloys. 1975. *Christ in Christian Tradition I: From the Apostolic Age to Chalcedon (A.D. 451)*. London: Mowbrays.

Hall, Stuart George. 1991. *Doctrine and Practice in the Early Church*. London: SPCK.

Hanson, R. P. C. 1988. *The Search for the Christian Doctrine of God*. Edinburgh: T. & T. Clark.

Kelly, J. N. D. 1960. *Early Christian Doctrines*. London: A. & C. Black.

———. 1972. *Early Christian Creeds*. London: Longmans.

Stevenson, James, ed. 1987. *A New Eusebius*. London: SPCK.

———. 1989. *Creeds, Councils and Controversies*. London: SPCK.

Wiles, Maurice. 1996. *Archetypal Heresy: Arianism through the Centuries*. Oxford: Clarendon.

Williams, Rowan. 1987. *Arius*. London: Darton, Longman & Todd.

Nietzsche, Friedrich von (1844–1900)

It cannot be denied that the philosophy of Friedrich Nietzsche was fervently atheistic. Beyond his familiar role as the enthusiastic proclaimer of the "death of God," Nietzsche styled himself as the "Anti-Christ," one who wrote "against the crucified," and to whom atheism was simply "obvious." The reasons for Nietzsche's unbelief are various, but it is his perception of Christianity as a pernicious "antiquity" that, more than anything else, explains his violent repudiation of the faith. For example, in *Human, All Too Human*, Nietzsche listed some prominent features of the Christian religion (belief in a virgin birth and in the imminent end of the world, the practice of drinking a god's blood, and so on) in order to suggest "how terrible all this appears to us, as if risen from the grave of the ancient past! Is it credible that such things are still believed?" If Christianity were simply a survival from a primal past, then it might be a harmless plaything, but Nietzsche's vitriolic attack arose from his conviction that, far from being innocuous, it is a threat to all that is valuable in life. Christianity has devalued the material world and has been suspicious of the life of the senses; Nietzsche claimed that in order to have rewarding lives we must embrace these and remain "true to the earth." Likewise, the emphasis on a life beyond the grave served to rob our lives here of seriousness and importance: the belief in an afterlife must be scrapped and replaced with the more life-enhancing myth of eternal recurrence, whereby one should live as though one's life would be repeated, exactly the same, time and again, for all eternity. And no less important, the *morality* of Christianity, such as that expounded in the Sermon on the Mount, was seen by Nietzsche to stem from the lowest of human motives: *ressentiment* (a term that he used to signify the vengefulness of the frustrated and impotent). This requires greater elaboration.

In *On the Genealogy of Morals* (1996 [1887]), Nietzsche claimed that moral values are not timeless absolutes, but are rather reflections of the concrete power interests of those who subscribe to them. The values of our culture—equality, justice, compassion, and so on—are the outcome of a struggle between an ancient aristocratic morality (which understood the word "good" to refer to strength and power, and the word "bad" to signify weakness and impotence) and the morality of the slaves rooted in a resentful response to their masters (which inverted the original aristocratic conception, reversing the meaning of the word "good" so as to signify humility, absence of power, and all the characteristics of the slave class). In what Nietzsche called "the slave revolt in morals," the aristocratic ideal is overturned and the qualities of strength and power—those things that Nietzsche thought of as being truly valuable and life-affirming—are treated with suspicion and regarded, even, as evils. Thus humanity turned its back on vivifying qualities and its decline began. The values of slavish *decadence* are exemplified in the beatitudes: "Blessed are the meek, for they shall inherit the earth." Nietzsche is horrified by this moral revolution, despairing that "what stems from slavishness and especially from the mob hotchpotch: *that* now wants to become master of mankind's entire destiny—oh disgust! disgust! disgust!" (1961 [1883–1884]).

Given the foregoing, one would expect Nietzsche's explicit comments about Jesus to be derogatory. And yet, the exact reverse is the case. Even in a book entitled *The Anti-Christ*, Nietzsche displayed a great respect for Jesus. That Nietzsche can thus surprise us is due to the firm distinction he drew between the Jesus of history and the Christ of faith. Once this was effected, Nietzsche found that there was much in the actions of the historical Jesus of which he could approve. He saw Jesus as a "free spirit" who uttered a *No* toward "everything that was priest and theologian." He "cares nothing for what is fixed," nor is he concerned with propounding dogmas of any kind. His message, rather, was his *life*, and he taught, not a new belief, but a new way of living. And this message is seen most memorably in his mode of dying: no resistance, no desire for revenge, no defending his rights, no ressentiment. So what is the character-type of Jesus? What is the "psychology of the redeemer"? Jesus is no hero; nor is he quite the "superman" that Nietzsche lionized, namely one with self-mastery, one who has control over his passions. For Nietzsche, Jesus seems to have had no passions to control. He attributed this to a case of "retarded puberty," echoed in Zarathustra's judgment: "He died too early." Jesus' complete lack of enmity, of rage, led Nietzsche to diagnose his psychology as that of "the idiot" (in the Dostoyevskian sense; perhaps also in the sense of the "holy fool" of Wagner's *Parsifal*). Jesus appears here as the "holy anarchist," and as such he died as a political criminal. And on this point Nietzsche was adamant: "He died for *his* guilt—all ground is lacking for the assertion that he died for the guilt of others."

Though Nietzsche found the historical Jesus somewhat admirable, the redeemer, he said, had been presented to us "in distorted form." There were several reasons why Jesus' type could not "remain pure." For a start, the milieu in which Jesus moved was "a strange and sick world," which must have left its mark on him. But more important, his followers—those who spoke and wrote about him—were incapable of following his existential example. The demands of the redeemer's mode of living were just too great for these people (described by Nietzsche as the "refuse of society"). Unable to follow the pattern of Jesus' life, they stressed instead faith *in* him and invented a doctrine that reversed all of Jesus' own thinking and was tragically characterized by the ressentiment so lacking in the redeemer himself. So whereas the concepts of sin, guilt, and punishment were absent from Jesus' teaching ("precisely this is the 'glad tidings'"), Nietzsche thought, by a cruel irony Christianity became *the* religion of sin, guilt, and punishment par excellence. And whereas Jesus implored people not to judge, Christianity became centered on that greatest judgment of all—the Last Judgment—so that Christianity shows itself to be "a hangman's metaphysics." The radical disjunction between the free, liberating teaching of Jesus and the resentful, punishing doctrine of the Church founded in his name led Nietzsche to call the Christian Church "a world-historical irony" and famously to declare: "In reality, there has been only one Christian, and he died on the cross."

Brian R. Clack

See also: Jesus, Teaching of; Glossary: *Jesus of history; Christ of faith*

References

Kaufmann, Walter. 1974. *Nietzsche: Philosopher, Psychologist, Antichrist*. Princeton: Princeton University Press.

Kee, Alistair. 1999. *Nietzsche against the Crucified*. London: SCM.

Nietzsche, Friedrich von. 1996 [1887]. *On the Genealogy of Morals*. Oxford: Oxford University Press.

———. 1968 [1888]. *The Anti-Christ*. Harmondsworth: Penguin.

———. 1961 [1883–1884]. *Thus Spoke Zarathustra*. Harmondsworth: Penguin.

Nonexistence Hypothesis

The argument that Jesus never existed, but was invented by the Christian movement around the year 100, goes back to Enlightenment times, when the historical-critical study of the past was born. Although mainstream New Testament scholarship has not paid attention to this argument in recent decades, debate on the existence of Jesus has been on the fringes of scholarship and popular religious discussion for more than two centuries.

By the end of the eighteenth century, a few radical Enlightenment thinkers had written that Christianity and its Christ were mythological, not historical, in origin. The English deist Lord Bolingbroke may have conceived this idea. In the 1790s, the radical French thinkers Constantin-François Volney and Charles François Dupuis suggested that Christianity was an updated conglomeration of ancient Persian and Babylonian mythology and that Jesus was its invented founder. Then this hypothesis remained quieter until Bruno Bauer (1809–1882), the most incisive writer in the nineteenth century against the existence of Jesus, began publishing his ideas. In a series of books from 1840 to 1855, Bauer attacked the historical value of the Gospel of John and the Synoptics, arguing that they were purely inventions of their early second-century authors. Bauer laid down the typical threefold argument that almost all subsequent deniers of the existence of Jesus were to follow (although not in direct dependence upon him). First, he denied the value of the

NT, especially the Gospels and Paul's letters, in establishing the existence of Jesus. Second, he argued that the lack of authentic reference to Jesus in non-Christian writings of the first century showed that he did not exist. Neither did the few mentions of Jesus by Roman writers in the early second century establish his existence. Third, he promoted the view that Christianity was syncretistic and mythical at its beginnings. Bauer's views were widely attacked by other historians, and refuted in the minds of most people, and they therefore gained no large or lasting influence.

Nevertheless, the nonexistence argument continued. Its most notable champions at the end of the nineteenth century and beginning of the twentieth were the Freethought advocate John M. Robertson and, in Germany, Arthur Drews. The most prolific and persistent contemporary advocate of the nonexistence argument has been George A. Wells (b. 1926). In his early works, Wells drew arguments from much recent Gospel scholarship concluding that the canonical Gospels were written at least forty years after Jesus' death by unknown authors who were not eyewitnesses to him. He argued that the Gospels contained much that was demonstrably legendary and that they were directed by theological (not historical) purposes. Furthermore, he said that earlier parts of the New Testament, notably Paul's letters, only presupposed that Jesus existed. Therefore, we need independent corroboration from other, "objective" sources to affirm his existence. Wells explained Jesus as a mythical figure arising from Paul's mysticism, for whom other late first-century Christians had to fabricate a life story.

Seven main arguments have been used against Wells's version of the nonexistence hypothesis. First, Wells misinterpreted Paul's silence about some details in the life of Jesus: the exact time of his life, the exact places of his ministry, that Pontius Pilate condemned him, and so forth. Most historians consider it wrong to suppose that what is unmentioned or undetailed did not therefore exist. Arguments from silence about ancient times, here about the supposed lack of biblical or extra-biblical references to Jesus, are especially perilous. Moreover, one should not expect to find exact historical references in early Christian literature, which was not written for primarily historical purposes.

Second, Wells argued that Christians invented the figure of Jesus when they wrote Gospels outside Palestine around 100. Not only is this dating far too late for Mark (which was probably written around the year 70), and for Matthew and Luke (both of which probably date to the 80s), it cannot explain why the Gospel references to details about Palestine are so plentiful and mostly accurate.

Third, Wells claimed that the development of the Gospel traditions, and historical difficulties within them, show that Jesus did not exist. However, development does not necessarily mean wholesale invention, and difficulties do not prove nonexistence.

Fourth, Wells could not explain to the satisfaction of historians why, if Christians invented the historical Jesus around 100, no pagans and Jews who opposed Christianity denied Jesus' existence. Successfully to deny his existence would have dealt a mortal blow to the Christianity they opposed, but they all (to judge from the surviving evidence) accepted the fact that he existed.

Fifth, Wells and his predecessors were far too skeptical about the value of non-Christian witnesses to Jesus, especially Tacitus and Josephus. They pointed to well-known text-critical and source-critical problems in these witnesses, arguing that these problems rule out the entire value of these passages and ignoring strong consensus that most of these passages are basically trustworthy.

Sixth, Wells and others advanced the nonexistence hypothesis not for objective scholarly reasons, but for highly tendentious, antireligious purposes. It has been a weapon of those who oppose the Christian faith in almost any form. They have correctly assumed that to prove this hypothesis would put an end to Christianity as it is known, but it remains unpersuasive.

Seventh, Wells and his predecessors failed to advance other, credible hypotheses to account for the birth of Christianity and the fashioning of a historical Christ. The hypotheses they advanced, based on an idiosyncratic understanding of ancient mythology, had little independent corroborative evidence to commend them to others.

A final argument against the nonexistence hypothesis comes from Wells himself. In his most recent book, *The Jesus Myth* (1999), Wells has moved away from this hypothesis. He now accepts that there is some historical basis for the existence of Jesus, derived from the lost early "gospel" "Q" (the hypothetical source used by Matthew and Luke). Wells believes that it is early and reliable enough to show that Jesus probably did exist, although this Jesus was not the Christ that the later canonical Gospels portray. It remains to be seen what impact Wells's about-face will have on debate over the nonexistence hypothesis in popular circles. Among New Testament scholars and historians, the theory of Jesus' nonexistence remains effectively dead as a scholarly question.

Robert E. Van Voorst

See also: Enlightenment; Jesus as a Historical Figure; Jesus in Social Context; Josephus; Paul

References

Van Voorst, Robert E. 2000. *Jesus outside the New Testament: An Introduction to the Ancient Evidence*. Grand Rapids, MI: William B. Eerdmans.

Wells, G. A. 1971. *The Jesus of the Early Christians*. London: Pemberton.

———. 1975. *Did Jesus Exist?* London: Pemberton.

———. 1996. *The Jesus Legend*. Chicago: Open Court.

———. 1999. *The Jesus Myth*. Chicago: Open Court.

O

Old Age

In Western society particularly, there is an increasing proportion of elderly persons as life expectancy increases. In a relatively short time, this trend may well extend to the human race as a whole. On what terms can the figure of Jesus have force for the elderly? Jesus died in his early thirties and his mission of preaching and teaching was that of a young man, with its natural enthusiasm and vigor. Even at a wholly natural level, it is easy to see some of his teachings, such as the one against anxiety in Matthew 6.25–34, as the thought of ardent and idealistic youth. We know that there are other ways of seeing such ideas—for example, in terms of their belonging to a tradition of "wisdom" teaching or as expressing Jesus' style of relationship with God. All the same, one may feel that this outlook is what might be expected of a movement of and for young people—and scarcely of other people. In the same vein, we can think of the call to forsake family and property (e.g., Mark 1.16–20; 10.17–30).

Now it is evident that very soon the Christian movement began to attract supporters who either at the time of their joining or by surviving were by no means in the bloom of youth (see 2 Tim. 1.5; Titus 2.2–3). And ever since, the Church has at best included people of all ages, and frequently the aged have been in a majority, even the means of its survival. One thinks of the apparently constant stream of old women, others seemingly ready to step in when death took its toll, who largely maintained the ordinary life and worship of the Church in Russia during the era of Stalin and his successors. At the same time, although the Church often came to admire celibacy, and indeed to enforce it for its clergy, partly on the example of Jesus, Christian family life patently became the normal and natural model for most Christians, bringing with it the acquisition and stabilizing of property from generation to generation. Nothing could be much further from the teaching of Jesus, whose literal observance became the special duty and aspiration of the religious life in its monastic and other forms from the fourth century onward. And naturally, the Church's standing as a most blatant property owner, notably in European societies from early medieval times, has often been open to easy attack on the grounds of its falling foul of the clear example of Jesus.

Yet in modern secular terms, Jesus was the leader of a youth movement (to exaggerate!) with a message. The question then arises of how far he can truly appeal to the aging. It is undeniable, of course, that the aged are often only too pleased to relate to the young, precisely because of their vigor and idealism. But it is one thing to admire these qualities, another to follow and obey. Classically, the difficulty has scarcely been felt, simply because the teaching of Jesus has often in practice been subordinated to his position in Christian belief and doctrine. Yes, in human terms he died young. But he is exalted by God and, in his divinity, is and always was beyond limitations of age, culture, and so on. In other words, we should say that he is the route to whatever God is and whatever God purposes, at one with God in will and love for the human race—at one, therefore, in the way human beings—of any age—should relate to him. In this context, old age immediately loses its disadvantage, and its own particular manner of relating to God (for example, in contemplation of death) comes properly into view.

In the writings of the important second-century Christian writer Irenaeus, there is an interesting pointer, characteristic in its reasoning more of his time than ours, in this direction (see *Adversus Haereses* 2.22.5). It was in the context of deciding the date of Jesus' death, and his view (placing it as late as the reign of Claudius) was a flash in the pan, soon extinguished; but intriguing nonetheless. He noted the statement in John 8.27: "the Jews therefore said to him: thou art not yet fifty years old." Must Jesus then not have been close to that age? Moreover, we may think, there was the belief that human life, in its full and desired span, was forty-nine years, seven years each of the seven "ages of man" (infancy, childhood, and so on, ending in old age). To be perfectly human, to be one of us, Jesus must surely have reached that final patch. In fact, though it is impossible to know the statistics in any given community of the period, the usual view is that in the first century, it was good to reach one's forties (and the psalmist's aspiration to a norm of seventy, in Ps. 90.10, was probably audacious even when it was written some centuries earlier). Incidentally, this observation puts Paul's recommendation in 1 Timothy 5.9 for Church provision for widows once they had reached the age of sixty in a new light: it is unlikely to have been onerous, and wholly different from what might be the situation in a modern Christian congregation, at least in the West. We can also see that the only really old person the Gospels record Jesus to have encountered, Anna, aged eighty-four or, on some readings of the text, even 103 or more (Luke 2.37), was truly a phenomenon, reminiscent of the long-surviving early characters in the Old Testament. She is then in line with the general scriptural ethos of the opening chapters of Luke's Gospel.

What is clear is that modern Christian attitudes about the elderly must rest, not on an appeal to specific NT texts that may seem to bear on the matter, but on a more general understanding of the nature of God and moral duties that ensue.

Leslie Houlden

See also: Family; Luke, Gospel of, and Acts of the Apostles

Old Testament

See Hebrew Bible

Origen (c. 185–254)

Origen was to prove to be the most influential—and the most controversial—theologian of the third century. He was from Alexandria and a man very much at home in the heady philosophical and cultural traditions of that great melting pot of the ancient world. After running into trouble with his bishop, Demetrius, he was forced to leave Alexandria in 231 and found refuge in Caesarea in Palestine, taking his great library with him. He died in Caesarea around 254, after being imprisoned and tortured during the Decian persecution. He was greatly admired by Eusebius of Caesarea, who devoted most of the sixth book of his *Church History* to Origen's life.

Origen's theology was the subject of bitter controversy even during his lifetime, and he was to be condemned as a heretic—300 years after his death—by the Fifth Ecumenical Council, at Constantinople, in 553. Reaction to Origen has rarely been dispassionate. Criticism of him down the centuries has centered on the heavy influence of Platonic categories on his thought. Thus, the great historian of dogma Adolf von Harnack (1851–1930) saw Origen as an archetypal Hellenizer whose speculative metaphysics distorted the original, pure gospel. The modern rediscovery of Origen owes much to the interests of the "new theologians" in France before Vatican II—men like Henri de Lubac and Jean Daniélou—who put a new spin on the study of Origen: they found a contemporary relevance in his thought as they deployed its almost poetic richness and speculative flexibility as a counter to a seemingly rigid scholasticism. The tendency of Origenian scholarship over the past few decades, exemplified above all in the work of Henri Crouzel, has been to emphasize Origen the man of the Church.

Origen's picture of Jesus can be approached from what at first glance seems like an idiosyncratic aspect of his thought. Origen repeatedly said that different people, looking at the earthly Jesus, saw different things: "he did not appear in the same way to onlookers, but rather in accordance with their capacity" (*Contra Celsum* 2.64). Why would Origen want to say that?

He is *not* saying that the Incarnation is in some sense unreal or illusory. Rather, he specifically said that a "whole human being," a human being like us, was conjoined to the Son or Word *(Logos)* of God, and "The soul and body of Jesus became one (indeed, 'one compound thing') with the Word of God" (*C Cels*. 2.9, with 1.66). Moreover, he reasoned, "The whole human person would not have been redeemed had he not assumed the whole human being" (*Dialogue with Heracleides* 70.17–19).

In this process the human soul of Jesus acts as a mediating principle between God and the body. Underlying that principle is the strongly Platonic, hierarchical ordering of Origen's mental world. His thought is shaped by a contrast between the stable realm of intelligible reality and the flux and impermanence belonging to materiality. In this chain of being, the human soul in general occupies an intermediate position. On the one hand, it is "not contrary to its nature to assume a body," while, on the other, as a "rational substance," it has a certain affinity with the mind, which is God (*De Principiis [On First Principles]* 2.6.3).

The human soul of Jesus occupies a special position. For Origen, in the beginning, before there was a material world, rational spirits or "souls," disembodied and all alike, contemplated God. The Son, who is (at this stage) the invisible image of the invisible God, let them "participate" in himself insofar as they clung to him in love. But these rational spirits became bored and looked down, falling to different degrees—some becoming angels, some human souls, and some demons, depending on the extent of their fall. Or rather, all but one fell, the one that would become the human soul of Jesus. That one "from the beginning of creation and thereafter clung to him inseparably and indissolubly" (*De Prin.* 2.6.3). To express the conjunction of that soul with the Logos—the Word of God—Origen used the analogy of iron made red-hot in the fire. The iron in fact remains iron, but it looks like fire and has the effect of fire: "we say that the whole has been made fire because nothing other than fire is seen in it, but if anyone attempts to touch it or handle it, he will feel the force not of iron but of fire" (*De Prin.* 2.6.6).

The rational spirits that entered into materiality (including the angels and demons, who became clothed in "bodies," albeit bodies of tenuous stuff). Indeed, the very physicality of our material world enables the articulation of diversity. Throughout the whole history of the world, or rather of successive world ages, a drama of restoration is played out as the refractory rational spirits are led back to the contemplation of God. In the end they will all be restored, including, perhaps, even the Devil himself.

Such is the sweep of Origen's spiritual vision. The world exists more as a school than a penal colony. In it and through it we are meant to reach out with the mind's eye, to try to work our way back up to a glimpse of the God who lies beyond. The whole of human history, the whole of our human life, is exercise, practice, and training in noetic ascent. That task is, and is meant to be, hard work, but we are not left to our own devices.

God himself is a single, undifferentiated light, inaccessible to our minds, but he has a Son—he is timelessly and eternally begetting a Son—who acts as a sort of prism, breaking up that light into facets that give us access to the mystery of the divine. These are the *epinoiai*, "aspects" or "conceptions," which express different modalities of his activity. He is first of all Wisdom, then Word, then Light and Truth. After that come titles expressive of his work of restoration—feeding, healing, leading the creation back to God; thus he is Life, Bread, Door, Physician, Shepherd, and much more (*Commentary on John* 1)—all images Origen found in Scripture, especially the Gospel of John, which he read through Platonist eyes.

In this work of restoration, the preexistent soul of Jesus has an abiding role—a role that reaches back to the very beginning of the drama of restoration. As the iron in the fire transmits heat, so "to all the saints a certain heat of the Word of God must be reckoned to have come, and in this soul that divine fire, we believe, rested substantially, from which any heat comes to the others" (*De Prin.* 2.6.6). There is, then, a cosmic role for Jesus in Origen's scheme of things.

It is now possible to see how the changing appearance of the earthly Jesus coheres with fundamental aspects of Origen's thought. In the first place, like all of Origen's theology, it is—or is at least intended to be—deeply scriptural. Just as the material world both conceals and reveals God, so does Scripture, the written Word. Beneath its hard surface lies an uncharted depth of meaning; to explore that depth is itself a part of the disciplined exercise, the intellectual and spiritual training, by which we learn to reach out toward God.

Behind the notion of Jesus' changing appearance lie texts such as Isaiah 53.2 ("without form or comeliness"), on the one hand, and Psalm 45.2 ("fairest among the sons of men"), on the other, which were both regularly applied to Christ. And Origen appealed (in *C Cels*. 2.64) to details that he thought showed that Jesus could not always be recognized: Judas had to give a sign to those who came to arrest him (Matt. 26.48); though Jesus had been teaching daily in the Temple, he could not be arrested there (Matt. 26.5). Above all, Origen pointed to the Transfiguration narrative, stressing the fact that the text says of Peter, James, and John "he was transformed *before them*" (Matt. 17.2).

More fundamentally, as Jesus can be said to have many epinoiai—those aspects of the Son's creative, sustaining, and restorative activity manifested throughout history—so does he have a multiplicity of earthly appearances (*C Cels*. 2.64). And in each case, that multiplicity is adapted to the needs of those on various rungs of the ladder of noetic ascent, that rising with the eyes of the mind from the confusion and unreality of gross materiality to the vision of the divine. He is Shepherd for those who have gone astray; Physician for those who are ill. But it is possible for rational spirits to pass beyond the need of those aspects of his activity. Similarly, not all have the strength to perceive his earthly glory. His appearance is in accordance with "what the onlookers are capable of" and what is "useful, as it was necessary for each to see him" (*C Cels*. 6.77).

Thus, Origen's picture of Jesus has much in common, formally, with what would come to be identified as orthodoxy two centuries later. His Jesus is "one," though a "composite" that has become one (*C Cels*. 2.9), and the "composition" comes from the fact that the Word has assumed a human being, consisting of soul and body. But all that is part of a vast, overarching scheme of restoration, which gives Jesus a cosmic significance. Jesus' body is a real, human body, but it shares the plasticity of a world in process of transformation.

Paul Parvis

See also: Alexandrian Theology; Harnack, Adolf von; John, Gospel of

References

Primary

Chadwick, Henry, trans. 1953. *Origen: Contra Celsum*. Cambridge: Cambridge University Press.

Butterworth, G. W. 1936. *Origen on First Principles, Being Koetschau's Text of De Principiis*. London: SPCK.

Scherr, Jean, ed. and trans. 1960. *Entretien d'Origène avec Héraclide*. Paris: Éditions du Cerf.

Secondary

Bigg, Charles. 1913 [1886]. *The Christian Platonists of Alexandria*. Oxford: Clarendon.

Chadwick, Henry. 1966. *Early Christian Thought and the Classical Tradition, Studies in Justin, Clement, and Origen*. Oxford: Clarendon.

Crouzel, Henri. 1989. *Origen*. Translated by A. S. Worrall. Edinburgh: T. & T. Clark.

Grillmeier, Aloys. 1975. *Christ in Christian Tradition*. Vol. 1 of *From the Apostolic Age to Chalcedon (451)*. Translated by John Bowden. London: Mowbrays.

Lyman, Rebecca. 1994. *Christology and Cosmology: Models of Divine Activity in Origen, Eusebius, and Athanasius*. Oxford: Clarendon.

McGuckin, John A. 1987. "The Changing Forms of Jesus" in *Origeniana Quarta, Die Referate des 4. Internationalen Origeneskongresses (Innsbruck, 2.–6. September 1985)*. Edited by Lothar Lies, Innsbrucker theologische Studien 19. Innsbruck: Tyrolia-Verlag.

Orthodox Tradition

Within the Orthodox tradition, Jesus Christ is understood as one person—the eternally begotten, fully divine Son of God the Father—who at the Incarnation also became fully human. Any Orthodox Christology must hold together both the unity of the personal subject of Christ and the duality of his "natures": he is one person who is at once both divine and human. This is the Christ made known in the Scriptures, as the Church itself (through the Fathers, the liturgy, and the councils) reads and understands them. This is the Christ who, to paraphrase the Nicene-Constantinopolitan Creed, "for us and for our salvation was incarnate and became human, was crucified and buried, and rose again according to the scriptures." This is the savior and redeemer of the world.

The Tradition

The Orthodox Church is a family of autocephalous (i.e., independent) churches that sees itself in unbroken continuity with the early Church established by Christ and his apostles. The Orthodox are historically based in Asia Minor and Greece (erstwhile Byzantium—the primatial see is still Constantinople, with headquarters in modern-day Istanbul), Syria and the wider Middle East, the Balkans, and Russia. Yet, particularly with the increase in the movement of peoples in the past century, the combined Orthodox presence is felt worldwide, with significant communities and thriving missions on six continents.

Another family of churches, known as the "Oriental" or "non-Chalcedonian" churches, are also widely known as "Orthodox." This family split with the Chalcedonian Orthodox Church in the fifth century in the aftermath of the Council of Chalcedon (451) over issues that involved a blend of theological, political, and cultural factors. The non-Chalcedonian churches have been historically located in Armenia, Asia Minor, Egypt, Ethiopia, the Middle East, and India. The split over the Council of Chalcedon had important implications for Christology and to this day formally separates this family of churches from communion with the Orthodox Church.

The Orthodox tradition draws neither on "Scripture alone" nor merely on the "two sources" of Scripture and tradition. In Scripture is found the normative revelation concerning God and his acts for us and for our salvation; in Scripture is found the Gospel of Jesus Christ. But the reading of Scripture can yield a wide variety of interpretations. St. Irenaeus of Lyons (second century) likened it to the tiles of a mosaic, which can be arranged either to portray a king (viz. Christ) or a dog or fox. Scripture therefore is read within the Church, which identifies a canon of truth, an interpretive framework operating in turn within several other particular sources: the writings of the Church Fathers; the theological definitions and creeds of the ecumenical councils; the Church's canons; the Church's liturgy; church art (notably the icons) and architecture; the lives of the saints.

Much of this legacy is shared by different Christian traditions, yet there is a particularity to the synthesis effected within the Orthodox tradition. That tradition represents an interpretive framework that leads to assertions about Jesus Christ being both God and man, and yet a single person. Part of its particularity lies in its close fidelity to the conciliar definitions and its refusal to relativize their content. But it also rests in the ways in which the scriptural and conciliar witness sees expression through the total life of the Church. The etymology of "Orthodox"—right praise, right glorification—is something to which "Orthodox tradition" is preternaturally faithful, so that its theology is never a dry or abstract pursuit. It is integrated into, and receives life and expression in, the Church's worship of God—in both the experience and the sung texts of that worship.

Jesus Christ Is the Content of Faith

Scripture as understood in tradition reveals that Christianity is not a philosophical or metaphysical system; it is not an ethical code, nor is the Church a society or club. Christianity is about the person of Jesus Christ. The central question posed to humanity is the question posed by Jesus: "Who do you say that I am?" The Orthodox interpretation of Scripture limits the range of possible answers to this question: it is impossible to see Jesus Christ's nature or his role in the world in equivocal terms. He is either "the Son of the living God," "the way, the truth, and the life," the sole one by whom we come to the Father, or he and the scriptural authors are utterly deluded.

The Son of God becomes the Son of Mary—God becomes man—for no other reason than "for us and for our salvation," as asserted in the Nicene-Constantinopolitan creed. Jesus Christ is the savior of the world, and the Orthodox tradition about Christ is firmly rooted in soteriology. In order to save, Jesus must be fully divine, but this divine salvation must reach the point of human need. Therefore, Jesus must be involved with, and *become*, everything that it means to be human.

Jesus Christ Is God

The most frequent explicit allusion to Jesus Christ in Orthodox liturgical life is by way of the formula "Our Lord and God and Savior Jesus Christ." At matins, Orthodox sing, "The Lord is God and has revealed himself to us." To say "Jesus is Lord" is to say "Jesus is God," which in turn is to say that he is divine—he shares with God the Father all the attributes of divinity.

Throughout the Gospels, Jesus is called "the Son of God" or "the Son of Man" (with reference to Dan. 7.13f.); he is also called "God" (John 20.28; 2 Pet. 1.1). In St. John's Gospel particularly, Jesus often refers to himself as "I Am" (*ego eimi*—like the Septuagint's translation of YHWH). The same Gospel reveals Jesus as the Logos who was "with God" and who "was God," through whom all the universe was created (cf. John 1.1–3)—who also "became flesh and dwelt among us" (John 1.14).

The fourth-century Arian controversy—the debate about the full divinity of the Logos/Son of God—showed that Christology immediately spills into Trinitarian theology. Once the identity of Jesus is established as that of the only begotten Son of God, it becomes necessary to assert that this Logos/Son is in no way less than the Father. In response to the Arian position, the Nicene Creed asserts that the Son is "Light from light, true God from true God." The Son is not a creature of the Father but is "begotten," as befits a father-son relationship, and is therefore *homoousios*—"consubstantial with" or "of the same essence/substance as" the Father.

The consubstantiality of the Son with the Father, and that of the Holy Spirit with the Son and the Father, therefore has cosmological implications. The Church Fathers asserted (contrary to the classical Greek philosophers) that there was a sharp division between the uncreated godhead and the created world. God the Father eternally begets his Son and Spirit by his very nature, but he creates the world ex nihilo of his own free will. The created world therefore is utterly contingent upon the uncreated God. And God creates the world through the Logos/Son (John 1.3; Heb. 1.2); all that exists is held together in the Logos/Son (Col. 1.17).

This, then, is the "cosmic Christ": the one who established the world upon its foundations, the one who revealed himself to Moses on Mount Sinai (Orthodoxy understands the whole of Scripture in terms of Christ), the Logos who is the truth and "logic" of the world, the one who in time is made known as Jesus of Nazareth, who is also crucified for us.

Scripture has many ways of indicating this continuity of personhood—the divine Son of the Father also becomes the human son of Mary. The prologue of John's Gospel is understood in these terms, as is the farewell discourse, notably John 17.5, in which Jesus speaks of the glory that he had with the Father before the world was made. The ancient hymn recorded in Philippians 2.5–11, and the opening of the letter to the Hebrews, testify to the same.

These passages of Scripture are often used by the Fathers and find their way into the doctrinal definitions produced by the ecumenical councils. They are a part of Orthodox liturgical life, found in the lectionary, and their meaning is also interpreted and elaborated in hymnography.

The "monogenēs" hymn, dating from the sixth century and attributed to the emperor Justinian, is sung at every divine liturgy to testify that one of the Trinity was crucified in the flesh: "O only-begotten Son and immortal Word of God, who accepted for our salvation to take flesh from the Holy Mother of God and Ever-Virgin Mary, and without change became man; you were crucified, Christ God, by death trampling down death, being one of the Holy

Trinity, glorified with the Father and the Holy Spirit; save us!" At the feasts of Christ, the Church often enjoys the language of paradox to express this same continuity of person. At Good Friday matins, the Church sings: "He who hung the earth upon the waters is hung upon the tree." At Jesus' Presentation in the Temple, the Church sings: "Today Simeon receives in his embrace the uncircumscribed Word." And at the feast of the Nativity (Christmas): "Today the virgin gives birth to the transcendent one and the earth offers a cave to the unapproachable one . . . for to us has been born a little child, God before the ages."

The continuity of personal identity in Christ from his eternal begottenness through the Incarnation is one of the main assertions of St. Cyril of Alexandria; the same principle was reflected in the Fourth Ecumenical Council, chiefly through the repeated insistence that the one who is homoousios with the Father and the one who is homoousios with us is the same person *(ho autos)*. The Fifth Ecumenical Council took up this formula of the "double birth" of the same person, a formula that in turn is also sung in several of the Church's vesperal hymns. The One who was begotten timelessly of God the Father is the same One who is born in time of the virgin mother.

It is likewise significant that the Orthodox refer to the Virgin Mary almost exclusively by her Christological title *Theotokos* or "mother of God," since the one whom she bore was none other than the divine Son himself. Indeed, the Christological reason for her virginity has uniquely to do with the fact that when Jesus was conceived in her womb, no new person came into being (as happens in the case of a normal human conception); instead, the preexisting person of the divine Logos took human composition.

The divinity of Christ is thus attested, recited, and sung in Orthodox tradition, both through the recognition of his divine acts and sayings as recorded in Scripture, and through the recognition of his identity as the incarnate Son of God, the second person of the Holy Trinity.

Jesus Christ Is Man

To assert that Jesus Christ is "consubstantial" with God the Father, sharing in all the attributes of divinity, is but one pole of Christology. It is incomplete without a second pole. Jesus Christ is equally consubstantial with us humans, sharing in everything that it means to be human. It is as vital to assert this "double consubstantiality" as it is to assert the "double birth."

Jesus Christ's divinity as well as his humanity were called into question from the beginnings of Christianity (cf. 1 John 4.1–2; 2 John 1.7). As a result, his humanity required explicit defense by the Fathers and councils of the Church. Yet the very same scriptural passages that bespoke Christ's being truly human (Matt. 4.2, 21.18; Mark 4.38; Luke 2.52; John 11.35; 19.28) also bolstered the Arian arguments that Christ was created, weak, and less than God. The challenge faced by Orthodox theologians was to account for how Christ could be simultaneously "true God from true God" and an infant born of a woman, someone who could "grow in wisdom and stature," be tempted, experience hunger and thirst, ask the Father to "glorify him," and die on the cross.

As was the case for Christ's divinity, the solution was found in a harmony of scriptural evidence and patristic and conciliar synthesis, expressed in turn in the liturgy. The classical patristic formulation finds expression in hymnody, particularly at the feast of the raising of Lazarus, on the eve of Palm Sunday: "You are God and man, proving by your actions the true reality of both your natures. In the flesh you came to the tomb, O Word, and as God you raised up the man four days dead." The one person, Jesus Christ (existing eternally as the divine Son), acts both "as God" and "as man." Alternately, the Fathers also speak of Christ doing some things "in accordance with his divine nature," or "insofar as he is God," and other things "in accordance with his human nature," or "insofar as he is man," or "as incarnate." It is important to stress that the one person is the subject of all that happens to Christ and of all that he says and does—for only a person, and not a nature, is capable of action and experience.

The terminology, adapted from the classical tradition, is critical in the formulation both of Christ's duality (God and man) and his single identity. Other than the language of the homoousios of Christ with us humans, the tradition invokes the language of nature *(phusis)*—in this case expressing the sum total of characteristics that make something what it is. Therefore, to speak of Christ as possessing human nature means he is everything that it is to be human.

Reflection on Christ's humanity therefore beckons for a reflection on our own humanity. In the humanity of Christ, we see an icon of humanity as it was meant to be: maintaining a freely chosen harmony with God's will, in freely chosen and loving communion with God himself. What is remarkable is that Christ's humanity, although without sin (that is, in complete harmony with God's will), is lived out not in quarantine but in the existential conditions of a fallen world. In the striking words of St. Gregory of Nazianzus, "[H]e was actually subject as a slave to flesh, . . . and to our human experiences; . . . held captive as we are by sin, he was subject to all that he saved. . . . He has united with himself all that lay under condemnation, . . . all that death pervades" (*Oration* 30, iii; xxi).

Christ's humanity, which incorporates a human soul and a human will, therefore indicates that sinlessness and perfection do not mean freedom from temptation. Christ is tempted in every respect that we are, yet he does not sin (Heb. 4.15). His humanity—sinless humanity—reveals not the overpowering of the human will by the divine—for the human will chooses uncompelled—but rather the restoration of human nature to its authentic state, where the human person freely, but naturally and spontaneously (that is, without deliberation), chooses communion with God.

The soteriological necessity of Christ's being fully human has to do with the Church's clear sense that the Incarnation had to be comprehensive. Many previous and subsequent patristic affirmations were summed up in Gregory of Nazianzus's brief *dictum*, "[W]hat is not assumed is not healed" (Epistle 101). This does not mean that Christ's divinity is a kind of alchemic force that changes everything that it touches into itself. Instead, the assumption by God of everything that it is to be human, "all that death pervades," means nothing less than Christ's having to suffer all of the physical, psychological, and moral trials that fallen humans do—and being victorious.

In assuming the totality of what it means to be human, under the conditions of the Fall, Christ reveals not only the true vocation of humanity but also the fact that God has "dwelt among us" (John 1.14), and "because he himself has suffered and been tempted, he is able to help those who are tempted" (Heb. 2.18).

Jesus Christ and the Holy Spirit

The Orthodox tradition celebrates the particular relationship that exists between Christ and the Holy Spirit. That the Spirit of the Lord rests upon the Son is testified by the prophecies (Isa. 11; 42; 61) and resurfaces in the Gospels. It is by the Spirit that Jesus is recognized as Lord (1 Cor. 12.3). He is the Spirit of the Son (Gal. 4.6).

Particularly when challenged by the *filioque* addition to the Nicene-Constantinopolitan Creed, Orthodox theologians have been firm in reiterating that, although the Son sends the Spirit in a temporal, "economic" sense, the Spirit eternally proceeds from the Father alone, not from the Son. Here Orthodox tradition remains faithful to the full content of John 15.26, which speaks both of the temporal sending and the eternal procession.

Jesus Christ Is Sacrament

The intertwining of theology and Church life so characteristic of the Orthodox tradition is further present in its sacramental theology. "Sacrament" refers to the union of the divine with the human, the unseen with the seen, the timeless with the temporal. This union is experienced in the bread and wine of the Eucharist and in the waters of baptism—the two fundamental sacraments. And if Christ is truly God and truly human, then Christ himself is the ultimate sacrament.

The unity of the divine and human natures in Christ is understood and expressed in the Chalcedonian definition of their being "without confusion, without change, without division and without separation." This means that the two realities in Christ retain their integrity and also experience a thorough and organic union, so that Christ is a single, whole, and unschizophrenic being.

The necessity of affirming both the union and the integrity of these two natures has repercussions. The Church itself, as the Body of Christ, as a divine/human ("theandric") reality, is itself a sacrament. In the sacraments celebrated in the Church, the integrity of "natures" is preserved as well. The consecrated elements do not cease being bread and wine, the Holy Church does not cease being lived out in history in particular contexts, and Christ does not cease to be fully human—even as each instance of his presence presents a unified whole. As in the person of Christ, human nature and will are not consumed by the divine, so it is in the being and life of the Church. And so human persons, following the pattern of Christ, are called to live in communion with God. We are ultimately made "partakers of the divine nature" (2 Pet. 1.4), even as our human nature is not overcome.

Peter Bouteneff

See also: Alexandrian Theology; Chalcedon; Coptic Christianity; Creeds; Ethiopian Christianity; Holy Spirit; Icons and the Icon Tradition; Irenaeus; John, Gospel of; Nicea; Russian Christianity; Second Person of the Trinity; Son of God; Son of Man

References

Athanasius, Saint. *On the Incarnation*. This fourth-century text is available in several English translations: London: Mowbray, 1982; Crestwood, NY: SVS, 1989.

Behr, John. 2001. *The Way to Nicea*. Crestwood, NY: SVS.

Meyendorff, John. 1974. *Byzantine Theology: Historical Trends and Doctrinal Themes*. New York: Fordham University Press.

Pelikan, Jaroslav. 1971–1974. *The Christian Tradition: A History of the Development of Doctrine*. Vols. 1–2. Chicago: University of Chicago Press.

Schmemann, Alexander. 1973. *For the Life of the World: Sacraments and Orthodoxy*. Crestwood, NY: SVS.

Thunberg, Lars. 1995. *Microcosm and Mediator: The Theological Anthropology of Maximus the Confessor*. 2d ed. Chicago: Open Court.

P

Pannenberg, Wolfhart (b. 1928)

Wolfhart Pannenberg was professor of systematic theology in the University of Munich from 1968 to 1994. He has been a leading figure in twentieth-century systematic theology in both Europe and North America.

Pannenberg sees Jesus both as a historical figure of first-century apocalyptic Judaism and as God incarnate and the second person of the Trinity. Jesus is first of all a figure within apocalyptic Judaism who preached the imminent coming of the kingdom of God, announced the coming of the end of time, and provoked responses in the lives of those who heard his message. Pannenberg constructs his picture of Jesus by identifying authentic sayings of Jesus from the Synoptic Gospels. Although Jesus fits partly into the prophetic tradition of Israel, he cannot adequately be summed up as a prophet. Rather, he is a sinless human being whose life and death have universal significance and typify the human capacity for openness to God. The central event in Jesus' life is his resurrection from the dead, which Pannenberg sees as a historical event by which God confirmed Jesus as divine. In this sense, Jesus is a revelation of God. Pannenberg's thinking about Jesus proceeds "from below" (an expression that his work in English popularized), that is, from the historical, human Jesus, and only then moves on to use the language of Incarnation and Trinity in relation to him.

Pannenberg combines historical, theological, and philosophical concerns in his understanding of Jesus. He sees him as the representative human being whose life, death, and Resurrection constitute his status as God's Son. Jesus' life was lived in freedom before God, not in that he had a capacity for aimless arbitrary acts, but in the sense of his total dedication to God's will. Jesus typified the general human capacity for openness to God and therefore fulfilled human destiny. Central to constructing Jesus' historical identity for Pannenberg is Luke 12.8: "And I tell you, everyone who acknowledges me before men, the Son of Man also will acknowledge before the angels of God." Although Jesus did not think of himself as the Son of Man, he was later shown to be that figure by God's confirmation of his role in raising him from the dead. Within the context of a notion of God revealing himself in history, Pannenberg sees Jesus bearing the sins of all people in his death, which thus has a vicarious significance for the whole human race. Jesus' own sinlessness, for Pannenberg, is to be thought of not in the sense that he was free from all sinful acts, but in the sense of his dedication to God's will and personal unity with God. Pannenberg also sees Jesus as Lord and King, both of which are to be understood in terms of his role in establishing the lordship and kingship of God in the setting up of the kingdom of God.

The central event of Jesus' life, for Pannenberg, was his Resurrection from the dead. The notion of general Resurrection from the dead was fundamental to the worldview of apocalyptic Judaism, with its expectation of God's action at the end of time. Pannenberg claims that Jesus' Resurrection had a retroactive power by which God confirmed Jesus' human life and showed that he had had divine status all along. For example, the Resurrection constituted God's confirmation of Jesus' pre-Easter claims to personal unity with him. The Resurrection of Jesus, therefore, has universal significance for all people in that it foreshadows the general resurrection of the dead at the end of time. In this sense, the Resurrection of Jesus was a decisive revelation of God. Although Pannenberg sees the Resurrection of Jesus as a historical fact, he also understands the language of Resurrection as metaphorical.

Although Pannenberg insists that modern thinking about Jesus must begin "from below," he is also happy to use the traditional Chalcedonian "two natures Christology." Thus, Jesus is "truly God" and "truly man" as established by the Resurrection. Such notions of Incarnation, however, must be seen as part of the logical outworking of Christology rather than as presuppositions in the process of establishing Jesus' identity. Pannenberg also uses Trinitarian categories: Jesus is related to God the Father in that he is the Son, but the Son is also distinct from the Father. This relation indicates a distinction within God himself but places Jesus firmly in relation to the Trinity. Pannenberg also speaks in terms of the Son's preexistence, on the grounds of his association with the Father in creation. Overall, incarnational and Trinitarian language arises naturally out of the historical investigation into Jesus' human life and death as seen in the light of the Resurrection.

Stephen W. Need

See also: Chalcedon; Christology, Modern; Jesus, Death of; Kingdom of God; Lord; Preexistence; Resurrection; Son of God; Son of Man

References

Galloway, Allan D. 1973. *Wolfhart Pannenberg*. London: George Allen & Unwin.
Pannenberg, Wolfhart. 1968. *Jesus—God and Man*. London: SCM.
———. 1994. *Systematic Theology*. Vol. 2. Edinburgh: T. & T. Clark.

Paranormal

Of many different interpretations of the Gospel records, one type of explanation concerns the paranormal. The word is used to describe phenomena and activities that cannot be explained by normal causation but do not indicate acts of God directly interfering in the regularities of nature. Some events, which are usually explained as either unhistorical or supernatural in origin, may in fact be paranormal, according to this view.

People taking this approach believe there is good evidence that telepathy exists. Did Jesus enjoy telepathic powers? On certain occasions, he is recorded in the Synoptic Gospels, in connection with his opponents, as "knowing their thoughts" without any communication between them. For example, he seems to have realized by some unknown means that a man's paralysis was caused by guilt (Mark 2.5), and he is also recorded as knowing, without being told, that a widow had put into the temple treasury all that she had (Mark 12.41–4). Jesus' remarkable discernment of a shoal of fish could be explained by clairvoyance (Luke 5.4–6).

In St. John's Gospel it is emphasized that Jesus "knew what was in man" (2.25). He knew without being told the past history of the Samaritan woman at the well (4). He knew (at a distance) that a nobleman's sick son was alive (4.50), and that Lazarus was dead (11.14). He knew, too, that his own disciples were complaining about his teaching and that they wanted to question him about an enigmatic saying. An earlier occasion, when he told Nathanael that he had seen him earlier "under the fig tree," might also be a case of clairvoyance (1.48).

These incidents may all be explained in other ways. Some may be due to the evangelists' insertions, or the accounts themselves may not have been historical but were felt to be appropriate to Jesus. There could have been unrecorded conversation, or nonverbal communication. Some hold that Jesus had supernatural knowledge, despite his own admission of his limitations. But a paranormal explanation cannot be excluded.

Precognition is a well-attested paranormal phenomenon. Some forty years before the event Jesus is seen as having foretold the fall of Jerusalem and the destruction of the temple; he also foretold his own death. He knew the whereabouts of a colt for his entry to Jerusalem, and he knew where his disciples, in preparing for the Last Supper, would meet a man carrying a jar. He predicted on the night of his arrest that Peter would deny him before cockcrow. These incidents, too, may have explanations that exclude the paranormal, though other explanations can barely account for the prediction of Peter's denial, as a defamatory legend about the chief of the apostles seems improbable.

The story of Jesus' temptations could be regarded as *haggadah* (legendary development to convey a message) rather than history. But periods of fasting, for which no normal explanation can be given, have been attested for longer than forty days (e.g., St. Catherine of Siena). And psychic powers might have made his three temptations real options.

The luminous phenomena of mysticism, for which no natural explanation can be given, are well attested in the history of the saints, and also among psychics. The Transfiguration of Jesus has been explained as a myth or legend read back into the story of Jesus, but if it was historical, the brightness of Jesus could be classed as a paranormal phenomenon. The apparition of Moses and Elijah might even be a veridical hallucination.

There have been many explanations of Jesus' mighty works as recorded in the Gospels. For his healings he seems to have employed various means, some of which appear similar to those employed by spiritual healers whose powers seem not to be susceptible to medical explanation. As for his exorcisms, "possession," although very rare, does occur, and when all psychological or pharmaceutical remedies have failed, exorcism has been found effective. His nature miracles strain credulity today and have been explained as haggadah; but some may have a paranormal explanation. The feeding of the multitudes can be paralleled by a large number of well-attested cases that cannot be lightly dismissed as phenomena belonging merely to the domain of legend. Possibly the sight of Jesus apparently walking on water can be explained as bilocation, the visible projection of personality, which is a rare paranormal phenomenon nevertheless evidenced, for example, in the life of Padre Pio, now raised to sainthood.

Jesus' repeated identification of John the Baptist with Elijah, and the crowds' identification of Jesus with one of the prophets, usually interpreted as the assumption of their spiritual role, may also be interpreted as references to reincarnation.

Jesus' resurrection appearances bear some resemblance to a paranormal phenomenon recognized in the annals of the Society for Psychical Research in which a loved one appears to (or speaks to) a spouse or close relative around the time of death; in such cases, like Jesus, the deceased rarely consents to be touched. Jesus' appearances, as recorded in the Gospels, were somewhat different. They lasted longer, there was extended conversation, the number of those who witnessed them was exceptional, and they were given mostly not for reassurance but to issue words of command. Nonetheless, the similarities are such that it is possible to classify them as paranormal.

All the phenomena and activities mentioned above are either susceptible to a natural explanation or may be regarded as supernatural resulting from the divine nature of Jesus. They can also be interpreted as paranormal. Their number suggests that this interpretation should not be lightly disregarded, especially as the paranormal seems apparent elsewhere in the Scriptures, both in the Old Testament and in the writings of St. Paul. There seems a mysterious connection between sanctity and paranormal phenomena, although the one does not necessarily involve the other. In Jesus' case, the paranormal phenomena could result not from the effects of his divine nature but from the remarkable gifts of his human nature, and thus might have no particular doctrinal significance.

Hugh Montefiore

See also: Jesus, Miracles of; Jesus, Teaching of

References

Gurney, E., F. W. Myers, and F. Podmore. 1886. *Phantasms of the Living*. London: Trubner.

Oates, Burns, and Michael Perry. 1959. *The Easter Enigma*. London: Faber and Faber.

Thurston, Herbert. 1952. *The Physical Phenomena of Mysticism*. London: Burns Oates.

Passion Narratives

See Jesus, Death of

Pastoral Theology, Modern

In Christian pastoral care, the carer works within a framework that has as its basis the belief that the person is made in the image of a God, who orders creation (Gen. 1.27, 28). The outworking of this belief understands pastoral care as involvement in the caring response of God to humanity, humanity to humanity, and humanity to God (Luke 10.27). Pastoral care, then, is carried out in the context of the whole work of God and draws on the Bible as a resource for the practical expression of this acknowledged involvement in the responsiveness of God. This task involves skill in uncovering what will be the best response for the particular situation.

Pastoral care is one of the major activities and concerns of those who follow Jesus, but the use it makes of the person of Christ and sayings attributed to him is often curiously unexciting. It is hard to avoid the feeling that, in recent times and even in Christian circles, Jesus does not feature as a resource in this area at a very profound level and that much of the inspiration for pastoral care and its works comes from secular sources. It is fair to draw attention to the huge influence in the past for Christian caring work of the model of Jesus as healer, of the Good Samaritan parable, and, of course, of the works of mercy based on Matthew 25.31–46. It is this Jesus model and this teaching that have made the Church so strong a vehicle of pastoral care down the centuries. However, the case of Jesus may not be untypical of the way in which the Christian tradition is interpreted in relation to many areas of modern life. In this sense, it is far from being insignificant for those interested in the practical impact of biblical interpretation, as distinct from its preoccupation with its own internal life, where profundity and sophistication are available in plenty.

There are two broad ways in which the figure of Jesus has had significance for pastoral care. First, Jesus is understood in terms of his significance to the believer, the one to whom a Christian turns for care, in the struggles of life and for ultimate salvation beyond sin and death. The Christ of faith is described as Savior, Redeemer, and Physician of the soul. Theologically expressed, Jesus as the Christ is the one through whom the redemptive love and care of God are made known and available to us. In sacramental terms, Jesus is described as the true sacrament of God and the primal source of all sacramental and nonsacramental ministries of care. In some Roman Catholic theologies of pastoral care, Jesus is the true source and end of all love and acts of care both inside and outside the Church.

When pastoral theologians have reflected on the historical Jesus, some have attempted to articulate his historical personality in terms of the ideal pastor, the Good Shepherd, who demonstrates the multiplicity of ways within which God cares. The encounters of Jesus with people in the Gospels have been taken as ideal instances of care demonstrating unbounded compassion and profound insight into human nature.

With the advent of historical criticism, for those who took it seriously, this unity and cohesion of thought have become problematic. It became difficult for thoughtful Christians to utilize the Gospel records of the life of Jesus in a direct way, and troublesome difficulties emerged for grounding contemporary pastoral care in the ministry of Jesus. The difficulties lie in part over miracles, but also in the fact that society has changed so significantly over the centuries. So the question arises today of whether the figure of Jesus in the Gospels can be related to contemporary need and to the practice of pastoral care in the Church.

However whole, the diversity, even inconsistency, in the portraits of Jesus in the Gospels has been viewed by some to be a threat to faith, but for pastoral theologians this diversity has provided an expression of the richness and mystery of the figure of Jesus, who can be grasped by no single portrait or conception. In this light, we may be able to find within the richness of the portraits of Jesus in the Gospels multiple resources for pastoral theology and its application.

Some writers on pastoral care have placed the use of the Bible and the portrait of Jesus in a wider theological context or drawn out significant biblical themes in the life of Christ. Thus, Matthew Fox (1983) explored the Scriptures as God's responsiveness to the world made clear in continuous acting through blessing, above all in the life of Christ. God blesses people in a privilege of care and love and in this blessing reveals his presence in life and growth. Fox argued that it is through our response to the blessing of Christ that we become most fully human. Blessing is the inner strength of the soul and the happiness it creates.

Rather than using isolated biblical verses to comfort or challenge, pastors who are aware of the diversity of story in the portraits of Jesus might consider helping people to relate to the distinctive affirmations they express about Jesus in ways appropriate to their own concerns. For instance, a person who may feel alienated or marginalized, or who suffers from shame or guilt, may experience the liberation of Jesus with particular power through Luke's Gospel, in which Jesus has a special concern for the alienated and marginalized. Or those experiencing a measure of moral confusion and uncertainty—or perhaps a general sense of lostness, may find Matthew's portrait of Jesus helpful as it portrays a figure of loving authority who calls people to follow through discipline, service, and responsibility.

This is not to suggest that offering a particular interpretation of the figure of Jesus through the Gospel portraits can offer any magical or immediate remedy for the human predicament. Rather, it suggests that ways can be found in which the figure of Jesus can be made present in situations of need, with both intellectual honesty and pastoral relevance. The stories of the love of God in Jesus, as the Christ, for such a wide range of people and groups, can be expressed and viewed as affirmations. Each episode can allow theological power to speak in its own particular and unique way to the multifaceted contours of human need.

Stephen Pattison (1988) suggested that the Bible and pastoral care must be related in this way with critical integrity. The starting point is to allow the Bible to shape and form the consciousness and character of people by allowing them to be in a constant dialogue with the text in traditional mode. We may take the Bible's themes, stories, and images and reflect upon their meaning in the experience of our lives. The Bible may contribute imaginatively to the task of formation and perform a background function with regard to meeting specific pastoral needs. But we should always be very careful about laying down the biblical line on any matter in pastoral care. There is no one view or theology in the Bible; pluralism and diversity characterize its message. Contemporary (postmodern) pastors will be aware that our concrete knowledge of Jesus is both limited and persuasively colored by the theological affirmations of the Church.

However, the themes dealt with in the Gospel portraits do point to enduring features of the pastoral task. The experience of being misunderstood, in a global perspective, the predicament of the weak, the poor, and the marginalized, the experience of being subject to things we cannot control, and the need to see beyond the material to that which is eternal are some of the themes relevant and essential to pastoral ministry in any age, however embodied in differing historical epochs.

It may, however, be that in the twenty-first century, insights from psychology, sociology, psychotherapy, and other disciplines of culture are likely to be predominant influences in pastoral theology. It is necessary to continue to articulate the gaps, the confusions, and the uncertainties with both humility and courage as a faithful response to the working out of God's love through care. A certain creativity of faithful response to this love, appropriate to the contemporary experience, is a key feature of pastoral theology. Creative approaches to the Christ of the Bible allow a freedom to challenge the perceptions of the past and to discern the Spirit of God in the present.

James Woodward

See also: Jesus, Miracles of; Jesus in Social Context; Kingdom of God

References

Fox, Matthew. 1983. *Original Blessing*. New York: Bear and Company.
Oates, Wayne. 1974. *The Bible in Pastoral Care*. Philadelphia: Westminster.
Pattison, Stephen. 1988. *A Critique of Pastoral Care*. London: SCM.

Patristic Thought

See Adoptianism; Alexandrian Theology; Antiochene Theology; Apollinarianism; Chalcedon; Gnosticism; Irenaeus; Nestorianism; Nicea; Serapion

Paul

Paul the Apostle—the greatest of all the early Christian missionaries and theologians, and one of the key writers of the New Testament—has done more than any other individual to shape the history of the Jesus movement. Radically converted to Christ as a young man, Paul devoted the rest of his life to proclaiming him as the Savior and Lord of the world. The passionate Christ-centered letters he wrote to the early Christians reveal to us his understanding of Jesus as the messianic redeemer whose atoning death and resurrection offer salvation and life-transforming power to all who put their trust in him. For Paul, the real significance of Jesus lies not in his earthly life and teachings, but in his death and resurrection, through which God brings salvation to the world.

Paul's Conversion to Christ

According to Luke's account (Acts 22.1–16; 23.6; cf. Phil. 3.5), Paul was raised in a traditional Jewish home and educated in Jerusalem as a Pharisee by one of Judaism's leading rabbis, Gamaliel. As a zealous young Jew, Paul actively persecuted the early Christians. But as a result of a visionary encounter with the resurrected Jesus (Acts 9.3–19; 1 Cor. 9.1), he came to realize that Jesus is the long-awaited Jewish Messiah and that salvation is mediated through him—not through careful observance of the law of Moses, as most Jews thought. (This understanding, he later emphasized, did not originate in the mind of some human, but was revealed to him by Christ himself, Gal. 1.12, 15–17.) It is his understanding of Jesus—as Messiah, Son of God, Savior, and Lord—that sets Paul apart from his Jewish contemporaries. Everything else—his distinctive views of the law, salvation, and the Christian life—is shaped by this insight.

Christ as Savior of the Gentiles

As a result of his visionary experience of Jesus, Paul came to understand salvation as now available to all people, Gentiles as well as Jews, just as the prophets of the Hebrew Scriptures had predicted. Through Christ, Gentiles now have the same access to God as Jews (Rom. 2.29f.; Eph. 2.11–3.6). In the new family of Christ, where Jews and Gentiles are united as God's forgiven people in a single messianic community, ethnic distinctions are no longer significant. One's identity as a person of God is defined only by his or her relation to Christ (Col. 3.11). (This is part of the "mystery" of God's ways that is now revealed in Christ; Eph. 1.9f.; 3.3–6; cf. Rom. 16.25f.) Convinced that God had called him to proclaim this "good news"—the message of salvation through Christ—to the entire Gentile world (Gal. 1.15f.), Paul devoted the rest of his life to this mission.

Salvation through Christ, Not the Law of Moses

Because salvation is for all people, Christ spells the "end of the law" for Paul. No longer is the law of Moses to be understood as the way of salvation or the primary guide for life (Rom. 10.4), as it was in traditional Judaism. Salvation is received personally by faith—that is, by putting one's trust in Christ as Savior—quite apart from one's observance of the law. And a believer's life is now understood as directed and empowered by the Spirit of Christ who lives within, not by the hundreds of stipulations prescribed in the law of Moses (Rom. 7.4–6).

As a result, Paul no longer reads the Hebrew Scriptures in a traditional Jewish way; instead, he reads and interprets them Christologically. Many texts in the Hebrew Scriptures are understood as referring to Jesus and the message of salvation in him, or as fulfilled in Jesus (Rom. 10.6–9; 1 Cor. 10.1–4; Gal. 3.16; Eph. 4.9f.). The sacred writings as a whole are now understood as intended to teach readers about "salvation through faith in Christ Jesus" (2 Tim. 3.15).

For believers, then, the focus of life has shifted from the law of Moses to Christ as Savior (Gal. 2.19f.). Jesus himself is spoken of as believers' "wisdom," "righteousness," "sanctification," and "redemption"—categories traditionally linked with the Torah in Jewish thinking (1 Cor. 1.30; cf. 6.11; Col. 2.2f.). To be saved, people must come to be "in Christ," a status they receive when they put their faith in Christ to save them. (The phrase "in Christ" or "in the Lord," common in Paul's letters but nowhere else in the New Testament—though the parallel phrase "in him" occurs frequently in the Gospel of John and 1 John—generally refers to God's saving work through Christ or to the new life of believers as saved people, living in dependence on Christ. When Paul speaks of Jesus, he prefers to speak of him as "Lord" or as "Christ"—a Greek term meaning "anointed one," that is, Messiah.) Paul's desire is that young believers become well rooted, built up, and firmly established in Christ, with their whole life thoroughly centered on him (Col. 2.6f.).

Accordingly, "righteousness"—a right standing with God—is defined no longer by observance of the law of Moses, but by faith in Christ. (A minority of scholars, taking the Greek phrase *pistis tou Christou* literally, would say "by the faith *of* Christ," that is, the faith of Christ himself.) By assuming the burden of human sin, Christ has made it possible for those who trust in him to be granted the gift of righteousness (2 Cor. 5.21). This is what Paul calls the "righteousness of God," the "righteousness of faith"—the righteousness God attributes as a free gift to those who believe in Christ (Rom. 5.15–17). Trust in Christ as Savior is what now makes people right with God (Rom. 1.16f.; 3.21–26; Gal. 2.16). Christ has redeemed believers from the "curse" of the law (that is, from God's judgment on their disobedience) by assuming the curse for them, in order that believers may receive all the blessings God has promised to those who are forgiven (Gal. 3.13f.). As a result of the gift of righteousness, believers now have peace with God (Rom. 5.1) and are reconciled to God (Rom. 5.10f.; 2 Cor. 5.18–21; Col. 1.20–22; cf. 1 Tim. 2.5). As redeemed people they are assured their sins are forgiven (Rom. 4.6–8; Eph. 1.7; Col. 1.14). By God's grace they will be rescued from God's wrath on the final day of judgment and given eternal life (1 Thess. 1.10; Rom. 6.23; cf. the emphasis of the pastoral letters on Jesus as the one who "abolished death and brought life and immortality to light," 2 Tim. 1.10; Titus 1.1). By believing in Jesus they are made "children of God" (Gal. 4.4–7), hence brothers and sisters of Jesus, fellow "heirs" with him of God's eternal gifts (Rom. 8.14–17, 29). In Christ they are fully assured that God's love and blessing are upon them and that nothing can ever separate them from that love (Rom. 8.31–39); they are safe in his hand. Their life has been transferred to a different dimension; they now live as people with one foot already in heaven (Eph. 2.6).

But this is only possible because of the grace of God working in a person's heart. Thus, believers are spoken of as those "chosen" to be in Christ before the world was ever created, those "destined" by God to become his adopted children and to receive his salvation (Eph. 1.4f., 11; 1 Thess. 5.9; 2 Thess. 2.13; cf. 2 Tim. 1.9; 2.10; Titus 1.1). Believers are those to whom God himself has granted the privilege of believing in his Son (Phil. 1.29). Throughout Paul's letters lies an emphasis on God's sheer grace as the effective cause of believers' salvation.

Unbelieving Jews, on the other hand—Paul's own people—stand under the judgment of God because of their rejection of Christ, a fact that leaves

Paul in agony (Rom. 9.1–3). Unable to see beyond the demands of the law of Moses, they continue to pursue "their own" righteousness, not the righteousness God freely offers in his Son (Rom. 9.30–32; 10.1–4). They fail to understand that real "circumcision" (the traditional Jewish mark of being under God's covenant) is a matter of the heart and can only come about by accepting God's chosen Messiah (Rom. 2.29; Col. 2.11). But because they have historically been the people of God, Paul continues to try to persuade them of the truth of Christ wherever he goes, frequently emphasizing that the good news of Christ is directed "to the Jew first" (Rom. 1.16; cf. 2.9f.). And one day, when the full quota of Gentiles have come to Christ, Paul is convinced that the whole of Judaism ("all Israel") will be saved (Rom. 11.25f.)—presumably by turning to their long unrecognized Messiah—because God will be faithful to the promises he made to them long ago. But the traditional Jewish way of thinking about relating to God—by observing the law of Moses—he sees as fundamentally irreconcilable with the good news of Christ. Those who rely on their obedience to the law for their salvation therefore exclude themselves from the saving grace of Christ (Gal. 5.1–6).

Jesus as Lord

As a result of his dramatic encounter with the living Christ, Paul also understands Jesus to be the Lord—the Lord of his people, the Lord of the Church, the Lord of the universe. And it is those who confess Christ as the resurrected Lord who will be saved (Rom. 10.9f., 13; cf. 1 Cor. 12.3). But the confession of Jesus as Lord is more than an abstraction. It must be a personal confession of what is true in a believer's life. For as Lord, Jesus is the master of every individual believer (Eph. 6.9); hence Paul speaks of himself as a "slave" of Christ (Rom. 1.1). Everything a believer does or says, then, is to be done "to the Lord" (Rom. 14.7–9; Col. 3.17), "out of reverence for Christ" (Eph. 5.21). Even slaves are to do their work "to the Lord," not merely to their masters (Eph. 6.5–7; Col. 3.22–24). This is why, generally speaking, Paul considers the single life preferable to marriage—it frees a believer to live more wholly "to the Lord" (1 Cor. 7.32–35). As Lord, Jesus deserves the single-minded worship and devotion of all his followers; he has claimed them wholly for himself. And one day, "every knee"—of the living and dead alike—will bow before him and acknowledge that he is the Lord of the entire universe (Eph. 1.20f.; Phil. 2.9–11).

Since he shares the title of Lord with God, Jesus stands in intimate relationship to God himself and deserves the same reverence. As Lord and Son of God, there is a divine dimension to Jesus in Paul's understanding. Frequently he attributes functions to Jesus that are normally attributed to God. For example, all of his letters (except 1 Thess.) begin with an invocation of grace and peace "from God our Father and the Lord Jesus Christ" (e.g., Rom. 1.7)—or some variant—and most close with the common benediction, "The grace of our Lord Jesus Christ be with you" (Rom. 16.20, 24; 1 Cor. 16.23; 2 Cor. 13.13; Gal. 6.18; Phil. 4.23; 1 Thess. 5.28; 2 Thess. 3.18; Philem. 25; the Pastoral Epistles close more simply with "Grace be with [all of] you"). As an apostle, Paul speaks of himself as commissioned "through Jesus Christ and God the Father" (Gal. 1.1); he speaks of "the kingdom of Christ and of God"

(Eph. 5.5); and he refers to both Christ and God as the final judge (Rom. 14.10; 2 Cor. 5.10). The eschatological "day of the Lord" becomes "the day of Christ" (1 Cor. 1.8; 2 Cor. 1.14; Phil. 1.6, 10; 2.16). With God, Jesus existed before anything else; he is the one through whom and for whom the entire universe was created and by whom it is sustained (1 Cor. 8.6; Col. 1.15–17). His authority transcends that of all other spiritual powers (Col. 2.10, 15). Jesus shared in the nature of God before his coming to earth (Phil. 2.6f.), voluntarily gave up his privileged position to come and die for human sin (Phil. 2.7f.), and then, by his Resurrection, returned to his glorified position in the presence of God (Phil. 2.9–11; Col. 3.1). There he lives to intercede for his people, just as his Spirit does in their hearts (Rom. 8.26f., 34; cf. Heb. 7.25; 1 John 2.1f.). As the living embodiment of all that God is, Christ is preeminent in everything (Col. 1.18f.) and all-sufficient for salvation (Col. 2.9f.). All other religions and their human teachings are mere "shadows" of the ultimate divine reality, Christ (Col. 2.9f.). However, even with such an exalted status, Christ is to be understood as ultimately subordinate to God (1 Cor. 3.23; 11.3)—he is the *Son* of God (Rom. 1.4)—and in the end he will acknowledge his subjection to God (1 Cor. 15.24, 28).

Christ as Head of the Church

As Lord, Jesus is the only true foundation of the Church (1 Cor. 3.11); he is the "cornerstone" (Eph. 2.20). He is also considered the "head" of the Church, and the Church is correspondingly viewed as his "body" (Eph. 1.22f.; 5.23; Col. 1.18). Every member of the Church is thus considered part of Christ's body (Eph. 5.29f.), with work to do for him—the work of building up the rest of the body, using the individual gifts that Christ himself gives (1 Cor. 12.12–27; Eph. 4.7, 15f.). One of the reasons sexual immorality is denounced is that believers are to regard their bodies as "members of Christ" (1 Cor. 6.15–17) and therefore devoted to him. Thus, to sin against fellow believers is to sin against Christ (1 Cor. 8.12), the head of the body. As the body of Christ, the Church is to submit to its head in everything, and its calling is to be the manifestation of Christ in this world that is made by and for him (Eph. 1.22f.).

Using related imagery, Paul also speaks of the Church as the "bride" of Christ (cf. Rev. 21.2). It was Christ's sacrificial love for his bride that took him to the cross, to make the Church holy and pure before him (Eph. 5.25–27). And it is the same love that motivates his continued tender care and nurture of the Church (Eph. 5.29). In turn, the Church is to keep herself a "chaste virgin," pure in her devotion to Christ (2 Cor. 11.2f.). This sacrificial love of Christ for his bride, the Church, becomes the model of love to be shown by Christian husbands to their wives (Eph. 5.25–30).

Occasionally Paul draws a rather unusual comparison between Jesus and Adam, who serves as his prototype (Rom. 5.12–21; 1 Cor. 15.21–22, 45–49). Both are thought of as "founders of a new humanity," and the actions of both have long-lasting consequences for those who follow them—but the results are vastly different. Whereas Adam, "the first man," was human and earthly, Christ, "the second man," was the Son of God from heaven. And whereas the sin of Adam brought death and God's judgment on all who followed him,

Christ's free gift of righteousness brings forgiveness and eternal life to all who believe in him. And one day, just as believers have experienced a mortal, physical body like that of "the first man," so they will receive an immortal, spiritual body—a resurrection body—like that of "the second man." Christ reverses the tragic direction set for humankind by Adam and opens up a whole new existence that transcends sin and death—resurrection life—for those who embrace him.

The Life-Transforming Power of the Spirit of Christ

As Messiah, Jesus inaugurates the coming kingdom of God. He brings the eschatological power of the messianic age—the "age to come"—into the lives of those who receive him, by his Spirit (the Holy Spirit) within them. By the power of his Spirit, believers are freed from the enslaving power of the law (Gal. 5.18) and enabled to live a life that transcends the all-dominating power of sin in this age (Rom. 8.2–4; cf. Titus 3.5f.). Filled with his love, goodness, and peace, their lives increasingly come to reflect the glory of God himself (2 Cor. 3.18; Gal. 5.22f.; Phil. 2.11; Col. 3.15). The ultimate goal of the Spirit's work is for believers to be transformed into the likeness of Christ himself (Rom. 8.29; Col. 1.27). And collectively, by the power, guidance, and ministry of the Spirit, the whole Church is to become like Christ its "head," and thus like God himself (Eph. 4.13, 15). This process, too, is part of God's saving work through Christ. The Spirit, then, is the life-transforming power of the kingdom of God, and the coming of the Spirit marks the inauguration of the kingdom brought about by the death and Resurrection of Jesus—though its full expression awaits the future "day of the Lord." Apart from the experience of the Spirit, people have no share in Christ or the kingdom of God (Rom. 8.9), no power over sin, and no hope of eternal life.

Because God's ultimate goal for his people is that they become like Christ, believers are called to "put on the Lord Jesus Christ" (Rom. 13.14), to "clothe" themselves with "the new self" (Eph. 4.24) and the characteristics of Christ (Col. 3.12). They are actively to imitate Christ in how they live, just as Paul does (1 Cor. 11.1)—especially in the area of love. When Paul speaks of the imitation of Christ, his emphasis is almost always on the sacrificial love expressed in the death of Jesus, not on the love expressed in his earthly life. Believers are to have the same kind of sacrificial love for one another (Rom. 15.2f., 7; Eph. 4.32; 5.2; Phil. 2.3–8). This selfless, Christlike love is the primary characteristic of the Christian life—the single most important virtue for believers to seek (Col. 3.14). Without it, Christian witness and ministry accomplishes little (1 Cor. 12.31–13.13). Love is the primary ethical expression of Christian faith ("The only thing that counts is faith working through love," Gal. 5.6). For Paul—as for Jesus—the law of love is the most important of all the moral commandments in the Hebrew Scriptures (Rom. 13.8–10; cf. Mark 12.31); this principle is what he means by the "law of Christ" (Gal. 6.2). So it is not surprising that love occurs first in his list of character traits produced by the Spirit of Christ in a believer (Gal. 5.22f.; cf. Phil. 1.8). Sacrificial love, above all, is the mark of a life transformed by the Spirit, a Christ-like life.

The Presence of Christ in Believers

Though Paul usually speaks of the Spirit of God as the one who inhabits a believer's life, at times he speaks of Christ himself as living in the believer (Gal. 2.20; Col. 1.27; Eph. 3.17; 2 Cor. 13.5; cf. 1 Cor. 6.19f.). This is possible because the Spirit of God *is* the Spirit of Christ (the two vary freely in Paul's vocabulary), and Paul identifies Christ ("the Lord") himself with the Spirit (2 Cor. 3.17)—another indication of the divine nature of Jesus in his thinking. This is why Paul can speak of being in the pain of childbirth until "Christ" is formed in his young converts (Gal. 4.19).

Christ's presence in believers gives them not only power over sin but also power for ministry. Indeed, Paul understands Christian ministry—on the deepest level—not so much as the work believers do for Christ as the work Christ does through believers (Rom. 15.18f.; cf. 1 Cor. 15.10; 2 Cor. 10.4f.). So when Paul speaks as an apostle of Christ, he sometimes speaks of Christ communicating directly through him (2 Cor. 13.3; cf. 1 Cor. 5.3–5; 2 Thess. 3.6, 12; Philem. 8, where he claims to speak with the authority of Christ). The suffering he experiences as an apostle provides an opportunity for Christ to manifest his life and power through him (2 Cor. 4.10f.; 12.9f.). Paul's goal, in all his hard work among the churches, is to "present everyone mature in Christ"—but the inspiration and energy for his work comes from Christ himself, who lives within him (Col. 1.27ff.). "It is no longer I who live," Paul says, "but it is Christ who lives in me" (Gal. 2.20).

The Death and Resurrection of Christ

In Paul's thinking, then, the real significance of Jesus lies not so much in his unique life and teachings—to which he rarely refers explicitly (1 Cor. 7.10f.; 9.14; cf. 11.23–25)—as in his death and resurrection (Rom. 4.25; 1 Cor. 15.3f., 12–21). Here is the focal point of God's work in Jesus to bring about the salvation of the world—just as it is in the four Gospels, all of which culminate in the account of these two momentous events. But it is Paul, not the Gospel writers, who spells out most fully the significance of the cross and resurrection.

Jesus' death, interpreted in light of the suffering servant described in Isaiah 53 (as it commonly was among the early Christians), is understood as an atoning sacrifice for the sins of the world. "Christ died for our sins" (1 Cor. 15.3). Because Christ died for undeserving sinners (Eph. 2.1–5; cf. 1 Tim. 1.15), those who believe in him are reconciled with God and saved from the wrath of God's coming judgment that will fall on all unbelievers (Rom. 5.6–10). This is the heart of the "good news" Paul preaches—and he is convinced that the simple message of Christ's death has a power in itself to convert hearts. (Hence, he emphasizes that when he preaches the "good news" his reliance is not on his own ability to persuade people but on the power of the message itself, the message of the cross, 1 Cor. 1.17f., 23f.; 2.1–5.) And it is this love of Christ expressed in the cross that provides the deepest motivating power for Paul's ministry, for by that love, Paul knows himself to be wholly claimed by Christ for his service (2 Cor. 5.14f.). And by coming to know that immeasurable love, believers can now be filled with "all the fullness of God" (Eph. 3.18f.).

But the resurrection of Jesus is as significant as his death. The two are tied together in Paul's thinking as a single expression of God's great saving work; both are of central importance. The resurrection is an essential element of the Christian gospel. "If Christ has not been raised, your faith is futile and you are still in your sins" (1 Cor. 15.17). If the death of Jesus achieves atonement, the resurrection accomplishes several things: it validates the identity of Jesus as the divine Son of God (Rom. 1.4) and confirms the message of salvation through him; it proclaims the defeat of the final enemy, death (1 Cor. 15.25f., 54–57), and victory over all the powers of evil (Eph. 1.20–22; Col. 2.15); it guarantees that his people will one day also be resurrected and receive the eternal blessings he has promised them (1 Cor. 15.20f.; Eph. 1.13f.); and it opens the door to the experience of resurrection life for those who receive him (Rom. 6.4–13). Those who embrace Jesus and become joined to him receive his Spirit (the Holy Spirit) and thus begin to experience the eschatological power of the kingdom of God—resurrection existence—in their own lives, here and now (Rom. 8.9–11).

As symbolized in their baptism, when believers become joined to Christ, they enter into the experience of Jesus' death and resurrection and come to partake of the benefits of that death and resurrection. Holy Communion also symbolizes this participation in Christ's death (1 Cor. 10.16; cf. 11.27–30). Like him, they "die"—to sin and the "world"—and "rise"—to live a new life, a spiritual one focused on the "heavenly" realities, by the power of his resurrected life within them (Rom. 6.3–11; Gal. 5.24; 6.14; Col. 2.20; 3.1–4). Raised with Christ and given "the mind of Christ" (1 Cor. 2.16), they become new and different people (2 Cor. 5.17), with their minds set on "things that are above, not on things that are on earth" (Col. 3.1–4). Their eyes are fixed on the hope of Christ's return (1 Thess. 1.3, 10; cf. 2 Tim. 4.8; Titus 1.2). The resurrected Christ now defines their identity and focus. And one day, like him, they too will rise with a new and different kind of body—a spiritual body—in the final resurrection, to live and reign forever with him (Phil. 1.21; 1 Cor. 15.12–23, 42–57; cf. 6.2–3). In the meantime, because they have "died" with Christ, they may be called to suffer for him (cf. 2 Tim. 3.12)—and Paul considers that a "privilege" (Phil. 1.29).

Christ as the Motivation of Christian Living

For Paul, the Christian life is not motivated simply by a divine code or set of rules, as it was in much of Judaism. At its deepest level, the Christian life—just as Christian ministry—is a response to the grace that God has shown believers in the saving work of Christ. It is a response of gratitude—a way of saying "thank you"—for the mercy God has shown in sending Christ to die. This is why his view of the Christian life is often marked by an emphasis on "thanksgiving" and "joy" (Eph. 5.18–20; Phil. 3.1; 4.4–6; Col. 2.6f.; 3.15–17; 1 Thess. 5.16–18). Thus, Paul's practical instructions on Christian living are generally preceded by an emphasis on God's saving grace in Christ and often introduced by the word "therefore" (Rom. 12.1; Eph. 4.1; Col. 3.5). In other words, Christian ethics, in his understanding, are always based on Christian theology—the good news of God's forgiving grace. This is also why Paul's ethical instructions frequently appeal to the believers' status "in Christ" (on "in the Lord") for their motivation (Phil. 4.2; Col. 3.18, 20).

The Return of Christ

At the end of the age, Christ will return—for two purposes. He will gather to himself those who acknowledge him, and he will decree judgment on those who do not (2 Thess. 1.6–10; 2.8). Just as he is the Savior now, so he will be the final judge then. Paul calls Christians to live holy lives in anticipation of that day so that they will have nothing of which to be ashamed when he returns (1 Cor. 1.8; Phil. 1.10; 1 Thess. 3.13; 5.23). Paul himself fixes his focus clearly on that future day and lives in light of it (Phil. 3.13f.). He knows that his real "citizenship" lies in heaven, and he eagerly anticipates the return of Christ to take him there and transform him fully to the Savior's likeness (Phil. 3.20f.).

Claimed by Christ

As one who knows that he is wholly indebted to Christ for his salvation, and that his whole life is therefore claimed by the Savior, Paul's greatest desire is to bring honor to Christ—to live and die for Christ alone (Phil. 1.20f.). For the sake of Christ, he has given up everything else, and he considers it all of little value—"worthless"—compared with the importance of gaining Christ and the righteousness of Christ. As a convert whose whole life has been revolutionized by Christ, Paul's all-consuming desire is to experience—as deeply as he can—Christ and his Resurrection power in his own life, to share in the sufferings of Christ, which he views as "completing" the sufferings of Christ (Col. 1.24), and ultimately to die for his sake (Phil. 3.7–10). "It is my eager expectation and hope . . . that by my speaking with all boldness, Christ will be exalted now as always in my body, whether by life or by death. For to me, living is Christ and dying is gain" (Phil. 1.20f.). And according to early Christian tradition, because of his faithful proclamation of Christ, he was given his wish: after a life of suffering for Christ, he was killed in the persecution of Nero about A.D. 65.

Roger Mohrlang

See also: Church; Holy Spirit; Jesus, Death of; Jesus, Origins of; Kingdom of God; Messiah; Resurrection

References

Beker, J. Christiaan. 1980. *Paul the Apostle*. Philadelphia: Fortress.
Bornkamm, G. ET1971. *Paul*. London: Hodder and Stoughton.
Bruce, F. F. 1977. *Paul: Apostle of the Heart Set Free*. Grand Rapids, MI: William B. Eerdmans.
Bultmann, Rudolf. ET1955. *The Theology of Paul*. Vol. 2 of *Theology of the New Testament*. New York: Charles Scribner's Sons.
Cerfaux, L. ET1959. *Christ in the Theology of St. Paul*. New York: Herder.
Dunn, J. D. G. 1998. *The Theology of Paul the Apostle*. Edinburgh: T. & T. Clark.
Gager, John G. 2002. *Reinventing Paul*. Oxford: Oxford University Press.
Hooker, Morna D. 2003. *Paul: A Short Introduction*. Oxford: Oneworld.

Ladd, George E. 1974. *A Theology of the New Testament*. Grand Rapids, MI: William B. Eerdmans.
Martin, Ralph P. *Reconciliation: A Study of Paul's Theology*. Atlanta: John Knox Press.
Ridderbos, Herman. ET1975. *Paul: An Outline of His Theology*. Grand Rapids, MI: William B. Eerdmans.
Sanders, E. P. 1977. *Paul and Palestinian Judaism*. London: SCM.
———. 1991. *Paul*. Oxford: Oxford University Press.
Stewart, J. S. 1954. *A Man in Christ: The Vital Elements of St. Paul's Religion*. New York: Harper and Brothers.
Wenham, David. 1995. *Paul: Follower of Jesus or Founder of Christianity?* Grand Rapids, MI: William B. Eerdmans.
Whiteley, D. E. H. 1974. *The Theology of St. Paul*. Oxford: Basil Blackwell.
Ziesler, John. 1990. *Pauline Christianity*. Rev. ed. Oxford: Oxford University Press.

Pentecostalism

Pentecostalism is the word used to describe the movement amongst Christians who believe that Jesus is the one who baptizes in the Holy Spirit, usually in a second spiritual experience subsequent to conversion, the evidence of which is often that of speaking in other tongues. Various sets of statistics suggest a worldwide figure of around 500 million Pentecostals. Growth of the movement in the twentieth century was phenomenal. Lesslie Newbigin was among those who saw it as a major force in Christendom alongside Catholicism and Protestantism.

Pentecostals would claim that, historically, the experience goes back to the Day of Pentecost (see Act 2) but was largely forgotten by the Church until the twentieth century, except for its reappearance amongst the second-century Montanists and the nineteenth-century Irvingites. However, the nineteenth-century holiness movement, which has its roots in eighteenth-century Methodism, centered its theology in a second experience of the Holy Spirit subsequent to new birth, the nature of which was perfect love, or entire sanctification. Pentecostalism may be seen as a development of this teaching, especially in Pentecostal holiness churches such as the Church of God, which lays emphasis on a clean heart but regards speaking in tongues as initial evidence of baptism in the Spirit. In the twentieth century, the roots of Pentecostalism may be found in a number of revivals in the United States and Europe. Arising directly or indirectly from these came the founding of churches such as the Assemblies of God, the Apostolic Church, and the Elim Church. Generally, Charles Parham and William J. Seymour are regarded as the founding fathers of Pentecostalism because of their ministries in Topeka and Los Angeles. Other important figures in the initial decade of the twentieth century included Evan Roberts in Wales, Thomas Ball Baratt in Norway, and Alexander Boddy in England.

The term "classical Pentecostals" is used to describe this early group of churches; "neo-Pentecostals" refers to charismatics who emerged in the latter half of the twentieth century. The charismatic movement began when people within the historic churches of Christendom, both Catholic and Protestant, experienced what classical Pentecostals described as baptism in the Spirit. Although many remained within their own churches, some left to form what were at first called "house churches" but later became independent community churches, fellowships, or organizations, such as the Ichthus Christian Fellowship and Team Ministries, Harvestime Fellowship and Covenant Ministries International, Team Spirit, Pioneer Team, and Vineyard Fellowship and Ministries International. Early leaders of these new churches included Roger Forster (Ichthus), John Noble (Team Ministries), Bryn Jones (Harvestime), Gerald Coates (Pioneer Team), and John Wimber (Vineyard). In some instances, those staying in their own denominations did so because charismatic renewal took place in their local churches, which became neo-Pentecostal in practice. Roman Catholics, Anglicans, Baptists, Lutherans, and Methodists were involved in varying degrees. Early leaders in the historic churches included Kevin Ranaghan and Francis MacNutt (Roman Catholic), Dennis Bennett and Graham Pulkingham (Episcopalian), Michael Harper and David Watson (Anglican), Larry Christenson (Lutheran), Tommy Tyson and Charles Clarke (Methodist), and David Du Plessis (Pentecostal). In recent years, impetus has been given to neo-Pentecostalism by the Alpha courses, arising from the ministry of Nicky Gumbel at the Holy Trinity Church, Brompton (England). Para-Church organizations that serviced neo-Pentecostal renewal included the Fountain Trust (England), the Fort Lauderdale Holy Spirit Teaching Mission (Florida), the Full Gospel Businessmen's Fellowship International, and the Women's Aglow Fellowship International.

Baptism in the Spirit is central to Pentecostalism. Although Jesus is the one who baptizes Christians in the Holy Spirit, neo-Pentecostals would argue that this doctrine in no way undermines the statement of the Nicene Creed that the Holy Spirit "proceeds from the Father and the Son." On the question of the nature of Christ, all Pentecostals accept the orthodox belief that Jesus is both human and divine; the Elim Churches, as part of their declaration of faith, state also that Jesus is savior, healer, baptizer, and coming king. Pentecostals are Trinitarians, although the Jesus Only communities in the United States and the Caribbean, which broke away from the Assemblies of God, do not use the Trinitarian formula in baptism but baptize only in the name of Jesus, their motive being that of avoiding tritheism. Most classical Pentecostals expect speaking in tongues to accompany baptism in the Spirit, but this is not so with neo-Pentecostals, who believe that other gifts and fruit of the Spirit may be accompanying evidence of the baptism without necessarily speaking in tongues. Classical Pentecostals were very definite in their doctrine of two crisis experiences, at new birth and baptism in the Spirit, but some neo-Pentecostals have interpreted baptism in the spirit in the light of their own Church doctrines. For example, charismatic Roman Catholics believe baptism in the spirit to be a working out in experience of their regeneration at water baptism; for evangelical Protestants, baptism in the Spirit is a fuller development of what happened at their new birth or conversion. Classical and neo-Pentecostals have different teachings about ordained ministry, but both would affirm that fruit and gifts of the Spirit are to enable the whole Church to be the body of Christ. Fruit of the Spirit such as love, joy, peace, patience, kindness, goodness, faithfulness, gentleness, and self control (Gal. 5.22) are to enable the believer to be more Christ-like in living. Gifts of the Spirit such as serving, teaching, encouraging, giving, leading, governing (Rom. 12.6–8), wisdom, knowledge, healings, miracles, prophecy, discernment, tongues, and interpretation (1 Cor. 12.8–10) are meant to build up the Church and continue the ministry of Christ in the world in the power of his Spirit. Because not all are gifted in the same way, each member complements the others. Using spiritual gifts is described as body ministry in which all members have a share alongside traditional ordained ministries.

Within the context of Pentecostal worship, spiritual gifts are used to build up believers and minister to personal needs. Such worship is exuberant and not dependent upon any written liturgy but may operate within a liturgical order, for example, at the time given for intercessions. Ideally, it follows the pattern of free worship described in 1 Corinthians 14.26–33. Singing, clapping, arm raising, and dancing are ways in which worshipers express themselves. Neo-Pentecostalism has been marked by a plethora of new hymns and songs that are now used also by classical Pentecostals, who traditionally used the *Redemption Hymnal* (1951, London: Elim Publishing House). Many of the new songs are found in publications such as *Complete Mission Praise* (1999, London: Marshall Pickering) and *Songs of Fellowship* (1998, Eastbourne: Kingsway Music). As dreams, visions, and prophecies are recounted and as tongues are spoken and interpreted, God speaks to his people as he does through the biblical expositions. There is often a time of ministry when prayers are offered for worshipers to receive the Spirit or to be healed. Ironically, in many neo-Pentecostal churches, what began as free worship has become structured into a threefold order: a time of praise, a time of preaching, and a time of ministry. In the 1990s, the Toronto Blessing (so called because of the worldwide attention that was drawn to it in the Airport Vineyard Fellowship in Toronto, Canada) was experienced amongst some Pentecostal groups, though it was greeted by others with suspicion. It included phenomena such as laughter, falling (resting in the Spirit), weeping, and crying out in various ways as the Spirit touched people. Within the Pentecostal scene there is a wide range of activities in worship. The expected result of worship is that Jesus has been glorified and believers have been blessed and built up to be the body of Christ in order to serve God in both the Church and the world.

With regard to serving in the world, W. J. Hollenweger and Jean-Jacques Suurmond have given evidence of Pentecostals being involved in the struggle against unjust policies and social structures, not least in Latin America, Asia, and Africa as well as parts of Europe. They attribute the success of Pentecostalism amongst different nationalities to its capacity for acculturation so that people can become Christians without having to abandon their own cultural identity. Issues such as opposition to sexism, racism, poverty, misery, and dictatorships have all figured on this Pentecostal agenda, although more with black than white Pentecostalism. There has been an increasing awareness of the social responsibilities of Christians amongst most

Pentecostals. The needs of the poor and a concern for social righteousness in the nation as well as the quest for personal holiness of life have been expressed in some of the more recently published renewal songs and in the teaching ministry.

There have been different ways of viewing Pentecostalism. Some have seen it as a reaction against the liberal biblical scholarship of the nineteenth and twentieth centuries, although not all Pentecostals are biblical literalists or fundamentalists. Others have pointed to a lack of the transcendental and miraculous within the worship of traditional churches to explain why many have sought and found this experience amongst the Pentecostals. More recently, there have been, on the one hand, those who have found Pentecostalism to be a reaction against a postmodernist culture, and yet others who have thought that an emphasis on the freedom of the Spirit in certain ways reflected it. Pentecostals themselves would see it as God renewing his people, restoring all the spiritual gifts found in the early Church, and enabling the Church to be the body of Jesus in the world.

William R. Davies

See also: African Christianity; American (North) Christianity; American (South) Christianity; Creeds; Holy Spirit; Hymns; Welsh Christianity

References

Bruner, F. D. 1970. *A Theology of the Holy Spirit: The Pentecostal Experience and the New Testament Witness*. Grand Rapids, MI: William B. Eerdmans.

Dunn, J. D. G. 1970. *Baptism in the Holy Spirit: A Re-examination of the New Testament Teaching on the Gift of the Spirit in Relation to Pentecostalism*. London: SCM.

Hocken, Peter. 1997. *Streams of Renewal: Origins and Early Development of the Charismatic Movement in Great Britain*. Exeter: Paternoster.

Hollenweger, Walter J. 1972. *The Pentecostals*. London: SCM.

Newbigin, L. 1953. *The Household of God: Lectures on the Nature of the Church*. London: SCM; New York: Friendship.

Suurmond, Jean-Jacques. 1994. *Word and Spirit at Play: Towards a Charismatic Theology*. London: SCM.

Walker, Andrew. 1985. *Restoring the Kingdom: The Radical Christianity of the House Church Movement*. London: Hodder and Stoughton.

Pilgrimage

Although the scallop shell has now become almost synonymous with pilgrimage, and more specifically, pilgrimage within the Christian tradition, the motivation to travel great distances for religious purposes predates the events surrounding Jesus by many centuries. Hinduism, arguably the most ancient of all the major world faiths, has had a continuing pilgrimage tradition that has been more central to its life than regular worship patterns like those to which Christians have been devoted. The focal part played by the oracle at Delphi in the life of the Ancient Greeks is another example of the practice of pilgrimage in antiquity. At the heart of pilgrimage has been the practice of journeying for religious reasons either in a foreign land or to a place outside one's home area and realm of everyday experience. Contemporary anthropologists would describe it as a "threshold experience" and as such would include the journeys necessitated in Judaism by the centralized cult following the Deuteronomic reforms.

The distinguishing mark of Christian pilgrimage is its Christocentric character. Even where the focus was upon the shrine of a saint, echoes of the life of Jesus were often central. So, for example, the cult of Thomas Becket from the later twelfth century onward related particularly to the saint's martyrdom and to resonances with the death of Jesus. Conflict with worldly power and the vested interests of the state were seen as common ground with the struggles of Christ, despite the ambiguities in Becket's life and his own manner of exercising power.

As historians of late antiquity have indicated, Christianity grew slowly and unevenly within the Roman Empire. Nevertheless, Christians had taken to pilgrimage early in their history and, notably, visited sites relating to Jesus and his ministry. Even early in the second century, a site referred to as "the cave of the nativity" was being visited in the Holy Land. Origen's commentaries manifest a detailed interest in the history of the Holy Land, including a journey in which he checked out the village where John had baptized Jesus. The only fact known about Melito of Sardis (died c. 190) is that he traveled to the holy places in Palestine (see his *Homily on the Passion*, ed. S. G. Hall).

Pilgrimage helped the early Christians to pinpoint places and events in the Gospels. The shift in fortunes of the Christian religion in the fourth century, marked particularly by the Emperor Constantine's conversion to Christian faith, meant an increase in those making pilgrimage to the places associated with Jesus. The legend of the discovery or "invention" of the true cross by St. Helena, the mother of Constantine, did much to institutionalize pilgrimage to the Holy Land. This legendary event was chronicled as happening in 326 during a visit to Palestine in which Helena founded basilicas both on the Mount of Olives and at Bethlehem. The first church on the site of the Holy Sepulchre also dates from the time of Constantine, being dedicated in 335. Despite the historical uncertainty of the events surrounding the so-called discovery of the true cross, there is clear evidence of patterns of pilgrimage relating to the sites associated with Jesus in the Gospels.

Historical evidence confirms that in the early Christian centuries pilgrims were traveling to the Holy Land to walk the Via Dolorosa, the path assumed to have been taken by Jesus on his way to the cross. The narrative of the devout woman, Egeria, probably a nun from Gaul, traveling throughout Asia Minor and the Middle East, describes a pilgrimage probably between the years 381 and 384. This pattern of pilgrimage to Palestine, exemplified classically in Egeria's travels, continued and became more popular during the later Middle Ages and focused on the sites related to the life of Jesus as recounted in the Gospel narratives. It has even been suggested (cf. Trocmé) that the Gospel narrative of the Passion was itself formed by such visiting of the sites. A minor English mystic of the late fourteenth and early fifteenth centuries, Margery Kempe, described journeys to the Holy Land, as well as other pilgrimages to Assisi, Rome, and Compostela, in her book.

In the Western Church, the practice of pilgrimage developed within two broad and differing patterns relating to the Irish-Celtic and Roman traditions. Both contrasting patterns related in different ways to the life and ministry of Jesus. The Irish-Celtic motivation for pilgrimage was for pilgrims to proclaim Christ as missionaries in a foreign land. St. Columba was thus a pilgrim for the gospel in his mission to the Pictish peoples. In the Roman pattern, pilgrimage was generally centered on the shrine of a local saint. Here pilgrimage mirrored the path of those who journeyed to the sites mentioned in the Gospels. In Jerusalem (as indeed elsewhere), the relics of the true cross were the focus; in Durham the incorrupt remains of Cuthbert; at Hailes in Gloucestershire a vial of the holy blood; and at Walsingham the site of a vision of Mary, the mother of Jesus. The relics were believed to convey the grace obtained for humankind in the Passion and death of Jesus. In that context, the typically medieval (in origin) Jesus-centered cult of the shroud of Turin has attracted great attention in recent years.

In the present day, the practice of pilgrimage has again become popular. The pilgrimage is sometimes used as a metaphor for the whole of human life—a pilgrimage from birth to death. There is also an anthropological rationale for pilgrimage, inasmuch as pilgrimage is seen as a "rite of passage," a liminal experience. This term implies the crossing of a threshold into a strange land or strange territory by means of the journey. The effect of experiencing "difference" is to change the religious consciousness of the pilgrim; through this liminal or threshold experience, the pilgrim returns home transformed. Christian interpretations frequently link this transformation with existential reflection upon the life, teaching, and Passion of Jesus.

Stephen Platten

See also: English Christianity, Medieval; Holy Sepulchre; Jesus, Death of; Roman Catholicism

References

Brown, Peter. 1981. *The Cult of the Saints*. London: SCM.

Davies, J. G. 1988. *Pilgrimage: Yesterday and Today—Why? Where? How?* London: SCM.

Hall, S. G., ed. 1979. *Melito of Sardis: On Pascha*. Oxford: Clarendon.

Hunt, E. D. 1982. *Holy Land Pilgrimage in the Later Roman Empire, A.D. 312–460*. Oxford: Oxford University Press.

Lane-Fox, Robin. 1986. *Pagans and Christians*. London: Penguin.

Platten, Stephen. 1996. *Pilgrims*. London: Fount.

Trocmé, Etienne. 1983. *The Passion as Liturgy: A Study in the Origin of the Passion Narratives in the Four Gospels*. London: SCM.

Turner, Victor, and Turner, Edith L. B. 1995. *Image and Pilgrimage in Christian Culture*. New York: Columbia University Press.

Wilkinson, John, trans. 1981. *Egeria's Travels to the Holy Land*. Jerusalem: Ariel; Warminster, England: Aris & Phillips.

Political Issues

See Ethics, Modern; War; Wealth; Work

Pontius Pilate

See Jesus in Social Context

Power

This brief article can do no more than indicate some of the complexities and contradictions that link the figure of Jesus to the subject of "power." We inhabit a world where the more power is a huge and technologically effective reality, the more it often seems morally repugnant and, at both theoretical and devotional levels, hard to associate unequivocally with God. At the very least, it invites careful unpacking.

The NT, however, came from a context where to associate Jesus with power (Greek *dunamis*) was no problem at all, just as the very word could be a synonym for God himself (Mark 14.62). As an attribute of Jesus, it was a wholly positive word, describing his strength and authority both in his lifetime and ultimately in God's final purpose: he preaches the kingdom of God now and will return "in power" in the day of its consummation (Mark 13.26). Commonly, the abstract noun is made concrete—for "acts of power" that Jesus performs (e.g., Matt. 11.21; 13.54; Mark 6.2), as do his disciples as his emissaries (Matt. 7.28) and John the Baptist (Matt. 14.2). The devils who invade humans and dominate so much of the world are seen as evil "powers," so that the world is a battleground where "power" is the prize (Matt. 13.25; Rom. 8.38). Those who recoil from struggle and violence should not, it seems, look for support to the case of Jesus or early reflections on him (Acts 2.22; 4.7; 10.38).

But there is a crucial qualification to be made to this account. In his Passion and death, Jesus was involved in a wholly "non-power" situation; though presumably it might be seen as simply an incident on a journey, morally striking and in itself tragic, the cross seems plainly a "powerless" episode where God is concerned. Yet already in Paul, the first Christian thinker and writer, it is presented quite differently, as part of the key to the whole Jesus story—indeed to his power. The simplistic association of Jesus with power is then in trouble. The key statement sees "power made perfect in weakness" (2 Cor. 12.9). And the summary statement of faith in Phil. 2.5–11 sets Jesus' death as the purpose of his coming, en route to his exaltation to heavenly glory. Paul is conversant with the ambiguity of power: normatively because of Jesus, but also in his apostolic experience. Power, that is, naked power, of whatever kind, has for him no place in the Christian understanding of things. Not that Paul denies it to God (e.g., 2 Cor. 4.7; 6.7), or indeed to Jesus' mission as a whole (Rom. 1.4; Phil. 3.10), but he puts it in a context of qualification, which has the effect of altering the shape of the whole.

Though of course no mainstream Christian thinkers, much less Christian believers, have formally "disempowered" the death of Jesus, there is little doubt that the classical formulation of Christian doctrine in the early centuries gave pride of place to him as a figure of divine power: he was God in human form, but divine without interruption or diminution, with "power" unmitigated, though restrained and assaulted. Jesus was preeminently regal, and in many liturgical and artistic contexts, so he has remained—despite all the crucifixes and nativity scenes of subsequent times that show a vulnerable Jesus. Where the two contrasting images meet, it is often in a spirit of wonder or of paradox.

As a number of articles in this book make plain, the medieval period introduced a note that was not formally at variance with what went before but still culturally and devotionally quite different. Jesus as a gentle, "sweet" lover or friend, pitiable in weakness or suffering, was a figure evincing anything but power in a straightforward sense. It was precisely the weakness and simplicity of the all-powerful savior that was the source of his attractiveness, practical efficacy—and paradoxical "power." With ups and downs, perhaps more in Catholicism than in at least the more manly kinds of Protestantism, this style of Christianity has persisted, though more in devotion than in theology. But as far as power is concerned, the paradox has remained unresolved: is God "really" omnipotent or not? Only in recent times the theme of divine weakness has, in an amended form, chimed in with at least two pressures in Christian thinking itself. Experiences such as the Holocaust in the 1930s and 1940s have put under pressure as, it seems, never before, belief in the power of God to defeat evil. Perhaps, believers have concluded, God's power was simply a beautiful idea that has been made incredible by experience. If he exists, he is certainly not endowed with "power" for good in any intelligible or effective sense. He is a God of weakness; or at any rate he gives his creatures the longest possible leash at the end of which we are free to do our worst as well as our best. Of such a God, the Jesus of the Passion is the best possible human icon, and the Jesus of the resurrection is a figure of dreams.

Christian feminism, and other kinds of "liberation" thinking (black, gay, etc.), are also moved to deny that "power" in any conventional form is an attribute of God—or else, as metaphor, it is not of primary value. Power is a male attribute, and its long reign as a key image for God is an outcome of male dominance in Christian (as in other) affairs. Power implies control and submission, both of them strong features of traditional Christianity and church structures. If God is not to be seen as male, the dynamic changes. It is not clear, however, that the more feminine attributes of God amount to the drastic passivity referred to above. But this line of reflection may join hands with the "servant Jesus" of earlier times, though eschewing the sentimental tendencies sometimes associated with him. In Christian thought and living, it seems at the least that power as an attribute of Jesus needs rescuing from both denial and simplistic assertion.

Leslie Houlden

See also: Alexandrian Theology; Feminist Theology; Great War; Jesus as Emperor; Jesus as Servant; Kenoticism; Kingdom of God; Liberation Theology

References

Caird, G. B. 1956. *Principalities and Powers*. Oxford: Oxford University Press.

Carr, Wesley. 1983. *Angels and Principalities*. Cambridge: Cambridge University Press.

Coakley, Sarah. 2002. *Powers and Submissions*. Oxford: Blackwell.

Prayer

This article is concerned not with prayer relating to Jesus in the wide or general sense but with what may be said about Jesus of Nazareth's practice and example in this matter.

All the Gospels in their different ways refer to Jesus engaging in prayer or give examples of him praying, and some tell of his teaching on prayer. There is, of course, nothing in the least surprising about this; indeed, it would be astonishing if this subject were absent from the stories of his life. Jesus' proclamation of the kingdom of God, and his acts that embody or express God's rule, are grounded in his relationship with God, expressed in converse with him. In any case, he was reared in a Jewish context where forms of prayer were normal parts of personal, family, and communal life—daily, at Sabbath, and on holy days and in relation to life's occasions of crisis, including death. One such bedrock form of prayer, the Shema (from Deut. 6.4–5), appears at Mark 12.29–30, though in the context not of prayer but of a question about the "first commandment of all" (indeed punctilious Matthew, at 22.37, "edits" the quotation to conform more specifically to that question).

We now trace what the Gospels have to say about Jesus' praying and his teaching of prayer; and it seems that the evangelists' own input into the treatment of the matter is not insignificant, though there is room for disagreement on how far it goes and where we should identify it. That contribution indicates the importance of the subject in the churches for which they were writing: Christians would look to Jesus for guidance in their own praying. It is as if the evangelists' various publics had said, "We wish to pray as Christians: how did Jesus pray and how would he have us pray?"

That is commonsensical generality. When we turn to specific evidence, first in the Gospel of Mark, as the earliest, there can be some disappointment. It would be hard to say that Mark felt much of a need to face these questions head-on. As if it were an obvious thing to say, however, he does twice speak of Jesus praying: at 1.35, in the wilderness, and at 6.46, on the mountain, both traditionally numinous places. With regard to the former, we recall the "temptation," or, better, "testing" of 1.13–14, where prayer is implicit. That episode itself looks ahead to the climactic test of the cross, faced in prayer in Gethsemane (14.32–42), where Jesus, perhaps unusually, is said explicitly to kneel rather than standing, as was more customary. Also, there is in Mark brief teaching on praying: there is assurance of positive outcomes for prayer (11.24), and, in the next verse, instruction to forgive people when standing before God, in order to be eligible for divine forgiveness for oneself. At 9.29, we learn that exorcism, to succeed, requires prayer, presumably for enlisting the power of God against that of the devil. And at 11.17, the temple is called by Jesus "a house of prayer" (quoting Isa. 56.7), animal sacrifice being seen as a vital form of prayer. Less important, when the end is near, we are to pray that it may not occur in winter, which reads like an almost maternally fussy piece of prudence. Finally, there is Jesus' enigmatic and horrifying final prayer on the cross, "My God, my God, why hast thou forsaken me?" (15.34, quoting Ps. 22.1), left wholly without comment by Mark, yet surely the extreme moment of the evangelist's persistent starkness and his refusal of reassuring solutions. It takes the prayer of Gethsemane to an even more drastic conclusion.

Matthew reproduces, with adjustments, most of these passages, but adds his own. These take mostly a didactic direction, though sometimes there is what we might see as the adding of a touch of piety, as at 19.13: where Mark said that Jesus was asked to touch young children brought to him (10.13), Matthew adds "and pray." Possibly (but far from certainly), the passage reflects and authorizes the conduct of the baptism of children in a setting of prayer. But much more illustrative of Matthew's concerns is the teaching that he gives, first at 5.44 on prayer for one's persecutors, the concomitant of loving one's enemies; we may suppose that prayer for one's friends and neighbors is taken for granted. More crucially, in 6.5–13, we have extensive instruction on prayer, alongside that on the other two pious duties of Judaism, fasting and almsgiving. Here, convention is adjusted in the direction of simplicity and single-mindedness: one must not pray with an eye on fostering a reputation for devoutness. As throughout Matthew, the intended audience was Jewish Christians, who are bidden to a trimmed-down and purified practice of religion: no long-windedness, no public parade. In this interest, a normative form of prayer is provided (the Lord's Prayer), to be discussed below.

Luke, however, is the evangelist who extends himself to depict Jesus as a man of prayer, and so, surely, an example to his followers who read the book. Though he can actually drop one Marcan reference to Jesus praying (4.42; cf. Mark 1.35), Luke commonly adds a reference to Jesus praying in passages, mostly particularly significant ones, taken over from Mark: at the baptism (3.21), after the healing of a leper (5.16), at the call of the disciples (6.12), at Caesarea Philippi (9.18), and at the transfiguration (9.28). Moreover, on the cross, Jesus indeed prays, but along lines very different from those in Mark: for the forgiveness of his torturers (23.34). It is wholly appropriate that in Acts Jesus' followers also pray, often at important junctures in the development of the mission, especially at the authorization of new groups or new leaders (1.14, 24; 2.42; 6.6; 7.59–60; 8.15; 9.11; 10.9; 13.3; 14.23; 20.36). Oddly, there is no reference to praying at the crucial meeting in Jerusalem described in chapter 15.

It is time to turn to the Lord's Prayer, whose context in Matthew has already been described. In Luke (11.1–4), that context is different: Jesus himself is praying and his disciples ask him to teach them to pray. The teaching is therefore more immediately personal and directed to followers—and the prayer itself meant to be more imitative: Jesus gives the model of prayer (as, says Luke, without elaborating, John the Baptist had also done for his followers). Thus we have two versions of the prayer, Luke's being shorter and, it may seem, trimmed down. The truth, however, may be more complex, and there is no agreement on its terms. It depends on one's general view of the way in which Matthew and Luke went about their work, following from Mark. If their shared, non-Marcan material (including this passage) came from a common source (labeled, for convenience in scholarship, Q), then discussion arises whether Matthew or Luke has stuck more closely to the Q version. The common view is that Luke's briefer version is more original, with Matthew having added a number of words and phrases, mostly, as it happens, typical of his writing. If, instead, Luke made use of Matthew as well as Mark, it follows that Luke has, in this passage, simplified Matthew's version of the prayer. It has even been suggested, more radically yet not without sense, that Matthew himself did not inherit the prayer (from tradition, going back, it may be supposed, to Jesus himself) but derived it from passages in Mark (sparse as they may seem) that speak of or point to Jesus' prayer. Thus, the first clauses easily typify Jesus' preaching of the kingdom: of course, then, we must pray for its coming. The doing of God's will and even the receiving of his bread (the latter a metaphor, with associations of manna in the wilderness and then of the Eucharist, rather than a matter of bodily need) follows the same theme in different forms. The prayer for forgiveness derives from Mark 11.25, which, in its place, Matthew omits (as if to say, "Already used in chapter 6"), and where Mark himself had been speaking of prayer in v. 24. (A symptom of Luke's alleged dependence on Matthew is a slip he then made: changing "debts" to "sins," but then forgetfully retaining Matthew's "debtors.") The last, eschatological clauses would then depend on the general perspective of Mark, but more closely on the Gethsemane prayer—the example of Jesus at his hour of crisis: Christians must adopt it for their everyday use. Luke then dropped the "testing" note but retained the prayer for release from evil (or the Evil One). Which way of reading the prayer is correct must be left here, but there is much to be said for the general view that the prayer represents Jesus' praying and Jesus' teaching in the context of the Gospels and the needs that they were written to meet. On any showing it was a prayer that conveys the crisis nature of Jesus' ministry and mission: the end is not long to be delayed, and here are the rudiments of a Christian's disposition toward God, the prime object of love (Mark 12.30).

In John's Gospel, chapter 17, the extended prayer of Jesus at the supper before the trial and death has been seen as itself a kind of extended meditation, in Johannine idiom, on the Lord's Prayer, which, it would then seem, the evangelist knew in one of its forms. (The prayer may also have helped to shape the discourse on Jesus as the bread of life in John 6.) In this case, words as well as ethos have been "Johannized" (as Luke may have "Lucanized" Matthew, or Matthew may have correspondingly done with Luke or Q)—for example, "hallow" has become "glorify." Certainly John shares the prayer's insistence on the believers' union in life and purpose with Jesus, as seen in the Gospels, and there is the same narrow concentration on essentials, and implicitly on the believers' sharing in the "prayer" of Jesus. That prayer is itself a way of referring to his utter union with the Father, now enfolding his own followers. Indeed, chapter 17 can even be read as bringing about that which it describes, as a kind of verbal enactment of the mission of Jesus, Son and Word, that will be achieved in deed at his death (19.30).

At Acts 7.59–60, 1 Corinthians 16.22 and Revelation 22.20, we see evidence of a development that would not be clear from the Gospels: that is, Christians praying to Jesus. To what extent this implies his being regarded as divine is open to discussion. It raises the relevant question of how much is implied by the "worshiping" of Jesus that is found a number of times in Matthew (the magi, 2.11, and the disciples, 14.33; 28.17). The word can signify any kind of reverencing (literally, "bending the knee"), and Matthew can use it without any hint of theological connotations (18.26). People hoping for healing are said to act thus before Jesus (8.2; 9.18; 15.25); so does the mother of James and John, seeking a favor (20.20). It is highly unlikely that Matthew has considered the theological implications of using the word: it expresses simply his sense of Jesus as messianic king, sent by God and now at his right hand, and as future judge (25.31–46) on God's behalf, with the aid of his chief followers (19.28). Of course Jesus is approached with reverence. Later questions and distinctions have simply not arisen, and Matthew's Jewish monotheism is not in question. In any case, we go here beyond the strict bounds of "prayer." What is plain is that, like any object of devotion, Jesus was soon seen as one to whom one could pray as the known mediator with God and whose power and status had, by his resurrection, been shown to be of the greatest. Hebrews (7.25; cf. Rom. 8.34) takes Jesus' praying, for us, into Heaven itself—it is his role. What lies ahead is development in formal, conceptual theology, as also in liturgy, where, with conservatism, typical Christian prayer came to be offered to God "through Jesus Christ our Lord," as it generally remains until this day—though of course Christians readily pray to Jesus himself both formally and informally.

Leslie Houlden

See also: Hebrews, Letter to the; John, Gospel of; Liturgy; Luke, Gospel of, and Acts of the Apostles; Matthew, Gospel of; Spirituality

References

Evans, C. F. 1987 [1963]. *The Lord's Prayer*. London: SCM.
Houlden, J. L. 1992. "The Lord's Prayer." Pp. 356–362 in *Anchor Bible Dictionary*. Vol. 4. New York and London: Doubleday.
Jeremias, J. 1978. *The Prayers of Jesus*. Philadelphia: Fortress.

Preexistence

A number of the historical articles in this book refer to the context of Jesus' life and of early beliefs about him within the Judaism of his time. That religious culture, diverse as it was, has to be understood (even reckoned with) if we are to get on terms with aspects of what was said and thought that are now foreign to our own ways of looking at the world. This rule applies most obviously to the area of eschatology and apocalyptic imagery and to the ways old Scriptures were then interpreted.

It applies also (and perhaps even more strangely) to matters concerned with the origins of Jesus. In Judaism, one of the ways of expressing a sense of the importance in God's scheme of things of various entities such as the Law, the design of the temple, or the identity of the Messiah was to see them as having existed "from the beginning," in the mind and context of God, before ever they had any earthly manifestation. In part, this mythological belief was a way of asserting and safeguarding the permanence, from all eternity and forever, of these key elements in the thought, life, and activity of God, especially in relation to his people. If they were really vital, how could it be otherwise? Scriptural texts lent ancient support to this belief; for example, at

Exodus 25.40, where Moses is being instructed in the design and furnishing of the tabernacle, which is seen as the ancestor of the Jerusalem temple, he is told that he must "make them after the pattern for them, which is being shown you on the mountain"—that is, in a revelation of what already exists in heaven. It is as if heaven lies just beyond a screen, which can, on occasion, be removed, so that chosen persons can see what lies within, and has always done so. The vision of Isaiah at his call (6.1–8) comes into this category, as does Jacob's vision of the ladder up to heaven thronged with angels who bridge the gap with earth (Gen. 28.10–17).

These ideas had been developed by the time of Jesus, together with the somewhat more philosophical sense of qualities within God, expressed outwardly toward the world and often personified, that had been his from all eternity, notably, his "word" (God "spoke" in the act of creating the world, Gen. 1; and see Ps. 33.6; Isa. 55.10f.) and his "wisdom" (Prov. 8.22–31; Wisd. of Sol. 9.1; 18.15; Eccles. 24). In these ways, the ideas were conveyed of, on the one hand, God's sovereign power to act, and, on the other hand, the rationality and orderliness of his activity—the world, and God's work toward it, is not a chaos, does not proceed "anyhow," never has and never will. We may, not unfairly, see this as a kind of poetic theology, though that would not do justice to the (as it seems) literalism with which it has often been treated as factually descriptive.

It is then not surprising that Christians, seeing in Jesus the key working out of God's purposes and the fulfillment of earlier foreshadowings, applied these ideas to him, especially those described in the previous paragraph. The article on "Jesus, Origins of" describes some of their main appearances: in Paul (e.g., 1 Cor. 8.6), in Hebrews (1.3), and, above all, in the Gospel of John (especially 1.1–18).

In subsequent Christian thought, this belief in Jesus' "preexistence" became entrenched and indeed seen as vital to orthodoxy. If Jesus were truly identified with God, then this must be true from all eternity, and so he existed from "the beginning." The article on "Nicea" shows how this point became a matter of keen discussion and controversy in the fourth century, and the Nicene Creed's central clause on Christ demonstrates how sensitive a matter it was and how vital it was for those Christians to state true belief carefully and clearly. Indeed, it is not much of an exaggeration to say that, in that period above all, more attention was paid to the "period" of Jesus' preexistence than to his lifetime on earth, which a naive person might think his more important aspect, all that we could and, even needed to, know about. So, enshrined in the creed, and fought over and therefore embedded in orthodox Christian consciousness, the belief in Jesus' existence, coequal with the Father, from all eternity has remained central to formal Christian belief. At its root in Christian documents is the prologue of the Gospel of John, where the Word (identified with Jesus—originally what we might see as a striking image, but soon turned into concrete "fact") is God's agent in the whole work of creation. High above a doorway at Chartres Cathedral in France is a carving of what the ordinary observer might suppose to be Jesus healing a young man, perhaps raising from death the son of the widow of Nain in Luke 7. It is clear from the carvings close

A carving at Chartres Cathedral, Chartres, France, depicts God creating Adam; Father and Son (Word) are one, and the formal doctrine finds itself expressed, with a natural human realism, through the aesthetic medium of sculpture. (Photo courtesy of Leslie Houlden)

by in the sequence that it is in fact a depiction of God creating Adam. Father and Son (Word) are one, and the formal doctrine finds itself expressed in the beauty of sculpture, with a natural human realism.

In more recent times, there has been much dispute over the status of the language and thought-forms used in the formal theological formulas. Some have discarded them wholly as false, or at any rate as not necessary to credible Christian statement and belief. Partly, the NT has come to be read more closely and imaginatively in the light of its own times and people have come to relativize old ways of perceiving, including the philosophical context in which these concepts were originally formulated. For others, with perhaps a more diagrammatic (as one might put it) sense of theological truth, the old doctrines remain important as the best or only way to safeguard vital truths about God—and, more immediately, about the person of Jesus, who was no simple human out to do good or to stand (and die) for certain causes but the plainest and fullest manifestation of God's very being. The question, then, is, Are there ways of holding to that conviction, lying at the heart of the Christian faith, which do not necessitate modes of expression and formulation that defy (for many in the present and a now longish past) a credible sense of the truth about Jesus? After all, the Synoptic Gospels and many Christians of the early centuries did not see him thus.

Leslie Houlden

See also: Adoptianism; Alexandrian Theology; Creeds; Jesus, Origins of; John, Gospel of; Nicea; Origen; Paul; Son of God

References

Dunn, James D. G. 1999. "Jesus: Teacher of Wisdom or Wisdom Incarnate?" Pp. 75–92 in *Where Shall Wisdom Be Found?* Edited by S. C. Barton. Edinburgh: T. & T. Clark.

Hurtado, Larry W. 1998. *One God, One Lord*. London: SCM.

Kuschel, Karl-Josef. 1992. *Born before All Time?* London: SCM.

Prophets, Prophecy, Jesus in

See Hebrew Bible

Psychotherapy

The disciplines of psychotherapeutic psychology and those of Christian theology and spirituality have been characterized, during much of their history, by mutual suspicion. From the point of view of psychotherapists, the roots of the mistrust lie in the prime means by which we identify with other people, that is, in the psychological mechanism of projection. Projection is often thought of as a neurotic phenomenon in which "disowned" parts of oneself are perceived in the person of another—and then feared, rejected, or condemned. But projection is not only neurotic. We may often be accurate in our (projective) perception of another person's strengths and weaknesses and, through this mechanism, we believe we can understand something of what it must be to live that person's life. It is the closest we can get to being in another person's place and feeling what they might be feeling and is therefore the means of our sympathy and compassion.

There are some fundamental consequences arising from this way of looking at the limits of human perception and our understanding of others. The mechanism of projection forms the infrastructure of our apprehension of God and our understanding of Jesus, so that the Christian tradition can be understood as formed in part by the personal, inherited, shared, and examined projections of many generations of Christians. This is not, of course, the same as saying that God cannot exist independently of our projections—rather, that we cannot transcend our humanity to ascertain it.

This simple fact about the limits of human perception has sometimes been used in a reductive fashion by psychotherapists. Sigmund Freud, in his "[The Man] Moses and Monotheism" (1990 [1939]), understood the perceptions of God he found in his patients to be made up in large part of neurotic projections. Much of the projected material consisted of negative experiences of punitive fathers that the sufferers linked in their minds with God, so that God was seen as a punitive father. In the same way, other psychotherapists have examined their patients' perceptions of Jesus—both positive and negative—as made up of projected material. What this means in practice is that those who consider themselves followers of Jesus tend to see in him the personification of all that they consider good. Christians with low self-esteem are apt to "disown" their good traits and project those traits onto Jesus. A corollary of this mechanism is that such believers are likely to "own" or retain only those aspects of themselves of which they disapprove. Such people tend, understandably, to see themselves as bad and as miserable sinners.

Another founding figure in modern psychotherapy, Carl Gustav Jung, is thought by some Christians to be more positive than Freud was in his view of religious experience and belief. Jung's early life as a child of the manse contrasts sharply with Freud's upbringing as a nonobservant Jew. Christians should nevertheless treat with caution Jung's positive references to Jesus, as his treatment of Christianity—for example, his reductive tendency in linking religious figures to archetypes (1978)—is highly eclectic and syncretistic. Neither Jung nor Freud was concerned to deal with theology in an interdisciplinary way: like all psychotherapists, they came across a great deal of damage that had been done to their patients by people and organizations with religious beliefs. Like many writers before and since, they took what they found useful to their own writing without regard to how representative it was of those religious systems.

Since the founding days of modern psychotherapy, psychotherapeutic psychology has entered most areas of human discourse, including theology, and has undoubtedly enriched the theological quest. For example, Caroline Walker Bynum, in her examination of theology and spirituality among women in the European Middle Ages (1982), noted how some male clerics tended to project onto Jesus feminine aspects of themselves. These traits did not fit easily with their culture's negative valorization of femininity but were acceptable as gracious aspects of Jesus.

There is a tradition in Christian mysticism not only of a feminine Jesus and Jesus as mother, but also of Jesus as lover. This tradition was and continues to be important to both men and women. In this tradition, it is the soul (the "I" of the adoring worshiper) that is stereotypically feminine, open, receptive, and longing for the entry of the sensitive, strong lover. The language of the tradition owes much to celibate writers (for example, Dame Julian of Norwich) whose sexuality is strongly engaged in their worship. From the psychotherapeutic point of view, they are projecting feminine and masculine aspects of themselves (regardless of their sex) onto Jesus. Although such projective mechanisms can undoubtedly constitute a neurosis (for example, a disgusted and fearful avoidance of intimate encounter with people), it would be an unimaginative (and, presumably, neurotic) psychotherapist who concluded that such mystical experience is intrinsically neurotic. The Christian disciple is using the means available to a human being to encounter Jesus intimately. Jesus' own approach, that is, examining the fruits of the encounter, might produce indications of healthiness (Matt. 7.20).

There is therefore a positive place for Jesus in the psychotherapeutic encounter. Understandings of what constitutes that encounter vary greatly. In practice, many people in therapy have found that their lives are going so badly that they feel a need to make some radical change. They need to assess their present position, discover how they come to be as they are, and find some way forward that promises a life with either less pain or, at the least, some sense of how the pain can be lived with creatively. For a Christian believer in therapy, Jesus could be part of the problem or part of the solution (Lyall 1995; Lynch 1999). From the psychotherapist's point of view, it may be important for the patient to reassess the relationship with Jesus. This process could entail setting aside neurotic ideas from childhood, such as the notion of Jesus as an all-seeing busybody who is trying to catch out the unwary believer, and allowing another Jesus to emerge. That Jesus might be, for example, the protective older brother the patient never had, or a companion in the struggle for justice, or a loving friend who does not need to be told what's wrong but is there with understanding, compassion, and encouragement. In such a task, the psychotherapist may need to help the patient "re-own" good, projected parts of the patient's self, that is, help the patient in a journey to "incarnation." The "scandal" of incarnation, from a Christian viewpoint, means that all who are born are potentially the sons and daughters of God and contain something of the fullness of God that is revealed in Jesus. We can trace the origins of this idea to Paul (Rom. 8.14–21) and John (1.12–13).

A healthy use of our projective mechanisms neither proves nor disproves the existence of a living and contactable Jesus: that question lies beyond the remit of psychotherapy. The agnostic position of psychotherapy as a discipline concerning questions about the nature or existence of God and of Jesus is neither encouraging nor discouraging of religious belief and practice. It is simply respectful of the beliefs and practices of patients and intellectually open to possibilities. It is also true to say that, in many societies in the twenty-first century, psychotherapists are open to discussion of "spirituality" in whatever form that takes. The risk now is not that references to Jesus will be unwelcome, but that anything vaguely "spiritual" may be thought to be of equal value with an examined Christian (Jewish, Muslim, Hindu, etc.) life.

Barrie Hinksman

See also: Bernard of Clairvaux; English Christianity, Medieval; Francis of Assisi; Interfaith Thought and Relations; John of the Cross; Julian of Norwich; Teresa of Avila

References

Bynum, C. W. 1982. *Jesus as Mother: Studies in the Spirituality of the High Middle Ages*. Berkeley, Los Angeles, and London: University of California Press.

Freud, S. 1990 [1939]. "[The Man] Moses and Monotheism." In *The Penguin Freud Library*. Edited by A. Dickson. London: Penguin.

Jung, C. G. 1978. "Man and His Symbols." In *Man and His Symbols*. London: Picador.

Lyall, D. 1995. *Counselling: The Pastoral and Spiritual Context*. Buckingham, UK: Open University Press.

Lynch, G., ed. 1999. *Clinical Counselling in Pastoral Settings*. London: Routledge.

Q

Quaker Thought

Quakers (Friends) offer a unique and paradoxical form of post-Reformation Christian spirituality and thought. They emerged in northern England in the early 1650s at the cusp of the transition between the late Reformation and the early liberal Enlightenment. Perhaps owing to the timing of that birth-moment, Friends have been susceptible to the gravitational fields of those two dominant cultural systems, which have pulled them in different directions over time. But early Quaker Christology was apocalyptic in character and not reducible to either Protestant or liberal understandings.

The early movement's central figure, George Fox (1624–1691), gathered groups of Seekers, Baptists, and other radicals, proclaiming the day of the Lord and announcing that Christ had come to teach his people himself, freeing them from obeisance to clerical teaching and authority (Gwyn 1986). This message emphasized Christ's Parousia in both senses of that word: presence and return. Christ's presence was preached by the early Quaker prophets as the light, or Spirit, of Christ in each person's conscience. This universally available knowledge of Christ had strongly egalitarian implications: it drew men and women from various classes and social locations into communities waiting together in silence upon divine teaching and leadership. Christ could speak through anyone moved by his Spirit to prophesy, pray, or exhort the group. Early Friends (they called themselves "Friends in the Truth" or "Children of the Light") asserted that this same light had always been present in all people, had inspired the prophets and apostles of old, and was preeminently incarnated in the person of Jesus of Nazareth. But they also asserted that Christ was being revealed with particular historical moment among them. Thus, Christ was appearing in a decisive new way as incarnated in the Quaker movement. This was an apocalyptic revelation (the Greek *apokalupsis* means "revelation") in that Friends saw it fulfilling the promises and prophecies of Scripture in their personal experience and in the new social order breaking forth among them. They did not rule out other, future fulfillment of Scripture; but they refused to speculate, choosing instead to remain attuned to the revelatory presence of Christ here and now.

Early Quaker preaching and spirituality had roots in the Radical Reformation. Quakers drew some of their egalitarian values, their countercultural ethos, and their martyrological impulse from the Anabaptist tradition. Their spirituality was influenced more by the Spiritualist Reformation, where the sacramental realities of communion and baptism in Christ are inwardly experienced on the heavenly/spiritual plane, obviating the necessity of outward elements. But the apocalyptic urgency and radical politics of the Quaker movement gave all these aspects a more acute sense of historic moment. Drawing upon images from the Book of Revelation, Friends called their campaign "the Lamb's War," a nonviolent offensive against the state-sponsored religion, economic injustice, and political repression of England's Puritan regime in the period after the Civil War. They understood themselves to be the faithful standing on spiritual Mount Zion, following Christ the Lamb into apocalyptic warfare against the forces of the Dragon (Rev. 13–14).

The apocalyptic impetus of early Quaker witness gave way to a more sectarian logic by the 1670s as the Restoration of monarchy and the Church of England (1660) foreclosed on the larger religious and political hopes of Friends. But their silent, inwardly sacramental worship and nonprofessional approach to ministry in Christ's presence continued to be refined. Struggling for toleration, Fox and William Penn (1644–1718, founder and first governor of Pennsylvania) reframed their Christianity as the radical and logical culmination of the Protestant Reformation. But they still portrayed themselves as the true Church restored after 1,600 years of apostasy.

Sectarian withdrawal and refinement continued throughout the eighteenth century. The rarefied, mystical Christian spirituality of Quakers in this classical period continued to be balanced with a radical social ethic, as exemplified by the writings of the New Jersey Quaker John Woolman (1720–1772). The Spiritualist Christology of early Friends remained normative, as seen in the writings of the Rhode Island minister Job Scott (1751–1793). Friends persisted in resisting creeds, believing that all affirmations of the Bible's witness (the words of God) are only notional, unless confirmed by inward experience in Christ's light (the Word of God). Hence, forensic interpretations of Christ's atoning death were eschewed in favor of the inward experience of dying and rising with Christ and a concrete ethic of taking up his cross in the countercultural lifestyle and morality of Friends. Various Quaker behavioral codes were understood to be living *testimonies* to the lordship of Jesus Christ in individual lives and in corporate witness to the wider world.

Quakers resisted the word "Trinity" as nonbiblical and tending to separate God into "persons" too distinctly. Nevertheless, their Christology is often manifestly Trinitarian, as seen in statements such as Fox's own testimony that "the Father drew me to his Son by his Spirit" (Fox 1952 [1694], 11). Traditional Quaker ministry fluidly utilized an array of biblical images—light, seed, anointing, measure, word, etc.—to provoke the hearer's awareness of Christ's presence and activity; that is, to open a variety of metaphorical spaces, helping the hearer locate and center the self in Christ's inward teaching. Given the primitivist and noncredal style of their faith, Friends traditionally have relied primarily upon a narrative style of theology. The religious journal, or spiritual autobiography, has been a principal genre of Quaker spiritual formation literature, and Friends have shown a strong penchant for preserving records and writing their history since the seventeenth century.

The nineteenth century saw the reversal of Quaker sectarian withdrawal as Friends began to absorb cultural influences and make alliances with outside groups. This new phase found Friends moving in two different directions: evangelical and liberal. Some Friends found allies for social reform among evangelicals and were drawn to their more explicit Protestant orthodoxy. Others continued the strong polemic of traditional Friends against mainstream Christianity and its doctrines of imputed righteousness, finding their allies in the secular realms of liberal humanism. These diverging tendencies created conflict among Friends on both sides of the Atlantic, and outright schism among American Friends (Ingle 1987; Kennedy 2001). Evangelical renewal was strongest in the nineteenth century, mainstreaming Quaker Christology, inspiring hybridizations of Quaker and evangelical forms of worship and ministry, and even leading in some cases to a renunciation of the universal light of Christ (Hamm 1988). Liberal renewal dominated the twentieth century, forging more secular alliances, especially in pacifist activism. Liberal renewal reaffirmed the primacy of personal experience (albeit premised on modern, then postmodern understandings of human spirituality); in many cases, the result has been a diminution or even rejection of a Christian understanding of the universal light (Dandelion 1996).

Douglas Gwyn

See also: English Christianity, 1500–1750; Enlightenment

References

Barbour, Hugh, and J. William Frost. 1988. *The Quakers*. New York: Greenwood.
Dandelion, Pink. 1996. *A Sociological Analysis of the Theology of Quakers: The Silent Revolution*. Lewiston, NY: Mellen.
Fox, George. 1952 [1694]. *The Journal of George Fox*. Edited by John L. Nickalls. Cambridge: Cambridge University Press.
Gwyn, Douglas. 1986. *Apocalypse of the Word: The Life and Message of George Fox*. Richmond, IN: Friends United Press.
Hamm, Thomas. 1988. *The Transformation of American Quakerism: Orthodox Friends, 1800–1907*. Bloomington: Indiana University Press.
Ingle, H. Larry. 1987. *Quakers in Conflict: The Hicksite Reformation*. Knoxville: University of Tennessee Press.
Kennedy, Thomas C. 2001. *British Quakerism, 1860–1920: The Transformation of a Religious Community*. Oxford: Oxford University Press.

R

Rabbis

The early rabbinic writings have been a main focus in the study of the ancient Jewish view of Jesus. Preserved in the Mishnah (c. A.D. 200) and the earliest, Tannaitic layer (pre-200) of the Babylonian Talmud, these traditions testify that Jesus was a "magician and deceiver" who founded a movement that continued to trouble the Jewish people. References to Jesus are of two types: by a code name, and by his actual name. Research into rabbinic traditions on the historical Jesus has largely been restricted to the earliest layers, on the supposition that they contain the best information.

Some scholars have argued that early hostility to Christianity led to numerous references to Jesus within rabbinic writing by insulting pseudonyms such as "Ben Stada," "Balaam," and "a certain one." The key Ben Stada texts are in *baraitoth* ("commentaries" on the Mishnah) from the Talmud and the Tosefta. The first two present Ben Stada as a worker of evil magic (*Babylonian Talmud* [hereafter *b.*] *Shabbat* 104b, *Tosephta* [hereafter *t.*] *Shabbat* 11.15). The last two parallel passages describe an ancient Torah-enforcement "sting operation" (*b. Sanhedrin* 67; *t. Sanhedrin* 10.11; cf. *Jerusalem Talmud* [hereafter *y.*] *Sanhedrin* 7.16). As an example, here is the first of these four passages, which shows the complexity of the Ben Stada traditions:

> It is taught that Rabbi Eliezer said to the Wise, "Did not Ben Stada bring spells from Egypt in a cut in his flesh?" They said to him, "He was a fool, and they do not bring evidence from a fool." Ben Stada is Ben Pantera. Rabbi Hisda said, "The husband was Stada, the lover was Pantera." The husband was [actually] Pappos ben Judah, the mother was Stada. The mother was Miriam [Mary] the dresser of women's hair. As we say in Pumbeditha, "She has been false to *[satath da]* her husband." (*B. Shabbat* 104b)

Other passages are said to present Jesus as Balaam, the non-Israelite prophet who figures rather positively in Numbers 22–24, but negatively in Numbers 31.16 and thereafter in Jewish tradition. The first two Balaam passages, from the Mishnah, have been thought by a few scholars to speak of Jesus' exclusion from the people of Israel (*Mishnah* [hereafter *m.*] *Sanhedrin* 10.2, *m. Abot* 5.19). The third Balaam passage is the Dantesque "Jesus in Hell" account from the Talmud (*b. Gittin* 56b–57a), and the fourth, also from the Talmud, deals with the age of Balaam at his death (*b. Sanhedrin*

106b). On the question of which Israelites will be excluded from the world to come, the Mishnah relates, "Three kings and four commoners have no part in the world to come. The three kings are Jeroboam, Ahab, Manasseh. . . . The four commoners are Balaam, Doeg, Ahitophel, and Gehazi" (*m. Sanhedrin* 10.2).

Still other texts speak of "a certain person" *(peloni)* who has been identified by some with Jesus. A key reference to "a certain person" occurs in a discussion of the definition of a "bastard," who, according to Jewish law, has restricted rights (*m. Yebamot* 4.13 and *b. Yoma* 66d; cf. *t. Yebamot* 3.3–4): Rabbi Shimon ben Azzai said, "I have found a family scroll in Jerusalem, and in it is written, 'A certain person *[peloni]* is a bastard through [a transgression of the law of] the kinsman's wife'" (*m. Yebamot* 4.13).

Modern historical scholarship has largely settled on the following consensus in evaluating these three putative code words. First, "a certain one" as a reference to Jesus is so intentionally vague in itself as to refer to almost anyone. Some have translated it "so-and-so," but this English translation misleadingly leaves a negative impression. *Peloni* has no inherently negative connotation in postbiblical Hebrew. The Mishnah section on "bastards" in which it appears, *m. Yebamot* 4.13, deals not just with any bastards, but with those who are offspring of "near of kin, which is forbidden." The "certain one" whom Rabbi Joshua mentions as an illustration is the offspring of such a violation. Since Jewish polemic against Jesus never claimed that he was an offspring of such a sin, this is not likely to be a cryptic reference to Jesus.

The specific application of "Balaam" to Jesus is also untenable for the earliest stage of rabbinic tradition. The wide field of Balaam references in the New Testament, Philo, and rabbinic Judaism reflects a long polemical tradition that typologically identifies many people as "Balaam." Moreover, Balaam was not an Israelite, despite the inexplicable identification of him as an "Israelite commoner" in *m. Sanhedrin* 10.2. The rabbinic tradition everywhere knows that Jesus was Jewish. Moreover, nothing else in the passage allows one to suspect Jesus. Other rabbinic texts (*b. Gittin* 56–57) manifestly present Balaam and Jesus as two separate people, and their attitudes to Judaism are also opposed. All this makes it highly unlikely that Jesus is understood by Balaam in these earlier passages. Since "Balaam" was a traditional prototype of the deceitful prophet from outside Israel, it was natural that Jesus, whose movement now opposed Judaism from the outside, would come to be associated with him. However, the evidence points away from concluding that "Balaam" was used as a code name for Jesus in Tannaitic times.

Neither can Ben Stada be a code name for Jesus. The first explicit identification of Jesus as Ben Stada comes in the later Amoraic layer. Moreover, information given about Ben Stada disagrees at almost every point with more certain data from the New Testament. Further, the portrait of Ben Stada does not fit other, more certain rabbinic traditions about Jesus, especially the one in *b. Sanhedrin* 43a relating to his trial and death. The passage also reflects confusion over the identity of Stada: is he Mary's husband, or Mary herself? This passage settles on the latter, using a pun to illustrate the point. She is called "Stada" because she has been false to *(satath da)* her husband. In another passage, the only telling connection to the Jesus traditions of the Talmud—the statement in *b. Sanhedrin* 67, "[T]hey hanged him [Ben Stada] on the day before the Passover"—is in all likelihood tacked on later to apply polemic against Ben Stada to Jesus.

In the second type of proposed Talmud passages on Jesus, he appears under his own name. Because the name Jesus (Yeshua) was a common one, the content must indicate that the Jesus being spoken of is Jesus of Nazareth. The first is a passage discussing Israelites who have no place in the world to come:

> When King Jannaeus [d. 76 B.C.E.] was killing our rabbis, Rabbi Joshua ben Perahiah and Jesus escaped to Alexandria, Egypt. When peace was restored . . . he set off (for home), and came to a certain inn, where he was given a warm welcome. He said, "How lovely is the *aksania* [inn, innkeeper]!" He [Jesus] replied, "Rabbi, she has narrow eyes." Rabbi Joshua said, "You villain, is that what you are thinking about?" So he sounded four hundred trumpets and excommunicated him. Many times Jesus came and pleaded to be allowed back, but he would not listen. But one day, when Rabbi Joshua was reciting the Shema, Jesus approached him. Deciding to welcome him back, he made a gesture to him. However, Jesus thought he was ordering him to leave, and he went and set up a brick and worshiped it. "Repent," he [Rabbi Joshua] told him, but he answered, "I have learned from you that no chance of repentance is given to one who sins and leads others into sin." And a teacher has said, "Jesus the Nazarene practiced magic and led Israel astray." . . . Our rabbis taught: Let the left hand push away, but the right hand always invite back, not like Elisha who pushed Gehazi away with both hands, and not like Joshua ben Perahiah who pushed Jesus away with both hands. (*B. Sanhedrin* 107b; cf. *b. Sotah* 47a; this passage has an earlier parallel in the Jerusalem Talmud that does not mention Jesus, *y. Hagigah* 2.2; cf. *y. Sanhedrin* 23c)

Other texts characterize the ministry of Jesus and his disciples negatively (*b. Sanhedrin* 43a, cf. *t. Shabbat* 11.15; *b. Shabbat* 104b; *b. Sanhedrin* 103a, cf. *b. Berakhot* 17b, and *b. Sanhedrin* 43a).

Also, Jesus' trial and death are treated in a passage from the Talmud (*b. Sanhedrin* 43a). Here Jesus is explicitly named, and again there is little doubt that Jesus of Nazareth is meant. This has rightly been called the most important reference to Jesus in the rabbinic literature:

> It was taught: On the day before the Passover they hanged Jesus. A herald went before him for forty days [proclaiming], "He will be stoned, because he practiced magic and enticed Israel to go astray. Let anyone who knows anything in his favor come forward and plead for him." But nothing was found in his favor, and they hanged him on the day before the Passover. (*B. Sanhedrin* 43a)

This one Tannaitic passage on the trial and death of Jesus not only names Jesus explicitly but it gives other information that confirms Jesus as the subject. This short narrative is the only surviving rabbinic treatment of the death of Jesus beyond a simple reference to it. On the whole, it seems to be an inner-Jewish explanation and justification of how one famous criminal,

Jesus of Nazareth, was put to death, and implicitly a warning to stay away from his movement.

As has been seen, most passages of the Tannaitic period that have been argued to refer to Jesus cannot be held to do so. Only the passages that cite Jesus by name, and perhaps by the code "Ben Pantera," are from this period. Further, we can discern information from the rabbis about Jesus that accords with reliable traditions in the New Testament: Jesus was born of Mary, was claimed to have Davidic descent, worked miracles, had disciples, and was executed. Rabbinic tradition is negative from the start of its Jesus references and consistently portrays Jesus as a magician and deceiver. Good evidence from the more certain references to Jesus suggests that what the rabbis say about Jesus is largely a polemic reaction to Christian traditions, either written or oral.

All this raises the question of how the rabbis gained this information about Jesus. The third-century rabbis seem to have had no traditions about Jesus that originated in the first century. Some rabbinic traditions concerning Jesus may represent responses to Christian preaching from the end of the first century, not from the time of Jesus. The presentation of Jesus' trial and death in *b. Sanhedrin* 43a likely presents a Jewish rebuttal to Christian traditions about Jesus' death. It cannot be claimed to represent early, independent information about Jesus, even though according to the Synoptic accounts some leading scribes were present at the trial of Jesus. The more specific information given here by the rabbis diverges from reliable traditions in the New Testament and shows no signs of being from the first century. It proceeds instead from polemical imagination, which ran free in rabbinic storytelling: Jesus was a failed rabbinical student, whose own teacher excommunicated him; he was tried after a forty-day period of inquiry and executed by Jews alone.

Perhaps the most telling indication that the rabbis had no independent, early traditions about Jesus is their failure to place him in the right century. Some place him in the first century B.C., others in the second century A.D. A chain of tradition from the first century would have set this error straight. The better explanation of all the rabbinic information on Jesus is that it originated in the second and third centuries. Although it reflects traces of Jewish polemic against Christians at that time, its main use in the rabbinic writings was, no doubt, to remind Jews that Jesus was a deceitful apostate and that his followers were still in error.

Robert E. Van Voorst

See also: Hebrew Bible; Jewish Perspective

References

Herford, R. Travers. 1903. *Christianity in Talmud and Midrash*. London: Williams & Norgate.

Meier, John P. 1991. *A Marginal Jew: Rethinking the Historical Jesus*. Vol. 1. New York: Doubleday.

Twelftree, Graham, 1982. "Jesus in Jewish Traditions." Pp. 290–325 in *Jesus Traditions outside the Gospels*. Edited by David Wenham. Sheffield: Sheffield University Press.

Van Voorst, Robert. 2000. *Jesus outside the New Testament: An Introduction to the Ancient Evidence*. Grand Rapids, MI: William B. Eerdmans.

Race

See American (North) Christianity; American (South) Christianity

Radical Orthodoxy

Radical orthodoxy as a theological movement dates back to the early 1990s and particularly to the publication of John Milbank's *Theology and Social Theory* (1990). John Milbank, Catherine Pickslock, and Graham Ward have been most influential in developing this pattern of thought, although others have either adopted the approach or have been influenced by it. The aim of this school, as implied by its name, is to produce a radical critique of theology. The analysis is rooted in a preliminary critique of secular philosophy; theological analysis is effectively required to turn the secular philosophical critique inside out. The argument for such a method is based on the premise that skeptical philosophers themselves are deemed to have been insufficiently self-critical with regard to their own presuppositions. A universal narrative of experience can no longer be taken for granted. The movement thus issues from the postmodernist assumption that criticizes so-called "meta-narratives"; there is no one all-embracing description of reality. Instead, such postmodern approaches attempt to describe a fragmented cultural world where these fragmentary subcultures are themselves only internally self-consistent; they cannot be tied to externally objective reference points. Adopting the Christian doctrinal pattern is thus a decisive and all-embracing choice that one believes makes sense of reality.

In adopting this particular form of postmodern analysis, radical orthodoxy criticizes other approaches to Christian theology that, it is argued, have been influenced by the presuppositions of various skeptical and autonomous secular philosophies. The requirement of radical orthodoxy is to explore reality only through the laws of the specifically Christian narrative. Even here, however, external reference points are suspect, and so it does not assume a return to the historical Jesus. There is no close analysis or reference to the New Testament text and thus no integration with the critical methods of biblical scholarship, for in this scholarship, once again, secular philosophy will already have influenced method by assuming that one can build a Christology on a neutral, universally accepted foundation of pure history. So, liberal Protestantism's search for the original kernel of the gospel in the historical Jesus is rejected. The structure that relates radical orthodoxy to Jesus is instead a theological structure rooted in the Incarnation and in a sacramental approach to the world. So only as God is encountered and made known in Christ through this sacramental relationship can humanity engage with Jesus. God's purpose made known through the Incarnation is embodied within the created world.

The theological significance of the figure of Jesus is focused in radical orthodoxy's desire to recover the irreducible particularity of divine redemption in Christ, as set out in the Augustinian tradition. Christ's redemptive purpose structures a theological view of the natural world, history, human desire, and truth. Nevertheless, despite this focus upon the redemptive role of Christ, there remains in radical orthodoxy's method an ambivalence about the concrete particularity of the figure of Jesus. Milbank's use of biblical material thus moves from the particular to a more conceptual or speculative approach to Jesus. The Gospel stories become allegories that are placed at the center of a participatory metaphysics, rooted in the sacraments. This conceptual approach is very obvious in attitudes toward the atonement. Milbank writes of our speculative grasp of sin as negation and the refusal of pure love itself. He notes: "The speculation is only occasioned by the horrifying and sublime compulsion of Jesus' death, whose concrete circumstance makes us feel that here we really 'see' sin, and at the same time the essence of human goodness" (Milbank 1990).

The radical orthodoxy approach to Jesus has thus a more Pauline feel to it than one rooted in Gospel narrative. It is what is accomplished in Jesus' death that shapes the redemptive process. Jesus unlocks a redemptive pattern that we may grasp through speculative reflection upon it. Milbank sees the Gospel stories as internally dividing into two different conceptual areas. These two areas include the proclamation of the coming kingdom of God and a pattern of redemption issuing from Jesus' rejection, suffering, and death. He argues, however, that there is also an "absence" in the biblical text of a fully worked-out picture of the savior. This absence, Milbank argues, allows the Church to produce its own conceptual picture of the savior in and through its participatory sacramental activity.

Critics argue that in spite of radical orthodoxy's analysis of modern theology, ironically it still finds itself trapped by the same difficulties. This critique of radical orthodoxy argues that ultimately the metaphysic itself and the pattern of redemption mapped in that metaphysic still become alienated from any clear scriptural authority. It is thus no more effective than other "modern" theologies at relating directly to the person of Jesus in Scripture. Moreover, it has effectively distanced itself from the established methods generated by the various schools of biblical criticism and thus obfuscates attempts to relate the person of Jesus directly to theological method.

Radical orthodoxy, then, is a highly conceptual metaphysical construct rooted purely in the Christian narrative without taint from secular philosophy but also without any deliberate rooting in the historical Jesus. Jesus is only mediated to humanity through Scripture and tradition, but there is a fundamental assumption that Christ is entirely and sufficiently adequate to human salvation. Effectively, the historicity of the story of Jesus holds a purely aesthetic function in shaping the pattern of the metaphysics at the heart of radical orthodoxy. No dependence is placed upon the New Testament narrative itself. Aesthetics stands at the heart, and Christ becomes the controlling metaphor within the total theological and sacramental structure.

In conclusion, then, the importance of the figure of Jesus theologically stands close to the heart of radical orthodoxy but only in a metaphysical sense. The impact that both the man and his teaching had on generating "orthodoxy" is essential, but that impact seems detachable from the man Jesus himself. For it is this orthodoxy, radicalized by a new critique, that gives the purity of the Christian narrative its power. Jesus remains elusive but still central to the whole radical orthodoxy enterprise.

Note: it is important to know that radical *orthodoxy* is quite different from radical *theology*, which is virtually its opposite. For the latter, see Glossary.

Stephen Platten

See also: Augustine of Hippo; Eucharist; Jesus, Achievement of; Kingdom of God; Liturgy; Paul

References

Milbank, John. 1990. *Theology and Social Theory*. Oxford: Blackwell.
Milbank, John, Catherine Pickslock, and Graham Ward. 1999. *Radical Orthodoxy: A New Theology*. London: Routledge.

Rahner, Karl (1904–1984)

A German Jesuit, philosopher, and theologian, Rahner developed an interpretation of Jesus Christ based in terms of transcendental Thomism, combining insights from the philosophy of Thomas Aquinas, Immanuel Kant, Joseph Maréchal, and Martin Heidegger with ideas derived from the Christian mystical tradition. Since he never wrote a general study of Christology, his ideas must be gathered from a number of writings of more restricted scope. His starting point is anthropological: analysis of our consciousness reveals that our knowledge, inquiry, hope, and freedom are possible only with reference to one who is an infinite, holy mystery and an "absolute saviour" whom we name as "God," who creates by communicating *himself* to his creation, emptying himself (cf. Phil. 2.7) by virtue of an eternal decision, and who realizes this decision in the events of human history. We can then reflect on our nonconceptual experience of this divine communication, define it as best we can in necessarily inadequate human terms, and recognize its definitive fulfillment in the life and person of Jesus Christ.

The evolutionary nature of the history of the human race points in the same direction: Jesus Christ is the perfect fulfillment of God's self-communication to his creation, lying at the point of intersection between the divine creativity and human development. This dynamism is the background or horizon of all human existence, and the Church's dogmas concerning the Incarnation must be related to it. Although God's entry into creation is the work of all three persons of the Trinity, it is only the second person, God's self-expression, who identifies himself with a creature in the person of Jesus Christ. His genuine humanity necessarily implies human limitations, including the psychological: though he enjoyed in his human mind the direct vision of God, the concepts in which he expressed this nonverbal, underlying awareness to himself and to others were subject to the limitations of human psychology and language. Those who are not Christians or even believers in God still express the dynamism toward the infinite mystery in their free choices, even though they do not identify the object of this tendency with the historic Jesus Christ; they therefore know him without naming him and can thus be called "anonymous Christians." Salvation comes about through the whole of Jesus' life, death, and resurrection, so that he is the original sacrament of our salvation, as both its sign and its cause.

The best starting point for Christology is human experience: Christology is the beginning and end of anthropology (Rahner 1978, 225). The analysis of consciousness reveals that in every free act one transcends oneself, that is, reaches beyond one's own limitations to an unlimited goal, to "a Thou who is absolutely trustworthy" (ibid., 209) and who forms the background or horizon to the human action; this is true not only of our knowledge but also of our hopes and our inquiries. (One is reminded of Robert Browning's words: "A man's reach should exceed his grasp, / Or what's a heaven for?" ["Andrea del Sarto," 1855].) In other words, these experiences are grounded in a nonconceptual apprehension *(Vorgriff)* of Infinite Being. In his doctoral dissertation, later published as *Geist in Welt* (*Spirit in the World,* 1968), Rahner associated this insight with St. Thomas Aquinas's theory (derived ultimately from Aristotle) that a person's knowledge is gained by abstraction from the data of the senses; this passage he interpreted in the light of Heidegger's conception that to exist in the world is to raise the question about Being, which lies behind finite beings.

The Belgian philosopher Maréchal pointed the way to a deepening of this insight: whereas Kant had sought to identify the "transcendental" ideas that make knowledge possible by imposing a shape upon it, thus making it impossible to know things as they are in themselves, Maréchal argued that the transcendental ideas that underlay all knowledge is of an objectively existing God. Rahner followed this lead when he identified God with the incomprehensible mystery or horizon of human knowing and seeking. The transcendental divine self-communication underlies all conceptual knowledge and therefore is itself not apprehended conceptually ("categorically"); it underlies all history and therefore is in itself outside history. Nevertheless, it needs to be reflected on and expressed as well as possible in human categories, and to be mediated "categorically" in history. This "orientation" toward the infinite, which forms the hidden basis of human striving, is supernatural in the sense that it takes us beyond any natural capacities; it can therefore be described as a "supernatural existential." Rahner found confirmation for this movement from the transcendental to the categorical in classical spiritual writers such as Bonaventure, who believed that the divine Word provides the light on which all natural and supernatural knowledge depends, and Ignatius Loyola, who regarded particular decisions as (categorical) realizations of a (transcendental) decision for or against God. (Rahner himself followed the same line in seeing every particular moral choice as the realization of a "fundamental option" for or against God.)

The definitive (eschatological) mediation in history of God's self-communication is Jesus Christ. By the free offering of his death, and by his resurrection, which manifests God's acceptance of the offering, he constitutes in history the victorious outcome of God's self-offering to the world. Thus the incarnate Jesus of Nazareth is the meeting point between the infinite extension of human self-transcendence or orientation toward God and God's communication of himself to his creation.

Rahner recognized problems of language in the traditional Christological formulas. The traditional confession "Jesus is God" is true only if the word "is" is given a distinctive meaning so that it conveys not the identity of the predicate with the subject, but "a unique, otherwise unknown and deeply mysterious unity between realities that are really different and which are at an infinite distance from each other" (Rahner 1978, 290). Again, the term "person" has one sense when applied to the Trinity to denote distinctness, and another when applied to Jesus Christ to express unity. Moreover, to ascribe to Christ one "person" bearing the divine and human natures is false if the word "person" is understood in the modern sense of a psychological or moral center, for Jesus in his human reality has a created center distinct from the divine and of an infinitely different order from it.

The full humanity of the incarnate Word is taught in the New Testament and the councils of the Church and is implied by the divine Word's entry into created history. It follows that Jesus Christ was truly subject to human limitations, including limitations to his knowledge: there were things that he genuinely did not know. This was true of his awareness of himself as God: though possessing the direct vision of God throughout his life in a transcendental, nonconceptual way—Rahner spoke of "direct" rather than "beatific" vision in view of Jesus' openness to suffering—Jesus needed to learn how to express that consciousness in categorical, conceptual terms. "New and surprising experiences," as well as "crises of self-identity," provided occasions for such growth in self-understanding (ibid., 249).

Transcendental Christology, as outlined above, Rahner believed, has a pastoral value in that it meets some contemporary concerns and presuppositions. It accords with the general acceptance of the theory of evolution without being entailed by it, for the natural cannot entail the supernatural. In addition, rooting the discussion of Jesus Christ in human experience avoids the danger of making the Gospels and the dogmas of the Church appear to be mere "mythology" and indicates the possibility of expressing the classical Christological dogmas in alternative forms. The essential requirement seems to be the affirmation of an "absolute savior," one who brings salvation eschatologically, that is, *irreversibly*. This is what is affirmed by traditional belief in the Incarnation, death, and resurrection of God the Son. Rahner suggested three "creeds" that express this truth less explicitly in terms of God's self-communication in fulfillment, respectively, of human transcendence, love of neighbor, and orientation toward the future. Thus, Jesus Christ is the "eschatological [i.e., irreversible] climax of God's historical self-communication"; second, in him, "the self-communication of God to man by which man's love for neighbour is borne has its eschatological, victorious and historical climax"; third, in him, God, who is the "absolute [as opposed to incomplete] future" of mankind, irreversibly accomplishes his will to give himself in his own reality by self-communication (ibid., 454–458). The possibility of alternative categorical formulations of the transcendental truth about the absolute savior indicates that people can in effect believe in Jesus Christ "anonymously," that is, without knowing his name. Thus any act of freedom that is open to the truth involves an implicit faith not only in God but in an incarnate savior who in his own person communicates God's irreversible saving presence to mankind. To the objection that talk of "anonymous Christians" fails to respect the convictions of non-Christians, who would object to being described in this way, Rahner replied that it was not intended as the language of evangelization but to help Christians to explain to themselves how God's saving grace can be operative among those who have no explicit faith in Jesus Christ.

As traditional theology recognized, God's action in the sphere of created things and in the process of creation itself is necessarily the work of all three persons of the Trinity; Rahner saw, however, that the same relations between the three persons that exist in God's inner nature are also present in his action outside himself. This truth he expressed in his "basic axiom" of Trinitarian theology: "the 'economic' Trinity is the 'immanent' Trinity." Rahner rejected the theory of St. Thomas that the Father or the Holy Spirit could have become incarnate instead of the Son (*Summa Theologiae* 3.3.5; it was, however "more appropriate" that the Son should do so: 3.3.8) because, Rahner maintained, it would follow from this teaching that the Incarnation would reveal nothing of the relation between the three persons. Nevertheless, all three persons are involved in this external divine action, but each in his own distinctive way. Jesus *is* the Father's revelation of himself to the created world just as he is the Father's expression of himself in the inner life of the Trinity; the descent of the Holy Spirit necessarily forms part of this single divine self-utterance as the one who brings it about that the world accepts it in faith, hope, and love (Rahner 1970, 86).

As we have seen, Rahner defined Jesus Christ as the "absolute saviour." This understanding accords with the profession in the Nicene Creed that God the Son became human "for us and for our salvation." The grace he won by his incarnation, death, and resurrection was offered by anticipation to all mankind from the beginning of history. Rahner was not satisfied with St. Anselm's satisfaction theory of redemption, according to which God forgives sinners in view of Christ's loving obedience; nor was he content with Abelard's teaching that we are saved by Christ's cross because we are moved by its attestation of God's love. Rather, salvation is effected when the history of salvation reaches its irreversible culmination, which is achieved when God accepts world history, to the extent of making it his own, and humanity definitively accepts this divine self-communication, which occurs in the life, death and resurrection of the God-man Jesus Christ, of which his Sacred Heart is the symbol. Because Jesus' humanity is part of the single dynamism of the world, it is the beginning of the transformation of all creation. The grace that we receive is derived from his humanity (as the life of a body was once thought to be derived from its head).

Underlying this explanation of salvation is Rahner's theological understanding of death. Since it is true of the whole human race, including Jesus, that death is not a purely passive event but an "act of consummation" that sums up the acts of one's whole life (Rahner 1961, 51), it is above all Jesus' death that establishes an order of salvation for the whole race. Christ's resurrection is both the saving fulfillment of his death and the manifestation of God's acceptance of it as a sacrifice for the world.

The Church is the community of faith in the crucified and risen Jesus Christ. It is through and in the Church that the victorious Jesus Christ remains permanently and invincibly present in history and offers salvation to the individual in a concrete and social way. The Church is thus the sign not just of God's *offer* of himself to mankind but also of the *success* of that offer; God's "yes" in Jesus Christ cannot be undone by humanity's "no." Accordingly, as the efficacious sign of grace, the Church can be called the basic sacrament of Jesus Christ; the seven sacraments are the means by which the Church fulfills its sacramental role according to the needs of the basic moments of a human life.

Edward Yarnold

See also: Anselm; Aquinas, Thomas; Bonaventure; Creeds; Ignatius of Loyola; Interfaith Thought and Relations; Kenoticism; Radical Orthodoxy; Resurrection; Second Person of the Trinity

References

Endean, Philip. 2001. *Karl Rahner and Ignatian Spirituality*, esp. chap. 8. Oxford and New York: Clarendon.

Lehmann, Karl, and Albert Raffelt, eds. 1994. *The Content of Faith: The Best of Karl Rahner's Theological Writings*. Translated by H. D. Egan. New York: Crossroad.

Marshall, Bruce. 1987. *Christology in Conflict: The Identity of a Saviour in Rahner and Barth*. Oxford and New York: Blackwell.

Pedley, C. J. 1984. "An English Bibliographical Aid to Karl Rahner." *Heythrop Journal* 25: 319–365.

Rahner, Karl. 1961. *On the Theology of Death*. Translated by C. H. Henkey. New York: Herder & Herder; London: Burns & Oates.

———. 1961–1992. *Theological Investigations*. Translated by C. Ernst et al., vols. 1–23. London: Darton, Longman & Todd; Baltimore: Helicon Press.

———. 1968. *Spirit in the World*. Translated by W. V. Dych. London: Sheed & Ward; New York: Herder & Herder.

———. 1970. *The Trinity*. Translated by J. Donceel. London: Burns & Oates; New York: Herder & Herder.

———. 1978. *Foundations of Christian Faith*. Translated by W. V. Dych. London: Darton, Longman & Todd; New York: Seabury Press.

Wong, Joseph H. P. 1984. *Logos-Symbol in the Christology of Karl Rahner*. Rome: Libreria Ateneo Salesiano.

Redemption

See Schleiermacher, F. D. E.

Reformation

See Anglicanism; Calvin, John; English Christianity, 1500–1750; Luther, Martin; Spirituality

Reimarus, Hermann Samuel (1694–1768)

By profession Reimarus was professor of Hebrew and Oriental languages in Hamburg. His intellectual bent was strongly scientific, and he was in many ways an exemplar of the spirit of the Enlightenment: rational and nonsupernatural in his search for explanations in many areas, including religion. Typically, however, he sought to defend natural religion and to oppose atheism.

Reimarus's claim to fame came through Albert Schweitzer, who began his classic study of the life of Jesus with him. Its English title is *The Quest of the Historical Jesus* (1910), but its original German title meant "From Reimarus to Wrede," spanning the period (largely in Germany) from the middle of the eighteenth century to the end of the nineteenth.

The story of the self-censorship of Reimarus's ideas on Jesus and the Gospels strike many as sad, though it would still not be inadvisable in principle in some German universities, where the training of the clergy is the dominant purpose of undergraduate programs in theology. In the latter part of his life, Reimarus became convinced, by reading the skeptical and critical works of, chiefly, English thinkers of the period, that the orthodox doctrine of Jesus was not sustainable. However, prudently, he did not publish his writings on the subject, and it was left to G. E. Lessing (1729–1781), who brought out some "fragments" of his work half a dozen years after his death—concealing the author's name—to bring his ideas out into the open. These works are usually known as "the Wolfenbüttel Fragments." They set about seeing Jesus in his Jewish setting and make an early attempt to interpret his claims and his apocalyptic preaching against that background. Thus historical realism started to assert itself against the decisive voice of Church dogma.

Moreover, Reimarus saw that we should read the Gospels as containing different layers of material representing a variety of reactions to Jesus. In particular, he believed that the early followers of Jesus, after his death, were responsible for his beginning to be seen in supernatural terms. Notoriously, Reimarus came to believe the truth of the story that is found near the end of the Gospel of Matthew telling of the disciples' theft of Jesus' body from the tomb and their fraudulent announcement of his resurrection. Matthew claimed that this was a wicked Jewish slander. Reimarus wanted to expose what really happened. In this way, though not many would now accept his judgment in this particular matter, he can stand as a pioneer of those who have approached the Gospels and the life of Jesus with "a hermeneutic of suspicion" and who believe there is a gap between what "really" happened and what we read, often itself notoriously contradictory: what it gives to us is all, at one level or another, later interpretation biased (by faith). In this way, he is rightly seen as a prime actor in the story of the historically critical study of the life of Jesus.

Leslie Houlden

See also: Christology, Modern; Enlightenment; Jesus as a Historical Figure; Resurrection; Schweitzer, Albert; Strauss, D. F.

References

Morgan, R. 1992. "Reimarus, H. S." Pp. 585–586 in *A Dictionary of Biblical Interpretation*. Edited by R. J. Coggins, and J. L. Houlden. London: SCM.

Schweitzer, Albert. 2000 [1910]. *The Quest of the Historical Jesus*. London: SCM.

Religious Education in British Schools

Since Jesus is central to Christianity, it would seem reasonable to expect teaching about him to play a major part in British religious education (RE). It is arguable that no subject on the British school curriculum has done more to reinvent itself over the past three decades than RE. Once the forlorn and lonely Cinderella of the timetable, the subject now commands widespread respect, supported as it is by professional organizations, resource centers, regular in-service training, and a vigilant inspectorate. Increasingly, pupils are coming to realize that the RE teacher is there to help them think more clearly about religion and about their own values and beliefs, not to advocate her or his own opinion. Year by year, at the age of fifteen or sixteen, more students take the subject at General Certificate of Secondary Education and Advanced Level. Given all this, it might seem reasonable to hope that the topic of Jesus would be taught in a manner that was scholarly and inspiring. Sadly, it has to be acknowledged that all too often this is not the case. Statute requires that Jesus appear on the curriculum, and there are excellent resources available, yet it seems that, for a number of reasons, particular difficulties attach to this part of the RE curriculum, which, as a result, tends either to be taught superficially or avoided altogether.

From the 1920s until the early 1960s, RE in Britain was effectively Christian education. In the thinking that lay behind the great Education Act of 1944, the purpose of the subject was unashamedly confessional: to produce Christian children in what was still considered a Christian country. The life and teaching of Jesus was the single most important element in the agreed syllabuses that followed the 1944 act. Children were to be fed a staple diet of biblical knowledge, with particular emphasis on the life of Christ as conveyed in the Gospels. Not surprisingly, given the unashamedly confessional nature of such an approach, Christ's divinity, atoning death, and resurrection were taught as articles of faith, to be accepted without question rather than subjected to critical scrutiny. However, as Britain became less homogeneously Christian, agnosticism, humanism, and materialism were more openly espoused, especially amongst the young, and the radical theology of the 1960s questioned the hitherto unquestionable. Moreover, psychological research into the development of children's religious thinking cast doubt on the wisdom of an unvaried diet of Bible study, and new theories of how religion might be learned and understood began to take hold. In the1960s, the ideas of Ronald Goldman and others, influenced by Piagetian theories of child development, led to a departure from traditional methods of RE teaching in favor of a themes-based approach. However, the methodology was still essentially confessional, inasmuch as the themes would generally lead the student toward some aspect of the Jesus story. Thus, for example, a study of "Hands" would lead to the caring hands of Jesus; "Bread" to the feeding of the multitude or the institution of the Eucharist; and so on. Thus, the centrality of Jesus was preserved, albeit in a manner that must have seemed artificial and contrived to the more discerning student.

However, a revolution of Copernican proportions was soon to overtake the subject. It has been claimed that, with the publication of the 1971

Schools Council Working Paper on Religious Education, a new educational subject was born, whose aim would be to teach children about religion rather than to make them religious. Influenced in particular by the thinking of Ninian Smart and John Hick, the aims and objectives of RE moved decisively from the confessional to the educational. The study of world religions, from being at best a peripheral part of sixth-form RE, became central to the subject from the primary level onward. Henceforth, the teacher's task would be to help pupils understand the nature of religion—as a worldwide phenomenon—and what it might mean to be a committed believer. The pupil's own faith, or lack of it, was no longer the teacher's concern. Christian nurture, it was argued, belonged in the Church, not the classroom.

The educational advantages of such a transformation were undeniable. Not only had the subject become more interesting and relevant, both to teachers and pupils: it was also able to make a valuable contribution toward furthering the aims of a pluralist and tolerant society. Shorn of its confessional peculiarities, it could take its place in the curriculum on educational merit alone. However, the outlook for the teaching of Jesus was less obviously promising. Here was a figure about whom there already existed, in the minds of both pupils and teachers, a degree of familiarity, a familiarity often tinged with pious accretions. Such familiarity could easily breed, if not contempt, then at least a lack of curiosity that did not apply in the case of such apparently more exotic figures as the Buddha, Muhammad, and Guru Nanak. Jesus continued to appear on the curriculum, often as one of a number of "Founders of Religion"; it is questionable how far such a description did him justice. Another, more promising, approach was to investigate Jesus through the eyes of other faiths. But though students might profitably learn about Jesus the rabbi, or Isa (Jesus), second greatest prophet of Islam, a study that shied away from the vexed question of divinity scarcely enabled them to have much idea why it was that this man should hold the central and unique position he did in the Christian faith.

Alarmed by the spread of multifaith approaches, the Conservative governments of the 1980s attempted to reinforce the central place of Christianity in RE syllabuses. The complaint was made that in going for a multifaith approach (caricatured by Archbishop Robert Runcie as the "credal smorgasbord"), RE was deserting the Gospels. After the Education Act of 1988, the law required syllabuses to be "in the main Christian" and thus to reflect the mainly Christian traditions of the country. As a result, a good deal of new and innovative material on teaching Christianity has appeared over the past decade, including textbooks, videos, and interactive computer software. Some of this material relates to the teachings of Jesus, with particular attention to understanding him in his first-century Jewish setting. Furthermore, in 1995, the Schools Curriculum and Assessment Authority produced sets of model syllabuses in which it is clearly stipulated that, throughout the various key stages of the curriculum, children should be given a thorough grounding in the subject of Jesus and his significance for the Christian faith. For example, at key stage 1, as well as learning the outline of Jesus' life, children should be taught that Jesus is a special person for Christians and that he changed, and continues to change, people's lives. This emphasis on both the Jesus of history and the Christ of faith continues throughout the four key stages: thus, at key stage 2, children should learn about the kingdom of God in parables and miracles; at key stage 3, about Jesus as fulfillment of Old Testament prophecies; and at key stage 4, about, inter alia, the Parousia, Eternal Life, and Judgment, as well as "The relevance of Jesus' teaching for all time."

However, model syllabuses do not necessarily translate into classroom practice. Research conducted by Karen Walshe and Terence Copley, of Exeter University, into actual syllabuses currently in use, suggests that a large number do not do justice even to the most basic beliefs about the person of Jesus. For example, only one of the twenty-four syllabuses surveyed made explicit reference to the term "Christ," only two to "God Incarnate," and only three to "Son of God." Walshe and Copley suggested that what is frequently being presented is a Jesus without theology, who may be little more than a vehicle for the transmission of Western values. Teachers, especially in primary schools, may talk enthusiastically about Jesus as a person of immense charisma who inspired feelings of respect and awe; all too often pupils are left wondering why.

Problems, not found in other parts of the RE syllabus, undoubtedly do arise in the teaching of Jesus. One of these, noted already, is familiarity—often with aspects of the man and his story that are peripheral to his religious significance. For example, children who have taken part in Nativity plays may have a disproportionate sense of the importance of the Christmas story and may be more familiar with the apocryphal innkeeper of Bethlehem than with Caiaphas or Pontius Pilate. Another problem arises from the piety of some teachers who still, consciously or not, attempt to evangelize in the classroom. Thus, children may repeat, parrot-fashion, that Jesus "died to save us from our sins," without understanding what such a formula might mean to the believer, or what they themselves are supposed to make of it. Equally unhelpful is the teacher so determined *not* to evangelize that he conveys an image of Jesus so bland and innocuous as to have prompted neither offense nor discipleship. Yet another problem may arise from the fact that Christianity, having drunk deeply of the spirit of the Enlightenment, is more obviously self-critical than most other religions. Biblical criticism, presented skillfully and at the right stage, can be inspiring, but the unwary teacher who attempts a little Gospel criticism may simply succeed in convincing his class that the entire story is an invention. This is especially the case when it comes to miracles; the adolescent mind is not always open to the subtleties of demythologizing. Finally, there is the matter of public examinations; the new syllabuses are undoubtedly attracting large numbers, but the most popular units are ethics and philosophy of religion, with relatively few candidates taking biblical papers.

None of the above need be taken as a counsel of despair. The figure of Jesus still has the potential to fascinate and attract the young, whether because, or in spite, of RE; and there are various ways in which such fascination may be harnessed and lead to deeper understanding and appreciation. It may be helpful to teach Jesus through art, drama, poetry, film, and so on, as well as through the biblical texts. Paintings from a wide variety of cultural backgrounds will positively and provocatively challenge the archetypal view of a mildly submissive and conformist figure. For example, the image of an angry Christ, painted by a victim of torture in Latin America, may lead to a study of liberation theology and of the God who liberates through self-identification with the marginalized and oppressed. After Monty Python's *Life of Brian* (1979) the traditional Jesus epic (such as *King of Kings* [1961] or *Jesus of Nazareth* [1977]) may inspire hilarity rather than admiration. But a film such as *Jesus of Montreal* (1989) in which a group of actors put on a new and radically challenging Passion play, and gradually find the events of their own lives mirroring those of the Passion, can lead to thoughtful reappraisal of the significance of Jesus. The message of Jesus, calling as it does for the ultimate in self-sacrifice, and thereby contradicting everything valued by a materialistic culture, may seem hopelessly out of touch with the times. Yet, to those young people, whether Christian or not, who find themselves disillusioned with, and alienated from, contemporary culture, the challenge to discover their true selves through self-loss in the service of others may prove to have enduring relevance and validity. Jesus is a part of the inheritance of anyone growing up in what is even nominally a Christian culture, regardless of personal faith, and those who go through their education learning little, if anything, of real value about him must be considered deprived. Students of all ages should be helped to understand what Jesus means for those alive today, as well as to understand the events recorded in the Gospels; teachers must not shirk the challenge of Christology. For the Christian, God is revealed most fully through the person and work of Jesus. If some, at least, of the implications of belief in, and worship of, such a God are to make any sense outside the confines of the Church, then adequate teaching in our schools about the meaning and significance of Jesus is essential.

David Lindsay

See also: Art; English Christianity, Modern; Film; Jesus, Miracles of; Jesus, Teaching of

References

Cole, W. Owen, and Ruth Mantin. 1994. *Teaching Christianity*. London: Heinemann.

Copley, Terence, and Karen Walshe. 2000. *Teaching about Jesus in Religious Education*. Exeter: University of Exeter School of Education.

Goldman, Ronald. 1965. *Readiness for Religion*. London: Routledge and Kegan Paul.

Shannon, Trevor. 1987. "Jesus." Pp. 39–47 in *Teaching Christianity: A World Religions Approach*. Edited by Clive Erricker. Cambridge: Lutterworth Press.

Renan, Ernest (1823–1892)

See Christology, Modern; English Christianity, 1750–1940; Enlightenment; French Christianity; German Christianity

Resurrection

For many, Christian faith stands or falls with the resurrection of Jesus of Nazareth from the dead, and such a conviction finds support in Paul's arguments that faith and the life of faith are pointless if Christ has not been raised (1 Cor. 15.14–19). This point raises a whole range of questions, however, about the nature of the resurrection that is presupposed, and how one decides whether it has taken place, for Paul's understanding is not necessarily that of other NT writers. In view of the central importance for the Christian faith with which this event has been invested, it is not surprising that the arguments for and against its reality and concerning its nature have been hotly debated.

Witnesses to the Resurrection of Jesus

Besides the accounts in the canonical Gospels, which contain glaring differences, there are, above all, the testimony of Paul (1 Cor. 15.4–8), our earliest witness to this tradition, and moreover the only one claiming to have seen the risen Jesus himself (cf. also 1 Cor. 9.1), as well as the fragmentary account in the apocryphal and later Gospel of Peter, which some (e.g., J. D. Crossan) nevertheless regard as preserving early traditions, earlier indeed than those contained in the canonical Gospels.

The Gospels mostly contain both the indirect witness of the empty tomb and the direct witness of appearances of the risen Jesus to his disciples. Mark's Gospel is here the exception. Although it obviously presupposes the resurrection tradition (8.31; 9.31; 10.34; 14.28; 16.6), this work probably ended originally, and enigmatically, at 16.8 with the fear and the silence of the women who had discovered the empty tomb; no subsequent appearances are described, and the accounts in some textual traditions that attempt to make good this gap are in all probability to be regarded as secondary additions by early Christians baffled by this open and inconclusive ending. It is clear that the tradition common to Matthew and Luke ends with Mark 16.8, and thereafter they diverge drastically from one another.

All four Gospels tell of the visit of women to Jesus' tomb early on the Sunday morning after his crucifixion; the accounts differ as to which women were involved (they only agree in naming Mary of Magdala), but the fact that women are given this role is striking, in view of the little value attributed to women's testimony at that time (cf. Luke 24.11). They discover that the tomb is empty but encounter a figure or figures by whom they are informed that Jesus is risen.

The sequel to this discovery differs in the various Gospels. Mark anticipates a reunion of Jesus with his disciples in Galilee (14.28; 16.7), and Matthew depicts this, but only after Jesus has already encountered the women on their way back from the tomb (28.9). Luke, in contrast, goes out of his way to avoid any return to Galilee and appearances there, even altering Mark 16.7 so that it refers to a past word of Jesus in Galilee (24.6), and stresses that the disciples must remain in Jerusalem until power (that of the Spirit given at Pentecost) is bestowed upon them (24.49). John begins with appearances of Jesus to Mary of Magdala and to the disciples in Jerusalem (20.14, 19, 26) but then continues in chapter 21 with an account of appearances in Galilee, which seems to show no knowledge whatsoever that anything has happened previously in Jerusalem. In view of the fact that Jerusalem was the place of

In Matthias Grünewald's oil-on-wood painting, the serene and transcendent figure of Christ resurrected contrasts sharply with the evidently stunned figures of the soldiers tumbling at his feet. *Panel from* Isenheim Altarpiece, *sixteenth century. Unterlinden Museum, Colmar, France. (Erich Lessing/Art Resource)*

Jesus' death and the later center of earliest Christianity and focus of the earliest Church's life, whereas we have no firm evidence of Christianity in Galilee during this phase of the Christian movement, it is hard to account for these stories of resurrection appearances in Galilee except by saying that the disciples did eventually return home after Jesus' death and there experienced something that they then interpreted as encounters with the risen Jesus.

The tradition that the resurrection took place "on the third day" (already mentioned in 1 Cor. 15.4) is a persistent one, but it is only compatible with something that happened and was witnessed in Jerusalem, for there is no way the disciples could have fled from Jerusalem to Galilee, particularly in view of the intervening sabbath, in time to encounter Jesus there so soon; in Luke 24 and John 20 they are indeed still in Jerusalem on that Sunday, which is intrinsically plausible. Moreover, it is difficult to dismiss the report of an appearance in Emmaus in Luke 24 as pure invention, for one must first account for the reference to this place. Some, however, see the dating on the third day as dependent on the OT Scriptures alone and not on historical events. Hosea 6.2 could be responsible for this tradition (even though that text is phrased in the first person plural, and 6.1 seems to speak of those who need to "return" to God; furthermore, this OT text appears nowhere in the NT as a testimony to Jesus' resurrection). The Hosea text is likelier than the other possibility, the experiences of Jonah, for that prophet's "three days and three nights" in the belly of the great fish (1.17) does not accord with the timing of a resurrection on Sunday morning (but see Matt. 12.40). The persistence of this tradition is further confirmed by the early Church's observance of Sunday as its special day, even though this must have created problems because of its divergence from the Jewish Sabbath tradition. One has, therefore, to ask whether this traditional dating arose, not from the desire to fulfill Scripture, but from something that happened on that Sunday that in turn led early Christians to seek prophetic confirmation of it, however tenuous, in the OT. What that event was is, however, open to question: it could be an appearance of the risen Jesus, the finding of the empty tomb, or simply the failure to find the body of Jesus.

Our earliest account (1 Cor. 15) is a summary one and lacks certain elements of the Gospel stories: there is no mention of the empty tomb or of the women as witnesses. Peter (Cephas) is named as the first witness (15.5), although an encounter with him alone is never described in the Gospels, though it is alluded to in Luke 24.34. James, too, is singled out as a witness (15.7; an appearance is described in the apocryphal Gospel of the Hebrews), presumably reflecting the prominence of this brother of Jesus as leader of the church in Jerusalem (cf. Gal. 1.19; 2.9). Besides these appearances, Paul mentions those to "the Twelve" and to "the apostles" as well as to himself and to "more than 500 brethren at one time, of whom the majority are still alive, although some have died" (15.6). Some have identified this last reference as a variant account of that event that Acts describes as the outpouring of God's Spirit at Pentecost, which would imply that a "resurrection appearance" need not be so corporeal and tangible an encounter with an earthly being as the Gospel accounts suggest and that an encounter with the risen Jesus was not so different from an ecstatic spiritual experience.

Resurrection as the Continuation and Vindication of Jesus' "Career"

The Gospel accounts of the appearances of the risen Jesus to his disciples give the impression of a resumption of their former contact with Jesus, even though certain elements in the descriptions of these appearances indicate that they are unlike the disciples' previous experience of Jesus. Above all, the recurrent motif of nonrecognition (e.g., Luke 24.16; John 20.15) suggests that something is now different, even though other features of the stories suggest that Jesus appears in a normal human form (e.g., in Luke's Emmaus story, 24.13–32). Luke's account, in particular, is marked by the apologetic concern to show that the risen Jesus was a real physical being and no ghost (24.37, 39–43; cf. also John 20.25–27). Matthew is also characterized by an apologetic concern to rebut the Jewish charge that the disciples had faked a resurrection by removing the body of Jesus; this Gospel, like the Gospel of Peter, tells of the posting of a guard at the tomb to prevent just such an attempt (27.62–66; 28.11–15). In contrast, the return of Jesus to life after his crucifixion was claimed by the early Christians as his vindication by a divine intervention, a reversal of the humiliation of the death that the Jewish leaders, in collusion with the Romans, had inflicted upon him (especially in Acts: for example, 3.15; 10.40; 13.30), a reversal that demonstrated that he was indeed God's Son (e.g., Rom. 1.4): the one whose crucifixion had apparently discredited him and his claims had been raised by God from the dead, in Paul's eyes, as the prototype of redeemed humanity (1 Cor. 15.20–22, 45–49).

Although the Gospels portray the resurrection appearances as if the disciples had encountered an earthly figure, Paul lists his own conversion experience as part of the same sequence (1 Cor. 15.8), and his experience is depicted in Acts as an encounter with a glorious heavenly being (Acts 9.3–5; 22.6–8; 26.13–15). That fits in with Paul's stress (in 1 Cor. 15) on the discontinuity between the old human nature that must die and the new, glorious, qualitatively different nature ushered in by the risen Christ as last Adam and life-giving Spirit (15.45).

"Resurrection" in the New Testament World

In claiming that God had raised Jesus from the dead, the early Christians were claiming something new and unparalleled. Both the Greco-Roman and the Jewish world knew of stories of dead persons being miraculously raised in the sense of being restored to life in this world, that is, being rescued from a premature death to resume their life and to die again in the fullness of time; such stories were associated with the OT prophets Elijah and Elisha as well as with Jesus himself. What was claimed to have happened to the crucified Jesus was, however, qualitatively different: it was believed that he had been raised from the dead, never to die again; he had died once and for all and would never again be subject to death (Rom. 6.9). This point takes up another tradition of resurrection that first emerges clearly in the latest writings of the OT, above all in Daniel: resurrection is part of the events of the end time, whether these take place on a renewed earth or in a new heaven and earth, and leads to everlasting life (or, in the case of the wicked, to everlasting death, 12.2). There, resurrection is part of a cosmic final event ushering in a new, or at least renewed, world. In the case of Jesus, however, only one individual seemed to have been affected and the old world continued otherwise unchanged. The novelty of this claim again raises the question of why and how Jesus' followers could come to make it, for there can be little that could have predisposed them to expect anything quite like this, apart from the predictions of his resurrection attributed to Jesus; despite these the disciples are portrayed as totally unprepared for the course of events and in particular for Jesus' resurrection. Nevertheless, some have suggested that what the disciples claimed to have happened was predictable and fully to be expected. One would then have to question the accounts of the disciples' dismay and bewilderment at Jesus' arrest and death; on the whole, it seems likelier that these reflect the actual situation, rather than that they were composed simply to heighten the dramatic effect of the resurrection stories.

The language of "resurrection" presupposes that something basically physical had happened affecting Jesus' body, either restoring it or transforming it; talk of a "spiritual resurrection" is problematic if it means the raising of something other than the body. On that basis the Greco-Roman world in general regarded "resurrection" as an impossibility; one could instead survive beyond death in a disembodied form or one could bypass death by being transformed into an immortal being. In those circles where the physical body was viewed negatively, a bodily resurrection would naturally be viewed with disfavor and could play no part in hopes for immortality. That some later Gnostics, despite their negative view of the body, came to spiritualize the term "resurrection" may be attributed as much as anything to their desire to appear to belong still to a Christian tradition, for which belief in "resurrection" was an indispensable article of faith. Although some Jews, including those most influenced by the surrounding Greco-Roman world, expressed their future hope in other ways, others regarded resurrection as a possibility that they attributed to the creative power of God, who would restore the old body, fashion a new one, or both, the one after the other (2 Baruch 50–51). Above all, belief in resurrection seems to have been a hallmark of the Pharisaic movement to which Paul had belonged (cf. Acts 23.6–8).

However, it is clear that for Paul, the resurrection, though bodily, involves a different kind of body from that which we now have; flesh and blood cannot inherit God's kingdom (1 Cor. 15.50), and it would be a reasonable inference that this principle applied also to Jesus' resurrection in his eyes. In this respect, those Church Fathers and their successors who clung to a "resurrection of the flesh" were less true to Paul's vision than those Gnostics who spoke of a qualitatively different resurrection body.

Interpreting the Resurrection of Jesus

At first sight, the accounts of the resurrection describe a historical event, but the truth of historical events, particularly those so far in the past and of the controversial and mysterious nature of these ones, is notoriously hard to gauge and can at any rate only be established with greater or lesser probability. It is, moreover, in essence an unwitnessed event, since prior to the

Gospel of Peter there is no claim by anyone to have witnessed the raising of Jesus itself, but only the consequences that are attributed to this event, the empty tomb and the appearances of the already risen Jesus. It is clear that the assertion that God has raised Jesus from the dead has the status of interpreting the traditions of the empty tomb and the appearances, is an inference from them, and is meant to provide an explanation of them. The intractability of this event for historical research and questioning has led some to postulate a special status for it as "historical" in a different sense to the usual one and not subject to the same criteria for historical probability as others; one can then attain by other means to that certainty that Christian dogma requires. However, the rise of belief in Jesus' resurrection among his disciples is a firm historical datum, indeed our primary historical datum, and a historian may legitimately ask how this belief arose and how well founded it is.

The tradition of the empty tomb, whether it be early or late, admits in itself of more than one interpretation, as is shown by Matthew's mention of the Jewish accusation that the disciples had stolen the body. Equally ambiguous is the failure to find the body of Jesus, for the likelihood that one executed as a criminal was given the right to his own grave (even by an admirer's generosity, Mark 15.46–6, and parallels) rather than being simply thrown into a mass grave has been questioned. Perhaps to counter this possible explanation of the failure to find the body, the women are shown as witnessing where Jesus' body was laid (although one would normally expect them to play a leading role at his burial). But if, in fact, they could identify neither the grave nor the body, then one can more easily explain the lack of any cult connected with Jesus' grave in the first Christian centuries.

Of uncertain value, too, are the traditions of the appearances. On the one hand, we have the seemingly very tangible appearances in the Gospels; on the other, the thoroughly otherworldly experience that the account in Acts of Paul's conversion depicts, which seems to square with Paul's own expectations for a resurrection life qualitatively different from the one that preceded it. A shift from the otherworldly to the tangible can more easily be accounted for than a shift in the opposite direction, for this tangibility is sometimes clearly apologetically motivated; it has, however, been suggested that the experiences were indeed of two different kinds. The suggestion that these were all originally visionary experiences opens the way to a purely psychological explanation, and some have therefore sought to distinguish between "subjective" and "objective" visions, although this is a distinction that only the external observer can draw, not the person experiencing the vision, who is unable to decide whether the vision is self-induced or stems from some external cause.

Inherently problematic in the accounts depicting a more concrete encounter with a corporeal Jesus is the motif of nonrecognition. This difficulty is linked to the philosophical problem of the identity of the person who is thus resurrected, if personal identity is linked to one's bodily existence: it is difficult to conceive of a self that can exist independently of the bodily identity that we now have, particularly if one upholds the integrity of the person as a psychosomatic entity and rejects the notion of a "soul" or some noncorporeal entity that is the real bearer of identity and can be transferred from body to body. Here Paul is of no help, since his entire argument (1 Cor. 15.35ff.) seeks to show the qualitative difference between the old and the new; in fact, his characterization of the new largely consists in stating that it is not like the old ("immortal" instead of "mortal," etc.). The two-stage resurrection of 2 Baruch 50–51 does, however, tackle the problem of identity: restoration of the old to enable continuity and recognition, followed by transformation so that the resurrected can live forever.

In view of the difficulty in establishing what actually happened or of conceptualizing what is supposed to have happened, it is not surprising that some have concentrated on the hard facts of the disciples' belief in Jesus' resurrection or their spiritual experiences and the subsequent coming into being of the early Christian community with its message. Others are prepared merely to talk of the rise of "resurrection faith," although this phrase is ambiguous: it could mean either the faith that Jesus is risen or the faith that came into being as a result of what was believed to have been Jesus' resurrection, but which has its own validity regardless of whether Jesus actually was raised from the dead or not; the phrase is then all the more misleading if the "resurrection faith" is shaped more by the traditions of the earthly life of the crucified Jesus. These uncertainties are difficult if the resurrection is held to be so central for the validity and tenability of the Christian faith and raise the questions whether Christian faith can nevertheless exist and have value without the undergirding of certainty about this event, and indeed whether faith is really faith if it must depend upon this undergirding, quite apart from questions about the view of God's nature and God's relation to this world that this event presupposes.

A. J. M. Wedderburn

See also: Crossan, J. D.; Jesus, Family of; John, Gospel of; Luke, Gospel of, and Acts of the Apostles; Mark, Gospel of; Matthew, Gospel of; Paul; Reimarus, Hermann Samuel

References

Avis, Paul, ed. 1993. *The Resurrection of Jesus Christ*. London: Darton, Longman & Todd.

Barton, Stephen C., and Graham N. Stanton, eds. 1994. *Resurrection: Essays in Honour of Leslie Houlden*. London: SPCK.

Evans, Christopher F. 1970. *Resurrection and the New Testament*. London: SCM.

Lüdemann, Gerd. 1995. *The Resurrection of Jesus*. London: SCM.

Marxsen, Willi. 1970. *The Resurrection of Jesus of Nazareth*. London: SCM.

McDonald, J. Ian H. 1989. *The Resurrection: Narrative and Belief*. London: SPCK.

Perkins, Pheme. 1984. *Resurrection: New Testament Witness and Contemporary Reflection*. London: Geoffrey Chapman.

Perrin, Norman. 1977. *The Resurrection Narratives: A New Approach*. London: SCM.

Wedderburn, Alexander J. M. 1999. *Beyond Resurrection*. London: SCM; Peabody: Hendrickson.

Wright, N. T. 2003. *The Ressurection of the Son of God*. London: SPCK.

Ritschl, A.

See Ecclesiology; Essence of Christianity; German Christianity; Harnack, Adolf von

Roman Catholicism

The following article has very specific limits and aims. The very title may appear slightly tendentious and leaves it quite unclear when Roman Catholicism achieved the status of a distinct group of believers. For the purpose of this article I shall assume that it refers to those who acknowledge the primacy and infallibility of the pope and their understanding of the origins and tradition of Christianity. It is therefore clearly distinct from the various Eastern Orthodox churches, on the one hand, and from the many Protestant churches, on the other.

The article also assumes, at the outset, the truth of the Christological formulae worked out, above all, at Ephesus in 431, with its insistence on the title of "Mary Mother of God" for Our Lady, and at the Council of Chalcedon in 451, with its affirmation of the two natures of Christ. It is not primarily concerned with examining any subsequent efforts at exploring the inner theological sense to be given to the dogmatic truths they expressed at the second and third councils held at Constantinople in 553 and 681, respectively. Both of these endeavored to articulate the faith of Chalcedon by doing justice to the unity and true humanity of Christ.

The interest is rather in the way popular devotion has expressed itself toward the person of Jesus. Although the main accent falls on post–A.D. 1000 devotions, it should not be assumed either that there was no devotion in the first millennium of the history of the Church or that theology, properly so called, was totally silent on the person of Jesus. As we shall see, although in one sense many of the devotions received their final expression after 1000, their history stretches back much further. Popular piety is often neglected in the writings of more literate theologians. As in secular history, so also in religious matters, our present knowledge of the past is controlled by those who "won," or by those who were more articulate in their faith.

Even so, two brief introductory remarks are in place. First, although little will be said about modern Roman Catholic Christology, it would be quite misleading to infer from that shortcoming that it is either nonexistent or trivial. The German Jesuit Karl Rahner (1904–1984), among others, endeavored to present a credible picture of Jesus in the light of a modern understanding. Second, it is instructive to consider the varying ways in which the figure of Christ and of the cross have been portrayed in Western art. In the very earliest years, all we have is a bare cross of the type discovered in the ruins of Pompei. Later on, the cross, again without a figure, is attended by the sun and moon. This representation, as well as the lifting up from the earth, is doubtless intended to express the victory of the Word over the powers of this world. Later on still, the figure begins to appear. Initially it was adorned with the robes of the priest and the crown of a king, to illustrate his dual role. Such representations date back to the eighth century. Then and finally, we find the most well known depictions of Christ with cruel realism in great pain. The most famous of these pictures, by Matthias Grünewald (1475–1528), occurs in the *Isenheim Altarpiece*.

If we inquire what it was that influenced the changing expressions of the lordship of Jesus, various answers may be offered. It was partly theology. It is always instructive to note that the interest of the early Church was focused on the divinity of Christ, a truth that was expressed at Nicea in 325 with the affirmation of the "consubstantiality" of the second person with the Father. For Augustine, the human nature was the means through which we travel to his divinity (*Tractate on John* xiii.4). Only later did the importance of the human nature call for emphasis in 431 and 451. The human Christ became more and more central, above all in the West, the divinity being recognized rather by the reaction of others to Christ than by any particularly divine elements in his representation. Finally, it may be suggested that the desire to identify Christ with human degradation was aided by the various catastrophes that struck Europe in the Middle Ages. We need a Christ who shares our nature in all its many aspects.

It is of course true that the Jesus Prayer was in circulation from the earliest days of Diadochus of Photike (mid-fifth century), above all in the East. It is also true that we find a passionate intensity in the devotion to the person of Jesus of such disparate writers as St. Paul, whose Christ mysticism finds expression in his letters to the Galatians (2.20 and 6.14) and to the Philippians (2.21), St. Ignatius of Antioch (died c. 107) in his letter to the Ephesians, and St. Jerome (345–420). But they originated no particular, distinctive form of devotion to Christ. We have to wait until the beginning of the eleventh century for this development.

The Medieval Period

We may begin with the life and work of St. Bernard of Clairvaux (1090–1153), "the last of the Fathers." In his writings, he endeavored, unsuccessfully, to limit the place of reason in theology. He also displayed an intense devotion to the person of Christ (especially in his sermons on the Song of Songs). This attitude had not been entirely absent in the earlier period, but it received a far greater degree of prominence from 1100 onward. It is notably distinct both from the "Platonic" tendency manifest among the great third- to fifth-century Fathers and from the drier approach of the great Scholastics, which owes something to Aristotle. The more devotional approach is connected with the devotion to the name of Jesus, finding expression in the hymn *Jesu dulcis memoria* ("Jesu, the very thought is sweet," popularly but erroneously ascribed to St. Bernard).

It was the same saint's intense devotion to the humanity of Christ and to his Passion that prompted devotion to the Five Sacred Wounds, one in the side and two each in the hands and feet, based upon the accounts of the Passion and the resurrection appearances of Christ, above all in Luke 24.39 and John 20. 27. The stigmata of St. Francis helped to further this devotion. The side of Christ was held to be particularly significant as it was believed to be the source of Christ's life in the Church through the two sacraments of baptism (the water) and the Eucharist (the blood). The members of the Pilgrimage of Grace in Northern England (1536–1537) wore the emblem of the five wounds on their sleeves.

It is, however, with St. Francis of Assisi (1181/2–1226) that popular and enduring devotion to the person of Christ really begins, though in some of its features it picks up earlier themes. This is true, for example, of devotion to the crib. There was a crib in Rome from the sixth century onward in the basilica of Santa Maria Maggiore. Franciscan devotion to the crib dates to 1223, in which year St. Francis is thought to have made one in Greccio, filling a manger with straw and introducing into the scene an ass and an ox, neither of which appears in the account of the Nativity in the New Testament. They were added in deference to the words of Isaiah 1.3, "The ox knoweth its owner and the ass his master's crib."

The Stations of the Cross in the form used today, with the fourteen representations depicting Jesus' last journey from the house of Pilate through his entombment, followed at some uncertain date not long afterward. The credit for "inventing" the Stations of the Cross belongs to Jan van Paesschen, prior of the Carmelites at Malines, though the extension of the devotion owes much to the eighteenth-century Franciscan St. Leonard of Port Maurice. It used to be the case that only Franciscan priests could erect and bless the stations. However, this devotion, too, had earlier roots and goes back to the time when devout pilgrims, particularly in the fourth century, followed the path traced by Christ on his way to Calvary. Egeria recounted her involvement in the various celebrations sometime between 381 and 384, and these included retracing Christ's sorrowful journey to Calvary.

The devotion to the blessed sacrament was encouraged by Blessed Juliana of Liège (1192–1258), an Augustinian nun. Her labors as champion of the feast of Corpus Christi began in 1206. The flowering came about subsequently through the theological genius of St. Thomas Aquinas (1224/5–1274), and the establishment of the Feast of Corpus Christi in 1264 by Pope Urban IV, who had previously been archdeacon of Liège, on the Thursday following Trinity Sunday. Although the doctrine of transubstantiation was "defined" at the fourth Lateran council of 1215, it owes its classic formulation to St. Thomas.

It is perhaps surprising, therefore, when one considers the amazing speculative powers of St. Thomas, that he could express so evident a personal feeling toward the Blessed Sacrament. This apparent contrast has even led people to suspect—wrongly as it turns out—the authenticity of his works of devotion. It is to St. Thomas that we owe the great office hymns, above all the *Lauda Sion*, set to music by Mendelssohn in 1846; the *Verbum supernum prodiens*, with its well-known last stanzas beginning "O salutaris hostia," and the *Pange Lingua*. The last two verses of this latter hymn, beginning "Tantum ergo"—"Therefore we before him bending this great sacrament adore"—are regularly used in the service of Benediction. The hymn *Adore Te* has been beautifully put into English by the Jesuit priest-poet Gerard Manley Hopkins (1844–1889) in the poem beginning with the words, "O godhead here in hiding."

The Rosary, whose invention is often erroneously ascribed to St. Dominic (1172–1221) as a weapon against the Albigensian heresy, came about considerably later. Its ascription to St. Dominic owes much to the revelations said to have been received by the Dominican Alain de la Roche. The devotion was given a great boost by the Dominican pope St. Pius V, who, in 1572, instituted the Feast of the Holy Rosary in thanksgiving for the Christian victory over the Turks at Lepanto on 7 October 1571. As a form of prayer, it consists of fifteen decades, with one Our Father, ten Hail Marys, and one Glory Be to the Father per decade, and is made up of three distinct groups of mysteries, Joyful, Sorrowful, and Glorious, beginning with the Annunciation and ending with the Coronation of Mary in heaven and the glory of all the saints. The recitation of the prayers helps to fix the mind and heart on the actual mystery in question.

This effect is also true of the devout meditation on the Life of Christ we find in the Carthusian, Ludolph of Saxony (1300–1378), a work that, at a later date, probably exercised a marked influence on St. Ignatius Loyola (1491–1556). The similarities between the biblical text of the *Exercises* of Ignatius and that of Ludolph are remarkable.

The culmination of this medieval devotion to Jesus is to be found in *The Imitation of Christ* by Thomas à Kempis (1380–1471), a work that, for all its power, marks an insistence on the relative unimportance of the mind in religious inquiries and may reflect a reaction against the austere logic of later scholastic thought. We find statements such as "I had rather feel compunction than know its definition" (1.1.3) and "What good is it to know the whole of the Bible from outside and yet have no humility and so displease God?" (1.1.1). The anti-intellectual and individualistic tone of the *Imitation* had the important result of distancing yet more the life of piety and religion from the life of learning and theology and effected a distance between theology and spirituality that had been foreign to the life of the patristic period, when great theologians such as Origen and Augustine had combined the two.

The Reformation and Later

The great saints of the Counter-Reformation, above all St. Ignatius of Loyola, the founder of the Society of Jesus, and Sts. Teresa of Avila (1515–1582) and John of the Cross (1542–1591), the reformers of the Carmelites, are all remarkable for their insistence on devotion to the historical, physical reality of the person of Jesus. The tendency to abstraction, evident, for example, in the writings of Evagrius (345–399), and the consequent reserve toward representations of Christ, is wholly absent from them. Even the Baroque style of architecture, used, for example, by the Jesuits in the mother Church of the Jesu in Rome, expresses by its use of color and statues the importance attached to outward beauty in its effort to lift the mind and heart to God. The spiritual exercises of St. Ignatius also invite those who make them to use the imagination in order to appreciate more fully the mysteries of the life of Christ. To that end they invite the user to meditate on the life of Christ by using the Synoptic Gospels rather than the more divine John. So, too, St. Teresa, in chapter 22 of her *Life*, wrote that "we must approach to the most

Jan de Heem's oil painting Eucharist in a Fruit Wreath, 1648, *exemplifies a genre of religious still lifes with fruit. The Eucharist motif, including a luminous rendition of the host, reflects the Catholic Counter-Reformation's response to the Protestant doctrine that bread and wine played only a symbolic role during communion. (Kunsthistorisches Museum, Vienna)*

exalted contemplation by way of Christ's humanity." The same attitude is found in the works of St. John of the Cross.

Further than this, the Church of the Counter-Reformation retained many of its pre-Reformation devotions, but it added to them at least two further ones, the devotion to the Infant of Prague and the more universally used devotion to the Sacred Heart. The former of these two refers to a statue of the child Jesus, holding in his left hand a globe with a cross on it, with his right hand extended in blessing. Since 1628 this statue has stood in the church of Our Lady of Victories in Prague, which belongs to the Discalced Carmelites. It came to Prague from Spain in the sixteenth century, but as to its previous history, nothing is known.

Devotion to the Sacred Heart, which has medieval roots in the writings of Saint Gertrude (c. 1256–1302), and is therefore not technically novel, owed its expansion to the visions between 1673 and 1675 of the Visitandine St. Margaret Mary Alacoque (1648–1690) at Paray-le-Monia. In 1765, Pope Clement XIII approved the office and feast for the whole Church. The devotion to the Sacred Heart was entrusted to the Society of Jesus, initially in the person of St. Claude la Colombière (1641–1682), and it is possible to see in it a challenge to the austere view of Christ and his salvation furthered by the Jansenists. It insisted both on the importance of devotion in religion and on the universal character of Christ's love against the somber doctrine of the "fewness of the elect," illustrated by the so-called Jansenist crucifix, where the arms are not outstretched to embrace all. The Feast of the Sacred Heart is kept on the Friday after the first Sunday after Trinity Sunday.

On 11 December 1925, Pope Pius XI (1857–1939) instituted the title feast of Christ the King, which is now observed on the Sunday before the first Sunday of Advent. Its express purpose was to lead the human race to "seek the peace of Christ" in the "Kingdom of Christ." It was, as it were, the answer of the Church to, and in, a Europe overshadowed by the First World War, and soon to undergo a second, while at the same time it labored under the ever-increasing threat of communism.

The last important, and now immensely popular, devotion to the Divine Mercy was revealed to Sister, now St., Faustina Kowalska (1905–1938) on 22 February 1931. She saw a vision with rays of mercy streaming from the area of the heart. She was instructed to have an image painted, underneath which was to be written, as a sort of signature, the words "Jesus, I trust in you." The message of Jesus to Faustina was, "Tell ailing mankind to draw close to my Merciful Heart and I will fill it with peace. . . . [M]ankind will not find solace until it turns with confidence to My Mercy." This, in many ways, is an extension of the devotion to the Sacred Heart, though there the accent falls on the importance of reparation, and here it is on the need of the human race for divine love and forgiveness. Perhaps the change in tone reflects the differing worlds in which the two saints received their respective revelations.

All these devotions insist upon aspects of Christ's relationship to us rather than on particular events in the course of his earthly life. Margaret Mary came from the society of seventeenth-century France, which was still basically Christian; the devotions to Christ the King and to the Divine Mercy reflect a less evidently Christian set of values and environment.

By way of conclusion, two points deserve mention. First, in all the cases that depend for their promotion on particular revelations, these revelations have been invariably accorded to women. This is true of devotions to the Blessed Sacrament (see above on Corpus Christi), to the Sacred Heart, and to the Divine Mercy, seemingly a reflection of the fact, evident in the Gospels, that the earliest post-resurrection appearances of Jesus were also made to women (cf. Matt. 28.1–10, Mark 16.1–8, Luke 24.1–11, and John 20.11–18). Even as the apostles found it hard to accept the message of the women, so, too, none of the later women in question found an easy or speedy acceptance within the Church. Second, there was a marked tendency, in the medieval period, to concentrate on the childhood and Passion of Christ. The devotion to the five wounds, to the Stations, to the crib, and to the Infant of Prague exemplify this. Perhaps the very frailty of Christ and his hidden divinity fostered this devout attitude. By contrast with most medieval devotions, the more modern period is a witness to a concentration on perpetual truths about Christ, such as his Sacred Heart, his Divine Mercy, and his Kingship.

Anthony Meredith

See also: Aquinas, Thomas; Art; Augustine of Hippo; Bernard of Clairvaux; Chalcedon; English Christianity, Medieval; Eucharist; Francis of Assisi; French Christianity; Ignatius of Antioch; Ignatius of Loyola; Jesus, Name of; Jesus as Emperor; John of the Cross; Kempis, Thomas à; Mary; Orthodox Tradition; Pilgrimage; Prayer; Rahner, Karl; Spanish Christianity; Teresa of Avila

References

Cross, F. L., and E. A. Livingstone, eds. 1997. *The Oxford Dictionary of the Christian Church*. Oxford: Oxford University Press.
Duffy, Eamon. 1992. *The Stripping of the Altars*. London: Yale University Press.
Kosicki, George W. 1996. *Revelations of Divine Mercy*. Ann Arbor, MI: Charis.
New Catholic Encyclopedia. 1967. New York: McGraw-Hill.
Rubin, Miri. 1991. *Corpus Christi: The Eucharist in Late Medieval Culture*. Cambridge: Cambridge University Press.
Southern, R. W. 1970. *Western Society and the Church in the Middle Ages*. Harmondsworth, UK: Penguin.
Walsh, Michael. 1993. *A Dictionary of Devotions*. London: Burns and Oates.

Russian Christianity

The Christ of the Byzantine Liturgy

Christianity reached Kievan *Rus'* in the tenth century with a considerable library (including the liturgical texts) written in a language very close to the vernacular: Old Slavonic. Originally, this was one of the dialects of southern Slavs that was used by the missionaries for translating sacred books from the Greek.

The availability of the Christian literature in the vernacular turned out to be a mixed blessing. The texts for translation were chosen normally from the libraries of the Greek monasteries, which did not contain secular literature. The rich libraries of Constantinople were hardly known to the Russians. The circle of available literature was therefore limited: more than half of all known Russian manuscripts are scriptural or liturgical texts. That may explain the absence of rational scientific investigation in theology almost up to the nineteenth century. "For seven centuries—that is, until the seventeenth—we know of no scientific work in Russian literature, not even a dogmatic thesis. . . . Russia, in fact, did not receive together with Greek Christianity the classical culture of Greece."

For this reason, liturgy, and not teaching, became the center of Russian Christianity. Jesus was known primarily as the Lord of common worship, the Pantocrator ("Lord of all"), the monarch of the heavenly court surrounded by angels and saints, his courtiers. His monarchical heavenly glory overshadows his sufferings, which remain peripheral and are interpreted in an abstract way rather than with human realism.

To the ruling classes, Christianity opened the way to the "civilized" world without any danger for the established social and political order. However, in the agricultural communities, any religion was judged primarily by its ability to influence the elemental natural forces.

The Christ in the Context of Slavic Archaic Religion

The basic myth of the Slavic archaic religion, which can be traced back to its Indo-European origins, describes the contest between the God of Thunder (Slavic "Perun") and his adversary (the God of the Earth, Slavic "Veles"). Both deities are important and alternate their influence over the course of the agricultural cycle. No Christian interpretation, with its moral focus, could introduce Christ into that dual structure: his adversary was the Antichrist who was completely evil and could bring only disaster to those who invoked him. In practice, St. Nicholas took the place of Veles and Elijah the prophet that of Perun. This explains why the importance of St. Nicholas is so disproportionate in Russian folk Christianity: his feasts still gather more worshipers than any other festivities, even Easter or Christmas. In this "non-official" mythology, St. Nicholas sometimes completely overshadows the Trinity: as the saying goes, "[I]f God dies, Nicola [St. Nicholas] will receive his power and succeed him."

Christ Pantocrator was connected to another archaic context. The cross on top of the onion-shaped dome of any Russian church is often coupled with a crescent. This tradition can be traced back to the twelfth century. Pagan Slavs wore crescents as amulets, sometimes also combined in one piece with a pectoral cross. Cross and crescent are symbols of the Sun and Moon, respectively. In Christian interpretation, the Sun stands for Christ, the Moon for the Mother of God. In the Byzantine liturgy, this symbolism is employed, for example, in the services of Christmas, Good Friday, and Holy Saturday. The same symbols could also be popularly interpreted as representing the "old" Indo-European deities: the custom of making the sign of the cross facing the Sun (or the Moon) is mentioned (and severely condemned) by Christian preachers as late as the end of the seventeenth century.

The cross became the main symbol representing Christ, and the cross and Christ are effectively identified in many texts of Byzantine liturgy. In Russian, the very words "cross" and "Christ" sound alike in most grammatical cases (e.g., genitive: *Khrist'a* and *krest'a*). No wonder that in fourteenth-century Novgorod the anticlerical movement of *strigol'niki* introduced the tradition of confession to the cross.

At the same time, the mythology of the cross/Christ is undoubtedly connected to the archaic mythology of the cosmic tree. The cross takes the place of the paradisal Tree of Life (another "type" or foreshadowing of the cross), and its four arms consecrate the "four-cornered earth," as in many archaic models of the world. The cross, like the traditional cosmic tree, is seen as the center of the world, providing the foundational support for the whole

Church of the Transfiguration, Kizhi, Karelia, Russia (The Art Archive/Nicolas Sapieha)

universe and serving as a way to heaven. The "action" of the cross consists in the fact that it guarantees victory over both demons and the enemies of the Church.

This complex amalgam of Byzantine Christianity and Slavic traditional religion remained alive and active for a very long time. In 1860, A.N. Afanas´ev published his all-embracing anthropological study that described pagan customs and rituals in Russian villages. The lethal blow to folk Christianity was given by Stalin's regime in the 1930s, when the traditional agricultural communities, which were also the grassroots communities of the Orthodox Church, were destroyed.

The Christ of the Nonconformist Religious Movements

The first large-scale attempt to "purify" the folk-tradition was made in the seventeenth century. By that time, after the fall of Constantinople, Moscow had become the center of the Orthodox world: it had *the* Orthodox monarch, the tsar ("Caesar"), in 1547, and *the* patriarch, in 1589, both titles that were officially validated by the senior Orthodox patriarchs. The new status of Moscow obliged Patriarch Nikon in 1653 to undertake a reform of existing practices so that Moscow would be worthy of the name of New Constantinople, the Third Rome. Liturgical texts had to be revised and corrected in accordance with the Greek originals. Christ of the liturgy became the central issue of the debate.

The new Slavonic spelling of the name Jesus made it closer to the traditional Greek pronunciation: instead of "Isus" it became "Iisus." But within the context of mythological consciousness, the change of the signifier led inevitably to the change of the signified. It is beyond human power to change verbal or any other signs in a sacred text, ritual, or custom, opponents said. So the "new" name of Jesus could not be received as the name of Christ, the object of faith. The wrong name could belong only to a wrong Christ, the Antichrist. Another novelty also concerned Christ: a newly adapted way of making the sign of the cross. Finally, new prescriptions for the order of processions in the liturgy were published: instead of going clockwise, "with the Sun" in Russian, they now had to go counterclockwise, "against the Sun." To go against the Sun meant, for many, to go against Christ the Sun of Justice. As processions were an important element in the sacraments and sacramentals, the "wrong" processions made the sacraments "wrong," that is, not merely invalid but sacrilegious. All of these things instigated a schism in the Russian Church.

For the Old Believers, as they came to be called, the traditional sacred history had come to an end. The only way to be with Christ was to suffer with him, not symbolically through the Church's sacraments, now seen as sacrilegious, but in real life. They were subjected to merciless persecution. Avvakum, their leader, introduced a new element into their Christ-centered devotion: self-sacralization through sufferings and death, including suicide. Collective suicides by fire (about 20,000 by the end of the seventeenth century) demonstrated the popularity of his teaching.

Self-sacralization inspired another movement that emerged in the late sixteenth century: that of *khristy* ("christs," in plural), known also by its later name *khlysty* ("scourges," probably because of the practice of self-flagellation). Little is known about the original ideology of the movement, and much was done by the official Church (and state) to discredit it. During court trials (1745–1756), the most terrible accusations (for example, infanticide, cannibalism, and sexual promiscuity) were based on confessions obtained by torture: indeed, to call somebody with unusual behavior "a christ" was normal in the peasant milieu in the eighteenth century. The immediate presence of the Holy Spirit in the soul brought about the likeness to Christ, indeed was seen as turning one into another christ. Liturgical gatherings had ecstatic elements and were understood as ascension to another world. The central theme of khristy hymns was the Last Judgment. There was no fear, however, as the members of a community knew they had been already justified and that they lived, as it were, in Paradise.

Although the khristy movement disappeared from view in the Soviet period, an interesting parallel to it emerged in the post-Communist decade of the 1990s. "The Church of the Last Testament" was founded in 1991 in Siberia by a former policeman who, after his dramatic conversion, took the name of Vissarion Christ. In less than five years, the movement attracted about 40,000 devotees, mostly well-educated urban intelligentsia in their thirties. Vissarion Christ called his followers to build "the City of the Sun" in the middle of West Siberian forest land, or *taiga*. It is supposed to be an oasis of "new humankind" living in harmony with themselves, with society and with nature, a self-sufficient economic unit. The response has been enormous, and the city is being built in spite of opposition from the local authorities and lack of money. Vissarion Christ preaches the "one unifying faith" embracing all religions. He himself is the center of the new humankind, and without him full union with God is not possible. His Last Testament consists of sixty-one commandments, but real guidance comes from the "voice of one's heart." There are also some elements of New Age ideology, theosophy, yoga, and the like.

The Tsar as Christ

The Slavonic word "tsar" is derived from "Caesar," originally a proper name and then a title of the Roman and Byzantine emperors (also, later, under Tartar rule, for the khan). In Slavonic translations the same word is used in the Bible and liturgical books for the kings of Israel (e.g., David) as well as for Christ. Ivan IV ("the Terrible") used the title for the first time at his inauguration (1547) in order to demonstrate that from now on, in spite of the fall of Constantinople, the Byzantine emperor would have a successor in the New Constantinople, Moscow. Indeed, it seemed obvious to Byzantine theologians, together with their Russian followers, that Orthodox Christianity was deficient without an Orthodox emperor as the central figure of the Orthodox world.

In this Russian context, the relations of the word "tsar" to the Greek "basileus" (king or emperor) or the Tartar "khan" were no longer relevant and it was the biblical connotations that came to the fore. During the inauguration ritual, the sacrament of confirmation was administered to the tsar for the second time, turning him into someone with a unique status. He received a special charisma of power and could also exercise certain sacramental rights otherwise reserved for ordained priests. That charisma was understood as a sacred gift of Christ's kingship. The monarch became the Christ (literally "anointed one") of today, the successor of Christ the King, the living image of God. From the beginning of the eighteenth century, the name "Christ" was used increasingly as the title of Russian monarchs. Thus, in Russian custom, the anniversaries of major military victories became liturgical feasts—for example, in 1709, after Peter the Great won the battle of Poltava, defeating the Swedish army. In the *liturgical* text for the feast, Peter is called "Christ," his military commanders are called "apostles," and the treacherous ally Mazepa is called "Judas." In the same way, the events of the tsar's life (birthday, name day, coronation) entered the Church calendar as feast days. The denial of the sacred character of the monarchical power was punished by excommunication. Many prominent theologians, such as Pavel Florenskii (1882–1937), considered the Russian tsar's sacred prerogatives a dogma of Orthodox religion.

The Christ of the Monastic Tradition

The Byzantine legacy received by Russia always had a strong monastic aspect. Most of the translations into the Slavonic language were made in the Greek monasteries and reflected the interests and horizons of the monastic community.

The first monastic communities of the Kievan period developed their own original tradition of *kenosis*, "self-emptying," imitating Christ, who "emptied himself to assume the condition of a slave" (Phil. 2.7). Poverty, manual labor, humility, obedience, forgiveness and love of enemies, and service to one's neighbors were held in high esteem and led to many canonizations (that is, declarations of sainthood). The Slavophiles of the nineteenth century romanticized kenoticism as a uniquely Russian spiritual tradition. In Fedor Tiutchev's poem (1855), Christ, laden with the burden of the cross, wanders over Russia like a servant blessing its poor, humble people.

In the Moscow period, Russian monasticism came into contact with a more sophisticated version of the Byzantine spiritual tradition that affirmed the concrete possibility in this life of beholding the vision of God through his divine energies. Byzantine theology described this union with the term *theosis*, "divinization," partaking in the divine nature. Divinization comes through contemplative prayer, and especially through the hesychastic ascetical method (from *hesychia*, "stillness"). It combined repetitive prayer formulas with bodily postures and controlled breathing (and was opposed by both Latin Christians and Byzantine humanists). An important element of it was the continual invocation of the name of Jesus, as in the "Jesus Prayer": "Lord Jesus Christ, Son of God, have mercy on me, a sinner."

The decline of monasteries in Greece under the Turkish rule and in Russia as a result of massive secularization (two-thirds of monasteries were closed during the eighteenth century) delayed the assimilation of hesychast spirituality. Its revival came with the publication of the anthology of the writings of the Desert Fathers known as the *Philokalia* (1782; Slavonic translation,

1793; Russian translation, 1877). This anthology, 1,207 pages of spiritual writings dating from the fourth to the fifteenth centuries, became *the* textbook of Russian spirituality. The role of the *Philokalia* is manifest in the book written by an anonymous layman, *The Way of the Pilgrim* (1884), which became a classic. The author describes how he learned step-by-step to pray the Jesus Prayer unceasingly.

It is difficult to imagine how the doctrine of stillness and unceasing prayer can lead to civil unrest, but it happened in 1913 among the Russian monks of Athos (in northern Greece). The issue was *imiaslavie* ("the worship of the name"), a doctrine imported from Russia. According to it, salvation is possible only by Jesus' name. This name itself contains God's energy, which is inseparable from God's essence and therefore *is* God himself. Opponents found in that doctrine only pagan pantheism and magic. The latter view was supported by the Church hierarchy in both Greece and Russia. In the end, a Russian bishop, accompanied by a military task force, was sent to Athos to stop the conflict. About 1,000 adherents of imiaslavie were arrested, removed from Athos, and dispersed over Russian monasteries.

Jesus as the Human Ideal and the Prophet of Justice

The Russian educated elite of the late eighteenth century could only accept religion, if at all, in the shape of deism, especially in connection with the freemasonry that was widespread and influential in Russia. Gradually, the humanist ideals of the Enlightenment led the same elite to give Christianity "a human face" by separating it from the Orthodox religion. Henri de Saint-Simon's *New Christianity* (1825), in which the French socialist proclaimed that religion's goal was "improving as quickly as possible the conditions of the poorest class," stimulated the return of the human Christ as a moral example to the center of the Russian cultural scene.

Vissarion Belinskii (1811–1848), a follower and correspondent of Saint-Simon's, wrote to Nikolai Gogol in 1847:

> What have you found in common between Christ and any church, least of all the Orthodox Church? He was the first to bring to people the teaching of freedom, equality, and brotherhood and to set the seal of truth to that teaching by martyrdom. . . . The Church, on the other hand, was a hierarchy, consequently a champion of inequality, a flatterer of authority, an enemy and persecutor of brotherhood among men—and so it has remained to this day. But the meaning of Christ's message has been revealed by the philosophical movement of the preceding century. And that is why a man like Voltaire, who stamped out the fires of fanaticism and ignorance in Europe by ridicule, is, of course, more the son of Christ, flesh of his flesh and bone of his bone, than all your priests, bishops, metropolitans, and patriarchs—Eastern or Western.

The painter Aleksandr Ivanov (1806–1858) gives us a good illustration here. He went to Rome to work at his major painting, *The Appearance of the Messiah* (1835–1857): Jesus approaching the bank of the Jordan for his baptism by John. The original idea was to show the moral renewal of the people inspired by the divinity of Jesus. He radically reassessed these plans after reading *Life of Jesus* (1835) by D. Strauss, where a clear distinction was made between the historical fact of Jesus and its mythical interpretation by his followers. Ivanov meticulously studied the book and even consulted Strauss. Now, Ivanov thought it preferable to portray a human Jesus who fulfills God's will completely and thereby becomes God-like, so that after his death the unenlightened masses would divinize him, whereas the enlightened few would respect him. Every character of this huge painting (now in the Tretiakov Gallery in Moscow) is synthesized from sketches of ancient sculptures and real-life models: ideal beauty merged with concrete reality. Thus, for the prototypes of his Jesus, Ivanov chose the face of Apollo Belvedere, a mosaic of the Byzantine Pantocrator from Sicily, combined with the faces of many simple men, and even women, of Italy.

By the 1860s, a social activist who was to suffer for bringing historically realistic truth to the people became typically associated with Jesus. Nikolai Nekrasov (1821–1878) wrote in 1874 about Nikolai Chernyshevskii, who had just been sent to internal exile for his socialist writings: "They have not crucified him, not yet, But come the hour, he will be on the cross. The God of sorrow and anger has sent him To remind the tsars of the earth of Christ." Here tsars are not at all "living Christs" as the Orthodox religion would claim but rather the opponents of Christ; on the contrary, Chernyshevskii is the true successor of Christ, to be crucified by them.

The most consistent ideology of Russian social Christianity was produced by Leo Tolstoy (1828–1910). In his *Gospels Translated, Compared, and Harmonised* (1880–1882), he presented his own "corrected" version of the Gospel story, which ends simply with the death of Jesus. For Tolstoy, Jesus is not the Son of God but only a wise man whose teaching could change the world if only the people would understand it and try to live by it. Tolstoy's "translation" is in fact a very convincing and powerful exposition of ethical religion that critics routinely have compared to Buddhism. Together with Tolstoy's other works on religion and ethics, it made a strong impact on Russian society and influenced even very distant countries and cultures (for example, Gandhi in India).

The radicalization of Christ's image probably reached its peak in *The Seven Who Were Hanged* (1908) by Leonid Andreev. In this novel, seven individuals—five terrorists and two common criminals—are condemned to death. The portrayal of the terrorists alludes strongly to the crucifixion of Jesus as they are arrested, tried, and then slowly transported to the place of their execution together with two common criminals. Tanya, one of the terrorists, is an example of someone willing to give up her own life to create a better society, and her selflessness becomes a model for action.

Jesus and the Grand Inquisitor

A challenging alternative to Saint-Simon's "new Christianity" was raised by a former adherent (and martyr) of it, Fyodor Dostoyevsky (1821–1881). "The Legend of the Grand Inquisitor" is a part of his novel *The Brothers Karamazov* (1880). The story is set in Spain in the sixteenth century. Jesus is visiting the sites of auto-da-fé where the flames are crackling around the heretics. He blesses the people and raises a child from the dead. Seeing that, the Grand Inquisitor has Jesus arrested and then comes to prison to talk to him. Jesus remains silent. The Inquisitor interprets his silence as his respect for human freedom, the same respect that Jesus showed in the desert when he rejected the temptation to turn stones into bread. What is freedom worth if obedience is bought with bread?

Freedom without bread is not worth much either. The Inquisitor prophesies that the time will come when religion and morality will be rejected: "There is no crime, and therefore no sin; there is only hunger. Feed people, and then ask of them virtue!" However, all the attempts to build this new society where everybody has enough bread would inevitably fail because "freedom and bread enough for all are inconceivable together, for never, never will they be able to share between them!" (See in Book 5, ch. 5).

The Inquisitor holds Jesus responsible for raising unrealistic expectations among the people, who can never be free because they are "weak, vicious, worthless, and rebellious." Jesus thought "too highly" of humankind. By showing people so much respect, he asked far too much of them, leaving them only his image as their guide. At some point, the burden of free choice proved unbearable, and they could not have been left in greater confusion and suffering than Jesus had caused, laying upon them so many cares and unanswerable problems.

The Inquisitor reminds Jesus that only a few noble souls were able to follow him in the course of history. Does Jesus care only for the elect, while the millions, numerous as the sands of the shore, must exist only for the sake of the great and strong? Against that, the Church sought to make all people happy by relieving them of the burden of freedom. Jesus could only disturb this work. That is why he should die in fire. Jesus suddenly approaches the old man in silence and gently kisses him. That is his answer. The old man opens the door of the prison cell: "Go, and come no more . . . come not at all, never, never!" Jesus disappears in darkness.

This enigmatic and disturbing parable formulated the central problem for Russian religious thought from the 1880s onward. V. S. Soloviev, N. A. Berdiaev, M. A. Bulgakov, and V. V. Rozanov, among many others, tried to give it a philosophical interpretation. Dostoyevsky put a question mark over the humanistic social project of the new Christianity (and socialism in general). Could social harmony be combined with material prosperity without loss of freedom? Would the destitute majority not prefer it to poverty? Would the masses not keep their religion that claims to have final answers rather than strive for a genuine faith that can only ask ultimate questions?

The Revolution of 1905 demonstrated that Dostoyevsky's legend might become a political scenario of the future. The anthology *Vekhi* (Landmarks), published in 1909, severely criticized the Russian intelligentsia for its irresponsibility, self-indulgence, intolerance, and thoughtless activismand for the superficial character of its beliefs. The authors suggested a reconsideration of the spiritual tradition of Orthodox Christianity in the light of religious philosophy, as Vladimir Soloviev had done before. The general trend in society was for an "alternative" Christ. Theosophy and anthroposophy became popular in the educated classes together with the revival of mystical sects, such as the above-mentioned *khristy/khlysty*. Grigorii Rasputin found his way to the tsar's palace precisely as a representative of this "genuine" folk Christianity.

After the Revolution of 1917, Jesus became the object of many mock trials; he was charged, in accordance with the legend, with indifference to the sufferings of the poor. Typically, he was sentenced to death. However, V. I. Lenin's death caused the return of the Christ image *incognito*, now applied to Lenin. Vladimir Maiakovskii (1893–1930), in a poem of 1924, depicted Lenin after the style of Byzantine liturgy, contrasting his visible human nature with his superhuman role in history, and his bodily death with his ascension to a higher level of life. Then Stalin's rule brought back the imperial image of Christ the tsar. After years of oppression, in 1944, in the war against Hitler, Stalin ordered the restoration of the Russian Orthodox Church, to be a focus of patriotism. In return, the newly elected Patriarch Sergius gave him a monarchical title "Our God-appointed Leader." In hymns, even in the state anthem of the time, Stalin was compared typically to the Sun, thus appealing to the most archaic layer of folk religion.

Jesus: Myth or Reality?

In 1922, however, all religious books, from the Bible to "idealist" philosophy, had been removed from public libraries and bookshops. Atheism became part of the state ideology. One of its most important components was the theory of Arthur Drews (1865–1936). According to him, the Jesus of the Gospels was a fiction, the product of a long tradition related to the ancient cult of a dying and rising Oriental deity. The Soviet propaganda machine elevated this theory to the rank of objective scientific truth, including it in textbooks for schools and universities.

Severe censorship meant there was no opportunity for a proper response to this propaganda. Russian émigré Dimitrii Merezhkovskii (1865–1941), in *Jesus the Unknown* (1931) agreed with Drews in finding many similarities between the Jesus of the Gospels and the deities of archaic myths but found the denial of the historicity of Jesus totally groundless. Merezhkovskii's theological framework, however, was full of fantastic elements, making references to Atlantis, the heavenly "Mother" of Jesus, and the like. His work remained little known in Russia.

Few significant attempts to respond to the claim of Soviet atheism were made in the 1960s. In 1966, *The Master and Margarita*, a novel by Mikhail Bulgakov (1928–1940), was published. He relied heavily on *The Life of Christ* (1874) by F. W. Farrar (1831–1903), and his interpretation of the Gospels is close to Strauss's. On the last day of his life, Jeshuah (his Jesus character) appears as an ordinary looking man bearing the signs of physical violence, fearful and anxious, and he dies because the mob misunderstands him and Pilate is too much of a coward to protect him.

Bulgakov's novel raised a new interest in Christianity among the Soviet intelligentsia brought up in the atheistic period. However, it did not tell much about Jesus, and the biblical texts remained largely unavailable or incomprehensible. The man who did make the Gospel story a part of the cultural scene of the 1970s was Alexandr Men' (1935–1990), an Orthodox priest and an author. His book *The Son of Man*, published in Brussels in 1968, later became widely disseminated in typewritten copies all over the USSR. In genre it is a "biography" of Jesus. The author did not assume a "matter of fact" attitude but openly confessed his faith in Christ in a humble and convincing way. Nonetheless, the basic results of modern New Testament criticism formed an organic part of the book. That stood in strong contrast to the official theology of the Russian Orthodox Church, which generally rejected Western biblical scholarship.

The Post-Communist Christ

After the raising of the Iron Curtain, Russia became the magnet for foreign missionaries. The Unification Church of Sun Myung Moon and the Church of Scientology have spread all over the country. The communities of Jehovah's Witnesses, criminalized by the Communist regime, have grown dramatically. Evangelicals claim that their communities in Russia are growing at a rate of a hundred every month. The traditional Western denominations, such as Roman Catholics, Lutherans, Anglicans, and Baptists, also have restored their positions in Russia lost after 1917. The Russian Orthodox Church has considerably increased its influence. The bookshops provide a huge spectrum of books, from modern biblical studies to propaganda pamphlets. The post-Communist Christ is a fluid mosaic.

Vladimir Nikiforov

See also: Enlightenment; Icons and the Icon Tradition; Jesus, Name of; Jesus as Emperor; Kenoticism; Marxism; Messiah; Orthodox Tradition; Strauss, D. F.

References

Copleston, Frederick C. 1986. *Philosophy in Russia: From Herzem to Lenin and Berdyaev*. Notre Dame, IN: Search Press, University of Notre Dame.

———. 1988. *Russian Religious Philosophy: Selected Aspects*. Notre Dame, IN: Search Press, University of Notre Dame.

Dostoyevsky, Fyodor. 1958 [1880]. *The Brothers Karamazov*. Translated by D. Mayarshack. 2 vols. London: Penguin.

Fedotov, George P. 1975 [1966]. *The Russian Religious Mind*. 2 vols. 1: *Kievan Christianity: The 10th to the 13th centuries*; 2: *The Middle Ages: The 13th to the 15th centuries*. Edited, with a foreword, by John Mayendorff. Vols. 3 and 4 in *The Collected Works of George P. Fedotov*. Belmont, MA: Nordland.

Gardavsky, Vitrslav. 1973. *God Is Not Yet Dead*. Harmondsworth, UK: Penguin.

Gasparov, Boris, and Olga Raevsky-Huges, eds. 1993. *Slavic Cultures in the Middle Ages*. Vol. 1 of *Christianity and the Eastern Slavs*. Berkeley, Los Angeles: University of California Press.

Nakhimovsky, Alexander D., and Alice Stone Nakhimovsky, eds. 1985. *The Semiotics of Russian Cultural History: Essays by Iurii M. Lotman, Lidiia Ia. Ginsburg, Boris A. Uspenskii*. Translated by Boris Gasparov. Ithaca, NY: Cornell University Press.

Shukman, Ann, ed. 1984. *The Semiotics of Russian Culture*. Ann Arbor: Dept. of Slavic Languages and Literatures, University of Michigan.

Zernov, Nicholas. 1963. *The Russian Religious Renaissance of the Twentieth Century*. New York: Harper & Row.

S

Sanders, E. P. (b. 1937)

American scholar E. P. Sanders published a biographical study of Jesus in the mid-1990s that became especially popular in the United States. An expert on first-century Judaism, Sanders's study successfully revived the thesis of Albert Schweitzer that Jesus was an ultimately mistaken eschatological prophet. As such, Sanders's work constituted the first major challenge to what had become the dominant paradigm in American studies, namely, the presentation of Jesus as a this-worldly sage, evident in the work of M. Borg, J. D. Crossan, R. Funk, the Jesus Seminar, and others. In many respects, Sanders's brief study presaged the more comprehensive work of both J. Meier and N. T. Wright.

A Methodist who is proud to identify himself with the theological tradition of "liberal Protestantism," Sanders has taught at both Oxford and Duke Universities. In 1977, he published *Paul and Palestinian Judaism*, a groundbreaking book that challenged construals of Palestinian Judaism that, he claimed, provided a false context for understanding the writings of Paul. He would follow this with a book on *Jesus and Judaism* (1985) but continued to be known primarily as a Pauline scholar. His book on *The Historical Figure of Jesus* (1993) is relatively brief and is aimed at nonspecialists. It eschews copious footnotes, detailed source analysis, or any discussion of methodological presuppositions—standard features for most works of its kind. It relies instead on commonsense arguments suggesting likely scenarios that explain the biblical traditions in light of historical knowledge of the times.

Sanders started with a skeletal list of what he calls "almost indisputable facts" about Jesus, points on which he thought there would be little scholarly argument. He then used the biblical narratives to fill out this scheme, accepting as authentic whatever seemed to fit with the known facts and to explain their development. Sanders tended to accept the basic reliability of the canonical witness (especially where there is multiple attestation), while allowing for exaggeration and elaboration of details. He did not, then, ask whether Jesus said *this* particular aphorism, told *this* particular parable, or performed *this* particular deed. Rather, he was content to indicate what the "preponderance of evidence" revealed about what constituted Jesus' general concerns—the *types* of things he said and did.

Sanders ended up presenting Jesus as an exponent of Jewish "restoration eschatology," a prophet who declared that God was going to act decisively and soon to restore Israel to unsurpassed greatness. The current temple would be destroyed and replaced by a new one built by God (Jesus' overturning of the tables in the temple court was a prophetic act predicting this event). The twelve tribes of Israel would also be reconstituted (symbolized in Jesus' selection of twelve key disciples). The central theme of Jesus' preaching, according to Sanders, was that God was about to establish a divine kingdom on earth. Sanders noted that Jesus told his disciples that a heavenly Son of Man would descend from the heavens and gather the elect in anticipation of a final judgment that would determine who would gain admission to the new kingdom. Jesus also taught that entrance to the kingdom would be granted as an act of God's covenantal grace; he encouraged obedience to the law but promised sinners a place in the kingdom even if they did not repent or live in accordance with the law. Notably, Jesus predicted that the Son of Man would come within the lifetime of his own followers; indeed, he expected to see it happen himself and his cry of dereliction from the cross (Mark 15.34) revealed that he may have ultimately despaired of hope, realizing that he had been wrong.

Criticism of Sanders's view dwells primarily on the proposal that Jesus was actually in error with regard to the central and best-known aspect of his mission. Many scholars think it unlikely that the early Christian movement could have survived the realization that Jesus had been, in effect, a false prophet. Other American scholars (J. M. Borg, J. D. Crossan, and the Jesus Seminar) have challenged the authenticity of eschatological sayings attributed to Jesus, believing that these come from an apocalyptic mindset incompatible with the wisdom perspective reflected in the bulk of the Jesus tradition.

Mark A. Powell

See also: Borg, J. M.; Crossan, J. D.; Funk, Robert; Jesus Seminar; Kingdom of God; Meier, J. P.; Paul; Schweitzer, Albert; Son of Man; Wright, N. T.

References

Sanders, E. P. 1977. *Paul and Palestinian Judaism*. Philadelphia: Fortress.
———. 1985. *Jesus and Judaism*. Philadelphia: Fortress.
———. 1993. *The Historical Figure of Jesus*. London: Penguin.

Savior

See Jesus, Achievement of; Jesus, Death of

Scapegoat

Any understanding of Jesus' mission that stresses that by his death he shouldered and took away the sins of the world brings us face to face with the idea of the scapegoat. A scapegoat is one who suffers vicariously, one who bears the blame for others. Within the Bible, the origins of this idea are found in Leviticus 16, in which a ritual for the Day of Atonement involves killing one goat as a sin offering and expelling into the wilderness another, which "shall bear all their iniquities upon him to a solitary land" (16.22). Although this particular rite is rarely viewed by early Christian writers as a precursor to

Jesus' death, other Old Testament passages relating comparable ideas were believed to herald his vicarious suffering. Uppermost here should be noted Isaiah's depiction of the Lord's suffering servant, the "man of sorrows" (53.3) who was "wounded for our transgressions" (53.5): "[T]he Lord has laid on him the iniquity of us all" (53.6). In the New Testament, scapegoat imagery is implicitly applied in descriptions of Christ's atoning death. Paul, for example, speaks of Christ as a blood sacrifice (cf. Rom. 3.25) who "died for all" (2 Cor. 5.15). It is, however, in the letter to the Hebrews that the imagery of the sacrificial victim is most explicitly employed to describe the death of Jesus. Stressing that there can be no forgiveness without the shedding of blood (Heb. 9.22), the author of the letter claims that, while the blood of goats can never take away sins (10.4), the blood of Christ is a perfect sin-offering (9.13–14) and that the people have therefore been sanctified through his blood (13.12). Jesus is thus the priest who offers up, not animal sacrifices, but himself (7.27).

In more recent times, consideration of the idea of the scapegoat has led thinkers to entertain deeply radical understandings of the significance of the death of Jesus. This is most spectacularly seen in the second edition of Sir James Frazer's classic study *The Golden Bough* (1900). Stinging criticisms of his chapter dealing with Christ's death led Frazer to relegate this section to an appendix in the third edition, and to abandon it altogether in the widely read abridged edition of 1922. A recently published new abridgment (by Robert Fraser, 1994) has reinstated the chapter to its (rightful) position of prominence. Although there are very few explicit references to Jesus in its pages, *The Golden Bough* has to be seen as offering a most subversive understanding of the origins of Christianity, and the force of Frazer's suppressed chapter on the crucifixion gains much weight from the implicit points in the argument that precedes it. For Frazer, the origins of Christianity could be understood only within the context of the religions of the ancient Near East as a whole. These, he maintained, were focused on the theme of the yearly decay and revival of vegetation. In the worship of Adonis and Attis, this process was personified through the idea of a god who died and rose again from the dead. The attempt to assist the growth of the crops and hasten the return of spring would take the form of sacrificing a man who personated a god. A sacrificial victim of this kind would serve a dual purpose: s/he would act out the aforementioned role of a dying and rising god but (crucially) would also serve as a scapegoat: "The accumulated misfortunes and sins of the whole people are sometimes laid upon the dying god, who is supposed to bear them away for ever, leaving the people innocent and happy" (1900, 3:1; 1994, 557). Frazer showed how the idea of the transference of evil and sin onto some other thing (inanimate, animal, human, or man-god) who is subsequently expelled or slaughtered has occurred in many cultures, arising, he claimed, from a confusion between the material and the immaterial: "Because it is possible to shift a load of wood, stones, or what not, from our own back to the back of another, the savage fancies that it is equally possible to shift the burden of his pains and sorrows to another, who will suffer them in his stead" (ibid.).

These claims alone sufficiently constitute a serious challenge to some of the most cherished of Christian beliefs: the belief in Jesus as a dying and resurrected god is just one among many such beliefs found in the ancient Near East and is essentially a poetic means of depicting the decay and rebirth of vegetative life in the spring (think here of all our familiar imagery surrounding the celebration of Easter); the belief in his atoning death, whereby our guilt is (as Augustine said) "purged, abolished, and extinguished," is a doctrine born of savagery and conceptual confusion. This line of argument is subversive enough, but in the second edition Frazer went still further, contending that Jesus' crucifixion took place as part of a barbaric rite. His theory rested upon his account of the Jewish festival of Purim, which he contended to be a continuation of the Babylonian festival known as the Sacaea. At the Sacaea, a condemned prisoner was invested with the insignia of royalty, and after a period of license, was scourged and subsequently hanged or crucified as a scapegoat. Purim was a wild bacchanalian revel, and its origins, as described in the book of Esther, are as a commemoration of the Jews' deliverance from a great danger that threatened them while in Persia. Frazer contended that it was customary at Purim to enact a Passion play nominally based upon the events depicted in the book of Esther and to employ two prisoners to act the parts of the vizier Haman (representing the failing energies of the past year) and the Jew Mordecai (representing the vigorous energies of the coming year). Both men would parade in royal garments, but their fates were different: the prisoner playing Mordecai would be set free, whereas the one playing Haman, having enjoyed a temporary period of royal license, would be crucified.

This play, like other sacred dramas, should not be seen as a mere entertainment but rather as a magical ceremony intended to hasten and strengthen the growth of the crops. Frazer's contention was that beneath the pious descriptions of the trial and crucifixion found in the Gospels, we can see the reality of the sequence of events. In that particular year's Purim celebrations, the role of Mordecai was played by Barabbas, while it fell to Jesus to masquerade as Haman. After a period of being treated as a king (witness the triumphant ride into Jerusalem), he was mocked, scourged (scourging being a standard cross-cultural method of transferring evil), and crucified. Frazer concluded: "The sceptic . . . will reduce Jesus of Nazareth to the level of a multitude of other victims of a barbarous superstition, and will see in him no more than a moral teacher, whom the fortunate accident of his execution invested with the crown, not merely of a martyr, but of a god" (1900, 3: 198; 1994, 676).

For obvious reasons, Frazer's musings have not proved popular with theologians, and the general opprobrium that has of late been poured on *The Golden Bough* has provided a convenient excuse for his worrying thoughts to be passed over. This is perhaps to be regretted, because, while certainly flawed, Frazer's lines of inquiry are worthy of serious consideration and further development.

A more recent scapegoat-oriented Christology, which has found greater favor in theological circles, is the account of the meaning of the Gospels offered by the contemporary French cultural theorist René Girard. In contrast to Frazer, Girard's understanding of scapegoat Christology was predicated on the contention that the similarity between Christian origins and the sacrificial practices of pagan religions is more apparent than real; that whereas the scapegoating involved in these other religions is hidden, the Bible always makes explicit the innocence of the victim and thereby reveals the injustice of what Girard called the "surrogate victim mechanism." His analysis began with a consideration of the violence that he thought inevitable in any society, and almost impossible to stop once unleashed: violence breeds violence. How does a society manage to preserve itself in the face of such engulfing violence? Girard's answer was that the stability of any society has typically been maintained by concentrating its violent impulses upon an arbitrarily chosen scapegoat upon which it can vent—as with a punchbag—all its violent impulses. (Recent history shows this is not an implausible hypothesis.)

Girard went on to maintain that "all mythical and biblical dramas, including the Passion, represent the same type of collective violence against a single victim" (2001, 1). This victim, because his or her death has permitted society to escape from its perilous feuding, is subsequently (though perhaps only temporarily) elevated to the divine status of a savior. The success of the mechanism depends upon its injustice being hidden: for example, the victim must be believed to be guilty and not arbitrarily chosen. This principle can be seen in the myth of Oedipus. Oedipus is expelled for crimes he has really (though, in this case, unwittingly) committed. With the Passion narrative, we find something altogether different: in presenting Jesus as God, the Gospels declare that he is a totally innocent victim (witness Pilate's pivotal words: "I find no case against this man"), and with his execution the whole cycle of violence and scapegoating is revealed. The uniqueness of the Christian message is thus preserved in Girard's account, and the brilliance of Christianity brings with it something else: a great concern for all victims of injustice, and a hope for a future free from mimetic violence. Although the views of Frazer and Girard are radically opposed, they are equally promising as ways of understanding the death of Jesus by placing the Passion within the context of real ritual practice instead of becoming enmeshed in what some might see as rarefied doctrinal formulae.

Brian R. Clack

See also: English Christianity, Medieval; Hebrews, Letter to the; Jesus, Death of; Jesus as Servant; Paul; Resurrection

References

Frazer, J. G. 1900. *The Golden Bough*. 2d ed. 3 vols. London: Macmillan.
———. 1994. *The Golden Bough*. A new abridgment by Robert Fraser. Oxford: Oxford University Press.
Girard, René. 2001. *I See Satan Fall Like Lightning*. Leominster: Gracewing.
———. 1986. *The Scapegoat*. London: Athlone.
———. 1977. *Violence and the Sacred*. Baltimore: Johns Hopkins University Press.
Schwager, Raymund. 2000. *Must There Be Scapegoats?* Leominster: Gracewing.

Schillebeeckx, Edward (b. 1914)

Edward Schillebeeckx, a member of the Dominican Order of Preachers, did not really develop an interest in the historical Jesus until after the Second Vatican Council (1962–1965), in which he played a key role, not only advising the Dutch bishops but also interpreting the council to a wider audience. Prior to that, his theology, arising out of academic lectures given in Leuven and Nijmegen, Netherlands, had followed the traditional topics of Roman Catholic systematic theology, though his existentialist interpretation of the Eucharist and his regular practice of thoroughly investigating the historical background to major issues (notably marriage and, later, ministry) pointed toward the way he was eventually to take. The substance of his thought about Jesus is to be found in *Jesus: An Experiment in Christology* (Dutch 1974; English 1979), though it is amplified in other books. He seems to have been led to write the book by a hermeneutical concern, namely, how to interpret Jesus to the wide international audience with which his post–Vatican II prominence confronted him, an audience that could no longer understand the traditional dogmatic categories. *Jesus* is the first major work by a Roman Catholic dogmatic theologian to introduce the results of scholarly exegesis of the New Testament into dogmatic theology in an attempt to answer the question "What does salvation in Jesus, coming to us from God, mean to us now?"

Schillebeeckx's long portrayal of the life and teaching of Jesus is not dissimilar to that to be found in contemporary New Testament studies (on which he has drawn widely). The discussions of the parables, miracles, and Jesus' identification with the outcast and intimacy with the Father are fairly conventional for their time; it is striking, though, that the kingdom of God and the death of Jesus are passed over relatively quickly (1979, 140–154, 272–319). Schillebeeckx remarked that "kingdom of God" expressed the conviction that God's cause is man's cause and pointed out that the term was presupposed as a concept familiar to Jesus' contemporaries (ibid., 143). Jesus' death is seen as an inevitable consequence of his lifestyle and a prelude to his resurrection; indeed, in *Christ: The Christian Experience in the Modern World*, Schillbeeckx was to say that humankind was redeemed "despite" it (1980a, 749). Perhaps the most controversial feature of the earlier book was his choice of the term "eschatological prophet" (1979, 475–499) to describe Jesus. The passage was criticized because it was thought to represent too "low" a view of Jesus; by giving it pride of place, Schillebeeckx seemed to be bringing all the honorific titles given to Jesus down to this level. Schillebeeckx's retort in his *Interim Report on the Books* Jesus *and* Christ, was that his critics had failed to understand the term "eschatological" (1980b, 67), which implied a significance for the whole of subsequent history.

What marks Schillebeeckx's approach was the hermeneutical context in which he put these exegetical findings. Whereas in the classical quest of the historical Jesus, Jesus was played off against the Church, here the Gospels were firmly considered within the context of the Church's community and faith, the original interplay and bond between the text and its readers. *Jesus* begins with an unusually long discussion of method, hermeneutics, and criteria: there can be no evasion of the need for academic study of the Bible; modern men and women have lost their first innocence and cannot regain it. But it is possible to strive for a second innocence. Once the complex problems of exegesis have been tackled, readers should be stimulated by the interplay between the text and their own approach to it to achieve greater personal liberation in the light of the message of the kingdom of God as presented through Jesus. The world in which Jesus lived and its expectations of salvation may have been very different from ours, but by following Schillebeeckx's approach it should be possible to learn more about "salvation in Jesus, coming from God" (1979, 115–178).

The notorious complexity of Schillebeeckx's literary style and his tendency to keep beginning again or changing his points of reference do not make his work easy to follow. After presenting what he acknowledged could be seen as a "Christology" from below, in the fourth and final part of *Jesus* he produced a synthesis that is much closer to the world of classical Christology (ibid., 573–674). His reason for inserting it, given in the *Interim Report,* was frankly pastoral. Had there been no reflection on the Chalcedonian Definition, readers would have been disturbed in a quite irresponsible way (1980b, 98ff.). In *Christ,* he continued an investigation into the second half of the New Testament along the lines of *Jesus*. However, again, he began with a long hermeneutical introduction about the significance of authority and experience (1980a, 27–79), which proved to be an important preparation for the discussion of suffering and salvation that ended the book (ibid., 670–839).

Despite its difficulties and somewhat rambling structure, Schillebeeckx's account of Jesus as the Christ is full of new and important insights too numerous to detail and may be said to be among the most creative Christological studies of the twentieth century.

John Bowden

See also: Chalcedon; Jesus, Achievement of; Jesus, Death of; Jesus, Miracles of; Jesus, Parables of; Kingdom of God

References

Schillebeeckx, Edward. 1979. *Jesus: An Experiment in Christology.* London: Collins; New York: Crossroad.

———. 1980a. *Christ: The Christian Experience in the Modern World.* London: SCM; New York: Crossroad.

———.1980b. *Interim Report on the Books* Jesus *and* Christ. London: SCM; New York: Crossroad.

———. 1987. *Jesus in our Western Culture*. London: SCM; New York: Crossroad.

Schleiermacher, F. D. E. (1768–1834)

Friedrich Schleiermacher, professor in Halle and Berlin, offered the most influential systematic treatment of Protestant theology since John Calvin. His radically new methodology allowed him to confront the challenges of the Enlightenment without being driven to defend every position that was exposed to its critique. Owing much to the influence of Pietism in his early life, he turned inward to the immediacy of experience and feeling as the starting point for theological reflection. He thus freed himself from the revelatory authority of Scripture or Church doctrine as traditionally understood and was able to recognize the achievements of science, to give full weight to historical and social factors, to accept a critical approach to the Scriptures, and to recognize the symbolic and contextual character of religious language. His aim was to find a middle way between supernaturalism and naturalism, and in so doing to embrace the whole of life and to relate Christ's person and work to that whole while maintaining his uniqueness.

There are anticipations of Schleiermacher's later thinking, mainly in his *On Religion: Speeches to Its Cultured Despisers* (1996 [1799]) and in *Christmas Eve: A Dialogue on the Incarnation* (1991 [1806]). The importance he attached to the authentic humanity of Jesus was apparent from his pioneering lectures on the *Life of Jesus* (1975 [1864]; first given in 1819 but not published until 1864 from his own and student notes).

In contrast to many who followed him, from F. C. Baur and D. F. Strauss to Martin Kähler and Rudolf Bultmann, Schleiermacher refused to separate the historical Jesus and the Christ of faith. His attempt to uncover not only the life but also the inner life of Jesus was helped by his acceptance of the historical reliability of the Gospel of John. His fully worked out Christology appeared in *The Christian Faith* (1928 [1821]), to which most attention will be paid here.

Schleiermacher's Christology cannot be appreciated without some reference to the wider framework of his thought and understanding of religion. From his earliest days, his aim was to reestablish the universality of religion, not, however, as an external institution, or in terms of ecclesiastical doctrine, but as inescapably present in the depths of human subjective experience as the "feeling of absolute dependence," or as he later called it, "God-consciousness." The key to his methodology is found in his claim that dogmatic propositions arise solely out of logically ordered reflection upon the immediate utterances of the religious self-consciousness.

By starting with experience as the basis for interpreting religion and redemption, Schleiermacher opened himself to misunderstanding and much misplaced criticism from idealist opponents and others. In the first place, for Schleiermacher, any reflection on being human in the world revealed an awareness of being free and yet of being contingently dependent on the world in a reciprocal relationship. With this comes the feeling of the nonreciprocal absolute dependence of the self and world. God is not to be inferred from this feeling but is rather discovered as the "Whence" (1928 [1821], 16) of it, its "codeterminant." Thus Schleiermacher could say that the essence of piety is "the consciousness of being absolutely dependent, or, which is the same thing, of being in relation with God" (ibid., 12).

However, God-consciousness can only realize itself through self-consciousness, and self-consciousness can only realize itself in response to stimuli of the senses and in a social context. In other words, God-consciousness must be earthed in history and society, and from this basis arises the diversity of religion. The particular historical determination that distinguishes Christianity from other religions is that in it "everything is related to the redemption accomplished by Jesus of Nazareth" (ibid., 52).

Redemption is needed because of sin. Like Irenaeus, Schleiermacher held that human beings are not created ready-made, but are meant to grow to perfection, which for Schleiermacher meant attaining perfect God-consciousness (ibid., 280). Sin manifests itself in the individual in yielding to the flesh and opposing Christ; or simply in the failure of the God-consciousness to develop. At the same time, it is at work through the corporate life of sin—humanity as a whole, symbolized by the old Adam—affecting or infecting all who are born into it.

Before sin has developed, there may be present only the "germ" of sin, but with increasing God-consciousness, not only is sin more clearly recognized, but also the impossibility of overcoming it; hence the misery of sin and the longing for redemption. Aiming to rule out any hint of Pelagianism, Schleiermacher concluded, "Sin is in every case a complete incapacity for good, which can only be removed by the influence of Redemption" (ibid., 282).

The misery of sin exists precisely because we cannot overcome it ourselves, yet the second phenomenon Schleiermacher addressed is the fact, the inward fact, of Christian experience of redemption. There must therefore be a cause or source external to ourselves that could bring this about; there must have been "a development of power of the God-consciousness that has proceeded continuously from its earliest manifestation to a state of absolute strength, that is, a condition of human perfection evolved without sin." Such a manifestation of the triumph of the God-consciousness and the defeat of sin can also bring about the same condition in us, and this is the role of the Redeemer, that is, Christ. It is indeed "only from the absolute sinlessness and the perfect spiritual power of the Redeemer that we gain the full knowledge of sin" (ibid., 278f.).

The inward certainty of faith rests on the "incipient satisfaction of that spiritual need [of redemption] by Christ; there can be . . . diverse ways of experiencing the need and succour, yet they will all be faith." In fact the consciousness of need may only be fully awakened by its satisfaction. "'Faith in Christ' . . . relates this satisfaction, viz. the state of redemption as effect, to Christ as cause" (ibid., 68f.). It is clear that for Schleiermacher, Christ's person cannot be separated from his work.

His critics might object, but for Schleiermacher, the argument from the present effect, redemption, to its efficient cause in one historical figure lies at the heart of his Christology. The question then arises as to what conditions must be met by the cause for it to be efficient. In particular, how was it possible for Christ to be the cause of redemption? And second, how can the redemptive power of that historical figure be continued into the present? For a start, Schleiermacher acknowledged that it cannot be proved that the "Christ is the only one who can work redemption" (ibid., 69); he simply addressed those who participate in the Christian communion through faith in Jesus as the Redeemer.

In addressing the first question, Schleiermacher dispensed with the traditional Chalcedonian terminology of two natures in one person, arguing that two natures cannot be postulated in one person without confusion. He therefore spoke of the divine in Christ in terms not of a divine being or nature, but of the perfect relationship between the divine and human becoming actual in history for redemption (an idea to be developed later by Paul Tillich).

Schleiermacher argued that for Jesus to fulfill his redemptive role, he himself had to be truly and completely human and at the same time absolutely sinless. To be sinless means that "he cannot simply have come out of the old corporate life of sinfulness," else he would have been tainted by sin like all other human beings. So one must postulate supernatural procreation or origin in some sense, a "miracle" insofar as it points to a "creative divine act," but not a literal virgin birth. The "miracle" extends to the unique "spiritual content of Christ's life" (his God-consciousness), which "cannot be explained by the [sinful] content of the human environment to which he belonged, but only by the universal source of spiritual life" (ibid., 381).

The creative, divine act of Christ's appearing does not, for Schleiermacher, detract in any way from his complete and authentic humanity. To "cause" what he did and does (redemption), he must, for one thing, have been truly human, a "truly historically conditioned individual" (ibid., 380) who could only speak and think in the language of his day. To attribute an empirical omniscience to him could only "mean the loss of true humanity"—the error of docetism (ibid., 382). (Yet despite Schleiermacher's protestations, his reliance on the Fourth Gospel and on the "creative divine act of his appearing" opened him to the charge of docetism and a lingering supernaturalism.)

It was important for Schleiermacher's argument that Christ was "ideal" in every moment of his life, else he would only have been an example to some people and not others, or in some respects and not others; he must have been the ideal "in order to establish a new corporate life within the old [corporate life of sin] and not out of it" (ibid., 381). Once again, the argument moves from the Christian experience of redemption to the necessary precondition of it, not from a mere idea (pace Strauss), but from an antecedent living historical reality, the second Adam and source of the new corporate life.

The matter becomes clearer once Christ's idealness is seen not in terms of static concepts of human or divine nature but in relation to the God-consciousness and as the fruit of it. Christ's God-consciousness cannot be thought of as fully formed at birth, Schleiermacher argued (opposing docetism once again), because if this had been the case, "his whole earliest childhood must have been mere appearance." On the contrary, the germ of God-consciousness was in Christ as in any other human being. It "had to develop gradually in human fashion into a really manifest consciousness." The fact of its development, however, did not detract from its constancy. Because of that, Christ could never be disturbed by inner conflict, such as must arise in human beings torn by sinful desires. An illustration might be a truly loving mother who could not entertain the desire of harming her child. So, in the case of Christ, no action could "ever proceed from the sense-nature and not from the God-consciousness" (ibid., 381ff.).

It is in Christ's perfect God-consciousness that Schleiermacher saw the presence of God in him. To quote his most famous (or notorious) Christological pronouncement: "The Redeemer, then, is like all men in virtue of the identity of human nature, but distinguished from them all by the constant potency of his God-consciousness, which was a veritable existence of God in him," or again, "[T]o ascribe to Christ an absolutely powerful God-consciousness, and to attribute to him an existence of God in him, are exactly the same thing." This nature contrasts with the "darkened and imperfect God-consciousness" in all other human beings, which cannot, therefore, by itself be "an existence of God in human nature" (ibid., 385ff.).

Against any suspicion of adoptianism or even Arianism—of a redeemer empowered by but yet at one remove from God—Schleiermacher wrote, "Of the Redeemer we must hold that the ground of his sinlessness was not external to himself" (as it is in us), "but that it was essentially grounded in himself, if he was to take away, through what he was in Himself, the sinfulness of the corporate life" (ibid., 386) in which we are submerged.

Schleiermacher was insistent that redemption is the work of God, and not just of an ideal human being with perfect God-consciousness. He accepted that he must show that in the twofold activity of Christ, in redemption and reconciliation, "the creation of human nature is . . . really fully accomplished" (ibid., 437). This comes about simply as a "continuation of the same creative act which first manifested itself in time by the formation of Christ's person." The creative act that made Jesus what he was continues in the believer and is the work of God in Christ, imparting the God-consciousness and its receptivity. All is grace.

The God who was active in the formation of the Redeemer continues, through him, the person-forming or re-forming work in redeemed believers, and through them is world-forming, too (ibid., 427). A rare hint of "judgment" appears in Schleiermacher's account when he recognizes that for believers, person-forming means that "an old man is put off and a new man put on" (ibid., 433). This is not so for Christ, who was perfect.

Schleiermacher expressed the importance of Christ's redemptive work in terms of the contrast between misery and blessedness. Misery is not simply the result of sin, of being self-centered or governed by desires of the flesh; it results at the same time from the growing awareness of sin arising from the developing God-consciousness. The distinction between misery, on the one hand, and pain and suffering, on the other, was important for Schleiermacher. Pain and suffering were real for Christ, and so are real, too, for the redeemed, but for Schleiermacher they are not "simple misery for they do not as such penetrate into the inmost life" (ibid., 432). They are misery only for the person who "clings to his own personality" and so, in a state of sin, experiences them as hindrances, not as new opportunities for action governed by the God-consciousness.

Christ's willingness to accept suffering reveals his perfect God-consciousness and conformity to God's will in the activity of redemption—the way God was in him to reconcile the world to himself. It proves that nothing can frustrate his purpose of founding the new corporate life, not even his own death. "Here accordingly the perfection does not lie properly and immediately in the suffering itself, but only in his giving up of himself to it" (ibid., 436). Schleiermacher saw no value in "suffering for suffering's sake." If Christ's suffering was just part of an external deal, some transaction with God or victory over the devil, unrelated to the "foundation of the corporate life," it would remain a "magical caricature."

By contrast, it was in order to assume us into his fellowship that he who was without sin entered the fellowship of our sinful life and suffered the painful consequences of *our* sin, not his own. Schleiermacher resisted any hint of Christ's experiencing misery, because for him, misery is self-centered. Therefore, Christ's "miserylessness" was as important as, indeed the same as, his "sinlessness." He concluded, "The climax of his suffering, we hold then, was sympathy with misery" (ibid., 436); or again, it was "a sympathetic feeling of the world's sin," which he carried all the time, "so that this suffering accompanies him throughout His whole life" (ibid., 453).

Christ's suffering was proof of his love: "His suffering in this fellowship, if occasioned by sin—and from merely natural evils he never suffered [!]—was suffered for those with whom he stood in fellowship, that is, for the whole human race, to which he belongs" (ibid., 457). That he could suffer in the extreme without lapsing into misery reveals that imperturbable and unconquerable blessedness that is the goal of the sinner's longing for salvation. Whoever sees it made real in Christ is drawn into vital fellowship with him, which was the purpose of his coming, in which Christ "so animates us that we ourselves are led to an ever more perfect fulfilment of the divine will" and "in which we are moved by him, that is, His motive principle becomes ours also." In other words, Christ's sinless perfection imparts "the perfect consciousness of sin" and at the same time the consciousness of sin overcome, and so the removal of the misery brought about by the consciousness of sin. A redemptive transformation is effected from the inside, not from the outside. This process parallels the fact that our condemnation does not result from Adam's sin, which lies outside of us, but "only in so far as we, being in natural life-fellowship with him and moved in the same way, all sin ourselves" (ibid., 456f.).

The question then arises of how later generations can move into life fellowship with Christ. Here Schleiermacher attached enormous importance to the Church on earth, not least because of his determination to rule out any kind of "magical" intervention, and his insistence that human life is set within history and community, as against any individualistic or unembodied spirituality. Hence, he argued, there is no other way of arriving at faith in Jesus as the Redeemer except through participation in the Christian communion, the "new divinely effected corporate life, which works in opposition to the corporate life of sin and the misery which develops in it" (ibid., 358). As in Christ himself, so also in the Church, he saw the supernatural mediated by the natural, not overriding it; were it otherwise, the Incarnation would not have been necessary.

Though the Incarnation lies in the past, Schleiermacher postulated that "it must still be possible [for us] to have the same experiences" as the first

Christians, else the unity of the Church and the relevance of the original Christians would be imperiled. The passage of time would render any historical witness to the perfection of Christ increasingly unreliable. Therefore, "The recognition of the sinless perfection in Christ, definitely constraining us to the new corporate life, must in the same way be still His work. But there is given to us, instead of His personal influence, only that of his fellowship, in so far as even the picture of Him which is found in the Bible also originated in the community and is perpetuated in it" (ibid., 363).

In human beings, generally self-consciousness, and so God-consciousness, develops gradually. The perfect God-consciousness reached in Christ cannot develop further; from him it must simply overflow into the rest of the world. The channel through which it is to overflow is the Church. Meanwhile, already, "Christendom as a whole, as the human race already united to the Redeemer, stands to the rest of humanity in the relation in which priests stood to the laity. For it is only in so far as there exists a real vital fellowship with Christ in at least one part of the race that there is also a relationship between Him and the rest. Hence in this sense, the Christian community, as inseparable from Christ, appears before God for the whole race and represents it" (ibid., 465).

It remains to be said that despite the Barthian counterblast against Schleiermacher's turn to the subject, Karl Barth himself acknowledged Schleiermacher to be "a hero, the like of which is but seldom bestowed on Theology" (2001, 413). At the same time, Barth's critique rests on a not entirely accurate reading of Schleiermacher, in particular in relation to Schleiermacher's acknowledgment of divine transcendence and his Christocentric, or at least "Christomorphic," emphasis. Schleiermacher's reliance on the historical reliability of the Fourth Gospel sets him apart from most subsequent scholarship, yet his emphasis on the inwardness of religion and his concern with the relationship of the historical Jesus to the Christ of faith set the agenda for generations of Protestant theologians. His methodological principles became and remain the stock-in-trade of critical theology.

Trevor Williams

See also: Adoptianism; Barth, Karl; Bultmann, Rudolf; Calvin, John; Chalcedon; Enlightenment; Irenaeus; John, Gospel of; Strauss, D. F.; Tillich, Paul.

References

Barth, Karl. 2001. *Protestant Theology in the Nineteenth Century*. Translated by Brian Couzens and John Bowden. London: SCM.

Christian, C. W. 1979. *Friedrich Schleiermacher*. Waco: Word Books.

Clements, Keith W., ed. 1987. *Friedrich Schleiermacher: Pioneer of Modern Theology*. London: Collins.

Gerrish, Brian A. 1984. *A Prince of the Church: Schleiermacher and the Beginnings of Modern Theology*. London: SCM.

Niebuhr, Richard R. 1965. *Schleiermacher on Christ and Religion*. London: SCM.

Schleiermacher, Friedrich. 1996 [1799]. *On Religion: Speeches to Its Cultured Despisers*. Translated by Richard Crouter. Cambridge: Cambridge University Press.

———. 1991 [1806]. *Christmas Eve: A Dialogue on the Incarnation*. Translated by T. Tice. Richmond, VA: John Knox.

———. 1928 [1821; revised 1830]. *The Christian Faith*. Translated by H. R. Mackintosh and J. S. Stewart. Edinburgh: T. & T. Clark.
———. 1975 [1864]. *The Life of Jesus*. Translated by S. Maclean Gilmour. Philadelphia: Fortress.
Spiegler, Gerhard E. 1967. *The Eternal Covenant: Schleiermacher's Experiment in Cultural Theology*. New York: Harper and Row.
Williams, Robert R. 1978. *Schleiermacher the Theologian: The Construction of the Doctrine of God*. Philadelphia: Fortress.

Schweitzer, Albert (1875–1965)

Albert Schweitzer, born in Alsace, was a distinguished German theologian and organist whose last four decades were spent as a physician in equatorial Africa. To understand his account of Jesus and the way it was received, it is necessary to set it against the background of earlier accounts. The orthodox account, unquestioningly accepted by both Catholics and Protestants for some fifteen centuries, pictured Jesus as the second person of the Trinity incarnate in the world. He was therefore taken to be timeless, and, as such, as readily intelligible and acceptable in one century and culture as in any other. There was little or no awareness of cultural development or of any of the problems associated with it.

This orthodox account was first seriously questioned in the seventeenth century; in his best known scholarly book, *The Quest of the Historical Jesus* (1910), Schweitzer chronicled the various discussions of the matter by critical scholars (mainly German) from H. S. Reimarus (1694–1768) to William Wrede (1859–1906) (the original German version, published in 1906, was entitled *Von Reimarus zu Wrede*). Paradoxically, these "liberal" scholars also pictured, if not a timeless Jesus, at any rate one who was primarily a teacher, and a teacher, what is more, whose teaching and way of life were immediately intelligible and attractive to people with a modern mindset. As Schweitzer pointed out, they could do this only by—quite unconsciously—reading back a lot of their own outlook and assumptions into the scanty data afforded by the New Testament.

Schweitzer dissented strongly from all this. He accepted the argument of Johannes Weiss in his book *Jesus' Proclamation of the Kingdom of God* (German 1892; English translation 1971) that Jesus was not primarily a teacher but an eschatological figure, that is, one who believed himself to have been sent by God to bring history to an end and to usher in what was known as the "rule" (or "reign," better translations than "kingdom") of God—a radically new state of affairs, brought into being entirely by the power of God, in which everything would be in exact conformity with God's will. As Schweitzer pointed out, the expectation of such a state of affairs in the near future was common to a number of Jewish writings of the time, and some of them forecast the appearance on earth of a divine agent ordained or "anointed" by God to bring it about—a "messiah." (The Greek for "anointed" is *christos*.)

According to Schweitzer, it was such a divinely anointed figure that Jesus believed himself to be. His public activity, Schweitzer claimed, lasted for only a short time, and when, quite early in it, he sent out his disciples to proclaim the arrival of God's rule, he expected it to come there and then. When it did not, he had to rethink his understanding of things. Many Jews of the time believed that the coming of God's rule would be preceded by a period of terrible sufferings, sometimes described as "the birth pangs of the new age," and Jesus, according to Schweitzer, shared this expectation (cf. Matt. 24.8 and Mark 13.8, where he uses the term). Uncertain whether the faith of his disciples would withstand such a momentous "time of trial" (*peirasmos*, cf. Matt. 6.13, where the disciples are to pray, "do not bring us to the [time of] trial"), he came to believe that it was his vocation, as God's anointed agent, to bear this suffering entirely himself, and so to spare others: "the pre-messianic tribulation is set aside for others, abolished, concentrated upon himself alone, and that in the form that is fulfilled in his own passion and death at Jerusalem. That was the new conviction that had dawned upon him. He must suffer for others that the kingdom may come" (1910, 347; cf. Mark10.45, "to give his life as a ransom for many").

The necessity for such eschatological suffering was simply taken as a given by Jesus and the New Testament writers, who make no attempt to explain it. They say simply "such things must be" (Mark 13.7, and cf., for example, 8.31 and Luke 17.1). With that in mind, Jesus set his face to go up to Jerusalem, in the full realization that he would meet persecution and terrible suffering there, but convinced that this suffering would prove redemptive and would herald the immediate arrival of God's rule. Indeed, he had predicted as much when he let the disciples into the secret of his status and mission at Caesarea Philippi (Mark 8.27ff. and parallels). What happened next is described in some of Schweitzer's best-known words: "Jesus, in the knowledge that he is the coming Son of Man lays hold of the wheel of the world to set it moving on that last revolution, which is to bring all ordinary history to a close. It refuses to turn and he throws himself upon it. Then it does turn; and crushes him. Instead of bringing in the eschatological conditions, he has destroyed them. The wheel rolls onward, and the mangled body of the one immeasurably great man, who was strong enough to think of himself as the spiritual ruler of mankind and to bend history to his purpose, is hanging upon it still. That is his victory and his reign" (1910, 368–369; the words are omitted in later editions).

Such an account was obviously unlikely to find acceptance with the orthodox, especially as Schweitzer went out of his way to emphasize the cultural and religious gulf that separates the historical Jesus from the modern world. Jesus will never again "be a Jesus Christ to whom the religion of the present can ascribe . . . its own thought and ideas. Nor will he be a figure that can be made by a popular historical treatment so sympathetic and universally intelligible to the multitude. Jesus of Nazareth will not suffer himself to be modernised as an historical figure. He refuses to be detached from his own time." He is, in fact, "a stranger and an enigma to our time" (ibid., 478).

There were other elements in Schweitzer's account that challenged widely held beliefs. He claimed, for example, that Jesus had been a complete predestinarian who taught that only a small body of people, specially foreordained by God, would be admitted to the new age when it came, and that this group would be exclusively Jewish (Matt.10.5, 23; 15.24). As for Jesus' teaching, apart from a call to repentance as a condition of entry into the new age, it consisted mainly of inculcating a morality that Schweitzer described as an *Interimsethik* ("morality for the interim"), that is, a way of behaving appropriate to the very short and testing period that was to elapse before the end came. This, Schweitzer thought, accounted for the character of the moral teaching found in the Sermon on the Mount, much of which seems impractical and too extreme, if understood as an ethic for an indefinite future in this world.

Though Schweitzer emphasized so strongly the gulf between Jesus' outlook and our own, he by no means took the figure of the historical Jesus, as he understood him, to be irrelevant to the modern world. His rather high-flown and romantic prose is not always easy to interpret, but he seems to have felt that Jesus' understanding of the world as being on the point of passing away can help us to evaluate it as the transient phenomenon it really is, and to concentrate on inwardness and communion with God. Jesus' love of the world, even to the point of suffering and dying for it, shows us how much we, too, must love it and do our best to serve all life in it. "The essence of Christianity," Schweitzer wrote, "is world-affirmation which has gone through a period of world-negation. In the eschatological world-view of world-negation Jesus proclaims the ethic of active love!" (1954, 55–56; the whole passage from which these words are taken is worth consulting). "The true relation to Jesus is to be taken possession of by him. Christian piety of any and every sort is valuable only so far as it means surrender of our will to his" (ibid., p. 56; see chapter 6 of that work and also the famous concluding paragraph of the *Quest*).

Schweitzer's account was unpopular in Germany because it was seen as ruling out such modern-friendly pictures of Jesus as that given in Adolf von Harnack's best-selling book *What is Christianity?* (German 1900; English translation 1901). In America Schweitzer was largely ignored, and though a number of English scholars welcomed the *Quest* (for example, F. C. Burkitt and William Sanday), the general attitude in England has been to ignore it. At any rate, Schweitzer's impact on the churches, whether measured by the content of individual sermons or of official pronouncements, has been negligible; but only to a very limited extent has that been because his arguments have been weighed and found wanting: they have simply not been taken into account.

It is true that since his time scholarship has uncovered a number of serious flaws in his arguments. It is, for example, ironic that one whose review of earlier *Lives of Jesus* exposed the extent to which they had attempted to make bricks without straw should himself have tried to build so much on the basis of scanty New Testament data. Nor did he take sufficient account of modern findings about the character of those data. He virtually ignored form-criticism and seriously underestimated the large element of *Tendenz* (bias, spin) that F. C. Baur, Wrede, and others had rightly detected in the Gospels. He took the view that once the centrality of eschatology had been recognized, the content of the Gospels could be accepted more or less as it stood. "The progressive recognition of the eschatological character of the teaching and action of Jesus carries with it a progressive justification of the Gospel tradition. . . . [T]horoughgoing eschatology . . . is able to accept and explain as historical on the whole everything which is contained in the two earliest Gospels about Jesus' activity." This view is now generally regarded as wrong: in particular, Schweitzer is widely agreed to have exaggerated the importance and trustworthiness of Matthew 10.5–23, especially the last verse. These were serious mistakes, and they lay precisely in the area that has mainly preoccupied Gospel scholarship since his time. Consequently, his approach to the Gospels, and with it his more speculative and theoretical ideas, has tended to be written off, and his writings about Jesus given less than their due. This is a pity, for it has meant that even where his views have been justified, they have still not generally been taken on board.

Subsequent work has fully justified Schweitzer's insistence that Jesus saw himself primarily as an eschatological figure, and, what is more, an eschatological figure of the sort expected by many at the time—one sent to bring history to an end and inaugurate God's rule. Efforts have been made to refute such a conclusion, but they have not met with much success. Attempts to show that Jesus had quite a different idea of the rule of God from his contemporaries, and believed that in part it had already come during his lifetime, have foundered from lack of evidence for any such radical reinterpretation on his part (cf., for example, Schweitzer 1914, 85; 1954, 38). In contrast to those who thought Jesus believed in such "realized" eschatology, Schweitzer stood for what he called "thoroughgoing" *(konsequent)* eschatology: Jesus expected that the world would end and that he would be revealed as Messiah (Hebrew for *christos*, the anointed one) in his own lifetime, and he was wrong. What is more, his eschatological expectations colored the whole of his outlook.

A small number of distinguished scholars have doubted whether eschatology was as central to Jesus' outlook as Schweitzer and most scholars since have supposed, but their arguments have not won much support; and in any case, even they would not dispute the general conclusion Schweitzer drew from his studies, namely, that whatever else Jesus may have been, he was essentially a figure of his own time, whose thinking and teaching were formulated in first-century Jewish categories. He was thus a culturally conditioned figure who cannot be assumed to speak directly to our condition. Since Schweitzer, many scholars who have recognized the truth of all this have suggested ways in which Jesus' teaching and activity may be interpreted, "translated," or "demythologized" for modern minds. Whatever may be thought of such attempts, no one has confronted modern Western readers more starkly than Schweitzer did with the sheer fact of the strangeness of Jesus by our standards, and the need to recognize and deal with it, if he is to continue to be an object of faith. Schweitzer is still eminently worth reading, both for these reasons and also for the many wise and challenging observations he makes *en passant*. In his rather grand and romantic prose, he has faced theologians—and, indeed, believers generally—with a question they are far from having answered.

D. E. Nineham

See also: Harnack, Adolf von; Jesus, Teaching of; Jesus as a Historical Figure; Kingdom of God; Messiah; Reimarus, Hermann Samuel; Second Person of the Trinity

References

Primary

Albert Schweitzer. 1910. *The Quest of the Historical Jesus*. Translated by W. Montgomery. London: A. & C. Black.

———. 2000. *The Quest of the Historical Jesus*. 2d ed. Translated from the latest German edition. Edited by John Bowden. London: SCM.

———. 1914. *The Mystery of the Kingdom of God*. Translated by W. Lowrie. London: A. & C. Black.

———. 1954. *My Life and Thought*. 2d ed. Translated by C. T. Campion. London: Guild Books.

———. 1968. *The Kingdom of God and Primitive Christianity*. Translated by L. A. Garrard. London: A. & C. Black.

Secondary

Mozley, E. N. 1950. *The Theology of Albert Schweitzer*. London: A. & C. Black.

Scottish (Gaelic) Christianity

Despite the claims that are sometimes made nowadays for an independent form of "Celtic Christianity" in Ireland, Scotland, and Wales, Christianity in the Gaelic west was essentially an imported faith. It shared its doctrines with the wider world of Western Christendom. This was true of the Scottish Highlands and Islands. Nevertheless, it is equally true to say that, after the waning of the Latinity of the medieval Church, and even in the heyday of that Latinity, the figure, person, and work of Christ were indigenized and expressed in terms of Gaelic language and culture. Christological doctrine and imagery were presented in forms that were meaningful to the Gaelic people across the centuries. Gaelic Scotland, however, has never had an indigenous or independent tradition of learned theological exposition. Consequently, there have been no novel or distinctively Gaelic views of the person and work of Christ, and there have been no major Christological debates within the Gaelic sectors of the churches, although there were differences of view on the nature and extent of the Atonement in the Reformed churches. Calvinist and Arminian positions are evident, but the overall balance is tilted toward a Puritan understanding of the work of Jesus Christ, made accessible through the abundant translation of Puritan prose works into Gaelic from 1750.

Translation of religious texts into Gaelic began some 200 years earlier, shortly after the Reformation. Gaelic printing was initiated by the publication in 1567 of a Classical Gaelic version of the *Book of Common Order*, a key text of the Scottish Reformation. The translation was undertaken by John Carswell (c. 1520–1572), superintendent of the Reformed Church in Argyll. The Roman Catholic Church in the Highlands and Islands has been part of the wider Catholic communion, and its priests, like their Protestant counterparts, have translated some mainstream Christological texts into Gaelic, most notably Thomas à Kempis's 1418 *De Imitatione Christi*, translated by Fr.

Robert Menzies of Aberfeldy, Perthshire, in 1785, and again by Fr. Ewen MacEachen in 1836. Similarly, the Scottish Episcopal Church has depended on the translation of liturgies from English to Gaelic. In the absence of original doctrinal treatises, poets, preachers, and prose writers had a major role in presenting the figure and person of Jesus Christ and in making him accessible to the wider community.

The presentation of Jesus Christ within the work of the Gaelic poets can be traced back into the Middle Ages through the classical—and Catholic—tradition of bardic verse shared by both Ireland and Scotland. Christ is often mentioned, but seldom is there extensive sketching. Poets in personal distress, through the loss of leaders, companions, and friends, invoked and beseeched his name. Affrica MacCorquodale, for example, composed a deeply moving elegy on the death (c. 1470) of her husband Neil son of Torquil. Neil was a MacNeill from the island of Gigha (off the west coast of Kintyre) and had been the constable of Castle Sween in Knapdale:

Mar thá Giodha an fhuinn mhín,
Dún Suibhne do-chím gan cheól,
faithche longphuirt na bhfear bhfial:
aithmhéala na Niall a n-eòl . . .
Má bhrisis, a Mheic Dhé bhí,
ar bagaide na dtrí chnó,
fa fior do ghbhais ar ngiall;
do bhainis an trian ba mhó.
(Sad is the state of smooth-soiled Gigha;
the fort of Sween I see without music,
the greensward of a stronghold of generous men;
the sorrow of the MacNeills is known to them,
If Thou, son of the living God,
hast made a breach upon the cluster of three nuts,
true it is that thou hast taken our choice hostage;
Thou hast plucked the greatest of the three.) (Watson 1937: 60–65)

The bardic—and thoroughly Gaelic—image of the "three nuts" appears to refer to Neill and his two sons, but the Trinitarian resonance is obvious. Here Christ is portrayed, in a slightly paradoxical way, as the spoiler of a closely knit human trinity, though at the end of the poem the poetess beseeches his protection and that of his mother, Mary.

The Roman Catholic tradition of Gaelic Scotland preserved a deeply human picture of Jesus Christ, and it was much more willing than the Protestant tradition to present him in the context of a physical body (including portraiture in paint, sculpture, and stained glass), earthly possessions, and human emotions. A homely and distinctly maternal approach is evident in the work of the seventeenth-century Gaelic poetess Sìleas NicDhòmhnaill (Giles or Cecily MacDonald, c. 1660–c. 1729), who belonged to the Keppoch branch of the MacDonalds. Her "Laoidh Mhoire Mhaighdean" (Hymn to the Virgin Mary) envisaged Christ making his way through Mary's birth-canal and into a world without any comfort :

'S éibhinn an sealladh a fhuair i
'Nuair thàinig E nuas à colainn;
Rothaill i 'n anartaibh bàna
An Slànair thàinig g' ar ceannach.
Cha d'iarr Macan na h-uaisle
Cuision na cluasag na leabaidh,
Gus an d' éirich leis a' mhàthair
'Ga chur 's a' mhainnseir 'n a chadal.
(Wonderful was the sight she saw
when he came down out of her body;
she wrapped in white clothes
the Saviour who had come to redeem us.
The child of nobility asked
for no cushion, pillow or bed,
till his Mother managed to put him
to sleep in the manger.) (Ó Baoill 1972, 94–101)

The poetess compliments the Virgin on her faithful mothering of the Christ child. In contrast to the more delicately maternal images of female poets, the fully grown Jesus, the joiner of Nazareth, is depicted by Fr. Allan MacDonald (1859–1905), parish priest of Eriskay, as a Hebridean boat-builder who builds the boat of his Church and appoints Peter as her captain (Campbell 1965, 21–24). Seagoing imagery is also found in Protestant verse composed in the Hebrides down to the present day, as can be seen in the hymns of Caitrìona MacDonald of Staffin, Skye, who presented Christ as "Fear a' Bhàta," the ferry-man who will take her and other Christian believers across the ocean of death (NicDhòmhnaill 1987, 47–48).

Although male and female poets can use similar imagery in depicting Christ, female poets often have a wider range of imagery at their disposal because of their ability to deploy their feminine instincts. This is evident in both Catholic and Protestant verse. Perhaps the most daring presentation of Jesus Christ in the entire corpus of Scottish Gaelic verse is found in a small song composed by an otherwise unknown female poet, Anna NicEalair (Anna MacKellar), apparently in Argyll in the first quarter of the nineteenth century. The translation of the Bible into Scottish Gaelic, completed in 1801, allowed the Gaelic people to transplant images from the Old and New Testaments into Gaelic soil. In times of spiritual revival, when entire communities were gripped by a desire for an intimate knowledge of Jesus, the expression of such intimacy could become remarkably physical as biblical imagery interacted with folksong motifs. The erotic images of the Song of Solomon were repossessed by Anna MacKellar to express her own experience of being ravished by Christ's love:

'S ann a thug thu dhomh do ghaol
Fo dhubhar craobh an aiteil;
Is co-chomann do rùin
Ann an gàradh nan abhall.
(In fact, you gave me your love

in the juniper's tree's shadow,
and the fellowship of your desire
in the garden with trees of apples.) (Meek 2003, 270–271)

Anna concluded her song by alluding to Christ's triumphant resurrection and his continuing work in preparing a place in heaven for her soul. These concepts hint at another, much harder, image commonly found in Gaelic religious verse, namely Jesus as warrior, surpassing all human heroes because of his divine power and ascension. This is the theme of the original Gaelic version of the carol well-known in its English translation as "Child in the Manger / Infant of Mary." It was composed by Mary MacDonald (1789–1872) of Mull. By putting its primary emphasis on the infant, it was not intended to be a Christmas carol but to convey the contrast between the humble Jesus, born in a manger with no earthly pomp (cf. the verse of Giles MacDonald), and all other earthly heroes, who, despite their luxury and human prowess, are unable to rise from the dead:

'S iomadh fear treubhach, gaisgealach, gleusda
Chaisg air an steud 's nach èirich dhiubh,
A-chaoidh gus an sèidear trompaid Mhic Dhè,
Ag àrd-mholadh Dhè 's a' seinn a chliù.
(Many a hero, warlike and skilful,
died on his steed, and never will rise,
until Christ's trumpet issues a summons,
praising our God, with song in the skies.) (Meek 2003, 266–269)

In these lines, Christ's second coming as judge of the world is anticipated, and it is he who turns the tables and rouses the dead warriors. The Day of Judgment is one of the most persistent themes in the Gaelic poetic corpus, in both Catholic and Protestant forms. It is most fully represented in the verse of Dugald Buchanan (1716–1768), a schoolmaster in Kinloch-Rannoch, Perthshire, who is generally regarded as the supreme Christian poet of the Protestant Highlands. His lengthy epic poem "Là a' Bhreitheanais" (The Day of Judgment) portrays Jesus Christ as the Christ of both the cosmos and the Highland glens:

Tha 'm bogha-frois mu'n cuairt d'a cheann,
'S mar thuil nan gleann tha fuaim a ghuth;
'S mar dhealanach tha sealladh shùl,
A' spùtadh as na neulaibh tiugh.
(The rainbow forms a circle round his head,
and like the torrent of the glens is the sound of his voice;
and like lightning is the glancing of his eyes,
spouting out of the thick clouds.) (MacLean 1913, 18)

Buchanan also composed a hymn on "Fulangas Chrìosd" (The Suffering of Christ), in which he dwelled on Christ's passion in considerable detail (ibid., 5–13). Reflections on Christ's death, his suffering, and his victorious ascension are also very common in nineteenth-century Gaelic hymnology, but they are treated much more subjectively, notably in the immensely popular hymns of the Rev. Peter Grant (1783–1867), Baptist minister at Grantown on Spey (MacDougall 1926). Though deploying pastoral and biblical images that resonate with rural life in the Highlands (e.g., the Good Shepherd), Grant's pictures of Jesus use comparatively few "earthly" and nonbiblical images. As Highlanders became more familiar with the Gaelic Bible, it influenced poetic expression, and "the things of this world" were eschewed (Meek 1996).

Gaelic poets provided the greatest range of pictures of Jesus Christ, drawing on day-to-day experience and also on Scripture. Prose composers and writers, predominantly Protestant, were more often concerned with the presentation of doctrine, but this focus offered less scope for creativity. Some works, such as the Rev. John MacRury's *Eachdraidh Beatha Chrìosd* (Account of the Life of Christ), published in Glasgow (1893), attempted to harmonize New Testament accounts of Jesus' life and death. Within the Protestant tradition, preachers often covered the same themes as the poets, but with less in the way of metaphorical interpretation. It is, however, common to find a biblical emblem providing a theme for a sermon, as can also happen with a hymn. Thus, the collection of Gaelic sermons by the Rev. Malcolm MacLeod, *An Iuchair Oir* (The Golden Key) (MacCalmain 1950), takes its title from its first piece, a meditation on Christ as "the key of David" (Rev. 3.7), and subsequent sermons in the collection likewise use emblematic themes (The White Stone, The Memorial Stone) representative of Christ. Sermons generally adhere closely to the words of Scripture and specifically to its teachings. In his moving account of a Communion service held out of doors in his native district of Morvern, the Rev. Dr. Norman MacLeod (1783–1862), the foundationally important Gaelic prose writer of the nineteenth century, depicted the preacher's message to the assembled multitude as follows:

> *B' iad na briathran a ghabh am ministeir mar stéidh a theagaisg air an là so, Luc. xxii. 19: 'Dèanaibh so mar chuimhneachan orm-sa.' O'n cheann-teagaisg so, leig e ris doibh ciod e Crìosd a chuimhneachadh; labhair e mu'n eòlas, mu'n ghràdh, agus mu'n chreidimh a tha fillte steach anns a' chuimhne so a chumail; agus ann an cainnt nach faodadh drùghadh air gach cridhe, leig e ris na sochairean lìonmhor a tha 'sruthadh o chuimhne cheart a chumail air Iosa.*
>
> (The words that the minister took as the foundation of his teaching on this day were Luke 22.19: "This do in memory of me." From this text, he expounded to them what it was to remember Christ; he spoke about the knowledge, the love, and the faith that are interwoven in keeping this remembrance; and in language which could not but affect every heart, he expounded the abundant benefits that flow from keeping a proper remembrance of Jesus.) (Clerk 1910, 491)

Yet even at times of Communion, with its strict ritual and strong doctrinal emphasis, personal envisaging of Jesus Christ was encouraged, mainly through the *Coinneamh Cheist* (Question Meeting) on the Friday of the Communion season, at which elders and male members of the churches were given the opportunity to relate their spiritual experiences by responding to a specific biblical text. Thus, at the meeting held at the time of Communion in Stornoway High Church in 1963, Donald MacLeod, Knock, spoke as follows (1963, 3):

> *Bha mi turus a bha seo a muigh anns an eithir air oidhche dhorcha fhiadhaich, agus fear eile còmhla rium. Cha robh fhios agam càit an robh sinn a' dol. Nach ann a dh' éirich solus air an fhairge. Có a bha ann ach m'athair air tìr agus torch aige a chum ar treòrachadh gu cladach, ach shaoil leinn gum b'aithne dhuinn fhìn an t-slighe, agus chaidh an eithir air a tarsaing! Tha an Tighearna ag iarraidh oirnn a bhith a' gluasad anns an t-solus. Is esan an Tì as urrainn ar treòrachadh ceart.*
>
> (I was on one occasion out in the boat on a wild dark night, and another man was with me. We did not know where we were going. Didn't a light appear on the sea. Who was it but my father and he had a torch in order to guide us to the shore, but we thought that we ourselves knew the way, and the boat capsized! The Lord asks us to walk in the light. He is the one who can guide us properly.) (*Na Dulleagan Gàidhlig*, 4)

This simple but vivid parable obliterates the distinction between prose and verse in the portrayal of Jesus Christ in Gaelic Scotland.

Donald E. Meek

See also: Calvin, John; Jesus, Achievement of; Kempis, Thomas à; Scottish (Lowland) Christianity; Welsh Christianity

References

Campbell, John Lorne, ed. 1965. *Bàrdachd Mhgr Ailein*. Edinburgh: Constable.

Clerk, Archibal, ed. 1910. *Caraid nan Gàidheal: The Friend of the Gael: A Choice Selection of Gaelic Writings by Norman MacLeod, D.D.* Edinburgh: John Grant.

MacCalmain, T. M., ed. 1950. *An Iuchair Oir: Searmoinean leis an Urramach Calum MacLeòid*, M.A. Stirling: Stirling Tract Enterprise.

MacDougall, Hector, ed. 1926. *Spiritual Songs by Rev. Peter Grant, Strathspey*. Glasgow: Alexander MacLaren.

MacLean, Donald, ed. 1913. *The Spiritual Songs of Dugald Buchanan*. Edinburgh: John Grant.

MacLeod, Donald. 1963. *Na Dulleagan Gàidhlig*, 4 (An Giblean [April]).

Meek, Donald E. 1996. "Images of the Natural World in the Hymnology of Dugald Buchanan and Peter Grant." *Scottish Gaelic Studies* 17: 263–277.

———, ed. 2003. *Caran an t-Saoghail: The Wiles of the World: An Anthology of Nineteenth-Century Gaelic Verse*. Edinburgh: Birlinn.

NicDhòmhnaill, Caitrìona. 1987. *Na Bannan Gràidh: Laoidhean*. Stornoway: Stornoway Religious Bookshop.

Ó Baoill, Colm, ed. 1972. *Poems and Songs by Sìleas MacDonald, c. 1660–c. 1729*. Edinburgh: Scottish Gaelic Texts Society.

Watson, William J., ed. 1937. *Scottish Verse from the Book of the Dean of Lismore*. Edinburgh: Scottish Gaelic Texts Society.

Scottish (Lowland) Christianity

The figure of Jesus has had a significant presence in the religious, social, cultural, and political life of the Scottish Lowlands, lying below the Highland Line, since at least the sixth century, and possibly earlier. Lowland Scotland is itself an area of regional diversity. It includes the more rural North East, Borders, and South West, as well as what was to become in the modern era the more urban and populated Central Belt between the Clyde and the Forth estuaries. The centers of power in Church and state, the universities, and other national institutions have been located in Lowland Scotland from the Middle Ages onward. The story of Scottish Lowland Christianity is therefore a twofold narrative. In part, it is the dominant strand of a national narrative of a Christian nation within pre-Reformation Catholic and post-Reformation Protestant Christendom, and in part it is the local account of a particular linguistic, social, and spiritual experience within Scotland, in distinction but not separation from Highland and Gaelic-speaking Christianity. It is also a story that is inseparable from the religious and cultural life of the British Isles and continental Europe as well as of those parts of the world linked to Lowland Scotland through trade, empire, and mission. The Jesus of Scottish Lowland Christianity is thus a distinctive local figure of faith and controversy, as well as a derivative configuration of currents of understanding and representation of Christ flowing from Europe and the wider world.

Along with the record of Celtic missionaries spreading out from Columba's Iona across the area now designated by Lowland Scotland from the later sixth century, there is evidence of an earlier Christian missionary presence among the Southern Picts in Galloway in the later fifth or early sixth centuries, associated with Ninian and centered on Whithorn. One of the earliest surviving "Lowland" representations of Jesus can be found on the Ruthwell Cross (c. 700), a preaching station in this same South West region of Scotland, by then part of the Anglian kingdom of Northumbria. The standing cross is inscribed with scenes from the life of Christ and the Runic inscription of part of an Anglo-Saxon poem, "The Dream of the Rood" (c. ninth century), framed by vine scrolls representing the tree of life. The full text of the poem describes Jesus as a brave warrior: "Then the young hero who was King of Heaven / Strong and steadfast, stripped for battle / Climbed the high gallows, his constant courage / Clear in his mission to redeem mankind" (Bateman, Crawford, and McGonigal 2000, 19). This Jesus of the Northumbrian missionaries in southern Scotland both appealed to and challenged the warrior codes of a pagan society, according to modern translator of the poem Robert Crawford. So the first Jesus of Lowland Christianity is a biblical savior, a crucified and risen God with a cosmic mission, firmly set within this local cultural context of militant heroism and the artistic celebration of the natural world.

As the Celtic Church of Iona and Northumbria gave way throughout Scotland to the institutional authority of the Western Church, centered in Rome, so the Jesus of Scottish Lowland Christianity became the figure represented throughout Europe in medieval Catholic piety and devotional practice. As Leslie Macfarlane has noted, the liturgy and devotion to the Eucharist kept that Scottish piety centered on Christ, even as the cult of the Blessed Virgin Mary was being introduced to Scotland by the incoming religious orders between the eleventh and thirteenth centuries. The devastating effects of war and plague in the fourteenth century increased the appeal of the suffering

Jesus of the Cross, "as may be seen in the introduction into Scotland of new feasts like the Crown of Thorns, the Holy Blood, the Five Wounds, and the Compassion of the Virgin at the Foot of the Cross, and their visual representation in prayer books, painted ceilings and banners" (Macfarlane 1993, 148–149). As in the rest of Christendom, Jesus was the object of both liturgical adoration and private devotion in medieval Scotland, and works like *The Imitation of Christ* by Thomas à Kempis (1418) were widely read. But he was also a national figure.

The founding document of medieval Scottish nationhood, *The Declaration of Arbroath* (1320), was both a work of international diplomacy appealing to the pope to recognize Scotland's independence from England and a contextual work of Christian political theology. It invokes the crucified and risen Lord Jesus Christ in biblical terms as "the King of Kings," a cosmic ruler who mythically honors the geographically remote Scots by their early (alleged) conversion through his apostle Andrew. However, this political Christ not only served the cause of Scottish nationhood but could also be invoked as a radical figure on the side of the poor. In a play by the courtier Sir David Lindsay, *Ane Satyre of the Thrie Estaitis*, first performed in 1552 and written in the Lowland Scots that was then flourishing as a literary language, the corruption of Church, state, and society and neglect of the poor in late medieval Scotland were exposed and the case for reform made through appeal to the words of Christ in the vernacular New Testament and the appearance on stage of the Christ-like figure of the representative Poor Man, John the Commonweal. When the poor are assured that their complaints of injustice will be heard, John cries out: "Thankit be Christ that buir the croun of thorne / For I was never sa blyth sen I was borne!"

Despite the profound changes to Scottish religious and national life brought on by the Scottish Reformation of 1560, this dual political figure of Christ the King, sovereign over the nation and yet friend of the poor and humble, remained as a dominant if sometimes contradictory trope of Jesus in the Scottish Protestant imagination from the sixteenth into the twentieth centuries. The Calvinist theology and piety of the Reformed Kirk and its early leaders, such as John Knox, emphasized the lordship and rule of Christ in both personal and public life in ways that shaped the consciousness of generations of Lowland Scots. In a collection of Protestant religious songs written in Scots and published for popular use in 1567, *The Guide and Godlie Ballates*, it is an everlasting King who is praised. In a ballad on "The Conceptioun of Christ," for example, ordinary Scots adhering to the new Reformed faith would have sung to a popular tune: "Jesus his name ye call / Quhilk salbe Prince ouir all / His Kingdome sall haue nane end." In their anti-Roman polemic, these same Protestant ballads could employ arresting everyday images of Christ from contemporary experience, such as "Jesus, our King, is gane in hunting." This Reformed Jesus is imagined as the hunter of the papal fox, with Peter and Paul as his hounds.

However, the militant and regal figure of Jesus found in post-Reformation theology and popular piety, especially in the covenanting movements of the seventeenth century, must be balanced by the erotic and emotional representation of Jesus in the letters of the leading Presbyterian minister and divinity professor, Samuel Rutherford (1600–1661). In these outpourings of Rutherford's heart and pastoral concern, Jesus is portrayed as the beloved Bridegroom filled with holy desire for his Bride, the Church. James Whyte (1983) has wondered whether this intimate figure of spiritual longing may also reflect the anxious mental state of seventeenth-century Scottish covenanters like Rutherford. By the mid-eighteenth century, a very different Jesus had emerged in Scottish Presbyterianism, the teacher of the Christian Stoic virtues, as represented in the sermons of the moderate ministers of the Scottish Enlightenment such as Hugh Blair. Along with the suffering and yet triumphant king of more orthodox Calvinist preaching, this stoic Christ is an austere and remote figure who failed to meet all the emotional needs of frail Scottish Lowland peasant believers. It is significant that in the later eighteenth-century poetry and songs in Lowland Scots of Robert Burns, this vacuum of religious feeling is filled by the Deil (devil), who appears as the more human and almost comic figure; while God is represented in the patriarchal and Old Testament figure of the male head of the peasant household gathered for family prayers.

Lowland Scottish Protestantism in the nineteenth century witnessed the rise of a number of competing understandings of Jesus to fill that same vacuum, reflecting the emerging tensions of an increasingly urban society undergoing rapid industrialization. The resurgent evangelical movement in and beyond the national Kirk encouraged fervent commitment to Jesus as a personal savior who rescued people from a sinful world. This trend was matched in the growing immigrant, and largely Irish, Catholic population by a disciplined devotion to the Sacred Heart of Jesus and by an emphasis on the eucharistic worship of an aesthetic Christ in the much smaller but socially more upper-class membership of the Scottish Episcopal Church under the influence of Anglo-Catholicism.

But the Scottish political Christ also appeared in the nineteenth century. Again the portrayal of Jesus as King and Lord over the Church and the nations is central to the documents and controversies that led to the Disruption of the Church of Scotland in 1843 and that followed in its wake. However, this militant Christ in Church-state affairs was not seen by the Disruption evangelicals as the political savior of the oppressed working class. As Donald C. Smith has observed, "Without noticing it, the [Scottish Presbyterian] Church preached a kind of docetic Christ" (Smith 1987, 61). A radical and more fully human Jesus could only be found in the minority views of a few Protestant laymen and ministers, such as the deported lawyer and Friend of the People Thomas Muir in the 1790s, the working-class rebels of the minor 1820 Insurrection, such as John Baird and Andrew Hardie, and the Chartist supporter and Church of Scotland parish minister Patrick Brewster. Nineteenth-century theological controversy about the nature of the Incarnation and atonement caused by the writings and ministry of John Macleod Campbell and Edward Irving, deposed ministers of the Church of Scotland, centered on their more doctrinal and experiential rather than political emphasis on Christ's full humanity.

In the later nineteenth and throughout the twentieth centuries, with the success of modern science, there was a return to the distinctive Scottish emphasis on the Cosmic Christ of creation. Henry Drummond, the popular scientist and evangelistic colleague of D. L. Moody, preached a Savior who was the fulfillment of an evolutionary process in nature and religion. Inspired by the work of a Presbyterian science professor, J. Y. Simpson, speculating on parallel universes, Hugh MacDiarmid wrote a poem in Lowland Scots on "The Innumerable Christ": "On coontless stars the Babe maun cry / An' the Crucified maun bleed" (Grieve and Aitken 1978, I, 32). The theologian Thomas F. Torrance has argued for the intellectual links between the Christocentric faith of the Scottish physicist James Clerk Maxwell and his scientific discoveries; Torrance explored in his own work on science and religion the space-time dimensions of the Incarnation and resurrection of this Cosmic Christ. The strange images of Crucified Fish in the paintings of the Scottish artist John Bellany, inspired by his evangelical upbringing in East Coast fishing villages, brings this Scottish Cosmic Christ into the center of contemporary Scottish art. But the crucified and cosmic figure of the "The Dream of the Rood" and Bellany's art, so central to Lowland life over 1,200 years, is no longer at the heart of the religious quest for most Scots, where even postindustrial villages have their alternative therapies and New Age shops. Jesus is competing with other gods in twenty-first-century Lowland Scotland.

William F. Storrar

See also: Celtic and Early English Christianity; English Christianity, Medieval; Enlightenment; Eucharist; Kempis, Thomas à; Kingdom of God; Mary; Roman Catholicism; Scottish (Gaelic) Christianity; Torrance, T. F.

References

Bateman, M., R. Crawford, and J. McGonigal, eds. 2000. *Scottish Religious Poetry.* Edinburgh: St. Andrews Press.

Donaldson, G. 1990. *The Faith of the Scots*. London: Batsford.

Grieve, Michael, and W. R. Aitken, eds. 1978. *The Complete Poems of Hugh MacDiarmid*. (2 vols.) London: Martin Brian and O'Keeffe.

Macfarlane, L. 1993. "Catholic Devotion (Pre Reformation)." In *Dictionary of Scottish Church History & Theology*, edited by N. M. de S. Cameron. Edinburgh: T. & T. Clark.

Smith, Donald C. 1987. *Passive Obedience and Prophetic Protest*. New York: Peter Lang.

Storrar, W. 1990. *Scottish Identity*. Edinburgh: Handsel Press.

Whyte, J. 1983. "Scottish Spirituality." Pp. 351–353 in *A Dictionary of Christian Spirituality*. Edited by G. S. Wakefield. London: SCM.

Scotus, Duns

See Bonaventure; Franciscan Thought and Piety

Second Coming of Jesus, in Current Belief

Expectation that Jesus will one day return to the earth has long been a central Christian tenet. Certainly it is there already in the New Testament, and given this biblical support, it is no surprise to find that it quickly found expression in the Church's creeds.

Despite what one might instinctively think, 2,000 years of belief in the literal return of Jesus shows little sign of falling from favor. Thus, for example, according to a 1983 Gallup poll, some 62 percent of all Americans had "no doubts" that Jesus will come to earth again, and a more recent American poll indicated that some 40 percent of all Americans answered yes to the question "Do you believe that the world will end, as the Bible predicts, in a battle at Armageddon between Jesus and the Antichrist?" and half of those said that they expected it to happen in their lifetimes. Thus, it seems, some 20 percent of American adults think that Jesus will be back within their lifetime to wage war with Antichrist, whom, of course, he will ultimately defeat. Statistics can lie; the figure may be lower (or higher). But even allowing for the possibility of major error, it is still clear that in America, at least, belief in the literal return of Jesus to this earth still runs high.

But it is not just in America that such views seem to be popular. To the statistics given above one may add those relating to the staggering growth of groups such as the Seventh-day Adventists, who, as their name suggests, place great emphasis upon the expected "Second Advent" of Christ. The Adventist Church is currently growing at nearly 7 percent net per year, and most of that growth is outside the United States. If this rate is maintained, the church will soon see an increase of 1 million new members every year. By 2015, it will be a major world religious force of some 25 million baptized members; by 2030 there could be 50 million.

The simple statement "Jesus will come again," however, masks a much more complex array of quite different beliefs. These range from rather poorly focused understandings of the "the second coming" found in some of the more established churches to really quite exceptionally detailed schemes that one finds elsewhere. Central to this discussion is the place of the millennial period described in Revelation 20, and in particular the question of whether Jesus will come back before or after the events there described. Those who think that Jesus will come back after it are generally known as "postmillennialists."

Historically, postmillennialism has been a force to be reckoned with, but it has now rather lost its appeal. Part of this may be a decline in collective self-confidence, for according to the postmillennialist it is really up to human beings, empowered by the Spirit of God, to "prepare the way of the Lord and make his pathways straight" (cf. Isa. 40.3; Matt. 3.3, and parallels). Humankind, so it is argued, will progress and develop to the point where something approaching a perfect society exists worldwide. This era will last 1,000 years (often understood figuratively) and it is after this period, and only then, that Jesus will return.

The other view, that Jesus will come back before the millennial period, is usually called "premillennialism." Among those who take a view on biblical prophecy, it is this premillennial understanding that seems currently to dominate. Those who hold to such a view, and there are countless millions who do, generally argue also that the world as we know it will decline further and further into moral and spiritual chaos until the coming of Christ, whose advent is the only hope of the world's salvation. Human beings individually, and the whole of human society, will not, so the premillennialist generally argues, progress to a state of perfection in preparation for the Lord's return, but rather slip into a state of total moral bankruptcy and wickedness. Hence, complex apocalyptic schemes, which often include the prediction of the coming of an individual, personal Antichrist and a time of great tribulation for those who would remain faithful, are very much a part of current premillennial belief.

Seventh-day Adventists, for example, hold to a fairly simple form of this belief. According to them the world is currently set for the great eschatological drama. That which will spark the final catastrophic chain of events is the passing of a Sunday law in America that will have the effect of forcing individuals to obey either God or Satan. Sunday observance, they argue, is the "Mark of the Beast" spoken of in Revelation 13.16–17, for it is the setting up of the first day of the week, Sunday, as a counterfeit Sabbath that challenges God's status as lawgiver and creator. This substitution is the work of the Roman Catholic Church, the Antichrist, but in the last days Romanism and the American government (symbolized by the lamb-like beast of Rev. 13.11ff.) will work together effectively to enforce worship of Satan, for it is he, ultimately, who is the driving force behind both. Sabbath-keepers will be persecuted in a time of trouble such as there never was; the days will be cut short, however, when Christ returns to redeem his own. (The word "Antichrist," or anti-Messiah originates in 1 John 2.18.)

There are many variations on this theme. The Jehovah's Witnesses, for example, argue that Jesus did return spiritually in 1914 to direct the work of the preaching of the coming kingdom in all the world (cf. Matt. 24.14). He will return visibly after the battle of Armageddon, at which point the world will be cleansed of all sin and wickedness, and the 144,000 (cf. Rev. 7.4; 14.1–3—understood by Witnesses to be a literal number), together with Christ, will reign over a restored earth inhabited by the great multitude (cf. Rev. 7.9; 19.1–6). The statistics given by the Jehovah's Witnesses for their membership are conservative in the extreme since they include only those who are "actively involved in the public Bible educational work." Even according to this very strict count, the 2001 report claims an active membership of just over 6 million (an increase of 1.7 percent over 2000); if one includes young people, those not baptized, and those who do not engage in witnessing activity to an extent to make them eligible for "active member" status, the figure is much higher. Indeed, the same report of 2001 indicates that the total number of persons attending the memorial service (the annual commemoration and Communion service held on the evening of Maundy Thursday) was 15,374,986.

Some premillennial schemes for the end of the world and the return of Jesus are much more complex. All, however, contain the same basic elements of further decline in society in general, perhaps to the point where law and order simply collapse and wickedness and chaos rule. Some, such as the Adventists and the Jehovah's Witnesses, maintain the much older view that the Antichrist is an institution (the Roman Catholic Church, perhaps, or the United Nations); others argue for an individual man. In any case, Christ comes to destroy this institution or individual, but not before it or he has ruled for a period of time, often thought to be either seven or three and a half years. The battleground for such exegetical dispute is found in passages such as Daniel 7, Revelation 13, and above all, 2 Thessalonians 2.

But among some interpreters of biblical prophecy, things can get more complicated still. A passage that is of particular interest to many is Luke 17.34–35. Here one finds the biblical foundation of belief in "the rapture":

> I tell you, in that night there shall be two men in one bed; the one shall be taken, and the other shall be left. Two women shall be grinding together; the one shall be taken, and the other left. Two men shall be in the field; the one shall be taken, and the other left. And they answered and said unto him, Where, Lord? And he said unto them, Wheresoever the body is, thither will the eagles be gathered together.

This passage is taken together with the words of 1 Thessalonians 4.15–17:

> For this we say unto you by the word of the Lord, that we which are alive and remain unto the coming of the Lord shall not prevent them which are asleep. For the Lord himself shall descend from heaven with a shout, with the voice of the archangel, and with the trump of God: and the dead in Christ shall rise first: Then we which are alive and remain shall be caught up together with them in the clouds, to meet the Lord in the air: and so shall we ever be with the Lord.

Few verses in the Bible can have had so profound an impact on popular prophecy belief as these. According to many interpreters, these verses speak of the sudden and unexpected return of Christ and the instantaneous gathering of the saved—so sudden and instantaneous, in fact, that some hopeful believers have invested in bumper stickers reading, "Warning: in the event of the rapture, this vehicle will become driverless." The righteous dead, too, will rise at this time and go to be with Christ, but the unrighteous will be left on earth to fend for themselves. (Some of these believers go on to say that final salvation will still be possible for those left behind so long as they do not receive the "Mark of the Beast," often thought to be a literal mark on the skin, and there are "left behind" survival booklets and Internet sites designed to advise those who are not taken how they may yet attain salvation.)

According to these "rapturists," this second coming of Christ will be unseen by unbelievers. The only thing they will know is that suddenly millions of people will have disappeared from the earth. Once the saved have been taken, the rest will be left to the ravages of Antichrist. At the conclusion of the period, Christ will return again (with the previously raptured saints). The wicked dead will be raised at this point. The judgment will take place, and all the wicked—including those who lived through the tribulation and received the Mark of the Beast and the wicked dead, now raised to life once more—will be slain after hearing their judgment. The saints will then rule on earth with Christ for 1,000 years, after which they will be taken to heaven.

No better current example of the influence of such thinking, and the scale of it, is seen than that of the phenomenally successful Left Behind series. These novels, with sales topping 50 million, give a graphic account of life on earth after the rapture, including the rise of the Antichrist, Nicolae Carpathia. Underpinning the account is a reading of several parts of the Bible, but especially the book of the Revelation of John, put forward by two of the most influential of all evangelical authors, Jerry B. Jenkins and Tim LaHaye. Although these books are fiction, there can be no doubt that the message they present is taken very seriously indeed both by the authors and by many of their readers. For example, on the launch of the website for the series, Jenkins wrote, "It is our hope that the new leftbehind.com will become your online home for spiritual growth, stimulation, support and close-knit fellowship as you strive to live and share the message of eternity with others while living every day in light of Christ's imminent return." Elsewhere on the website there appears a short video of LaHaye explaining what "the rapture" means.

Those who believe in schemes such as those presented by Jenkins and LaHaye may be referred to as "pretribulationist rapturists"—that is, they believe that the second coming of Christ and the concurrent "rapture" of the saints (dead and alive) will occur before the great tribulation and the coming of Antichrist. The redeemed are safe in heaven while the earth goes further and further into chaos and Antichrist grows in power and influence. This process is not over until the "third" coming of Christ at the end of the tribulation period. To many, such thinking seems strange. However, even the shallowest of trawls of the Internet will quickly reveal just how live an issue this is to many millions of people across the globe. To be sure, there are some sites that seem to be one-person outfits, but there are others that are massively backed and suggest huge followings. These currently include http://www.leftbehind.com and sublinks from http://www.virtualchurch.org.

This pretribulationist position appears to have been largely a development in eschatological thinking that took place during the nineteenth century. It is characteristic of dispensationalism, the system created largely by the Irish Anglican clergyman John Nelson Darby (1800–1882), according to which God's dealings with humankind may be divided into various periods, or "dispensations." It was Darby also who first argued for a secret rapture. Dispensationalism became particularly influential, especially so after the publication in 1909 of the Scofield Bible, the notes appended to which reflect the dispensationalist (rapturist, pretribulationist) position. Before that, most, if not all, premillennialists were "post-tribulationists," that is, they argued that the coming of Christ would take place only after the tribulation. Not just the wicked, then, but the righteous, too, would go through the period of tribulation and face the possibility of having to resist getting the dreaded "Mark of the Beast." Such people, and again one should not underestimate the numbers involved, may prepare for the period of tribulation in a number of ways, perhaps, for example, by storing up food and other necessities that they expect not to be able to buy without submitting to Antichrist (cf. Rev. 13.7). Very shortly before the actual appearance of Christ, they argue, they will be caught up together with the resurrected faithful to meet Christ in the air (cf. 1 Thess. 4) and return to earth with him, both to destroy the wicked and to reign during the millennial period.

There has developed also a "mid-tribulationist" school. According to this view, the living saints do have to go through the tribulation, but not all of it. The "mid-tribs" posit that the rapture will take place halfway through the seven-year period, perhaps coinciding with the sounding of the seventh trumpet of Revelation 11.15 and the event described in 11.12: "Then they heard a loud voice from heaven saying to them, 'Come up here!' And they went up to heaven in a cloud while their enemies watched them." Like the pretribulationists, the "mid-tribs" then argue that the saints will return with Christ to witness the judgment and destruction of the wicked and begin the millennial rule on earth.

There are other views of course. As was hinted above, many mainstream churches shun the kind of speculation and extremism (as they see it) that has been outlined. The official Roman Catholic view, for example, is that the millennium is a period of peace brought in by the establishment of the Church. Like most Anglicans, Catholics in general are rather shy of engaging in discussion relating to the kinds of issues that seem so important in much of American popular belief. Methodism, too, would now (though perhaps not when it was founded) prefer to think in terms of God working in, through, and with human beings and human institutions to bring a gradual transformation of the world into a more perfect state. Members of such ecclesial bodies might well, if pressed, indicate that they do believe, as they often confess in the recitation of the creed, "that he will come again to judge the living and the dead," but not many choose to dwell upon it or are able to put much flesh on those very bare confessional bones. Nevertheless, as Paul Boyer (1992) and others have demonstrated beyond all reasonable doubt, "out there . . . in the darkness beyond the scholarly campfire," millions, it seems, are looking heavenward in eager anticipation of the time when the heavens roll back and, to the believer at least, Christ appears to take his faithful out of the world, even if only shortly thereafter to return once more to witness the destruction of evil and the banishment of sin.

Kenneth G. C. Newport

See also: American (North) Christianity; Creeds; John, Revelation of; Seventh-day Adventism

References

Boyer, Paul. 1992. *When Time Shall Be No More: Prophecy Belief in American Culture*. Cambridge: Harvard University Press.

Cohn, Norman. 1970. *The Pursuit of the Millennium: Revolutionary Millenarians and Mystical Anarchists of the Middle Age*. London: Paladin.

Garrett, Clarke. 1975. *Respectable Folly: Millenarians and the French Revolution in England and France*. Baltimore: Johns Hopkins University Press.

Harrison, J. F. C. 1979. *The Second Coming: Popular Millenarianism, 1780–1850*. London: Routledge and Kegan Paul.
Newport, Kenneth G. C. 2000. *Apocalypse and Millennium: Studies in Biblical Eisegesis*. Cambridge: Cambridge University Press.
Popkin, Richard H., ed. 1988. *Millenarianism and Messianism in English Literature and Thought, 1650–1800*. Leiden: Brill.
Wainwright, Arthur W. 1993. *Mysterious Apocalypse*. Nashville: Abingdon.
Weber, Timothy P. 1987. *Living in the Shadow of the Second Coming: American Premillennialism, 1875–1982*. Chicago: University of Chicago Press.

Second Coming of Jesus, Origins of

Belief that Jesus, now risen from the dead and departed to heaven, would return to the world in triumph, to judge and to rule forever, goes back to the earliest known Christian writings. It has remained in statements of Christian belief down to the present day. It comes as the final clause of the central section of the creeds, that relating to belief in and about Jesus. We have in the Apostles' Creed, for example, "He shall come to judge the living and the dead," and the Nicene Creed is similar.

The oldest evidence for the belief comes in what is probably Paul's earliest letter, the first to the Thessalonians, where he is concerned to reassure his readers about the fate of Christian believers who have already died before the Lord's expected return has taken place. They are not to worry, for such believers will, when the day comes, be raised from death and join Jesus and the Christians still living, sharing in his triumph (1 Thess. 4.13–18). We have to understand the greatly restricted picture of the universe (compared with our sense of "space") prevailing in Paul's day and the inherited Jewish belief in the heavenly exaltation of great servants of God (such as Enoch, Moses, and Elijah), and then the possible role of such figures in the ultimate assertion of God's sovereignty and the judgment of humankind at "the end of the world" as it was commonly called (see Dan. 7). For those who saw Jesus as the center and climax of God's revelation of his saving purpose, it was natural that he should step into these roles.

Modern readers may find such a belief extraordinary (though see the preceding article), putting it down to the extreme confidence and enthusiasm of the members of a new religious movement expressing their faith by way of the conventions of their Jewish culture. They will feel this partly because its working out raises so many hard questions: how can such a future be envisaged in practice? How can or could a single person exercise rule and judgment on such a scale, and how can "heaven" and "earth" relate in such a way? We can, of course, make allowances for the smaller scale of the first-century picture of things and for the doubtless restricted view of an individual like Paul in the Eastern Mediterranean world of the time. But lest we should think of this teaching as a short-term enthusiastic manifestation, which later sobriety would modify, we should note immediately that in 1 Corinthians 15, written a few years later (in the mid-fifties), Paul repeats it, with refinements relating to practical implications that have come to his attention. Would people rise in their bodies? What then would happen to the Christians surviving on that day? All would be transformed, says Paul, to appear as "spiritual bodies," so that all will be on the same footing (vv. 42–55). These ideas, too, have precedents in Jewish speculation, for example, 2 Esdras 2.45. On the central issue, an even later Pauline letter renews similar doctrine (Phil. 3.20–21).

The belief is naturally part of a complex of eschatological ideas (i.e., concerning the end of things) in which Jewish thought had long been rich. So, in 1 Corinthians 15, notably, it is bound up with belief in the resurrection of the dead; the resurrection of Jesus makes him a pioneer guaranteeing a similar future to his people.

What Paul so clearly displays is found also in the Gospels, written after Paul's time, on the lips of Jesus. There, at least in Matthew (24.3, 27, 37, 39), as indeed occasionally in Paul (1 Thess. 2.19; 1 Cor. 15.23), we find what was to become the technical term in Christian vocabulary for the return or "second coming" of Christ: *Parousia*. In itself it is an ordinary Greek word meaning "presence" or "appearing" (e.g., in Phil. 1.26; 2.12), but in the relevant contexts it has virtually become an English technical term, to be printed without italics. But it is salutary to have in mind its usual sense: it refers to the "appearing" of some valued or revered figure whose arrival is the occasion of excitement and joy. That is the atmosphere that surrounds its application to Jesus' second coming, a hope so often dulled over the many Christian centuries. Indeed, all the Synoptic Gospels were beginning to react to this factor, urging constant vigilance for that Parousia (e.g., Mark 13; Matt. 24; Luke 21).

So, in the face of its nonfulfillment, the lively hope for Jesus' return was already being adjusted within the period of the writing of the NT books themselves. The easiest solution to a consciously felt problem was simply to cast the eyes further and further forward, or at least, so to provide institutions and teaching for the practicalities of Christian life that one could (so to speak) manage if the hope were delayed, even indefinitely, in its fulfillment. In writings such as the pastoral epistles (1 and 2 Tim., Titus), written probably by a later follower of Paul's, there is keen attention to matters of Church organization and discipline. The writing of Acts, as a history of the Church's mission in the first few decades, may itself be seen as a testimony to a concern with the development of the institution within the life and history of the world as it is. More profoundly, however, the Gospel of John goes a long way toward seeing the reality of Christ's presence as filling the community of believers in the here and now: they are one with him, and he dwells in them, so that their acts and words are his acts and words (see especially chapters 14–17), and the Spirit is his guarantee and continuator. In line with this perspective, there is a minimum of attention here to the coming end of things or a future resurrection (5.24–27; 6.39–40; but see 21.23; 14.3). On this understanding, a literal Parousia is, spiritually at least, inessential.

Both ways of dealing with the fact that Jesus had not returned in anything like the expected sense have persisted and are understandable. The first has been, presumably, more general (see the clause in the creeds); the latter is more constructive, demanding and ultimately fruitful for Christian life. But there has been a third reaction: the revival from time to time, perhaps especially in times of crisis and often in small or marginalized groups, of the full-blown doctrine in all its urgency—only to relive the discouragement of the earlier period, or sometimes happily to survive the letdown, repeating in some form one or another of the previous ways of accommodating. However, for many modern Christians, especially in the United States and the developing world, the belief remains literal, vivid, and strong.

We should notice that the final book of the NT, the Revelation of John, is unique in the intensity of its vision, though it ends with the return of Jesus as still ahead: "Surely I am coming soon" (22.20). Its function then is to renew the earthly Church's orientation toward heaven and the living majesty of God in the face of whatever fills its life on earth (see chapters 2–3): the book is a restorer of easily distorted proportions, whereby God is reduced to an adjunct of earth rather than being the source, center, and purpose of all else. At the same time, the Revelation, so outlandish to many now in its imagery, teaches another lesson about this idiom of thought. As was noted above, reference is often made to the goal as "the end of the world." But here we read of "a new heaven and a new earth": that is, a renewal and restoration of the created order in full. In that way, what is involved is faith in an ultimate hope for God's creation, and not at all its destruction in some act of ultimate barbarism.

Leslie Houlden

See also: Creeds; John, Gospel of; John, Revelation of; Resurrection; Second Coming of Jesus, in Current Belief; Seventh-day Adventism

References

Glasson, T. F. 1963. *The Second Advent*. London: Epworth.

Lincoln, A. 1981. *Paradise Now and Not Yet*. Cambridge: Cambridge University Press.

Rowland, C. 1982. *The Open Heaven*. London: SPCK.

———. 1985. *Christian Origins*. London: SPCK.

Second Person of the Trinity

The formal and official terminology for representing Jesus Christ, God the Son, in the context of the long-authorized doctrine of the Holy Trinity, names him as the "second person" of the triune God. That doctrine may be found succinctly expressed, or at any rate witnessed to, in the Nicene Creed. In that doctrine, Jesus is seen as from all eternity coequal with, though derived from, the Father, who is the fount of all deity, and coequal also with the Spirit, who, again from all eternity, proceeds from the Father (and, in the dominant Western Christian tradition, equally from the Son). This kind of conceptualizing (except for the actual terms "Father," "Son," and "Spirit") does not appear in the NT, apart from rudimentary statements (e.g., Matt. 28.19; 2 Cor. 13.14) that could later be seen as foreshadowings, but developed in the first four centuries of the Church, largely within a scripturally conditioned version of Platonist philosophical reflection.

As a way of thinking about Jesus, the term seems, as far as its ethos and language are concerned, to be very different from the simpler, more image-based thinking of the Gospels and other early writings. It can also seem to be at a distance from the basic business of Christian devotion and behavior. It has nevertheless been of crucial importance in the tradition of Christian theological thought, that is, in attempts to formulate faith in the most profound and comprehensive possible way. But adherence to a given formulation does not necessarily mean identity of thought or mental imagery, and in fact there have been several ways of trying to conceptualize (even visualize) what this language should mean with regard to Jesus. For example, in the early period, some emphasized the image of "Word," seen as utterance, speech, God's mode of self-expression in creation and redemption. On this view, only with the statement "the Word was made flesh" (John 1.14) is there any question of personal identity being reached, and only later, at Jesus' exaltation to heaven, can we be fully ready to think of him as "second person of the Trinity" (and we cannot tell how far the mind of John the evangelist had gone along this path of personifying the image he had inherited from the OT). But such simple, history-based imagining soon gave way before the consideration that God must be eternally one and the same. So the eternity of the Trinitarian being of God came to be accepted. But there could still be emphasis on either the "coming together" (as it were) of three persons, or the oneness of God expressing itself in various aspects, either outwardly toward the world or within his own inner life (of which our inner consciousness, as his creatures, might be a mirror, for we are made in his image, according to Gen. 1.26). So Christ as second person might be envisaged as the collaborator of the Father and Spirit in creation and salvation, or as the prime receiver of the Father's creative love. "God is love" (1 John 4.8), and here we see, in the reciprocal love of Father and Son, bonded by the Spirit, the mode of its inner working, then its outpouring in creation, in relation especially to humanity. A number of these lines of reflection are to be found in the fertile and varied thought of Augustine, who was hugely influential in later, chiefly Western theology (Catholic and Protestant alike).

Speculation concerning the Holy Trinity, and the place of Jesus in that context, is to be found in all periods of Christian history, and in many of the articles in this book. It is worth recording that, despite its never being formally modified, Christian imagination and devotion have often taken rather different turns. For example, the twelfth century and then the past few centuries have seen an emphasis on the humanity of Jesus, for devotion and for practical example. In the former period (for example, in the work of St. Bernard), this focus in no way meant a doctrinal rebellion: indeed, the fact that a *divine* humanity was involved added to the wonder of contemplation of the person of Jesus in all the events of his earthly life. Christian art came to express precisely this sense of human realism shot through with divinity. In more recent times, however, attention to Jesus in this world has often meant a virtual discarding of his place in the Trinitarian framework.

In other circles, notably in seventeenth-century English radical thought, the emphasis shifted to Jesus within the individual believer: we should turn our attention not only from formal doctrine but even from the outward Jesus of history to his presence within those who believe in him. So "Jesus" took the role more traditionally taken by the Spirit, or, in other circles of the period, by the "inner light" of God within those who believed in him (a theme particularly associated with the Quakers). Thomas Webb, active in the period of the English Civil War and the subsequent regime of Oliver Cromwell (1642–1658), expressed his belief about Jesus thus: "We did look for great matters from one crucified at Jerusalem 1600 years ago; but that does us no good; it must be a Christ formed in us." (Formal orthodox doctrine would deny the negative while emphasizing the positive.) Certainly, the bonds of traditional doctrine have often been loosened, especially at the levels of personal faith and devotion, and its concerns could even fade from view entirely, even in many of the activities of practical Church life.

Leslie Houlden

See also: Alexandrian Theology; Art; Augustine of Hippo; Bernard of Clairvaux; Creeds; John, Gospel of; Nicea; Quaker Thought

References

Houlden, J. L. 1992. *Jesus, a Question of Identity*. London: SPCK.
Kelly, J. N. D. 1958. *Early Christian Doctrines*. London: A. & C. Black.

Serapion (d. after 360)

Serapion, a friend of Antony's and Athanasius's, was first a monk, then bishop of Thmuis in the Nile Delta (c. 339–359); in both roles he was prominent in his time. His main extant works are the tract *Against the Manichees* and *The Sacramentary*, a collection of liturgical prayers. At the heart of all his thinking, but set out most clearly in the first of these works, lay his view of Jesus' relationship with God and his understanding of Jesus as Savior.

In *Against the Manichees*, Serapion conceived of Jesus' relationship with God primarily in terms of sonship: a status—rather unusually—that he never ascribed to Christians, and thus one that demonstrated exclusive intimacy. Basing his thought on Scripture (notably, the Gospel of John), he considered that God is a unity, but that, before the creation of the world, he begat an offspring from the depths of himself who is unique—only begotten, legitimate, and precisely like the one who begat him—his image, his exact expression, his radiance—so that anyone looking upon the Son looked upon the Father, and further, that the Son had full knowledge of the Father. The Son, however, does not only know the Father, he makes him known, perceiving and expounding his will as both messenger and prophet, speaking in the prophecies concerning himself in the Old Testament. Consequently, the Son's earthly life is viewed as willed by the Father. This description of the Son carries echoes of the debate with Arius's theology: the term "offspring" is frequent in Athanasius's *Against the Arians*, and Serapion's chosen scriptural texts to indicate the Son's generation from the Father are those fundamental to this debate. In addition, Serapion's stress on the Son's knowledge of the Father and of his will refutes ideas found in Arius's *Thalia*. As well as being concerned with the Son's relationship with the Father, Serapion was also keen to ensure that the Son was seen as being served by the forces of heaven, and as having all things subjected to him except God himself. Important, too, was the Son's role in creation: Serapion described him both as the one through whom the Father made all things and as Maker (in his own right), a lack of precision that indicates his position as between that of Origen and that of Athanasius.

Against the Manichees speaks eloquently of Jesus as Savior, the one who acts to set right the functioning of human beings. His ability to be effective in this task arises partly from his role as the agent of creation and revealer of the Father, but also—more significantly, in Serapion's view—from the fact of the Incarnation. Bearing a normally functioning, mortal human body, in communion with other human bodies, Jesus automatically set these bodies free from negligence, raised them up, and restored them to what they had been originally. Showing the way of perfection and purity, he enabled human bodies to become sufficiently temperate for Father and Son to dwell in them, just as God dwelt in the perfectly virtuous body of Jesus. The action of Jesus the Savior in the human soul and mind, set out in the most beautiful passage in the whole work, is to knock upon the door of the human disposition; as the Word (characteristically speaking through the Old Testament), he offers the invitation of the Song of Songs 5.2 (Casey 1931, 47, 52–67). If allowed entry (probably in baptism), Christ comes to dwell in a person, destroying evil, restoring the original relationship of friendship with the Father, and hiding in the soul the generous benefits he brings. As a result, the soul and mind are exalted, ready for a higher sort of life, able to praise God perfectly and experience silent joy.

The most important and frequently occurring aspect of Jesus the Son in *The Sacramentary* is his only-begottenness: it is through the only begotten, for example, in the anaphora (the central prayer of the Eucharist) and the prayer of blessing of the baptismal waters, that God the Father is made known and salvation given to created nature, and it is the only begotten's healing power that causes the oil used to anoint the sick to be effective. In contrast with *Against the Manichees*, in *The Sacramentary* the term "Savior" is generally reserved for God the Father: the Son's role is that of mediator. It is of note also that the principal agent of sacramental causality in both Eucharist and baptism is the Word and not the Holy Spirit: Serapion's eucharistic epiclesis (part of the eucharistic prayer, calling on God's action) is an epiclesis of the Logos, rather than, as is more commonly done, of the Holy Spirit.

Maxine West

See also: Alexandrian Theology; John, Gospel of; Manichaeism; Nicea; Origen; Son of God

References

Casey, Robert P. 1931. *Serapion of Thmuis against the Manichees*. No. 15, Harvard Theological Studies. Cambridge: Harvard University Press.

Johnson, Maxwell E. 1995. *The Prayers of Sarapion of Thmuis: A Literary, Liturgical, and Theological Analysis*. No. 249, Orientalia Christiana Analecta. Rome: Pontificio Istituto Orientale.

West, E. Maxine. 2001. "The Law, a Holy School: Serapion of Thmuis and Scripture." Pp. 198–201 in Vol. 35, *Studia Patristica*. Edited by Maurice F. Wiles and Edward J. Yarnold. Leuven: Peeters.

Seventh-day Adventism

The Seventh-day Adventist Church is a hugely successful organization that currently looks set for a period of rapid expansion from its present 12 million–member base. The Church is often lumped together conceptually with the Church of Jesus Christ of Latter-day Saints (the Mormons) and the Jehovah's Witnesses, since it is often assumed that the views of all three groups sit only uneasily with more established Christian teaching. In fact, much of Seventh-day Adventist theology is either simply not known outside of its own immediate context or else misunderstood, and popular suspicion of the organization is unwarranted and more often than not ill-informed. This said, however, it is true that members of the Seventh-day Adventist Church do hold to some highly distinctive doctrines. Not the least of these is the claim that the writings of Ellen G. White (1827–1915), often referred to as "the Spirit of Prophecy" in Seventh-day Adventist literature, are to be considered inspired. Seventh-day Adventist observance of the Jewish Saturday Sabbath rather than the Christian Sunday and of Old Testament food laws, and their fervent eschatological expectation, including their rather negative understanding of the rest of Christendom (at least in their literature, if not in actual practice), also mark them out as somewhat distinctive against the general Christian backdrop. Seventh-day Adventists themselves, however, at least those who produce its academic literature, see things rather differently and align themselves clearly with the evangelical Protestant tradition. Such an alignment is not entirely inappropriate, for on many central points Seventh-day Adventists and the wider Christian body find themselves in agreement. This is certainly true (now) of their Christology.

The Seventh-day Adventist Church is extremely conservative with regard to the biblical text. This view results in the promotion of the belief that whatever Jesus is credited with saying or doing in the Gospels, he must have said or done. Seventh-day Adventist academic work on the historical Jesus hence sometimes gives the appearance of being rather outdated, despite the fact that those writing it have often been trained to doctoral level outside of the Seventh-day Adventist education system. Careful attention is paid to the Greek words used in the text, and perhaps even the Aramaic underlying it, but in general Seventh-day Adventist scholars seem not to be concerned with the kinds of issues that dominate much of contemporary Jesus research. Again, this position stems from an uncompromised confidence in the reliability of the biblical text, a confidence that renders such issues as seeking to establish criteria of authenticity pointless. Needless to say, the Gospel of John, no less than the Synoptics, is seen by Seventh-day Adventists as an accurate account of what Jesus actually did and said.

The Church confesses Jesus as Lord, at once both fully human and fully divine. Like other Christians, Seventh-day Adventists have trouble in explaining how this is possible, insisting that, despite the apparent incongruity, since the Bible teaches it, we must believe it. The Church is also fully Trinitarian in its broader formulation, confessing the full equality of Father, Son, and Holy Spirit, three persons, one God. Concerning the work of Christ, too, the Church falls into line with conservative evangelical thinking. There is great emphasis placed upon the sacrificial death of Jesus on the cross. This is often put in the context of penal substitution, and thus we read in one standard Seventh-day Adventist work, "In His death Jesus took our place, identifying Himself with sinners" (Froom 2000, 177). According to the Church, Jesus' work was also to reveal the Father, to be an example, to heal the weak and the sick, and in other ways to put into effect the promises of God, but above all it was by his sacrificial, substitutionary death that he brought peace between a holy God and a sinful human race. Given the suspicion in which the Seventh-day Adventists are often held by other Christians, it is of little surprise to find that members of the Church, especially the professional academics, are keen to stress the extent to which both their Trinitarianism and their Christology are in keeping with standard evangelical doctrine, which indeed it is. Jesus, fully God and fully human, whose words and works are accurately recorded in the Bible, died a substitutionary death upon the cross to save each one of us individually from the consequences of our own sin.

Internally, however, Christology has always been something of an issue in Seventh-day Adventism and the cause of much, sometimes heated, debate. (The same is true, of course, of many other ecclesial bodies.) To be sure, the Church has not always uniformly held to the kind of Christology to which it has come now in its more mature years. This is true in terms of the way in which Seventh-day Adventists have understood both the nature of Christ and his work.

It is reasonably clear, for example, that a number of very important early Seventh-day Adventist figures were Arian. Such figures included Uriah Smith (1832–1903), longtime editor of the Church's principal publication, the *Review and Herald*, and author of two very influential books on Daniel and Revelation (books that were edited by the Church in later times to expunge Arian statements). Commenting on Revelation 3.14, Smith wrote that Jesus was "not the beginner, but the *beginning*, of the creation, the *first created being*, dating his existence far back before *any other created being or thing*, next to the self-existent and eternal God" (Froom 2000, 159). Other confessed Arians included J. H. Waggoner (1820–1889), who was also, like Smith, a very influential early figure and editor of another of the Church's publications, *The Signs of the Times*. Understandably, Seventh-day Adventist writers who treat this part of their history are concerned to stress that these two men (and others like them), although in central positions, were expressing only their own views and not the established view of the Church. This may be so, but anyone who has read some of the other Seventh-day Adventist literature from the period could easily be forgiven for thinking that subordinationism at least, if not straightforward Arianism, was actually fairly firmly entrenched therein. Ellen White, for example, though stressing the equality of Christ with God in some places (and of course the equality he had could have been bestowed rather than inherent), in others wrote about Christ in ways that suggested she was thinking from within a subordinationist framework. For example, she wrote of Satan: "Instead of seeking to make God supreme in the affections and allegiance of His creatures, it was Lucifer's endeavor to win their service and homage to himself. And coveting the honor which the infinite Father had bestowed upon His Son, this prince of angels aspired to power which it was the prerogative of Christ alone to wield" (White, 494). This statement looks subordinationist at the very least: the "infinite Father" has a Son upon whom he "bestowed" honor. James White, Ellen White's husband, also had some Arian leanings, at least in the early years of the Church's development.

This difficulty is complicated further by the fact that Seventh-day Adventists take the view that Christ is to be equated with Michael the Archangel. Hence, commenting on Daniel 10.21 ("But I will shew thee that which is noted in the scripture of truth: and there is none that holdeth with me in these things, but Michael your prince"), White wrote: "The words of the angel, 'I am Gabriel, that stand in the presence of God,' show that he holds a position of high honor in the heavenly courts. When he came with a message to Daniel, he said, 'There is none that holdeth with me in these things, but Michael [Christ] your Prince'" (White, 99). This equation of Michael the Archangel with Christ is almost unique in the Christian tradition and is probably a vestige of Seventh-day Adventism's earlier reluctance fully to embrace a Trinitarian theology.

One further very important issue in the Seventh-day Adventist understanding of Jesus has involved a question over the nature of the humanity that Christ took on at his Incarnation: in brief, was it that of unfallen Adam or that of fallen humankind in general? Seventh-day Adventists do not believe in original sin in the Augustinian sense, but they do believe that after the Fall humankind inherited a "bent" for sinning. According to Seventh-day Adventist writers, the image of God had been marred within us, and it is with the restoration of this image that much of Seventh-day Adventist practice is concerned. So, to repeat, was Jesus like pre-Fall Adam or like us?

The most recent authoritative statement on the issue steers a careful path: "His humanity did not correspond to Adam's humanity before the Fall, nor in every respect to Adam's humanity after the Fall, for the Scriptures portray Christ's humanity as sinless" (Froom 2000, 164). Seen in a Seventh-day Adventist context, this assessment carefully walks a theological tightrope, for the Church has long suffered internal dispute on the issue of the nature of Jesus' humanity. Ellen White herself, it seems, took the view that Jesus was born with a post-Fall human nature and was consequently subjected to the inherited weaknesses that this state brought. She wrote: "Jesus accepted humanity when the race had been weakened by four thousand years of sin. Like every child of Adam He accepted the results of the working of the great law of heredity. What these results were is shown in the history of His earthly ancestors. He came with such a heredity to share our sorrows and temptations, and to give us the example of a sinless life" (White, 49; Bull and Lockhart, 71).

Some in the Church were later to reject this view. In 1957, the book *Seventh Day Adventists Answer Questions on Doctrine* was published. This book was a conscious attempt by Church theologians to align Seventh-day Adventists with the evangelical tradition and in particular to answer the questions on the Church's doctrines that had been raised during discussions with Walter Martin and Donald Barnhouse. Here an alternative to White's view was put forward very forcefully: "[I]n His human nature Christ was perfect and sinless," being "exempt from the inherited passions and pollutions that corrupt the natural descendants of Adam" (Bull and Lockhart, 70–71). These may seem like minor issues to many, but not to Seventh-day Adventist theologians, for what one thinks about this subject may impact upon the understanding one has of the process of salvation and sanctification (with which, as has been said, much of Seventh-day Adventist practice is concerned). If Jesus was indeed like us in every respect and yet did not yield to temptation, then it ought to be the case that we, too, could, in theory, live a sinless life. Jesus did it; Jesus was like us; therefore, we ought to be able to do it. If, however, Jesus had an advantage, in that he did not have the "bent" for sinning that comes with being a natural descendant of Adam, then perhaps what he managed, perfect obedience to the law of God, is not in fact possible for the rest of humanity and was only achieved by him by virtue of the fact that he had a stronger starting position. It would not be unfair to say that, for the Seventh-day Adventist Church, which has been remarkably successful in avoiding a major schism throughout its history, this issue of the nature of Jesus' humanity (and the concurrent implications for the doctrine of sanctification) is the one that has most significantly rocked the boat.

Closely connected with this issue is that of the atoning work of Christ. It is certainly the case that Seventh-day Adventists, in common with evangelicals, argue that Christ died a sacrificial death upon the cross. The question is: was this death all that is needed to bring atonement? Again, this has been a major issue in Seventh-day Adventist thinking about Jesus. From an early point in the Church's history it has been argued that Jesus' death on the cross, as important and essential as it was, is not the only thing necessary for atonement, for without the application of the benefits of Christ's death through the medium of his high priestly ministry in the heavenly sanctuary, the death of Christ is of no benefit.

This view ties in with what some have seen as the hub of Seventh-day Adventist theology: the sanctuary doctrine. Seventh-day Adventists think that they know pretty well what Jesus has been doing for the past 2,000 years: he has been interceding on behalf of humankind in the heavenly sanctuary (see Rom. 8.34; Heb. 7.25). Upon his ascension (which Seventh-day Adventists believe is accurately described in the writings of Luke), Christ entered into the heavenly "holy place" (the antitype of the "holy place" of the earthly temple), there to intercede on behalf of humankind. This intercession is as much a part of the process of atonement as was Christ's death; at least, that was what Ellen White said: "The intercession of Christ in man's behalf in the sanctuary above is as essential to the plan of salvation as was

His death upon the cross. By His death He began that work which after His resurrection he ascended to complete in heaven" (White, 489).

Again, this problem has been a real issue in Seventh-day Adventist thinking about Jesus. One of the most bitter disputes within Seventh-day Adventism was that which took place in the 1970s and was centered upon the person of Desmond Ford, an Australian Seventh-day Adventist academic who, for various reasons, came to the conclusion that the heavenly ministry of Christ was superfluous and that the atonement had been completed on the cross. The Church went to great lengths to deal with the theological storm to which the Ford controversy gave rise but in the end dismissed him from his post as a lecturer at Pacific Union College in California, one of the Church's higher education institutions. Ford had touched a raw nerve, and not just because he had brought into question the view that the atonement was something that was ongoing and had not been completed on the cross. Indeed, such a view had been brushed aside already in *Questions on Doctrine*, and one could argue that all Ford was doing was taking the principles laid out in that book to their logical conclusion. But more was at stake: by denying outright not just the theological need but the actuality of the ministry of Jesus in the heavenly, antitypical sanctuary, Ford had in effect called into question the Church's raison d'être.

The Church can trace its origins to 22 October 1844, the day upon which some 50,000 believers expected Jesus to return visibly to this earth. The date was set on the basis of Daniel 8.14 and the statement that after the passing of "2,300" days (understood as years) the sanctuary would be cleansed. Following the nonfulfillment of the expectation, some of the disappointed took the view that the "sanctuary" spoken of by Daniel was not the earth, as William Miller, a preacher who had launched the movement, had thought, but rather a heavenly sanctuary. On 22 October 1844, these believers argued, Jesus had begun to cleanse that sanctuary by moving from the Holy into the Most Holy Place (that is, the center of the heavenly temple, which was the antitype of that in ancient Jerusalem), there to begin the work of the antitypical high priest on the antitypical day of atonement. The ones who came to this conclusion were the later Seventh-day Adventists and saw it as their God-given mission to announce this message to the world. As Jesus moved from the Holy to the Most Holy Place, so the argument ran, God had raised up a Church to tell the world about it: the Seventh-day Adventists. If, as Ford was now arguing, this idea of the high priestly ministry of Christ was superfluous, as the atonement had been completed on the first Good Friday, the Seventh-day Adventist Church lacked a prophetic role, the very reason for its existence.

Seventh-day Adventists have hence explored some relatively neglected theological territory with regard to the person and work of Jesus, and to date it has been Christology rather than any other issue that has most obviously threatened the theological unity of the Church.

Kenneth G. C. *Newport*

See also: Hebrews, Letter to the; Jesus, Achievement of; Jesus as a Historical Figure; John, Revelation of; Lord; Nicea; Second Coming of Jesus, in Current Belief; Second Person of the Trinity

References

Ball, Bryan, and William Johnsson, eds. 2002. *The Essential Jesus*. Boise, ID: Pacific Press Publishing Association.

Bull, Malcolm, and Keith Lockhart. 1989. *Seeking a Sanctuary: Seventh Day Adventism and the American Dream*. San Francisco: Harper & Row.

Froom, Le Roy Edwin. 1971. *Movement of Destiny*. Washington, DC: Review and Herald Publishing Association.

———. 2000. *Handbook of Adventist Theology*. Hagerstown, MD: Review and Herald Publishing House.

Webster, Eric Claude. 1992. *Crosscurrents in Adventist Christology*. Berrien Springs, MI: Andrews University Press.

White, Ellen. 1911 (1986). *The Great Controversy between Christ and Satan*. Brookfield, IL: Pacific Press.

Sexuality

First, there is the historical question. The Gospels, our only relevant source of information, are famously lacking in any clear evidence bearing upon either the nature of Jesus' sexuality or what would usually be described as sexual behavior on his part. This difficulty has not prevented people from clutching at straws. Thus, much has been made of the dealings between Jesus and Mary Magdalene (often fused—or confused—with other women in the narratives who may or may not be identical with her), and novelese stories relating to the saint's later life and even beyond have emerged onto the literary scene and into public consciousness from time to time: the subject retains titillation value.

Various episodes in the Gospel of John come into discussion. The first is the anointing of Jesus' feet in 12.1–9. The woman is named as Mary and identified (cf. 11.2) as the sister of Martha and Lazarus. It is pure surmise (and characteristic of the merging of persons prevalent in later Christian legend-making, reminiscent of the multiple part-assigning of an economical play or opera director) to identify her with Mary Magdalene. But whoever anointed the feet of Jesus in John 12, it is alleged that her action could not but have been highly stimulating sexually. Each to his taste, of course, but it is equally plausible to see it as repellent or neutral in that regard. A readiness to make much of this episode is, in any case, deterred by the fact that in Mark (14.3–9), and then in Matthew (26.6–13), the woman is unnamed and apparently a stranger, and she anoints not Jesus' feet but his head. And Jesus sees the purpose as being a kind of burial-anointing-in-advance: it is, as it were, a recognition of Jesus' kingship, a kind of coronation, even as he comes to his death. No hint of sexual content appears. Finally on this subject, a story of an anointing of Jesus by a woman—again unnamed—appears in Luke, but much earlier (at 7.36–50): he omits such an episode at the start of the Passion. Here the woman's notoriety and patent devotion evoke teaching by Jesus, common in Luke (cf. Zacchaeus, 19.1–10; the Pharisee and the publican, 18.11–14; and the penitent thief at the crucifixion), on the welcome that awaits the penitent sinner. Again, the mention of Mary Magdalene shortly after, in 8.2, has given rise (without justification) to the identifying of the two: another case of exegesis out of control. As in John 12, however, the anointing in Luke 7 is of the feet and gives rise to the same speculations as the John 12 story. What is more, much is made of the greatness of her love for Jesus (7.47). But, alas for any bearing the story might have on our present subject, it is, as we have seen, a typically Lucan episode in its theme and in its telling: a Pharisee is shown up, in the typical context of a meal, as outclassed religiously by the penitent fervor of the woman who performs a servant's act of hospitality to a visitor, which the Pharisee-host had omitted—and she receives the reward, like so many of Luke's characters, of willing forgiveness. (For the gist of the theme, see Luke 5.31.)

Mary Magdalene really does appear, however, in John 20.1–18, and the "Touch me not" of v. 17 has given rise (whether it is taken to be "do not now touch" or "do not go on touching"—the Greek verb can bear either sense) to suggestions of an intimacy of some kind. But this is to suppose that what we read is a literal and historical account, devoid of Johannine theological motifs at this point, hard though they may be now to identify with certainty but whose presence we ought surely to expect. The encounter between Jesus and the Samaritan woman in chapter 4 gives rise to comparable speculations, and here the theologically laden character of the conversation is easier to see. For whatever reason, this Gospel gives a central place to women, in a number of ways, with the confession of faith in 11.27 standing out.

Something of the same situation arises with the (again in John's Gospel alone) alleged special relationship between Jesus and the unnamed beloved disciple (though legend, and countless readers, have known for sure that he is the apostle John!), which has given rise to suggestions of Jesus' homosexual disposition, suggestions that, however discreetly and tentatively proposed, are likely to give rise to protest (see end of essay). But there is every reason to think that "the disciple whom Jesus loved," mentioned only in this Gospel, is, quite apart from any identity that the original readers may have known, a symbolic figure. In this sense, he would probably represent the ideal Christian, which the Johannine Church saw in the mode of faith held by its own members: their version of Christian understanding being truer and deeper than that of other followers of Jesus, giving them a unique intimacy with him.

It may be added that Morton Smith, followed more recently by Dominic Crossan (1992, 411–416), has proposed religio-erotic involvement of Jesus, in the light of what is taken to be an episode in the Gospel of Mark, involving the young man who appears (uniquely in Mark) in 14.51–52 and 16.5–7. The thesis is that it was part of the original text, preserved in Gnostic circles (in one of whose manuscripts it was discovered in 1958), then later suppressed, and so was absent from what became (and of course remains) the standard version of Mark. The story, coming after Mark 10.34, tells of Jesus raising the young man from death and loving him, and staying overnight, in a kind of initiation episode. There are, however, many reasons for seeing this passage as a sectarian addition to Mark rather than a suppression. (It only remains for Jesus to be seen as pedophiliac in tendency on the basis of Mark 10.13–16!)

It is apparent that the Gospels do not afford the kind of cinematic or gossip-column evidence that could help us in our inquiry. But can an exception be made for the question of whether Jesus was married? We know that it was unusual to remain single in Jewish society of the time, and the lack of reference to a wife does not rule out the existence of one. After all, as far as the Gospels go, telling of Jesus' time of ministry in Galilee, we only know of Peter's marriage because his mother-in-law was healed by Jesus (Mark 1.29–31), though later, according to 1 Corinthians 9.5, Peter took his wife with him on his gospel-spreading travels. Could it not be the case that, as in so many trades and emergencies down the ages, in very many societies, Jesus and his disciples (the Twelve) left wives at home, because of the special and urgent demands imposed by the preaching of the kingdom of God (cf. Matt. 8.19–22)? So it may be, though we should note that in Mark 10.29 (and its parallel in Matthew, though not in Luke), wives are not included in the list of those to be left behind by those who follow Jesus. We know so little of the detailed procedures of Jesus' mission. But the Gospels give us no positive warrant at all (unless we think Peter's case entitles us to generalize) for supposing that Jesus had a wife at home. Even in Judaism, marriage might be forgone by charismatic prophetic leaders (as good a "job description" for Jesus as any) intent on the message that demanded all. John the Baptist and Paul may stand as parallels (though a case has been made for the latter's being a widow), and we may cite the instance of at least the core members of the Qumran community, who shared with the Christians a lively expectation of imminent divine intervention and the dawn of a new age. Only Matthew 19.10–12, however, in the teaching ascribed to Jesus points in the direction of urging voluntary celibacy on Christians in appropriate cases.

Then there is the legacy of Jesus in this regard in terms of doctrine and spirituality, by comparison a huge and diffuse subject. The "unmarriedness" of Jesus has been a weighty factor in the tendency, in the greater part of Christian life down the centuries (and almost universally until the Reformation), to give a spiritual preference to the single state. Yes, marriage may be good, but celibacy is better. The psychological ethos, however, soon changed from that of Jesus' own setting. The urgency of the kingdom of God that he preached involved no wholesale policy of asceticism—in fact, Jesus is said to have given scandal for his unascetic lifestyle (unlike John the Baptist) (Matt. 11.18f.); nor does Jesus' teaching include any disparagement of marriage or sex in itself. Indeed, by contrast with the NT letters, the Gospels contain very little teaching on sexual matters at all (see Matt. 5.27–30; 19.10–12). Jesus' teaching on divorce, narrowing down its scope or even forbidding it for his followers, in fact gave a positive boost to marriage and the family in both Jewish and Gentile settings. And, once the Church expanded into the Gentile world, it seems to have organized itself into households, so that its very structure encouraged and generally depended on families, in both the narrow and the wider sense. No favoring of celibacy there.

It is nevertheless often felt that the NT exhibits a bias against the physical aspects of life. Early Christianity, notably in the writings of Paul, exalted "spirit" at the expense of "flesh," but it was far from being the case that the latter term always signified the body, as opposed to the "higher" self of the soul; rather, in most cases it was a matter of the twin lordships under which human beings might live, with "flesh" pointing to the tendency to live and act in one's own selfish and "non-God" interests. As in Judaism, sexual sins figure prominently in the routine lists of moral ills that appear in the NT letters (e.g., 1 Cor. 6.9–10; Gal. 5.19–20); but, though the presence of some of them is now sometimes regretted for a variety of modern reasons, they are mostly the commonplace immoralities of almost any culture's basic teaching, and strongly so in Jewish ethics. And they certainly imply no disparagement of our sexuality in itself. One might say that disorders are the more condemned when order is greatly esteemed. That would certainly be the case with Jewish morals in this respect.

No, it was in the post-NT Christian movement, and especially, to begin with, on some of its fringes, that asceticism and the taming of the body came to the fore as the higher Christian ideals, notably in the monastic movement that became so powerful a trailblazer for serious Christians from the fourth century. No doubt, Jesus was seen as the monk's model and champion: the fasting in the wilderness (Matt. 4.1–11), with its struggle against Satan and its victory, was a potent model and inspiration. And Jesus' virgin life (as was assumed) fortified his role; indeed, it became a vital element in the mystery of his being as the incarnate Word or Son of God. And the Transfiguration (Mark 9.2–8) gave a model of pure spiritual hope to those who endured the rigors of self-denial. Gradually, Jesus' immunity from ordinary humans' sexual processes, from his conception on, came to seem wholly fitting. This image was then enhanced by beliefs not warranted from the Gospels, for example, in his mother Mary's perpetual virginity, and hence in the theory that his alleged "brothers" (e.g., Mark 6.1–6; Gal. 1.19) were in fact cousins. The story of his conception and birth in the Gospels of Matthew and Luke, where the apparent noninvolvement of Joseph is on grounds of prophecy now fulfilled and has ample OT models, was now read in an ascetic, sex-denying sense. In such a case, sex now seemed inappropriate.

These beliefs, then, derived from powerful cultural forces whereby the "spiritual" was seen as altogether higher and better than the "physical" and sex seemed more a potential disorder than a beneficent gift. It showed itself in a variety of aspects of religious and philosophical thought in the Hellenistic world in which early Christianity soon found its main home—for example, in much of Gnosticism, a speculative (and for a time powerful) Christian manifestation, and among the often mystically inclined heirs of the philosophy of Plato and its developments.

The effect was to transmute radically the image of Jesus, not just with regard to sexuality but his very status in the order of things. In the changed ethos, his Jewishness gave way to a transnational, or at any rate one kind of Greco-Roman, identity. Even more profoundly, his basic humanness (however unusual and indeed unique it was) tended to fade from view. If he was truly the One from heaven, united with the Father and himself divine, then plainly he was not a man as other men are. This was not so much a necessary corollary of pure doctrine as the outcome of a spiritual preference, a different placing of weight in one's response to the world and to life within it. The divine savior simply could not be "one of us," except by acts of condescension, of which the greatest and most beneficial was his coming here at all. And certainly, sexuality, seen (at least as experienced) as part of the inferior inheritance of the children of fallen Adam, could form no practical part of his life. Perhaps sexuality in itself need not have been so disastrous and sin-laden a feature of human existence, but its bond with irrational desire and loss of control made it the very core of the human race's fallen state. It was the role of Augustine of Hippo (354–430) both to probe the subtleties of this matter and to naturalize it in the mainstream of, at any rate, Western Christianity.

In early medieval times, these assumptions came to be somewhat modified as the "perfect human nature" of Jesus, always part of orthodox faith alongside and at one with his divine nature, came to be seen in more affective terms. It was not exactly that he became more "one of us" in a way that modern secular people would recognize, but rather that his divine humanity came to be seen as more tender, more to be loved and empathized with, in its simplicity and purity. It is the Jesus of the crib of Francis of Assisi, of hymns such as *Jesu, dulcis memoria* ("Jesus, the very thought is sweet"), and of devotion to the holy name of Jesus. But still it remained that the life of chastity, in monk, friar, nun, and priest, was the closest to the Christ ideal.

We should explore this theme further. At a number of levels, ranging from the highly intellectual, normally in a Platonist tradition, to the plainly erotic, we have a long tradition of "Jesus mysticism" centering on the relationship between Jesus as lover or bridegroom and the believer, or, as it is often put, the soul, so accentuating perhaps not just the asexual interiority but also the intense individualism involved. Its expressions range from the writings of Pseudo-Dionysius in the sixth century, through twelfth-century Cistercians such as Bernard of Clairvaux, Aelred of Rievaulx, and the Spanish Carmelites of the sixteenth century, on to Charles Wesley in the hymn "Jesu, lover of my soul, let me to thy bosom fly.". Behind all we can see the inspiration of the Song of Solomon in the Old Testament, something of a maverick in the Jewish canon, but a gift to this particular Christian tradition of—mainly monastic—spirituality. To sense the force of its erotic quality, with the two sexes working in a variety of combinations, one has only to conduct an experiment with the hymn *Jesu, dulcis memoria,* referred to above. Take one of its numerous translations: "Jesu, the very thought of thee with sweetness fills my breast; but sweeter far thy face to see, and in thy presence rest." Substitute, for "Jesu" a modern name, and pop music for hymn tunes, and the point is made: we have a powerful, if rather conventional, love song.

The later Middle Ages, at least in some parts of Europe, especially Italy and the German Empire, saw a development of this consciousness in the area of the sexuality of Christ that is at first sight surprising, particularly in some of its manifestations in Church art, and that will seem distasteful even to many moderns. Not only is Jesus frequently depicted nude (and, despite Luke 2.21, in a tradition going back to early representations of Jesus' baptism, uncircumcised—otherwise his humanity would be marred, rendered "imperfect," and doctrine forbids), he is also, in the conventional depiction of "the man of sorrows" painted or sculpted for Church use, shown sitting in the most abject misery, wearing a crown of thorns, yet plainly in a state of sexual excitement. Why should this be? Certainly not, as we might suppose, out of pornographic humor or crudity, but out of doctrine: Jesus suffered, in his perfect, divine humanity, for mankind, out of pure but passionate love, and his human body must manifest that love. There is nothing modern about this: it is pure late medieval Christology in visual form.

It is all a far cry from modern post-Freudian perceptions of Jesus, which will tend to start from the assumption that of course he shared ordinary human sexuality, however "virtuous" its manifestation may have been. But then, we insist on asking, what exactly would being virtuous involve? Repression? Sublimation? And then what price of character might that exact? Who is exempt from the price (if we must put it so) of our sexual nature? Is the monk still the more perfect Christ-like Christian, and is the family, not to speak of other sexual lifestyles, still second-grade in a Christian scale? And should our judgment depend on how Jesus actually lived in Palestine so long ago, or should we argue from our present spiritual and moral principles about the nature of humankind and the divine image in which we are created?

There is, of course, a fine modern Western ideal of celibacy, with a number of styles of manifestation, and it is bound to "feel" countercultural in a particularly modern way. We cannot believe that it "felt" the same for Jesus in his quite different world. How he felt or thought in this respect is beyond our knowledge and our grasp. And as far as the "perfection" of his humanity is concerned, is the idea of perfection sufficiently understandable and univocal for it to make much useful sense? All this leaves on one side the dominant modern perception, for good or ill, that sex is a great and joyful gift, of which one may hope Jesus was not unaware. The early Christian writings also lack any trace of the modern romantic perception of sex, with loving or ecstatic delight as normal (Berger 2003, 232–237).

In the survey of New Testament material that opened this article, attention was given to speculation in recent times about the possible homosexuality of Jesus, and it was apparent that no such inference can be drawn from the Gospels. The same applies to similar speculation about Jesus' opinion on the moral status of the homosexual condition and of homosexual activity. There is no material in the Gospels bearing on the subject; though it would be extraordinary, in the Jewish setting of his life, if (supposing the question had arisen in anything like the modern form) Jesus had taken a liberal view. As is well known, early Christian writers, both Paul and his heirs, were not sparing in their condemnation (Rom. 1.21–25; 1 Cor. 6.9; 1 Tim. 1.10). However, gay apologists have in recent years adopted a more promising way of appealing to Jesus for support that represents a striking development from the point of view of traditional teaching about his relationship with sexuality and sexual morals. One can legitimately point to Jesus' willingness, even determination, to go for unfetteredness in human relationships and to challenge conventional taboos. One points to his willingness to have dealings of acceptance and affection with tax collectors, prostitutes, and others who were the receivers of social disapproval (see, for example, Matt. 21.31–32;

Luke 19.1–10; 7.36–50). It can be claimed that, in view of the traditional (and, by comparison, stuffy) attitudes taken by early Church writers, this depiction of Jesus must surely be true to history. Is it not then in the highest degree likely that Jesus would have subscribed to an open approach to gay relationships, if social conditions had put the subject on the public agenda, and would have opposed the repressive and sometimes hypocritical attitudes of present-day Church authorities? It is of course precarious to assert what Jesus "would have thought," and dangerously anachronistic, but that applies equally to the protagonists of the opposing view; there is certainly strength in the argument from congruity, so far as it goes. And this line of thought may be supported by arguments of a more doctrinal kind about Jesus' acceptance and inclusion of humanness in its plain diversity and refusal to conform to a single mold and structure. So it is that the subject of Jesus and sexuality continues to take new forms and to explore new questions, prompted by the agenda of the times.

Leslie Houlden

See also: Alexandrian Theology; Augustine of Hippo; Dead Sea Scrolls; English Christianity, Medieval; Francis of Assisi; Hymns; Jesus, Name of; Jesus, Origins of; Julian of Norwich; Mary; Spanish Christianity; Wesley, Charles, and Wesley, John

References

Alison, James. 2001. *Faith Beyond Resentment*. London: DLT.
Berger, Klaus. 2003. *Identity and Experience in the New Testament*. Minneapolis: Fortress.
Brown, Peter. 1989. *The Body and Society*. London: Faber.
Brown, R. E. 1970. *The Community of the Beloved Disciples*. Dublin: Chapman.
Crossan, John Dominic. 1991. *The Historical Jesus: The Life of a Mediterranean Jewish Peasant*. San Francisco: HarperSan Francisco.
Steinberg, Leo. 1984. *The Sexuality of Christ in Renaissance Art and Modern Oblivion*. London: Faber.
Vasey, Michael. 1995. *Strangers and Friends*. London: Hodder and Stoughton.

Son of God

From the earliest Christian writers onward, "Son of God" has been one of the leading ways of referring to Jesus. According to context, the term may be called a description, a title, a claim, an expression of devotion, even, almost, a name. It can easily be understood wrongly, especially if its origins are to be our guide. For example, it is often taken to be equivalent to saying that he is divine, or, crudely, to refer to his origins, with God for father and Mary for mother. The background of the term leads us into many and varied paths, some of them perhaps surprising, but all leading round to the way Jesus was described and acclaimed.

Two metaphors have always dominated human thought about deity: the first is that of a monarch over his realm; the other that of a father in a household. The first speaks of power, authority, and judgment, the second (in modern Western culture, anyway) of nurturing, relationship, even love, though in very many cultures, with their ethos of strong paternal authority, the distinction is not always very marked and the one merges with the other. In the context of this second metaphor, all (male) members of a particular people are "sons" of the deity. In more developed religious settings with a belief in the one God of the whole world, all (male) humans may be seen as "sons," for the deity is "father" in being the creator of all and the word gets unwittingly "degenderized."

Against this general background, how can it be that any particular human being comes to be called "Son of God"? In two ways: first, the king, often felt to embody or sum up his people, may be seen to have special access to and intimacy with the deity for the good of all—he is a representative figure, so he is, in a special or concentrated way, his "son." Second, as moral aspirations mature in particular groups in society, those who aim at or achieve a notable degree of virtue may see themselves, with a particular sense or even right, as "sons of God." We should note that in none of these cases does any claim to divine status arise in relation to the term. Nor, generally, at least in the case of the latter category, will there be any story of supernatural conception or birth.

There is a further dimension. In many premodern cultures that hold a picture of the universe lacking the sheer, stunning vastness of modern astronomy as it has grown in the West in recent centuries, the "space" between God and his earthly created realm was also under his authority and peopled by invisible creatures (angels or perhaps half-deities); they, too, were part of the divine "household" or "realm" and could be called "sons of God."

To illuminate the case of Jesus, we draw chiefly on usage among Jews of his time, in particular their authoritative Scriptures (represented in the Christian Old Testament), though it is also relevant to recognize, especially as the Christian movement developed in the later first century beyond its Jewish origins into the wider Greco-Roman world, that "son of (a) god" might be used of heroes, emperors, and other great men, as well as, of course, appropriate members of "clans" of deities, such as proliferated in the mythology of the time. It is not always easy to tell how many people took many of these attributions as more than gaudily honorific or as giving one a religious frisson rather than as ingredients in a serious conceptual theology.

So what of usage in the Jewish traditions? Virtually every one of the categories mentioned above is to be found in the Jewish Scriptures. God is father of Israel (Exod. 4.22; Hos. 11.1; Isa. 63.8); father of the angels, who are his sons (Job 38.7); father to the king (2 Sam. 7.14), and so to a future or longed-for king or "anointed one" (as perhaps in due course in Ps. 2.7); and, later, father of righteous persons, seen as particular "sons of God" (Wisd. of Sol. 2.13–18). In Israel, as its monotheistic faith and hatred of idolatry became more and more the distinctive mark, there is no doubt that in none of these cases was "divinity" being attributed to those being called God's sons, above all by the turn of the eras. At the same time, there were styles of Judaism by this time in which the aura of God's presence could be seen as diffused among those close to him—by "physical" proximity in the heavens, by receiving a special role in his service, or by the leading of a holy life devoted to God's service.

The metaphorical (as opposed to "hard" conceptual) nature of this language is illustrated by the fact that, in admittedly only a few instances, God's parental role is put in feminine terms: he is like a mother to Israel (Isa. 42.14; 66.13), and though (unacceptably to the modern reader) there is no tradition of "daughters of God," the people of Jerusalem and Israel are themselves often referred to in feminine, "daughter" terms (Mic. 4.8, 10, 13; Lam. 1.6; Zech. 9.9).

Every one of these aspects of Jewish usage and belief is to be found among early Christians and in their first writings, the New Testament. In the terms we have been using, sonship to God was one among a host of metaphors or images that sprang to mind as they sought to express their sense of the central importance of Jesus. But first, more widely, in Ephesians 3.14–15, God is the "father, from whom every family in heaven and on earth is named." In Romans 8.14, and implicitly elsewhere (Matt. 6.1, 4, 6, 9; Mark 11.25; Luke 6.36; 11.2), Christian believers, not only Jesus, are "sons of God," and God is readily described as their "father."

The Gospel of John is the first Christian writing actually, and probably deliberately, to make the verbal distinction between Jesus as "Son" (Greek *huios*) and Christians as "children" (Greek *tekna*) of God (e.g., John 1.12). In fact, in this Gospel, the unique relationship of God and Jesus as Father and Son is the doctrinal axis on which everything rests (see, especially, chapters 13–17), though at the same time, no NT writing goes further in integrating Jesus and his followers. We may note how Matthew, by contrast, solid in his belief in Jesus' unique role, can show Jesus referring to God frequently as "my," "your," and "our" Father, apparently finding no difficulty in not insisting on "son" as special for himself. Seen as Israel's messiah-king, he is addressed as "Son" by God at his baptism (Mark 1.11, referring back to Ps. 2.7). In Luke 20.36, "sons of God" appears as a term for angels, and in Revelation, Jesus is seen in just such a heavenly guise and called God's Son (2.18; see also 21.7).

The upshot is twofold. First, "Son of God," in line with senses found in the Jewish background and in the early Christian usage, is a term referring not only to Jesus but also to Christians, and only in the late first-century Gospel of John was a start made on confining the term to Jesus to signify his uniqueness, though Romans 8.29 may be an attempt by Paul to show how he saw the connection: Jesus as "the firstborn among many brethren." As we have seen, this is not to say that the status of Jesus was underplayed in the earlier years, only that the established senses of this term were such that its wide range of applications was, it seems, taken in the early Christian stride. Looked at from another angle, when it was applied to Jesus, it contributed to a belief in his "specialness" as God's prime agent for human good, as one of a galaxy of terms and images, each with its own Jewish pedigree; what was new was their intense concentration. And second, when applied to Jesus, "Son of God" stems (it seems likely) from a number of aspects of its established range: he was Israel's messiah, he was a righteous servant of God (cf. Luke's amendment of "Son of God" in his source, Mark 15.39, to "righteous one" in 23.47), he was God's chosen and beloved agent, with the highest status in God's eyes, eligible for exaltation in heaven.

It is in this whole context that we should read the infancy stories, where, especially in Luke, Jesus is depicted as "Son of God" (1.35). But it is not a case of any kind of asexual union between God, as father, and Mary, as virgin mother; rather, it is a story telling of God's choice of Jesus right from his very conception by an act of divine power (Spirit). The model is a number of Old Testament stories of the divinely accredited birth of great agents of God, such as Isaac (Gen. 21), Samson (Judg. 13), and Samuel (1 Sam. 1–2). Jesus is, from the beginning, the messiah of God, and this way of narrating his origin plays its part in making the point plain. We note that, without any such element, his status had already been made perfectly plain by Paul and Mark, and was soon to be made so again, in an even more cosmic manner and under different imagery, by John in the Fourth Gospel.

So much for the New Testament. What followed? Once the Jewish context of thought had become largely lost in Christian thinking, and new intellectual questions about Jesus had arisen, it is not surprising that "Son of God" came to play a different role. The relevant question was how we are to understand the person of Jesus. Christians believe him to be both divine and human, but how exactly are these two elements (or aspects) related? Did they coexist as equals in the one Jesus of Nazereth? Or did they come to the fore alternately as Jesus moved, for example, from dinner with his followers to the miraculous healing of a leper? Was his every word "divine," or only certain statements? This is not the place to discuss the complexities of this area of controversy (which had not occurred to the New Testament writers, who nevertheless furnished the only basic evidence available for its discussion, and which may strike modern readers as arid or bizarre). But in this context, "Son of God" came to signify Christ's "divine nature," whereas the New Testament term "Son of Man" signified his "human nature." It is ironic that this move, insofar as it was based on the Gospels, was wholly misjudged, in that in its earlier use, as we have seen, "Son of God" was a term chiefly for humans, and so for Jesus as human (however exalted in significance), and "Son of Man," among a number of senses, could signify a heavenly (though still not divine) figure. In later theological discussion about the term in its own right, it has tended, in a whole variety of conceptual frameworks, to stand for Jesus as God's decisive agent or as his veritable Incarnation in the conditions of this world.

It remains to deplore the frequent modern use of the expression as a simple equivalent for oversimplified statements that "Jesus was God" and the modern appeal to the birth stories as "proof" of its truth, often met of course by its scornful rejection. Neither comes anywhere near being true of the usage and sense of the term in the New Testament.

Leslie Houlden

See also: Christology, Modern; Jesus, Origins of; John, Gospel of; Mary; Messiah; Son of Man

References

Borgen, P. "God's Agent in the Fourth Gospel." In *The Interpretation of John*. Edited by J. Ashton. London: SPCK.

Byrne, B. 1979. *"Seed of Abraham"—"Son of God."* Rome: Biblical Institute Press.
De Jonge, M. 1977. *Stranger from Heaven and Son of God*. Missoula, MT: Scholars Press.
Meeks, W. A. 1986. "The Man from Heaven in Johannine Sectarianism." In *The Interpretation of John*. Edited by J. Ashton. London: SPCK.

Son of Man

In the Gospels, though scarcely ever elsewhere in the New Testament writings, Jesus is very frequently referred to as "Son of Man," or rather, he refers to himself in this way: in all but one of the uses in the Gospels (John 12.34), the term is found on his own lips. Down the centuries, though with different nuances, it has generally been taken to refer to Jesus' humanness. Naturally, the exact sense has varied with the interests of Christians (and others) who have used it. Thus, in the early centuries, when there was much theological discussion about the way the divine and the human were related in the one person of Jesus, "Son of Man" was taken to refer to his humanity, just as "Son of God" was taken as an expression for his divinity. Indeed, the two phrases formed the natural bedrock in the Gospels for this dual identification of Jesus and gave fundamental evidence for its correctness. More recently, in times of lesser interest in theological precision and greater concern with wide social and political implications of Christianity, "Son of Man" has often been used to express a conviction, perhaps in a left-wing tone of voice, of Jesus' solidarity with the human race: he is "one of us," or, in Dietrich Bonhoeffer's (1906–1945) famous phrase, "the man for others."

Now that scholars have become much better equipped to understand first-century expressions in their original senses and (as the essential prerequisite) more interested in their cultural context, it has become apparent that, as in the case of "Son of God," the term "Son of Man" originally carried meanings that were quite other than those later attributed to it, and even when they seem to get near, the "tone of voice" is very different indeed. Indeed, it is not too much of an exaggeration (to be used rhetorically and with caution) to say that the original senses of the two expressions were the opposite of what has generally been supposed. "Son of God" was most often a title for certain categories of human beings, and "Son of Man" often (though by no means always) carried heavenly connotations.

To turn to the use of "Son of Man" in the Gospels, the fact that, unlike other expressions or titles, it appears so frequently, and virtually exclusively, on Jesus' lips has naturally led even cautious critics to feel that it must have been his characteristic way of describing himself. Naturally, there has been a search for precedents in Jewish usage. The most obvious place to turn is the Book of Ezekiel, where the term occurs many times as God's way of addressing the prophet. It seems minimally technical, with the force of "You fellow, . . ." and it is quite uncertain that it carries any further implication, such as labeling Ezekiel as spokesman to his people. But more broadly, "Son of Man" is a Hebrew idiom (with other counterparts, such as "sons of the prophets") to speak of a member of a particular class or group, in this case the human race: Psalm 8.4 is a clear example, where "man" and "Son of Man" (both in common gender) are in parallel.

Is this then what Jesus meant by it? And if so, is it devoid of theological sense—or does it carry some implicit claim to prophetic status after the manner of Ezekiel? Certainly there are sayings of Jesus where he seems to mean no more than "myself—as [mere] man," most obviously Matthew 8.20, where Jesus says "the Son of Man has nowhere to lay his head." Even so, does the expression carry any sense of typicality ("one such as I"), or is it personal to Jesus himself? In recent years, thanks chiefly to the work of Geza Vermes, it has come to be thought that in Jewish usage it might carry idiomatic force whereby a person could refer to himself with a sense of self-effacing modesty. It would then be like the use by a certain sort of English person of "one" when others might say "I": someone rescues a drowning child and is complimented, only to reply, "What else would one do?" A difficulty with this attractive interpretation is that the parallels adduced in Semitic usage belong to a somewhat later period; so the scrupulous are deterred.

It is, however, apparent that though such a sense might explain a number of the sayings, it does not explain all of them. It is also apparent that by the time the Gospels were written, all sense of Semitic idiom had been overshadowed by the Greek writers (and no doubt Greek-speaking Christian use), who treated the expression as a title for Jesus, one way of referring to him among others, so that it carries a definite article (see Matt. 8.20, above). However, some of the uses of "Son of Man" plainly have a link (whether going back to Jesus or depending on subsequent Christian reflection) with another scriptural passage: Daniel 7.13. In this passage, which refers to a future heavenly scene at the time of the consummation of God's purposes, "one like a Son of Man" comes before God and receives universal and everlasting authority. There is nothing surprising in this text chiming in with and fortifying early Christian belief about Jesus after the resurrection (rather like Psalm 110.1). In its context, the expression simply means "one in human form" (by contrast with various symbolic animals that figure in earlier phases of the vision). But once the term moved into Greek and began to be applied to Jesus, the Aramaic (that is, the Semitic vernacular) sense was lost and it acquired personal titular force, with the definite article: Jesus was "the Son of Man." So it appears in the trial scene in Mark 14.62, and then frequently in numerous apocalyptic passages in the Gospels (and Acts 7.56). Sometimes, indeed, it may have lost any technical sense and turned into simply a way of referring to Jesus, a kind of alternative name, just as "Christ" seems quickly to have lost its force as the Greek for "Messiah" and become, in effect, a proper name (as perhaps in Matt. 16.13, modifying Mark 8.27).

This observation leads to other perspectives on our inquiry. It is natural to begin with the attempt to identify a possible background in Semitic usage, despite the difficulties just noted. It is then also natural (and much scholarly discussion has been devoted to this aspect) to go on to see which of the sayings that use "Son of Man" are more likely to be original to Jesus and which are best seen as coming from early Christian development. Thus, it has often been thought that those sayings that show Jesus prophesying his own Passion and resurrection are best taken as unlikely to be from his own lips (see Mark 8.31; 9.31; 10.32–34). They were written after the event to show that he had foreseen his fate and held it in his control: it was his God-given destiny. So, too, those sayings that speak of the Son of Man as in Daniel, in an apocalyptic role, may be doctrinal constructions of the Church. That leaves the third category of sayings, those, such as Matthew 8.20, which refer in this way to Jesus the earthly figure: they have the best claim to bring to us, albeit in translation and with the use of the definite article (coming from Christian technical usage), the living voice of the Master.

Whatever the force of such analysis, it has now to be overshadowed or complemented by awareness that perhaps each evangelist uses this term as part and parcel of his theological portrait of Jesus; the more important one supposed "Son of Man" to have been, the more likely it is to act as a doctrinal vehicle. So in Mark, one can see "Son of Man" operating first to express Jesus' authoritative role in his ministry on behalf of God, but semi-anonymously, so that we as readers see what others cannot (2.10, 28); second, to foretell his coming ordeal, his God-given role, which, again, the readers know to be the theologically essential stage toward his triumph (8.31ff.; 10.45); and finally, to speak of his vindication as God's chosen one, destined to carry out his universal purpose of judgment and salvation (13.26; 14.62). On such a view, "Son of Man" carries the weight of Mark's theological program, step by step, and is a vehicle of continuity and identity in the career of Jesus amid a variety of scriptural themes and texts that illuminated what had occurred.

Matthew, then, certainly developed the use of the term in a titular direction, and, as we saw, almost simply as a way of referring to Jesus. For him, the apocalyptic usage is further emphasized and "Son of Man" is sometimes a means whereby the message is further centered on Jesus' person (compare Mark 9.1 with Matt. 16.28). John's (lesser) use of "Son of Man," though not wholly clear, seems not to be out of line with what is found elsewhere, as John 5.27 indicates.

One may move still more widely, surveying "Son of Man" in the overall early development of the expression in Christian thought about Jesus. Thus, Michael Goulder has suggested that more attention should be paid to the early Christian reflection on Psalm 8, both v. 4, with its use of "Son of Man," and v. 6, with its obviously relevant statement of triumph. It was a scriptural passage that both shouted for and received early Christian attention (see 1 Cor. 15.20–28; Heb. 2.5–9). The latter passage uses the psalm to back the essence of the early Christians' sense of the Christological story: Jesus came to our lowly state, but temporarily, and, via the Passion, is "clothed with glory and honor." It may then be possible that, with such a strategy in mind, we may understand the use of "Son of Man" in Mark, where it was able, as we saw, to carry out such a wide-ranging and essential theological "job." Thus it came into its own first in scripturally based doctrinal statement and then in theologically formed narrative. And we find ourselves a long way from both questions of Semitic background and of Jesus' speech. A long way, too, from the later theological use of this term, down to our own day, with which we began.

Leslie Houlden

See also: Bonhoeffer, Dietrich; Hebrews, Letter to the; Mark, Gospel of; Matthew, Gospel of; Son of God; Vermes, Geza

References
Borsch, F. H. 1967. *The Son of Man in Myth and History*. London: SCM.
Burkett, D. 1999. *The Son of Man Debate*. Cambridge: Cambridge University Press.
Hooker, M. D. 1967. *The Son of Man in Mark*. London: SPCK.
Vermes, G. 1973. *Jesus the Jew*. London: SCM.

Spanish Christianity

The history, culture, and thought of Spain are inseparable from Christianity, which became established by the third century. The rise of Marian devotion from the tenth century gave particular prominence to the relationship between the virgin and her son, and the religious controversies of the sixteenth century heightened the importance of sacramental devotion to the consecrated body of Christ. Popular traditions, both local and national, expressed through processions and other festive celebrations, especially at Passiontide and Corpus Christi, have always been important and have happily coexisted with more cultured expressions of faith.

Among the earliest writers is Prudentius (348–c. 410), one of whose lyrical poems, on the Incarnation, "Corde natus ex parentis" (Of the Father's Heart Begotten), remains in use as a Christmas hymn. Though the Moorish invasion of 711 put an end to Christian dominance, the gradual progress of the reconquest, completed in 1492, saw more and more of the peninsula return to Christian rule. The Mozarabic rite developed in Christian areas; at the Fraction the Host is broken into seven pieces and placed on the paten in the form of a cross to represent the mysteries of Christ. Death, Nativity, and Resurrection form the cross piece (from left to right); Incarnation, Nativity, Circumcision, Epiphany, and Passion the vertical (in descending order).

The virgin and child, the crucifixion, and the resurrection are the commonest subjects of the carvings and sculptures of the Romanesque period. Their stylized, austere representations endow them with mystery, in contrast with later Renaissance and Baroque scenes from the Passion intended to appeal more directly to the emotions. The tympanum over the entrance to the Cathedral of St. James in Santiago de Compostela, known as the Portico of Glory (1188), is the work of Maestro Mateo and greets pilgrims with its portrayal of Christ enthroned on high, surrounded by the twenty-four elders of the Apocalypse.

The Majorcan philosopher Ramón Llull (1232–1316) sought to persuade Jews and Muslims of the truth of Christianity. His *Felix (Book of Wonders)* contains a series of exemplary tales intended to overcome their reservations about the Incarnation and the Passion. Llull presented the Incarnation as the best way by which God is known and loved, through union with his Son, whose humility, poverty, and sufferings became the means by which God suffered in the world he had created so that he might be more greatly honored. Llull' s *Book of the Lover and the Beloved* is steeped in the affective mysticism associated with exegesis of the Song of Songs, in which the Lover is the human soul and the Beloved, Christ. Llull himself remarked that his work was based on similar examples in Sufi teaching.

In the one surviving Spanish epic, the *Poema de mio Cid* (early thirteenth century), the hero's wife Ximena prays for her husband to be protected in his exile through an appeal to God's saving acts, with some confusion of the Persons of the Trinity. She addresses the "glorious Lord, Father who art in heaven" (line 330), who was incarnate of Mary, worshiped by the shepherds and the wise men (named), walked the earth for thirty-two years, turned water into wine and stones into bread (a further confusion, of the temptation narrative with the multiplication of the loaves), raised Lazarus from the dead, was arrested, crucified, and placed between two thieves. The conversion of the centurion Longinus occupies six lines, and the prayer concludes with the resurrection, the harrowing of hell, and a final reference to "Thou that art king of kings and Father of all the world" (line 361).

The *Libro de buen amor* (Book of Good Love, c. 1330), by Juan Ruiz, archpriest of Rita, intersperses the amorous adventures of the author/protagonist with religious lyrics in a way modern readers find disconcerting. It begins with an invocation to the Lord God to deliver the author as he delivered saints in times past; Jesus, invoked by his name Emmanuel, is remembered for telling his followers that they would be persecuted. Among the poems are four sets of "Joys of Mary" and a gloss on the Ave Maria, both of which focus on her son and belong to popular tradition. The ironic tone of the work is well illustrated in Juan Ruiz's handling of the traditional *planctus*, or complaint to Death: from stanzas 1556 to 1564 the verse remembers Jesus Christ and his victory over death, with particular reference to his descent into hell and his ransoming of Adam and Eve and many prophets and patriarchs, who are taken by him to paradise. But then Juan Ruiz turns to mourn the death of the go-between who has procured women for him, imagining her seated in glory with Christ as a reward for all her labors.

The sixteenth and seventeenth centuries (the Golden Age) represent the high point of Spanish Catholic culture. Works of spirituality in the vernacular, influenced by the *devotio moderna*, the *De imitatione Christi* (1418) of Thomas à Kempis, and the writings of the Rhineland mystics, began to be printed in Spain from 1500. These exerted considerable influence on monastic communities and the growing reading public, as did the *Philosophia Christi* of Erasmus (c. 1466–1536). The Erasmian call for a simpler form of Christianity, with an emphasis on an interior discipleship, at first found a ready response, but it came to be viewed with increasing suspicion. Spanish spirituality, however, continued to be molded by devotion to Christ's Passion: the influence of the *Spiritual Exercises* of Ignatius of Loyola (c. 1491–1556) can scarcely be overestimated. They established a pattern of meditative prayer in which the exercitant is encouraged to participate imaginatively in scenes from the life of Christ as recorded in the Gospels and to engage in dialogue with Christ crucified, so that sins may be confessed and the grace of God received. One of the most famous (but anonymous) poems of the sixteenth century is a sonnet (now familiar as a hymn) addressed to Christ crucified expressing the need to love God for God's own sake, not out of fear of hell or hope of reward for heaven ("My God, I love thee—not because / I hope for heaven thereby").

The Golden Age saw a flowering of mystical teaching. The first of the two Carmelite mystics, St. Teresa of Avila (1515–1582), believed that meditation on the humanity of Christ should never be abandoned, however lofty an experience of contemplative prayer the soul might enjoy: "I tried as far as I could to hold Jesus Christ, our good and our Lord, present within me. My manner of prayer was this: if I was thinking about a moment in the Passion I pictured it within me" (*Life* 4.8). In one of her early visions, she saw "the most sacred Humanity [of Christ] risen, as he is painted, in great beauty and majesty" (ibid., 28.3). Though her faith was theocentric, Teresa's spirituality was strongly incarnational, focused on the life of Christ, his sufferings, his death, and his resurrection. She insisted that prayer and good works must go hand in hand, using the story of Christ in the house of Mary and Martha to drive the point home. By contrast, St. John of the Cross (1542–1591) taught that such meditation must be abandoned for the soul to enter the dark night, a painful but creative process of reordering life to prepare for divine union. Though his teaching may appear individualistic, he set it firmly within the Trinity's expression of love in creation and redemption. To those who sought visions and revelations, St. John asserted the full sufficiency of God's gift in Christ, and to those who desired consolations, he offered only the way of the Cross. His lyrical poems, intensely sensuous in expression, use the nuptial imagery of the Song of Songs to recount how the bride (the soul) searches for the hidden bridegroom (Christ) and is found by him. They have been admired by many twentieth-century poets and writers.

The most Christocentric writer of the period was the Augustinian Fray Luis de Leon (1527–1591), whose *De los nombres de Cristo (Concerning the Names of Christ)* explores the nature and purpose of Christ through exposition of a series of his biblical names, drawn largely from the Old Testament but concluding with the name Jesus, the bread of life who kneads the poverty and suffering of humanity with the grace and wisdom of divinity to satisfy human hunger and heal human sickness. He placed Christ at the heart of the cosmos, and his account of Christ's healing and reconciling work was primarily Pauline in inspiration. He was drawn to the position associated with John Scotus Eriugena that the Incarnation would have happened regardless of the Fall, in order to bring human beings to their divinely ordained perfection. Another Augustinian, Malón de Chaide (c. 1539–1589), wrote a devotional treatise, *La conversión de la Magdalena (The Conversion of the Magdalen)*, which uses Luke 7.36–50 to explore the nature of sin, repentance, and redemption.

Religious drama also flourished during the Golden Age. The dramatic form most closely associated with Christ is the *auto sacramental*, a late development of older morality and mystery plays performed in the streets at Corpus Christi, often with music, dancing, and elaborate stage sets. Biblical and classical stories are used alongside more abstract subjects: Christ, for example, is the Good Shepherd or the divine Orpheus, and allegorical devices and a highly developed typology climax in adoration of the continuing presence of Christ in the consecrated Host.

The Council of Trent's decree on sacred images (1563) encouraged painting, and many artists of the period received commissions to paint works for churches and monasteries. Episodes from the life of the infant Jesus and from the Passion predominated. El Greco (c. 1548–1616; Domenikos Theotocopoulos, a native of Crete and trained as an icon painter) painted many such scenes, but also less common subjects such as the *Baptism of Christ*, the *Cleansing of the Temple*, the *Agony in the Garden*, and the *Disrobing*, which hangs in Toledo Cathedral. Diego de Velazquez (1599–1660) painted fewer religious works; among them are his early *Jesus in the House of Mary and Martha* (1618), *Christ at Emmaus* (1622–1623), and two Crucifixions, both showing Christ nailed to the cross with four rather than the customary three nails, following the recommendation of his father-in-law, the painter Francisco Pacheco, whose discursive *Arte de la pintura* (1649) makes many observations on how particular scenes from the life of Christ were to be portrayed. Alonso Berruguete (c. 1485–1561), Luis de Morales (c. 1509–c. 1585), Juan de Juanes (c. 1510–1579), Juan Femimdez de Navarrete (c. 1540–1579), Jusepe de Ribera (1590–1652), Francisco de Zurbaran (1598–1662), and Bartolome de Murillo (1617–1682) produced many paintings that reflect the devotional spirit of the age: among the latter's works are *Multiplication of the Loaves and Fishes* and *Healing of the Paralytic at the Pool of Bethesda*, *Marriage of Cana*, and a fine series representing the *Parable of the Prodigal Son*.

In music, too, large numbers of Masses, motets, and other devotional music for services, especially for Christmas, Passiontide, and Corpus Christi, were composed. The works of Tomás Luis de Victoria (1548–1611) have passed into the repertoire, but more recently composers for the liturgical year, such as Francisco de Peñalosa (c. 1470–1528), Cristóbal de Morales (c. 1500–1553), and Francisco Guerrero (?1528–1599), have gained increasing recognition.

Spanish culture is generally regarded as having entered a long period of decline by the end of the seventeenth century. Antonio Soler (1729–1783) continued to write music for the Church's year, but the outstanding figure of the eighteenth and early nineteenth century is Francisco de Goya (1746–1828). Though chiefly a painter of secular subjects, some of his earlier works are religious paintings, such as his dark-toned *Arrest of Christ* (1788–1798).

In the nineteenth century one detects a shift of interest toward the figure of Jesus as an ethical exemplar. In the later novels of Benito Perez Galdós (1843–1920), Jesus assumes increasing importance as Galdós engages critically with Leo Tolstoy's presentation of the Gospel. Like many of his contemporaries, he was influenced by a liberal view of Christianity, with its roots in Ludwig Feuerbach and Ernest Renan, which emphasized the practical application of the teaching of Jesus over doctrinal affirmations as to his nature. In novels such as *Nazarin*, *Halma*, and *Misericordia* (1895–1897) the ethical exemplarity of Christ is central. In the first of these a connection is made between Christ and Don Quixote in the figure of a protagonist who seeks to live according to the folly of Christ in the modern age. Another figure who wrestled with issues of belief and ethics was the writer and philosopher Miguel de Unamuno (1864–1936). At the heart of his struggles lay the conflict between reason and faith, philosophy and science, especially in respect of the resurrection of Jesus and the human hunger for eternal life, most evident in his *Del sentimiento trágico de la vida (The Tragic Sense of Life)* (1913). His long sequence of meditative poems, *El Cristo de Velazquez* (The Christ of Velazquez, 1920), addressed to the famous painting of the crucifixion by the artist, blends traditional devotional language with a wide range of biblical imagery, but it also raises existential questions. The disjunction between doctrine and life finds fictional form in his short story "San Manuel Bueno, mártir" (1933), in which a devoted village priest cares in an exemplary manner for his flock while confessing to his closest friend that he believes in nothing.

The figure of Jesus has continued to be represented in Spain throughout the twentieth century, though often in less orthodox ways than in the past. The unfinished Catedral de la Sagrada Familia (Cathedral of the Holy Family) by Antoni Gaudí (1852–1926) in Barcelona devotes its eastern portal to the Nativity. The best-known visual image is the *Christ of St. John of the Cross* (1951) by Salvador Dalí (1904–1989). The unusual angle of the crucifixion was inspired by a pencil sketch drawn by St. John of the Cross, although Dalí turned the figure, which hangs above the bay of Port Lligat, around ninety degrees so that it faces the viewer. He explained that it derived from a cosmic dream and reflects the unity of the universe.

Religious concerns are not the explicit focus of the plays and poems of Federico García Lorca (1898–1936), but because these are deeply rooted in Andalusian culture the presence of Christian motifs is constant, usually in local dress. In his *Romancero gitano (Gipsy Romance)* (1928), he retold the story of the Annunciation in gypsy guise and linked the sufferings of gypsy characters such as Antoñito el Camborio with those of Christ. His "Oda al santísimo sacramento" ("Ode to the Most Holy Sacrament") (1929) combines his own original poetic voice, full of sensual imagery, with popular traditions to contrast the stillness and the smallness of the Host with the world of change and flux, interpreting its innocence, purity, and simplicity as a sign for human consolation. More recently, the poetry of José Ángel Valente (1929–2000) contains many allusions to the Gospel story: one of his collections is entitled *Poemas a Lázaro* (1960).

In the later period of Franco's dictatorship, liberation theology, with its emphasis on the revolutionary Christ, attracted some support; at the same time, the more conservative Opus Dei promoted an active apostolate based on personal discipleship and holiness. Since the death of Franco (1975), the Church has lost some of its power and influence, but popular traditions still flourish. However much the processions of Holy Week have become a tourist attraction, they express the human response to the sufferings of Christ, and

Christ of St. John of the Cross *by Salvador Dalí. 1951; oil on canvas (Glasgow Museums: The St. Mungo Museum of Religious Life and Art)*

Corpus Christi is marked by a public holiday and processions devoted to the presence of Christ in the sacrament.

Colin Thompson

See also: American (Hispanic) Christianity; American (South) Christianity; Art; Ignatius of Loyola; John of the Cross; Kempis, Thomas à; Liberation Theology; Mary; Music; Roman Catholicism; Teresa of Avila

References

Carr, Raymond. 1980. *Modern Spain, 1875–1980*. Oxford: Oxford University Press.
Elliott, J. R. 1963. *Imperial Spain, 1469–1716*. London: Edward Arnold.
Gies, David T., ed. 1999. *The Cambridge Companion to Modern Spanish Culture*. Cambridge: Cambridge University Press.
Martin, Melquiades Andres, and Santiago Fernandez Ardanaz. 1983–1987. *Historia de la teologia espanola*. 2 vols. Madrid: Fundacion Univerisitaria Espanola.
Russell, P. E., ed. 1973. *Spain: A Companion to Spanish Studies*. London: Methuen.
Stanton, Edward F. 1999. *Handbook of Spanish Popular Culture*. Westport, CT, and London: Greenwood Press.

Spirituality

Although Jesus is central to Christian devotion, the corporate prayer of the Church, in particular the eucharistic liturgy and the divine office, has, from early times, been addressed to God the Father *through* Jesus Christ. The early Christian writer Origen (died c. 254) even insisted that there should be no prayer actually directed to Jesus. Certainly most (though not all) of the "official" prayers of the liturgy (such as collects) are addressed to God the Father and end "through Jesus Christ our Lord." We can say that corporate prayer in Christian churches is theocentric (God-centered) rather than Christocentric (Christ-centered).

Yet this statement, without modification, is confusing. For there has been much prayer directed to Jesus throughout Christian history, and this practice continues to the present. The name of Jesus has a central place in Christian spirituality. There are twenty major references to the name of Jesus in the first ten chapters of the Acts of the Apostles, and devotion to the "Holy Name" developed in the early Middle Ages. In Western Catholicism, "Holy Name" is a common dedication of churches, and the Litany of the Holy Name has been a popular devotion for centuries. In the Eastern Church, the Jesus Prayer ("Lord Jesus Christ, Son of God, have mercy on me, a sinner") has been a central feature of devotion since the time of the Desert Fathers. It is a prayer of contemplative repetition, linked with attention to breathing, and its aim is the attainment of *hesychia,* inner quietude.

Invocation of the name of Jesus was recommended by Nilus of Ancyra (died c. 430), and the first explicit reference to the Jesus Prayer occurs in the life of Abba Philemon, an Egyptian hermit of the seventh century. John Climacus (570–649) urged his followers to "flog your enemies with the name of Jesus" and to "let the remembrance of Jesus be united with your breathing," and Philotheos of Sinai in the ninth century urged his followers: "Through the remembrance of Jesus Christ, gather together your scattered mind." The

Jesus Prayer spread to Russia in the fifteenth century through Nil Sorsky, and it was popularized in the West in the twentieth century.

However, spiritual writers in all periods have warned of a focus on the name of Jesus, and on worship of Jesus, to the neglect of practical discipleship, of following Jesus, recognizing and serving him in the persons of the "little ones," the poor, naked, hungry, and imprisoned. (Matt. 25.31–46 is certainly the basis for much early reflection on this theme.) Ignatius of Antioch wrote of his desire to "become the pure bread of Christ" and to "imitate the passion of my God" (Ignatius, Rom. 6.3) but equally stressed the importance of following Jesus in love for the widow, the orphan, and the hungry. John Chrysostom (c. 347–407) warned of praising Jesus within the Church while he himself was starving outside the door in the persons of the afflicted.

This emphasis on "following" and "discipleship" was emphasized in later centuries by the Anabaptists and, in the twentieth century, by Dietrich Bonhoeffer (1906–1945) and by liberation theologians such as Jon Sobrino and Segundo Galilea. The contemporary evangelical writer Jim Wallis has warned that neglect of the actual teachings of Jesus can lead to a situation where "all that remains of Jesus is his name." The idea of "spirituality" apart from practical discipleship is alien to mainstream Christian practice and thought.

Early Christian liturgy was marked by a sense of triumph in the victory of Jesus over sin and death. The earliest portrayals of the Cross (c. 430) were triumphal, and liturgical hymns, such as those of Venantius Fortunatus (c. 530–c. 610), stressed the victory of the Cross. Jesus was seen as king, triumphing over the powers of evil through his death and resurrection. There is an objective character to these hymns that is quite different from the individualism of later centuries. Jesus himself is described as the Tree of Life by Ephrem the Syrian (c. 306–373) and Cyril of Alexandria (d. 444), and his identity as a new "Passover" occurs as early as Paul. The theme was greatly developed by Melito of Sardis in the late second century. The Old English text *The Dream of the Rood* (eighth century) still reflects this sense of victory. The joy of the resurrection is particularly marked in the Eastern Orthodox tradition, as in the Paschal liturgy and the hymns of St. John of Damascus. The Paschal vigil is dominated by the recurring and ever mounting chant: "Christ is risen from the dead, trampling down death by death, and upon those in the tombs bestowing life."

Theologically, it is Christ, Word and image of God, more than the human Jesus, who has been the focal point of Christian spirituality. In the New Testament, solidarity with Christ is central. The word "Christ" occurs 500 times in the New Testament, including 379 times in Paul. To be a Christian is to be part of the body of Christ, the organism created by the Incarnation. The entry of the Word into flesh is of critical importance. The claim that "every spirit which does not confess that Jesus Christ has come in the flesh is not of God" (1 John 4.2–3) is undoubtedly the first diagnostic test of Christian spirituality. The flesh is central to the life of the Spirit: spirit is communicated through matter, matter the vehicle of spirit. The New Testament has no faith in "spirituality" as such.

The New Testament sees the purpose of the coming of Jesus Christ to be that of uniting all things in him (Eph. 1.10). By the blood of Jesus, his disciples have been brought near to God and a new humanity has been created (Eph. 2.13–16). The aim is that, through the work of Jesus, Christians might be filled with the fullness of God and become sharers in the divine nature, thus to be restored to the divine likeness. Unity, fullness, and the breaking down of human divisions are central to the "spirituality" of the early Christians. There is also an emphasis throughout early Christian spirituality on love. God is love, and the person who loves is born of God and knows God (1 John 4.7ff.). It is impossible for Christians to be separated from the love of God in Christ (Rom. 8.38). Against those who emphasized "knowledge" *(gnosis)*, Paul stressed that, whereas knowledge puffs up, love builds up. Thus, the practice of love is central to Christian life and to the nature of the Christian community.

Two things follow from this emphasis: the fundamentally social character of Christian spirituality, and the impossibility of separating "spirituality" from "ethics." (The widespread use of the word "spirituality" to describe a separate zone of Christian existence and thought is very modern indeed.) In the devotional life of early Christianity, the dominant theme is that of communion with God in Jesus Christ. The idea of being "in Christ," a term used 164 times in Paul's letters (excluding the pastorals), is central. At the heart of life in Christ is the moment of baptism, in which the disciple puts on Christ and is clothed with Christ. Christ lives both in the Christian community and in individual Christians (Phil. 1.21; Gal. 2.20). He is in the midst of the community as the "hope of glory" (Col. 1.27). Christians have died and been raised with Christ, and their lives are hidden with Christ in God (Col. 3.1–4). As a result of being grafted into Christ, there is a new creation (2 Cor. 5.17). To know Christ and the power of his resurrection is linked with sharing his suffering and becoming like him in his death (Phil. 3.10). New Testament spirituality is rooted in these themes of solidarity and communion.

Another important theme in early Christian writing was that of feeding on Christ. The symbolism of eating and drinking occurs frequently. Jesus was seen as grapes-producing vine, living water, living bread, and so on. Ambrose, in the fourth century, urged his hearers to "drink Christ," seeing him as fountain and river. This language is common throughout Christian history and appears in many modern hymns, such as "Rock of Ages" (referring to the water-yielding rock in Numbers 20).

In Eastern Orthodox spirituality, the stress is on triumph. Icons of Jesus show the baptism, transfiguration, and resurrection. There is a focus on deification *(theosis)*, the divinizing of humanity, which begins with Irenaeus and Athanasius and is central to the theology of the Greek Fathers. In Roman Catholic and Anglican theology it appears in Augustine, Aquinas, Richard Hooker, and later writers. Another feature of Eastern spirituality is that of the "holy fools," those who followed and manifested the humiliated Christ, and who were signs of contradiction. To follow the crucified Jesus was to be a fool for Christ's sake.

The "imitation" of Christ occurs in the New Testament in relation to the Cross chiefly (for example, Mark 8.34). Ignatius of Antioch spoke of imitating "the passion of . . . God," greeted his readers "in the blood of Christ," and described them as "branches of the cross." The theme of imitation as a general aspect of personal devotion only became important in the fifteenth century through Thomas à Kempis's *The Imitation of Christ*. Said to have been more popular than the Bible among Roman Catholics before the Second Vatican Council, it is utterly individualistic and devoid of social content.

The Passion (suffering) of Christ became a central focus of devotion in the West after the eleventh century through the influence of Bernard of Clairvaux (1090–1153) and the Cistercians. Bernard spoke of "the richness of God's mercy in the open wounds of Christ." Devotion to the wounds of Christ and the idea of the folly of the Cross were emphasized within the Cistercian tradition, particularly in the work of William of St. Thierry (1085–1148), and were further developed by Bonaventure (c. 1217–1274). The period from the eleventh to the thirteenth centuries was critical for the shift from a corporate to an intensely personal devotion to the Cross.

Francis of Assisi (1181–1226), described by Bonaventure as *insignia secator crucifixi Iesu* ("the outstanding follower of Jesus crucified"), was a key figure in the development of devotion to the crucified Jesus. According to Thomas of Celano, Francis was "always thinking about Jesus. Jesus was in his mouth, in his ears, in his eyes, in his hands. Jesus was his whole being." In Francis, the Cross became central, and in Franciscan spirituality, there is, in Bonaventure's words, "no other path but through burning love of the Crucified." Bonaventure's works *The Tree of Life* and *The Mystical Vine* are important examples of this style of affective devotion.

The Pietà, a sculpture or painting of Mary lamenting over the dead body of Jesus, appears in the thirteenth century, with clotted blood and concentration on sorrow. The mystery plays, with their dramatic style, and the Stations of the Cross, a devotion associated in the Western Catholic tradition with Lent and Passiontide, also date from these years. The stations have been a way in which, through movement and concentrated attention, communities identify with, and enter into, the road to Calvary. This devotion, often dramatized through streets and upon mountains, has become particularly valued in recent years in Central and South America. The theme is expressed in late medieval paintings of the Passion, and Hieronymus Bosch's *Christ Carrying the Cross*, finished before his death in 1516, is a powerful example.

In the work of fourteenth-century mystics, there is a stress on union with God in the depths of the soul, the point where the birth of God occurs. Meister Eckhart (c. 1260–c. 1328) wrote of "the feast of the eternal birth." Jesus may have been born in Bethlehem, but "if it takes not place in me, what avails it?" In these writers there is a warmth and intensity of devotion, though in some of them the figure of Jesus becomes a little distant. What matters is "the Godhead." An important figure in this period is Julian of Norwich (c. 1342–after 1416), who brings up the theme of "Jesus our Mother" (though it is the climax of a line going back to St. Anselm). More central in

Julian is the centrality of the Passion of Jesus and the concentration on the flesh of Jesus, which also occurs in Richard Rolle (c. 1300–1349). The fourteenth century was also a time when devotion to the wounds of Jesus intensified, the popular prayer *Anima Christi* ("Soul of Christ, sanctify me") being first cited in 1344.

The growth of eucharistic devotion outside the Mass also took place in the Middle Ages, and the creation of the feast of Corpus Christi in 1317, with its processions and focus on adoration of the sacrament, was a critical moment. Devotion to Jesus in the sacrament became central to Western Catholic spirituality and is brought out powerfully in Thomas Aquinas's hymn "Adoro te devote" ("Thee we adore, O hidden Savior, thee"). Although eucharistic spirituality and devotion to Jesus in the sacrament may have declined in the late twentieth century, it was a central feature of the spirituality of Charles de Foucauld (1858–1916) and the order he founded, the Little Sisters and Brothers of Jesus.

Within Protestant spirituality, from Martin Luther to the evangelical revivals of the nineteenth century, the Cross is central. Luther coined the term *theologia crucis* ("theology of the cross") in 1518. The focus on conversion and on a holy life almost always includes a strong emphasis on friendship with Jesus (such as in the hymn declaring, "What a friend we have in Jesus"). There are close parallels between Catholic hymns to the Sacred Heart of Jesus and evangelical hymns about the Blood of the Savior. In both, there is an intensity of feeling and of personal devotion to the human Jesus. Hymns reinforce feeling, and frequently feeling related to the figure of Jesus; thus, famous hymns include the lines "Blessed assurance, Jesus is mine," "Jesus, keep me near the cross," and the like.

Much of the devotional material associated with this personal focus on Jesus is world-denying. Charles Wesley's hymn "Jesus, Lover of My Soul" calls upon Jesus to hide him "till the storm of life is past." More recent hymns tend to focus entirely on the relationship of the individual with Jesus. Some of this devotion has lacked any real creational and incarnational basis. So it has been common in some evangelical circles to speak of "bringing Jesus into the situation"—as if he were not there already.

Jesus as the Word made flesh has also been a key theme in linking worship and action in the world. The Incarnation, and its social consequences, was central to Anglican thought from the time of F. D. Maurice in the 1840s. Christian socialists were among those who stressed the service of Jesus in feeding and clothing human beings. In taking up this work, they argued, one is feeding and clothing Jesus Christ himself. The "social implications" of the doctrine of the Incarnation have been at the heart of Anglican social thought since Maurice, strengthened by Charles Gore's Bampton Lectures of 1891.The nineteenth-century "slum priest" of Portsmouth, Robert Dolling, said that it was because of his belief in the Incarnation that he campaigned for the drainage of the district.

Several features of twentieth- and twenty-first-century spirituality are important. The experience of two world wars was an important factor in the revival of the theme of "the suffering God," expressed, for example, in Edward Shillitoe's poem from the Great War: "But to our wounds only God's wound can speak, / And not a God has wounds but thou alone." Although this theme is explicit in the works of the Congregationalist P. T. Forsyth (1848–1921), who wrote that there was "a Calvary above which was the mother of it all," it is most marked in the writings and poems of Wilfred Owen (1893–1918), and of G. A. Studdert Kennedy (1883–1929), whose influence is evident on Jürgen Moltmann's *The Crucified God* (1974).

Within the Western Catholic tradition, there has been a remarkable revival of the Ignatian Exercises, a method of meditation on one's life in the light of the gospel with an emphasis on following Jesus. There has also been a focus on the "dangerous memory" of Jesus, a theme stressed by J. B. Metz and developed by feminist theologians.

The figure of Jesus has been at the heart of many movements of oppressed and marginalized people. There has always been a fascination with, and devotion to, the figure of Jesus among people outside Christianity and the churches. Often seen as a rebel figure, Jesus has inspired many movements of resistance, not least among black people and other groups suffering oppression. Since the 1960s, a cluster of groups that have gone under the general heading of "the Jesus Movement" has attracted many young people by its countercultural vision. Some of this has been sentimental and idealist, but much of it has led to a real attempt to follow Jesus, to take his teachings seriously, and to live a new kind of life. Many young people have been attracted by the movements that have developed from this nonecclesial devotion to Jesus of Nazareth.

Kenneth Leech

See also: Alexandrian Theology; Anglicanism; Augustine of Hippo; Baptism; Bernard of Clairvaux; Bonaventure; Bonhoeffer, Dietrich; Eucharist; Feminist Theology; Francis of Assisi; Great War; Hymns; Ignatius of Antioch; Ignatius of Loyola; Irenaeas; Jesus, Name of; Julian of Norwich; Kempis, Thomas à; Liberation Theology; Liturgy; Luther, Martin; Mary; Orthodox Tradition; Roman Catholicism; Russian Christianity; Syriac Tradition

References

Bennett, J. A. W. 1982. *Poetry of the Passion*. Oxford: Clarendon.
Bynum, Carolyn Walker. 1982. *Jesus as Mother*. Berkeley: University of California Press.
Hussherr, Irenee. 1978. *The Name of Jesus*. Kalamazoo: Cistercian Publications.
Louth, Andrew. 1981. *The Origins of the Christian Mystical Tradition*. Oxford: Clarendon.
Miles, Margaret R. 1981. *Fullness of Life: Historical Foundations for a New Asceticism*. Philadelphia: Westminster.
Schreiter, R. J. 1988. *In Water and in Blood*. New York: Crossroad.
Ward, Benedicta. 1976. *The Influence of St. Bernard*. Oxford: SLG.
Ware, Kallistos. 1974. *The Power of the Name*. Oxford: SLG.
Williams, Rowan. 1979. *The Wound of Knowledge*. London: Darton, Longman and Todd.

Spirituality (Protestant)

The Protestant reformers of the sixteenth century brought to Christian spirituality a new and fundamental emphasis on Jesus' death. As such, that emphasis was not new: it is found in innumerable paintings, crucifixes, and writings from the Middle Ages. What was new was a shift in focus from seeing that death as something to be contemplated and mourned to seeing it as something to be celebrated and believed in: Jesus died, not to share my death, but to set me free. The consequences of this shift of focus for the Christian's spiritual life are considerable: the stress is put less on the life of Jesus than on his death, less on Jesus as exemplar and more on Jesus as savior. On the cross, and without any help from us, Jesus set us free from sin and death, and those who choose (rather, are chosen) to believe this are adopted as God's children and invited to share a new relationship with God through Christ in which they are assured of the free gifts of God's love and acceptance (for example, John 3.16 and Rom. 8.12–7).

For Protestants, it follows that the Christian's life is a response to what God has done for us in Christ, to the discovery and the experience of God's love and forgiveness, rather than a means by which that love and forgiveness may be won. Martin Luther wrote: "Christians are not made righteous in doing righteous things, but being now made righteous by faith in Christ, they do righteous things" (*Commentary on Galatians* 3.10). We are saved by a process that is entirely external to us: the question of who is to be saved and who is not is a matter entirely for God, and nothing we can do will make any difference to it. The way we live as Christians will not affect the outcome of our salvation, but it will show others whether we have been saved or not, making manifest to us and to others the fruits of all that God in Christ has done for us.

This emphasis led Protestant spirituality to conceive of Christ's death more as something to celebrate than as something to grieve, which had been the case in much late medieval Catholic piety. Visually, the bare cross sufficed: the crucifix showing Christ suffering was abandoned. Protestant hymnody, which has played a vital part in Protestant spiritual life, has always stressed the unworthiness of the sinner, but only in order to underline the need to celebrate what God has done for each individual Christian through the death of Jesus. When the Lutheran composer J. S. Bach wrote his setting of the *St. John Passion*, he marked the death of Christ with the slow and moving aria "Es ist vollbracht" (It is finished), after which the evangelist announces "Und neigte das Haupt und verschied" (And he bowed his head and died) in tones of solemn grief. But immediately after Christ's death, grief is abandoned, and there follows a bright and hopeful aria in the key of D major, which includes a prayer to the dead Jesus asking whether the person praying is set free by Christ's death, to which Christ simply replies "Ja" (yes). Where a Catholic setting of Christ's death would have concentrated much more intensively on its pathos and tragedy, Bach sought to emphasize what Christ did for us in dying: he set us free. It is a vivid example of a fundamental change in how Jesus' death was understood.

It follows from this basis that one of the fundamental ingredients of Protestant spirituality is the doctrine of assurance, the conviction that we can be certain of our salvation provided we believe that Christ has died for our sins (Rom. 5.8; Gal. 2.20; Tim. 7.15). We know ourselves to be forgiven and loved unconditionally; we are declared to be God's children by an outright act of divine forgiveness revealed to us on the Cross, where Jesus suffered in our place, and then, like the Prodigal Son (Luke 15.11–32), we find ourselves transformed from guilty outsiders to children restored and welcomed home. But each of us must accept this new status for ourselves, and that gives Protestant spirituality a strongly individualistic tone. It is my relationship with Jesus (and, through Jesus, with the Father), not the Church, which is primary. And that relationship is as direct as it is personal: no other mediator, no priest or canonized saint, is needed. We stand alone before God, even though, in the fellowship of our fellow believers ("the godly"), we need never be lonely.

The uncompromisingly Christ-centered nature of Protestant theology had other important implications for Christian spiritual life, and for the role of Jesus within it. Holiness came to mean less a desire to live *like* Christ, in the sense of imitating his recorded deeds, and more a desire to live *with* Christ, in the Pauline sense of becoming one body with him. Protestants frequently celebrated the beauty and attractiveness of Christ, a beauty we can share once we accept for ourselves the truth of his saving death. Both Martin Luther and John Calvin maintained that we are called to grow into an ever deeper union with Christ, and both made use of marital imagery in describing that union. In this they were at one with their Catholic forebears, though where Catholic spiritual writers tended to emphasize love as the primary content of our relationship with Christ, Protestants tended to emphasize faith.

This understanding of the Christian life as directed toward an intimate union with Christ has much in common with Catholic spirituality, but it is not the same thing. For Protestants, our union with Christ is always a partnership between two persons, not the fusion of those persons into one: it is a moral and personal union, not an ontological one, for Christ and the Christian remain distinct. And it comes about through Christ's death, not through anything we do or through initiatives we take. By believing that Christ died for us, we begin to participate in his death and to appropriate the dynamic of his self-giving love so that it becomes the mainspring of our own lives. Yet this appropriation by us is never a repetition of what Christ did, once for all, on the Cross: rather, it is the means by which, as we grow in an ever deeper awareness of what his death means for us, we begin to experience something of its power and beauty within ourselves.

In Protestant spirituality, prayer is always mediated through Christ, for only Christ makes access to God possible. Prayer that is not founded upon faith in Christ is not likely to be heard. Protestants have tended to prefer extemporaneous prayer, as coming "from the heart," rather than formal liturgical prayer; they have understood all genuinely Christian prayer as being in reality a part of Christ's continuing prayer to the Father, so that Christ prays in us and ensures that our prayer is heard (John 16.23–4). This understanding allows us to be bold in our prayer, for through our assurance of salvation and our adoption as children we may be confident that God hears us and may bring the whole of ourselves into our prayer, so that our prayer, as well as our lives, begins to bear witness to the truth of our redemption. Protestants, like Catholics, have valued meditative and reflective prayer focused on Jesus, but here, too, Protestants have been much more likely to contemplate the saving work of Christ on the Cross than the details of his human life.

Jesus plays a further important role in Protestant spirituality as intercessor. Following the writer of the letter to the Hebrews (7.25), Protestants believe that Christ's continued intercession for us in the presence of the Father is precisely what enables us to persevere in the Christian life when we are tempted to abandon it or when we are afflicted by suffering. The intercession of Christ imparts a dynamism to the spiritual life of the Christian, which might otherwise appear as a static affair since the entire work of salvation is accomplished already, and externally. Christ's continuing prayer on our behalf is what leads us on beyond the Cross to behold the glory of God in the face of the risen Christ: it helps to make the life of prayer become, not just a struggle, but an adventure, too.

That brings us to a further important role that has been played by Jesus in Protestant spirituality as the one who will return. An active expectation of the second coming of Christ is found in much Protestant belief and practice, linked with a firm, even defiant, conviction that he will vindicate those who believe in him. Numerous Protestant groups and sects, from the Reformation onward, have exhibited a strongly eschatological character: some foresaw the return of Christ as leading to the subversion of the established political order and its replacement with Christ's kingdom, others as precipitating the final judgment and the separation of the saved from the damned, the sheep from the goats. Pentecostal choruses and black Christian spirituals celebrate the second coming of Christ as though it were happening now, visualizing with vivid and often apocalyptic imagery the glories of the life to come.

Gordon Mursell

See also: Art; Calvin, John; English Christianity, Medieval; Jesus, Achievement of; Jesus, Death of; John of the Cross; Luther, Martin; Pentecostalism

References

McGrath, Alister E. 1985. *Luther's Theology of the Cross: Martin Luther's Theological Breakthrough*. Oxford: Oxford University Press.

———. 1993. *Reformation Thought: An Introduction*. 2d ed. Oxford: Blackwell.

Raitt, Jill, ed. 1988. *Christian Spirituality II: High Middle Ages and Reformation*. New York: Crossroad.

Rupp, E. G. 1984. "Protestant Spirituality in the First Age of the Reformation." Pp. 155–170 in *Popular Belief and Practice: Papers Read at the Ninth Summer Meeting and the Tenth Winter Meeting of the Ecclesiastical History Society*. Edited by G. J. Cuming and D. Baker. Cambridge: Cambridge University Press.

Tamburello, Dennis E. 1994. *Union with Christ: John Calvin and the Mysticism of St. Bernard*. Louisville, KY: Westminster John Knox Press.

Strauss, D. F. (1808–1874)

From a long-term point of view, David Friedrich Strauss was perhaps the most influential nineteenth-century critic of the Gospels and of approaches to the life of Jesus. So his became one of the first "boo" names that caused German biblical criticism to be seen as scandalously dangerous by many in Germany itself, and certainly among English-speaking Christians, who were only just beginning to embark upon historical criticism of the Scriptures in any significant way. The spread of Stauss's reputation was much helped by the fact that, as early as 1846, his *Life of Jesus Critically Examined* (1835) was published in an English translation by George Eliot, thereby illustrating her own intellectual position ahead of the herd. It was something of a bombshell.

Strauss was trained, under F. C. Baur, at the theological seminary in Tübingen, already notorious for its avant-garde criticism of received opinion on the history of early Christianity. Strauss was particularly important for combining the impact of historical work sponsored at Tübingen with theological revision stemming particularly from the work of F. D. E. Schleiermacher (1768–1834) a generation earlier. His impact was therefore wider and more devastating than, for example, that of Hermann Samuel Reimarus (1694–1768), whose heir he could be said to be in the sphere of skeptical criticism of the Gospels and the study of the life of Jesus.

For Strauss, the combination of approaches led not only to further doubts about the historical veracity of the miraculous or supernatural elements in the stories about Jesus but also to a rejection of doctrines that had been developed in the early centuries of the Church on the basis of them. For example, the classical doctrine of the Incarnation, worked out in the fourth and fifth centuries, philosophical in the mode of its formulation, involved, in practice, a positive view of the birth narratives opening the Gospels of Matthew and Luke.

Strauss, though rationalistic in the tradition of the Enlightenment, did not reject religious faith, but he did reinterpret it drastically. The supernatural element in the Gospels, books that he thought dated from the second century, was "myth," the fruit of the religious imagination, conditioned by the thought forms of the times, of devout followers of Jesus in the early period: understandable, but not reliable as history. Much of this material was modeled on OT stories, such as those relating to Moses, Elijah, or Elisha. Strauss's case was furthered by his insistence that long-observed inconsistencies between the Gospels should be taken seriously and not simply "harmonized" out of significance. It is not surprising that in 1835 he was immediately dismissed from his Tübingen post.

How have Strauss's ideas fared in the light of history? Some of them have not stood the test of time, notably his view of the late dating of the Gospels. But his idea of reading the Gospels, and their various ingredients, in the context of their times has come to be so widely accepted that to think otherwise, even among those who may be uncomfortable with some of the effects of the method, is hardly tolerable academically. True, Strauss's Hegelian philosophical framework, important for him, has disappeared, but his "placing" of the more wondrous elements in the story of Jesus into the context of the ideas and conventions of the time has remained, and scholars who reject it must argue for their rejection. In much of the West, the boot has, academically at least, shifted to the opposite foot from the days when pioneers like Strauss wrote their books and suffered in consequence.

Whether he deserved it or not, Strauss is one of the first of a line of (mainly German) figures who became the bêtes noires of more orthodox opinion for their far-reaching rejection of the historical accuracy of so much of the Gospels. In the twentieth century, Rudolf Bultmann came for many to occupy a similar role. It can be argued that despite their demonization, they have never had a fair hearing in Church circles, and doctrinal thinkers, Protestant or Catholic, have scarcely come to terms with these aspects of their ideas and the implications that they carry. It is then a matter of the degree of development that Christianity can sustain—assuming, of course, that Strauss and his successors had significant truth on their side.

Leslie Houlden

See also: Bultmann, Rudolf; Enlightenment; Keck, Leander E.; Reimarus, Hermann Samuel; Schleiermacher, F. D. E.; Schweitzer, Albert

References

Keck, L. E. 1977. *The Christ of Faith and the Jesus of History: Introduction.* Philadelphia: Fortress Press.

Strauss, D. F. 1972 [1835]. *The Life of Jesus Critically Examined.* Edited by P. C. Hodgson. Translated by George Eliot from the 4th German ed. Philadelphia: Fortress; London: SCM.

Syriac Tradition

Syriac is one of the main dialects of Aramaic (the language spoken by Jesus), and the Syriac tradition is represented today by those churches for which Syriac is, or was, their literary and liturgical language. Early Christian tradition is often spoken of as having two strands, Greek East and Latin West. This dichotomy neglects an important third element, the Syriac Orient, for which Syriac (which began as the local Aramaic dialect of Edessa, modern Urfa, Southeast Turkey) served as the literary language. In the fourth century, this Syriac tradition produced the greatest poet-theologian of the patristic period, St. Ephrem (d. 373), and it lives on in the several different churches of Syriac liturgical tradition to be found today, not only in their ancestral homes in the Middle East and south India, but also in their diaspora, all over the world.

The fifth-century controversies concerning how best to define the relationship between the divinity and humanity in the incarnate Christ produced a three-way split in Syriac Christianity. The Definition of Faith produced at the Council of Chalcedon (451), which has always been normative for the Greek East and Latin West (both Catholic and Reformed), was rejected by many in the East, largely as a result of the ambiguity of two of the key technical terms used ("nature" and "hypostasis"), which meant different things to different people. Today this three-way split within the Syriac tradition is represented by (1) the Syrian Orthodox Church (which rejects Chalcedon, along with the other Oriental Orthodox Churches—Armenian, Coptic, and Ethiopian); (2) the Maronite Church, along with the Eastern Rite Chaldean and Syrian Catholic Churches, which all belong to the Chalcedonian tradition; and (3) the Church of the East, which, having grown up outside the Roman Empire, never took part in any of the councils of the Roman Empire. In the polemical literature of the mainstream Chalcedonian Churches, the misleading names of "Monophysite" and "Jacobite" were given to the Syrian Orthodox, and "Nestorian" to the Church of the East (the Chalcedonian Churches were themselves called "Nestorian" by the Syrian Orthodox). The Arab invasions of the seventh century effectively fossilized these doctrinal divisions, and it is only in recent decades that ecumenical dialogue has clarified how the misunderstandings of the past arose, showing that beneath the verbal conflict between the doctrinal formulations of the three traditions, there is a fundamental agreement that the historical Jesus is the incarnate Son of God.

The Incarnate One

Early Syriac writers normally used the phrase "[the Word] put on a body" as a metaphor for the Incarnation, positing a movement from one "womb," or "staging post," to another. Thus, Jesus, starting out from the "womb" of the Father (this being the Syriac translation of John 1.18, usually translated "bosom" in English), proceeded to the womb of Mary, the womb of the river Jordan, and the womb of Sheol (the underworld); these three "staging posts" were seen as the effective focal points that brought about salvation.

The paradox of the infant Jesus, who is at the same time "the fashioner of infants," caught the imagination of numerous Syriac poets from Ephrem onward. In a series of poems, Ephrem has Mary address her child; in the following typical stanza, Mary acknowledges that the presence of Jesus in her womb has served as her baptism:

> O Son of the Most High,
> who has come and resided in me
> so that I have become your mother,
> as I bore you—your second birth—
> so too you have given birth to me a second time:
> you have put on your mother's robe—your body,
> whereas I have put on your glory. (*Hymns on the Nativity* 16.11)

The early Syriac tradition has a number of distinctive features in its portrayal of Jesus. One of these is the prominence it gives to Jesus as a physician and healer. In his *Church History* (I.13), Eusebius recounted the (legendary) story of how king Abgar the Black of Edessa wrote to Jesus, "the good Savior," asking him to come to Edessa to heal him of a disease; Jesus replies that he will send a disciple after his Ascension. The expanded Syriac form of the story (dating from the early fifth century) characteristically has Abgar address Jesus as "the good physician" rather than "Savior." This motif accords with the frequent description of Jesus as physician in the two main fourth-century Syriac authors, Aphrahat and Ephrem. In keeping with this title, Jesus is often described as providing the "medicine of life" (the phrase could equally be translated "medicine of salvation"); this is usually identified as the Eucharist. This emphasis on Jesus as healer leads many writers (but above all Aphrahat) to portray sin and repentance in medical rather than juridical terms. Thus Aphrahat addressed priests, "You who are doctors and disciples of our glorious doctor should not withhold healing from the person who needs to be healed: to the person who shows you his abscess, provide him with the medicine of repentance" (*Demonstration* 7.4). This imagery still frequently features in liturgical texts, as in the following prayer used in the Maronite rite at Vespers for Sunday: "O Christ our Savior, the doctor who heals all our illnesses, heal what disfigures us with the medicine of your mercy; bring our sick state to the wholeness of recovery, using the overflowing compassion of your grace, for you are the true doctor."

Another very characteristic term applied to Jesus is "bridegroom." The parable of the virgins (Matt. 25.1–12) was particularly influential, and in v. 10 the wise virgins are often portrayed as entering, not the marriage feast, but the bridal chamber (the reading may go back to Tatian's *Diatessaron*, or *Harmony of the Gospels*, in the second century). This version allowed for an understanding of Jesus as bridegroom not just for the personified Church but also for the individual wise virgin, or soul. For the former, betrothal to Jesus was usually seen as taking place at his baptism in the Jordan; for the latter it was at Christian baptism—with the actual entry into the bridal chamber (for those who had kept their wedding garment pure) only at the eschaton. The terms "bridal chamber of light" or "of joys" are recurrent ones for the kingdom of heaven in the liturgical texts of all the Syriac churches.

Along with the baptism of Jesus, the piercing of his side on the Cross (John 19.34) also frequently served as a paradigm of the betrothal of Jesus to the Church, the water and blood that issue from his side representing his bridal gift to the Church, namely baptism and the Eucharist. The following passage, from the East Syriac Breviary, is characteristic: "Give thanks, O Church, to the King's Son who has betrothed you, in order to be his queen; he has brought you in to his bridal chamber, making flow the blood from his side as a wedding gift, clothing you in the glorious [baptismal] Robe of Light that does not fade away" (Bedjan, III: 430; *Breviarium Chaldaicum* III). Surprisingly, the Song of Songs does not become influential in the development of this bridal imagery until the sixth century, perhaps owing to the Syriac translation of Gregory of Nyssa's commentary on that book. A good example of this influence is provided by an Epiphany hymn from this period, in which the Church speaks:

> Jesus is mine and I am his. He has desired me:
> he has clothed himself in me, I am clothed in him;
> with the kisses of his mouth has he kissed me
> and brought me to his Bridal Chamber on high.
> (*Parole de l'Orient* 15 [1988/1989], 176)

A profusion of further titles accorded to Jesus can be found in Syriac liturgical texts and poetry. Some of these are based on biblical sources and their subsequent interpretation (for example, "Coal of Fire," from Isa. 6:6; "Fatted Ox," from Luke 15.23; and "Hidden Power," from Luke 1.35); others have looser biblical roots, including "Athlete," "Companion," "Farmer," "Fashioner of Infants," "Fountain of Life," "Heavenly Eagle," "Liberator of all," "Lifegiver," "Merchant," "Pearl," and "Provisioner of all."

The Syriac churches are extremely rich in eucharistic prayers; though the majority of these are addressed directly to the Father, the earliest of them were once addressed to Jesus as the Christ. The invocation in several of them, a prayer that the Spirit of Jesus "come" and be present, can be traced back, by way of prayers in the third-century Acts of Thomas, to the Aramaic phrase *Maranatha*, "our Lord, come!" cited by Paul (1 Cor. 16.22). Prayers addressed to Christ in other liturgical contexts are of course common, but only rarely is he addressed simply as "Jesus," as in the following, from the *Syrian Orthodox Night Office for Thursdays:* "Jesus, Son of the Father, be our help; Jesus, Son of Mary, be our protection; Jesus, strengthen us; Jesus, guard us; Jesus, drive away the evil one from us; Jesus, forgive us our offenses and sins; Jesus, have pity on us when you judge us." An unusual case of a prayer put into the mouth of Jesus (at the time of his baptism) is to be found in *Commentary on Luke* by the Syrian Orthodox theologian Philoxenos (d. 523), where Jesus requests his Father to send the Spirit "to sanctify the womb of baptism so that it may give birth to new children, making them your sons and daughters and my brothers and sisters, and heirs of the Kingdom." The baptism of Jesus is seen as the source, alongside John 19.34, for Christian baptism (Watt, 59).

As in other traditions, the ideal of the Christian life is seen as the imitation of Christ: Christians "put on Christ" at their baptism, which is often taken as conforming to his way of life. According to Philoxenos, Jesus observed the "lesser commandments" (of outward acts of charity and the like) until his baptism, after which he kept the "greater commandments" (of total renunciation, for example). Imitation of the former is required of all Christians, but the latter are only for those who have dedicated themselves to the ascetic life.

The name of Jesus in Syriac begins with Y (YSHW'), the tenth letter of the alphabet. The poet Ephrem plays on this in several of his hymns, linking it with the date of the conception of Jesus as identified in early Syriac tradition:

> Y is placed at the beginning of your name;
> with the number ten that it indicates
> it is placed in Nisan (=April):
> on the 10th you entered the womb.
> Your conception thus coincides with the symbolic number of perfection.
> (*Hymns on the Nativity* 27.2)

Tenth Nisan as the date of the Annunciation was arrived at by identifying Zachariah (John the Baptist's father) as the high priest, placing his vision in the temple (Luke 1.9) on the Day of Atonement, 10th Tishri (October), and then adding the six months mentioned in Luke 1.26. Elsewhere, Ephrem spoke of the name of Jesus as "a hidden bridge that conveys from death to life" (*Hymns on Faith* 6.17), and the seventh-century mystic Isaac the Syrian prays "O name of Jesus, key to all gifts, open up for me the great door to your treasure-house so that I may enter and praise you" ("Second Part" 5.5). Though brief "arrow prayers" addressed to Jesus are to be found in a number of Syriac monastic writers, no close Syriac counterpart to the Greek and Russian Orthodox "Jesus Prayer" ever developed.

Different cultures have different attitudes about naming their children after Jesus. In the East Syriac tradition, from the fifth century onward the element "Jesus" appears frequently in compound names, such as in Abdisho, "servant of Jesus"; Isho'yahb, "Jesus has given"; Shubhalisho', "praise to Jesus," and so on. In modern times, Jesus (West Syriac Yeshu', East Syriac Isho') is occasionally used alone, and in certain areas this may even be in the Muslim form, 'Isa.

According to the Syriac version of the Abgar legend, Abgar's emissary to Jesus took the opportunity to paint his portrait, and by the sixth century this portrait had materialized as an icon "not made by hands," only to be transformed a couple of centuries later into a mandylion, or scarf, on which Jesus' face had been miraculously imprinted. It was this precious relic that the Byzantine Emperor Romanos had transported from Edessa to Constantinople in 944. (King Abgar and the mandylion are already portrayed on a tenth-century icon at St. Catherine's Monastery, Sinai.) The fate of the mandylion subsequent to the sack of Constantinople by the Venetians in 1204 is unknown. According to some, it ended up in La Sainte Chapelle in Paris, only to fall victim to the French Revolution; others identify it as the miraculous icon in the Church of St. Bartholomew in Genoa, or even as the Turin shroud.

A detailed written description of the appearance of Jesus is given in the apocryphal *Letter of Lentulus*, where the mention of a forked beard fits with a number of icons that may derive ultimately from the Edessa icon/mandylion.

An important early portrayal of Jesus is to be found in an illustrated Syriac Gospel manuscript dated A.D. 586 (the *Rabbula Gospels*); in this one finds Jesus as an infant in the arms of Mary (standing) and various marginal illustrations of episodes in the life of Jesus, including his baptism by John, where flames are shown going up from the Jordan, a feature frequently mentioned in Syriac liturgical poetry. Both the crucifixion and ascension receive full-page treatment; in the former, Jesus is unusually depicted with his eyes open, and in the latter, he appears standing in a mandorla (i.e., an almond-shaped enclosure of light) held up by angels, above the standing apostles, with Mary prominently in the center.

The Syriac tradition in fact never developed any distinctive artistic tradition of its own; instead, in different areas and at different times, Syriac pictorial art adopted (and sometimes adapted) other artistic traditions. Thus in the Middle Ages Jesus would be portrayed sometimes in a provincial Byzantine style; at other times, it might be Islamic or Mongol. In India, the pre-Portuguese artistic tradition of the Syriac Church followed local Indian styles, and this practice has now been revived in some circles, replacing the nineteenth-century Italianate style of portraying Jesus that has unfortunately proved so pervasive in many of the Syriac (and other) churches in modern times.

Sebastian Brock

See also: Alexandrian Theology; Baptism; Chalcedon; Coptic Christianity; Ethiopian Christianity; Eucharist; Indian Christianity; Nestorianism; Orthodox Tradition

References

Bedjan, P., ed. *Breviarium Chaldaicum*. Rome: Congregatio Pre-Ecclesia Orientali.

Brock, Sebastian. 1992. *The Luminous Eye: The Spiritual World Vision of Saint Ephrem the Syrian*. Kalamazoo: Cistercian.

Cameron, Averil. 1996. "The History of the Image of Edessa: The Telling of a Story." In *Changing Cultures in Early Byzantium*. Aldershot: Variorum.

Koonammakkal, Thomas. 1997. "Ephrem on the Name of Jesus." *Studia Patristica* 32.

Leroy, Jules. 1964. *Les manuscrits syriaques a peintures, I-II*. Paris: Paul Geuthner.

McVey, Kathleen. 1989. *Ephrem the Syrian: Hymns*. New York: Paulist.

Murray, Robert. 1975. *Symbols of Church and Kingdom*. Cambridge: Cambridge University Press.

Watt, J. W. 1978. *Philoxenos of Mabbug. Fragments of a Commentary on Matthew and Luke*. Leuven: Peeters.

T

Temple of Jerusalem

See Jesus in Social Context

Teresa of Avila

The Jesus of St. Teresa of Avila is he who acts within, showing just how risen he is in the Church by transforming the heart of the believer. Prayer, and founding communities of prayer, was Teresa's response to an age of religious strife. When she wrote of Jesus, it was above all the Jesus she came to know in prayer: the living Christ whose gospel life is available now because he is risen. Teresa therefore fought to affirm the centrality of this Jesus in the mystical journey. Her love for him, and so for his cause, made her communities places of gospel living, a living text revealing Jesus' virtues. This mystic, then, confirmed Jesus' risen vitality and revealed the gospel as a perennial source of transformation in the world.

Teresa of Jesus

Teresa's life (1515–1582) divides into three phases: her years of growth and spiritual struggle; her mystical flowering following conversion (1554), which led to the creation of a small praying community in her native Avila; and her last fifteen years as foundress of further convents around Spain. The lifestyle she instigated was marked by her assuming a new religious name: "Teresa of Jesus." Her writings, spanning her last twenty years, comprise her autobiography, *The Life;* the spiritual charter for her communities, *The Way of Perfection;* the record of her founding journeys, *The Foundations;* her mature mystical work, *The Interior Castle* (1577); shorter spiritual and administrative writings; and thousands of letters, of which 450 are extant.

Teresa's Christological formation came through homely Spanish paintings and statues, popular piety, homilies, and conversation. Some reading, notably the Castilian version of Ludolph of Saxony's *Vita Christi* (c. 1300–1378), shored up the biblical, liturgical basis. But it was above all in her personal journey that her word on Jesus took shape.

The Centrality of Christ's Humanity in Teresa's Journey

The Interior Castle describes spiritual growth as progressive surrender to divine action, a passage through a series of dwelling places until the person reaches her center, the seventh dwelling, where the Trinity abides. On the threshold of this complete union, the author insisted on the role, in this progress, of the human Jesus (*Castle* 6.7). As union with the divine intensifies, is not the particularity of Jesus an obstacle in prayer? Teresa had thought so, following Francisco de Osuna and Bernadino de Laredo. But she came to qualify this belief as "a great betrayal" (*Life* 22.3). Growth in prayer means growth in receptivity; hence prayer may indeed become less tied to images and concepts, and so less dependent on Gospel words and scenes. But Teresa was adamant that forcing this independence would be a mistake, and that where mystical stillness does supervene, this does not imply dispensing with Christ's mediatorship. It means, rather, that his presence is more encompassing, less over-against. There (the seventh dwelling), "continuously, in a wonderful way, she never ceases to walk with Christ our Lord; he, divine and human, is her constant companion" (*Castle* 6.7.9).

The passion with which Teresa affirmed this centrality of Jesus suggested that more was at stake than mystical theory. The same passion characterized her denunciation of thirst for prestige *(honra)* and her plea that, despite one's sinfulness, one never abandon prayer. The three—Jesus, *honra*, prayer—are connected in her own history. In earlier life, her dependence on what people thought of her had enslaved her, which had resulted in a pitiful struggle with her thirst for affection lasting some twenty years. She attested that what changed her was prayer—prayer as frequent contact "with him who we know loves us" (*Life* 8.5). And what enabled her to return to this prayer, the space of personal encounter with the Other, was precisely the welcome she found in the humanity of Jesus. "I would try to represent Christ within me, and it seems to me I got on better in those situations where I could see he was most alone. It seemed to me that being alone and afflicted, as a person in need, he had to accept me" (*Life* 9.4). Jesus' humanity thus made prayer possible; it was he who released Teresa for a total surrender. Indeed, this process took sacramental, Hispanic form: the sight of a statue of the bleeding Savior was the catalyst for her renouncing self-reliance and putting all her confidence in him (*Life* 9.1–3).

This conversion marked the onset of her mature mystical—gifted, unmerited, unconstrained—experience of God. Although the Inquisition was denying access to spiritual writings, with the publication of the Index of Forbidden Books in 1559 under Pope Paul IV, Teresa encountered Christ as her "living book" (*Life* 26.5). She struggled to explain this to her confessor, who asked how she knew that what she experienced was Christ: "I told him I didn't know how I knew, but that I could not but be aware that he was close to me and that I saw and felt this clearly, and that my soul was much more recollected, in a long-lasting prayer of quiet with effects unlike those I had normally experienced; and that this was something very clear" (*Life* 27.3). Teresa's mystical experience was a declaration of the lordship of Christ, in which he increasingly claimed her as his. It was a testimony to the resurrection, attesting to the validity of the Incarnation: the sight of his beauty liberated her, while confirming his human closeness. She wrote: "Seeing this Lord, and relating to him in such a continuous way, I began to love him and to trust him much more. I could see that, though he was God, he was human, and he is not shocked by people's weaknesses. He knows how wretchedly feeble we naturally are, liable often to fall thanks to the first sin which he came to remedy. I can be with him as with a friend, even though he is Lord. For I can see he is not like those we call lords here, whose whole lordship consists just in posing" (*Life* 37.5).

Teresa was passionate about the human Christ because only he in his humanness had been able to untangle her enslavement. Accordingly, when Teresa in *Life* and *Castle* affirmed Jesus' centrality in the spiritual journey, her word carried unassailable conviction.

Jesus, "the Way"

In defense of her belief in Jesus' centrality, Teresa offered two explanations and an intuition (*Life* 22). The first explanation was this: actively to dispense with the human Jesus in search of a more ethereal prayer smacks of pride. The gospel is for the little, and spiritual growth comes through taking the lowest place. Put otherwise, to anchor prayer in the humanness of Christ testifies to the primacy of grace. Spiritual growth is a gift bestowed on the Lord's poor, not the attainment of a religious élite. Second, Christ's humanness keeps faith earthed: "We are not angels; we have a body. To want to become angels while we are on this earth—and as much on the earth as I was—is ridiculous! Normally, the mind needs some support. . . . When we are busy, or being badly treated, when life is hard, or we cannot get that much quiet, and when prayer is dry, we have a very good friend in Christ. We look at him as man, we see him in weakness and difficulties, and he is company for us. Once we have acquired the habit, it is very easy to find him at our side" (*Life* 22.10).

These are her reasonings: Jesus means humility; and he blesses our bodiliness. But more central is her intuition: that one of the Trinity died on the cross and lives in risen flesh, and is worthy of a person's life: "In seeing you near me, I have seen all blessings. With so good a friend present, so good a leader who came forward first of all to suffer, we can bear everything. He helps us; he gives us strength. He never fails. He is a real friend" (*Life* 22.6).

Earthly Jesus and Risen Christ

Teresa's language of "friendship" indicates that what she sought in prayer was not an image or thought, but the living person. The key to prayer, then, is awareness of persons: knowing who you are and who the Other is (*Way* 22.1; *Castle* 1.1.7). Her "representing" Christ denotes re-presenting, attending to his presence. Her interest was not in history but in communion. Jesus' past is available and relevant, because it is risen in him. So one can seek him in Gethsemane, or at Sychar, or at supper, or on Easter morning, all settings enabling personal encounter.

The language of mutual gaze served Teresa here: "I am asking you only to look at him"; he never "turns his eyes away from you" (*Way* 26.3; see *Life* 13.22). The language, too, of interiority: prayer takes place "within," in "recollection"; that is, where the person is most available, most herself (*Way* 28).

When Teresa wrote of the Eucharist the same vocabulary occurred—gazing, entering within (*Way* 33–35). The Eucharist epitomizes Jesus' accessibility: available as Bread, "he is on easy terms" (*Way* 34.9). Teresian prayer, encounter with the risen Christ who carries his earthly history within him, finds its source and highest expression in the Eucharist: intimate communion with a living Jesus in his bodily presence.

The tenderness of Teresa's regard for the Eucharist accords with the most delicate aspect of her Christology: Jesus' humanity permits reciprocity. Not only can the person approach him in her weakness; she can support him in his weakness. His risen presence makes available now the vulnerability of his flesh then: "Or look at him burdened with the cross, not even given the chance to draw breath. He will look at you with such beautiful, compassionate eyes, eyes full of tears. He will forget his sufferings to console you in yours, just because you have gone to be with him and console him, and are turning to look at him. 'Oh Lord of the world, my true Spouse,' you can say to him . . . 'are you in such need, my good Lord, that you accept me as your companion and want me there with you? I can see in your eyes that my presence has brought you comfort'" (*Way* 26.5–6).

Window onto the Father

For Teresa, mystical fullness is life in the Trinity; if Jesus is the "way," he is the way to that (*Castle* 7.1). This insight receives homely expression in the *Way of Perfection*, where Teresa set out a pattern of life and prayer for her nuns. They were invited to find in Jesus a companion who would teach them, precisely, to call God "Father" (*Way* 26). The Lord's Prayer became a privileged entry into the delicacy of love between Son and Father, a realm where the Father's name, the soul's consent, and the Son's body are gifts exchanged in a circle of trust. In the sanctuary of the soul where the Father dwells, we are invited to offer to the Father the suffering Son (*Way* 28.4). The Lord's Prayer makes us at home in the divine exchange: "Between such a Son and such a Father there cannot but be the Holy Spirit" (*Way* 27.7). Teresa's human Christ is not an ending, but a window opening onto the divine family.

The Eucharist, then, is given precisely to enable us to do the will of the Father. In showing "the extreme love he [the good Jesus] has for us," it awakens the person daily to love (*Way* 33.1–2). The Eucharist kept open the thoroughfare to the Father's heart set up on Calvary, encouraging Teresa to offer the eucharistic Christ to the Father to sanction her petitions (*Way* 35.5). This offering was given breathtaking expression in her more personal *Spiritual Testimonies:* "Once when I had received Communion I was given to understand how his Father receives this most holy Body of Christ within our soul, present there where I understand and have seen that these divine Persons are; and I realized how much this offering of his Son pleases him, for he delights and finds joy in him" (*Testimonies* 57 [52]).

Window onto the World

For Teresa, Jesus opens also onto the world. Commitment to him means commitment to his cause. She identified this cause with the mission of her Church, which at root involved the conquest of evil in the world (see *Life* 32.6; *Foundations* 1.7). She asked her sisters to hold this mission as the raison d'être of all their prayer and asceticism. Jesus' friends, though few, must be good ones, who so resonate with his crucified love that they are wholly turned to the world he came to save (*Way* 1, 3). Hence, the style of her enclosed communities, small groups of women living in poverty and sisterhood, had an apostolic rationale. The nuns were to be free from dependency, preoccupation, and people-pleasing so that they could serve real issues. "The world is on fire. . . . No, my sisters, this is no time to be treating with God of matters of small importance" (*Way* 1.5).

They served Christ's cause, and furthered his Church, principally through prayer. But since this meant relationship, not mere ritual, it entailed a consistent lifestyle. "What kind of people will we have to *be?*" Teresa asked in the *Way of Perfection*, if prayer was really to serve the Church. In answer, she highlighted three virtues: fraternal love, mortification, and humility. With motherly finesse she discussed each (*Way* 4–15) and in so doing revealed her attentiveness to Jesus. For instance, fraternal love, which does not look for payoffs but gives itself, makes sacrifices, and so elicits love in the other, imitates "the captain of love," the "good lover," Jesus (*Way* 6.9; 7.4). His poverty, humility, freedom from dependence, and obedience through to death (*Way* 2; 12–15; 10; *Foundations* 5) were to encourage the sisters in their struggle to become a gospel community, a new "college of Christ" (*Way [Esc.]* 20.1).

Christ-like service defined the holiness of the seventh dwelling places. What was the point, Teresa asked, of all the mystical favors described so far? The Father can do us no greater "favor" than conform us with his Son, bestowing strength to imitate him in his suffering (*Castle* 7.4.4). "This is what prayer is for, my daughters; this is the point of this spiritual marriage: that it always give birth to deeds, deeds" (*Castle* 7.4.6). The aging Teresa, affectionate, keen-witted, a prodigy of courage and common sense, is proof of the rightness of her focus on the human Christ. And her communities, intended to be a fresh space for gospel living, would themselves display Jesus' transforming power.

Iain Matthew

See also: John of the Cross; Roman Catholicism; Spanish Christianity; Spirituality

References

Alvarez, Tomás. 1980. *Living with God: St. Teresa's Concept of Prayer.* Translated by Christopher O'Mahony and Dominica Horia. Manchester: Koinonia.

———. 1996. "Jesucristo en la experiencia de Santa Teresa." Pp. 1–43 in vol. 3 of *Estudios Teresianos*. Burgos: Editorial Monte Carmelo.

Goedt, Michel de. 1993. *Le Christ de Thérèse de Jésus*. Paris: Desclée.

McIntosh, Mark A. 1998. *Mystical Theology*. Malden, MA, and Oxford: Blackwell.

Teresa of Avila. 1985–1987. *The Collected Works of St. Teresa of Avila*. Translated by Kieran Kavanaugh and Otilio Rodriguez, OCD. Washington, DC: ICS.

Williams, Rowan. 1991. *Teresa of Avila*. London: Geoffrey Chapman.

Textual Criticism

This may be the first article on Jesus in textual criticism ever to be written. And so the first question is one of scope. The area to be explored should be the presentation of Jesus in the Gospels rather than the Christology of the early Church. As a matter of fact, the distinction is rather an artificial one, however, since the texts are received only through the medium of early Christian interpretation of Jesus as the Christ, that is, the chosen agent of God for our salvation. This interpretation may be searched for in two ways. The first is through an examination of the physical evidence of the manuscripts. The second is in the text contained by the manuscripts. After that, it will be necessary to explore the relationship between textual criticism and Christology. Finally, the significance of textual theory for the study of Jesus will be discussed.

The Physical Presentation

The most obvious source is illuminations. Much could be said, especially with regard to Byzantine miniatures. The reader is referred to the articles discussing the portrayal of Jesus in art and in icons. But it is worthwhile for this discussion to draw attention to one interesting feature of the sixth-century Rossano Gospels. The miniature of the story of the Good Samaritan depicts the Samaritan as Christ. This feature, described as unique by K. Weitzmann, provides a full theological interpretation of the passage. Its significance will become more fully apparent in a moment. Instead, I wish to discuss certain features of scribal practice.

The *Nomina Sacra*

Nomina sacra (sacred names) is a term used by paleographers to describe the practice in Greek and Latin Christian (and especially New Testament) manuscripts of writing certain words in an abbreviated form, with a horizontal line above them. In the earliest manuscripts, four are used: *Theos* (God), *Kurios* (Lord), *Iesous* (Jesus), and *Christos* (Christ). By and large, three evidently refer to Jesus. One of them, Kurios, has considerable significance, for it is found in the New Testament writers referring to God, to Jesus as Lord, and as a polite form of address to Jesus ("Lord" in the AV, often "Sir" in modern versions), and to various figures in parables. By treating all three forms as nomina sacra, the written texts place every reference to Jesus as Kurios on the same theological level as references to God. Moreover, in the visual distinctiveness of the phenomenon, the presence of Jesus stands out on the page. And stands out in the company of God. It is a strong visual claim for his status as within the story and yet above the story. This preeminence was lost when the canon of names was extended to include, not only *Uios* (Son), *Pneuma* (Spirit), and *Stauros* (Cross), but also *Anthropos* (man), *Ouranos* (Heaven), *Israel, Dauid,* and the like.

The presentation of the nomina sacra in purple manuscripts can be especially dramatic. These manuscripts use silver ink (even gold, as in the example of one magnificent ninth-century purple minuscule manuscript now in St. Petersburg, no. 565 in the list of Greek New Testament manuscripts) to be more easily read and more impressive. It looked splendid, and was certainly not neutral. The practice angered Jerome, who said that the Church would find Christ naked and hungry at the gate, not in the glitter.

The use of nomina sacra can have some other interesting theological results. At Hebrews 4.8, the Israelite leader Joshua, Iesous in Greek, is given in the nomen sacrum form in the famous fourth-century manuscript Codex Sinaiticus. It is hard not to suspect a typological intent, one that most modern interpreters would say was lacking from the author's thought. More significant still is the use of nomina sacra in Matthaean and Lucan parables featuring lords, for example, in those featuring the lord of the vineyard (Matt. 20.8); the lord of the house (Luke 14.21, 22); and the lord who distributed the talents (Matt. 25.19, 20ff.; Luke 19.15ff.). These examples do not necessarily occur in all manuscripts.

At one time I thought of these cases as due to the force of scribal habit, but I began to suspect that they may be interpretative, especially since there are also "lords" found written out in full. There may be an analogy between the nomina sacra and the practice in many Syriac manuscripts of adding "our Lord" where the name Jesus appears. Whatever the scribal motivation, the effect on the *reader* is to make these parables involving lords into stories in which there is a straight correspondence between the boss and the Christian Kurios. What about the *listener?* Was there any way in which a nomen sacrum (at least those in the original four) was marked by a response, a bowing of the head perhaps? It is perhaps noteworthy that in the temple service for Yom Kippur, at the point at which the high priest pronounced the divine name, those present bowed down.

Just as the space within which Jesus was worshiped changed with the Church's fortunes, from private room to grand basilica to Byzantine splendor or Gothic magnificence, so the copies of the Gospels changed. They began as simple papyrus codices. They became, at least on occasion, sumptuous parchment volumes with the Peace of Constantine. And in the Byzantine period they acquired a neat and convenient format, with a range of useful guides for the reader, illuminations of the evangelists, and a consistent and safe text form.

Textual Variation

This huge field may be divided into smaller groups:

1. Passages whose inclusion or removal add to or diminish information about Jesus in the Gospels. The larger examples are John 7.53–8.11, Luke 22.43–44, Luke 23.34, Mark 16.9–20, and Luke 6.4 D. Curiously enough, the first three of these belong among the most significant defining moments of history's perception of Jesus: a deeper justice towards a woman; his agony before death, receiving divine comfort; the prayer for his enemies' forgiveness.

It is hard to see this linkage as coincidence. It is more likely to be evidence of the way in which early Christianity responded to the Gospel stories and to the arguments about faith and practice that they implicitly contained or were seen to contain. At least the majority of these stories appear to have originated by the middle of the second century.

2. The history of harmonization. Down to the modern critical era, the

Gospels were extensively harmonized. In early Christianity, the existence of four divergent accounts of Jesus was rather embarrassing, since their differences were used as evidence by detractors of Christianity. On the whole, the tendency was to treat the four versions as a single account. In the middle of the second century, Tatian produced his Diatessaron, a harmony of the four Gospels into a single narrative. This was to prove enormously influential, both directly and through the many other harmonies in many tongues of the Middle Ages. In fact, it is fair to say that most people have been most familiar with a composite image of Jesus. For example, the birth narratives of Matthew and Luke and the prologue of John are taken as a sequence of complementary readings at most Christmas carol services. Until the introduction of the Common Lectionary in 1999, in England it has been only in the practice of reading the entire Passion narrative of a single evangelist in Holy Week that the coherence of the separate writers has been maintained in the lectionary. For nearly two centuries, however, critical scholarship has moved in a different direction. Since the editions of Karl Lachmann and Brooke Foss Westcott and Fenton John Anthony Hort (1881), harmonization has been to a considerable extent removed from the actual text, with the obvious corollary that the number of differences between the portrayals of Jesus in the four Gospels has increased significantly. The rule of thumb for editing the text is that the reading that is different from that of the other Gospels is more likely to be authentic. Thus, a small number of manuscripts preserve a different version of the Lord's Prayer in Luke 11.2–4 from Matthew 6.9–13, while the vast majority have very similar texts in both places. Only since 1881 has the distinctive Lucan form gained currency as the form found in most editions and translations.

The same Karl Lachmann separately produced convincing evidence for Marcan priority. This work led to the recognition that Mark was not (as had always previously been supposed) simply an abbreviated version of Matthew, but an independent voice. The hitherto unknown greater degree of variation from the other Gospels that was being found in manuscripts of Mark could be interpreted within this framework. In fact, the study of the distinctiveness of each Gospel has been an important contribution of modern scholarship. Within it, textual criticism has contributed in two ways: first with the raw materials, in the form of rediscovery of the variations, which, though often slight individually, have together made up the distinctive profile of each Gospel. Second, textual scholarship has more recently demonstrated how textual variation continued to arise from early Christian responses to the traditions about Jesus, so that the kinds of factors that led Matthew to revise Mark, and led Luke probably to revise both of them, also led later readers and copyists to modify the text further.

3. The third area spills over into Christology. It used to be claimed that textual variation did not influence any significant element of Christian belief, including beliefs about the person of Jesus. A single example shows how far this is from the case. At the baptism story in Luke 3.22, according to a manuscript copied in about 400 and some Latin witnesses, the words from heaven were "You are my Son, today I have begotten you." In all other wit-

nesses it is found in the form "You are my beloved Son, in you I am well pleased." There is a strong case for arguing that the former version was older but was displaced under orthodox influence because it played into the hands of the adoptianists.

In fact, it is difficult to separate theologically motivated variation from other kinds of variants, since the evangelists were writing under the influence of theological questions, and the texts were preserved in highly charged theological environments. Another example is the question whether Jesus was angry or compassionate at the plight of the leper (Mark 1.41). The anger, if it was original, could have been removed on either theological or moral grounds. Other passages that show signs of alteration on Christological grounds are:

Mark 1.1: insertion of title "Son of God" again avoids adoptianism at 1.11; Jesus was already God's Son.
Mark 15.34: "forsaken" changed to "reviled" in order to avoid separationism (that is, making a gap between Father and Son).
Luke 2.43: removal of reference to "his parents": Jesus had no human father.
John 1.18: "God" rather than "Son" seems to show a more advanced Christology.

Outside the Gospels, one of the most interesting readings is found in Hebrews 2.9, where the author originally wrote "apart from God," a reading surviving only in two Greek manuscripts. Because of the use to which this idea, paralleled elsewhere in the book, was put by separationists, it was changed to the anodyne "by the grace of God," a usage of the word "grace" atypical of the writing.

Textual Theory

Although it is sometimes assumed that the role of textual criticism is to recover the original text of a writing, there has never been agreement on this aim among practitioners in either the practice or the theory. With regard to the Gospels, it is generally agreed that it is not possible to recover a form of their texts older than the late second century, though it is arguable that the task of the editor of Paul is to reconstruct the oldest recoverable text of the collection of letters, not of the separate writings. On the theory there is especially fierce debate today. Textual scholars have interest in witnesses and text forms of all periods, and it is important to realize that all these witnesses and texts represent Jesus as he has been understood and portrayed at a particular time and in a certain place. This is true of every witness that we have, just as it is true of the original writings. The contribution of textual criticism is not to provide a window in time to an authentic original Jesus. It is not even to provide a window to four authentic portrayals of Jesus in four Gospels. It is to provide a window to an almost innumerable number of Jesuses in different manuscripts, and thus in different communities and theologies.

Conclusion

Textual criticism's contribution to the study of Jesus lies in the following areas.

1. The study of the Greek manuscripts and manuscripts of the versions in other tongues (especially Syriac, Latin, and Coptic as well as Gothic, Old Slavonic, Armenian, Ethiopic, and Georgian), showing how the narratives about Jesus were graphically presented in the early centuries and what impact those presentations had on views about him.

2. The study of variation between the witnesses, showing the sum of different interpretations of the Gospels and the relationship between them, and the theological and other reasons that gave rise to them.

3. The study of the history of the text, including the social and theological locations within which views of Jesus changed and developed, demonstrating that the oldest Gospels do not exist in a time capsule. The truth is very different. They have survived only through the medium of Christian interpretation of them.

D. C. Parker

See also: Adoptianism; Art; Icons and the Icon Tradition; Lord

References

Ehrman, B. D. 1993. *The Orthodox Corruption of Scripture*. New York: Oxford University Press.

Gamble, H. Y. 1995. *Books and Readers in the Early Church: A History of Early Christian Texts*. New Haven and London: Yale University Press.

Parker, D. C. 1997. *The Living Text of the Gospels*. Cambridge: Cambridge University Press.

Trobisch, David. 2000. *The First Edition of the New Testament*. Oxford: Oxford University Press.

Weitzmann, K. *Late Antique and Early Christian Book Illumination*. New York: George Braziller.

Williams, C. S. C. 1951. *Alterations to the Text of the Synoptic Gospels and Acts*. Oxford: Blackwell.

Theodore of Mopsuestia

See Antiochene Theology

Thomas, Gospel of

The Gospel of Thomas, cited occasionally by Hippolytus and Origen, was discovered in 1945 among the Nag Hammadi documents in Egypt. This document contains, by modern scholarly division, 114 sayings of Jesus. Its sayings come in several forms: proverbs and other wisdom sayings, parables, prophetic sayings, and very brief conversations. The Gospel of Thomas is the most important second-century noncanonical source we possess in the study of the historical Jesus.

About a quarter of the sayings in the Gospel of Thomas, typically the shortest ones, are virtually identical to Synoptic sayings. For example:

> The disciples said to Jesus, "Tell us what the Kingdom of Heaven is like." He answered them, "It is like a mustard seed, the smallest of all seeds. But when it falls on plowed ground, it grows into a large shrub and becomes a shelter for the birds of heaven" (20).
>
> Jesus said, "You see the sliver that is in your brother's eye, but you do not see the log in your own eye. When you take the log out of your eye, then you will see to remove the sliver from you brother's eye" (26).
>
> Jesus said, "Blessed are the poor, for yours is the Kingdom of Heaven" (54).

About one-half have partial parallels in the canonical Gospels. For example,

> And he said, "The [wise] man is like a wise fisherman who threw his net into the sea. When he drew it up from the sea, it was full of small fish. The fisherman found among them a large, good fish. He threw all the small fish back into the sea; with no trouble he chose the large fish. He who has ears to hear, let him hear" (8).
>
> Jesus said, "Behold, the sower went out. He filled his hand [with seed], and he threw. Some fell on the road. The birds came, and they gathered them up. Others fell on the rock and did not send roots into the earth and did not send ears toward heaven. Others fell among thorns. They choked the seed, and the worm ate [it]. And others fell on good earth, and it raised up good fruit to heaven. It bore sixty and one hundred twenty per measure" (9).

The final group, making up approximately one-quarter to one-third of the sayings, are manifestly gnosticizing sayings with a different theological outlook from the rest:

> The disciples said to Jesus, "Tell us how [the] end will occur." Jesus said, "Have you found the beginning that you search for the end? In the place of the beginning, the end will be. Blessed is he who will stand at the beginning, and he will know the end, and he will not taste death" (18).
>
> Jesus said, "If the flesh exists because of spirit, it is a miracle, but if spirit [exists] because of the body, it is a miracle of miracles. But I am amazed at how this great wealth established itself in this poverty" (29).
>
> Jesus said, "The images are manifest to man, and the light in them is hidden in the image of the light of the Father. He will not reveal himself, and his image will be hidden by his light." (83).
>
> Jesus said, "When you see your likeness, you rejoice. But when you see your images which came into being before you, [which] do not die nor manifest, how much will you bear!" (84).

The Gospel of Thomas has no Christological titles, no narrative material, and no reference within its sayings to any action of Jesus or any event in his life. It is dated after 70 and before c. 140, the date archaeologists have determined for its papyri. Within this range further precision is difficult, although most interpreters place its writing in the second century, understanding that many of its oral traditions are much older. Most place its composition in Syria, where traditions about the apostle Thomas, the fictional author of this book, were strong. It also shows a Jewish-Christian origin, with its praise of James the brother of Jesus:

> The disciples said to Jesus, "We know that you will leave us. Who will become our ruler?"" Jesus said, "Wherever you may be, go to James the righteous one. Heaven and earth came into being for him" (cf. also 27).

However, *Thomas* has since moved beyond this setting into Gentile Christianity:

> His disciples said to him, "Is circumcision profitable or not?" He said to them, "If it were profitable, the father would beget them circumcised from their mother. But true circumcision in the Spirit is completely useful" (53).

Of all the extracanonical gospels, the Gospel of Thomas is the one most likely to have a claim to preserve a significant number of authentic sayings of Jesus. The argument for the independence, and hence the value, of the traditions of Jesus' sayings in the Gospel of Thomas is based on three main factors. The first is genre: as a collection of sayings, the Gospel of Thomas represents the genre in which the early Jesus material is thought to have been collected and passed down, such as is found in Q (hypothetical source for Matthew and Luke). No such collections are to be found later than about A.D. 150, the sayings genre having been absorbed into the dialogue genre. So it is likely that the roots of the Gospel of Thomas are in an early collection that dates to the first century. The second argument is the order of the sayings, which in the Gospel of Thomas is independent of the order of the Synoptic Gospels. The order of sayings in the Gospel of Thomas is due to its catchword composition (typical of oral tradition), completely nonnarrative structure, and other factors. The differing order makes it unlikely that Thomas was literarily dependent on the Synoptics. Occasionally the Gospel of Thomas and Luke agree in order against Mark, but this probably does not mean that Thomas used Luke; it can be explained as a variant of the Q tradition common to Luke and Thomas. Third, a history-of-traditions argument states that the Gospel of Thomas often gives the sayings of Jesus in an earlier form than that found in the Synoptics. For example, the parables of Jesus are far less allegorized than the parallels in the Synoptics, as in the parable of the wicked husbandman:

> He said: "A good man had a vineyard. He rented it to some farmers so that they could work it; he would receive its profits from them. He sent his servant to get from the farmers the profits of the vineyard. They seized his servant, beat him, and almost killed him. The servant went back and he told his master. His master said, 'Perhaps they did not know him.' He sent another servant,

> and the farmers beat him also. Then the master sent his son. He said, 'Perhaps they will respect my son.' Those farmers seized him, and they killed him, because they knew he was the heir of the vineyard. He who has ears, let him hear" (65).

The form in Thomas is simpler and shorter than in the Synoptic form (Mark 12.1–12 and parallels), has no allusions to Isaiah 5.1–2, and shows no trace of allegory. Thus, it is arguably closer to the earliest probable form of the parable as given by Jesus.

The treatment of the sayings of Jesus in the Gospel of Thomas is governed by its theological aims, which can be characterized as "semi-Gnostic," or "gnosticizing," that is, on the way to Gnosticism (sayings 18, 29, 83–84). Not yet present are the formal Gnostic cosmology and mythology that we see in full-blown Gnostic systems of the second century. Also, the short narrative contexts of a few sayings (22, 60, 100, below; 12 and 55, above) show that Thomas does not have an overall postresurrectional setting, as almost all other Gnostic gospels do.

> Jesus saw babies being nursed. He said to his disciples, "These babies being nursed are like those who enter the Kingdom." They said to him, "We are children, [and] shall we enter the kingdom?" Jesus said to them, "When you make the two one, and when you make the inner as the outer and the outer as the inner and the upper as the lower, so that you will make the male and the female into a single one, so that the male will not be the male and the female [not] be female; when you make eyes in place of an eye, and a hand in place of a hand, and a foot in the place of a foot, [and] an image in place of an image, then shall you enter [the kingdom]" (22).

> [They saw] a Samaritan carrying a lamb; he was going to Judea. He said to his disciples, "Why does he carry the lamb?" They said to him, "That he may kill it and eat it." He said to them, "As long as it is alive he will not eat it, but only when he has killed it and it has become a corpse." They said, "Otherwise he cannot do it." He said to them, "Seek a place for yourselves in rest, lest you become a corpse and be eaten" (60).

> They showed Jesus a gold coin, and they said to him, "Caesar's men demand taxes from us." He said to them, "Give Caesar's things to Caesar, give God's things to God, and give to me what is mine" (100).

Jesus is exclusively a revealer of secret teaching who brings salvation by his teaching alone. As the first saying of *Thomas* relates, "Anyone who finds the interpretation of these words will not taste death." And the world and the human body are unqualifiedly and irredeemably evil:

> If you do not fast [against] the world, you will not find the Kingdom. If you do not keep the Sabbath as the Sabbath, you shall not see the Father (27).

> Jesus said, "The heavens and the earth will roll up in your presence, and he who lives by the Living One will not see death" (111).

As in later Gnostic systems, femaleness is equated with fallenness, and "every woman who makes herself male will enter the kingdom of God" (114). This today is the most controversial saying in this document, and for its interpretation should be compared with other gender-symbolic sayings such as saying 22 (above) and this one:

> Simon Peter said to them, "Let Mary leave us, because women are not worthy of Life." Jesus said, "Look, I shall guide her so that I will make her male, so that she also may become a living spirit, being like you males. For every woman who makes herself male will enter the Kingdom of Heaven" (114).

The eschatology is "realized"; the kingdom of God is beyond time and place, yet always present, and people enter it by self-knowledge:

> Jesus said, "If the ones who lead you say, 'There is the kingdom, in heaven,' then the birds of heaven shall go before you. If they say to you, 'It is in the sea,' then the fish shall go before you. Rather, the kingdom is within you and outside you. If you know yourselves, then you will be known, and you will know that you are sons of the living Father. But if you do not know yourselves, then you are in poverty, and you are poverty" (3).

> Jesus said, "Blessed are the solitary and the chosen, because you will find the Kingdom. Because you come from it, you will return there" (49).

> Jesus said, "If they say to you, 'Where did you come from?' say to them, 'We come from the light, where the light came into being through itself. It stood and reveals itself in their image.' If they say to you, '[Who] are you?' say to them, 'We are his sons and we are chosen of the living Father.' If they ask you, 'What is the sign of your Father who is in you?' say to them, 'It is movement and repose'" (50).

> His disciples said to him, "On what day will the Kingdom come?" [He said,] "It will not come by expectation. They will not say, 'Look here,' or, 'Look there,' but the Kingdom of the Father is spread out on the earth and men do not see it" (113).

Discipleship is an individual, not a community matter; the "you" in the *Gospel of Thomas* is typically singular, while in the Synoptics it is typically plural. The individual must journey through this life by rejecting all ties to possessions, to family, and to formal religious acts such as fasting, prayer, sacrifice, cleansing, and circumcision:

> His disciples asked him, "Do you want us to fast, and how shall we pray, and shall we give alms, and what food regulations shall we keep?" Jesus said, "Do not lie, and do not do what you hate, because all is revealed before Heaven. Nothing is hidden that will not be revealed, and nothing is covered that shall remain without being revealed" (6).

> Jesus said to them, "If you fast, you will bring sin upon yourselves and, if you pray, you will be condemned and, if you give alms, you will do evil to your spir-

its. If you enter any country and wander through [its] regions, if they receive you, eat whatever they set before you. Heal the sick among them. For that which goes into your mouth will not defile you, but that which comes out of your mouth will defile you" (14).

Jesus said, "Be wanderers" (42).

Jesus said, "He who does not hate his father and his mother cannot be my disciple, and [he who] does not hate his brothers and his sisters and [does not] carry in my way will not be worthy of me" (55).

Jesus said, "Why do you wash the outside of the cup? Do you not know that he who made the inside is also he who made the outside?" (89).

The disciples said to him, "Your brothers and your mother are standing outside." He said to them, "Those here who do the will of my Father are my brothers and mother; they will enter the Kingdom of my Father" (99).

"He who does not hate his [father] and his mother in my way will not be able to be my [disciple], and he who does [not] love his father and his mother in my way, will not be able to be my [disciple], for my mother . . . [?], but [my] true [mother] gave me life" (101).

They said [to him], "Come, let us pray today, and let us fast." Jesus said, "Why? What sin have I committed, or by what have I been conquered? But after the bridegroom has left the Bridal Chamber, then let them fast and pray" (104).

The Gospel of Thomas offers much to the study of the historical Jesus. It does not offer anything of narrative value on the life, death, and resurrection of Jesus; however, its rich collection of sayings, many of which may go back to early stages of Jesus tradition, sheds light on parallel passages in the Synoptic Gospels. Many scholars see an independent stream of tradition in these sayings, and this is the primary value of Thomas in Jesus research. But these sayings must be analyzed individually, and it is hard to draw an overall judgment on their value. Their distance from Jesus, theologically and temporally, must also be taken into account. Obviously, sayings that reflect an explicit gnosticizing tendency will usually be discounted. What remains is of potential value in understanding the teaching of Jesus, its individual sayings, and overall meaning. For example, the lack of Christological titles in the Gospel of Thomas may indicate that Jesus did not claim these for himself. Also, if we eliminate the Gnostic overtones from Jesus' teachings to his followers, more evidence comes forward for the radical itinerant charismatics who preached the earliest Jesus message. The radical social stance of some segments of early Christianity may have found a new home in gnosticizing Christianity in the second century.

Robert E. Van Voorst

See also: Gnosticism; Jesus, Family of; Jesus, Parables of; Jesus Seminar; Kingdom of God; Origen

References

Chilton, Bruce. 1982. "The Gospel of Thomas as a Source of Jesus' Teaching." Pp. 155–175 in *Jesus Traditions outside the Gospels*. Edited by David Wenham. Sheffield: Sheffield University Press.

Franzmann, Majella. 1996. *Jesus in the Nag Hammadi Writings*. Edinburgh: T. & T. Clark.

Meyer, Marvin. 1988. *The Nag Hammadi Library in English*. 3d ed. San Francisco: Harper.

Tuckett, Christopher. 1986. *Nag Hammadi and the Gospel Tradition*. Edinburgh: T. & T. Clark.

Van Voorst, Robert E. 2000. *Jesus outside the New Testament: An Introduction to the Ancient Evidence*. Grand Rapids, MI and Cambridge, UK: Eerdmans.

Tillich, Paul (1886–1965)

Paul Johannes Tillich, a German philosopher-theologian who fled the Nazi regime in 1933 to teach in the United States, understood the historical person Jesus of Nazareth not as the figure reconstructed on scanty evidence by scholars but as the one received by his disciples, and by the Church, as the Christ (that is, the object of faith). We, too, are called to acceptance of, transformation by, and participation in "the new being in Jesus as the Christ." Tillich developed this Christology in the context of a theology of existence influenced by F. W. J. Schelling, Søren Kierkegaard, and Martin Heidegger, with references to depth psychology and a theology of culture. The fullest statement of his position is found in his three-volume *Systematic Theology*, published in 1948, 1957, and 1963, respectively.

The historical actuality of Jesus Christ is critical to Tillich's thought. He wrote: "If the factual element in the Christian event were denied, the foundation of Christianity would be denied" (1957a, 107). But the term "historical Jesus" can have two meanings. It can, first, mean the person who can be determined by historical and critical means to stand behind the Gospel reports. But the documents give little reliable information about the actual character and life of the one thus portrayed. What information exists is fragmentary, hypothetical, subject to criticism as regards the methods of obtaining it, and tending to change in particulars as well as in essentials from one researcher to the next. At best one can achieve some degree of probability. Or, second, the term "historical Jesus" can mean that the event in which Jesus is received as the Christ must include, as a matter of faith, a factual element not dependent on historical research. Faith points to a factual transformation of reality in the personal life standing at the center of the New Testament's depiction.

But Tillich rejected Kierkegaard's famous statement that it is sufficient for the Christian faith nakedly to assert, without further detail, that in A.D. 1–30 God sent his Son to earth. For Tillich, the power that has created and preserved the community of the New Being is not reducible to such an abstract statement about its appearance. That power is conveyed in a rich "picture" of him in whom the power has appeared. No special trait of this picture can be verified with certainty. But there is an *analogia imaginis* between the picture and the actual personal life that lies behind it. It was this personal reality, when encountered by the disciples, that generated the picture. This picture, elaborated in the scriptural narratives, still mediates the transforming power of the New Being (that is, the new life available to believers). As Tillich wrote, "[T]he mediated material which is given to us in the biblical picture of the Christ is the result of the reception of the New Being and its transforming power on the part of the first witnesses" (1957a, 115). It follows, then, that Jesus is the Christ in virtue of being received as such by the Church.

The notion of a "picture" of the historical figure behind the Gospels opened the way for Tillich to make ample use of the symbolism this picture contains. "Symbol" became a key category in this writer's thought. He distinguished symbols from mere signs and explained that true symbols participate in the realities they convey. Christological symbols are thus the expressive medium in which the historical fact called Jesus of Nazareth is received by those who consider him to be the Christ. Symbols must be understood as symbols. They lose their meaning if taken literally. Symbols should be criticized only on the basis of their power to express what they are supposed to express.

This approach saves the riches of the biblical text, not to speak of the whole tradition of Christian and other art, for the believer, and in the process authorizes imaginative rather than merely philosophical preaching. Tillich thus offered us, not a "demythologization" of biblical discourse, but a "deliteralization." Myths are an important kind of symbol and they have their place in conveying the message. This move distinguishes Tillich's method from Rudolf Bultmann's. Bultmann moved from the bare assertion that "God has acted" to the expectation of our radical response in faith, seemingly ignoring the expressive power of the mythic and symbolic. "Demythologization," for Tillich, meant the mistaken cancellation of myth altogether as a means of religious expression, depriving religion of its language and silencing the experience of the holy.

One may illustrate the power of symbol at work in Tillich's reading of the Cross and Resurrection narratives. The moment of the disciples' acceptance of Jesus as the Christ is also the moment of his rejection by the powers of history. He who is the Christ has to die for his acceptance of that title. And those who continue to call him the Christ must assert the paradox that he who is supposed to overcome existential estrangement must participate in it and its self-destructive consequences, yet not be bound by those consequences.

Cross and Resurrection are symbols indeed, yet they are grounded in historical events. Tillich wrestled with the resulting paradoxes. "Is it perhaps wiser," he asked, "to follow the suggestions of those scholars who understand the Resurrection as a symbolic interpretation of the Cross without any kind of objective reality?" Or could one say that "in the minds of the disciples and of the writers of the New Testament the Cross is both an event and a symbol and that the Resurrection is both a symbol and an event . . . ? The certainty that he who is the bringer of the new eon cannot finally have succumbed to the powers of the old eon made the experience of the Resurrection the decisive test of the Christ-character of Jesus of Nazareth" (1957a, 153–154).

The Jesus so pictured becomes the Christ by being received as a response to questions implied in human existence. Here Tillich deployed his "method of correlation," which he had developed in the first volume of the *Systematic Theology*. Questions inherent in the human situation are formulated in such a way that they call forth theological answers. Theological responses then interpret the deposit of Christian truth so as to respond to these existential questions. Questions and answers relate to one another in mutual interdependence.

Yet the answers cannot be *derived* from the questions. The *substance* of the answer is independent of the question because the answer derives from revelatory experience. The answer, "the Christ," cannot be created by man. But the *form* of the theological answer is *not* independent of the form of the question. Man can receive the answer and express it according to the way he has asked for it in the first place.

The fundamental human question seeking theological response has to do with anxiety in confronting our finitude. Such anxiety is the product of an "existential shock" at the contemplation of the possibility of our not-being, that is to say, our contingency. Finitude is the condition that existentially unites being with not-being. We would, of course, not form a notion of finitude were there not in us already the notion of an infinity beyond our grasp. Hence we come to an existential awareness of "that which concerns us ultimately." Being able to name that which is of "ultimate concern" places us on the brink of naming the "ground of being": in Christian terms, "God."

Yet the movement from "ultimate concern" to naming "God" is not easy. The expression "God above God," appearing in *The Courage to Be* (1952), "takes seriously the radical doubt experienced by many people. It gives one the courage of self-affirmation even in the extreme state of radical doubt. In such a state the God of both religious and theological language disappears. But something remains, namely, the seriousness of that doubt in which meaning within meaninglessness is affirmed. The source of this affirmation of meaning within meaninglessness, of certitude within doubt, is not the God of traditional theism but the 'God above God,' the power of being which works through those who have no name for it, not even the name God" (1957a, 12).

Tillich thus affirmed that God is "being-itself," not *a* being among other beings. God is the "ground of being," the foundation of the very being of each being. We have our power to be by participation in the ground of being. We are able to speak about God because there are analogies between our finite being and God's infinite being. Tillich's doctrine here resembles the *analogia entis* of St. Thomas, except for the vital difference that, in Tillich, God is not merely the necessary being, or the being than which no greater can be conceived, standing at the apex of a great chain of being. God, rather, is the unexpected, unpredictable response to the question implied in our finitude.

Tillich reserved the uppercase "G" for the dimension of transcendence *in* the courageous encounter with this question, which always has a concrete, historical dimension. The transcendent *meets* us in Jesus Christ yet does not deliver itself over to us. There is no being-to-being relationship here. God remains God. At this point we meet the basis of Tillich's affirmation of a Trinitarian monotheism as well as his dynamic, existential version of what Chalcedon called, in an inevitable but not wholly successful appropriation of Greek categories, the two natures united in the one person of Jesus Christ.

For Tillich, patristic formulations fail to some degree both in their substance and in their conceptual form. Yet he thought it unfair to criticize the Church Fathers for their use of Greek concepts. No others were available at the time. And at least the notion of *Logos* served them well. But now the Church faces the task of reconstructing its Christology: "The assertion that Jesus as the Christ is the personal unity of a divine and a human nature must be replaced by the assertion that in Jesus as the Christ the eternal unity of God and man has become historical reality" (1957a, 148).

Lewis S. Mudge

See also: Aquinas, Thomas; Bultmann, Rudolf; Chalcedon; Christology, Modern; Jesus, Death of; Kierkegaard, Søren; Messiah; Resurrection

References

Adams, James Luther, Wilhelm Pauck, and Roger L. Shinn, eds. 1985. *The Thought of Paul Tillich*. San Francisco: Harper and Row.

Kegley, Charles W., and Robert W. Bretall, eds. 1964. *The Theology of Paul Tillich*. New York: Macmillan.

Kelsey, David H. 1967. *The Fabric of Paul Tillich's Theology*. New Haven and London: Yale University Press.

Tillich, Paul. 1948, 1957a, 1963. *Systematic Theology*. 3 vols. Chicago: University of Chicago Press.

———. 1952. *The Courage to Be*. New Haven and London: Yale University Press.

———. 1957b. *Dynamics of Faith*. New York: Harper and Row.

Torrance, T. F. (b. 1913)

T. F. Torrance was born in China in 1913 of Church of Scotland missionary parents. Subsequently he became professor of Christian dogmatics at the University of Edinburgh (1950–1979), but he never lost the missionary, almost pietistic, outlook of his early years. He has maintained throughout his life the Christocentrism of his early teacher, H. R. Mackintosh, and Karl Barth, whose *Church Dogmatics* (1932) he helped to translate from 1956 to 1976. A student and later a friend of Karl Barth's, Torrance became convinced that Barth was the greatest Christian theologian since John Calvin. With Barth, Torrance has sought to insist upon a complete oneness between Jesus Christ and the inner being of God, a theme that resounds throughout all his writings.

Although clearly located in the Reformed tradition, and with a particular debt to Calvin, Torrance has written extensively on the Greek Fathers, especially Athanasius and the Alexandrian school. A staunch defender of

Athanasius, Torrance regards the Nicene *homoousion* ("of one substance") as the cornerstone of Christian theology, securing the genuine revelation of God in Jesus Christ, as against Arian dualism. This is explained in a doctrine of the Trinity that portrays the monarchy of God the Father as located in the mysterious *perichoresis* (or "co-inherence") of all three persons. He prefers to reject both the late Orthodox distinction between the energies and essence of God and the Cappadocian location of the person of the Father as the source or origin of the Son and Spirit. In this way, Torrance claims to have overcome the older antagonisms over the Filioque clause in the Nicene Creed. In proceeding from the being of the Father, the Holy Spirit proceeds from the one being which all three persons fully share, together and separately, in a holistic perichoresis. The immanent and economic Trinities are thus one: by God alone may God be known, to cite an expression that Torrance often employs, and which he derives from Athanasius and Irenaeus.

Torrance was well aware of the limits of human understanding in these matters and has also written widely on questions of hermeneutics and theological method. There is an emphasis here upon an epistemological realism, but subject always to the primacy of worship in Christian knowledge and experience.

His interest in the philosophy of realism led him into a deep debate with the philosophy of science, which he regarded as providing a bulwark against both the objectivizing positivism and the subjectivizing existentialism, extremes he detected in much twentieth-century theology. *Theological Science* (1969a) established Torrance's reputation and set the agenda for much of his later writing. He developed a fascination with modern physics, particularly the field theories of electromagnetism and gravitation. Torrance became convinced that there were deep links between the patristic exploration of Trinitarian relations and their created analogues in the field theory of modern physics. Just as patristic theology sought through the doctrine of the Trinity to overcome the dualism between God and the world, which was a commonplace of Greek philosophy, so modern physics had overcome the Newtonian dualisms between space, time, and physical events, that is, between mathematics and physics.

Torrance regards the constancy of the speed of light as the scientific equivalent to the homoousion: the uncreated invariance of God's eternal being. The rationality of the created world, as brought to expression by scientists, mirrors in a contingent way the rationality of God. Science, for Torrance, has a redemptive hue, as the ministry of reconciliation meets the wider creation. The scientist is seen almost as high priest of creation. The knowability of the created world parallels the inherent, if always mysterious, knowability of God.

The scientist-philosopher Michael Polanyi provided Torrance with a metaphysics in which these theological themes could be brought to expression. Although emphatically a realist—science genuinely expresses the nature of created reality—Polanyi insisted that scientific concepts were always revisable and had an inherent personal element embedded in them, due to the deep structures of nature, to which science could only ever approximate. For Polanyi this meant that science was necessarily a communal activity, as the extravagance of one scientist was limited by his responsibility to others in the scientific community. For Torrance this situation exactly mirrors the proper ecclesial and doxological context of theology.

By relating patristic theology, understood from within the Reformed tradition, to the science of Michael Faraday and Albert Einstein, and the social metaphysics of Polanyi, Torrance has asserted a proper if subsidiary place for natural theology within a Barthian universe. Many have seen this as his greatest achievement. His book *Space, Time and Incarnation* (1969b) sought to expose the use of outmoded container notions of space, from Aristotle to Newton, in sacramental and incarnational theology. These underlay the Reformation disputes on the sacraments, both between Protestants and Catholics, and within Protestantism itself. Although theologically conservative by instinct and conviction, Torrance rejected the modern phenomenon of fundamentalism as based on an empiricist rationalism that science itself was now abandoning.

The missionary zeal with which Torrance has addressed this broad canvas has brought both admirers and critics to a sharper degree than is inspired by most modern theologians. The critics have pointed to the uncertain transference of scientific models to theology and the limited tradition of the philosophy of science upon which he has relied. Others would like to have seen a wider application of Torrance's methodology to the dogmas of theology themselves, and less concentration upon methodological and hermeneutical issues. This direction might have resulted in greater revision to the theologies of Athanasius, and especially Calvin, than Torrance was instinctively prepared to consider. It is significant that Torrance is largely silent in relation to those areas of Barth's theology where Barth most explicitly set out a different understanding from that of Calvin. The exception is Barth's sacramental theology, where Torrance was highly critical, from a more traditional Reformed perspective. Torrance at this point even accused Barth of the dualism between God and the world that he believed Barth had generally succeeded in avoiding, but which had regularly beset modern theology.

Peter R. Forster

See also: Alexandrian Theology; Barth, Karl; Calvin, John; Creeds; Eucharist; Holy Spirit; Nicea; Orthodox Tradition

References

Primary

Torrance, T. F. 1969a. *Theological Science*. Oxford: Oxford University Press. 2d ed.; 1996, Edinburgh: T. & T. Clark.

———. 1969b. *Space, Time and Incarnation*. Oxford: Oxford University Press.

———. 1981. *Divine and Contingent Order*. Oxford: Oxford University Press.

———. 1984. *Transformation and Convergence in the Frame of Knowledge*. Belfast: Christian Journals.

———. 1996. *The Christian Doctrine of God*. Edinburgh: T. & T. Clark.

Secondary

McGrath, Alister E. 1999. *T. F. Torrance: An Intellectual Biography*. Edinburgh: T. & T. Clark.

Transfiguration

The earliest appearance of the episode in the life of Jesus traditionally called "the Transfiguration" comes in the Gospel of Mark at 9.2–8. There are parallel versions, differing in detail but not in substance, at the comparable points in Matthew (17.1–8) and Luke (9.28–36). It is then to Mark that we should look in the first place for a sense of its meaning. Apart from the closely related baptism of Jesus at 1.9–11, it is virtually unparalleled in its content within the life of Jesus in its supernatural character (but see the mysterious walking on the water in Mark 6.45–52); therefore it is likely that it was seen as rich in significance. That view is strengthened when we recognize that the account is reminiscent of OT stories in the lives of the great servants of God, those who had been crucial as intermediaries between God and his people. The notable examples are those of Moses, above all, at Exodus 24.12–18, and the theophany to Isaiah (6.1–8), and in some ways the heavenly vision of Elisha at 2 Kings 2.9–12. For such great ones, there was a ready path of communication with God. In itself, then, the story is at root an affirmation of Jesus' central place in God's great purpose.

Such a story is, so to speak, made desirable in the context of the largely unrecognized character of Jesus as presented in the general flow of Mark. That lack of recognition, at least with regard to the real nature of his mission and destiny, is even true of his closest followers, as is demonstrated by the immediately preceding episode of Peter's failure to accept the coming death of Jesus as something he must undergo.

The manifestation of divine "glory" is characteristic of stories of this kind. The sense is of light and splendor, that which shows conclusively the status of the one who manifests it—whether a great king or even God himself (as in the OT examples). Here, Jesus himself is, as it were, clothed with the glory of God, communicated to him as God's "Son," his fully accredited agent and representative. In this way, the story reasserts the message of the baptism, which virtually begins Mark's narrative and established for us his understanding of Jesus, and also transcends it, going a step further in its assertion of Jesus' true role.

It is typical of Mark to show that even such a sight scarcely has the desired effect as far as the three disciple-witnesses are concerned—their plan to build booths or shelters seems fatuous, or perhaps it is meant as a mistaken attempt to make permanent that which is, for the time being, only a signal of the future. Matthew (17.6–8) makes them more responsive: they are moved to venerate and are rewarded for their devotion by Jesus ("Rise, and have no fear"). It is also possible that the booths are meant to refer us to the Jewish Feast of Booths (or Tabernacles), commemorating Israel's wandering in the wilderness, where the people were led by pillars of cloud and light, means of God's guidance.

In any case, the story also goes beyond the baptism in making clear that God gives to Jesus a role akin to and apparently above that of Moses and Elijah, supreme mediators of God's purposes to Israel and standing for the Law and Prophecy, respectively, twin pillars of the people's life and identity. This allusion must surely be the core of Mark's message in the episode, and it is made much more explicit in the Gospel of Matthew, with his numerous examples of Jesus both fulfilling the prophets and building upon the Mosaic law. In both Matthew and Luke, it is not hard to see the Transfiguration as a kind of foreshadowing of the Resurrection stories, where Jesus' appearances have a similar miraculous character and validate him; in Mark, lacking such stories, it may appear as a kind of substitute for the discerning.

It is often said that in the Gospel of John, where the story does not occur (though see 12.27–30 for what may be a reminiscence of it), it is absent because the whole depiction of Jesus is suffused with "glory" from start to finish. It is certainly the case that glory is one of John's key words, pointing us to Jesus' reality as God's reproduction on earth, in a relationship that is now accessible to us, and so making his glory, or God-given splendor (albeit visible only to the eye of faith), available also to us. This language is one of John's chief ways of making his central doctrinal case: that the shared life and reality of Father and Son are, by his love, opened up to all those who will receive them (see, for example, 1.14; 2.11; 17.22).

There is not much sign that the Transfiguration was reflected upon in early Christianity, though the theme of glory, together with its relationship to Moses' reception of the Law on the holy mountain (mountains are everywhere the scene of theophanies), had already been established in the writing of Paul: see 2 Corinthians 3.7–18, where the contrast is between the fading splendor of Moses' face, when he was in proximity to, and then left, the divine presence, and the ever-growing and permanent splendor now open to Christians. In other words, the theme provides Paul with a striking image, and he constantly draws the contrast between the dispensation associated with Moses and that now available as a result of Christ. This interpretation is not so far from the sense that Mark's story would carry.

There is, however, one passage in early Christian writing that does reflect on the story in the first three Gospels: 2 Peter 1.16–21 has its own different thoughts on the subject. Written in the persona of Peter the leading apostle, whose behavior in Mark's story was so typically unsatisfactory, the passage sees the event on the mountain pointing ahead, as prophecy, to the future consummation assured to Jesus' people. It gives a message of hope and confidence. And, in its character as an event, it enables the writer to use it to counter other smart tales that his readers will have heard. Its role now is to help keep Christians on the true path. In this way, this probably pseudonymous writing is, like others from the later NT period, concerned by all means to fight off false versions of the truth that has been committed to the true followers of the Lord, and the Transfiguration story serves as the vehicle for the message.

Leslie Houlden

See also: Mark, Gospel of; Son of God

References

Chiltern, B. D. 1987. *God in Strength*. Sheffield: Sheffield Academic Press.
Ramsey, A. M. 1949. *The Glory of God and the Transfiguration of Christ*. London: SPCK.

Trinity

See Holy Spirit; Liturgy; Nicea; Second Person of the Trinity

Troeltsch, Ernst (1865–1923)

Among theologians Ernst Troeltsch remains the foremost advocate of a thoroughly historical approach to the figure of Jesus. As a Christian thinker, Troeltsch wished to affirm Jesus' enduring religious significance. But he also insisted that theology must come to terms with what he called "historicism": the realization that our ethical and religious norms are products of particular historical contexts and that we therefore cannot assume they are universally binding. Troeltsch attempted to reconcile these two convictions by appealing to the impact of the personality of Jesus and by insisting that communal religious life requires the focus and inspiration that only a historical figure can provide. At least for Christians, that figure is Jesus.

Troeltsch was not only a theologian but also a philosopher, historian, and pioneer sociologist of religion. Since his intellectual interests were so broad, he devoted a relatively small proportion of his work to questions of Christology. But insofar as he remained a theologian, he could hardly avoid discussing the significance of Jesus. Along with many nineteenth-century thinkers, Troeltsch rejected the traditional Christology of the Councils of Nicea (A.D. 325) and Chalcedon (A.D. 451), which he regarded as internally incoherent, incompatible with the historical method he advocated for theology, and unjustifiably exclusivist in its deification of Jesus. But while insisting on a rigorously historical approach to Jesus, Troeltsch did not think Christianity could be based on particular, allegedly extraordinary facts about its founder. For it is of the very nature of historical research to deprive such facts of their apparently extraordinary character. First, the historian understands Jesus as a product of his own time and place, namely, the world of first-century Palestinian Judaism. Jesus' ethical teaching, for instance, was strongly (even "one-sidedly") apocalyptic in tone (Troeltsch 1991b, 276), a fact that Troeltsch first confronted reluctantly but was eventually able to regard positively. Second, the historian regards the origin of Christianity as no different in principle from the origin of other religions. Christianity must now be understood within the context of the history of religions; it must measure its claims against the similar claims made by other religious communities. Jesus may be a unique historical figure, as all figures of history are, but he is "cut of the same cloth" (as it were) as the founders of other great religions and must be understood by analogy with them.

Having recognized the limits imposed by our modern historical consciousness, Troeltsch attempted to reaffirm Christianity's traditional veneration of the figure of Jesus. Echoing the very followers of his Göttingen teacher Albrecht Ritschl (1822–1889), whom he so often criticized, Troeltsch first of all appealed to the marvelous personality of Jesus, which he saw as the true point of origin of Christianity and the ongoing foundation of Christian faith. In *The Absoluteness of Christianity* (1929), for instance, Troeltsch claimed that among religious teachers Jesus is unique in his appeal to the unconditional will of God as it is known spontaneously in the human heart. In an essay on "Historical and Dogmatic Method in Theology," he wrote that, although in one sense Jesus is part of the spiritual history of humanity, in another sense he breaks through its usual limitations, insofar as the goals for which he strives are transcendent goals (Troeltsch 1977).

Troeltsch argued that a theological focus on the personality of Jesus is compatible with a historical approach to Christianity. It is true that the personality of Jesus lies hidden beneath the layers of early Christian tradition that constitute the New Testament. But we can still know enough about the historical Jesus to sustain Christian faith. In any case, Troeltsch insisted, Christian faith is not based on the historical Jesus alone; we fully understand Jesus' personality only through its impact on later generations. In our own time, believers may legitimately create images of Christ that answer current concerns, images that are related to but not identical with a historical depiction of Jesus. Finally, the bridge between history and theology was provided by Troeltsch's idealist metaphysics, which he saw as inseparable from Christian thought. If history as a whole is "a disclosure of the divine reason" (Troeltsch 1991a, 27), then the insights achieved by key religious personalities are nothing less than divine revelation. The adoption of an idealist metaphysics is itself an act of faith, but one that Troeltsch argued was philosophically defensible.

The second major theme in Troeltsch's discussions of Jesus is developed in the one extended essay he wrote on this topic, entitled "The Significance of the Historical Existence of Jesus for Faith" (Troeltsch 1991a). Troeltsch admitted that the modern doctrine of redemption does not, strictly speaking, require the figure of Jesus. In Troeltsch's thought it is God himself, rather than Jesus, who is appropriately described as Redeemer. But he argued that Jesus remains important, not just because of the impact of his personality on the individual, but also because of the communal nature of religion. Religion requires a communal cult, the focus of which is generally the founding personality of the religion. This is not a theological necessity, but it is a law of "social psychology." Moreover, a mythical figure will not do: believers need the assurance that "a real man thus lived, struggled, believed and conquered" (Troeltsch 1977, 197).We may not know much about Jesus, but we do know enough to grant us this assurance.

The dialectical theologians of the twentieth century, led by Karl Barth (1886–1968), were dismissive of a theology that rests on such apparently flimsy arguments. It is true that Troeltsch was much better at highlighting the difficulties facing Christianity than he was at solving them. But the difficulties with which he grappled were not his alone; they face anyone who confronts the challenge of history to Christian faith. Despite the often violent theological reaction to Troeltsch's work, the questions he raised have not yet been satisfactorily answered.

Gregory W. Dawes

See also: Barth, Karl; Chalcedon; Jesus as a Historical Figure; Nicea

References

Coakley, Sarah. 1988. *Christ without Absolutes: A Study of the Christology of Ernst Troeltsch*. Oxford: Clarendon.

Troeltsch, Ernst. 1972 [1929]. *The Absoluteness of Christianity and the History of Religions*. 3d ed. Translated by David Reid. Library of Philosophy and Theology. London: SCM.

———. 1977. *Ernst Troeltsch: Writings on Theology and Religion*. Translated and edited by Robert Morgan and Michael Pye. London: Duckworth.

———. 1991a. *Religion in History: Essays Translated by James Luther Adams and Walter F. Bense*. Edited by James Luther Adams and Walter F. Bense. Edinburgh: T. & T. Clark.

———. 1991b. *The Christian Faith*. Translated by Garrett E. Paul. Fortress Texts in Modern Theology. Minneapolis: Fortress.

V

Vermes, Geza (b. 1924)

Geza Vermes is a native of Hungary, the child of a Jewish family who was ordained as a Roman Catholic priest, escaped to the West in 1946, and eventually became an English academic and, for the past almost forty years, a lecturer and subsequently professor at the University of Oxford. Over the years he returned more and more to his Jewish roots. His greatest achievement has been to make known, edit, and translate the Dead Sea Scrolls. This, and explicating the life of the Qumran community in the period around the turn of the eras, has been his claim to fame.

But he is also widely known for his writings on Jesus of Nazareth. Indeed, he has been perhaps the foremost influence in recent years, and in current academic circumstances, in getting across the lesson of the Jewishness of Jesus. It is a message often recognized in theory, but neglected on the many occasions when imagination or rigor of mind slip, or else when it is found more convenient for religious or theological reasons quietly to ignore it. There are many Christian attitudes toward Jesus, both in past and present, which accord ill with a rigorous perception of Jesus as a Jew, and the long history of Christian anti-Semitism has only encouraged such amnesia. Particularly in this aspect of his work, there has often been an element of the gadfly about Vermes, and there is a feeling that he relishes the tweaking of conventional noses—all the more so when their owners can be shown simply to be ill-informed. In his memoirs, he confesses to surprise that his views have not caused more outrage. At the same time, in some of his opinions (for example, about Gospel criticism) he can be relatively conventional and not chase after the avant-garde. Perhaps these matters interest him less than his main focus on historical background.

He first came to prominence in relation to the study of Jesus in the mid-1960s because of his work on the term "Son of Man," so commonly applied to Jesus in the Gospels, and indeed virtually always found on his own lips. Placing it in what Vermes held to be the most appropriate Jewish context, he saw it not as a quasi-theological affirmation or a title, drawn perhaps from Daniel 7.13 and signifying the coming triumph of Jesus, but rather as a perfectly ordinary term in popular usage, an idiom often indicating self-reference on the part of its user, but in a spirit of modesty or reticence. The evidence was not great in quantity, but, as forcibly promoted by Vermes, it took the apparently endless study of the subject into a new phase, though it has not, it seems, brought discussion to a conclusion.

More broadly, after articles in the 1960s, Vermes's chief contribution to the study of Jesus has been through a series of three volumes (1973, 1983, 1993) presenting Jesus as a remarkable but not totally astonishing teacher who, like others of his time, came up against the Jewish and Roman authorities of the day and suffered the predictable penalty. So, while his wonderful teaching is recognized, Jesus is seen as being far from meriting (how could anyone *merit* them?) the claims made for him in subsequent Christian faith. It is of course undeniable that Vermes's insistence on Jesus' Jewishness was a healthy counterblast to the often almost intuitive perception of him against a quasi-Hellenistic backdrop, which so soon became the dominant context for the Christian movement and for its developing theology. Rather, for Vermes, Jesus takes his place "in the venerable company of the Devout, the ancient Hasidim." Moreover, we should not see him as having suffered for anything outrageous or intolerable in his teaching, but out of the sheer jumpiness of the authorities toward any hints of possible insurrection. In a situation where terrorism exists, rulers can see it around every corner—and act to eliminate any possible threat, however unjustly. In reality, Jesus was a moving preacher of the kingdom of God, conveyed vividly by way of parabolic images.

Leslie Houlden

See also: Dead Sea Scrolls; Jewish Scholarship; Son of Man

References

Vermes, G. 1973. *Jesus the Jew*. London: SCM.
———. 1983. *Jesus and the World of Judaism*. London: SCM.
———. 1993. *The Religion of Jesus the Jew*. London: SCM.
———. 1998. *Providential Accidents: An Autobiography*. London: SCM.

W

War

Although this article discusses what may be said on "Jesus and war," many of the factors that arise and much of its argumentation apply, in a variety of ways, to "Jesus and . . ." other political issues and indeed some other kinds of ethical questions. So the article is in this way paradigmatic and does not just apply to the subject of war and human conflict.

A difficulty with subjects of this kind is that we are required to take a view about Christian doctrine concerning Jesus. Are we to "hear" him as a human being, a man of his time and place, or as divine, speaking, in some way, timelessly, instructing us for all times and all places? Christian belief is that he was both divine and human, but questions such as those raised in this article compel us to decide how to "place" his teaching and conduct.

If he was a man of his time and place, limited by his experience, it is no good expecting from him wisdom on the detailed ethical issues relating to modern nuclear warfare. Indeed, as a man of the Galilee of the early first century, he had no direct experience of warfare at all, though he may have known about it from the history of his people, or perhaps from rumors from remote parts of the Roman Empire. He will also have known of the part played by war, between God and his enemies, in prophecies of the crisis that would usher in the end of the age (e.g., Ezek. 38–39; Dan. 9.26). Indeed, his recorded teaching includes references to such wars and rumors of wars (e.g., Mark 13.7), though we should remember that the Gospels containing such prophecies were written later in the century, during or after the period of warfare in Palestine arising from the Jewish revolt against the Roman power (A.D. 66–73): for some of those involved in the writing or the tradition that led up to it, war had become a matter of closer experience. There is also the question of how far special humans may have inspired insight taking them beyond their mere experience.

But if Jesus, whether as divine or even as an inspired prophet, was not wholly limited by the knowledge appropriate to a person of his time and place, then we may look to him for insights applicable, no doubt with many variations, to this and indeed to all kinds of comparable situations. To whatever degree and in whatever way, his humanity would not be like ours, earthbound and practical. It is now less common and less easy than in former times to see Jesus in this way, at least in the stronger, most "timeless," and utterly "divine" way: historical imagination (or common sense) is too strong.

We may of course say that the Spirit of God, indwelling and guiding his people, may now guide us to apply Jesus' teaching, first-century in ethos though it was, appropriately to our day. Then we find that, on this and other matters, Christian people disagree, perhaps for good reasons, perhaps through the influence of their political or national allegiance: when conflict threatens, God is often found to be on one's own side! We try, then, to make our decisions on such rational arguments as may apply. In the case of war, we turn to the Christian tradition of theory about the "just war," outlining a set of principles and conditions under which war may or may not be legitimate for Christians. The price then paid is that any teaching of Jesus himself is pushed some way into the background—and the strict terms of this article are left behind. What will emerge is not "what Jesus taught (or even teaches)" but "what the Church teaches." Fine, but let us know what we claim to be saying.

Even if, for good reasons, we follow the path of a developing tradition of Christian reflection, it may still be worth our while to see what bearing the teaching of Jesus may have on our subject. Even if we end up rejecting it as inapplicable to our circumstances, so far away in time and character from first-century Galilee, we may still be moved—and shamed or puzzled—by what he taught, and perhaps led to modify our reasonable reflections that have slid, unnoticed, into mere worldly common sense. We may come to think that it may be better, morally, to act in an imperfect way regretfully (yet inevitably) than to feel no regret for what we feel obliged by circumstance to do, immoral as it is. We shall then at least recognize that the lesser of two evils is still evil and not a kind of good. We may think of the bombing of Dresden in World War II and numerous other warlike acts in the years since, all justified by national interest or by the alleged need to prevent worse evils.

We turn from this position-taking to what Jesus is reported as teaching in relation to war. As we saw, he took it as part of the "woes" that will preface the end of the age. Of the how, when, and where, there is nothing precise. In any case, it did not occur. The teaching, though vivid, is formulaic (Mark 13, with parallels in Matt. 24 and Luke 21). The topic is to a degree brought down to earth when we read of future Christian victims (Mark 13.9f.). But none of this is the balanced and sober wisdom of a "world statesman." It is in fact the fervent (and conventional) preaching, real or supposed, of a Jewish apocalyptic prophet of the period.

We turn away from the apocalyptic idiom to Jesus' moral teaching, apparently for life in the here and now: he forbids hostility toward enemies and commands us to love them (Matt. 5.43–48). But does this notion have any bearing on the affairs of nations or is it only about interpersonal relations?

The question about the tribute-money (Mark 12.13–17) need not lead us to see Jesus as giving carte blanche to all government policies whatsoever and as placing no limits on his followers' acquiescence. It is about taxpaying, in the particular context of the Roman occupation of Palestine, and we may decide that its point is not to neatly apportion obligations but to shake us into realizing that all things are God's and we owe all to him: what else could Jesus' preaching of the kingdom of God possibly entail?

It is easy to refer to Matt. 10.34 ("I come not to bring peace but a sword"), but this statement cannot be held to back all kinds of bloodthirsty behavior by Christians. It relates, vividly, to the divisions inevitably provoked by Jesus' mission—in the immediate setting. And at the arrest of Jesus (Matt. 26.52), ordering Peter to put away his sword is hardly a statement of eternal and universal principle commanding pacifism. It belongs in its setting. The Gospels are not rule books to ransack for skillfully formulated general principles, and Jesus was not uttering eternally applicable truths at every opening of his mouth.

All the same, it is hard to find in the reported teaching any support for war as a considered policy for nations to adopt. Whether that is a decisive (even sole) determining factor when Christians reach a view about the ethics of war is another matter. Historically, they have not mostly found it so but have taken more general and philosophical paths; also, very often, paths encouraged by expediency. It is hard to think it sensible to take such scattered material as the Gospels contain as determinative for all times and circumstances. At the same time, whatever terrible situations and decisions nations and their rulers have to face, it would be repellent if Christians were not to feel moved by those fellow believers (such as some early Christians, then sixteenth-century Anabaptists and then the Quakers) who, for whatever reason, have felt the straight moral force of the command to love not just one's neighbor but one's enemy as well and to turn the other cheek (Matt. 5.38–48; cf. Also 5.9): it is the closest we can get to a justification of unconditional pacifism, and we have to decide whether it is high idealism, hoping that we shall at least try to go some way in its direction, or the straight command that it seems to be, not to be played with. What is the point of a revealed religion if it simply tells us to do what we would do anyway? The force of that passage is unequivocal and universal. But then, even if Jesus commands perfection (v. 48), he is also gracious to those who fall short. So wider questions of the place of commands in the Christian scheme of things immediately come into play: about failure, penitence, and absolution being a good deal preferable to bumbling mediocrity throughout. Grace carries the day over law.

In practice, argument about war has centered less on the few possibly relevant sayings of Jesus than on (1) moral principles governing the theory of the just war and (2) the teaching of Paul (Rom. 13.1–7) enjoining obedience to the ruler, whatever he commands and whoever he may be. This passage has been the occasion of much anguished discussion, especially at the time of the Reformation, when Catholic Christians found themselves fighting a novelty, Reformed or Protestant Christians. How could it be justified to fight even dissident fellow believers? The Crusades against the infidels of Islam had at least seemed to raise fewer qualms, even to be praiseworthy; though then, too, Jesus the figure of peace receded from view, as he so often has through the centuries as fanaticism, greed, local interest, or sheer barbarism have prevailed. But sometimes Christians have fought not out of greed but to hasten the Last Days, and so for Christ. Constantine, however, the first

Christian emperor of Rome, took, not Jesus, but his Cross, as his badge—to fight his rivals for sole power.

Leslie Houlden

See also: Ethics, Modern; Family; Great War; Jesus, Teaching of; Quaker Thought; Wealth; Work

References

Bainton, R. H. 1996. *Christian Attitudes to War and Peace: A Historical Summary and Critical Re-evaluation*. New York and London: Abingdon.

Chadwick, Owen. 2001. "Resistance Justified." Pp. 315–350 in *The Early Reformation on the Continent*. Oxford: Clarendon.

Raven, C. E. 1938. *War and the Christian*.

Shiels, W. J., ed. 1983. *The Church and War*. Studies in Church History 20. Oxford: Blackwell.

Tooke, J. D. 1965. *The Just War in Aquinas and Grotius*. London: William Clowes.

Wealth

"Rich" and "Poor" in the Teaching of Jesus

The teaching on wealth and possessions attributed to Jesus in the Gospels is best approached via an understanding of the essential social features of the preindustrial, agrarian society in which he lived. This society, in fact, shows great similarity to the agrarian and industrializing agrarian societies of two-thirds of the world today, particularly in massive wealth differentiation between the elite and the mass of the population, in the limitation of the majority of the population to a subsistence diet, and in the absence of a large and influential middle class such as is characteristic of industrialized nations. The agrarian society of antiquity manifested the essential social bifurcation typical of all agrarian societies between a narrow governing class (numbering less than 1 percent of the population: "the few" [Greek *hoi oligoi*], "the notables," "the rich," "the powerful") and the large mass of small tenant farmers, laborers, and artisans ("the many" [Greek *hoi polloi*], "the people," "the poor"). Most people lived in rural villages and were engaged in agricultural production. Pressing socioeconomic problems, including overpopulation, land shortage, and land exhaustion, led to a meager (subsistence) diet, and sometimes worse, for some 90 percent of the population.

In neither Jewish history nor the Greco-Roman period were long-standing structural problems of peasant debt and land accumulation by the rich, which arose because of the tightness of economic resources, ever solved. Smallholders, whose land-lots had often been divided down to subsistence parcels through inheritance over the generations, tended to lose their frequently mortgaged land to larger landholders through the problem of too many mouths to feed, especially when the crux moment of a bad harvest came. The elite asserted absolute control of all economic resources through a strong military machine, financed by rents and taxation, and were much given to conquest. The governing class was supported by a small but well-rewarded administrative "retainer" class numbering less than 5 percent of the population. Petty officials, estate stewards, and lower military officers ensured the operation of the machinery of taxation and the collection of rents and were required to give absolute loyalty to the governing class. High taxation, usually from a half to two-thirds of all agricultural production, kept most of the population at subsistence level and led to the marginalization of a degraded "underclass." These losers in the socioeonomic competition usually numbered between 5 and 10 percent of the population; their diet fell below subsistence level, and their lives, in consequence, were often brutal and short.

The Judgment of the Rich in Jewish Tradition

Uniquely in the ancient world, the Mosaic covenant of the Hebrew Bible offered full preservation of a free peasantry through laws that prohibited the charging of interest on debt and permanent loss of land, required the release of debt in the Sabbath year, and prohibited the unreasonable pursuit of debt (Exod. 22.25; 23.6–12; Lev. 25; Deut. 15.1–18; 23.19–20; 24.6, 10–15, 17–22). Both the Israelite prophets of the eighth century B.C. and postexilic figures such as Ezra and Nehemiah had sought to maintain the mutual social covenant at the heart of Israelite religion. Nonetheless, an oppressive super-rich class is evident in Palestine from the third century B.C. in the activities of such figures as the murderous and rapacious Joseph son of Tobiah (Josephus, *Antiquities of the Jews* 12.4.1–5, §§154–185), who exacted a very heavy burden of taxation on behalf of Greek overlords. Moderate Jewish leadership was displaced, and the mass of the population progressively impoverished.

The development of large estates by the rich at the expense of smallholders, who were reduced to landless tenants paying high taxes and rents or laborers eking out an existence on pitiful wages, cut clean across the essential Jewish tenet that the land and its fruits belonged to God and were to be justly distributed. The Jewish wealth-elite, by transgressing the divine sanction that protected the free peasantry, placed itself outside the divine covenant. There remained for it only judgment and terrible punishment when God, through his Messiah, reestablished justice in Israel, returning the land to the poor. Thus sections of 1 Enoch dating from the second to first centuries B.C. protest keenly against the luxuriously living, land-robbing governing class (91–92; 95.7; 96.3–8; 97.8–11; 98.1–2; 99.11–15; 100.6–7; 107). In the apocalyptic vision of God's great coming judgment, these powerful rulers confess that "our souls are satiated with unrighteous *mammon* [cf. Luke 16.9, 11; on this Aramaic term see further below], which could not save us from being cast into fiery She'ol" (63.10). The pious and upright poor, who "love God" and "have loved neither gold nor silver, nor all the good things that are in the world, but have given over their bodies to suffering," receive from God eternal reward (108.8–15).

Jesus and the Poor

Most of Jesus' followers were drawn from amongst those who struggled to eke out a subsistence diet; hence, he instructed them to pray each day to receive a "daily ration of bread" sufficient for survival (Greek *arton*, "bread," and *epiousion*, perhaps "daily," "needful," Matt. 6.11; Luke 11.3). He was remembered for his striking willingness to dine with prostitutes (Luke 5.27–32), those brutalized women of the Jewish underclass who had only their bodies to sell to gain bread. Prostitution was the common fate of the women of the ancient world's underclass; Herodotus even wrote that the lower-class women of Lydia earned money for their dowries by prostitution (*Histories* 1.93).

Jesus' teaching was framed in language that reflected the essential social bifurcation between unjust rich and struggling poor in ancient agrarian society. He promised the kingdom of God to the poor and hungry of the present age; against the well-fed rich, who were responsible for the plight of the poor, he pronounced woes (Luke 6.20–26). Matthew is often accused of "ethicizing" Jesus' promise that the poor will inherit the land when God's kingdom comes, for he confirms this inheritance to the "poor *in spirit*" and "meek" (Matt. 5.3–5). Indeed, Jesus did not press his concern for the poor to the point of political rebellion. Though an immensely popular figure, he refused to stir the masses to violent revolt; nor would he speak against the payment of Roman taxes (Mark 12.13–17). The poor must in humility accept their lot, embracing the present suffering and sharing amongst themselves. Their heavenly Father is able to provide for all their needs (Matt. 6.25–34), perhaps through the generosity of pious patrons.

The Poverty of the Disciple

In Jesus' teaching, property (Aramaic *mammon*) is virtually demonized because of its potential to draw the soul away from the exclusive worship of which only God is worthy: "You cannot serve God and mammon" (Luke 16.13; Matt. 6.24). The "deceitfulness of wealth" (Mark 4.19) may choke Jesus' word of repentance. Those he chose for the spiritual calling of teaching, healing, and wielding authority over the demonic world were to renounce property. Such disciples were to give up all that they had, selling their possessions and giving away the proceeds to the poor (Luke 12.32–34, 14.33). They left all to follow him (Mark 1.16–20, 2.13–17; Luke 5.1–11). Like Jesus on his preaching tours, their connections with the ordinary world were in effect to be severed (Matt. 8.19–22; Luke 9.57–62). During peripatetic mission they were to travel without purse, money, or provisions (Mark 6.8–9; Matt. 10.9–10; Luke 9.3–4, 10.4, cf. 22.35–36).

This ideal of renunciation has deep roots in forms of piety that had developed during the era of the Jewish people's impoverishment. In order to avoid calamity in the coming judgment, the faithful must fully embrace the suffering of the present evil age. Indeed, the coming of God's kingdom would be hastened by such perfect obedience, explored in close-knit conventicles of teachers and students (disciples) that arose within the ordinary mass of the population, such as that led by Jesus (the son of a worker in wood and stone, Mark 6.3). Within such circles were generated, perhaps as early as the late third century B.C., ideals of celibacy and the renunciation of property. The social context in which these ideas developed is observable in the fragmentary work 4Q *Instruction* from the Dead Sea Scrolls, dating from c. 200 B.C. Both teacher and student are reduced to subsistence level or worse. Nonetheless, despite such dire circumstances, to taint the soul by avoiding the consequences of economic deprivation through any dishonest act in a matter of property (such as theft breach of trust concerning a deposit) remains unacceptable and immoral and is to be avoided at all costs. Indeed, heightened consciousness concerning the woes caused by economic injustice means that dishonesty in money matters is presented as the nemesis of existence. God's coming judgment upon present economic dislocation meant that the faithful must be scrupulous to keep far from their souls any stain of dishonest dealings in property (cf. Acts 5.1–11). The student's economic poverty may seem to render problematic his desire perfectly to know and obey God's Law: "You are poor. Do not say: I am poor, I cannot become wise." The teacher who commented "You have taken a wife in your poverty" could easily advise that time be made for study, leading to perfect obedience, by restraint in procreating children (which meant less time would be needed for garnering wages) or even through celibacy (cf. Matt. 19.10–12). This work recasts the fifth commandment (Exod. 20.12; Deut. 5.16) in order to stress that limited material means do not excuse the support of parents in their old age: "Honour your father in your poverty, and your mother in your low estate" (4Q416 frag. 2, col. III, lines 12–13, 15–16, 20). Similar thinking is expressed in Jesus' refusal to allow the legal fictions of the Pharisees to circumvent material care for parents and other social obligations, sullying the human heart (Mark 7.1–16, cf. Luke 16.10–15).

Supporters of Jesus Who Retained Property

Jesus allowed those not called to wield spiritual authority to retain private property. Such supporters were to be generous and unostentatious in their almsgiving and to lend willingly to those who asked (Matt. 5.42; 6.2–4). Implicit in the Gospel narratives are local supporters who offered hospitality to Jesus and his traveling party. Their homes often became the venue for teaching. Such local figures of good standing (Matt. 10.11, cf. Mark 6.10) also hosted those disciples sent out by Jesus in pairs (Mark 6.7; Luke 10.1) to preach, heal, and exorcise demons.

Jesus and the Rich

According to Luke (who has sometimes been suspected of heightening associations with the elite in both his Gospel and Acts), Jesus was supported on his own preaching tours by the patronage of women of means who were part of his traveling party. These included Joanna the wife of Chuza, senior steward of the estates of Herod Antipas, ruler of Galilee (Luke 8.1–3). Jesus demanded that those with wealth generously assist the destitute and undernourished. Thus his parable of the rich fool (Luke 12.16–21, cf. Gospel of Thomas 63) laments the greed of a farmer who selfishly hoards surplus grain and other goods, looking forward to a life of easy luxury. In the parable of the rich man and Lazarus (Luke 16.19–31), an owner of great estates has indulged himself in the fine garments and rich feasting of the elite. However, despite the strictures of the Law and the Prophets, he has ignored the needs and appeals of a poor sick man who has languished at his gate. He is condemned to unmitigated torment, while awaiting resurrection and final judgment, in a fiery corner of the place of the dead (cf. 1 Enoch 21–22).

Jesus' parable of the laborers in the vineyard (Matt. 20.1–15) reflects both the dire circumstances of the age and the kind of behavior Jesus expected of the wealthy. The generous vineyard owner assists laborers who have walked the rural roads but found no work. He knows the plight of the wandering poor and seeks out as many as possible, visiting the local marketplace repeatedly during the day to hire them as workers. He rewards each at evening with a full day's wage so that they will be able to buy enough food for both themselves and their families on their return. The parable illustrates both the gracious character of God, who seeks out the undeserving, and the generosity that those who repent and receive his mercy must display (cf. Matt. 18.21–35 on forgiveness of debts).

Jesus welcomed the rich who were prepared to be generous with their wealth. He accepted invitations to dine with the wealthy, urging them to provide for the poor who could not reciprocate their generosity (Luke 14.1–12). He could also seek out contact with the wealthy, as in the case of the immoral senior tax-collector Zacchaeus (Luke 19.1–10). When Zacchaeus repents of his wickedness, determining to distribute half his wealth to the poor and make restitution fourfold to those whom he has defrauded, Jesus declares that salvation has come to his house. Jesus accepted the gift of a costly tunic, woven, like that worn by the high priest, in one piece (John 19.23–24, cf. Josephus, *Antiquities* 3.7.4 §161). He defended the wealthy Mary of Jerusalem's anointing of him as royal Messiah with costly perfumed oil (Mark 14.3–9) at Bethany. This village was probably the poorhouse of Jerusalem (Greek *Bethania;* Aramaic *Beth 'anya,* "house of the poor"), where the destitute who accumulated in and around the city gathered to receive alms, and where poor pilgrims who had made the arduous journey from Galilee could be intercepted and offered aid. Jesus made it his place to stay when visiting Jerusalem, demonstrating his identification with the poor and proximity to those wealthy who cared for them.

On the road to Jerusalem, Jesus commanded a wealthy man to sell all that he had, distribute the proceeds to the poor, and follow him (Mark 10.17–29). He intended that the man should become his student; but he also had in view the good of the man's soul and the pressing needs of the poor. Jesus demonstrated in the temple against the avarice of the established religious hierarchy, protesting against the Jewish temple tax (additional to Roman taxation) and the expense of the sacrificial offerings by overturning the tables of the moneychangers and driving out the expensive sacrificial beasts sold only by the temple monopoly (Mark 11.12–18; John 2.12–22). This action probably led to his execution. The sharing that characterized the life of the early community of Jesus' post-Easter followers (Acts 2.42–47, 4.32–35.11, 6.1–6) is an important index of his social concern.

Brian J. Capper

See also: Jesus in Social Context; John, Gospel of; Kingdom of God; Luke, Gospel of, and Acts of the Apostles; Mark, Gospel of; Matthew, Gospel of; Prayer

References

Bauckham, R. J. 1988. "Jesus' Demonstration in the Temple." Pp. 72–89 and 171–176 in *Law and Religion: Essays on the Place of the Law in Israel and Early Christianity.* Edited by Barnabas Lindars. Cambridge: James Clarke.

Blomberg, Craig L. 1999. *Neither Poverty nor Riches: A Biblical Theology of Material Possessions*. Leicester: Apollos.

Capper, Brian J. 1995. "The Palestinian Cultural Context of Earliest Christian Community of Good." Pp. 323–356 in *The Book of Acts in Its Palestinian Setting*. Edited by R. J. Bauckham. Grand Rapids, MI: William B. Eerdmans.

———. 2001. "Two Types of Discipleship in Early Christianity." *Journal of Theological Studies* 52: 105–123.

———. 2002. "The Church as the New Covenant of Effective Economics: The Social Origins of Mutually Supportive Christian Community." *International Journal for the Study of the Christian Church* 1.

Hengel, Martin. 1973. *Property and Riches in the Early Church*. London: SCM.

Horsley, Richard A. 1993. *Jesus and the Spiral of Violence*. Minneapolis: Fortress.

Schmidt, Thomas E. 1987. *Hostility to Wealth in the Synoptic Gospels*. Sheffield: Sheffield Academic Press.

Stegemann, Ekkehard W., and Wolfgang Stegemann. 1999. *The Jesus Movement: A Social History of Its First Century*. Edinburgh: T. & T. Clark.

Welsh Christianity

From the early Middle Ages the person of Jesus has played a central role in Welsh Christianity. Sparse but significant evidence suggests a strong emphasis on the Trinity in early Welsh Christianity. Franciscan and Dominican influences led to a concentration on the incarnate Christ. Religious art, particularly as expressed in carvings of the Rood, helped to influence popular and poetic views of Christ during the late medieval period. A tradition developed of religious carols stressing the salvific role of the incarnate Christ. The significance of a personal relationship with Jesus was a central theme of the great hymn writers of the eighteenth-century Methodist Revival in Wales. Their influence remained central in shaping popular Welsh Christianity until well into the twentieth century. In the mid-nineteenth century the Calvinist consensus that had dominated Welsh theology from the post-Reformation period began to break up under the pressure of new ideas from outside Wales. Welsh Christianity remains strongly Christocentric.

The earliest known religious poetry in the Welsh language consists of a sequence of nine *englynion* (verses in traditional meter) in the margins of the Cambridge University Juvencus Manuscript, dating from the first half of the tenth century. These verses, addressed to the "Almighty Creator," make repeated reference to the Trinity. They conclude, however, with a reference to the need to praise *map Meir* ("Mary's son").

In the thirteenth century the advent of the Franciscans and Dominicans led to a much sharper focus on the person of the incarnate Christ. An anonymous Dominican wrote *Ymborth yr Enaid* (The Nourishment of the Soul), an original work of religious prose including a detailed meditative description of the twelve-year-old Jesus in the temple. Brother Madog ap Gwallter, a Franciscan, composed a poem on the birth of Jesus that is generally regarded as the first Welsh Christmas carol. It stresses the paradox of the Incarnation, yoking contrasting adjectives together to underline the combination of the apparent weakness and poverty of the child in the manger with the strength and wealth of his divine status.

A poem by Dafydd ap Gwilym, the major Welsh fourteenth-century writer, reflects on a painting of Christ and his apostles on a wooden panel. This subject matter indicates the significance of religious art in shaping popular perceptions of Jesus during the pre-Reformation period in Wales. Dafydd ap Gwilym also addressed verses to *y Grog* (the Rood, or crucifix), which became a particular focus of devotion in the fourteenth and fifteenth centuries. Poems were addressed both to particular examples of the Rood (at Chester, Brecon, and elsewhere in Wales and the Marches) and to the Rood itself. In one such poem, Lewys Glyn Cothi (c. 1420–1489) described the Rood as the living, suffering image of the man on the Cross. He portrayed Calvary as a hill of light before nightfall, where the crucified God-man is both harsh judge and abundantly merciful savior.

With the Reformation, visual representations of Jesus almost entirely disappeared from Welsh churches. An image that survives from the pre-Reformation period is the exquisite thirteenth-century gold figurine of Christ in Majesty attached to the cover of the twelfth-century *Book of Llandaf* (National Library of Wales MS 17110E). This piece shows a seated Christ with one hand raised in admonition and the other holding a Book of the Gospels. The contrast with the most significant modern Welsh statue of Christ is significant. In 1957, Sir Jacob Epstein's massive aluminum *Majestas* was unveiled in Llandaff Cathedral. In this huge sculpture, Christ is standing, his hands by his side, their empty palms facing those who move toward the figure as they enter the building. The gesture is one of compassion and welcome rather than of judgment.

The Welsh New Testament and Prayer Book appeared in 1567, and the complete Welsh Bible in 1588. Only a very small proportion of the population was literate, and they had to wait until 1630 for a Welsh Bible that could be bought by the general public. During this period, easily remembered free-meter poetry became an essential vehicle for Christian teaching. These poems took the form of *cwndidau* (sometimes described as "sermons in song") and carols.

Welsh Christmas carols both before and after the Reformation described the complete movement of God's saving action in Christ rather than confining themselves to Jesus' birth at Bethlehem. Thus, a carol attributed to Huw Dafydd, written to be sung on Christmas morning in 1520, begins by praising the newborn son of the virgin and goes on to describe his crucifixion, resurrection, and ascension; it ends with an exhortation to charity, pious devotion, and penitence. A carol "exhorting belief in Christ" composed by the Anglican layman Huw Morus (1622–1709) in 1668 has a similar pattern. As might be expected, it contains a much wider range of scriptural references, and the final stress is on repentance, faith, and confidence in the blood of Christ. A late but powerful (and still extremely popular) example of the genre is "Ar gyfer heddiw'r bore" (For Early This Morning), a carol composed for the predawn Christmas *Plygain* service by Dafydd Hughes (1792–1860), "Eos Iâl." This dramatic description of Christ's willing self-sacrifice for sinful humanity draws on a wealth of biblical imagery.

The greatest of all the popular didactic religious poets was a Jacobean Anglican cleric. Rhys Prichard (1579–1644), vicar of Llandovery in Carmarthenshire, used carols and other simple verse forms to teach his parishioners about Jesus. Prichard's most famous carol starts with an invitation to his congregation to join him on a cheerful journey to Bethlehem to see their kindly newborn savior. He emphasized the fact that the child in the manger was to suffer on the Cross. The paradox of the God-man is stressed as strikingly by Prichard as it had been by Madog ap Gwallter in the thirteenth century. The infant in Mary's lap is the one who keeps the world from falling into oblivion. The baby lying in the stable is the architect of the sun and the planets. Rhys Prichard's poems were published after his death in a volume that helped to shape popular Welsh piety for over two centuries.

In the early 1730s, Griffith Jones, a country rector, appalled by continuing widespread illiteracy in Wales, began to establish a system of circulating schools. These taught both children and adults to read using the Prayer Book Catechism and the Bible as textbooks. Shortly afterward, the Methodist Revival began under the leadership of Daniel Rowland (1713–1790), curate of Llangeitho in Cardiganshire, and Howel Harris (1714–1773), a lay exhorter from Breconshire. The poet of the movement was William Williams of Pantycelyn (1717–1791). In the elegy that he wrote after Rowland's death, Williams described him as a champion of Trinitarian orthodoxy. Howel Harris was strongly influenced by the Moravians and this led him to use language about the crucified Jesus that Rowland regarded as heretical. He accused his fellow leader of Patripassianism (the belief that God the Father himself suffered in the suffering of Christ), and in 1750, Welsh Methodism split into two factions.

William Williams backed Rowland in this doctrinal disagreement, composing a religious epic, *Golwg ar Deyrnas Crist* (A View of the Kingdom of Christ) to support his cause. In 1762, he produced a new collection, *Caniadau y rhai sydd ar y Môr o Wydr* (Songs of Those Who Are on the Sea of Glass), which became the songbook of a renewed Methodist Revival in Llangeitho that healed the division between Rowland and Harris and their respective followers. Many of Williams's hymns express an intense personal relationship with Jesus that reflects the emphasis on spiritual experience that was at the heart of early Welsh Calvinistic Methodism. They became a part of popular Welsh-language religious culture until well into the twentieth century.

Ann Griffiths (1776–1805), another significant Welsh Methodist hymn writer, came from an area of Montgomeryshire where the tradition of composing carols for the Plygain service was very strong. Her hymns are centered on her love for the person of Jesus and reflect a profound knowledge of Scripture and an interest in Christian doctrine. She regarded the humanity of Christ as the source of his sympathy with human weakness, and his divinity as the means by which he could defeat the world, the flesh, and the devil on our behalf.

The handbook of Welsh-language theology during the nineteenth century was the hugely popular *Geiriadur Ysgrythyrawl* (Scriptural Dictionary) compiled by the Calvinistic Methodist leader Thomas Charles of Bala (1755–1814). It appeared between 1805 and 1811, and by 1904 it had reached its seventh edition. Charles's view of Jesus was based on the traditional creeds and reflects a doctrinal orthodoxy that was characteristic of nineteenth-century Welsh Christianity, apart from a small Unitarian minority. By the closing years of the Victorian era, new ideas about Jesus began to have an impact in Wales. Thomas Charles Edwards (1837–1900), great grandson of Thomas Charles of Bala, published *The God-Man* in 1895 (a Welsh translation appeared two years later). His presentation of a kenotic Christology led to widespread debate. One of his most incisive critics was Roland Sawil Thomas (1844–1923), author of a substantial volume entitled *Undod personol y Duwddyn* (The Personal Unity of the God-Man). Another was the popular preacher John Cynddylan Jones (1840–1930), who condemned the doctrine of kenosis as a modern attempt to humanize God.

A more radical approach to the person of Jesus came from the Welsh Independent theologian David Miall Edwards (1873–1941). In *Crefydd a bywyd* (Religion and Life, 1915) he attempted to redefine teaching about Christ in the light of contemporary knowledge and philosophy. Edwards concluded that the key to Jesus' nature was the relationship between Father and Son. There could not be an eternal Father without an eternal Son. Jesus was supremely conscious of his *mabol* ("sonly") relationship with God.

Doctrinal tensions within Welsh Calvinistic Methodism came to the fore when the radical preacher Tom Nefyn Williams (1895–1958) was expelled from the ministry in 1929. Williams saw Christ as a perfect example of a human being, made so by his unique sense of the divine. He denied the Trinity, the Incarnation, the deity of Christ, his miracles and resurrection, and any form of the atonement. However, by 1932, he had returned to the orthodox fold and was readmitted to the ministry of his denomination.

Poets and hymn writers have often tended to be more influential than theologians both in shaping and reflecting the Welsh religious consciousness. Evan Rees (1850–1923) won the chair at the Chicago International *Eisteddfod* (1893) with a poem about Jesus of Nazareth that contained nothing to offend conventional Welsh nonconformist piety. An English hymn by Timothy Rees (1874–1939), a Welsh-speaking Anglican monk who became bishop of Llandaff, spoke of the "crucified Redeemer" whose anguished presence he had sensed in the suffering both of the Flanders trenches and of the South Wales valleys during the Great Depression. The poetry of David Gwenallt Jones (1899–1968), who returned to Christianity after a period of Marxist agnosticism, stressed the sacramental significance of the incarnate Christ. The most distinguished English-language religious poet in Wales during the second half of the twentieth century was Ronald Stuart Thomas (1913–2000), an Anglican cleric in whose work Christ is an absence rather than a presence.

The continuing importance of the person of Jesus for what remains of Welsh-language Christianity was shown by two books that appeared in 2000, both written by Welsh Presbyterian ministers. *Iesu'r Iddew a Chymru 2000* (Jesus the Jew and Wales 2000) by Pryderi Llwyd Jones was a controversial presentation of recent scholarship aimed at a popular audience. It placed particular emphasis on Jesus' humanity and his Jewish background. *Iesu Grist, Ddoe, Heddiw ac am Byth* (Jesus Christ, Yesterday, Today and Forever) by

Elfed ap Nefydd Roberts was written to stimulate discussion about the person and place of Jesus in Christian belief and practice.

Patrick Thomas

See also: Calvin, John; Franciscan Thought and Piety; Kenoticism; Wesley, Charles, and Wesley, John

References

Allchin, A. M. 1991. *Praise above All: Discovering the Welsh Tradition*. Cardiff: University of Wales Press.

Ap Gwilym, Gwynn. 1999. *Gogoneddus Arglwydd, Henffych Well: Detholiad o ryddiaith a barddoniaeth Gristnogol Gymraeg drwy'r Canrifoedd*. Llandysul: Churches Together in Wales.

Jones, Pryderi Llwyd. 2000. *Iesu'r Iddew a Chymru 2000*. Talybonk: Gwasg y Lolfa.

Jones, R. Tudur. 1981–1982. *Ffydd ac Argyfwng Cenedl: Hanes Crefydd yng Nghymru, 1890–1914*. Swansea: Ty John Penry.

Morgan, D. Densil. 1999. *The Span of the Cross: Christian Religion and Society in Wales, 1914–2000*. Cardiff: University of Wales Press.

Morgan, Derec Llwyd. 1988. *The Great Awakening in Wales*. London: Epworth.

Roberts, Elfed ap Nefydd. 2000. *Iesu Grist, Ddoe, Heddiw ac am Byth*. Caernarfon, UK: Gwasg Pantycelyn.

Williams, Glanmor. 1976. *The Welsh Church from Conquest to Reformation*. Cardiff: University of Wales Press.

Wesley, Charles (1707–1788) and Wesley, John (1703–1791)

The figures of John and Charles Wesley are among the most important in the history of Christianity, and their vision of a heartfelt "methodical" religion, which takes seriously the Bible, reason, tradition, and personal experience, is one to which many millions have been drawn. (For example, despite a recent, rapid, and substantial decline in numbers, the United Methodist Church is still the second largest Protestant organization in the United States, with some 8.5 million members.) Both John and Charles were Anglican priests, and both maintained a firm allegiance to that body until their deaths (John perhaps more in word than in deed). Both received their initial education at home from their mother Susanna, a "convert" to Anglicanism from a Puritan background, and both came under the influence also of father Samuel, himself an Anglican priest and longtime rector of the Parish of Epworth in Lincolnshire. Both attended Oxford University, and it was here, in 1729, that Charles established the "Holy Club" from which the ethos and structures of Methodism were later to grow. Anglicans then the brothers were; working as they did within the context of the eighteenth century, however, meant that the surface of their fundamentally Anglican theology was significantly disturbed by the strong and often turbulent religious undercurrents operative in England during that time. This can be seen in their understanding of Jesus no less than in other areas.

During the evangelical revival of the eighteenth century, of which the Wesleys were a significant, but not the only, part, more and more emphasis came to be placed upon the efficacy of Christ's blood and the individual application of what Christ had accomplished on the cross, and it is not surprising that the Wesleys echoed this wider concern. This emphasis can be seen throughout the better-known works of the Wesleys, both the hymns of Charles, that is, and the prose of John. But important though this concentration upon the blood of Christ was, it does not appear always to have been uniformly there. One can see it developing and finally being fully espoused in, for example, Charles's preaching, a body of material that predates the bulk of his poetic work.

In 1735, Charles and John had gone to America to work, they hoped, for the conversion of the Native Americans. A number of examples of Charles's preaching have survived from this period, and hence we may gain some insight into the form and content of his homiletic work during these early years. It is important to note, however, that most of the sermons that have survived from this period are sermons composed by Charles using his brother's sermons as a base (Charles indicated the same at the end of each such manuscript by noting, in shorthand, "from my brother's copies," followed by a date). There is evidence to suggest that in the process of copying, Charles was a creative editor (Newport, 78–81). It is entirely reasonable to argue, therefore, that in these early sermons one gains a glimpse of the relatively early work of both John and Charles, for what we have here in effect is a creative edition of a number of John Wesley sermons as edited by Charles. Importantly, one suspects, these sermons never came to publication in the lifetime of the Wesleys and survive only in manuscript form. They therefore give us a glimpse not just of what the brothers were in later life willing to place in the public domain in published form, but what they were actually preaching at the time.

In a number of these sermons Christ is most noticeable by his absence, but where he does appear it is generally (there are a few exceptions) as a hard and inescapable judge who looks down upon sinful humanity not so much with compassion and love as with anger and expectation. There is little here of what will later become so important, especially to Charles: the sufficiency of Christ's sacrifice upon the cross and the infinite love extended by Christ to even the most miserable and wicked of sinners (amongst whose ranks Charles never tired of counting himself). In a sermon on Philippians 3.14–15, for example, Charles argued that God demands perfection (or at least perfect obedience, that is, a perfect obedience to the law insofar as we can in our sinful state attain it). The road to salvation is long and hard, and he that stops to rest along the way may find that he has stopped short of the glory of God; he may be caught unawares by the sudden return of Christ and as a result lose his place in the eternal kingdom. Other sermons from the period reflect the same basic pessimism, where again there is a very noticeable lack of focus on what God in Christ (according to the doctrine of the later Wesleys) has done. To be sure, Christ will step in and make up any deficiency, but only once that person has done everything that is in his or her power to do (there is an echo here back to the medieval notion of the necessity for everyone *facere quod in se est*, "to do that which is within one"). The system is far from Christocentric.

This was to change, however. Both John and Charles underwent an intense religious experience during the period following their return from America (in March 1738 and December 1736, respectively). During the next several months, both came under the influence of the Moravians, a lively evangelizing church newly arrived in London from Germany. Although they could not let go of their Anglicanism, both were deeply impressed with the sense of assurance of salvation and personal experience of it that the Moravians seemed to exhibit. The influence of the Moravians and other factors led to the watershed of May 1738 when first Charles and then John had an experience sometimes referred to as their "evangelical conversion." Quite what happened is unclear, but both express it in terms of a "warming," or, in Charles's case, a "palpitation," of heart. Charles wrote a number of hymns in celebration of this event. The one written at the time may well have been "Christ the Friend of Sinners"; a year later he wrote "O for a Thousand Tongues to Sing." Reflection on the experience may also have prompted the composition of one of the most famous of all of Charles's hymns, namely "And Can It Be," a hymn that expressed an absolute confidence in the work of Christ. The first stanza of that magnificent hymn reads:

> And can it be, that I should gain
> An interest in the saviour's blood?
> Died he for me, who caused his pain?
> For me who him to death pursued?
> Amazing love! How can it be
> That thou, my God, shouldst die for me?

What is found here in poetic form is echoed in the sermon material. From this point on, though he never escaped his own depressive personality, Charles nevertheless exuded an air of confidence that by the blood of Christ the salvation of humankind in general, and of each individual in particular, was accomplished. Christ is now not the harsh judge, but the friend of sinners, the person and means by which God has put into effect a plan of salvation that will encompass all. John, too, reflected such thinking, thinking that was so central to the broader evangelical movement of which the brothers were a part. John's view can be seen in his sermon "Free Grace," first published in 1739, and also in "Salvation by Faith" (1738). (In the context of the brothers' disputes with Calvinism within their ranks, they were both keen to express the universal application of what Christ had done on the cross and the consequent potential salvation of all humankind.)

In the wider corpus of the brothers' work, the atonement theory advanced is unquestionably "satisfaction," more precisely, penal substitution. Each sinner is deserving of death, but Christ in his mercy and love suffered that death on our behalf and accomplished thereby both the satisfaction of that which the justice of God required and the fullest expression of the mercy of God who himself bore the penalty that we should individually pay. (See, for example, Charles's *Hymns on God's Everlasting Love* [1741] and *Hymns on the Lord's Supper* [1745] and John's *Notes on the New Testament* [1755] on Rom. 3.25; 5.6; 1 John 2.2.)

For the Wesleys, the person of Christ was important, too, in that it was in Christ that God had revealed himself to humankind. Charles was perhaps more insistent than John on this point, for though John did see the self-revelation of God in the person of Christ, he also took the view that God could be known, incompletely at least, through other means (tradition, reason, and of course Scripture). Charles also thought these things important, but in his hymns at least he put much more stress on the perfect revelation of God that comes in and through Christ. One may literally see God as one sees Christ, as in the line from one of his most famous compositions, "Hark, the Herald Angels Sing" (the popular version of which is not quite what Charles actually wrote), a part of which reads, "veiled in flesh the Godhead see, hail incarnate deity."

Such emphasis upon the self-disclosing divinity of Christ is a part of the even broader theme of the Incarnation as found in the works of the brothers. That both were incarnational in their understanding is clear enough. John's views can be seen in his comments on John 1.1–18 and Colossians 1.15–20. Charles gave great expression to this view, not fearing to call Jesus "God" in many places: "the immortal God for me hath died, Jesus the Lord is crucified" (as quoted in Rattenbury, 154). So clear is this identification that at times Charles's Christology perhaps borders on being patripassionist (that is, the view that in Christ, the Father himself suffered). This tendency has already come across in the two hymns quoted above and in one of his sermon manuscripts; to note but one further example, Charles wrote, "God hath died," which he then corrected, lest he be misunderstood, to "Christ hath died" (Newport, 57).

This perhaps unintentional blurring of the edges between Father and Son (a blurring condemned as heretical early on in the Church's doctrinal formulation) is perhaps a result of the Wesleys' uncompromising Trinitarianism, which comes across, for example, in Charles's *Hymns on the Trinity* (1767). Indeed, Charles seems to have had a particular burden with this subject and composed perhaps as many as 300 hymns upon it (though his lines "The Unitarian fiend expel / and drive his doctrine back to hell" are often inappropriately applied: in fact, they were more probably addressed to Muslims than to "Unitarians" as such). John's views on the subject can be seen in his mature treatment presented in his sermon "On the Trinity" dated 8 May 1775. Here John argued that though one might not be able to comprehend it, one ought nevertheless to believe that God is three yet one. The argument, put in the context of one's inability to understand things such as the speed of light and the way in which the heavens are ordered, urged an unquestioning acceptance of the words of 1 John 5.7, "For there are three that bear record in heaven, the Father, the Word, and the Holy Ghost: and these three are one." (John Wesley, of course, was fully aware of the textual problems associated with this verse but did not let such matters get in the way of his presentation of Trinitarian doctrine.)

In the works of the Wesleys, then, Jesus appears as fully God who died to save each individual from the penalty of sin by dying for them. The powerful, uncompromising presentation of this doctrine, especially in the hymns of Charles, has led some to wonder (as Ernst Käsemann did of the author of

John's Gospel) whether the Wesleys might even be charged with docetism (the view that Jesus was not actually a human being at all, though he might have appeared as such to the unspiritual eye). If the Wesleys did fall afoul of this charge, it was (again in terms borrowed from the academic debate of the Gospel of John) "naively." That is, they so emphasized the divine nature of Christ that, as an unintentional consequence, they allowed the human Jesus to disappear.

Against such a view one could cite some obvious lines, such as those found in a later stanza from "And Can It Be":

> He left his Father's throne above
> (So infinite, so free his grace)
> Emptied himself of all but love
> And bled for Adam's helpless race.

On an abstract level, one might wish at this point to discuss the kenotic Christology of these lines. More important for the Wesleys, however, was the act of Christ in bleeding "for Adam's helpless race." Great emphasis is placed upon the reality of the suffering of Christ. Again and again this point comes across in Charles's work, so much so that it seems that John was alerted not to the danger of docetism but the very opposite. In 1789, John wrote and preached a sermon that contained the following words (the sermon was published the following year):

> And are we not then especially apt to speak of him [Christ] as a mere man? Particularly when we are describing his sufferings, how easily do we slide into this! We do well to be cautious in this matter. Here is not room for indulging a warm imagination. I have sometimes almost scrupled singing, (even in the midst of my brother's excellent hymn,) "That dear disfigured face," or that glowing expression, "Drop thy warm blood upon my heart," lest it should seem to imply the forgetting I am speaking of "the Man that is my fellow, saith the Lord of Hosts." Although he so "humbled himself as to take upon him the form of a servant, to be found in fashion as a man;" yea, though "he was obedient unto death, even the death of the cross;" yet let it ever be remembered, that he "thought it no robbery to be equal with God." And let our hearts still cry out, "Thou art exceedingly glorious; thou art clothed with majesty and honor." (*Sermons* 4.102–103)

The fact that John felt constrained to speak so directly on this point suggests that focusing with great realism on Christ's humanity at the expense of recognizing his divinity was indeed a real danger in the circles in which he moved. It is interesting to note that Charles's hymns came directly into question on this point. Elsewhere in this same sermon, John made it clear that in talking about Christ he had always sought to avoid "fondling" terms—the very reason, in all probability, that he excluded Charles's hymn that begins "Jesu lover of my soul / let me to thy bosom fly" from the Great Hymnbook (as it is commonly known) of 1780.

In the work of the Wesleys, then, one detects some of the recurrent Christological problems. Christ is God yet man, and when one talks about

Christ it is difficult, perhaps impossible, to avoid emphasizing one part of this equation over the other. There can be no doubt, however, that both John and Charles (after 1738) put Christ at the very heart of their religion and saw him as the means by which God had brought about the salvation of humankind. Nothing remarkable about that, perhaps. What is more remarkable, however, is the sense of duty that both John and Charles felt to tell others about this act of God in Christ, and how they were so driven by this conviction that they set about playing their part in the more general evangelical revival of their day.

Kenneth G. C. Newport

See also: American (North) Christianity; Calvin, John; English Christianity, 1750–1940; Hymns; Jesus, Achievement of; Kenoticism

References

Primary

Wesley, Charles. 1741. *Hymns on God's Everlasting Love*.

———. 1745. *Hymns on the Lord's Supper*.

Wesley, John. 1755. *Notes on the New Testament*.

———. *Sermons*. Edited by Albert Outler. 4 vols. Nashville: Abingdon Press, 1984–1987.

Secondary

Newport, Kenneth G. C., ed. 2001. *The Sermons of Charles Wesley: A Critical Edition with an Introduction and Notes*. Oxford: Oxford University Press.

Rattenbury, J. Ernest. 1941. *The Evangelical Doctrines of Charles Wesley's Hymns*. London: Epworth.

Westcott, B. F. (1825–1901), Lightfoot, J. B. (1828–1889), and Hort, F. J. A. (1828–1892)

The so-called Cambridge "Triumvirate" were biblical scholars who worked together on a commentary scheme for the whole of the New Testament in order to show that it was possible to respond constructively to the challenge of German critical scholarship. Their understanding of Jesus therefore grew out of their exegetical work. They are part of a movement in the later nineteenth century that moved the center of gravity in English theology from the Atonement to the Incarnation, from a "theology of the cross" to a "theology of the cradle."

Brooke Foss Westcott took the Johannine writings in the scheme, and his commentary on the Gospel of John is still valued for its theological insight. He was profoundly influenced by St. John's portrait of Jesus. For him, St. John's declaration that "the Word became flesh" (John 1.14) was the Gospel in a nutshell and the central fact in the history of the world. In this momentous act, God had bridged the gulf between the human and the divine and had made possible a new solidarity between human beings.

Western theology since Augustine had taught that this act was a direct response to the Fall, but Westcott followed the medieval theologian Duns Scotus in insisting that even if human beings had never sinned, God would still have become incarnate, simply to unite humanity with himself. The love of God alone, Westcott believed, explained the Incarnation, and to express the concept he coined the term "the Gospel of Creation." The optimism about human nature in his social and ethical teaching may derive from this shift of emphasis from human sinfulness to divine love.

Westcott's imagination was fired by St. John's claim that Jesus was the preexistent Logos, or Word, of God (John 1.1–4). Like the Alexandrian fathers, he saw the Logos at work in the Greek philosophers, who prepared the way for the greater revelation in Jesus. He regarded Plato as an unconscious prophet of the gospel. This reasoning became the basis for his very positive view of the relationship between Christianity and other world faiths. At a time when missionaries were encountering pre-Christian religions such as Hinduism and Buddhism, he believed the Logos concept enabled Christians to speak of the presence of Christ in those other faiths. Through this unusually affirmative view of other religions, he had a lasting influence on a whole generation of missionaries, especially in India, which was his special interest. One of his prophecies was that Indian thinkers would best be able to interpret St. John.

Westcott shared the Johannine insight that the essence of the Christian faith is a personal relationship with a living Lord. He showed no interest in the historical Jesus, the subject of numerous "lives" in the mid-nineteenth century, and was aware of the limitations of theology, where knowledge of a body of dogma could take the place of a living relationship. It is significant that the resurrection of Jesus has a special resonance in his thought. It was the subject of his first theological work, *The Gospel of the Resurrection* (1866). He linked the creation with the resurrection and regarded the risen Jesus as the first representative of the created order to attain the God-given goal, perfect manhood. The empty cross, not the crucifix, was for him the supreme symbol of the Christian faith.

A title he frequently used in speaking of the risen and ascended Jesus was "Christus Consummator," or "Christ the Fulfiller." He found this concept in the letter to the Hebrews, where Jesus is seen as the archetype of the human race who realized human life as it was meant to be and offered a perfect life to God (Heb. 2.10). Westcott took this concept further and argued that through Jesus the whole of creation reaches its goal; Jesus' acts as "Fulfiller" include all living creatures and not human beings alone. This line of argument enabled him to make a positive response to the challenge to faith presented by the theory of evolution. There are similarities between Westcott here and the twentieth-century Jesuit Pierre Teilhard de Chardin (1881–1955), who saw Jesus as the "omega point" or consummation of the cosmos.

In the last two decades of his life, Westcott devoted all his energies to working out the social implications of the doctrine of the Incarnation. As canon of Westminster (1883–1890) and bishop of Durham (1890–1901), he taught that the new solidarity between human beings, which the Christ-event had created, must be embodied in every aspect of life. He spoke of the need for cooperation rather than competition in social and industrial life, and of the need for people to acknowledge their interdependence in national and international life. He himself exemplified this spirit in identifying himself with the Christian Socialist movement when he became president of the Christian Social Union in 1889, and in his mediation in the Durham coal strike of 1892.

Joseph Barber Lightfoot, the historian of the trio, took the Pauline epistles in the commentary project. Like Westcott, he believed that the Incarnation was the leading idea of Christianity. The coming of Jesus was the center of history: all that preceded it was a preparation for it, and what followed was its realization, chiefly in the life of the Church.

He saw Christ as the "image of God" who entered history to show how human life should be lived and to reveal the Father. An important aspect of faith was imitating the earthly pattern of the life of Jesus. He was emphatic that Christianity was essentially a life, and not adherence to doctrines or obedience to rules. In his view, personal influence was always more important than what systems or organizations might achieve. History showed that it was the life and personality of individuals that led to the greatest triumphs of the human spirit.

He drew inspiration, as Westcott did, from St. John's doctrine of Jesus as the preexistent Logos, a concept that was important in his understanding of history. For him, the indwelling Word causes, directs, and sustains history as a whole, which he frequently described as "the increasing purpose of God." This emphasis was also important in that it enabled him to respond positively to the new discoveries in science and historical research, which were troubling the faith of many in the second half of the nineteenth century. Science and history, no less than the Bible and theology, were the inheritance of the Christian.

Like Westcott, Lightfoot believed that God in Christ had entered history in order to bridge the gulf between heaven and earth. There is a strong emphasis in his teaching on the unity of the sacred and the secular. He was Westcott's predecessor as bishop of Durham but did not become as deeply involved as the latter in the social and industrial life of the diocese.

Fenton John Anthony Hort worked for twenty-eight years with Westcott on a new critical edition of the Greek New Testament, but he produced only three fragments of his portion of the commentary scheme and did not even commence work on the Synoptic Gospels, which were his responsibility. He shared his colleagues' conviction that the Incarnation was the pivotal moment in human history and the central affirmation of Christian theology. He recognized the paradox of God become man: Jesus is Son of Man and Son of God, a human being and yet also savior and lord.

The doctrine had practical consequences in that it joined together heaven and earth, the spiritual and the material. Hort strongly affirmed the material world as God-given. As a trained natural scientist, he maintained a lifelong interest in botany and geology. He took a close interest in the Christian Socialist movement of 1848–1854, and he was always an admirer of F. D. Maurice. When appointed a lecturer, and later professor, at Cambridge, he fought hard to prevent the separation of theology from secular studies.

His most profound reflections on the significance of Jesus for contemporary life and thought are found in *The Way the Truth the Life* (1893), the Hulsean lectures for 1871, which are a sustained theological meditation on the well-known words of Jesus in John 14.5–6. He related those words to the challenges facing the Church from Darwin's *Origin of Species* (1859), on the one hand, and from the development of historical criticism, on the other. He saw the living Christ calling his Church to a deeper faith in his universality and sovereignty. It need not fear the future with all its uncertainty because his "way" runs through past and future alike. Since he is also "the truth," every addition to truth is to be welcomed, not feared, for all truth enriches our knowledge of God and the gospel of Christ. The challenge is to receive Christ as "the life," but not in isolation from the whole of life. The lectures, never completed for publication, were delivered in the same year that Hort was an examiner for the Cambridge Natural Science tripos. They reflect the controversies of the 1860s, yet have a timeless quality in their call to Christians to respond positively to the challenges of the day and to follow the living Christ into the unknown future.

Graham Patrick

See also: Alexandrian Theology; Hebrews, Letter to the; Interfaith Thought and Relations; Jesus, Achievement of; Jesus as a Historical Figure; John, Gospel of; Preexistence; Resurrection

References

Olofsson, Folke. 1979. *Christus Redemptor et Consummator: A Study in the Theology of B. F. Westcott*. Uppsala: University Press.
Patrick, Graham. 1988. *F. J. A. Hort: Eminent Victorian*. Sheffield: Almond Press.
Treloar, Geoffrey. 1998. *Lightfoot the Historian*. Tübingen: Mohr Siebeck.

Wiles, Maurice (1923–2005)

In the title of an early essay, Maurice Wiles posed the challenging question, "Does Christology rest on a mistake?" (1972, 3)—the mistake of supposing that the redeeming work of Christ requires "the underpinning of a distinct divine presence in Jesus" (ibid., 10). Over the years, he has worked out his own Christological views, not in any single work of systematic theology but in a series of rigorously argued books and articles. In these he has questioned not only the necessity of the doctrine of the Incarnation for Christian faith, but its intelligibility. Throughout he has shown himself intensely aware, and intent on making others aware, of the mystery of God and of the limitations of language about God. He is equally conscious of the extent of historical and cultural change and of the ultimate inaccessibility of the past, not least of that figure of the past, Jesus of Nazareth. Questions about God and about Jesus in relation to God are, he insists, distinct, but must always be allowed to interact on each other.

Wiles's more recent work *The Archetypal Heresy* concludes with the words that one important outcome of historical study "is its capacity to free us from the restrictive shackles that history is liable to impose on us" (1996, 186). Ever since his early and sympathetic work on Arianism, Wiles has repeatedly exercised that freedom to challenge long-held beliefs about how to understand the figure of Christ "in relation to the ultimate reality of God" (ibid., 185). Although not defending Arianism as a source of lived faith for today, Wiles argues that an orthodoxy shaped in reaction against it, or rather against misrepresentations of it, is equally questionable. We cannot assume axiomatically that Jesus was God and man; that could only "conceivably be the conclusion of our inquiry" (1974, 43). However, in the light of biblical criticism and of the fact that "modern historical consciousness has made historical relativists of us all" (ibid., 45), he doubts the possibility of finding sufficient evidence to justify that conclusion.

Historical issues aside, Wiles recognizes that the wider question of God's relationship to the world must interact with the question of Incarnation (and closely related issues such as miracles, providence, and the problem of evil). Though ready to affirm his faith in a personal God, Wiles rejects, on the basis not only of a modern scientific understanding of the world, but on moral grounds, the idea of God's direct action in the world in terms of efficient causation. Wiles's defense against a crude charge of deism is to affirm the language of divine *presence,* rather than of divine *action*—a presence that was exceptional but not absolutely unique in Jesus of Nazareth (thus Wiles opens the way to a positive, pluralist approach to other faiths). Nevertheless, Wiles can speak of the unique vision of God that permeated Jesus' life and impacts on his followers through his story. Against the accusation that his Jesus is simply a revealer of eternal truths, Wiles engages in a rigorous analysis of how religious language works, arguing that symbol and parable do not simply reveal, but *create,* new reality, and thus Jesus' story can have life-transforming effect. It is this, Wiles maintains, that Christian doctrines and beliefs seek to express, and for which, contrary to the Church's ancient but mistaken belief, the underpinning of the Incarnation is not necessary.

However, Wiles accepts that the language of Incarnation may still serve to symbolize basic Christian convictions. Thus continuity with Christianity's past is not lost, and a third way is opened up between having to accept traditional formulations of faith with all attendant difficulties or abandoning it altogether. Wiles offers four brief statements on what "Incarnation" symbolizes, which he believes most Christians can agree upon: (1) That "Jesus Christ is the focal point of God's dealing with the world . . . and of central significance in determining the content of our beliefs about God," that is, about how our lives should be lived and be transformed through faith in God; (2) Incarnation "symbolizes the intimacy of God's involvement with the world," with all that follows from that; (3) The impact of Jesus' death "implies that unlimited self-giving love is at the heart of the nature of God," and that no wickedness or suffering can remove us from his presence; and (4) "The story of Christ's resurrection symbolizes the conviction that wickedness, suffering and death do not have the final word about human life" (1999, 45).

The weight Wiles attaches to divine presence and the life-transforming impact of Christ may indeed make it easier to dispense with the Incarnation as traditionally understood, but the challenge facing Wiles is whether such an interpretation can bear the weight of Christian faith or do justice to its language. He argues, for example, that the apocalyptic ideas of Jesus' day served (mistakenly in his view) to secure an absolute status for him (1974, 63), but perhaps they served as much to provide a language in which to express absolute commitment to Christ as the object of his followers' "ultimate concern."

Wiles argued that "to ask for some further ontological justification of that vision [of divine redemption at work in Christ] would be to succumb to the category mistake of confusing the human historical story with the divine mythological story" (1972, 11). However, if Jesus is confessed as Lord in the fullest sense, or even as the focal point of God's dealings with the world, the question of the ontological corollary of this confession may be raised, not in order to justify it, but in the rational pursuit of understanding what must be true about God, about Jesus, and about the world and humanity for that confession to be rightly made. There may be more at stake here than asking what must be true to make sense of the distinctive nature of Christian experience as whole (1974, 61), or even of religious understanding of the world as a whole (ibid., 50), even if, as Wiles argues, Christians in the past have been too ready to use religious language and imagery too literally, or to treat what is culturally conditioned as divinely ordained.

Trevor Williams

See also: Christology, Modern; Interfaith Thought and Relations; Jesus, Miracles of; Jesus, Parables of; Jesus as a Historical Figure; Nicea; Radical Orthodoxy; Tillich, Paul

References

Wiles, Maurice. 1972. "Does Christology Rest on a Mistake?" Pp. 3–12 in *Christ, Faith, and History*. Edited by Stephen Sykes and John Clayton. Cambridge: Cambridge University Press.

———. 1974. *The Remaking of Christian Doctrine*. London: SCM.

———. 1982. *Faith and the Mystery of God*. London: SCM.

———. 1986. *God's Action in the World*. London: SCM.

———. 1996. *Archetypal Heresy: Arianism through the Ages*. Oxford: Oxford University Press.

———. 1999. *Reason to Believe*. London: SCM.

Wittgenstein, Ludwig (1889–1951)

Although one should not expect to find in his writings any systematic (or even extended) treatment of the nature and person of Jesus, a consideration of the work and subsequent theological influence of Ludwig Wittgenstein may be fruitful for Christological inquiry. Two things here are worthy of reflection: the comments that Wittgenstein himself made about Jesus; and the application of his wider thoughts on religion to the matter of Christology. With regard to the first of these, there are passages in the posthumously published collection of remarks entitled *Culture and Value* in which Wittgenstein reflects on what it might be that inclines "even" him to believe in Jesus and in his resurrection. His answer takes the form, not of any historical or metaphysical speculation, but of an almost childlike desperation: if Jesus did not rise from the dead then he decomposed like all other men "and can no longer *help*; and once more we are orphaned and alone" (Wittgenstein 1980, 33). This sentiment coheres with an earlier remark in which he muses that not to have heard of Christ would be like feeling "left alone in the dark" (ibid., 13). One may feel that there is something infantile about such remarks, but they chime with the simplicity of Christianity as Wittgenstein (influenced in this respect by Leo Tolstoy) understood it. Such an understanding attracted Wittgenstein to the Gospels, the humble and egalitarian message of which contrasts sharply with (what he sees as) the proud and hierarchical nature of the epistles of St. Paul: in the Gospels "you find huts; in Paul a church" (ibid., 30).

This emphasis on a "simple faith" is a constant feature of Wittgenstein's reflections on religion and can be most explicitly seen in the early period of his philosophy. In the *Tractatus Logico-Philosophicus* (1921), Wittgenstein had expounded a minimal conception of language whereby its sole purpose was to depict (possible or actual) factual situations in the world. This theory entailed that the only viable use of language was that to which it was put within the natural sciences, and consequently the language of theology (as well as that of metaphysics, of aesthetics, and of ethics) was illegitimate. But rather than dismiss religious faith as worthlessly nonsensical—as the logical positivists were subsequently to do—Wittgenstein's actual purpose was to retain a crucial role for religious belief, and he elaborated what Paul Engelmann later referred to as "wordless faith," a faith in which doctrines (exposed as lacking sense owing to their failure to connect with the objects found in the world) are replaced by appropriate life conduct. Even when the overarching semantic framework of the *Tractatus* had been fatally undermined by the criticisms leveled in the later (and posthumous) *Philosophical Investigations* (1953) (in which his earlier monolithic conception of language had been replaced by a more open-textured one in which language was described as a motley collection of diverse linguistic practices, each governed by its own set of rules), Wittgenstein still maintained that an emphasis on doctrinal formulae ran counter to the spirit of the gospel and was to that extent unacceptable: "I believe that one of the things Christianity says is that sound doctrines are all useless. That you have to change your *life*" (1980, 53). The emphasis here is once more on *action*, an emphasis made explicit in a comment on the theology of Karl Barth, which, Wittgenstein implied, merely "gesticulates with words." The lesson to be drawn: "*Practice* gives the words their sense" (ibid., 85).

In view of the foregoing, it would be right to assume that Wittgenstein would be unimpressed by the desire to produce some precise Christological formula. At worst, such an enterprise might be seen as an instance of language idling (para. 132), although appeal to his (albeit undeveloped) notion of "Theology as grammar" (ibid., para. 373) could preserve a place for such abstract work. What we might then call "grammatical Christology" would consist of an elaboration of the rules concerning what can and cannot be said about the being and work of Jesus within the linguistic practices of the Christian faith. Other aspects of Wittgenstein's thinking on this matter suggest other—though still undeveloped—lines of inquiry. Consonant with his claim that religious belief only *appears* to be propositional but is in reality "a way of living" (1980, 64), Wittgenstein's ideas about Jesus can admit of an interpretation whereby to "believe in the Lord Jesus Christ" and to express a belief in his divinity should be regarded as expressions of a manner of living (consisting of self-denial, service to others, and so on) from which such linguistic pronouncements cannot be divorced, and only within which they have life. Wittgenstein's musings can thus be placed within the tradition of those thinkers—such as Tolstoy and Friedrich Nietzsche—who, while impressed by the manner of life of Jesus, are less favorable to the abstract speculations of theologians, stressing instead that the only way to be a Christian is to follow the life-example of Christ. A truly "Wittgensteinian Christology"—as yet unattempted—would need to incorporate both these elements: a grammatical elaboration of the nature and being of Jesus and an emphasis on simple Christian *practice*.

Brian R. Clack

See also: Barth, Karl; Christology, Modern; Jesus as Servant; Nietzsche, Freidrich von; Paul; Resurrection

References

Clack, Brian R. 1999. *An Introduction to Wittgenstein's Philosophy of Religion*. Edinburgh: Edinburgh University Press.

Engelmann, Paul. 1967. *Letters from Ludwig Wittgenstein with a Memoir*. Oxford: Basil Blackwell.

Kerr, Fergus. 1986. *Theology after Wittgenstein*. Oxford: Basil Blackwell.

Sherry, Patrick. 1977. *Religion, Truth and Language-Games*. London and Basingstoke: Macmillan.

Wittgenstein, Ludwig. 1953. *Philosophical Investigations*. Edited by G. E. M. Anscombe and Ruth Rhees. Oxford: Blackwell.

———. 1961 [1921]. *Tractatus Logico-Philosophicus*. Translated by D. F. Pears and B. F. McGuinness. London: Routledge and Keegan Paul.

———. 1980. *Culture and Value*. Oxford: Basil Blackwell.

Women and Jesus

See Feminist Theology; Jesus, Family of; Mary; Roman Catholicism; Sexuality

Word

See Bonaventure; John, Gospel of; Preexistence

Work

When in 1955 the Roman Catholic Church wanted to embrace what is commonly called "the world of work," surely with more than an eye on the arch-enemy and competitor of the period, Russian-led communism, with its stress on "workers" and toil as the road to social good, it selected as the devotional symbol St. Joseph the Worker, spouse of Mary, with his feast on (no coincidence) the first of May, with its strong "workers" associations.

This link between Joseph and work rested formally on a single biblical text, Matthew 13.55, where the people of Nazareth refer to Jesus, visiting and astounding them, as "the carpenter's son." In fact, Matthew was adapting Mark 6.3, where the people say, "Is not this the carpenter?" referring to Jesus himself. Matthew's little alteration may be of no more than trivial significance, but it would not be out of character for him to have felt that carpentering would represent a certain indignity for the Messiah and that explicit reference had better be transferred to his parent. Luke says only: "Is this not Joseph's son?"—with no reference to either as workmen (4.22). Perhaps he, too, was avoiding taking action, but more discreetly.

There is, in fact, no reason to suppose that both Joseph and Jesus would not have engaged in work to earn their daily bread, though the precise social level implied by the Greek *tekton* (conventionally rendered "carpenter," though it could also mean a worker in stone or a builder) is not wholly clear. It might indicate a rather special or key place in the village hierarchy, or, by contrast, point to loss of land (the real sign of a stable living) in uncertain times and virtually reduction to "odd-jobbing."

In any case, Jesus abandoned the life of stable daily work and became an itinerant preacher. What is more, he urged others to do the same (Mark 1.16–20; 2.13–14). And there is no hint anywhere that this was somehow a dereliction of basic human duty, an abandonment, even a scorning, of a dignity that comes from work: no sign of anything like a Protestant work-ethic. Rather, the preaching of the kingdom, the furthering of the cause of God and the urgent completion of his purposes take precedence.

Indeed, there is in the preaching of Jesus a lightness of touch that may reflect a sense of the kingdom as a return to Eden, the paradisal state where human life was free of toil (see Matthew 6.25–34). Here is a doctrine of almost reckless abandon, urging simple reliance on God for the meeting of one's needs. It is a reversal of the curse of Adam, whereby hard work is a punishment for disobedience (Gen. 3.17–19), and is in tune with other texts that see the dispensation inaugurated by Jesus in "new creation" terms (e.g., 2 Cor. 5.17). Everything is becoming brand-new. Once more, modern ideas about the dignity of work and even about human creativity in craftsmanship do not feature in this springtime of the Christian movement. Where itinerant apostolate is in view and local support is to be looked for, there is no interest in the logic that other people's work is being relied on to provide for the preacher (e.g., Matt. 10.11, 41–42): the needs of the kingdom dominate all. Of course, work figures in several of Jesus' parables (e.g., Matt. 20.1–16; Luke 16.1–8), but it is not treated in its own right and is merely a vehicle of a message that has nothing to do with the status of work in itself.

In the earliest Christian communities of the next period, urban not rural, settled not itinerant, it is not surprising that we find what we would no doubt see as a more sober, more practical approach. Paul was a tentmaker and content to work to support himself, even defiantly so, in defense of his economic independence, perhaps in relation to the more wealthy of his converts (1 Cor. 9.8–18). And giddy apocalypticism is firmly put down: "If anyone will not work, let him not eat" (2 Thess. 3.10). More comforting, wiser values emerge and we feel more at home.

As far as Jesus himself is concerned, then, there is little basis for a "theology of work" in anything like a modern sense. If biblical roots are sought, then they are more likely to be found in the Old Testament rather than the New, especially in the creative energy of God displayed in passages such as Genesis 1–2, Proverbs 8, and Psalm 104, though the new creation doctrine of Paul and the vision laid out in Revelation 21–22 are potent indeed. We may, however, note the attention given to our theme in John 5: "My Father is working still, and I am working" (v. 17). But what is referred to is not work in general, rather the life-giving, "saving" work of healing, just exemplified in the curing of the man ill for thirty-eight years. This is indeed about new creation, or the removal of the evils that have assailed the old. The work of Jesus is the giving of life. That example can, of course, serve as a springboard for all kinds of good work in his name. It may, indeed, provide the poetic impetus to vivify many kinds of ordinary work that humankind is engaged in, though there are forms of toil where it would take an extraordinary depth of soul or imaginative power to do so. And then sociopolitical visions may begin to join hands with religious faith for the world's healing.

Leslie Houlden

See also: Jesus in Social Context; Kingdom of God

Wright, N. T. (b. 1948)

N. T. Wright has argued that Jesus was an apocalyptic prophet who understood himself to be Israel's messiah and, in some sense, the very embodiment of Yahweh. Jesus received the call to act as Israel's messiah (or confirmation of such a call) at his baptism by John the Baptist and announced that the long-awaited kingdom of Israel's God was coming to birth. This kingdom involved the return from exile, the defeat of evil, and the return of Yahweh to Zion. The agenda of Jesus involved not a military victory of God over evil but a victory involving turning the other cheek, going the second mile, taking up the cross. Israel was warned, therefore, that her present ways of advancing the kingdom were counterproductive and would result in a great national disaster.

Jesus drew matters to a head in one particular trip to Jerusalem. Prophecies detailing the return from Babylonian exile (Isa. 40–55 in general, and 52.13–53.12 in particular) shed light on that trip—events in the temple, the upper room, and the hill outside the city gate. And Mark 13 sheds light on Jesus' understanding of the significance of the coming fall of Jerusalem in A.D. 70. Jesus interpreted his death and vindication after death as the defeat of evil; this was the way that Yahweh would return to Zion. The destruction of Jerusalem thus "proves" that Jesus was right and the nation wrong.

Jesus, however, knew that his followers would be muddled and ambiguous—as he also knew that the nation as a whole would not repent. It was, therefore, within Jesus' intention that his followers would return to his summons after failing to heed it during his lifetime. They would reuse Jesus' teachings, his challenge to Israel, as a basis for their understanding of themselves as the renewed community of Yahweh's people.

In order to understand the historical Jesus, however, the Gospels must be studied from the context of the life of Jesus within first-century Judaism. Jesus affirmed the basic Jewish paradigm that offered a long-awaited renewal and restoration, but he provided new terms and new goals—as other Jewish sects had done (including the followers of John and the Essenes).

The metanarrative (or paradigm) for Israel was exile and restoration. Wright saw this theme as central for Jesus and used the parable of the prodigal son as the template for understanding and presenting Jesus' career. This story of a son who goes off into a far country, and returns to find his welcome challenged by another son who has stayed put, is the story of Israel's exile and restoration. At a deep level (the level of "narrative grammar"), it is the story of the exilic prophets, the books of Ezra and Nehemiah, and a good deal of subsequent Jewish literature. The story of the prodigal says that the hope of Israel is now being fulfilled. But Jesus' retelling of the story is subversive. Israel went into exile because of her own folly and disobedience, and the return is the result of the fantastically generous love of her God. Moreover, the real return from exile is taking place in Jesus' own ministry.

The way that Jesus is related to Judaism in both a positive and negative fashion provided Wright with his major criteria for authenticity. To make historical sense, Jesus' proclamation of the kingdom must be clearly understood within its Jewish context *and* it must challenge some prevailing assumptions within that Jewish context. In addition, Jesus' proclamation must be clearly understood as the presupposition for the very different resonance of "kingdom" in the early Church *and* retain a focus characteristic of Jesus' career, not simply the work of Jesus' post-Easter followers. Wright called these the criteria of double similarity and double dissimilarity.

Wright did not apply these criteria to individual sayings but to the Gospels' story line about Jesus in light of other prevailing Jewish narratives concerning the end of the exile. The criteria, then, do not function as criteria for authenticity function in Rudolf Bultmann, the New Quest, and the Jesus Seminar (authenticating a limited number of isolated sayings and actions of Jesus). In fact, no tradition of the Synoptic Gospels is called into question with the use of the criteria used by Wright. The criteria validate the agenda of a "Third Quest" that fits Jesus into first-century Judaism. And the criteria allow the Synoptic traditions to be accepted as historical as they fit comfortably within the ministry of Jesus as apocalyptic prophet. The criteria are useful as they show how the data of the Synoptic Gospels fit into the large-scale narrative Wright constructed.

Wright began his story of Jesus' career with the story of the prodigal son, and he brought his story to a conclusion with a use of that story to summarize the epistemological assumptions followed in the book and to ridicule other assumptions. He reversed the judgment of Albert Schweitzer that Jesus comes to us as one unknown. Rather, Wright said, "*We* come to *him* as ones unknown, crawling back from the far country, where we had wasted our substance on riotous but ruinous historicism" (1996, 662). The swinehusks are the assured results of modern criticism that reminded us of the knowledge that we had nearly extinguished, and so we began the journey home. "But when we approached, as we have tried to do in this book," Wright declared, "we found him running to us as one well known, whom we had spurned in the name of scholarship or even of faith, but who was still patiently waiting to be sought and found once more" (ibid.).

E. V. McKnight

See also: Baptism; Bultmann, Rudolf; Jesus in Social Context; Jesus Seminar; John the Baptist; Kingdom of God; Messiah; Schweitzer, Albert

References

Primary

Wright, N. T. 1992a. *The New Testament and the People of God*. Vol. 1 of *Christian Origins and the Question of God*. London: SPCK; Minneapolis: Fortress.

———. 1992b. *Who Was Jesus?* London: SPCK; Grand Rapids, MI: William B. Eerdmans.

———. 1996. *Jesus and the Victory of God*. Vol. 2 of *Christian Origins and the Question of God*. London: SPCK; Minneapolis: Fortress.

———. 2003. *The Resurrection of the Son of God*. Vol. 3 of *Christian Origins and the Question of God*. London: SPCK.

Secondary

Newman, Carey C., ed. 1999. *Jesus and the Restoration of Israel: A Critical Assessment of N.T. Wright's "Jesus and the Victory of God."* Carlisle, UK: Paternoster Press; Downers Grove, IL: InterVarsity Press.

GLOSSARY

Note: cross-referenced topics appearing in bold type in the glossary text refer the reader to articles in the body of this encyclopedia. Terms appearing in italic type refer to other glossary entries.

Apocalyptic: as an adjective, the term refers to a style of thought, imagery, and writing concerned with the coming end of the present world and so of human history. Often, this material also refers to the present invisible world of heavenly realities, which is described in continuity with the future state of affairs. *Apocalyptic*, together with the related noun, *apocalypse*, has the literal sense of "revelation" or "revelatory," and the root is the Greek word-family bearing this sense. The fund of imagery of this kind, with all its richness and fecundity, came into Jewish circles in the final centuries before Christ from Persian sources, and, in intermarriage with existing Jewish mythological forms, developed into a rich tradition, with many written productions, for example, the latter part of the Book of Daniel. In early Christianity, it took fresh forms, notably in the Revelation (or Apocalypse) of John and in parts of the Gospels (for example, Mark 13; Matt. 24; Luke 21; cf. also 1 Thess. 4.13–17). In this writing, Jesus, now exalted to heaven, was incorporated—and took central place—in the pattern of what was to come, and there is little doubt that in the Church's early days (and probably in Jesus' own mind) the future was soon to be unfolded. In the second century, this style of Christian belief faded and ideas that were more philosophically based came to be the favored idiom, even though belief in a coming end as not too far distant remained. Language and imagery of this sort have enjoyed vigorous revivals at various times in the Church's history and in particular circles, removed as they are from its original base. In much of Christianity, however, the nonarrival of what was foretold has meant that the emphasis has shifted to other, less dramatic aspects of faith, to spirituality in the here and now, and to practical ethics. This can either be seen as an abandonment, however understandable, of an essential part of Christian faith, or as a legitimate development, itself also foreshadowed from the earliest days, notably in the Gospel of John. But "apocalyptic" enshrines a vital sense of movement and purpose. (See **American [North] Christianity; John, Revelation of; Kingdom of God; Second Coming of Jesus, Origins of; Second Coming of Jesus in Current Belief;** see also *Eschatology*.)

Atonement: the event and process whereby God, through Jesus, and chiefly through his death, brought a new status of acceptance and forgiveness to the human race, whether in terms of an offer that may or may not be accepted; or in terms of a gift freely available to all; or, on some views, one available only for a chosen minority. It may be seen as, in effect, a new policy on the part of God, a revision of his legitimate condemnation of a fallen race, or rather as a dramatic and costly disclosure of his eternal purpose for the good of his creation, especially humankind. Such an act is designed to make us "at one" with

God, which may even be seen as our being raised to a status alongside Christ (Rom. 8. 14–21; John 1.12–14). One might see the whole concept as stemming from a kind of spiritual euphoria to which Jesus gave rise.

Many images are used to describe this divine act, for example, reconciliation with God (2 Cor. 5.18–20), or new creation (2 Cor. 5.17; Gal. 6.15). They represent a vivid sense of transformation and newness. In later times, some of the quasi-poetic images found in the early days developed into full-blown theories, often in the light of prevailing social or intellectual conditions: thus, Anselm's picture of Christ as offering "satisfaction" for us all to God, whose "honor" has been insulted by our sin, assumes the framework of feudal relationships in early medieval European society. Similarly, Abelard's emphasis on the moral nature of Jesus as, by his life and death, an example that is to move us to return to God, reflects a sense of moral and spiritual quest as found in the religious life of the same period.

New Testament imagery, derived from Jewish practice of the period, sometimes took up the institutions of animal sacrifice, as detailed in the Book of Leviticus. Such allusions certainly captured the dramatic sense of Jesus' death having brought about a revolution. This image itself could take a variety of forms, both in the New Testament (Rom. 3.25; John 1.29) and later, when it could harden into quasi-literal schemes. Colossians 2.15 may be seen as the seed of another line of imagery, that sees Jesus as having vanquished the devil. And the Letter to the Hebrews works out an elaborate story line of Jesus taking up and fulfilling the ceremonies of the Jewish Day of Atonement (Yom Kippur). Those who feel uncomfortable with both the rigor and the incompatibility of the more formal "theories of the atonement" may prefer to see them as luxuriant growths from what are better seen as quasi-poetic images, each perhaps playing its part in helping our understanding but failing when taken into hard, intellectual elaboration. The heart of the matter may lie in the conjunction of God's love and human response, with its varied levels of adequacy and perception. And Jesus' death brings home the utter tragic seriousness of what is at stake. (See **Hebrews, Letter to the; Jesus, Achievement of; Paul.**)

Baptism: derived from the Greek for "dip," the term came into Christian use from Judaism. There, ceremonial washings were a constant feature of life and used also (as in the case of John the Baptist's mission) to symbolize a more radical recommitment, as well as probably in relation to conversions to Judaism. As far as we can go back in Christian life, such "dipping" was used as the rite of initiation into the Christian community—or rather, for many, for example Paul, into Christ himself. It could be seen as indeed a washing (1 Cor. 6.11), or, more radically, as a drowning of the old self and a rising to new life in Christ (Rom. 6.3–11); it could also be seen as making one a possession of Jesus (Acts: baptism "into the name of Jesus"). One of its most fruitful aspects was that it could be used for males and females alike (unlike circumcision, the basic rite of entry into Judaism). Thus Christianity had a built-in sexual equality or gender-indifference that has not always been recognized (see Gal. 3.28), and the prominence of women converts in Acts and in the text of the Gospel of John reflects this equality. Once established, the rite has remained, with variations of use and controversies over its proper applicability (for example, whether or not one should baptize infants), and it has been the basic act of Christian initiation ever since. (See **Baptism; John the Baptist; Son of God.**)

Catechesis: Greek for "instruction." Almost confined to technical reference to Christian instruction, oral or written. But "catechisms" (that is, handbooks, whether short or long) continue to appear from the churches to serve as the bases for Christian teaching. They were much favored among the Reformers in the sixteenth and seventeenth centuries, and the Roman Catholic Church has recently issued a sizable new catechism containing official guidance and exposition of belief and conduct.

Christology: words, ideas, thought, or teaching concerning Jesus Christ, from Greek *Christos* ("Messiah"). At root, there is the belief that he is central in the saving purpose of God, first in relation to the people of Israel (for he stems from their history and is one of them), then to the human race (to which he also belongs). That this belief about Jesus came to center formally on the idea of his being "Messiah" is in a way accidental, but it was this term to describe his status and role that (though oddly applied to such a one as he—nonpolitical, unmilitary, proletarian) quickly became so central that "Jesus Christ" rapidly came to be, in effect, one form of his proper name, with its technical sense usually lost.

Ideas about his status appeared in a series of terms that expressed some aspect of common response to or evaluation of him. Each has its own pedigree in Jewish (and Old Testament) usage and obtained a new twist through being applied to him: hence, "Son of God," "Son of Man," "Lord"—as well as "Messiah" (see the encyclopedia articles that cover each of these terms for detailed discussion). These terms quickly lost their original sharpness and their original sense from Judaism, and some of them took new senses to express aspects of developing ways of understanding Jesus. By the second century, and then with increasing sophistication, discussion came to center on the twin Christian conviction that Jesus was (in some sense—but what sense?) both divine and human. As many people then thought these two aspects of reality to be mutually exclusive, it was hard to see how anyone could be both—yet that Jesus was such a one was precisely the wonder of what God had done. In the following three centuries, there was unceasing discussion and disagreement as churches tried to work out a satisfactory statement of the matter, culminating in the Council of Chalcedon in 451. (See the blind entry at **Christology** in this encyclopedia for a list of relevant articles; the **Chalcedon** entry for the nearest to an agreement achieved in the period; and the glossary listing covering the word pairs *Divinity-Humanity; Divine nature–Human nature; Son of God–Son of man.*)

In recent centuries, since the Enlightenment and the development of a strong historical sense, in general and in relation to the Bible, as well as sensitivity to the diversity of cultures in which people have thought about this matter, there has been a tendency for the old controversy's terms to fade and the old settlement to be questioned—not because it was "false" but because it seems off target. In particular, in the early centuries, it seemed most natural to see Jesus as certainly divine (how otherwise could he "save" us?), and then to inquire how and in what ways he could also be human; now, it has come to be felt that he must certainly have been a man of his time and place, however exceptional and wonderful, and then we must try to see how to understand his being divine. In this quest, some of the New Testament terms, seen as striking images, have come (for those who attend) to resonate through to our culture, and people may see what it may mean to take the man Jesus as "God-for-us."

Two pairs of expressions are, as a result, common in discussing Christology: first, "high" and "low," and second, "from above" and "from below." The former contrast refers to twin approaches such as we have just described. Is Jesus to be seen as at root divine, with his humanity as a kind of instrument in his hand ("high"), or as basically a man, one of us, but God's agent ("low")? Then, and similarly: Does one start the discussion from Jesus' "heavenly" status and then work out how to see his "visit" to the world ("from above"); or does one start from this world, Galilee of the first century, and then work out how we might see this insignificant figure from an insignificant place as God's chosen one ("from below")? (If the latter, how does he really differ from other alleged prophet-like figures and what happens to the traditional idea of his "uniqueness"—and then how far does that matter—perhaps he is "unique *for us*"?) People may vacillate and see virtue in both emphases, feeling that it is foolish to place Jesus as "no more than" a mere man (what man has a 450,000-word book about him, and it could be bigger!); yet equally foolish to see him as a "visitor" from elsewhere, not deeply akin to us, as if in some television drama or ancient myth. The question of dealing with the subject in a way that evacuates neither the factuality nor the wonder that faith cannot renounce (and which reason may support) remains. (In addition to the encyclopedia articles already mentioned, see **Christology, Modern; Enlightenment; Interfaith Thought and Relations; Lord; Messiah; Son of God; Son of Man.**)

Church: the actual English word is rooted in the Greek for "the Lord's *(kurios)* place" but this has no relation to the word it translates, *ekklesia,* an assembly or gathering, probably with overtones from the Greek version of the Jewish Scriptures (the Old Testament), where it is used in some places for the assembled people of Israel. This origin remains in many European languages, for example, *église* in French and *eglwys* in Welsh. With whatever precise associations, Old Testament, civic, or otherwise, this was the dominant term that the Christian community took for itself (others, such as "the Way," found a few times in Acts, soon faded). It can signify that community as a whole, wherever found; or, in due course, one form of it among others, perhaps regarded by its adherents as uniquely authentic, for example, the Roman Catholic Church or the Methodist Church; then, by extension, a building where the community assembles. (See **Church**.)

Council: gatherings, chiefly of bishops, from either one geographical area or the Church as a whole, whether by church initiative or at the instance of the emperor (as often after Constantine's conversion). The best-known ancient church councils bearing on the subject of Jesus were at Nicea (325) and Chalcedon (451). Their purpose was to arrive at guidance and rules for both belief and practice. From the third and especially the fourth centuries councils have been a constant feature of Christian life, varying in form, frequency, importance, and competence—down to the present. (See **Nicea; Chalcedon.**)

Counter-Reformation: the common name for the movement of Catholic rejuvenation that took place in the second half of the sixteenth century and whose influence continued in the succeeding period. Its official springboard was the Council of Trent, a gathering of bishops under the papacy that met spasmodically from 1545 to 1563. In addition to doctrinal "tightening," it had a profound influence on matters such as the training of the clergy, leading to the establishment of a coherent system of seminaries.The Counter-Reformation reinforced the Catholic position on matters, such as the doctrine of the Eucharist, that the Reformers (for example, Martin Luther and John Calvin) had questioned in their different ways. Its work was furthered by new religious orders, such as the Jesuits and the Oratorians (see **Ignatius of Loyola**).

It is a mistake, however, to see this movement as purely a reaction to the Protestant Reform (see *Reformed*), and for this reason the word *counter* is misleading. In the late fifteenth and sixteenth centuries, there was in Europe a general movement to reform much in Christian thought and practice, and though its strong effect was first felt in North Germany, Swiss cities, and then England and parts of France, others closer to Rome (in power and geography) also felt the need for change. The two related manifestations, which, tragically, led to widespread European war in the first half of the seventeenth century (the Thirty Years War), shared some of their aims at heart and sprang from shared roots. Only since the second half of the twentieth century has there begun to be serious rapprochement between the two sides of the former single Western Church, with some of the issues that arose at the Reformation coming to be seen in a fresh light. This tendency has perhaps been especially felt in relations between the Roman Catholic and the

Anglican Churches, but also between Catholics and Lutherans. The Second Vatican Council of the 1960s made a major push in this direction (for example, through bringing in the use of local languages instead of Latin for Catholic liturgy, just as the Reformers had done, and in making ecumenical relations much more open and positive). So people long estranged have begun to discover that that they belong to one family. And of course the effects now spread far beyond Europe.

Creed: a summary of belief, often emphasizing matters in dispute at the time of its formation, but originally meant for the profession of faith by converts at baptism, then serving disciplinary purposes. Related adjective: creedal. (See **Creeds**.)

Divinity-Humanity; Divine nature–Human nature; Son of God–Son of man: these pairs of words are often used to refer to the dual character or the two aspects of Jesus as understood down the centuries in Christian faith (see *Christology*). The first two pairs of words are hardly prominent in ordinary Christian speech, or even in hymns, liturgies, sermons, or the creeds (statements of belief) in regular use. They are the words used in technical discussion and definition: this is what is to be safeguarded if we are to say what we believe about Jesus. So the two pairs belong together in the more technical kind of Christian speech. The third pair is used more popularly to express the same truth: Jesus unites God and humankind. Not that he is a hybrid; rather, he spans the divide between God and his creatures. His marvel lies precisely in his being the bridge-figure, the point of attraction for humans uncertain of their standing before God or bereft of him (through sin, failure, or suffering). Jesus is the one who gives hope and "rescue." (see *Atonement; Redeemer; Salvation*). But these two familiar expressions from Paul and the Gospels, "Son of God" and "Son of man," have a complex history, going back into pre-Christian Judaism, and began by having senses other than those they later acquired: see **Son of God** and **Son of Man**. The first two pairs are by contrast products of the Church, as it sought to express its faith in the context of the prevailing Platonist-style philosophical climate.

In the first four centuries, the great weight of Christian theological discussion and dispute centered on the question of the terms on which Jesus' "two-ness" might properly be understood. The risk lay in somehow underplaying the one aspect or the other or else positing such a strange being that he hardly belonged in any comprehensible category at all. Much of the problem arose because of the assumption of his preexistence, before ever he came into the world, on the basis of poetic Jewish symbols and New Testament texts (see **Preexistence**). Not surprisingly, there were those who unbalanced or confused the situation by over-weighting one aspect or the other, the divine or the human. Was Jesus human? Yes, of course; but he was, more than any other human who has ever been, inspired and empowered by God, so that in him we truly meet God: God, in that sense, has been among us, and we can grasp the lifeline. Others, taking as given his "divinity"—he was from all eternity one with God in "being" or "nature"—ask: how may we make sense of his coming into this world of transience, evil, and suffering? It must have been done by nothing less than a supreme act of condescension, a visit (a royal visit?) from one who truly belonged elsewhere—and only because of that was in a position to raise us to be with and even like him. For many, that was the Christian dream—only no dream, for it was the sober reality. But questions arose: did he then truly have a human "nature" like ours, or was that of no purpose for him (for he was divine), so that he was, in effect, of one nature only (see **Chalcedon,** re Monophysitism and Monophysite)? And was he in any case *truly* divine, or only secondarily so or analogically so? For surely there is only one God: Christians are not polytheists, worshipers of several gods, as pagans taunted in the early centuries. (See article on **Nicea,** for Arius' sense of this difficulty.) No, they said, only God can save us—we are saved—so he must indeed be truly divine.

"Of one substance with the Father" was the formula in the creed (see article) of Nicea in 325. But was that to say that the two are made of the same "stuff," as two bars of chocolate are made of "the same substance"? Or was it to say they are "one entity," as a substance can mean an "object"?—for there was only one "thing" to see and relate to: God is God and there could be no tampering with that oneness.

The root of some of these strange difficulties and dilemmas (as they may now seem, at least to the newcomer to them) lay in part in the language available for their discussion. It was the language of highly rational, technical prose; but was the subject one perhaps more appropriate to poetry and the language of relationships? At all events, this technical language is, among modern Christians or unbelievers, either taken for granted or else left aside, hardly suitable for discussion. Once one goes below the surface, the terms we are discussing here are likely to be found intractable, and image-speech may be more helpful. We are speaking the language of faith, doing its best to make sense of itself: but was this the best sense forever and ever? Or will other, less tight, images serve? For Christians still feel that the central truth must be somehow retained.

Ecclesiastical: a formal term for "relating to the Church." It is the adjective from *ekklesia*, the Greek word for "assembly" that lies behind "church" in English (see *Church*). It tends to be used in official contexts: for example, one speaks of ecclesiastical titles, customs, law, usage, music, and so on.

Ecumenism: from Greek *oikoumene*, "the inhabited world." It is the name given to the movement from the early years of the twentieth century especially, to develop better relations between the plethora of different Christian churches everywhere, most of which owed their origin to quarrels or disagreements of one sort or another. The Ecumenical Movement was inspired by an acute sense of the scandal of Christian disunity, perhaps most notably in countries where rival churches engaged in missionary activities, as it seemed, like rival firms touting for business. The ultimate aim was the reunion of the churches, seen as authorized by Jesus' prayer in John 17, "that they all may be one." In the meantime, negotiations could be entered into in different kinds of areas, both theological and ethico-practical.

The concrete fruits of the great endeavors of the past eighty years or so may be thought meager—a few reunion schemes in India and elsewhere for example, but the climate has undoubtedly been transformed. The Orthodox Church, hitherto often isolated from other churches, has been a full member of the central ecumenical agency, the World Council of Churches, centered in Geneva; and since the 1960s (the Second Vatican Council), the Roman Catholic Church has taken a number of important steps of an ecumenical kind, hitherto improbable, though they are often seen as grudging. In recent years, the movement is perceived as having lost some of its momentum, but in some countries this is partly because at local levels as well as among church leaders a good deal of cooperation and interaction is now taken for granted. (The adjective "ecumenical" is also used to refer to church councils attended by bishops from the whole Church, as distinct from more local gatherings; for example, those of **Nicea,** 325, and **Chalcedon,** 451.)

Eschatology: Literally, the study of thought about '"the last things" (Greek *eschata*), traditionally categorized as "death, judgment, heaven, and hell." (See also *Apocalyptic*.)

Ethics: the study and practice of morality or good behavior; the mode of argument and reflection on questions of human conduct. (See discussion in articles including **Family, War,** and **Wealth.**)

Eucharist: from Greek *eucharistia*, "thanksgiving": the central act of worship in all the mainstream Christian churches from the beginning (though not all Protestant bodies use it with great frequency). The act is rooted in the Last Supper and consists centrally in the blessing of (or "giving thanks" for) bread and wine, and receiving them as the great expression of unity with both fellow Christians and with God-through-Christ. It has attracted to itself, not surprisingly, both richness of devotion and imagery as well as controversy. (See **Eucharist; Hymns.**)

Evangelical: from Greek *euaggelion*, literally, "good news"; the word used in Paul and two of the Gospels (Mark and Matthew) for the Christian message, and in due course brought into common Christian use. The term has come to bear a variety of applications: (1) to refer to Protestant Christians in the early days of the Reformation in the sixteenth century (and to the German Lutheran Church to this day): they sought to recall people to the "good news" of early Christianity as revealed in the New Testament; (2) to refer to Christians who adhere to a "Bible only" message, as opposed to those who favor dependence also on church tradition and more Catholic styles of worship and church life—especially in English and American Christianity in the nineteenth, twentieth, and twenty-first centuries; (3) to refer to "gospel values," as in evangelical poverty or evangelical lifestyle, that draw on the Gospels for models of Christian life—common in Roman Catholic usage. In the second century, the related word "gospel" came to be used for books that were seen to give an account of the "good news"—"according to" a particular writer (Mark or Matthew, for example). English usage has made the related words diverge in application: strictly and linguistically, "evangelical" persons are "gospel" people, though many who are uncomfortable to be called "evangelicals," given the word's associations with particular ideas and policies, may wish to adopt the latter name for themselves. "Evangelism" is the activity of making this gospel known.

Heresy: from the Greek *hairesis*, "party," "faction"; in Christian usage, *heresy* came to refer less to people than to ideas and beliefs. It meant a belief at variance with "right belief" (see also *orthodoxy*). Sometimes this variance has been on a particular point of doctrine—the nature of the Eucharist, for example, or the person of Christ; sometimes it has been more comprehensive, as in the case of the Protestant groups and churches of the sixteenth century and since—from the point of view of Catholicism. Although it has tended to be a term chiefly known from its use by the "big" churches in relation to breakaway groups, it has also been used in smaller contexts and indeed by the breakaways about the parent bodies. It is an easy charge to level, for the human mind is fertile, inescapably, and resistance to its movement is endemic in those with authority. But there is a serious issue about the "management" of development and change in the statement of belief in changing cultures and other circumstances. Though the cry of "heresy" is still easily raised, the phenomenon in question tends now to be treated with more patience and caution, whether wisely or weakly is not for a glossary to say.

Hypostasis: one of the technical words, derived from Greek thought of the period, that were prominent in discussion of the Trinity and of the truth about Jesus during the early centuries of the Church. It is often translated "substance," but its basic sense is "reality" as opposed to illusion. A difficulty was that another word (*ousia*, literally "being," from the Greek verb "to be") carried the same sense of "substance," and there was scope for confusion. In due course, it settled down as the word used to signify the "threeness" in God (each of the "persons," Father, Son, and Spirit, was a distinct *hypostasis*), while *ousia* served for that which they shared, the essential oneness of God. (See also the glossary listing for the word pairs *Divinity-Humanity; Divine nature–Human nature; Son of God–Son of man*).

Incarnation: the act of becoming "flesh" (Latin *carnis*) or human, starting from some higher level, in Christian use, "the divine": so used to describe Jesus' coming into the human sphere (see *Christology*). The term stems from John 1.14: "[T]he Word was made flesh and dwelt among us." It tends to focus on the wonder of the action by God, or else its sheer factuality. But as a term it is not confined to the figure of Jesus. (See **Interfaith Thought and Relations.**)

Jesus of history; Christ of faith: the two expressions have come to be used as a kind of shorthand to express, one might say, the dilemma raised for many believing Christians by the spirit (even more than the findings) of the critical study of the New Testament. The more candidly and vividly Jesus is seen in his historical setting, the less natural it seems to view him as the object of faith in anything like the traditional way and under traditional terms. In that sense, faith becomes a bigger leap than in former times. But the expressions can also refer to the twin response from the earliest days. For many, Jesus was, in his own day, simply one man among others; for others, he was the object of faith (under a number of verbal expressions, such as "messiah," "son of God," and "lord"). On any showing, faith being faith, there can be no way of "proving" that the one evaluation can lead to the other: it is a matter of attachment, loyalty, conviction, of its very nature unprovable (though many have sought to demonstrate it along various lines of argument that tend to assume what they seek to achieve). Of course, many modern scholars, while understanding the difference between the two "tones" of evaluation, see no reason why the move to faith should not be made by modern persons, probably in different ways from the first Christians but with a shared conviction that Jesus is central to the self-disclosure of God and the carrying out of his purpose for humankind. (See **Christology, Modern** and **Jesus as a Historical Figure;** see also *Christology* in this glossary.)

Johannine, Lucan, Marcan, Matthean, Pauline: standard adjectives used to describe the thought and writings that bear the corresponding names (John, Luke, Mark, Matthew, Paul), the form of the adjective, where it seems strange, deriving from the Greek or Latin form of the name.

Liberal theology: a term widely used to point to a range of theological ideas and attitudes stemming generally from the Enlightenment in the eighteenth century, and from movements going back even further. It is marked by a readiness to question the traditional authorized doctrines, for example concerning Jesus, in the light of changing ways of thought that have come to seem compelling. In that sense, liberal theology tends to be out of tune with the official deliverances of the churches. Whether it is popular or not varies from time to time. As far as Jesus is concerned, its effects show in a willingness to face historical study realistically and with imagination, and not to suppress its results in the interests of ways of thinking that stem from earlier days when historical attitudes were undeveloped. There is also a sense that the technical theological terms used to "define" Jesus in the early centuries were derived from a philosophical framework that can no longer be sustained. So there is likely to be felt a need to take traditional creeds as documents of their time but now serviceable as symbols of belief rather than quasi-legal statements to be accepted as they stand. However, liberal theology believes that it is loyal to the essence of faith and indeed is liberating it from worn shackles to become more understandable in new times. The heyday of liberal theology was in some universities in nineteenth-century Germany and in some British and American circles. Karl Barth pioneered a reaction against liberal theology in the years after the Great War, with considerable success, and its later popularity in the twentieth century was more in America and Great Britain than in Germany. (See **Barth, Karl; Creeds; Enlightenment; Harnack, Adolf von; Schleiermacher, F. D. E.**)

Mariology: literally, "word" (Greek, *logos*) concerning Mary; but like all "-logy" words, the sense relates to thought and investigation about the particular subject (cf. "biology" = the study of *bios*, "life"). Just as "Christology" means "thought, doctrine, concerning Christ/Jesus," so, as a dependent subject, there is teaching concerning Mary, the Blessed Virgin, mother of Jesus, and, notably from the early fifth century, "mother of God." The doctrines or beliefs concerning Mary depend upon her role in relation to Jesus. The earliest derives from the Gospels: the belief that she was unmarried at the time of Jesus' conception and that this was a divine act (see **Jesus, Origins of**). There can be little doubt that in Matthew 1 and Luke 1–2 this assertion was intended less as a testimony to remarkable biology than as an attempt to portray Jesus' birth as a work of God, appropriate to the unique role he would play in God's purposes. In this way it was not unlike some other significant births in the Old Testament.

Subsequent developments of doctrine, however, though they have been thought to follow logically from the "mystery" of the *incarnation* (see glossary term) are not to be obviously derived from Scripture. The earliest to develop, the belief that Mary remained virgin forever, is indeed hard to reconcile with references in the New Testament to brothers and sisters of Jesus (see **Jesus, Family of**). It arose (as did the title "mother of God") from the weight of emphasis placed on the *divinity* (see glossary term) of Christ: it was felt appropriate that a "fence of specialness" must be placed around the extraordinary privilege accorded to us in his coming among us, and so around the means by which this took place. Later, congruous, developments include the belief that Mary herself was conceived without inheriting the taint of original sin inherited by all from Adam's Fall, thus further strengthening the fence. This belief in her Immaculate Conception (the term is often used in error for the virginal conception, or Virgin Birth, of Jesus) has roots in the second century (Mary is a new Eve, as Jesus is a second Adam, 1 Cor. 15.22, 50; Rom. 5.12ff.), and its feast was kept from the early Middle Ages, but controversially; the doctrine (or dogma) was only promulgated officially by the Pope in 1854. Her specialness is rounded off by the doctrine of Mary's Assumption, that is, the theory that she did not die as we all die, but was taken body and soul to heaven in triumph. This, too, is a belief dating from early medieval times, in both Eastern and Western Churches, with variety of detail and with some controversy. It was finally "defined" by the Pope in 1950, as far as the Western (Roman) Catholic Church is concerned. These beliefs (apart from the first, evidently grounded in the Gospels) are not generally entertained among Protestants, even though there is a measure of congruence in devotion to Mary as an ecumenical (see *Ecumenism*) spirit develops. The doctrines may thus be distinguished from the devotion. (See **Mary.**)

Mediator: a term applied to Jesus in his role as a bridge between God the Father and the human race. The idea formally derives from Scripture (1 Tim. 2.5; Heb. 8.6; 9.15; 12.24), but it is a natural metaphor for what Christians believe Jesus accomplished through his death and resurrection in reconciling sinful man to God (see glossary listing for the word pairs *Divinity-Humanity; Divine nature–Human nature; Son of God–Son of man*). It may be seen as having the advantage of relative simplicity: it makes the necessary point without elaboration and conceptual complication. Whatever the precise manner of its happening, this is what Jesus achieved, this is the purpose of his life and death. (See **Jesus, Achievement of.**)

Missiology: this term denotes a fairly recently developed branch of theology relating to the Christian "mission," in its complex history and huge variety down the centuries; also in its current position in an age of *ecumenism* (see glossary term above) and interfaith relations, when the Church no longer has the boost once available from European governments as imperial and colonial powers. All the mainstream churches are involved in study and reflection on these issues. (See **Interfaith Thought and Relations.**)

Monophysite: From Greek *monos* ("sole," "only") and *phusis* ("nature"). the term denotes a party of Eastern Christians who, under the championship of Eutyches, became distinct and articulate in the mid–fifth century (though with clear antecedents, see listing for word pairs *Divinity-Humanity; Divine nature–Human nature; Son of God–Son of man*). They supposedly held that in Christ there was only one nature, the divine, and his apparent humanness was itself suffused with divinity; but the doctrine was held with varied degrees of rigor over the centuries, and in recent years there have been numerous conciliatory moves between churches of this tradition (see **Armenian Christianity; Coptic Christianity; Ethiopian Christianity**) and, for example, Pope Paul VI in 1973 and Pope John Paul II in 1984. What is to be noted is that the full literal meaning of "monophysite" ("one nature-ite") is a misleading description (virtually a kind of insult) of those originally tarred with its brush—they did not believe Jesus had been a sort of phantasm who had flown in from the other world. On the other hand, they did seriously underplay the human reality of his experiences in a way that now strikes many as an improbable account of Jesus, the man of Nazareth in the Galilee of the first century. (See also **Alexandrian Theology** and **Chalcedon.**)

Neoplatonism: a new surge of Platonist thought, chiefly in the work of Plotinus (c. 205–270), in the third century A.D. Plato himself died in 347 B.C., and after his time there were numerous attempts to revive and develop the main lines of some aspects of his teaching. Philo, the Jewish thinker in Alexandria in the first century A.D., is an example. With its strong religious tendencies, Neoplatonism had profound effects on many in the Roman world, including a number of Christian thinkers, most notably Augustine (see **Augustine of Hippo**) in the late fourth century. Its most congenial home among Christians of the period was Alexandria (see **Alexandrian Theology**), where Origen (c. 185–c. 254) was reared in pre-Plotinus Platonist circles and had a crucial effect on the development of the speculative theology of the East in his time (see **Origen**). The philosophy was profoundly metaphysical, that is, speculative, and more concerned with the invisible realities of the spiritual world than with the empirical world of our experience. Christians of this persuasion or tendency found inspiration (with limited plausibility) in the Gospel of John (see **John, Gospel of**). They believed that the "divine" (the One) is knowable by contemplation, and so by spiritual ascent from the things of this world and by purification from its ties. It is, of course, hard to relate such a philosophy in its purity to the Christian gospel, centered on the incarnation of God in Christ within the world of everyday experience. But we can see the force of this tendency especially in Alexandrian theology and in aspects of the monastic movement, including the concentration on contemplative prayer (see **Benedict; John of the Cross; Spirituality**), though it has always been tempered by the central features of Christian faith, however much it has owed to some aspects of a Platonist outlook.

Orthodoxy: literally, Greek for "right opinion." In Christian use, it is the opposite of "heresy," literally a faction—and then the ideas that mark it (see *Heresy*). But the term has also come to be the common name for the Church of the East, "the Orthodox

Church," in effect a number of independent but associated churches, centered from the fourth century on Constantinople (or Byzantium; now Istanbul), but now widespread, especially in Russia, Greece, and other Balkan lands. (See **Orthodox Tradition.**)

Patristic: from *pater* ("father") in Greek and Latin. It is the adjective applied to the period, thought, and theology relating to the leading thinkers ("the Fathers") of the early centuries of the Church. (See **Nicea; Chalcedon;** see also listing for word pairs *Divinity-Humanity; Divine nature–Human nature; Son of God–Son of man.*)

Pelagianism: this has become a common term to denote a tendency, supposedly prominent among recent Anglo-Saxons (Pelagius himself was a Briton of the late fourth and early fifth centuries), to see self-generated virtue and achievement as the road to "salvation," however that might be seen. It is, in other words, allegedly the death of true Christianity, which centers on salvation or atonement (see glossary listings *Salvation* and *Atonement*) as an act of the gracious God, done out of love for helpless humankind in and through Christ. Pelagianism is then a serious heresy. Such a simplistic account, however, fails to do justice to Pelagius himself, who entered into a subtle and prolonged controversy in a series of writings, batted to and fro with Augustine (see **Augustine of Hippo**). Pelagius's undoubted emphasis on moral seriousness, preached in a context of Roman moral laxity, was not at all intended to undermine the Christian gospel, but it seemed to do so to one of Augustine's radical temper of mind and particular intellectual history, which made the gravity of the human heritage of sin and the fact and necessity of divine grace, free and unearned, central to his awareness. Pelagius was declared a heretic by 420.

Pietism: strictly, a movement chiefly in German Protestantism in the eighteenth century that concentrated on the inner experience of religion and the devotional life. It may be seen as a reaction against the overintellectualized ethos of some German religion, and its influence can be seen in the church music of J. S. Bach. Pietism had effects in other countries (see **Wesley, Charles, and Wesley, John**). But the word is used more widely, often pejoratively, to describe religious attitudes that are seen as less than rigorous intellectually and perhaps wandering into emotional self-indulgence.

Puritan: the term given to the people, the movement, and the teaching, chiefly in line with the Reformed tradition as it developed in England (see *Reformed*). Its roots go back to developments in Cambridge and elsewhere during the reign of Henry VIII, under Lutheran influences from Germany, but later it developed a more strongly Calvinist turn as a result of the influence of scholars and preachers who went as exiles to Geneva and other Swiss and German cities where the Reformation had taken hold during the reign of Mary Tudor (1553 to 1558). Returning in Elizabeth's reign, 1558 to 1603, these scholars and preachers acted as a pressure group seeking to radicalize the English Reformation Settlement in both worship and doctrine. Government pressure kept a lid on the movement, but it eventually won through to success after the fall of Charles I in the 1640s, and in the 1650s the existing Church of England, with its system of bishops and a measure of Catholic-style worship, was abolished. The change lasted only until 1660, and the Puritan movement was removed from power, in due course leading to the formation (and in part the toleration) of "non-conformist" churches alongside the established Church of England. Earlier in the seventeenth century, many Puritans, seeking freedom, had emigrated to New England, and it is this tradition that lies at the root of many of the Protestant churches in the United States. (See **American [North] Christianity; English Christianity, 1500–1750.**)

Radical theology: the name for a group of ideas or tendencies developed in recent decades to take further (and, from a traditional church point of view, disloyally) the tendencies of liberal theology. In England, though it looks back a few years to "death of God" thinking in the United States and elsewhere, it stems largely from the thought of Don Cupitt of the University of Cambridge, who in a long series of short books has shown what he believes to be the unsatisfactory and incredible character of traditional Christian ideas, including belief in any kind of "objective" deity. Naturally, Jesus is seen as purely a man of his time, to whose teaching one might react with warmth or with a measure of critical skepticism. A number of present-day biblical critics work, in effect, with these tendencies in mind. (See **Jesus Seminar** and the very different **Radical Orthodoxy.**)

Redeemer: one of the best-known terms for Jesus, thanks to some well-known hymns, such as "Guide Me, O Thou Great Redeemer" (where in fact the reference is chiefly to the God of the Old Testament rather than to Jesus), and, above all, to the aria from Handel's *Messiah,* "I know that my redeemer liveth" (where the reference is certainly to Jesus, though the text comes from Job 19.25). In the New Testament, however, the noun never appears, though other members of the same word-family occur a few times: for example, the English verb, "redeem" occurs eight times in relevant contexts, and "redemption" appears, relevantly, in a small handful of texts.

Behind these terms we have two different families of Greek words, expressing two different images: that of purchase and that of release. It is not difficult to see the appropriateness at any rate of the second image as one way of speaking of Jesus' achievement on behalf of humankind, which had been "enslaved" to sin, suffering, evil powers, and death. The other image, of purchase (in, for example, Rev. 5.9; 14.3, 4; and Gal. 3.14; 4.5), may involve more of myth or story, of our being held by diabolical powers who demand "payment" for our release (see also Rom. 3.24; 8.23; 1 Cor. 1.30). The idea of a price paid is probably not absent from the other image of release, so that the two word-groups may coalesce. It is hard to know in a given instance how far the words retain much of their original story-content, though they reacquired it in later (fourth century) Christian myth-making about Christ being in debt to the devil for us, his legitimate captives.

Behind the language, which is common in the Old Testament, lie humdrum social customs about buying back that which has been alienated in some way, or else the paying of a ransom. Inherent is the idea of paying a price for something of value that has been lost from one's possession and can now be regained. In the Old Testament, the aptness of the idea to illuminate and express God's generous intent for his people was well grasped. As applied to Jesus, the "redeemer" picture is best seen as one among a number of images that come under the heading of atonement or salvation, ways of speaking of the achievement of Jesus, or, better, expressing people's conviction of their relationship with God having been revitalized or restored, with purifying effect, as a result, directly or indirectly, of a transforming experience of Jesus and what he has done, especially in his act of self-sacrifice on the cross. (See **Jesus, Achievement of;** see also *Atonement* and *Salvation.*)

Reformed: may be applied to churches, notably those with a Calvinist history and doctrine, often now called Presbyterian (found for example, in Switzerland, France, Scotland, and the United States); or to theologians such as Karl Barth and their style of theology. Sometimes, the term is used more generally to refer to churches and thinkers affected or brought into being by the Reformation in the sixteenth and seventeenth centuries. Originally, the term was "the reform," meaning attempts, originally in various parts of northern Germany, to amend the existing Catholic Church (for which there was no alternative of any importance in Western Europe), in respect of some of its ideas and some of its long-standing practices.

The Reform was inspired by a new ability to study the Scriptures in the original Greek and Hebrew and a new flexibility of thought. This inspired a belief that the celibacy of the clergy, the practice of giving Communion to the laity only under the form of bread, the giving of special status to monks, friars, and nuns, the passivity of laypeople in the conduct of worship, and the sale of indulgences, among other ideas and customs, ought to be changed. One major effect was a more lively sense of Jesus in his time, not yet carried very far, but beginning to be felt. It was rare, however, to question the traditional doctrines about him, even though he might be believed in with a fresh sense of his work in the soul, stemming especially from a revived perception of the writing of Paul. (See **American [North] Christianity; Barth, Karl; Calvin, John; Chalcedon; Luther, Martin;** see also *Counter-Reformation*.)

Resurrection: chiefly used, in our context, of Jesus' return to life by God's act, as told in the Gospels. The idea of restoration to life was deep in the Jewish psyche, initially as a kind of symbol or aspiration rather than a belief about one's own or the people's literal future (for example, Ezek. 37). It surfaces among the features of apocalyptic hope in the period around that of Jesus and figures in the stories of his acts (for example, the daughter of Jairus, Mark 5.21–43; Lazarus, John 11.1–44), then is central to the post-crucifixion Christian hope and restoration (1 Cor. 15.3–7), not just for Jesus but for his people (1 Cor. 15). (See **Resurrection;** see also *Apocalyptic*.)

Revelation: sheerly as a word, it is barely distinguishable from *apocalypse*, but in practice it is a broader term, referring to the idea of God's self-disclosure, by whatever means, including, for example, in human minds as they come to discern various truths about him. In that sense, it is a broad term, applying also to the vehicles of that disclosure, including the words of prophets and the writings of Scripture, and, centrally, the person of Jesus. It is related to the idea of God as "light," making himself available and intelligible (cf. John 1.3–9). (See also *Apocalyptic*.)

Sacrament: a term in Christian usage for a number of rites wherein some act, usually involving a physical element, is a covenanted (that is, guaranteed by God) means of gracious, beneficial encounter with him. Two such acts have always been seen as Christ's bequest to his Church, enjoined on his followers for them to retain and observe. The first is baptism (see **Baptism**), the rite of initiation into Christ and the Church from earliest times (see Matt. 28.19); the second is the Lord's Supper, Holy Communion, Eucharist (see **Eucharist**), or Mass, derived from the Last Supper (see 1 Cor. 11.23–25: "do this in remembrance of me"). The former is administered once only to a particular person (though since Reformation times, some of those baptized in infancy and brought to lively faith in adulthood have undergone a second, "real" baptism); the second is the repeated rite of Christian observance, seen as sustenance for the Christian life or as the God-given, visible encapsulation of Christian faith, centered on Christ's sacrifice. From medieval times, other rites have been given the name of "sacrament," as having aspects of the same character: confession of sin in the presence of a priest, confirmation, marriage, ordination, and anointing of the sick and dying. At the Reformation, these were demoted from this category by Protestants (though Luther accepted confession) as not warranted to have such a status by Scripture. (See also *Baptism* and *Eucharist*.)

Salvation: related to atonement, but a broader term referring to God's acts to restore his people, of which "Atonement" is a particular form or set of images; "salvation" itself (from Latin, *salvatus*), stems from the idea of being "made safe"—in the face of, for example, the devil, sin, disaster, suffering, or sickness. So Jesus is seen as "savior," the agent of salvation, the term being particularly important in Luke (for example, 2.11; 19.10) and the Pastoral Epistles (1 Tim., 2 Tim., and Titus). It is a central perception, whatever the precise language, of the effect of Jesus from the start, not to be spiritualized away from his healing acts and other restorative actions. (See also *Atonement*.)

Spirituality: now often an omnibus term for the perception of the self as more than a merely eating, reproducing, money-making being, but as having other capacities—toward beauty, a sense of the mystical (whatever that may be taken to mean), love of people, and other noble aspirations, personal and artistic. Among these, many recognize a sense of God or at least of "the divine" or "the other," however conceived. In Christian usage, it is a term for the "feeling for" prayer, the "desire for" God and hope for developing intimacy with him, together with the practice of prayer with that end in view. It is also used for the formal study of the subject, with "liturgy" being its near cousin, dealing with formal prayer and worship, with "liturgiology" as the stricter term for the academic subject. (See **Prayer; Spirituality.**)

Theology: literally, "discourse about God," or the study of God and ideas concerning him. The word is used more loosely—for example, in "the theology of animal life" or "the theology of education,"—to mean thought about a given subject in the light of ideas about God.

Word; Wisdom: in the Old Testament, God is constantly represented as "speaking," uttering his word(s) to a variety of people in a variety of contexts. Sometimes, as when God speaks to Abraham in Genesis 12ff. or to Moses in Exodus, the picture is simply anthropomorphic: God behaves as if he were a superior kind of man. In many religious contexts, of course, God's speech is a metaphor for his communication by whatever means, his being "sensed" as meaning or intending something, perhaps especially to his chosen ones, such as prophets or leaders of the people. But sometimes, the metaphor has more of a philosophical sense. When God creates the heavens and the earth in Genesis1, he does it by commanding utterance, which is unfailingly successful, beginning with "Let there be light." Here, there is a sense that intelligible speech produces orderly results; so that the created "order" (note the word) is not at all a chaos, in fact, quite its reverse (cf. Psalm 33.6). In Jewish thought, this metaphor was often conjoined or twinned with that of God's "wisdom." Once more, God was not irrational in his deeds, notably in creation (Prov. 8.22–31): they exhibit perfect sense. Wisdom of Solomon 9.1 brings the two images together, and 18.14–16 sees "wisdom" (divine intent, rational purpose) as determining the exodus from Egypt—it was no impetuous, ill-considered act.

In the first century A.D., the Jewish thinker Philo was developing this idea, under Platonist impulse (as indeed its prominence in the Judaism of the just-earlier period may have been indebted to Greek influences). There is therefore nothing surprising in our finding this kind of imagery applied to Jesus: in creation and indeed in all he does, he represents God's rationally purposive will. John made the most of it (1.1–14), making it a kind of foundation concept. But Paul has strong traces of it as well (1 Cor. 1.24; 8.6). And perhaps it is being applied to Jesus in less obvious texts, such as Matthew 11.19 and Luke 7.35; 11.49, though with what degree of intent is unclear. In the subsequent period, the Platonist associations of "word" *(logos)* to signify the orderly exercise of power and purpose came more strongly to the fore, with, as it were, the Johannine blessing in the background and the Johannine texts often in the foreground, to describe the activity and being itself of Christ. Later, "wisdom" and some of its associated texts came to be applied to the Virgin Mary, perhaps partly because *sophia*, the Greek noun for "wisdom," is feminine, as is the Latin *sapientia*. (See also *Christology*.)

INDEX

Note: page numbers in **bold type** refer to encyclopedia entries devoted to that topic.

G

M